Qq

is the 17th letter of our alphabet. It was also a letter in the alphabet used by the Semites, who once lived in Syria and Palestine. They named it *qoph* which may have been their word for *ape* or *monkey*, and they wrote it with a picture symbol that may represent a monkey. The Greeks later took the letter into their alphabet for a time, calling it *koppa*. The Romans adopted it from the Greeks, and gave it its present capital *Q* form. They also originated the usage of following *q* with *u*. See ALPHABET.

Uses. *Q* or *q* is about the 25th most frequently used letter in books, newspapers, and other printed material in English. *Q* is used as an abbreviation for Quebec. In titles, *Q* may indicate *queen*, as in *Q.C.* for *Queen's Counsel*, and it can mean Quarter as in *QMC* for *Quartermaster Corps*, a military unit. The lower case *q* is used to abbreviate *quart*, *quarter*, *quarterly*, and *question*. A Latin phrase, *quod vide*, or *which see*, is represented by *q.v.*, and is used in footnotes and other citations.

Pronunciation. *Q* followed by *u* in English has the sound of *kw* as a rule. A person makes this sound by narrowing and rounding his lips. The back of his tongue touches or is near his velum, or soft palate. His vocal cords do not vibrate. Final *que* as in *unique* has the sound of *k*. The combination *qu* also has the sound of *k* in such words as *liquor* and *croquet*. This combination has the sound of *k* or *kw* in French, of *kv* in German, and of *k* in Spanish. The Romans pronounced it like *kw*. See PRONUNCIATION. — I. J. GELB and J. M. WELLS

The 17th letter may have taken its shape from an ancient symbol used to show a monkey. Its sound may have come from the Semitic word *qoph*, which means *ape* or *monkey*.

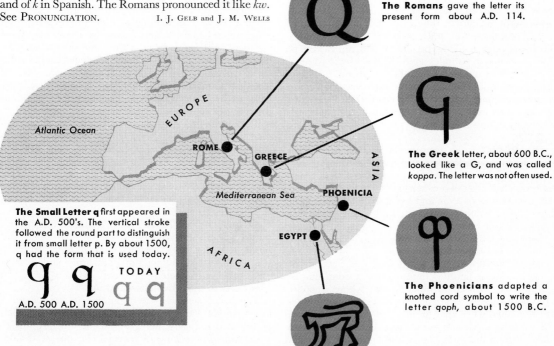

The Romans gave the letter its present form about A.D. 114.

The Greek letter, about 600 B.C., looked like a G, and was called *koppa*. The letter was not often used.

The Small Letter q first appeared in the A.D. 500's. The vertical stroke followed the round part to distinguish it from small letter p. By about 1500, q had the form that is used today.

A.D. 500   A.D. 1500   TODAY

The Phoenicians adapted a knotted cord symbol to write the letter *qoph*, about 1500 B.C.

The Egyptians, about 3000 B.C., drew a picture of a monkey.

I

QATAR, *KAH tuhr,* is an Arab sheikdom on a low, sun-baked peninsula jutting into the Persian Gulf from the eastern side of Saudi Arabia. It has a population of about 135,000, and covers about 8,500 square miles. Its exact size is unknown because Qatar and neighboring Saudi Arabia disagree on the exact location of their borderline. Qatar, an unusually barren desert, consists of nearly flat limestone with a little sand blown on top. Doha, on the eastern coast, is the capital (see DOHA).

Qatar is one of the leading oil-producing areas in the Middle East. Many of its people work for the Iraq Petroleum Company which owns the Qatar petroleum rights. The oil comes from the Dukhan field on the western side of the peninsula. Oil was first discovered in 1939. Because of the shallowness of the Persian Gulf, oil tankers cannot reach its western shore. A pipeline crosses the desert to Umm Said, on the eastern side of Qatar. Here the gulf is deep enough for tankers.

Qatar has an average annual rainfall of less than 4 inches. There are very few wells for irrigation. As a result of the shortage of water, agriculture in Qatar is severely limited. A few people make their living by pearling and fishing. Others herd camels and goats for a living.

Qatar

Qatar is an independent and British-protected sheikdom. Great Britain has controlled Qatar's defense and foreign affairs since 1916. But in 1968, Britain announced it would withdraw from Qatar by the end of 1971. DOUGLAS D. CRARY

QATTARA DEPRESSION, *cot TAH rah,* is a sunken, pit-shaped region of Egypt, about 130 miles west of Cairo and about 40 miles south of the Mediterranean Sea. It covers an area of 7,000 square miles. At its deepest point, it lies 436 feet below sea level. The region is almost rainless, but spring waters feed parts covered by dense marshes. In places, the Qattara Depression is walled by impassable cliffs. GEORGE H. T. KIMBLE

Q.E.D. See ABBREVIATION.

QUADRANT is an instrument used for measuring altitudes in navigation, surveying, and astronomy. The instrument gets its name from the mathematical quadrant, which consists of one-fourth of a circle. It is shaped like one quarter of a pie and has a scale marked on its curved edge. Another instrument, the sextant, has largely replaced it (see SEXTANT). JOHN J. FLOHERTY

QUADRATIC EQUATION. See ALGEBRA (Quadratic Equations in One Unknown).

QUADRILATERAL, *KWAHD rih LAT er ul,* is the name given to a plane figure with four straight sides, that is, a four-sided *polygon.* A quadrilateral whose opposite sides lie parallel is a parallelogram. The opposite sides are also equal when they are parallel, and in that case, the opposite *angles* are equal, too. If the angles of a parallelogram are right angles, the figure is a *rectangle.* If the rectangle has equal sides, it is a *square.* The figure is a *rhomboid* if it is a parallelogram without right angles. When all the sides of a rhomboid are equal, it is a

rhombus. The area, *A,* of any parallelogram with base *b* and altitude *h* is given in the formula $A = bh$.

A *trapezoid* is a quadrilateral with one set of parallel sides of unequal length. The trapezoid is *isosceles* if the nonparallel sides are equal. HARRY C. BARBER

See also RECTANGLE; RHOMBUS; SQUARE.

QUADRILLE. See DANCING (The 1800's).

QUADRILLION is a billion millions in the United States and France. One quadrillion is written with 15 zeros: 1,000,000,000,000,000. In Germany and Great Britain, a quadrillion has 24 zeros. See also DECIMAL NUMERAL SYSTEM (Larger Numbers).

QUADRIVIUM. See EDUCATION, HISTORY OF (In Ancient Rome).

QUADROON. See MULATTO.

QUADROS, JÂNIO. See BRAZIL (The 1960's).

QUADRUPLE ALLIANCE, *quad ROO p'l,* is an alliance between four countries. Many quadruple alliances have been formed. Perhaps the most important were those formed by Great Britain, France, Holland, and Austria in 1718, and by Great Britain, Austria, Prussia, and Russia in 1815. Great Britain, France, Spain, and Portugal formed a Quadruple Alliance in 1834.

QUADRUPLETS, *KWAHD roo plets,* are four children born to a mother at one time. They occur more often than quintuplets, but less often than triplets. According to one theory, quadruplets are born once in every 884,736 births. But some authorities believe they occur less than once in every million births. In the United States from 1933 to 1958, however, 110 sets of quadruplets were born in which at least one of the children was born alive. This is an average of one quadruplet set in 663,470 births.

Identical quadruplets are born from the cell mass of a single egg which became separated. An example of identical quadruplets were the Morlok girls. There also are four possible combinations of identical and fraternal quadruplets. The Badgett family in Texas had three identical triplet girls born at the same time as another sister. She came from a different cell mass, and is a *fraternal* quadruplet. Another possibility is two pairs of identical twins born together from two fertilized egg cells, each of which divided. The Derner girls of Germany were two such sets of identical twins born together.

Two of the four Keys sisters of Texas were born identical twins from one egg cell, while the other two quadruplets were fraternal, each born from a separate cell mass. The Schense children are examples of the fifth possibility, four fraternal quadruplets born at the same time but from different egg cells. G. W. BEADLE

QUADRUPLEX TELEGRAPHY. See TELEGRAPH (Faster and Better Service).

QUAESTOR, *KWES tur,* was a financial administrator in ancient Rome. Quaestors collected taxes and supervised the state treasury and records. In each Roman province, a quaestor paid army and government officials, collected taxes, and served as second in command to the provincial governor.

The first quaestors were appointed to assist Roman kings. In the early republic, a quaestor assisted each of the two *consuls* (chief government officials) in investigations, especially of crimes. The quaestors later came to specialize in finance. The office became elective in 447 B.C. By the 40's B.C., the number of quaestors had increased to 40. FRANK C. BOURNE

The
World Book
Encyclopedia

Q·R   Volume 16

Field Enterprises Educational Corporation

Chicago London Paris Rome Stuttgart Sydney Tokyo Toronto

The World Book Encyclopedia

Copyright © 1973, U.S.A.
by
Field Enterprises Educational Corporation

QUAHOG. See CLAM.

QUAI D'ORSAY, *KAY DAWR SAY*, is the name of a street in Paris which runs along the left *quay* (bank) of the Seine River. The offices of the French Ministry of Foreign Affairs front on the Quai d'Orsay. The offices, and even the foreign policy of the French government, are sometimes given the name of the street. *Quai d'Orsay* means *Quay of Orsay*. The street was named for a French general.   ROBERT E. DICKINSON

QUAIL, *kwayl*, is a name given to several different kinds of birds. In Europe, it refers to several kinds of game birds of the pheasant family. Americans use the name for several birds of the grouse family. The best known of these is called the *bobwhite*. The bobwhite is called a quail in northern and eastern United States and in Canada. Southerners call it a partridge.

The bobwhite gets its name from its clear whistling call, which sounds like *ah bob WHITE*. This bird is the only kind of quail native to the area east of the Mississippi River. It usually lives in the region from the Gulf states to southern Ontario. The bobwhite is a plump bird, 10 inches long. It has reddish-brown feathers with black, white, and buff markings. These marks make the bobwhite look as if it had a speckled jacket.

The bobwhite builds its nest on the ground, and lives in the grass. A brood may include from 10 to 18 eggs or more. Weed seeds provide half the bobwhite's food. The rest is grain, wild fruit, and insects. The bobwhite also eats insect pests, such as chinch bugs, grasshoppers, boll weevils, army worms, and cutworms. The bobwhite is a friend of farmers because it eats insects.

Quail flesh is a popular food. Hunters have killed so many of the birds that many states have hunting laws to protect them. Quail scatter at the approach of an enemy. Then they sound a *gathering call*. Bird authorities believe quail gather together this way.

Other kinds of American quail are the *California quail, Gambel's quail, mountain quail, scaled quail*, and *Mearn's quail*. The mountain quail is the largest, and Mearn's is the smallest. All except Mearn's have crests that stand out from their heads. Their feathers usually are slate blue, olive brown, and black and white. These birds live in the western and southwestern states.

Scientific Classification. Quails belong to the pheasant family, *Phasianidae*. The bobwhite is genus *Colinus*, species *C. virginianus*.   JOSEPH J. HICKEY

See also BIRD (table: State Birds; color pictures: Birds That Help Us, Game Birds); FRANCOLIN.

QUAKER CITY. See PHILADELPHIA.

QUAKER-LADIES. See BLUET.

QUAKER POET. See WHITTIER, JOHN GREENLEAF.

QUAKER STATE. See PENNSYLVANIA.

QUAKERS is the popular name for members of the RELIGIOUS SOCIETY OF FRIENDS. Quakerism developed in England in the 1600's. Today, a majority of its followers live in the United States. England and Kenya also have large Quaker populations. Smaller Quaker groups exist elsewhere in the Americas, in northern Europe, Asia, Africa, Australia, and New Zealand.

Quakers have been known throughout their history for their humanitarian activities. They reject war and stress peace education. They have been pioneers in removing barriers to racial equality and have been among the leaders in prison reform and in the humane treatment of mental patients. Quakers have always been concerned with education, and the high quality of their many schools and colleges has been widely recognized.

History. George Fox of England founded Quakerism. His spiritual experience led him to witness to what he called the *Inner Light* of Christ that dwells in the hearts of ordinary people. Those who followed that Inner Light were considered truly spiritual and following God's will. Fox began preaching in 1647 and attracted a variety of religious seekers during that period of social and political revolution in England. The word *Quaker* was originally meant as an insult to Fox, who told an English judge to "tremble at the Word of the Lord." The judge called Fox a "quaker."

From the beginning, the Quakers emphasized inward spiritual experiences rather than specific creeds. The early Quakers, or Friends, developed radically fresh forms of worship and business proceedings. These forms were based on a trust in the Holy Spirit and faith that ordinary laymen were capable of receiving the Spirit.

In 1682, a Quaker, William Penn, founded the colony of Pennsylvania as a haven for the continually persecuted English Quakers who wished to emigrate to the New World. Penn gave the colony a constitution that was a model for safeguarding the religious liberties of its citizens. While the Quakers governed during the period from 1682 to 1756, Pennsylvania had no militia and only a modest police force.

Worship. Quakers regard all life as sacramental and observe no special sacraments. Business and worship are conducted in monthly, quarterly, and yearly meetings. Originally, Quakers worshiped by gathering together in whatever place was available for periods of group silence. During the silence, the faithful attentively waited for the Lord to exercise His power upon their lives; to lay on them "the burden of the world's suffering" and their responsibility to respond to it. Anyone could speak at the meeting, if he felt a message had been given him during the silence.

Quaker business meetings are guided by a *clerk*. After a period of silent waiting, he states a particular problem and listens to the members' suggestions. Then, without being bound to any member's specific suggestion, the clerk presents for the group's consideration a *minute* that seeks to resolve the problem in an acceptable way. No votes are taken, but the process continues until even opposing minorities are at least satisfied that their position has had a hearing and that it has been given consideration.

The loose organizational structure of the Religious Society of Friends has always given a great deal of liberty to its regional yearly meetings. This liberty has resulted in a variety of worship and spiritual patterns in different parts of America, Europe, and other parts of the world. The Friends World Committee for Consultation in Birmingham, England, is a communications center for many regional yearly meetings in the world. For Quaker membership in the United States, see RELIGION (table).   Critically reviewed by DOUGLAS V. STEERE

Related Articles in WORLD BOOK include:

Dyer, Mary
Fox, George
New Jersey (English Control)

Penn, William
Prison (Early Reforms)
Whittier, John Greenleaf

QUAKING ASPEN. See ASPEN.

3

QUALITATIVE ANALYSIS

QUALITATIVE ANALYSIS. See CHEMISTRY (Chart).

QUANTA. See QUANTUM THEORY.

QUANTICO MARINE CORPS DEVELOPMENT AND EDUCATION COMMAND, in Quantico, Va., is the principal center for training officers of the United States Marine Corps. The Marine Corps also develops and tests new weapons, amphibious craft, and tactics and techniques at Quantico. Quantico lies about 35 miles south of Washington, D.C. Schools at Quantico include the Basic School for commissioned officers, the Command and Staff College, the Commissioned Officer Candidate School, the Communications Officers' School, the Extension School, the Physical Fitness Academy, and the Woman Officer School. The center also has schools for amphibious warfare, computer science, instructor training, and ordnance. Part of the Federal Bureau of Investigation Academy is at Quantico. Quantico was founded in 1917.   JOHN A. OUDINE

QUANTITATIVE ANALYSIS. See CHEMISTRY (Chart).

QUANTRILL, *KWAHN trill,* **WILLIAM CLARKE** (1837-1865), was the leader of a Confederate guerrilla band during the Civil War. Born in Ohio, he went to Kansas in 1857 and started farming. The next year, he rode west with a wagon train and became a gambler at Fort Bridger, Wyo. He returned to Kansas in 1859, and taught school for one term. Quantrill was accused of stealing cattle and horses and of killing several persons, but he managed to escape arrest.

From *Gray Ghosts of the Confederacy* by Richard S. Brownlee, Courtesy LSU Press and State Historical Society of Missouri

William C. Quantrill

At the start of the Civil War, Quantrill formed a band of guerrilla troops. He led his men on raids against Kansas and Missouri farmers and townspeople who favored the Union. Quantrill's band was mustered into Confederate service in 1862, but continued to operate independently. On Aug. 21, 1863, he and his men burned most of the town of Lawrence, Kans., and killed about 150 people. Frank James, Jesse James' brother, rode with the band that day. Quantrill was killed during a raid in Kentucky.   WAYNE GARD

QUANTUM MECHANICS. See QUANTUM THEORY.

QUANTUM THEORY is a theory of physics. It states that energy, such as light, is given off and absorbed in tiny definite units called *quanta* or *photons.* Light appears to be a steady stream, or a continuous flow, of energy. Actually, light is not given off or absorbed in one continuous process, but it is a series of many small actions that may be compared to the filming of a motion picture, in which each movement is photographed in many small pictures. But, when shown on the screen, the motion picture appears as one continuous movement.

Radiant Energy. The quantum theory of energy applies only to the kind of energy that is transmitted, or carried, by waves. This type of energy is called *radiant energy,* and includes heat, light, ultraviolet rays, infrared rays, X rays, radio waves, and cosmic rays. It also in-cludes the gamma radiation given off by radioactive elements and atoms that are being split. Each type of radiant energy is transmitted in waves that are in a certain range of frequencies. For convenience, each range of frequencies has been arranged in a sort of table, from the lowest to the highest frequency. This arrangement of the frequencies is called a *spectrum.* Just as there is a large spectrum of radiant energy, there is a smaller spectrum of light waves, found in the rainbow, and a similar spectrum of each of the other types of waves.

When a substance radiates or absorbs energy, all the atoms of that substance are disturbed and begin to vibrate. If the substance is radiating energy, each atom loses or gives off a certain amount of energy. If the substance is absorbing energy, each atom gains a certain amount of energy. As the atoms vibrate, they give off light in a color pattern that differs for each element.

The first experiment which showed that a radiating body gives off light was made by the German physicist Max Planck in 1900. He bored a hole through a metal box painted black on the inside and outside. The hole appeared to be the blackest part of the box. Then he put the box in a flame and found that the hole was no longer the blackest part but was glowing brighter than the rest of the box. As the box was heated to different temperatures, the amount of brightness changed. It was learned that the amount of radiance coming from a black body changed as the fourth power of the absolute temperature of the box (see ABSOLUTE ZERO). A spectroscopic view through the box showed all the colors of the rainbow, from the deepest red to violet.

The Structure of Matter. To understand the quantum theory, it is necessary to know something about the structure of matter. All matter is composed of tiny units called *atoms.* In the midst of each atom is a *nucleus,* which is made up of protons and neutrons. Around this nucleus are *electrons* that move about in *orbits* (paths) much the same as a planet orbits around the sun.

As long as an atom remains undisturbed, the electrons go on revolving, just as the earth revolves, and no energy is let off or taken in. But, if some outside force acts upon the atom, the electron is forced to change its orbit. If the electron must change to a smaller orbit, it makes the jump, and a *quantum* of energy is *given off* by the atom. If the electron is forced to a larger orbit, it jumps quickly, and a quantum of energy is *absorbed* by the atom. This is the action of *radiation* and *absorption.*

According to the quantum theory, every substance that radiates energy contains a certain amount of quanta, depending upon the type of substance. The value of the quanta depends upon the number of vibrations per second of the substance. It also depends upon a certain quantity that is the same for all substances, known as *Planck's constant.* The value of the quanta of a substance, then, can be found by multiplying the number of vibrations per second by Planck's constant. The mathematical formula for this relation is: $E = h\nu$, where h is Planck's constant and ν is the number of vibrations per second. The value of h equals 6.62×10^{-27} erg-seconds.

Quantum Mechanics. In 1913, the Danish physicist Niels Bohr explained how electrons jump their orbits and either absorb or radiate energy. He also explained how a group of hydrogen atoms always radiates light in a limited number of definite frequencies. In the 1920's and 1930's, other mechanical theories of the atom were

4

developed to explain the heavier elements. After repeated experiments, scientists discovered that the quantum theory is more than a mere theory. It has definite and accurate applications to the physical world. Therefore, the quantum theory is now called *quantum mechanics* by physicists and other scientists.

Quantum mechanics, or the quantum theory, has been an extremely important development in science. It has brought a much more complete understanding of the way atoms are held together, and has helped explain many phenomena of atomic research. The information provided by quantum mechanics has also been applied in the photoelectric cell.   ROBERT F. PATON and RALPH E. LAPP

Related Articles in WORLD BOOK include:

Atom	Photon
Bohr, Niels	Planck, Max K. E. L.
Electric Eye	Proton
Feynman, Richard P.	Radioactivity
Heisenberg, Werner	Radiometer
Light (Quantum Mechanics)	Relativity
Mechanics	Schrödinger, Erwin

QUAPAW INDIANS, *KWAW paw*, were a Plains tribe of North America. They belonged to the Siouan language group. They are also called *Arkansas Indians.* The account of Hernando de Soto's expedition from 1539 to 1543 records the first mention of the Quapaw. Today, about 600 Quapaw live in Oklahoma.

QUARANTINE, *KWAHR un teen*, means to *isolate* (shut off from others) certain persons, places, and animals which may carry danger of infection. The period of quarantine depends on the amount of time necessary for protection against the spread of a particular disease. The word *quarantine* comes from the Latin *quadraginta*, meaning 40. In early times, officials held a ship outside of port for 40 days if they suspected it carried infection among its passengers or freight.

International Quarantine is held in three types of stations. They are maritime, aircraft, and border places of entry. All ships entering ports from foreign areas are subject to quarantine. The officer in command of the ship gives a statement to a port inspection officer about the health status of crew and passengers. The ship is allowed to dock if it is free from infectious disease. If such disease is present, the ship must stay in the harbor flying a yellow flag until it completes a period of quarantine. Heavy penalties result from false statements or for concealing facts about disease.

The quarantine station is always located at some distance from the landing places. In the United States, the Public Health Service controls the quarantine service. The diseases over which the United States maintains a quarantine are Asiatic cholera, yellow fever, smallpox, typhus fever, leprosy, psittacosis (parrot fever), plague, and anthrax.

Aircraft quarantine differs from the maritime quarantine because of the speed of air transport. Passengers are allowed to go to their destinations. But health officials keep them under check until it is certain that they do not have any infectious disease.

States, cities, small communities, single households, and even individuals are subject to quarantine laws. Officials enforce these laws to prevent the spread of contagious diseases. They post notices on houses where infectious diseases are known to be present. Doctors and nurses remain isolated with the patient or take special measures of disinfection to prevent carrying germs.

Quarantine laws have proved effective in reducing death rates and in checking the spread of epidemics.

Plant and Animal Quarantine. Harmful insect pests have been brought into the United States and Canada by diseased plants and animals. The governments of both nations have laws that provide for the inspection of all plants entering the country. Some states have quarantines to keep out diseased plants and animals or insect pests. Local areas may be quarantined to prevent the spread of such animal diseases as the foot-and-mouth disease, which affects cattle and other livestock.   THOMAS PARRAN

Related Articles in WORLD BOOK include:

Bill of Health	Insect (Insect Control)	Public Health
Epidemic	Plant Quarantine	Service
Fumigation		Sanitation

QUARK is an atomic particle that exists only in theory. Some scientists believe that all the known atomic particles may be combinations of three basic bits of matter. They call these supposed bits of matter *quarks.* Physicists try to prove the existence of quarks by producing them in atom smashers. Scientists also study cosmic rays in the hope of identifying quarks that may exist deep in space. But no experimental evidence of the existence of quarks has been found.

Scientists were led to the idea of the quark by the discovery of many kinds of atomic particles. Particles that once were thought to be basic were found to *decay* (break down) into two or more other particles. As scientists improved atom smashers and detecting instruments, they discovered more and more atomic particles. They discovered so many that it became unlikely that any of the known particles could be a basic bit of matter. In the mid-1960's, it was suggested that the basic particles had not yet been discovered.

Many of the particles discovered in atom smasher experiments carry an electrical charge. The charge may be positive or negative, but it is always a whole multiple of the charge carried by an electron. If quarks exist, they differ from known particles in the charges they carry. In theory, quarks carry electrical charges that are only fractions of the charge of an electron. Some quarks would have a charge one-third that of an electron, and others would have a charge two-thirds that of an electron.   KAZUHIKO NISHIJIMA

QUARLES, BENJAMIN ARTHUR (1904-   ), is an American historian. Quarles has written many books about Negroes and their role in United States history. His books include *Frederick Douglass* (1948), *The Negro in the Civil War* (1953), *The Negro in the American Revolution* (1961), and *The Negro in the Making of America* (1964). Since 1953, he has been a professor and head of the department of history at Morgan State College in Baltimore, Md.

Quarles was born in Boston. He graduated from Shaw University in 1931, and received a doctor's degree in American history from the University of Wisconsin in 1940. From 1934 to 1939, he was instructor of history at Shaw. He became professor of history at Dillard University in 1939, and was dean of the university from 1946 to 1953.   EDGAR ALLAN TOPPIN

QUARRYING is a method of taking large solid blocks or broken masses of stone from the earth and preparing

QUARRYING

them for construction projects. A *quarry* is a large pit in the earth from which the stone is taken. Kinds of stone taken from quarries include basalt, granite, limestone, marble, sandstone, slate, and travertine.

Some quarries are dug into the sides of mountains. Most are open at the surface, and they may be hundreds of feet wide and over a hundred feet deep. Stone is quarried by the plug and feather method, the explosive method, or channeling by machinery.

Plug and Feather Method. Rocks can be split along smooth lines by exerting constantly increased pressure evenly on all parts of the rock's surface. With this pressure, workmen can break the rock into any size and shape. Evenly cut blocks are called *dimension stone*.

The principal tools are a *plug* (wedge), which is flat on its two opposite surfaces, and two pieces of steel which are rounded on one side and flat on the other. These are called the *feathers*. The first step is to drill a series of small holes about three-fourths of an inch in diameter into the rock in a straight line. The wedge is placed between the two feathers and all three are inserted in a hole. When all the holes in the line are filled with the tools, the workmen drive the wedges and feathers downward, eventually splitting the rock.

The mass of rock that is broken off is turned over to other workmen. They may split the rock into smaller pieces by the plug and feather method, or with such hand tools as saws, drills, picks, hammers, and wedges.

Explosive Method. This method is not suitable for breaking stones into definite shapes, for the explosive shatters much of the stone. The explosive method is generally used to break off huge masses of rock from their place in the earth. Strong explosives are best if *crushed stone* (finely broken pieces) is desired. Crushed

At an Indiana Limestone Quarry, workmen cut huge slices of rock with a channeling machine, and lift them by hoists.

Indiana Limestone Co.

stone is widely used in paving roads and making concrete. When stones of large size and more regular shape are desired, a milder explosive is used. In both cases, holes are drilled deep into the solid mass. The explosive is put into the holes and the charge is set off by slow-burning fuses or by electric firing. All the explosions may go off at once, or delay blasting may be used. Sometimes hundreds of tons of stone are forced out of the earth in a few huge pieces. See BLASTING.

Channeling by Machinery. Most large quarries use a channeling machine to make the first cut into a solid bed of rock. It looks somewhat like a small locomotive with long chisels on the sides. A track is laid along the smooth surface on top of the rock, and as the machine moves along the track, it forces the chisels downward. Little by little, the chisels cut the rock to any depth from 1 to 10 feet. The rock is broken off below by blasting or by the plug and feather method.

The Quarrying Industry. Quarries in the United States are constantly being opened and shut down. It is not possible to state the exact number of them at any given time. There have been as many as 2,200 operating in one year, but there are usually about 1,900. Of these, about 900 are limestone quarries, 400 granite quarries, 300 sandstone quarries, and fewer than 100 marble quarries. In the late 1960's, over 800 million tons of stone were quarried annually in the United States. Only 2 million tons were dimension stone. The remainder was crushed stone.　　GEORGE B. CLARK

QUART is a measure of capacity used in the United States and Canada to measure both dry and liquid substances. In the United States, the liquid quart equals $\frac{1}{4}$ of a gallon, and .9463 liter in the metric system. It contains 57.75 cubic inches. The dry quart equals $\frac{1}{32}$ of a bushel and 1.111 liters, and contains 67.2 cubic inches. Quarts in both measurements are divided into two pints. A vessel $4 \times 4 \times 3.6$ inches will hold about a liquid quart. Canadians use the imperial quart, dry and liquid. It contains 69.3185 cubic inches, or 1.136 liters. See also WEIGHTS AND MEASURES.　　E. G. STRAUS

QUARTER. See MONEY (United States Money).

QUARTERDECK. See SHIP (Nautical Terms).

QUARTERING ACT. See REVOLUTIONARY WAR IN AMERICA (The Quartering and Stamp Acts).

QUARTERMASTER. See ARMY, U.S. (Quartermaster).

QUARTET. See BARBERSHOP QUARTET SINGING; MUSIC (Chamber Music).

QUARTO. See BOOK (Parts of a Book); FOLIO.

QUARTZ (chemical formula, SiO_2) is a common mineral that is found in many rocks. It can easily be recognized because it looks like pieces of broken glass. It is also found in small grains in sandstone, where calcite or mica holds it together. Quartz is the hardest of all common minerals. Only rare minerals such as topaz, corundum, and diamond are harder than quartz. It is also very stable, which means that it is not easily changed by weather conditions or moisture.

Types of Quartz. There are many varieties of quartz. Quartz may come in six-sided crystals or in one mass. A pure quartz crystal is one which contains no substance besides silicon and oxygen, and has a clear glassy appearance. This type of crystal, called *rock crystal*, is sometimes cut for gems. All other kinds of quartz may be colored. *Amethyst* is probably the best-known colored quartz. Other kinds are *false topaz*, or *citrine*, which

6

Elmer R. Nelson

Quartz glistens in the light like a jewel. This mineral is used to make high-quality lenses for many kinds of optical instruments.

is pale yellow; *rose quartz*, which is rose-colored; and *smoky quartz*, which is brown or black. Some types of quartz do not come in crystals but in a mass of fine grains. These include *chalcedony*, *flint*, and *jasper*.

Quartz is a useful mineral. Its most important uses are in the fields of radio, short-wave sound production, television, and radar. Quartz plays this important part because it possesses an unusual *property* (power) known as the *piezoelectric effect* (see PIEZOELECTRICITY). For this type of use a quartz crystal is cut into *plates* (slices). Each plate has two flat *faces* (surfaces). If a plate of crystal is put in some sort of a vise and the two faces are squeezed together, one face will develop a positive electric charge and the other face will develop a negative electric charge. A voltage will then be created across the crystal. Pierre Curie, the physicist, discovered this in the 1880's. The action will also take place in reverse. If a voltage is applied to the faces of the crystal, the crystal will contract and expand. This action, known as *vibration*, will take place as rapidly as the change in the polarity of the voltage.

The Quartz Crystal, or any crystal that has the piezoelectric effect, has a rate of speed at which it naturally vibrates. This rate is known as *frequency*. The natural frequency of vibration of a crystal depends upon its thickness. The thinner the crystal, the higher the frequency of vibration. Some crystals can be cut so thin that they vibrate millions of times each second. If a crystal were connected to a source of voltage, such as a generator, which would alternate in polarity at the same rate as the natural frequency of the crystal, the crystal would begin to contract and expand with tremendous force. At this point, the crystal and the generator would be in *resonance* (see SOUND [Resonance]).

The property of piezoelectric effect has made the quartz crystal an important part of the transmitting equipment of a radio. The quartz crystal is used in that part of the transmitter which produces the radio wave that is transmitted over the air. This part of the circuit is known as the *oscillator*. In the oscillator, the crystal is made to vibrate at its natural frequency. With the aid of a vacuum tube and other parts, this vibration is changed into a radio wave of the same frequency and is finally sent out over the air. In order to change the frequency of a transmitter, then, just change the crystal.

Quartz is also used in making sandpaper and grindstone. Quartz sands are used in the manufacture of glass and mortar. Rock quartz makes excellent lenses. Quartz will transmit ultraviolet rays that will not pass through any other kinds of glass. Many ultraviolet-ray tubes are made of quartz.   RICHARD M. PEARL

Related Articles in WORLD BOOK include:

Abrasive	Cairngorm	Flint	Onyx
Agate	Carnelian	Hardness	Opal
Amethyst	Chalcedony	Jasper	Sardonyx

QUARTZITE is a rock composed chiefly of quartz. The quartz is found both as individual crystals and as the cementing material holding the crystals together. Quartzite is a strong rock. When breaks occur in it, they cut across the quartz crystals as well as through the cementing material. Quartzite can be *sedimentary* or *metamorphic*. Sedimentary quartzite is formed when the cementing material is deposited between loose quartz crystals and then crystallizes. Metamorphic quartzite is formed when quartz sandstone recrystallizes under high pressure and temperature.   WILLIAM C. LUTH

QUASAR, *KWAY sahr*, is the farthest object in the universe that man has ever seen. Quasars are small *galaxies* (groups of stars) located billions of light-years from the earth. A typical quasar has about 10 million times as much *mass* (amount of material) as the sun. Its diameter may be as small as one light-week or as large as 12,000 light-years. A quasar radiates light and radio waves at a rate about 100,000 billion times as fast as the sun. The radiation is estimated to continue at this rate for at least 100,000 years. Astronomers cannot explain how quasars produce so much energy.

The first quasar to be discovered was identified first as a radio source and then as a light source. In 1959, astronomers at the Mullard Radio Astronomy Observatory in Cambridge, England, included it in a catalog of radio sources. In 1960, astronomers using the 200-inch optical telescope at Palomar Observatory in California found a faint, starlike object at the same spot in the sky. The object was named a *quasi-stellar* (somewhat starlike) *radio source*. The name was later shortened to *quasar*. By the mid-1960's, more than 200 quasars had been found.   HAROLD F. WEAVER

See also RED SHIFT.

QUASIMODO, *kwah SIH moh doh*, **SALVATORE** (1901-1968), an Italian poet, won the 1959 Nobel prize for literature. Until about 1942, Quasimodo belonged to the *hermetic* school, a group of poets who wrote in a difficult, personal style that seemed sealed off from everyday life. Largely because of World War II, Quasimodo turned to a style that dealt with the events of his time. Beginning with *Day after Day* (1947), his poetry became an accurate reflection of the grief and destruction that the war had brought to mankind.

Quasimodo was born in Modica, near Syracuse, Sicily. In 1918, he moved to northern Italy. He published his first poems in literary magazines in Florence. These verses were published as a collection called *Waters and Lands* (1930). Quasimodo also wrote many essays on literature, and translated the work of such writers as E. E. Cummings, Molière, Sappho, and William Shakespeare.   SERGIO PACIFICI

QUATERNARY PERIOD. See EARTH (table).

QUEBEC

QUEBEC (*kwee BECK*), or QUÉBEC (*kay BECK*), is the largest province of Canada. It has more people than any other province except Ontario. Over 80 per cent of the people have French ancestors, and most of this group speak only French. These French Canadians write the name of the province as *Québec*. Montreal is the largest city in Quebec, and in all Canada. The capital of the province is also named Quebec, but it is often called Quebec City.

The strong French influence in Quebec makes the province quite different from the rest of Canada. The people largely follow customs and traditions of France, rather than of Great Britain. For example, almost 90 per cent of the people of Quebec belong to the Roman Catholic Church. Most Quebec schools teach the Roman Catholic religion and use French as the language of instruction. The province's older buildings are French in architecture. Colorful French-style homes, mills, and outdoor ovens can still be seen in some parts of the countryside. Almost every village has a Catholic church, and crosses and shrines stand by the roadsides.

The early French settlers in the Quebec region were interested chiefly in the fur trade. They found the climate harsh, and settlement and economic development came slowly. Rapid economic growth during the 1900's has placed Quebec among the great industrial regions of North America. Today, manufacturing is the province's chief source of income. Thriving factories and mills operate on the power provided by hydroelectric plants on Quebec's many rivers. No other region of North America produces so much electric power.

Quebec produces about a third of all the goods manufactured in Canada. The Montreal area ranks second to the Toronto area among Canada's leading manufac-

Château Frontenac in Quebec City

WORLD BOOK photo

Percé Village and Harbor on the Gaspé Peninsula

W. R. Wilson, FPG

turing centers. Oil refineries there produce about a third of Canada's gasoline. Other important products of Quebec include clothing and processed foods and metals. Quebec leads all North American regions in the production of aluminum and paper.

The province's vast natural resources provide its industries with huge supplies of valuable raw materials. Quebec mines produce about 85 per cent of Canada's asbestos. The province also is a leading producer of copper, gold, and zinc. The far northern wilderness of Quebec, mostly unpopulated, has vast deposits of iron ore. Much of northern Quebec is too cold for trees. But forests cover about three-fifths of the province. They provide balsam firs, spruces, and other trees for Quebec's great logging and paper industries.

The St. Lawrence River Valley and the rolling Eastern Townships, south of the river, have rich soils. Quebec ranks among North America's leading producers of apples and dairy cattle and milk, and leads in the production of maple syrup.

Quebec's great St. Lawrence River is one of the most important waterways in North America. The word *Quebec* came from the Algonkian Indian word *kebec* (*the place where the river narrows*). The French explorer Samuel de Champlain heard the Indians use this word for a place on the St. Lawrence River. He founded Quebec City there in 1608. It was the first permanent settlement in Canada. The battlefield on which France lost Canada to Great Britain in 1759 lies within the city. Because of its rich historical background, Quebec is sometimes called the *Storied Province*.

For the relationship of Quebec to the other provinces of Canada, see CANADA; CANADA, GOVERNMENT OF; CANADA, HISTORY OF.

The contributors of this article are Michel Brunet, Professor of History at the University of Montreal; Pierre Dagenais, Professor at the University of Montreal; and Raymond Dubé, Editor-in-Chief of Le Soleil *of Quebec City.*

--- FACTS IN BRIEF ---

Capital: Quebec (Quebec City).

Government: *Parliament*—members of the Senate, 24; members of the House of Commons, 75. *Provincial Legislature*—members of the National Assembly, 108. *Counties*—74. *Voting Age*—18 years.

Area: 594,860 square miles (including 71,000 square miles of inland water), first in size among the provinces. *Greatest Distances*—(north-south) 1,222 miles; (east-west) 965 miles. *Coastline*—9,879 miles.

Elevation: *Highest*—Mount Jacques Cartier, 4,160 feet above sea level. *Lowest*—sea level.

Population: *1971 Census*—6,027,764, second among the provinces; density, 10 persons to the square mile; distribution, 78 per cent urban, 22 per cent rural.

Chief Products: *Agriculture*—beef cattle, chickens, eggs, hay, hogs, milk, oats, potatoes. *Fishing Industry*—cod, eels, herring, lobsters, redfish, scallops. *Forest Products*—fuelwood, logs and bolts, pulpwood. *Manufacturing*—chemicals and chemical products; clothing; electrical machinery; fabricated metal products; food and beverage products; paper and paper products; primary metals; transportation equipment. *Mining*—asbestos, copper, gold, iron ore, sand and gravel, stone, titanium dioxide, zinc.

Entered the Dominion: July 1, 1867; one of the four original provinces.

Motto: *Je me souviens* (I remember).

Montreal Harbor, a Chief Port of Entry to Canada
George Hunter, Publix

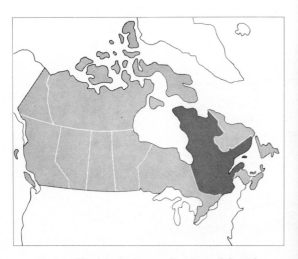

Quebec (Blue) Is the Largest Province of Canada

Lieutenant Governor of Quebec represents Queen Elizabeth in the province. He is appointed by the governor-general-in-council of Canada. The lieutenant governor's position, like that of the governor-general, is largely honorary.

Prime Minister of Quebec is the actual head of the provincial government. The heads of the other provinces are called *premiers*. Quebec, like the other provinces and Canada itself, has a *parliamentary* form of government. The prime minister is a member of the National Assembly, where he is the leader of the majority party. The voters elect the prime minister as they do the other members of the Assembly. The prime minister receives a salary of $22,000 a year, in addition to the allowances he gets as a member of the Assembly. For a list of all the prime ministers of Quebec, see the *History* section of this article.

The prime minister presides over the executive council, or cabinet. The council includes 28 other ministers chosen by the prime minister from among his party's members in the legislature. The ministers direct the 21 departments of the provincial government. The council resigns if it loses the support of a majority of the legislature.

Legislature. Quebec has a one-house legislature called the *National Assembly*. Each of its 108 members is elected from an electoral district. The members serve terms that may last up to five years. However, the lieutenant-governor, on the advice of the prime minister, may call for an election before the end of the five-year period. If he does, all Assembly members must run again for office. The legislature meets at least once a year, usually in November, and stays in session until it completes its business.

Quebec formerly had a two-house legislature. The lower house was called the *Legislative Assembly* and the upper house the *Legislative Council*. But in 1968, the Legislative Council was abolished, and the Legislative Assembly became the National Assembly.

Courts. The highest court in Quebec is the court of queen's bench. It consists of a chief justice and 11 *puisne* (associate) judges. The superior court has a chief justice, an associate chief justice, and about 60 associate judges. It meets in the major cities of nine judicial districts. The governor-general-in-council appoints all judges of the court of queen's bench and the superior court. The judges hold office until the age of 75. Lower courts of Quebec include courts of the sessions of the peace, provincial courts, municipal courts, and social-welfare courts. Provincial authorities appoint the judges of all these courts.

Quebec is the only province in which judges do not decide cases chiefly on the basis of *common law*. Under the common-law system, developed in England, rulings are determined by previous court decisions and the customs of the people. In Quebec, the French system is used. Judges decide cases chiefly on the basis of a *code* (set of rules). The judges can disregard the decisions of other judges in similar cases.

Local Government is based on Quebec's 74 counties, which include the areas of cantons, parishes, and townships. The mayors of these communities make up the county council. The members of the county council appoint its head, called a *warden*. All of Quebec's cities, towns, and villages have the mayor-council form of government.

Taxation. Taxes levied by Quebec account for about 65 per cent of the provincial government's income. Quebec is the only province that collects its own provincial personal income taxes, instead of having them collected by the federal government. The province also taxes corporation income and sales. The chief source of income is a gasoline tax. The provincial government receives about a fourth of its income from federal-provincial tax-sharing arrangements. Most of Quebec's other income comes from license and permit fees and from the sale of liquor. The sale of liquor is under government control.

Politics. Since 1867, the Quebec provincial government has been controlled by one of three parties—Conservative, Liberal, and Union Nationale. The Conservatives held power during the first 30 years, except for two brief Liberal administrations. In 1896, Wilfrid Laurier, a Liberal from Quebec, became the first French-Canadian prime minister of Canada. His victory helped bring the Liberals to power in Quebec in

Office of the Lt.-Governor, Province of Quebec

The New Official Mansion has been the home of Quebec's lieutenant-governor since 1966. Fire ruined the old mansion, and took the life of Paul Comtois, then lieutenant-governor of the province.

The Provincial Coat of Arms

The Provincial Flag

Symbols of Quebec. The provincial coat of arms combines the emblems of France, Great Britain, and Canada. The three *fleur-de-lis* represent the coat of arms of the French kings. The British lion stands across the center. The three maple leaves at the bottom symbolize Canada. The seal was adopted in 1939. The flag, adopted in 1948, bears a *fleur-de-lis* in each corner. The white cross stands for the cross planted on Quebec's soil by Jacques Cartier, who discovered the Gulf of St. Lawrence in 1534.

1897. The Liberals controlled the provincial government until 1936.

The Union Nationale party, led by Maurice Duplessis, came to power in 1936. Duplessis strongly opposed any federal control over Quebec, and fought hard to protect French-Canadian rights—economic, political, and social. This French-Canadian nationalism became very popular in Quebec. Duplessis led the government for a combined total of 18 years, longer than any other prime minister. The Liberal party, which also declared itself for freedom from federal control, returned to power in 1960. Since 1960, power has shifted between the Liberal and Union Nationale parties.

Several small political groups that favored Quebec's complete withdrawal from the federal union also developed during the 1960's. A small minority of nationalist extremists used bombings, robberies, and other violence to promote their aims. These groups make up only a tiny part of Quebec's population.

The Floral Emblem
White Garden Lily

The Parliament Buildings are in Quebec City, the capital since 1867. Earlier capitals were Quebec City (1608-1841), Kingston, Ont. (capital of combined Upper and Lower Canada, 1841-1844), Montreal (1844-1849), Quebec City and Toronto, Ont., alternately (1849-1865), and Ottawa, Ont. (1866-1867).
Office du Film du Quebec

The Provincial Tree
Sugar Maple

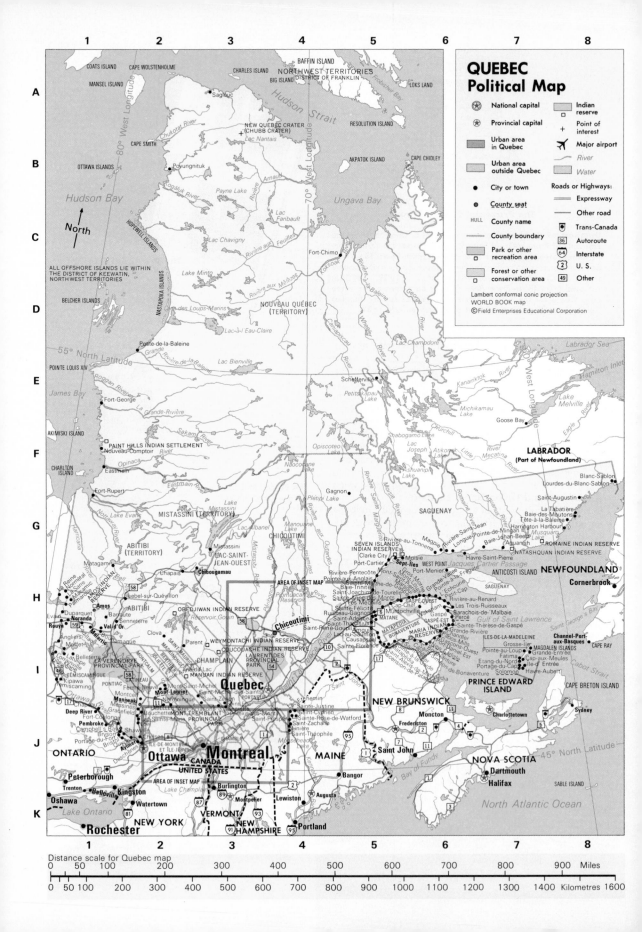

QUEBEC
Political Map

Legend:

- National capital
- Provincial capital
- Urban area in Quebec
- Urban area outside Quebec
- City or town
- County seat
- HULL County name
- County boundary
- Park or other recreation area
- Forest or other conservation area
- Indian reserve
- Point of interest
- Major airport
- River
- Water

Roads or Highways:
- Expressway
- Other road
- Trans-Canada
- 36 Autoroute
- 64 Interstate
- 2 U.S.
- 49 Other

Lambert conformal conic projection
WORLD BOOK map
© Field Enterprises Educational Corporation

Distance scale for Quebec map

0 50 100 200 300 400 500 600 700 800 900 Miles

0 50 100 200 300 400 500 600 700 800 900 1000 1100 1200 1300 1400 1500 1600 Kilometres

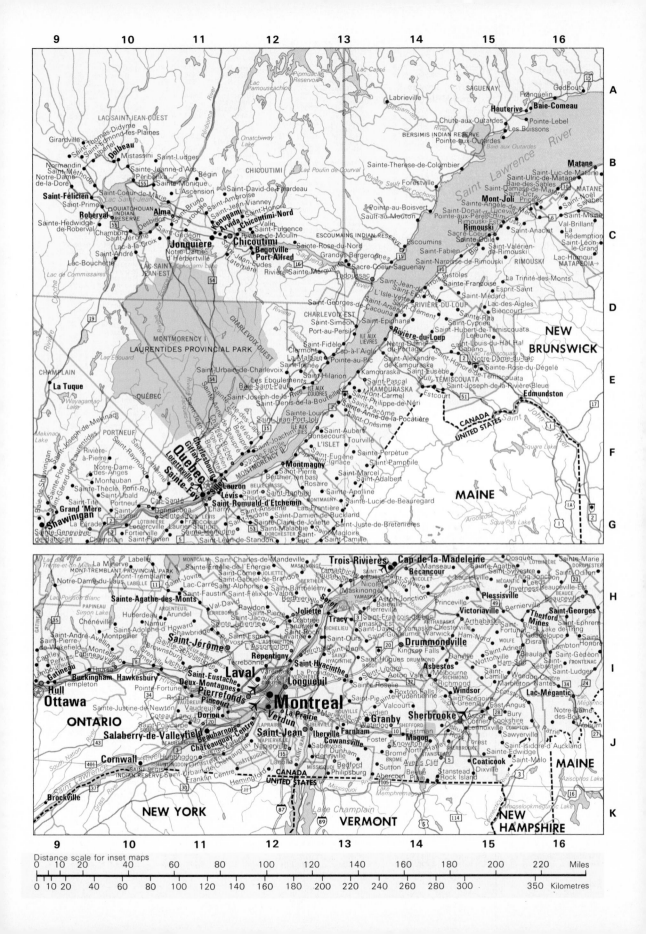

Population

6,027,764	..Census..	1971
5,780,845	.. " ..	1966
5,259,211	.. " ..	1961
4,055,681	.. " ..	1951
3,331,882	.. " ..	1941
2,874,662	.. " ..	1931
2,360,510	.. " ..	1921
2,005,776	.. " ..	1911
1,648,898	.. " ..	1901
1,488,535	.. " ..	1891
1,359,027	.. " ..	1881
1,191,516	.. " ..	1871

Metropolitan Areas

Chicoutimi-Jonquière ..131,924
Montreal ..2,724,889
Ottawa-Hull ..596,176
(447,736 in Ontario; 148,440 in Quebec)
Quebec ..476,316

Counties

Abitibi ....112,244..H 2
Argenteuil ..31,319..H 11
Arthabaska 51,524..H 14
Bagot ....23,591..I 13
Beauce ..63,960..H 16
Beauharnois 52,137..I 11
Bellechasse 23,517..G 12
Berthier ....27,288..I 2
Bonaventure 41,701..I 5
Brome ....15,311..J 14
Chambly ..231,590..J 3
Champlain 113,150..I 3
Charlevoix-Est ....16,780..D 13
Charlevoix-Ouest ..13,650..D 12
Château-guay ....53,737..J 12
Chicoutimi 163,348..G 4
Compton ..21,367..I 15
Deux-Montagnes ..52,369..I 11
Dorchester ..32,473..H 16
Drummond ..64,144..I 14
Frontenac ..27,293..I 16
Gaspé-Est ..41,727..H 6
Gaspé-Ouest 18,754..H 6
Gatineau ..55,729..I 2
Hull ....109,946..I 9
Huntingdon 15,358..J 11
Iberville ..20,400..J 13
Île-de-Montréal et Île-Jésus ..2,187,153..J 3
Îles-de-la-Madeleine 13,303..I 7
Joliette ..52,088..I 2
Kamouraska 26,264..E 14
Labelle ..30,582..J 2
Lac-Saint-Jean-Est ..45,220..C 10
Lac-Saint-Jean-Ouest ..57,074..H 3
Laprairie ..61,691..J 12
L'Assomption ..62,198..I 12
Lévis ..62,776..G 11
L'Islet ..23,187..F 13
Lotbinière ..27,373..H 16
Maskinongé 21,257..I 2
Matane ..30,261..H 5
Matapédia 26,856..I 5
Mégantic ..58,020..H 15
Missisquoi 33,953..J 13
Montcalm ..21,546..I 2
Montmagny 26,307..G 13
Mont-morency I 20,401..D 11
Montmorency II (Île-d'Orléans) ....5,435..F 12
Napierville ..12,067..J 12
Nicolet ..30,004..H 14
Papineau ..31,793..H 10
Pontiac ..19,570..I 1
Portneuf ..51,540..I 3
Québec ..423,162..E 10
Richelieu ..47,093..I 13
Richmond ..41,044..I 15
Rimouski ..64,263..C 16
Rivière-du-Loup ..39,488..D 14
Rouville ..31,759..J 13
Saguenay ..111,272..G 6
Saint-Hyacinthe 50,494..I 13
Saint-Jean ..45,892..J 12
Saint-Maurice 108,366..I 2
Shefford ..62,361..J 14
Sherbrooke 101,470..I 15
Soulanges ..11,449..J 10
Stanstead ..36,266..I 14
Témiscamingue ..54,656..I 1
Témiscouata 23,189..E 15
Terrebonne 139,945..H 11
Vaudreuil ..36,593..J 11
Verchères ..35,273..I 13
Wolfe ......16,197..I 15
Yamaska ..15,206..H 13

Cities, Towns, and Villages

Acton Vale ..4,572..I 14
Adamsville* ..495..J 3
Aguanish ..638..G 7
Albanel ....781..B 10
Alençon* ..1,140..J 3
Alma ..22,353.°C 11
Amos ..6,845.°H 1
Amqui ..3,777.°I 5
Ancienne-Lorette* ..8,282..I 3
Andréville* ..446..I 4
Ange-Gardien .521..J 13
Angers* ..887..J 2
Angliers ..403..I 1
Anjou* ..33,842..J 3
Annaville ..463..H 14
Anse-St.-Anne-des-Monts* ..817..H 5
Armagh* ..982..I 4
Arthabaska ..4,483.°H 15
Arvida ..18,433..C 11
Asbestos ..9,760..I 15
Ascot Corner .595..J 15
Ayer's Cliff ..874.°J 14
Aylmer ..7,160..J 2
Bagotville ..6,019..C 12
Baie-Comeau .12,108..A 16
Baie-de-Shawinigan .848..G 9
Baie-des-Sables ....625..B 16
Baie-d'Urfé* 3,886..J 3
Baie-St.-Paul ..4,156.°E 12
Baie-Trinité .731..H 5
Baieville ..507..H 14
Barraute ..1,291..H 1
Beaconsfield* ..19,328..J 3
Béarn* ..509..I 1
Beauceville* ..2,084.°H 16
Beauceville-Est ..2,186..H 16
Beauharnois 8,138.°J 11
Beaulac ..514..I 16
Beaulieu* ..651..I 4
Beauport* .14,739..I 3
Beaupré ..2,853..F 12
Bécancour ..8,163.°H 14
Bedford ..2,789.°J 13
Beebe Plain 1,236..K 14
Bélair* ..4,485..I 3
Belleterre ..614..I 1
Bellevue* ..534..I 3
Béloeil* ..12,248..J 3
Bernierville ..2,405..H 15
Berthier (en bas) ..548..F 12
Berthierville 4,076.°H 13
Betsiamites* 1,425..H 5
Bic ..1,154..C 15
Biencourt ..504..D 15
Black Lake .4,140..H 16
Blainville* ..9,641..J 3
Bois-des-Filion* ..4,060..J 3
Boisville* ..631..I 7
Bonaventure 1,155..I 6
Bonsecours ..854..F 13
Boucherville* ....20,000..J 3
Bouchette ..425..J 2
Bourlamaque 4,122..I 1
Bromont* ..1,088..J 3
Brompton-ville* ..2,766..J 3
Brossard* ..23,421..J 3
Brownsburg 3,387..I 11
Bryson ..815..J 1
Buckingham 7,267..I 9
Bugeaud* ..583..I 6
Cabano ..3,055..E 15
Cadillac ..1,105..H 1
Calumet ..743..I 11
Campbell's Bay ..1,192.°J 1
Candiac* ..5,189..J 3
Cap-à-l'Aigle .684..E 13
Cap-aux-Meules ..836..I 7
Cap-Chat ..3,855..H 5
Cap-Chat-Est* ..1,323..H 5
Cap-de-la-Madeleine 31,120..H 14
Cap-St.-Ignace ..1,301..F 12
Cap-Santé ..598.°G 10
Caplan ..412..I 6
Carignan* ..3,333..J 3
Carillon* ..402..J 2
Carleton ..614..I 6
Carleton-Centre ..1,016..I 5
Causapscal ..2,974..I 5
Chambly* ..11,466..J 3
Chambord ..1,103..C 10
Champlain ..633..G 10
Chandler ..3,842..I 6
Chapais ..2,906..H 2
Chapeau ..516..J 1
Charette ..624..J 3
Charlemagne*4,174..J 3
Charlesbourg33,484..F 11
Charny ..5,192..G 11
Château-guay ..15,759..J 3
Châteauguay-Centre ..17,897..J 12
Châteauguay Heights* ..1,238..J 12
Château-Richer ..3,099.°F 12
Chénéville ..725..H 10
Chibougamau 9,741..H 3
Chicoutimi .32,990.°I 4
Chicoutimi-Nord ..14,058..C 12
Chute-aux-Outardes ..1,934..B 15
Clarke City ..713..H 5
Clermont ..3,386..E 13
Coaticook ..6,566..I 15
Coleraine* ..1,171..J 4
Como-Est* ..1,025..J 2
Compton* ..498..J 3
Contrecoeur* 2,688..J 3
Cookshire ..1,490.°I 15
Coteau-du-Lac* ..838..J 11
Coteau-Landing ..850.°J 11
Côte-St.-Luc* ..24,358..J 3
Courcelles* ..707..J 4
Courville* ..6,217..I 4
Cowansville 11,906..J 13
Crabtree ..1,683..H 12
Danville ..2,589..I 15
Daveluyville ..1,002..J 3
Deauville ..757..J 14
Dégelis* ..3,049..I 1
Delson* ..2,930..J 3
Desbiens* ..1,831..C 10
Deschaillons-sur-St.-Laurent* ..1,174..I 3
Descham-bault* ..994..I 3
Deschênes* ..1,802..J 2
Deux-Montagnes 8,598..I 12
Disraëli ..3,394..I 16
Dixville ..545..K 15
Dolbeau ..7,656..B 10
Dollard-des-Ormeaux* 25,284..J 3
Donnacona ..5,846..G 10
Dorion ..6,195..J 11
Dorval* ..20,471..J 3
Dosquet* ..481..H 15
Douville* ..3,288..J 3
Drummond-ville ..31,537.°I 14
Drummond-ville-Ouest* ..2,682..J 3
Drummond-ville-Sud* ..9,003..J 3
Duberger* ..8,489..I 4
Dunham ..488..J 13
Duparquet* ..771..H 1
Durham-Sud* ..464..J 3
East Angus .4,747..I 15
East Broughton* 1,250..J 4
East Broughton Station* ..1,118..J 4
Eastman ..527..J 14
Escoumins ..2,241..C 14
Estcourt ..652..E 14
Étang-du-Nord 891..I 7
Évain ..609..H 1
Farnham ..6,462..J 13
Fatima ..1,060..I 7
Ferme-Neuve ..2,003..I 2
Forestville ..1,617..B 14
Fort-Chimo ..666..C 5
Fort-Coulonge ..1,785..J 1
Fort-George ..1,300..E 1
Fort-Rupert ..542..J 1
Fortierville ..521..G 10
Frampton* ..634..J 4
Francoeur ..1,193..G 11
Franquelin ..499..A 16
Gagnon ..3,773..G 5
Gascons-Ouest 542..I 6
Gaspé ..16,842..H 6
Gatineau ..22,356..I 9
Gethsémani* ..522..G 7
Giffard ..13,087..F 11
Girardville ..1,068..B 9
Godbout ..671..A 16
Gracefield ..1,049..J 2
Granby ..34,385..J 13
Grande-Entrée 772..I 7
Grande-Rivière ..1,216..H 6
Grande-Vallée 830..H 6
Grandes-Bergeronnes 804..C 14
Grandes-Piles 540..J 3
Grand'Mère 17,144..G 9
Greenfield Park* ..15,277..J 3
Grenville ..1,464..I 11
Gros-Morne ..473..H 6
Guigues* ..596..I 1
Ham-Nord ..501..I 15
Ham-Sud ..58.°I 15
Hampstead* .7,035..J 3
Harrington Harbour ..402..G 8
Hauterive .13,204..A 16
Havre-Aubert .459..I 7
Havre-St.-Pierre ..2,687..G 6
Hébertville-Station* ..1,162..I 3
Hemingford ..802..J 12
Henryville ..665..J 13
Hérouxville* ..536..J 3
Howick* ..575..J 3
Huberdeau ..505..H 11
Hudson* ..4,320..J 2
Hudson Heights* ..1,543..J 2
Hull ..62,842.°I 9
Huntingdon ..3,069.°J 11
Iberville ..9,300.°J 13
Île-Perrot* ..4,043..J 3
Inverness ..359.°H 15
Jacola* ..727..I 1
Jacques-Cartier* ..591..J 3
Joliette ..19,497.°H 12
Jonquière ..28,080..C 11
Jouvence* ..1,236..I 3
Kamouraska ..505..E 13
Kénogami .10,955..C 11
Kingsey Falls .562..I 14
Kirkland* ..2,920..J 3
Labelle ..1,492..H 10
Labrieville ..421..A 14
Lac-à-la-Croix ..586..C 11
Lac-à-la-Tortue* ..668..J 3
Lac-au-Saumon ..1,307..I 5
Lac-aux-Sables* ..882..I 3
Lac-Bouchette 944..C 10
Lac-Brome* .4,071..J 3
Lac-Carré ..660..H 11
Lac-des-Aigles 599..D 15
Lac-des-Écorces* ..595..I 2
Lac-Etchemin2,789..J 4
Lac-Mégantic ..6,756.°I 16
Lachine* ..44,345..J 3
Lachute ..11,789.°I 11
Lacolle ..1,226..J 12
Lafontaine* ..2,976..J 2
La Guadeloupe 1,923..I 16
La Malbaie .4,032.°E 13
Lambton ..766..I 16
L'Ange-Gardien ..1,483..F 11
L'Annonciation ..2,148..J 2
Lanoraie ..1,157..H 13
La Patrie ..446..I 16
La Pérade ..1,125..G 10
La Prairie ..8,310.°J 12
La Providence 4,671..I 13
La Reine ..430..H 1
Larouche ..577..C 11
LaSalle* ..72,916..J 3
La Sarre ..5,095..H 1
L'Ascension ..1,123..B 11
L'Ascension-de-Patapédia ..471..I 5
L'Assomption 4,885.°I 12
La Station-du-Coteau* ..883..J 2
La Tabatière ..412..G 8
Laterrière ..581..C 11
La Tuque .13,071..E 9
Laurentides* .1,745..J 3
Laurier-Station ..945..G 11
Laurierville ..922..H 15
Lauzon .12,744..G 11
Laval* ..704..I 4
Laval 228,101..I 12
Lavaltrie ..1,265..I 13
La Vernière* ..605..I 7
Lawrence-ville* ..549..J 3
Lebel-sur-Quévillon ..2,935..H 2
L'Échourie ..488..H 6
Leclercville ..417..G 10
Leeds ..440..H 16
LeMoyne* ..8,162..J 3
Lennoxville ..3,867..I 15
L'Épiphanie 2,757..J 3
Léry* ..2,243..J 3
Les Becquets* .493..J 3
Les Caps* ..684..I 7
Les Cèdres* ..434..J 3
Les Chenaux* ..565..I 4
Les Éboulements 573..E 13
Les Hauteurs-de-Rimouski* 576..I 5
Les Méchins .708..H 5
Les Saules* .6,242..I 3
Les Trois-Ruisseaux ..600..H 6
Lévis ..16,566..G 11
Limbour ..605..I 9
Limière* ..1,231..J 4
L'Islet* ..1,187..I 4
L'Islet-sur-Mer* ..883..I 4
L'Isletville ..1,234..I 4
L'Isle-Verte ..1,356..D 14
Longue-Pointe-de-Mingan ..420..G 6
Longueuil ..97,483.°I 12
Loretteville 11,646.°G 11
Lorraine* ..3,134..J 3
Lorrainville ..906..I 1
Lotbinière ..543..J 3
Louiseville ..4,015.°H 13
Lourdes-du-Blanc-Sablon 543..F 8
Luceville ..1,410..C 15
Lyster* ..871..J 3
Macamic ..1,675..H 1
Magog ..13,280..I 14
Malartic ..5,357..H 1
Manic 5* ..1,541..H 5
Maniwaki ..6,457.°J 2
Manseau ..742..H 15
Maple Grove* ..1,705..J 3
Marbleton ..620..I 15
Marieville ..4,521..I 13
Marsoui ..601..H 6
Mascouche* ..8,783..J 3
Maskinongé ..995..H 13
Masson* ..2,348..J 2
Massueville* ..631..J 3
Matagami ..2,350..H 1
Matane ..11,826.°B 16
Matapédia ..515..I 5
McMaster-ville* ..2,502..J 3
Melbourne ..457..I 14
Melocheville* ..1,592..J 3
Mercier* ..4,007..J 3
Micoua* ..1,064..H 5
Millerand* ..501..I 7
Mistassini ..3,607..B 10
Mistassini ..1,048..G 3
Moisie ..538..H 5
Mont-Albert* ..1,030..H 5
Mont-Carmel ..857..E 13
Mont-Joli ..6,707..C 16
Mont-Laurier ..8,196.°I 2
Mont-Louis ..512..H 6
Mont-Rolland* ..1,416..J 2
Mont-Royal* .21,470..J 3
Mont-St.-Hilaire ..5,966..J 3
Mont-St.-Michel ..477..J 2
Mont-St.-Pierre ..364..H 6
Montebello ..1,289..I 10
Montmagny 12,378.°F 12
Mont-morency* ..4,947..I 3
Montreal 1,197,996..J 3
Montréal-Est* ..5,048..J 3
Montréal-Nord* ..88,030..J 3
Montréal-Ouest* ..6,364..J 3
Morin Heights* 599..J 2
Murdochville 2,858..H 6
Napierville ..1,993.°J 12
Nazareth* ..1,965..I 5
Neuville* ..797..J 3
New Carlisle ..1,213.°I 6
New Richmond* 3,942..I 6
Newport* ..589..H 6
Newport West* 572..H 6
Nicolet ..4,716..H 14
Nitro* ..176..J 2
Nominingue ..702..J 2
Noranda ..10,670..H 1
Normandin ..1,794..B 9
Normétal ..2,110..H 1
North Hatley .726..J 15
Notre-Dame-de-la-Doré ..1,208..B 9
Notre-Dame-de-Lorette ..5,691..I 3
Notre-Dame-des-Agnes ..800..F 10
Notre-Dame-des-Lauren-tides* ..5,087..I 4
Notre-Dame-d'Hébert-ville ..1,516..C 11
Notre-Dame-du-Bon-Conseil* ..1,057..J 3
Notre-Dame-du-Lac ..2,116.°E 15
Notre-Dame-du-Laus ..559..H 9
Notre-Dame-du-Nord* ..606..I 1
Omerville* ..1,109..J 3
Ormstown ..1,517..J 11
Orsainville* 12,561..I 4
Otter Lake* ..663..J 2

Otterburn Park* ....3,506..J 3
Ouiatchouan* 1,464..I 3
Outremont ..28,402..J 3
Pabos-Mills ...679..H 6
Palmarolle .....450..H I
Papineauville 1,407.°I 10
Parent ....452..J 2
Percé .....5,598.°H 6
Perkins .....587..J 9
Petit-Cap ...1,028..H 6
Philipsburg ....388..K13
Pierrefonds 33,046.°I 12
Pierreville .1,456..H13
Pincourt ...5,903..J 11
Plaisance* ....589..J 2
Plessisville .7,224..H15
Pointe-au-Pic .....1,228..E 13
Pointe-aux-Outardes ..836..B 15
Pointe-aux-Trembles 35,521..J 3
Pointe-Basse* 511..I 7
Pointe-Calumet* .2,226..J 2
Pointe-Claire* ..27,310..J 3
Pointe-des-Cascades* ..683..J 3
Pointe-du-Lac* ..1,329..J 3
Pointe-Gatineau* 15,607..J 2
Pointe-Lebel .....751..A 16
Pont-Rouge .3,226..G 11
Port-Alfred .9,191..C 12
Port-Cartier .3,738..H 5
Port-Menier ..463..H 6
Portage-du-Cap .....733..I 7
Portage-du-Fort .....431..J I
Portneuf ...1,300..G 10
Portneuf-Station* .1,386..I 3
Poste-de-la-Baleine ...849..E 2
Povungnituk ..602..B 2
Préville .....1,299..J 3
Price ......2,752..C 16
Princeville .3,827..H15
Proulxville* ..689..J 3
Quebec ...182,502..J 3
Quyon ......874..J 2
Rawdon ....2,752..H12
Repentigny .19,441..I 12
Restigouche* 1,105..I 5
Richelieu ..1,762..J 3
Richmond ..4,275.°I 14
Rigaud ....2,145..I 11
Rimouski ..26,546.°C 15
Rimouski-Est 2,069..C 15
Ripon* ......588..J 2
Riviera ....3,552..J 2
Rivière-à-Pierre .....788..F 10
Rivière-au-Renard ..1,833..H 6
Rivière-au-Tonnerre ..646..G 6
Rivière-Boisclair* ..586..J 3
Rivière-du-Loup ...12,423.°D 14
Rivière-du-Moulin ..4,341..C 12
Rivière-Pentecôte ..647..H 5
Robertsonville* ...1,293..J 4
Roberval ..8,286.°C 10
Rock Island .1,346..K14
Rosaire ....463..G 13
Rosemère* .6,727..J 3
Rougemont* ..866..J 3
Rouyn ....17,804..H I
Roxboro* ..7,654..J 3
Roxton Falls 1,139..I 14
Sacré-Coeur .1,923..C 15
Sacré-Coeur-Saguenay .1,258..C 13
St.-Adalbert ..483..F 13
St.-Adelphe* ..721..I 3
St.-Adolphe-d'Howard ..416..H11
St.-Adrien ...407..I 15
St.-Agapitville* ...1,493..I 3
St.-Alban* ...765..I 3
St.-Alexandre-de-Kamouraska 408..E 14
St.-Alexis-de-Matapédia ..455..I 5
St.-Alexis-des-Monts ..2,050..J 3
St.-Amable* ..959..J 3
St.-Ambroise 1,627..C 11
St.-Ambroise-de-Kildare* ..619..J 3
St.-Anaclet ..645..C 15

St.-André .....602..C 10
St.-André-Avellin ..1,090..I 10
St.-André-Est* .....1,160..J 2
St.-Anselme .1,412..G 12
St.-Antoine* .5,828..J 2
St.-Arsène ....563..D 14
St.-Aubert ....752..F 13
St.-Barnabé-Nord* ....526..J 3
St.-Barthélémy ....636..H 13
St.-Basile-le-Grand* ..4,383..J 3
St.-Basile-Sud* ....1,692..I 3
St.-Benjamin* 554..J 4
St.-Benoît-Labre* ....539..J 4
St.-Bernard* ..577..J 4
St.-Boniface-de-Shawinigan* ....2,586..I 3
St.-Bruno ..1,282..C 11
St.-Bruno-de-Montarville* ...15,822..J 3
St.-Calixte-de-Kilkenny* ..583..J 3
St.-Camille ....689..G 13
St.-Canut* ....750..J 2
St.-Casimir .1,227..G 10
St.-Casimir-Est* .....466..I 3
St.-Césaire* .2,273..J 3
St.-Charles ...968..G 12
St.-Charles-de-Drummond* ..2,232..J 3
St.-Charles-de-Mandeville ....919..H13
St.-Chrysostome* ..1,073..J 3
St.-Coeur-de-Marie .1,225..C 11
St.-Côme .....981..H12
St.-Constant 3,444..J 3
St.-Cyprien ...445..J 4
St.-Cyprien ...639..D 15
St.-Cyrille* .1,129..J 4
St.-Cyrille-de-L'Islet ..565..I 4
St.-Damase .1,119..J 3
St.-Damien-de-Buckland ....1,436..G 12
St.-David-de-Falardeau ..576..B 11
St.-David-de-l'Auberivière* ...3,808..J 4
St.-David-d'Yamaska ..478..I 13
St.-Denis ....898..I 13
St.-Dominique* ..1,732..J 3
St.-Donat-de-Montcalm* 1,525..H 11
St.-Donat-de-Rimouski ..436..C 16
St.-Édouard-de-Maskinongé* ...457..H13
St.-Éleuthère* ...1,035..I 4
St.-Élie .....629..J 3
St.-Elzéar* ...519..I I
St.-Émile ...2,636..I 4
St.-Éphrem-de-Tring ..954..H16
St.-Épiphane ..653..D 14
St.-Esprit ...862..I 12
St.-Étienne-des-Grès* ..719..J 3
St.-Eugène ....666..F 13
St.-Eustache 9,464..I 12
St.-Fabien ..1,497..C 15
St.-Félicien .4,955..C 10
St.-Félix-de-Valois ...1,455..H 12
St.-Féréol ....629..F 12
St.-Fidèle ....525..E 13
St.-Flavien ...653..G 11
St.-François-du-Lac ...987.°H13
St.-Frédéric* ..437..J 4
St.-Fulgence ..994..C 12
St.-Gabriel-de-Brandon ..3,362..H 12
St.-Gabriel-de-Kamouraska* ...551..I 4
St.-Gédéon ...884..C 11
St.-Gédéon .1,180..I 16
St.-Georges* 2,036..I 3
St.-Georges .7,570..H16

St.-Georges-de-Cacouna ....991..D 14
St.-Georges-Ouest* ..6,002..J 4
St.-Gérard* ..629..J 3
St.-Germain-de-Grantham* 1,109..I 14
St.-Gervais* ..556..I 4
St.-Gilles* ....695..I 3
St.-Grégoire* ..666..J 3
St.-Grégoire-de-Greenlay ....694..I 15
St.-Guillaume 803..I 13
St.-Henri* ..1,161..I 4
St.-Hilarion ..449..E 12
St.-Honoré .1,053..C 12
St.-Honoré .1,040..I 16
St.-Honoré-de-Témiscouata ....506..E 14
St.-Hubert 36,789..J 3
St.-Hubert-de-Témiscouata ....744..D 14
St.-Hugues ..1,463..I 13
St.-Hyacinthe* .24,192.°I 13
St.-Isidore ...738..G 11
St.-Jacques .1,973..H 12
St.-Janvier* 2,477..J 2
St.-Jean ...32,484.°J 13
St.-Jean-Baptiste-Rouville* ..751..J 3
St.-Jean-Chrysostome* ..1,911..I 4
St.-Jean-de-Boischatel 1,678..F 11
St.-Jean-de-Dieu ...1,175..D 14
St.-Jean-de-Matha* ..892..J 3
St.-Jean-Eudes ...2,721..C 11
St.-Jean-Port-Joli ..1,741.°F 13
St.-Jean-Vianney ...177..C 11
St.-Jérôme ..1,931..C 10
St.-Jérôme .26,131.°I 11
St.-Joachim ..891..F 12
St.-Joachim-de-Tourelle ...931..H 5
St.-Joseph* .4,944..J 3
St.-Joseph-de-Beauce* ..2,886..J 4
St.-Joseph-de-la-Rivière-Bleue* ..1,411..E 14
St.-Joseph-de-Sorel* ..3,279..J 3
St.-Jovite ..2,844..H11
St.-Jude* ....500..J 3
St.-Juste-de-Bretenières .418..G 13
St.-Lambert* ...18,590..J 3
St.-Lambert-de-Lévis* ..619..I 4
St.-Laurent*63,067..J 3
St.-Laurent-d'Orléans* ..597..I 4
St.-Lazare* ...591..I 4
St.-Lazare-de-Vaudreuil* ..607..J 2
St.-Léon-de-Standon ..457..G 12
St.-Léon-le-Grand ....799..C 16
St.-Léonard* ..52,013..J 3
St.-Léonard-d'Aston* ..995..J 3
St.-Léonard-de-Portneuf* ....542..I 3
St.-Liboire ...667.°I 13
St.-Louis-de-Champlain* .635..J 3
St.-Louis-du-Ha! Ha! ...655..E 15
St.-Luc* ...4,852..J 3
St.-Ludger ...268..B 10
St.-Magloire ..582..J 3
St.-Marc* ....539..J 3
St.-Marc-des-Carrières* 2,664..I 3
St.-Martin-de-Tours* ...1,447..J 4
St.-Méthode-de-Frontenac ..736..J 4
St.-Michel-de-Bellechasse* 903..I 4
St.-Michel-des-Saints 1,771..I 3
St.-Moïse .....466..C 16
St.-Narcisse ..746..I 3
St.-Narcisse-de-Rimouski 536..C 15
St.-Nazaire* ..877..G 4
St.-Nicéphore 961..J 3
St.-Nicolas* .1,969..I 4
St.-Noël .....904..C 15

St.-Odilon ....636..H 16
St.-Omer ....664..I 5
St.-Ours .....843..I 13
St.-Pacôme .1,171..E 13
St.-Pamphile 3,553..F 13
St.-Pascal ..2,491.°E 13
St.-Patrice-de-Beaurivage* ..466..J 4
St.-Paul* ....574..J 3
St.-Paul-du-Buton* ...850..J 4
St.-Paul-l'Ermite* .3,175..J 3
St.-Paulin* ...808..J 3
St.-Philippe-de-Néri ...683..E 13
St.-Pie .....1,695..I 13
St.-Pierre* ..6,762..J 3
St.-Polycarpe ..528..J 11
St.-Prime ..2,327..C 10
St.-Prosper .1,525..J 4
St.-Raphaël 1,220.°G 12
St.-Raymond 4,000..F 10
St.-Rédempteur* ...1,655..J 4
St.-Rémi .....2,297..J 3
St.-Roch .....614..I 13
St.-Roch-de-l'Achigan* ..729..J 3
St.-Romain* ..903..J 4
St.-Romuald-d'Etchemin 8,439.°G 11
St.-Samuel-de-Gayhurst* ..466..I 16
St.-Sauveur-des-Monts* ..1,827..J 3
St.-Sébastien ..419..I 16
St.-Siméon .1,184..D 13
St.-Stanislas* ..562..J 3
St.-Sylvestre ..465..H 16
St.-Théophile ..469..J 4
St.-Thomas-de-Joliette* ...614..J 3
St.-Timothée* ...1,572..J 2
St.-Tite ....3,136..G 9
St.-Tite-des-Caps ....1,190..F 12
St.-Ubald ....811..G 10
St.-Ulric-de-Matane ...920..B 16
St.-Urbain-de-Charlevoix 1,014..E 12
St.-Vallier* ...571..I 4
St.-Victor* .1,014..J 4
St.-Wenceslas* 410..I 4
St.-Zacharie 1,394..J 4
St.-Zénon ....503..J 3
St.-Zotique* .1,230..J 2
Ste.-Adélaïde-de-Pabos* ..782..I 6
Ste.-Adèle* .2,675..J 2
Ste.-Agathe-des-Monts 5,525..H 11
Ste.-Agathe-Sud* ....963..J 2
Ste.-Angèle-de-Mérici ..693..C 16
Ste.-Anne-de-Beaupré* .1,778..F 12
Ste.-Anne-de-Bellevue* .4,932..J 3
Ste.-Anne-de-la-Pocatière ..4,246..E 13
Ste.-Anne-des-Monts .5,577.°H 5
Ste.-Anne-des-Plaines* .1,389..J 3
Ste.-Anne-du-Lac ...382..I 2
Ste.-Aurélie* ..559..J 4
Ste.-Catherine 677..F 10
Ste.-Claire-de-Joliette 1,408..G 12
Ste.-Croix ..1,559.°G 10
Ste.-Émélie-de-l'Énergie ..697..H 12
Ste.-Famille 1,016.°F 12
Ste.-Félicité ..814..H 5
Ste.-Flore ....679..G 9
Ste.-Foy ...67,834..G 11
Ste.-Françoise ..399..D 14
Ste.-Geneviève* ..2,847..J 3
Ste.-Geneviève-de-Batiscan ..769.°G 10
Ste.-Hedwidge-de-Roberval 502..C 10
Ste.-Hélène-de-Kamouraska* ...567..I 4
Ste.-Hénédine 640.°G 12
Ste.-Jeanne-d'Arc ....926..B 10
Ste.-Julie* ..2,552..J 3
Ste.-Julienne .858.°H 12
Ste.-Justine ..932..J 4

Ste.-Louise ...510..F 13
Ste.-Madeleine* ...1,106..J 3
Ste.-Marie ..4,308..H 16
Ste.-Marthe-de-Gaspé ..434..H 6
Ste.-Martine 1,786.°J 12
Ste.-Mélanie* ..590..J 3
Ste.-Monique ..727..B 10
Ste.-Perpétue .760..F 13
Ste.-Pudentienne ....799..J 14
Ste.-Rosalie .2,202..I 13
Ste.-Rose-de-Watford .403..J 4
Ste.-Rose-du-Dégelé .2,067..E 15
Ste.-Scholastique ..14,778.°I 11
Ste.-Thècle .1,723..G 9
Ste.-Thérèse* ...17,161..J 3
Ste.-Thérèse-de-Gaspé ..551..H 6
Ste.-Thérèse-Ouest* ..7,282..J 3
Salaberry-de-Valleyfield ...29,776..J 11
Sandy Beach Centre* ...531..H 6
Sault-au-Mouton ...954..C 14
Sawyerville ..851..J 15
Sayabec ...1,799..C 16
Schefferville .3,277..E 5
Scotstown ...918..J 16
Scott-Jonction* ..658..I 4
Senneterre ..4,305..H I
Senneville* .1,418..J 3
Sept-Îles ..24,289..H 5
Shawbridge ..963..I 11
Shawinigan 27,502..G 9
Shawinigan-Sud* ...11,452..J 3
Shawville ..1,746..J 2
Sherbrooke .80,457.°J 15
Sillery ....13,950..G 11
Solomon .....462.°I 7
Sorel ....19,371.°H 13
Soulanges* ...446..J 2
Squatec* ..1,017..I 4
Stanstead ..1,195..K 14
Sullivan* ..1,108..H I
Sully ....807..E 14
Sutton ....1,694..J 14
Tadoussac ..1,004.°D 13
Temiscaming 2,430..I I
Templeton ..3,696..I 9
Terrasse-Vaudreuil* 1,555..J 2
Terrebonne ..9,208..I 12
Terrebonne-Heights* .1,540..J 3
Thetford Mines ...21,662..H 16
Thurso ....3,243..I 10
Tingwick* ....580..J 3
Touraine* ..9,649..J 2
Tourville ....928..F 13
Tracy .....11,845..H 13
Tring-Jonction ..1,286..H 16
Trois-Pistoles ..4,654..D 14
Trois-Rivières .55,240..H 14
Trois-Rivières-Ouest* ..8,071..J 3
Upton* .....814..J 3
Val-Barrette* ...527..J 2
Val-Brillant ..698..C 16
Val-David .1,625..H 11
Val-d'Or ..17,419..H I
Val-St.-Michel* ..2,063..I 4
Valcourt ...2,505..J 14
Vallée-Jonction* .1,276..J 4
Vanier* ....9,716..J 4
Varennes ..2,368..I 12
Vaudreuil ..3,831.°J 11
Verchères .1,843.°I 12
Verdun ...74,520..J 12
Victoriaville* ...22,088..H 15
Ville-Marie .1,995.°I I
Villeneuve* .4,044..I 4
Wakeham ...470..H 6
Warwick ...2,841..I 15
Waterloo ..4,949.°J 14
Waterville .1,435..J 3
Weedon-Centre* ..1,429..I 15
Westmount 23,570..J 3
Wickham* ...520..J 3
Windsor ...6,047..I 15
Woburn .....498..J 16
Wottonville* ..682..I 15
Yamachiche .1,135.°H 13

*Does not appear on map; key shows general location.
°County seat

Source: Latest census figures (1971 census where available or 1966 census).

QUEBEC / People

The 1971 Canadian census reported that Quebec had 6,027,764 persons. The population had increased 4 per cent over the 1966 figure of 5,780,845.

Seventy-eight per cent of the people of Quebec live in cities and towns. About 45 per cent live in the metropolitan area of Montreal. Quebec has three other Census Metropolitan Areas as defined by Statistics Canada. They are Chicoutimi-Jonquière, Ottawa-Hull, and Quebec. For the population of these metropolitan areas, see the *Index* to the political map of Quebec.

Montreal, the largest city in Quebec, is also the largest city in Canada. It ranks second in population only to Paris among French-speaking cities in the world. Twelve other cities in Quebec have populations of over 50,000. They are, in order of size, Laval, Quebec City, Longueuil, Montréal-Nord, Sherbrooke, Verdun, La Salle, Ste.-Foy, St.-Laurent, Hull, Trois-Rivières, and St.-Léonard. See the separate articles on the cities of Quebec listed in the *Related Articles* at the end of this article.

Most of the people of Quebec are French Canadians. Nearly all are descendants of the French settlers who came to the Quebec region during the 1600's and 1700's. The emigration from France stopped almost completely after the French colony came under British rule in 1763. By that time, the colonists had developed a strong sense of their own nationality. They considered themselves *Canadiens* (French Canadians), not Frenchmen. Not many British settlers arrived until the early 1800's. They soon controlled the colony economically as well as politically. But the French Canadians lived apart and continued to follow their own ways of life and traditions.

Today, French Canadians make up 81 per cent of Quebec's population. People of English, Irish, or Scottish descent form 11 per cent. French is the only tongue spoken by two-thirds of the people. A fourth of the population speaks both French and English. Most of the rest speak only English.

Ninety-three per cent of Quebec's population was born in Canada. The others came from France, Great Britain, Italy, the United States, and other countries.

Roman Catholics make up 88 per cent of the province's population. Other large religious groups include members of the Anglican Church of Canada, the United Church of Canada, and the Jewish faith.

Corpus Christi Religious Festival is celebrated by Quebec children. Girls in first communion dresses and boys wearing satin bandoliers parade to a temporary altar called a *reposoir.* Almost 9 of every 10 Quebec residents are Roman Catholics.

POPULATION

This map shows the *population density* of Quebec, and how it varies in different parts of the province. Population density means the average number of persons who live on each square mile.

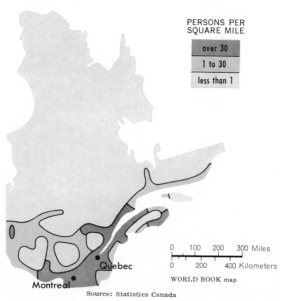

PERSONS PER
SQUARE MILE

over 30

1 to 30

less than 1

Quebec

Montreal

| 0 | 100 | 200 | 300 Miles |
| 0 | 200 | | 400 Kilometers |

WORLD BOOK map

Source: Statistics Canada

Crowds of Christmas Shoppers hurry along a main street in downtown Montreal. About 4 of every 10 persons in Quebec live in or near Montreal. The stores offer merchandise brought into the city's port by ships from many parts of the world.

Schools. During the 1600's, Roman Catholic priests and missionaries from France established the first schools in the Quebec region. They taught Indian and white children. Priests provided the only schooling for many years. During that period, nearly all the settlers were French Roman Catholics.

British colonists began arriving during the late 1700's. They were Protestants, and wanted their own schools. In 1801, the provincial legislature set up a system of free public education under Protestant control. But the French Canadians blocked this system by refusing to organize schools under the new law. In 1846, the colony established two separate school systems under church control, one for Roman Catholics and the other for Protestants.

The separate school systems, headed by a superintendent of education appointed by the lieutenant-governor, lasted until 1964. That year, the provincial government combined the two systems. The province created the cabinet post of minister of education, and gave him control of the school program. The minister is advised on educational policies by the superior council of education. This council of 24 members must include at least 16 Roman Catholics, 4 Protestants, and 1 member of neither faith. Roman Catholic and Protestant committees supervise religious teaching.

Most Roman Catholic schools teach in French, and most Protestant schools use English. Quebec also has nonreligious schools. Quebec law requires children between 6 and 15 to attend school. For the number of students and teachers in Quebec, see EDUCATION (table).

Libraries. French Canadians and British Canadians established Canada's first public library in 1779, in Quebec City. The province now has more than 250 public libraries. Laval University, McGill University, and the University of Montreal have outstanding libraries. The provincial government operates the Legislative Library in Quebec City and the Saint Sulpice Library in Montreal.

Museums. The Montreal Museum of Fine Arts has excellent collections of ancient glass, European handicrafts, and primitive art. It also displays Canadian and European paintings. The Château de Ramezay, built in 1705 by Governor Claude de Ramezay in Montreal, includes a fine historical museum. In Quebec City, the Museum of Numismatics of Laval University has a famous collection of old and rare coins. McGill University operates two museums in Montreal. One, the Peter Redpath Museum, specializes in geology and mineralogy. The other, the McCord National Museum, concentrates on Canadian history and North American archaeology. The Provincial Museum in Quebec City displays works by Quebec artists.

--- **UNIVERSITIES** ---

Quebec has seven degree-granting universities, listed below. See the separate articles on these institutions. For enrollments, see CANADA (table: Universities and Colleges).

Name	Location	Founded
Bishop's University	Lennoxville	1843
Laval University	Ste. Foy	1663
McGill University	Montreal	1821
Montreal, University of	Montreal	1876
Quebec, University of	*	1969
Sherbrooke, University of	Sherbrooke	1954
Sir George Williams University	Montreal	1929

*For the campuses of the University of Quebec, see CANADA (Education).

Laval University in Ste. Foy was established in 1663. It began as a seminary in the buildings at the right. It later moved to another location. The province has seven universities. The Roman Catholic Church operates two French-language universities, Laval and Sherbrooke. Classes at the universities of Montreal and Quebec are also conducted in French. Three nondenominational universities— McGill, Sir George Williams, and Bishop's—teach in English.

The Citadel Overlooks Quebec City

QUEBEC/A Visitor's Guide

Quebec attracts about 7 million tourists yearly. Probably no other Canadian province is so rich in places of historical interest. Vacationers find the charm of Old France as they wander through the winding cobblestone streets of 300-year-old Quebec City. Every year, pilgrims visit the many religious shrines.

The rugged Gaspé Peninsula attracts artists, hikers, and mountain climbers. The lovely lakes and rolling farmland of the Eastern Townships have given the area the nickname *Garden of Quebec*. Many tourists take canoe trips down the rushing rivers of the Laurentian Mountains. Baseball fans visit Montreal during the summer to see the Expos of the National League.

In winter, thousands of skiers from all parts of Canada and the United States speed down Quebec's fine ski trails. Many sports fans come to Montreal to watch the Canadiens of the National Hockey League and the Alouettes of the Canadian Football League.

PLACES TO VISIT

Following are brief descriptions of some of Quebec's many interesting places to visit.

Bonaventure Island, off the Gaspé Peninsula near Percé, is one of the largest water-bird refuges that people can visit. More than 60,000 gannets, gulls, and other birds nest on the island in summer.

Chubb Crater, officially called Le Cratère du Nouveau-Québec, is one of the world's largest known meteor craters. It lies between Hudson and Ungava bays, and can be reached only by airplane. The crater is about 11,000 feet in diameter and 1,350 feet deep.

Ile d'Orléans rises in the middle of the St. Lawrence River near Quebec City. About 4,000 French Canadians live on the island. Old Norman-style houses, many churches, and religious shrines dot the island.

Man and His World, a cultural exhibition in Montreal, is a continuation of Expo 67, the 1967 international exhibition. Several countries continue to present national exhibitions.

Mount Royal Park, in Montreal, is a lovely wooded area. Only horse-drawn vehicles are allowed in most of the park. The top of 769-foot-high Mount Royal offers a magnificent view of Montreal and the St. Lawrence.

See MONTREAL (Cultural Life and Places to Visit).

Percé Rock, about 200 feet off the Gaspé coast, rises straight out of the water to a height of 154 to 290 feet. The rock is 1,565 feet long and 300 feet wide.

Quebec City, founded in 1608, is known as the cradle of French civilization in North America. The Citadel, a walled fortress, overlooks the city. See QUEBEC (city).

Ste.-Anne-de-Beaupré, in Montmorency County, is a Roman Catholic shrine. Shipwrecked French sailors built a chapel there in 1658. See SAINTE ANNE DE BEAUPRÉ.

National Parks. Quebec has two national parks, Forillon and La Mauricie. It also has two national historic parks, Fort Chambly and Fort Lennox. The province has five national historic sites. For the area and chief features of these parks and sites, see CANADA (National Parks).

Provincial Parks. Quebec has 33 provincial parks. They include large areas of the Canadian Shield and Gaspé Peninsula. For information on the provincial parks of Quebec, write to Parks Branch, Department of Tourism, Fish, and Game, Parliament Building, Quebec, Que.

Miller Services Ltd.
Man and His World

ANNUAL EVENTS

On June 24, French Canadians honor their patron saint, Jean Baptiste (John the Baptist). The province observes this day as a legal holiday, with solemn ceremonies followed by gay festivities and art and sports events. Other annual events in Quebec include the following.

January Through Spring: Tommycod Fishing Festival in La Perade, January-February; Laurentian Snow Festival in Sainte-Agathe-des-Monts, February; Quebec Winter Carnival in Quebec, early February; International Pee Wee Hockey Tournament in Quebec (Canadian and U.S. boys), early February; Du Maurier International and World Cup Ski Competitions at Mont Sainte-Anne in Beaupre, mid-March; Montreal International Music Competition in Montreal, first two weeks in June.

July-September: Valleyfield International Regatta (speedboat races) in Valleyfield, second weekend in July; International Swimming Relay Race in La Tuque, third weekend in July; Lake Saint Jean Swim Marathon, first weekend in August.

Basilica of Sainte Anne de Beaupré
Canadian Gov't. Travel Bureau, Ottawa

Canoes Race Across the St. Lawrence River
George Hunter, Publix

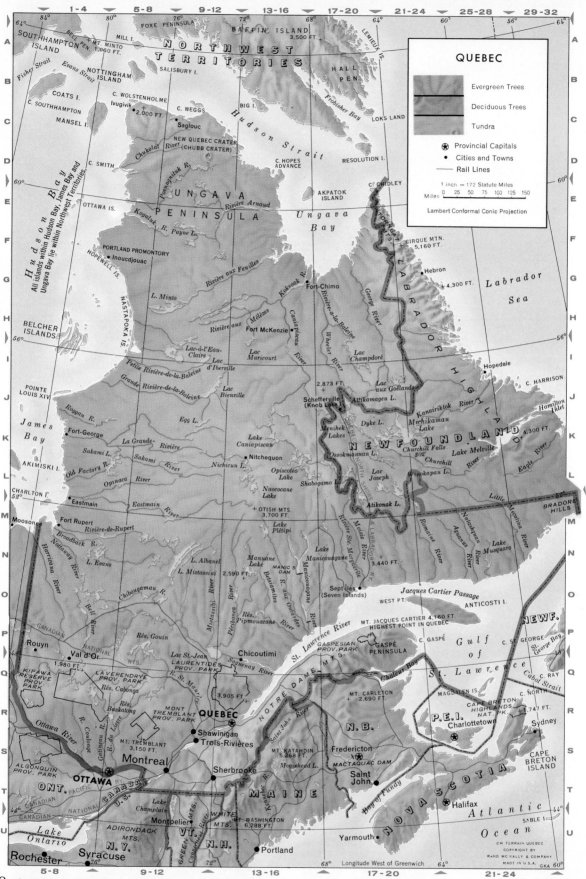

QUEBEC

Evergreen Trees

Deciduous Trees

Tundra

⊛ Provincial Capitals
• Cities and Towns
— Rail Lines

1 inch = 172 Statute Miles

Miles 0 25 50 75 100 125 150

Lambert Conformal Conic Projection

Specially created for **World Book** Encyclopedia by Rand McNally and World Book editors

Land Regions. Quebec has four main land regions: (1) the Canadian Shield, (2) the St. Lawrence Lowland, (3) the Appalachian Region, and (4) the Hudson Bay Lowland.

The Canadian Shield is a vast, horseshoe-shaped region. It covers almost half of Canada and dips into the northern United States. In Quebec, this rough, rocky plateau lies north of the St. Lawrence Lowland and Appalachian regions, and covers about nine-tenths of the province. It includes the North Shore, which extends along the St. Lawrence River from the Saguenay River to Labrador. Through the ages, the Canadian Shield was scraped by glaciers, and much of its soil was worn away by wind and water. In many sections, the ancient rocks have no soil at all. Most of the region has remained a wilderness of forests, lakes, rivers, and streams. Treeless tundras with mosses and lichens cover the northern part of the Canadian Shield (see TUNDRA). The region has little land that can be farmed, but it has a variety of great mineral deposits.

The Laurentian Mountains, or Laurentides, form the southeastern edge of the Canadian Shield in Quebec. The highest ranges rise in the Laurentides Provincial Park and Mont Tremblant Provincial Park areas. Mont Tremblant, northwest of Montreal, rises 3,150 feet above sea level. See CANADIAN SHIELD.

The St. Lawrence Lowland consists chiefly of the St. Lawrence River Valley and the Montreal Plain. It also includes Anticosti Island and small islands in the river's broad mouth. The level lowland is about 10 miles wide near Quebec City, and broadens to about 100 miles at Montreal. The land lies less than 500 feet above sea level. Some rocky hills break the flatness of the plain. Eight hills called the Monteregians rise in the southwestern part of the lowland. The best known is 769-foot-high Mount Royal, which overlooks Montreal.

The St. Lawrence River Valley has always been the most important part of the province. Its fertile soil supports most of Quebec's farming. The many cities and towns in the valley make it one of the most heavily populated regions of Canada.

The Appalachian Region is the northeastern extension of the Appalachian Mountains of the eastern United States. It extends from Vermont along the province's southeastern boundary. This region consists of three main sections: (1) the Eastern Townships, between the St. Lawrence River Valley and the United States border; (2) the South Shore, which extends along the mouth of the St. Lawrence from the Eastern Townships to the Gaspé Peninsula; and (3) the Gaspé Peninsula, north of New Brunswick. The land is broken by lakes, mountains, and streams.

In the gently rolling Eastern Townships, the Notre Dame Mountains form an extension of the Green Mountains of Vermont. The South Shore has two separate areas. The Piedmont Region along the St. Lawrence estuary is a rich farming area, and the inland plateau has thick forests. The Gaspé Peninsula is also heavily forested. Mountain ranges in the interior of the peninsula make transportation between the northern and southern coasts difficult. Mount Jacques Cartier, the highest point in Quebec, rises 4,160 feet in the Gaspé Peninsula. See GASPÉ PENINSULA.

The Hudson Bay Lowland extends into Quebec from Ontario. It covers a small strip of land about 25 miles wide and 70 miles long, south of James Bay.

Coastline. Water forms most of Quebec's boundaries. The province has a coastline of 9,879 miles, including bays, inlets, and offshore islands. The main bodies of water that surround Quebec are James and Hudson bays on the west, Hudson Strait and Ungava Bay on the north, and the Gulf of St. Lawrence on the southeast and south.

North of the Gulf of St. Lawrence, the coastline is uneven. Many bays cut into the land, and rocks rise along the water's edge. To the south, along the Gaspé

Land Regions
of Quebec

HUDSON BAY LOWLAND

CANADIAN SHIELD

St. Maurice R.

Ottawa R.

St. Lawrence R.

APPALACHIAN REGION

ST. LAWRENCE LOWLAND

Beaumont Hydroelectric Project stands across the St. Maurice River on a rough and rocky plateau, part of the Canadian Shield.

Bourg Royal, above, is laid out in the wheellike trait-carré plan—a church as the hub and farms as spokes.

Farm on the Gaspé Peninsula, right, lies among thickly forested mountains in the Appalachian Region.

Peninsula, the coastline is more regular. The waters along the northern and western coasts remain frozen much of the year, usually from the end of December to May.

Rivers, Waterfalls, and Lakes. Inland waters in Quebec cover 71,000 square miles. Quebec has a greater total area of fresh water than any other province. Its many rivers help make it the leading producer of hydroelectric power in Canada and the United States.

Quebec's principal river is the 1,900-mile-long St. Lawrence. It enters Quebec at the point where the province, New York, and Ontario meet. The river then flows northeast into the Gulf of St. Lawrence. Ever since the French explorer Jacques Cartier sailed up the St. Lawrence in 1535, this important trade route has influenced the life and development of Quebec and Canada. The river has been called the *Mother of Canada*. Its importance increased greatly in 1959, when the St. Lawrence Seaway was completed. The seaway allows large ocean-going ships to travel up the river and to the Great Lakes. See SAINT LAWRENCE RIVER; SAINT LAWRENCE SEAWAY.

All the other important rivers in Quebec flow into the St. Lawrence. Most of them, including the Saguenay, St. Maurice, and Ottawa, rise in the Canadian Shield and join the St. Lawrence from the north or

northwest. The principal rivers south of the St. Lawrence include the Chaudière, Richelieu, and St. Francis.

Rivers flowing east, north, or west into James Bay, Hudson Bay, Hudson Strait, and Ungava Bay drain more than half the province. Much of northern Quebec is undeveloped and has no people, so these rivers have never been important. Many of them are more than 200 miles long. The longest is the 660-mile Koksoak River.

Most of Quebec's rivers have waterfalls and rapids. Many of the rapids, such as Rapide Blanc on the St. Maurice River and Rapide des Quinze on the Ottawa River, are used to produce hydroelectric power. Some of the falls are quite beautiful. The best known ones include Shawinigan Falls, which drops 146 feet on the St. Maurice River; 114-foot Joffre Falls on the Chaudière River; and 273-foot Montmorency Falls on the Montmorency River.

Countless lakes lie throughout the province. More than 20 of them cover more than a hundred square miles each. The rugged Canadian Shield has the largest lakes, of which 840-square-mile Lake Mistassini is the biggest. Other lakes in this region include Lac-à-l'Eau-Claire, Lac St.-Jean, and Lakes Bienville, Caniapiscau, and Minto. Some of the loveliest lakes are in the Laurentian Mountains. Lake Megantic, just north of Maine, is famous among fishermen.

The climate of Quebec varies greatly throughout the vast area of the province. For example, the average annual temperature ranges from 44° F. in the far south to 17° F. in the far north. Quebec's highest recorded temperature, 104° F., occurred in Ville Marie on July 6, 1921. The lowest temperature, −66° F., was recorded in Doucet on Feb. 5, 1923.

Quebec's winters are long and cold, especially in the north. This section has almost no summer. Much of the area has permanently frozen soil beneath the surface of the ground. The January temperature in the north ranges from −5° F. to −15° F. In July, the temperature there averages between 45° F. and 55° F.

In southern Quebec, the January temperature ranges from 3° F. to 15° F. Much of the St. Lawrence River, and other rivers and lakes, are frozen from December to mid-April. Summers in the south are warm, and sometimes hot, but short. The July temperature averages between 54° F. and 68° F.

The province's annual rainfall and snowfall decrease toward the north. In the southern region, *precipitation* (rain, melted snow, and other forms of moisture) ranges from 34 to 45 inches a year. The north receives from 15 to 31 inches annually. All Quebec has heavy snowfall in winter. The south gets from 97 to 166 inches of snow yearly, most of it between late November and mid-March. Northern Quebec has from 69 to 129 inches of snow a year.

SEASONAL TEMPERATURES

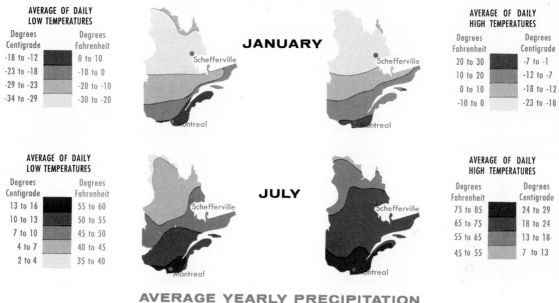

AVERAGE OF DAILY LOW TEMPERATURES

Degrees Centigrade	Degrees Fahrenheit
-18 to -12	0 to 10
-23 to -18	-10 to 0
-29 to -23	-20 to -10
-34 to -29	-30 to -20

JANUARY

AVERAGE OF DAILY HIGH TEMPERATURES

Degrees Fahrenheit	Degrees Centigrade
20 to 30	-7 to -1
10 to 20	-12 to -7
0 to 10	-18 to -12
-10 to 0	-23 to -18

AVERAGE OF DAILY LOW TEMPERATURES

Degrees Centigrade	Degrees Fahrenheit
13 to 16	55 to 60
10 to 13	50 to 55
7 to 10	45 to 50
4 to 7	40 to 45
2 to 4	35 to 40

JULY

AVERAGE OF DAILY HIGH TEMPERATURES

Degrees Fahrenheit	Degrees Centigrade
75 to 85	24 to 29
65 to 75	18 to 24
55 to 65	13 to 18
45 to 55	7 to 13

AVERAGE YEARLY PRECIPITATION
(Rain, Melted Snow, and Other Moisture)

Inches	Centimeters
40 to 50	102 to 127
30 to 40	76 to 102
20 to 30	51 to 76
10 to 20	25 to 51

0   200   400   600 Miles
0   300   600 Kilometers

WORLD BOOK maps

MONTHLY WEATHER IN MONTREAL AND SCHEFFERVILLE

	JAN	FEB	MAR	APR	MAY	JUNE	JULY	AUG	SEPT	OCT	NOV	DEC	Average of:
MONTREAL	23	24	35	50	64	74	79	76	67	55	41	27	High Temperatures
	8	9	21	34	47	57	62	60	52	41	30	15	Low Temperatures
	13	15	15	14	13	13	13	10	12	12	15	16	Days of Rain or Snow
	12	9	21	14	14	18	23	16	13	17	22	16	Days of Rain or Snow
SCHEFFERVILLE	-3	4	17	30	43	58	64	59	49	37	22	8	High Temperatures
	-21	-17	-3	12	25	39	46	43	36	25	9	-8	Low Temperatures

Temperatures are given in degrees Fahrenheit.

Source: Meteorological Branch, Canadian Department of Transport

23

Many early settlers of Quebec earned their living by fishing or by trapping fur-bearing animals. Logging became important in the early 1800's, and manufacturing and mining began developing rapidly during the early 1900's. Today, manufacturing is Quebec's largest industry and its greatest source of income.

The values given in this section are in Canadian dollars. For the value of Canadian dollars in U.S. money, see MONEY (table).

Natural Resources of Quebec include rich soils, vast mineral deposits, great forests, much wildlife, and plentiful supplies of water.

Soil. The St. Lawrence Lowland has the province's richest soils. They are composed chiefly of *sediments* (material that settles to the bottom of liquid). The sediments were deposited by the sea and various lakes and streams that covered the region after the Ice Age. The soils include clays, loams, sands, and silts.

Material deposited by the Ice Age glaciers, and some lake sediments, cover most of the Appalachian Region. These soils include clays, limestone and slate loams, sands, and sandy loams. Stony soils occur in much of the Eastern Townships. The Gaspé Peninsula has sandy soils broken by boulders. Heavy loams occur on the southern shores of the peninsula.

Granites, schists, and other kinds of stone are found in most of the Canadian Shield. The soil covering is generally thin and not suitable for agriculture. But the region has some areas of good soil covering. This soil consists chiefly of clays, loams, and sands developed from clay deposits and river sands. A rock and clay soil covers the Hudson Bay Lowland.

Minerals. The largest known beds of asbestos in the Western Hemisphere lie in the Eastern Townships. The northern tip of Quebec also has large asbestos and nickel deposits. The Canadian Shield has most of the province's iron ore and copper deposits. The most important iron ore deposits are on the Labrador border and at Ungava Bay, in the Mount Wright and Mount Reed areas. The largest copper deposits lie just east of the Ontario boundary, at Chibougamau, Noranda, and Val d'Or. The Gaspé Peninsula and the Appalachian Region near Sherbrooke also have large copper deposits. The most important gold-bearing ores are near Noranda and Val d'Or. This area of Quebec also has deposits of tungsten and zinc.

Another rich mining territory lies west and northwest of Montreal. It provides a great variety of minerals, including feldspar, granite, graphite, kaolin, magnesite, mica, molybdenum, and quartz.

Besides asbestos and copper, the Eastern Townships have chromite, industrial limestone, lead, marble, nickel, and soapstone. The Gaspé Peninsula has deposits of copper, granite, lead, oil, tungsten, and zinc.

Forests cover about 378,000 square miles, or more than three-fifths of Quebec. No other province has a greater total forest area. Nearly all the commercially valuable trees grow south of 52° north latitude, because most trees cannot grow in the cold climate farther north. The southern part of the Canadian Shield has important stands of balsam fir and spruce, the province's most valuable trees. Maples, pines, and white and

PRODUCTION OF GOODS IN QUEBEC

Total value of goods produced in 1969—$7,517,701,000

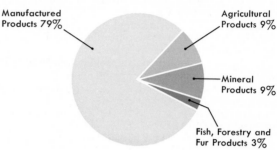

Manufactured Products 79%

Agricultural Products 9%

Mineral Products 9%

Fish, Forestry and Fur Products 3%

Note: Percentages are based on farm cash receipts, value added by forestry and manufacture, and value of fish, fur, and mineral production.

Sources: *Canada Year Book, 1970-71*, Statistics Canada; and other government publications

EMPLOYMENT IN QUEBEC

Total number of persons employed in 1970—1,905,200

		Number of Employees
Manufacturing	🧍🧍🧍🧍🧍🧍🧍🧍🧍🧍	522,100
Community, Business & Personal Services	🧍🧍🧍🧍🧍🧍🧍🧍🧍🧍	503,600
Wholesale & Retail Trade	🧍🧍🧍🧍🧍	269,600
Transportation, Communication & Utilities	🧍🧍🧍	180,500
Government	🧍🧍	105,400
Agriculture	🧍🧍	105,000
Finance, Insurance & Real Estate	🧍🧍	86,000
Construction	🧍	82,600
Mining	🧍	25,500
Forestry & Fishing	🧍	24,900

Sources: *Estimates of Employees by Province and Industry*, Jan., 1971, Statistics Canada; Labor Division, Statistics Canada

yellow birches also grow in the region. Small stands of balsam, birch, black and white spruce, dwarf aspen, and willow trees grow north of latitude 52°. The region west of Ungava Bay and Hudson Strait has mosses and lichens, the tundra type of vegetation.

The Appalachian Region has thick stands of timber, especially on the higher mountain ridges. The Eastern Townships provide most of the maple trees for Quebec's important maple-sugar industry. Balsam firs are the most common trees of the Gaspé Peninsula.

Plant Life. Forest wild flowers that bloom in May include bellworts, bloodroots, dogtooth violets, spring beauties, squirrel corn, and trilliums. In early summer, buttercups and daisies brighten the prairies, and the hawkweed blooms in drier areas. Prairie strawberries and raspberries provide an important commercial source of fruit in summer, especially in the St. Jean area. Autumn brings out asters, joe-pyes, and goldenrods. The area west of Hudson Strait and Ungava Bay has the tundra type of plant life.

Animal Life. Many kinds of fur-bearing animals live in Quebec. The region north of the commercial forest zone provides most of the province's valuable pelts. Beavers, foxes, martens, minks, muskrats, and seals are the most numerous fur-bearing animals. Bears and foxes

Quebec Lumber Mills process millions of tons of logs every year. Manufacturers use the wood to make pulp, paper, and paper products. More paper is produced in Quebec than anywhere else in North America.

Workers Make Asbestos Insulation in the town of Asbestos. Quebec produces about half of the world's asbestos. Mines in the province also produce large amounts of copper, gold, iron, and zinc.

Photos, National Film Board

are found throughout the province. The largest numbers of deer, moose, and raccoons live in the southern regions. Caribou graze on the Gaspé Peninsula and in central Quebec. During the summer, central and southern Quebec provide a nesting ground for black ducks. Other game birds include geese, ruffed grouse, Wilson's snipes, and woodcocks.

Cod accounts for about a third of Quebec's saltwater seafood catch. The remainder includes eels, herring, lobsters, mackerel, salmon, and smelt. Eels, minnows, and pickerel are the leading products of the inland commercial fisheries. Game fish are plentiful in the lakes and rivers. Several kinds of trout—chiefly brook, gray, and rainbow—thrive in these waters. Striped bass swim in the St. Lawrence River, and smallmouth bass are found in the lakes farther north. The inland waters also have walleyed and great northern pike, muskellunge, and salmon.

Manufacturing. Products manufactured in Quebec have an annual *value added by manufacture* of about $5,963,000,000. This figure represents the value created in products by Quebec's industries, not counting such costs as materials, supplies, and fuel. More people of Quebec earn their living in manufacturing than in any other kind of work.

The province's vast raw materials and hydroelectric power have helped the industries develop. Quebec's 11,000 factories, mills, and refineries account for about a third of Canada's total industrial production. Most of Quebec's production occurs in the more than 5,500 plants of the Montreal area. The Montreal area ranks second only to the Toronto area among Canada's leading manufacturing centers.

The food and beverage industry, with an added value of about $811 million yearly, is the major manufacturing activity. Most of the food and beverage plants are in the St. Lawrence Valley, between Montreal and Quebec City. Quebec is a leader among the provinces and states in the production of cheese. Other major products include alcoholic beverages, butter, canned fish and vegetables, flour and bread, and meats and meat products.

Quebec's second most important manufacturing industry is the production of pulp, paper, and paper products. The industry has a value added of about $586 million a year. Quebec has about 55 pulp and paper mills, most of which are in Trois-Rivières and other cities of the St. Maurice River Valley. These mills use over half the timber cut in the province. They account for about a third of the total earnings of Canada's pulp and paper industry. Quebec leads the provinces and states in the production of paper. *Newsprint* (paper used for newspapers) is its most valuable paper product. Quebec produces about 3,700,000 tons of newsprint a year, and provides almost half of Canada's newsprint exports. Quebec's paper mills also produce paperboard, wallboard, wrapping paper, and other paper products.

The production of transportation equipment is Quebec's third most important industry. This industry's products have an annual value added by manufacture of about 445\frac{1}{2}$ million. Factories in Argenteuil, Gatineau, and Quebec City manufacture aircraft and aircraft parts. Lévis, Montreal, and Quebec City have shipbuilding and repair facilities. Railroad equipment is produced in Montreal and St.-Hyacinthe. Quebec factories also produce motor vehicles and motor vehicle parts.

Quebec's fourth-ranking manufacturing activity is the production of electrical equipment, with an annual value added by manufacture of about $444 million. The production of electrical communication equipment is centered in Montreal, Rimouski, and Roxboro. Electrical appliances are manufactured in Montreal and Quebec City.

Other important industries in Quebec include the production of primary metals and of chemicals and chemical products. The province is a leading producer of clothing. The metal fabricating industry is also an important manufacturing activity in Quebec.

Agriculture. Quebec farm products provide an annual income of about $678 million. Farms cover about 11 million acres, or about 3 per cent of the province. The farms average about 175 acres in size. About 10 per cent of the people live on farms. Most of the farmland lies along the St. Lawrence River.

Milk production accounts for about 40 per cent of Quebec's farm income. Quebec ranks among the leading provinces and states in milk production and in the number of dairy cattle. The province's farmers own more than a million milk cows. More than half the milk goes into the manufacture of such products as butter, cheese, and ice cream. The farmers sell most of the rest of the milk for drinking.

Hogs are the most valuable meat animals raised in Quebec. But beef cattle provide most of the meat eaten in the province. Farmers in the Montreal area raise the largest number of beef cattle, hogs, and poultry. Sheep grazing is important in Matane, Matapédia, and Rimouski counties. Quebec's poultry farmers raise about 75 million chickens and about $3\frac{3}{4}$ million turkeys annually. The province produces eggs worth about $36\frac{1}{2}$ million annually.

Nearly all the farmers, especially those near large cities, raise some vegetables. Potatoes are the leading crop in acreage. Other important vegetables include carrots, cauliflower, cucumbers, lettuce, onions, sweet corn, tomatoes, and turnips.

Apples, Quebec's most important fruit, are grown chiefly in the Montreal area and in Missisquoi County. Quebec ranks among the leading provinces and states in apple production. Farmers also raise blueberries, raspberries, and strawberries.

Quebec farmers feed most of their field crops to their livestock. Oats rank second to hay in value among field crops. Farmers also raise corn for cattle feed and for grain, hay, mixed grains, oats, spring wheat, sugar beets, and tobacco.

Quebec leads the provinces and states in the production of maple syrup. About 90 per cent of Canada's maple syrup, sugar, and taffy comes from Quebec. The annual maple harvest provides an average of about 2 million gallons of syrup, some of which is made into sugar and taffy.

Mining in Quebec has an annual value of about $678 million. Copper is the greatest source of this income. Most of the copper ores contain gold and silver as well as copper. Quebec is a leading copper and gold producer among the provinces and states. The richest copper-producing regions lie near Chibougamau and

Noranda, and on the Gaspé Peninsula. Gold mines operate around Noranda, Malartic, and Val d'Or. Some of the gold ore also contains silver.

Quebec produces about 85 per cent of Canada's asbestos. Asbestos mining is centered around the towns of Thetford Mines and Asbestos in the Eastern Townships. Mining companies in this region produce about $1\frac{1}{3}$ million tons of asbestos each year. This is about half the world's output.

Iron mining increased rapidly in Quebec in 1954, when deposits on the Quebec-Labrador border were developed. The Schefferville and Gagnon mining areas supply most of Quebec's iron ore, and make the province a leading iron-producing region. In 1965, a $50 million iron-ore processing plant began operating in Pointe Noire.

Quebec is a leader among the provinces in zinc production. Northwestern Quebec, the Chibougamau area, and the Lake Mattagami region have large deposits of zinc. The Lake Allard ilmenite deposits rank among the world's largest. They provide most of Quebec's titanium ore. Mines in this area send the ore to an electric smelter at Sorel. Quebec is also a leading molybdenum-producing province. It produces about $3\frac{1}{2}$ million pounds of molybdenum a year.

Mining in a uranium-columbium field at Oka began in 1961. Production has been low for uranium but high for columbium. The St. Lawrence Lowland region supplies clay, limestone, and silica sand for the manufacture of cement. Mines and quarries in Quebec also produce gold, sand and gravel, stone, and titanium dioxide.

Forestry. Timber cut in Quebec has an annual value of about $185 million. This figure places Quebec among the leading logging provinces and states. Lumberjacks cut about $12\frac{3}{4}$ billion board feet of wood yearly. Balsam firs and spruce trees provide most of the timber. More than half the wood is used by the province's pulp and paper industry.

Electric Power. Quebec leads the provinces and states in hydroelectric power, both developed and potential. The province produces more electric power per person than any other region in North America. It probably produces this power more cheaply than any other region because it has such great water resources.

Hydroelectric plants supply almost all of Quebec's power. The other plants operate on steam. In 1963, the provincial government took over all the hydroelectric plants. It operates them under the Quebec Hydro-Electric Commission (Hydro-Quebec). The largest plant is at Beauharnois on the St. Lawrence River near Montreal. For Quebec's kilowatt-hour production, see ELECTRIC POWER (table).

Transportation. Montreal is Canada's chief transportation center. All early highways in French Canada were called *les Chemins du Roi* (the King's Highways). The first one linked Montreal and Quebec City in the 1700's. Canada's first major canal, the Lachine Canal, by-passed Lachine Rapids on the St. Lawrence River near Montreal. This canal was opened in 1825. It was closed in 1970 after ships began using the new South Shore Canal. A 15-mile railroad, the first one in Canada, began operating between Laprairie and St. Jean in 1836.

Quebec has about 160 private and public airports, of which 80 are seaplane bases. About 15 major com-

FARM, MINERAL, AND FOREST PRODUCTS

This map shows where the province's leading farm, mineral, and forest products are produced. The major urban areas (shown in red) are the province's most important manufacturing centers.

0   100   200   300 Miles

0   100   200   300   400 Kilometers

WORLD BOOK map

Copper Mines on the Gaspé Peninsula help make Quebec a top producer of the metal.
George Hunter, Publix

mercial airlines serve Montreal. The international airport in Dorval near Montreal is one of Canada's chief ports of entry by air.

Quebec has about 5,000 miles of railroad tracks, mainly in the St. Lawrence Lowland and the Appalachian Region. Branch lines reach the mining areas to the north.

Provincial highways and roads total more than 44,-000 miles. About 34,000 miles of them are paved.

More than 45 ports handle water transportation in Quebec. Most of the chief ports, such as Montreal, Quebec City, Sept-Îles, Sorel, and Trois-Rivières, lie along the St. Lawrence River. The ports of Baie-Comeau, Quebec City, Sept-Îles, and Trois-Rivières are kept ice-free all year around. Montreal is at the gateway to the St. Lawrence Seaway. Ocean ships moving up the St. Lawrence River use the seaway to reach the Great Lakes. Sorel is at the head of a waterway leading south to New York City. From its harbor, boats and small barges can travel to the Hudson River by way of the Richelieu River and Lake Champlain. The Richelieu and Ottawa rivers, like the St. Lawrence Seaway, have systems of canals.

Communication. Quebec has about 200 magazines and 200 newspapers, including 14 dailies. Most of them are printed in French. Publishing in the province began in 1764 with the founding of the Quebec City

Gazette. This newspaper was published in both French and English until 1842. That year, it began publishing only in English. In 1884, the newspaper became the *Quebec Chronicle-Telegraph.* In 1776, a French printer, Fleury Mesplet, came to Montreal with Benjamin Franklin. They published propaganda material for the 13 American Colonies during the Revolutionary War. In 1778, Mesplet began publishing *La Gazette du Commerce et Littéraire, pour la Ville et District de Montréal,* which is now *The Gazette* of Montreal.

La Presse and the *Star,* both published in Montreal, have the largest daily circulations in the province. Other large Montreal newspapers include *Le Devoir* and *Le Petit Journal.* The major daily newspapers in Quebec City are *Le Soleil* and *L'Action.*

In 1919, the Canadian Marconi Company made the first radio broadcast in Canada, from Montreal. Its station, CFCF, began regular broadcasts in 1920. The government-owned Canadian Broadcasting Corporation introduced television broadcasting in the province in 1952. Station CBFT of Montreal began broadcasting that year, chiefly in French. Today, Quebec has about 70 radio stations and more than 20 major television stations. Most of the stations broadcast in French. A number of smaller television stations rebroadcast programs from the major stations to distant areas of the province.

27

United Empire Loyalists were colonists who remained loyal to Great Britain and moved from the United States to Quebec after the Revolutionary War.

Chubb Crater ●

Quebec Nearly Doubled in Size in 1912, when its northwestern boundaries were extended to Hudson Bay and Hudson Strait. The shaded area on the map, *left*, shows the province from 1867 to 1912. The map on the *right* shows present-day Quebec.

Chubb Crater in northwestern Quebec, one of the world's largest meteor craters, was explored in 1950. It has a diameter of more than two miles.

The Great Paper Industry, one of Quebec's most important businesses, began in 1803 in a small paper mill just outside the city of Montreal.

HISTORIC QUEBEC

The First Steam Locomotive in Canada began to operate along a 15-mile line between Laprairie and St. Jean in southern Quebec in 1836.

France Lost a Colonial Empire in America when the British Army stormed Quebec Heights and captured the city of Quebec in September, 1759.

QUEBEC ★

Montreal ● Laprairie
● St. Jean

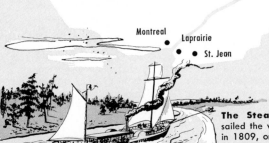

The Steamboat *Accommodation* sailed the waters of the St. Lawrence in 1809, only two years after Fulton built his first successful steamer.

The First Permanent Settlement in Canada was founded at the city of Quebec by Samuel Champlain in 1608. Settlers built a fort and trading post.

Indian Days. Eskimos and several Indian tribes were living in what is now Quebec when the first white settlers came. The Eskimos lived in the far north, chiefly west of Ungava Bay and along the shores of Hudson Bay. The Naskapi Indians hunted in the eastern part of the Quebec region. The members of this tribe who lived toward the south, between the St. Maurice River and present-day Sept-Îles, were called *Montagnais* (mountaineers) by the French. Five tribes of the Iroquois nation made permanent homes along the Richelieu River and west of it.

The Cree Indians roamed between the Naskapi and Eskimo lands and south of James Bay. Other tribes in the Quebec region included the Algonquin, Huron, Malecite, and Micmac. See INDIAN, AMERICAN (Table of Tribes).

From the discovery of the Gulf of St. Lawrence by Jacques Cartier in 1534 to the creation of the Dominion of Canada in 1867, the history of Quebec parallels that of Canada. For details, see CANADA, HISTORY OF.

Early Years as a Province. The British North America Act of 1867 created the Dominion of Canada (see BRITISH NORTH AMERICA ACT). It recognized French, in addition to English, as one of Quebec's two official languages. The act also gave the province direct control over education and civil law. In 1867, Pierre-J.-O. Chauveau, a Conservative, became the first prime minister of Quebec.

French Canadians had resented British rule in Canada from the time it began in 1763. The federal system that was established in 1867, and the rights it granted the French Canadians, partly satisfied them. The British North America Act had guaranteed the school rights of Canada's two major religious groups. In Quebec, the Protestant, English-speaking minority received provincial funds for its schools. But the French Canadians of Quebec soon discovered that French Canadians in the other provinces could not use public funds to establish Roman Catholic, French-language schools.

Ill feeling between French and British Canadians came to a head after the *métis* (persons of mixed white and Indian ancestry) of Saskatchewan rebelled in 1885. British troops captured their leader, Louis Riel, and he was hanged later that year. Riel's execution further split the two peoples of Quebec. French Canadians considered Riel a hero who had been unjustly killed for a noble cause. British Canadians regarded him as a traitor. See SASKATCHEWAN REBELLION.

Tension between the two peoples rose again in 1899. That year, Great Britain went to war against the Boers in South Africa. French Canadians opposed fighting in the Boer War. But British Canadians considered it Canada's duty to send troops to support England.

Sir Wilfrid Laurier of Quebec, the Dominion's first French-Canadian prime minister, sided with the majority and sent troops to South Africa. Laurier had a hard time calming the anger that this policy stirred up in Quebec. During the next several years, he did much to convince French Canadians that all Canada was their homeland, not just Quebec. Laurier also helped lay the foundation for gradual Canadian independence. See LAURIER, SIR WILFRID.

IMPORTANT DATES IN QUEBEC

1534 Jacques Cartier discovered the Gulf of St. Lawrence and claimed the Quebec region for France.

1608 Samuel de Champlain of France established Quebec City, the first permanent settlement in Canada.

1663 King Louis XIV of France made the Quebec region a royal province.

1759 The British captured Quebec City during the French and Indian War.

1763 Great Britain acquired the Quebec region by the Treaty of Paris.

1774 The British Parliament approved the Quebec Act, extending Quebec's borders and establishing French-Canadian political and religious rights.

1791 The Constitutional Act divided Quebec into Upper Canada and Lower Canada.

1840 The Act of Union joined Upper Canada and Lower Canada under one government.

1867 The British North America Act created the Dominion of Canada, forming the province of Quebec.

1912 Quebec nearly doubled in size by acquiring territory east of Hudson Bay.

1927 The British Privy Council set the present Quebec-Labrador boundary.

1950 Mines near Havre-St. Pierre began producing the important mineral ilmenite, a titanium ore.

1954 The world's largest asbestos fiber mill opened in Asbestos.

1960 Huge deposits of asbestos were discovered in the Ungava Peninsula of northern Quebec.

1963 The provincial government bought all privately owned electric power companies.

1967 Expo 67, an international exhibition, was held in Montreal as part of Canada's centennial celebration.

1972 A strike by over 200,000 Quebec public employees closed most schools and limited hospital and government services throughout the province for 11 days.

In 1912, Quebec nearly doubled in size. Its northwestern boundaries were extended to Hudson Bay and Hudson Strait. Interest in the region's natural resources grew, and Quebec and Newfoundland disputed the Quebec-Labrador boundary. The British Privy Council settled this question in 1927 in favor of Newfoundland, a decision still resented in Quebec.

World War I. Relations between Quebec and the other provinces became bitter during World War I (1914-1918). Most French Canadians believed that the British Canadians were more interested in defending the British Empire than in promoting Canada's welfare.

In 1917, when Canada began drafting men into the armed forces, the split between the French and British Canadians deepened greatly. Many English-speaking Canadians accused Quebec of sabotaging the war effort. This charge caused great bitterness in the province, and led to some talk of withdrawing from the Dominion. Nevertheless, French-Canadian troops served heroically in the war. The French-Canadian Royal 22nd Regiment fought with especial heroism in the Battle of Vimy Ridge in France.

Between the Wars. After World War I, industry expanded rapidly in Quebec. As a result, more persons from rural areas found work in the cities. Until this

29

time, they had been moving to Ontario, the western provinces, or the United States.

Many French-Canadian leaders resented the industrial expansion, which was controlled by British Canadians and Americans. They claimed that the growth of big business would destroy the French-Canadian way of life. But the people wanted the new industry with its improved wages and living standards.

World War II. During World War II (1939-1945), Quebec was of great value to the Allies. The province had a large labor force, plentiful electric power, and huge deposits of asbestos, copper, and zinc. Quebec's industrial production nearly tripled.

Tension between French and British Canadians developed again during the war. The federal government, under the Liberal Party, set up a military draft for service overseas, in spite of repeated promises made to Quebec voters not to do so. Prime Minister Adélard Godbout reduced the people's bitterness over the draft and cooperated with the federal government. But the voters elected the Union Nationale Party to power in 1944. The new government, under Prime Minister Maurice Duplessis, emphasized French-Canadian political rights in Quebec and opposed control by the federal government.

The Mid-1900's. The economic growth in Quebec that followed World War II extended into the 1950's and 1960's. In 1950, mines near Havre-Saint-Pierre began to produce ilmenite, a titanium ore. The world's largest asbestos fiber mill opened in Asbestos in 1954. In 1960, huge asbestos deposits were discovered in the Ungava Peninsula.

During the 1960's, Quebec and other provinces became dissatisfied with joint federal and provincial social programs and division of taxes. Quebec exercised the provinces' right to withdraw from these pro-

grams and to administer its share of taxes without federal supervision. Quebec then gained control of its pension plans, social security programs, and student loans. In 1962, Quebec voters approved a proposal for the province to take over the ownership of privately owned electric companies. The Liberals, led by Prime Minister Jean Lesage, won the election by a large majority, and the province bought all privately owned electric companies in 1963.

The result of the 1962 election reflected an upsurge of strong French-Canadian feelings among some of Quebec's people. This upsurge began at the end of the Duplessis Administration in 1960. A number of French Canadians wanted Quebec to *secede* (withdraw) from the Canadian confederation and form a separate nation. Some extremists used demonstrations, raids, and bombings to promote secession. In 1969, many separatist groups joined forces and formed the Parti Québécois.

In 1967, President Charles de Gaulle of France visited Expo 67, a world's fair held in Montreal as part of Canada's centennial celebration. During his visit, De Gaulle shouted the secessionist slogan, "Vive Québec libre" (Long live free Quebec). His action strained relations between Canada and France.

In 1969, the National Assembly passed the Quebec language bill. This measure made French the major language of Quebec and gave parents the choice of educating their children in either French or English.

Quebec Today. In the 1970's, Quebec is working to match its economic growth with its growing labor market. Unemployment in Quebec is second highest among the Canadian provinces and territories, and it continues to rise. To provide more jobs, the provincial government is attempting to develop new and different kinds of industry and to attract new investment in Quebec.

In April, 1970, Quebec voters returned the Liberal Party to power. Robert Bourassa became prime minister. The Parti Québécois won about a fourth of the popular vote.

In October, 1970, members of the *Front de Libération du Québec* (FLQ), a separatist group, kidnaped British Trade Commissioner James R. Cross and Quebec Labor Minister Pierre Laporte. Bourassa requested the aid of federal troops to protect other government officials and public buildings. Canadian Prime Minister Pierre E. Trudeau then sent thousands of soldiers to major cities in Quebec. Provincial police made about 3,000 raids and arrested about 450 persons. Laporte was later murdered, and four FLQ members were charged with the crime. The Canadian government allowed Cross's kidnapers to go to Cuba in return for the release of Cross.

The violent tactics of the FLQ frightened many Quebecers and, for a time, hurt the separatist movement. But the violence lessened in the early 1970's, and an increasing number of Quebecers became sympathetic to the movement. In 1972, several large Quebec labor unions voted to support the separatist campaign.

The largest strike in Canadian history broke out in Quebec in 1972. More than 200,000 public employees left their jobs in a dispute over wages and related matters. The 11-day strike closed most schools and limited hospital service and government operations throughout the province.   MICHEL BRUNET,

PIERRE DAGENAIS, and RAYMOND DUBÉ

——————— THE PRIME MINISTERS OF QUEBEC ———————

	Party	Term
1. Pierre-J.-O. Chauveau	Conservative	1867-1873
2. Gédéon Ouimet	Conservative	1873-1874
3. C.-B. de Boucherville	Conservative	1874-1878
4. Henri-G. Joly	Liberal	1878-1879
5. J.-Adolphe Chapleau	Conservative	1879-1882
6. J.-Alfred Mousseau	Conservative	1882-1884
7. John Jones Ross	Conservative	1884-1887
8. L.-Olivier Taillon	Conservative	1887
9. Honoré Mercier	Liberal	1887-1891
10. C.-B. de Boucherville	Conservative	1891-1892
11. L.-Olivier Taillon	Conservative	1892-1896
12. Edmund J. Flynn	Conservative	1896-1897
13. F.-Gabriel Marchand	Liberal	1897-1900
14. S.-Napoléon Parent	Liberal	1900-1905
15. Lomer Gouin	Liberal	1905-1920
16. L.-Alexandre Taschereau	Liberal	1920-1936
17. Adélard Godbout	Liberal	1936
18. Maurice Duplessis	Union Nationale	1936-1939
19. Adélard Godbout	Liberal	1939-1944
20. Maurice Duplessis	Union Nationale	1944-1959
21. J.-Paul Sauvé	Union Nationale	1959-1960
22. Antonio Barrette	Union Nationale	1960
23. Jean Lesage	Liberal	1960-1966
24. Daniel Johnson	Union Nationale	1966-1968
25. Jean-Jacques Bertrand	Union Nationale	1968-1970
26. Robert Bourassa	Liberal	1970-

QUEBEC/*Study Aids*

Related Articles in WORLD BOOK include:

BIOGRAPHIES

Abbott, Sir John J. C.	Lemelin, Roger
Bourassa, Henri	McGill, James
Brock, Sir Isaac	Montcalm, Marquis de
Carleton (Sir Guy)	Papineau, Louis J.
Cartier, Sir Georges-É.	Roy, Maurice Cardinal
Cartier, Jacques	Saint Laurent, Louis S.
Champlain, Samuel de	Taché, Sir Étienne-P.
Drummond, William H.	Trudeau, Pierre E.
Fitzpatrick, Sir Charles	Vanier, Georges P.
Laurier, Sir Wilfrid	Wolfe, James
Laval de Montmorency, François	

CITIES AND TOWNS

Arvida	Montreal	Sherbrooke
Hull	Montréal-Nord	Sorel
Lachine	Quebec (city)	Trois-Rivières
Laval	Saint-Laurent	Verdun
Longueuil	Shawinigan	Westmount

HISTORY

Acadia	Quebec Act
British North America Act	Revolutionary War in
Canada, History of	America
French and Indian Wars	United Empire Loyalist
Plains of Abraham	War of 1812

PHYSICAL FEATURES

Anticosti	James Bay	Ottawa River
Canadian Shield	Lake Champlain	Richelieu River
Chaudière River	Lake Memphre-	Saguenay River
Gaspé Peninsula	magog	Saint Lawrence
Gulf of Saint	Magdalen Islands	River
Lawrence	Montmorency	Ungava
Hudson Bay	River	

PRODUCTS

For Quebec's rank among the provinces and states in production, see the following articles:

Aluminum	Forest and Forest	Maple Sugar	Textile
Cattle	Products	Milk	Titanium
Cheese	Gold	Paper	
Copper	Lumber	Silver	

UNIVERSITIES

Quebec's degree-granting universities have separate articles in WORLD BOOK. They are listed in a table in the *Education* section of this article.

Outline

I. Government
  A. Lieutenant Governor
  B. Prime Minister
  C. Legislature
  D. Courts
  E. Local Government
  F. Taxation
  G. Politics
II. People
III. Education
  A. Schools
  B. Libraries
  C. Museums
IV. A Visitor's Guide
  A. Places to Visit
  B. Annual Events
V. The Land
  A. Land Regions
  B. Coastline
  C. Rivers, Waterfalls, and Lakes
VI. Climate
VII. Economy
  A. Natural Resources
  B. Manufacturing
  C. Agriculture
  D. Mining
  E. Forestry
  F. Electric Power
  G. Transportation
  H. Communication
VIII. History

Questions

Why is Quebec called the *Storied Province?*

What percentage of Quebec's people are French Canadians?

What is Canada's largest city and chief transportation center?

How did the execution of Louis Riel affect relations between French and British Canadians?

How much of Canada's asbestos comes from Quebec?

Who was the first French Canadian to serve as prime minister of Canada?

How did Quebec receive its name?

What is Quebec's chief manufacturing activity?

How was Quebec's school system changed in 1964?

Why did relations between Quebec and the other provinces become bitter during World War I? During World War II?

Books for Young Readers

BARBEAU, C. MARIUS. *The Golden Phoenix and Other French-Canadian Fairy Tales: Retold by Michael Hornyansky.* Oxford (Don Mills, Ontario), 1958; Walck (New York City), 1958.

CARLSON, NATALIE S. *The Talking Cat, and Other Stories of French Canada: Retold.* Harper (New York City), 1952. Fiction. *Jean-Claude's Island.* 1963. Fiction.

ROCKWELL, ANNE F., ed. *Savez-Vous Planter les Choux? and Other French Songs.* World Publishing Co. (New York City), 1969.

SCHULL, JOSEPH. *Battle for the Rock: The Story of Wolfe and Montcalm.* Macmillan (Toronto), 1960; St. Martin's (New York City), 1960.

SWAYZE, J. FRED. *Frontenac and the Iroquois: The Fighting Governor of New France.* Macmillan (Toronto), 1959.

SYME, RONALD. *Champlain of the St. Lawrence.* Morrow (New York City), 1952.

TOYE, WILLIAM. *Cartier Discovers the St. Lawrence.* Oxford (Don Mills, Ontario), 1970; Walck (New York City), 1970.

Books for Older Readers

BISHOP, MORRIS G. *Champlain: The Life of Fortitude.* McClelland (Toronto), 1963.

COSTAIN, THOMAS B. *The White and the Gold: The French Regime in Canada.* Doubleday (Garden City, N.Y.), 1954.

ECCLES, WILLIAM J. *Canadian Society During the French Regime.* Harvest (Montreal), 1968. Written in English and French.

LEACOCK, STEPHEN B. *Leacock's Montreal.* Rev. ed. John Culliton, ed. McClelland (Toronto), 1963.

McLEAN, ERIC D., and WILSON, R. D. *The Living Past of Montreal—Le Passé Vivant de Montréal.* McGill-Queen's Univ. Press (Montreal), 1964.

MARIE DE L'INCARNATION, MÈRE. *Word from New France. The Selected Letters of Marie de l'Incarnation.* Joyce Marshall, ed. and trans. Oxford (New York City), 1967.

PALARDY, JEAN. *The Early Furniture of French Canada.* Macmillan (Toronto), 1963.

ROBERTS, LESLIE. *Montreal: From Mission Colony to World City.* Macmillan (Toronto), 1969.

TOYE, WILLIAM. *The St. Lawrence.* Oxford (Don Mills, Ontario); Walck (New York City), 1959.

TRENT, WILLIAM. *Northwoods Doctor.* McClelland (Toronto), 1962.

TRUDEL, MARCEL. *An Atlas of New France.* Laval Univ. Press (Quebec), 1968.

31

City Crest

Quebec, famous for its Old World atmosphere, is called the only walled city in North America. A stone wall encircles part of the upper section of the city. The tallest landmark is the Château Frontenac, a hotel, shown in the center foreground.

Office Municipal de Tourisme

QUEBEC, *kwee BECK,* or *kay BECK* (pop. 182,502; met. area, 476,316), is the capital of the province of Quebec and one of the largest cities in Canada. Its churches, ancient stone houses, and crooked cobblestone streets give it the charm of an old European city. The Château Frontenac, a French-Renaissance style hotel with red brick walls, a steep copper roof, and towers and turrets, stands out in the city's skyline.

Quebec is the only walled city in North America, although most of the modern city lies outside the walls. Visitors come to Quebec chiefly for its Old World atmosphere. But the city is a busy transatlantic shipping terminus and manufacturing center.

Most of Quebec's people are of French descent. Sir Wilfrid Laurier, the nation's first French-Canadian prime minister, once said "Quebec is to French-Canadians what Mecca is to Arabs, the most sacred city."

Quebec is sometimes called the *Gibraltar of America,* because of the Citadel. This mighty fortress stands on a steep-sided cliff above the St. Lawrence River. France lost Canada to Great Britain in a battle on the Plains of Abraham just west of the Citadel in 1759. The city also is called the *Cradle of New France,* because Samuel de Champlain founded his first log settlement in New France here in 1608.

Location, Size, and Description

Quebec lies at the point where the St. Lawrence and St. Charles rivers meet. The city is about 400 miles from the Gulf of St. Lawrence. The St. Lawrence River suddenly narrows to about a mile in width close to the

Jean-Charles Bonenfant, the contributor of this article, is former Chief Librarian, Legislative Library of the Province of Quebec.

city. The word *Quebec* comes from an Algonkian Indian word meaning *the river narrows here.* Quebec covers nine square miles.

The Citadel overlooks Quebec from the summit of Cape Diamond, 347 feet above river level. The cape drops sharply toward the St. Lawrence, but slopes more gradually to the St. Charles. The British government completed building the fortress in 1832. Massive walls and a maze of gun emplacements and other fortifications surround the Citadel and its 140 acres of parade ground. Troops of the Royal 22nd Regiment guard the Citadel. The official summer residence of the Canadian Governor-General is the Citadel.

The Dufferin Terrace, with its 60-foot-wide planked promenade, extends about a quarter of a mile from the Citadel to the Château Frontenac. It offers an excellent view of lower parts of Quebec. See CITADEL.

Upper Town lies north of the Citadel on the high ground above the rivers, 305 feet above sea level. It includes some of the city's most beautiful homes, public buildings, and churches. A stone wall built at the same time as the Citadel encircles part of Upper Town. Three of its old gates—St. Louis, Kent, and St. Jean—have been rebuilt and provide passage through it. Quebec's walls average about 35 feet in height.

Lower Town is the commercial section. It lies 19 feet above sea level on the narrow strip of land north-

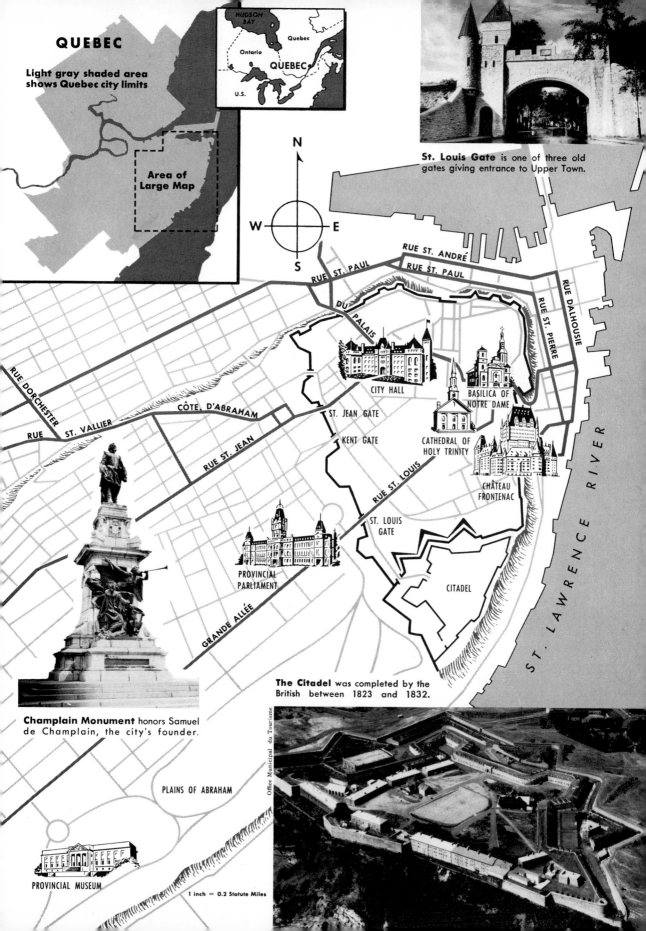

QUEBEC

Light gray shaded area shows Quebec city limits

HUDSON BAY

Ontario

Quebec

QUEBEC

U.S.

Area of Large Map

St. Louis Gate is one of three old gates giving entrance to Upper Town.

N

W E

S

RUE ST. ANDRÉ

RUE ST. PAUL

RUE ST. PAUL

DU PALAIS

RUE ST. PIERRE

RUE DALHOUSIE

CITY HALL

BASILICA OF NOTRE DAME

CATHEDRAL OF HOLY TRINITY

RUE DORCHESTER

RUE ST. VALLIER

CÔTE D'ABRAHAM

ST. JEAN GATE

KENT GATE

RUE ST. JEAN

CHÂTEAU FRONTENAC

ST. LOUIS GATE

RUE ST. LOUIS

CITADEL

ST. LAWRENCE RIVER

PROVINCIAL PARLIAMENT

GRANDE ALLÉE

The Citadel was completed by the British between 1823 and 1832.

Office Municipal du Tourisme

Champlain Monument honors Samuel de Champlain, the city's founder.

PLAINS OF ABRAHAM

PROVINCIAL MUSEUM

1 inch = 0.2 Statute Miles

east of Upper Town. Large stores and factories fill the area. Some of the streets, such as Sous le Cap and Champlain, have the reputation of being the narrowest in North America. They are only eight feet wide. Many of the homes are hundreds of years old and have gray or white stone walls, steep tin roofs, and small dormer windows.

What to See and Do in Quebec

Many visitors enjoy sight-seeing tours in *calèches*, or horse-drawn buggies. The city's Winter Carnival just before Lent features skating, tobogganing, skiing, and other sports. The 10-day provincial fair is held in September in Exposition Park.

The provincial legislature meets in a French-Renaissance building completed in 1878. The central tower soars 172 feet high. Sixteen bronze statues of great Canadians decorate the main façade.

More than 50 churches serve the people of Quebec. The present Roman Catholic Basilica of Notre Dame, erected in 1922, includes the original walls of 1647. Other Roman Catholic buildings include Notre Dame des Victoires Church, with its paintings by Rubens and Van Dyck; and the Ursuline Convent, founded in 1639. The Marquis de Montcalm, the French commander who died in the 1759 battle against the English, lies buried in the convent. The Anglican Cathedral of the Holy Trinity, opened in 1804, was the first cathedral of the Church of England built outside Great Britain. The English oak pews have doors and locks.

The Provincial Museum is in National Battlefields Park. Its collection of Canadiana includes historic documents, models of old houses, and paintings.

The People and Their Work

About 93 of every 100 persons in Quebec have French ancestors. Most of the rest come from a British background. French is the dominant language of Quebec, but signs and other public notices appear in both French and English. About 97 of every 100 persons belong to the Roman Catholic Church.

Professional persons, office workers, and people who offer personal services make up more than half of the working population. Over 400 manufacturing establishments operate in Quebec. Most of the industrial sites lie along the St. Charles River. The leading factories include a pulp and paper mill; shipyards; and clothing, meat-packing, shoe, and tobacco plants.

Transportation and Communication

Quebec's large harbor provides docking space for ocean-going ships. The shipping season lasts from May to December for most ships. But in the late 1950's, a few began using the harbor all year. The six-mile water front, which has about 40 berths, extends along both sides of the cape and into the mouth of the St. Charles River. Ferry boats link Quebec and Lévis, a town across the St. Lawrence River. The Quebec airport is at Ancienne Lorette, 10 miles west of the city. Several railroads and a private bus line also serve Quebec.

Of the four daily newspapers published in Quebec, three are printed in French: *L'Action Catholique*, *L'Évènement-Journal*, and *Le Soleil*. The *Chronicle-Tele-graph* appears in English. Four radio stations and one television station broadcast in French, and one radio and one TV station in English.

Schools and Libraries

Schools. Students attend more than 70 Roman Catholic schools and 4 public schools. The province manages both systems through locally elected boards (see the Schools section in the article on the province of QUEBEC). Jesuit College, Ursuline College, Quebec Seminary, and the School of Fine Arts are located in Quebec. Laval University, the oldest university in Canada, is located in Sainte-Foy, near Quebec. It was founded in 1663 as the Seminary of Quebec, and received a royal university charter in 1852.

Libraries. Quebec has nine public libraries, including the libraries of the legislature, Canadian Institute, and Literary and Historical Society. Other libraries include those of Laval University and the Franciscan Fathers, rich in early printed books.

History and Government

The French Period began in 1535, when the explorer Jacques Cartier spent the winter near the Indian village of Stadacona. Samuel de Champlain established a permanent settlement there on July 3, 1608, and named it Quebec. Louis Hébert, the first Canadian farmer, set up his household at Quebec in 1617. Three years later, Champlain built Fort St. Louis on the present site of the Château Frontenac.

Quebec underwent the first of several attacks in 1629, when David Kirke captured it for England. France regained the city in 1632 by the Treaty of Saint-Germain-en-Laye. Monsignor François de Montmorency-Laval arrived in 1659 to become the first bishop of Quebec. He and his Roman Catholic Church helped make Quebec the center of New France.

The French controlled Quebec until 1759, in spite of two more British attempts to capture it. Sir William Phips, who later became governor of Massachusetts, tried to recapture Quebec in 1690, but governor Louis Frontenac repulsed him. Another expedition, led by Admiral Sir Hovenden Walker, turned back in 1711 because of a storm on the St. Lawrence. On Sept. 13, 1759, General James Wolfe defeated French forces under the Marquis de Montcalm on the Plains of Abraham. The British captured Quebec five days later (see QUEBEC, BATTLE OF). The Treaty of Paris, which ended the French and Indian War in 1763, gave Quebec to the British.

The English Period. American troops led by Benedict Arnold and Richard Montgomery besieged Quebec during the winter of 1775-1776. They suffered a disastrous defeat in which Montgomery was killed.

When Upper and Lower Canada (present-day Ontario and Quebec provinces) were established in 1791, Quebec City became the capital of Lower Canada. Quebec received its city charter in 1832. After Upper and Lower Canada were united in 1841, Quebec served as the capital of United Canada from 1852 to 1855, and from 1860 to 1867. Delegates from British North American colonies met in Quebec in October, 1864, to lay plans for confederation. This conference resulted in the creation of the Dominion of Canada in 1867. Quebec became the capital of the province of Quebec.

Recent Developments. Prime Minister Winston Churchill and President Franklin D. Roosevelt met in the Citadel in 1943 and 1944, during World War II. The decision to invade Normandy was made there.

Quebec has seen rapid progress in commerce and industry during the 1900's, much of it due to expanding port and warehousing activities.

A mayor and 16 aldermen administer Quebec. All are elected to three-year terms.   JEAN-CHARLES BONENFANT

QUEBEC, BATTLE OF, settled the fate of the French empire in America. France's defeat at Quebec in 1759 led to the Treaty of Paris of 1763 that gave Canada and all French territory east of the Mississippi River to Great Britain.

About 2 million British colonists were living along the eastern seaboard when the Seven Years' War began in 1756 (see SEVEN YEARS' WAR). About 60,000 French lived in America, mostly in Canada. Skirmishes between the British and French had taken place for about two years before war broke out. The British wanted to expand westward, but a chain of French posts blocked their move. Without a formal declaration of war, the British attacked French settlements in Ohio. The Marquis de Montcalm took command of French troops in 1756, and swept through Forts Oswego, William-Henry, and Ticonderoga. But finally, after 1758, his army of about 5,000 regulars had to fall back on Quebec. The city stood on heights dominating the Saint Lawrence River, and seemed impregnable to attack. French cannon covered all ship movements.

In 1758, the British seized Louisbourg, a French fortress protecting the mouth of the Saint Lawrence. They assembled a huge fleet of ships and set sail for Quebec in May, 1759. The 250 ships carried 8,000 soldiers under the command of General James Wolfe. For three months, the British urged the French in the fortified city to surrender. Wolfe could not decide whether to attack the French positions at Beauport, east of Quebec, or to climb the steep cliffs leading to the wide plateau called the *Plains of Abraham*, west of the city. He feared that his ships would be unable to pass before Quebec under the fire of French batteries.

Bombardment of Quebec. British troops landed on the Isle d'Orleans, five miles east of Quebec, in June. Other forces occupied Pointe Lévis on the south bank. Protected by cannon fire, a few British ships sailed past the city on July 18 and anchored at Anse des Mères. Wolfe then decided to attack Beauport. Under Montcalm and General François de Lévis, French, Canadian, and Indian soldiers repelled the attack.

Wolfe, depressed by the loss, vowed to make a last attempt by assaulting Quebec from the west. Montcalm believed that the British could not land at Anse au Foulon, located at the foot of the cliffs leading to the Plains of Abraham. But he wanted French troops at Cap Rouge farther west to occupy the Plains of Abraham. The Marquis de Vaudreuil, governor of Canada, ordered these troops to stay at Cap Rouge.

The Attack on Quebec began during the cloudy, calm night of Sept. 12-13, 1759. The tide bore British flatboats to the Anse au Foulon. The men climbed silently to the Plains and surprised a larger enemy post. By dawn, 5,000 British regulars had scaled the cliffs and were ranged for battle on the Plains. Montcalm had expected an attack at Beauport. He quickly moved

up 4,000 militiamen and Indians to meet the enemy. They arrived about 10 that morning.

The French fired too quickly at the British, who advanced in closed ranks and held their fire. When the French were near at hand, the British fired, reloaded, fired again, and then charged with bayonet and sword. The French retreated in disorder. Wolfe was wounded mortally in the first shots. Montcalm, who had been trying to rally his men, was wounded about the same time. His men brought him back to Quebec, where he died a few hours later. In 15 minutes, the fate of the French empire in America had been settled. General Jean-Baptiste Ramezay carried out the request of the townsmen by surrendering Quebec to General George Townshend on September 18.

The French tried to recapture Quebec in April, 1760. They defeated the British at Sainte Foy. This proved to be a useless victory. The British fleet arrived in the river below Quebec soon after the battle, and the British army coming up from Lake Champlain forced the surrender of Montreal in September. The Treaty of Paris of 1763 reduced all French possessions in North America to two small islands off the coast of Newfoundland, St. Pierre and Miquelon. In 1908, the site of the battles of Quebec and Sainte Foy became the National Battlefields Park.   P. B. WAITE

Related Articles in WORLD BOOK include:

Acadia	Paris, Treaties of
French and Indian Wars	Plains of Abraham
(The French and Indian War)	Wolfe, James
Montcalm, Marquis de	

QUEBEC, UNIVERSITY OF, is a coeducational university with campuses in Chicoutimi, Montreal, Quebec, Rimouski, and Trois-Rivières. All courses are conducted in French. The university program includes courses in biological sciences, commerce and administration, education, engineering, fine arts, liberal arts, mathematics, physical sciences, and social sciences. The university's Quebec campus is the site of the National School of Public Administration, a graduate school; and of the National Institute for Scientific Research.

A board of governors administers the University of Quebec. Each campus is administered by its own board of directors. The university was founded in 1969. For enrollment, see CANADA (table: Universities and Colleges).   ALPHONSE RIVERIN

QUEBEC ACT was a group of laws passed by Great Britain in 1774. It guaranteed the use of French civil law in Quebec, then a British colony with a largely French population. It also guaranteed the French Canadians the right to practice Roman Catholicism, and allowed the Catholic Church in Quebec to collect a tax from its members. The act enlarged Quebec to include much of what is now Quebec, Ontario, and the Midwestern United States.

Great Britain passed the act to settle questions about law and government in Quebec. Britain also had a more selfish reason. It faced a possible revolution in its 13 American Colonies to the south. Britain hoped to have some French support if the revolution began, or, at least, to keep the French in Quebec from joining it.

In the same year it passed the Quebec Act, Britain

passed four acts designed to punish Massachusetts. The Americans bitterly resented all five acts, and called them the *Intolerable Acts* (see INTOLERABLE ACTS). The Americans invaded Quebec shortly after their revolution began in April, 1775, but were turned back. Most French Canadians remained neutral during the invasion, because they considered it mainly a quarrel between Britain and British colonies.   P. B. WAITE

QUEBEC CONFERENCE was a meeting at which Canadian leaders completed plans for forming a united Canada. It was held in the city of Quebec from Oct. 10 to Oct. 27, 1864. At that time, eastern Canada consisted of five self-governing colonies of Great Britain. It was made up of United Canada, which consisted of Lower Canada and Upper Canada; and the Maritime Provinces of New Brunswick, Newfoundland, Nova Scotia, and Prince Edward Island. The Hudson's Bay Company, a fur-trading firm, controlled most of central and western Canada. British Columbia and Vancouver Island were two British colonies in the far west.

Three chief factors made union desirable. (1) Britain believed the Canadians could better defend themselves if they were united. (2) Union could help economic growth. (3) Union might help end friction between the French people of Lower Canada and the English people of Upper Canada.

The delegates to the conference, now called the Fathers of Confederation, proposed a union of all the eastern provinces under a central government. They also made provision for future admission of the western territories. Within two years, Lower Canada, Upper Canada, New Brunswick, and Nova Scotia agreed to the plan. Lower Canada became Quebec and Upper Canada became Ontario. Quebec, Ontario, New Brunswick, and Nova Scotia were the provinces when the British North America Act formed the Dominion of Canada in July, 1867.   P. B. WAITE

See also CANADA, HISTORY OF (Confederation; table).

QUEBRACHO, *kay BRAH choh,* is a South American tree that grows in Argentina and Paraguay. Its wood contains 20 per cent tannin. Workers extract the tannin and export it to the United States for use in tanning leather. The name *quebracho* comes from the Spanish language and means *ax-breaker*. The tree has hard and tough wood, called *quebracho colorado* wood.

Scientific Classification. Quebracho belongs to the cashew family, *Anacardiaceae.* It is classified as genus *Schinopsis,* species *S. lorentzii.*   HAROLD NORMAN MOLDENKE

QUECHUAN. See INDIAN, AMERICAN (Indians of the Andes); INCA.

QUEEN, the insect. See ANT (The Ant Colony; Life of the Ant); BEE.

QUEEN is the title of a woman who rules a kingdom in her own right, or who is the wife of a king. If she rules in her own right, she is called a *queen regnant.* She has the same powers that a king would have, depending on the constitution of the country she rules.

If the queen is the wife of the king, she is called a *queen consort.* The mother of the ruling monarch is the *queen mother,* and the widow of a king is a *queen dowager.* Each queen has her own household, but none exercises any official power in the government.

Kings or queens of Great Britain and other constitutional monarchies have few powers of government, but they can influence public opinion.   I. J. SANDERS

For names of queens, see names of individuals; for example, ELIZABETH II. See also CORONATION; KING; PRINCE CONSORT; ROYAL HOUSEHOLD OF GREAT BRITAIN.

QUEEN, ELLERY, is the pen name of two cousins, Frederic Dannay (1905-   ) and Manfred B. Lee (1905-1971), who became successful detective-story writers. Ellery Queen is also the name of their chief fictional character. They also published under the name of BARNABY ROSS. Dannay and Lee published their first detective novel, *The Roman Hat Mystery,* in 1929. They took turns developing plots and writing their mystery stories.

Dannay and Lee were both born in Brooklyn. They became full-time writers after they won a detective-story contest in the 1920's. In 1941, Dannay and Lee founded *Ellery Queen's Mystery Magazine,* which publishes current detective fiction and reprints detective fiction classics.   PHILIP DURHAM

QUEEN ANNE'S LACE. See WILD CARROT.

QUEEN ANNE'S WAR. See FRENCH AND INDIAN WARS.

QUEEN CHARLOTTE ISLANDS lie in the north Pacific Ocean, about 60 miles off the coast of British Columbia. This group of islands forms part of British Columbia. They are separated from the mainland by Hecate Strait on the east, Dixon Entrance on the north, and Queen Charlotte Sound on the south. About 3,739 people live on the Queen Charlotte Islands, which cover about 3,705 square miles. Captain George Dixon explored the islands in 1787 and named them for his ship, the *Queen Charlotte.* The three largest islands in the group are Graham, Moresby, and Kunghit. Lumbering, fishing, farming, and cattle raising provide the main occupations on the islands. The Indians of the islands are known as the Haida.   RODERICK HAIG-BROWN

QUEEN CITY OF THE ADRIATIC. See VENICE.

QUEEN CITY OF THE WEST. See CINCINNATI.

QUEEN EMMA SUMMER PALACE. See HAWAII (Museums).

QUEEN OF SHEBA. See ETHIOPIA.

QUEENS, N.Y. (pop. 1,987,174), is the largest of New York City's five *boroughs* (districts). Queens covers all of Queens County, 127 square miles.

Mainly a residential area, Queens Borough has several well-known sections. These include Flushing, Forest Hills, and Kew Gardens. La Guardia Field and John F. Kennedy International Airport are located in Queens. The site of present-day Queens was settled by the Dutch in 1635. It became part of the British province of New York in 1683, and was named for England's Catherine of Braganza, Queen of Charles II. Queens became part of New York City in 1898.   WILLIAM E. YOUNG

See also NEW YORK CITY (Queens; map).

QUEENS COLLEGE. See UNIVERSITIES AND COLLEGES (table [New York, The City University of]).

QUEENS COLLEGE (North Carolina). See UNIVERSITIES AND COLLEGES (table).

QUEENS MIDTOWN TUNNEL runs 85 feet under the East River to connect midtown Manhattan and Queens. For location, see NEW YORK CITY (color map). Construction of the tunnel began in 1936, and was completed in 1940, at a cost of $53 million. It has twin tubes, each with 21-foot-wide roadways. Each tube is over 6,000 feet long. The tunnel can handle over 22 million automobiles and trucks a year.   GEORGE E. SPARGO

QUEEN'S UNIVERSITY AT KINGSTON is a coeducational school at Kingston, Ont. It is privately supported, and also receives grants from the federal and provincial governments. It has faculties of arts and science, law, engineering, and medicine. There are schools of business, nursing, physical education, and graduate studies, and an institute of local government. Queen's was founded in 1841. Queen's Theological College is affiliated with the university. For enrollment, see CANADA (table: Universities and Colleges).   J. A. CORRY

QUEENSBERRY, MARQUIS OF (1844-1900), JOHN SHOLTO DOUGLAS, a British sportsman, sponsored the modern boxing code that bears his name (see BOXING [From Bare Knuckles to Gloves]; QUEENSBERRY RULES). The rules were actually written by John Graham Chambers of the Amateur Athletic Club. They first appeared in 1867. Douglas became marquis when only 14. He served in parliament from 1872 to 1880.   LYALL SMITH

QUEENSBERRY RULES are a set of rules for boxing matches. They were drawn up under the supervision of the Marquis of Queensberry in 1867, when matches were fought with bare fists. The Marquis and John Graham Chambers, an English athlete, framed rules to replace the Revised London Prize Ring Rules then in effect.

The new rules, as applied in a London tournament in 1872, called for a fair stand-up match, rounds of three minutes, classification of boxers by weight, and the wearing of gloves. The Queensberry Rules were first used in America in a heavyweight title fight in 1892, when James J. Corbett defeated John L. Sullivan in New Orleans. Later, the Amateur Athletic Union adopted these rules.   JAMES POWERS

See also BOXING (From Bare Knuckles to Gloves).

QUEENSLAND is the second largest state in Australia. It occupies the entire northeastern part of the continent, and has 3,236 miles of seacoast. One of the wonders of Queensland is the Great Barrier Reef. This is a coral ridge which rises out of the sea some distance from the shore and follows the coastline for 1,200 miles. It encloses a broad bay.

Location, Size, and Surface Features. Queensland covers 667,000 square miles in northeastern Australia. For detailed maps, see AUSTRALIA.

The eastern section of the state is rugged and mountainous. The Great Dividing Range runs in a north-south direction through this section. The highest peak in the state is 5,287-foot Mount Bartle Frere. Western Queensland is a treeless, grassy plain broken by a spur of mountains. Central and western Queensland have vast grazing areas. Artesian wells supply this otherwise dry region with water. Farther south, the Warrego and Condamine rivers flow southward and join the Darling River. There are mangrove thickets along the streams, and dense tropical forests.

Queensland (shown in black)

Most of Queensland's rivers flow south and west from the Great Dividing Range. Cooper's Creek

Black Star

Tall Modern Buildings tower over tropical palm trees in the busy, prosperous city of Brisbane, capital of Queensland.

and the Diamantina River run southwest from this range to Lake Eyre in central Australia.

Natural Resources. Forests thicker than most tropical jungles grow on the mountain slopes of southern Queensland. The state is rich in bauxite, bismuth, coal, copper, gold, iron ore, silver, and tin.

Climate. Temperatures in Queensland rarely rise above 95° F. Temperatures average 60 to 70° F. in July and 90° F. in January. The rainfall on the eastern coast of Queensland is heavy, especially in the north where it averages 160 inches a year. In the extreme west, as little as six inches of rain may fall in a year.

The People. Queensland has 1,732,280 persons, including 19,003 aborigines. Most of the people were born in Australia or in the British Isles. About one-third of the people live in the capital, Brisbane (see BRISBANE). Townsville is Queensland's second largest city.

Agriculture. Queensland is an agricultural state, and depends on crops and herds for its wealth. Sugar cane is the chief crop. Other important crops include barley, oats, wheat, and several kinds of hay. Many kinds of tropical fruits thrive on the well-watered coast. Cotton, peanuts, and tobacco are also grown in Queensland. The state raises nearly half of Australia's cattle. Sheep raising is also important to the state.

Manufacturing. Queensland's chief industries are brewing, meat packing, sugar refining, and tanning. Queensland exports large amounts of wool, fruit, meat, sugar, and hides.

Education. Primary education is free and compulsory. Queensland University was set up in Brisbane in 1911, and a university college was founded at Townsville in 1961. Various technical and secondary schools receive government support.

Government. A governor appointed by the British Crown on the advice of the Queensland government serves as the chief executive in Queensland. An executive council of 11 ministers assists the governor. The state parliament has most of the governing power in

QUEENSLAND NUT

Queensland. The parliament consists of 78 members in a single assembly who serve three-year terms. Eighteen representatives and 10 senators represent Queensland in the federal parliament. All adults can vote.

History. The English navigator, James Cook, explored the coast of Queensland in 1770 and took possession of the region. Cook called it New South Wales. See COOK, JAMES; NEW SOUTH WALES.

The first settlement in Queensland was a *penal* (prison) colony, established on Moreton Bay in 1824. After 1840, free settlers entered the region.

Queensland was a part of New South Wales until 1859, when it became a separate colony. In 1867, the discovery of gold brought a rush of immigration. In January, 1901, Queensland and the other Australian colonies became states when they united to form the Commonwealth of Australia. C. M. H. CLARK

See also BRISBANE; GREAT BARRIER REEF.

QUEENSLAND NUT. See MACADAMIA NUT.

QUEENSTON HEIGHTS, BATTLE OF. See WAR OF 1812 (Chief Battles of the War).

QUEENSTOWN. See COBH.

QUEIRÓS, *kay ee RAWSH,* **PEDRO FERNANDES DE** (1565-1615) was a Portuguese pilot who served Spain. He took part in the discovery of the Marquesas Islands. Queirós believed that a great continent existed in the South Pacific and was allowed to make a voyage from Peru in search of it in 1605. But he found only a few Pacific islands. Queirós was born in Évora, Portugal, and died in Panama. CHARLES EDWARD NOWELL

QUEMOY, *kee MOY,* is the name of a group of islands about 5 miles off the coast of China, in the Formosa Strait. *Quemoy* is also the name of the largest island in the group. The Chinese call this island *Kinmen.* For location, see TAIWAN (map).

The Quemoy islands have a population of about 56,000 and an area of 68 square miles. The Chinese Nationalist government continued to control the islands after the Chinese Communists conquered mainland China in 1949. The Communists heavily bombarded the islands with artillery fire in 1958, but only occasional shelling occurred during the 1960's. RALPH N. CLOUGH

QUERÉTARO, *kay RAY tah roh,* is a mountainous state in central Mexico. It has a population of 485,523, and covers 4,544 square miles. For location, see MEXICO (political map). Farm products include wheat, corn, beans, and lentils. Mines there produce opals, silver, gold, lead, and copper. The city of Querétaro is the capital. The Mexican constitution was drafted in the city in 1916 and 1917. Querétaro is one of the original Mexican states. CHARLES C. CUMBERLAND

QUESTION MARK. See PUNCTUATION.

QUETZAL, *ket SAHL,* is a brilliantly colored bird of the trogon family, found in Central America. The head, back, and chest are glittering emerald-green, and the under parts are crimson. The head has a wide crest of golden-green, hairlike feathers. The upper tail feathers are enormously developed and form a train about 3 feet long. The brown and buff-colored female has no long tail feathers. As in trogons, the quetzal's feet are small and weak. This inactive bird sits quietly for long periods on a perch in the dense forest. It builds its nest in a hole in a tree. Ancient Maya chiefs used the long

tail feathers as a symbol of authority. There are still many legends about this bird. One legend says that the quetzal loves freedom so much that it cannot survive captivity. The quetzal is the national bird of Guatemala, and appears on the postage stamps and coins.

Scientific Classification. The quetzal belongs to the trogon family, *Trogonidae.* It is classified as genus *Pharomacrus,* species *P. mocinno.* RODOLPHE MEYER DE SCHAUENSEE

See also BIRD (color picture: Birds of Other Lands).

QUETZAL is a silver coin used as the currency unit of Guatemala. The coin is named for the quetzal, the national bird of Guatemala shown on the coin. The quetzal equals 100 centavos. See also MONEY (table: Values).

The Quetzal Is a Silver Coin of Guatemala.

Chase Manhattan Bank Money Museum

QUETZALCOATL. See AZTEC (Religion); MYTHOLOGY (American Indian Mythology; picture).

QUEUE, *kyoo,* is the name of the long braid of hair once worn by Chinese men. It is also used to mean a line of waiting persons or vehicles.

QUEVEDO, *kay VAY do,* **FRANCISCO DE** (1580-1645), was the leading Spanish humanist of the 1600's. He wrote extensively on social, political, religious, and aesthetic problems of Spanish Renaissance life. His works include *Life of the Swindler* (1626), a cruelly ironic picaresque novel; *Visions* (1627), a satirical prose portrait of Spanish society; and hundreds of poems on moral and sentimental themes. His political ideology, expressed in the *Politics of God* (1626) and other works, was modeled on the life and teachings of Christ and contrasted with the harsh realities of Spanish court intrigue. Quevedo's theological and philosophical essays generally reflect an ascetic and stoic point of view.

Quevedo was born in Madrid. His bitter satires caused him much personal trouble. He was jailed from 1639 to 1643 as the supposed author of verses ridiculing corruption in the court of King Philip IV. PETER G. EARLE

QUEZALTENANGO, *kay SAHL tay NAHNG goh* (pop. 45,195; alt. 7,872 ft.), is a trade center in western Guatemala. It is the country's second largest city. It markets such Indian products as blankets and pottery. *Quezaltenango* is an Indian word meaning *place of the quetzal.* The quetzal is the national bird of Guatemala.

QUEZON Y MOLINA, MANUEL LUIS (1878-1944), served as the first president of the Philippine Commonwealth from 1935 until his death. In 1934, the U.S. Congress passed the Philippine Independence Act, which established the Philippine Commonwealth. The next year, Quezon was elected president. The Japanese invasion of the Philippines drove Quezon to Corregidor. He escaped from Corregidor by submarine in 1942.

Quezon headed a Philippine government in exile

This Inspired Quiltwork is now a permanent exhibit in the Smithsonian Institution. It was made in the late 1800's, and its many bright colors center their patterns around the central star, or rising sun, design which dominates the piece.

Florence Peto

until his death. He was buried in Arlington National Cemetery. After World War II, his body was returned to the Philippines.

Quezon was born in Baler, Luzon, on Aug. 19, 1878, and studied law at the University of Santo Tomás in Manila. He served under the patriot Emilio Aguinaldo as a major in the Spanish-American War. After the war, he joined the United States territorial government. Quezon began his political career as governor of Tayabas province in 1905. From 1907 to 1909, he served as a member of the Philippine Assembly. As head of the Nacionalista Party, he worked for independence. From 1906 to 1915, Quezon was Philippine commissioner in the U.S. Congress. From 1916 to 1935, he was president of the Philippine Senate.

QUEZON CITY, *KAY sawn* (pop. 482,400; alt. 40 ft.), capital of the Republic of the Philippines, is a beautiful city 10 miles northeast of Manila (see PHILIPPINES [color map]). It is named for Manuel Luis Quezon, first president of the Commonwealth of the Philippines. Stately government buildings stand along Quezon City's palm-lined boulevards. The sprawling campus of the University of the Philippines lies in the city.

The Philippine government in 1939 purchased the land where Quezon City now stands. The land was part of a large private estate and was bought chiefly to serve as a residential area. Many Filipinos moved to the city from Manila after World War II. The government officially transferred the capital from Manila to

Quezon City in 1948. But Manila is the chief governmental center.   RUSSELL H. FIFIELD and CARLOS P. ROMULO

QUICK FREEZING. See FOOD, FROZEN.

QUICKLIME. See LIME.

QUICKSAND is a deep mass of extremely fine sand. It usually forms on the bottoms of streams and on the sand flats along seacoasts. When dry, quicksand looks like powder. The grains are either jagged or round. When water is forced upward through the sand, the grains are pushed apart and the sand swells. The sand loses firmness and cannot support heavy weight. Many persons have lost their lives by sinking into quicksand.

A person caught in deep quicksand must remain calm. He should fall flat on his back with his arms stretched out at right angles to his body. In this position, he will float on the sand. He should then roll slowly off the quicksand to firm ground. Building on quicksand is a difficult engineering problem that requires special types of building foundations.   RICHARD M. PEARL

QUICKSILVER. See MERCURY (metal).

QUILL. See FEATHER (Parts); PEN (History).

QUILT is a padded needlework covering, made of three layers of fabric. Silk, cotton, wool, or a similar fabric may be used for the front and back layers. The *interlining* (middle layer) may be of wool, cotton, kapok, or down. Quilting is usually used for bed coverings. But it also makes warm linings for winter clothing.

Quilting. When a bed quilt is sewed together, the three layers are stretched over a round or rectangular

QUINACRINE

The Hard, Golden-Yellow Quince puckers the mouth when tasted raw, but it has a delightful flavor when it is cooked.

quilting frame to keep the fabrics smooth and in shape. The stitches follow a design marked on the top layer. Small stitches are used so that the interlining will not slip. The edges are bound with bias strips of cloth.

Colorful geometric or floral patterns may decorate the top of a quilt. Two common methods of design are piecing and appliqué. The top of a *pieced* quilt is made of many small pieces of fabric sewed, or pieced, together to form a pattern. A jumble of odd-shaped patches, sewed together haphazardly, forms a "crazy quilt." In an *appliquéd* quilt, cutout cloth designs are sewed or embroidered on the quilt top (see APPLIQUÉ).

History. Quilting has been practiced for thousands of years. Soldiers of the Middle Ages wore padded and quilted coats and hoods under their armor. The Dutch and English colonists brought quilts to America to protect themselves from the severe cold of the winters. Quilting was a favorite art in American colonial and frontier homes. Women and girls wore quilted petticoats. Quilts covered the backs of chairs and fireside benches as a protection against drafts of cold air. At quilting *bees* (parties) in small towns, women and girls quilted in the afternoon. Their families joined them in the evening for supper and dancing.

Interesting and beautiful quilt designs were developed and passed on from generation to generation. Some quilt patterns portrayed historical events. Others had sentimental significance. Figures of lovebirds often decorated the quilts of young brides. Other popular designs included the *Wedding Ring*, the *Flower Garden*, and the *Dresden Plate*. Many early quilts were handed down as heirlooms, and a number can be seen on display at museums. Making quilts is still a popular hobby. HELEN MARLEY CALAWAY

QUINACRINE. See ATABRINE.

QUINARY NUMERALS. See NUMERATION SYSTEMS (The Quinary System).

QUINCE is an attractive shrub or small tree that is closely related to the apple and pear. It has many large, pinkish-white flowers and twisted branches. The flowering *Japanese quince* has showy red flowers, many branches, and a very sour fruit. The fragrant, fuzzy fruit is round to pear-shaped, and is golden-yellow. Its flesh is very hard, but bruises easily. The fruit has an acid taste, and is almost never eaten while fresh. It is used in marmalades and jellies. It is often combined with other fruits in preserves. Botanists call this type of fruit a *pome*. It bears many seeds in its core.

Quince can be grown from hardwood cuttings. A part of a young branch is placed in the soil, with its tip above the ground. It then sprouts roots and shoots. Buds from pear trees sometimes are *grafted* (joined) to a part of the quince. The result is a dwarf tree that yields pears (see PEAR).

Quince was originally grown in central Asia, and has been cultivated since ancient times. Most of the trees in the United States are grown in California, Michigan, New York, and Pennsylvania. New York grows most of the United States quince crop.

Scientific Classification. Quinces belong to the rose family, *Rosaceae*. Edible quinces are genus *Cydonia*, species *C. oblonga*. The Japanese flowering quince is genus *Chaenomeles*, species *C. japonica*. REID M. BROOKS

QUINCY, *KWIN see*, Ill. (pop. 45,288; alt. 490 ft.), on the east bank of the Mississippi River, is the westernmost city in the state (see ILLINOIS [political map]). In the mid-1800's, river transportation and early industries made Quincy a city second only to Chicago in commercial importance. Fortunes were made there in pork packing, river shipping, flour milling, brewing, and the manufacture of plows, stoves, and wagons. Quincy has about 80 industrial plants producing a wide range of products. The sixth of the Lincoln-Douglas debates was held there on Oct. 13, 1858. Quincy has a mayor-council government. PAUL M. ANGLE

QUINCY, *KWIN zee*, Mass. (pop. 87,966; alt. 140 ft.), an industrial city bordering on Boston Harbor, lies about 8 miles south of Boston. It covers about 16 square miles (see MASSACHUSETTS [political map]).

Quincy, Mass., is a shipbuilding and industrial center. Two United States Presidents, John Adams and John Quincy Adams, were born in Quincy. Both men are buried there.

Large shipyards are located in the city along Quincy Fore River, an inlet of Boston Harbor. They produce atomic-powered cruisers and other warships, as well as merchant vessels and yachts. Factories in the city manufacture gears, television tubes, rivets, packaging machinery, detergents, and food products.

Granite quarrying was a major industry in Quincy during the 1800's. One of the first railroads in the United States was built in Quincy, in 1826. Cars carried the granite for the Bunker Hill Monument from Quincy quarries to the waterfront. Barges then transported the granite to the site of the monument in Charlestown.

Captain Wollaston, an Englishman, settled Quincy as a trading post in 1625. It received a town charter in 1792 and a city charter in 1888. John Adams, the second President of the United States, and John Quincy Adams, the sixth President, were born and are buried in Quincy. The Adams house, home of the Adams family for 160 years, is a national historic site. Quincy has a mayor-council government.   WILLIAM J. REID

QUINCY COLLEGE. See UNIVERSITIES AND COLLEGES (table).

QUININE, *KWY nine* or *kwih NEEN,* is a bitter substance that is taken from the bark of the cinchona tree. It is used to treat malaria and other diseases. The trees from which it comes first grew along the eastern slopes of the Andes Mountains in South America. Indians there used the bark as medicine even before the Spanish came in the 1500's. The trees began to die out during the mid-1800's, but other cinchona trees were planted in India and Indonesia, especially Java. Most of the quinine used today comes from Java.

Doctors have used quinine chiefly to suppress attacks of malaria. It reduces the fever during attacks, but does not cure the disease. Quinine is used to treat malaria in many tropical regions where the drug is cheap and easy to obtain. In the United States, however, quinine has largely been replaced by *synthetic* (man-made) drugs such as quinacrine (atabrine), chloroquine, and primaquine. These drugs are more expensive to produce, but they are much more effective and less dangerous to use against most types of malaria than quinine. In Vietnam, however, doctors have found a type of malaria resistant to modern synthetic drugs. As a result, doctors there are again using quinine.

Doctors today still use the drug *quinidine* to treat

Quinine Comes from the Bark of the Cinchona Tree.
Field Museum of Natural History

and correct certain disorders of heart rhythm. Quinidine has the same chemical formula as quinine, and differs from it only in the way the atoms are arranged in the molecule. Doctors believe quinine and quinidine may cause abnormalities in unborn children. For this reason, pregnant women should not take these drugs without first consulting a doctor.   SOLOMON GARB

See also ALKALOID; CINCHONA; MALARIA.

QUINNIPIAC COLLEGE. See UNIVERSITIES AND COLLEGES (table).

QUINSY, *KWIHN zih,* is an abscess that forms in the region of the tonsils, causing sore throat. Doctors rarely use the word. They usually call this condition a *peritonsillar abscess.* It frequently follows attacks of acute tonsillitis (see TONSILLITIS). As a result of the infection, pus gathers about the diseased tonsils, forming an abscess. The abscess causes pain, and the patient's throat swells. The abscess may break open itself. If it does not, the doctor may open it to let the pus drain out.   ALBERT P. SELTZER

QUINTANA ROO, *keen TAH nah RAW oh,* is a territory of Mexico. It has a population of 91,044, and covers 16,228 square miles on the Yucatán Peninsula. For location, see MEXICO (political map). The territory occupies a jungle-covered plain. The hot, humid climate has discouraged settlement, and Quintana Roo is the most thinly settled region in Mexico. Hardwoods grow in the rich forests, but the land is poor for farming. Quintana Roo became a territory in 1902. Chetumal is the capital.   CHARLES C. CUMBERLAND

QUINTET. See MUSIC (Chamber Music).

QUINTILIAN, *kwin TILL yun* (A.D. 40?-95?), was a Roman instructor of public speaking and rhetoric. His full name in Latin was Marcus Fabius Quintilianus. He is best known for his 12-volume *The Training of an Orator.* It tells of the experience Quintilian gained in 20 years of teaching oratory and rhetoric. It deals with the training of a would-be orator from infancy, and with the practice of public speaking. The work also contains some of the best ancient literary criticism.

Quintilian was born in Calagurris, Spain. Little is known of the early years of his life. But it is believed that his family moved to Rome when he was young and that he grew up there.   THOMAS A. BRADY

QUINTILIS. See JULY.

QUINTILLION is a billion billions in the United States and France. One quintillion is written with 18 zeros: 1,000,000,000,000,000,000. In Germany and Great Britain, one quintillion has 30 zeros. See also DECIMAL NUMERAL SYSTEM (Larger Numbers).

QUINTUPLETS are five babies born to the same mother at one time. Scientists estimate that quintuplets occur only once in every 85 million births. The first quintuplets known to have lived more than a few hours after birth were five girls born to Elzire and Oliva Dionne on May 28, 1934. The Dionne quintuplets were born near Callander, Ont., Canada. The Fischer quintuplets were the first set of quintuplets born in the United States to survive early infancy. The four girls and a boy were born to Andrew James and Mary Ann Fischer on Sept. 14, 1963, in Aberdeen, S. Dak.

See also DIONNE QUINTUPLETS; MULTIPLE BIRTH; INCUBATOR (picture).

QUIPU. See INCA (Education; color picture: Inca Indians); INDIAN, AMERICAN (Writing).

QUIRE. See WEIGHTS AND MEASURES (Paper Measure).

QUIRINAL HILL, *KWIR ih nal,* is the northernmost of the famous seven hills of Rome. It was named for the god Quirinus (see QUIRINUS). It was originally the home of the Sabines (see SABINE). Evidence of their ancient settlement has been found on this hill. There were many famous temples on the hill, including the oldest shrine of the god Jupiter. Julius Caesar had large gardens on the edge of the hill, and the emperor Constantine built a famous public bath there. In the A.D. 1500's, a large palace and garden were built on the hill for the popes. These were later used by the kings of Italy. HERBERT M. HOWE

QUIRINAL PALACE was the residence of the kings of Italy. It stands on the Quirinal Hill in Rome. Before 1870 the palace was the summer residence of the popes. Gregory XIII began it for that purpose in 1574. In 1948 it became the official residence of the president of the Italian Republic. TALBOT HAMLIN

QUIRINUS, *kwih RYE nus,* was the third most important god in early Roman mythology. Only Jupiter and Mars were more important. After Romulus, the founder of Rome, died, the Romans made him a god called *Quirinus.* The festival of Quirinus was held on February 17. See also ROMULUS AND REMUS. JAMES F. CRONIN

QUISLING, *KWIZ ling,* **VIDKUN ABRAHAM LAURITZ** (1887-1945), was a Norwegian traitor of World War II. The word *quisling* came to stand for *traitor* because of his aid to German occupation forces. At the end of the war, he was convicted of treason and shot.

Quisling was born in Telemark. He joined the army and rose to the rank of captain. In 1931, he formed his own political party, the National Union. He contacted German Nazi leaders, and conferred with Adolf Hitler in 1940. Shortly afterward, the Germans attacked Norway. Quisling served briefly as head of the puppet Norwegian government. RAYMOND E. LINDGREN

QUITCLAIM. See DEED.

QUITO, *KEE toh* (pop. 551,163), is the capital of the Republic of Ecuador. It is Ecuador's second largest city and its principal textile center. Quito lies almost on the equator, 9,350 feet above sea level in the Andes Mountains. See ECUADOR (map; picture).

The name *Quito* comes from the word *Quitus,* the name of an ancient people who lived in Ecuador long before Spanish conquerors arrived in 1534. The Spaniards ruled Quito until 1822, when General Antonio José de Sucre defeated them in the Battle of Pichincha on a mountain slope overlooking the city. The victory helped Ecuador become an independent republic.

Under Spanish rule, Quito was a great center of religious art. Today, many of the city's old churches and monasteries have paintings and sculptures from that period. MURDO J. MACLEOD

QUIVIRA. See KANSAS (Exploration).

QUIXOTE, DON. See DON QUIXOTE.

QUMRĀN. See DEAD SEA SCROLLS.

QUO VADIS. See SIENKIEWICZ, HENRYK.

QUO WARRANTO is a Latin phrase which means *by what authority.* Today a quo warranto is a legal term applied to a writ or proceeding used by a court to inquire if an individual has the right to hold an office or franchise. The term *individual* may mean a person, company, or corporation. See also WRIT. THOMAS A. COWAN

QUOITS, *kwoits,* is a game of tossing a metal ring, called a *quoit,* over a peg. It was played as early as the 1300's in England, where it may have developed from the game of horseshoes (see HORSESHOE PITCHING).

Any number may play quoits at one time. Championship rules provide for two pegs that stand 1 inch above the ground and 18 yards apart. The quoits have a rim 2 inches wide, with a 4-inch hole in the center. Rubber, rope, or wooden quoits are often used for indoor games. Each player stands beside one peg and throws two quoits at the other peg. A *ringer* is a quoit that encircles the peg, and counts three points. A *leaner,* or *hobber,* is a quoit that leans against the peg, and counts two. If there are no ringers or leaners, the quoit closest to the peg counts one point. The game usually ends when one player has 21 points. DOROTHY DONALDSON

QUONSET HUT, *KWAHN sut,* is a corrugated steel building made in the shape of a half cylinder. The flat side forms the floor. The building is usually about 50 to 100 feet long, and 20 to 40 feet high. The first quonset hut was built for the navy in 1941 at Quonset Point, R.I. The huts have both military and civilian uses.

QUONSET POINT NAVAL AIR STATION, R.I., serves as headquarters for the U.S. Fleet Air Quonset. The activities of this command range from Antarctic exploration to air research and development. Its commander operates as the northern representative of the commander of naval air forces of the Atlantic Fleet. Several antisubmarine helicopter, utility, air development, and air service squadrons have bases here. The station covers 2,559 acres, and lies 20 miles south of Providence. It takes its name from the Indian word *Seconiquonset* (land jutting into the water). It was a recruiting depot in the Spanish-American War and a training center in World War I. The post became a naval air station in 1941. JOHN A. OUDINE

QUORUM, *KWOH rum,* is a certain number, or proportion, of members of an organization required by parliamentary law to be present before the group can transact business. In social organizations, the quorum is usually fixed by the constitution or by-laws, and may be less than a majority of the total membership. But if the assembly is a legislative body, such as a city council or a state senate, a majority of the members is required to form a quorum. No action of the members can change this requirement. A majority is also usually required if the body is a board of managers or trustees elected by a corporation to carry on its business. A quorum is not needed to debate legislative measures. But a quorum is required for a vote to be legal. PAYSON S. WILD

QUOTA INTERNATIONAL is a service club of women executives, organized to advance the interests of women in all career fields. Its motto, "We Share," is from the Latin word *quota,* meaning *a share.* The organization was founded in Buffalo, N.Y., in 1919. It has more than 12,000 members in about 400 clubs in the United States, Canada, Australia, and Mexico. Headquarters are at 1145 19th Street NW, Washington, D.C. 20036.

QUOTA SYSTEM. See IMMIGRATION AND EMIGRATION (Limits).

QUOTATION MARK. See PUNCTUATION.

QUOTIENT. See DIVISION.

Rr

is the 18th letter of our alphabet. It was also a letter in the alphabet used by the Semites who once lived in Syria and Palestine. They named it *resh*, their word for *head*, and adapted an Egyptian *hieroglyphic*, or picture symbol, for a human head to represent it. The Greeks later called the letter *rho*. When the Romans adopted the letter, they gave it its present capital *R* form. See ALPHABET.

Uses. *R* or *r* is about the sixth most frequently used letter in books, newspapers, and other printed material in English. *R* is used to stand for *Respond* or *Response* in prayer books and liturgies. *R* indicates *radius* or *ratio* in mathematics; *radical* in chemistry; and *resistance* in electricity. In titles, *R* may mean *royal* as in *R. N.*, for *Royal Navy*, or *registered* as *Registered Nurse*. *R* may mean *regular* as in *R.A.* for *Regular Army*, or *reserve* as in *USNR* for *U. S. Naval Reserve*. In some countries, *r* is the abbreviation for a unit of money, for *ruble* in Russia and for *rupee* in India. It is also an abbreviation for *rook* in chess.

Pronunciation. In English, a person pronounces *r* by placing the sides of his tongue against his molars, with the point of his tongue toward the hard palate. He contracts his tongue to form the *r* and the vowel that follows it. His velum, or soft palate, is closed, and the vocal cords vibrate. In some dialects, the *r* is trilled. In some regions in the United States, *r* is not pronounced in such words as *farm* or *here*. See PRONUNCIATION.   I. J. GELB and JAMES M. WELLS

The 18th letter took its shape from an ancient Egyptian symbol used to show a human head. Its sound came from the Semitic word *resh*, which means *head*.

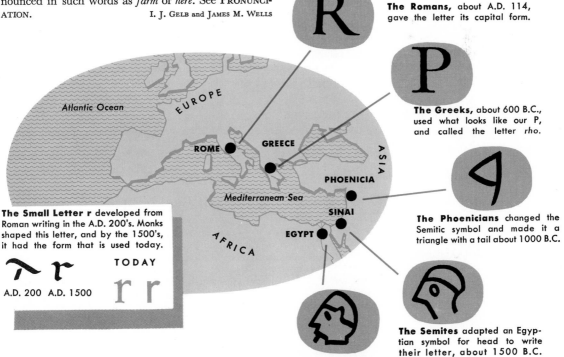

The Romans, about A.D. 114, gave the letter its capital form.

The Greeks, about 600 B.C., used what looks like our P, and called the letter *rho*.

The Phoenicians changed the Semitic symbol and made it a triangle with a tail about 1000 B.C.

The Small Letter r developed from Roman writing in the A.D. 200's. Monks shaped this letter, and by the 1500's, it had the form that is used today.

A.D. 200   A.D. 1500   TODAY
r r

Atlantic Ocean
EUROPE
ROME   GREECE
ASIA
PHOENICIA
Mediterranean Sea
SINAI
AFRICA   EGYPT

The Semites adapted an Egyptian symbol for head to write their letter, about 1500 B.C.

The Egyptians, about 3000 B.C., wrote with a symbol that represented a human being's head.

43

℞ is a symbol used on prescriptions written by doctors. It is generally accepted as representing the Latin word *recipe*, which means *take*. ℞ is traceable to ♃, the sign of Jupiter, which was placed on ancient prescriptions to appeal to that god for favorable action of the medicine. A more recent explanation of the cross at the end of the R, is that it is merely a substitute for a period. See also PRESCRIPTION.

RA. See RE.

RABAT, *ruh BAHT* (pop. 266,000; alt. 225 ft.), is the capital of Morocco. Rabat is in the northern part of the country. It lies on the Atlantic coast at the mouth of the Bou Regreg, a shallow river. The Bou Regreg separates Rabat from Salé, a city of about 89,000 persons. See MOROCCO (color map).

Rabat is divided into old and new sections. The old section, called the *medina*, is in the central and northern parts of the city. It has many small, white, flat-roofed houses and several *mosques* (Moslem houses of worship). The new section spreads out around the medina. It has broad streets and modern European-style buildings.

Rabat exports canned fruits and vegetables and has textile and cork-processing industries. Craftsmen in the city make baskets, carpets, embroidered fabrics, leather goods, tapestries, and other handicrafts. Asbestos products, bricks, and flour are other products of Rabat.

Mohammed V University was founded in Rabat in 1957. With more than 3,000 students, it ranks among Morocco's largest universities. Rabat's Museum of Antiquities exhibits objects from prehistoric and Roman times.

The Romans occupied the site of present-day Rabat in the first century after Christ. Ruins of buildings built by the Romans stand in southeastern Rabat. The Moorish leaders Abd-el-Mumin and Yacoub-el-Mansour founded the present city in the 1100's. France made Rabat the headquarters for a protectorate established in 1912 over most of Morocco. When the French gave up their protectorate in 1956, Rabat became the capital of Morocco's new, independent government.

RABAUL. See NEW BRITAIN.

RABBI, *RAB eye*, is the title of the spiritual leader of a Jewish congregation. The word is Hebrew for *my master*. Rabbis conduct religious services and are leaders in the educational and social life in Jewish communities.

The title of rabbi first came into use sometime between the birth of Jesus Christ and A.D. 100. It originally referred to teachers who were members of the *Sanhedrin*, a Jewish governing council in Palestine in Roman times (see SANHEDRIN). During the Middle Ages, rabbis held great power in Jewish communities in Europe. They carried on scholarly and religious activities and also served as political leaders of these communities.

In the United States, most rabbis are trained at one of three seminaries. Each seminary serves a major branch of Judaism. The Hebrew Union College trains reform rabbis, the Jewish Theological Seminary of America prepares conservative rabbis, and Yeshiva University trains orthodox rabbis.　　WILLIAM A. CLEBSCH

See also JUDAISM (The Rabbi).

RABBIT is a furry animal with long ears and a short, fluffy tail. Rabbits do not walk or run, as most other four-legged animals do. A rabbit moves about by hopping on its hind legs, which are much longer and stronger than its front legs. The animal also uses its front legs when it moves. A rabbit balances on its front legs much as a person balances on his hands when he plays leapfrog. When chased by an enemy, a rabbit can hop as fast as 18 miles an hour. Many children have pet rabbits. Pet stores sell tame rabbits that have been raised to be pets.

Rabbits live in Africa, Europe, North America, and other parts of the world. They make their homes in fields and prairies where they can hide their young under bushes or among tall grasses. A female rabbit usually has four or five young at a time, and may give birth several times every year. Rabbits in the southern United States, where the weather is warm most of the year, may have babies more than five times a year. In the northern part of the country, rabbits may give birth two to four times between April and September.

For thousands of years, men have hunted rabbits for meat and for skins. Today, most rabbits used for food and fur are raised by man, but sportsmen still hunt wild rabbits. Many people enjoy rabbit meat, which is sold fresh or frozen. Rabbit skins are used for making fur coats, or as trimming for cloth coats and hats. The skins can be cut and dyed to look like mink, beaver, or some other more valuable fur. A stiff cloth called *felt* may be made by squeezing rabbit fur together with other kinds of fur. The long fur of Angora rabbits is spun into a soft, warm yarn used for sweaters.

Rabbits and hares look much alike, and are often mistaken for each other. Some are even misnamed. For example, the Belgian hare is a rabbit, and the jack rabbit is a hare. Most rabbits are smaller than hares and have shorter ears. The animals can be told apart most easily at birth. A newborn rabbit is blind, it has no fur, and it cannot move about. A newborn hare can see, it has a coat of fine fur, and it can hop a few hours after birth. In addition, the bones in a rabbit's skull have a different size and shape from those in a hare's skull.

Rabbits and hares belong to the same *order* (main group) of the animal kingdom. The name of this order, *Lagomorpha*, comes from two Greek words meaning *hare-shaped*. To learn where the order fits into the animal kingdom, see ANIMAL (table: A Classification of the Animal Kingdom).

The Body of a Rabbit

Wild rabbits have soft, thick brownish or grayish fur. The fur of pet rabbits may be black, brown, gray, white, or combinations of these colors. An adult wild rabbit grows 8 to 14 inches long and weighs 2 to 5 pounds. Pet rabbits may grow about 8 inches longer and weigh 5 pounds more. Most female rabbits are larger than males. Among most other kinds of mammals, the males are larger. Few rabbits live more than a year in the wild because they have little protection against enemies. Many pet rabbits live as long as five years.

Charles M. Kirkpatrick, the contributor of this article, is Professor of Wildlife Biology at Purdue University.

A rabbit's eyes are on the sides of its head. As a result, the animal can see things behind or to the side better than in front. Rabbits can move their long ears together or one at a time to catch even faint sounds from any direction. Rabbits also depend on their keen sense of smell to alert them to danger. A rabbit seems to twitch its nose almost all the time.

Rabbits were once classified as *rodents* (gnawing animals). Like beavers, mice, and other rodents, rabbits have chisel-like front teeth for gnawing. But unlike rodents, rabbits have a pair of small teeth behind the upper front teeth.

A rabbit's tail is about 2 inches long, and is covered with soft, fluffy fur that makes it look round. The fur on the underside of the tail of most kinds of rabbits has a lighter color than that on top. American cottontail rabbits are named for the white or light gray fur on the underside of their tails. When a cottontail hops, its tail looks somewhat like a bouncing ball of white cotton.

The Life of a Rabbit

Rabbits of the United States and Canada live in fields, prairies, marshes, and swamps—wherever they can find bushes or clumps of tall grass in which to hide. They seldom live deep in a forest.

Homes. Most rabbits live in a shallow hole called a *form*. Shrubs, weeds, grasses, or leaves hide the bowl-shaped form from sight. Some rabbits live in a form throughout the year. Others, especially those of the northern United States and Canada, find a better protected home in winter. The winter den may be in a burrow, or under a pile of brush, rocks, or wood. Most rabbits do not dig their own burrows. They move into ones abandoned by such animals as badgers, prairie dogs, skunks, or woodchucks. Most rabbits live alone, but several may make their dens in the same pile of brush or wood.

Food. Most rabbits eat and play from dusk to dawn, and spend the day resting and sleeping. A rabbit eats many kinds of plants. In spring and summer, its foods are green leafy plants, including clover, grass, and weeds. In winter, the animal eats the twigs, bark, and

---
FACTS IN BRIEF

Names: *Male*, buck; *female*, doe; *young*, kit or kitten.

Gestation Period: Cottontails, 26 to 30 days; European rabbits, 28 to 33 days.

Number of Young: 2 to 9, usually 4 or 5.

Where Found: Africa; Australia; Europe; New Zealand; North, Central, and South America.

Scientific Classification: Rabbits belong to the order *Lagomorpha*, and to the rabbit and hare family, *Leporidae*. Cottontails belong to the genus of New World rabbits, *Sylvilagus*. European rabbits belong to the genus of Old World rabbits, *Oryctolagus*.

A Young Cottontail Sits Motionless to Escape Hunters, But Hops Away Quickly If They Come Near.

RABBIT

Ronald Thompson, APF

Angora Rabbits are raised for their fur. The long, white hairs are plucked from the animals' coats and spun into soft yarn.

Small Stock Magazine

A Belgian Hare, trained for shows, poses stiff-legged to display its shiny coat. Belgian hares are a breed of European rabbit.

fruit of bushes and trees. Rabbits sometimes damage crops because they nibble the tender sprouts of beans, lettuce, peas, and other vegetables. They also damage fruit trees by gnawing the bark, and may kill berry bushes by eating the sprouts.

Young. A female cottontail rabbit carries her young inside her body for 26 to 30 days before birth. She usually has four or five young, called *kits* or *kittens*, at a time, but she may have only two or as many as nine. The kits cannot see or hear, and they have no fur. The mother keeps them in a nest she has dug in the ground. She does not stay in the nest, but remains nearby. She lines the nest and covers the kits with grass and with fur that she pulls from her chest with her teeth. The cover hides the newborn rabbits and keeps them warm. By the time the kits are about 10 days old, they can see and hear, and have a coat of soft fur.

About two weeks after birth, when the kits are about

THE BODY OF A RABBIT

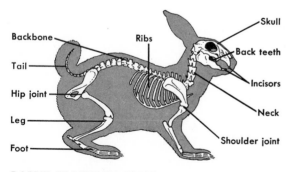

Backbone · Ribs · Skull · Back teeth · Tail · Incisors · Hip joint · Neck · Leg · Shoulder joint · Foot

RABBIT TRACKS IN SNOW

Hind feet

Front feet

WORLD BOOK illustration by Tom Dolan

46

as big as a man's fist, they leave the nest and hide in long grass and leaves. They usually dig their first forms near the nest. The mother seldom feeds her young for more than a few weeks after birth. Some female cottontails leave to start their own families when less than six months old.

Enemies. Man is the greatest enemy of rabbits. Every year, hunters kill millions of rabbits for sport. Farmers also kill many rabbits to protect crops. Other enemies of rabbits include coyotes, foxes, mink, and weasels. Hawks, owls, and some other birds hunt rabbits for food. Many dogs and cats also kill rabbits.

Rabbits usually try to hide from their enemies. If a rabbit is in the open when an enemy approaches, it may sit still and wait for the foe to go away. If the enemy comes too close, the rabbit dashes for safety. A frightened rabbit can leap 10 feet or more, and can travel as fast as 18 miles an hour. But it can go only a short distance because it tires quickly. The rabbit tries to confuse its enemy by zigzagging left and right. It sometimes circles back and follows its own trail for a short distance, and then leaps off in another direction. The rabbit may dive into a burrow or a pile of brush to escape.

Kinds of Rabbits

There are two chief kinds of rabbits: (1) cottontails, and (2) European rabbits.

Cottontails are the wild rabbits of Canada, the United States, and Mexico. There are several species of cottontails, including desert cottontails, mountain cottontails, and New England cottontails. Perhaps the most common species is the eastern cottontail, sometimes called the Florida cottontail. This rabbit lives in southeastern Canada, in the United States as far west as the Rocky Mountains, and in eastern Mexico.

European Rabbits, often called Old World rabbits, originally lived in southern Europe and northern Africa, and on some western Mediterranean islands. From these places they spread throughout Europe, including the British Isles. Man brought European rabbits to many other parts of the world including Australia, New

Rabbit Hutches are special cages that provide light, airy homes for pet rabbits. They are easy to keep clean and have troughs that hold hay and other food. Hutches can be bought at pet stores, or they can be built of wood and wire.

WORLD BOOK photo by E. F. Hoppe

Zealand, and South America. Rabbits have become pests in all these regions. The animals have few natural enemies there, and are a constant threat to plant life. Groups of European rabbit families may live near one another and share a system of burrows called a *warren*.

Man domesticated European rabbits hundreds of years ago, and developed many different varieties. Rabbits sold as pets in the United States and Canada are varieties of European rabbits. So are those raised for fur or meat. Among them are the albino, Angora, Belgian hare, chinchilla, and Flemish giant.

Pet Rabbits

Many rabbits are raised to be pets. Few wild rabbits live long in captivity.

Most rabbits do not like to be held or petted too often. Never lift a rabbit by its ears or legs. Grasp the loose skin over the animal's shoulders with one hand, and place the other hand under the rump to support the rabbit's weight.

WHERE RABBITS LIVE

The black areas in the map, *below*, show where rabbits are found.

Pet rabbits and wild rabbits both can get a disease called *tularemia* (rabbit fever). Anyone who handles a sick rabbit can get the disease and become severely ill with high fever, headaches, and sores on the body. Do not touch a rabbit that seems ill. If your pet is sick or injured, call a veterinarian for advice.

Cage. You can buy a *hutch* (rabbit cage) at a pet store, or you can build one. Place the hutch outdoors in a shady place. It should stand on a platform about 3 feet off the ground so it will not be flooded during a storm. The platform also keeps the rabbit from trying to dig burrows under the hutch. A rabbit needs plenty of fresh air, but must be kept warm and dry. In winter, the hutch should be put in a well-lighted basement or in a sun-warmed shed to protect the animal from the cold.

The hutch must be cleaned thoroughly every day. Fresh hay should be put in the rabbit's sleeping box at least twice a week.

Food. Pet rabbits eat such whole grains as barley, oats, and wheat. At noon, you can also give your pet beets, carrots, turnips, fresh-cut clover, or grass. You can give the animal some hay at night. Hay helps the rabbit's digestion, and biting the hard stalks helps wear down the front teeth, which grow continuously. If you feed the rabbit cabbage, give the animal only small amounts or it may get sick. Keep a bowl of fresh water in the hutch at all times.

Do not overfeed your rabbit. A rule of many rabbit raisers is to give the animals only as much food as they will eat in half an hour. All green foods should be removed as soon as the rabbit has finished eating because they spoil quickly. Some grain can be left in the trough at night.   CHARLES M. KIRKPATRICK

See also HARE; FUR (Rabbit); JACK RABBIT; TULA-REMIA.

RABBIT FEVER. See TULAREMIA.

RABELAIS, *rab uh LAY*, or *rah BLEH*, **FRANÇOIS** (1494?-1553?), a French humorist, wrote the comic satire *Gargantua and Pantagruel*. Gargantua and his son Pantagruel are giants with enormous appetites. Through their fantastic adventures, Rabelais ridicules the politics, justice, education, and religious institutions of his day. For example, the comic descriptions of Gargantua's education really satirize the educational methods of the time and express Rabelais' own ideas on the subject. Though famous for the earthy quality of his humor, Rabelais wrote earnestly about a wide range of serious subjects.

Rabelais was born near Chinon in the province of Touraine. He became a Franciscan monk in 1520, and received a bachelor of medicine degree in 1530 from the University of Montpellier. He practiced and lectured on medicine from 1532 to 1546.

In 1532, Rabelais published *Pantagruel*, a continuation of an anonymous popular work, *Chronicles of the Giant Gargantua* (1532). While preserving its popular tone, Rabelais added much learned material, and showed extraordinary gifts as a satirist and story-teller. *Pantagruel* was condemned for obscenity by the Sorbonne, the theological college of the University of Paris. In 1534, Rabelais published *Gargantua*, his own version of the episodes preceding *Pantagruel*. This book, which introduces the mischievous monk Frère Jean, was also condemned by the Sorbonne. In 1546, Rabelais published Book Three, which the Sorbonne condemned for heresy. He published Book Four in two parts, in 1548 and 1552. Rabelais wrote only parts of Book Five, which appeared in 1562 and 1564, after his death.

With his linguistic creativity, Rabelais invented many words, some of which remain in the French language. His emphasis on laughter and wine was surely an exaggeration, for scholars agree that though his love of life was genuine enough, he was a serious observer and thinker. His verve, his optimism, his delightful story-telling, and his ability to become involved in both fun and ideas, have made him one of the greatest and most loved French writers. ABRAHAM C. KELLER

See also FRENCH LITERATURE (The Humanists).

RABI, *RAH bih*, **ISIDOR ISAAC** (1898-), an Austrian-American physicist, won recognition for his studies of molecular beams. He also studied the magnetic properties of atomic nuclei. This study produced new information about how atoms are made, and what constitutes an atomic nucleus. It won for him the 1944 Nobel prize in physics. Rabi made many other studies in nuclear physics, atomic physics, and magnetism. In 1967, he received the Atoms for Peace Award.

Rabi was born in Austria, and earned degrees from Cornell and Columbia universities. He joined the physics department at Columbia in 1929, and later became head of the department. From 1940 to 1945, he served as assistant director of the Radiation Laboratory at the Massachusetts Institute of Technology, where he supervised the development of radar devices. He joined the Office of Scientific Research and Development in 1946, and became a member of the general advisory committee of the Atomic Energy Commission the same year. CARL T. CHASE

RABIES, *RAY beez*, or HYDROPHOBIA, *hy droh FOH bih uh*, is an infectious disease that destroys the nerve cells of part of the brain and causes death. Human beings and all warm-blooded animals are susceptible to the disease.

Rabies is a Latin word, meaning *rage* or *fury*. It probably received its name because infected animals often become excited and attack any object or animal in their way. Because one of the symptoms of rabies is an inability to swallow water, the disease often is called *hydrophobia*, which means *fear of water*.

Cause. Rabies is caused by a virus that lives in the saliva of a *host* (carrier). Most mammals can carry the rabies virus. If the host bites another animal or a human being, or if some of its saliva enters an open wound, the victim may get rabies. Animals have also developed rabies after breathing the air in caves that contained millions of bats. The virus can enter mucous membranes, such as those lining the nose, but it cannot invade unbroken skin. Dogs and wild animals are the most common source of infection for human beings.

When the virus enters the body, it travels along nerves to the spine and brain, producing inflammation. Once symptoms appear, death is inevitable. The symptoms develop about 10 days to 7 months after exposure.

Symptoms in Man. Among the first symptoms are pain, burning, or numbness at the site of infection. The victim complains of headaches and is unable to sleep. Muscle spasms make the throat feel full, and swallowing becomes difficult. Sometimes, the sight of water creates such painful throat contractions that drinking is dreaded. Later, the patient may have convulsions. But after a day or two, he lapses into a quiet period, which progresses to unconsciousness and, finally, death. The disease lasts from 2 to 12 days.

Symptoms in Dogs. The disease follows the same pattern as in man. During the period of excitation, the dog may wander great distances. It is aggressive, growling and barking almost constantly, and will attack without reason. From this stage the disease usually progresses to general paralysis, then death. Some rabid dogs never show signs of the excitative phase but only of the paralysis. This form of the disease is sometimes called *dumb rabies*. Paralysis of the jaw and throat muscles are characteristic of this type of rabies.

Treatment. The most important treatment is to prevent the disease by vaccinating all dogs. A person bitten by any animal should immediately wash the area thoroughly with soap and water. The animal should be penned up and watched by a qualified person for symptoms of rabies. If these develop, the doctor begins to vaccinate the victim at once. He gives injections of vaccine daily for 14 days or longer. If the animal cannot be found, the physician gives the injections to the victim as a safety measure. ERNEST S. TIERKEL

See also PASTEUR, LOUIS.

RABINOWITZ, SOLOMON. See SHOLOM ALEICHEM.

RACCOON, *ra KOON*, is a small furry animal related to the panda, kinkajou, and coati. It is called "coon" for short. All the different kinds of raccoons live in the two Americas.

The common raccoon is about 32 inches long from its nose to the end of its tail. It weighs from 20 to 25 pounds. It has a stout body covered with long, coarse hair that is grayish, with black tips. The underfur is pale brown.

Hobart V. Roberts

Raccoons Climb Trees to Escape from Dogs When They Are Hunted.

The raccoon has a bushy, grayish-white tail, with black rings. Its face looks like that of a fox. The nose is sharp and delicate. A black patch around each eye has a ring of white hair around it. This gives the raccoon a cunning look that fits its mischievous nature.

Their Habits. Raccoons have long legs and strong claws. They are famous tree climbers, and like to live in hollow trees. In cold climates, they sleep there during the winter, but do not hibernate. Raccoons also make their homes in dens in rocky ground or ledges.

Like bears, coons eat almost anything that comes their way. Among their favorite foods are frogs, crayfish, turtles, and other fresh-water animals. They are fond of all berries and other fruits. They eat corn greedily, and ruin corn crops with their visits. If water can be found nearby, they wash their food before they eat it. They also like to paddle in the water. Perhaps their worst faults are robbing birds' nests and raiding chicken coops.

Most raccoons have three or four young at a time. The baby raccoons are blind and helpless at first, and the parents care for them for several months. The cry of a baby raccoon sounds like that of a human baby. Most raccoons live from 10 to 12 years.

Their Uses. If captured when young, coons are easy to tame, and make amusing pets. In the Southern States, coon hunts are a favorite sport on moonlight nights. People eat roast raccoon more in the South than in other parts of the country. In colonial days, coonskin caps, sleigh robes, and overcoats were popular. Today, raccoon coats for women are made from the original long-haired pelt, or the hairs are plucked out, leaving the pale-brown underfur. This is called *sheared raccoon*.

From 1838 to 1844, the raccoon was the emblem of the Whig party in the United States. Members of that party were popularly called *coons*. The famous log cabins of the Harrison and Tyler campaign of 1840 always had coonskins nailed to the outside.

Scientific Classification. Raccoons are in the raccoon family, *Procyonidae*. The common raccoon is genus *Procyon*, species *P. lotor*.   E. LENDELL COCKRUM

Related Articles in WORLD BOOK include:
Animal (color picture)   Kinkajou   Trapping
Coati   Panda   (picture)
Fur

RACEME, *ruh SEEM*, is a term used in botany for a type of flower cluster. Each flower on a racemose plant grows on its own short stem, called a *pedicel*. All the flower stems are on the same stalk, or *peduncle*. There is no flower or terminal blossom at the exact end of the stalk. More flowers appear as the stalk grows longer. Therefore there is no definite number of flowers on a racemose plant. This kind of flowering is called an *indeterminate inflorescence*. The stems of the individual flowers grow in the axils of small modified leaves, called *bracts*. The lily of the valley is an example of a racemose plant. See also INFLORESCENCE.   ARTHUR W. GALSTON

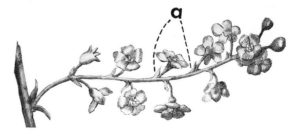

(a) Indicates Bracts On a Racemose Flower Cluster.

Crowd Watching a Parade in Honolulu, Hawaii

AMERICAN INDIAN
Group of Bolivian Indians

MELANESIAN
New Guinea Mother and Child

MICRONESIAN
Yap Islanders

RACES OF MAN

The Major Races of Man. All human beings belong to the same species. But mankind consists of many races, and the members of each resemble one another in some ways. The Honolulu crowd scene above includes people of several races and shows part of the huge range of human variation. The other illustrations show members of the major geographical races.

RACES OF MAN. All human beings have a common ancestry. In this sense, all people are related to one another. But many groups of mankind have lived apart for long periods of time and have come to differ from one another in various ways. Members of the same group, or *race*, resemble one another more than do members of different races.

Race has been used as a major basis of telling one group from another. Some members of some races can be identified easily by the color of their skin, the color of their hair, or the shape of their eyes. But some mem-

Stanley M. Garn, the contributor of this article, is Professor of Health Development at the University of Michigan and the author of Human Races.

bers of the same race—and even the same family—have widely differing body features. Some are short and others are tall. Some have light complexions, blue eyes, and straight blond hair. Others have dark complexions, brown eyes, and dark curly hair. Today, many scientists use blood groups and other characteristics of body chemistry in comparing different races.

Races are major *subdivisions* (parts) of a species. All existing races of man—that is, all people living today—belong to the species *Homo sapiens*. These two Latin words, meaning *man* and *wise*, separate man from other manlike species that once existed but are now extinct.

Species of plants and other animals also consist of groups that differ from one another. Such groups are sometimes called *races*, but they are usually referred

Dan Budnik, Woodfin Camp, Inc.

POLYNESIAN
Tahitian Woodcarver

Marc Riboud, Magnum

ASIAN
Chinese Schoolchildren

J. Alex Langley, DPI

AUSTRALIAN
Australian Aborigine

A. Lawrence, Pix

AFRICAN
Young Girls of Tanzania

Irving Schild, DPI

EUROPEAN
Italian Family

Robert Pastner, FPG

INDIAN
Shoppers on a Ceylon Street

to as *natural populations, breeds, varieties,* or *subspecies.* A natural population is a group of animals or plants of the same species that live in a certain area and reproduce largely within their own group.

Human races also are natural populations. Some natural populations of man have lived in the same general area for thousands of years. Some of these populations are extremely large and have hundreds of millions of members. Others are small and have only a few thousand members. Some natural populations, such as the Apache and Navaho Indians, have moved to their present locations to improve their climate or food supply. Others, such as the Cherokee and Seminole Indians, have been forced onto their present lands. Still other populations, including the peoples of Northwest Europe and West Africa, have multiplied greatly, and many of their members live on continents far from their original homeland.

Human races, like all other natural populations, are

based on *heredity,* the passing on of characteristics from parents to offspring. All hereditary characteristics are determined by tiny particles called *genes.* A child inherits half his genes from his father and half from his mother. Members of the same race have more genes in common than do members of different races. Closely related races also have more genes in common than do distantly related races, just as cousins have more genes in common than do members of different families. For further information on how characteristics are inherited, see the WORLD BOOK articles on HEREDITY; CELL; and GENE.

All the genes in a population are sometimes called the group's *gene pool.* The degree to which a particular gene is present in a group is called the population's *gene frequency.* When we say that races change, we mean that their gene frequencies change.

The idea of race has often been misunderstood, and the term has sometimes been misused on purpose. Race

51

has often been confused with culture, language, nationality, or religion. Differences in physical appearance have led some people to mistakenly conclude that members of some races are born with superior intelligence, talents, and moral standards. Race has also been a major basis of discrimination by one group against another. See MINORITY GROUP; SEGREGATION.

This article tells how races are classified. It describes racial differences and how races develop and change. It also discusses some mistaken ideas about race and how the term is misused.

How Races Are Classified

The number of races of mankind varies according to the classifier and the purposes of his classification. At one time, many scholars divided human beings into three major races—Caucasoid, Mongoloid, and Negroid. Today, many *anthropologists* (scientists who study man) distinguish between larger and smaller population units. Some call these units *geographical races* and *local races*. They recognize 9 or 10 geographical races and hundreds of local races.

The Three-Race Theory. During the Middle Ages—from the A.D. 400's to the 1500's—Europeans knew about the darker-skinned, curly-haired peoples of Africa. They also knew about the peoples of Asia, most of whom were shorter and had light-brown skins. These eastern peoples had straight hair, pads of fat over their cheekbones, and folds of skin extending from their eyelids over the inner corners of their eyes. This limited picture of the peoples of the world suggested that there were three "original" races—European, or "white"; African, or "black"; and Asian, or "yellow."

For many years, scholars attempted to explain all human populations in terms of the three "original" races. They believed that all people belonged to one of those races or to some combination of them.

Increased contacts between people of different cultures revealed that the number of large geographically isolated human groups was far larger than three. During the 1900's, scientists have learned much about blood types and their relation to races. Studies of blood types have greatly changed the scientific outlook on races. Such information tends to rule out the simple three-race theory. This evidence shows that no possible combination of African, Asian, and European groups could produce the aborigines of Australia, the Micronesians of the Yap Islands, or the Negritos of the Philippines. A more complicated explanation than simple race mixture became necessary to explain such populations.

Today, scholars know that the larger and smaller groupings of mankind are the products of evolutionary change. They know that race differences result from a group's common ancestry, thousands of years of living in the same area, and exposure to common selective forces. These forces will be discussed in this article in the section called *How Races Develop and Change.*

Geographical Races—sometimes called *major races* —are collections of similar races. In general, they extend throughout major continental areas, such as Africa and Asia, and large island chains, such as Micronesia and Polynesia. Geographical races do not correspond exactly to the continents. For example, the European geographical race includes populations throughout Europe, in the Middle East, and north of the Sahara in Africa. This article recognizes nine geographical races: (1) African, (2) American Indian, (3) Asian, (4) Australian, (5) European, (6) Indian, (7) Melanesian, (8) Micronesian, and (9) Polynesian. For some of the main characteristics of these races, see the table with this article called *Geographical Races of Man.*

Geographical races exist because of such natural barriers as oceans, mountains, and deserts. For thousands of years, these barriers isolated groups of people and

THE GEOGRAPHICAL RACES OF MAN

This map shows where the major geographical races of man lived before the great period of overseas exploration began in the late 1400's. The color areas indicate the approximate extent of each race. The map does not show the present-day distribution of races.

WORLD BOOK map

slowed down migrations into and out of regions. India, for example, has been partly isolated from the rest of Asia by the Himalaya. Australia, an island continent, was largely cut off from the rest of the world until the British established a prison colony there in 1788. The British found only scattered tribes in Australia and called these people *aborigines*, which means *natives*. The tribes had developed for many generations with only a slight introduction of genes from groups who had made their way into Australia from New Guinea. The American Indians also remained isolated from the rest of the world for thousands of years. See ABORIGINE; INDIAN, AMERICAN (The First Americans).

Europeans were less isolated from other geographical races than were the American Indians or the Australian aborigines. During the Middle Ages, the invading Moors brought genes into Europe from Africa, and the Tartars brought genes from Asia. On the other hand, little or no migration occurred from the African Congo to Denmark or from Finland to Sumatra.

Since the 1500's, people have increasingly migrated to lands occupied by other geographical races. Today, about half as many people of European descent live outside Europe as in Europe. Most of them live in Australia, New Zealand, North or South America, or South Africa. Millions of people from India live in other parts of Asia, in Africa, or in North or South America. In the United States, thousands of Japanese, Korean, and Vietnamese war brides have added new genes to those of the population. In Hawaii, many people have mixed Portuguese-Hawaiian-Chinese-Japanese ancestry.

Local Races are smaller population units than are geographical races. They are subcategories of geographical races.

Each geographical race consists of local populations that differ *genetically* (according to their genes). However, the gene pools of local populations of the same geographical race are more alike than are the gene pools of different geographical races. Before white men came to the New World, the American Indians consisted of hundreds of local groups, or *local races*. Even today there are such distinct North American groups as the Apache, Blackfoot, Creek, Dakota, Iroquois, and Seminole. Local races in Latin America include the Araucanian, Arawak, Cayapo, Jivaro, Lacandon, and Yucatec.

Some local races, such as the Northwest European, have millions of members. This group includes the "white" peoples of Scandinavia, Germany, Belgium, The Netherlands, Great Britain, and Ireland. It also includes peoples who emigrated—or whose ancestors emigrated—from those countries. Smaller local races include the Basques, who live on the slopes of the Pyrenees between France and Spain, and the Lapps, who live in extreme northern Europe.

Within local races, there are sometimes more or less distinct subpopulations that some anthropologists call *microraces*. However, microraces—and even local races—are not always clearly distinguished. Especially within the same broad geographic area, there has always been some intermarriage between members of different subpopulations.

Studying Races. Scientists study the large or small racial groupings, depending on the questions they are trying to answer. For example, researchers might want to compare the frequency of the Rh-negative blood group in members of the European geographical race and the African geographical race. More often, scientists study a local race. They might want to know the effects of climate on the evolution of the Bushmen of

---
GEOGRAPHICAL RACES OF MAN

African, frequently called *Negroid*, is a collection of related races in Africa south of the Sahara. Members have curly or tightly coiled hair, thick lips, and large amounts of melanin in the skin, hair, and gums. They have changed genetically to meet such diseases as malaria. American Negroes are mostly of African origin.

American Indian, sometimes called *Amerindian* or *American Mongoloid*, is related to the Asian geographical race but differs in various blood-group frequencies. For thousands of years, American Indians were the only people in the Western Hemisphere. Their skin ranges from light to dark brown, and they have straight, dark hair.

Asian, sometimes called *Mongoloid*, includes populations in continental Asia, except for South Asia and the Middle East. It also extends to Japan, Taiwan, the Philippines, and the major islands of Indonesia. Members have straight hair, inner eyefolds, and pads of fat over their cheekbones. Most of them are shorter than Europeans and have light brown skin.

Australian, also called *Australian aborigine* or *Australoid*, is a group of local races in Australia. Members have large teeth, moderate to heavy skin coloring, narrow skulls, and a moderate amount of body hair.

European, sometimes called *Caucasoid*, includes populations throughout Europe, in the Middle East, and north of the Sahara. Members have lighter skins than the people of any other geographical race, with

blondness increasing from south to north. The "whites" of Australia, New Zealand, North and South America, and South Africa are members of the European geographical race.

Indian includes populations in South Asia and extends from the Himalaya to the Indian Ocean. Skin color ranges from light in the north to dark in the south. The Indian and European geographical races both have high frequencies of blood group B, but they differ in several other blood groups.

Melanesian, or *Melanesian-Papuan*, includes the dark-skinned peoples of New Britain, New Guinea, and the Solomon Islands. They resemble Africans in skin color but are unlike Africans in blood-group frequencies.

Micronesian occupies a series of islands in the Pacific, including the Carolines, Gilberts, Marianas, and Marshalls. Members are dark-skinned and most are small. Micronesians have wavy to woolly hair. Their blood-group frequencies resemble those of the Polynesians, but they have higher frequencies of blood group B.

Polynesian consists of Pacific Island peoples living far apart, ranging from Hawaii in the north to New Zealand in the south and from Easter Island in the east to the Ellice Islands in the west. Members are tall and many are stout. Polynesians have light to moderate skin color. Like other Pacific populations, they have low frequencies of blood group B.

RACES OF MAN

HUMAN VARIATION

No two human beings—not even identical twins—are exactly alike. But members of the same geographical race tend to show certain physical resemblances, just as members of the same family resemble one another. The illustrations on this and the next page show some of the likenesses and variations in features among individuals and populations.

– SOME GENETICALLY DETERMINED RACE DIFFERENCES –

ABO Blood-Group System. Blood-type O is the most common, followed by type A. Type B is common among members of the African and Asian geographical races, but it is rare or completely absent among American Indians and Australian aborigines.

Rh Blood-Group Factor. The Rh-negative gene *r* is relatively common among Europeans, especially among the Basques, but is extremely rare elsewhere.

MNS Blood-Group System. Blood-group M is common among American Indians. But it is rare among Australian aborigines and populations in the Pacific. Most of these peoples belong to group N. Both the M and N groups are common among Asians and Europeans.

Lactase Deficiency. In many parts of the world, older children and adults lack the intestinal enzyme *lactase*. As a result, they cannot drink more than 8 ounces of milk a day without discomfort.

Missing Third-Molar Teeth. Many people of Asian origin lack the third molar, or wisdom, teeth. Between 9 and 20 per cent of all adult Europeans also lack some or all of these four teeth. Almost all West Africans have the third molars.

Wrist-Bone Fusions. The *triquetral* and *lunate* bones of the wrist are *fused* (joined) in 6 per cent of all West Africans and 1.2 per cent of American Negroes, but only 0.1 per cent of people of European descent.

Color Blindness. Only a few persons are truly blind to all colors. The inability to distinguish red from green is rare among most groups but is more common among some populations of the Middle East.

Sickle Cell Gene. In parts of Africa, up to 40 per cent of all individuals in some populations carry the sickling hemoglobin gene. But in parts of the world where malaria is rare, the frequency of the sickling gene is close to zero.

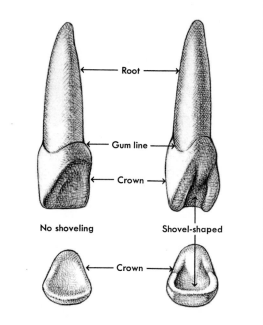

WORLD BOOK illustrations by Neil O. Hardy

The Upper Front Teeth, called *incisors*, of many American Indians are shovel-shaped on their back surfaces, shown by the arrows. Among some Indian populations, the back surfaces are almost tubular-shaped. Tooth size and shape vary greatly from one race to another.

southern Africa. Or, investigators might concentrate on a very restricted population, such as that of Easter Island, to study the effects of mating between closely related persons.

Racial Differences

Early descriptions of human races were based on physical differences that could be easily seen. Such differences included the color of the skin and the color and texture of the head hair and beard. People also noted differences in body size and proportions and in the shape of the nose, lips, and eyelids. During the 1800's, some scholars used these differences to develop simple systems of comparison and analysis.

Many physical features not only are complicated genetically but also are affected by the environment. Skin color, for example, involves the combined effect of many genes and is also affected by exposure to sunlight. Thus, a well-tanned Swedish farmer may be darker than an Italian office worker.

Scholars use *simply-inherited traits* for more useful information on races and how they differ. Such traits are determined by a single set of genes and are not directly affected by the environment.

Obvious Physical Differences, to some extent, can be used today in making racial comparisons. For example, the amount of the blackish or brownish substance called *melanin* in the skin largely determines the skin's lightness or darkness. Dark-skinned races have more melanin in their skin than do light-skinned races (see SKIN). Inner eyefolds are characteristic of the peoples of Asia and of many American Indian groups. Most Eskimos, Filipinos, and Japanese have short legs in proportion to their body height. Thick lips are common among Africans and some peoples of the Pacific. Heavy beards are common among members of the European geographical race and of the Ainu local race in Japan.

Blood-Group Differences. Blood groups are the most important simply-inherited traits for racial comparisons. Every person's red-cell characteristics are deter-

54

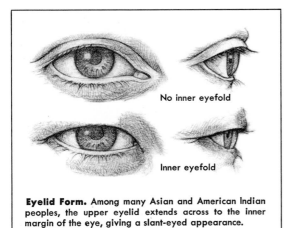

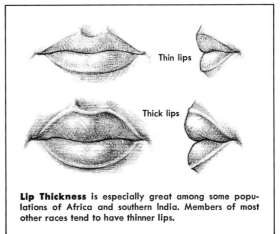

Eyelid Form. Among many Asian and American Indian peoples, the upper eyelid extends across to the inner margin of the eye, giving a slant-eyed appearance.

Lip Thickness is especially great among some populations of Africa and southern India. Members of most other races tend to have thinner lips.

Warren Garst, Tom Stack & Associates

Rohn Engh, Van Cleve Photography

Hair Form Varies Widely among individuals and populations. Many African Bushmen have peppercorn hair, *left*, which is tightly coiled and grows in small patches. American Indians have coarse, straight hair, *right*, which is also common among members of the Asian geographical race.

mined by the genes he inherits from his parents. Studies of blood groups show a gradual change in the frequencies of some blood groups from one area to the next. The best-known blood-group system is the ABO system. In this system, type O is the most common throughout the world, followed by type A. Type B is common among members of the Asian and African geographical races, less common among Europeans, and rare among Australian aborigines and American Indians. The Rh-negative type is relatively common among Europeans but rare among other races. Other blood-group systems used in comparing human populations include the Diego, Kell, Kidd, Lutheran, and MNS systems. Many of these systems are named for the person in whom the blood-group factor was first discovered. See BLOOD (Blood Groups).

Knowledge of blood groups helps scientists determine relationships between races. For example, the Australian aborigines were once considered "primitive Caucasoids." But they differ so much from Europeans in

blood-group frequency that it is unlikely that either geographical race was derived from the other. The dark-skinned peoples of Australia, southern India, and the Pacific all differ in blood-group frequencies. Their blood groups also set them apart from the peoples of Africa. The American Indians, who came from Asia 10,000 to 40,000 years ago, resemble the peoples of Asia to some extent. But they have also come to differ from Asians, particularly in lacking blood group B and having a low frequency of group N.

Medical uses of blood and the treatment of blood diseases have led to increased knowledge of genetic differences between populations. Much information on blood-type frequencies comes from blood-bank records. In addition, persons who receive blood transfusions must first have their blood type identified. See BLOOD BANK; TRANSFUSION, BLOOD.

Other Simply-Inherited Traits are also used in the study of race. For example, Africans and Europeans have soft, sticky earwax. The Japanese and many

55

American Indian groups have the dry, crumbly type. People of Asian descent have large amounts of a certain type of amino acid in their urine. Europeans, on the other hand, have only small amounts. People of African origin may have some *fused* (joined) wrist bones. Some people of Asia and Central and South America have a reduced middle section of the little finger.

Race and Disease. Races differ in the frequency of certain genes that are involved in disease and resistance to disease. A hereditary blood disorder called *sickle cell anemia* occurs mainly in members of the African geographical race. Individuals who inherit the sickling hemoglobin gene from both parents suffer from sickle cell anemia. Most cases of this disease are fatal. Persons who inherit the sickling gene from only one parent do not get the disease. But they can transmit the abnormal gene to their children.

Genetic carriers of sickle cell anemia are relatively immune to malaria. For this reason, the abnormal hemoglobin gene has come to be an advantage in some parts of Africa, southern Europe, and the Caribbean. Populations that have been exposed to malaria for the longest time have the most abnormal hemoglobin genes. This is an example of how the genetic makeup of races changes to meet the pressures of the environment.

Many other genetically determined disorders also occur more frequently in one population than in others. The hereditary disease *phenylketonuria* (PKU) occurs among the European geographical race more often than among Asians or Africans. The bodies of people with this disease cannot properly transform one kind of amino acid into a related amino acid. The disorder results in mental retardation unless treated early. Many adult Africans, Asians, and American Indians have *lactase deficiency*. They lack the enzyme necessary to digest the milk sugar *lactose*, so milk may not be a good food for them. In some populations, a protein in wheat prevents food from being absorbed into the blood stream. This condition leads to a disease called *sprue*, which involves several digestive disorders.

Race and Climate. The genetic makeup of races may change to meet changes in climate. Dark and light skin color, for example, are adaptations to different climates. The amount of melanin that colors the skin, hair, and eyes differs greatly from one person to the next. Large amounts of melanin help protect the skin from sunburn and improve vision in bright sunlight. Therefore, dark skin and dark eyes are helpful adaptations for people who live in hot climates with much sunlight. But in cloudy climates with long winter nights, dark skin may interfere with the production of vitamin D.

Races also differ in response to cold. Eskimos respond by keeping a high blood flow in their arms, legs, fingers, and toes. They keep their body temperature up by burning more energy. As a result, they require more food during the Arctic winter. Certain physical features also keep Eskimos warm. For example, their stocky bodies hold warmth better than do the bodies of tall, thin people. The Australian aborigines meet cold in a different way. The body temperature in their legs and feet drops during sleep, and they burn less energy than

SICKLE CELL ANEMIA

Sickle cell anemia is a hereditary blood disease that is common in central Africa. Individuals who inherit the sickling hemoglobin gene from both parents suffer from the disease.

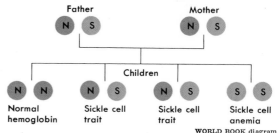

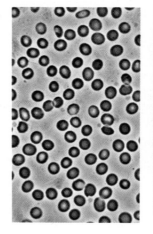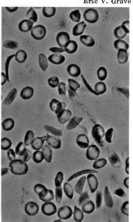

WORLD BOOK diagram

In the chart above, each parent carries one normal hemoglobin gene and one sickling gene. A child of such parents has one chance in four of inheriting the sickling gene from both parents, and thus developing sickle cell anemia. Persons who inherit the sickling gene from only one parent do not get the disease. But they can transmit the abnormal gene to their children. The magnified blood samples below show normal red blood cells, *left*, and the abnormal cells of a person with sickle cell anemia, *right*.

Eric V. Gravé

do other peoples. The only part of their body that remains warm in the cold desert night is the trunk.

The Australian aborigines, who may sleep in below-freezing night temperatures, and the Eskimos of the Arctic have both adapted to cold. The aborigines have a generally warm climate and a limited food supply. They have no extra food to burn for body heat when the temperature drops below freezing. Instead, they adapt by saving energy. But this method of adapting to cold would not be possible in the Arctic. The Eskimos are adapted to extreme cold—temperatures as low as 40 to 60 degrees below zero. Their adaptation depends on the availability of food to supply energy and body heat.

How Races Develop and Change

Human races, like all natural populations, change continually. Several processes play an important part in the formation and change of races. They include (1) natural selection, (2) mutations, (3) genetic drift, and (4) race mixture. Social factors, as well as technological and medical advances, also produce racial changes.

Natural Selection is the process by which individuals that best fit their environment tend to survive and pass their characteristics on to their offspring. Persons with a favorable genetic makeup for a specific environment are likely to survive and have children. Those who are least well adapted are unlikely to live to adulthood and reproduce. As a result, advantageous genes increase in frequency, and disadvantageous ones decrease. Many scientists believe that differences in skin color, body build, and many other traits represent genetic adaptations to different environments. If the environment of a region were to change, the race populations of the region would adapt with changes in their genetic makeup through many generations. See NATURAL SELECTION.

Mutations. A mutation is a change in a gene. The changed gene produces a different inherited trait and is passed on to the following generations. Mutations result from a change in the order of units of DNA (deoxyribonucleic acid), the chief chemical compound of genes. Scientists can change the order of DNA units with radiation and chemical treatments, but they cannot tell in advance which genes will mutate.

Most mutations are harmful, but some are beneficial. A favorable gene may make a person stronger, healthier, or better suited to his environment. Mutations provide a major source of new genes in a population's gene pool. Beneficial genes increase in frequency from generation to generation through natural selection. On the other hand, harmful mutations tend not to increase in a population, because they do not help individuals adapt to their environment. See MUTATION; HEREDITY (Heredity and Evolution); NUCLEIC ACID.

Genetic Drift refers to chance changes in the gene frequencies of a population from generation to generation. Such changes have little importance in large populations, but they may greatly affect the genetic makeup of small populations. In a small primitive society, for example, a rich man or a tribal chief may have many wives and many children. Thus, his genes may greatly increase in the population. On the other hand, a man or woman with a rare gene may have no children, and the gene may disappear from the population.

Race Mixture. The entire history of mankind involves the gradual elimination of small populations called *isolates*, each of which mates largely within its own group. Such populations are continually being blended into larger ones.

The greatest amount of race mixture occurs between populations that live next to one another. These populations tend to resemble one another and to differ from those separated by great distances. Such resemblances do not occur if one of the groups has migrated from a distant region. For example, the Apache and Navaho Indians differ considerably from other tribes of the Southwestern United States. Those two tribes migrated from the Canadian Northwest only a few hundred years ago and still resemble the Indians of that region.

Race mixture may also result from various cultural practices. Since earliest times, people have moved from one place to another and have chosen mates from other groups. Such practices as exploration, warfare and con-quest, bride capture, colonization, and enslavement of other peoples have brought individuals of various races together. The result in many cases has been change in the genetic makeup of the populations involved.

Some races are the products of interbreeding within the past few hundred years between members of two or more geographical populations. The Coloureds of South Africa are the descendants of the Hottentots and other peoples who mated with the first European settlers in South Africa. American Negroes, though mostly of African origin, have mixed racial ancestry. In the United States, a person with any known Negro ancestry is usually considered a Negro—even if he has white skin. But a person of Caribbean ancestry may be considered "white"—even if he has a high proportion of African genes.

Other Factors have also produced changes within races. Many agricultural or technological changes have contributed indirectly to race change. For example, the Irish potato famine of the mid-1840's had a tremendous influence on the genetic makeup of certain populations. Thousands of people starved to death, and at least a million persons emigrated from Ireland. They settled in England, Scotland, the United States, and other countries—and created new genetic combinations in those lands.

In North and South America, the populations that raised corn first expanded first. Elsewhere, population expansion and genetic change followed the introduction of wheat, the yam, the deep plow, fertilizers, and insecticides.

Advances in military technology have likewise influenced changes in racial patterns. Iron swords and axes and the use of horses in battle contributed to military success and resulted in racial mixture between the conquerors and the conquered. Military and administrative skills helped the ancient Romans conquer half the then-known world. English talent for shipbuilding contributed to the start of the British Empire and resulted in gene flow from England into India, Africa, Australia, and the Americas.

Mistaken Ideas About Race

Many people misunderstand what race is—and consequently use the term incorrectly. For example, some people speak of the "English-speaking race." But people of many races speak English. Language is a cultural trait and is not determined biologically. Confusion also exists about race and nationality, race and culture, and race and intelligence.

Race and Nationality. People often speak of the "German race," the "Italian race," or the "Welsh race." There are no such races, though there may be more or less distinct subpopulations in those countries.

There is no single Jewish race, though most Jews of Europe and the United States are of Mediterranean origin. The Jews of Egypt, Greece, Iran, Morocco, Russia, and Western Europe differ considerably from one another because of their differing histories.

Neither is there a single Negro race. For example, the people of Dahomey differ genetically from those of neighboring Upper Volta. Because of shifting national

RACES OF MAN

boundaries, a close relationship between any race and any nationality would be merely coincidental.

Race and Culture. The people of different countries have different accomplishments, customs, interests, and values. All these elements—and many more—make up a people's culture and have no relation to race (see CULTURE). Such elements are sometimes misunderstood, with the result that people view other groups in terms of *stereotypes.* That is, they have oversimplified, uncritical beliefs about other groups. At various times, for example, certain groups have been described as dirty, dishonest, sly, humorless, or dull. These judgments have often been confused with racial traits though they have nothing to do with race. Many such judgments have nothing to do with culture either, but only with the opinions or prejudices of those who make them.

Race and Intelligence. In general, conquering people believe they are smarter than those they have conquered. They often attempt to justify their conquests by claiming superiority. The ancient Romans believed they were smarter than the Greeks, but they used Greek slaves to educate their children. In the 1930's, the leaders of Nazi Germany preached that Germans belonged to the "superior Nordic race," and that Jews and all other non-Nordic peoples were inferior. But there is no scientific basis to such claims.

Many scientists believe that a person's intelligence is partly inherited and partly determined by his environment. But they disagree over the relative importance of heredity and environment. The problem of comparing races by intelligence is extremely difficult because few such comparisons can be considered equal. A better-educated group, for example, will score higher on tests that measure education. A group with more language skills will do better on tests that measure language. Groups that value mathematical skills or technical ability will do better on tests involving such skills or knowledge. Expectations also play an important part in comparison of intelligence. Most children who expect to go to college and to enter professions that require academic training do better in schoolwork and on school tests.

Scientists are trying to develop *culture-free* tests that minimize the effects of environmental differences on test scores. Until such tests are perfected, many experts believe it is impossible to say whether some races are more intelligent than others.　　STANLEY M. GARN

Related Articles in WORLD BOOK include:

RACIAL GROUPS

Ainu	Hamite	Malay
Aleut	Hottentot	Maori
Bushman	Igorot	Negrito
Dyak	Indian, American	Negro
Eskimo	Kalmuck	Pygmy

OTHER RELATED ARTICLES

Adaptation	Heredity
Africa (People)	Latin America (The People)
Asia (People)	North America (The People)
Australia (The Aborigines)	Pacific Islands
Cephalic Index	Prehistoric Man
Europe (People)	World (The Races of the
Evolution	World; pictures)

Outline

I. How Races Are Classified
  A. The Three-Race Theory
  B. Geographical Races
  C. Local Races
  D. Studying Races

II. Racial Differences
  A. Obvious Physical Differences
  B. Blood-Group Differences
  C. Other Simply-Inherited Traits
  D. Race and Disease
  E. Race and Climate

III. How Races Develop and Change
  A. Natural Selection　　D. Race Mixture
  B. Mutations　　E. Other Factors
  C. Genetic Drift

IV. Mistaken Ideas About Race
  A. Race and Nationality　　C. Race and
  B. Race and Culture　　　　Intelligence

Questions

What is a natural population?

How do mutations lead to changes in races?

Why do groups that live next to one another tend to be more genetically alike than groups separated by great distances?

What is natural selection? How does it cause races to change?

What are geographical races? How do they differ from local races?

How does knowledge of blood groups help scientists determine relationships between races?

Why do American Indians resemble the peoples of Asia in many ways?

What blood disease afflicts mainly members of the African geographical race?

How can large amounts of melanin be helpful under some conditions and harmful under others?

How do Eskimos and Australian aborigines differ in their adaptation to cold?

RACHEL, *RAY chul,* was the favorite wife of Jacob. Jacob served her father, Laban, seven years to win her, and his love was so great, "they seemed to him but a few days" (Genesis 29:20). But then Laban tricked him and gave him Rachel's older sister, Leah, instead. Jacob married Rachel a week later, but had to work another

Brown Bros.

Leah and Rachel, *left and second from left,* the daughters of Laban, both married Jacob, *right.* Rachel was Jacob's favorite.

seven years for her. Rachel's first child was Joseph, who became his father's favorite. At the end of the journey from Mesopotamia back to Canaan, Rachel died after giving birth to Benjamin. Rachel was considered the ancestress of the northern Israelite tribes of Ephraim and Manasseh, which claimed descent from Joseph. A century after the Assyrians deported part of the tribes in 721 B.C., Jeremiah described Rachel as mourning over her lost children (Jeremiah 31:15).   JOHN BRIGHT

See also JACOB.

RACHMANINOFF, *rahk MAH nuh NAWF,* **SERGEI VASSILIEVICH** (1873-1943), was a Russian composer. He also won fame as a conductor and one of the greatest pianists in history.

In general, Rachmaninoff composed in the romantic style of the late 1800's. Throughout his career, his works were hardly touched by modern trends. Rachmaninoff's music is filled with passion and power, combined with a feeling of melancholy. He greatly admired the Russian composer Peter Ilich Tchaikovsky, and much of his music reflects Tchaikovsky's influence.

The New York Times
Sergei Rachmaninoff

Rachmaninoff composed many works for the piano. He wrote his famous *Prelude in C sharp minor* for solo piano when he was only 19. One of his best-known works is the *Second Piano Concerto* (1901). Some of the melodies in this composition have been arranged as popular songs, such as "Full Moon and Empty Arms." Among Rachmaninoff's later works, the best known is *Rhapsody on a Theme by Paganini* (1934) for piano and orchestra. Rachmaninoff also composed short compositions that display his talent for writing for solo piano.

Rachmaninoff's compositions for orchestra include three symphonies. Of the three, his *Second Symphony* (1907) is performed most often. His other orchestral works include the symphonic poem *The Isle of the Dead* (1909) and *The Bells* (1913) for chorus and orchestra. He based *The Bells* on a poem by the American poet Edgar Allan Poe. Rachmaninoff also composed many beautiful songs, including "Lilacs" (1902) and the wordless "Vocalise" (1912).

Rachmaninoff was born in Oneg, near Novgorod. He received most of his music education at the Moscow Conservatory, where he studied piano and composition. When he graduated in 1892, he received a gold medal for a one-act opera, *Aleko.*

Rachmaninoff's *First Symphony* (1897) was unsuccessful, which depressed him deeply. He finally overcame his discouragement and composed the *Second Piano Concerto,* which was a great success. For years, Rachmaninoff divided his time among composing, conducting, and touring as a concert pianist. He first performed in the United States in 1909 when he appeared as soloist at the première of his *Third Piano Concerto* in New York City.

From 1910 to 1917, Rachmaninoff lived in Moscow. He left the country in 1917 after the Russian Revolution broke out. He never returned to his homeland, and his urge to compose seemed to diminish after he left Russia. Instead, he concentrated on a career as a concert pianist and guest conductor. He made many recordings as pianist and conductor with the Philadelphia Orchestra, his favorite symphony orchestra.

For about 18 years, Rachmaninoff spent almost all his time making annual tours of western Europe and the United States. He settled in the United States in 1935. Rachmaninoff became an American citizen in 1943, a few weeks before his death.   BORIS SCHWARZ

RACIAL SEGREGATION. See SEGREGATION.

RACINE, *ruh SEEN,* Wis. (pop. 95,162; met. area 170,838; alt. 630 ft.), is the third largest city in the state, and the second most important industrial center, after Milwaukee. It lies on Lake Michigan at the mouth of the Root River (see WISCONSIN [political map]). Racine is about 25 miles south of Milwaukee, and 70 miles north of Chicago. It has many people of German and Scandinavian descent.

Racine has more than 200 industries. Leading products include farm tools, malted milk, floor waxes, luggage, electrical appliances, automotive parts, and printing products. Racine was founded in 1834 and became a city in 1848. It has a mayor-council government. Racine is the seat of Racine County.   JAMES I. CLARK

See also ARCHITECTURE (picture: S. C. Johnson Co.).

RACINE, JEAN (1639-1699), ranks among the greatest French playwrights. Racine wrote during the French Classical Age. He followed the classical rules for composition, including the use of a single concentrated plot. The outstanding feature of Racine's art is its simplicity. He used a limited vocabulary and his plots contain very little action. He said his artistic ideal was "to construct something out of nothing."

Almost all of Racine's important plays are tragedies. All of his tragic heroes follow the same pattern. They are victims of violent passions which they cannot control, and they ignore reality and try unsuccessfully to impose their wills on other persons. In the process, most of them cause the death of those they love most. In the end, the heroes recognize their illusions and accept the misery of the human condition as unavoidable. In this respect, Racine is close in spirit to the Greek playwright Sophocles. Racine's theory of tragedy has much in common with Aristotle's literary essay, *Poetics.*

Racine wrote in 12-syllable couplets, as did his rival Pierre Corneille. But Racine used a simpler style.

Racine was born in La Ferté-Milon, near Meaux, and was educated by the strict Jansenist religious sect. He showed promise of a literary career at an early age. In 1664, Racine staged *La Thébaïde,* his first tragedy to be produced. It met with little success. His next play, *Alexandre* (1665), enjoyed considerable acclaim.

With the production of *Andromaque* (1667), Racine became known as one of the greatest dramatists of his time. His next seven plays are masterpieces. They are *Les Plaideurs* (1668), his only comedy; and the tragedies *Britannicus* (1669), *Bérénice* (1670), *Bajazet* (1672), *Mithridate* (1673), *Iphigénie* (1675), and *Phèdre* (1677). In 1677, Racine retired from the stage. Later, he wrote *Esther* (1689) and *Athalie* (1691), tragedies based on stories from the Old Testament.   JULES BRODY

See also FRENCH LITERATURE (The Classical Age).

Horse Racing is one of the most popular forms of racing. Fans thrill to the excitement as sleek horses and their colorfully dressed jockeys speed toward the finish line.

RACING is a trial of speed in running, rowing, swimming, riding, driving, flying, and many other kinds of physical activity.

Contests of speed of both men and animals have excited keen interest from the earliest times. The successful runner in the early Greek games was crowned with a wreath of laurel, and was honored by all the people. Various kinds of racing games were also popular with the people of ancient Rome.

In modern times, contests of speed have become a regular part of the rivalry among colleges, especially in the United States and Canada. The Olympic Games, held in ancient times, are popular in their revived modern form. They include many races, among them the famous marathon run. See OLYMPIC GAMES; TRACK AND FIELD (table).

Man has invented machines that give him greater speed. Bicycle, motorcycle, automobile, and airplane races were added to trotting, pacing, and running races as popular sports. Automobile racing is one of the most exciting sports because of the great speeds reached by the drivers. Many persons also enjoy the thrill of sailing and rowing races (see ROWING). Bicycle racing was once a rival of horse racing in America. Although it has lost some of its popularity, it is still a favorite amateur sport. For many years before World War II, the six-day bicycle race was one of the chief sports attractions in the United States. In Europe, especially in Italy, France, and Belgium, bicycle racing is a major sport. Important races are held every year. The famous races Tour of France and Tour of Italy cover more than 2,000 miles each.

Dog Racing has been a sport since the days of ancient Egypt. The chief dogs used for racing are the Saluki (an Egyptian breed), the greyhound, and the whippet (see GREYHOUND; WHIPPET). There are only about 30 American dog tracks, but these have great popularity. England is the most important dog-racing country in the world, and each year the famous greyhound race for the

Foot Races are fun and good exercise. These boys are set to dash away from the starting line in a race at a park. The world's fastest runners can cover 100 yards in less than 10 seconds.

Waterloo Cup is held at Liverpool. The popularity of dog racing greatly increased in 1919 with the invention of a mechanical rabbit which the dogs chase. The mechanical rabbit runs along the edge of the dog track on an electric rail, serving as a lure to draw the dogs around the race course as fast as they can run.

Horse Racing has long been called *the sport of kings.* Many early horse races were *fixed.* That is, the winner was decided on before the race and the riders knew it. But this dishonest practice was corrected, and the sport has become one of the most popular in the world. Horses are matched in trotting, pacing, and running races. They are divided into classes according to their speed and age.

Harness racing developed chiefly in America, and the early trotters and pacers of the United States had no equals. The mile has been the standard distance for harness races. The famous pacer Dan Patch paced the one-mile race in 1 minute $55\frac{1}{4}$ seconds in 1905. This record was matched by Greyhound, a trotter, at Lexington, Ky., in 1938. Billy Direct, a pacer, set a new mile record of 1 minute 55 seconds at the same park that same year. Another famous pacer, Adios Harry, equaled the record established by Billy Direct in a race at Vernon Downs, N.Y., in 1955. In 1960, Adios Butler broke this record by pacing the mile in 1 minute $54\frac{3}{5}$ seconds at Lexington, Ky.

In England, running races have always been more popular than harness races. One of the greatest horse-racing events of the world is the English Derby, held at Epsom Downs, near London. The Grand National Steeplechase in England and the Grand Prix de Paris in France are other famous running races. This type of horse racing also has regularly scheduled seasons in Mexico, Canada, and South America.

In America, the most famous running race is the yearly Kentucky Derby at Louisville. Three-year-olds compete in this race. The Kentucky Derby, the Preakness at Pimlico, Md., and the Belmont Stakes near New York City are called the *Triple Crown.* The Mary-

John G. Zimmerman, Alpha

Dog Races often feature greyhounds, the fastest of all dogs. The dogs chase a mechanical rabbit that moves along an electric rail.

land Hunt Cup Race in April is the outstanding steeplechase in the United States. The *purses* (amount of money offered as prizes) for these races often total $100,000 or more. A few purses total over $200,000.

Among records set for the running races is that of Citation at the Golden Gate Fields in Albany, Calif., in 1950. Citation ran one mile in 1 minute $33\frac{3}{5}$ seconds. Swaps lowered the time to 1 minute $33\frac{1}{5}$ seconds in

Ferenc Berko, DPI

Ski Racing includes the slalom event, *above,* in which each skier tries to speed over a marked course in the least possible time.

Wide World

Sailboat Racing is an exciting water sport. Crewmen need skill to move the boats across the open sea at high speeds.

The Powder Puff Derby, *above,* is an annual transcontinental air race in which all the pilots are women. The derby's official name is the All-Woman Transcontinental Air Race.

The Indianapolis 500, *below,* is the most famous American automobile race. More than 300,000 persons attend this annual 500-mile race over a paved oval track in Indianapolis.

The Olympic Games have long featured racing events. These runners competed in a 100-meter race in the 1896 Olympics.

1956. In 1959, the horse Intentionally tied the record established by Swaps.

Automobile Racing has been a popular sport since the earliest days of the automobile. The popularity of this sport has grown enormously in the United States. Many types of cars and different lengths of track are used for the races (see AUTOMOBILE RACING). Boys compete in the All-American and International Soap Box Derby held each year at Akron, Ohio. See SOAP BOX DERBY.

Air Races. The greatest speed records of all time have been set by the airplane. In the United States, pilots compete in the Bendix Trophy Race and other air races. For airplane speed records, see AIRPLANE (table: Speed Records).   WALTER HAROLD GREGG

Related Articles in WORLD BOOK include:

Derby	Horse Racing	Rowing
Dog Racing	Motorcycle	Running
Harness Racing	Olympic Games	Track and Field

RACISM is the belief that members of one or more races are inferior to members of other races. Usually, this attitude also involves the belief that one's own race is superior to other races. People who believe in or practice racism are called *racists.* They claim that members of their own race are mentally, physically, morally, or culturally superior to those of other races. Because racists assume they are superior, they believe they deserve special rights and privileges.

Groups, as well as individuals, differ. But there is

no scientific evidence to support claims of superiority or inferiority for these differences. Social scientists emphasize that no two groups have exactly the same environment. As a result, many group differences are largely the result of different environments. Scientists have long disagreed over the relative importance of heredity and environment in determining these differences. For a discussion of such a disagreement, see the articles on INTELLIGENCE (Controversy over Intelligence) and RACES OF MAN (Race and Intelligence).

Racism is widespread and has caused major problems, even though no scientific proof supports racist claims. Claims of racial superiority and inferiority have been used to justify discrimination, segregation, colonialism, slavery, and even *genocide* (mass murder).

Racism is a form of prejudice. Many people tend to consider their own appearance and behavior as normal and therefore desirable. They may distrust or fear people who look or act differently. When differences are obvious—such as in skin color, shape of eyes, or religious worship—the distrust becomes greater.

Such attitudes can lead to the belief that people who look or act differently are inferior. Many people do not bother to look for the same qualities in other races that they admire in their own. Also, they do not recognize the different but equally good qualities that members of other races possess.

Racism in the United States has been directed mainly by the white majority against racial or ethnic minority groups. Such groups include Negroes, American Indians, Mexican Americans, Puerto Ricans, and persons of Chinese or Japanese ancestry. These minorities have been discriminated against in such areas as housing, education, and employment. For a detailed discussion of such discrimination, see the articles on SEGREGATION; MINORITY GROUP; ETHNIC GROUP; NEGRO; CHICANO; and INDIAN, AMERICAN.

Individual and Institutional Racism. In the United States, sociologists distinguish between individual and institutional racism. Individual racism refers chiefly to the prejudicial beliefs and discriminatory behavior of whites against Negroes and other minority groups. It is based on racial assumptions of superiority and inferiority.

Institutional racism, on the other hand, refers to the policies of communities, schools, businesses, and other groups and organizations that restrict the opportunities of minority groups. Institutional racism may or may not intentionally practice discrimination. Regardless, it has produced harmful results. For example, a company may hire only college graduates for work that does not require a college degree. But far fewer blacks than whites have had the opportunity to earn a degree. Thus, the company policy lessens the job opportunities of blacks even though the firm might not have intended to do so.

History. Racism has existed since the beginning of history. More than 2,000 years ago, for example, the ancient Greeks and Romans made slaves of people whom they regarded as inferior. The Jews considered themselves the chosen people of God and have themselves been persecuted on religious and cultural grounds. For hundreds of years after Marco Polo's travels to China in the 1200's, the Chinese regarded Westerners as "hairy white barbarians."

Between the 1700's and early 1900's, Europeans gained control of large parts of Asia and Africa. They justified their domination on the grounds that the black-, brown-, and yellow-skinned inhabitants had to be "civilized" by the "superior" whites. This civilizing mission was called the "white man's burden." By the mid-1900's, most colonialism had ended. But its effects on the world are still felt today. For details, see the articles on AFRICA (The 1960's) and ASIA (Results of Colonialism; The Spread of Communism).

From the 1600's to the mid-1800's, many whites in the United States held Negroes in slavery. Slavery was a major cause of the Civil War (1861-1865). The slaves were freed during the 1860's, but segregation and discrimination against blacks continued. In the mid-1900's, the U.S. government passed laws designed to give equal opportunities to blacks. Even so, severe racial problems—which began with slavery and were fostered by discrimination and segregation—continue to plague the United States today.

Genocide is the most extreme result of racial hatred. Adolf Hitler, the ruler of Nazi Germany, preached that Germans belonged to the "superior Nordic race," and that Jews and other non-Nordic peoples were inferior. Hitler's belief in German superiority and his hatred of Jews resulted in Nazi policies that brought the murder of about 6 million Jews during the 1930's and 1940's. See JEWS (Nazi Persecutions).

Since the late 1940's, the government of South Africa has followed a racial policy called *apartheid*, the world's most complete system of racial separation. It calls for separate institutions, jobs, and residences for whites and nonwhites.   THOMAS F. PETTIGREW

Related Articles in WORLD BOOK include:

Apartheid	Oriental Exclusion Acts	Races of Man
Genocide	Prejudice	Slavery

RACK. See HORSE (Gaits).

RACK was an instrument of torture often used in the Middle Ages. The victim was bound on an oblong wooden frame with a roller at each end. If he refused to answer questions or to confess, the rollers were turned until his joints were pulled out of their sockets. The rack was used by the Romans, and was a favorite tool of the Spanish Inquisition.   MARVIN E. WOLFGANG

RACKHAM, ARTHUR (1867-1939), an English artist, won wide recognition for his illustrations for children's books. His illustrations were filled with gnomes, elves, witches, fairies, and kindly human creatures.

Rackham drew and painted these figures with delicacy and rich detail. He made details of wood grain, tree bark, and lines in faces and hands important parts of the whole design. He even gave his trees personalities. His imaginative and skillful pictures brought to life the characters in many favorite stories, including *Peter Pan*, *Grimm's Fairy Tales*, *Aesop's Fables*, *Midsummer Night's Dream*, *Rip Van Winkle*, and *The Wind in the Willows*.

Rackham was born in London. He became interested in drawing while he was young. But it was not until he began working in an insurance office that he could afford to continue his art studies. He attended evening classes at the Lambeth School of Art. Rackham's drawings were published for the first time in the English humor magazine, *Punch*.   NORMAN L. RICE

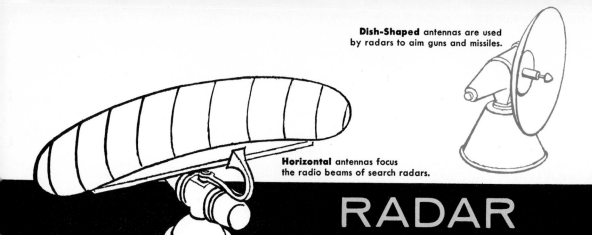

Dish-Shaped antennas are used
by radars to aim guns and missiles.

Horizontal antennas focus
the radio beams of search radars.

RADAR

Radar Antennas focus radio
waves into beams. The size and
shape of the antenna depends
on the way the radar is used.

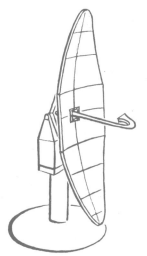

Vertical antennas enable
radars to find the heights of planes.

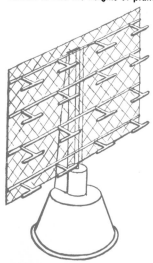

Square antennas are also
widely used by search radars.

RADAR, *RAY dahr,* is an electronic device that can "see" hundreds of miles despite fog, rain, snow, clouds, and darkness. It can find and accurately locate missiles, aircraft, ships, cities, rainstorms, and mountains. Radar uses radio waves instead of light waves, which the human eye uses in seeing. This makes it possible for radar to locate many kinds of objects at far greater distances than the eye can see, even in perfect weather.

Radar became an important military device during World War II. Today, networks of radar lookout stations guard the United States and Canada 24 hours a day against long-range missiles and airplanes. Patrol planes and ships search the oceans with radar for hostile ships and aircraft. Airports use radar to guide planes safely to earth in fog or storms. Ships use it to enter safely into fog-bound harbors, and to steer clear of other vessels or icebergs. Radar helps weathermen warn of approaching hurricanes and tornadoes.

The name *radar* comes from the phrase *Radio Detection and Ranging.* Radar sends out pulses of radio waves in a beam. As the waves strike objects, they are reflected like echoes back to the radar. Reflected waves picked up by the radar antenna cause dots of light called *blips* to appear on a fluorescent screen similar to a television screen. By watching the blips, an observer can tell the direction and distance to an object. On some radars, he can learn the object's height, speed, size, and even what it is.

The Uses of Radar

Aviation. Radar on the ground and in airplanes makes flying safer. In an airport control tower, a man called a controller watches the paths of approaching planes on a radar screen. He assigns each pilot by radio a direction and altitude to approach the runway. This type of radar is called *Ground Controlled Approach* (GCA). Pilots guided from the ground by a controller using GCA radar can make perfect landings even in fog.

Large passenger planes often carry *weather radar* with which to detect storms. A pilot uses the radar to "look through" the clouds to the heart of a storm, and flies a course that avoids the roughest weather.

Most large commercial and military planes that fly over oceans have *radio altimeters.* The radio altimeter is a radar that tells the pilot his altitude above the earth. See AIRCRAFT INSTRUMENTS (Altimeters).

Ships, including freighters on the Great Lakes, usually have radar. In fog, rain, or snow, a ship's radar can spot other ships or icebergs in time to prevent collisions. Near shore, a ship's radar detects large landmarks, such as cliffs or lighthouses, and shows the vessel's position. The buoys that mark the entrance channels of harbors often have radar reflectors so they can be seen more easily by a ship's radar. Some large ports, such as New York City, have radar that shows a maplike picture of the harbor with its ships, piers, and bridges. The harbor master can guide ships in or out of port in all kinds of weather.

National Defense. Radar has become an important military tool of many uses. *Early Warning* radar helps prevent surprise air attacks by detecting approaching enemy aircraft. *Ballistic Missile Early Warning System* radar guards against missile attacks. *Ground Controlled Interception* (GCI) radar directs

Weathermen spot storms with radar. A dome usually protects the radar's antenna. Blips on the radar screen, *lower right,* show rain clouds and a spiral hurricane. The hurricane lies 25 to 60 miles from the radar. The rings on the screen mark off the distance from the weather radar station in intervals of 20 miles.

fighter planes against enemy bombers. Warships use *Ship Controlled Interception* (SCI) radar for the same purpose. *Fire Control* radar accurately aims and fires guns and missiles such as rockets.

Fighter planes often have *Airborne Intercept* (AI) radar. It detects enemy aircraft, guides the fighter to them, and aims and fires the fighter's guns or missiles. Bombers with radar bombsights can drop bombs accurately on targets at night or in bad weather. Patrol planes search the oceans with *Airborne Early Warning* (AEW) radar for enemy ships and aircraft. Naval escort ships use radar to keep blacked-out convoys in position at night and to warn of enemy ships and aircraft.

Radar alone does not show whether a plane or a ship is hostile or friendly. Therefore, planes and ships of a friendly nation or of allied countries use a radio system similar to radar called *Identification, Friend or Foe* (IFF). The heart of IFF is an automatic answering radio device called a *transponder.* When triggered by searching radar, the transponder signals whether the plane or ship is a friend. The signal shows as a special blip.

Radar directs many kinds of guided missiles to their targets from planes, ships, or firing stations on the ground (see GUIDED MISSILE). The tips of some shells and bombs have tiny radars called *variable time* (VT), or *proximity,* fuses. These radars explode the shells or bombs in the air near the target, and can often cause more damage than a direct hit. *Mortar Locator* (ML) radar tracks enemy mortar shells in flight and plots the position of the mortars for defending forces.

Law Enforcement. Traffic policemen in many parts of the United States and Canada use radar to enforce speed laws. A radar-equipped police team places its radar set alongside a highway. The radar views approaching cars and shows their speeds on a meter.

Weather. Forecasters can look into a storm with radar and learn its size, shape, speed, direction of travel, and rate of development. Tornadoes, hurricanes, and storm clouds filled with rain, hail, or snow can be spotted over 200 miles away. This usually gives weathermen time to warn communities lying in the path of a storm. In the late 1950's, the U.S. Weather Bureau (now National Weather Service) bought radars for a storm-warning system covering almost the entire country.

Radar provides ships with far-seeing "eyes." At night, or in fog and storms, radar-equipped ships can locate shore lines and avoid collisions with icebergs and other ships.

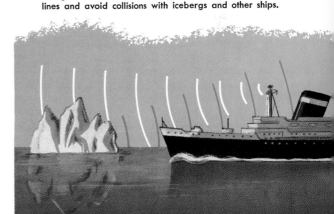

Radar-Guided Missiles guard the United States against hostile planes. The missiles may be equipped with radar or be directed from radar sets based on the ground or on ships.

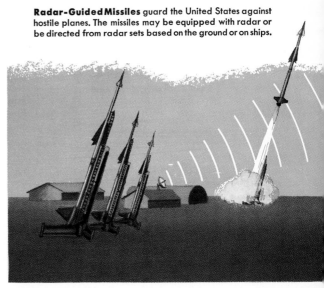

65

HOW RADAR WORKS

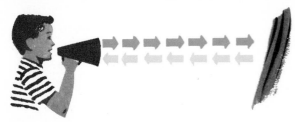

Echoes make it possible for radar to detect distant objects. When you shout toward a cliff, the sound waves of the shout bounce back as an echo. Objects such as airplanes reflect radio waves just as they do sound waves. Radar sends out pulses of radio waves and listens between the pulses for echoes, or reflected radio waves bounced back from objects.

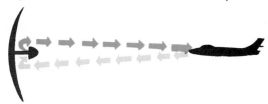

Science. Astronomers have used radar to measure the distance to the moon, and have received echoes from Venus and the sun. These distances must be known accurately to plan space flights and to provide a check on calculations of distances to other planets. Radar also provides information on the size of mountains and craters on the moon, and on the motions of the moon. Zoologists use radar to study how birds fly and to count migrating birds. Radar can detect large birds in flight more than 10 miles away. Oceanographers measure wave heights with radar. Surveyors use radar to map wilderness areas accurately. Physicists study the aurora borealis, lightning flashes, meteorites, and the ionosphere with radar.

How Radar Works

Detection. Radars are complicated devices, but the way they work is quite simple. Objects echo, or reflect, radio waves much as they do waves of light or sound. Most radars send out short, intense pulses of radio waves with transmitters, and "listen" between pulses with radio receivers for the reflected waves. The radar shows the echoes as blips on the screen of a cathode-ray tube (see CATHODE RAYS).

The principle of detecting objects by means of echoes is much older than radar itself. Bats use echoes to avoid obstacles while flying (see BAT [How Bats Navigate]). Sailors once used echoes to navigate in foggy weather near land. A sailor stationed in the

PARTS OF A RADAR SET

Radar measures the time it takes a pulse of radio waves to go out to an object and return as an echo. Radio waves travel 186,282 miles a second. Therefore, the distance to an object is 164 yards for each millionth of a second. The radar indicator has a timing device that figures out the distance.

1 The modulator signals the transmitter when to produce a pulse of radio waves. Then it stops the transmitter while the radar listens for an echo.

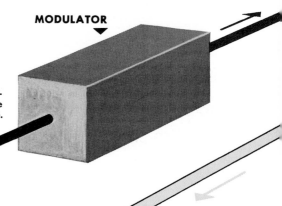

MODULATOR

◀ **INDICATOR**

5 The indicator shows the echoes as dots of light called *blips* on a fluorescent screen similar to a television screen. It tells the direction and the distance to an object causing a blip.

bow of a ship would shout, or strike a bell. If an echo returned, he knew that an obstacle was nearby.

Distance. Radio waves, like light waves, travel at a constant speed of 186,282 miles a second. A radar has a sensitive electric timer that measures the time it takes a pulse to travel to an object and the echo to return. By using the speed of radio waves, the timer figures out the *range*, or distance to an object.

Direction. The radar antenna focuses the outgoing pulses of radio waves into a beam, much as a flashlight focuses a light beam. Only targets or objects in the beam can be seen. The direction the antenna points when the radar receives an echo shows the direction to the target or object. Most radars cannot see objects below the horizon, because their beams bend only slightly in the atmosphere. For this reason, low-flying airplanes do not show up on ground-based radar until they are much closer than high-flying airplanes.

Other Radars include *Doppler*, or *Continuous Wave* (CW), radar. It is used chiefly to determine the speed of moving objects. For example, traffic policemen detect speeders with Doppler radar. It sends out continu-

ANTENNA

The antenna focuses the outgoing pulses of radio waves into a beam and collects the returning echoes. The duplexer switches the transmitter to the antenna so a pulse can go out and then connects the receiver to the antenna so the radar can listen for an echo.

3

2 The transmitter generates the pulses of radio waves. Radar uses *microwaves*, or waves that are only a fraction of an inch to a few inches long.

TRANSMITTER

DUPLEXER SWITCH

RECEIVER

4 The receiver is the radar's listening device. It *amplifies* the weak echoes to make them strong enough to show on the radar's indicator.

ous radio waves instead of pulses. When radio waves strike a moving object, the reflected waves have a different *frequency* (number of vibrations a second) than the outgoing waves. This difference in frequency indicates the object's speed. See DOPPLER EFFECT.

Moving Target Indication (MTI) radar sends out pulses of radio waves, but it works somewhat like Doppler radar to distinguish between fixed and moving objects. MTI radar shows only moving objects.

Frequency Modulation (FM) radar sends out radio waves whose frequency is continuously *modulated* (varied). By using the rate at which the frequency is varied, FM radar determines the distance to an object. Radio altimeters are FM radars.

Laser radar sends out a narrow, intense beam of light instead of radio waves. Portable laser radars can be used by troops in battle and by surveyors in rough terrain. See LASER (picture, Laser Range Finder).

The Radar Set

Radar sets range in size from small, 35-pound units used by police to large missile-warning sets that weigh

many tons and fill entire buildings. The main parts of a radar set include the antenna, transmitter, modulator, duplexer switch, receiver, and indicator.

Antenna sends out the pulses of radio waves in a beam and picks up echoes reflected by objects. It is usually shaped like a dish. A motor rotates the antenna so that the beam of outgoing radio waves sweeps completely around the radar station. Radars designed to find the height of objects have antennas that tilt back and forth as they rotate.

Transmitter generates the pulses of radio waves sent out by the antenna. The pulses are thousands or even millions of watts in power, but each pulse lasts only a few millionths of a second. The radar spends a much longer time listening between pulses for echoes than it does sending out pulses. Most radars use *microwaves* (see MICROWAVE). Their transmitters use tubes such as the *multicavity magnetron, klystron,* and *traveling-wave,* to generate microwaves. Some long-range radars use longer radio waves than microwaves and have triode or klystron tubes. See ELECTRONICS (Microwave Tubes).

Modulator is a device that tells the transmitter what to do and when to do it. It makes the transmitter give a short powerful pulse during the sending intervals, and stops the transmitter when the radar is listening.

Duplexer Switch, or transmit-receive (TR) switch, makes it possible to use only one antenna. In a millionth of a second, it automatically switches the transmitter or the receiver onto the antenna line as each is needed. If both the transmitter and receiver were connected to the antenna at the same time, the powerful pulses from the transmitter would burn out the receiver.

Receiver takes the weak echoes collected by the antenna and *amplifies* them, or makes them strong enough to show on the indicator. The sensitive receiver easily picks up tiny echoes of much less than a millionth of a millionth of a watt in power.

Indicator is the key part of a radar system. It shows the operator the information the radar has gained about an object. The indicator is usually the fluorescent

A Radar Operator in an airport radar room keeps track of planes flying near the terminal by watching their blips on a plan position indicator.

TWO IMPORTANT RADAR INDICATORS

Range Height Indicator (RHI) shows the height and distance to airplanes. The RHI screen, *left*, shows the blip of an airplane flying at a height of 10,000 feet 65 miles away.

Plan Position Indicator (PPI) locates objects. The PPI screen, *right*, has a compass scale and rings showing the direction and distance to the blips of three airplanes.

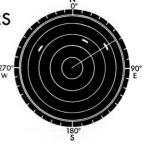

screen of a cathode-ray tube. But it may also be a bell that rings or a light that flashes when an object is detected. Some radars have color indicators that show echoes from different kinds of objects in different colors. For example, moving objects might appear as red blips and fixed objects as yellow blips.

Plan Position Indicator (PPI) is the most common kind of indicator. A PPI screen might be compared with the face of a watch. A compass scale runs around the edge of the screen like the numbers on a watch. As the antenna rotates, a thin line of light called the *trace* sweeps around the screen like the second hand of a watch. Echoes from objects appear as bright, arc-shaped blips. When the trace passes through a blip, the direction to the object can be read on the compass scale just as one would tell the time on a watch.

The distance of the blip from the center of the screen shows how far away the object is. Concentric circles on the screen mark off this distance in miles. For example, the blip of an object 60 miles away appears on the 60-mile range circle. Some PPI screens have a movable line, called a *cursor*, similar to the minute hand of a watch. When the PPI operator lines up the cursor with a blip, the direction and range appear on special dials.

A PPI operator can also determine the direction in which a moving object is traveling, and its speed. Each time the rotating antenna beam hits a moving object, the operator marks the position of the blip on the screen with a grease pencil. The pencil marks show the object's direction of travel. The operator determines the speed of the object by the amount of time it takes the blips to cover a certain distance on the screen.

Range Height Indicator (RHI) radar measures the height of an object, such as an airplane. The indicator of this radar has a trace that looks like a horizontal *V*. Lines on the screen mark off the height in feet and the range in miles. Some RHI radars also have dials that show the range and height when cursors are lined up with the blips.

Other Kinds of Indicators include the A-scope and B-scope. The A-scope has either a horizontal or vertical trace, and shows the distance to an object and the strength of the echo signal. It is used mainly to obtain more details about close-spaced objects, such as a fleet of planes. The B-scope has a vertical trace and a square scale on its screen that shows both the range and direction to an object. It also gives more detailed information such as the number of planes in an air fleet.

Fire Control Radar differs from search type radar chiefly in the precision with which it locates targets. It looks at a single target, measures its position, and follows it automatically. The antenna sends out a pair of slightly separated beams that bracket the target. A computer takes the radar measurements and makes the calculations to aim guns or missiles to hit the target.

Radar Warning Systems

Radar plays a vital role in the defense systems of North America, Europe, and Asia. Powerful long-range radars have been organized into such systems as the

68

Ballistic Missile Early Warning System, the Distant Early Warning line, and the Space Surveillance system.

Ballistic Missile Early Warning System (BMEWS) provides warning against surprise attack by an intercontinental ballistic missile (ICBM). Such a system requires mighty radars. The entire flight of a 5,000-mile ICBM may last less than 40 minutes. To allow 20 to 30 minutes warning time, the radars must detect the tiny warhead at distances of more than 1,000 miles away.

The first BMEWS radar post was built at Thule, Greenland, in the late 1950's and early 1960's. It has four superpowerful search radars—each equipped with an antenna larger than a football field. Each antenna sends out two radar beams with a range of more than 3,000 miles. The power for the beams comes from 20 transmitters housed in buildings the size of a large school. Computers analyze the echoes received to determine which are from missiles, and then feed the information to defense centers in the United States over two separate communication systems. The information received is displayed on illuminated panels.

BMEWS posts similar to the one at Thule were completed at Clear, Alaska, and Fylingdales Moor, England, in 1963. The Thule, Clear, and Fylingdales posts form a *BMEWS line*. This line guards against possible ICBM enemy attacks from across the arctic regions.

The line helps keep watch over Russia and part of China.

Distant Early Warning (DEW) line consists of about 60 radar stations built at about 100-mile intervals across the arctic regions of North America. The line stretches from the Aleutian Islands across Alaska and Canada to the east coast of Greenland. It provides warning chiefly against aircraft.

Space Surveillance (SPASUR) radar system detects silent artificial satellites that might be used for spying, such as those that broadcast only on command from the ground. The system detects an unknown satellite on its first passage over the United States and determines its orbit. SPASUR consists of two large complexes of transmitters, receivers, and antennas installed by the navy in the southern United States. One complex extends from Georgia to Mississippi. The other is in California and Arizona. SPASUR uses continuous-wave radars with separate antennas for the transmitters and receivers. The antennas look like fences and may be as much as 1,600 feet long.

History

Radar developed only after years of research in physics and radio. Physicists and mathematicians made

WHAT RADAR SHOWS FROM THE AIR

A map, *below*, shows how the New York City area looks from the air. The pictures, *right*, show how a radar screen would present the area from an airplane in flight at three different positions.

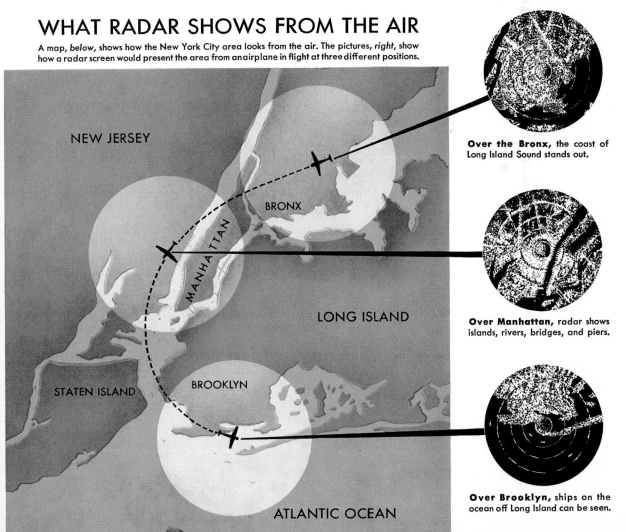

NEW JERSEY

BRONX

MANHATTAN

LONG ISLAND

STATEN ISLAND

BROOKLYN

ATLANTIC OCEAN

Over the Bronx, the coast of Long Island Sound stands out.

Over Manhattan, radar shows islands, rivers, bridges, and piers.

Over Brooklyn, ships on the ocean off Long Island can be seen.

RADAR IN NATIONAL DEFENSE

United Press Int.

Official NORAD Photo

 On Land. Long lines of radar stations stretch across Canada. These stations form part of the North American defense system, guarding the arctic skies 24 hours a day.

 From the Air. Radar planes patrol the skies over North America to warn against surprise air attack and to guide fighter-interceptor planes to their targets.

many of the most important discoveries leading to radio and radar in the 1800's and early 1900's. Men who made important contributions included Heinrich R. Hertz, Guglielmo Marconi, Karl Ferdinand Braun, and Lee De Forest. Hertz discovered radio waves in the 1880's and showed that they could be focused into a beam and be reflected from objects. In the 1890's, Marconi developed the first radio-sending equipment. Braun invented a cathode-ray oscilloscope in 1897. In 1907, De Forest invented the radio amplifier tube.

Early U.S. Experiments. Scientists at the Naval Research Laboratory did much of the early work in the United States on radar. In 1922, A. H. Taylor and L. C. Young detected reflections from a boat on the Potomac River while studying short-wave radio. Young and L. A. Hyland observed similar reflections from aircraft in 1930. These scientists used a system of continuous radio waves called the *beat* method. This method did not give the range of an object, but it could detect aircraft as far as 50 miles away.

In 1934, Young proposed using pulses of radio waves, the method most widely used today. R. M. Page, another navy scientist, developed a radar of this type, and observed echoes from aircraft in December, 1934. By early 1936, pulse radar with a range of 25 miles had been developed, and by 1938, a pulse radar had tracked a small aircraft 100 miles. The navy installed models of this radar on 20 major warships before the Japanese attacked Pearl Harbor on Dec. 7, 1941.

Beginning in 1936, navy scientists showed their equipment to the Army Signal Corps and engineers from the electronics industry. Parallel work had been underway by the Signal Corps and it demonstrated working pulse radar not long after the navy did. The army had two excellent types of radars ready by 1941. An army radar unit in the Hawaiian Islands detected the Japanese air fleet approaching Pearl Harbor, but thought the blips were caused by American bombers.

British Developments. The British became active in radar early in 1935 when the Air Ministry asked physi-

HOW RADAR CATCHES SPEEDERS

Police in many parts of the United States and Canada use radar to enforce speed laws. The radar set is mounted on a car parked near a highway, *left*. The set sends out radio waves. A moving car reflects the waves and gives them a different number of vibrations per second than the outgoing waves. The radar measures this difference to find the car's speed and record it on a meter, *right*.

WORLD BOOK photo

WORLD BOOK photo

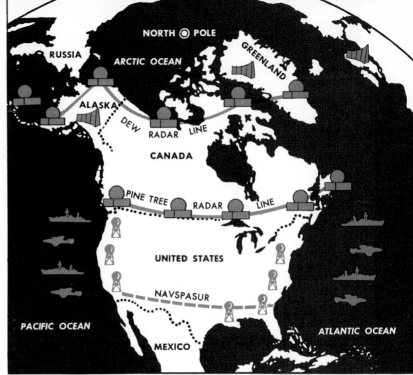

At Sea. Radar picket ships range many miles from the coasts of the United States to watch for unfriendly ships and planes.

NAVSPASUR (Naval Space Surveillance System) along the southern coast of the United States guards against attack from the south.

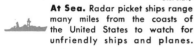
Coastal radar stations also guard the United States shoreline.

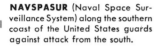
BMEWS radar posts watch for ballistic-missile attacks.

Radar Is the Heart of the North American Defense System. Networks of radar stations stretch across Canada and girdle the United States, ready to alert defense forces and guide them to the target if hostile planes, missiles, or ships try to attack.

cist Robert Watson-Watt to work on antiaircraft weapons. By June, 1935, Watson-Watt and a group of scientists working with him had developed a pulse radar capable of detecting aircraft at ranges up to 17 miles. Spurred by the growing threat of war, the British quickly recruited many of their best scientists. They developed Plan Position Indicator radar and an efficient multicavity magnetron to generate microwaves. Before

A policeman farther down the highway stops speeding motorists. He has received a description of the speeder's car by radio from an officer in the car with the radar. Police radar can determine the speed of a vehicle within 2 miles an hour.

WORLD BOOK photo

World War II began in September, 1939, the British had installed a chain of large radar-warning stations on their shores. They also developed Ground Controlled Interception radar and Airborne Intercept radar for night fighter planes. These radars were ready for the Battle of Britain and were credited with enabling a small force of British fighter planes and antiaircraft artillery to fight off the massive German air attacks.

France and Germany also began work on radar during the 1930's. The French installed a beat-type collision-warning radar on the ocean liner *Normandie* in 1936, and had developed pulse-type radar by 1940. German scientists were working on radar by 1935, and had good wartime radar for early-warning, for antiaircraft gun control, and for ships. But the Germans did not develop microwave radars and so failed to obtain the accuracy that the Allies did. Russia had developed a warning radar by 1941 and Japan by 1942. But no other countries developed as good radar, or used it as widely and effectively in the war as did the British and Americans.

During World War II, United States and British radar scientists cooperated closely. American scientists gave the British the duplexer switch, and the British gave the United States the multicavity magnetron. The Allied scientists scored a big achievement by developing receivers, high-power transmitters, and antennas to operate with microwaves. Microwaves made it possible to develop narrow-beamed, highly accurate radars with small antennas for aircraft, ships, and mobile ground stations. American scientists did much of their radar work at the Radiation Laboratory, located at the Massachusetts Institute of Technology.

Radar became so effective in aiming antiaircraft

71

RADAR

guns that each side tried to jam the other's radar. Allied bombers carried radios to send signals that confused or blanked out enemy radar. They also dropped tons of aluminum foil strips called *window*. These strips reflected false echoes on enemy radar indicators. In the Pacific Ocean, radar gave the U.S. Navy superiority over Japanese forces in night naval battles. In the Atlantic, airborne radar enabled the Allies to inflict crippling losses on the German submarine fleet.

Recent Developments. Among important technical advances of the late 1950's and early 1960's was the development of a radar system that can "see" over the horizon. The beams of regular radars go out in straight lines and cannot detect targets below the horizon. The new system is called MADRE after *magnetic drum receiving equipment*, a key part of the radar. MADRE has a range of 800 to 2,000 miles. It uses radar waves with frequencies similar to short-wave radio. At these frequencies, the radar waves bounce off the layer of the atmosphere called the ionosphere and return to earth just like radio waves. In this way, the waves can detect low-flying targets. The beams of microwave radars would be 200 miles high at the ranges MADRE reaches.

The Naval Research Laboratory developed MADRE through a suggestion made by R. M. Page. It accurately preserves the characteristics of the outgoing signal and sorts out wanted echoes by comparing them with the signal sent out. Plans call for the first MADRE post, located on Chesapeake Bay, to cover the North Atlantic Ocean from the Azores to Nova Scotia.

The navy also developed a radar communication system that uses the moon as a relay station. The highly dependable system bounces signals off the moon to provide communication from shore stations to ships. The wave bands used by ordinary radio are so busy that it is easier to transmit a microwave signal to Europe, for example, by the half-million-mile path to the moon and back than by regular radio.

The military services announced development of a superaccurate mapping radar and a sentry radar for use by ground forces in the late 1950's and early 1960's.

Mapping radar is a special airborne radar which makes a map of the ground over which it is flown. Cities, lakes, rivers, bridges, fields, mountains, and airports stand out clearly. The radar presents a picture nearly equal to aerial photographs, and the mapping can be done at night and in bad weather. The radar even "sees" through camouflage. Mapping radar sends

A Radar Map of Dallas, Tex., shows details of the city with startling clarity. *Mapping radar* also spots moving targets and even "sees" through camouflage. The radar maps strips of ground up to 20 miles wide. It may be used on piloted or unmanned aircraft flying at speeds up to 2,500 mph. Unlike aerial photography, radar mapping can be done at night and in bad weather.

Texas Instruments, Inc.

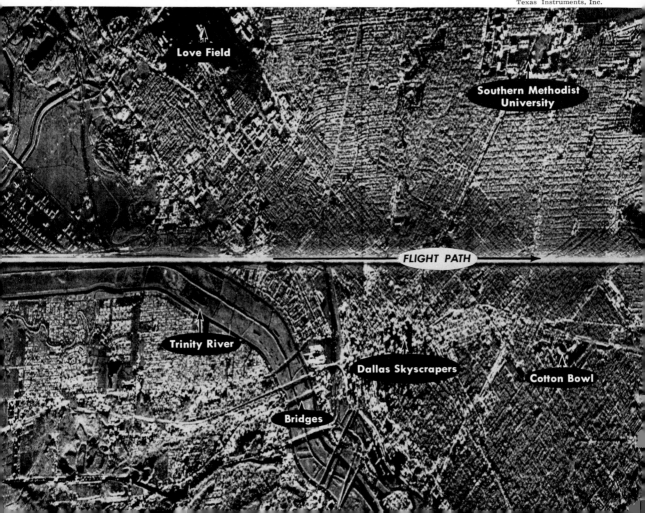

Love Field

Southern Methodist University

FLIGHT PATH

Trinity River

Dallas Skyscrapers

Cotton Bowl

Bridges

out short pulses of radar waves in a very narrow beam to avoid distortion. The antenna is mounted on the side of the aircraft, and the beam scans the ground as the plane flies along. The radar set inside the plane has a special type of indicator. A movie camera photographs the indicator to record the map picture.

Sentry radar is used by ground troops to detect the movement of enemy troops and vehicles. The indicator makes a different sound for each type of target detected. In this way, a trained operator can tell the difference between foot soldiers, tanks, trucks, and jeeps. This radar can detect a crawling soldier at a range of 2 miles.

The U.S. Army developed an antenna with no moving parts, for scanning radar. Scanning radars, such as those used to detect missiles, require large antennas which are difficult to turn. The antenna points the radar beam in different vertical directions by shifting the frequency of the radar waves.   ROBERT C. GUTHRIE

Related Articles in WORLD BOOK include:

Aircraft Instruments (Altimeters)	Microwave National Defense
Airport	Navigation
Antenna	Radio
DEW Line	Range Finder
Electronics	Shoran
Guided Missile	Ultrahigh Frequency
Hurricane (picture)	Wave
Measurement (picture: A Radar Telescope)	Watson-Watt, Sir Robert A.

Outline

I. The Uses of Radar
   A. Aviation   C. National Defense   E. Weather
   B. Ships   D. Law Enforcement   F. Science
II. How Radar Works
   A. Detection   C. Direction   D. Other Radars
   B. Distance
III. The Radar Set
   A. Antenna   D. Duplexer Switch   G. Fire Con-
   B. Transmitter   E. Receiver   trol
   C. Modulator   F. Indicator   Radar
IV. Radar Warning Systems
   A. Ballistic Missile Early Warning System
   B. Distant Early Warning
   C. Space Surveillance
V. History

Questions

How can radar see around the curve of the earth?
What animal uses the principle of radar?
How is radar used for national defense?
How can radar tell whether a plane is friendly?
What is the key part of a radar set? Why?
How can you demonstrate the principle of radar?
Why do some radars have antennas that tilt back and forth?
How did Allied fliers "fool" enemy antiaircraft radar in World War II?

RADAR ASTRONOMY. See ASTRONOMY (Radio Telescopes).

RADCLIFFE-BROWN, SIR ALFRED REGINALD (1881-1955), a British anthropologist, helped develop present-day American and British anthropological theories. He was born in England and was graduated from Cambridge University. After many years of research and teaching in London, Australia, and the Union of South Africa, he taught at the University of Chicago from 1931 to 1937. He then became the first professor of social anthropology at Oxford University.   DAVID B. STOUT

See also CULTURE (Theories About Culture).

George M. Cushing, Jr.

Radcliffe College is a woman's school affiliated with Harvard University. Most girls live in the dormitory quadrangle, above.

RADCLIFFE COLLEGE is a private liberal arts college for women in Cambridge, Mass. It is affiliated with Harvard University, and was founded in 1879 as a result of women's demands to attend courses given by Harvard instructors. In 1943, the entire curriculum of Harvard's College of Arts and Science was opened to Radcliffe students. The Harvard faculty provides all instruction and Radcliffe graduates receive their degrees directly from Harvard. But Radcliffe maintains its own administrative board. Until 1963, degrees were awarded by Radcliffe. The Radcliffe Yard, which includes classrooms and a library, is across the Cambridge Common from Harvard. For enrollment, see UNIVERSITIES AND COLLEGES (table).   MARY I. BUNTING

RADFORD, ARTHUR WILLIAM (1896-   ), an admiral in the United States Navy, served from 1953 to 1957 as chairman of the Joint Chiefs of Staff. Born in Chicago, he graduated from the U.S. Naval Academy, and served during World Wars I and II. Radford won recognition as an expert on naval aviation and aircraft-carrier warfare. He was commander in chief of the U.S. Pacific Fleet from 1949 to 1953.   DONALD W. MITCHELL

RADFORD COLLEGE. See UNIVERSITIES AND COLLEGES (table).

RADIAL ENGINE. See GASOLINE ENGINE (Kinds).

RADIAL SYMMETRY. See SYMMETRY; ECHINODERM.

RADIAN. See WEIGHTS AND MEASURES (Circular).

RADIANT ENERGY. See QUANTUM THEORY (Radiant Energy); LIGHT (Electromagnetic Waves).

RADIANT HEATING. See HEATING.

RADIATION

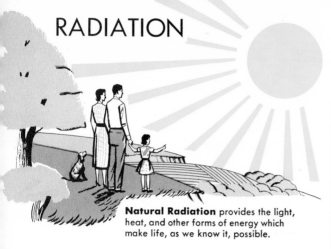

Natural Radiation provides the light, heat, and other forms of energy which make life, as we know it, possible.

Wide World

Man-Made Radiation gives us new means of improving our way of life. This vault contains radioactive medicines.

RADIATION. When you feel the warmth of sunshine you are sensing what scientists call *radiation*. The sun gives off heat, or *thermal radiation*. It also gives off light rays, or *visible radiation*. Everything you see reaches the eye through light rays. Heat and light are just two of the many kinds of radiation which affect our lives.

What Radiation Is

Radiation comes to us in an amazing way. Imagine a particle much too small to be seen even with the most powerful electron microscope. Imagine also that this tiny particle moves in a wavelike fashion and goes so fast that it would circle the earth more than seven times in one second. This high-speed particle you have imagined actually exists. It is called a *photon*. Light rays, heat radiation, radio waves, X rays, cosmic rays, and the gamma rays produced by splitting atoms are all streams of photons. *Radiation* is the term used to describe any stream of photons. It also describes the particles shot out when atoms decay or split.

As you read this page, photons emitted from the sun, an electric light, or some other radiating source are hitting the encyclopedia page. The black print absorbs most of these tiny, vibrating "bullets" and their energy is converted into heat. The white parts of the page reflect most of the photons they receive. Some of these photons go right through the pupils of your eyes. The lens of your eye focuses the photons so that they form on the light-sensitive retina of the eye the same pattern of light and dark places that exists on the printed page. When you see different colors, your eyes are being hit by streams of photons which differ in their rates of vibration.

But radiation is not confined to visible light. When we go out in the sunlight, we may sunburn or tan. This condition results from the action of photons which have so high a frequency that they are invisible. These photons are *ultraviolet rays*. Other invisible photons, vibrating even more rapidly than ultraviolet rays, can pass through objects that visible light cannot penetrate. These are the X rays which we use in medicine and in industry. As atoms split or decay in natural radioactivity, they give off very fast vibrating, or ultrahigh-frequency, photons, called *gamma rays*. The highest frequency photons known are the *cosmic rays* that bombard the earth from outer space.

Even this is not the whole story of radiant energy. All radiation can be arranged in a special table, or *electromagnetic spectrum*. The photons which vibrate the fastest are at one end of the spectrum, and those which vibrate the slowest, at the other. We started with light and moved up this table to cosmic rays. Starting again with light, which is about at the middle of our table, and going down the spectrum to the photons of lower frequency, we find first the photons that produce radiant heat. These are the *infrared rays*. Any warm object, even your body, gives off these rays. Special photographic plates which are sensitive to infrared rays can take a dim picture of a person in complete darkness.

As we move on to photons of lower frequency, we reach a place in our table where we find the streams of short-wave photons that are used in short-wave radio communication. We speak of them as "short-wave" or "high-frequency" radio waves, but they are much too long and occur at much too low a frequency to affect our eyes as light does. The term *short wave* is used to distinguish the radio waves used by amateurs, aircraft, and police from the longer waves and lower frequency of the photons used in regular radio broadcasting.

All these radiations are produced by photons which travel 186,282 miles a second. They differ only in the frequencies of their vibrations. Photons at the radio-broadcasting end of the table, or spectrum, move in giant waves that must be measured in miles. These are the low-frequency photons. The high-frequency cosmic rays at the other end of the spectrum move at the same speed but in waves so short that they must be measured in fractions of a millionth of an inch. In between the high-frequency and low-frequency photons are all the other forms of radiant energy.

How Radiation Affects Life on the Earth

The importance of radiation in our lives is tremendous. An automobile moves down the highway, while high above it a jet plane, burning a different fuel, zooms across the sky. Radiant energy is the final source

HOW ATOMIC WORKERS ARE PROTECTED AGAINST RADIATION

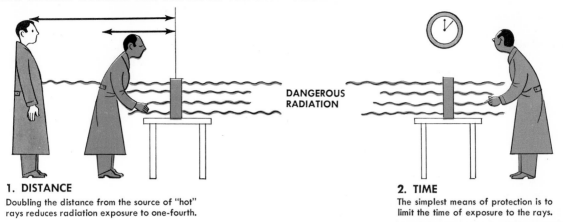

DANGEROUS RADIATION

1. DISTANCE

Doubling the distance from the source of "hot" rays reduces radiation exposure to one-fourth.

2. TIME

The simplest means of protection is to limit the time of exposure to the rays.

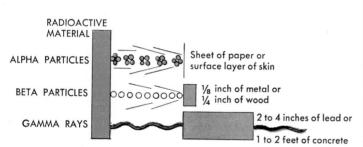

RADIOACTIVE MATERIAL

ALPHA PARTICLES — Sheet of paper or surface layer of skin

BETA PARTICLES — ⅛ inch of metal or ¼ inch of wood

GAMMA RAYS — 2 to 4 inches of lead or 1 to 2 feet of concrete

3. SHIELDING

Shields, or barriers, of sufficient thickness will stop deadly rays.

Remote Control "Hands" pick up and move a bottle of radioactive isotopes at an atomic plant. A thick shield protects the operator from radiation exposure. He watches his control tongs through a mirror above him.

of the power that moves them both. A breeze blows in your backyard, while, in a neighboring state, a violent thunderstorm blows down trees, brings torrents of rain, and creates an awe-inspiring display of lightning. Radiant energy is the cause. You get a drink of water from the faucet in your kitchen. That water was once— no, many times—a part of the great oceans that surround the continents of the earth. Radiant energy lifted ocean water into the sky and then produced the rain that dropped to the earth to be collected and piped to your house. You turn on the radio and listen to a broadcast from London. Radiant energy traveled from the transmitter to your loudspeaker in so short a time that you could hear the speaker's voice before a man at the back of the auditorium in which he spoke could hear him. A giant four-engined airplane lets down to a safe landing at an airport in a fog so dense that the pilot could not see the wings of his airplane. Radar, using radiant energy, guided him down.

In a large hospital a patient is moved into position under a *cobalt bomb*. This "bomb" is being used to save the patient's life, not to destroy him. The cobalt had earlier been placed in a nuclear reactor and the bombarding neutrons in the reactor had made the cobalt give off gamma rays. This radioactive cobalt now

radiates a tremendously powerful beam of these rays into the cancer tissue of the patient to destroy the cancer and save a life. Somewhat longer but similar rays shoot out of the dentist's X-ray machine. These rays are used to take a picture of your teeth so that the dentist will know what cavities there are in your teeth.

A green plant traps the radiant energy of the sun and changes it into food. The food you ate today contained energy earlier stored by a plant—energy that was once a stream of photons given off by the sun. The coal with which houses are heated is *fossil radiation* which was trapped by ancient plants from the radiating sun and changed over long periods of time into coal. Scientists believe that oil was produced in a similar fashion. Even the electricity that you use is energy that can be traced directly or indirectly to the sun. Without the sun, our earth would be a cold, barren, weatherless planet. See SUN (How the Sun Affects the Earth).

How Man Puts Radiation to Work

Suppose that the atomic fires in our sun were suddenly put out and we were forced to use the world's supply of coal, oil, natural gas, peat, tars, and wood in order to keep the earth warm enough for us to live. If we were to provide the same energy that our dead sun had

RADIATION

been providing, we would use up every scrap of these fuel materials on earth in about one year. This would include all the known deposits of gas, oil, and coal, and all the timber yet uncut. We would have but one source of energy left on the earth—atomic energy. If we were to provide the same amount of energy the sun had given us by using all of the atomic fuels that we have, we would again be out of fuel in less than a week.

Radiant Energy as a Direct Source of Power. We need not worry about the sun going out. But scientists have become increasingly interested in the possibilities of using the sun's vast source of energy for the direct production of power. All man's present fuels together give us each year only about three thousandths of 1 per cent of the energy from sunlight that bathes the earth each year. Man uses radiation indirectly for power production in harnessing wind in windmills and falling water in turbines. Solar batteries have been developed which can convert sunlight into electrical power. See SOLAR ENERGY.

The Electromagnetic Spectrum and Its Uses. We have learned that natural radiation is composed of photons which are alike except in the frequency with which they vibrate. In 1860 the English physicist, James Clerk Maxwell, suggested that light resulted from vibrating electrical charges that set up alternating electric and magnetic effects. Since Maxwell's time, light waves have been called *electromagnetic waves*. But more recent studies have shown that all radiations are basically the same. Electromagnetic waves range from the slowly vibrating, long-wave photons produced by an alternating electric current to the extremely short-wave, high-energy photons of gamma rays shot out by splitting atoms, and the even shorter waves of cosmic rays.

All these rays or waves are transmitted through space with the same speed. This speed is the velocity of light, which is 186,282 miles per second. On a sunny day, when you feel the warmth of the sun, you must realize that the light and infrared rays which just struck your skin took slightly over 8 minutes to travel the 93,000,-000 miles from the sun.

Besides having a definite wavelength, a wave also has a definite number of vibrations per second for this wavelength. We call this the *frequency* of the wave and express it in terms of *hertz* (cycles per second). We can always find the frequency of a wave if we know its wavelength. Or, if we know the frequency, we can find its wavelength. The reason is that the frequency multiplied by the wavelength of a wave must always give a product equal to the velocity of light. This is true of all electromagnetic waves. For example, all radio stations have an assigned frequency on which they transmit their programs. See RADIO (Radio Waves).

At the other end of the spectrum, far removed from radio waves or light waves, are the extremely high-frequency radiations. X rays, which are very penetrating, have a wavelength of 0.1 Angstroms and a frequency of 30 billion billion hertz. Cosmic rays contain gamma rays of even higher frequency, but we customarily talk of their energy rather than their frequencies because the frequencies are astronomic.

Other Kinds of Rays. Not all rays are electromagnetic. Not all rays move with the velocity of light.

Strictly speaking, we should not call a stream of electrons coming from a radioactive source, *rays*. They are simply fragments of atoms that shoot out like tiny bullets. The only photon emitted by atoms is the gamma photon, which has the same radiation as that produced by X-ray machines. But any particle, photon or not, that travels at a very high rate of speed, takes on a vibratory motion. We speak of such atomic particles as radiations. See ATOM; RADIOACTIVITY.

Learning to Live with High-Energy Radiation

However necessary radiation may be for life on the earth, it can also destroy life. Even the relatively small amounts of ultraviolet radiation that penetrate the atmosphere can cause painful, and in some cases serious, sunburn. In ordinary experience a person may never come in contact with radiation much more dangerous than the ultraviolet rays from the sun or a mercury-vapor "sun" lamp. But the last few years have brought increased uses of X rays, and since 1945 we have had to contend with the even higher-energy radiations produced by splitting atoms. Radioactive atoms spray out particles and radiations that can kill.

Protecting Ourselves from High-Energy Radiation. Anyone who has had an X ray taken knows that the X rays penetrate the body without producing any sensation. When you have a dental X ray you do not feel the passage of the X rays. But you know that they have penetrated through your cheek and your teeth from their effect on the photographic film. When you have your teeth X-rayed, the dentist stands aside from the X-ray machine when he turns it on. He also has *you* hold the film inside your mouth. He does this to make sure that he does not suffer any ill effects which could occur from *repeated* exposure to the X rays. The dentist may take a hundred X rays a week, whereas you may have one or two per year, or even less. Such infrequent X rays do not hurt you, but if the dentist were exposed to hundreds of X-ray "shots" he would certainly be harmed. He would suffer *radiation damage*.

In Laboratories and Hospitals where radium and other radioactive substances are used, the persons entrusted with their use are trained to protect themselves and others from injury. Normally, radium is kept inside a lead safe or vault. The lead shielding offers protection from the gamma rays. Whenever the radium is taken from the safe it is picked up either with long-handled tongs or by remotely-operated equipment.

Occasionally, through carelessness or oversight, some tiny "needles" of radium may be lost in a hospital. These may be located with a Geiger counter, which detects the gamma rays given off by the radium.

In Atomic Energy Projects, very large quantities of radioactive material must be handled every day. These materials are produced from the fission of uranium. When the U-235 atom splits in two, fragments are produced which are highly radioactive, and destructive to living tissue. Men working in atomic plants have to deal with large quantities of these *fission fragments*. For safety, remote control devices are used to operate the reactors and handle the radioactive materials which are produced. Thick concrete shields are used as barriers to protect the workers. With so much radioactive material around, the question "How can you be sure that no one gets too much radiation?" becomes important. The answer is that authorities set up rules for working safely so that no one is exposed to too much radiation. All workers must carry radiation meters with them at all times. These automatically record how much radiation each person is getting. The simplest of these meters is a piece of photographic emulsion or film sealed in black paper so that light will not strike it. X and gamma rays striking the film produce tiny specks of blackening. The amount of blackening on the developed film indicates the amount of radiation the person carrying it has received. Another instrument is called a *pocket-chamber*, or *electroscope*. It is a plastic chamber that carries a charge of electricity. Passage of gamma rays through the chamber discharges it. By measuring the loss of electrical charge one can tell how much radiation passed through it.

Effects of Exposure to Radiation. In the early days of the use of radium for making luminous watch dials, there were a number of deaths resulting from lack of proper health protection in this industry. Some young women who worked in dial-painting plants used to point the tips of their brushes by touching them to their lips. In the process, they took into their mouths a small amount of the radioactive compound on the brush. This compound was taken into the body, where it was deposited in the bone structure. Alpha particles given out by the radium bombarded the bone marrow and destroyed tissues which form the red blood cells. Some of these persons died a lingering death.

The *roentgen* (*r*) is a measure of radiation. It is named for the discoverer of X rays, Wilhelm Konrad Roentgen. Workers in atomic plants are allowed to take no more than 0.3 roentgen of radiation each week. Scientists believe that this quantity of radiation will not harm a person even over a period of years. If a person receives more than 100 roentgens over the entire body in a single exposure, radiation damage might result, but the person would not die. It takes about 500 roentgens to kill a human being.

It is not yet entirely clear what happens to living tissue subjected to high-energy radiation. It is known, however, that such radiation *ionizes* any substance it hits, including living cells (see ION AND IONIZATION). The chief effects of such radiation on the cells are probably indirect. Radiation ionizes water in the cells. This forms electrically charged atoms of hydrogen and hydrogen peroxide that oxidize the *enzymes* of the cells. Enzymes are chemicals that cells need in order to burn fuels to get the energy necessary for their life activity. When the enzymes are oxidized, the cells probably starve to death. In addition, radiation may break the chemical bonds holding proteins together. It may kill cells directly by destroying their *nuclei* (centers). See RADIATION SICKNESS; FALLOUT.

How Radiation Can Change Living Things. It sometimes happens in nature that sudden changes occur in a species of plant or animal. We say that a *mutation* occurs in the species (see MUTATION). In many cases these mutations make the animal or plant less able to live in its environment and the new species dies out. Such mutations are harmful. In some cases, however, the change may help the animal adapt itself better to its environment. In other words, the mutation is beneficial. Such changed species should prosper and in some cases replace the unchanged species.

People engaged in breeding animals take advantage of natural mutation to breed superior types of animals. The same is true of scientists who seek to develop new varieties of plants, such as corn, that will be more resistant to plant diseases.

Mutations may be induced by radiation, especially by the penetrating radiation emitted in radioactivity. Studies have been made which show that the rate of occurrence of mutations in a species is increased if the species is irradiated with X rays or gamma rays. This fact is responsible for the fear that radiation from atomic weapons may produce mutations in human beings. These mutations—possibly harmful ones—would be passed on to future generations. This subject is being carefully investigated by *geneticists*, or scientists who study the mechanism of inheritance.

Producing High-Energy Radiation

Scientists have devoted much of their time in recent years to perfecting methods for producing radiation of very high energy. In general, there are two methods which can be used to accelerate nuclear particles to very high speed. Both methods depend upon having a source of charged particles, because neutral atoms cannot be accelerated. The particles called protons may easily be produced by *ionizing*, or stripping the electrons from, ordinary hydrogen gas. *Deuterons*, the nuclei of heavy hydrogen atoms, are produced by ionizing heavy hydrogen or deuterium gas. Alpha particles are likewise produced by ionization of helium gas. In this case two electrons are stripped from the helium atom. Electrons are easily produced by emission from a heated filament.

One acceleration technique is to pull the charged particles down an *evacuated* tube, or one in which a vacuum exists, in a straight line, giving the particles more and more energy as they speed down the tube. Machines of this type include Van de Graaff generators, linear accelerators, and microwave accelerators.

In the second type of accelerator, the charged particles are bent in a circular path by a suitable magnetic field. Then they are made to whirl in an orbit, picking up energy with each trip around until they reach their final energy. Machines of this kind include the cyclotron, the betatron, the synchrocyclotron, and the synchrotron. See ATOM SMASHER with its list of Related Articles.

Laws and Theories of Radiation

Planck's Theories. In 1900 the great German scientist Max Planck took the first major step in explaining radiation. He was studying the problem of what causes heated objects to give off light.

Before Planck's time, scientists had believed that the heat and light radiated from a heated object was a stream of energy that was as continuous as a stream of water flowing down a river bed. They believed that this stream had a wavelike or vibratory motion. This viewpoint helped them to explain many such things as rainbows. But they had rejected Sir Isaac Newton's earlier notion that light was a stream of bulletlike particles shot out from the radiating source.

But light seems also to act as if it is composed of such

tiny bullets. For one thing, light produces a definite pressure when it falls on an object. As a comet moves around the sun, its great gaseous tail is always streaming out away from the sun. This can be satisfactorily explained only by assuming that the light from the sun pushes the tail away. This pressure of light is quite small, but it has been measured.

Planck's theories gave us a start in accounting both for the wavelike motion of light and for the pressure effects of light. He assumed that the motion of atoms and of the vibrating electrons within atoms caused tiny, vibrating particles to be shot out into space. We now know that these particles vibrate with a frequency that varies according to the energy of the atoms or electron vibrations which cause them to be shot out. Planck developed the now famous *quantum theory* of energy transmission in which he suggested that any heated body gives off light in tiny, separate packages, or *quanta*, which we now call photons. See QUANTUM THEORY.

Particle-Wave Relationship. In 1924, the French physicist Louis de Broglie first showed that there is a precise relationship between matter (particles) and waves. He said that every moving particle, such as an electron, has its definite wavelength, which depends only upon the particle's mass and its speed. The greater the particle's mass, the shorter its wavelength. Likewise, the greater its speed, the shorter the wavelength. As the speed of all photons in the electromagnetic spectrum is the same, it is clear that the photons of greatest mass would have the shortest wavelength, or the highest frequency. These are the high-energy cosmic and gamma rays. Relatively high energies are required to produce these photons. But toward the other end of the scale, the relatively low energy of burning wood will produce the low-energy, low-frequency photons of yellow light.

We no longer worry about trying to pin down a radiation and ask whether it is a wave or a particle. We know that it may behave as both. We know, too, that there is not just one color or wavelength of light given off by a glowing body. Rather, a whole spectrum is given off.

Our sun gives off separate and distinct wavelengths of light. These sharp wavelengths, or lines, are rays of light given off by atoms of individual elements. Each element emits its own special groups of light lines. Simple elements like hydrogen and helium emit only a few groups of lines, and they are distributed in a regular fashion—in what is called a regular series. The regular intervals between the spectral lines of any element suggest that there must be some regularity inside the atom which accounts for these lines.

Excited Electrons. Niels Bohr of Denmark explained the regularity of the spectral lines in his planetary theory of the atom in 1913. And he gave us the picture that scientists today believe explains the origin of radiation or photons. He pictured the atom as a miniature solar system. At the center of the atom was a heavy nucleus, like our sun in the solar system. Spinning around the nucleus, like planets, were electrons whirling in a never-ending path at a dizzy speed. Treating the simplest atom of hydrogen as a proton nucleus and a

single electron, Bohr was able to calculate the orbits for the electron. He showed that the mutual attraction between the positively-charged nucleus and the negatively-charged electron was held in exact balance by the counter-effect of the electron's centrifugal force. Except for the centrifugal force due to its circular motion, one would expect that the proton and electron would be drawn together. Bohr assumed that the normal hydrogen atom consisted of the proton, with the electron whirling around it in a fixed orbit a constant distance away. When energy was added to the atom, as by collision with electrons, the electron might be knocked out of its number one, or normal, orbit to one farther away. In this number two orbit, the electron is in an "excited" state. See ATOM (Electronic Structure).

But actually the electron is always unstable in this excited condition, and soon it dives back to its number one orbit, and the atom is back in its normal or undisturbed state. In the process of returning to its normal condition from the excited state, the atom loses energy. This energy is emitted in the form of a quantum, or photon, of light. The color or wavelength of the emitted photon is determined by the change which the electron makes in going from one orbit to another. There are many excited states for an atom, and for each orbit there is a definite amount of energy. When the atom is de-excited, this energy is liberated as a photon of the corresponding energy.   RALPH E. LAPP

Related Articles in WORLD BOOK include:

Outline

I. **What Radiation Is**
II. **How Radiation Affects Life on the Earth**
III. **How Man Puts Radiation to Work**
   A. Radiant Energy as a Direct Source of Power
   B. The Electromagnetic Spectrum and Its Uses
   C. Other Kinds of Rays
IV. **Learning to Live with High-Energy Radiation**
   A. Protecting Ourselves from High-Energy Radiation
   B. Effects of Exposure to Radiation
   C. How Radiation Can Change Living Things
V. **Producing High-Energy Radiation**
VI. **Laws and Theories of Radiation**

Questions

How widely may radiation differ and still be radiation?
Is radiation produced by particles or by waves? What is the reason for your answer?
What is a *photon?* How fast does it travel? How do photons differ?
What is the difference between light and heat? How are light and heat alike?
How has man put the sun's radiation to work?
What is the *electromagnetic spectrum?*
How does radiation affect weather?
In what three ways do atomic workers protect themselves from high-energy rays?
What uses do we make of high-energy radiation?

RADIATION BELT. See Van Allen Radiation.

RADIATION DETECTOR. See Geiger Counter.

RADIATION SICKNESS is the illness that follows a person's exposure to damaging amounts of certain types of radiations. These radiations may come from atomic explosions, radioisotopes, atom smashers, or X-ray machines. Ionization from the radiations causes changes in the atoms of living tissue (see Ion and Ionization). Thus the function of vital substances is lost. Such changes kill or damage the body cells and tissues and may cause death or lasting injury.

Some cells are more easily injured than others, but scientists do not know why. Most sensitive are the cells of the blood-forming organs (bone marrow), the lining of the stomach and intestines, the skin, and the sex glands. Most resistant to radiation are the cells of the brain and muscles.

There are several different kinds of radiation sickness, each differing from the others in the amount of radiation received by the individual. Small amounts kill, or severely damage, the cells of the blood-forming organs and also do some damage to the cells of the intestines and skin. Persons exposed to this amount of radiation may die in 16 to 60 days. Larger amounts severely damage the intestinal cells, and death may occur in 4 to 10 days. Tremendous amounts of radiation damage the brain, and death occurs in a few hours. Doctors have found no treatment for radiation sickness, other than transfusions and antibiotics. Joe W. Howland

See also Fallout; Radiation (Effects).

RADIATOR is a set of pipes or tubes that gives off heat to its surroundings. Steam or hot-water radiators in homes transfer heat to the air in a room. When warmed, the air next to the pipes expands, becomes lighter, and rises. Cooler air from the room streams in to take its place, creating a constant circulation of air. This process is called *convection*, and certain types of radiators are called *convectors*. Radiators also heat room air by direct *radiation*. See Heat (How Heat Travels).

An automobile radiator works in the same way. Water carries heat from the engine to tubes at the front of the radiator. Air rushing past the tubes absorbs heat from the water and cools it. An engine-driven fan helps move air through the radiator. Ira M. Freeman

See also Automobile (color diagram: Cooling System); Heating (Central Heating Systems).

RADICAL, in chemistry, is a group of two or more atoms which act and remain together as a single unit in chemical reactions. For example, OH is the hydroxyl radical and it appears in all hydroxides. Most radicals combine with other atoms or radicals to form compounds or ions. However, they may exist for relatively short times unbound to any other group. Such radicals are called *free radicals*. Stanley Kirschner

RADICAL REPUBLICAN. See Reconstruction (Congress Takes Control).

RADICAL SIGN. See Root.

RADICALISM is a political philosophy that emphasizes the need to find and eliminate the basic injustices of society. The word *radicalism* comes from the Latin word *radix*, meaning *root*. Radicals seek what they consider the roots of the economic, political, and social wrongs of society and demand immediate and sweeping changes to wipe them out.

In the United States, many people regard radicals

as political extremists of either the left or right wing. But the meaning of the word *radical* varies from country to country and from time to time. For example, French radicals generally support moderately liberal left wing policies. On the other hand, Yugoslav radicals are regarded by some people as extreme right wing conservatives. In addition, the people whom one generation considers radicals may differ greatly in viewpoint from the radicals of the previous or next generation.

In Europe, the term *radical* came into general use in Great Britain during the early 1800's. It described reform demands by such political leaders as Charles James Fox. In 1797, Fox had demanded what he called "radical reform" to make Britain's political system more democratic. During the 1800's, the British philosopher Jeremy Bentham led a group called "philosophical radicals." Bentham believed that all legislation should aim to provide the greatest happiness for the greatest number of people.

Radicalism developed in France after the French Revolution (1789-1799) had made that nation a republic. During the 1800's, many European radicals took the French Revolution as their model and tried to establish republics in their own countries.

Several European radicals established the socialist movement and demanded the total reconstruction of society. During the late 1800's, the movement split into moderate and radical factions. The moderate socialists sought change through gradual reform. The radical socialists insisted that only revolution could reform society. In Russia, the moderates were called *Mensheviks* and the radicals *Bolsheviks*. The Bolsheviks seized power in 1917 and established a Communist government.

In the United States, the followers of Alexander Hamilton, the first secretary of the treasury, opposed the French Revolution. They used the term *radicals* for the pro-French followers of Thomas Jefferson.

In the years before and during the Civil War (1861-1865), radical abolitionists called for an immediate end to slavery. Other radicals demanded cheap land, prohibition of alcoholic beverages, voting reforms, and women's rights. After the Civil War, Radical Republicans sought a "hard peace" for the defeated South (see Reconstruction). During the late 1800's and early 1900's, left wing radical groups included the Knights of Labor, the Populists, and the Socialists.

American radicals, unlike European radicals, have never been able to establish a major political party. However, radicals in the United States have influenced national politics through their writings and speeches. They also have organized third parties that demanded reforms. These parties have often gained enough support to force the major parties to pass reform legislation. Such legislation has included the income tax, government regulation of industry, and social welfare programs.

During the 1960's and early 1970's, many radicals of the New Left demanded a reformation of society to end segregation and war (see New Left). Some women radicals joined the women's liberation movement. Right wing radicals included white racists and those who believed strongly in states' rights. Christopher Lasch

See also Left Wing; Right Wing.

Entertainment

Motor Traffic Control

RADIO

RADIO is one of the most important means of communication. People throughout the world can speak to each other across great distances by radio. Soldiers in the Arctic, lonely ranchers in Australia, and explorers in the jungles of South America can keep in touch with civilization by radio. Sailors use radio to contact the shore, and airplane pilots use it to talk to their bases. Radio broadcasting serves as an important means of information, education, and entertainment.

Have you ever been in a home that had no radio? If so, it was an unusual home, because about 95 of every 100 homes in the United States have radios—more than have automobiles or telephones. There are now almost four radios per family in the United States. About 95 of every 100 Canadian homes have radios.

People wake up to clock radios, ride to their jobs with car radios, do their work while listening to radio, and spend leisure hours hearing favorite programs. Portable radios are popular at the beach and on picnics. Sports fans even take them to baseball and football games. Thousands of persons have discovered the fun of building and operating amateur radio stations.

To broadcast a program, a radio station changes ordinary sound waves into radio waves. The radio waves *radiate out* into space, or go in all directions. The phrase "radiate out" gives us the word *radio*. Your radio set changes the radio waves back into ordinary sound waves so you can hear the program.

Guglielmo Marconi, an Italian inventor, proved the possibility of radio broadcasting when he first sent radio waves through the air in 1895 (see MARCONI, GUGLIELMO). The first regularly scheduled programs began a relatively short time ago—in 1920. Since then, research to improve radio has led to radar, television, and

Arthur Hull Hayes, the contributor of this article, is a former President of CBS Radio.

other electronic wonders. The development of television in the 1940's and 1950's brought many changes in radio programs. But television itself depends on radio waves to carry the sound and picture.

Uses of Radio

Programming. Suppose that in one day you wanted to: (1) learn the news of your town, state, country, and the world, (2) listen to a lecture about a famous book, (3) go to a major league baseball game, and (4) listen to the music of your favorite orchestra. To do all this, you could buy newspapers, books, and magazines, tickets to the ball game and lecture, and phonograph records made by the orchestra. All this would be inconvenient and expensive. But all this and many other programs and services are on radio at a cost of a few pennies a day.

Radio brings outstanding events within reach of almost everyone. Lectures, concerts, and sports events can usually be found only in big cities. But radio takes these attractions to small towns and farm areas. Through radio, people have come to appreciate good music and follow world events.

Public Services regularly provided by radio stations include frequent weather reports, news broadcasts, educational programs, round-table discussions, and religious services. Farmers await daily reports on price trends and the number of hogs and cattle shipped to various markets. Advertising by various companies pays for some of these programs. But radio stations and networks regularly broadcast public-service programs at their own expense. Such broadcasts range from fire-prevention and safe-driving campaigns to health information, appeals for welfare organizations, reports from local and national legislators, and speeches by the President.

Advertising supports radio broadcasting in the United States. Retailers and manufacturers pay for radio commercials, because these broadcasts often reach millions

Emergency Communication

Air Traffic Control

of prospective buyers. Advertisers spend an estimated $764 million a year to broadcast their sales messages. An advertising "jingle" may become as familiar as the latest tune. See ADVERTISING (Ways of Advertising).

In Business and Industry. Some public-address systems in factories and business offices work like small broadcasting stations. News services use radio to transmit photographs to newspapers (see FACSIMILE). Many taxi companies install two-way radios in their cabs to provide fast service. Dispatchers use the radios to tell drivers where to pick up passengers. In turn, the drivers can tell the dispatchers where they are. Police cars and fire-department cars use similar equipment.

Many persons use the Citizens Radio Service, also called the Citizens Band Radio, to communicate over short distances. For example, a rancher using this system can talk to his helpers on another part of his ranch. There are about 1,400,000 such transmitters in the United States. The Federal Communications Commission regulates transmitter operating procedures.

Passengers on ships and trains make long-distance calls by radiotelephone. Radiotelephone is the use of radio waves in combination with ordinary telephone hookups. Salesmen and deliverymen use radiotelephones in their cars and trucks to keep in touch with their offices.

Navigation. Ship-to-shore radio provides ships with weather forecasts and harbor reports. Radio waves are used by radar sets on ships and airplanes to determine the direction and distance of icebergs, ships, airplanes, and shorelines. Radio beams keep airplanes on their courses, and pilots receive weather reports and take-off instructions by radio. Commercial airlines could not operate without radio to direct planes flying in and out of crowded airports. See RADAR (The Uses of Radar).

National Defense. Armies use radio to keep their troops in touch with headquarters. They also use it to communicate across battlefields. See WALKIE-TALKIE.

Television and most FM stations would go off the air in case of an enemy attack. But the *Emergency Broadcast System (EBS)*, established in 1963, allows AM stations and certain FM stations to broadcast on their own frequency during an attack. The stations would not use call letters, because all stations in a given area would broadcast the same material from a single source. EBS

--- RADIO TERMS ---

Affiliate is a radio station that carries some programs provided by a *network*.

AM stands for *amplitude modulation*, a broadcasting method in which the sound changes the power of the wave.

Call Letters are the initials that identify a radio station, such as WBBM in Chicago.

Channel is the radio frequency assigned to a station.

Clear Channel is a frequency used for nighttime broadcasts by only one high-powered station.

E. T. stands for *electrical transcription*, a phonograph record produced especially for broadcasting.

FM stands for *frequency modulation*, a static-free radio broadcasting method in which the sound changes the frequency of the wave.

Frequency is the number of *cycles* (vibrations) a radio wave or sound wave completes in a second. It is measured in *hertz*. Frequency is also used to mean *channel*.

Network is a group of stations joined together by telephone lines to carry the same programs.

Remote Pickup is a radio program that originates outside the studio.

Signal is a radio wave broadcast by a station and picked up by a receiving set.

Signature, or **Theme,** is the song or sound effect that identifies a program when it comes on or goes off the air.

Station Break is a pause to identify a station by its call letters and location.

Wave Length is the distance between two crests of a radio wave. *Short-wave* lengths are shorter than 200 yards.

Wireless is the original word for radio. It is still occasionally used in Great Britain.

would be used to transmit information and reports from: (1) the President, (2) local authorities, and (3) state and regional civil defense officials. EBS would also be used to give national reports, instructions, and news.

Governments use radio to inform and influence the people of other countries. The Voice of America, an agency of the United States government, broadcasts to countries throughout the world, including Russia and its Communist satellites. Radio Free Europe, an unofficial enterprise supported privately by United States citizens, broadcasts from Western Europe to Communist countries in the East. The Voice of America and Radio Free Europe sponsor programs that express the freedom and benefits of democracy.

A Visit to a Radio Station

Most radio stations look like ordinary office buildings. They have offices for employees who plan the broadcasts, sell the advertising, and perform the many administrative tasks connected with any business. But radio stations also have libraries, tape rooms, storage rooms, repair facilities, and broadcasting studios.

The Studio. Everything about a radio studio is designed to control sound. Unwanted noises and vibrations are kept out, and the best quality is assured for sounds that are broadcast. The studio may be a large auditorium with seats for an audience, or it may be a small room used for newscasts and dramatic shows.

Most radio studios are suspended on cables attached to the frame of the building. This keeps out vibrations from traffic, construction work, and other disturbances. Studios have two sets of doors. The space between the doors makes a *sound lock* that helps shut out noise.

Studio ceilings and walls are often wavy or irregular. Their side walls are not parallel with each other. The wavy surfaces and uneven walls keep sound waves from *reverberating*, or bouncing from one to another. Bouncing sound waves would create a blurring noise or even an echo on the broadcast.

The broadcast originates from a stage or special area in the studio. Performers speak their lines or play musical instruments into a microphone. Some microphones hang from a *boom*, or overhead rod.

The Control Room. The producer of a radio show works from the control room while the program is on the air. A soundproof glass wall separates the control room from the broadcasting area. The producer coordinates the different elements that go into the program. He has a clear view of what happens, because the control room is several feet above the studio floor. The director sits in

A VISIT TO A RADIO STUDIO

A radio station broadcasts programs from a soundproof *studio*. The studio walls absorb echoes, and shut out noises from the outside.

Music may be played by musicians or produced from recordings. Here, a group of musicians plays music that is being recorded on tape.

The Technician controls the loudness and quality of the studio sounds. During the broadcast, he works in the control room behind soundproof glass.

Performers await their cues to start a variety program. Unlike most television performers, radio performers may read from a script.

CBS Radio

The Producer plans the show, chooses the performers, and coordinates all the different elements which go into the program. He sits in the control room while the program is being broadcast.

The Director sits in the studio. He holds up cue cards which give the different performers their signals to go on the air. He also provides cues for the commercials on the program.

the studio. He signals the performers to go on the air and provides cues for the commercials on the program.

The *audio* (sound) technician works at a *console*, a large instrument containing electronic tubes. The console has controls connected with all the microphones in the studio. The technician uses these controls to regulate the volume of each microphone. Another control connects the studio with the tape room, for any part of the program recorded on tape. The console also has a switch that puts *electrical transcriptions* (phonograph records) on the air. Transcriptions often carry *commercials* (advertising).

Near the console is a *jack field*, which looks much like a telephone switchboard. Wires called *patch cords* are plugged into the jack field. By shifting the patch cords about, the technician makes all kinds of connections between the microphones. For example, he can hook up the microphones that are outside the studio or in other parts of the building.

Sound Effects. In past years, when many dramatic programs were on radio, the sound-effects man played an important part in radio production. This technician is still important in broadcasting some drama programs, many radio commercials, and in some other types of broadcasts.

The sound-effects man works at a table in the studio. To create his sounds, he uses special devices or plays phonograph records of the sound needed. Suppose you are listening to a commercial about automobiles. You hear a car driving and then braking to a stop (record); the car door slams (record); you hear footsteps on a gravel path (the sound-effects man may shuffle his feet in a gravel-filled box); and a doorbell rings (the sound-effects man has many bells, buzzers, and chimes).

Master Control in a large network station has switches that put the broadcast on wires leading to many stations across the country. The master-control operator works at a huge console, with thousands of connections.

Tape Room. Many programs are recorded directly on spools of magnetic tape. Stations may use the tape for later broadcasts or for repeat broadcasts. Tape provides good reproduction and easy storage. It can be edited by cutting and splicing. Magnetic tape can be erased and reused many times.

News Room. News comes in on teletype from the news services and by telephone from the radio station's reporters. The news staff edits the news and prepares it for broadcast. The news room is usually near a studio, so the news commentator can quickly broadcast the latest events. Radio broadcasters sometimes interrupt a regular program to put an important news bulletin on the air.

Library. Large stations may have a reference library for writers, researchers, newsmen, and advertising staffs. Thousands of phonograph records may be stored in a record library. Some stations also have libraries for sheet music. A sound-effects library, or stock room, stores special sound-making devices and recordings of special sounds used to make broadcasts true to life.

How a Radio Program Is Broadcast

Radio Waves travel at the speed of light: 186,282 miles a second. But sound moves at a speed of only about one-fifth of a mile a second. A radio listener in California can actually hear the sounds of an orchestra sooner than an audience in a New York City concert hall where the broadcast originates!

When broadcast, a radio wave goes two ways—along the ground and into the sky. The *ground wave* is very powerful, but it loses its strength as it moves farther and farther away from the transmitter. While it remains strong, the wave can blanket the area it reaches, and can be received easily.

The *sky wave* shoots up into space until it comes to a layer of electrically charged atmosphere called the *ionosphere* or the *Kennelly-Heaviside layer* (see IONOSPHERE). When a sky wave hits the ionosphere, several things happen. Part of the wave diffracts and bends away from the ionosphere in the direction of the earth. Part of it is absorbed into the ionosphere. If the bent wave is strong enough, it will be received thousands of miles from the place where it started.

In short-wave radio, the sky wave easily bends earthward. For this reason, short-wave radio is used for long-distance messages. Short-wave operators often communicate with stations halfway around the world. See SHORT WAVE.

Wave length is the distance between one peak of a wave to the next peak. In radio, wave lengths are measured in meters, the standard international unit of length. One meter is equal to 39.37 inches, or slightly more than one yard. The *frequency* (rate of vibration) of the wave determines its length. For example, a frequency of 550 kilohertz produces a wave length of 545.1 meters.

Microphone. The first step in a broadcast takes place when the sounds of the program go into the microphone. The microphone changes the sound waves into electrical waves. The electrical waves have the same frequency as the sound waves. To change the sound vibrations into electrical waves, some microphones have a metal ribbon or coil that vibrates. Others may have crystals or particles of carbon. See MICROPHONE.

Studio Controls. The electrical "image" of the sound goes from the microphone on wires to the control room. In the control room, the technician *mixes* and *balances* the sound, or blends the voices, music, and sound effects into a harmonious relationship. He also strengthens the electrical waves. The technician does all this as the waves pass through *audio-frequency* vacuum tubes. He can make a watch tick sound like a thunderclap, or a thunderclap like the tick of a watch.

Transmitter, or sender, consists of electrical equipment that changes the electrical waves into radio waves, and then sends them out into the air. To do this, the transmitter strengthens the weak incoming audio frequencies from the studio, and combines them with powerful radio-frequency *carrier waves*.

The audio frequency and the carrier wave form a *modulated wave*. Stations use either of two kinds of modulated waves. In an *amplitude-modulated* (AM) wave, the sound changes the power of the wave. In a *frequency-modulated* (FM) wave, the sound changes the frequency (see FREQUENCY MODULATION).

An AM wave covers a great distance, because it is long and follows the curve of the earth. Its wide range is obviously an advantage. But most static and man-made interferences are also AM, and can disturb radio

RADIO

reception. The advantage of FM is its full frequency and relatively noise-free reception. But FM waves do not follow the curve of the earth. They can be received only as far as the horizon.

FM stations and low-power stations are often located in the middle of a city, in order to reach many listeners within their limited range. But high-power AM stations build their transmitters in thinly populated areas. Otherwise, their strong signals might drown out neighboring stations.

Stations build powerful transmitters as far as possible from high buildings, gas tanks, and power installations, because such obstructions might distort the radio waves. The surrounding ground must be a good conductor of electricity if the strongest possible signal is to be attained. Some of the best transmitter locations are on marshy ground or near large bodies of water, because water is an excellent conductor.

Listeners can receive powerful radio stations hundreds of miles from their transmitting point. For example, a 50,000-watt, clear-channel station in Chicago may regularly be heard at night by listeners as far away

as Florida. A 5,000-watt station in a small town reaches only the neighboring area.

Sending Antenna. The transmitter feeds the radio waves to a broadcasting antenna. The *antenna system* is usually a tower reaching high into the air. From the tower, the radio waves spread out into space in ever-widening circles, like the ripples made by a stone dropped in still water.

The height of an antenna is related to the length of the radio wave being transmitted. The antenna is usually one-half, one-fourth, or one-eighth the length of the wave. A station operating on a frequency of 1,000 kilohertz produces a wave length of 300 meters, or about 983 feet. The station would probably have a tower about 496 feet high.

This relationship of a tower size to the length of the radio wave is much like the relationship of the length of a piano string to the frequency of the tone it produces. A short piano string produces a tone with a high frequency. A long string has a low frequency.

Some transmitters have antenna systems that use two or more towers. With two towers, the station can send its broadcast in only one general direction. One of the towers blocks the waves from spreading into the area which

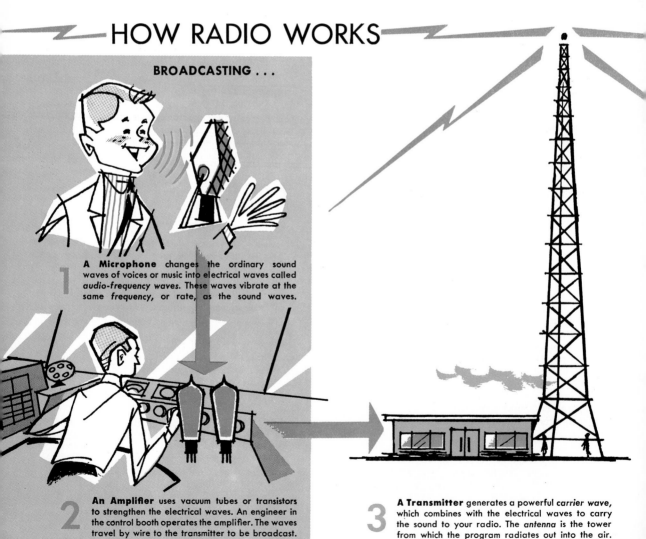

HOW RADIO WORKS

BROADCASTING . . .

1 A **Microphone** changes the ordinary sound waves of voices or music into electrical waves called *audio-frequency waves*. These waves vibrate at the same *frequency*, or rate, as the sound waves.

2 An **Amplifier** uses vacuum tubes or transistors to strengthen the electrical waves. An engineer in the control booth operates the amplifier. The waves travel by wire to the transmitter to be broadcast.

3 A **Transmitter** generates a powerful *carrier wave*, which combines with the electrical waves to carry the sound to your radio. The *antenna* is the tower from which the program radiates out into the air.

the station seeks to avoid. Such an arrangement is called a *directional antenna system*. Transmitters often use directional antennas to prevent interference with the broadcasts of a station that may be located nearby.

How a Radio Program Is Received

Radio waves move through the air around us all the time. These waves cannot be seen, and they cannot be heard. But a radio receiver turns them into sounds like those broadcast into the microphone. You then can hear the program.

Receiving Antenna is like an ear, listening for radio waves and vibrating to them. Most radios have built-in antennas, but an outside antenna provides better reception for weaker signals. The radio wave striking the antenna sets up a small electric pressure. As a result, a tiny electric current trickles into the set. This tiny current carries the radio carrier wave along with the audio frequency from the microphone.

Tuner. The government assigns each radio station a wave length. Wave lengths correspond to certain frequencies. A radio dial shows the frequencies of the stations which may be tuned in. For example, station WBBM in Chicago broadcasts on a frequency of 780 kilohertz. To tune in WBBM, the listener sets the pointer on his radio dial to the number 780.

The tuner selects a frequency put out by one radio station. The tuner has two parts. One part is a coil of wire or a loop of wire that may also serve as a built-in antenna. The other part is a *variable capacitor*, which consists of two sets of semicircular metal plates.

These two sets mesh closely together. One set never moves. The other set shifts its position when you twist the tuning knob on your radio receiver and tune to a station. The tuner matches your receiver to an incoming radio frequency.

Vacuum Tubes and Transistors. A typical radio set has five or more vacuum tubes or transistors and uses a *superheterodyne* circuit. In a superheterodyne hookup, the incoming wave from the station is changed to a lower frequency and then amplified. This circuit has five major sections: (1) converter, (2) intermediate frequency amplifier, (3) detector, (4) audio amplifier, and (5) rectifier. Each section contains at least one vacuum tube or transistor.

When radio waves enter a receiving set, they are

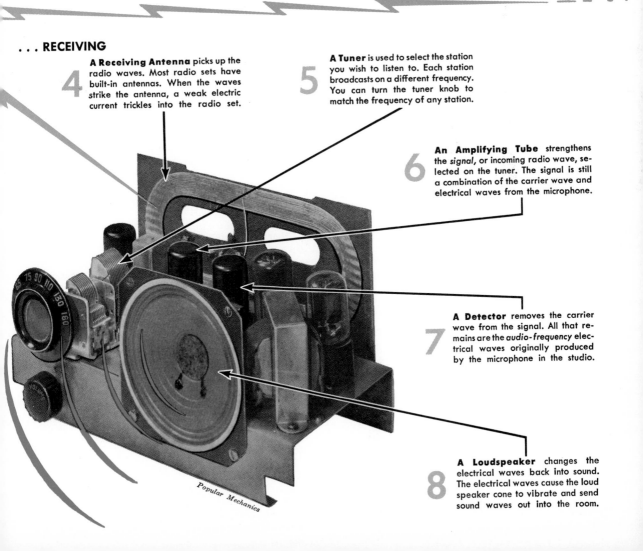

... RECEIVING

4 **A Receiving Antenna** picks up the radio waves. Most radio sets have built-in antennas. When the waves strike the antenna, a weak electric current trickles into the radio set.

5 **A Tuner** is used to select the station you wish to listen to. Each station broadcasts on a different frequency. You can turn the tuner knob to match the frequency of any station.

6 **An Amplifying Tube** strengthens the *signal*, or incoming radio wave, selected on the tuner. The signal is still a combination of the carrier wave and electrical waves from the microphone.

7 **A Detector** removes the carrier wave from the signal. All that remains are the *audio-frequency* electrical waves originally produced by the microphone in the studio.

8 **A Loudspeaker** changes the electrical waves back into sound. The electrical waves cause the loud speaker cone to vibrate and send sound waves out into the room.

Popular Mechanics

In 1920, earphones were needed to hear the first radio programs. Early radio sets used batteries for their power. Few listeners heard the broadcasts.

In the Mid-1920's, loudspeakers replaced earphones. Sets still used outside *aerials* (antennas).

By the 1930's, radios had built-in aerials and loudspeakers. Programs reached millions of listeners.

changed to the lower frequency by a circuit called a *converter*. The weak signal is then amplified by the *I.F.* (intermediate-frequency) amplifier. The signal next goes to a *detector*. This removes the radio carrier wave, which has remained with the signal all the time. All that remains is the *audio frequency* (electric pulse put out by the microphone). An *audio amplifier* strengthens the audio frequency signal before it flows into the loudspeaker.

The *rectifier* in a radio changes *alternating* (two-way) current into *direct* (one-way) current. Household electricity usually has an alternating current, but direct current is needed to operate the vacuum tubes in a radio set.

Some radios work from batteries. Many radio sets use transistors instead of vacuum tubes. Some circuits may be a combination of transistors and vacuum tubes. Transistors are much smaller than vacuum tubes, but they serve the same purpose. See TRANSISTOR.

Loudspeaker is the final link between the broadcasting studio and the listener. Its basic parts are a powerful *magnet* and a coil of wire called the *voice coil*. The voice coil is attached to a cone, which is usually made of paper. When the varying currents from the amplifiers pass through the coil, they exert varying pulls against the magnet's field. The cone then vibrates in time with the audio frequencies flowing through the coil. The cone's vibrations create waves of air exactly like those that first went into the microphone. And out comes sound! See LOUDSPEAKER.

Government Regulation of Radio

If anyone who felt like broadcasting could transmit on any wave length, with any power, and at any time he chose, the result would be so much confusion that nobody would receive the benefits of radio. Therefore, governments have found it necessary to regulate broadcasting.

In the United States. Congress established the Federal Radio Commission in 1927 to control radio broadcasts. The Federal Communications Commission (FCC) replaced the Radio Commission in 1934. The FCC licenses broadcasters, assigns frequencies, designates

station call letters, and controls station power. See FEDERAL COMMUNICATIONS COMMISSION.

The FCC grants station licenses "to serve the public interest, convenience, and necessity." A license is good for three years, and then must be renewed. The United States government takes the position that the air belongs to all the people, and should be used in the interest of everyone. But it does not decide what kind of programming should be done.

In Great Britain, radio is controlled by the British Broadcasting Corporation (BBC), a nonprofit agency chartered by the government as a public service. Listeners pay yearly license fees to hear BBC programs. There are no advertising commercials.

In Canada, features of the United States and British systems are combined. The government set up the Canadian Broadcasting Corporation (CBC) in 1936, because privately owned stations could not serve the country's vast, sparsely settled areas. The CBC operates an English-language network and a French-language network. The CBC operates over 35 stations. It gets about 70 per cent of its revenue from the government and 30 per cent from advertising. Many independent stations carry CBC programs. Canada has about 220 privately owned AM stations and 35 privately owned FM stations.

Other Countries have developed radio broadcasting in various ways. Some stations are under government control, and others are partly supervised by the government. Some are partly commercial. For example, France's 90 AM and FM stations are directed by a government agency and are devoted largely to educational and cultural programming.

The Radio Industry

Over 5,100 commercial AM and FM radio stations broadcast in the United States. All are privately owned. Almost one-third of these stations are affiliated with national radio networks. Affiliate stations are individually owned, and carry both local and network programs. A low-powered station in a small town may have an audience of only a few thousand persons. But a large, clear-channel station in a big city reaches millions of listeners in several states.

Four nationwide networks broadcast in the United States. They are the American Broadcasting Company

AND PRESENT

Zenith Radio Corp.

A Clock Radio can start an electric coffee maker, then awaken you with your favorite program.

A Car Radio makes it possible for you to hear programs while driving anywhere in the city or country.

CBS Radio

A Pocket-Size Portable can be carried wherever you go. It uses transistors in place of vacuum tubes.

————FAMOUS FIRSTS IN RADIO————

1864 James Clerk Maxwell discovered that electrical impulses travel through space at the speed of light.
1888 Heinrich Hertz demonstrated the wave theory, and established a relationship between electrical waves and light waves.
1895 Guglielmo Marconi sent radio signals over a mile.
1900 R. A. Fessenden broadcast voice by radio.
1901 Marconi received the first overseas radio message, from England to Newfoundland.
1904 Radio was used in the Russo-Japanese War.
1904 John Ambrose Fleming discovered that a vacuum tube can be used to detect radio signals.
1907 Lee de Forest patented the *triode*, or three-element vacuum tube.
1909 Passengers and crew of the S. S. *Republic* were saved in the first sea rescue using radio.
1912 Edwin H. Armstrong developed the superheterodyne circuit.
1919 President Woodrow Wilson became the first President to use radio when he spoke from a ship to World War I troops aboard other vessels.
1920 Stations KDKA of Pittsburgh and WWJ of Detroit made the first regular commercial broadcasts.

1923 Frank Conrad pioneered short-wave radio.
1923 The first permanent station hookup, or network, was established, and became the National Broadcasting Company in 1926.
1933 Armstrong constructed the first FM station.
1941 The largest audience in radio history, estimated at 90,000,000 listeners, heard President Franklin D. Roosevelt address the United States two days after the Japanese attack on Pearl Harbor.
1947 Bell Telephone Laboratories developed the transistor.
1952 The Federal Communications Commission and the United States Air Force established *Conelrad* (replaced in 1963 by the *Emergency Broadcast Service*).
1957 Scientists developed atomic-powered batteries for use in portable radios.
1959 Radios in Russian and United States rockets sent information to earth from beyond the moon.
1960 The first radio and television debates between two candidates for the Presidency took place between John F. Kennedy and Richard M. Nixon.
1961 Scientists held the first radio talks with a man in space, Russian cosmonaut Yuri Gagarin.

(ABC), the Columbia Broadcasting System (CBS), the Mutual Broadcasting System (MBS), and the National Broadcasting Company (NBC). In addition, regional networks serve various areas.

Commercial stations sell time to advertisers. Stations reaching the largest audience receive the highest fees. For example, a big-city station may charge as much as $150 for a single one-minute commercial, while a small-town station may receive only $12 for the same message broadcast three times in one day. Fees for sponsoring full-length shows are much higher.

History

Beginnings of Radio. Scientists in several countries took part in the development of radio. A Princeton University professor, Joseph Henry, and a British physicist, Michael Faraday, experimented separately with electromagnets in the early 1800's. Each arrived at the theory that a current in one wire can produce a current in another wire, even at a distance (induction theory). Another British physicist, James Clerk Maxwell, suggested in 1864 that electrical impulses travel through space at the speed of light. Heinrich Hertz, a German physicist, proved Maxwell's theory between

1886 and 1888. In 1892, Édouard Branly, a French physicist, invented a device that could receive radio waves and cause them to ring an electric bell.

In 1895, Guglielmo Marconi of Italy put all this thinking together, added ideas of his own, and developed the first *wireless* telegraph. Reginald A. Fessenden, an American physicist, demonstrated the first radio-voice transmission in 1900. Until then, radio messages had been sent only in "dot-dash" code. By 1906, Fessenden broadcast phonograph music.

In 1904, John Ambrose Fleming, an English electrical engineer, invented a vacuum tube that could detect radio signals. His tube had two electrodes, the *plate* and the *filament*. It is called a *diode* tube, because it has only these two elements. Lee de Forest of the United States modified the vacuum tube by adding a third element, the *grid*. The grid represented an improvement, because it controls the flow of electrons through the tube. The De Forest tube, patented in 1907, is a *triode* (three-element tube). It is also called an *audio tube*, because it increases the radio signal. Later, engineers developed tetrodes and pentodes. The *tetrode* tube has two grids and the *pentode* tube has three. See ELECTRONICS (Vacuum Tubes).

87

A SIMPLE RADIO SET

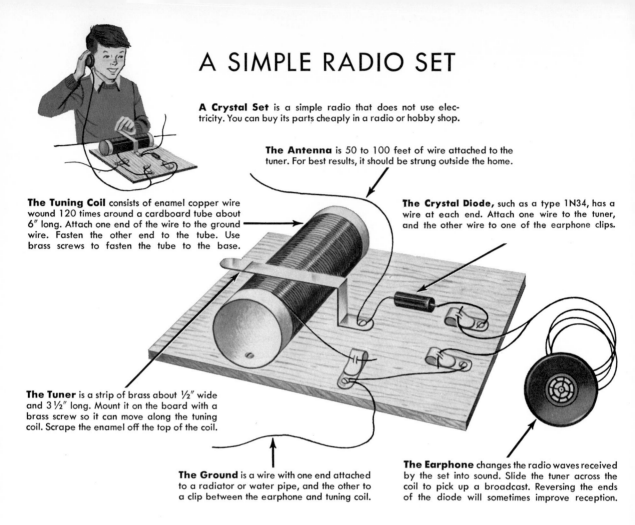

A Crystal Set is a simple radio that does not use electricity. You can buy its parts cheaply in a radio or hobby shop.

The Antenna is 50 to 100 feet of wire attached to the tuner. For best results, it should be strung outside the home.

The Tuning Coil consists of enamel copper wire wound 120 times around a cardboard tube about 6" long. Attach one end of the wire to the ground wire. Fasten the other end to the tube. Use brass screws to fasten the tube to the base.

The Crystal Diode, such as a type 1N34, has a wire at each end. Attach one wire to the tuner, and the other wire to one of the earphone clips.

The Tuner is a strip of brass about ½" wide and 3½" long. Mount it on the board with a brass screw so it can move along the tuning coil. Scrape the enamel off the top of the coil.

The Ground is a wire with one end attached to a radiator or water pipe, and the other to a clip between the earphone and tuning coil.

The Earphone changes the radio waves received by the set into sound. Slide the tuner across the coil to pick up a broadcast. Reversing the ends of the diode will sometimes improve reception.

Commercial Broadcasting in the United States began in 1920 when stations KDKA in Pittsburgh and WWJ in Detroit went on the air. Broadcasting started in the way that many programs are broadcast today—with phonograph records. KDKA's broadcast of the Harding-Cox election returns in 1920 has been celebrated as the first great popular event in broadcasting history. Radio advertising began on a summer day in 1922 when a suburban real-estate firm in Jackson Heights, N.Y., sponsored the first commercial broadcast.

The names of radio personalities became household words in the 1920's. Graham McNamee became the first well-known radio reporter. The Happiness Boys won popularity as a comedy team. The Clicquot Club Eskimos first used sound effects.

In the 1930's and 1940's, radio blossomed with important stars and programs. Probably no radio performers ever created so much excitement as did Amos 'n' Andy. Soon came Bing Crosby, Kate Smith, Eddie Cantor, Burns and Allen, Ed Wynn, Rudy Vallee, Jack Benny, and the ventriloquist Edgar Bergen with his dummy Charlie McCarthy.

During this period, radio became a national and international influence. While other American Presidents before him had spoken on radio, Franklin D. Roosevelt was the first to grasp fully the great force of the medium and the opportunity it provided for taking government policies directly to the people. His "fireside chats" became important radio listening. In Europe, Adolf Hitler and Benito Mussolini used radio to militarize Germany and Italy and to soften up neighboring countries for conquest.

Singers, orchestras, comedians, election reports, and play-by-play descriptions of sports events gave radio a mass appeal. Radio also helped develop the dance band era in the 1930's. Millions of persons listened to the music of Tommy Dorsey, Benny Goodman, Wayne King, Guy Lombardo, and Glenn Miller.

Because of radio's importance as a news source, many news reporters became as famous as the musicians and entertainers. By the time the United States entered World War II in 1941, radio listeners could readily identify the voices of such newsmen as Elmer Davis, Gabriel Heatter, H. V. Kaltenborn, Edward R. Murrow, Lowell Thomas, and Walter Winchell.

Wartime kept people close to their radios—not only to keep abreast of the news, but to find relief in their favorite entertainment. Such names as Bob Hope, Fibber McGee and Molly, Red Skelton, Arthur Godfrey, Frank Sinatra, and the Lux Radio Theatre became famous in the 1940's. During the war years, radio produced great documentary programs which helped spotlight the goals to be achieved by the war and the peace that followed it.

88

Radio Today. The rise of television caused many changes in radio programming. Dramas and "soap operas" almost disappeared from the air. Music, news, and sports became more important. Many stations specialize in playing distinct types of music. Some play music that is popular with teen agers. Many FM stations emphasize classical music.

By 1950, about 40,700,000 homes in the United States had a radio set. By 1960, there were almost that many sets installed in automobiles. By the early 1970's, the number of radio sets in homes, automobiles, and public places was about 336 million. During this time, the public bought about 50 million radio sets each year.

Radio became increasingly important to scientists in the mid-1960's. Radio telescopes make it possible for astronomers to broaden their knowledge of outer space (see TELESCOPE [The Radio Telescope]). Radio signals from weather balloons help meteorologists learn about the atmosphere (see BALLOON). Special transmitters make it possible to track the paths of rockets and guided missiles. Artificial earth satellites contained radios that broadcast information on conditions in space. In December, 1958, a United States artificial satellite picked up and recorded a radio message from earth. A radio in the satellite then rebroadcast the message. This marked the first two-way broadcast to a space vehicle. See COMMUNICATIONS SATELLITE (History).

Careers in Radio

Over 54,000 persons work full time or part time for U.S. radio stations and networks. Like any business, radio needs administrative personnel and office workers. Stations and networks employ advertising, sales, and public relations specialists. To produce programs, stations and networks need persons with creative interests, artistic talents, and journalistic skills. Radio also depends on skilled technicians.

Performing and Production. Jobs as reporters, announcers, writers, directors, producers, musicians, and other entertainers are the hardest to find. Stations and networks simply do not have enough such jobs to go around. Performers and writers often start by taking part in public-service programs on local stations, without pay. Experience on a small station is almost always a requirement for a network job or a position on a big-city station.

Technical Work. Radio technicians must have an FCC license and a certificate from a recognized radio technical school. Many large stations require a college degree in electrical engineering for top positions in their engineering departments. But technicians often move through the ranks into supervisory jobs. The engineers and technical assistants keep equipment in repair, and work in a control booth and at the transmitter while a show is on the air. Many technically trained men work for radio-repair shops. Radio servicemen often enter this field after becoming amateur radio operators. The radio repairman often owns his own shop.

Opportunities and Advancement. Some radio stars earn high salaries, comparable to those of television and motion-picture actors. Radio news writers generally receive higher pay than newspaper reporters, and station advertising salesmen often attain substantial incomes. But most radio people have picked their careers not necessarily to become wealthy. They have entered radio because they believe it is livelier and more exciting than any other occupation.   ARTHUR HULL HAYES

Related Articles in WORLD BOOK include:

BIOGRAPHIES

Armstrong, Edwin H.	Lodge, Sir Oliver J.
De Forest, Lee	Marconi, Guglielmo
Hertz, Heinrich R.	Maxwell, James Clerk

PARTS OF THE RADIO

Antenna	Microphone	Transistor
Loudspeaker	Quartz	

RADIO EQUIPMENT

Direction Finder	Radar	Television
Facsimile	Radio Control	Walkie-Talkie
Public Address System	Radio Telescope	

OTHER RELATED ARTICLES

Advertising	Kilohertz
American Broadcasting Companies	Monitoring Station
	Mutual Broadcasting System
Columbia Broadcasting System, Inc.	National Broadcasting Co.
	Radio, Amateur
Electronics (Science Project: A Candle-Powered Radio)	Radiogram
	Radiosonde
	RCA Corporation
Federal Communications Commission	Reflection
	Short Wave
Frequency Modulation	Static
Invention	Ultrahigh Frequency Wave
Journalism (Journalism in Radio and Television)	Voice of America
	Wave Band

Outline

I. **Uses of Radio**
II. **A Visit to a Radio Station**
    A. The Studio
    B. The Control Room
    C. Sound Effects
    D. Master Control
    E. Tape Room
    F. News Room
    G. Library
III. **How a Radio Program Is Broadcast**
    A. Radio Waves
    B. Microphone
    C. Studio Controls
    D. Transmitter
    E. Sending Antenna
IV. **How a Radio Program Is Received**
    A. Receiving Antenna
    B. Tuner
    C. Vacuum Tubes and Transistors
    D. Loudspeaker
V. **Government Regulation of Radio**
VI. **The Radio Industry**
VII. **History**
VIII. **Careers in Radio**

Questions

Why do radio stations sometimes record their programs on magnetic tape?

How does broadcasting in the United States differ from radio in Canada?

Why must broadcasting be controlled by a government agency?

What happens to a sound wave when it enters a microphone?

What is a network? An affiliate station?

What is the purpose of the receiving antenna?

Why do many stations put their broadcasting antennas on the outskirts of a city?

Why do some people prefer radio to television?

What are some important applications of radio?

How would your life be different without radio?

Reading and Study Guide

For a *Reading and Study Guide on Radio*, see the RESEARCH GUIDE/INDEX, Volume 22.

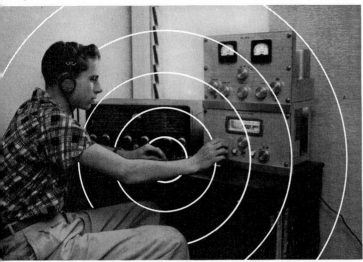
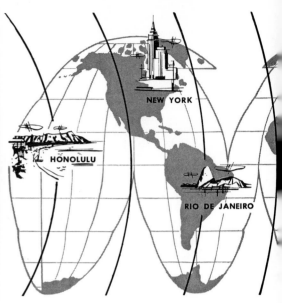

American Radio Relay League

Amateur Radio Operators often build their own *transmitters* (sending sets) on which they can send messages thousands of miles. They make friends with other *hams* (amateurs) in many lands.

RADIO, AMATEUR. Thousands of persons enjoy the useful and interesting hobby of amateur radio. These radio *hams* (amateurs) send messages on their home radio stations to new friends in the next block or halfway around the world. Seven-year-old boys and girls have become amateur radio operators. Many successful electronic engineers first learned the basic facts about electronics by becoming interested in ham radio.

The governments of most countries encourage radio amateurs because trained radio operators are needed in emergencies. Hams provide emergency communications during floods, fires, tornadoes, and hurricanes. The Federal Communications Commission (FCC) has often praised hams for their voluntary work in emergencies. To make further use of this stand-by reserve, the FCC has provided rules for the Radio Amateur Civil Emergency Services (RACES). The rules would assure orderly ham radio communications if the United States were attacked. Most states issue special automobile license plates to identify ham operators.

The Air Force, Army, and Navy recognize the value of amateur radio as training for future skilled technicians. They sponsor special training activities that encourage personnel to earn amateur radio licenses.

Sending Messages. Amateurs send messages either by voice or in International Code (see MORSE CODE [illustration: The International Code]). Hams use a language that the untrained listener cannot understand. Part of this special language consists of three-letter groups starting with the letter Q. Hams call these groups *Q signals*. For example, the signal *QRA* means "What is the name of your station?" The Q signals have been agreed upon internationally, and enable hams who do not speak a common language to understand each other. The Q signals also save time. When sending code, hams often omit vowels to save time.

Stations. An amateur radio station includes an *antenna*, a *transmitter* (sending set), and a *receiver* (see RADIO [How a Radio Program Is Broadcast]). Some hams have large stations that occupy an entire room. Others operate small stations in a corner of a room. Hams often build their own sending equipment from do-it-yourself kits. Some hams design and build their sending stations without kits. But most amateurs buy their receivers already assembled. Complete amateur stations cost from $50 to $25,000.

Licenses. Amateur radio is the only hobby regulated by international treaty. Amateur *bands* (transmitting channels) agreed upon by most nations, are sandwiched in among the short-wave radio frequencies assigned to ships, aircraft, international broadcasting stations, armed forces, police, and others (see RADIO [How a Radio Program Is Received]; SHORT WAVE).

To operate an amateur station in the United States, an amateur must first obtain a license from the FCC. There are five classes of licenses: (1) novice, (2) technician, (3) general, (4) advanced, and (5) extra class. An amateur may operate only on the portions of the bands assigned to his class of license.

Amateurs usually obtain a *novice* license first. It does not require much technical radio knowledge. The applicant must be able to send and receive code at the rate of five words a minute. The novice license is good for two years and may not be renewed. It permits only the use of code and lets the amateur gain experience.

When the ham feels ready to advance, he applies for either a technician or a general class license. These are five-year, renewable licenses. Both licenses require additional technical knowledge, but the *technician class* license requires no increase in code speed. To qualify for the *general class* license, an applicant must send and receive code at a speed of at least 13 words a minute. *Advanced* and *extra class* licenses, both good for five years, require a thorough understanding of how radio works and increased code ability. A fee is charged for all five-year licenses.

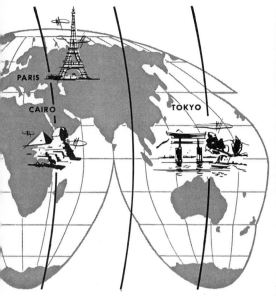

PARIS

CAIRO

TOKYO

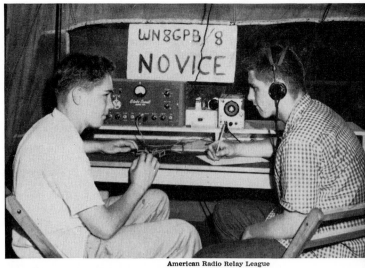

American Radio Relay League

Hams in the United States must obtain licenses. They identify themselves with their license number, such as WN8GPB/8, when talking to other amateurs. Beginners usually get a novice license first.

Amateur Organization. Hams in the United States have their own organization, the American Radio Relay League (ARRL). Its headquarters are at 225 Main St., Newington, Conn. 06111. The league encourages hams to serve the public in such activities as emergency communications. It also publishes *QST*, the oldest radio magazine in the country. It gives information to beginners, and sponsors contests and operating activities.

One of the most popular activities, the annual Field Day, is held during the third weekend in June. Hams with portable equipment meet in remote areas to send "emergency" messages to as many stations as they can. In another contest, the DX (distance) Test, hams compete in contacting as many stations in other lands as they can within a specified time limit.

History. Amateur radio began shortly after Guglielmo Marconi successfully received radio signals in Newfoundland from across the Atlantic Ocean in 1901 (see MARCONI, GUGLIELMO). Many young scientists became interested in amateur radio. By 1912, there were so many stations on the air that a radio law became necessary to prevent interference. Amateurs and other private stations were restricted to wave lengths that were considered of little value. But soon amateurs were sending messages from coast to coast. Amateur radio operators founded the ARRL in 1914. Their original purpose was to help each other relay messages beyond the range of individual sets. Soon the league and its magazine served in exchanging technical information.

During World War I, 4,000 of the 6,000 hams in the United States served as radio operators in the armed forces. A few years later, hams were using short-wave radio for transatlantic broadcasts.

In 1920, a ham in Pittsburgh used his station to play phonograph records for the entertainment of neighbors listening on small crystal sets. This use of an amateur station led to commercial radio broadcasting.

Amateurs have contributed to many major radio developments. In 1956, Gus Fallgren of Chelmsford, Mass., first used a transistor radio to send messages to transatlantic stations (see TRANSISTOR).

Ham operators built *Oscar* (Orbiting Satellite Carrying Amateur Radio), the first nongovernment satellite. Launched in 1961, it broadcast greetings in code to hams throughout the world. Hams also bounce experimental signals off the moon.

More than 255,000 amateurs operate radio stations in the United States. About 13,000 new hams take up this hobby every year.   WILLIAM I. DUNKERLEY, JR.

See also MORSE CODE; RADIO.

RADIO AND MACHINE WORKERS OF AMERICA. See ELECTRICAL, RADIO AND MACHINE WORKERS, INTERNATIONAL UNION OF.

RADIO ANNOUNCER. See RADIO (Careers).

RADIO ASTRONOMY. See ASTRONOMY (Radio Telescopes; Studying Radio Waves); RADIO TELESCOPE.

RADIO BEACON is a radio sending station that broadcasts signals to help guide aircraft and ships.

Radio range beacons mark the route of an airway with radio signals. The earliest radio range beacons sent out patterns of signals approximately like a four-leaf clover, with the leaves overlapping. On two opposite loops, or leaves of the clover, the pilot would hear the Morse signal A (· —). On the other two loops he would hear the signal N (— ·). In the overlapping area the two signals would merge into a monotone. So the pilot flying toward the transmitter, or away from it, on any one of the four courses marked by the overlapping of the A and N signal areas, would hear a monotone, and know that he was on course. If the pilot got off course, he would hear only the A signal on one side or the N signal on the other side of the course.

This early radio range beacon was improved so that it would show whether the aircraft was on course by means of a needle on an instrument-panel dial. This relieved the pilot of the task of listening for the radio signals while flying an airplane.

The *very high frequency omnidirectional radio range station* was developed after World War II. It also is called *VOR* or *Omnirange*. The Omnirange, instead of sending four courses only, sends a series of courses, called *radials*, that radiate from the transmitter like spokes from the hub of a wheel. Signals indicate to the pilot his exact position with relation to the sending station. With VOR equipment, the pilot can set his destination on dials and the equipment will constantly tell him his position and in what direction to fly.

RAY O. MERTES, JOHN H. FURBAY, and GEORGE GARDNER

See also BEACON.

RADIO CITY. See NEW YORK CITY.

RADIO COMPASS. See DIRECTION FINDER.

RADIO CONTROL is a method of controlling machines from a distance with radio waves. It is one of the most useful and modern types of remote control.

Radio-Controlled Airplanes were known as far back as 1924, when a group of United States Navy experimenters converted a navy seaplane to radio-control operation. They flew the plane, without a pilot, through turns and dives before the control failed and the plane crashed. The next navy experiment took place in 1936, when a radio-controlled biplane called the N2C-2 was built. This plane was flown successfully as the first target *drone*, and was shot at by the gun crews of the aircraft carrier U.S.S. *Ranger* in 1938. Model-airplane builders began building successful radio-controlled

Chamberlain Manufacturing Corporation

Radio Remote Control makes it easy for a driver to open his garage door without leaving his car. A signal from the control device starts an electric motor that opens the door.

models about 1937 (see AIRPLANE MODEL). By the time of World War II, all the large nations had radio-controlled airplanes.

One type of pilotless plane can be run from a motor truck on the ground or from another airplane. It has been in use since 1944. One form of this plane uses a combination of telemeter and television. The *telemeter* takes a record of the plane's stresses and strains while flying, and radios the information to the ground station (see TELEMETRY). The robot plane has two types of television equipment. The first takes pictures of the instrument panel and sends them to the control. The second takes pictures of the horizon through the windows of the plane. All this information is received by the control station in the truck on the ground. The operators guide the pilotless plane with a tiny control stick, just as if they were in it. One stick is mounted on the regular control stick of the "mother" plane, and another is on the chair of the operator. An automatic pilot actually flies the radio-controlled plane. It receives radio signals from the control unit and contains two gyroscopes that remain stable even in fast maneuvers.

Uses of Radio Control. The United States Army and Navy use radio-controlled planes for target practice. The latest planes, with their measuring instruments, are also "flying laboratories" for testing planes in flight. They offer a safe way to test planes moving at speeds near the speed of sound. Radio-controlled planes have already proved their value in dangerous types of observation. Such planes photographed the second atomic test at Bikini.

World War II brought radio-controlled tanks and flying bombs. One German tank enabled the driver to step out as the vehicle neared its target, and guide it farther with a portable sending set. After stopping it and dropping its time charge, he could call the tank back and drive away. In 1942, the United States built a radio-controlled cargo ship of steel and concrete. It was designed to solve the problem of dangerous shipping in wartime. In 1947, an Air Force transport plane, guided entirely by automatic radio controls, flew a round-trip transatlantic flight between the United States and Great Britain. Some railroad yards use radio-control systems to regulate traffic. With the aid of an electronic computer, the trainmaster can transfer rolling cars to the desired track so they will hitch up with other railroad cars. WALTER A. GOOD

Related Articles in WORLD BOOK include:
Automation
Guided Missile
Gyropilot
Radar
Servomechanism
Telemetry

RADIO CORPORATION OF AMERICA (RCA). See RCA CORPORATION.

RADIO DIRECTION FINDER. See DIRECTION FINDER.

RADIO ENGINEER. See RADIO (Careers in Radio).

RADIO STAR. See ASTRONOMY (Studying Radio Waves from Space).

RADIO TELESCOPE is a device used to collect and study radio waves from space. All telescopes collect electromagnetic waves, but different types of telescopes collect different forms of these waves. The optical telescopes gather the electromagnetic waves that make up the visible light spectrum (see ELECTROMAGNETIC WAVES). Radio telescopes, on the other hand, collect the electromagnetic waves that are known as *radio*

The World's Largest Radio Telescope, 1,000 feet in diameter, is in the hills near Arecibo, Puerto Rico. Scientists use the telescope to study the sun, moon, planets, natural radiation, and the earth's outer atmosphere. Steel cables support the wire mesh reflector that gathers radio waves from space.

waves (see RADIATION [The Electromagnetic Spectrum]).

Radio telescopes use antennas to collect and focus electromagnetic waves while optical telescopes use mirrors. Most antennas are *parabolic* (bowl-shaped). They focus the radio waves on other antennas that feed them as electrical impulses into radio receivers. The impulses are reproduced as wavy lines on paper.

The world's largest radio telescope, with an antenna 1,000 feet in diameter, stands in the hills south of Arecibo, Puerto Rico. It collects radio waves the same way the mirror of the Hale telescope collects light waves at the Palomar Observatory in California.

A telescope relies on its ability to "see" details. This ability depends on the diameter of the mirror or antenna used and the *frequency* (rate of vibration) of the electromagnetic waves collected. Radio telescopes receive frequencies that are about a million times slower than the slowest visible light vibrations.

For this reason, radio telescopes have much larger structures than optical telescopes. But radio telescopes do not even begin to approach the quality of optical telescopes. To achieve results comparable to those of the Hale telescope, a radio telescope would need an antenna about 60 miles in diameter.

Radio telescopes locate and map sources of radio waves in space. The chief sources of radio waves are *nebulae* (clouds of dust, gas, and stars) outside the Milky Way, *quasars* (extremely bright, distant objects), *pulsars* (celestial objects which send out precisely timed pulses of radio waves), and the remnants of *supernovae* (unusually bright stars). Radio waves from space were first identified in 1931 by Karl Jansky, an American engineer.   GORDON J. STANLEY

RADIO WAVE. See ELECTROMAGNETIC WAVES; RADIO (Radio Waves).

RADIOACTIVE FALLOUT. See FALLOUT.

PARTICLES GIVEN OFF BY RADIOACTIVE ATOMS

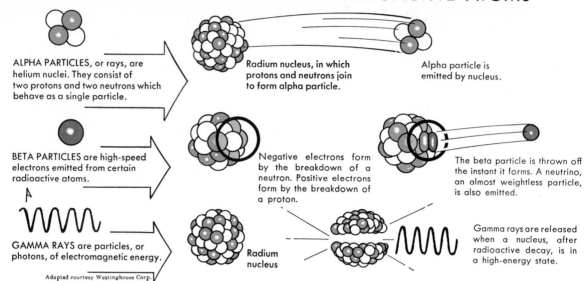

ALPHA PARTICLES, or rays, are helium nuclei. They consist of two protons and two neutrons which behave as a single particle.

Radium nucleus, in which protons and neutrons join to form alpha particle.

Alpha particle is emitted by nucleus.

BETA PARTICLES are high-speed electrons emitted from certain radioactive atoms.

Negative electrons form by the breakdown of a neutron. Positive electrons form by the breakdown of a proton.

The beta particle is thrown off the instant it forms. A neutrino, an almost weightless particle, is also emitted.

GAMMA RAYS are particles, or photons, of electromagnetic energy.

Radium nucleus

Gamma rays are released when a nucleus, after radioactive decay, is in a high-energy state.

Adapted courtesy Westinghouse Corp.

RADIOACTIVITY is the process by which atoms emit *radiation*, or atomic particles and rays of high energy, from their *nuclei* (cores). Of more than 1,500 different kinds of known atoms, almost 1,200 are radioactive. Only about 50 radioactive types exist in nature. Scientists make the rest artificially. Henri Becquerel of France discovered natural radioactivity in 1896.

Kinds of Radiation

There are three kinds of radiation: alpha rays, beta rays, and gamma rays. Becquerel, Ernest Rutherford of New Zealand, and Marie and Pierre Curie of France identified them (see ATOM [Development]).

Alpha Rays have a positive electrical charge. They consist of two protons and two neutrons, and are identical with the nuclei of helium atoms. Alpha rays are *emitted* (given off) with high energies, but lose energy rapidly when passing through matter. One or two sheets of WORLD BOOK paper can stop them. See ALPHA RAY.

Beta Rays are electrons. Some radioactive nuclei emit ordinary electrons, which have negative electrical charges. But others emit *positrons*, or positively charged electrons. Beta particles travel with almost the speed of light. Some can penetrate half an inch of wood. See BETA RAY.

Gamma Rays have no electrical charge. They are the same as X rays (see X RAYS). These rays are *photons* (particles of electromagnetic radiation) and travel with the speed of light. They are much more penetrating than alpha and beta particles. See GAMMA RAY.

Properties of Nuclei

To understand what happens inside a radioactive atom, we must know what the nucleus is like. The number of protons in the atom's nucleus is called the *atomic number*. Each element has a different atomic number. Hydrogen, which has one proton, has atomic number 1. Uranium has atomic number 92, because it has 92 protons. The *mass number* of an atom is the total of protons and neutrons in its nucleus. Ordinary hydrogen has one

proton and no neutrons, so it has mass number 1. Heavy hydrogen, or *deuterium*, has mass number 2, because it has one proton and one neutron. A radioactive form of hydrogen, *tritium*, has mass number 3. It has one proton and two neutrons. But all three types of hydrogen have the same atomic number. Atoms with the same atomic number but different mass numbers are called *isotopes*. Ordinary hydrogen, deuterium, and tritium are isotopes of hydrogen. Scientists usually write them $_1H^1$, $_1H^2$, $_1H^3$. The lower number is the atomic number and the upper number is the mass number. All the isotopes of an element have the same chemical properties. See ATOM; ISOTOPE.

Emission of Radiation

Radiations originate in the nuclei of radioactive atoms. Alpha particles, which consist of protons and neutrons, are fragments of the nuclei that emit them. But no electrons exist in the nucleus. In beta radiation, an electron is created by the change of a particle in the nucleus. When atoms emit alpha or beta radiation, they *transmute* (change) into atoms of another element. Emission of gamma rays does not result in transmutation. See TRANSMUTATION OF ELEMENTS.

Alpha Radiation. When a nucleus emits an alpha particle, it loses two protons and two neutrons. For example, alpha radiation occurs in U^{238}, an isotope of uranium that has 92 protons and 146 neutrons. After losing an alpha particle, the nucleus has 90 protons and 144 neutrons. The atom with atomic number 90 is no longer uranium, but thorium. The isotope formed is $_{90}Th^{234}$.

Beta Radiation. When a nucleus emits a beta particle, it also emits a neutrino. A *neutrino* has no electric charge and almost no mass (see ATOM [Neutrinos]). In radiation of negative beta particles, a neutron in the nucleus turns into a proton, a negative electron, and a neutrino. The electron and neutrino are emitted the instant they form, and the proton remains in the nucleus. This means that the remaining nucleus contains one more proton and one less neutron. For example, an isotope of carbon, $_6C^{14}$, gives off negative electrons. C^{14} has eight neutrons and six protons. When it breaks down, a neutron changes into a proton, an electron, and a neutrino. After emission of the electron and the neutrino, the nucleus contains seven protons and seven neutrons. Its mass number remains the same, but its atomic number increases by one. The element with atomic number 7 is nitrogen. Thus, $_6C^{14}$ changes to $_7N^{14}$ after emission of a negative beta particle.

When a nucleus emits a positron, a proton in the nucleus turns into a neutron, a positron, and a neutrino. The positron and neutrino are emitted the instant they form, and the neutron remains in the nucleus. A carbon isotope, $_6C^{11}$, emits positrons. C^{11} has six protons and five neutrons. When it emits a positron, one proton changes into a neutron, a positron, and a neutrino. After emission of the positron and the neutrino, the nucleus contains five protons and six neutrons. The mass number remains the same, but the atomic number drops by one. The element of atomic number 5 is boron. Thus, $_6C^{11}$ changes into $_5B^{11}$ after emission of a positron and a neutrino.

Gamma Radiation may occur in several ways. In one process, the alpha or beta particle emitted by a nucleus does not carry off all the energy available. After emission, the nucleus has more energy than in its most stable state. It rids itself of the excess by emitting gamma rays. No transmutation takes place by gamma radiation.

Half-Life

The number of particles emitted in a given length of time by a sample of a *radioisotope* (radioactive isotope) equals a definite percentage of the number of atoms in the sample. For example, in any sample of C^{11}, 3.5 per cent of the atoms break down each minute. At the end of a minute, only 96.5 per cent of the sample will remain. At the end of a second minute, only 96.5 per cent of the previous 96.5 per cent, or 93.1 per cent of the original amount, will remain. At the end of 20 minutes, only half of the original quantity will remain. This shows that the *half-life* of C^{11} is 20 minutes. This dying away of a substance is called *radioactive decay*. Different radioisotopes have different half-lives. They may range from fractions of a second to billions of years. With a few exceptions, the only radioisotopes found in nature in detectable quantities are those with half-lives of many millions or even billions of years. Scientists believe that when the elements that made up the earth were formed, all possible isotopes were present. Generally, those with short half-lives have decayed to undetectably small amounts. But some naturally occurring short-lived radioisotopes have been formed by the decay of long-lived radioisotopes. For example, thorium-234, which has a short half-life, is produced from uranium, which has a long half-life. Another short-lived isotope, carbon-14, is produced continually by cosmic rays (see COSMIC RAYS). Long-lived radioisotopes found on the earth include potassium-40, thorium-232, uranium-235, and uranium-238.

Hundreds of short-lived radioisotopes are produced artificially by bombarding nuclei with neutrons and other fast nuclear particles in atomic reactors (see ATOMIC REACTOR). When a neutron or other particle strikes an atom's nucleus, the nucleus is likely to capture

it. In some cases, a nucleus captures a particle and immediately gives off some of its own particles.

Uses of Radioisotopes

In Industry, radioisotopes have many uses. Gamma rays can be used to examine metallic castings or welds in oil pipe lines for weak points. The rays pass through the metal and darken a photographic film at places opposite the weak spots. Manufacturers may place a radioisotope that emits beta particles above a sheet of material. A beta-particle detector on the other side measures the strength of the radiations coming through. If the sheet thickness increases, fewer particles reach the detector. The detector can control rollers and keep the sheet at desired thicknesses. Radioisotopes help study rate of wear on rubbing surfaces. One surface is made radioactive. Then the amount of radiation in the lubricating oil or on the other surface indicates the wear.

In Research, scientists use radioisotopes as *tracers*, to determine how chemicals act in the bodies of plants and animals. All isotopes of an element are chemically the same, so the radioisotope can be used in the same way as the ordinary isotopes. For example, to trace the course of phosphorus in a plant, a botanist may mix radioactive phosphorus with the ordinary phosphorus. To learn when the phosphorus reaches a leaf, he may place a *Geiger counter*, which detects radioactivity, on the leaf. To find where the phosphorus lodges in the leaf, he may place the leaf on a photographic plate. In the developed plate, called a *radioautograph*, darkened regions show the position of the radioisotope.

A radioisotope of carbon, C^{14}, has been widely used to date materials that are older than written history. Geologists use other radioisotopes to date rocks. See RADIOCARBON; RADIOGEOLOGY.

In Medicine. Radioisotopes can detect abnormal behavior of certain organs of the body, such as the thyroid gland. The rate at which this gland accumulates iodine indicates its health. A doctor may determine the rate of activity by giving his patient some radioactive iodine. He measures the rate at which the gland accumulates this isotope by placing a Geiger counter near the gland.

Radioisotopes may be used to treat cancer. Radiation in large doses destroys living tissue. It seems to damage cells most during cell division. Cancer cells divide more often than normal cells, so radiation kills more cancerous cells than normal ones.

Dangers of Radiation

Radiation damages living tissue, so persons working with radioactive material must be shielded from the radiations (see RADIATION [Learning to Live with High-Energy Radiation]; RADIATION SICKNESS). Alpha and beta rays are absorbed rather easily, but gamma rays are very penetrating. Elements of high atomic number absorb gamma rays better than those of low atomic number (see ELEMENT, CHEMICAL). K. B. FENTON

Critically reviewed by SIR JOHN COCKCROFT

"DETECTIVE RAYS" TELL AGE OF ONCE-LIVING THINGS

All living plants and animals, including man, take in radiocarbon from the air. This substance is *radioactive*, or gives off rays. After the living thing dies, the radiocarbon in its remains loses radioactivity at a fixed rate over thousands of years.

An ion counter picks up and counts the rays given off by radiocarbon. By this means, scientists can determine the age of once-living material up to about 40,000 years.

A living man gives off 918 disintegration rays per hour from the radiocarbon atoms in each gram of carbon.

After death, the radiocarbon gives off rays at a known rate. It loses half its radioactivity in the first 5,750 years, and half the remainder each 5,750 years that follow.

459 RAYS per hour
5,750 years old

229 RAYS per hour
11,500 years old

ABOUT 7 RAYS per hour
40,250 years old

RADIOCARBON, or CARBON 14, is a radioactive *isotope*, or form, of carbon (see ISOTOPE). It may be used for finding how old things are. By means of radiocarbon dating of ancient objects, scientists have gained much new knowledge about prehistoric man, prehistoric animals, and changes in the earth's climate. W. F. Libby of the University of Chicago and his collaborators discovered carbon 14 in nature in 1947. They developed it as an archaeological and geological calendar.

Formation of Radiocarbon. Radiocarbon is formed by cosmic rays. When these streams of atomic particles reach the earth's atmosphere, they smash several different kinds of atoms in the air, breaking them down into neutrons, protons, mesons, and other particles. Some of the neutrons that result from this atom-smashing strike atoms of nitrogen. This causes the nucleus of the nitrogen atom to disintegrate and give off a proton. The atom then becomes radiocarbon, which has an atomic weight of about 14. Radiocarbon is heavier than ordinary carbon, which has an atomic weight of about 12.

The radiocarbon atoms, like all radioactive substances, immediately begin to decay by giving off particles. This process is called *radioactivity*. The atoms decay at an exact and uniform rate. Radiocarbon is half gone in about 5,750 years. Therefore, scientists say that it has a *half-life* of that length of time. After about 11,500 years, only one fourth of the original amount of radiocarbon is left. After another 5,750 years, only one eighth remains. See RADIOACTIVITY (Half-Life).

There is one atom of radioactive carbon 14 for every trillion atoms of ordinary carbon in the air we breathe. Human beings, animals, and plants constantly absorb radiocarbon from the atmosphere. The radiocarbon in their tissues keeps disintegrating, but it is continually renewed from the air as long as they live.

Using Radiocarbon. When a tree is cut down, it dies and stops taking in radiocarbon. But the radiocarbon already in its wood goes on decaying at its constant rate. Perhaps wood from a certain tree was used in a coffin for an Egyptian king. We can measure the radiations from the radiocarbon left in the wood, and learn how old the wood is. This tells us about when the king died.

In dating an object by its radiocarbon content, the scientist first heats and burns a sample of it to convert it to carbon dioxide. The carbon dioxide is purified, and reduced to pure carbon by hot magnesium metal. After this reduction, the amount of radioactivity remaining in the carbon is measured with a Geiger counter (see GEIGER COUNTER).

There are many other uses of artificially produced carbon 14 to trace the element carbon through biological and industrial processes. The isotope was first made artificially by Samuel Ruben and Martin D. Kamen in 1939. RALPH E. LAPP and JAMES R. ARNOLD

See also ARCHAEOLOGY (Absolute Chronology); LIBBY, WILLARD F.

RADIOCHEMISTRY. See CHEMISTRY (Branches).

RADIOGEOLOGY is the science that deals with the relation of radioactivity to geology. The earth and the waters of the sea as well as the air we breathe contain small amounts of radioactivity. This radioactivity is caused (1) by the products of the heavy radioactive elements uranium and thorium, (2) by radioactive potassium, (3) by radiocarbon which is continually produced by cosmic rays striking our atmosphere, and (4) by small amounts of less important elements such as samarium and rubidium.

The earth's surface contains on an average five parts of uranium per million parts of rock. Uranium in the earth has been there since the earth was formed and is constantly disintegrating, finally becoming lead. Lead consists of four isotopes of mass 204, 206, 207, and 208. Lead isotope 206 is formed from uranium isotope 238. Lead-207 is formed from uranium-235, which decays more quickly. When uranium atoms decay to form lead, they also form helium. By measuring the amounts of these isotopes in a uranium-bearing mineral, scientists can calculate its age from several ratios: the ratio of lead-206 to uranium-238; the ratio of lead-207 to uranium-235; the ratio of lead-206 to lead-207; and the ratio of helium to uranium. Similar calculations can be made for thorium-bearing minerals.

On the basis of the ratios of lead isotopes in ancient rocks and in meteorites, scientists estimate that the age of the solar system, and therefore of the earth, is about 4½ billion years. This figure agrees with calculations based on the decay of radioactive potassium to argon, and of rubidium to strontium.

The uranium-to-lead process is like a great clock that measures time in billions of years instead of in hours. The clock also has a "second hand" that measures thousands of years. This is radiocarbon, or carbon-14. Analysis of radiocarbon content makes it possible to determine the age of such materials as wood, bone, and fossilized pollen. The age of specimens is of great importance to geologists, archaeologists, and other scientists who try to determine when certain things and living creatures existed.   RALPH E. LAPP

See also RADIATION; RADIOACTIVITY; RADIOCARBON.

RADIOGRAM is a wireless telegram, or a telegram sent by radio. The word *radiogram* generally denotes messages between ship and shore, to and from airplanes in international flight, and wireless messages from country to country. The rates charged are the same as those for a cablegram. If the message is *full rate*, it is to be delivered at once. If the message is sent as a *letter telegram*, it is usually delivered the next day.   FRANKLIN M. RECK

RADIOISOTOPE. See RADIOACTIVITY; ISOTOPE.

RADIOLARIA. See PROTOZOAN (The Sarcodina).

RADIOLOGICAL WARFARE. See CHEMICAL-BIOLOGICAL-RADIOLOGICAL WARFARE.

RADIOLOGY. See MEDICINE (table: Kinds of Medical Specialty Fields); X RAYS.

RADIOMETER, *RAY dee AHM uh tur*, is a device for measuring the intensity of radiant energy. A radiometer converts radiation of mostly unknown composition into heat and measures it.

A common form of radiometer consists of a glass bulb which encloses a rotation shaft carrying vanes. Almost all air is removed from the bulb. One side of each vane is painted black, and the other, silver. When radiant

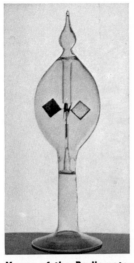

Vanes of the Radiometer turn when radiant energy heats their blackened sides.

energy falls on the vanes, it heats the blackened side more than the silvered side. Air molecules meeting the heated black side take up more energy than those meeting the silvered faces. The molecules on the vane's blackened side recoil harder than those on the silvered side. This causes the blackened sides of the vanes to move away from the radiation.

If all air were removed from the bulb and the friction at the ends of the rotary shaft were reduced, the silvered side of the vanes would move away from the radiation. This would happen because radiation has a slight pressure. The speed at which the vanes of the radiometer spin shows the intensity of the incoming radiant energy.

Some tiny astronomical radiometers use flies' wings for vanes. In electrical forms called *bolometers*, the heating of a tiny piece of metal varies the resistance of a circuit (see BOLOMETER). Astronomical radiometers measure the heat radiation of the planets. MARCEL SCHEIN

RADIOSONDE, *RAY dee oh SAHND*, is an instrument used by meteorologists to take *soundings* (measurements) of the upper air. A radiosonde consists of devices that measure temperature, relative humidity, and air pressure, combined with a radio transmitter. The parts

A Radiosonde is used by meteorologists to measure atmospheric conditions. The device relays the information to earth by radio.
Bendix, Friez Instr. Div.

are enclosed in a small, lightweight box that is carried aloft by a balloon filled with helium or hydrogen.

The radio transmits the information recorded by the measuring instruments to ground stations. In addition, radio direction finders track the radiosonde to determine the speed and direction of the wind at various levels. This is computed by measuring the elevation angle and direction of the radiosonde while the balloon is ascending at a known rate of speed.   G. D. DUNLAP

See also WEATHER (Weather Forecasting).

RADIOTELEGRAPHY. See RADIOGRAM.

RADIOTELEPHONE. See RADIO (In Business and Industry); TELEPHONE (Overseas Service; Mobile Telephone Service).

RADISH is an annual plant grown for its edible root. There are many different kinds of radishes. Those most often grown in the United States are called *spring* radishes. The roots vary in shape, size, and color, according to the variety. Gardeners plant the seeds in spring. Sometimes they space the plantings by about 10 days to obtain a continuous supply. In mild, cool climates, radishes may grow throughout the year. The roots are ready for harvest in four or five weeks. They are used as an appetizer and in salads. In China and Japan, people grow a winter radish called *daikon*. They use it as a vegetable or make pickles from it.

Crisp White Radishes, *top,* and glistening scarlet ones, *bottom,* have a sharp taste that adds flavor to salads.
W. Atlee Burpee Co.

Scientific Classification. Radishes belong to the mustard family, *Cruciferae.* They are classified as genus *Raphanus,* species *R. sativus.* The large winter radishes are *R. sativus,* variety *longipinnatus.* JOHN H. MACGILLIVRAY

See also HORSERADISH.

RADISSON, *RAH DEE SAWN,* **PIERRE ESPRIT** (1636?-1710?), was a French explorer and fur trader in North America. He and his brother-in-law, Médart Chouart, Sieur de Groseilliers, were probably the first white men to explore areas west of the Great Lakes.

Radisson was born in France, and went to Canada in 1651. The next year Iroquois Indians captured him, but he escaped. In 1659 and 1660, he and Groseilliers explored the area west and southwest of the Great Lakes. In 1661, they explored north of Lake Superior. In 1665, Radisson quarreled with the French authorities. He went to England and offered to lead a trading expedition to Hudson Bay. Out of this offer grew Hudson's Bay Company in 1670.   WILLIAM R. WILLOUGHBY

See also HUDSON'S BAY COMPANY; MINNESOTA (History).

RADIUM (chemical symbol, Ra). Radium is a very rare and precious element. It is especially important because it gives off intense radiations that are useful in medicine and the physical sciences. Radium's most stable isotope has a mass number of 226. The atomic number is 88.

The discovery of radium, which came just three years after the discovery of X rays, marked a turning point in the history of modern physics. It led to further investigation of the nature of the atom and it also was one of the early steps that led to the release of the energy of the atom.

Discovery and Occurrence. In 1898, Pierre and Marie Curie announced in Paris their discovery of a new element, which they named *radium.* They obtained this element from *pitchblende,* an ore containing uranium. Scientists had previously discovered that uranium gave off radiation. Radiations from radium, however, were far more intense than those from uranium. The Curies extracted a few grains of radium chloride, a salt of radium, from a ton of pitchblende. This radium chloride, weight for weight, gave off rays that were nearly a million times as intense as the rays that had been observed to be given off from uranium.

Radium is found in the minerals and ores that contain uranium. In general, one part by weight of radium is found for every three million parts of uranium. In a ton of high-grade ore that is 50 per cent uranium, only 150 milligrams of radium (equal to about one two-hundredth of an ounce) will be found.

There are over a hundred uranium-bearing minerals, but most of the world's uranium comes from pitchblende. Zaire uranium deposits are generally considered to be the richest in the world. Deposits of lower grade ores are also found in Czechoslovakia, in the Great Bear Lake region of Canada, and in the Colorado Plateau in the western United States. Important uranium ores besides pitchblende include *uraninite, carnotite,* and *autunite.*

The price of radium has steadily decreased. Until 1922, Colorado carnotite was the principal source. However, the high-grade pitchblende ores of Zaire were found to be a much more valuable source. Radium costs between \$25 and \$50 per milligram ($\frac{1}{1000}$ gram). One ounce at these prices would cost between about \$709,000 and \$1,418,000.

Properties. Radium is a silver-white metal. It is difficult to obtain in its pure form. It is generally sold in the form of radium chloride or radium bromide. However, when you speak of buying a milligram of radium, the milligram refers to the total amount of radium in the salt, and does not include the other elements. Some radium compounds are white and resemble table salt.

Radium has much the same chemical behavior as do other elements, such as calcium, strontium, and barium, which belong to the alkaline-earth family. It oxidizes rapidly in air. It has a melting point of 700° C. (1292° F.). It has a boiling point of about 1737° C. (3159° F.).

How Radium Breaks Down. Radium is not a stable element. It is constantly giving off rays and changing into other elements. At the same time, it is a product of a similar process that began with uranium. This process of giving off rays is called *radioactivity.*

Radium gives off three kinds of radiation. First, there is the radiation called *alpha particles,* or *alpha rays.* An alpha particle is the nucleus of the helium atom. Alpha particles are deflected, but not very greatly, by a magnetic field. They are stopped by a sheet of

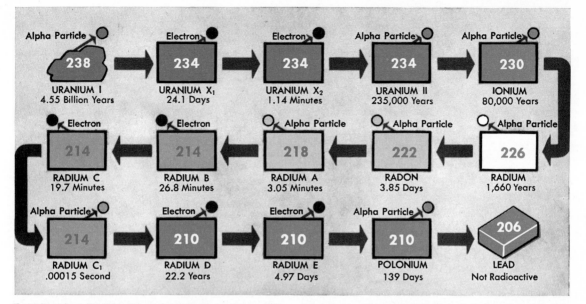

How Uranium Breaks Down into Radium. The uranium atom gives off an alpha particle and begins the series of atomic changes that pass through radium and end up as lead. The figures in the boxes are the atomic weights of the various elements. The time below each box is the half-life period of the element. In some radioactive changes, an electron is given off that does not change the atomic weight. Giving off an alpha particle reduces the atomic weight.

paper or by two inches of air. They are positively charged, and move at a speed of about 10,000 miles a second. Alpha particles also affect a photographic film in much the same way that light does.

Beta particles are high-speed electrons and are greatly deflected by electric and magnetic fields. *Gamma rays* are the third kind of radium radiation. They are not affected by an electric field. Gamma rays are electromagnetic radiations, and therefore are related by light, ultraviolet rays, X rays, heat rays, radio waves, and the other electromagnetic radiations. A gamma ray and an X ray of the same energy cannot be told apart. See BETA RAY; GAMMA RAY; X RAYS.

It is possible to see the effect of alpha rays for yourself, because they are responsible for the luminous glow of certain watch dials. If you look at such a watch face in the dark with a magnifying glass, you will see that the light is not continuous but, rather, is made up of tiny pinpoints of light. Each one of these tiny pinpoints is caused by an alpha particle given off by the radioactive substance in the paint. This particle strikes special crystals in the paint and causes them to fluoresce. See ALPHA RAY.

The breakdown of radium takes place beyond man's control. It is unaffected by temperature, pressure, or chemistry. The first product of the breakdown of radium is a heavy, inert gas called *radon*, also known as *radium emanation*. The radium atom gives off an alpha particle when it changes to radon. Radium A is produced when radon gives off an alpha particle. Radium B is produced when Radium A gives off an alpha particle. Radium B gives off a beta particle and changes to Radium C. Radium C gives off alpha and beta particles and gamma rays, and changes into another series of radium-decay products, including Radium D, Radium E, and Radium F. Radium F is

the chemical element *polonium*. Polonium changes into lead, which is not radioactive. See POLONIUM.

The rate at which radium breaks down is constant. So, too, are the rates at which the other members of this radium series break down. Scientists know that about one in every hundred billion atoms of radium breaks down each second. In any given sample of radium, half the atoms will break down in the course of about 1,660 years. This figure of 1,660 years is called the *half-life* of radium (see RADIOACTIVITY [Half-Life]). In another half-life of 1,660 years, half the remaining radium will decay, and so forth.

The other elements of the radium series have varying half-lives. The half-life of radon is slightly under four days, while the half-life of uranium is over four and a half billion years. The number of atoms of radium found in connection with the atoms of uranium remains the same, about three million atoms of uranium for each atom of radium. The proportion remains the same because as quickly as the atom of radium breaks down, a new atom of radium is supplied by the breakdown of an atom of uranium. See URANIUM.

In speaking of radium, we often apply the name *radium* to the various products of radium such as radon, Radium A, Radium B, and Radium C, as well as to the element itself. One gram of radium together with its short-lived products produces about 130 calories of heat every hour.

Uses of Radium. The gamma rays given off by radium have proved extremely useful in treating certain forms of cancer, tumors, and skin diseases. Radium is widely used in treating cancer. Radium is kept in sealed glass or metal tubes that are often very small. In shipping, the tubes of radium are enclosed in heavy walled tubes of lead to protect persons handling them.

Because of the small size of the containers of radium,

radium is often lost—thrown away in bandages or washed down the drain. Special methods of searching for lost radium with an ion counter have been developed. The ion counter can detect the gamma radiation given off by the radium. See ION COUNTER.

Dangers of Radium. Radium can produce severe burns, much like those produced by X rays. Careless exposure to the radiations of radium may cause such burns. The burns do not appear immediately after being exposed. Several days may pass before the tissue which has been affected becomes inflamed. Bad burns from radium often cause sores which are hard to heal. Radium taken into the body becomes deposited in part of the bone. This is called *radium poisoning.*

Preparation. In removing radium from the uranium ores, radium must at first be kept closely connected with barium. Radium is removed from the barium by a process called *fractional crystallization.*

The quantity of radium obtained is determined by testing the number of gamma rays it gives off with those given off by a sample of radium bromide, which is a standard in the U.S. Bureau of Standards. In the United States, there are about two pounds of purified radium in use today. MARCEL SCHEIN and RALPH E. LAPP

See also CURIE (family); PITCHBLENDE; POLONIUM; RADIOACTIVITY; RADON.

RADIUM INSTITUTE is a department in the University of Paris, founded in 1912 with Marie Curie as director. It has two parts. The Curie Institute of Physics and Chemistry conducts scientific research only. The Pasteur Institute of Radium Pathology experiments in the medical application of radium. The French government pays part of the school's operating costs.

RADIUS. See CIRCLE; SPHERE.

RADIUS, in anatomy. See ARM.

RADON, *RAY dahn,* is a radioactive chemical element. Traces of radon are found in the air in various amounts, depending on the weather. Doctors use it to treat certain types of cancer. Friedrich Ernst Dorn, a German chemist, discovered radon in 1900.

Radon is a colorless gas. It is classed as an *inert gas* because it does not react readily with other chemicals. Radon is formed by the radioactive decay of radium in the earth's crust, and has at least 17 known isotopes. Its symbol is Rn, and its atomic number is 86. Its most stable isotope has a mass number of 222, and a half-life of 3.8 days (see RADIOACTIVITY [Half-Life]). FRANK C. ANDREWS

RAEBURN, SIR HENRY (1756-1823), became perhaps the most famous Scottish painter. He painted only portraits, and was generally considered better at portraying men than women. Raeburn's portraits are skillful, honest, and frank. But they lack the fashionable grace and charm of the English painters Thomas Gainsborough and Sir Joshua Reynolds.

He painted members of the Scottish aristocracy, their wives and children, and famous literary men like Sir Walter Scott and James Boswell. Raeburn's conversational ability and good sense made him welcome in literary society. He became wealthy and joined the Royal Academy. He was born in Edinburgh and lived there all his life. Shortly before his death, he was knighted by King George IV. LESTER D. LONGMAN

RAFFIA is a fiber made from the leafstalks of certain varieties of palm trees. One of these palms, the *Raphia ruffia,* grows abundantly on the northeastern coast of the Malagasy Republic. Another, the *Raphia taedigera,* grows on the islands of Japan. Residents of the Malagasy Republic make clothes from raffia fiber, and weave baskets, mats, and small fancy bags from it. Large amounts of raffia are exported for use in greenhouses as a wrapping to protect plants from cold, and to tie buds and grafts in tree and plant surgery. Raffia is used in schools as a weaving fiber for baskets. See also BASKET WEAVING. ELIZABETH CHESLEY BAITY

RAFFLES, SIR STAMFORD. See SINGAPORE (The City; History).

RAFFLESIA, *ra FLEE zhih uh,* is the name of a small genus of plants which have huge flowers but no leaves or stems. The flowers grow as parasites on the stems and roots of several Cissus shrubs in Malaya. One species of rafflesia produces flowers more than 3 feet wide. The stamens and pistils grow on separate flowers, and require some agent to pollinate them. The flowers have five wide, fleshy lobes and usually have a bad odor.

Scientific Classification. The rafflesia belongs to the rafflesia family, *Rafflesiaceae.* It is classified as genus *Rafflesia,* species *R. arnoldii.* MARCUS MAXON

See also FLOWER (color picture: Giant Rafflesia).

RAFT is one of the simplest kinds of watercraft. It may be made of logs lashed together with ropes, or of any other material that floats. Rafts are usually square or rectangular, but they may be built in any shape. Poles, paddles, or sails can be used to propel a raft across the water. Sometimes river and ocean currents alone move a raft to its destination. Modern rafts often are wooden platforms fastened atop floating barrels. Many are anchored and used as floats for swimmers.

The Art Institute of Chicago

The *Boy with Rabbit* by Sir Henry Raeburn shows the fine romantic qualities of this Scottish artist's work.

Early man built rafts of logs, reeds, or inflated animal skins lashed together with vines. Such rafts provided a means of using the currents of waterways. A raft drifting with a river's current could carry passengers and goods downstream to the sea. For this reason, ancient seaports were frequently located at the mouths of rivers, where they could easily receive goods from areas farther inland. During the 1800's, *flatboats* (large rafts) served as an important means of transportation on the Ohio and Mississippi rivers (see FLATBOAT).

In 1947, Thor Heyerdahl of Norway and five companions drifted on the balsa-wood raft *Kon-Tiki* for about 4,300 miles. They sailed from Peru to the Tuamotu Islands in the central Pacific. In 1963 and 1964, 70-year-old William Willis of the United States sailed for 10,850 miles on the *Age Unlimited*, a steel pontoon raft. He went from Peru to Australia—with a stop in Samoa for repairs—in 204 days.　　　　ROBERT H. BURGESS

See also HEYERDAHL, THOR.

RAFTER. See HOUSE (The Roof).

RAGNARÖK. See ODIN.

RAGTIME is a kind of music that uses strongly syncopated melody and a regularly accented accompaniment. Originally a *piano rag* had a regular rhythmic bass for the left hand and a highly complex melody for the right hand. The term *ragtime* gradually came to be applied to early forms of jazz, such as Irving Berlin's "Alexander's Ragtime Band." See also JAZZ.

RAGWEED is the name of several weeds that grow in the United States and Canada. These weeds grow along roadsides, and in pastures, fields, and vacant lots. Many persons are allergic to ragweed pollen. The pollen is produced in great amounts and the wind spreads it. Persons allergic to the pollen may get symptoms of hay fever when there are about 25 grains of pollen for each cubic yard of air. The air may contain much more than this during the ragweed blooming season.

USDA
Ragweed

The *common ragweed*, sometimes called *bitterweed* and *hogweed*, is a coarse annual plant with finely divided leaves. It usually grows 1 to 3 feet tall, but sometimes may grow taller. Its small, hard fruit has several short, sharp spines near the end. *Giant ragweed*, sometimes called *kinghead*, is also an annual. It commonly grows 3 to 6 feet tall, but some plants grow to 10 feet. Its leaves usually are divided into three broad parts. *Perennial ragweed* looks something like the common ragweed, but is a perennial. It grows from long, spreading roots. Unlike the common ragweed, its fruit has blunt tubercles instead of spines.

Ragweed grows quickly in any untended spot. It is so ordinary looking and its flowers are so inconspicuous that efforts to eradicate it have failed.

Scientific Classification. Ragweeds are in the composite family, *Compositae.* The common ragweed is genus *Ambrosia,* species *A. artemisiifolia.* The giant ragweed is *A. trifida.* Perennial ragweed is *A. psilostachya.*　　　ARTHUR CRONQUIST

See also HAY FEVER.

RAIKES, ROBERT (1735-1811), an English publisher, first developed Sunday schools on an extensive scale. He knew many "little miserable wretches" in his home city, Gloucester, who worked six long days in the factories and had no chance for education. He opened his first Sunday school there in 1780. Sunday schools helped train children in reading and arithmetic as well as in the Bible, because there were no public schools. Before Raikes died, his system had spread throughout England.　　　　F. A. NORWOOD

RAIL. See RAILROAD (Rails).

RAIL is the common name of a family of marsh birds that live throughout most of the world. The family includes the rails proper, the gallinules, and the coots or mud hens. The birds called rails live in grassy marshes. They run swiftly over the mud, seeking worms, insects, snails, floating seeds, and plant sprouts to eat. Rails vary in length from 5 to 19 inches. They have long, narrow bodies, short wings and tails, long legs and toes, and loose plumage of mixed black, brown, and gray feathers. The shape of their bodies helps them to slip through the reeds and grasses. The expression "thin as a rail" is said to come from their appearance. Rails migrate hundreds of miles, but they are seldom seen in flight except when chased from cover. They build nests of grasses or reeds on the ground. They lay from 6 to 15 buffy-white eggs, speckled with reddish-brown.

The rails most common in Europe are the *water rail* and the *corn crake*, or *land rail*, which frequents fields. The *king rail, yellow rail, black rail, clapper rail, Virginia rail,* and *sora* (or *sora rail*) are found in America. The clapper rail is hunted in the southern United States.

Scientific Classification. Rails make up the rail family, *Rallidae.* King rail is genus *Rallus,* species *R. elegans;* the clapper is *R. longirostris;* the Virginia, *R. limicola.* The yellow rail is *Coturnicops noveboracensis;* the sora, *Porzana carolina;* the black, *Laterallus jamaicensis.*　GEORGE E. HUDSON

See also COOT; GALLINULE.

The Virginia Rail lives in reedy lakes and marshes, where its protective coloration makes it hard to see.

John H. Gerard, N.A.S.

Freight Trains are essential to the economy of the United States. Long freight trains carry mail and thousands of products every day. Freight accounts for about 90 cents of every dollar of income earned by U.S. railroads.

Chicago and North Western Railway

RAILROAD

RAILROAD. Every day, thousands of trains thunder along railroad tracks throughout the world. Huge, streamlined diesel locomotives haul long strings of passenger or freight cars. These trains carry people, mail, and many of the things we eat, wear, or use in building.

The "iron horse" came as the first great transportation achievement of the machine age. The early wood-burning locomotives with their big smokestacks puffed and tooted across the countryside, pulling one or two cars. They carried heavy loads faster, and over longer distances, than any previous means of transportation.

As railroads were built across the United States, they opened up wide farming and ranching areas. They tapped rich forest and mineral resources. They brought better health to the people by hauling a greater variety of foods than ever before had been available. Railroads connected the newer regions of the West with the older and more settled parts of the East. Towns sprang up along the tracks, and cities grew where rail lines met.

Today, automobiles, trucks, buses, airplanes, river barges, and pipelines compete with railroads as means of public and private transportation. But the railroads still make up the backbone of the transportation system of the United States and of most other large countries.

How Railroads Serve the Public

Railway service takes four forms: the transportation of (1) passengers, (2) freight, (3) express, and (4) mails.

Passenger Service. Millions of Americans travel on the railroads each year, even though passenger train travel has been declining in the United States. Large numbers of people use railway commuter trains to travel daily to and from work.

In the United States, the railroads operate hundreds

Thomas J. Sinclair, the contributor of this article, is Special Assistant to the Vice-President of the Association of American Railroads.

of passenger trains daily. Some of these trains run many hundreds of miles, as, for example, between Chicago and San Francisco, or between New York and Miami. Others run for shorter distances.

Many different passenger-train accommodations are available. A typical long-distance, de luxe passenger train may consist of a baggage car, three day coaches, six or eight sleeping cars, a dining car, and a lounge car —12 or 14 cars in all. The train may be powered by a two- or three-unit diesel-electric locomotive.

Passenger trains in the United States travel fast. There are more than 250 station-to-station passenger runs of 70 miles an hour or faster. Some runs average up to 85 miles an hour, from the start of the run to the stop. In 1969, an electric train called the *Metroliner* began operating between Washington, D.C. and New York City. It reached speeds greater than 100 miles an hour. Its planned top speed was 150 miles an hour.

Freight Service earns about 90 cents of every dollar that the railroads take in. Railroad freight trains carry all sorts of products, including lumber, coal, grain, livestock, automobiles, and all types of food.

Each day of the year, on the average, the railroads of the United States operate about 10,000 freight trains. The average freight train has 71 cars, not including the caboose, and carries more than 1,700 tons of freight. Each serviceable freight car in the United States travels about 19,000 miles a year.

Express Service. The railroads of the United States provide a special kind of transportation service through the Railway Express Agency (REA Express), which they own. This agency has about 6,000 offices throughout the United States. It handles over 56 million parcels of surface and air express yearly in the U.S. and other countries. It also offers fast door-to-door pickup and delivery service. See RAILWAY EXPRESS AGENCY.

Mails. The transportation of United States mails is the fourth important service performed by the railroads. In the United States, railroads carry most of the *bulk mail*, which includes all mail except first class. The railroads use trailers and special containers carried on flatcars for first class, and mail storage cars for the bulk mail.

What Makes Up a Railroad

A railroad is a system by which trains of cars, usually drawn by diesel electric, steam, electric, or gas turbine locomotives, run upon tracks of steel rails. The railroad is different from other means of transportation. First, it is the only form which makes use of the flanged wheel on the steel rail. Second, it is the only form of transportation in which a large number of cars is pulled by one power unit operated by one crew.

Right of Way. The land upon which the railroad is built is called the railroad *right of way*. It is usually between 75 and 200 feet wide.

Roadway. The roadway consists of the entire structure supporting and forming the railway track or tracks. It includes land, bridges, trestles, culverts, embankments, ballast, crossties, tie plates, and rails.

Ballast. Gravel, crushed rock, cinders, slag, and other materials are placed on the roadbed beneath and around the crossties. These materials, called *ballast*, improve drainage, lessen dust, and keep down weeds. They also add to the strength and stability of the track, and provide a smoother ride.

Crossties, or simply, *ties*, are the sills, or crosspieces, which support the rails. Ties may be made of wood or concrete. They are usually spaced 21 inches apart, center to center, and run about 3,000 to the mile.

Tie Plates are thin steel plates which support the rails on the crossties. Spikes driven into wooden crossties through the tie plates hold the rails in place.

Rails. The modern steel rail is designed to stand many years of duty under the impact of heavy locomotives and trains. Rail weighs from 60 to 174 pounds to the

yard. The standard length of rail is 39 feet. But some railroads use rails ranging up to 45, 60, and even 78 feet in length at highway-railway grade crossings, station platforms, and other special places. On some railroads, standard-length rails are welded together end to end to form continuous rails. Many stretches of continuous rails are several miles long. Welded rails give a smoother ride and last longer.

Rails which may be imperfect and contain hidden flaws are detected before they fail, by means of the *detector car*. This car travels over the rails and discovers flaws with an electric detecting device.

Rail Fastenings. Rail ends are joined together by means of two pieces of steel called *angle bars*, or *rail joints*. These are firmly held in place by bolts which pass through openings in the rails.

Gauge. The distance in feet and inches between the rails in a track is called the *gauge*. At one time in the United States there were 23 different railroad gauges. Widths between rails ranged from 3 feet to 6 feet. As a result, cars of one railroad could not operate over many other railroads. Finally, in the 1870's, railroad managers began to convert their lines to a standard gauge of 4 feet 8½ inches, the gauge most used in Great Britain.

By 1886, practically all railroads in the United States and Canada had adopted this standard gauge—a move which greatly speeded the shipment of freight as well as passenger travel by rail. Most of the railroads of Mexico are also standard gauge. A car can be loaded at any station in the United States, Canada, or Mexico, and sent to any other station in these countries without reloading or disturbing its contents.

When the first Russian railroads were built, the Russian rulers insisted on 5-foot gauge. They knew

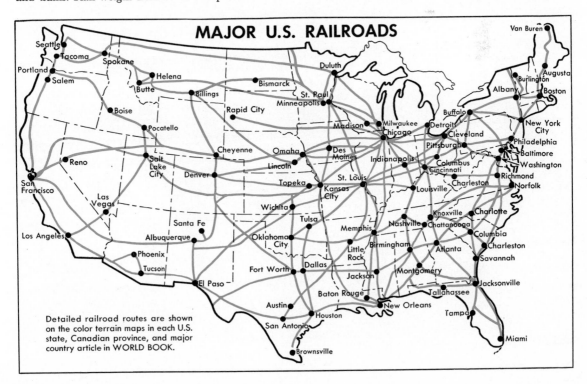

MAJOR U.S. RAILROADS

Detailed railroad routes are shown on the color terrain maps in each U.S. state, Canadian province, and major country article in WORLD BOOK.

RAILROAD

Inside a Diesel Locomotive, *above,* the engineer, aided by a fireman, runs a passenger train. On a train with a dining car, the chef, *below,* can prepare a wide variety of meals in the little kitchen.

Santa Fe Railway

A Modern Chair Car has two levels. Passengers ride in the upper level. Baggage space and washrooms are on the lower level.

The Dining Car of a passenger train serves snacks and full meals. The waiter serves food prepared in the car's kitchen. Passengers can eat in the dining car or in their rooms.

Santa Fe Railway

The Lounge on the upper level of this car is a friendly meeting place for passengers. Magazines, games, and beverages are available. A stairway leads to a coffee shop on the lower level.

A Bedroom on a Train is large enough for four persons. The room has four beds, chairs, two toilets, and two washstands.

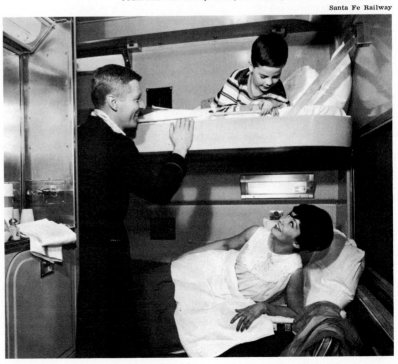

The Conductor, *above,* punches tickets, announces station stops, and helps make passengers comfortable. The brakeman, *below,* makes sure the train is running safely. He also assists the conductor.

TYPES OF FREIGHT CARS

BOXCAR
Common length, 40½ ft.
Average capacity, 54.5 tons

FLATCAR
Common length, 53.6 ft.
Average capacity, 59.1 tons

HOPPER
Common length, 40 ft.
Average capacity, 73 tons

that if Russia were invaded, the broad gauge would keep locomotives and cars of other countries from being used there. That 5-foot gauge has never been changed in Russia.

Tracks. Modern railway tracks are usually laid with a track-laying machine. This machine can lay several miles of track in a day. The ties are automatically dropped in their proper places along the roadbed. The track-laying machine moves forward rapidly, as the rails are put in position and temporarily spiked down. A crew of workmen completes the job.

Many railroad lines have 2 tracks beside each other. Trains can run in one direction on one track, and in the other direction on the other track. On some lines where traffic is very heavy, there are more than two parallel tracks. Along some lines, there may be only one track. A signaling system called Centralized Traffic Control (CTC) makes two-way traffic on one track possible. But single-track lines must be provided with sidings, or passing tracks, where one train may turn off the main track and allow another train to pass.

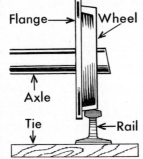

Flanged Wheels hold railroad cars on the track. Early railways used flanged rails.

Grades and Curves. The *grade* of a track is the rate of climb or descent. A perfectly level track has what is called a zero grade. A rise of 1 foot in 100 feet of track is known as a 1 per cent ascending grade; a rise of 2 feet in 100 feet is a 2 per cent ascending grade, and so on. Grades up to 1 per cent are common in America.

Curves permit a railroad to follow a course which requires the least expense in construction, in operation, or in both. By winding around instead of going in a straight line, a railroad can often avoid hills, rivers, and ravines and be made to follow a comparatively level route.

Railway curves range all the way from a fraction of 1 degree ($\frac{1}{360}$ of a circle) to as high as 6 degrees. In rare instances in mountain regions, railroads have curves as great as 10 or 11 degrees.

Bridges make it possible for railway trains to cross rivers and ravines and to run from one point to another by more direct routes than would be possible otherwise. Altogether, there are about 192,000 railroad bridges in the United States.

The oldest railway bridge in use in the United States is a stone-arch structure on the Baltimore & Ohio Railroad in Maryland, completed in 1829.

Tunnels. There are more than 1,400 railway tunnels in the United States. The longest of these is the Cascade Tunnel, which is 7.79 miles long. It is in the Cascade Mountains of Washington. See TUNNEL (Railroad Tunnels).

Railway Stations. Most of the railroads' business with the traveling and shipping public is carried on through passenger and freight stations located in cities and towns throughout the country. In addition, the railroads have many thousands of sidings and spur tracks for use in loading and unloading freight cars. Railroads have stock pens that are used for loading, unloading, and caring for livestock. Railroads also maintain extensive terminal and dock facilities at the seaports.

A *union station* is a station which is used by more than one railway company. But not all jointly-used stations are called union stations.

Freight stations are sometimes huge structures, where many freight cars are loaded and unloaded each day. The floor of the station and its platforms are usually the same height as the freight-car floor, so that hand trucks or mechanical trucks can move easily between station and car.

Engine Houses and Shops. When a locomotive completes its run, either in passenger or freight service, it is brought to the *locomotive yard* for inspection and refueling. Locomotives are kept in *engine houses* (or *roundhouses*, as they are still often called). These buildings have many stalls for locomotives. Each stall is fitted with a pit beneath the track. Crews of workmen stand in the pits while they do repair work beneath the locomotives.

Only light repairs are made in the engine houses.

TYPES OF PASSENGER-TRAIN CARS

MAIL BAGGAGE CAR and EXPRESS CAR
65 ft.—Common length—81 ft.

DINER
Common length, 82 ft.
Capacity, 36 persons

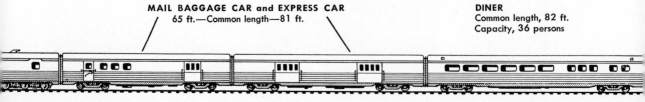

GONDOLA CAR Common length, 53 ft.
Average capacity, 67.6 tons

STOCK CAR
Common length, 44 ft.
Average capacity, 40.3 tons

TANK CAR
Common length, 45 ft.
Average capacity, 55.4 tons

REFRIGERATOR CAR
Common length, 50 ft.
Average capacity, 61.3 tons

CABOOSE
Length varies

But in the *locomotive erecting shops*, an engine can be taken apart and rebuilt if necessary. Some large *railway shop plants* are equipped to build as well as to overhaul and repair locomotives.

Rolling Stock. An operating railroad is divided into two major parts. These are the immovable, or fixed, plant and the *rolling stock*. Thus far we have been discussing the *fixed plant*, which includes right-of-way, roadway, track, bridges, tunnels, terminals, stations, shops, roundhouses, and so on. Equally important are the movable parts of the plant, or the rolling stock. This includes locomotives, passenger cars, mail cars, express cars, and freight cars.

Locomotives. Steam locomotives provided the only power to move trains until 1895. In that year the first electric locomotive was placed in service. This type of locomotive receives its power from overhead transmission wires. In 1925 the first diesel locomotive, with its self-contained power plant, was placed in service on a United States railroad. Diesel locomotives burn fuel oil. See LOCOMOTIVE.

Passenger-Train Cars. There are many different kinds of passenger cars. *Coaches* have seats for 50 to 90 passengers. Double-decked coaches on commuter trains seat more than 170 persons. *Dining cars* offer fine meals. *Lounge, tavern, club,* and *observation cars* have reclining chairs or sofas. They may also have large windows so passengers can enjoy the scenery. *Sleeping cars* provide a variety of sleeping accommodations. *Dome cars* have seats on top of the car under a glass roof or dome, so passengers may comfortably watch the countryside through which they pass.

Passenger-train cars also include *baggage cars, express cars,* and *railway-mail cars.* Many railroads operate combination mail-and-express cars, or combination express-and-baggage cars, or express-baggage-mail cars.

Freight Cars. *Boxcars* are completely housed in, with sides, ends, and roofs. Boxcars are used to carry such merchandise as grain, flour, dried and canned fruits, coffee, sugar, salt, and packaged goods. A boxcar usually has a large sliding door on each side. Sometimes, the entire side is a door. Boxcars are made of steel and lightweight alloys.

Flatcars, also known as *platform cars*, are merely open platforms mounted on wheels. They are used widely to transport lumber, logs, bridge girders, heavy machinery,

military equipment, tractors, and other commodities which are too large or too bulky to be loaded in a boxcar. There are also flatcars that are fitted to carry big truck trailers or specially built containers. This service has come to be known as *piggyback* service.

In *well-type* and *depressed-center* flatcars, the center sections are lower than the ends. The cars are extra long, and may have 10, 12, or even 16 wheels instead of the usual 8. They are designed to carry very heavy shipments such as machines, engines, and other large products.

Gondola cars are equipped with steel sides and end walls that rise about 4 feet above the platform floor. Gondola cars are used to carry coal, lumber, sand, gravel, sulfur, iron ore, cinders, and other bulk commodities.

Hopper cars are usually all-steel cars. They are equipped with high sides and ends. At the bottom are the hopper doors. These may be closed for loading, and sprung by mechanical means for dumping contents. Hopper cars are used for transportation of coal, sand, gravel, earth, slag, cinders, sulfur, phosphate, crushed stone, and other commodities dumped by trip door. Some hopper cars are covered and fitted with bins. They are designed to carry flour, grain, cereals, and other bulk products.

Stock cars are quite similar in design to boxcars, except that side walls are slatted to admit air for ventilation. They are used for shipments of cattle and other livestock.

Auto-rack cars, which have several levels, are used to carry new motor vehicles from the automobile factories to the dealers. Auto-rack cars with three levels can carry 12 regular size automobiles or 15 compact models each.

Tank cars are fitted with cylindrical steel tanks lined with metal, porcelain, or glass. Every tank car has a safety dome to provide for expansion of its contents. Tank cars are used for shipments of crude oil, fuel oil, gasoline, naphtha, kerosene, and various other liquids.

Milk cars are made of steel or aluminum, with a horizontal cylindrical tank fitted with glass, porcelain, or other protective lining. These cars are used by shippers to transport large quantities of fresh milk and cream.

SLEEPING CAR
Common length, 78 ft.
Capacity, 23 passengers

PASSENGER COACH
Common length, 69 ft.
Capacity, 76 passengers

DOME COACH
Has "upstairs" dome for viewing scenery
Common length, 85 ft.
Capacity, 76 passengers

Prepared in cooperation with
Assoc. of American Railroads; Pullman Co.;
Milwaukee Rd.

Container cars are flatcars and gondola-style cars fitted with four or five metal waterproof and fireproof containers, some with special linings. These cars are used for transportation of a wide variety of commodities such as drug and medical supplies, and chemicals. The containers can be transferred to or from motor trucks.

Compartmentizer cars are boxcars fitted with several rooms or compartments where less-than-carload shipments can be placed, loaded, and carried to destination under lock and key.

Refrigerator cars look like boxcars, but they contain insulated walls, floors, and ceilings, and are fitted with ventilators and airtight doors to keep desired temperatures inside. Refrigerator cars are fitted with bunkers for storage of ice, or have mechanical refrigeration units. Refrigerator cars may also have heaters to keep the contents from freezing in cold weather. They are used to transport fresh meats, sea foods, fresh fruits and vegetables, dairy products, cut flowers, and other commodities which require uniform or controlled temperatures.

The Caboose. At the end of every freight train is the usually red caboose, familiar to millions of Americans. The caboose is the office of the conductor, and the traveling home of the freight-train crew.

A caboose usually has a glassed-in enclosure, called *a crow's nest, watch tower, lookout,* or *cupola,* that sticks up about two feet above the roof. Some cabooses have bay windows instead. The conductor or one of the brakemen usually sits in the cupola or in the bay window and watches to see that the train is running satisfactorily.

On most freight cars, the wheels are fastened rigidly to the axles and the axles turn when the wheels turn. The ends of the axles turn in *journal boxes,* which contain lubricating pads to cut down friction. When there is not enough lubrication in the journal box, the axle may overheat. Railroad men then say a *hotbox* has developed. Many car wheels turn on roller bearings.

Signals and Safety Devices

There are three major types of railway-signal systems governing the safe movement of trains. By watching the signals, the locomotive engineer knows when to stop his train, when to slow down, and when to go ahead.

The *block-signal system* controls train movements within *blocks* or *zones.* No train should enter or leave a block without the proper signal.

A signaling device is placed at the head of every zone. This device can signal a train to stop because the track in the block ahead of it is occupied by another train. It can also signal the approaching train to slow down, or it can allow it to proceed at its own speed. The signaling is done by means of *semaphores* or colored lights. A green light indicates *go ahead,* a yellow light indicates *caution,* and a red light indicates *stop.*

Railroad signals can be operated by a man in a tower along the track. In the automatic block system, signals are operated by an electric current flowing through the rails. Trains entering the block short-circuit this current, causing the signal to change to *caution* and *stop.* When the train leaves the block, the

signals return to *clear track.* Signals can also be controlled by electrical means from the train itself.

A system of signals also may operate from the cab of the engine. These signals appear on a small panel in the engine cab.

In the *interlocker signal system,* track and switches at a specific location are set and "locked" against all except one train movement at a time.

The newest signaling system is *centralized traffic control,* which is called CTC by railroad men. Today, there are more than 47,000 miles of railway track in the United States where train movements are controlled by CTC.

With CTC, a single operator can signal any train crew within the controlled zone to halt, go slowly, proceed, back up, take a passing track, meet or pass a train, or contact operator by telephone or radiophone. The CTC operator even throws the switches for trains to meet and pass whenever and wherever desired. CTC makes it possible for trains to move along in both directions on a track without stops to wait for meeting or passing orders. This has had the effect of making the traffic capacity of single-track railroad nearly equal to the capacity of double-track.

In both the block-signal system and CTC, the switches on the various signals are so arranged that the operator can never put on signals which would admit two trains to the same place on the track.

In the early 1960's, many railroads began installing an electronic safety device called an *Alertor* in their engine cabs. The Alertor automatically applies the train's brakes within 20 to 30 seconds, if the engineer does not perform his normal functions for any reason.

Many other safety devices have been developed. One of the most important of these is the Westinghouse air brake. See BRAKE.

Railroads in the Arts

From the start of railroading, the majesty and power of the "iron horse" captured the imagination of the people. They made up songs and stories about railroads and railroad workers. From the Irish immigrants who were brought to America to help build the railroads in the 1840's came such folk songs as "Paddy Works on the Erie." And during the 1880's railroad workers were singing "Drill, Ye Tarriers, Drill." The mighty Negro folk hero John Henry was a driller on the railroad (see HENRY, JOHN).

Other popular railroad songs include "Casey Jones," "I've Been Workin' on the Railroad," and "The Gandy Dancers' Ball." A rollicking railroad song in South African folklore is "Train to Kimberley."

Painters, too, have found inspiration in railroads. Painters who have used the railroads as subject matter for their pictures include Thomas Hart Benton, Charles E. Burchfield, George Inness, Yasuo Kuniyoshi, and Charles Sheeler.

Some good books about railroads, and transportation books with chapters on railroads, are listed at the end of the TRANSPORTATION article.

History of Railroads

Beginnings. Roads of rails were being used in Europe as early as 1550. At first, these primitive *tramways*

RAILROAD "TALK"

AUTOMATIC BLOCK SIGNALS
are "traffic lights" for the engineer.

COLOR LIGHT TYPE
These lights are duplicated on a panel in some locomotives.

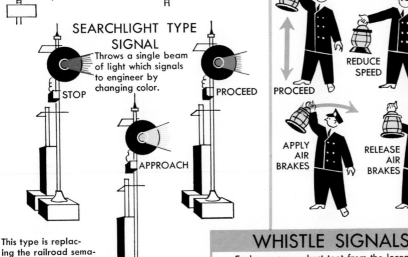

STOP SIGNAL

APPROACH SIGNAL—proceed at reduced speed, prepared to stop at next signal.

STOP AND PROCEED SIGNAL—stop, then move ahead at a restricted speed into an occupied block of track.

CLEAR SIGNAL —go ahead.

SEARCHLIGHT TYPE SIGNAL
Throws a single beam of light which signals to engineer by changing color.

STOP

PROCEED

APPROACH

This type is replacing the railroad semaphores, which were used for many years.

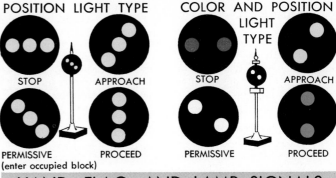

POSITION LIGHT TYPE

STOP

APPROACH

PERMISSIVE (enter occupied block)

PROCEED

COLOR AND POSITION LIGHT TYPE

STOP

APPROACH

PERMISSIVE

PROCEED

HAND, FLAG, AND LAMP SIGNALS
Like "traffic cops," members of the train crew can signal to the engineer.

PROCEED

REDUCE SPEED

STOP

BACK

APPLY AIR BRAKES

RELEASE AIR BRAKES

WHISTLE SIGNALS

Each ● means a short toot from the locomotive horn or whistle. Each ▬ means a long toot.

- ● Apply brakes. Stop.
- ▬ ▬ Release brakes. Proceed.
- ▬ ▬ ● ● ● Flagman go back and protect rear of train.
- ▬ ▬ ▬ ● ● Flagman return from west or south.
- ▬ ▬ ● ● ● Flagman return from east or north.
- ● ● ● Protect front of train.
- ● ● Answer to any signal not otherwise provided for.
- ● ● ● When standing, back up. When running, stop at next passenger station.
- ● ● ● ● Call for signals.
- ▬ ▬ ● ▬ Approaching highway grade crossing.
- ▬ ▬ Approaching station, junction, or railroad crossing.
- ▬ ▬ ● Approaching a meeting or waiting point for trains.

A number of short toots is an alarm for persons or livestock on the track.

TRAIN SIGNALS
DAY   NIGHT

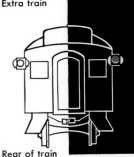

Section following

Extra train

Rear of train

FIXED SIGNALS
are like highway markers.

STATION 1 MILE.

STATION WARNING SIGN tells the engineer that he is approaching a station.

WHISTLE POST tells the engineer to start blowing the locomotive whistle or horn for a grade crossing.

RAILROAD CROSSING ONE MILE

YARD LIMIT

YARD LIMIT SIGN shows limits of railroad yard where switch engines may work in making up trains and other switching movements.

Passenger train speed limit

SPEED LIMIT SIGN

30
15

Freight train speed limit

Adapted courtesy of Union Switch and Signal Div., Westinghouse Airbrake; Southern Railway System

RAILROAD

(wagonways) consisted of wooden rails over which horse-drawn wagons or carts might be moved with greater ease than over muddy or rutted dirt roads. To prevent wear and to provide a smoother surface, iron strips were later fastened on the tops of the wooden rails.

The first all-iron rails were cast in 1767 by the Colebrookdale Iron Works in England. These rails were about three feet long and were flanged to keep the wagon wheels on the track. Many years later, the flange was transferred to the wheel.

Meanwhile, men were harnessing steam power. Thomas Newcomen invented a crude steam engine in 1712. James Watt produced a greatly improved steam engine in 1769, and a better one in 1774. William Murdock's steam vehicle of 1784 was another milestone. But it was not until 1804 that the Englishman Richard Trevithick built the first crude steam railway locomotive.

In 1814, George Stephenson of England built a steam locomotive, the *Blucher*, which actually drew a train of eight loaded cars, weighing thirty tons, at a speed of four miles an hour. By 1825, Stephenson had improved his locomotives, and in 1829, he built *The Rocket*, the first really successful steam locomotive. Ever since, he has been honored as the *father of the steam locomotive*. See ROCKET, THE.

Meanwhile, in 1815, John Stevens of Hoboken, N.J., had obtained from the state of New Jersey the first railroad charter ever issued in America.

By this time, there were several short, horse-powered railroads in the United States, including one on Beacon Hill, Boston, built by Silas Whitney and opened in 1807, and one owned by Thomas Leiper in Delaware County, Pennsylvania, built in 1809.

First Application of Steam Power to Track. The first known application of steam locomotion to railway track in America occurred in 1825, when a small locomotive with an upright boiler was run on a circular track at

RAILROAD BEGINNINGS AROUND THE WORLD

Each date indicates the year in which the first railroad in the country was opened for public business:

1825	Great Britain
1830	United States
1832	France
1834	Ireland (Eire)
1835	Belgium, Germany
1836	Canada
1837	Cuba, Russia
1838	Austria
1839	Czechoslovakia, Italy, The Netherlands
1844	Switzerland
1845	Jamaica, Poland
1846	Hungary, Yugoslavia
1847	Denmark
1848	Guyana, Spain
1850	Mexico
1851	Chile, Peru
1853	India
1854	Australia, Brazil, Egypt, Norway
1855	Panama
1856	Portugal, Sweden, Turkey
1857	Argentina
1859	Luxembourg
1860	South Africa
1861	Pakistan, Paraguay
1862	Algeria, Finland
1863	New Zealand
1864	Indonesia
1865	Ceylon
1866	Bulgaria
1869	Greece, Honduras, Romania, Uruguay
1871	Ecuador
1872	Japan
1874	Colombia
1876	Tunisia
1877	Burma, Venezuela
1880	Guatemala, Nicaragua
1882	El Salvador, Réunion
1883	Congo
1885	Malaysia, Vietnam
1886	Angola, Mozambique
1889	Bolivia
1890	Costa Rica
1891	Israel
1892	Iran, Philippines
1893	Thailand
1895	Lebanon, Syria
1897	Rhodesia
1898	Congo
1899	Korea, Sierra Leone
1900	Ethiopia, French Somaliland, Sudan
1901	Ghana, Nigeria
1903	Madagascar
1905	Togo
1907	Malawi
1909	Cameroon
1911	Morocco
1912	Libya
1927	Nepal
1947	Albania

WORLD MILEAGE OF RAILROADS

There were 748,473 miles of railroad in the world in 1970, distributed as follows:

	Miles	Per Cent of Total
North America	273,734	37
Europe	232,172	31
Asia	107,954	14
South America	59,446	8
Africa	46,915	6
Australia and New Zealand	28,252	4
World	748,473	100

The 10 countries having the greatest railway mileage were:

United States	209,000
Russia	80,927
Canada	43,613
India	37,004
Australia	25,240
Argentina	24,741
France	22,705
China	*21,750
Brazil	19,893
Japan	16,953

Source: *Railway Directory & Year Book, 1972*
*Estimate

Hoboken, N.J. Both locomotive and track were built by John Stevens, who had been an officer in the American Revolutionary War.

In 1828, the Delaware & Hudson Canal Company of Pennsylvania decided to build a railroad and sent Horatio Allen, a young engineer, to England to buy locomotives. He brought back three. The first and only one of these that was used was the *Stourbridge Lion*, which made its trial run in 1829 with Allen as engineer. Allen opened the throttle, and, in a cloud of dust and hissing steam, moved down the track at the amazing speed of ten miles an hour! But the six-ton *Lion* proved too heavy for the flimsy track, and, after running a few miles under Allen's direction, it was removed from the rails and used as a stationary power engine. Many years later, what was left of the *Lion* was placed in the Smithsonian Institution in Washington, D.C., where it is today. It was the first full-size locomotive ever to run on a regular railroad in America.

Race of *Tom Thumb* and the Horse. In 1830, an exciting race took place near Baltimore. Peter Cooper, a New York ironmaster, had built a little locomotive which he called the *Tom Thumb*. It was so small that its boiler tubes were made of gun barrels.

The operator of a stagecoach line challenged Cooper to race his locomotive against one of the stage line's horses. Cooper accepted the challenge. Many Baltimoreans turned out to witness the race. At first, the real horse and the iron horse ran neck and neck. But Cooper built a hotter fire and applied more steam. Gradually, the engine began to gain. It crept ahead of the horse yard by yard, and soon it was out in front.

The Winning of the West. Railroads played a leading part in the development of the western United States. They brought eastern markets within a few days of the western grain and cattle lands, and eventually helped create great cities in the West itself. Early railroad builders faced many dangers, including unfriendly Indians and stampeding buffalo.

As victory seemed to be within Cooper's grasp, a belt slipped and the engine came to a dead stop. While Cooper was desperately trying to replace the belt and get back in the race, the stagecoach horse ran past the engine. Finally Cooper got the engine running, but it was too late. The horse reached the goal line well ahead of the *Tom Thumb*.

Before many years had passed, however, other "iron horses" were winning victories over the stagecoaches.

A few months after the famous race of the *Tom Thumb* and the horse, a new locomotive arrived by ship in Charleston, S.C. This was the *Best Friend*, made at the West Point Foundry in New York. It began regularly scheduled service on the South Carolina Railroad in December, 1830. Its boiler exploded early in 1831. But the *Best Friend* still was the first locomotive to pull a train of cars in regular service in the United States. The *West Point*, built in the same foundry, replaced the *Best Friend* in 1831.

After 1830, locomotives and railroads multiplied rapidly. Historic milestones of progress were the first runs of (1) the *De Witt Clinton* on the Mohawk & Hudson Railroad in New York in 1831, (2) the *John Bull* on the Camden & Amboy Railroad in New Jersey in 1831, (3) *Old Ironsides* out of Philadelphia in 1832, and (4) the *Pontchartrain* out of New Orleans in 1832.

Opening of the Railway Era. The opening of the first few miles of the Baltimore & Ohio and the South Carolina railroads in 1830 marked the real beginning of the railway era in the United States. These railroads, crude as they were, proved the value of steam-railway transportation.

By 1835, more than 200 railway charters had been granted in 11 states and more than a thousand miles of railroad had been opened for operation.

Era of Expansion. By 1850, the United States had really entered the railway era in earnest. At many points, canals and stagecoaches were beginning to give way to steam-railway transportation. America was on the threshold of its greatest era of expansion.

At that time the federal government was the owner of vast areas of wild lands in the West and South. For years, much of this land had been offered to settlers at $1.25 an acre. But there were no buyers, because the lands were far from transportation and markets. In 1850 the government, largely through the efforts of Stephen A. Douglas, Henry Clay, and other statesmen, adopted the policy of granting lands to the states to help develop the railroads.

The first federal land grant for railroads was made to aid in the construction of the Illinois Central and Mobile & Ohio railroads, forming a through rail route from the Great Lakes at Chicago to the Gulf of Mexico at Mobile. The congressional grant was to Illinois, Mississippi, and Alabama. It consisted of alternate, even-numbered sections for six miles on either side of the proposed rail routes. These even-numbered sections might be compared with the black squares on a checkerboard. The odd-numbered sections would correspond to the red squares. The government kept every other section.

When the Land-Grant Act was passed, the government advanced the price of the odd-numbered sections to $2.50 an acre, or double the price it had asked before. But with the promise of a railroad, the lands were quickly taken up by settlers. In this way the government received as much for the odd-numbered sections which it had kept, as it had asked before for the entire area.

This experiment was so successful and the pouring-in of settlers along the Lakes-to-Gulf route was so great that the federal government continued its policy of granting lands to aid in the building of pioneer railroads through unsettled areas.

Of the total existing railway mileage in the United States today, 9 per cent received federal land grants

111

in construction aid. In return for these federal grants, all the railroads for many years carried government troops and property at half of standard rates, and United States mails for four-fifths of established rates. Congress repealed the land-grant rates, effective in 1946. The railroads estimated they had paid the government 10 times the value of the lands at the time they were granted.

Railroad to the Pacific. The gold rush of 1849, coupled with the newly adopted railroad land-grant policy and the prospect of expanding trade with the Far East, speeded the development of the West.

During the 1850's, there was much agitation for a railroad along the 32nd parallel—from Charleston, S.C., to San Diego, Calif., through Montgomery, Vicksburg, Shreveport, and El Paso. The federal government bought from Mexico 29,640 square miles of land in southern New Mexico and Arizona, known as the *Gadsden Purchase*, to provide a route entirely within United States territory for such a railroad. But when the Civil War broke out, the 32nd parallel route was temporarily abandoned. Planners adopted the central, or 42nd parallel route, extending westward from Omaha, Nebr., along the Platte River and through Wyoming, Colorado, Utah, and Nevada to the West Coast at San Francisco Bay.

In 1863, President Abraham Lincoln issued an executive order fixing the eastern boundary of the Union Pacific Railroad on the Iowa border, near Omaha. The state of California had previously chartered the Central Pacific Railroad to build a line eastward from Sacramento to meet the Union Pacific. In July, 1865, the first rail of the Union Pacific was laid near Omaha.

Rails and crossties had to be shipped from the East and Midwest. Rails, locomotives, and other equipment for building the Central Pacific from Sacramento eastward had to be sent by ship around Cape Horn.

The Wedding of the Rails. Thousands of Chinese *coolies* (laborers) toiled to push the railroad eastward from Sacramento around and through rugged mountain ranges and across the desert lands of Nevada. Other thousands of hardy Irishmen, Scots, Germans, and Scandinavians, along with thousands of veterans of the Civil War, carried the rails of the Union Pacific westward at a speed never before equaled. There was intense rivalry between the two great construction forces as they approached Utah. Each day they came several miles closer to their meeting.

Finally, on May 10, 1869, the tracks of the Union Pacific and the Central Pacific were joined at a point called Promontory, in the Promontory Mountains north of Great Salt Lake (see UTAH [picture: First Railroad]). Then, between the noses of two locomotives, a dramatic scene took place. A golden spike was driven

---

IMPORTANT DATES IN RAILROADING

1767 The Colebrookdale Iron Works in England made the first iron rails.

1769 James Watt of Scotland patented the first efficient steam engine.

1804 Richard Trevithick of England built the first steam railway locomotive.

1814 George Stephenson's locomotive pulled the first train of cars, in England.

1825 The first regularly operated steam railroad, the Stockton & Darlington of England, began operating. The first locomotive to run on rails in the United States was built by John Stevens. It was first run at Hoboken, N.J.

1830 The first successful steam locomotive in the United States, the *Best Friend of Charleston*, began operating out of Charleston, S.C. Peter Cooper's *Tom Thumb*, the first steam locomotive built to burn coal, operated from Baltimore. The first United States railroad to haul passengers, the Baltimore & Ohio, ran a horse-drawn passenger car a few miles out of Baltimore.

1831 The first railway-mail service in the United States was begun on the South Carolina Railroad out of Charleston, S.C. Isaac Dripps of the Camden & Amboy (N.J.) Railroad invented the locomotive cowcatcher.

1833 Andrew Jackson became the first United States President to take a train ride.

1835 The first railroad to Washington, D.C., was opened from Baltimore.

1836 The first locomotive with an engineer's cab, the *Samuel D. Ingham*, was built at Philadelphia for the Beaver Meadow R.R. (now Lehigh Valley). The first locomotives with whistles were built at Lowell, Mass., by George Washington Whistler.

1837 The world's first sleeping car, a rebuilt coach, operated between Harrisburg and Chambersburg, Pa.

1839 William F. Harnden started the first long-distance railway-express service in America between Boston and New York City.

1850 President Millard Fillmore signed the first railroad land-grant act.

1851 The telegraph was first used for directing train movements on the Erie R.R.

1859 The first Pullman sleeping car operated between Bloomington, Ill., and Chicago.

1863 Dining cars were used between Baltimore and Philadelphia. Kitchens were added in 1868.

1866 Automatic block signals were introduced.

1868 The first railroad refrigerator car was introduced.

1869 The Westinghouse air brake was patented. The first transcontinental rail route was completed.

1872 The first electrically-lighted passenger car, the sleeping car *Olga*, began operating on the New York Central Railroad. The first electric locomotive headlight was tried out in 1881. Electric lights were introduced in coaches in 1882.

1881 The first steam heating was used in passenger cars.

1885 The transcontinental Canadian Pacific Railroad was completed.

1887 The first oil-burning locomotive was tested in Pennsylvania. The Pullman Co. patented the first vestibule car.

1893 *Locomotive 999* made the world's first 100-mph run.

1895 The first successful electric locomotive was run by the B & O.

1904 The Pennsylvania R.R. placed in service the first all-steel passenger cars.

1925 The first diesel-electric locomotive went into service.

1931 The first air-conditioned Pullman car was put in service between Chicago and Los Angeles.

1945 The domed observation car was introduced.

1948 The first gas-turbine electric locomotive was tested.

1955 An electric locomotive running between Bordeaux and Dax, France, made the world's first 200-mph run.

1965 Congress passed a bill providing for a $90 million, three-year development and research program.

1968 The Pennsylvania and New York Central railroads merged to form the Penn Central Company.

1969 Penn Central's high-speed electric train, the *Metroliner*, began operating between New York City and Washington, D.C., at speeds over 100 miles an hour.

1970 The U.S. Congress authorized creation of the National Railroad Passenger Corporation (Amtrak) to operate passenger trains between cities.

"Old No. 9," *below,* the first Pullman sleeping car, was rebuilt from a wooden day coach in 1859. Today, travelers have a choice of several kinds of private sleeping accommodations for long railroad trips. They range in size from a roomette to a suite for a family of four.

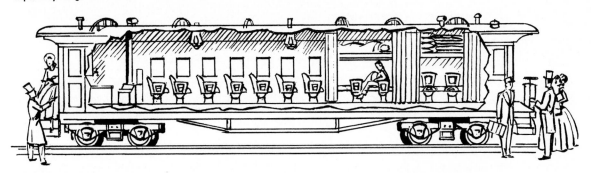

Types of Sleeping Rooms

Every kind of private room in a modern sleeping car is air-conditioned and has a closet, a toilet and washstand, and a bell to call the porter. The porter sets up the bed for each passenger.

A **Compartment,** *right,* is a room for two. The lower bed serves as a sofa by day, and the upper bed swings down from the wall.

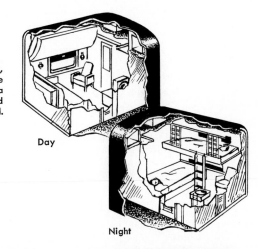

Day

Night

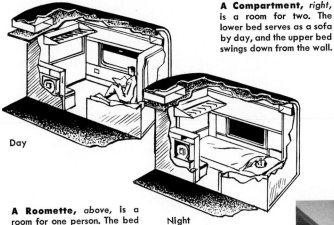

Day

Night

A **Roomette,** *above,* is a room for one person. The bed swings down from the wall.

A **Drawing Room,** *below,* has three beds. The folding chairs slide under the beds at night.

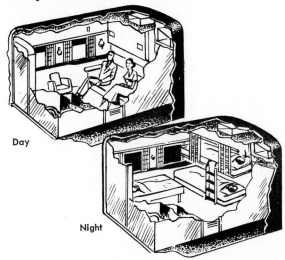

Day

Night

A **Lounge by Day—A Sleeping Room at Night.** The sofa in a roomette folds up, and a mattress is placed on top. A closet and a washbasin with a toilet below it are at the right.

RAILROAD

as a symbol of the completion of the first chain of railroads to span the North American continent. (This spike is now owned by Stanford University and kept at Palo Alto, California.) The railroad brought the Atlantic and Pacific coasts within a few days' journey of each other.

The linking of the Santa Fe from the East and the Southern Pacific from the West at Deming, N.Mex., in 1881 completed a second rail route to the Pacific. Other transcontinental railroad routes soon followed. There are now seven in the United States. In 1885, the Canadian Pacific line was completed from Montreal and Toronto to Vancouver, B.C.

Increased Capacity and Efficiency. By 1915, the United States was covered with a network of railroads. A period of adjustment followed, in which the railroads cut out unprofitable branches. They increased capacity and efficiency by building additional main-line and yard tracks, larger shops, more powerful locomotives, larger cars, and automatic signal and routing systems.

Total railway mileage has decreased about 46,000 miles since 1920, but railroads carry more than three-fourths again as much freight today as in 1920. U.S. railroads still operate about 206,400 miles of main track.

Railroads in the United States and Canada

The United States has about 28 per cent of the world's railroad mileage and handles about 24 per cent of the freight that moves on the railroads of the world. The combined freight capacity of all the railroad cars in the United States totals over 119 million tons. More railroad cars transport manufactured goods than any other freight. Other commodities, in order of the number of freight cars used, are coal, grain and grain products, ore, and forest products. The average freight train carries over 1,800 tons of freight in 70 cars.

In 1970, the United States Congress established the National Railroad Passenger Corporation (Amtrak) to operate passenger trains between cities. Amtrak is a private corporation that is partly financed by government funds. Private railroad companies, under contracts with Amtrak, run the trains owned by the corporation.

Canada has two great railway systems. The Canadian National Railways, with about 23,000 miles of railroad, is owned by the Canadian government. The Canadian Pacific Railway, with about 16,000 miles of railroad, is owned by private investors.

Leading Railroad Companies

Railroads in the United States represent an investment of more than $37 billion. About 52 per cent of this investment is in fixed property. About 48 per cent is in rolling stock. Over 530 companies comprise the railroad system of the United States. The following are the largest, in total miles of track operated:

Penn Central Transportation Company, commonly known as *Penn Central*, was formed in 1968. The company is the result of mergers between the New York Central Railroad, the Pennsylvannia Railroad, and the New York, New Haven and Hartford Railroad. Penn Central, with assets of about $4½ billion, operates over 42,000 miles of track between the Atlantic Ocean and the Mississippi River. Headquarters are in Philadelphia.

Burlington Northern, Inc., was formed in 1970 by the merger of the Great Northern; Northern Pacific; Chicago, Burlington & Quincy; and the Spokane, Portland & Seattle railroads. Burlington Northern operates almost 35,000 miles of track from Illinois and Minnesota, through the Northern Great Plains, to the Pacific Northwest. It has the longest route, 23,600 miles, of any U.S. railroad. The company has assets of almost $3 billion. Headquarters are in St. Paul, Minn.

Atchison, Topeka, and Santa Fe Railway, commonly known as the *Santa Fe*, was founded by Cyrus K. Holliday in 1859. It operates 21,500 miles of track between its Chicago headquarters and the Gulf States and the Pacific coast. Its assets total almost $2 billion.

Southern Pacific Company was formed by joining other railroads together in 1884. One of these railroads was the Central Pacific, which was organized in California in 1861. The Southern Pacific has more than 18,300 miles of track between the Midwest and the Pacific coast. Its assets total $2¼ billion. Southern Pacific headquarters are in San Francisco.

Union Pacific Railroad was organized in 1862 by Thomas C. Durant. It has about 16,000 miles of track in

--- RAILROADING TERMS ---

Back Shop. Shop for heavy repairs to locomotives.
Bad Order. Car or locomotive needing repairs. Also called *cripple*.
Bend the Iron. Change the position of the switch.
Board. See *Paddle*.
Captain. Conductor.
Car Knocker. Car inspector.
Clock. Steam or air gauge on locomotive.
Cripple. See *Bad Order*.
Crummy. Caboose.
Deadhead. Person riding free on a railroad pass. Also a locomotive or a car being hauled "dead" on a train.
Drag. Slow freight train.
Drop. Switching movement. "Drop cars on track 3."
Frog. An X-shaped device to enable the wheels running on one track to cross the rail of another track.
Fusee. Red flare used for signaling purposes.
Gandy Dancers. Section men who work on the roadbed.
Goat. Yard, or switch, engine.
Green Eye. Clear signal.
High Iron. Main-line track.
Highball. Signal to "come ahead" or "pick up speed."

Hog. Locomotive. Also called *jack*.
Hotshot. See *Redball*.
In the Color. Train standing in the signal block waiting for a clear board, or signal to proceed.
Jack. See *Hog*.
Main Line. The principal route of a railroad.
Manifest. See *Redball*.
Matching Dials. Comparing time on watches.
Paddle. Semaphore signal. Also called *board*.
Piggyback Train. Flatcars carrying truck trailers.
Red Board. Stop signal.
Redball. Fast freight train. Also called *manifest* or *hotshot*.
Reefer. Refrigerator car.
Shoofly. Temporary track built around a flooded area, a wreck, or some other obstacle.
Switch. Connection between two lines of track to permit cars or trains to pass from one track to the other.
Timetable. The authority for the movement of regular trains, and schedules of such movement of trains.
Wiping the Gauge. Stopping suddenly.
Wye. Tracks running off the main line, forming a huge Y—used for turning cars or engines where no turntable is available.

HOW FREIGHT TRAINS ARE MADE UP

The Yardmaster, *above,* controls cars pushed by switch engines, *right,* up and over the *hump,* a man-made hill. As the cars coast down the hump, he switches them to different tracks in the classification yard, *background,* according to their destination.

Photos: Santa Fe Railway, Union Pacific Railroad; artwork, courtesy Penn Central

1
The Hump Conductor gives orders to the yard engineers by two-way radio.

2
The "Pin-Puller" uncouples the cars before they are pushed over the hump.

3
Coupling-Up. Carman connects airbrake line between cars lined up in the yard.

4
Hanging "Markers." When flagman hangs signal lanterns, called markers, on rear of caboose, a string of cars officially becomes a train.

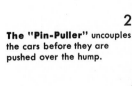

LIFE IN THE CABOOSE

The caboose is an office on wheels for the freight conductor, who is shown at *left* talking by two-way radio with his engineer fifty cars ahead. Here the conductor keeps records of the contents of each car and its destination. The brakeman sits in the cupola above the conductor's head and watches cars ahead. The caboose is "home" to these and other members of the train crew. They often cook meals on the caboose stove.

Northern Pacific;
Penn Central

13 states west of the Mississippi River. It operates from Iowa and Missouri to the Pacific coast. The company has assets of nearly $2 billion. Its headquarters are in Omaha, Nebr.

Other Large Railroads in the United States, with their approximate track mileage include the Chicago & North Western (16,545 miles); the Chicago, Milwaukee, St. Paul & Pacific (15,400 miles); the Norfolk & Western (14,864 miles); the Seaboard Coast Line (14,232 miles); and the Missouri Pacific (13,318 miles). The Baltimore & Ohio Railroad is the oldest U.S. *common carrier railroad* (one that offers service to the public for a fee). It was organized in 1827, and is now controlled by the Chesapeake and Ohio Railroad.

During the 1960's, several railroads applied to the Interstate Commerce Commission for permission to merge. The trend toward mergers was spurred by rapidly rising costs of operation. By merging, the railroads hoped to improve service and reduce costs.

U.S. Railroad Regulation

For many years, each railroad fixed its own freight and passenger rates. The first federal act to regulate the railroads was the Interstate Commerce Act of 1887, which set up the Interstate Commerce Commission. This act was strengthened by other laws adopted in 1906, 1910, 1920, 1933, 1940, and 1958.

The Interstate Commerce Commission was given the power to set rates for the railroads and revise them from time to time. The Commission has the responsibility of maintaining reasonable and nondiscriminatory rates for railroad services. See INTERSTATE COMMERCE COMMISSION.

Careers in Railroading

Although the number of persons working for the railroads has declined since 1950, railroads still rank among the leading employers in the United States. They provide employment for about 660,000 men and women, and they pay out more than $5¼ billion in wages every year.

Most railroading jobs are held by members of railroad unions, some of which are called *brotherhoods*.

Engineers and Train Crews. All locomotives are operated by an *engineer*. The engineer runs the locomotive and is responsible for its proper operation. Until the mid-1960's, the engineer was assisted by a *fireman*. The fireman aided the engineer in various duties, such as watching and checking signals, ringing the bell, and checking engine performance.

But under a ruling made by an arbitration board appointed by the United States Congress in 1963, the railroads were permitted to eliminate most firemen's jobs over a period of time. However, the fireman, or fireman-helper, remains on passenger locomotives. Railroads and railroad unions also began bargaining over the size of "train crews." Members of the train crew, other than the engineer and the fireman, included a *conductor* and one or two *brakemen*. This was true on both passenger and freight trains. On important passenger trains, the crew also included a *baggageman*.

Other train-service employees, though not members of the train crew, are sleeping-car conductors, sleeping-car porters, dining-car stewards, dining-car waiters, cooks, stewardesses, and persons with similar jobs. Other train-service employees include Railway Express Agency employees.

The conductor is in charge of the train. On a passenger train, the conductor collects tickets or fares from the passengers. The conductor, as well as the engineer, takes train orders from the *dispatchers*. He supervises the work of the train crew. Brakemen assist the conductor. The *head-end brakeman* looks after the operation of the cars at the front of the train, and the *rear brakeman* looks after cars at the rear of the train. A brakeman operates warning lights or red flags when the train makes a forced stop. He thereby tries to protect the train against any train which may be following or approaching. Brakemen also couple and uncouple cars as directed by the conductor.

On a freight train, the conductor looks after the freight which is carried in the cars. He must check on the cars in the train and see to it that they are dropped off at the proper places, and that loaded or empty freight cars are picked up.

Jobs in the Operating Department. The operating department is responsible for the operation of stations, trains, yards, and terminals, and for the upkeep of the property. Usually included in this department are the Mechanical Department, under a *chief mechanical officer* or a *superintendent of motive power*, and the Engineering Department, under a *chief engineer*. The Mechanical Department keeps locomotives, cars, and other equipment in serviceable condition. The Engineering Department has charge of the design, construction, and maintenance of all fixed property.

Each of the larger railroads is made up of two or more divisions for operating purposes. Each division may consist of from one hundred to several hundred miles of track. Operation of the division is under the control of a *division superintendent. Trainmasters* working under the division superintendent direct train and switching operations in terminals, stations, and yards. The movements of trains on the various sections of the division are controlled by *train dispatchers*, who work under the general direction of the division superintendent and trainmasters. The train dispatcher on duty must know where each train should be at all times.

Freight cars are assembled into trains in freight yards. When the trains reach their destinations, their cars are separated, or broken up, in the freight yards. The operation of modern push-button freight yards requires the services of *switchmen* and *yard tower operators*. The *terminal superintendent*, or *yardmaster*, supervises operations in the freight yards.

Many kinds of workers are required to keep the tracks in good condition and to keep the locomotives running. Along the tracks, the workers help repair the roadbed, renew rails and crossties, rebuild and repair bridges and crossings, keep the rails in proper position, place ballast on the roadway, remove weeds, and generally keep the road in good condition. These workers include the *section foreman* and the *section men. Signal maintainers* and their helpers take care of signal systems along the roadway.

In engine houses and shops, locomotive and car repair work requires *blacksmiths, machinists, steel workers, carpenters, painters,* and *laborers*.

Various other workers are needed by the railroad to handle the many details of passenger service and to attend to the details of the railroad as a business. Each large passenger station, for example, has a *station agent* or *stationmaster*, a *ticket agent, ticket sellers, gatemen, baggagemen,* and many other types of special workers.

Jobs in Other Departments. The traffic department has charge of getting freight and passenger business, and publishes price schedules (called *tariffs*), timetables, and advertising material. It also promotes activities, such as forestation, that promise to increase the railroad's business. Railroads also have departments dealing with such business matters as accounting, finance, law, personnel, public relations, purchasing, research, safety, sales, systems management, and tax problems.   THOMAS J. SINCLAIR

RAILROAD, ELEVATED

Related Articles. See the Transportation section of the various state, province, and country articles. See also:

BIOGRAPHIES

Baldwin, Matthias W.	Huntington (family)
Bryant, Gridley	Jones, Casey
Cooper, Peter	Pullman, George M.
Flagler, Henry M.	Stanford, Leland
Gould (family)	Stephenson (family)
Harriman (family)	Trevithick, Richard
Henry, John	Vanderbilt (family)
Hill, James J.	Westinghouse, George

OTHER RELATED ARTICLES

Air Rights	Locomotive
Altoona	Monorail Railroad
Andes Mountains	National Mediation Board
Brake (diagram)	Post Office
Caboose	Pullman Strike
Canada, History of (picture)	Railroads, Association
Common Carrier	of American
Credit Mobilier of America	Railway Express Agency
Diesel Engine	Railway Labor Act
Electric Railroad	Refrigeration (picture)
Gadsden Purchase	Standard Time
Highball	Streamlining
Interstate Commerce	Tom Thumb
Iowa (The Coming	Transportation
of the Railroads)	Trans-Siberian Railroad
Japan (picture: Railroads)	Western Frontier Life

Outline

I. **How Railroads Serve the Public**
  A. Passenger Service   C. Express Service
  B. Freight Service   D. Mails
II. **What Makes Up a Railroad**
  A. Right of Way   K. Bridges
  B. Roadway   L. Tunnels
  C. Ballast   M. Railway Stations
  D. Crossties   N. Engine Houses and
  E. Tie Plates   Shops
  F. Rails   O. Rolling Stock
  G. Rail Fastenings   P. Locomotives
  H. Gauge   Q. Passenger-Train Cars
  I. Tracks   R. Freight Cars
  J. Grades and Curves
III. **Signals and Safety Devices**
IV. **Railroads in the Arts**
V. **History of Railroads**
VI. **Railroads in the United States and Canada**
VII. **Leading Railroad Companies**
VIII. **U.S. Railroad Regulation**
IX. **Careers in Railroading**

Questions

What four types of service do the railroads provide?
How many freight trains operate daily in the U.S.?
What is the difference between passenger cars and freight cars? What is a gondola car? A hopper car?
What makes the railroad different from any other form of transportation?
What is the right of way? The roadway? Ballast?
What are the main types of railroad signals?
What is standard gauge, and why is it important?
What is an engine house?
What is meant by rolling stock?
What are the four leading kinds of freight carried by railroads of the United States?

Reading and Study Guide

For a *Reading and Study Guide on Railroads*, see the RESEARCH GUIDE/INDEX, Volume 22.

RAILROAD, ELECTRIC. See ELECTRIC RAILROAD.
RAILROAD, ELEVATED. See ELEVATED RAILROAD.

117

American Cyanamid Co.

MODEL RAILROAD

RAILROAD, MODEL, is a small railroad copied after full-sized railroads. It has many of the same features, including miniature switches, stations, towns, tunnels, bridges, main lines, yards, and scenery. Model railroads differ from toy trains. Toy trains are purchased complete, and ready to run. Model railroads must be assembled from homemade or ready-built parts. Cars, locomotives, and other equipment often come in kits that can be assembled at home. The builder lays and wires his own track, and furnishes his model railroad with his own realistic design. All the equipment can be made to run by remote control.

Model railroading is a favorite pastime, chiefly for adults and teen-agers. Many families work on models together. The father may handle the more difficult tasks, such as building locomotives. The son makes the cars and works out the signal and control circuits. The mother and daughter often work on scenery and structures surrounding the railroad.

Model railroading offers a variety of activities to suit many kinds of skills and interests. The hobby is broad enough so that a person can work on the parts he especially enjoys. For example, if he likes mechanical and electrical work, he may build his own locomotives and electrical circuits. He can buy the other parts ready-made if he wishes.

Size. A model railroad may cover as little as 9 to 12 square feet, or it may occupy a large part of a basement or attic. All railroad models are built to an exact *scale*. This is the relation in size between the model and the *prototype*, or full-sized railroad. The most common scale is 3.5 millimeters to 1 foot, making each part of the model $\frac{1}{87}$ the size of the prototype. These model trains use a *gauge* or track width, called *HO*. This width equals 16.5 millimeters, or about $\frac{5}{8}$ of an inch. The next most popular scale is $\frac{1}{4}$ inch to 1 foot. This makes the model $\frac{1}{48}$ the size of the prototype. It runs on *O*-gauge tracks that are $1\frac{1}{4}$ inches wide.

Track is usually purchased in straight or curved sections. The track resembles toy train track, but it has more ties. This makes it look like full-sized railroad track. Sometimes the rails and the ties come separately, so that the builder can spike them together for even greater realism. Other track comes in three-foot strips that can be adjusted to a curved or straight course. Curves of model railroads are not so sharp as the curves of toy trains. The switching tracks also branch off at less-sharp angles. This makes model trains run more smoothly and appear more realistic when they go around curves.

A model railroad is usually wired so that the track can be laid with two rails, like real railroad track. One rail carries the electric current to the locomotive. The other rail carries the current away from the locomotive. Models of some electric railroads use an overhead trolley wire or a third rail to provide a means of carrying current to the locomotive.

Cars for model railroads usually come in kits that can easily be assembled on a table or work bench. The outside parts are already colorfully painted, and the sides often have the official lettering of real railroads. The material varies, according to the parts. The bottom and frames may be wood, and the sides and roof may be metal. Sometimes the entire assembly is made of plastic.

Paul Larson

Realistic Scenery makes up an important part of model railroad sets. The trackside buildings, *above*, were copied from actual small towns. A miniature railroad, *below*, built according to scale, carries visitors around Disneyland in Anaheim, Calif.

Disneyland

The model builder always makes sure that the wheels of the cars have the correct gauge for the track.

Locomotives are either purchased already assembled or they are built from kits. They receive their power from household electric current that passes through a transformer. Most model-railroad locomotives resemble steam or diesel prototypes.

Steam-Type Locomotives are favored by most model-railroad builders, chiefly because they have a great variety of styles and have many moving parts that show. Steam locomotives also offer the builder a greater challenge than do other styles. Many builders find their biggest thrill in trying to duplicate such intricate parts as the running gear, air compressors, water heaters, and piping that show on the outside of a steam locomotive. Some models use pill-like pellets that give off smoke from the locomotive. The drive motors are usually placed in the firebox. A set of gears connects the motor to the drive axles.

Diesel Locomotives have a fairly simple construction and are relatively easy to build. They have become popular among persons who are building their own locomotives for the first time. The drive motors are usually located in the center of the locomotive cab. Many diesel models use two or more locomotives to make them look more like real diesel trains.

Other Equipment depends largely on the individual builder and on how complete he wishes his railroad system to be. This is especially true of control wiring and signaling equipment. The simplest wiring hookup allows only one train to run at a time. More complicated setups make it possible to run two trains at once. Some

An Old-Time Steam Locomotive Can Be Built from a Kit.
Lindberg Products Inc.

Visible Moving Parts Make Steam Locomotives Popular.
A. L. Schmidt, *Model Railroader*

Most Model Trains Have the Traditional Red Caboose.
A. L. Schmidt, *Model Railroader*

Cars Carry the Names of Nationally Known Railroads.
A. L. Schmidt, *Model Railroader*

Revell, Inc.

Both Adults and Children enjoy model railroading. Diesel locomotives, run by remote control, come with some kits. The popular HO model size is exactly 1/87 full size.

systems are designed to run a number of trains at the same time. These systems often use an automatic train control that prevents collisions. Signals add to the realism of the model by changing from green to red as the trains pass.

Much of the realism of a model railroad depends on how thoroughly the builder designs the scenery of the system. He may build his system so it goes over a complicated route that takes it through freight yards and tunnels, over bridges and highways, and into passenger terminals.

Unlike locomotives and cars, the basic scenery of the countryside cannot be purchased. Most scenery is built by forming wire screening into the desired shape of the ground. The wire is then covered with plaster, and painted.

The builder can make his own trees, shrubbery, and fences. He usually inserts these before the plaster dries. He may also buy additional equipment, such as farm buildings, skyscrapers, and terminals.

History. Model railroading became a well-known hobby as a result of the model railroads shown at the Chicago world's fair of 1933 and 1934. The public interest in these models caused manufacturers to offer model-railroading kits. In 1935, the National Model Railroad Association was organized to establish uniform standards for tracks, wheels, and other model railroad equipment.

In the early 1960's, the *Model Railroader* magazine estimated that about 175,000 adults had model railroading as their hobby. Today, there are more than 300 model-railroad clubs. The members work as a group to build a more elaborate railroad system than they could construct individually.   A. C. KALMBACH

RAILROAD RETIREMENT BOARD (RRB) administers a retirement pension system for retired railroad employees, their spouses, and their survivors. It also administers an unemployment insurance system, together with a re-employment service. The board was established by the Railroad Retirement Act of 1935. Its three members are appointed by the President of the United States, with the consent of the Senate. Headquarters are in Chicago. Railroad Retirement Board

See also Social Security (Railroad Retirement).

RAILROAD WORM. See Apple Maggot.

RAILROADS, ASSOCIATION OF AMERICAN, is the central coordinating and research agency of the American railroad industry. It deals with matters of common concern in railroading. It also publishes pamphlets for schools about the history and development of railroads. It was organized in 1934. Members include railroads in the United States, Canada, and Mexico. It has headquarters and a library of about 385,000 volumes on railroading in the American Railroads Building, 1920 L Street NW, Washington, D.C. 20036.

Critically reviewed by Association of American Railroads

RAILWAY is the term used in Britain and other Commonwealth countries for a railroad. See Railroad.

RAILWAY BROTHERHOODS were unions of railroad workers in the United States and Canada. Many persons used the term for the "big four" railroad labor unions. These were the Brotherhood of Locomotive Engineers, the Brotherhood of Locomotive Firemen and Enginemen, the Brotherhood of Railroad Trainmen, and the Order of Railway Conductors and Brakemen. In 1969, the last three merged with the Switchmen's Union of North America to form the United Transportation Union. The new union has about 280,000 members.

Railroad unions did not develop as other unions did. They started as insurance agencies for their members. Insurance companies considered railroading so hazardous that they would not insure the workers. Locomotive engineers formed the first brotherhood in 1863, followed by the railway conductors in 1868, the firemen and engineers in 1873, and the railroad trainmen in 1883.

The railway brotherhoods faced problems that did not confront other labor unions. The railroads operated under strict government controls, and the unions usually used collective bargaining, rather than strikes, to win their ends. The brotherhoods remained independent of the organized labor movement until the late 1950's. Then the trainmen and the firemen and enginemen joined the American Federation of Labor and Congress of Industrial Organizations (AFL-CIO).

RAILWAY EXPRESS AGENCY (REA EXPRESS) is a domestic and international package-shipping service. It provides rapid, door-to-door deliveries for businesses and individuals. The agency operates on more than 425,000 miles of rail, air, and highway routes in the United States. It also uses ocean vessels and airlines in all parts of the world. Each year it speeds more than 100 million parcels to and from thousands of cities. It carries farm produce, vacation baggage, animals, merchandise for retail stores, and many other items.

William F. Harnden, a young railway conductor, began the service on March 4, 1839. He carried bundles, money, and valuable papers in a carpetbag between Boston and New York City. Harnden traveled by railroad and on Long Island Sound steamboats. Soon other men, including Alvin Adams, Henry Wells, and William G. Fargo, organized similar companies.

The express service expanded with the railroads, which had reached St. Louis by 1849. From St. Louis, the Overland Mail and Wells, Fargo & Co. carried

cargo, mail, and passengers across the 2,000 miles of wilderness to San Francisco, making the trip in 26 days. The famous Pony Express was later organized to provide a faster mail and express service. See Pony Express; Wells, Fargo & Company.

In 1918, the seven major express companies in the United States merged to form the American Railway Express Company. The large railroads purchased this company in 1929, and changed its name to the Railway Express Agency. In 1959, the railroads began a reorganization of the agency to increase its operating efficiency. Large terminals have replaced many tiny railroad station offices. Highway trucks now carry goods in areas where railroads do not run or where train service is not convenient. In 1960, the agency adopted the trade name REA Express. Company headquarters are in New York City. Critically reviewed by REA Express

RAILWAY LABOR ACT is a U.S. federal law that deals with labor disputes between railroad and airline companies and their employees. Its main purpose is to prevent strikes that might endanger the economy or create a national emergency. The act was designed to bring about settlements through negotiation, mediation, arbitration, or, if necessary, through the investigation and recommendations of an emergency fact-finding board appointed by the President. The act has no provision that can force the parties to reach an agreement. However, it does require that employees not strike for a period of 60 days after the appointment of a fact-finding board. If the employees reject the board's recommendations, they are free to strike after the 60 days.

Two federal agencies administer the Railway Labor Act. The three-member National Mediation Board can invoke the act on its own or upon the request of employers or employees. The board also handles disputes concerning railroad and airline employee representation and negotiation of new contracts. The 36-member National Railroad Adjustment Board decides disputes involving grievances or the interpretation of existing agreements. It has jurisdiction only over railroads and their employees.

The Railway Labor Act was passed by Congress in 1926, and has since been amended several times. The original act applied only to railroads. The railway industry received early Congressional attention because its unions were strong, and it was feared that a series of railroad strikes might be dangerous for the economy. In 1936, the act was amended to apply also to labor relations between airlines and their employees.

The Railway Labor Act proved successful in helping avoid major strikes until the early 1940's. In 1941, the railroads prevented a strike by granting wage increases that were much higher than the emergency board's recommendations. It soon became common for companies and unions to reject board recommendations. Since the early 1960's, most railroad and airline strikes have been prevented by emergency actions outside the Railway Labor Act. During a railroad dispute in 1963, Congress passed an emergency measure demanding compulsory arbitration. There has since been increasing pressure for revision of this act, which was once considered a model labor law. Gerald G. Somers

See also National Mediation Board.

RAIN

The map shows average annual *precipitation* (rain, snow, sleet, and other forms of moisture) throughout the world. Most areas of heavy rainfall lie near the equator. However, there are other factors besides location that affect the amount of rain an area receives.

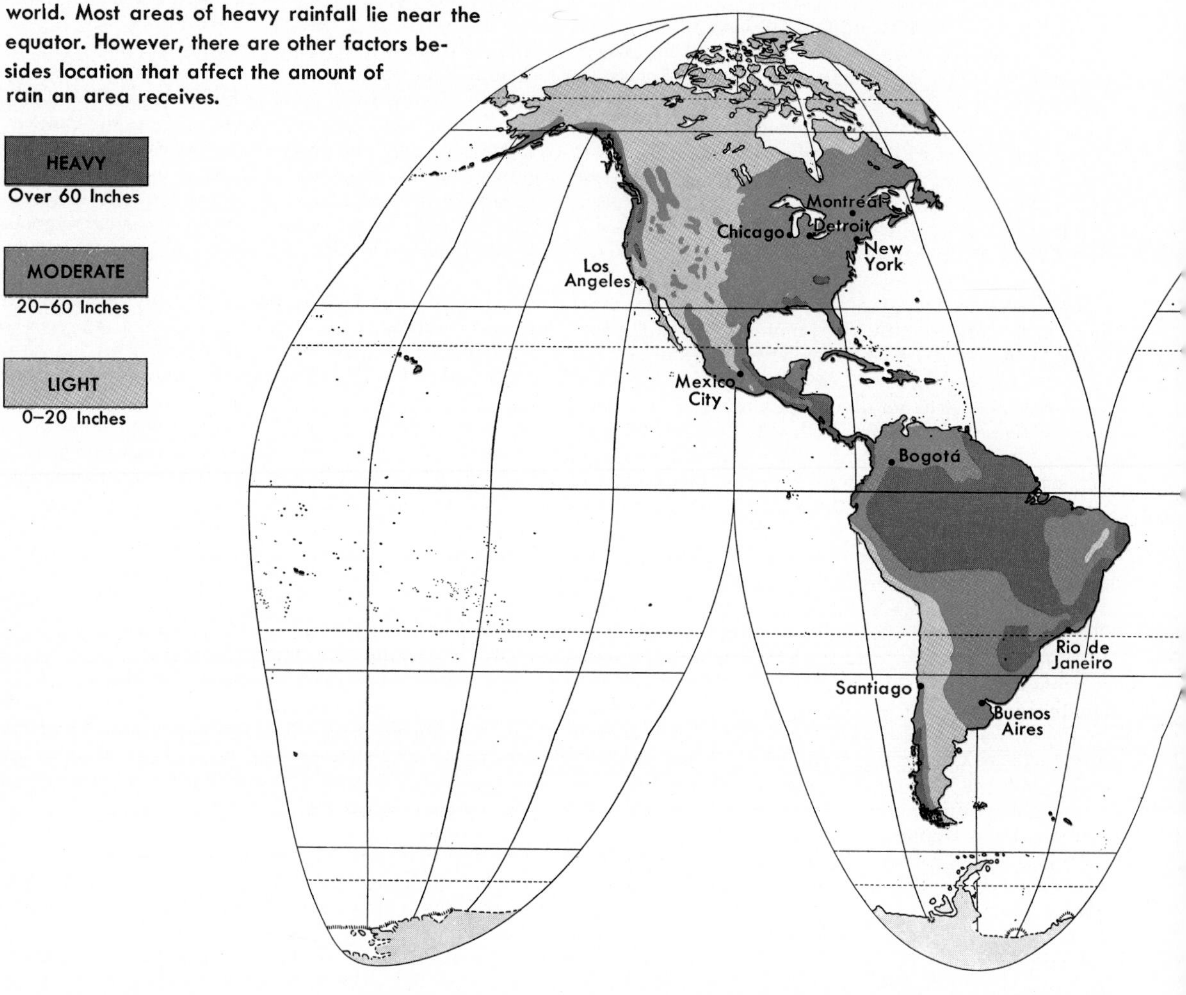

HEAVY
Over 60 Inches

MODERATE
20–60 Inches

LIGHT
0–20 Inches

Montreal
Chicago Detroit
New York
Los Angeles
Mexico City
Bogotá
Rio de Janeiro
Santiago
Buenos Aires

RAIN. Rain is a necessity for all life. When city dwellers mutter objections during a shower or thunderstorm, they do not realize that millions of both men and animals are gladdened by the falling drops. When rain falls after a long dry spell, all nature undergoes a revival of life. Withering plants and trees become green again, and farmers who had been afraid they would lose their crops have hopes for a harvest. Streams baked almost dry by the summer sun refill and make it possible for the fish and other water animals to live and multiply. Birds drink gladly from the pools of water.

But there can be too much rain. Then swollen rivers overflow their banks. The waters rush over the river valleys, uprooting trees, sweeping away homes and buildings, destroying crops, and causing loss of life.

But generally a renewal of life follows rain. Wherever there is plenty of rain during the growing season, life of all kinds is abundant. Where little or no rain falls, the land is barren and there are few forms of life. Great deserts form when such a lack of water continues.

Rain is always falling somewhere on the earth. The record for the entire surface of the earth, according to computations at thousands of widely scattered weather stations, is 45,000 thunderstorms a day, or 1,800 an hour. The island of Java is the world's most thunderous spot. It has no fewer than 223 storm days a year.

How Rain Falls

What Is Rain? A child who is asked this question will probably say that rain is water that falls out of clouds in drops. Such an answer would be correct. But it does not explain why the clouds form or why they sometimes lose their moisture in the form of rain, or at other times are carried away by the winds without causing rain.

The formation of rain depends upon several interesting processes of nature. Moisture is constantly being

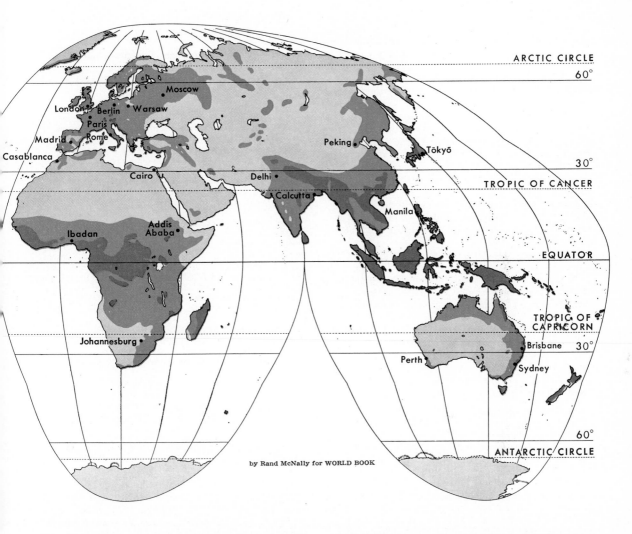

ARCTIC CIRCLE
60°

Moscow

London Berlin Warsaw
Paris
Madrid Rome
Casablanca

Peking
Tōkyō

30°

Cairo
TROPIC OF CANCER
Delhi
Calcutta

Manila

Addis
Ibadan Ababa

EQUATOR

TROPIC OF
CAPRICORN

Johannesburg
Perth
Brisbane 30°
Sydney

60°

ANTARCTIC CIRCLE

by Rand McNally for WORLD BOOK

taken up into the air from the earth's surface, especially from the warmer parts of the ocean. The process whereby this moisture is picked up is called *evaporation*. The moisture, called *water vapor*, cannot be seen. It is mixed with the other gases in the air and is carried upward by the wind. When the moisture-loaded air is rising, it cools at the rate of 1° F. for about every 180 feet of its rising. This is because the air expands as it rises. Once the air starts to rise it will continue to do so until its temperature is the same as that of the air surrounding it. When the temperature is equalized, the upward movement of that mass of air is halted.

As air rises and cools, the amount of water vapor it can hold decreases. If the rising and cooling continues long enough, the air will become saturated. If the air is then cooled below that point, it is said to have reached the *dew point*. When air reaches the dew point, some of the water vapor the air contains condenses into tiny

particles of water, so fine that they might be called *water dust*. This water dust is known as clouds or fog, according to whether it is high in the air or near the surface of the earth. A still greater cooling of the air will cause the tiny cloud particles to unite into drops so large and heavy that they fall.

Floating particles in the air, called *condensation nuclei*, are very important in rain formation. The condensing vapor collects on these tiny particles. But the basic condition necessary for the formation of rain is the lowering of the temperature to a point where the air can no longer hold all the moisture in it.

The rate of rainfall within a certain period of time, usually an hour, determines the intensity of rain. When the weather forecaster speaks of a *trace of rain*, he means that the rainfall is so slight that it cannot be measured. A *light rain* is a rain that measures from a trace to .10 of an inch per hour. A *moderate rain* falls at a rate from

123

RAIN

.11 to .30 of an inch per hour. A *heavy rain* refers to a rain that falls faster than .30 of an inch per hour.

A cylindrical instrument called a *rain gauge* measures the actual accumulation of rain. The gauge is so constructed that the rain falls into a long tube inside the gauge, which has markings that show the depth of the rain (see RAIN GAUGE). Scientists have many other instruments that help them predict the probable rainfall. See WEATHER (What Makes Up Weather?).

Raindrops vary greatly in size and in the swiftness with which they fall to the earth. The largest drops of rain that have been measured were about one-fourth of an inch in diameter. They dropped at the rate of from fifteen to twenty-five feet a second. The smallest drops ever measured were not more than one-twentieth of an inch in diameter. They fell at a much slower rate, probably about five feet a second.

Raindrops are often pictured as being shaped like a teardrop. However, this is false. Raindrops are always perfectly round. The pull of gravity on the falling raindrop does not change this round shape into a teardrop shape, as is often believed.

When raindrops fall through the atmosphere, they help wash all sorts of impurities from the air, including dust, soot, pollen from plants, and many other solid substances. It has been estimated that a rain lasting five days in London, England, which is a very smoky city, will wash tons of solid impurities from the air. Sometimes these dust particles are so thick that they actually color the rain. So-called "blood showers" and "red rain" have been known to fall in various parts of the world where the rain water was colored as it fell through clouds of volcanic dust. "Brown snow," or "black snow," is really rain which has been darkened by the same process.

Rain Around the World

Tropical regions usually have a heavy rainfall because a great amount of moisture is evaporated from the warmer parts of the ocean. The tropics generally have a yearly average of at least a hundred inches of rain. The temperate zones average about one-third as much rain, and the polar regions about one-eighth as much. The highest rainfall for one year in any *area* was 1,041 inches, in Cherrapunji, India. The highest in one *spot* was over 600 inches on Mount Waialeale, Kauai Island, Hawaii. The lowest rainfall ever recorded was three one-hundredths of an inch in Arica, Chile, which has maintained this average over a period of fifty-nine years. The chief causes for variation in rainfall are the location of a given region, its height above the sea, its distance from the sea, and the character of the land. On slopes that are exposed to ocean winds, rainfall is generally abundant. But regions shut off from the sea by high mountains are often almost rainless. Because mountains enclose most of the Great Basin in western United States, it seldom rains there. See GREAT BASIN.

Lands That Always Have Rain. The southern slope of the rugged Himalaya in India is the area that has the heaviest average rainfall in the world. It ranges from two hundred to six hundred inches a year. Most of it falls during the summer when the warm winds from the Indian Ocean, heavily laden with moisture, lose nearly all of it as they strike the mountains and are forced to rise. On the Himalayas' northern slopes the annual rainfall is less than ten inches because practically no moisture is carried across their tops. The vast Amazon region in South America also has heavy rainfall, because it lies in the equatorial belt of rising air.

Lands That Have Little or No Rain. The Sahara is an example of a nearly rainless region. In this desert, the lack of rain is due to the location of Northern Africa, which lies in the belt of the trade winds. These winds, which blow from the great land mass of Asia toward the equator, contain little moisture. Even when

---

——— INTERESTING FACTS ABOUT RAIN ———

Driest State is Nevada, which has an annual yearly rainfall of 8.8 inches.

Earth's Average Yearly Rainfall is 32 inches. If all this rain fell at once, the world would be covered with 3 feet of water.

Heaviest Rainfall in the United States was recorded in 1950 at Yankeetown, Fla., where 38.7 inches of rain fell on a 10-square-mile area within a 24-hour period. Mount Waialeale, Hawaii, has the highest local rainfall in the United States. It has an annual average rainfall of 460 inches.

Heaviest Rainfall in the World was recorded at Cherrapunji, India, where 1,041 inches of rain fell between August, 1860, and July, 1861. The heaviest rainfall for a 24-hour period was 73.62 inches at Cilaos on the island of Réunion in the Indian Ocean on March 15-16, 1952.

Lowest Rainfall in the United States was recorded in Death Valley, California, which has an annual rainfall of 1.78 inches.

Lowest Rainfall in the World was recorded at Arica, in northern Chile. The annual average, taken over a 59-year period, is only .03 of an inch. At Iquique, in northern Chile, no rain fell for 14 of the years during the period from 1899 to 1919.

Thunderclouds each hold an average of 100,000 tons of water, or about 6 trillion raindrops.

Wettest State is Hawaii, which has an average yearly rainfall of 70 inches.

---

they are warmed at the surface and begin to rise, rain seldom results. Similar deserts are rainless in southwestern United States, especially Death Valley, California, and in Western Australia. There are almost desert tablelands in west-central Asia.

California furnishes an example of a coastal region where one season is very dry. During the summer months, winds blow from the southwest over a cold ocean current, called the *California Current*. Moisture already in the air as it blows over the cold water condenses near the ocean surface to form the well-known California summer fogs. The moisture in these fogs is quickly evaporated as the sun warms the air. But no rain falls, because neither the winds nor the sea breeze is strong enough to force the air to rise to heights great enough to cause condensation.   WALTER J. SAUCIER

Related Articles. See the article on CLIMATE; the Water Cycle color diagram with the WATER article; and the *Climate* section of the continent, country, state, and province articles. Other related articles in WORLD BOOK include:

Barometer	Dust	Rainbow
Cloud	Evaporation	Sleet
Cloudburst	Humidity	Storm
Desert	Rain Gauge	Weather
Dew	Rain Making	

RAIN CROW. See CUCKOO.

RAIN DANCE. Many primitive tribes living in arid regions have held special dances with the hope of producing rain. The Papago Indians of Arizona held a rain dance before they planted their crops. First, the women gathered jars of cactus juice. Then for two nights, while the liquid fermented, men and women danced around a fire and sang songs about rain. Next morning, they drank the cactus juice. They believed that, as they filled themselves with this juice, so would the earth become filled with rain. The masked dances of the Pueblo Indians and the Hopi snake dance were also rain dances (see SNAKE DANCE).   JOHN C. EWERS

RAIN FOREST. See TROPICS (Plant Life); FOREST AND FOREST PRODUCTS (Tropical Rain Forests); ANIMAL (color picture: Animals of the Tropical Forests); SELVA.

RAIN GAUGE is an instrument used to measure the amount of rain that falls in a certain place or region during a certain period of time.

Among the many types of rain gauges made, the United States Weather Bureau uses the simplest kind. It is shaped like a cylinder, and has a removable cover. Inside the cylinder is a long narrow tube, where the rainfall is measured. The top of the tube is connected with a funnel. The rain falls into the funnel and flows into the tube. The mouth of the funnel has an area 10 times that of the tube. This means that if an inch of rain falls into the funnel, it would fill 10 inches of the tube. The rain in the tube is measured by a special "ruler." With this ruler, a depth of 10 inches gives a reading of 1 inch of rainfall.

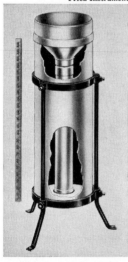

Rain Gauge
Friez Instrument

In case the rainfall becomes so heavy that the water in the tube overflows, this extra rain flows into the space between the outside of the cylinder and the tube. After the rain in the tube is measured, it is poured out and the extra rain is placed in the tube and measured. The total amount of rainfall would then equal the sum of these two measurements.

To insure accuracy, the rain gauge usually stands on the ground, away from buildings and trees.   JOHN VERNOR FINCH

RAIN MAKING. Until the late 1940's, the only men who attempted to "make rain" were Indian medicine men and "rain doctors" who claimed to work by magic. Today, scientists know much about why and how nature produces rain and snow. Under certain special conditions, they can cause rain to fall on a small area.

Scientists can make rain only if clouds are present. The clouds must be almost ready to produce rain or snow. With these conditions, scientists cause the water drops or ice crystals in the clouds to collect and fall to the ground. Sometimes this is easy, but sometimes it is impossible. The fluffy *cumulus* clouds that often form over mountains in winter and spring consist of water droplets cooled to below their normal freezing point. Scientists drop crystals of *dry ice* (solid carbon dioxide) into the clouds from an airplane. This causes the water drops in the clouds to change into large ice crystals and snowflakes, which fall as snow.

Under favorable conditions, rain or snow can be produced in the same kind of clouds by putting silver iodide into the clouds from below. Scientists produce silver iodide smoke by means of special generators on the ground. They allow the smoke to rise into the clouds. The tiny crystals of silver iodide act as *nuclei* (tiny centers) for the ice crystals to grow on. Other methods of rain making have been used, based on the same principles. Scientific rain making can be done only with special kinds of clouds and under special conditions.   GEORGE F. TAYLOR

See also SNOW; WEATHER (Attempts to Control the Weather).

RAIN-TREE. See MONKEYPOD TREE.

In Rain Making or Snow Making, meteorologists "seed" a cloud. To make rain, they may spray water into the cloud. For snow making, they may use silver iodide crystals or dry ice as "seeds." Droplets of supercooled water in the clouds join both kinds of "seeds." Either snowflakes or raindrops may result from this cloud seeding, depending on the temperature near the ground.

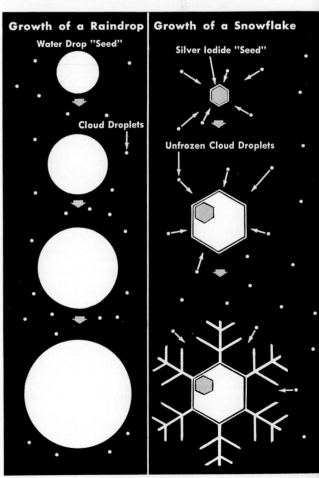

Growth of a Raindrop

Water Drop "Seed"

Cloud Droplets

Growth of a Snowflake

Silver Iodide "Seed"

Unfrozen Cloud Droplets

Photo by Gilbert F. Fernandez

HOW RAINBOWS ARE FORMED

Raindrops act as tiny prisms and mirrors to break up sunlight into colors of the spectrum and send colored light back to our eyes. Each raindrop forms many colors. But the color that reaches our eyes from a particular raindrop depends on the angle between it and the line formed by the sun's rays. Many raindrops, each sending colored light at certain angles, form a complete rainbow.

Diagrams by Arnold Ryan Chalfant & Associates for WORLD BOOK.

WHY A RAINBOW IS AN ARC

You see a rainbow as an arc when the sun is behind you and the sky in front of you is filled with moisture. Each band of color occurs at a certain angle. The raindrops in each band lie in an arc. In the red band, for example, all the points of the arc measure about 42° from the line formed by the sun's rays. The other colored bands occur at angles less than 42° from the sun's rays.

RAINBOW is an arch of brilliant colors that appears in the sky when the sun shines after a shower of rain. It forms in that part of the sky opposite the sun. If the rain has been heavy, the bow may spread all the way across the sky, and its two ends seem to rest on the earth.

The reflection and refraction of the sun's rays as they fall on drops of rain cause this interesting natural phenomenon. "All the colors of the rainbow" is an expression that means a brilliant display of color.

The seven colors that appear in each rainbow are violet, indigo, blue, green, yellow, orange, and red. But these colors blend into each other so that the observer rarely sees more than four or five clearly. The amount of space each color takes up varies greatly and depends chiefly upon the size of the raindrops in which any particular rainbow forms.

How Rainbows Form. Sunlight is a combination of the seven colors named. Each color has a particular range of wave lengths. You see the rainbow when the sun is behind you and the rain is falling in front of you. As a ray from the sun passes into a drop of rain, the water acts like a prism.

The ray is *refracted* (bent) as it enters the drop, and is dispersed or separated into different colors. As it strikes the inner surface of the drop, it is *reflected* (turned back). On leaving the drop, it is further refracted and dispersed. Many drops of rain produce the natural spectrum seen in the heavens. Each color is formed by rays that reach the eye at a certain angle, and the angle for a particular color never changes.

A complete bow shows two bands of colors. The inner and brighter one is called the *primary* bow. The outer and less distinct one is known as the *secondary* bow. The primary bow has the red coloring on the outside and the violet on the inside of the arch, while in the secondary bow, the colors appear as just the opposite.

In the secondary bow, two reflections form within the drop. The higher the sun, the lower the bow, and if the sun rises higher than 40 degrees, no bow can be seen. When the sun is near the horizon, an observer on a high mountain or in a balloon might see the whole circle of the rainbow.

Rainbows are often observed in the spray that flies from a garden hose or a sprinkler. Beautiful rainbows often may be seen on sunny days at Niagara Falls.

Lunar Rainbow. Occasionally, the light of the moon forms a rainbow. The feebleness of the light paints the glowing bow in faint colors, which are difficult to observe. The moon's rainbow differs from the sun's only in intensity of color.

Names Around the World. The rainbow is known by many different names. Italians call it "the flashing arch." In Sanskrit, it is "the bow of Indra." The people of Annam call a rainbow "the little window in the sky."

North African tribes greet the rainbow as "the bride of the rain." In the various languages of central Europe, the rainbow is called "the arch of Saint Martin," "the bridge of the Holy Spirit," "the crown of Saint Bernard," and "the girdle of God."   WALTER J. SAUCIER

RAINBOW BRIDGE NATIONAL MONUMENT is in southern Utah. It contains one of the world's best-known natural bridges. This bridge is 309 feet above the bottom of a gorge, and has a 278-foot span. Some trails to the bridge have been blocked by the waters of Lake Powell, created by Glen Canyon Dam. But the

bridge can be reached by boat. Congress made the area a national monument in 1910.

RAINBOW FOR GIRLS is a character-building organization for girls between the ages of 12 and 20. Its official name is SUPREME ASSEMBLY INTERNATIONAL ORDER OF THE RAINBOW FOR GIRLS. Members must be recommended by a member of the Masonic Order or the Eastern Star, but need not be related to a Mason (see MASONRY). The organization has about 215,000 active members in about 3,300 assemblies in the United States, Canada, and several other countries. Its international headquarters are at 315 E. Carl Albert Parkway, McAlester, Okla. 74501.   LETA SEXSON

RAINIER, MOUNT. See MOUNT RAINIER.

RAINIER III (1923-   ), RAINIER LOUIS HENRI MAXENCE BERTRAND DE GRIMALDI, became prince of Monaco in 1949. His marriage to actress Grace Kelly in 1956 aroused international interest. The birth of their daughter Princess Caroline the next year delighted Monaco. As long as the royal family continues, Monaco remains independent from France. The couple also has a son, Prince Albert, and a daughter, Princess Stephanie Marie Elisabeth.

Wide World
Rainier III

As prince, Rainier has provided low-cost housing, expanded schools, and tried to balance the budget of his government.   J. CARY DAVIS

RAINY LAKE lies on the boundary between Ontario and Minnesota, about 125 miles north of Duluth, Minn. For location, see MINNESOTA (physical map). It covers about 350 square miles, and is shaped roughly like a capital L. Each arm is about 40 miles long and from 3 to 8 miles wide. Thousands of islands lie scattered throughout the lake. For this reason, the longest stretch of open water is only about a mile wide. The Canadian National Railway crosses the lake almost at its center on trestle bridges that link islands.

Stands of spruce and pine cover the rocky shores of Rainy Lake. Many of these trees are cut for paper mills at Fort Frances and International Falls, located at the west end of the lake. A dam at Fort Frances harnesses water for power. Sportsmen catch pike, pickerel, and other kinds of fish in Rainy Lake. Whitefish taken from the lake are sold commercially. The region around the lake is noted for bear, moose, and other wild game. The Rainy River carries overflow waters westward to Lake of the Woods.   HAROLD T. HAGG

RAINY RIVER. See RAINY LAKE.

RAISA, *rah EE suh*, **ROSA** (1893-1963), a dramatic soprano, was popular for many years with audiences of the Chicago Opera Company. Born in Bialystok, Poland, she fled from there at the age of 14. She went to Italy and studied singing at the Conservatory of Naples. She was discovered and trained by the soprano Eva Tetrazzini. Miss Raisa also sang in Italy. In 1913, she made her American debut in Chicago in the title role of Verdi's *Aida*.   MARTIAL SINGHER

RAISIN

RAISIN is a sun-dried grape. Varieties of yellow grapes that have tender skin, rich flavor, and high sugar content are especially suited for making raisins.

Raisins were once an expensive food, and only the wealthy ate them. Today, everyone can enjoy them. Raisins are used as an ingredient in puddings, cakes, candies, cookies, and bread. They are also sold as sweets in small boxes.

Raisins have been a food delicacy since ancient times. The Egyptians first discovered that drying fruit preserved it, made it sweeter, and improved its flavor. The Bible mentions that an Israelite brought cheese and raisins to pay his taxes to King David. In Rome during the time of Nero, the wealthy always had raisins on the menu at their feasts. Growing, drying, and selling raisins was an important trade in Armenia as early as 400 B.C. Asia Minor was the center of the raisin industry about the time of Christ. The climate and soil of the Mediterranean countries made them famous for raisin growing during the Middle Ages.

The raisin industry of California was started by priests, the Jesuit friars and the Franciscan padres. The padres planted fruit trees and vines around the missions to help supply the Indian settlements with food.

After the Civil War, some of the gold hunters of the central California valleys soon discovered that the hot, dry summers and mild winters of California made the valleys ideal places for growing raisins. By 1892, California was growing more raisins than Spain, and raising a crop of over 60 million pounds. California produces approximately 525 million pounds of raisins a year. California is the only U.S. state that produces raisins commercially.

Varieties of Raisins. There are four main varieties of raisins. The two most common varieties are the Thompson seedless and the muscat. Seedless raisins first came from Turkey. In 1879, a man named Thompson brought the first seedless-grape cuttings to California. The muscat is a large, seed-bearing raisin. Muscats were brought to America by the Spanish missionaries. A third variety is the sultana, which is seedless, and has a distinctive flavor. The sultana is used mainly in bakeries. The fourth variety is the Corinthian raisin. Corinthians, also known as currants, are small. They are used mainly to flavor bakery goods.

Raisin Growing. Grapevines are all much alike, and the same planting and care is given to the different raisin varieties, although the raisins and grapes are harvested at different seasons. The vines are planted in rows spaced far apart to allow space for drying the fruit and to permit thorough cultivation. Vines begin bearing grapes in three or four years, and may produce fruit for 100 years with proper care. Four and a half pounds of grapes produce about one pound of raisins.

Preparation for Market. Seedless grapes are allowed to ripen on the vine. When they are ripe, workers pick them by hand, and place clusters of them on trays between the rows of vines. The raisins dry in the sun for 10 to 15 days. After drying, the raisins are stacked and dried again. Then they are stored in great bins, called sweat boxes, to equalize their moisture content. Next, the fruit is sent to the packing houses.

In the packing house, workers stem and grade the raisins by passing them over screens of different sized mesh. Machines remove stem caps as the fruit passes between revolving screens. A machine that whirls them through a fine spray of water gives the raisins a final cleaning. The cleaned raisins are then pressed into sealed packages.

Raisins with seeds go through a slightly different process. Muscat raisins are larger and softer than the seedless variety, and they receive additional drying before they are passed through the stem-removal machine. After drying, the muscats are softened again, and washed in hot water. They are fed between rubber rollers which press the seeds to the surface. A saw-tooth roller catches the seeds between its teeth and removes them. The seeds are carried away, while the raisins go to machines that pack them.

Food Value. Raisins are well known as a nourishing food. They contain 24 per cent moisture, 2.3 per cent protein, .5 per cent fat, 71.2 per cent carbohydrates, and 2.0 per cent ash. A 100-Calorie portion of raisins contains .75 grams of protein, .019 grams of calcium, .038 grams of phosphorus, .00139 grams of iron, and .114 grams of ash.

Raisins contain 10 minerals of important food value. The iron and copper in raisins have given them the name of blood builders. The sugar in raisins gives quick energy because the body absorbs it immediately. Raisins are a source of vitamins A and G, and a good source of vitamin B_1. They contain enough alkali to help balance the acids in the body.   Leone Rutledge Carroll

See also Grape; Fresno.

RAISIN RIVER MASSACRE. See War of 1812 (Chief Battles of the War).

RAJAH, *RAH juh,* is a title taken from the Sanskrit word *rajan,* which means *king.* Ruling princes of native states in India were once the only persons known as rajahs. But under the British Empire the title of rajah was also given to certain other high-ranking Hindus. Native princes who kept some authority under British rule were called *maharajah* (great king).

RAJPUT, *RAHJ poot,* is a person in India who claims to be a descendant of people who made up the military and ruling class in ancient India. The word *Rajput* means *son of a king* in the Sanskrit language of ancient India. Most Rajputs are noted for fierce pride and great courage in battle, and many serve in India's armed forces.

Rajput kingdoms flourished in northern and central India between A.D. 700 and 1200. The kings followed strict rules of courtesy in their battles with one another. The Rajputs also defended the Hindu culture against Moslem invaders from Afghanistan and Persia. The Moslems eventually conquered the Rajput territory, and many Rajputs retreated into the deserts of what is now the state of Rajasthan.   J. F. Richards

RAKE is a machine used to gather mowed hay and place it in long piles called *windrows.* The windrows are then gathered by a hay loader or baler. The first rakes were wooden hand rakes. People still use hand rakes to rake leaves from lawns. Modern rakes are usually pulled by, or mounted on, a tractor. Rakes can also be used to gather straw, green forage, and seed crops.

The Dump Rake consists of curved steel teeth mounted on an axle between two wheels. The teeth slide over the ground and rake hay as the machine

A **Side-Delivery Rake** gathers mowed hay and drops it in long rows called *windrows*. As the machine moves forward, rows of rotating teeth brush the hay to one side, leaving it in a windrow.

International Harvester Co.

moves forward. When the rake is full, the operator dumps the hay by pulling a lever that lifts the teeth from the ground. The machine goes back and forth across the field, leaving the hay in windrows.

The Side-Delivery Rake leaves the hay in a continuous windrow at the side of the vehicle carrying the rake. In one type of side-delivery rake, the teeth are attached to cylinders that roll along at an angle to the direction traveled. The teeth just clear the ground as the cylinder rotates. As the machine moves ahead, the teeth brush the hay to the side of the machine, leaving it in a windrow.

The *finger-wheel rake* consists of five or six wheels with toothlike spikes on the rim. The wheels are set at an angle to the direction traveled, and move the hay to the side. The *drag-type rake* has no moving parts. It has curved fingers that move the hay to one side, much as a snowplow moves snow.   A. D. LONGHOUSE

RALEIGH, *RAW lih*, N.C. (pop. 121,577; met. area 228,453; alt. 365 ft.), is the state capital and the trading center for a rich farming district. It lies near the center of the state (see NORTH CAROLINA [political map]). The city was founded as the capital in 1792. Workers completed the present Capitol in 1840 (see NORTH CAROLINA [color picture]). The state legislative building was completed in 1963. For the monthly weather in Raleigh, see NORTH CAROLINA (Climate).

Raleigh is the home of Meredith College, North Carolina State University at Raleigh, St. Augustine's College, and Shaw University. Raleigh also serves as the home of two junior colleges, Peace and St. Mary's. The city has more than 20 public schools. The North Carolina Museum of Art, opened in 1955, is said to have the most outstanding art collection in the South. The State Library and State Department of Archives and History are also in the city. Andrew Johnson, 17th President of the United States, was born there. Raleigh, the county seat of Wake County, has a council-manager form of government.   HUGH T. LEFLER

RALEIGH, SIR WALTER

RALEIGH, *RAW lih*, **SIR WALTER** (1552?-1618), is one of the most colorful figures in English history. He was a soldier, explorer, writer, and businessman. He spelled his last name RALEGH.

Raleigh was born at Hayes Barton, a family home in Devonshire, and attended Oxford University. He left school before graduating to join a band of gentlemen volunteers who were helping the Huguenots in France (see HUGUENOTS). In 1578, he returned to England and joined his half brother, Sir Humphrey Gilbert, on a voyage of discovery and piracy in America.

Raleigh and Elizabeth I. In 1580, Raleigh became a captain in the army in Ireland. There he distinguished himself by his ruthlessness at the siege of Smerwick. The next year he went to Queen Elizabeth's court with dispatches (see ELIZABETH I). There is a famous story about his meeting with Elizabeth. The queen was out walking, and stopped before a large mud puddle. Raleigh removed his coat and placed it over the puddle for her to walk on.

It is doubtful that this story is true. But in any

Sir Walter Raleigh, *right,* led several expeditions to South America. He also tried to establish a colony in North America. A famous legend tells how Raleigh placed his cloak over a puddle, *below,* so that Queen Elizabeth could cross it.

Brown Bros.; Culver

129

case, Raleigh soon became the queen's favorite. She granted him an estate of 12,000 acres in Ireland. It was on this land that he first planted the potato in 1596. She also gave him trade privileges and the right to colonize in America. In 1585, she made him a knight.

His Expeditions. Raleigh became deeply interested in exploration, like most prominent Englishmen of his day. He sent several expeditions to America, and spent a fortune trying to establish an English colony there. His settlers landed in what is now the state of North Carolina and explored the coast as far as present-day Florida. Raleigh named this entire region *Virginia* in honor of Elizabeth, "The Virgin Queen."

Raleigh's first colonizing expedition left Plymouth in April, 1585. It established a colony on Roanoke Island in Pamlico Sound. But sickness and fear of the unknown caused the survivors of this first English colony in North America to return home with Sir Francis Drake in 1586.

In 1587, Raleigh made a second attempt to colonize Roanoke Island, and 117 colonists, including 17 women, landed. On Aug. 18, 1587, the first English child was born in North America (see DARE, VIRGINIA). John White, the governor, went back to England for supplies. He was delayed by war with Spain, and when he returned to Roanoke in 1590, the settlers had mysteriously disappeared (see LOST COLONY).

Raleigh also took part in the victory over the Spanish Armada in 1588. He led other expeditions against Spanish possessions and returned with much booty. During the 1590's, his power reached its height, and he used his influence to do many great things. He obtained a pension for the poet, Edmund Spenser, and helped Spenser publish *The Faerie Queene* (see SPENSER, EDMUND). Raleigh also helped introduce the potato plant and the use of tobacco to Ireland.

His Fall. Raleigh lost the queen's favor by marrying one of her maids-of-honor. In an effort to recover his position and the money he had spent, he led an expedition to Guiana, in South America, to search for El Dorado, a legendary land of gold. But the expedition failed.

Elizabeth died in 1603, and the new king, James I, distrusted and feared Raleigh. He charged Raleigh with treason, and imprisoned him in the Tower of London. There Raleigh lived comfortably for 12 years with his family and servants, and wrote his *History of the World*. He was released in 1616 to lead an expedition to search for gold in South America. The king ordered him not to invade Spanish territory. But Raleigh's men attacked the Spaniards, and he had to abandon the project.

Upon his return to England, he was sentenced to death for disobeying orders. Raleigh met his fate calmly. He joked with the executioner, and even gave the signal for the ax to fall. JAMES G. ALLEN

RAM. See SHEEP; ARIES; BATTERING-RAM.
RAM, HYDRAULIC. See PUMP (Hydraulic Rams).
RAMA. See RAMAYANA.
RAMA, kings of Thailand. See THAILAND (History).
RAMADAN. See ISLAM (Customs and Ceremonies).
RAMAKRISHNA. See HINDUISM (History).
RAMAN, *RAH mun,* **SIR CHANDRASEKHARA VENKATA** (1888-1970), an Indian physicist, discovered that

when a beam of light passes through a liquid or a gas, it is scattered and the frequency of some of the scattered light is changed. This change in frequency, called the *Raman effect* provides a way to study the structure of the scattering molecules. For this discovery, Raman was knighted in 1929, and he received the 1930 Nobel prize for physics.

Raman was born in Trichinopoly (now Tiruchchirāppalli). He founded the *Indian Journal of Physics* and the Indian Academy of Sciences. After 1930, he worked principally on the structure of crystals. G. GAMOW

RAMAYANA, *rah MAH yuh nuh,* is one of the two great epic poems of India. It is partly historical and partly legendary and mythical. *Ramayana* tells the thrilling story of Rama, the king's son and heir. Rama is banished from his home through the trickery of his stepmother. The brave and honorable hero spends 14 years in wandering and adventure. His wife, Sita, is the Hindu ideal of pure devotion to duty, husband, and family. With the help of an army of apes, Rama rescues her from a wicked magician who had kidnaped her. See also MAHABHARATA; VISHNU. FRANZ ROSENTHAL

RAMBOUILLET. See SHEEP (Fine-Wooled Sheep).
RAMEAU, *ram OH,* **JEAN PHILIPPE** (1683-1764), was a French composer and music theorist. His *Treatise of Harmony* (1722) is considered a landmark in the development of modern theories of harmony (see HARMONY). Rameau's harmonic theories helped shift the emphasis in composition from counterpoint to a symphony style using chords. He wrote chamber music and works for the harpsichord, but he is best known for his stage compositions.

Rameau's chief dramatic works include the operas *Hippolyte and Aricie* (1733), *Castor and Pollux* (1737), and *Zoroastre* (1749), and the opera-ballet *Les Indes Galants* (1735). These works generally follow the emotional style of Jean Baptiste Lully, a French composer of the late 1600's, but Rameau added the novelty of extravagant staging. Although Rameau's stage works are seldom performed today, they were important in the development of opera and French music.

Rameau was born in Dijon. By the time he was a teen-ager, he could play the violin, harpsichord, and organ. Rameau worked as an organist in several French cities until about 1722, when he settled in Paris. In Paris, he joined a group of philosophers known as the *philosophes*. The group included Jean Jacques Rousseau and Voltaire. In 1752, Rameau became involved in the "War of the Buffoons," a fierce debate among Paris intellectuals over the merits of French versus Italian opera. One side, represented by Rameau, supported French opera. The other side, which included Rousseau, supported Italian opera. JAMES SYKES

RAMESES II. See RAMSES II.
RAMIE, *RAM ee,* is a perennial plant native to Asia, grown chiefly for its fiber. It is one of the oldest sources of fiber known to man. There are over 30 known varieties of ramie. The most common kind comes from China and Japan. Its thick, broad leaves are dark green on top, and white and woolly underneath. Another common variety grows in the tropics. Growers plant pieces of the roots, which grow into plants in about three months. The stalks grow to a height of from 3 to 7 feet.

In Asia, workers strip the tough ramie fiber from the stalks by hand. The fiber at this stage is often called

China grass. Then it is washed and dried several times to remove the gums, pectins, and waxes. In the United States, ramie is grown mainly in Florida. Machines harvest it and strip it of its bark and core. Chemicals remove gummy material and impurities from the fiber.

Ramie's strength increases greatly when it is wet, so it is suitable for life rafts, ropes, canvas, and nets. Other uses include surgical dressings, towels, air-conditioning filters, and fabrics. Farmers in Central America have used ramie as a high-protein fodder for pigs.

Scientific Classification. Ramie is a member of the nettle family, *Urticaceae.* It is classified as genus *Boehmeria,* species *B. nivea.*   HAROLD NORMAN MOLDENKE

See also BOEHMERIA.

RAMJET. See JET PROPULSION (Ramjet).

RAMOTH-GILEAD. See CITIES OF REFUGE.

RAMP, or WILD LEEK, is a wild onion that grows in moist woodland areas in the eastern United States. The flat leaves grow from the ground in spring and disappear by summer. Then a leafless flowering stem appears, bearing several greenish-white flowers at its tip. The plants smell and taste like onions. Some persons believe that the Indian word *checagou,* from which Chicago got its name, refers to the smell of the ramp.

Scientific Classification. Ramps belong to the lily family, *Liliaceae.* They are genus *Allium,* species *A. tricoccum.*   RICHARD W. POHL

See also ONION; LEEK.

RAMPART. See CASTLE.

RAMPOLLA, MARIANO CARDINAL (1843-1913), MARCHESE DEL TINDARO, became a cardinal of the Roman Catholic Church and papal secretary of state in 1887. He shared responsibility for Pope Leo XIII's policy of reconciling French Catholics to their country's republican form of government. His efforts displeased not only the French monarchists, but also Emperor Francis Joseph of Austria-Hungary. The emperor took extraordinary action in 1903, when the College of Cardinals met to elect a new pope. He registered a veto of Cardinal Rampolla. The exact effect of the emperor's veto cannot be known, because popes are elected by secret vote. But it seems likely it prevented the choice of Rampolla, whose ability was well known.

Rampolla was born in Polizzi, Italy. He was ordained a priest in 1866. During his education at the Vatican seminary, he showed such ability, particularly in Oriental languages, that he was chosen for a career in Vatican diplomatic service.   JOHN T. FARRELL and FULTON J. SHEEN

RAMSAY, SIR BERTRAM HOME (1883-1945), was a British admiral. During World War II, he commanded the naval phase of Allied landings in Normandy on D-Day, June 6, 1944. Earlier in the war, he had directed the evacuation of British forces from Dunkerque in 1940. He also commanded the naval planning and landings of Allied forces in North Africa and Sicily in 1942 and 1943.

Ramsay was born in London, the son of a brigadier general. During World War I, he served in the Dover patrol. He retired from the navy in 1938, but was recalled in 1939 to take command at Dover.   C. L. MOWAT

RAMSAY, SIR WILLIAM (1852-1916), was a Scottish chemist who, with Baron Rayleigh, isolated the first rare atmospheric gas, argon. Ramsay also discovered the other inert gases: helium, neon, krypton, and xenon. For this work, he received the 1904 Nobel prize

for chemistry. His explanation of the nature of these elements led to important ideas about atomic structure. The gases also have great practical importance. Each of these elements has a separate article in WORLD BOOK.

Ramsay was born in Glasgow and studied in Germany at Heidelberg and Tübingen universities. He taught at Glasgow and Bristol, and at University College in London. He was knighted in 1902, and in 1911, he became president of the British Association for the Advancement of Science.   HENRY M. LEICESTER

See also ELEMENT, CHEMICAL.

RAMSES II, *RAM seez* (reigned 1290-1224 B.C.), was a famous Egyptian *pharaoh* (king). Ramses came to the throne at an early age, ruling for a short time

P & A

Statues of Ramses II guarded the Abu Simbel temple near the Nile for more than 3,000 years. Construction of the Aswan High Dam made it necessary to move the temple to higher ground.

as coregent with his father, Seti I. During the early part of his reign, Ramses tried to end Hittite control of Syria. About 1285, he fought an indecisive battle against the Hittites at Kadesh and claimed a great victory. But about 1269, he made a treaty with the Hittite king which divided Syria between them (see HITTITE).

During the rest of his long reign, Ramses devoted his energies to a vast building program. He built a new capital in the Nile delta. He completed the *hypostyle* (columned) hall at Karnak (see EGYPT, ANCIENT [color picture: The Temple of Amon-Re]). He also built the mighty rock temples at Abu Simbel, and other temples in nearly every important Egyptian city. Ramses took credit for many buildings of his ancestors.

It has sometimes been said that Ramses was the pharaoh mentioned in the Biblical book of Exodus. The accuracy of this statement is doubtful. Ramses' mummy is preserved in the Cairo Museum.   RICARDO A. CAMINOS

See also CLEOPATRA'S NEEDLES; ABU SIMBEL, TEMPLES OF.

RAMSEY, ALEXANDER. See MINNESOTA (Territorial Days; table: The Governors of Minnesota).

RANCHING

Werner Stoy, Camera Hawaii; Ernst Peterson, Publix

Life on Cattle Ranches has changed greatly since they were founded in the 1800's in the American Southwest. Ranchers still use cow ponies occasionally to rope calves, *left*, and do other work. But now some ranchers also use helicopters, *above*, to check on herds in distant parts of the ranch.

RANCHING usually means raising cattle and sheep on large farms. Some fruit farms and farms that raise such small fur animals as mink are also called *ranches*. So are many places of 5 or 10 acres in California. But this article deals with cattle and sheep ranching. For information on *dude ranches*, the resorts where tourists get an idea of what life in the Old West was like, see DUDE RANCH.

Cattle and sheep ranches are very large because it takes many acres of grassland to feed a herd. An average ranch in the Western United States covers about 10,000 acres.

Most American ranches are found in the Western United States and Canada. There are some in the Southeastern States along the Gulf of Mexico. Australia, Argentina, Mexico, New Zealand, and African countries also have large ranches. But Australians and New Zealanders call them *stations*.

Most early ranchers in the United States raised cattle on unfenced land owned by the federal government called *open range*. Hired men called *cowboys* rode herd on the cattle. Today, a rancher generally owns much of the land in his ranch, and he and members of his family do most of the work themselves. Neighboring ranchers help each other when extra help is needed. Only the largest ranches still employ cowboys.

Life on a Cattle Ranch centers around raising calves that are sold as *feeder cattle* to men called *feeders*. After the animals are fattened, they are called *slaughter cattle* and are shipped to a *stockyard* (market) where they are sold and slaughtered for meat. The rancher usually keeps some calves to replace older cows.

The rancher starts his year in the fall after selling his calves. He prepares for winter by buying or harvesting a hay crop and such feed grains as barley and oats. When snow covers the ground during the winter, the cattle cannot find food by themselves. The rancher then carries feed out to his cattle in a truck and spreads it on the ground for them to eat.

Many of the cows give birth to calves in early spring, and the rancher must watch them closely then. If a calf becomes ill, he may move the calf and its mother in from the fields to the ranch headquarters to treat the calf. A month or two later, when the calves are active and strong, neighbors help the rancher round up the cattle and herd them into a small fenced area called a *corral*. There the calves are *branded* (marked) with a hot iron to show who owns them. They are also given medicine to prevent diseases. During the rest of the spring and summer, the herd *grazes* (eats grass) on the range.

The cattle follow a daily routine on the range. They graze very early in the morning, eating very rapidly. They chew their food only enough to moisten it and then swallow it. During the middle of the day, the cattle rest in a shady place. The food is returned to their mouths in the form of a *cud*, and they chew it again. In late afternoon, most of the cattle go to the watering hole to drink. They then graze until dusk.

During the day, the rancher mends fences, repairs machinery, and makes sure the watering holes contain enough water for his cattle. He also puts out blocks of salt that the cows can lick, because cattle need salt in their diet. He also plants and cares for his hay and

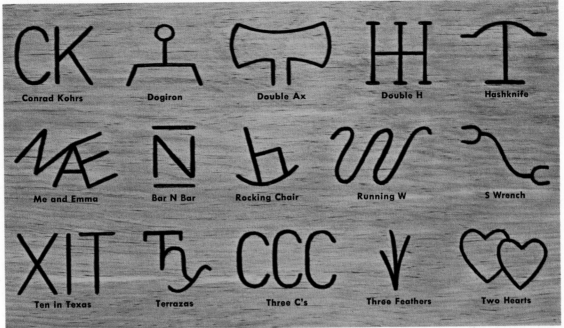

Conrad Kohrs	Dogiron	Double Ax	Double H	Hashknife
Me and Emma	Bar N Bar	Rocking Chair	Running W	S Wrench
Ten in Texas	Terrazas	Three C's	Three Feathers	Two Hearts

WORLD BOOK illustration by Walter Maslon

Famous Ranch Brands of the Old West. Branding cattle was very important in the 1800's, when cattle roamed on *open* (unfenced) range. The brand on each animal showed who owned it. Branding also made it difficult for *rustlers* (thieves) to steal cattle and sell them as their own.

grain crops. In the fall, his neighbors help him round up the cattle again. Then the calves that are old enough to be *weaned* (taken from their mothers) are sold.

Ranch life once was lonely. But the automobile, truck, and good roads have brought the rancher and his family closer to other people. Ranchers usually go to town at least once a week, and they visit their neighbors frequently. Most ranch children ride school buses to school in nearby towns. Ranch families now live in comfortable homes that have electricity, modern plumbing, a telephone, and, usually, a television set.

Life on a Sheep Ranch is different from life on a cattle ranch because sheep produce two crops—lambs and wool. In the spring, crews of men use power clippers to *shear* (cut off) the sheep's wool and the rancher sells it. Lambs are usually born in spring. They and the freshly sheared sheep are then branded with paint. In the fall, most of the lambs are weaned, shipped to stockyards, and sold. Sheep must be watched more closely than cattle, because they can be killed more easily by wild animals or sudden storms.

History. Ranching in the United States began in the mid-1800's. The ranchers raised cattle on the open range, and hired cowboys to guard and herd the cattle.

When the cattle were almost ready for slaughter, the ranchers formed big herds and drove them overland to the nearest railroad, in Kansas. A single trail herd had several thousand cattle and it moved from 10 to 15 miles each day. The ranchers sold the cattle in Kansas to buyers who shipped the cattle to the East.

During the 1870's and Early 1880's, large ranches developed in the West. One, the XIT ranch in northern Texas, was 200 miles long, 25 miles wide, and had 150,-000 cattle. Many cowboys worked on these big ranches, and they lived in buildings called *bunkhouses.* But in the mid-1880's, bad weather killed thousands of cattle, and ruined many ranchers. Many of the big ranches were sold and divided into smaller ranches.

Range Wars. Some of the best land was *homesteaded.* That is, men moved onto federal land under the terms of the Homestead Act, which gave a man up to 160 acres of land if he promised to live on it and farm it. The homesteaders built fences to protect their crops from the ranchers' cattle. Sheep ranching also began to develop. Sheep ranchers moved their sheep from one range to another, and the sheep occasionally grazed on ranges that cattle used. Soon, cattle ranchers, homesteaders, and sheep ranchers began to fight for the land and watering holes. Many of these disputes developed into bloody *range wars.* Unlimited use of the open range ended in 1934. Since then, ranchers have needed permits to graze herds on federal land.

Since the 1940's. Land prices increased in the 1940's, so ranchers had to develop new ways to make their land more productive. They developed more watering holes and planted better grasses for their cattle and sheep to eat. Ranchers also began to use new methods of handling livestock with less help. Horses are still necessary, but ranchers now also use jeeps, trucks, and even helicopters to get the most production.   JAMES R. GRAY

For a description of ranch life in the Old West, see COWBOY; WESTERN FRONTIER LIFE (Life in the Country). See also AUSTRALIA (Agriculture); CATTLE; CHUCK WAGON; SHEEP.

RAND CORPORATION

RAND CORPORATION is a nonprofit research organization that studies various policy problems of the United States, especially those involving national defense. The U.S. Air Force started Project RAND (*Re*search *AN*d *D*evelopment) in 1946 to conduct long-range studies of intercontinental warfare other than by ground armies. RAND became an independent corporation in 1948, but the military, particularly the Air Force, still finances most of its work.

RAND investigates such subjects as the military and economic strength of Russia and Communist China, and the air defenses of the United States. It also studies the design of weapons, uses of earth satellites, ways to supply the armed forces more efficiently, and military and political conditions in various parts of the world. Since 1967, RAND has increased its research on such nonmilitary problems as city transportation, water supplies, and housing. Most of RAND's reports on military matters are secret and are given directly to the Air Force or the Department of Defense. RAND has headquarters in Santa Monica, Calif.   HARVEY GLICKMAN

RANDALL, CLARENCE BELDEN (1891-1967), an American industrial leader, was an economic adviser to the United States government. He began his career as a lawyer, but became assistant vice-president of the Inland Steel Co. in 1925. He became president of the company in 1949 and chairman of the board in 1953. After 1956, he served the government in several advisory positions, and became special adviser to the President on foreign economic policy matters. Randall was born in Newark Valley, N.Y.   W. H. BAUGHN

RANDOLPH is the name of a famous Virginia family.

William Randolph (1651?-1711) was a planter and colonial administrator of Virginia. He was one of the founders of the College of William and Mary. He was born in Warwickshire, England, and settled in Virginia about 1673. From 1694 to 1698, he served as attorney general of Virginia.

Sir John Randolph (1693?-1737), the son of William Randolph, was educated at the College of William and Mary. He became noted as a lawyer and twice represented Virginia in England. He served as speaker of the Virginia House of Burgesses from 1734 until his death. He was born in Henrico County, Virginia.

Edmund Randolph (1753-1813), the grandson of Sir John Randolph, served as General George Washington's aide-de-camp during the Revolutionary War. He was born near Williamsburg, Va., and was educated at the College of William and Mary.

Randolph was attorney general of Virginia in 1776 and later became a member of the Continental Congress. In 1786, he was elected governor of Virginia and the next year attended the Constitutional Convention. There he proposed his famous "Virginia Plan," which favored the large states by calling for representation in Congress based on population or the tax contributions made by each state. Randolph refused to sign the Constitution when this plan was not followed, but he urged Virginia to accept it to unite the country.

In 1789, Washington appointed Randolph attorney general of the United States, and, in 1794, secretary of state. He resigned this position the next year when he was unjustly accused of obtaining money from France.

Randolph then practiced law. He was one of Aaron Burr's attorneys when Burr was tried for treason in 1807 (see BURR, AARON [Tried for Treason]).

John Randolph of Roanoke (1773-1833) was the great-grandson of William Randolph, and the most famous member of the Randolph family. As a statesman, he was more noted for his colorful personality than for his achievements. He did not hesitate to call his political enemies names. He had a cruel, biting tongue, and was the most feared orator of his time.

Randolph was born in Prince George County, Virginia, a descendant of Pocahontas and John Rolfe. He was mainly self-educated, but he studied for a short time at Princeton and Columbia colleges. He practiced law for a while, and in 1799 was elected to the United States House of Representatives.

Randolph was a champion of lost causes and opposed many popular measures. He was the Democratic-Republican Party's leader in the House, and supported Thomas Jefferson's purchase of Louisiana. But, later, he broke with the President over the intended purchase of Florida. Thereafter, he was almost always in the opposition. He upheld states' rights against expanding federal powers. Randolph opposed the war with England in 1812, the nationalistic tariffs, and the formation of the Bank of the United States. He led southern opposition to the Missouri Compromise in 1820, and became a bitter enemy of Henry Clay, who had been one of its chief supporters.

In 1825, Randolph was elected to the U.S. Senate. He used insulting language in the Senate regarding Clay's appointment as secretary of state, and Clay challenged him to a duel. It was a dignified, bloodless affair. Randolph insisted on wearing a dressing gown, and Clay shot through its enormous folds. Randolph fired into the air. Randolph later served in the Virginia Constitutional Convention of 1829-1830 and was U.S. minister to Russia in 1830 and 1831.   J. CARLYLE SITTERSON

George Wythe Randolph (1818-1867), a great-great-great grandson of William Randolph, served as Confederate secretary of war from March to November, 1862. He was particularly effective in coordinating the work of the field commanders. But President Jefferson Davis resented his energy, and he resigned.

Randolph was born at Monticello in Virginia, the home of his grandfather, Thomas Jefferson. He served as Virginia peace commissioner to the United States in 1861. He organized and commanded the Richmond Howitzers early in 1861. He also served in the Virginia secession convention.   FRANK E. VANDIVER

RANDOLPH, A. PHILIP (1889-   ), played a leading role in the struggle for Negro rights from the 1920's through the 1960's. He also became an important figure in the American labor movement. In 1925, Randolph founded the Brotherhood of Sleeping Car Porters, a union he headed until 1968. He became a vice-president of the American Federation of Labor and Congress

A. Philip Randolph
Wide World

134

of Industrial Organizations (AFL-CIO) in 1957.

Asa Philip Randolph was born in Crescent City, Fla., but moved to New York City as a young man. He held odd jobs during the day and attended City College of New York at night. A Socialist at the time of World War I, he later became convinced that unions offered Negroes the best hope for a fair wage. A group of Pullman car porters asked him to organize and lead a union for them. In 1941, Randolph threatened a march on Washington, D.C., to demand jobs for Negroes in defense industries. The threat was one reason why President Franklin D. Roosevelt set up the Fair Employment Practices Committee. Randolph helped organize the march in Washington in 1963 to protest injustice to Negroes.   RICHARD BARDOLPH

RANDOLPH, EDWARD (1632?-1703), was a British agent in colonial New England. In 1676, he carried royal instructions for the colonial governments to Boston. Curtly treated there, he returned to England and wrote two strongly critical reports. As a result, the British separated New Hampshire from Massachusetts.

Randolph took charge of customs for New England in 1679, and he inaugurated the new royal government of New Hampshire the next year. When Massachusetts resisted his authority, he had its charter annulled in 1684. He served the royal governor, Sir Edmund Andros, until 1689, when both were jailed during a rebellion in Boston. Randolph became surveyor general of customs for Great Britain in North America in 1691. He was born at Canterbury, England.   BRADFORD SMITH

RANDOLPH, PEYTON. See CONTINENTAL CONGRESS.

RANDOLPH AIR FORCE BASE, Tex., houses the headquarters of the United States Air Force Air Training Command. It covers 2,551 acres of coastal plain 15 miles northeast of San Antonio. The primary purpose of the base is to train jet pilots. During World War II, thousands of pilots received basic and primary flight training at the base, which became known as "The West Point of the Air." It was set up in 1931, and named for Captain William M. Randolph, a member of the committee selected to name the new air base. He was killed in a training flight.   RICHARD M. SKINNER

RANDOLPH-MACON COLLEGE. See UNIVERSITIES AND COLLEGES (table).

RANDOLPH-MACON WOMAN'S COLLEGE. See UNIVERSITIES AND COLLEGES (table).

RANDOM SAMPLE. See STATISTICS.

RANEY NICKEL. See HYDROGENATION.

RANGE FINDER is a device for measuring distances. The military uses range finders to determine the distance to a target. Ranging devices also include radar, which measures the time lapse of an electromagnetic echo, and optical range finders used on cameras.

The basis of a military range finder is a long tube with eyepieces at the center and an arrangement of lenses and prisms at each end. By adjusting the prisms, the range-finder operator can sight the target simultaneously from both ends of the tube. The difference in direction of the two lines of sight is called the *parallactic angle*. This angle depends upon the distance to the target. The angle will be large at short distances, and small at long distances. The parallactic angle is measured on a dial from which the range in yards can be read directly.

There are two principal types of range finders, the coincidence and the stereoscopic. The operator of a *co-incidence* instrument looks through a single eyepiece and sees two distinct images of the target. By turning a knob, he can make these two images move together and merge. When this happens, the distance can be read on the range dial. The operator of a *stereoscopic* instrument looks through a pair of eyepieces like binoculars, and sees a single image of the target. He also sees a marker that appears to be floating in space near the target. The operator moves a knob until the marker and the target appear to be at the same distance. Then he reads the distance on the range dial.

Since World War I, range finders have been used in naval gunnery as a part of *director systems* which aim the guns automatically. During World War II, the Army adopted director systems for antiaircraft fire. But radar, which can measure ranges more accurately, largely replaced the range finder in World War II.

See also RADAR.

RANGE LIGHTS. See NAVIGATION (Aids).

RANGELEY LAKE. See MAINE (Rivers and Lakes).

RANGERS were specialized infantry units of the U.S. Army. Rangers were given much tougher training than other infantrymen. The Rangers were organized in 1942 under the leadership of Colonel William O. Darby. The first regiment of 2,000 men was formed in Great Britain. It consisted of volunteers from the American Commando School. About 9 out of 10 of the first regiment lost their lives opening up enemy defenses before invasions. Separate Ranger units were disbanded in 1952, but individuals still receive Ranger training.

The *Connaught Rangers* make up a regular infantry regiment in the British Army. A colorful group called *Rogers' Rangers* fought with the British and American armies during the French and Indian Wars of the 1750's. They developed the stealthy, daredevil tactics of the Indian, which have since been associated with the name ranger.   JOHN J. FLOHERTY

See also COMMANDO; ROGERS' RANGERS.

RANGERS, FOREST. See FOREST AND FOREST PRODUCTS (Careers in Forestry); FOREST SERVICE.

RANGERS, TEXAS. See TEXAS RANGERS.

RANGOON, *rang GOON* (pop. 821,800; alt. 20 ft.), is Burma's capital and largest city. It lies on the Rangoon River, 21 miles north of the Bay of Bengal

A Range Finder measures the distance to an enemy target. The device is part of a system that aims the guns automatically.

RANJIT SINGH

(see BURMA [color map]). It is Burma's chief port. Rangoon is a modern city with many parks and wide boulevards. It has a library, museum, hospital, and the University of Rangoon, founded in 1920. The city also has many Buddhist shrines. The most famous of these shrines is the 2,500-year-old, 368-foot-high Shwe Dagon pagoda.

Teakwood and rice are the city's principal exports. Rangoon ranks among the world's leading rice markets. Factories manufacture pottery, and silk and cotton cloth. Alaungpaya, a Burmese king, founded the city in 1755, on the site of an old fishing village. During World War II, the Japanese occupied Rangoon from 1942 to 1945. JOHN F. CADY

RANJIT SINGH, *run JEET SING* (1780-1839), known as the *Lion of the Punjab*, was one of the most important figures in the history of India. He became the first Indian ruler to create a great Sikh kingdom (see SIKHISM).

Ranjit was the son of an important chief in the Punjab, a region in northwest India. His father died when he was 12. At first, Ranjit ruled only a small state. But he gradually conquered neighboring states and threw off the control of the powerful Afghans.

Ranjit wanted to unite all Sikhs in a great nation. He expanded to the north and west, and made his state the largest in the Indus valley. But the British prevented him from uniting all Sikhs. He signed treaties with the British that kept the peace and guaranteed his territories. T. WALTER WALLBANK

RANK IN ARMED SERVICES indicates a person's authority and standing. The terms *rank* and *grade* are usually synonymous, but officers are said to hold rank, and enlisted men and women to hold ratings or grades. Grade also refers to the authorized level of pay. These terms indicate rights, powers, and duties fixed by law. In the United States, Congress creates ranks and grades, and regulates appointments and promotions.

Under the U.S. Constitution, the President holds the rank of *commander in chief* of the armed forces. A *commissioned* officer holds a commission granted by the President with the advice and consent of the Senate. A *warrant* officer is a specialist in a particular field. He holds a warrant granted by the secretary of the army, navy, or air force. *Noncommissioned* officers are enlisted men who hold their grades for skill and long service.

A person is appointed to, or commissioned in, a rank

or grade. Among persons who hold the same grade, length of service and date of appointment to the grade determine rank. For example, one colonel outranks another if he has been in grade one day longer. This difference in rank can have considerable importance. If a group of servicemen without a designated commander suddenly faces a situation that requires command decisions, the highest ranking man takes command. He may later have to prove his right to command others.

Rank is a right granted an officer by law. It cannot be withdrawn except through legal processes. When an officer performs his official duty, his rank indicates his relation to other officers of the group involved. His rank is not a perpetual guarantee that he has the right to exercise command, but it normally indicates that he will. The President may relieve an officer of command.

During the Civil War period, the armed services used an honorary title called *brevet* to expand the officer corps. The brevet, a temporary commission, gave an officer a nominal rank higher than his regular one for a certain period or for a special assignment. At the end of the emergency, the officer could expect to return to his regular rank. During and after World War II, army officers held both *temporary* and *permanent* ranks.

GRADE AND PAY FOR OFFICERS
Monthly base pay for less than 2 years service
COMMISSIONED OFFICERS

Grade	Army, Air Force, and Marine Corps	Navy	Base Pay
O-10	General	Admiral	$2,263.50
O-9	Lieutenant General	Vice-Admiral	$2,006.40
O-8	Major General	Rear Admiral (upper half)	$1,817.10
O-7	Brigadier General	Rear Admiral (lower half) Commodore*	$1,509.60
O-6	Colonel	Captain	$1,119.00
O-5	Lieutenant Colonel	Commander	$894.90
O-4	Major	Lt. Commander	$754.80
O-3	Captain	Lieutenant	$701.40
O-2	First Lieutenant	Lieutenant (j.g.)	$611.40
O-1	Second Lieutenant	Ensign	$530.70

WARRANT OFFICERS

Grade	Army, Air Force, Marine Corps, and Navy	Base Pay
W-4	Chief (Commissioned) Warrant Officer	$714.30
W-3	Chief (Commissioned) Warrant Officer	$649.50
W-2	Chief (Commissioned) Warrant Officer	$568.50
W-1	Warrant Officer	$473.70

Source: U.S. armed services   *Wartime rank only

GRADE AND PAY FOR ENLISTED PERSONNEL
Monthly base pay for less than 2 years service

Grade	Army	Air Force	Marine Corps	Navy	Base Pay
E-9	Sergeant Major	Chief Master Sgt.	Sergeant Major; Master/Gunnery Sgt.	Master Ch. Petty Off.	$811.50*
E-8	Master Sgt.; First Sgt.	Senior Master Sgt.	First Sergeant; Master Sergeant	Sr. Chief Petty Off.	$681.00†
E-7	Sgt. 1st Class; Specialist 7	Master Sergeant	Gunnery Sergeant	Chief Petty Officer	$475.50
E-6	Staff Sgt.; Specialist 6	Technical Sergeant	Staff Sergeant	Petty Officer (1/C)	$410.40
E-5	Sergeant; Specialist 5	Staff Sergeant	Sergeant	Petty Officer (2/C)	$360.60
E-4	Corporal; Specialist 4	Sergeant	Corporal	Petty Officer (3/C)	$346.80
E-3	Private First Class	Airman 1st Class	Lance Corporal	Seaman	$333.60
E-2	Private	Airman	Private 1st Class	Seaman Apprentice	$320.70
E-1	Recruit	Airman Basic	Private	Seaman Recruit	$288.00

Source: U.S. armed services   *Over 10 years   †Over 8 years

The permanent rank was normally two or three grades lower than the temporary one.

Promotion to the next higher rank for officers is usually based on length of service in the grade they hold, satisfactory performance of their duties, and a vacancy in the next higher grade. Promotion boards consider officers for promotion. Boards usually consider officers within a certain *zone* (based on their time in grade), but truly outstanding officers below the zone may be selected for promotion. A person "passed over" for promotion twice when he is in the zone is discharged. During wartime, promotions may be given "on the battlefield."

Enlisted men and women must spend some time in a grade before they can be considered for advancement. The navy uses competitive written examinations, and the army uses an evaluation system.

Rank and Pay. Officers and enlisted personnel are paid according to their rank and length of service. The monthly rates shown in the tables refer only to *base pay* for less than two years' service. Increases are added to base pay after certain periods of service are completed. These increases are called *longevity pay.* All personnel begin to receive such pay after two years of service. The tables do not show allowances for quarters, food, or special duty. Officers above the rank of major general or rear admiral receive a personal allowance. The armed services also grant *proficiency pay* to persons whose skills are greatly needed.   THOMAS E. GRIESS

See also COMMANDER IN CHIEF; COMMISSION, MILITARY; FLAG OFFICER; MATE; and color pictures with AIR FORCE, U.S.; ARMY, U.S.; MARINE CORPS, U.S.; NAVY, U.S.

RANKE, *RAHNG kuh,* **LEOPOLD VON** (1795-1886), a German historian, persuaded historians to use critical methods and examine history objectively. He introduced the seminar method of teaching. After 1840, his methods were largely used in teaching German historians. Ranke was born at Wiehe, in Thuringia. His first book, *History of the Romance and Teutonic Nations* (1824), earned him a position as professor at the University of Berlin. He also wrote *History of the Popes* and *History of the Reformation in Germany.*   FRANCIS J. BOWMAN

RANKIN, JEANNETTE (1880-   ), was the first woman to be elected to the United States Congress. A Republican, she served from 1917 to 1919 as congressman at large from Montana. In 1940, she was elected to the House of Representatives for one term. She voted against United States participation in World War I, and was the only member of the House to vote against entering World War II. Jeannette Rankin was born near Missoula, Mont., and studied at the University of Montana and at the School of Philanthropy in New York City.   GEORGE M. WALLER

Harris & Ewing
Jeannette Rankin

RANSOM is money paid to recover something that is being held unlawfully. It also means the money paid to kidnapers to obtain the release of someone who has been imprisoned, concealed, or detained illegally. The term generally is used to describe the money demanded by kidnapers for releasing their victim or for promising to release him. See also KIDNAPING.   FRED E. INBAU

RANSOM, JOHN CROWE (1888-   ), is an American poet, critic, and editor. In his writing, Ransom describes what he considers an impersonal, spiritually barren society brought about by science and technology. Much of his work reflects his affection for the rural, aristocratic way of life in the South before the Civil War.

Ransom's poems seem to be quiet and gentle, but they are toughened by his ironic wit and his awareness of human frailties. A revised edition of his *Selected Poems* was published in 1969. Ransom helped lead the New Criticism movement, which emphasizes analysis of the text of a poem or story, rather than its author or social significance. *The New Criticism,* a collection of Ransom's essays, was published in 1941.

Ransom was born in Pulaski, Tenn. In 1914, he became a professor of English at Vanderbilt University. He joined the faculty of Kenyon College in 1937. Ransom founded the *Kenyon Review,* a literary magazine, and edited it from 1939 to 1958.   JOHN B. VICKERY

RANSOME, ARTHUR (1884-1967), was a British writer of children's stories. Camping and sailing are the subjects of *Swallows and Amazons* (1931) and *Swallowdale* (1932). In 1937, Ransome received the Carnegie medal for *Pigeon Post* (1936). He also wrote *Coot Club* (1935) and *We Didn't Mean to Go to Sea* (1938). He was born in Leeds.   GEORGE E. BUTLER

RANUNCULUS is a group of annual or perennial herbs. The best known are the crowfoot, buttercup, and spearwort. The plants bear white or yellow flowers. About 300 varieties grow in the temperate regions.

Scientific Classification. *Ranunculus* forms a genus of the crowfoot family, *Ranunculaceae.*   EARL L. CORE
Related Articles in WORLD BOOK include:
Adonis   Buttercup   Columbine Hepatica Pasqueflower
Anemone Clematis   Cowslip   Larkspur Peony

RAPA ISLAND, *RAH pah,* lies 600 miles south of Tahiti in the South Pacific Ocean. It is a rugged, volcanic island, rising to 2,077 feet. Rapa covers 8½ square miles and has a population of about 360. The people are Polynesians, and engage in fishing and farming (see PACIFIC ISLANDS). The early inhabitants of Rapa built hilltop forts and carved statues resembling those of Easter Island (see EASTER ISLAND). France governs Rapa Island. See also AUSTRAL ISLANDS.   NEAL M. BOWERS

RAPA NUI. See EASTER ISLAND.

RAPALLO, *rah PAHL loh,* **TREATIES OF.** There are two pacts known as the Treaty of Rapallo. The first agreement was signed by the governments of Italy and Yugoslavia on Nov. 12, 1920, at Rapallo, Italy. It settled a dispute over the ownership of territory belonging to Austria-Hungary before World War I. Both Italians and Slavs lived in this territory, located east and north of the Adriatic Sea. The treaty provided that part of the territory, Rijeka (Fiume), would be an independent state. Italy received part of Carniola and all of Istria, but gave up its claims to Dalmatia, except for Zara and most islands along the coast. But Italian nationalists wanted Rijeka under their control. In 1924,

Italy and Yugoslavia signed a new treaty, turning Rijeka over to Italy.

Most of the major European powers, along with Australia and Japan, attended a conference on economic and financial matters at Genoa, Italy, in the spring of 1922. At this meeting, a second Treaty of Rapallo was signed by Germany and Russia on Apr. 16, 1922. By its terms, the two countries restored diplomatic relations and agreed to discuss trade pacts.   DWIGHT E. LEE

RAPE is an annual plant cultivated for its leaves and used as temporary pasture crop for livestock in the United States. A small amount is grown for the production of its oil-bearing seeds. The succulent rape plant grows fast. It produces best under cool, moist conditions. It resists rather severe frosts, and is best seeded in the fall in the southern states and in the spring in the northern states. It produces a high yield.

USDA

Rape Plant

Scientific Classification. Rape belongs to the mustard family, *Cruciferae*. It is in the genus *Brassica*, and is classified as species *B. napus*.   ROY G. WIGGANS

RAPHAEL, *RAFF ay el* (1483-1520), an Italian painter, was one of the greatest artists of the Italian Renaissance.

Raphael's real name was Raffaello Sanzio. He was born at Urbino, and studied with the painter Perugino in Umbria. Raphael's early painting, *The Marriage of the Virgin* (at the Brera Gallery in Milan), is based on Perugino's painting of the same subject. Raphael further developed Perugino's balance of design, his light, pure colors, the poised grace and sweetness of his figures, and the spaciousness of their landscape settings. Raphael never forgot Perugino's art. This period in his career was known as his Umbrian period.

From about 1504 to 1508, Raphael worked in Florence. He learned from Masaccio how to group his figures and how to draw draperies. His friend Fra Bartolommeo taught him many secrets of modeling and coloring and developed Raphael's gift for the expression of spiritual beauty. From Leonardo da Vinci, Raphael learned how to paint gracefully, and from Michelangelo he learned anatomy. This period was known as his Florentine period. During this time he painted *The Entombment*, and many of his famous Madonnas.

Brown Bros.

Raphael

Raphael painted his masterpieces in Rome during the last 12 years of his life. For Pope Julius II, he painted a number of frescoes in the Vatican, including *Parnassus* and *The School of Athens*.

At this time, Michelangelo was painting the ceiling of the Sistine Chapel. Raphael was one of the most loved painters of his time. He was called "the Divine Raphael." His work was in such demand that he sometimes had assistants paint or finish painting his designs. Engravings and tapestries of his designs also helped spread his fame. In 1514, Pope Leo X appointed Raphael chief architect of Saint Peter's Church in Rome.

Raphael was and is most admired for his idealized and tranquil Madonnas. His *Madonna of the Goldfinch* appears in color in the PAINTING article. Raphael's whole view of nature, including man, was ideally beautiful and peaceful. His last great work, the *Transfiguration*, which is now at the Vatican Museums in Rome, was finished by his pupil Giulio Romano, who developed Raphael's late, darker, more dramatic style.

Raphael's great works also include the *Madonna Tempi* (Alte Pinakothek, Munich), *Portrait of Castiglione* (Louvre, Paris), and the fresco, *Galatea* (Farnesina, Rome).   ROBERT O. PARKS

For works by Raphael see GEORGE, SAINT; MADONNA AND CHILD; MIRACLE; PLATO.

RAPID CITY, S.Dak. (pop. 43,836; alt. 3,230 ft.), is the chief gateway to the scenic Black Hills. The city lies 25 miles northeast of Mount Rushmore National Memorial and 50 miles west of Bad Lands National Monument (see SOUTH DAKOTA [political map]).

Rapid City ranks as the second largest city in the state. It is the leading wholesale center for the Black Hills region. Industrial products include cement, flour, and lumber. The South Dakota School of Mines and Technology is at Rapid City. Ellsworth Air Force Base lies about 8 miles northeast of the city. Rapid City was founded in 1876. In 1972, a flood swept over Rapid City, causing more than 200 deaths and an estimated $100 million in damage. The city has a mayor-council form of government.   EVERETT W. STERLING

RAPIDS. See WATERFALL.

RAPP, GEORGE. See NEW HARMONY.

RAPPAHANNOCK RIVER, *RAP uh HAN uck*, is a waterway in Virginia. Much Civil War fighting took place along the Rappahannock. It rises in the Blue Ridge Mountains and flows southeast for 185 miles into Chesapeake Bay (see VIRGINIA [physical map]).

The Rappahannock is a tidal stream for nearly 100 miles below Fredericksburg. A waterfall at this city produces electric power. The Rapidan River is the Rappahannock's main branch.   RAUS M. HANSON

RARE EARTH is any one of a group of metallic elements with atomic numbers 58 through 71. The name *rare earth* is really incorrect, since they are neither rare nor earths. They received this name because chemists first isolated them in their oxide forms. These oxides somewhat resemble calcium, magnesium, and aluminum oxides, sometimes called *common earths*.

Rare earths have three electrons in the outer shells of their atoms that take part in valence bonding. Because of this structure, all rare earths have similar properties in water solutions, and all can exist in the *trivalent* (three electric charges per atom) state. The elements scandium, yttrium, lanthanum, and actinium

The Alba Madonna by Raphael is one of the most glorious examples of the rich religious art of this master of the Italian Renaissance. It is now one of the prized exhibits in the Mellon Collection of the National Gallery of Art in Washington, D.C.

also have three valence electrons. They are sometimes called rare earth elements, but they have somewhat different electronic structures.

The rare earth elements are called the *lanthanides* because they follow lanthanum in the periodic chart of elements. The elements following actinium are called the *actinides*. The lanthanides and actinides are placed in rows at the bottom of most periodic charts.

The true rare earths are silver-colored metals. In nature, they are always found together in combination with nonmetallic elements in the form of phosphates, carbonates, fluorides, silicates, and tantalites. The minerals monazite and bastnasite are the chief sources of the rare earths. The rare earths are not really rare. Even the

scarce rare earths, such as europium and lutetium, are more common than the platinum-group metals. Promethium does not occur naturally, but forms as a result of atomic reactions. Many rare earths form during the fission of uranium and plutonium (see FISSION).

The rare earths have many scientific and industrial uses. Tiny amounts of separated rare earths are used in lasers. Unseparated rare earths are added to various metals, including aluminum and magnesium, to make them stronger. The carbon electrodes used in motion-picture projectors have rare-earth cores. A mixed rare-earth alloy called *misch metal* is combined with iron to make flints for cigarette lighters.

Until 1945, processors had to use long and complicated chemical processes to obtain significant amounts of pure rare earths. This made them scarce and costly. Today, an *ion-exchange* process has made possible a rapid, inexpensive, and automatic separation that gives highly pure, low-cost rare earths.   FRANK H. SPEDDING

See also BERZELIUS, JÖNS JAKOB; ELEMENT, CHEMICAL (tables); LANTHANUM; SCANDIUM; YTTRIUM.

THE RARE EARTHS

Element	Chemical Symbol	Atomic Number	Atomic Weight
Cerium	Ce	58	140.12
Praseodymium	Pr	59	140.907
Neodymium	Nd	60	144.24
Promethium	Pm	61	145.00
Samarium	Sm	62	150.35
Europium	Eu	63	151.96
Gadolinium	Gd	64	157.25
Terbium	Tb	65	158.924
Dysprosium	Dy	66	162.50
Holmium	Ho	67	164.930
Erbium	Er	68	167.26
Thulium	Tm	69	168.934
Ytterbium	Yb	70	173.04
Lutetium	Lu	71	174.97

Each element listed in this table has a separate article in THE WORLD BOOK ENCYCLOPEDIA.

RARITAN RIVER is a waterway of northern New Jersey. Two branches that rise in the northern highlands of the state join to form the Raritan. It flows southeast for 75 miles into Raritan Bay, an inlet of Lower New York Bay. Boats can go up the river only as far as the fall line, near the city of New Brunswick (see FALL LINE). Perth Amboy, an important manufacturing center, lies at the mouth of the Raritan. Ships used the Delaware and Raritan Canal, between the Raritan and Delaware rivers, from 1834 to 1933. For location, see NEW JERSEY (physical map).   RICHARD P. McCORMICK

RASBORA. See FISH (color picture: Tropical Fresh-Water Fishes); TROPICAL FISH.

RASHT, or RESHT, (pop. 143,557), is the capital of Gilan province in Iran. It lies near the Caspian Sea at the western end of the Elburz Mountains (see IRAN [color map]). Rasht is one of Iran's chief silk-producing centers. Other products include glass, matches, and hosiery. Rasht was founded sometime before the A.D. 1000's. It became an important trading center during the 1600's. Most of Russia's trade with Iran in the 1800's came through Rasht.   RICHARD N. FRYE

RASMUSSEN, KNUD JOHAN VICTOR (1879-1933), was a Danish Arctic explorer and authority on Eskimos. Rasmussen influenced Denmark to improve its treatment of the Eskimos. In 1910, he founded a trading station, Thule, in Greenland. Later, Thule Air Base was built there. On Rasmussen's most famous expedition, described in his book *Across Arctic America* (1927), he visited Eskimos from Greenland to the Bering Strait. His many books include *Eskimo Folk Tales*. He was born in Greenland and was part Eskimo.   JOHN E. CASWELL

RASPBERRY, *RAZ bear ee*, is a thorny bush that grows in the Northern Hemisphere. It belongs to the rose family. The raspberry plant bears small, rounded berries that are much like blackberries. The berries grow from $\frac{1}{4}$ inch to more than 1 inch in diameter. Each looks like a cluster of tiny beads, colored red,

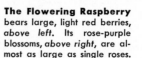

Roche

The Flowering Raspberry bears large, light red berries, *above left*. Its rose-purple blossoms, *above right*, are almost as large as single roses.

Wild Raspberry Bushes bear deep red berries that have a sharper flavor than cultivated kinds, *right*. The fruit is also smaller and juicier.

black, or purple. These beads are small cells, called *drupelets*. Each drupelet contains a tiny seed. The berries grow around a part of the plant called the *standard* (receptacle). When the fruit is ripe, it separates easily from the receptacle. Pickers remove the fruit entirely from its standard as well as from the branch. The blackberry does not separate from the standard. This is the principal difference between blackberries and raspberries. Raspberries are among the most popular of all bush fruits. Among the small fruits, they rank second in importance only to the strawberry.

The stems and branches of the raspberry bush bear only once, in their second year. Growers then cut off the branches at the ground. But they allow new stems that have grown from the roots to remain. These bear the fruit for the next year.

Kinds. Many kinds of raspberries have been developed by fruitgrowers. Those grown in the United States came from the *European red raspberry*, the *American red raspberry*, and the *American black raspberry*. A fourth type, the *purple raspberry*, is really a hybrid of the red and black raspberries. There are also a few yellow varieties of raspberries.

Cultivation. To obtain new red raspberry bushes, growers usually plant new shoots, called *suckers*, which

Raspberries grow in clusters on tall, sturdy stalks. The wrinkled, three-lobed leaves are often a silvery color underneath.

Frank Fenner

grow out of the roots of the old plant. But they grow black and purple raspberries from tip layers. In this method, the grower bends the tips of the plants over and covers them with earth. These tips develop roots, which the grower transplants the following season.

Raspberries grow best in fine, deep, sandy loam, and in regions where summers are cool. Only a few regions in the United States are suitable for growing raspberries, because of the extremes of climate. The best raspberry-growing regions are along the North Atlantic Coast, the Great Lakes region, and the Pacific Coast states.

Crop Production. Red raspberries ripen first, but produce the least fruit. Black raspberries ripen next, and the purple last. The purple varieties bear the most fruit. Black raspberries have larger seeds than the red. All raspberries are picked when they are ripe but still firm. People use them for canning, making pies and jams, and as a dessert fruit.

Diseases. Mosaic and virus diseases have greatly harmed and even ruined the red raspberry crop in some areas. Plants affected with these diseases must be destroyed and replaced by disease-free plants. *Anthracnose*, or *bitter rot*, forms dark, depressed areas on the canes and shoots. It is a serious disease of black raspberries. Growers control this disease by spraying the bushes and by pruning out all except the newest shoots immediately after harvest.

Scientific Classification. Raspberries belong to the rose family, *Rosaceae*. The European red raspberry is classified as genus *Rubus*, species *R. idaeus*. The American red is *R. strigosus;* the American black, *R. occidentalis;* the purple, *R. neglectus.*   ROY E. MARSHALL

See also BLACKBERRY; BRAMBLE.

RASPE, RUDOLPH ERICH. See MUNCHAUSEN, BARON.

RASPUTIN, *rass POO tin,* **GRIGORI YEFIMOVICH** (1872?-1916), a Siberian peasant, gained the reputation of a saint and exerted harmful influence on the last Russian czar, or emperor. He contributed to the downfall of the Russian empire (see RUSSIA [The February Revolution]).

Born in western Siberia, Rasputin, in his middle thirties, joined a religious sect and became known as a *holy man.* He went to St. Petersburg (now Leningrad), then the capital of Russia. In 1907, he was introduced to the czar and czarina in order to help heal their son, who suffered from hemophilia. His apparent success gave him great influence on the imperial couple, and he began to meddle in political decisions and ministerial appointments.

Rasputin had common sense, but he was selfish, greedy, and dissolute. A group of high noblemen feared that widespread hatred of Rasputin would turn against the czar himself. They assassinated Rasputin in December, 1916. But they did not save the empire. Revolution in Russia broke out within three months.   W. KIRCHNER

Grigori Rasputin
Culver

RASTATT, TREATY OF. See SUCCESSION WARS.

Fish and Wildlife Service
The Female House Rat May Bear 12 Litters in One Year.

George McClulan Bradt
The Pack Rat Collects Shiny Objects for Its Home.

Fish and Wildlife Service
The Roof Rat Often Lives in the Tops of Houses.

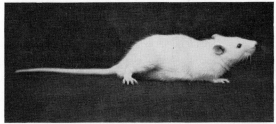
J. C. Allen
Scientists Use the White Rat for Medical Experiments.

RAT is a large member of the order of gnawing animals called *rodents*. It is in the same family as the house mouse. It looks like a mouse, but is two or three times as large. The two most common rats are the *black* and the *brown*, or *Norway*, rats. The brown rat lives in nearly all parts of the world. The black rat thrives best in the tropics and is not fitted for life in cold climates. The black rat is between 7 and 8 inches long, not including its naked, scaly tail of 8 or 9 inches. The brown rat is larger and much bolder and tougher than the black rat. It generally weighs about three-fourths of a

RAT

pound when grown, but may weigh up to 25 ounces. Few black rats live in regions where there are brown rats. The black rat came from Europe to the United States in ships with the first settlers. The brown rat came later, also by ship from Europe, and has driven the black rat from most parts of the United States.

The brown rat has thicker, shorter ears, a shorter tail, and a stouter body. The brown rat is grayish-brown, while the black rat is dusky black or gray. Both rats infest boats, wharves, dark and neglected buildings, barns, and houses. The brown rat likes to live in basements or under buildings. The black rat often inhabits the upper floors and one of its names is *roof rat*.

Rats Are Harmful. Rats are terrible pests, destroying stored grain, young poultry, fruits, vegetables, eggs, and other food products. The loss in the United States due to rats has been estimated at about $190 million a year. Their sharp teeth can gnaw through wood, plaster, or soft metal such as lead. They have a keen sense of smell and quickly detect an approaching danger. The *white rat* is the albino form of the brown rat. It is used in medical science, and makes an interesting pet.

Rats breed several times a year, and produce from 6 to 22 young in each litter. The average is 9 or 10. This rapid breeding, and the fact that rats carry bubonic plague, transmitted from rats to man by fleas, has forced man to fight constantly against rats. The ports of the western United States are especially active in this never-ending campaign, because the plague has its firmest foothold there. Rats on ships from tropical countries bring it into the United States. It is found in some native rodents, and then goes under the name *sylvatic plague*.

How to Get Rid of Rats. It is more important to keep rats from breeding than it is to destroy them after they have become numerous. All garbage should be kept in closed containers, and all buildings should be made rat-proof with wire netting and concrete. The rats are thus cut off from food and nesting places.

The best way to destroy rats is to use traps and poisons. Cage traps and the spring, or guillotine, traps are both used with some success. The traps should be washed and handled with gloves, for the rats are suspicious of anything that smells of human hands. After a rat has been killed in a spring trap, the trap should be washed and scorched briefly over a flame to remove traces of the dead rat.

Arsenic, barium chloride, and strychnine are good poisons. Red squill poison has recently been used more than all other poisons because it is harmless to man and to domestic animals which might accidentally eat it. Warfarin is also an effective poison. Ships and storehouses can be fumigated to destroy the rat population. Whole rat families may be destroyed in their homes by placing a cloth soaked with carbon bisulfide in the entrance to the burrow and sealing it with earth so the fumes cannot escape. Care must be taken to prevent fires and explosions when using carbon bisulfide.

Scientific Classification. Rats are in the Old World rat family, *Muridae*. The black rat is genus *Rattus*, species *R. rattus*. The brown is *R. norvegicus*. THEODORE H. EATON, JR.

See also BOUNTY; KANGAROO RAT; MOUSE; PACK RAT; VOLE.

RATCHET, *RACH it*, is a wheel or bar that can move in only one direction. It often consists of a notched wheel and two *pawls* (metal bars hung from a pivot). One pawl is attached to a lever. As the lever is moved, the free end of the pawl locks into a tooth of the wheel, causing the wheel to rotate. A second pawl prevents the wheel from turning backwards while the lever is being returned to begin another stroke.

A mechanical counter is a simple device that uses the ratchet-and-pawl combination. A ratchet-and-pawl mechanism locks a machine such as a hoisting winch so that it does not slip.   J. L. MERIAM

RATE-OF-CLIMB INDICATOR. See AIRCRAFT INSTRUMENTS (Altimeters).

RATE OF EXCHANGE. See ECONOMICS (Terms).

RATEL, *RAY tul*, is a small animal that lives in India, southwestern Asia, and Africa. It belongs to the weasel family, as do the badgers (see WEASEL; BADGER). The ratel has dark gray fur on its upper body and black fur

New York Zoological Society

The Ratel, Unlike Most Fur-Bearing Mammals, is light on top and dark below, reversing the usual coloration.

below. This combination is a strange coloring in mammals, whose darker fur is usually on the upper part. The African ratel has a distinct line around the body between the black and gray fur. This makes it look as though it were wearing a white-edged blanket. Its teeth are smaller and weaker than those of the Indian animal, but otherwise the two are almost entirely alike. The ratel eats insects, frogs, snakes, birds, and rats. It hunts by night and lives in a hollow tree by day. The ratel is a quick, nervous, active animal. It is fond of honey and bees, and is sometimes called the *honey badger*. The long, loose fur protects it from being stung.

Scientific Classification. Ratels belong to the weasel family, *Mustelidae*. The African ratel is classified as genus *Mellivora*, species *M. capensis;* the Indian ratel is *M. indica*.   E. LENDELL COCKRUM

RATHBONE, JUSTUS HENRY. See KNIGHTS OF PYTHIAS.

RATIO, *RAY shoh*, is another name for the quotient of two numbers of the same kind. The ratio of 8 to 4 is $\frac{8}{4}$ or 2. The ratio of 3 miles to 4 miles is $\frac{3}{4}$ or .75. The ratio of 2 miles to 5 gallons does not exist.

The ratio of a to b is $\frac{a}{b}$, that is $\frac{a}{b} = r$

Multiplying this equation by b gives $a = rb$

This is another definition of ratio: The ratio (r) of the two numbers is the number by which the second is multiplied to get the first.

Ratio is one of the most useful ideas in everyday mathematics, and it is used hundreds of times. Pi (π) is the ratio of circumference to diameter in a circle. Other ratios are specific gravity; the coefficient of expansion; the ratio of similarity; and the sine, cosine, and tangent in trigonometry.

Federal law says that the ratio of length to width for the official United States flag must be 1.9. This means that, no matter what the size of the flag, the length is 1.9 times the width.

Problems. If a flag is to be 5′ wide, how long should it be made? $5 \times 1.9 = ?$

A city gardener is to lay out a bed of ornamental plants in the form of a flag. It is 45.5′ wide. How long should the flag be?

If $L = 1.6\ W$, a flower bed 22′ long would be how wide?

$L = 1.6\ W$

$22 = 1.6\ W$. Now divide both sides by 1.6.

Some Facts About Ratio. There is no such thing as the ratio of two numbers unless the two numbers can be expressed in the same units. Such units might be inches, feet, meters, hours, or gallons.

A ratio is a *pure number* or an *abstract number*. That is, it has no units. The ratio of two numbers may be 5, but it cannot be 5 years.

An old method of expressing the ratio of a to b (or of expressing any fraction) is by means of a colon. This is written $a:b$ and is read a is to b. This method is no longer used for fractions, but it is still sometimes used for ratios.

Find, if possible, the ratios of:

(1) 12 to 6
(2) 6 to 12
(3) 7 miles to 18 miles
(4) 3 ft. to 5 in. (First change the feet to inches.)
(5) $3\frac{1}{2}$ days to 10 hours
(6) 144 ships to 18 ships
(7) 14 acres to 28 bushels
(8) 3 pints to 9 quarts
(9) 6 minutes to 20 seconds
(10) 18 feet to 9 yards.   HARRY C. BARBER

See also PERCENTAGE; PROPORTION.

RATION. See ARMY, UNITED STATES (A Typical Day); RATIONING.

RATIONALISM, *RASH un ul iz'm,* is an outlook that emphasizes human reason and its ability to answer basic questions. *Philosophical rationalism,* in the 1600's, stressed the power of reason as opposed to sense experience. René Descartes, Gottfried Leibniz, and Baruch Spinoza used deductive reasoning as the basis for their philosophical systems (see DEDUCTIVE METHOD). *Cultural rationalism,* in the 1700's, relied on reason rather than faith in creating a theory of man and his destiny. Voltaire and Thomas Paine led the movement. See also AGE OF REASON; PHILOSOPHY (The Tools of Philosophy; The Appeal to Reason).   JAMES COLLINS

RATIONING, *RAY shuhn ing* or *RASH uhn ing,* is a method of making sure that everyone receives his fair share of scarce goods, foods, or other items. Governments usually impose rationing only during emergencies, such as wars. During World War II, when supplies of almost every commodity grew scarce, the governments of most warring countries used rationing. Controls were severe in Great Britain, Russia, and other countries, and less strict in Canada and the U.S.

There are two primary reasons for rationing. First,

the government must take steps to conserve materials vital to its war effort, such as gasoline. Second, it must control the distribution of materials regarded as essential for a strong civilian economy or for good civilian morale, such as coffee. In both cases, rationed items are already in short supply or soon will be.

Rationing is directly related to price controls. Workers receive high wages during a war, and can afford items they might otherwise consider luxuries. If they can buy all the luxuries they want, they soon compete for scarce goods, driving prices rapidly upwards. The government sets legal limits on prices, and also sets legal limits on how much of a given item any consumer may buy, by rationing it.

How Rationing Works. There are two basic systems for rationing. In one, a civilian consumer proves to his local ration board that he really needs a particular item for work connected with the war effort. The board issues him a *certificate* to buy the item he needs. The board has only a limited number of these items available, and gives certificates on the basis of real need. If the man needs another item, he must apply to the board a second time, proving his need all over again. During World War II, ration boards used certificates for automobiles, tires, typewriters, and stoves.

The *coupon* system is used for items that consumers must buy again and again, such as foods, gasoline, and shoes. The ration board issues coupons to all consumers (or to all qualified consumers, such as automobile owners). The consumers then take their coupons with them when they shop, and surrender a certain number for each rationed item they buy. If they use up their coupons before the ration period ends, they cannot buy any more rationed items until the next period.

In World War II, rationed items in the United States included automobiles, bicycles, fuel oil, gasoline, kerosene, shoes, stoves, tires, typewriters, and many foods. Sugar was rationed longest, from May, 1942, to June, 1947. Most rationing ended in 1945.

See also BLACK MARKET; PRICE CONTROL; WORLD WAR II (Government Controls).

RATTAN, *ra TAN,* is a tough, stringy material. It comes from the reedy stems of different kinds of palms that grow in East India and Africa. These trees belong to the genus of palms known as *Calamus.* The stems of rattan palms sometimes grow to be several hundred feet long. The plants climb over other trees by means of little hooks on the leaves. In the countries where these palms grow, natives use the rattan stem to make ropes and mats. American and European countries import large amounts of the stems. Manufacturers use them to make umbrella handles, walking sticks, furniture, baskets, ship cables, and chair bottoms. Rattan is strong, bends easily, and lasts long. The finest grades come from the island of Borneo. Other good rattans grow in Burma, Ceylon, Malaysia, and Sumatra.

Workmen prepare the stems for shipment by cutting them into lengths of 5 to 20 feet. They then take the leaves and outer covering off the stems by pulling them through a notch in a tree or board. Some kinds of rattan palms have a fruit that can be eaten. The young shoots are eaten like vegetables.   ELIZABETH CHESLEY BAITY

See also BASKET WEAVING.

Interesting facts about RATTLESNAKES

General Biological Supply
The Rattlesnake's Backbone consists of about 200 ball-and-socket joints which make it extremely flexible.

Faubert, Fish and Wildlife Service
The Rattle on the tail consists of a set of loosely interlocking, horny segments.

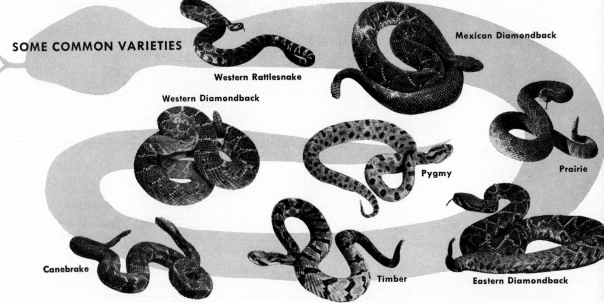

SOME COMMON VARIETIES

Western Rattlesnake

Western Diamondback

Mexican Diamondback

Pygmy

Prairie

Canebrake

Timber

Eastern Diamondback

Lee Passmore; N.Y. Zoological Society; Hugh S. Davis; Chicago Academy of Sciences; Fish and Wildlife Service; Harold M. Lambert; Zoological Society of Philadelphia.

RATTLESNAKE is any one of the poisonous American snakes with a rattle on the end of the tail. Rattlesnakes often give a warning sound with the rattle before they bite.

The rattlesnakes are classed among the pit vipers. Twenty-eight separate kinds of rattlesnakes live from southern Canada to Uruguay. By far the greatest number of rattlesnakes live in the dry region from the southwestern states of the United States through the Mexican highlands. One species is found over a large part of South America. Only one kind of rattlesnake lives in almost the whole of the northern United States west of the Mississippi Valley. A few other kinds appear in the valley and east of it.

It is easy to recognize a rattlesnake by its rattle, which is a set of horny pieces loosely joined together. It makes a clear sound when the snake shakes it. Many other snakes also have the habit of vibrating the tail. Certain harmless snakes, often mistaken for rattlesnakes, can make a sound with their tails in dry grass or leaves. But a careful observer can quickly tell whether a snake is a real rattler. The rattlesnake always lifts its tail when it sounds. The harmless snake must have its tail under something to make a noise.

There are large and small kinds of rattlesnakes. The diamondback rattler of the southeastern United States is the heaviest of all poisonous snakes, although not the longest. It gets its name because diamond-shaped blotches edged with yellow cover its body. Diamondbacks rarely grow more than 7 feet 4 inches long. A few other rattlers grow almost as large. Several small kinds of rattlers are ordinarily only 2 feet long when full grown. The horned rattlesnake, or sidewinder, found in desert regions, is one of these small rattlers. The ridge-nosed rattlesnake and the pygmy rattlesnake are even shorter than 2 feet.

The northern Pacific rattlesnake has young when it is 3 years old. It is thought that other kinds grow at the same rate. Naturalists know very little about their life span.

Many persons believe that it is possible to tell the age of a rattler by the number of segments, or "rattles," in its rattle. This is not true. Two to four new segments are added each year, one every time the skin is shed. But when about 10 segments accumulate on the end of its tail, they begin to fall off. The segments look like hollow rings, each partly fitting over the one behind. A young snake has a single small segment, and each new rattle is a little larger. Those which develop on a full-grown snake are all about the same size.

The Rattler's Forked Tongue Helps It Detect Odors.

Giant Diamondbacks Often Weigh 20 to 25 Pounds.

Rattler Skin Makes Fine Leather; the Flesh Is Eaten.

Most rattlesnakes eat birds and small mammals. A few also eat amphibians and reptiles. They destroy rodents and other harmful animals.

All rattlesnakes bear live young instead of laying eggs. The newborn snakes can take full care of themselves and give painful bites.

The larger rattlers rank among the most dangerous of snakes. They should be carefully avoided. They do not always rattle before striking.

The rattlesnake sends out poison through two long hollow teeth, or fangs, in its upper jaw. The poison forms in a pair of glands, one on each side of the jaw. The fangs can be folded back in the mouth when they are not in use. When an angry rattlesnake strikes, the fangs are erected and the mouth opened wide.

Scientific Classification. Rattlesnakes belong to the pit viper family, *Crotalinae*. The pygmy belongs to the genus *Sistrurus*. It is classified as *S. miliarius*. The ridge-nosed is in the genus *Crotalus*. It is *C. willardi*. The eastern diamondback is *C. adamanteus;* the sidewinder is *C. cerastes;* the northern Pacific is *C. viridis oreganus*. CLIFFORD H. POPE

See also SNAKE (color pictures: Eastern Diamondback, Timber Rattlesnake, The Mouth of a Pit Viper); SNAKE BITE; LIFE (table: Length of Life of Animals).

RATTLESNAKE PILOT. See COPPERHEAD.

RATTNER, ABRAHAM (1895-), is an American painter who is best known for works of a religious nature. His paintings are noted for their brilliant color, rich texture, and symbolism. They have been compared to stained-glass windows because of their glowing colors. Rattner often uses words and inscriptions in his works. He painted many familiar Biblical themes, including the Crucifixion and the Last Judgment. He also painted less familiar Biblical subjects, such as the Valley of Dry Bones. He developed personal symbolic themes that seem to speak directly to our time. For example, he painted a window cleaner removing dirt from a window. This is a symbol of the way God clears man's vision to enable man to see the brilliance and beauty of the divine. Rattner was born in Poughkeepsie, N.Y. ALLEN S. WELLER

RAUSCHENBERG, ROBERT (1925-), an American artist, was a founder of the pop art school. Many of his works include three-dimensional objects, such as stuffed birds and soda pop bottles. He calls these works *combine paintings*, or *combines*. His best-known combines are *Monogram* and *Bed*. The central figure of *Monogram* is a stuffed Angora goat with an automobile tire around its middle. *Bed* is a quilt and pillow splashed with oil paint. Rauschenberg is also known for his lithographs. He attracted attention in 1953 when he erased a draw-

Collection of Mr. and Mrs. Frank Titelman, Altoona, Pa.

Rauschenberg's *Tracer* reproduces unrelated realistic images with oil paint and the silk-screen printing process to achieve an unusual effect. The artist completed the picture in 1963.

145

RAUWOLFIA SERPENTINA

ing by artist Willem de Kooning and entitled it *Erased de Kooning Drawing*. Rauschenberg was born in Port Arthur, Tex. See also POP ART. ALLEN S. WELLER

RAUWOLFIA SERPENTINA is a snakeroot shrub found in India and Southeast Asia (see SNAKEROOT). The plant commonly is known as *Rauwolfia*. An extract from the juices of the plant, called *reserpine*, calms emotionally disturbed persons and makes them more responsive to treatment. Rauwolfia also is used to treat *hypertension* (high blood pressure). The root has been used as a medicine in India for hundreds of years.

RAVEL, *ruh VEHL,* **MAURICE** (1875-1937), was a French composer. He used a variety of musical forms, and his works show great precision and clarity. Some critics classify Ravel, along with the French composer Claude Debussy, as an impressionist. But Ravel relied heavily on the strong melodies and rich textures of classical music of the 1800's. Debussy experimented more in form and style.

Ravel was born in the seacoast town of Ciboure, near France's southwestern border with Spain. His works, including the comic opera *The Spanish Hour* (1911) and the music for the ballet *Bolero* (1928), reflect a Spanish influence. He wrote most of his compositions before World War I (1914-1918).

Ravel's major works include *String Quartet in F* (1903); *Shéhérezade* (1903), a group of songs; two piano works, *Mirrors* (1905) and *Gaspard de la Nuit* (1908); and a ballet, *Daphnis and Chloe* (1912). Most critics consider *Daphnis and Chloe*, with its expert orchestration and graceful melodies, to be Ravel's masterpiece.

Ravel's most notable compositions after World War I include the orchestral piece *La Valse* (1920) and *Bolero*. During the 1920's, Ravel toured the United States and Europe, conducting his own works and performing them on the piano. JOSEPH BLOCH

RAVEN is a large black bird that belongs to the same family as the crow. It lives in all parts of the Northern Hemisphere, from Greenland and Alaska on the north to Guatemala on the south.

Fish and Wildlife Service

The Raven Is a Larger Cousin of the Crow. Ravens were once common, but many have been killed by traps for fur-bearing animals and by poisoned wolf bait.

The raven may sometimes grow to be 26 inches long, and its wings may spread as wide as 3 feet. Its feathers have a slight purple luster, and there is often a touch of dull green on the belly. The feathers at the neck are usually dull gray at the base.

The raven usually builds its nest on cliffs, though some ravens build nests in trees. The nest is usually built in the late winter. Ravens make their nests of sticks and line them with bark, moss, cattle hair, wool, seaweed, grasses, or rabbit fur. The female usually lays from three to eight eggs of a light-greenish color with many brown spots. Ravens eat a wide variety of food. They may eat dead fish and frogs, mussels, grasshoppers, crickets, worms, clams, eggs of waterfowl, and young birds.

Three kinds of ravens live in North America: the *American raven*, the *northern raven*, and the *white-necked raven*. The American raven, which is the most common, lives in the western United States from the Rocky Mountains to the Pacific Coast, and in Canada. The northern raven resembles the American raven, except that it is larger and its bill is longer and heavier. It lives in Alaska, Greenland, and as far south as Washington. It has also been found in northern Michigan, New York, and Maine, and in the mountains of South Carolina. The white-necked raven lives from Texas to southern California, and from western Kansas to Mexico.

The black luster of the raven's feathers has given the word *raven* a special meaning. It is used to describe the color of hair that has a black luster, as in "raven hair." The raven is one of the first birds mentioned in early history and mythology. It is mentioned in the Bible as the first bird sent out from Noah's Ark.

Scientific Classification. Ravens belong to the crow family, *Corvidae*. The American raven is classified as genus *Corvus*, species *C. corax*, variety *sinuatus*. The northern raven is *C. corax principalis*, and the white-necked raven is *C. cryptoleucus*. HERBERT FRIEDMANN

See also BIRD (Interesting Facts [Longest-Lived]).

RAVENNA, *ruh VEN uh* (pop. 120,929; alt. 39 ft.), is a historic city in northern Italy, famous for its art treasures and architecture. It is also an agricultural and manufacturing center. A 6-mile canal connects it with the Adriatic Sea (see ITALY [political map]).

Ravenna's Mausoleum of Galla Placidia, built about A.D. 440, is one of the oldest examples of early Christian architecture. It has some of the most beautiful mosaics in Ravenna. The famous churches of San Vitale, Sant' Apollinare, and Sant' Apollinare in Classe, built in the 500's, also contain beautiful mosaics.

Ravenna served as the capital of the West Roman Empire from about 402 until the barbarian leader Odoacer seized the empire in 476. Then Theodoric, king of the Ostrogoths, murdered him and took over the city. Ravenna was part of the Byzantine Empire from about 540 until the 700's. It was one of the Papal States for many years, and in 1860 it became part of the kingdom of Italy.

See also ARCHITECTURE (pictures: Sant' Apollinare in Classe); BYZANTINE ART (pictures).

RAW MATERIALS are those from which finished articles are made. Raw materials are chiefly natural resources, but also include some synthetic chemicals.

Related Articles. See the articles on specific raw materials, such as COTTON; LUMBER. See also NATURAL RESOURCES; WORLD WAR II (Strategic Raw Materials).

RAWALPINDI, *RAH wul PIN dee* (pop. 340,175; alt. 1,726 ft.), served as the capital of Pakistan from 1960 until the mid-1960's, when Islamabad became the capital. Rawalpindi lies in northern Pakistan (see PAKISTAN [map]). The city has an oil refinery, steel mills, and furniture and chemical factories.

RAWLINGS, MARJORIE KINNAN (1896-1953), an American novelist, wrote books describing life in the Florida backwoods. She worked as a journalist but gave it up in 1928 to settle on a farm at Cross Creek, Fla. Her comfortless life there gave her the background for her novels. She became famous for sympathetic stories of children and animals. One of these stories, *The Yearling*, won a Pulitzer prize in 1939. Her other books include *South Moon Under* (1933), *Golden Apples* (1935), *When the Whippoorwill* (1940), *Cross Creek* (1942), *Cross Creek Cookery* (1942), and *The Sojourner* (1953).

Marjorie Kinnan Rawlings

Marjorie Kinnan was born in Washington, D.C., and graduated from the University of Wisconsin. She was married to Charles Rawlings. GEORGE J. BECKER

RAWLINSON, SIR HENRY. See ARCHAEOLOGY (The 1800's).

RAY. See SKATE; STING RAY; TORPEDO (fish).

RAY, JAMES EARL. See KING, MARTIN LUTHER, JR.

RAYBURN, SAM (1882-1961), served longer as speaker of the United States House of Representatives than any other man. He presided over the House from 1940 to 1947, from 1949 to 1953, and from 1955 until his death —almost 17 years. He also served 49 consecutive years as a member of the House of Representatives.

Rayburn was born in Roane County, Tenn. His full name was Samuel Taliaferro Rayburn. When Rayburn was 5, he moved to Texas with his family. He worked his way through

Wide World
Sam Rayburn

East Texas College and studied law at the University of Texas. Later, he practiced law before turning to national politics. He was elected to Congress in 1912 and quickly established himself as a hard worker with considerable ability. Rayburn soon became a Democratic leader in Congress, although he seldom made speeches. He presided over the 1952 and the 1956 national conventions for the Democratic Party. F. JAY TAYLOR

RAYLEIGH, BARON. See NOBEL PRIZES (table [1904]).

RAYMOND, HENRY JARVIS (1820-1869), brought political independence and moderation to American journalism through the newspaper he and two associates founded, *The New York Times*. He had two careers, one in journalism, the other in politics. As a journalist, he worked as an assistant to Horace Greeley, editor of the *New York Tribune*. After Raymond helped found the *Times*, they became political and journalistic rivals. The *Times* avoided sensationalism and concentrated on facts, and it soon became a leading newspaper. Raymond held public offices in New York, and served a term as a Republican member of Congress from 1865 to 1867. But he supported President Andrew Johnson's Reconstruction policies, and soon lost political power. Raymond was born near Lima, N.Y. I. W. COLE

RAYON, *RAY on*, is a man-made fiber produced from wood pulp or cotton linters. It is widely used to make industrial materials and clothing. Rayon fabrics can be manufactured warm or cool, shiny or dull, and elaborate or plain.

How Rayon Is Made. Rayon is manufactured from the cellulose fiber of wood pulp or cotton (see CELLULOSE). Various chemical processes reduce the cellulose to a thick liquid from which the rayon threads are made. The liquid cellulose is then forced through extremely small openings in devices called *spinnerettes* to form *filaments*, or tiny threads. The filaments are twisted together to form rayon yarn. The three chief methods for making rayon are (1) the viscose process, (2) the cuprammonium process, and (3) the acetate process.

The Viscose Process is the usual method of changing wood or cotton cellulose into rayon. This process begins by soaking sheets of white pulp in a weak solution of sodium hydroxide. After the soaked sheets are removed from the solution, they are put through rollers that squeeze out the excess solution. The sheets of cellulose then pass through shredding machines where they are made into fine pieces called *crumbs*. The crumbs are aged at high temperatures for about a day. Aging helps determine what type of viscose yarn will be produced.

After aging, the crumbs are treated with carbon disulfide, which turns them to *cellulose xanthate*, a deeporange substance. Then the crumbs are dissolved in a weak solution of sodium hydroxide. This turns the mixture to a thick, molasseslike solution, which "ripens" for four or five days at a low temperature.

When the solution has ripened, it is forced by compressed air into spinning frames that contain the spinnerettes. Small pumps force the solution through the spinnerettes to form filaments.

The Cuprammonium Process is a method of dissolving cotton cellulose in a copper-ammonia solution. A special spinning process produces yarns of ultrafine *denier*, or weight (see DENIER). This process produces about 5 per cent of the world's rayon.

The Acetate Process changes the properties of cellulose by treating it in acetic anhydride and acetic acid, with sulfuric acid. This treatment produces *cellulose acetate*, which is then dissolved in acetone to form a syruplike solution.

Spinning. All rayon-making centers about the spinnerette, which contains a plate with tiny holes. Pumps force the cellulose through these holes. The threadlike cellulose then flows into a chemical bath that hardens the liquid into threads. To produce cottonlike yarns, the threads are cut into short lengths, then combed and

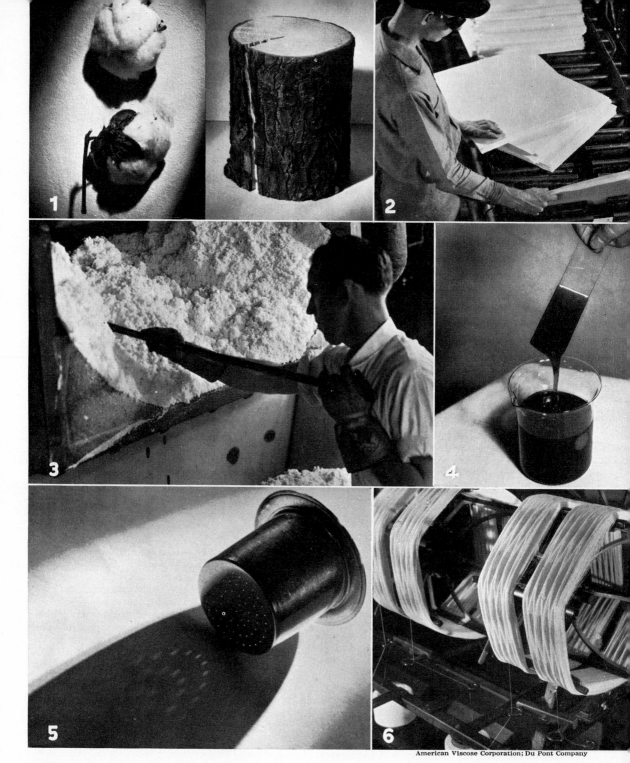

American Viscose Corporation; Du Pont Company

THE MANUFACTURE OF RAYON

In the Process of Making Rayon, (1) cotton bolls and spruce logs are reduced to a pulp from which cellulose is obtained. (2) When the cellulose has been produced it is formed into sheets. These are treated in sodium hydroxide. (3) The sheets are shredded after this chemical treatment. They come from the shredding machine in crumb form. (4) Further chemical treatment turns the cellulose crumbs into a viscose liquid about as thick as molasses. (5) Forcing this viscose through a spinnerette is the next step. The canlike spinnerette has many tiny holes in one end, and the viscose forms fine strands, or filaments, as it squirts out of them. (6) The numerous filaments are gathered together by a machine as they come from the spinnerette, and twisted into a single thread. The thread is wound into skeins on reels, from which it is unwound when it is woven into various rayon fabrics.

twisted. The yarns are woven into fabrics that look like cotton, wool, or spun silk.

Properties of Rayon. Viscose and cuprammonium rayons have much the same chemical properties. Both dye easily, and both lose their strength when wet. They regain their original strength when dry. Acetate rayon reacts to heat, and may easily be burned when ironing. Boiling water takes out its luster. But acetate rayon has special qualities, such as fineness, texture, and dyeability, that make it desirable. It can also be treated so the material has permanent pleats.

History. In 1884, the French inventor and industrialist Hilaire Chardonnet patented the first practical synthetic fiber (see CHARDONNET, HILAIRE). He called it *artificial silk.* The fiber was first manufactured in the United States in 1910. In 1924, it was named *rayon,* the *ray* indicating the sheen of the fiber, and the *on* showing that it was a cottonlike fiber.

Rayon ranks second only to cotton as the most widely used fiber. It is used in knit and woven fabrics for clothing, upholstery, drapery, and decorating fabrics. Large amounts of rayon are also used to make cord for automobile tires.　　　　　　　　　　　CHARLES H. RUTLEDGE

See also FIBER (Synthetic Fibers); PIQUÉ; VELOUR.

RAZOR, *RAY zer,* is a cutting instrument used to remove hair from the skin. The men of ancient Egypt used razors, because they liked clean-shaven faces better than bearded ones. Julius Caesar and many men of his time were entirely clean shaven.

Safety Razors have short rectangular blades. Their edges are protected by metal or plastic holders. This makes it almost impossible for a person to cut himself deeply while shaving. Blades for safety razors cost little. As the cutting edge becomes dull, the old blade is thrown away and replaced by a new one.

Stainless steel blades, permitting more shaves than earlier blades, became popular in the early 1960's. Stainless steel blades with chromium or platinum edges were introduced in the late 1960's. They gave even more shaves than a normal stainless steel blade.

Straight-Edged Razors have specially tempered steel blades about 3 or 4 inches long. The blade has a rounded back and slopes to a fine edge. It is usually fastened by a rivet to a handle of two pieces of metal, ivory, or bone. The blade rests in the handle when not in use. It closes like a springless knife. The best blades were formerly made in Sheffield, England, but a number of factories in the United States now make blades as fine as the best Sheffield razors.

A good straight razor will last a long time if given good care. The razor wears well if the shaver soaks his face with lather before shaving. During shaving, the blade cuts better if guided against the direction in which the hair grows. When a person shaves, the edge of the blade actually bends, causing it to become dull. The cutting edge should be smoothed with a leather strop before it is used. The blade must be *honed* (sharpened) regularly.

Electric Razors are widely used. These little machines are powered by small electric motors. The cutting head passes over the skin and clips the hair. The head may become dull after continued use, and may need either sharpening or replacing. The heads of many electric shavers can be adjusted for heavy, medium, or light beards.

Some shavers have built-in auxiliary clippers, such as a barber's clippers. They are used to trim long hairs and sideburns. Most cutting heads must be cleaned from time to time.　　　　　　　　　WALTER R. WILLIAMS, JR.

RCA CORPORATION is a leading electronics and communications company. Its many products include television sets, television cameras, phonographs, phonograph records, tape recorders, and computers and other data processing and high-speed communication equipment.

RCA is also an important producer of electronic parts, such as tubes, circuits, and transistors. The company played a major role in the development of black-and-white and color television. Its contributions to the United States space program include the design

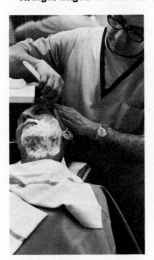

WORLD BOOK photos

People Use Three Main Kinds of Razors. A straight-edged razor, *left,* is used by most barbers. It must be handled skillfully to avoid cuts. A safety razor, *center,* has a shielded blade and can easily be loaded with a blade. Many men and women think an electric razor, *right,* is the easiest kind to use.

and construction of the *Tiros* weather satellites. The company is a major industrial contractor to the U.S. Department of Defense.

RCA owns the National Broadcasting Company (NBC) radio and television networks (see NATIONAL BROADCASTING COMPANY). It also owns Random House, Inc., a book publishing firm, and Hertz Corporation, an automobile and truck rental company.

Several divisions of RCA carry out special functions. *The RCA David Sarnoff Research Center* works to create new products and to improve existing ones. *RCA Communications, Inc.*, operates world-wide radio and leased communication channel services. *The RCA Service Company* operates and maintains electronics systems for the federal government, including the Ballistic Missile Early Warning System and Cape Kennedy tracking system. It also maintains computer systems for industry and services electronic instruments in homes. *The RCA Graphic Systems Division* develops electronic equipment that is used in the printing industry. *The RCA International Division* handles the corporation's overseas operations.

RCA was founded in 1919 as the Radio Corporation of America. It has headquarters in New York City. For its sales, assets, and number of employees, see MANUFACTURING (table: 100 Leading U.S. Manufacturers).

Critically reviewed by the RCA CORPORATION

See also SARNOFF, DAVID; ZWORYKIN, VLADIMIR K.

RDX is a powerful explosive also known as *cyclonite* and *hexogen*. During World War II, RDX was widely used as the chief explosive charge in bombs. It is still an important military explosive, and also has wide use in detonators and fuses. Manufacturers make RDX by the action of nitric acid on hexamethylene-tetramine, a product of formaldehyde and ammonia. When RDX is mixed with liquid TNT, an explosive called *composition B* is formed. This explosive is more powerful than TNT, and is replacing it in artillery shells. See also PLASTIC BOMB.   JULIUS ROTH

RE, *ray*, or **RA**, was the ancient Egyptian god of the sun. The word *re* means *sun* in the Egyptian language. Re was "the creator of all that is and is not yet, the father of fathers and the mother of mothers." As Osiris was the god of the dead, Re was the god of the living. The pharaohs, Egyptian rulers, considered themselves sons of Re. His main center of worship was at Heliopolis, the Sun City. Re was represented either in human form or with the head of a falcon and a human body. He carried the sun disk as his symbol.

Worship of Re reached its height during the reign of Amenhotep IV in the 1300's B.C. Amenhotep believed that Re was the god of the whole world, and the only god. This may be considered the beginning of *monotheism* (worship of only one god) in the ancient Near East. Amenhotep worshiped the sun-god in the form of *aton* (the sun disk), and changed his own name to Akhenaton (see AKHENATON). But when he died, the exclusive worship of the sun-god was abandoned.   I. J. GELB

See also EGYPT, ANCIENT (Religion).

REA. See RURAL ELECTRIFICATION ADMINISTRATION.

REA EXPRESS. See RAILWAY EXPRESS AGENCY.

REACTION, in physics. See JET PROPULSION (The Principle).

REACTION, CHEMICAL. See CHEMISTRY (Chemical Reactions).

REACTIONARY. See CONSERVATISM.

REACTOR, ATOMIC. See ATOMIC REACTOR.

READ, GEORGE (1733-1798), was a signer of the Declaration of Independence from Delaware. He served in the Continental Congress from 1774 to 1777 and voted at first against independence. During the Revolutionary War, he served for a time as president of Delaware. He was a member of the federal Constitutional Convention, U.S. Senator from 1789 to 1793, and chief justice of Delaware from 1793 to his death. Read was born at North East, Md.   RICHARD B. MORRIS

READE, CHARLES (1814-1884), was an English novelist and playwright. His *The Cloister and the Hearth* (1861) has been called by some critics the greatest historical novel in English. It is an exciting love story which also gives a good picture of life in the 1400's.

Many of Reade's 23 other novels attack social abuses of his day. He criticized harsh treatment of the insane in *Hard Cash* (1863) and British trade unions in *Put Yourself in His Place* (1870). *It's Never too Late to Mend* (1856) exposed terrible prison conditions. Reade wrote 20 plays. Several are adaptations of his novels.

Reade kept large files of clippings, and of his own notes about what he saw. He referred to these when writing and thus was able to produce highly realistic accounts of life in the 1800's.

Reade was born at Ipsden, Oxfordshire. He attended Oxford University and became a lawyer. He never practiced law, however.   JAMES DOUGLAS MERRITT

READERS' GUIDE. See LIBRARY (Using Magazines and Newspapers; picture).

READINESS. See HANDWRITING (Writing Readiness); LEARNING (Efficient Learning); READING (When Should Children Learn to Read?).

READING, *RED ing*, Pa. (pop. 87,643; met. area 296,382; alt. 265 ft.), lies on the Schuylkill River in southeastern Pennsylvania, 55 miles from Philadelphia (see PENNSYLVANIA [political map]). It is in the heart of the Pennsylvania Dutch region, surrounded by fertile valleys noted for fruit-growing and dairy farming.

While Reading is known as a hosiery-manufacturing center, it is also outstanding for the production of clothing, builders' hardware, optical goods, pretzels, paints, brick, candy, specialty steels, automobile frames, railroad equipment, textile machinery, and foundry products. Four out of 10 industrial workers in Reading work in the metal or textile industries.

The Schuylkill River and the Schuylkill Canal played an important role in the development of transportation for this center. Today the city is the hub of the Reading Railroad. Three major airlines provide air transportation. The city is served by an extensive system of highways, including the Pennsylvania Turnpike.

Reading was laid out in 1748 under the direction of two sons of William Penn. It was named for Reading, England, the home of some of its early settlers. During the Revolutionary War, military supplies for the Continental Army were stored in Reading. The city also served as a hospital center and prison camp. Reading became a borough in 1783 and a city in 1847. It has a commission form of government and is the seat of Berks County. Albright and Alvernia colleges are located in Reading.   S. K. STEVENS

Carol Ann Bales; WORLD BOOK photo

Reading Opens the Door to Learning and Enjoyment. Through reading, we can share the knowledge and the lives of people of today and the past throughout the world.

READING is the act of interpreting printed and written words. It is a basic tool of education and one of the most important skills in everyday life. We live in a world of printed words. Through reading we acquire new ideas, obtain needed information, add to our personal pleasure, and broaden our interests. All these achievements can lead to a happier, more successful life.

The average adult in a civilized country reads hundreds or even thousands of words every day. He may not look at a single book, newspaper, or magazine to do this. In addition to his mail, he reads street signs, traffic directions, advertisements on billboards, package labels, television commercials, and many other things with words that influence his life in one way or another. The ease and skill with which he is able to read all these words help him develop pride and self-confidence.

The Importance of Reading

High school and college students study for examinations by reading the notes they have taken in class. Doctors read professional journals so they can use the latest medical knowledge in treating their patients. Housewives read cookbooks before trying new recipes. Factory workers read union contracts to be sure they understand their job rights.

But people do not read only in school and at work. There are many other uses of this vital skill that provide continuous self-improvement and enjoyment.

In School. All the subjects of elementary school—arithmetic, social studies, spelling, and others—depend on the student's ability to read. In high school and college, a high level of competence in reading becomes even more important. Here, students are required to

make regular use of library books, current periodicals, and professional journals. Unless a person knows how to read quickly, easily, and accurately, he will be seriously handicapped in school.

On the Job. A person's ability to read has a direct bearing not only on his educational goals, but also on his choice of a career. In addition, good reading habits are an asset in almost every type of work. Many persons advance to more important and better-paying positions by acquiring additional knowledge and skills through reading. The number of semiskilled, skilled, and professional occupations that require high reading ability has increased rapidly during recent years. Today, a person who cannot read is virtually unemployable.

For Information. Reading is a continuous source of inspiration and pleasure. Books and other printed materials provide knowledge that is helpful in various ways. Many persons read to learn more about their special fields of interest, such as current events, European history, painting, flowers, philosophy, physics, or American Indians. A man who plans to build a garage might read a do-it-yourself manual. A farm girl with a pet calf wants to read all she can about the best way to raise it so she can enter it in a livestock show.

For Recreation. Reading for fun becomes more important as new labor-saving devices at home and in industry create more leisure time. The world of books offers endless hours of pleasant and varied enjoyment

Henry A. Bamman, the contributor of this article, is Professor of Education at Sacramento State College and co-author of Improving Reading Ability: A Manual for College Students.

Reading Plays an Important Part in Almost Everything We Do. At home, reading provides pleasure and relaxation. Almost all professions and jobs require the ability to read quickly and intelligently. On the street, reading helps us find our way and plays an important part in traffic safety. In fact, modern life could not exist without the printed word and the ability to read it.

Illustration courtesy of Standard Oil Co. of California

for the person who reads easily and swiftly. Reading about different lands can provide interesting armchair journeys to all parts of the world. Recreational reading often includes reading for information. But the most popular books for adult reading are travel and adventure stories, romances, and mystery and detective stories. The classics, biographies, and historical novels have a somewhat smaller audience of readers.

World Literacy. The way of life of any nation is influenced by the percentage of its people that can read. Yet only about 66 per cent of the world's population over the age of 15 can read and write.

About 99 per cent of all Canadians more than 15 years old are literate. About 99 per cent of all United States citizens over 14 can read and write. About the same percentage of all Russians between the ages of 9 and 49 can read and write.

More than 800 million persons over the age of 15 throughout the world cannot read and write. The regions with the greatest percentages of illiterate people include Africa, Asia, and Latin America.

The world illiteracy rate, however, is decreasing. In Latin America, for example, this rate dropped from about 32 per cent in 1960 to about 23 per cent in 1970. See ILLITERACY (map: Illiteracy Rate).

Kinds of Reading

A good reader uses many different patterns of reading and study. Each involves the use of a variety of skills and attitudes. The pattern used depends upon the type and complexity of the reading material, the purpose for reading, and the reader's familiarity with the kind of ideas expressed. For example, a different pattern would be used for reading a novel than for reading an electrician's manual to learn how to install a new fuse box.

The Reader's Purpose plays an important part in determining the kind of reading he does. Different persons may read the same book in different ways, because their purposes vary. The reader establishes his purposes by thinking and by asking questions about what he plans to read. Comprehension and speed vary according to the reader's purpose.

Survey Reading. Once a person has determined his purpose for reading, he should skim or scan the article, story, or textbook assignment to preview the ideas presented. This initial scanning, sometimes called a survey, provides an overview that will aid in interpretation when he reads more thoroughly. The reader also decides what he should cover thoroughly, what he may read hurriedly if at all, and what he can put aside and read at a later date. Many business executives must learn to survey what they have to read, because they have no time to cover in detail everything that comes to them.

Study-Type Reading involves a number of procedures. The reader should ask himself several questions about the material while skimming it. A word in the title of an article, a key word or phrase in the text, or a summary sentence may help him formulate thought-provoking questions. Then he reads to answer these questions. A person should read for central thoughts, then for significant details. Finally, he reconstructs the meaning to serve the purpose that originally led him to read the material.

Some readers grasp only the central thoughts and miss the details. Others examine only the details and miss the central thoughts. A good reader recognizes the author's plan of organization and reads both for significant ideas and details. He determines which ideas and details are worth remembering. He may scan examples and restatements but read carefully only those things that he regards as necessary to his understanding.

Essential Aspects of Reading

Learning to read can be an exciting experience, and it need not be difficult. But reading is not a simple skill that is learned once and for all. It involves a variety of steps that can always be improved, regardless of a person's age. As revealed through careful research, reading is a four-step process involving: (1) perception, (2) comprehension, (3) reaction, and (4) application or use. These occur more or less simultaneously in the act of reading.

Perception, or the recognition of the meaning and pronunciation of printed symbols, is the first step in reading. Through the use of word-attack skills, students can recognize many words correctly. Poor recognition ability may cause a person to read incorrectly. For example, he may read the word *window* as *widow*. See PERCEPTION (Factors Affecting Perception).

Comprehension is a person's ability to grasp the meaning of what he reads. His comprehension depends on his ability to recognize the uses of words and their relationship to one another. For example, the word *run* has many uses and meanings. *The batter drove in a* run. *Some people* run *to bargain sales. We try not to* run *out of money. She has a* run *in her hose.* When a person perceives words with ease, relates them to one another, and attaches meaning to them accurately, he is capable of comprehending what he reads. Comprehension includes recognizing and understanding main ideas and related details. A good reader recognizes that many ideas are implied and that he must "read between the lines" to get the full meaning.

Reaction in reading takes many forms. A person may feel agreement, doubt, enjoyment, or sorrow as he reads. He may reject what he reads as being impractical or un-

true. Or he may find beauty and pleasure in a story. A good reader's feelings, attitudes, or understandings are affected by what he reads as he reacts to the writer's ideas. Such readers often raise questions about the ideas expressed in articles or stories.

Application occurs as the information in the reading material fuses with the reader's previous experiences and corrects misunderstandings, provides new insights, broadens interests, or helps solve problems. For example, reading a magazine article may help a reader fix a broken window or figure out his income tax. Or the reading of a book may even change his entire philosophy of life.

Eye Movement. The eye begins the total reading process. The stimulus from the written page is carried through the eye to the brain, where recognition may or may not occur. Reading involves eye movements. A photographic camera can be used to record eye movements in reading. Such records help determine how rapidly a reader recognizes words or groups of words. As a person reads a printed page from left to right, his eyes alternately pause and move to the right. The number of words the reader sees at a *fixation* (pause) determines the extent of his eye span, or span of recognition. The wider the span of recognition, the more the reader will recognize at each pause.

The amount recognized at each fixation varies with the kind and difficulty of the material read. A poor reader pauses on every word, sometimes refixating on it two or three times. A good reader reads with fewer pauses, grasping larger phrases or complete ideas at each fixation.

Sometimes even a good reader rereads what he has already read. He looks backward to reread a word, phrase, or sentence. Such backward movements of the eyes are called *regressions*. At times, a good reader's eyes will move far ahead to clarify a doubtful point.

Well-developed eye movements also help in skimming material. The good reader is unaware of his eye movements. His mind is absorbed with the meaning of what he is reading, and he never realizes that his eyes move and pause as he reads.

When Should Children Learn to Read?

A person's readiness to learn how to read depends upon many factors. These factors include his mental maturity, personality development, previous experiences, emotional stability, and oral-language development. *Reading readiness* varies greatly among individuals. Not all children can start learning to read at the age of 6. On the other hand, many children have rewarding reading experiences by the time they are halfway through the first grade. Some children begin reading before entering first grade. Others may not be ready for reading until the end of first grade or even later.

Help at Home. Parents can help children develop reading readiness by providing them with simple, well-illustrated picturebooks. Parents should read good stories, books, and poems to their children. This reading must be on a level that the youngsters can understand and appreciate. Parents also must consider the maturity and interests of their children when selecting stories and books. Parents often read aloud what they enjoy, and fail to recognize that children may have strong likes and dislikes that are different. A youngster's questions about letters or sounds and words should be answered simply but accurately. Family discussions of the stories and books encourage further interest in reading at all ages. A child who has few words in his speaking and listening vocabularies when he enters school has a poor chance of learning to read well.

Help at School. School activities that develop reading readiness include reading to children, telling them stories, discussing experiences, providing new experiences, offering them many opportunities to express themselves orally, and writing down simple stories they dictate. Reading programs in the early elementary grades stress basic skills essential to developing independence in recognizing and understanding new words.

As children acquire small sight vocabularies, they learn simple skills of comprehension. They develop their ability to use reading skills with increasing effectiveness all through elementary and high school.

Word Recognition

Beginning readers learn various skills that are useful in recognizing words. These word-attack skills relate to (1) the forms of words, (2) context clues, (3) the use of phonics, (4) structural analysis, and (5) the use of the dictionary.

Sight Words. Most children probably first learn to recognize words by sight. They learn to recognize the forms of many words from television, street signs and billboards, labels on objects, and simple books. The beginning reader must acquire a basic sight vocabulary, including such words as *the* and *are*. The mature reader recognizes most words by sight.

Context Clues often aid in learning the meanings of new words. Readers are helped by relating new words to other information or pictures in what they read. Look at the picture and the sentence below.

"The proud father pushed the perambulator through the park."

Suppose the reader does not know what *perambulator* means. The picture and the words *proud father* serve as context clues to help him interpret *perambulator* as *baby carriage*. Without a picture, the reader must use the clues in the words near the unknown word.

Phonics. As a child acquires a sight vocabulary, he begins to realize that some words begin in the same way. He may notice, for example, that *car* and *cat* begin with the letter *c*. Instruction in phonics, or phonetic analysis,

begins at this time. It is an essential part of most reading programs.

The word *phonics* comes from a Greek word meaning *sound*. Through the use of phonetic principles, youngsters learn to give the correct sound to each part of a word, and to recognize and pronounce words.

Most teachers start instruction in phonics by helping children learn the sounds of the consonants (all letters other than *a*, *e*, *i*, *o*, and *u*). These are learned as they appear at the beginning, the end, or in the middle of words. Later, children are introduced to consonant combinations, such as *ch* and *gr*, as in *chair* and *grade*. Phonics instruction also includes learning vowel principles that are useful in analyzing and sounding new words and syllables. See PHONICS.

Structural Analysis involves the recognition of *morphemes* (units of meaning) in words. In the word *walked*, the child recognizes the word *walk* and the suffix *ed*. The number of syllables in a word is determined by the number of vowel sounds. For example, the word *different* has three vowel sounds and three syllables: *dif-fer-ent*. The ability to identify prefixes, suffixes, and roots in words is essential to understanding the meaning of words with many syllables. The word *undoubtedly*, for example, has the prefix *un*, the root word *doubt*, and two suffixes, *ed* and *ly*.

Using a Dictionary. Many teachers begin dictionary instruction in the first year of reading instruction. Using a dictionary combines the use of many word-attack skills, including phonics and structural analysis. A dictionary also helps a child expand the meanings of words he knows. See DICTIONARY.

Effective readers understand and use a wide range of words. Such a command of words helps improve reading. Some youngsters recognize words when reading without knowing what they mean. These children are referred to as "word callers."

Growth in vocabulary depends greatly upon an attitude of curiosity about words—a sensitivity and interest in the various shades and degrees of meaning that words may have. As children acquire meaningful vocabularies, they learn new concepts and ideas. Children also enrich their understanding of words as they have broader experiences. See VOCABULARY.

Reading a variety of materials—fiction, biography, science, travel, adventure, and history—provides opportunities for vocabulary development. Good listening also helps, as do opportunities for discussion and written expression. The more formal study of word origins and word parts such as prefixes, suffixes, and roots, stimulates increased interest in vocabulary development.

Parents can promote vocabulary growth by arousing interest in the meanings of new words that children hear in everyday life. Discussing words at home, collecting words of various types, providing a variety of materials to be read for pleasure, and sometimes even dramatizing the meaning of words help a child develop a broader, more useful vocabulary.

Comprehension and Speed

Efficient reading means reading with both understanding and speed. Most children first learn to grasp the sense meaning of a passage, and then the broader meanings, such as those that are implied. Soon, however, they learn to react thoughtfully to the ideas read.

Suzanne Szasz

Learning to Recognize Words is basic to reading. The use of context clues, such as the cards held by the teacher, *left*, aid in word recognition. The young readers relate words to the pictures on the cards. By the use of phonics, *right*, children learn to recognize words with similar sounds, such as those on the chalkboard. This helps them pronounce unfamiliar words.

The critical reader continuously questions the accuracy and value of information given in reading materials. But not all that we read needs to be read critically. The reader's purposes determine the degree of comprehension needed for each type of reading. For example, children should learn to skim when looking for specific information in reference books. They read and understand more thoroughly a topic in which they are interested. The English philosopher Francis Bacon once said; "Some books are to be tasted, others to be swallowed, and some few to be chewed and digested."

Reading Flexibility should develop as a student progresses through school. The way he reads a novel, for example, will differ from the way he reads a science text. His reading rate will vary with the type of reading material and the purpose of reading. The average rate of reading for adults is probably about 250 WPM (words per minute). This rate might cover a range from 150 WPM for difficult material to 350 WPM for easy material. Although most people can probably learn to increase their reading rate, it is impossible to say how fast a person should read. The best reader is a flexible reader who adapts his rate to the material and purpose.

Silent Reading is a two-step process involving the recognition and interpretation of printed words. In achieving most purposes, it is more efficient than oral reading. The need for silent reading increases as children grow older. As a child gains skill in silent reading, he achieves greater independence in personal reading and study. Independence in reading should be achieved as early as possible. A person who fails to develop the ability to read with ease and understanding turns to other ways of gaining information, such as motion pictures, television, or other people. The ability to read rapidly for meaning is an important factor in the rate of learning.

Oral Reading involves not only the recognition of words and the grasp of meaning, but also the oral interpretation of the author's ideas to others. The purposes for oral reading vary. Sometimes children and adults read aloud for appreciation of literature, such as reading a poem or a play. Or they may read to entertain an audience. Certain professions, such as the ministry and teaching, require oral reading. The purpose and occasion for oral reading affects the rate at which a person reads. A scientist, for example, may read a report to share the results of an experiment with other scientists more rapidly than he would read it to an audience untrained in his field.

The characteristics of effective oral reading include

155

proper pronunciation of words, rhythmic phrasing, a rate adjusted to the reader's purposes, good voice pitch, and fitting expression. An understanding of grammatical structures and punctuation marks also helps.

Many schools provide opportunities for *choral reading*. This consists of rhythmic reading of literary selections in unison to develop confidence in reading aloud and to heighten appreciation.

The Teaching of Reading

The methods and materials used in teaching reading should be challenging and interesting at all stages. The techniques and materials used by the teacher must be adapted to the reader's stage of development if instruction is to be most effective. They must also challenge the learner's interest and stimulate a desire to succeed.

Through the years, reading has been an important part of the elementary school program. Today, the importance of reading instruction in high schools, colleges, and universities, and in adult education, has been recognized. Industrial and government training programs also stress the improvement of reading. An increasing number of high schools and colleges provide daily instruction to help students become better readers. Teachers at all levels of education recognize the need to teach the specialized reading and study habits essential in such fields as science, social studies, and mathematics. But, regardless of what type of program an elemen-

tary school adopts, learning to read must be a cooperative venture between home and school.

A Well-Balanced School Program includes at least four approaches to helping youngsters become more effective readers. First, the *basic reading program* provides instruction in all the basic reading attitudes and skills. This instruction ranges from teaching fundamentals of word recognition and vocabulary improvement to helping children learn how and when to use different kinds of reading patterns. Second, the teachers of the various school subjects teach the *reading and study skills* needed by students in these courses. The third approach stresses reading to pursue a hobby or to develop an interest. This includes providing youngsters with opportunities to engage in personal *reading for pleasure and fun*.

The fourth approach provides special help to children with reading difficulties. Children are often called *retarded readers* if tests show that their achievement is one or more years below their age or grade expectancy. A better standard is a year or more below what might be expected in terms of their capacity to learn. Many effective techniques can help retarded readers. Children receive this help in *remedial reading* programs. Reading specialists identify children's reading difficulties and provide suitable help for overcoming them. Reading experts and other specialists such as physicians, psychologists, psychiatrists, and social workers may help identify reading problems. The children receive special

UNESCO; H. Bristol

Reading Is a Worldwide Skill. Children and adults in every land study their country's language. Women in a village in India, *opposite page,* learn to read in adult-education classes held in the evening. This is part of their nation's battle against illiteracy. Children in Burma, *above,* study their reading lessons in an open-air school. They sit on the ground using low benches as desks.

assistance in improving word-attack skills, vocabulary, comprehension, and study skills.

Individualized Reading Programs. Many schools have developed reading programs that give special recognition to the wide range of children's reading abilities and needs. An individualized reading program adjusts instructions and personal reading materials to the reading achievement, interests, and ability of each student. The class has books and other reading material covering many grade levels and fields of interest. These *multilevel* materials are used for recreational reading as well as for studying subject matter. Each child reads as much and as rapidly as he can. Teacher guidance is provided as the need arises.

Basal Readers serve as the basic reading textbooks in most schools. These textbooks usually contain carefully planned reading lessons, including provision for word-attack skills, vocabulary development, and comprehension improvement. Teachers who use basal readers usually separate the children into several groups according to reading ability. In this way, instructional materials and techniques are adapted more closely to individual needs.

Developmental Reading. Reading instruction starts in elementary school. But growth and refinement in reading interests, attitudes, and skills continue in high school, college, and even adult life. Developmental reading includes both vertical and horizontal growth.

In *vertical growth,* a child attains higher degrees of skill in specific aspects of reading according to his ability to learn. He attacks words efficiently, learns more words, and reads with greater understanding. But enrichment must occur at each stage of development. This *horizontal growth* includes the broadening of interests, knowledge, and attitudes learned through reading at given levels of advancement.

Reading Interests of a child change as he grows. Children vary in their reading interests early in life. Even children in the same family do not always develop the same interests and tastes in reading. Children become less alike as they grow older. Some prefer animal stories, while others enjoy folklore. Reading interests that are more or less popular among most children include animals, pets, adventure, sports, aviation, fairy stories, children from other lands, folklore, biography, autobiography, and historical fiction. Teen-agers often read about possible occupations and about the lives of successful persons in those fields. They also may read stories about young people like themselves.

Children can broaden their interests in reading by coming in contact with a wide range of subjects. Extensive reading on a variety of topics and with different types of materials helps stimulate a desire to read. Reading aloud, dramatizations, discussions, reports, trips to libraries and bookstores, and buying books are effective ways of sparking interest in reading.

Many firsthand experiences also lead children to books and other printed materials. Reading about airplanes after riding in one makes a book much more exciting and interesting. Teachers and parents can read aloud to show the rhythm and beauty of a poem, or to reveal how the plot of a story unfolds. Children may never learn to appreciate certain types of reading matter if these are not read aloud to them.

Developing Reading Habits. The habit of reading books and stories should be developed early in a child's life. At school and at home, youngsters should be surrounded with exciting books to read. A first-grade teacher can often tell whether someone has read to a child at home, because the youngster usually comes to school eager to learn and read. He shows a curiosity about books, which other children lack. Teachers and parents alike can help develop interest in reading by encouraging the habit of visiting the school library and the children's and young adults' sections of the public library. Letting children buy their own books, giving books for presents, dramatizing stories, and encouraging children to join a book club or to watch television programs about books all encourage their interest in reading.

How to Become a Better Reader

Almost everyone would like to become a better reader. The ability to read well is usually essential in efforts at self-improvement. A person generally knows if he reads well or poorly. Even children are aware of good and poor reading habits. But before anyone can improve his reading, he must have the desire to read more effectively. As a rule, the quality and variety of what he reads have a greater effect upon reading improvement than has the amount he reads.

READING

Selecting Materials. To be a better reader, a person must read what he can understand. Some people read things that are too simple to challenge effort. Others try to achieve better reading habits by reading things that are too difficult. Reading a variety of interesting and challenging material that is not too hard but requires some effort will improve one's reading ability.

Vocabulary Improvement. Almost anyone can improve his vocabulary. Vocabulary building continues throughout a person's lifetime. One can enlarge his vocabulary by reading a wide range of different types of materials, by using the dictionary frequently, by listening to others speak, and by writing. Vocabulary growth is promoted by the study of word parts and word origins, along with keeping a notebook of unfamiliar words to learn. Without a good vocabulary, comprehension and speed of reading are limited.

Meanings and Ideas. Reading is an active adventure in which the reader tries to discover exact meanings, to acquire new concepts, and to evaluate the ideas of the writer. He can improve his reading by asking himself what he wants to get out of it, then striving to achieve that end. He can make an outline and take notes on his reading as a check on his understanding of important points. He should reread any sections that may be unclear. An effective reader often reviews his outline immediately, and goes over it later for better understanding and retention. Less emphasis on memorization and greater attention to organization of ideas and to evaluation improve retention. If students take notes and review them systematically, they help eliminate the need for cramming before examinations. If a person discusses what he has read with someone else, it helps him become a more penetrating reader. It also gives him the opportunity to clarify his understanding by expressing what he has read in his own words. Discussion

Reading Speed can be improved with the help of mechanical aids such as the reading accelerator. This device limits the time for reading each line and can be adjusted for different speeds.

Chicago Public Schools

also helps him to review new concepts and ideas.

Improving Reading Speed. Most persons can easily improve their reading speed. Reading simple stories at faster rates provides excellent practice for increased reading speed. So does reading to answer questions and to locate main ideas. Setting time limits, reading with a stop watch, and eliminating all other thoughts from the mind also aid more rapid reading.

Many devices and materials provide more formal means for improving reading speed. Special reading selections with controlled vocabulary, sentence length, and idea difficulty are used as aids in evaluating reading rate and comprehension. Such an evaluation or score may be placed on a graph. Subsequent readings of similar material provide evidence of the reader's progress. Plotting the results on a graph serves as excellent motivation for reading improvement. Mechanical accelerators may also be used. A timing device on the accelerator regulates the time spent on each line of words, and helps develop faster and more flexible reading. Another device known as a *tachistoscope* operates like a film projector. It flashes words or phrases on a screen for a fraction of a second to help readers develop larger eye spans and reduced fixation times.

These devices should be used only if a study of individual reading difficulties suggests that they will provide help where it is needed. A student must learn to transfer his skills from a reading device to books and other printed materials. Otherwise, he may only improve his ability to use the device.

Common Reading Difficulties

Individual reading difficulties should always be diagnosed by a trained specialist. A child with reading problems should have his sight and hearing checked immediately. But most reading problems do not result from poor eyesight or hearing.

Unfamiliarity with Reading. Before trying to teach children to read, a teacher should be sure they are familiar with books and reading. Some children come from homes where adults do little or no reading. Such children should have classroom experiences with books and oral reading before actual reading instruction.

Dislike of Reading. An individual's attitude toward reading may contribute more to reading difficulty or efficiency than any other factor. Some children learn to dislike reading because of a poor start in developing elementary reading skills. Youngsters should enjoy happy, successful experiences with their first reading attempts.

Word Substitution and Letter Reversal. Some children have trouble learning to recognize words. They read *there* for *these*, *list* for *last*, and *bed* for *bet*. Some children reverse letters in words and read *saw* for *was*. Poor visual and auditory discrimination abilities may account for many such errors. These difficulties should be recognized and corrected as early as possible.

Vocalization. Overreliance upon the sounds of letters in words or too much oral reading can cause children and adults to acquire the habit of moving their lips, muttering, or whispering words in silent reading. Vocalization may also involve movement of the larynx muscles or "saying" the words in the mind with little lip movement. In any case, vocalization usually decreases reading efficiency.

Word-by-Word Reading also indicates a serious reading problem. Both speed and comprehension suffer by reading each word as a unit. Children who are given books too difficult for them often develop this problem. They may read each word separately without understanding the thoughts presented by the author.

Regression. Poor concentration, missing an idea, or not understanding a word can cause a person to reread material. Such backward movement of the eyes occurs most frequently when the materials read are difficult. Sometimes poor eye movements will cause regression.

Where to Get Help. Many specialists can help children who have serious reading problems. These experts include remedial reading teachers, other reading specialists, psychologists, learning-disabilities specialists, and eye specialists.

Readability

A person's reading success is determined not only by how well he reads, but also by how readable the material is. Important factors that influence the readability of any printed material include (1) the average number of words in sentences, (2) the number of commonly understood words, (3) the average number of syllables in the words, (4) the number of long complex sentences, (5) the number of abstract ideas, and (6) the use of personal pronouns.

Textbooks, reference books, newspapers, and magazines can be written at predetermined grade levels by controlling these factors. A number of readability formulas have been developed for estimating the readability of passages. The approximate reading level of the people who will read the material must be known.

The control of readability presents certain problems that affect both the reader and the writer. The use of simple language may make it difficult to convey unusual concepts and ideas as accurately as more complex words do. Patterns of writing used to control sentence structure may lack variety and interest even though the sentences become more readable. The writer may lose some of his creativity in trying to adjust his writing to readability controls. But careful use of such controls can result in materials that are both readable and interesting.   HENRY A. BAMMAN

Related Articles in WORLD BOOK include:

Book	Guidance	Literature for
Book Week	Illiteracy	Children
Curriculum	Initial Teaching	Perception
Dictionary	Alphabet	Phonics
Education	Language	Study
Elementary School	Library	Teaching
Encyclopedia	Literature	Vocabulary

Outline

I. The Importance of Reading
  A. In School   D. For Recreation
  B. On the Job   E. World Literacy
  C. For Information

II. Kinds of Reading
  A. The Reader's Purpose
  B. Survey Reading
  C. Study-Type Reading

III. Essential Aspects of Reading
  A. Perception   D. Application
  B. Comprehension E. Eye Movement
  C. Reaction

IV. When Should Children Learn to Read?
  A. Help at Home   B. Help at School

V. Word Recognition
  A. Sight Words   D. Structural Analysis
  B. Context Clues   E. Using a Dictionary
  C. Phonics

VI. Comprehension and Speed
  A. Reading Flexibility   C. Oral Reading
  B. Silent Reading

VII. The Teaching of Reading
  A. A Well-Balanced School D. Developmental
       Program   Reading
  B. Individualized Reading E. Reading Interests
       Programs   F. Developing
  C. Basal Readers   Reading Habits

VIII. How to Become a Better Reader
  A. Selecting Materials
  B. Vocabulary Improvement
  C. Meanings and Ideas
  D. Improving Reading Speed

IX. Common Reading Difficulties
  A. Unfamiliarity with   D. Vocalization
      Reading   E. Word-by-Word
  B. Dislike of Reading   Reading
  C. Word Substitution and F. Regression
      Letter Reversal   G. Where to Get Help

X. Readability

Questions

What four steps are involved in reading?
What factors contribute to a child's readiness for reading?
What are individualized reading programs? Basal readers?
How can adults improve their reading speed?
What important factors contribute to readability?
What common reading difficulties are found among children?
What are the four aspects of a well-balanced school reading program?
How are accelerators and the tachistoscope used for improving reading ability?

Books to Read

DURKIN, DOLORES. *Teaching Them to Read*. Allyn & Bacon, 1970. A practical guide for both teachers and parents, with many suggestions for helping children learn to read.

GRAY, WILLIAM S. *On Their Own in Reading: How to Give Children Independence in Analyzing New Words*. Rev. ed. Scott, Foresman, 1960. A thorough treatment of word perception as a part of the total reading process.

HARRIS, ALBERT J. *How to Increase Reading Ability: A Guide to Developmental and Remedial Methods*. 5th ed. rev. & enl. McKay, 1970. Detailed suggestions for helping children learn to read and learn to overcome reading disabilities.

HERBER, HAROLD L. *Teaching Reading in Content Areas*. Prentice-Hall, 1970. Application of reading skills to all areas of the curriculum.

HORN, THOMAS D. *Reading for the Disadvantaged: Problems of Linguistically Different Learners*. Harcourt Brace Jovanovich, 1970. Suggestions for helping economically and socially disadvantaged children learn to read.

McKEE, PAUL, and DURR, WILLIAM K. *Reading: A Program of Instruction for the Elementary School*. Houghton Mifflin, 1966. A detailed description of a balanced reading program.

STROUD, JAMES B., AMMONS, ROBERT B., and BAMMAN, HENRY A. *Improving Reading Ability: A Manual for College Students*. 3rd ed. Appleton-Century-Crofts, 1970. Suggestions for young people and adults who wish to improve their reading skills, with extensive practice materials.

WARDHAUGH, RONALD. *Reading: A Linguistic Perspective*. Harcourt Brace Jovanovich, 1969. Application of linguistic knowledge to the teaching of reading.

READING READINESS. See READING (When Should Children Learn to Read?).

REAGAN, JOHN HENNINGER (1818-1905), an American statesman, worked for government regulation of railroads. He was a United States senator from Texas from 1887 to 1891, and sponsored the bill to establish the Interstate Commerce Commission. Reagan served as postmaster general of the Confederate States, and in the United States House of Representatives from Texas from 1857 to 1861 and from 1875 to 1887. Reagan was born in Sevier County, Tenn., and died at Palestine, Tex.   ARTHUR A. EKIRCH, JR.

REAGAN, RONALD WILSON (1911-   ), a one-time motion picture and television star, was elected governor of California in 1966 and re-elected in 1970. Reagan entered national politics when he campaigned on television for Barry Goldwater in the 1964 presidential race. In his 1966 campaign for governor, he promised to reduce government spending and the role of government in society. Reagan was an unsuccessful candidate for the Republican nomination for President in 1968.

Reagan was born in Tampico, Ill. He was graduated from Eureka College in Illinois. He became a sports announcer in the 1930's and signed his first movie contract in 1937. During World War II, Reagan served as an officer in the United States Army Air Forces. During the 1940's and 1950's, he served as president of the Screen Actors Guild, and as head of the Motion Picture Industry Council.   CAROL L. THOMPSON

REAGAN DAM, once called PACOIMA DAM, is a flood-control project on Pacoima Creek near Los Angeles, Calif. It is a concrete dam of the arch type, and is 372 feet high with a crest length of 640 feet. When completed, the reservoir had a storage capacity of 4,714 acre-feet of water. Reagan Dam was built by the Los Angeles County Flood Control District. Completed in 1929, the project cost $2,466,738.   T. W. MERMEL

REAGENT is any chemical that reacts in a predictable way when mixed with other chemicals. The most common chemicals used at home, in industry, and in chemical laboratories are reagents. These include bicarbonate of soda (used in baking powder), industrial acids, photographic *hypo* (sodium thiosulfate), and laboratory indicators. Reagents are used to produce specific changes in substances and to test for the presence of various chemicals in mixtures.

Bicarbonate of soda, when mixed with acids, reacts to produce bubbles of carbon dioxide gas needed in baking (see BAKING POWDER). The reagents oxalic acid and hydrochloric acid clean metals by reacting with metallic oxides and removing the oxides from the surface of the metals. Hypo dissolves excess silver salts out of photographic film during developing. *Karl Fisher reagent,* a laboratory reagent that changes color according to the amount of water mixed with it, is used to measure the water in gasoline and in other substances in which water is an impurity.   JOHN P. FACKLER, JR.

REAL, *reel,* or, in Spanish, *ray AL,* was a coin used in Spanish-speaking countries for many years. Eight *reales* (reals) made up a Spanish milled *peso* (dollar) which became known as a *piece of eight* (see PIECE OF EIGHT). *Real* means *royal* in Spanish.   BURTON H. HOBSON

REAL ESTATE is land and all the things permanently attached to it, such as the trees and buildings upon it and any minerals such as coal, iron, or stone beneath the surface. Real estate is sometimes called *real property.*

A house is *real estate,* but the rugs and furniture in it are *chattels* (personal property). The line between real estate and personal property cannot always be easily drawn. For example, British law classes railway stocks and bonds as real property. The same things are classified as personal property in the United States.

An owner's right to real estate may be absolute, qualified, or limited. At his death, the right will descend to his lawful heirs, unless the property must be sold to pay the owner's debts. Real estate can be sold or given only by written contract.

The term *real property* came into use from the fact that, in case of contest over the title, the rightful owner received the *real* (actual) property. This was not necessarily true in a contest over the ownership of chattels, which might be settled by a payment of money.

The basic real estate vocation is that of a *broker,* who markets real property on behalf of owners. A typical broker has associated with him *salesmen,* who are responsible to him. A career in real estate usually begins with sales work. This sales work may involve long, irregular hours. But success may bring an excellent income. Over 950,000 persons in the United States are licensed as real estate brokers or salesmen. Many more work in building, mortgage finance, and related fields.

Recognized fields of specialization in real estate, other than brokerage, include *appraisal, property management,* and *counseling* on such real estate problems as industrial sites and farm purchases and sales.

Real estate work is rapidly moving toward professional status. About 60 universities and colleges now offer four-year courses. Over 350 colleges and universities offer at least one course. Real estate organizations encourage such formal training. The National Association of Real Estate Boards (NAREB) includes about 1,600 local real estate boards and 50 state associations. It coined the term *Realtor* to designate its active members who subscribe to the NAREB Code of Ethics. The term may not lawfully be used by others.   EUGENE P. CONSER

Related Articles in WORLD BOOK include:

Abstract	Fixture	Lien	Title
Air Rights	Heir	Mortgage	Torrens
Appraisal	Joint Tenancy	Primogeniture	System
Deed	Lease	Property	Will
Depreciation			

The Real Was Once Used in Spanish-Speaking Countries.

Chase Manhattan Bank Money Museum

REALISM, in the arts, is the attempt to portray life as it is. To the realist, the artist's main function is to describe as accurately and honestly as possible what he observes through his senses.

Realism began as a recognizable movement in the arts in the 1700's. By the mid-1800's, it was a dominant art form. In part, realism has been a revolt against *classicism* and *romanticism*—artistic movements characterized by works that idealize life. Classicists show life as being more rational and orderly than it really is. Romanticists show life as being more emotionally exciting and satisfying than it normally is.

The realist tries to be as objective as is humanly possible. He tries not to distort life by forcing it to agree with his own desires or principles. However, in the process of selecting and presenting his material, the realist cannot help being influenced by what he feels and thinks. Even the most thoroughgoing realism, therefore, is the result of both observation and personal judgment.

In Fiction. Realistic fiction has been primarily a revolt against the sentimentality and melodrama of romantic idealism. Characters in realistic fiction tend to be more complex than those in romantic fiction. Settings are more ordinary, plots are less important, and themes are less obvious. Most realistic fiction deals with probable, commonplace events and believable people. Much realistic fiction presents unpleasant, and even offensive, subject matter. This sordid quality is especially associated with *naturalism*, an outgrowth of realism.

The growing popularity of realism has been more than simply a reaction against the pretty worlds of romantic fiction. More fundamentally, its popularity has been due to two factors. One is the development of modern science, with its emphasis upon detailed reporting. The other is an increasing desire of writers and readers for a realistic understanding of social problems.

In English literature, realism first became important in the 1700's with the work of Daniel Defoe and Henry Fielding. In the 1800's, realism became much more important in the works of Jane Austen, Charles Dickens, Thomas Hardy, George Meredith, George Moore, William Makepeace Thackeray, and Anthony Trollope. Honoré de Balzac, Gustave Flaubert, and Émile Zola of France; and Leo Tolstoy and Ivan Turgenev of Russia were other outstanding European realists of the 1800's. See RUSSIAN LITERATURE (The Age of Realism).

Henry James, William Dean Howells, and, to some extent, Mark Twain were the first acknowledged realists in American literature. Stephen Crane, Frank Norris, and Theodore Dreiser were the first American naturalists. In their fiction, and in that of later writers such as Sinclair Lewis, F. Scott Fitzgerald, Ernest Hemingway, and John Steinbeck, realism became so generally accepted as to make romantic fiction seem outdated.

In Drama. As in fiction, realism in drama is an attempt to show life as it is. Realistic drama first developed in Europe as a reaction to the melodramas and sentimental comedies of the early and middle 1800's. It has taken many forms, from the light realism of the comedy of manners to the heavy tragedy of naturalism.

Realistic drama first became important in Europe with the plays of Henrik Ibsen of Norway. Ibsen examined the social issues of his time in such plays as *Pil-*

lars of Society (1877) and *A Doll's House* (1879). Anton Chekhov described Russia's fading aristocracy in *The Cherry Orchard* (1904). The English theater was slow to accept realism. George Bernard Shaw finally brought the movement to life with his long series of witty plays dealing with social problems, starting with *Widowers' Houses* in 1892. In Ireland, John Millington Synge blended realism and poetry in *Riders to the Sea* (1904). In a similar manner, Sean O'Casey explored the issues of Ireland's struggle for independence from England in *Juno and the Paycock* (1924) and other plays.

Realism did not make a permanent impact on the American theater until the production of Eugene O'Neill's *Beyond the Horizon* in 1920. Since then, most American drama has been realistic.

In Painting. Realistic painting developed as a reaction to two influential styles of the early 1800's—neoclassicism and romanticism (see PAINTING [The 1800's]). Aspects of realism can be seen in the work of Spanish painter Francisco Goya in the 1700's. Realism gained dominance in European painting in the 1800's with the work of such French artists as Camille Corot, Gustave Courbet, and Honoré Daumier. The French *impressionists* of the late 1800's developed a modified form of realism. In their paintings, realism was narrowed to the brightly lighted but restricted reality that can be seen at a momentary glance (see IMPRESSIONISM).

In the United States, the leading realists of the late 1800's included Thomas Eakins and Winslow Homer. They were followed in the early 1900's by a group of painters called the *Ashcan School* or *The Eight*. The Ashcan School opposed the sentimentality and academic quality then popular in American art. The group included William Glackens, Robert Henri, and John Sloan. They painted realistic street scenes, portraits, and landscapes. Other realists include George Bellows, regional painters John Steuart Curry and Grant Wood, and social critics Edward Hopper and Reginald Marsh.

Realism Today. In fiction and drama, realism has become so widespread that it scarcely has any identity as a distinct movement. The most common realistic themes include the importance of the subconscious, the role of racial minorities in society, and man's search for values in a hostile world. Beginning in the early 1900's, painters began rejecting realism in favor of various kinds of nonrepresentational and abstract styles. By the 1960's, realism was only a minor influence in painting.   JOHN C. GERBER

There is a separate biography in WORLD BOOK for each author and painter discussed in this article.

REAM. See WEIGHTS AND MEASURES (Paper Measure).

REAMER. See DRILLING TOOLS.

REAPING MACHINE is used to harvest grain. Before the invention of the reaping machine, a good reaper could cut about an acre of wheat a day using a hand sickle. But before he could cut all of his crop, part of it would probably rot and not be worth harvesting. Large crops would be impossible under such conditions. The present wheat crops produced in the United States, Canada, and other wheat-growing countries have been made possible to a large extent by the development of the reaping machine that was patented by Cyrus H. McCormick in 1834 (see McCORMICK, CYRUS HALL).

One of the First Reapers had a device that raked the cut grain from the platform, leaving it untied in the field.

The Self-Binder enabled one man to control the cutting and binding of the grain. The first model was built in 1876.

International Harvester Co.

The Improved Binder of 1888 tied up the bundles of grain with twine instead of wire. An adjustable canvas grain shield was added to the platform.

This Compact Combine performs all the steps in cutting and threshing the grain in one operation. There are more than 700,000 combines in use in the United States alone.

Self-Propelled Combines are streamlined machines whose built-in motors eliminate even the tractor.

Probably no other invention has contributed so much toward increasing man's food supply as the reaping machine. The largest factories making these machines are in and near Chicago. Harvesters are now found in every wheat-growing country. In the United States alone, more than 700,000 combines are in operation.

The First Reaper. McCormick's invention was a crude machine, but it completely changed the practice of growing grain. The reaper stood on two wheels. One was the main wheel, to which the gearing was attached. This wheel was of cast iron, and had projections on its outer rim to keep it from slipping. The cutting part consisted of a horizontal steel plate called the *cutter bar*, which was 6 feet long, about 5 inches wide, and ½ inch thick. Long steel points called *guards* were riveted to this bar. The cutting was done by triangular knives attached to a steel bar which slid forward and backward in a groove in the guards. A crank operated by the gearing attached to the main wheel gave the knife bar a rapid motion. A divider separated the grain that was to be cut from that left standing. A reel bent the grain back against the knives and picked up the stalks that were bent or lodged, so that all the grain was cut. As the grain was cut, it was laid on a platform. A man following the machine raked it off into piles.

The Modern Reaper, or Self-Binder, has been developed from the original reaper. The first improvement consisted of a self-raking device which raked the grain

from the platform and did away with the labor of the extra man. Following this improvement came the canvas belt which carried the grain over the main wheel to a box. Men riding on a platform attached to the machine took it from this box and bound it. Then came the knotting device, a clever piece of machinery which enabled the harvester to bind as well as cut the grain.

In the modern self-binder, the canvas belt carries the grain to the binder head, where it is packed until there is enough for a bundle. Then a trip sets the knotting apparatus in motion, and the bundle is firmly bound with twine. It is then moved from the binder head by revolving arms, and loaded on a platform or laid on the ground, according to the plan of the machine. An ordinary binder requires three or four horses to operate it successfully, and it will harvest 10 to 15 acres of grain a day. It can be used with equal success in harvesting wheat, oats, barley, and rye. On most farms today, tractors are used for operating the machines.

The *header* is a form of harvester used in regions where the grain is well dried before harvesting. It cuts the grain just below the heads, and carries them to a storage box on the machine, or to a wagon drawn beside it. The heads are stacked until dry enough to thresh.

The Combined Harvester-Thresher, or Combine, as it is commonly called, is a machine that cuts and threshes the grain, all in one operation. It has a cutting mechanism quite similar to that used on a self-binder. This mechanism is attached to the side of a small threshing machine. A wide, endless canvas belt carries the unthreshed grain from the cutting mechanism directly to the threshing cylinder of the combine.

The threshing mechanism is of the usual type, with some slight changes to adapt it for traveling over rough ground. The threshed straw is usually dropped from the rear of the machine. The grain goes directly into a motor truck or wagon which is drawn alongside of the machine, or else it is collected in a large bin mounted on the combine, and dumped into a truck or wagon when this is filled. In some grain regions, the grain is run directly into bags, which are sewed up and then dropped in groups of four or five on the field, to be collected at a later time.

The combine is pulled by a tractor or is self-propelled by a motor built into the machine. The first combine was used in Michigan in 1837, but combines did not come into general use until about 1917. By the 1930's a smaller combine had been developed.

The combine marks almost as great an advantage over the self-binder as the self-binder did over the cradle and the flail.   A. D. LONGHOUSE

See also BINDER TWINE; COMBINE.

REAPPORTIONMENT. See APPORTIONMENT.

REAR ADMIRAL. See RANK IN ARMED SERVICES.

REASON usually has three different meanings. (1) It can signify the mind, or an agency used in thinking. For example, we may ask someone to use his reason rather than his emotions. (2) Reason also refers to the evidence for a belief, opinion, or judgment. We may demand a reason for a person's liking contemporary music, or his belief that someone is a thief. (3) Reason may refer to a process of arriving at a decision or a conclusion. For instance, we may say that a jury was reasoning correctly when it decided a defendant was guilty. To reason with someone means to present evidence that will lead to a sound conclusion.

Reasoning can be inductive or deductive. A person uses *inductive reasoning* when he sees a puddle of water and infers that it has rained recently. A doctor uses inductive reasoning when, after learning that all his patients who had indigestion ate ham, he concludes that the ham caused the indigestion. Inductive reasoning is not conclusive. The evidence only makes the conclusion probable. See INDUCTIVE METHOD.

A person uses *deductive reasoning* when he asserts that, if life requires oxygen, then where there is life there must be oxygen. Deductive reasoning shows what must be true if the evidence is valid. See DEDUCTIVE METHOD.

Good reasons support the conclusions, but bad ones do not. A person's inability to do arithmetic is a good reason for refusing to hire him as a bank clerk. A person's nationality is a bad reason for saying that he is a thief. Correct reasoning requires good reasons that can be shown to be true. Correct reasoning also requires a knowledge of logic (see LOGIC).   LOUIS O. KATTSOFF

See also FALLACY; GEOMETRY (Assumptions); JUDGMENT; MIND.

REASON, AGE OF. See AGE OF REASON.

REBAB. See INDONESIA (Arts).

REBATE, *RE bayt,* in mercantile law, is a discount, or reduction of the amount to be paid. Giving a certain percentage off for cash is a rebate. Sometimes a rebate is

given to obtain favors or good will. It is unlawful for transportation companies to give rebates to shippers. Those who do are subject to heavy fines. See also ROOSEVELT, THEODORE (Domestic Problems).   JOHN H. FREDERICK

REBECCA. See ISAAC.

REBEKAH LODGES. See ODD FELLOWS, INDEPENDENT ORDER OF.

REBELLION OF 1837-1838 was an attempt to limit harsh British rule in Canada. The rebel leaders were William Lyon Mackenzie in Ontario and Louis J. Papineau in Quebec. Both were courageous, but their rebellion failed to win support among the people.

In Lower Canada. A party of discontented French Canadians arose in Quebec, or Lower Canada. This group grew in power after the War of 1812, and won many seats in the legislative assembly. For 20 years the legislative assembly demanded more liberal government from the British governor and his council. Questions of nationality and religion also entered into the quarrel. Later, the assembly demanded full control of government funds.

Rebellion began in Lower Canada after the British Government refused to allow the establishment of an elected legislative council. French Canadians held protest meetings and organized a group called the *Sons of Liberty.* Armed rebels gathered at the towns of Saint Charles and Saint Denis, but British troops scattered both forces. Smaller radical groups put up weak fights in villages north of Montreal. The rebellion was crushed almost before it began, and the rebel leader, Papineau, fled to the United States.

In Upper Canada. The political situation in Upper Canada was very much like that in Lower Canada. Mackenzie, the Radical leader, broke with the moderate Reformers and renounced allegiance to Great Britain. He called upon the people to revolt and capture the military supplies in the Toronto city hall. Four hundred rebels answered his call, but they were quickly defeated by a larger force of British troops.

Mackenzie and some of his followers fled to an island in the Niagara River just across the United States border. They called themselves *Patriots,* and set up a provisional government. They received supplies on the American steamer *Caroline* until British troops set the ship on fire and sent it over Niagara Falls. Mackenzie found many Irish-American sympathizers, but his rebellion ended hopelessly in 1838.

Results of the Rebellion. The rebellion failed because the Radicals did not have the full support of the French Canadians or the Reformers. But the uprising had one important result. It caused the British government to send the Earl of Durham to Canada. Durham's report on conditions in Canada resulted in the Act of Union in 1840. This act united the provinces of Upper and Lower Canada.   EDWARD R. ADAIR

See also DURHAM, EARL OF; MACKENZIE, WILLIAM LYON; UNION, ACT OF.

REBOZO. See MEXICO (Clothing).

REBUS, *REE bus,* is a word game in which the placement or size of numbers, letters, or words indicates names, phrases, or other words. A rebus can also have pictures, or words and pictures. For example, a picture of an eye, followed by "CA," followed by a picture of a

Benjamin Franklin Used Rebuses along with script writing in a short tract called "The Art of Making Money Plenty."

dog, could stand for "I see a dog." Or, using words and figures: stand you my I charged 4 shoes for "I understand you overcharged for my overshoes." AL could be *altogether* (*A L* together). WALTER H. HOLZE

RECALL enables voters to remove a person from office before his term is completed, and to elect a new public official. A special election is held for this purpose.

Before a recall election can be held, a petition must be filed that has been signed by a certain number of voters. Usually the number must equal 25 per cent of the votes cast for this particular office during the previous election. Candidates for the office may file petitions in the usual way. The special election then becomes a contest between the new candidates and the officer whose recall is sought. The person receiving the largest vote serves out the rest of the term.

The movement to provide for recall of state and local officials came with efforts to provide for more direct popular control over government generally. The modern use of recall in the United States began with the charter of Los Angeles in 1903. Seattle followed in 1906. Several hundred cities and twelve states have since adopted it. The states include Oregon (1908), California (1911), Colorado, Washington, Idaho, Nevada, and Arizona (1912), Michigan (1913), Louisiana and Kansas (1914), North Dakota (1920), and Wisconsin (1926). Some states that use the recall do not apply it to judges. Mayors of cities have often been recalled, but the recall of a state officer is unusual. North Dakota removed a governor by recall in 1921.

People who favor the recall argue that voters should have a direct way of removing an officer whom they consider dishonest, incompetent, or heedless of public opinion. Most state constitutions provide for the removal of an officer by impeachment. But people sometimes wish to remove from office someone who is not guilty of anything for which he could be impeached.

Opponents of recall point out that the practice may be abused. They say that able men and women may be unwilling to risk taking an office from which the voters may later remove them for no fault except the failure to go along with the public sentiment of the moment.

Some people expressed the fear that the threat of removal by recall, as applied to elected judges, would weaken judicial independence. But such fears have proved to be exaggerated, because recall has never been used in any case involving a judge of a supreme or superior court. MURRAY S. STEDMAN, JR.

See also INITIATIVE AND REFERENDUM.

RECALL, in psychology. See MEMORY (How Much Do We Remember?).

RECEIPT, *ree SEET,* is a written statement showing that one person has paid money to another. It may also be a written statement showing that goods, or property, has passed from the ownership or responsibility of one person to another. The receipt is proof that a transaction has taken place. The three kinds of receipts are *receipts in full, receipts on account* (when some of the amount due is paid), and *receipts to apply on special accounts.*

A receipt should always show whether payment is made in full, on account, or on the special account to which payment is made, when there is more than one account between two persons. A receipt should always be given when an account is paid. A bill marked *paid* and properly signed is as good as a receipt.

George Evans of Muncie, Ind., sold groceries to Charles Miller on account. Miller agreed to pay the account on the first of each month. On Dec. 1, 1972, Miller's account was $15.75, and when he paid in cash, Evans gave him this receipt:

```
$15.75        Muncie, Ind., Dec. 1, 1972
     Received of Charles Miller
   Fifteen and 75/100........Dollars
     In full of account to date.
              George Evans
```

A canceled check would also show that payment was made. JOHN H. FREDERICK

See also BILL OF LADING.

RECEIVER. See RADIO (How a Radio Program Is Received); TELEPHONE (How the Telephone Works); TELEVISION (How TV Is Received; Color Television).

RECEIVER is an individual, a bank, or a trust company appointed by a court to hold, manage, or dispose of property. The most common reason for appointing a receiver is bankruptcy (see BANKRUPT). If a person or company does not have enough assets to cover all debts, the court may name a receiver to protect the people or companies to whom the debts are owed.

The court also may appoint a receiver if the owner of the property is unable to handle it properly. For example, if a person under legal age inherits property, a receiver may be appointed to act for him. A receiver also may handle an insane person's property. But in most cases, a *guardian* acts for minors and a *conservator* acts for people unable to understand how to handle property. A receiver also may manage property involved in a lawsuit, such as a mortgage foreclosure.

A receiver is an officer of the court. He is limited in his authority and actions by the decree appointing him, and by the laws of the state and the nation. Ordinarily, the receiver must be a person who has no direct interest in the business or estate he handles. He also must administer the estate in the best interests of all parties concerned. In some states, a receiver may be appointed to take charge of the property of a husband who fails to support his wife or his children. After the receiver has finished his work, he is discharged by the court.

The court pays a receiver for his services. The fees of the receiver and the expenses of the receivership must be paid before any other obligations. The court requires the receiver to furnish bond. WILLIAM TUCKER DEAN

RECEPTOR. See PERCEPTION; NERVOUS SYSTEM (Nerve Impulses).

RECESSION. See ECONOMICS (table: Important Terms).

RECIFE, *ruh SEE fuh* (pop. 1,056,000; alt. 10 ft.), in northeastern Brazil, is the capital of the state of Pernambuco and the fourth largest city in the country. It lies at the mouths of Capibaribe and Beberibe rivers, partly on the mainland and partly on an island in the Atlantic Ocean (see BRAZIL [political map]).

Factories and mills of Recife produce textiles, ceramics, paper and leather goods, vegetable oils, and alcohol. The city's chief source of wealth comes from the exportation of bananas, coffee, cotton, hides, and sugar. Hundreds of students attend Recife's two universities.

The Portuguese settled the Recife region in 1535. During Dutch invasions of Brazil (1630-1654), Recife was the center of enemy operations. Recife became a Brazilian town in 1710, and a city in 1823.   MANOEL CARDOZO

RECIPROCAL TRADE AGREEMENT is an agreement between nations to exchange trade favors. Most countries have at one time or another signed reciprocal trade treaties with other countries. In effect, one nation says to another: "The tariffs of our country are as published. But if you will lower tariff rates for us on certain products, we will make corresponding reductions in tariffs for you. We have goods you must purchase, and you have things that we require. Why not arrange favorable tariff terms for both of us?"

As a common example of this arrangement, one country produces more wheat than it needs, but has to buy sugar because it does not raise this crop. Another country produces more sugar than it needs, but must buy wheat. So the first country agrees to sell wheat to the second country at a cheaper price than to other countries. In return, the second country agrees to send the first large quantities of sugar at a low price. Favors granted by a reciprocal trade treaty are sometimes called *most-favored-nation* privileges.

The United States government has signed many reciprocal trade treaties. In 1854, Canada and the United States signed the Elgin-Marcy Treaty. Under the terms of this treaty, each government agreed to reduce duties on goods imported from the other country. In 1875, the United States entered into a trade agreement with Hawaii. Under this agreement, Hawaiian sugar was admitted to the United States without any duty. A treaty with Cuba in 1902 admitted Cuban sugar to the United States at low tariff rates.

The Trade Agreements Act of 1934 made reciprocal trade treaties an important part of United States foreign policy. This act authorized the government to lower customs duties by as much as 50 per cent in negotiating reciprocal trade treaties with other nations. Secretary of State Cordell Hull made more than 20 such treaties under this act, principally with other American nations. The Reciprocal Trade Agreements Act of 1948, and others like it, have given the government the authority to continue its reciprocal trade policies.

The reciprocal trade treaties which the United States has made with Latin-American countries have usually strengthened good will. Sometimes, however, such treaties have led to tariff wars between countries. In such situations, both importers and exporters suffer great losses, and there is often much ill feeling among the nations concerned.   TELFORD TAYLOR

See also HULL, CORDELL; ROOSEVELT, FRANKLIN DELANO (Good Neighbor Policy); TARIFF.

RECIPROCATING ENGINE is an engine that works by means of a piston which *reciprocates*, or moves back and forth, in a cylinder. Gasoline engines and the steam

engines used on railroad locomotives are reciprocating engines. A fluid under pressure, such as air, steam, or a burning mixture of fuel and air, causes the piston to move back and forth. A connecting rod attached to the piston turns a crankshaft. This converts the reciprocating motion to rotary motion. See also GASOLINE ENGINE; STEAM ENGINE.   WILLIAM L. HULL

RECITATIVE, REHS *ih tuh TEEV,* is a recitation set to music. It is often used in opera for what would be a fairly long speech in a play. A recitative may have little or no melody, and it is usually loose in form. A recitative with an accompaniment is called *recitativo stromentato.* One without is *recitativo secco.* These Italian words mean *instrumental* and *dry.*

RECLAMATION, BUREAU OF, is a United States government agency that works to develop water and land resources in the Western States. The bureau plans projects to store and provide water for city drinking supplies, hydroelectric power, irrigation, outdoor recreation, and other purposes. It makes contracts with private companies to build such projects, which include dams and reservoirs, hydroelectric power plants, and irrigation canals. The bureau also administers a flood control program. The agency was established in 1902 as the Reclamation Service and is part of the Department of the Interior. Its name was changed in 1923.

Critically reviewed by the BUREAU OF RECLAMATION

See also IRRIGATION (Irrigation in the United States).

RECLAMATION ACT. See IRRIGATION (Irrigation in the United States).

RECLAMATION OF LAND. Much crop land that has become either too dry or too flooded for farming purposes can be *reclaimed* (restored to usefulness). Irrigation and drainage are two of the most common ways of reclaiming wasted lands. Removal of stumps from cutover forest lands and restoration of eroded land are also classed as reclamation.

Dry lands are reclaimed by building canals and ditches to carry water from a source to the dry land. Most irrigation projects use streams as a source of water (see IRRIGATION). Swamplands are usually reclaimed by digging drainage canals, and draining the water off the land into canals or ditches (see DRAINAGE).

In the United States, swampland reclamation has been done largely by individual communities. The federal program for irrigation began in 1902, when the Department of the Interior set up a Bureau of Reclamation. Most of the irrigation projects undertaken by the Reclamation Bureau are in the western states.

Other countries also have programs for reclaiming the land. Large irrigation works have been built in Australia, Canada, Egypt, and India. Many South American countries have irrigation programs. Mexico has a program to provide farm homes through the irrigation of dry lands. The Netherlands, Belgium, and Italy are among the many European countries that have reclaimed flooded lands through drainage (see NETHERLANDS [introduction; color map: The Long Battle Against the Sea]).   GLENN K. RULE

See also CONSERVATION; DRAINAGE; IRRIGATION.

RECOGNITION. See MEMORY.

RECONNAISSANCE PLANE. See AIR FORCE, UNITED STATES (Planes and Weapons of the Air Force).

RECONSTRUCTION was the period in American history that followed the Civil War. During the troubled years from 1865 to 1877, the people of the United States tried to deal with issues that have not been settled even today. Leaders were not always statesmanlike in handling the task of restoring the Union. Some of the mistakes they made resulted from the heritage of hate left by the war. But, more important, the American people had had no experience in meeting the problems that follow a great war. The situation was unusually difficult because they had fought among themselves.

Reconstruction originally meant the political process by which the defeated Southern States, which had seceded from the Union, again became part of the United States. It included the conditions that the victorious North imposed upon the South. This political phase of Reconstruction ended in 1877, when Southern whites overthrew the last Northern-controlled state governments in the South and regained local control.

From the beginning, however, Reconstruction had a social as well as a political meaning. The social aspect involved the touchy problem of race relations, particularly the fate of about 4 million freed Negro slaves. Should the national government decide their status and enforce it—even against the will of the whites? Or should the Southern white people be permitted to handle the problem themselves? These questions continued to disturb Americans long after 1877.

Reconstruction also had long-lasting political results. It intensified the sectional conflicts that the Civil War was supposed to have ended. The Southern States

united in a "solid South" that tended to split, rather than unite, the nation. Reconstruction also threatened to limit drastically the powers of the President, and left many unsolved problems about the relationships between the executive and legislative branches of the nation's government.

Aftermath of War

In the North. The economy of the North was bursting with wartime prosperity in 1865. The boom that had started during the Civil War continued during the years of peace that followed. Agriculture and industry greatly expanded production, and the era of big business began. Railroad mileage in the nation almost doubled between 1860 and 1870, with most of the growth in the North and in the West.

Some Northerners demanded that the leaders of the Confederacy be punished by imprisonment or even death. President Jefferson Davis of the Confederacy and a few civil officials were arrested. But they were never tried, because Northern authorities could find no legal grounds for trying them. Besides, few Americans liked the idea of revenge. Most Southern military leaders could not be arrested, because they were under military parole (see PAROLE). The government executed only one prominent Confederate official, Henry Wirz, commander of Andersonville prison in Georgia, where 12,000 Union soldiers had died.

In the South, unlike the North, the Civil War had brought terrible destruction. Cities and towns, plantations and farms lay in ruins. Railroads and roads had

RECONSTRUCTION

Pleasant Hill (Mo.) Post Office

The Destruction Caused by the War left thousands of Americans poor and homeless. In Tom Lea's mural, *Back Home, 1865*, Southerners survey the ruins of their farm.

The Problems of Peace troubled both North and South. Carpetbaggers, armed with money-making schemes, went south to improve their fortunes. They worked through newly freed Negroes to win control of Southern legislatures and carry out their programs.

Thomas Nast from Culver; from *The American Past* by Roger Butterfield, published by Simon and Schuster, Inc.

RECONSTRUCTION

been completely or partly destroyed. Thousands of Southerners faced the problem of finding enough food to stay alive until they could cultivate the land again. The national government took no direct action to relieve the distress of the South. Nothing in the nation's past had prepared it to provide mass relief for a large area (see RELIEF). The government did create the Freedmen's Bureau to help freed Negroes, or *freedmen*, make the change from slavery. The bureau aided both Negroes and whites. But its many opponents accused its agents of fraud and party politics. See FREEDMEN'S BUREAU.

The Southern States had the main responsibility for the Negroes. Most of them passed laws called "black codes." These laws tried to regulate Negro labor and to insure the higher social position of the whites. All the laws granted some civil rights to Negroes, but they also included restrictions. For example, Negroes could not bear arms, serve on juries, or attend schools with whites. Unemployed Negroes could be arrested for vagrancy and hired out to employers. The black codes convinced many Northerners that the South would not deal fairly with the Negroes. To some, the codes seemed to be an attempt to restore the essentials of slavery.

Plans for Reconstruction

Lincoln's Proposal. The first plan for Reconstruction came from President Abraham Lincoln during the Civil War. As Union troops occupied large areas of the South, Lincoln became anxious to begin the process of bringing the seceded states back into the Union. He wanted to restore the Union as soon as possible, and had no wish to punish the South.

Lincoln's plan, announced in December, 1863, offered a general *amnesty*, or pardon, to all who would take an oath of loyalty to the United States. The oath required Southerners to promise to support the Constitution of the United States and to obey federal laws concerning slavery. High Confederate civil and military officials were temporarily excluded from taking the oath. If one tenth of the number of 1860 voters in a state took the oath, they could re-establish the state government. Lincoln promised to recognize such a government. Louisiana, Arkansas, and Tennessee began to carry out Lincoln's plan in late 1864 and early 1865.

Congressional Schemes. A group of Republicans in Congress, called the Radical Republicans, opposed Lincoln's plan. They thought it treated the South too gently, and that it did not protect the rights of the freedmen. Through the efforts of the Radical Republicans, representatives from the newly reconstructed states were refused admission to Congress. In July, 1864, the Radicals presented a plan of their own, the Wade-Davis Bill. This measure required that a majority of the voters in a state take an oath of loyalty. A state also would have to abolish slavery before it could be readmitted to the Union. No one who had served as a Confederate or state official could vote for the state legislature. The bill passed a few days before Congress adjourned, and Lincoln disposed of it with a pocket veto. The bill's authors, Senator Benjamin F. Wade of Ohio and Representative Henry Winter Davis of Maryland,

then issued a violent denunciation of Lincoln, the Wade-Davis Manifesto. The manifesto condemned Lincoln's actions and insisted that Congress alone had the power to control Reconstruction.

Johnson's Efforts. Before the issue between Lincoln and the Radicals could be settled, the President was assassinated on Apr. 14, 1865. Vice-President Andrew Johnson, who succeeded him, was sincere and well-meaning. But he lacked Lincoln's skill in handling people, and did not know when and how to compromise.

Johnson announced his own Reconstruction plan in the spring of 1865. He proposed that the government should pardon all Southerners who took a loyalty oath, but should not extend amnesty to high Confederate officials or persons with property valued at more than $20,000. A state had to revoke its ordinance of secession and abolish slavery in order to rejoin the Union. Eight states accepted Johnson's plan and began to carry it out. Congress had adjourned for eight months, so the Radicals offered little opposition at this time. But they did not like Johnson's proposal any more than they had Lincoln's. Representatives from the reconstructed states were again denied admission when Congress reconvened in December, 1865.

Congress Takes Control

The Radical Republicans. Many members of Congress resented the fact that Johnson had gone ahead with Reconstruction plans without consulting them. His actions particularly angered the Radical Republicans, led by Representative Thaddeus Stevens of Pennsylvania. Prominent Radicals included Representative Benjamin Butler of Massachusetts, and Senators Oliver Perry Morton of Indiana, Benjamin Wade of Ohio, and Charles Sumner and Henry Wilson of Massachusetts.

The Radicals favored a "hard peace" for the defeated South. Several motives influenced them. Some blamed the South for starting the Civil War, and wanted to punish Southerners. Others worried about the future of the former slaves. They thought that the federal government had an obligation to see that the former slaves received their rights as free men.

But many Radicals viewed Reconstruction in political terms. They wanted a plan that would keep the Republican party in power. They were determined to retain the legislative gains made in the war. These gains included a high tariff, free homesteads, a banking system favorable to business, and subsidies to railroads. If the Democrats returned to power in the South, they would oppose the Republican program.

The Republicans wanted to create a Republican party in the South. Such a party would have to rest on Negro votes. So, for both idealistic and political reasons, the Radicals supported Negro suffrage. They had to proceed cautiously, because some Northern states still denied the vote to Negroes. But they gained control of Congress by skillful maneuvering, and won over a large section of Northern public opinion.

Sumner said the seceded states had committed "state suicide," and had ceased to exist as states. Stevens held that the results of the war had turned the former Confederate states into "conquered provinces." Both lines of reasoning led directly to the desired conclusion—that Congress could do whatever it pleased with the South.

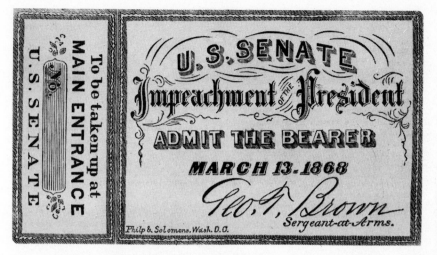

Culver

The Impeachment Trial of President Johnson aroused bitter controversy. Thaddeus Stevens, *right*, was in poor health and had to be carried into the Senate. But he and other Radicals worked tirelessly trying to obtain votes against Johnson.

The Radicals at first worked through the Joint Committee on Reconstruction, which they created in December, 1865, to study public opinion in the South. The committee gathered evidence supposedly showing that Southerners had not sincerely accepted the results of the war. Radical propaganda made the black codes seem worse than they were.

Civil Rights Measures. Radicals pushed through the Civil Rights Bill in April, 1866, to counteract the black codes. This act tried to prevent states from discriminating against citizens because of race. Johnson vetoed the bill, but Congress overrode his veto.

Encouraged by their success, the Radicals brought forward Amendment 14 to the Constitution later in 1866. This measure contained the first national definition of citizenship in U.S. history. It also attempted to protect civil rights against state interference, and declared that state representation in Congress and the Electoral College would be reduced if a state denied the vote to any adult men. Another provision disqualified prominent Confederate leaders from holding national or state office. See UNITED STATES CONSTITUTION (Amendment 14).

When the amendment went to the states for ratification, ten former Confederate states and two border states voted against it, because they would not approve a measure penalizing their leaders.

Only Tennessee ratified the amendment and rejoined the Union. The amendment was temporarily defeated, but this defeat hurt the South. Northerners generally favored the amendment.

Strengthening Radical Power. The Congressional elections of 1866 showed how the North felt about the South's actions. The voters returned an overwhelming Republican majority to Congress, and the Radicals gained more than the two-thirds majority necessary to override a presidential veto. They then moved to profit from their victory and enact their final program. They tried to make certain that Congress, rather than the President, would control the administration of their plans. In 1867, the Radicals passed two laws that were clearly unconstitutional. The Tenure of Office Act pre-

vented the President from dismissing certain officials, including Cabinet members, without the Senate's consent (see TENURE OF OFFICE ACT). The Command of the Army Act prohibited the President from issuing orders to the army except through the commanding general, who could not be removed without the Senate's approval. The army was important because the Radicals intended to use it to enforce their program.

The Reconstruction Acts of 1867 embodied the final Radical plan for Reconstruction. This series of bills divided the ten unreconstructed states into five military districts. A major general commanded each district. Each general had to prepare the states in his "province" for a return to statehood by arranging for a registration of voters. Election boards would register all adult Negro males, and any adult male whites who would take a complicated loyalty oath. In the 10 states, 703,000 Negroes and 627,000 whites registered. The voters were to elect a convention to prepare a new state constitution providing for Negro suffrage. As a final condition, the state had to ratify Amendment 14 to the Constitution. Johnson vetoed the Reconstruction Acts. But the Republican majority easily passed them over his veto, and they went into effect throughout the South.

The Impeachment of Johnson. The Radicals now set out to punish their enemy in the White House. They began impeachment proceedings against President Johnson in 1868 (see IMPEACHMENT). He had given them grounds for action by removing Secretary of War Edwin M. Stanton, in violation of the Tenure of Office Act. The charges against Johnson emphasized his dismissal of Stanton. They also accused the President of not enforcing the Reconstruction Acts and of treating Congress disrespectfully. But the charges offered no evidence that the President had committed "high crimes and misdemeanors," the only legal grounds for impeachment. The Radicals failed by one vote to muster the two-thirds majority in the Senate necessary to convict the President, and Johnson completed his term. If the Radicals had succeeded in convicting Johnson, the power of the President might have been permanently limited. Ulysses S. Grant succeeded Johnson in

Members of the Ku-Klux Klan, Dressed like Ghosts, Rode at Night to Frighten Negroes and Carpetbaggers.

1869. Grant generally supported the Radical program. See JOHNSON, ANDREW; GRANT, ULYSSES S.

The South During Reconstruction

Scalawags and Carpetbaggers. Republican state governments in the South depended on Negro voters. But white men usually provided the real leadership. Some Southern whites believed they could cooperate with the Negroes and direct their votes. These men became known as *scalawags*. Contrary to popular opinion, they were not all worthless scoundrels. Most scalawags were planters and businessmen who had long experience dealing with Negroes. But they could not control the Negro voters. They refused to grant all the Negroes' social and economic demands, and lost their leadership to a group of Northern whites, the *carpetbaggers*. These Northerners had come South for selfish or idealistic reasons, and were willing to give the Negroes what they wanted (see CARPETBAGGER). Many scalawags and carpetbaggers worked through the Union League, a Northern organization that tried to convince Negroes to vote Republican. Southern whites regarded the Democratic party as the only "white man's party."

Republican State Governments in the South had the support of United States Army regiments, sometimes composed of Negro troops. Without the presence of the soldiers, the Republicans would have been helpless before the Southern whites.

These state governments wrote a record full of contradictions. Their programs combined fraud with liberal, though sometimes impractical, social legislation. State budgets and debts reached figures previously undreamed of. Some of the money went into the pockets

of dishonest men. Some went for worthy purposes, such as public education. The Republican governments represented poor Negroes, and tried to provide public-works and poor-relief programs.

The corruption was not limited to the South. It spread throughout the entire nation during this period. City and state governments in the North were probably as bad as any in the South.

Southern Resistance took several forms. Southern whites formed secret societies such as the Ku-Klux Klan and the Knights of the White Camellia to prevent Negroes from voting. These organizations used various kinds of pressure, including violence. The federal government moved vigorously against them. In three force bills passed in 1870 and 1871, it authorized the use of troops to preserve civil rights. The secret societies disbanded, but they had had some success in forcing Negroes and carpetbaggers out of politics. See FORCE BILL; KU-KLUX KLAN.

Southerners then created semimilitary organizations such as the White League of Louisiana and the Red Shirts of South Carolina. The idea of such societies began in Mississippi, and was known as "the Mississippi Plan." Members carried firearms on election day, and attended the polls in a body. Negroes refused to vote in the face of such threats. Amendment 15 to the Constitution, adopted in 1870, tried to guarantee Negro suffrage (see UNITED STATES CONSTITUTION [Amendment 15]). But Southerners kept Negroes from voting by means of complicated literacy tests and poll taxes. When these requirements kept white voters from the polls, some states adopted "Grandfather Clauses." They set aside restrictions if a voter's grandfather had been qualified to vote. This provision effectively barred Negroes. See GRANDFATHER CLAUSE; POLL TAX.

Economic pressure was the most powerful weapon used by the whites. Negroes had gained their freedom, but they still worked as laborers and depended on white men for their living. Whites could easily force Negroes to vote as directed, or not to vote at all, by refusing to give them credit or jobs, or to rent them land.

The End of Reconstruction

Republican rule in the South lasted a comparatively short time. In some states, the whites overthrew it almost immediately. In others, white recovery progressed more slowly. Southerners got rid of the Republicans in Virginia, North Carolina, and Georgia as early as 1870. Texas returned to Southern control in 1873, and Alabama and Arkansas the following year. Whites in Mississippi won out in 1875.

Public opinion in the North gradually turned against the use of military force to support Republican rule. When Rutherford B. Hayes became President in 1877, he withdrew the last federal troops from the South. Republican governments promptly collapsed in the three remaining Southern States—Louisiana, South Carolina, and Florida. Reconstruction in the South had ended.   T. HARRY WILLIAMS

Critically reviewed by BRUCE CATTON

Related Articles in WORLD BOOK include:

Carpetbagger	Ku-Klux Klan
Civil War	Lamar, Lucius Q. C.
Force Bill	Negro
Freedmen's Bureau	Scalawag
Grandfather Clause	Sumner, Charles
Grant, Ulysses S.	Tenure of Office Act
(Reconstruction Policies)	United States Constitution
Johnson, Andrew	(Amendments 14, 15)

Outline

I. Aftermath of War
  A. In the North   B. In the South
II. Plans for Reconstruction
  A. Lincoln's Proposal   C. Johnson's Efforts
  B. Congressional Schemes
III. Congress Takes Control
  A. The Radical Republicans D. The Reconstruction
  B. Civil Rights Measures   Acts
  C. Strengthening Radical   E. The Impeachment
     Power   of Johnson
IV. The South During Reconstruction
  A. Scalawags and Carpet- C. Southern Resistance
     baggers
  B. Republican State Governments
V. The End of Reconstruction

Questions

Why did the Radical Republicans want a "hard peace" for the South?

Who were the *scalawags?* The *carpetbaggers?*

When did Reconstruction begin? When did it end?

Who was the only prominent Confederate official to be executed after the Civil War?

Why did the South object to Amendment 14 of the Constitution? How did Southern defeat of the amendment affect the North?

How did Lincoln's plan for Reconstruction compare with that of Johnson? With that of Congress?

Why were Confederate leaders never brought to trial?

What were the black codes?

How did Southerners regain control of their state governments?

What measures did the Radicals push through Congress to strengthen their control of Reconstruction?

RECONSTRUCTION FINANCE CORPORATION (RFC) was founded by Congress in 1932 as an emergency agency to operate during the depression. It had authority to lend money to banks, railroads, schools, business firms, public agencies, and other institutions. Through these loans, it kept many banks and businesses from failing. Although the agency was meant to last no more than 10 years, Congress extended its lifetime until 1957.

In 1951, a Senate investigating subcommittee accused the RFC of using favoritism and political influence in some of its dealings. Reorganization followed, and the RFC was placed under the supervision of a single administrator appointed by the President. In 1954, Congress assigned RFC loan powers to the Small Business Administration. Congress abolished the RFC in 1957 and transferred many of its functions to the Housing and Home Finance Agency.

The RFC raised funds by issuing bonds, notes, and other promises to pay. It played an important part in financing war industries during World War II. It operated a tin smelter, abacá plantations in Latin America, and several plants that manufactured artificial rubber.   ROBERT D. PATTON

RECORD is a word with several meanings. A *written record* keeps track of events and facts. A *phonograph record* plays sound. A *record* may also be a list of achievements in a certain field. For such records, see WORLD BOOK's articles on AIRPLANE; AUTOMOBILE RACING; BALLOON; BASEBALL; BOWLING; EARTH; HELICOPTER; OLYMPIC GAMES; SWIMMING; and TRACK AND FIELD.

RECORD PLAYER. See PHONOGRAPH.

RECORDER is a wooden flute with a whistle mouthpiece. The player changes notes by opening or closing a thumb hole and seven finger holes. Recorders won wide popularity in England in the 1600's. Four sizes popular today include *soprano* or *descant*, *alto*, *tenor*, and *bass*. Recorders can be played as solo instruments or in groups.

RECORDING MACHINE. See DICTATING MACHINE; PHONOGRAPH; TAPE RECORDER.

A Tenor Recorder, *left*, has a keyed bottom hole. The smaller soprano instrument, *center*, does not. Both have soft, mellow tones.

American Music Conference

RECREATION

WORLD BOOK photo by Ed Hoppe

RECREATION. The average adult must spend a certain number of hours daily at some kind of work in order to earn a living or to care for a family. The growing child must attend school regularly. Eating, sleeping, and other tasks usually take a definite amount of time each day. But it is seldom necessary for people to devote all their time to these occupations. Most of us have some time in which we can do things for the sole reason that we find pleasure in doing them. Such activities are called recreation.

The Importance of Recreation. Real recreation is something which not only gives us pleasure, but also helps to renew, or recreate, the mind and the body. Therefore, the kind of recreation we engage in is important to all of us. It becomes increasingly important as machines take over more of our work. Man now spends fewer hours earning his living than he did fifty or one hundred years ago. The trend toward shorter working hours continues. Thus man finds himself with more and more time for recreation. If he spends this time wisely, he can greatly enrich his life. His recreation can help him to discover new talents, and to improve himself both physically and mentally. Society in general reaches a higher level of culture when large numbers of persons have time to develop their personalities and interests to the fullest possible extent. For this reason, recreation is of social as well as individual importance.

Kinds of Recreation. Any activity that gives pleasure and is engaged in from choice and not from necessity can be considered recreation in a general sense. But the term is more specifically applied to those activities which call for physical or mental participation. For example, when we hike, swim, play baseball, or build a model airplane, we are engaging in active recreation. But when we watch a motion picture or a tennis match, we are engaging in passive recreation. Therefore, such leisure-time occupations are more aptly termed amusements. Recreations which give us something to do stimulate us more than amusements we merely look at or listen to. If a person is to gain the greatest benefit from his recreation, a large share of it should be active.

Recreation can help a person develop a well-rounded life. He can do this by choosing a recreation which offers a different type of activity from that pursued in his daily work. For example, a person who works at a desk all day may obtain great benefit and pleasure from some form of sport. But a factory worker engaged in monotonous operations may find more creative satisfaction in some kind of craft work.

Need for Guidance. Surveys show that most persons, especially young people, need guidance in the use of their free time. The home, the school, the church, and various organizations can provide such guidance in many cases. But families of low income often lack the means to give their children proper recreation. If the child has nowhere else to go, the street usually becomes his playground. There he joins others like himself, and together they form gangs.

The lack of wholesome outlet for energies and interests often leads these gangs to seek dangerous forms of amusement. For example, they may break into vacant houses, hitch rides on passing cars, or engage in fights with rival gangs. Lack of money sometimes drives them to commit petty thefts. Children subjected to such influences frequently become juvenile delinquents and eventually criminals. The cost to the community of dealing with such problems often far exceeds the cost of providing adequate recreational facilities.

Opportunities for Recreation

Opportunities for wholesome recreation are provided by private organizations and through municipal, state,

Skin Diving is an exciting form of recreation provided by rivers, lakes, and oceans. Skin divers explore the strange world beneath the surface. They enjoy watching fish, colorful plants, and mineral formations.

Bermuda News Bureau

AMF

Bowling provides exercise and enjoyment for all members of the family. It is a thrilling sport for beginners as well as expert bowlers.

Baseball is called the *national pastime*. Each year, millions of Americans attend exciting baseball games to cheer for their favorite teams and to relax in the outdoors.

WORLD BOOK photo

WORLD BOOK photo, courtesy Field Museum of Natural History

Museums provide recreation and education. At a natural history museum, visitors can view past and present wonders of nature. On display in the room at the right are the skeleton of a prehistoric dinosaur and realistic figures of elephants of today.

and federal agencies. Great progress has been made in this respect, especially since about 1900. But provisions still fall short of the needs, particularly the needs of people in small towns, rural areas, and congested city slums. More provisions for recreation are needed for people in the lower income levels. Such people usually cannot take advantage of free state or national parks, for example, because they cannot afford the costs of transportation to the parks. Their children often find themselves with nothing to do during summer vacation periods. Racial and social discriminations may bar them from using many recreational facilities.

Municipal Facilities. Nearly all cities and towns of any size now make some provision for recreation. But conditions vary considerably throughout the country.

Community facilities usually include parks, playgrounds, picnic sites, and sometimes swimming pools, tennis courts, and golf courses. Playgrounds serve recreational needs best when a trained supervisor is in charge of them. Some communities arrange for the use of school playgrounds, auditoriums, and gymnasiums in the evenings. Museums and libraries also provide means for recreation.

Many coastal cities have municipally owned bathing beaches which the residents may enjoy at little or no cost. Both coast and inland river cities often have municipal fishing wharves. Larger cities have zoos, aquariums, and sometimes concert halls, theaters, and stadiums. These also fill recreational needs.

State Facilities. States provide parks, camping grounds, and forest preserves for recreational activities. These may have ski runs, lodges, and other facilities available at minimum expense. States also maintain public beaches and boating and fishing areas along lakes, rivers, and coasts. Some states have planning boards or youth commissions to study the needs of the people and recommend legislative measures. Often such work is carried on through the board of education and the schools.

Federal Government Facilities. The oldest federal provision for recreation is the maintenance of public lands for recreation. The government provides national parks, forest preserves, and other areas. Citizens can camp, rent land for summer homes, hunt, fish, climb mountains, and engage in other outdoor activities in these areas which the government has set aside.

No single federal agency exists for the sole purpose of providing or recommending recreational facilities. But approximately 30 governmental agencies aid in some way to meet these needs. For example, both the Fish and Wildlife Service and the Public Health Service do work of this kind. Various welfare conferences called by the government have studied recreational problems.

Welfare and Private Organizations. A number of organizations have given outstanding aid to the recreational needs of the country. The United States has more organizations for this purpose than any other country.

Probably the oldest and most active organization is the National Recreation Association. This association trains recreation supervisors and administrators, advises communities on how to solve their recreational problems, and carries on other work.

The Young Men's Christian Association and the Young Women's Christian Association maintain hundreds of centers throughout the country. They provide young men and women with opportunities for sports, social activities, and many other forms of recreation.

The Boy Scouts and Girl Scouts of America and the Camp Fire Girls have very active recreational programs. These organizations offer opportunities for camping, nature study, sports, craft work, and numerous other activities.

The Boys' Clubs of America provide recreational facilities especially for boys in large cities. Many have gymnasiums and swimming pools in addition to club rooms. Some have classes in crafts, dramatics, and other subjects of interest to boys. Most of these clubs also maintain summer camps for their members.

Other organizations include the American Association for Health, Physical Education and Recreation, the Police Athletic Leagues, the Youth Hostels, the Salvation Army, the Junior Leagues, and the American Legion. Various fraternal organizations sponsor recreational activities for young people. The Masons have two organizations for this purpose, one for boys and one for girls. The Kiwanis and Rotary clubs and many Jaycee chapters take an active interest in such work. Churches also play a major role in recreation.

Rural children are aided by such organizations as the 4-H Clubs, the Future Farmers of America, the National Grange, and sometimes local farmers' cooperatives.

Careers in Recreation

Nearly all public, private, and voluntary organizations in recreation need trained workers to direct and operate their programs. Public and private recreational agencies employ more than 50,000 full-time recreation workers and thousands of part-time workers. Many employers require full-time workers to have at least a bachelor's degree with a major in recreation, social science, or physical education. Most part-time workers are college students or teachers. A recreation worker should be genuinely interested in people. He should also enjoy helping, teaching, and working with many types of people.   BERNARD S. MASON

Related Articles. See the section A Visitor's Guide in the various state and province articles. See also the following articles:

Amusements	National Park	Sports and
Camping	System	Sportsmanship
Collecting	Park	Television
Dancing	Photography	Theater
Game	Physical	Toy
Handicraft	Education	Tricks and
Hobby	Play	Puzzles
Leisure	Radio	Vacation
Model Making	Reading	Youth Hostel
Motion Picture		

RECREATION AND PARK ASSOCIATION, NATIONAL, is an organization which promotes better recreation opportunities in the United States. It helps communities obtain better playgrounds and other recreation facilities and services. More than 4,000 professional workers and volunteers work with the association. The association provides a national information service, maintains a recreation library, and publishes *Recreation* magazine. More than 1,900 recreation agencies are affiliated with it. The association was founded in 1906, and has headquarters at 1700 Pennsylvania Avenue NW, Washington, D.C. 20006.   JOSEPH PRENDERGAST

RECRUITING is a method governments use to obtain personnel for their armed services. They recruit men and women through voluntary enlistments. Or they may draft them for military service.

Early Roman legions included drafted men, and were called "the gathering of the clans." Later, the Roman emperors began hiring men for military duty. During the Middle Ages, lords had to provide men to defend the king's domain. Then the kings began hiring men, called *mercenaries*, from the nobles (see MERCENARY).

The Paris Commune set up the first citizens' militia during the French Revolution, and called it the *national guard*. The French Republic established the first military conscription system in 1792.

During the 1800's, some European countries used bands of hired thugs called "press gangs" to force men to fight for them. Most nations adopted some form of universal military service. But Great Britain continued to recruit men by voluntary enlistments. It did not adopt a military draft until World War I. In World War II, it extended the draft to include women.

Americans who fought in the Revolutionary War were citizen-soldiers. The Continental Congress did not draft men during the war. The basic idea behind recruiting developed from the Militia Act of 1792. This law called for "the enrollment of all white, male citizens of the respective states." Before the draft law of 1863, during the Civil War, men volunteered for duty in the United States Army. The draft law recruited other men.

The United States government used *selective service* to recruit military personnel in World Wars I and II. Each branch of the armed services had volunteers and drafted men. Peacetime conscription in the early 1940's spurred voluntary enlistments before and during World War II. The government also increased its enlistment activities after the Korean War began in 1950. Since then, the government has recruited about 8 of every 10 servicemen through enlistments.

See also DRAFT, MILITARY; SELECTIVE SERVICE SYSTEM.

RECTANGLE, *REK tangg'l*, is a four-sided plane figure with four right angles. A blackboard or an ordinary sheet of writing paper illustrates a rectangle. It is a parallelogram with right angles. Its opposite sides are parallel and equal. If all four sides are equal, the rectangle is a square.

The formula for the area (A) of a rectangle which is L units long and W units wide is $A = LW$. Its perimeter, P, is $2L + 2W$, or $P = 2(L + W)$.

If a room measures 12' by 15', its floor area is 12' × 15' or 180 square feet, and its picture molding, or perimeter, is 2 (12 + 15) or 54 feet.   HARRY C. BARBER

See also QUADRILATERAL.

Both (A) and (B) Are Rectangles, although (B) is ordinarily called a square.

RECTIFICATION. See DISTILLING.

RECTIFIER. See ELECTRONICS (Terms; Gas-Filled Tubes).

RECTO. See BOOK (Parts of a Book).

RECTUM. See ALIMENTARY CANAL; COLON.

RECYCLING. See ENVIRONMENTAL POLLUTION (Controlling Pollution).

RED is one of the three primary colors in pigments. The other two are yellow and blue. A primary color is one which cannot be made by mixing other colors. Some of the most common red coloring matters, or pigments, are carmine, vermilion, red ochers, madders, and certain coal-tar products.

The light coming from the sun seems to have no color, but actually it is a combination of seven colors. These colors are red, orange, yellow, green, blue, indigo, and violet. These seven colors are known as the *spectrum*. When one beam of sunlight strikes a drop of rain or a prism, the beam bends and separates into the seven colors of the rainbow. Each color is a light wave of a certain length. The longest light wave in the rainbow or the spectrum is red. See COLOR.

Red has various meanings. For example, it often is a sign of danger. Red is used as a stop signal on traffic lights, and as a danger signal on railroads. The expression "to see red" means to be very angry. Revolutionists in many countries have carried red flags as a symbol of opposition to their governments. They claim that red is the symbol of the common blood of humanity.

RED AND THE BLACK, THE, or, in French, *Le Rouge et le Noir*, is a novel by Stendhal (Marie Henri Beyle), published in 1831. In it, Julien Sorel, the main character, is determined to get ahead, whatever the cost. He begins his career as a tutor in the Rênal family. Mme. de Rênal, the mother of his pupils, falls in love with him, and Julien has to leave because of village gossip. Later he becomes secretary to a nobleman in Paris, and courts his daughter. Mme. de Rênal writes a letter to the marquis, revealing Julien's past. In revenge Julien shoots her, and is later executed. See also STENDHAL.

RED BADGE OF COURAGE, THE. See CRANE, STEPHEN.

RED BLOOD CELL. See BLOOD.

RED CEDAR. See JUNIPER.

RED CLOUD (1822-1909) was the most famous chief of the Oglala, one of the largest groups of Sioux Indians. He was not a chief by birth, but rose to leadership through his bravery in battle and wisdom in council. In 1865, he stopped U.S. soldiers from building a road through Wyoming. The next year, he joined in the attack on Fort Phil Kearny, in Wyoming. Many whites thought he planned the 1866 massacre of 81 U.S. soldiers commanded by Captain W. J. Fetterman. But scholars do not believe he was responsible for this event.

In 1868, Red Cloud forced the United States to give up three forts. The government also agreed not to build any more roads through Sioux territory. Red Cloud was later removed as head of the Oglala, because he threatened a government agent. Reduced in power, he spent the remainder of his life at peace with the United States government. Red Cloud was born in Nebraska at the fork of the Platte River. He died on the Pine Ridge Reservation in South Dakota. E. ADAMSON HOEBEL

RED CROSS

The Horrors of War, *left*, led Jean Henri Dunant to form the Red Cross to relieve human sufferings.

Serving in Wartime, *far left*, Red Cross workers in World War I served coffee to men near the front.

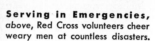

Serving in Emergencies, *above*, Red Cross volunteers cheer weary men at countless disasters.

Rare Blood, *left*, is sent by the Red Cross to doctors and hospitals throughout the world.

American National Red Cross

RED CROSS is an organization that works to relieve human suffering. Over 100 nations have Red Cross societies. Each national society carries on its own program. But Red Cross workers in all parts of the world are united in their aims. They try to prevent misery in time of war or peace, and serve all peoples, regardless of race, nationality, or religion.

The name *Red Cross* comes from the organization's flag, a red cross on a white background. The flag honors Switzerland, where the Red Cross was founded in 1863. The Swiss flag is a white cross on a red field. Societies in most Moslem countries use a red crescent on a white field, and call themselves Red Crescent societies. In Iran, the emblem is a red lion and sun. See FLAG (color pictures: Flags of World Organizations).

The American Red Cross

More than 36 million adult members belong to the American National Red Cross. In the early 1970's, the society spent an average of about $160 million a year on its programs. It raises money through voluntary contributions.

Services to the Armed Forces and Veterans make up the largest program of the American Red Cross. The organization spent an average of about $58 million a year on this program in the early 1970's. Red Cross services are available to U.S. military personnel wherever they are. The Red Cross helps solve personal and family problems and provides counseling, emergency communications, and financial aid. Red Cross volunteers serve in military medical facilities and in veterans' hospitals. A special Red Cross staff helps veterans and their dependents present claims before Veterans' Administration boards.

Disaster Services programs begin long before disaster strikes. Local Red Cross chapters help their communities develop year-round preparedness for disaster situations. Volunteer groups are trained to provide food, clothing, emergency first aid, and nursing and medical service; and to operate shelters for homeless families. All aid to disaster sufferers is free.

The Blood Program of the American Red Cross collects and distributes more blood than any other single agency in the United States. It collects about 3 million blood donations a year from voluntary donors. It gives blood to about 4,300 civilian and government hospitals, and supplies blood products that doctors need to treat patients.

The Red Cross is the coordinating agency for providing blood and blood products to the Department of Defense on request or in a national emergency.

Safety Programs include Red Cross courses in first aid and swimming. The society offers standard, advanced, and instructor courses in first aid. It also has a first aid course for young people. Safety information is included in each course. A program of first aid on the highway is carried on by trained Red Cross volunteers in mobile units and at first aid stations. Courses are also offered on the fundamentals of swimming, lifesaving, and handling small boats.

Nursing and Health Programs include courses in home nursing and mother and baby care. Reserve registered professional nurses are maintained for service in Red Cross and community activities, and in disasters.

Red Cross Youth. Elementary and secondary school students serve in the Red Cross. Activities range from volunteer hospital service to such international friendship projects as gift exchanging. Young persons also travel to other countries to teach health and safety.

International Activities. The American Red Cross maintains relations with other national Red Cross societies through the League of Red Cross Societies. It provides emergency help to disaster victims and refugees in other countries, and gives advisory aid to other Red Cross societies. It helps other Red Cross societies locate and reunite families separated by war, disasters, or other emergencies.

Organization. Volunteers and career staff members form the backbone of Red Cross activities in the United States. Red Cross workers belong to about 3,200 chapters that serve every county in the United States. The members of each chapter elect a volunteer board of directors to administer chapter programs. Volunteers make up the entire staffs of about 1,700 chapters. Some chapters have only one paid professional worker, who serves as executive secretary.

Four area offices give general supervision and technical assistance to individual chapters. They also direct field staff members assigned to armed forces installations in their areas. These offices are in Alexandria, Va.; Atlanta, Ga.; St. Louis; and San Francisco. Overseas area offices supervise work for servicemen abroad.

The American Red Cross has national headquarters at 17th and D Sts. NW, Washington, D.C. 20006. A 50-member board of governors develops national policies of the organization. All members of the board are volunteers. The President of the United States is honorary chairman of the American Red Cross. He appoints the organization's chairman and seven other board members. The board itself elects 12 more members. Chapter representatives elect 30 additional members at the organization's annual convention. The board selects the president of the American Red Cross.

The Canadian Red Cross

Health Services. The National Free Blood Transfusion Service is the major project of the Canadian Red Cross Society, which is made up of about 2,100,000 adult members and 900,000 junior members. The Blood Transfusion Service provides whole blood and blood products for all hospitals in Canada. The service is a four-way cooperative effort: (1) the provincial governments provide and maintain laboratories for processing the blood; (2) the Red Cross supplies technical staffs, equipment, and transportation; (3) Canadian citizens voluntarily donate their blood; and (4) hospitals administer blood and blood products to patients at no charge.

The Canadian Red Cross provides courses in water safety in all the provinces. In some areas, these courses are given to the handicapped, especially handicapped children. Mobile Red Cross dental clinics in Ontario serve isolated areas of that province.

The Red Cross in Canada has pioneered in many nursing projects. Its 37 outpost hospitals and nursing stations serve citizens in remote areas. Almost 600 communities benefit from its Sickroom Equipment Loan Service, which lends sickroom supplies to families free of charge. Registered nurses volunteer to teach basic home nursing.

Aid to Veterans. The Red Cross in Canada, as in the United States, devotes much of its activity to veterans. Volunteers visit veterans' hospitals and institutions to bring cheer to sick and disabled veterans. Seven Red Cross lodges and a recreation room provide homelike surroundings for thousands of patients near major veterans' hospitals.

Welfare Services. Trained Canadian Red Cross Homemakers visit homes where mothers are ill. They feed and care for the children and perform other tasks. The Canadian Red Cross Corps, a uniformed group of volunteer housewives and businesswomen, help veterans and perform community services. The Tracing and Reunion Bureau, another welfare service, obtains health and welfare reports on persons throughout the world. It also traces missing persons.

Relief Work. All provincial divisions of the Canadian Red Cross are prepared to give emergency disaster relief. Services include food, shelter, clothing, medical assistance, registration of victims, and answers to welfare inquiries during the emergency period.

The Women's Work Committee supplies clothing and emergency relief equipment to warehouses in Chile, Colombia, Curaçao, France, Kenya, Lebanon, and Singapore. Through this system of stockpiling, the Canadian Red Cross can send relief supplies to other lands within hours after a disaster strikes. The Canadian Red Cross sends professional and technical personnel to international disaster areas when requested to do so by the League of Red Cross Societies or the International Committee of the Red Cross.

The Canadian Red Cross Youth, made up of school children, raises money to support a Fund for Youth at Home and Abroad. This fund also provides hospital and medical care for thousands of handicapped and crippled children each year.

Organization. Volunteers perform more than 90 per cent of Canadian Red Cross work. The society has about 935 chartered branches in communities throughout the country. An office directs the work in each province and supervises each provincial division.

A Central Council of not more than 58 volunteers governs the national organization. The 10 provincial divisions elect three members each to the council. These 30 representatives appoint not more than 28 other members. The Central Council elects the officers of the society and the members of a national executive committee.

The Red Cross in Other Lands

The American and Canadian Red Cross societies belong to the international Red Cross movement, made up of about 115 national Red Cross, Red Crescent, and Red Lion and Sun societies in all parts of the world. Each society conducts a variety of humanitarian services according to the needs of its country's people. All societies operate under the fundamental principles of Red Cross, and most carry on extensive medical and health programs. Nearly all national societies have junior divisions and activities for the young.

National Red Cross societies cooperate internationally through their federation, the *League of Red Cross Societies*, which has headquarters in Geneva, Switzerland. The league encourages its members to work together, represents them in international discussions, and helps them develop their programs. The *International Committee of the Red Cross*, also located in Geneva, serves as a neutral intermediary during conflicts between nations for the protection of war victims. It works for the continual improvement of the Geneva Conventions, the treaty that provides for the humane treatment of prisoners during war. It also grants recognition to new Red Cross societies. The League and the International Committee shared the 1963 Nobel peace prize. The *International Red Cross Conference* is the highest deliberative body of the international Red Cross. Delegates from Red Cross groups and representatives of governments that signed the Geneva Conventions attend the conference every four years to discuss the Geneva Conventions

RED CROSS

A Young Earthquake Survivor hugs a gift provided for him by Red Cross members in the United States.

The Red Cross Helps Servicemen Overseas. A Red Cross representative helped this marine in South Vietnam get a leave to attend his brother's funeral.

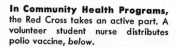

In Community Health Programs, the Red Cross takes an active part. A volunteer student nurse distributes polio vaccine, *below*.

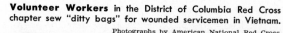

Volunteer Workers in the District of Columbia Red Cross chapter sew "ditty bags" for wounded servicemen in Vietnam.

Photographs by American National Red Cross

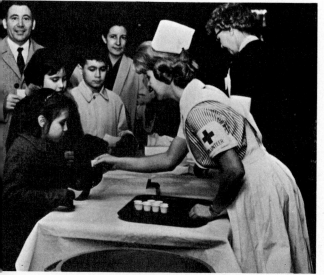

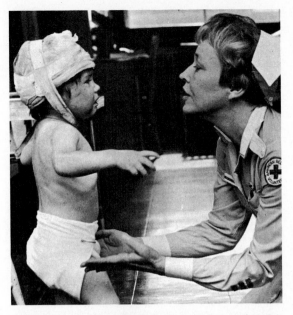

Red Cross Volunteers Help the Sick and the Injured in many ways. They work in hospitals, aid victims of accidents and disasters, and help handicapped persons.

Red Cross Help for Servicemen has spanned several wars. Red Cross units provide coffee and other refreshments for troops, arrange recreation, and help men with personal problems.

Photographs by American National Red Cross

and world humanitarian problems involving cooperation between Red Cross and governments.

History

Beginnings. Jean Henri Dunant, a Swiss philanthropist, founded the international Red Cross. He was touring Italy in 1859 during the Austro-Sardinian War. Dunant saw the field at Solferino the day after 40,000 men had been killed or wounded in a battle. Horrified at the suffering of the wounded, he formed a group of volunteers to help them.

In 1862, Dunant published a pamphlet called *Un Souvenir de Solferino (Recollections of Solferino)*. It ended with the plea, "Would it not be possible to found and organize in all civilized countries permanent societies of volunteers who in time of war would give help to the wounded without regard for their nationality?" The appeal won favorable response. On Oct. 26, 1863, delegates from 16 nations and several charitable organizations met in Geneva to discuss Dunant's idea. This conference laid the groundwork for the Red Cross movement and chose the organization's symbol.

Delegates from 12 European nations met in Geneva in August, 1864, on invitation from the Swiss Federal Council. Two observers from the United States attended. Out of this meeting came the *First Geneva* (or Red Cross) *Convention*. Later treaties amended and improved it.

In the United States, Congress did not ratify the Geneva Convention for 18 years, fearing foreign entanglements. The American Association for the Relief of Misery on the Battlefields was organized during this time. It adopted the red cross as its emblem. This group disbanded in 1871 because the United States had not yet ratified the Geneva Convention. Clara Barton worked to have the treaty ratified, and helped establish the American Association of the Red Cross in 1881. President Chester A. Arthur finally signed the treaty on Mar. 1, 1882. The Senate accepted it a few days later without a dissenting vote. The Red Cross association was later reorganized, and in 1905 Congress granted it a new charter that established the basic organization of today's American Red Cross.

The American Red Cross grew during World War I. It met the welfare needs of rapidly expanding military forces. Red Cross field directors and other workers served troops in the United States and overseas. In 1917, Home Service was established in many communities to provide a link between servicemen and their families. The Red Cross also organized and equipped 58 base hospitals, 54 of which went overseas. The Junior Red Cross, founded in 1917, gave American school children a chance to help the war effort. In 1965, the Junior Red Cross became Red Cross Youth.

After the war, the Red Cross aided millions of veterans and helped relieve war-caused suffering in many lands. During the 1920's, the Red Cross established 2,400 public health nursing services throughout the United States.

During World War II (1939-1945), the Red Cross Army-Navy Blood Donor Service collected more than 13 million pints of blood for the armed forces. Whole blood was flown from the United States to a warfront for the first time during the Korean War (1950-1953). Also during the 1950's, the Red Cross aided refugees of the Algerian and Hungarian revolts.

The Red Cross spent nearly $146 million during the 1960's for disaster relief and rehabilitation. It aided survivors of earthquakes in Chile (1960), Yugoslavia (1963), and Alaska (1964). The Red Cross also directed the shipment of $53 million worth of donated food and drugs to Communist Cuba in exchange for the release of about 1,100 prisoners and refugees (see CUBA [The Bay of Pigs Invasion]).

In the late 1960's and early 1970's, the Red Cross provided hospital and recreational programs for U.S. armed forces in Vietnam. It also sponsored a campaign to free American prisoners of war, and gave disaster relief to refugees of South Vietnam. In 1970, the Red Cross extended aid to survivors of a cyclone and tidal wave in East Pakistan (now Bangladesh).

In Canada. Major General G. S. Ryerson flew the first Red Cross flag in Canada during the Northwest Rebellion of 1885. He established the first overseas branch of the British Red Cross in 1896. The Canadian Red Cross Society developed from this small branch, and was incorporated by an act of the Canadian Parliament in 1909. The International Committee of the Red Cross recognized the Canadian Red Cross in 1927.

Critically reviewed by the AMERICAN NATIONAL RED CROSS and the CANADIAN RED CROSS SOCIETY

Related Articles in WORLD BOOK include:

Barton, Clara
Dunant, Jean Henri
First Aid

Geneva Conventions
Social Work
Swimming (Water Safety)

Outline

I. The American Red Cross
A. Services to the Armed Forces and Veterans
B. Disaster Services
C. The Blood Program
D. Safety Programs
E. Nursing and Health Programs
F. Red Cross Youth
G. International Activities
H. Organization

II. The Canadian Red Cross
A. Health Services
B. Aid to Veterans
C. Welfare Services
D. Relief Work
E. The Canadian Red Cross Youth
F. Organization

III. The Red Cross in Other Lands
IV. History

Questions

What kinds of services does the Red Cross provide in disaster areas?

Who founded the Red Cross? What led him to do so?

What types of educational programs does the American Red Cross sponsor?

What is the Sickroom Equipment Loan Service?

How are Red Cross activities financed?

Who is always appointed honorary chairman of the American Red Cross?

What is the League of Red Cross Societies?

What kinds of aid does the Red Cross offer to servicemen and veterans?

What is the major project of the Canadian Red Cross Society?

What emblems other than the red cross are used in some countries?

RED CROSS YOUTH. See RED CROSS.

RED DEER is a graceful and majestic animal, related to the American elk. About 20 kinds of red deer live in the forests of Europe, Asia, and northern Africa. They eat grass, moss, and tender twigs. Their smooth coats range in color from gray to yellowish-brown. All red deer have dark, shaggy collars and a yellow to orange patch on the buttocks. The *hart* (adult male) grows stately, branched antlers that are shed each year. A hart weighs between 250 and 350 pounds, and stands from $3\frac{1}{2}$ to $4\frac{1}{2}$ feet high. Most *hinds* (adult females) stand about 6 inches shorter than the harts, and have no antlers. They bear a single calf in late spring.

Scientific Classification. Red deer belong to the deer family, *Cervidae*. They are genus *Cervus*, species *C. elaphus*. VICTOR H. CAHALANE

See also ANIMAL (color picture: Animals of the Woodlands); DEER; ELK.

RED DRUM. See REDFISH.

RED FLAG LAW. See AUTOMOBILE (The Steam Car).

RED FOX. See FOX; FUR (Names of Furs [Fox]).

RED GUARD. See CHINA (Recent Events).

RED GUM. See SWEET GUM.

RED HAW. See HAWTHORN.

RED LEAD is a reddish-orange pigment, commonly used as a rust preventative for structural steel. It is made by heating lead monoxide in open air at a temperature of about 925° F. (496° C.). Red lead mixes easily with linseed oil and some synthetic resins to make protective finishes. Red lead is used in making storage batteries, glass, and matches. JOHN R. KOCH

RED MEN, IMPROVED ORDER OF, is a fraternal society with about 85,000 members in more than 1,300 lodges in the United States. They pay dues that entitle them to benefits in case of sickness, accident, or death. The full name of the society is GREAT COUNCIL OF THE UNITED STATES IMPROVED ORDER OF RED MEN. Its address is P.O. Box 683, Waco, Tex. 76703. CARL R. LEMKE

RED-OUT is the cloudy red vision which an airman may experience when flying certain maneuvers. It comes when flying outside loops, spins, or in other acrobatics where the flyer's head is farthest from the center of rotation. Forces that act in the seat-to-head direction cause blood to rush to the head and flood the eyes, face, and brain. These forces are called *negative acceleration*. Opposite forces drain blood from the head and cause the condition called *blacking out*. W. R. STOVALL

RED PEPPER. See CAPSICUM; CAYENNE PEPPER.

RED POWER. See INDIAN, AMERICAN (Indians Today).

RED PUCCOON. See BLOODROOT.

RED RIVER, so named because of the red-colored sediment it carries, is the southernmost of the main branches of the Mississippi. It is about 1,300 miles long. Its drainage basin covers about 90,000 square miles.

The Red River rises in northern Texas. Its north fork has its source east of Amarillo, Tex., and the Prairie Dog Town fork rises south of it. For most of its eastward course, the river forms the boundary between Oklahoma and Texas. Then it flows through southwestern Arkansas and into Louisiana. At Alexandria, La., it enters the flood plain of the Mississippi. The two rivers join 341 miles above the mouth of the Mississippi. See SOUTHERN STATES (color map). JOHN H. GARLAND

See also LAKE TEXOMA.

RED RIVER OF THE NORTH is a 533-mile waterway of the United States and Canada. It is one of the three great rivers which flow into Lake Winnipeg to form part

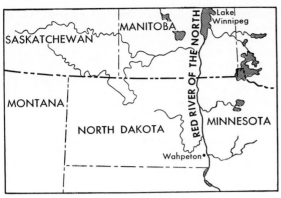

The Red River of the North Flows into Lake Winnipeg.

of the Saskatchewan-Nelson river system. Most of the course of the Red River runs through a level plain which was formerly the bed of Lake Agassiz, a glacial lake formed thousands of years ago (see LAKE AGASSIZ).

The Red River Valley is one of the richest farming areas in the world. Farmers raise wheat, flax, barley, potatoes, and sugar beets. Cities along the Red River include Fargo and Grand Forks, the two largest cities in North Dakota; Moorhead, Minn.; and Winnipeg and Saint Boniface, in Manitoba. Boats can sail from Grand Forks to Winnipeg on the river.

The Red River of the North is formed by the union of the Otter Tail and Bois de Sioux rivers at Wahpeton, N.Dak., opposite Breckenridge, Minn. The Red River flows north, and forms the boundary between North Dakota and Minnesota. The Otter Tail River rises in the west-central part of Minnesota, only a few miles west of the headwaters of the Mississippi River. The Bois de Sioux River begins in Lake Traverse. This is only 5 miles from Big Stone Lake, from which the Minnesota River flows. These lakes lie in the former outlet of Lake Agassiz.   HAROLD T. HAGG

RED RIVER REBELLION, or FIRST RIEL REBELLION, occurred when the settlers in the Red River Valley of Manitoba revolted against the Canadian government in 1869-1870. This uprising was called the Red River Rebellion. Most of the rebels were *métis* (persons of European and Indian descent), who opposed the extension of British rule into a region that had long been almost independent.

The Hudson's Bay Company had ruled the Red River Valley until 1869. It allowed the métis to live much as they pleased. But in 1869, the company turned its rights in Rupert's Land (including present-day Manitoba) over to the British government. In 1870, Great Britain gave the district to the Canadian government, and plans were drawn up for developing the region.

At this time, the only people who lived in the great Canadian Northwest were Indians, a few traders, and about 12,000 Red River Valley settlers. These settlers lived a simple life. They held no title to the lands they farmed. When they grew tired of a plot of ground, they moved on to some other spot which suited them. See MANITOBA (Places to Visit [Red River Valley]).

The Revolt. Road builders, surveyors, and officials of all kinds suddenly descended upon the settlers. Their lands had been arranged on the old French plan of strips reaching back from the riverfronts. The new officials decided to rearrange the farms into townships and sections. This alarmed and angered the settlers and caused great excitement.

A leader arose among the métis. He was Louis Riel, a settler of French, Irish, and Indian blood. The Canadian government soon sent out William McDougall as first governor of the new territory. When Riel heard of McDougall's approach, he determined to keep him from organizing the new government. Riel led the métis in an attack on Fort Garry, now the city of Winnipeg. They captured the fort, and Riel set up a "provisional government" there. The settlers prepared to resist the authority of the Canadian government. The métis met McDougall at the border of Rupert's Land and forced him to turn back.

McDougall wisely saw that the métis had a real grievance. He obeyed Riel in order to keep the peace. But at this point, Riel lost his head and doomed the rebellion. A group of loyalists made an attack on the métis at Fort Garry. The rebels drove the loyalists off and captured some of them. Riel imprisoned the captives as "enemies of the provisional government." A young English Canadian named Thomas Scott was one of those imprisoned. For some reason, the métis picked Scott as an example. They condemned him as a traitor to the provisional government and shot him.

Riel's Flight. The people of eastern Canada became extremely indignant at this cold-blooded murder. A force of 700 men, under the command of Colonel Garnet Wolseley, was ordered into the Red River Valley. They made the long, difficult journey westward by way of Lake Superior. As they approached Fort Garry, Riel fled into the United States. His flight from the Red River Valley ended the rebellion.

While Wolseley and his men were marching westward, the Dominion parliament admitted Manitoba as a self-governing province of the Confederation. The government set aside 1,400,000 acres of land for the use of the métis. But many of them were still dissatisfied and wandered westward into the present province of Saskatchewan. Riel also appeared in that territory some years later, and led another revolt known as the Saskatchewan Rebellion. Riel was captured and hanged for treason in 1885.   EDWARD R. ADAIR

See also RIEL, LOUIS; SASKATCHEWAN REBELLION; MANITOBA (History).

RED ROCKS PARK. See EASTER (picture: Sunrise Services).

RED SEA is an arm of the Indian Ocean that separates the Arabian Peninsula from northeastern Africa. Authorities give various reasons for the origin of the name *Red*. The surrounding hills and the coral reefs and seaweed are a reddish color. Thousands of tiny sea animals often color the water red. The hot winds often blow clouds of desert sand that settle on the surface in great reddish streaks.

The story of the passage of the Children of Israel across the Red Sea is one of the most famous Bible stories. It is told in Exodus 14.

The Red Sea is about 1,400 miles long and nowhere wider than 220 miles. Its average depth is about 2,000 feet. It covers 169,050 square miles, an area a little

RED SHIFT

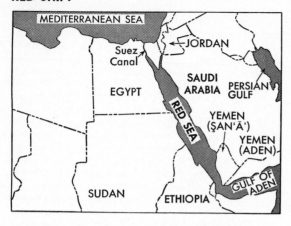

The Red Sea Links the Suez Canal and Indian Ocean.

larger than that of California. Large reefs make the sea dangerous for navigation even by small vessels, except for a central channel in the southern half. It is 20 miles wide.

The Red Sea has been the great water highway between Europe and the Orient since the opening of the Suez Canal. Before that time, trade goods had to be sent overland by caravan or be shipped around the Cape of Good Hope. Because of the sea's military importance, the British placed mines at its southern entrance during World War II. The British forces sank Italian ships and took Eritrea's key port of Massaua in 1941.

The Red Sea is really a great crack in solid rock that has filled with water. The shore is barren, and there are few harbors in the desert regions. High mountain ranges rise on the east. Low sand hills and rocky tablelands line the west coast of the sea, which contains many coral reefs.

Red Sea waters are salty because the high winds and extreme heat cause the sun to evaporate moisture rapidly. The temperature often rises to about 100° F. (38° C.). The sea has plant and animal life different from that of the Mediterranean Sea.   BOSTWICK H. KETCHUM

RED SHIFT is a shift in the *spectrum* (color pattern) of a galaxy or another astronomical object toward the longer (red) wave lengths. Light acts like a wave, and its *wave length* is the distance between crests of the wave. When red shift occurs, all wave lengths are lengthened by the same fraction. The red shift is expressed as a percentage of increase over the normal wave length. An

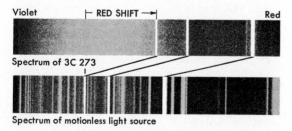

Red Shift of Quasar 3C 273 is measured by comparing bright lines in the quasar's spectrum with the same lines in the spectrum of a motionless light source. The difference in the positions of the lines indicates the quasar's speed away from earth.

example of red shift can be seen in the spectrum of a *quasar*. A quasar is a somewhat starlike source of radio and light waves (see QUASAR). A series of bright lines called the *Balmer lines of hydrogen* appear in the spectrum of Quasar 3C 273 (object 273 in the 3rd Cambridge catalog of radio sources). The wave length of each Balmer line in 3C 273 is 15.8 per cent longer than normal. Therefore the red shift of the quasar is 15.8 per cent.

Most astronomers believe red shift occurs in astronomical objects because the objects are speeding away from the earth. The amount of red shift indicates the speed of the object. Objects with very small red shifts are moving at a percentage of the speed of light equal to the red shift percentage. The speed of objects having larger red shifts must be calculated by using Einstein's special theory of relativity. The red shift of 3C 273 indicates a speed of about 27,000 miles per second, 14.5 per cent of the speed of light. Some quasars have red shifts of more than 200 per cent, indicating they are moving at more than 80 per cent of the speed of light.

In 1929, American astronomer Edwin Hubble discovered that the amount of red shift increased as the distance of distant galaxies from the earth increased, and therefore, red shift could be used to estimate their distance. This discovery also showed that every galaxy is moving away from every other galaxy, and therefore that the universe is expanding.   MAARTEN SCHMIDT

See also ASTRONOMY (Astronomers at Work); QUASAR.

RED SINDHI. See CATTLE (Other Dairy Cattle).

RED SPIDER. See MITE.

RED SQUARE. See MOSCOW (Famous Landmarks; picture); RUSSIA (color picture).

RED TAPE is a derogatory term used to describe the inefficiency of government or of business. The term originated in England during the 1700's. People used red string to tie legal and official documents together. Later, the term came to mean official routine in general. *Red tape* may describe an official's rigid observance of rules and regulations, or it may refer to the routing of requests and orders through various channels which result in delay. It may also include the many technicalities found in large business.   ROBERT A. DAHL

RED TIDE is a term used for brownish or reddish areas of ocean, river, or lake water. The color comes from tiny plants or animals that have suddenly increased by the millions. Red tides appear in waters in most parts of the world. In the United States, they are most often seen off the coasts of Florida, Texas, and southern California.

Most red tides are harmless. But some kill fish and other water animals, which then may float on the water or wash ashore in great numbers. The decaying bodies cause an unpleasant odor. Still other kinds of red tides do not kill sea life, but they make the shellfish that feed on them poisonous to eat. Harmful red tides are caused by several species of *dinoflagellates* (one-celled sea creatures). Some kinds of dinoflagellates secrete a poison that paralyzes and kills fish. Dinoflagellates may also kill fish during red tides by using up nearly all the oxygen in the water.

Scientists do not fully understand why the dinoflagellate population suddenly increases, causing harmful red tides. It is known that dinoflagellates grow fastest when the food, temperature, amount of sunlight, water currents, and amount of salt in the water suit their needs. They may decrease when other sea creatures eat the food or the dinoflagellates. When many favorable conditions occur at the same time, the dinoflagellates have a "population explosion" and red tides occur. The discolored areas may cover from a few square feet to several square miles. They last from a few hours to several months.   CADET HAND

RED-WINGED BLACKBIRD is a general name for 15 different kinds of such birds. The eastern red-winged blackbird lives in North America from the Rocky Mountains to the Atlantic Ocean. It grows about 9½ inches long. The birds nest in bushes or small trees in swamps and marshes. They build their nests of dried grass, cattails, or reeds. The female lays from three to five eggs that are light blue or olive, with black, brown, or purple scrawls. The birds eat grain, but they also devour injurious insects and weed seeds. The San Diego, Rio Grande, and Nevada redwings resemble this eastern bird. See also BIRD (color pictures: Other Bird Favorites, Birds' Eggs).

Scientific Classification. The red-winged blackbird is in the New World blackbird family, *Icteridae*. It is genus *Agelaius*, species *A. phoeniceus*.   LEON A. HAUSMAN

REDBIRD is the common name for all birds with red or mostly red plumage. In the United States, the name is often applied to the cardinal bird and occasionally to the scarlet tanager and summer tanager. The European bullfinch is also called a redbird. See also CARDINAL (bird); TANAGER.

REDBREAST. See ROBIN.

REDBUD, or JUDAS TREE, is any one of a group of small trees and shrubs native to North America, southern Europe, Asia, and Japan. Redbuds are particularly beautiful early in spring when the whole tree is covered with pink, delicate blossoms, each about 1 inch long. The flowers emerge from both the old wood and the new young twigs. They reach full bloom before the leaves appear. Some redbud trees grow 40 feet high. The reddish-brown bark is rather smooth, and the wood is hard and close-grained. The simple, heart-shaped leaves are quite handsome. Redbud trees bear many seeds every year. The seeds grow in flat, thin pods. They are a valuable source of food for wild game.

Gardeners value redbuds as ornamentals. These trees grow best in fertile, sandy soil. They are grown from seeds or cuttings. Growers transplant the trees when they are quite young and use them for hedges or lawn trees. The redbud is also called the Judas tree because of the belief that Judas Iscariot, the betrayer of Jesus Christ, hanged himself on a redbud tree.

Scientific Classification. Redbuds are in the pea family, *Leguminosae*. The redbud of the eastern United States is genus *Cercis*, species *C. canadensis*.   T. EWALD MAKI

See also TREE (Familiar Broadleaf and Needleleaf Trees [picture]).

REDCOAT. See REVOLUTIONARY WAR IN AMERICA.

REDEMPTORISTS. See RELIGIOUS LIFE (table: Some Leading Religious Orders).

REDFISH is a name applied to several different kinds of fish, but particularly to the *red drum*, or *channel bass*. This game fish is abundant in the Atlantic Coast waters of the southern United States. This handsome fish has a gray skin, with a coppery iridescence, or shine. The skin often turns red after death. The fish grows to be 5 feet long and may weigh up to 75 pounds, but red drums of more than 40 pounds are rare. This popular food fish is one of the valuable products of the Texas fisheries.

The term is also applied to a red fish of southern California, a richly colored fish with a thick body. This fish has a crimson body with blackish purple fins. It weighs up to 15 pounds. It is sometimes called the *fathead*, because of the fatty lump on its blunt forehead. Its flesh is prized, especially by the Chinese, who dry and salt it. *Redfish* is also the name given in Alaska to the red or blue-black salmon (see SALMON).

Scientific Classification. The red drum is a member of the drumfish family, *Sciaenidae*. It is genus *Sciaenops*, species *S. ocellata*. The California redfish is a member of the wrasse family, *Labridae*. It is genus *Pimelometopon*, species *P. pulchrum*.   LEONARD P. SCHULTZ

See also OCEAN (color picture: Life in the Ocean).

REDI, FRANCESCO. See SPONTANEOUS GENERATION; LIFE (Early Theories).

REDISTRICTING. See APPORTIONMENT.

REDLANDS, UNIVERSITY OF. See UNIVERSITIES AND COLLEGES (table).

REDMOND, JOHN EDWARD (1851-1918), an Irish leader, succeeded Charles Stewart Parnell as the political champion of Irish Home Rule. When Redmond became chairman of the Irish Nationalist Party in 1900, he healed the split in the party caused by Parnell's disgrace (see PARNELL, CHARLES S.). Redmond believed in moderation, and was shocked by the bloody Easter Rebellion in Dublin in 1916. But the Sinn Féin Party, which used violence, gradually displaced Redmond's party. He was born in Ballytrent.   JAMES L. GODFREY

REDOX PROCESS. See OXIDATION.

L. W. Brownell

Flowers of the Redbud Tree form showy masses. The wood of the tree has a beautiful black-veined design.

Eric Hosking

The Fluffy Little Redpoll Has a Bright Red Crown.

REDPOLL is a small bird related to the finches and sparrows. Both male and female have a red crown, black chin, and whitish underparts, with dark streaks on the sides. In addition, the adult male has a rosy-pink breast. Redpolls breed in the northern part of North America and migrate south as far as California, Kansas, and South Carolina. These birds build their nests in bushes or small trees. They construct them chiefly of grass stems and line them with feathers. The females lay from five to seven blue eggs speckled with reddish brown. Redpolls eat plant buds and some insects. In winter they commonly travel about in flocks.

Scientific Classification. Redpolls belong to the finch family, *Fringillidae*. They are classified as genus *Acanthis*, species *A. flammea*. GEORGE J. WALLACE

REDSKIN. See INDIAN, AMERICAN.

REDSTART is an active, graceful American warbler. Because of its agile movements and flaming orange-red and black plumage, people in Cuba call it *candelita*, which means *little torch*. In summer, the redstart lives throughout most of North America. In winter, it makes its home in Cuba, the West Indies, and northern South America. The adult male is black, with vivid salmon-red or orange-red markings. The female and young are brown with markings of dull yellow. The female lays four or five creamy-white eggs blotched with reddish

brown markings. The redstart feeds chiefly on insects.

Scientific Classification. The American redstart belongs to the wood warbler family, *Parulidae*. It is genus *Setophaga*, species *S. ruticilla*. GEORGE E. HUDSON

See also BIRD (color pictures: Birds That Help Us, Birds' Eggs).

REDSTONE ARSENAL, Ala., serves as headquarters of the U.S. Army Missile Command. It also houses the U.S. Missile and Munitions Center and School. The Redstone Arsenal covers 40,000 acres, and lies near Huntsville, Ala. It received its name from the red soil. The arsenal includes two free-flight rocket ranges and facilities for testing liquid and solid propellant rocket missiles. Redstone Arsenal was established in 1941 by combining the Chemical and Ordnance arsenals located there. In 1960, the George C. Marshall Space Flight Center was established at the arsenal. This center manages the research and development of high-power rocket boosters. SAMUEL J. ZISKIND

REDTOP, a kind of grass. See BENT.

REDUCING. See WEIGHT CONTROL.

REDUCTION has two meanings in chemistry. The term originally referred to any chemical process in which a substance either combines with hydrogen or loses oxygen. Today, the term also refers to the gain of electrons by a substance during a chemical reaction.

The combining of nitrogen with hydrogen to form ammonia (NH_3) is an example of the original meaning of reduction. Another example of this kind of reduction is the removal of oxygen from zinc oxide (ZnO) to form metallic zinc. This reduction is used in extracting zinc from its ore.

According to the newer meaning of reduction, a substance can be reduced without combining with hydrogen or losing oxygen. For example, copper *ions* (electrically charged atoms) in a solution are reduced to metallic copper when metallic zinc is added. The complete equation for this reaction is written:

$$Cu^{++} + Zn \rightarrow Cu + Zn^{++}.$$

In this reaction, copper ions gain electrons from the metallic zinc and are reduced. The equation for this half of the complete reaction can be written:

$$Cu^{++} + 2e^- \rightarrow Cu.$$

Giving up electrons is the opposite of reduction and is called *oxidation* (see OXIDATION). Reduction and oxidation always occur together. The combined processes make up the redox process. ESMARCH S. GILREATH

A Male Redstart Takes Its Turn Feeding Fledglings as They Cling to a Branch Near Their Nest.

Allan D. Cruickshank, National Audubon Society

REDWOOD is a magnificent forest tree that grows along the West Coast of the United States from central California to southern Oregon. It thrives in the foggy climate along the sides of the mountains that face the Pacific Ocean, and only rarely occurs more than 50 miles from the coast. The redwood is also called *coast* or *California redwood* to distinguish it from the giant sequoia to which it is closely related (see SEQUOIA).

The redwood tree has yellow-green needles that grow about an inch long and remain on the tree for several years. The fruit is a globe-shaped, scaly cone about 1 inch long. Tightly packed under each scale are several reddish-brown seeds. Each of the seeds produced by the redwood is about $\frac{1}{16}$ of an inch long. It would

REDWOOD

Rings of annual growth show the tree's age and indicate the changes in climates over the course of many centuries.

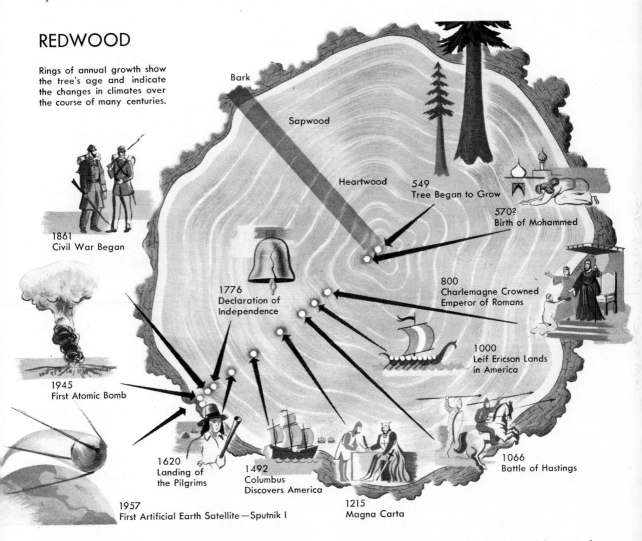

Bark

Sapwood

Heartwood

549
Tree Began to Grow

570?
Birth of Mohammed

1861
Civil War Began

800
Charlemagne Crowned
Emperor of Romans

1776
Declaration of
Independence

1000
Leif Ericson Lands
in America

1945
First Atomic Bomb

1620
Landing of
the Pilgrims

1492
Columbus
Discovers America

1066
Battle of Hastings

1957
First Artificial Earth Satellite—Sputnik I

1215
Magna Carta

Redwoods are among the world's tallest living trees. They commonly grow 200 to 275 feet high and often have trunks that are 8 to 12 feet in diameter. The tallest redwood known, which stands in Humboldt County, California, towers 368.6 feet in height.

The typical redwood forest is impressive. The massive trees grow close together, shutting out most of the sunlight. There is little underbrush, for few plants can survive in the cool, dim atmosphere. Even the trees themselves seem to be crowding one another. Often tight circles of young trees surround old stumps, completely enclosing them. The lowest branches of old trees may be 80 to 100 feet above the ground. But those of the young trees grow all the way to ground level.

take about 123,000 of these tiny seeds to weigh a pound.

Redwood bark may be 12 inches thick. Its fibrous texture gives it a deeply fissured appearance and makes it fire resistant. The wood is soft, red, and weak, but remarkably resistant to decay, disease, or insect enemies. Lumbermen prize it for siding or interior finish in buildings, and for other nonstructural uses when durability is important.

Great *burls* (lumps) often grow on trunks of older redwoods. They sometimes measure several feet across. These burls are highly valued for their beautiful grain and are often used for veneer. Small burls are sold for table decorations because of their ability to sprout when placed in water.

A Section of Bark, *above*; Redwood Leaves, *below*.

A Lone Redwood, *left*, dwarfs the California landscape. These gigantic trees may live to be thousands of years old.

Many redwood forests have been set aside as state or national parks in order to preserve the ancient beauty of these impressive trees.

Scientific Classification. Redwoods belong to the taxodium family, *Taxodiaceae*. They are classified as genus *Sequoia*, species *S. sempervirens*.   RICHARD J. PRESTON, JR.

See also FOREST AND FOREST PRODUCTS (picture: Forests of Giant Redwoods).

REDWOOD NATIONAL PARK covers about 58,000 acres in northern California. It is in the huge forest of redwood trees that grows along the Pacific Coast from central California to southern Oregon. The world's tallest known tree, a redwood about 367 feet high, is in the park. The park also includes 40 miles of scenic coastline. Three state parks lie within the boundaries of the national park. Congress established Redwood National Park in 1968. For location, see CALIFORNIA (political map).   GEORGE B. HARTZOG, JR.

See also REDWOOD.

REED is a common name for many kinds of tall, slender grass plants. The word also commonly refers to the stems of these plants, which are often jointed in many places. The stems may be as slender and fragile as straw, or they may be as thick and sturdy as bamboo. The pith that fills the center of the reed can usually be removed, leaving a hollow, jointed tube. The hollow stems have been used to make musical instruments.

The reed musical instruments have a mouthpiece containing a vibrating strip that was once made only of reed. Plastic, wood, glass, and metal are now used to make the "reed." Farmers in Europe thatch their houses with other types of reeds.

Reeds grow in almost all countries of the temperate and warm regions. Straw is sometimes called reed in England. The American Indians often made the roots, young leaves, and stems of various kinds of reeds a part of their diet.   HAROLD NORMAN MOLDENKE

REED, THOMAS BRACKETT (1839-1902), served as speaker of the United States House of Representatives from 1889 to 1891 and from 1895 to 1899. He was sometimes called *Czar Reed* because of the way he controlled the House. A Maine Republican, Reed served in the House from 1877 to 1899. In 1890, he won adoption of "Reed's Rules." These rules increased the speaker's power, but they made the House more effective. Many of the rules are still used by the House of Representatives. Reed was born in Portland, Me.   ROBERT M. YORK

REED, WALTER (1851-1902), a medical officer in the United States Army, helped show how to control typhoid fever and yellow fever. During the Spanish-American War in 1898, he became chief of a commission to study the origin and spread of typhoid fever in Army camps. Experiments showed that flies were the most important carriers of the infection, and that dust and uncleanliness helped spread it.

In 1900, Reed headed a commission to investigate an epidemic of yellow fever among American troops in Cuba. He and the other doctors, including James Carroll and Jesse Lazear, carried on a series of daring experiments. Several of the doctors, as well as a number of soldiers, volunteered to be infected by yellow fever germs to study the course of the disease. Two died as a result. The experiments established that the bite of a mosquito transmits yellow fever. They showed how the disease might be controlled. See YELLOW FEVER.

Walter Reed

Reed was born in Gloucester County, Virginia. He studied medicine at the University of Virginia and at Bellevue Hospital Medical College in New York City. He entered the Army in 1875. Walter Reed Army Medical Center in Washington, D.C., is named for him.   NOAH D. FABRICANT

REED COLLEGE. See UNIVERSITIES AND COLLEGES (table).

REEDBIRD. See BOBOLINK.

REEDER, ANDREW HORATIO. See KANSAS (History).

REEF. See ATOLL; CORAL.

REEL. See FISHING (Standard Fishing Equipment).

REELFOOT LAKE, in northwestern Tennessee, was formed by earthquake movements in 1811 and 1812. The lake and its surrounding area attract sportsmen because of the fresh-water fish, waterfowl, and other game. Reelfoot Lake State Fish and Game Preserve was established there in 1925.

REEVE. See BOROUGH; SHERIFF.

REEVE, the female ruff. See RUFF.

REEVE, TAPPING. See LITCHFIELD.

REFECTORY. See CLOISTER.

REFEREE. See FOOTBALL (The Officials).

REFERENCE BOOK. See ALMANAC; ATLAS; DICTIONARY; ENCYCLOPEDIA; LIBRARY.

REFERENDUM. See INITIATIVE AND REFERENDUM.

REFINING. See METALLURGY (Extractive Metallurgy); PETROLEUM (Refining Petroleum; color picture: Refining Petroleum); SUGAR.

REFLECTING GALVANOMETER. See CABLE (The Atlantic Telegraph Cable).

REFLECTION is the return of a wave of energy, such as light, heat, sound, or radio, after it strikes a surface. Reflection can be compared to the action of a ball rebounding from a wall. A ball thrown at right angles to the wall will bounce back in the same line. If the ball is thrown along a path that makes less than a right angle with the wall, its path on rebounding will make the same angle with the wall, but on the opposite side of the point where the ball hit the wall. Imagine a line drawn to make a 90-degree angle with the wall at the point where the ball struck. The angle formed by the path of the thrown ball and this line is the *angle of incidence*. The corresponding angle made by the rebounding ball is the *angle of reflection*. These two angles are always equal.

The principle of reflection has many applications in daily living. The mirror (a glass coated with silver) reflects most of the light that strikes it. Polished surfaces, such as chromium, reflect most of the light that strikes them. Clear surfaces, such as window glass, reflect little light. The best example of the reflection of sound waves is the echo. Radar uses the reflection of radio waves.   S. W. HARDING

See also LIGHT (Science Project: How Light Behaves; Reflection, Refraction, and Absorption); ECHO; KALEIDOSCOPE; MIRROR; RADAR.

REFLEX ACTION. If you accidentally touch a hot stove, you jerk away before you have time to think what you are doing. Actions of this kind, which are not planned or decided beforehand, are called reflex actions. Each reflex involves some stimulus that causes a response. In the above example, the hot stove was the stimulus and the jerking away was the response.

Reflex actions are quite common and easy to notice. If light is directed at a person's eye, the pupil of the eye will become smaller. When the light is removed and the person's eye is shaded, the pupil becomes larger again. The light acts as a stimulus, and the reaction of the pupil is the eye's response. Doctors often test a person's reflex actions. Frequently they test the *patellar reflex*, or knee jerk. The patient sits with his knees crossed and the doctor strikes a point just below the kneecap. This causes the patient's foot to kick suddenly.

Scientists call these kinds of reflexes *unconditioned reflexes*. They occur in all normal persons, and many animals also have some of them. Unlike most of man's behavior, unconditioned reflexes occur with no specific learning or experience. They are considered involuntary acts, because a response always occurs when a stimulus is presented.

How Reflex Action Occurs. Most reflex acts are very complicated. But in the simplest forms, four events are involved. Briefly, these could be called (1) reception, (2) conduction, (3) transmission, and (4) response. The stimulation is *received* by receptors, or sensitive nerve endings. These may be in the eye, ear, nose, tongue, or skin. Energy from the stimulus is changed into nerve impulses and *conducted* from the receptor to the central nervous system. From there, the nerve impulses are *transmitted* to the motor nerves, which control muscle action. The motor nerves conduct the impulses to the muscles and glands, causing them to *respond*, or act.

To illustrate the events in a reflex action, suppose a

HOW REFLEX ACTION WORKS

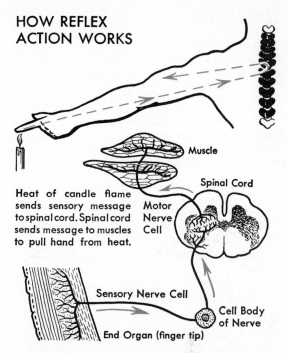

Muscle

Spinal Cord

Heat of candle flame sends sensory message to spinal cord. Spinal cord sends message to muscles to pull hand from heat.

Motor Nerve Cell

Sensory Nerve Cell

Cell Body of Nerve

End Organ (finger tip)

person touches the flame of a candle with his finger. The heat of the flame stimulates receptors in the skin of the finger. This creates a nerve impulse that travels along a sensory nerve to the spinal cord. In the spinal cord, the sensory nerve fibers interlace with motor nerve fibers. The nerve impulse passes from the sensory fibers to the motor fibers, which in turn relay it to the muscles, causing them to contract. When the muscles contract, the person's hand jerks back.

Most reflex acts are much more complicated than this. They often involve other parts of the nervous system, such as the brain. Reflex acts are quicker than voluntary acts. You jerk your hand away from a hot stove before you feel pain. You do not have to take the time to decide exactly what you are going to do.

People have many reflex reactions to emotional stimuli. These include changes in blood pressure and respiration. A lie detector measures certain body reactions to emotional stimuli. A person telling a lie usually has small emotional reactions that can be detected because of these reflex reactions. See LIE DETECTOR.

Conditioned Reflex, another kind of reflex action, works by association. For example, a dog's mouth begins to water when the animal smells food. The Russian physiologist Ivan P. Pavlov showed that the flow of saliva is a conditioned reflex, not an automatic reaction to the smell of food. Pavlov rang a bell each time he brought food to a dog. Eventually, the dog's mouth began to water when Pavlov merely rang the bell—with no food being present. The dog associated the ringing of the bell with the food, just as it associated the odor with the food.   RUSSELL M. CHURCH

See also NERVOUS SYSTEM.

REFORESTATION. See CONSERVATION (Forest Conservation); FOREST AND FOREST PRODUCTS.

REFORM BILLS, in England. See CHARTISM; GREAT BRITAIN (Era of Reform; Gladstone and Disraeli).

REFORM SCHOOL. See REFORMATORY.

REFORMATION

REFORMATION was a religious movement of the 1500's that gave birth to Protestantism. It had a tremendous impact on man's social, political, and economic life, and its influences are still felt today. The Reformation began in 1517 when Martin Luther, a German monk, protested certain practices of the Roman Catholic Church. About 40 years later, Protestantism was established in nearly half of Europe.

Before the Reformation, Europe had been held together by the universalism of the Catholic Church and by the claim of the Holy Roman Emperor to be the supreme *secular* (nonreligious) ruler. After the Reformation, Europe had several large Protestant churches and some smaller Protestant religious groups. All of them competed with the Catholic Church—and with each other—for the faith and allegiance of men.

Causes of the Reformation

Religious Causes. During the late Roman Empire and the early Middle Ages, missionaries had converted the peoples of Europe to Christianity. The pope gradually assumed greater importance and authority in the church and in relation to the secular rulers. In the early 1200's, Pope Innocent III claimed that "Ecclesiastical liberty is nowhere better preserved than where the Roman church has full power in temporal as well as spiritual matters." But about 100 years later, in 1303, King Philip IV of France humiliated Pope Boniface VIII by having him arrested (see PHILIP [Philip IV]). The secular rulers were growing in power.

During the 1300's and 1400's, the church suffered several serious setbacks. In 1309, a French pope, Clement V, moved the papacy from Rome to Avignon, France, where it remained for about 70 years. This period was called the *Babylonian Captivity*, in remembrance of the 70 years that the Jews had spent as captives in ancient Babylon. In 1378, after Pope Gregory XI moved the papal residence back to Rome, a small group of cardinals elected another pope, called an *antipope* (see POPE [The Troubles of the Papacy]). For nearly 40 years, there were two or three popes at a time. This split caused great confusion in the church. Some Catholic leaders believed that the church should be ruled by church councils rather than by a pope. Such councils met in Pisa, Italy, in 1409; in Constance, Germany, from 1414 to 1418; and in Basel, Switzerland, from 1431 to 1449. The councils called for a "reform in head and members."

Serious abuses also had appeared in the church. The large administrative structure of the church required a great deal of money to finance it. To obtain this money, the church used many devices that hurt its spiritual nature. These devices included selling important positions in the church. In Italy, the popes and higher clergy lived like secular princes. They built lavish palaces and indulged in corrupt financial practices. The religious life of the church suffered. The sacraments were often celebrated meaninglessly,

Lewis W. Spitz, the contributor of this article, is Professor of History at Stanford University and the author of The Protestant Reformation.

Wood engraving of the early 1500's by Jorg Breu the Elder; The Newberry Library, Chicago

The Sale of Indulgences caused Martin Luther to attack the church. This picture shows church representatives selling indulgences. The pope's authorization for the sale hangs on a cross.

and the church's spiritual message about God's mercy was weakened by an emphasis on man's good works, such as giving money to charity to earn salvation.

Critics of the church included the religious reformers John Wycliffe in England, John Huss in Bohemia, and Girolamo Savonarola in Italy. These men protested the abuses but could not stop them. Some thinkers within the church, including Johannes Eckhart and Thomas a Kempis, emphasized a mystical approach to Christianity. But no one could restore the church's spiritual health and moral purity.

At the same time that the church was neglecting its spiritual leadership, a tremendous increase in religious feeling was developing among the common people. The situation created great tension between the people and their church leaders during the 1300's and 1400's.

Cultural Causes. Beginning in the 1300's, a great revival of learning and art called the Renaissance developed in Italy and, to a lesser extent, elsewhere in Europe. The Italian author Petrarch pioneered in the revival of classical studies—the literature, history, and philosophy of ancient Greece and Rome. Renaissance humanists believed that by returning to the classics, they could begin a new golden age of culture.

The interest in ancient civilizations encouraged by the Renaissance had an important effect on religion. The study of Hebrew and Greek enabled scholars to read the Holy Scriptures in the languages in which they originally had been written. Also, in studying early Christian times, scholars saw how the church had changed through the centuries. The invention of movable type in the mid-1400's helped spread learning through printed books. As a result, an increasing number of laymen gained an education during the Renaissance and Reformation.

Political Causes. During the Middle Ages, the Holy Roman Emperor claimed to be the secular head of Christianity. Kings ranked beneath the emperor, followed by princes, dukes, and counts. But the broad authority of the emperor never really existed, and by the end of the Middle Ages, the empire consisted chiefly of the German territories of central Europe. Even there, the princes of many areas were independent. An imperial *diet* (council) consisting of representatives of the nobility and of the cities helped the emperor govern.

In western Europe, the kings were increasing their power over their own people and against the pope and the emperor. The monarchies in England, France, and Spain were growing stronger, organizing their finances, and building their armies. Some people regarded the pope as a political leader of a foreign state and opposed his control and influence in their own countries. After the Reformation began, some monarchs broke completely away from the pope.

Economic Causes. During the Middle Ages, Europe had an agricultural economy. Most people were peasants who lived in villages and tilled the soil with simple tools. Beginning in the 1100's, cities began to increase in size, especially in Italy and The Netherlands. Merchants traded woolen cloth, glassware, iron implements, and other manufactured goods for raw materials such as furs, wood, and wool. As the cities grew wealthy and independent, they threw off the control of local lords and prince-bishops. Many turned to the king or emperor for protection.

Development of the Reformation

Martin Luther. The Reformation began within the Catholic Church itself. On Oct. 31, 1517, Martin Luther, a monk and professor of theology, posted his Ninety-Five Theses on the door of the Castle Church in Wittenberg, Germany. The theses were a series of statements that attacked the sale of *indulgences* (pardon from some of the penalty for sins). Luther later criticized what he considered other abuses in the church.

Luther believed that men could be saved only through faith in Jesus Christ. His view of religion placed man directly before God, trusting Him and relying on His forgiving grace. Luther taught that God *justifies* men. By that he meant that God makes them righteous through His kindness to them. This doctrine of justification by faith in Christ alone was the heart of Luther's belief. It contradicted the church's teaching of grace and good works as a way to salvation.

In January, 1521, Pope Leo X excommunicated Luther and declared him a heretic. Emperor Charles V and members of the imperial diet ordered Luther to appear before the diet in Worms, Germany, in April. There, Luther was ordered to *recant* (take back) what he had said and written. Luther replied in a famous speech: "Unless I am convinced by the testimony of the Scriptures or by clear reason (for I do not trust either in the pope or in councils alone, since it is well known that they have often erred and contradicted themselves), I am bound by the Scriptures I have quoted and my conscience is captive to the Word of God. I cannot and I will not retract anything, since it is neither safe nor right to go against conscience. I cannot do otherwise."

In May, 1521, the emperor signed the Edict of Worms, which declared Luther to be an outlaw whom anyone could kill without punishment. But Frederick the Wise, Prince of Saxony, protected Luther, who led

Engraving of the 1500's by M. Herz and G. Köler; Bibliothèque Nationale, Paris

The Augsburg Confession summarized the religious teachings of Martin Luther. In this picture, the confession is being read to Charles V, Holy Roman Emperor, at the Diet of Augsburg in 1530.

the Protestant movement until his death in 1546.

The word *Protestant* (one who protests) dates from the diet of Speyer, Germany, in 1529. There, princes who supported Luther protested the anti-Lutheran actions forced on them by the emperor and the Catholic nobility. In 1530, the Lutherans presented the *Augsburg Confession* to the diet of Augsburg, Germany. The main author of the confession was Philipp Melanchthon, Luther's chief colleague in the Reformation. The confession became the basic statement of Lutheran doctrine. In the Peace of Augsburg, signed in 1555, the Holy Roman Empire officially recognized the Lutheran churches. See AUGSBURG CONFESSION.

The introduction of Lutheranism into Scandinavia was largely the work of the Swedish and Danish kings. In the 1520's, King Gustavus I of Sweden took over much church property and introduced Lutheranism in Sweden and Finland, then under Swedish control. In 1536, King Christian of Denmark and the National Assembly made Lutheranism the state religion. They also established it in Norway, then a Danish province.

Zwingli and the Anabaptists. In Switzerland, Huldreich Zwingli, a priest in Zurich, led the movement for religious reform. Zwingli was an eloquent preacher and a great Swiss patriot. Long after his death in 1531 in a war against Catholic forces, his ideas of reform continued to inspire the Swiss Protestant churches. In 1529, Zwingli and Luther met in Marburg, Germany, to discuss their disagreement over the interpretation of Christ's presence in the Lord's Supper. Luther regarded this sacrament as a means by which God gave people His grace. He believed in the real presence of Christ in the bread and wine. Zwingli considered the sacrament a thanksgiving to God for grace already given in other ways, especially through giving man the Gospel. He believed the bread and wine were mere symbols of Christ's body and blood. Their quarrel led to the first major split in Protestantism.

In Zurich during the 1520's, a group known as the Swiss Brethren, led by Conrad Grebel, decided that the Scriptures did not teach infant baptism. The Swiss Brethren favored adult baptism and were called *Anabaptists* (rebaptizers). The Anabaptists were not satisfied with Protestant efforts to reform Christianity, so they withdrew from religious and secular life and formed their own groups. They were persecuted by both Catholic and Protestant authorities. See ANABAPTISTS.

John Calvin helped establish Protestantism in Geneva, Switzerland. From there, he directed efforts to convert the people of France and other countries of western Europe. Calvin, a refugee from France, had studied law and the classics before becoming a Protestant. He was a frail man but had an iron will and a great gift for organization. Calvin's *Ecclesiastical Ordinances* (1541) established the structure of a *presbyterian* form of church government in which a council of elders rules each church. His influential *Institutes of the Christian Religion*, first published in 1536, offers a clear, systematic presentation of Protestant teachings.

Calvin's followers in France were called *Huguenots*. They came from all classes of society, including some influential noble families such as the Bourbons. Sup-

ported by Spain, France's Catholic kings attempted to suppress the Huguenots in a series of religious wars from 1562 to 1598. Beginning on Saint Bartholomew's Day, Aug. 24, 1572, the pro-Catholic party murdered thousands of Huguenots in Paris and in the French provinces. But Protestantism survived as a minority religion, even in France. See SAINT BARTHOLOMEW'S DAY, MASSACRE OF.

In England, as in Scandinavia, the Reformation was established by an act of state. The immediate cause for England's break with the Catholic Church was the refusal of Pope Clement VII to *annul* (cancel) King Henry VIII's marriage to his first wife, Catherine of Aragon. Catherine had not borne Henry a son, and the king wanted to marry Anne Boleyn in the hope that the marriage would produce a male heir to the throne.

In 1534, Parliament passed the Act of Supremacy, which made the monarch the head of the church in England. Henry VIII remained basically a Catholic, but Protestantism made great advances under his son, Edward VI. Queen Mary I, known as "Bloody Mary," succeeded Edward in 1553. She restored Catholicism as the state religion and suppressed the Protestants. But Queen Elizabeth I, who reigned from 1558 to 1603, established a moderate form of Protestantism that became known as *Anglicanism*. The *Thirty-Nine Articles*, issued in 1563, presented the teachings of Anglicanism. Englishmen who followed John Calvin were called *Puritans*. They opposed Anglicanism because it was *episcopal* (governed by bishops). The Puritans preferred the presbyterian form of church government. Catholicism was officially banned.

In Scotland, John Knox introduced Calvin's teachings and presbyterian system. In 1560, the Scots made Protestantism their state religion. England forced Ireland to adopt Protestantism as the state religion, but the Irish people remained loyal Catholics. Protestants colonized northern Ireland, also known as Ulster, and the conflict there between Catholics and Protestants is still a serious problem today.

Results of the Reformation

Religious Influences. As a result of the Reformation, Europe was divided between the Catholic countries of the south and the Protestant countries of the north. Many Protestant denominations developed, and they were organized in a variety of ways. In many parts of Europe, this diversity of religious life created a mood of religious toleration and a respect for the importance of the individual conscience. The Reformation also stimulated many reforms within the Catholic Church. The church gained new purity and strength during the late 1500's and the 1600's in a movement called the *Counter Reformation* (see COUNTER REFORMATION).

Political and Social Influences. The establishment of state churches, as occurred in England, contributed to the growth of nationalism. Lutheran regions tended to be conservative and supported strong central governments. Calvinist areas, where Protestants were often in the minority, tended to support democracy and argued for man's right to oppose tyranny by monarchs.

Luther and other Protestants regarded life in the world as the "sphere of faith's works." They idealized family life and participation in community activities. The Protestant stress on the holiness of man's role in daily life encouraged industriousness, thrifty living, and careful management of material things. This attitude became known as the *Protestant Ethic*. It contributed to the growth of industry and commerce during the 1700's and 1800's.

Protestant leaders also emphasized education. They promoted literacy, an educational curriculum based on ancient Greek and Roman literature, and a high respect for teachers and learning. Protestants and Catholics both contributed to great scientific achievements of the 1500's and early 1600's, including the discoveries of Galileo and Sir Isaac Newton. But after about 1640, advances in science were promoted more energetically in Protestant lands.   LEWIS W. SPITZ

Related Articles in WORLD BOOK include:

BIOGRAPHIES

Calvin, John	Mary (I)
Cranmer, Thomas	Melanchthon, Philipp
Eck, Johann	Ridley, Nicholas
Henry (VIII)	Tetzel, Johann
Huss, John	Tyndale, William
Knox, John	Wycliffe, John
Latimer, Hugh	Zwingli, Huldreich
Luther, Martin	

REFORM GROUPS

Albigenses	Huguenots	Presbyterians
Anabaptists	Lollards	Protestant
Anglicans	Lutherans	Waldenses
Covenanters		

OTHER RELATED ARTICLES

Augsburg Confession	Nantes, Edict of
England (The English Reformation)	Peasants' War
	Schmalkaldic League
France (Religious Wars)	Scotland (The Reformation)
Germany (The Reformation; The Thirty Years' War)	Thirty-Nine Articles
	Thirty Years' War
	Toleration Act

For a *Reading and Study Guide on the Reformation*, see the RESEARCH GUIDE/INDEX, Volume 22.

REFORMATORY is an institution for juvenile lawbreakers. Reformatories were originally intended to reform and educate young offenders, rather than to punish them. They also removed youths from contact with adult prisoners. But early reformatories were organized much like prisons. They proved so unsatisfactory that the term often has been dropped. Institutions for youthful offenders are now usually called training schools, forestry camps, or honor farms.

The United States Bureau of Prisons operates four reformatories and three juvenile and youth institutions. City, county, and state governments also finance some reformatories. The first reformatories to operate in the United States were established in the early 1800's in Boston, New York City, Philadelphia, and Elmira, N.Y.   HANS W. MATTICK

REFORMED CHURCHES IN AMERICA are incorporated as The General Synod of the Reformed Church in America, a Protestant organization. The doctrines of the church have their origin in the teachings of John Calvin. The minister, elders, and deacons are collectively designated the *Consistory* in each local church, and they run it. A group of churches make up a *Classis*, and a group of Classes make up a *Synod*. The *General Synod* is the highest judicatory of the Reformed Church.

The Reformed Church in America is an offspring of the Dutch Reformed Church in The Netherlands. The Reformed Church was organized on Manhattan Island in 1628 by Dutch and Walloon colonists. It received a charter from King William III of England in 1696.

The Reformed Churches founded Hope College in Holland, Mich.; Central College in Pella, Ia.; and Northwestern College in Orange City, Ia. They have seminaries in New Brunswick, N.J., and in Holland, Mich. For membership of the Reformed Churches, see RELIGION (table [Reformed Bodies]).   ARAD RIGGS

REFRACTION is the change in the direction in which waves travel when they pass from one kind of matter into another. Waves are *refracted* (bent) when they pass at an angle from one medium into another in which the velocity of light is different. A pencil standing in water looks broken at the water line because light travels slower in water than in air. The amount that a ray bends in passing from one medium into another is indicated by the *index of refraction* (*n*) between the two mediums for that wavelength. Finding *n* is a problem in trigonometry. It is a function of the sines of the angles of incidence and refraction, as $n = \dfrac{\sin i}{\sin r}$.

This is also called *Snell's Law* after the Dutch mathematician Willebrord Snell van Royen (1591-1626) who formulated the law.

Press Syndicate

A Pencil in a Glass of Water appears to be broken at the water's surface as a result of light refraction.

Common indexes of refraction depend on the angle in air as related to the angle in the medium, such as glass, quartz, or plastic. The different colors in light are never refracted in the same way. Because of this, refracted light beams often break up into the colors of the spectrum. A prism works on this principle to produce a spectrum.   SAMUEL W. HARDING

See also LENS; LIGHT (How Light Behaves; Science Project: How Light Behaves); MIRAGE; PRISM.

REFRACTOMETER, REE *frack TAHM ee tur*, is an instrument that measures the *refractive index* of a substance. This is a measure of the amount a light ray *refracts* (bends) when it passes through a substance (see REFRACTION). In one type of refractometer, the light passes through two substances. One has a known refractive index. The light passes through the substance with the unknown refractive index, then through the other one. The difference in the readings indicates the unknown refractive index.   CLARENCE E. BENNETT

See also INTERFEROMETER.

REFRACTORY is any nonmetallic material or object that can withstand high temperatures without becoming soft. Refractories are used to line blast furnaces, in crucibles for melting metals, and in other places where resistance to temperature and corrosion is required. One of the most widely used refractories is *firebrick*. It contains aluminum silicates and minor amounts of titanium and iron oxides. Other refractory substances are silica, magnesite, and graphite.   JAMES S. FRITZ

General Electric

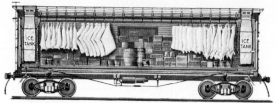

Railroad Refrigerator Car

Swift & Co.

REFRIGERATION is the process of producing low temperatures. It takes place when heat is removed from a substance. Cooling can be done by a natural method, such as by ice or snow, or by machines. For thousands of years, man has used some kind of refrigeration to keep food from spoiling and to cool beverages.

Housewives store foods in home refrigerators and freezers. Grocery stores and food companies use refrigerated display cases. They also have freezing rooms and cold-storage warehouses. Fresh foods are carried long distances in refrigerated trucks, refrigerated railway cars, and refrigerated compartments of ships.

Air conditioning depends on refrigeration to cool homes, offices, theaters, stores, and automobiles. Refrigeration makes it possible to store serums, vaccines, blood plasma, and other lifesaving medical supplies. Drug companies use refrigeration to make penicillin and other drugs. Cleaners and fur companies store furs in refrigerated vaults to protect them from moths and to keep the furs in good condition. Florists refrigerate cut flowers to preserve their fresh appearance. Drinking fountains supply cold water, and ice machines provide blocks, cubes, flakes, and chips of ice. Ice plants and skating rinks use refrigerating machines to manufacture ice. Industry uses refrigeration in the processing of rubber, lubricants, and steel, and in producing frozen fruit juices, candy, photographic films, ice cream, chemicals, and many other products.

Principles of Refrigeration

Refrigeration removes heat from solids, liquids, and gases. It is based on the second law of thermodynamics (see THERMODYNAMICS). This law states that heat flows only from warmer bodies to colder bodies, or from a sub-

stance at a certain temperature to a substance at a lower temperature. Heat cannot go from a colder substance to a warmer substance. When a warmer body *A* touches a colder body *B*, *A* becomes colder and *B* becomes warmer. The flow of heat from warmer bodies to colder bodies is called *heat transfer*. During refrigeration, heat transfer occurs when we place the substance we wish to cool near a *refrigerant*, or cooling agent.

Heat Transfer. Simple heat transfer takes place when a colder fluid flows through or over a warmer substance. The temperature rises in the colder fluid, and decreases in the warmer substance as heat is transferred. This simple type of refrigeration occurs when we cool a warm bottle of water in a running stream. The stream acts as a refrigerant. It absorbs heat and rises in temperature as it flows over the bottle.

All substances can absorb heat. But refrigerants absorb heat more quickly and in larger quantities. Common refrigerants include air, water, brine, ice, ammonia, carbon dioxide, sulfur dioxide, and many specially prepared substances such as Freon and Carrene.

Effects of Heat Transfer. Heat transfer produces several effects. It both cools (reduces the temperature of the warmer body) and heats (increases the temperature of the body that absorbs the heat). Heat transfer may also change the physical state of a substance. For example, removing sufficient heat causes a gas to change to a liquid. This process is called *condensation*. The reverse of condensation is *vaporization*, or the process of a liquid changing to a gas. Gases lose heat when they condense. Liquids absorb heat when they vaporize. The temperature at which a substance condenses or vaporizes at a given pressure is its *boiling point* (see BOILING POINT). Removing enough heat from a liquid causes it to *freeze*, or become solid. The temperature at which a substance freezes is called its *freezing point* (see FREEZING). The reverse of freezing is *melting*, the process of changing a solid to a liquid (see MELTING POINT). Liquids lose heat when they freeze. Solids gain heat when they melt.

All refrigeration systems depend on gains or losses of heat that occur during condensation, vaporization, freezing, or melting. The heat gained or lost during

Ancient Egyptians Cooled Water on Roof-Tops at Night.

Refrigerator Truck

Refrigerator Ship

these physical processes is called *latent heat* (see HEAT [Changes in State]).

Ice Refrigeration

People cool with ice if they lack convenient power to produce other methods of refrigeration. Natural ice, cut from lakes and ponds in winter, has long provided refrigeration during warm seasons. Campers and some farm housewives cool food in iceboxes similar to those used by millions of families before the development of mechanical refrigeration. Railroad refrigerator cars and some refrigerated motor trucks carry ice to keep foods cool during shipment.

Ice is one of the oldest methods of refrigeration. The Chinese cut and stored ice as long ago as 1000 B.C. Ice refrigerates because it absorbs heat when it melts. For example, this happens when we cool a warm drink by putting ice cubes in the glass. Ice makes a useful refrigerant because it has a constant melting temperature of 32° F. It absorbs large quantities of heat as it melts, but the unmelted ice always maintains the same temperature. Each pound of ice that changes to water at 32° F. absorbs 144 British Thermal Units (B.T.U.'s) or 36,288 calories of heat (see BRITISH THERMAL UNIT; CALORIE). Ice can be used to cool foods in iceboxes or to freeze liquids by *endothermic reactions*. These are chemical reactions that enable ice to produce freezing temperatures.

Iceboxes work because warm air rises. A cake of ice in the upper part of an icebox absorbs heat from the warm air. This cools the warm air and increases its weight. The heavier air flows downward to the food compartments. The air becomes warmer and lighter as it absorbs heat from the food. The warmer, lighter air rises to the upper compartment, where it again loses heat to the ice. The melting ice produces water that helps keep the icebox moist. Vegetables and other foods keep better in moist air.

Endothermic Reactions. By itself, ice could never absorb enough heat to reduce the temperature of a substance below its own melting point of 32° F. But endothermic reactions enable ice to produce freezing temperatures. Certain chemical compounds, particularly salts, produce a freezing action when mixed with ice or snow, or even

other compounds (see SALT, CHEMICAL). Such combinations are called *endothermic mixtures*. Some mixtures of ice and chemicals produce temperatures of −40° F. or lower. Endothermic mixtures include such combinations as calcium chloride and snow; ice, sodium chloride, and ammonium nitrate; and sodium sulfate, ammonium chloride, potassium nitrate, and diluted nitric acid. All these substances absorb heat during their chemical reactions.

The hand-operated ice-cream freezer is an example of the use of endothermic mixtures. Ice cream begins to freeze at about 28° F., or 4 degrees below the melting point of ice. To freeze ice cream, the ingredients are mixed in a container surrounded by crushed ice and salt. The endothermic reaction of the ice and salt absorbs latent heat from the ingredients, causing them to freeze.

Using chemicals to reduce temperature is not new. About 1550, the Italians found that a mixture of potassium nitrate (saltpeter) and water could be used to cool bottled liquors.

Dry Ice is solid carbon dioxide. As a refrigerant, it has two important advantages over ice made from water. Like water ice, dry ice undergoes change at a constant temperature. But, instead of changing to a liquid, dry ice *sublimes* (vaporizes) directly to a gas (see SUBLIMATION). For this reason boxes containing food packed in dry ice do not leak fluid as they would if packed with water ice. This characteristic gives dry ice its name.

Dry ice sublimes at −109.3° F., which is much lower than the melting temperature of water ice. Food processors find dry ice especially valuable for maintaining a freezing temperature in foods and ice cream, because it produces much lower temperatures than water ice. Dry ice must be handled carefully, because it can cause frostbite and severe burnlike injuries. See DRY ICE.

Mechanical Refrigeration

Mechanical refrigeration works on the principle that liquids absorb heat when they vaporize. You can demonstrate this by wetting your hands and waving them rapidly. The water evaporates quickly and causes a cooling sensation by lowering the skin temperature. A fan cools you because it evaporates the natural moisture

American Colonists Stored Ice for Summer Use.

Clippers Carried Ice Stored in Sawdust.

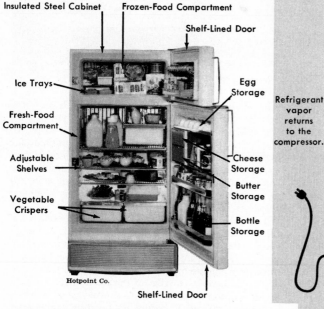

Insulated Steel Cabinet   Frozen-Food Compartment

Shelf-Lined Door

Ice Trays

Egg Storage

Fresh-Food Compartment

Adjustable Shelves

Cheese Storage

Butter Storage

Vegetable Crispers

Bottle Storage

Hotpoint Co.

Shelf-Lined Door

Refrigerant absorbs heat as it evaporates.

FREEZING UNIT (EVAPORATOR)

HEAT FLOW   THERMOSTAT BULB

REFRIGERANT CONTROL DEVICE

Refrigerant control device lowers refrigerant pressure.

Refrigerant vapor returns to the compressor.

"ON-OFF" SWITCH AND TEMPERATURE CONTROL

REFRIGERANT (VAPOR)

HEAT FLOW

REFRIGERANT (LIQUID)

COMPRESSOR   CONDENSER

Refrigerant leaves receiver as a liquid.

High-pressure gas loses heat in the condenser and becomes a liquid.

RECEIVER
Liquid refrigerant flows to the receiver.

on your skin. Mechanical refrigeration includes three principal systems: (1) compression, (2) absorption, and (3) steam-jet.

Compression and Absorption Systems refrigerate by changing a refrigerant from a liquid to a gas and back to a liquid again. These repeated operations make up the *refrigeration cycle*. In a compression system, a compressor brings about the refrigeration cycle. This system is widely used in industry and in most home electric refrigerators. In the absorption system, the refrigeration cycle is caused by the direct application of heat from gas, steam, or some other source. All home gas refrigerators and some industrial units use the absorption system. Jacob Perkins, a Massachusetts inventor, developed the first compression machine in 1834. Ferdinand Carré, a French engineer, developed the first absorption system between 1851 and 1855. Karl von Linde of Germany introduced the first successful compression system using ammonia between 1873 and 1875.

Electric and gas home refrigerators are hermetically sealed, or airtight and leakproof, refrigeration units that maintain cooling temperatures between 35° F. and 45° F. They usually have freezing compartments with temperatures between 0° F. and 10° F.

Steam-Jet Refrigeration uses water as a refrigerant. High-velocity steam brings about the refrigeration cycle. Steam-jet refrigeration is less common than the compression system because its temperature is limited to about 36° F. and above.

The Electric Refrigerator is a compression-type refrigeration unit powered by an electric motor. A home electric refrigerator consists of five basic parts: (1) the receiver, (2) the refrigerant-control device, (3) the evaporator, (4) the compressor, and (5) the condenser.

At the beginning of the refrigeration cycle, the refrigerant, usually Freon 12, leaves the *receiver*, or storage

tank, under high pressure. It travels through pipes to the *refrigerant-control device*. This mechanism reduces the pressure of the refrigerant as it enters the *evaporator*, or freezing unit. The evaporator consists of pipes or coils on the walls or sides of the cabinet, or surrounding the ice-tray compartment. At a low pressure, the liquid refrigerant evaporates inside these coils, and absorbs heat. This causes refrigeration to take place. The *compressor* pumps the refrigerant from the freezing unit as a vapor, and raises its pressure. It then discharges high-pressure gas into the air-cooled *condenser*. There the gas loses the heat it gained in the evaporator, and condenses into a liquid at the high pressure. The liquid refrigerant flows back to the storage tank.

The Gas Refrigerator works on the absorption principle. It uses heat energy as a source of power, and has no moving parts. A home gas refrigerator consists of five basic parts: (1) the generator, (2) the separator, (3) the condenser, (4) the evaporator, and (5) the absorber. Liquid ammonia usually serves as the refrigerant.

During the refrigeration cycle, heat from a gas flame is applied to the *generator*. This tank contains a strong solution of ammonia gas dissolved in water. The heat causes the solution to boil. Ammonia vapor and some of the solution rise to the *separator*, which removes the liquid. The hot gas continues its rise to the *condenser*, where it is cooled and liquefied. Since the water has been separated from the ammonia, the liquid is now almost pure ammonia. The liquid ammonia flows through a tube into the *evaporator*, or freezing unit,

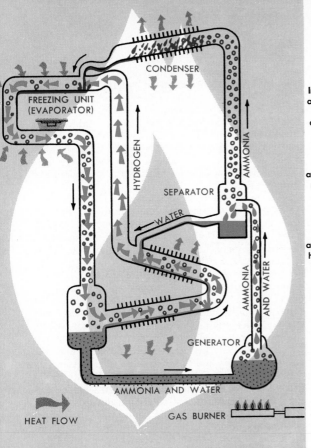

CONDENSER

FREEZING UNIT
(EVAPORATOR)

HYDROGEN

AMMONIA

SEPARATOR

WATER

AMMONIA
AND WATER

GENERATOR

AMMONIA AND WATER

HEAT FLOW

GAS BURNER

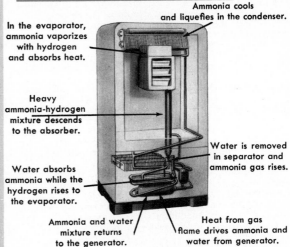

THE GAS REFRIGERATOR

Ammonia cools
and liquefies in the condenser.

In the evaporator,
ammonia vaporizes
with hydrogen
and absorbs heat.

Heavy
ammonia-hydrogen
mixture descends
to the absorber.

Water absorbs
ammonia while the
hydrogen rises to
the evaporator.

Water is removed
in separator and
ammonia gas rises.

Ammonia and water
mixture returns
to the generator.

Heat from gas
flame drives ammonia and
water from generator.

Courtesy Whirlpool Corp., St. Joseph, Mich.

where it vaporizes with hydrogen gas. The hydrogen equalizes the pressure between the condenser and the evaporator. The vapor absorbs heat and produces refrigeration. The heavy mixture passes downward into the air-cooled *absorber*, where the ammonia is absorbed by water. The light hydrogen gas separates from the solution, rises through a pipe above the absorber, and returns to the evaporator. The cool ammonia-water solution flows back to the generator.

Steam-Jet Refrigeration uses only water as a refrigerant. It works on the principle that water vaporizes easily under low pressure, such as that in a partial vacuum (see VACUUM). As the water evaporates, its temperature goes down. The lower the pressure, the faster the evaporation and the lower the temperature produced.

The water flows through a chamber with an opening, across which a high-speed jet of steam passes. The steam creates suction within the space above the water, and lowers the pressure in the chamber. Some of the water evaporates and absorbs heat from the liquid in the chamber. The cool water is pumped out through pipes that carry it to wherever it is to be used. The water vapor rising from the chamber combines with the steam and is removed from the system.

Steam-jet systems produce practically no noise or vibration, occupy little space, and have no moving parts except a pump. They require a constant supply of steam, but this may come from the exhaust of other machinery. Steam-jet refrigeration has wide use in industrial and shipboard cooling. Brewers and distillers also make use of this type of mechanical refrigeration.

Refrigerator Care

Defrosting is probably the most important part of caring for a refrigerator. The coating of frost that collects on the freezing unit acts as insulation and interferes with the cooling ability of the refrigerator. Because of this, the refrigerator should be defrosted regularly.

Automatic Defrosting works by means of clocks or by means of devices that count the number of times the door opens. Defrosting takes place at a certain time each day, or after the door has been opened a certain number of times. The controls open a valve that allows hot gas from the compressor to flow through the coils and melt the frost. During this time, refrigeration is stopped. In some refrigerators, the controls activate an electric heater close to the coils. Many automatic-defrosting refrigerators have drains that carry the drip water from the coils out of the cabinet through an opening close to the compressor. The heat from the compressor evaporates the water. Other automatic-defrosting refrigerators, and most semiautomatic and manual units, have drip pans under the freezing unit. Water collects in these pans and must be emptied after defrosting. Automatic defrosting takes little time, so there is no danger that the food will spoil.

Semiautomatic and Manual Defrosting. Refrigerators can be defrosted by turning them off. In a manual type, a hand-operated switch turns off the freezing unit and starts it again after defrosting. A semiautomatic refrigerator must be turned off manually, but starts automatically when defrosting is completed. Defrosting can be speeded by putting hot water in the ice trays.

Basic Rules for Refrigerator Care. To obtain the best service from a refrigerator, follow these basic rules:

1. Never use an ice pick or other sharp instrument to chip away the frost. This may damage the freezing unit.
2. Defrost regularly, before the frost on the freezing unit builds up to $\frac{1}{4}$ of an inch.
3. Cover food to decrease odors and reduce moisture.

4. Keep the door closed tightly to keep out heat and moisture. Open the door as seldom as possible.

5. Check the door gasket to see that it is tight and forms an effective seal against the cabinet.

6. Keep the temperature of your refrigerator within a safe range. The temperature in the chill compartment should be between 32°F. and 40°F. The temperature in the freezing compartment should be between 0°F. and 10°F. Check the temperature with a thermometer.

7. Do not crowd your refrigerator with food and dishes. It needs air circulation to cool properly.

8. Do not put hot food in the refrigerator. This makes steam which increases frosting. It also wastes refrigeration.

9. Clean the inside of the refrigerator regularly with borax or soda and hot water. This keeps your refrigerator smelling fresh.

10. Set your controls on the warmest setting before going on vacation. Less refrigeration is required, because the door will not be opened and closed.

11. Leave space behind the refrigerator so that air can flow over the condenser coils.   RAYMOND C. GUNTHER

Related Articles in WORLD BOOK include:

Air Conditioning	Dry Ice	Heat
Ammonia	Food, Frozen	Ice
Anhydrous	Food Preservation	Melting Point
Ammonia	Freezing	Railroad
Boiling Point	Freon	(Freight
Cold Storage	Gorrie, John	Cars)

Outline

I. Principles of Refrigeration
  A. Heat Transfer
  B. Effects of Heat Transfer
II. Ice Refrigeration
  A. Ice   B. Dry Ice
III. Mechanical Refrigeration
  A. The Electric Refrigerator
  B. The Gas Refrigerator
  C. Steam-Jet Refrigeration
IV. Refrigerator Care
  A. Defrosting
  B. Basic Rules for Refrigerator Care

Questions

Why does a fan cool your body?

Can heat flow from a cooler substance to a warmer substance? Explain.

How does a gas refrigerator work?

What are the advantages of steam-jet refrigeration?

How does a coating of ice on the freezing unit interfere with refrigeration?

How often should a refrigerator be defrosted?

How does automatic defrosting work?

What makes the air circulate in an icebox?

What are the five basic parts of the electric refrigerator?

What is meant by "refrigeration cycle"?

REFRIGERATOR CAR. See RAILROAD (Freight Cars); REFRIGERATION (picture).

REFUGE, BIRD. See BIRD (Refuges and Sanctuaries).

REFUGE, CITIES OF. See CITIES OF REFUGE.

REFUGEE, *REHF you JEE,* is a person who flees from one place to another to find *refuge,* or safety. Usually, a refugee will flee from one country to another to escape religious or political persecution. Since World War II, the name *displaced persons,* or DP's, has been applied to many refugees who refuse to return to their homes in countries taken over by communists. The term *refugee* comes from the Latin word *fugere,* meaning *to flee.*

Just before and during World War I, there were many Jewish refugees fleeing from *pogroms,* or persecutions, in Russia. There were also many Greek and Armenian refugees from Turkey. About 1½ million refugees fled from Russia during the Russian Revolution from 1917 to 1920. There were so many refugees in Europe after World War I that the League of Nations appointed the famous Norwegian explorer and scientist Fridtjof Nansen as a special commissioner to help the refugees. After Nansen died in 1930, the League established an international office for refugee problems. This office issued identification certificates, called "Nansen passports," to refugees who had lost their nationality.

The number of refugees increased again before and during World War II. Millions of Chinese fled westward after the Japanese invasion in 1937. About 340,-000 Spaniards moved to southern France during the Spanish Civil War from 1936 to 1939. Hundreds of thousands of Jews and other opponents and victims of the Nazis fled Germany and Austria between 1933 and 1938.

After World War II, the United Nations set up a Relief and Rehabilitation Administration (UNRRA) to help the nearly 8 million persons uprooted and displaced during the war. In 1946, the UN established the International Refugee Organization (IRO) to take over the work of UNRRA. The IRO aided many DP's in Europe as well as millions of others displaced by the partition of Palestine in the Middle East and the partition of India and Pakistan in Southeast Asia.

Refugees continued to receive aid in the late 1950's and early 1960's. International programs helped refugees from communist-controlled countries, from Africa, and from other areas. Besides contributing to United Nations aid programs, the United States took part in the Intergovernmental Committee for European Migration (ICEM), which moved more than 400,000 persons to new homes between 1952 and 1960. The United States has also aided refugees from Cuba. Between 1952 and 1961, the U.S. government also helped more than 600,000 *escapees,* or refugees, through the United States Escapee Program (USEP). Most of these escapees fled from Eastern Europe.   TELFORD TAYLOR

See also DISPLACED PERSON; GENOCIDE; MIGRATION (Migration in the 1900's); NANSEN, FRIDTJOF; WORLD WAR II (Population Changes); UNITED NATIONS (Aid to Refugees).

REGALIA. See TOWER OF LONDON.

REGELATION, *REE juh LAY shun,* is the process in which solid ice melts under pressure alone and refreezes as soon as the pressure is taken away. If two blocks of ice near 32°F. are pressed together for a while they will be found frozen together when the pressure is taken off. Squeezing snowballs to make them harder is another example of regelation.

When ice is not too cold it melts by pressure alone. A skate passing over ice melts a thin film of water, and the skater glides on this water. When ice is too cold it will not melt easily by pressure alone. For this reason, skating is not successful in extremely cold weather when the ice will not melt under the skate. A small object placed on ice will often bury itself in the ice. The ice will refreeze over the object.

A glacier moving along slowly melts and refreezes, slipping a little under pressure each day. In the Ice Age, regelated ice in central Canada pushed continental glaciers as far as 2,400 feet up the sides of the Rocky Mountains.   RALPH G. OWENS

See also FREEZING.

REGENERATION, in plants and animals, is the capacity to replace lost or damaged parts by growing new ones. Regeneration is common in plants. If a tree or shrub is cut off near the ground, new shoots may spring from the stump. Among animals, the sponges, coelenterates, and the simpler worms show remarkable power of regeneration. They can be cut in pieces and each piece can grow into a new animal. Starfishes can grow new arms. Crayfishes can grow new claws, eyes, and legs. Animals with a backbone—called *vertebrates*—have only limited powers of regeneration. But the lizard called the *glass snake* escapes from its enemies by breaking off the end of its tail. It later grows a new one. Salamanders can even regenerate lost limbs. Man and other mammals can regenerate only hair, nails, skin, and a few other tissues. In some cases, a different sort of tissue grows over the damaged area and forms a scar. RALPH BUCHSBAUM

See also FLATWORM; PLANARIAN.

REGENT, *REE junt,* is a person who rules a country when the rightful ruler cannot act, either because he is too young, out of the country, or ill. In some countries, a member of the royal family may be the regent. In others, a council may exercise duties of the ruler.

The British had no special arrangements providing for a regency until the Regency Act of 1937 was passed. This law provides for the appointment of a regent if the monarch is unable to rule. A council of state can act as regent for short periods of time. This council is composed of the husband or wife of the ruler and the next four persons in succession to the crown.

In the United States, members of the governing body of libraries, museums, school systems, and universities and colleges are called *regents.* I. J. SANDERS

REGENT DIAMOND. See DIAMOND (Famous Diamonds).

REGER, *RAY gur,* **MAX** (1873-1916), was a German composer and organist. His complex, unconventional music aroused controversy. He was born in Brand, Bavaria, and he studied with his father and other teachers. Reger wrote works for orchestra, chorus, piano, organ, and instrumental ensembles. He also wrote 260 songs. Little of Reger's music is played today. HALSEY STEVENS

REGICIDE, *REJ uh side,* is a person who kills a king. The name means, literally, *king killer.* The English officials who were responsible for the execution of Charles I of England were called regicides. The term *regicide* also is used for the crime of killing a king.

REGIMENT was once the largest unit in the infantry and armored divisions of armies. In most armies today, the regiment is mainly an administrative headquarters unit. In the United States Army, it has been replaced as a combat unit by the *brigade,* which is more mobile and adaptable than a regiment (see BRIGADE).

Today, the regiment serves as a headquarters unit with a number of battalions or squadrons grouped under it. A regiment does not fight as a unit. The battalions which are grouped under the regiment are assigned to divisions to perform their combat duties. For example, a battalion from the *505th Infantry Regiment* (airborne) may be assigned to the *82nd Airborne Division,* while another battalion from the *505th* may be assigned to the *101st Airborne Division.* The men of these battalions, while attached to various divisions, still consider themselves part of the *505th* regiment.

A regiment may have as few as one or two battalions in peacetime, or as many as 15 in war. Battalions have 500 to 1,200 men each. The only regimental organization in the U.S. Army today that has combat duties is the armored cavalry regiment. It is made up of three units called squadrons.

The U.S. Marine Corps maintains infantry regiments in its divisions. Each regiment has about 3,000 men under the command of a colonel. Infantry Marine regiments do not use the word regiment in their names. They are known by such names as the *Fifth Marines.* The name *regiment* is used chiefly in Marine service regiments that provide *logistical* (supply) support to Marine combat infantry units. CHARLES B. MACDONALD

REGINA, *ree JY nuh,* Sask. (pop. 137,759; met. area 138,956; alt. 1,896 ft.), is the capital of the province. It was named *Regina,* the Latin word for *queen,* in honor of Queen Victoria. Regina lies in southern Saskatchewan, about 100 miles north of the United States (see SASKATCHEWAN [political map]). Regina is an important manufacturing and distribution center. For information on the monthly weather in Regina, see SASKATCHEWAN (Climate).

The chief industries in Regina include oil refineries, bakeries, creameries, meat-packing and beverage plants, light and heavy sheet metal, chemicals, woodworking, and concrete-pipe factories. Regina is also the center of intensive gas and oil developments. The city ranks as a major distributing point for agricultural implements. The pipeline which links the Alberta oil fields with the Great Lakes runs through the city. Two transcontinental railway lines serve Regina. The city also has air and highway transportation facilities. A campus of the University of Saskatchewan is in Regina.

Regina was settled as the railroads developed in southern Canada. In 1882, the town became the headquarters for the North-West Mounted Police (now the Royal Canadian Mounted Police). Regina became the capital of the Northwest Territories in 1883. It gained its city charter in 1903. Regina became the capital of Saskatchewan when that province was created in 1905. Regina has a mayor-council government. F. C. CRONKITE

REGINA MEDAL is an award honoring a person for his lifetime contribution to children's literature. The award is sponsored by the Catholic Library Association, and is given regardless of nationality or creed. The face of the medal bears a crown superimposed on an *M,* signifying *Mary,* for whom the medal is named. The words "Regina Medal, Continued Distinguished Contribution to Children's Literature," encircle the symbols. On the reverse side of the medal, names of the

WINNERS OF THE REGINA MEDAL			
Awarded	Winner	Awarded	Winner
1959	Eleanor Farjeon	1967	Bertha Mahony Miller
1960	Anne Carroll Moore	1968	Marguerite de Angeli
1961	Padraic Colum	1969	Lois Lenski
1962	Frederic G. Melcher	1970	Ingri and Edgar d'Aulaire
1963	Ann Nolan Clark	1971	Tasha Tudor
1964	May Hill Arbuthnot	1972	Meindert DeJong
1965	Ruth Sawyer		
1966	Leo Politi		

winner, the sponsor, and the year encircle a shield which bears a quotation from Walter de la Mare's collection of poems, *Bells and Grass*. The quotation reads: ". . . only the rarest kind of best in anything can be good enough for the young."   M. Richard Wilt

REGION is an area with common characteristics that set it off from other areas. It may be a part of a city, county, state, province, nation, or the world. People do not agree on how to identify regions, draw their boundaries, or appraise their significance. Where the West, the East, the South, or the North begins depends upon where a person is standing.

A region generally has no distinct geographical or political boundaries. Its identity is usually one of character. For example, a region may have *natural* characteristics. It may be known for its mountains, rivers, climate, soil, minerals, forests, or crops. An *economic* region may include all or part of a natural region. *Cultural*, *historical*, and *political* regions are also divided along their particular lines, or according to their interests and purposes. Each region has conflicting as well as unifying interests.

Regional Differences have influenced national politics throughout United States history. The East, based on manufacturing, commerce, and banking, generally favored a high tariff. The South, exporting crops such as cotton and tobacco, opposed the tariff. The West, an always-moving frontier, favored easy money and protection against creditors. Persons in rural areas and small towns are usually more region-conscious than city dwellers. Bargains among regions remain a feature of congressional lawmaking.

Regional Problems must either be dealt with by the national government or be broken into fragments for separate handling by each state government involved. Federal departments and bureaus have regional headquarters in key cities. The Tennessee Valley Authority was established to serve a southern region. Compacts between states help solve other regional problems, including water pollution, oil production, education, and bridges across interstate streams.

Such factors as growth of cities, mobility of families, standardization through the press, radio, and television, and national economic measures have smudged if not erased lines denoting regions.   James W. Fesler

See also United States (table: Geographic Regions); Europe (Land Regions); Asia (Land Regions; Way of Life sections); Canada (The Land); Appalachia.

REGIS COLLEGE. See Universities and Colleges (table).

REGISTERED MAIL. See Post Office (Registry).

REGISTRATION OF VOTERS. The laws of many countries require all persons who plan to vote in a coming election to register themselves as voters at a stated time before the election. This serves to keep unqualified persons from voting.

See also Voting.

REGRESSION is a characteristic sign of certain mental illnesses. It comes from a Latin word meaning *to go backward*. Doctors use the word to mean a return to a way of thinking or behaving that would normally be characteristic of an earlier period of life. For example, if a 4-year-old child, after the birth of a baby brother or

sister, began to act like a baby himself, doctors would call his behavior regression. However, mentally healthy persons sometimes exhibit regression, as when they play games or daydream.   Charles Brenner

REGROUPING, in mathematics. See Addition (Regrouping); Numeration Systems (Working with Numeration Systems).

REGULATORS. See Westward Movement (Regional Conflicts).

REGULUS, a missile. See Guided Missile (Recent Developments).

REGULUS, *REG yoo lus*, is the brightest star in the constellation Leo. It shines 75 times brighter than the sun, and is about 55 light-years away from Earth. See also Astronomy (How to Use a Star Map [illustration]); Leo.

REGULUS, MARCUS ATILIUS (? -249? B.C.), was a Roman general who became a national hero. His life story was repeated as an example of true patriotism. As *consul* (chief government official) in 256 B.C., he commanded the victorious Roman invasion of Africa against Carthage in the First Punic War (see Punic Wars). But he demanded unconditional surrender. Instead, the Carthaginians raised more troops and hired Xanthippus, a Spartan general, who defeated the Romans and captured Regulus.

Carthage sent Regulus to Rome about 249 B.C. with peace terms. He promised to return if the Romans refused to make peace. Regulus urged the Roman Senate not to accept the terms, though he knew this meant his death when he returned to Carthage. Romans later said he was killed by torture by the Carthaginians, but this story may have been made up by his family. Regulus was an aristocrat, but he was not rich. Before the war, he lived a simple life on his farm.   Henry C. Boren

REHABILITATION. See Hospital (Professional Services Department); Handicapped; Medicine (table: Kinds of Medical Specialty Fields); Social and Rehabilitation Service; Speech Therapy.

REHAN, ADA (1860-1916), an American actress, was famous for her portrayal of Katherine in Shakespeare's *Taming of the Shrew*. She was the leading actress in Augustin Daly's stock company for 20 years. From 1879 until her retirement, she played over 200 parts. She was born Ada Crehan in Limerick, Ireland.

REHNQUIST, WILLIAM HUBBS (1924-   ), became an associate justice of the Supreme Court of the United States in 1972. President Richard M. Nixon nominated him to fill the vacancy created when Justice John M. Harlan retired.

Rehnquist's nomination sparked a heated debate in the Senate. The controversy centered on Rehnquist's philosophy, which his opponents termed "ultra-conservative." During Senate hearings on Rehnquist's nomination, several civil rights groups and liberals spoke against him. They objected to positions Rehnquist had taken in the past on such issues as school desegregation and wiretapping.

Rehnquist was born in Milwaukee. He attended Stanford University and graduated with highest honors from the university's law school in 1952. That same year, Supreme Court Justice Robert H. Jackson appointed Rehnquist his law clerk. From 1953 to 1969, Rehnquist practiced law in Arizona. He was a United States assistant attorney general from 1969 to 1971. In that post, Rehnquist served as a legal adviser to the executive branch of the government.   OWEN M. FISS

See also SUPREME COURT OF THE UNITED STATES (picture).

REICH, *rike,* is a German word meaning *empire* or *state.* Adolf Hitler, the German dictator, called his government the *Third Reich.* The first was the Holy Roman Empire. The second was the German Empire that lasted from 1871 to 1918. See GERMANY (History).

REICHSTADT, DUKE OF. See NAPOLEON II.

REICHSTAG, *RIKES TAHK,* was the lower house of the German parliament under the empire and the Weimar Republic. During the Republic, one deputy represented 60,000 persons. Membership in the Reichstag fluctuated from 475 to 600, according to the size of the popular vote. Men and women over the age of 20 could vote for the deputies. Under Adolf Hitler, the Reichstag lost its power. After World War II, the lower house of the West German parliament became known as the Bundestag.   JAMES K. POLLOCK

REICHSTEIN, *RIKE shtine,* **TADEUS** (1897-   ), a Swiss chemist, shared the 1950 Nobel prize for physiology and medicine for his research on hormones of the outer cover, or cortex, of the adrenal glands. He isolated cortico-sterone, or *cortisone,* in 1936 (see CORTISONE). In 1933, he synthesized ascorbic acid, or vitamin C. Reichstein was born in Włocławek, Poland. He studied at the Zurich State Technical College in Switzerland and became a university professor.   HENRY H. FERTIG

REICHSWEHR, *RIKES VAYR,* is the German term for *army of the state.* The German republic set up a Reichswehr in 1919 from volunteer units called *Free Corps.* It had about 300,000 men. But the Treaty of Versailles forced Germany to cut it to 100,000 men. Army leaders retained only outstanding men, and worked to develop an efficient general staff and *cadres* to train new troops. The Reichswehr became the nucleus of German armed forces in World War II.   THEODORE ROPP

REID, JOHN E. See LIE DETECTOR.

REID, WHITELAW (1837-1912), was an American journalist and diplomat. He bought control of the New York *Tribune* in 1872. From 1905 until his death he served as ambassador to Great Britain.

Reid was born in Xenia, Ohio. During the Civil War, he was war correspondent for the Cincinnati *Gazette*. In 1892, Reid was the Republican Party nominee for Vice-President of the United States, but he was defeated.   JOHN ELDRIDGE DREWRY

REIGN OF TERROR lasted from June 2, 1793, to July 18, 1794, during the French Revolution. Under Maximilian Robespierre's leadership, the Jacobins ruled France through committees of public safety and of general security, a revolutionary tribunal, and representatives in all parts of the country. The tribunal ordered the execution of about 3,000 persons. The representatives executed 17,000 others in the French provinces. The Reign of Terror ended with the death of Robespierre.   ROBERT B. HOLTMAN

See also FRENCH REVOLUTION (The Reign of Terror); MARAT, JEAN PAUL; ROBESPIERRE.

REIMS, *reemz* (pop. 152,967; met. area 167,830), is a fortified city of northern France. It lies on the Vesle River about 98 miles northeast of Paris (see FRANCE [political map]). The beauty of the city centers around a magnificent cathedral, which was begun in the 1200's.

The Art Institute of Chicago

The Cathedral of Notre Dame in Reims, France, was started in 1211. The beautiful structure was finished in 1430.

The church towers high above the surrounding homes.

During World War I, Reims was bombed daily for nearly four years. When the war ended the people rebuilt many homes and buildings. World War II brought more suffering to the city. The Germans occupied Reims from 1940 to 1944. Reims later became an important supply base for Allied troops. The Germans signed their surrender at Reims on May 7, 1945.

Reims lies in one of the important wine regions of France, and leads in the production of French champagne. The city is France's most important wool market. Reims has many dyeing and wool-manufacturing plants. Other factories produce machinery, chemicals, soap, paper, and wine bottles and casks.

Lovers of art and architecture have long admired the Cathedral of Notre Dame at Reims, one of the most beautiful examples of Gothic architecture. Nearly all the French kings were crowned in the cathedral. Heavy bombing during World War I badly damaged the cathedral, but it was repaired by 1937.   ROBERT E. DICKINSON

REINCARNATION, or **REBIRTH.** See TRANSMIGRATION OF THE SOUL; RELIGION (Life and Death).

REINDEER, *RAIN DEER,* is a deer of northern Europe and Asia, closely related to the North American caribou. It can be tamed, and has become one of man's most valuable possessions in the arctic regions. Reindeer and caribou differ from other members of the deer family in having large, deeply cleft hoofs, a hairy muzzle, and somewhat broader antlers, borne by both male and female. Reindeer stand about $3\frac{1}{2}$ feet high and weigh about 300 pounds. They are smaller, and have shorter legs than the caribou. This has probably come about as the owners sought to get an animal that could be managed.

199

YIla, Rapho-Guillumette

The Big Antlers of the Reindeer drop off intact every year. They are used to make knives and household utensils.

Reindeer provide the people of Lapland with the chief means of transportation in their cold barren country. These animals can draw their sledges over the snow at the rate of 12 to 15 miles an hour. Reindeer have endurance as well as swiftness, and can travel with a load of from 250 to 300 pounds for hours at a time. To the lowland Laplanders, the reindeer is horse, sheep, and cow, all in one. The animals furnish the people with clothing, meat, and milk, and if they live in tents, with shelter. In the summer, the people cure reindeer meat and make great quantities of cheese from the surplus milk, to be stored for use through the long winter. Many of the animals run wild, but are lured into traps by the use of trained decoy reindeer. They are given ownership marks by cutting or biting out notches from the ears, and are then trained. They wander about near their owner's home and find their food under the snow.

In order to provide a reliable source of food for the Eskimo of western Alaska, the United States Office of Education imported 1,280 reindeer from Siberia between 1892 and 1902. More than a million reindeer descended from these animals now range from Point Barrow to Kodiak Island. In 1935, the Canadian government established a large herd of reindeer near the mouth of the Mackenzie River in Yukon Territory.

Reindeer hides are used to make clothing and sleeping bags. The meat is jerked, smoked, or canned.

Scientific Classification. The reindeer belongs to the deer family, *Cervidae*. It is classified as genus *Rangifer*, species *R. tarandus*.   VICTOR H. CAHALANE

See also ASIA (picture); CARIBOU; DEER (picture).

REINDEER LAKE covers 2,444 square miles in central Canada. It lies on the border between northern Saskatchewan and Manitoba. For location, see SASKATCHEWAN (physical map). Some of its deep, clear waters drain south, into Reindeer River and the Churchill River. Its northern waters flow into the Cochrane River and on to Lake Athabasca. It has important fisheries.

REINDEER MOSS is a type of lichen that grows in the arctic regions and sometimes farther south. It is the main source of food for the caribou, or reindeer, of the Arctic. Sometimes, men eat reindeer moss. In Scandinavia, it has been used to make bread.

See also LICHEN.

Scientific Classification. Reindeer moss is genus *Cladonia*, species *C. rangiferina*.   ROLLA M. TRYON

REINER, FRITZ (1888-1963), was one of the great symphony orchestra and operatic conductors of his time. He became especially noted for his performances of the music of central European composers. Orchestras trained by Reiner gained fame for the precision as well as the excellence of their playing.

Reiner was born and educated in Budapest, Hungary. From 1914 to 1921, he served as musical director of the Dresden Royal Opera in Germany. He came to the United States in 1922 as director of the Cincinnati Symphony Orchestra and held that position until 1931. Reiner then taught at the Curtis Institute of Music in Philadelphia until 1941. From 1938 to 1948, he conducted the Pittsburgh Symphony. He was a major conductor at the Metropolitan Opera in New York City from 1949 to 1953. Reiner served as musical director of the Chicago Symphony from 1953 until his death in 1963.   ROBERT C. MARSH

REINFORCED CONCRETE. See CEMENT AND CONCRETE (Reinforced Concrete).

REINFORCEMENT, in psychology. See LEARNING (Classical Conditioning).

REINHARDT, *RINE hart*, **MAX** (1873-1943), a noted Austrian theatrical producer and director, became famous for his spectacular productions. He experimented with many new theatrical forms and styles. For his pantomime-pageant, *The Miracle*, he rebuilt the inside of a theater to resemble a cathedral. He staged this play successfully in the United States in 1924. He staged Shakespeare's *Midsummer Night's Dream*, and later made it into a motion picture.

Reinhardt was born Max Goldmann in Baden, near Vienna. In 1920, he founded the theater festival in Salzburg, Austria. When the Nazis came to power, he moved to the United States.   BARNARD HEWITT

REJA is an iron screen. See IRONWORK, DECORATIVE.

RELAPSING FEVER is an infectious disease that occurs chiefly in the tropics. It is caused by any one of several microorganisms called *Borrelia*, which are spirochetes. A person with relapsing fever develops chills, fever, headache, and muscular aches and pains. These may last for several days or a week. Then the patient seems to return to good health for about a week. Suddenly the symptoms return, and if the patient is not treated, he may have as many as 10 relapses.

Lice and ticks transmit the microorganisms to human beings. Like typhus, louse-borne relapsing fever is found in regions with poor living conditions (see TYPHUS). The two diseases often occur together. The tick-borne types are found in the Western United States as well as in other parts of the world. Doctors sometimes use antibiotics to treat the disease.   H. WORLEY KENDELL

RELATIVITY. The relativity theory, popularly called the Einstein theory, has caught the imagination of the average man more than any other physical theory in history. Yet the theory of relativity, unlike many other results of physical science, is not easily understood by the layman. We can understand the relativity theory fully only by means of the mathematical formulas which make it up. Without mathematics, we can only state some of its basic ideas and quote, but not prove, some of its conclusions.

The relativity theory deals with the most fundamental ideas which we use to describe natural happenings. These ideas are time, space, mass, motion, and gravitation. The relativity theory gives new meaning to the old ideas that these words represent. It is basically made up of two parts. One is the special, or restricted, relativity theory. This was published by Albert Einstein in 1905. The general relativity theory was put forward by Einstein in 1915.

Special Theory of Relativity

This theory is called the special relativity theory because it refers to a special kind of motion. This is uniform motion in a straight line, that is, with constant *velocity*. Suppose we are on a smoothly running railroad train which is moving at a constant velocity. In this train you may drop a book, play catch, or allow a pendulum to swing freely. The book will appear to fall straight down when it is dropped; the ball will travel directly from the thrower to the catcher. All these activities can be carried on in much the same way and with the same results on the ground outside the train. So long as the train really runs smoothly, with constant velocity, none of our mechanical activities will be influenced by the motion.

On the other hand, if the train stops or speeds up abruptly, our activities may be changed. A book may be jarred from a seat and fall without being dropped. A ball will travel differently.

One way of stating the principle of this theory is to say that the laws of mechanics are the same for an observer in a smoothly moving train as for the observer on the ground. Physicists would say: *if two systems move uniformly relative to each other, then all the laws of mechanics are the same in both systems.* This principle may be called the classical relativity principle. This principle is as old as the ideas of mechanics and physics.

Suppose we have a long train much like the train in the previous example. But instead of rolling along at a speed of 75 miles an hour, it will be moving uniformly at a speed of, let us say, 20,000 miles a second. Instead of having two boys playing catch on the train, we will have a radio antenna on the train sending out radio waves, or a flashlight sending out light signals. Observers on the train will measure the velocity of the radio waves and light signals. On the ground we will also have an antenna or flashlight, and observers measuring the velocity of the signals given off. Is the velocity of the radio or light waves the same for the men on the ground as it is for those on the train? If we had asked this question of a physicist in the late 1800's, he would have said no. He would have said that the classical relativity principle holds true for mechanical activities, but not for those of electromagnetic waves, that is, not for radio or light waves.

A physicist would have said that radio and light waves travel through *ether* at a velocity of 186,282 miles per second. Ether is a substance that scientists imagined to fill all space, to account for the transmission of light in outer space. The physicist would have said that the stars, sun, planets, and our imaginary moving train move through the ether sea at different speeds. Therefore, the velocity of light will be different for an observer on the sun, on the earth, and on the train. Just as the earth changes its velocity during the year in which it completes its journey around the sun, the speed of light for the observer should change too.

Scientists believed that the ether through which all objects of the universe were believed to move provided a nonmoving frame of reference. All other motions could be judged from this frame of reference. Ether was looked upon as a fluid or elastic solid. It was believed to occupy the spaces between the atoms that made up matter. It offered little resistance to the earth's movement through space.

It was Einstein who asserted that the relativity principle was true for all phenomena, mechanical or electromagnetic.

Among the many experiments which helped destroy the ether theory, the most famous is that of Michelson and Morley in 1887. Their measurements of the speed of light showed that the motion of the earth in regard to the sun had no influence upon the velocity of light. Therefore, light has a uniform velocity, regardless of the frame of reference.

The basic ideas of the special relativity theory are found in a mathematical formulation of two postulates. The first is that the relativity principle is valid for all phenomena. The second postulate is that the velocity of electromagnetic waves, or light, in empty space is constant, and furthermore is independent of the velocity of its source or observer.

The following deductions have been made from these postulates by mathematical means.

According to the special relativity theory, no material body can move with a velocity greater than that of light.

If a conductor on a fast-moving train compared his clock with the many clocks in the stations he passed, he would find that the rhythm of his clock is faster than the rhythm of the clocks on the ground. On the other hand, it will appear to the stationmasters that the rhythms of their clocks are faster than the rhythm of the conductor's clock on the train passing the station. This effect is small, and could be detected only if the velocity of the one clock that passes many others were not very small compared with the speed of light.

Two events judged as taking place at the same time by the observer in the train are not simultaneous for the observer on the ground.

The length of every object resting in the train appears to the observer outside to be shortened in the direction in which the train is moving.

Perhaps the most important of these deductions is the inconsistent fact that mass is not unchangeable. The mass of an object increases with its velocity. Theoretically, the mass of an object could become infinite if its velocity became the velocity of light. This mass increase has been observed with experiments. A small particle of matter accelerated to 86 per cent of the speed of light weighs twice as much as it does when it is at rest.

The interchange between mass and energy ($E = mc^2$) became of extreme practical importance in the liberation of the energy found in the nucleus of an atom. When energy is liberated from the nucleus of the uranium atom and atoms of other elements are formed, the total mass of these atoms is less than the total mass of the uranium atom. This means that some of the mass of the nucleus of the uranium atom has been transformed into energy. The $E = mc^2$ law shows that the energy in a single uranium nucleus is 220,000,000,000 electron volts, providing that all of its mass could be converted to energy. However, splitting the uranium nucleus, a process known as *fission*, releases only 0.1 per cent of the total energy content.

Various experiments have proved the truth of many of these conclusions about relativity. In 1938, N. E. Ives used a hydrogen atom as a moving clock. He found that a fast-moving hydrogen atom does slow down in its rhythm, just as Einstein predicted the moving clock would do. This slowing down could be shown by a change in the frequency of the line given off in its spectrum. The changes of mass as predicted by the special theory of relativity are observed in machines that are used to accelerate electrons and nuclear particles to the high speeds necessary in the studies of nuclear properties.

The mathematician H. Minkowski gave a mathematical form to the special relativity theory in 1907. A line involves only one dimension. We can locate any point on a sheet of paper by measuring from that point to any two sides of the paper that are perpendicular to each other. Therefore, we can say that any point on a sheet of paper involves two dimensions. All points in space involve the idea of three dimensions, height, length, and breadth. But there is one other important fact involved. In physics as well as history we must deal with events. When and where did the French Revolution start, for example? When and where does the earth have the smallest velocity in its movement about the sun? Events must be characterized by four numbers, bringing in the idea of a fourth dimension. Three of these numbers will answer the question *where;* one must answer the question *when.* Answering the question *when* involves the idea of time. Then we consider things in terms of four dimensions.

This question of answering when and where an event took place becomes more complicated, according to the theory of special relativity, because rods can change their lengths, and clocks change their rhythms, depending on the speed at which they operate when they are in motion. Therefore, we must answer the questions *when* and *where* an event took place in terms of a definitely moving system, or in terms of the relationships between two moving systems. For example, if we know when and where an event took place for an observer on our swiftly moving train, and if we know the velocity of the train, we can find out when and where the same event took place for an observer on the ground. The mathematical formulation of the theory of special relativity tells us how to find these four numbers, characterizing an event in one system from an event in another. It tells us that the question *when* has no absolute meaning, that the answer to the question depends on the system we choose.

General Relativity Theory

The mathematical formulas which make up this general theory are much more difficult than those which are concerned with special relativity. The general relativity theory attacks and changes the old ideas about gravitation which have dominated physics since the days of Isaac Newton. According to Newton, two bodies attract each other with a force depending upon their mass and their distance apart. The gravitational influence of a star is felt at the same moment throughout the entire universe, even though it decreases with the distance from the star. But for electromagnetic waves, action spreads through space with great but perfectly definite velocity, that of light. Because of our knowledge of electromagnetic radiation, we tend to reject ideas that disturbances and actions that travel through space have infinite speed. We tend to believe that though they may travel at a very high speed, that speed is not limitless.

Imagine that parallel straight lines are drawn on a rubber sheet. Then imagine that we pull the sheet so that the lines are no longer parallel. The rubber sheet will stand for the four-dimensional world of the relativity theory. The pull of our hands which changes the shape of the sheet shows what happens when moving material bodies influence each other. The relationship between time and space is thus influenced by matter and its motion. This gives a geometrical structure to the world. The mathematics used by the general relativity theory is drawn from geometries which have postulates which disagree with those of Euclid. In such geometries, the sum of the angles of a triangle will be greater or less than 180°. These geometries are called Riemannian geometries. Einstein applied Riemannian geometries to the description of what goes on in the physical world.

According to Newton's theory, a planet moves around the sun because of the gravitational force exerted by the sun. According to the theory of general relativity, the planet chooses the shortest possible path throughout the four-dimensional world which is deformed by the presence of the sun. This may be compared to the fact that a ship or an airplane crossing the ocean follows the section of a circle, rather than a straight line, in order to travel the shortest route between two points. In the same way, a planet or light ray moves along the "shortest" line in its four-dimensional world.

So far, three things have been discovered in which Einstein's theory of general relativity receives experimental proof as opposed to the theories of Newton. These differences are not great, but are measurable. In the first place, according to Newton's theory, the planet Mercury moves in an ellipse about the sun. According to Einstein's theory, Mercury moves along an ellipse, but at the same time the ellipse rotates very slowly in the direction of the planet's motion. The ellipse will turn about forty-three seconds of an arc per century (a complete rotation contains 360 degrees of an arc and $360 \times 60 \times 60$ seconds of an arc). This effect is rather small. Nevertheless, Mercury is nearest to the sun and the relativistic effect would be still smaller for other planets.

If we take a picture of part of the heavens during an eclipse of the sun and near the eclipsed sun, and then

Relativity and Time

150,000 MILES PER SECOND

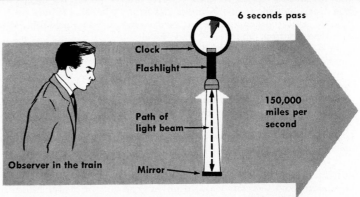

6 seconds pass

Clock

Flashlight

150,000 miles per second

Path of light beam

In the Train, a flashlight near the ceiling sends a beam of light down to a mirror on the floor. An observer measures the time it takes for the light to leave the flashlight, strike the mirror, and be reflected up to the flashlight. If the distance between the flashlight and the mirror is 560,000 miles, the beam travels 2 × 560,000 miles, or a total of 1,120,000 miles. The observer's clock shows that 6 seconds pass, and so the velocity of light is 1,120,000 miles divided by 6 seconds, or about 186,000 miles per second.

Observer in the train

Mirror

6 seconds pass

150,000 miles per second

A Stationary Observer sees the light beam travel 1,860,000 miles (not 1,120,000 miles) because the beam moves sideways as well as down and up. But according to the theory of relativity, the stationary observer must measure the same velocity as the observer in the train—about 186,000 miles per second. Therefore, while the clock in the train shows that 6 seconds pass, the stationary clock must show that 10 seconds pass. The measured speed is then 1,860,000 miles divided by 10 seconds, or 186,000 miles per second.

Path of light beam

Path of light beam

Stationary observer and clock

10 seconds pass

WORLD BOOK illustration by Richard Hennessy

take another picture of the same part of the heavens a little later, the two photographs will not show identical positions for all the stars. This is so because, according to general relativity, a light ray sent by a star and passing near the rim of the sun is deflected from its original path by 1.75 seconds of an arc.

Physicists have known for more than a hundred years that when some elements are heated to incandescence they give off a pattern of colored lines which can be examined through a spectroscope. According to the Einstein theory, if we examine the spectral lines of an element on our earth with the spectral lines given off by the same element on the sun or on a star, the spectral lines of the element on the sun or star should be very slightly shifted toward the red end of the spectrum, compared with the spectral lines of the same element on our earth. This is the Doppler effect. Sirius, the dog star, has a very dense companion star. According to the relativity theory, the red shift of a spectral line from Sirius should be 30 times greater than the red shift of the same line from the sun. Experiment has confirmed this shift. In 1960, two American physicists, R. V. Pound and G. A. Rebka, Jr., detected the red shift resulting from the earth's gravitational field. They measured the

effect of altitude in the frequency of gamma rays.

There seems little question that experimental evidence is favorable to the general relativity theory. But some scientists believe that the evidence is not yet decisive. One reason is that all the predicted effects which we have discussed lie very close to the amount of error that would normally occur in an experiment. However, experimental proof of the general relativity theory is still being sought. In January, 1947, Erwin Schrödinger announced that he had integrated the general theory with electromagnetic radiations.

Relativity and Man's Ideas

The ideas of relativity form a framework which can embrace all laws of nature. Relativity has changed the whole philosophical and physical notions of space and time. It has influenced our views and speculation of the distant worlds and stars and of the tiny world of the atom. Some of this speculation is still going on. Does our universe, regarded as a whole, resemble a plane

RELATIVITY

surface or a sphere? It is not possible to answer this question, because there are many different theories. All these theories try to describe the universe as a whole and are based upon the mathematical principles of general relativity. According to some theories, a light ray sent from an arbitrary point in space returns, after a very long time interval, to the point of departure, like a traveler in his journey around our earth. Thus, if you were to start from your home and travel into space along a straight line, you would eventually return to the point from which you started. According to other theories, however, a light ray or a traveler would continue an endless journey through space.

Such theories about the universe are developed to explain the motion and distribution of distant nebulas.

In spite of all these successes of the relativity theory, it is not right to say that Newtonian physics is wrong. Newtonian physics holds true if the velocities of the objects being studied are small compared with the velocity of light. Such objects are found every day in our own experience, and therefore classical physics can still be applied to our daily problems. Astronomers have found that Newton's theory of gravitation still holds true in their calculations. But the relativity theory does limit the area to which the Newtonian physics can be successfully applied.

The relativity theory is, like all our theories, an invention of the human mind. New theories may eventually show limitations of the relativity theory and deal with problems that the relativity theory does not cover. But no physicist doubts that the relativity theory has brought scientific progress.   RALPH E. LAPP

Critically reviewed by RUDOLF L. MÖSSBAUER

Related Articles in WORLD BOOK include:

Doppler Effect	Fourth Dimension	Interferometer
Einstein, Albert	Gravitation	Light
Electromagnetism		

RELAXATION. See HEALTH (Work and Play).

RELIEF, in art, is sculpture in which the figures or designs project from their background. It differs from *sculpture in the round,* in which the figures stand alone and have three full dimensions. In relief sculpture, the figures are only partly modeled, but they give an illusion of being fully modeled. They may stand out from the background surface, or they may be carved into it. If they are carved into it, the sculpture is called *hollow relief* or *intaglio.* Relief sculpture may be of three types: high relief; low relief; and half relief, or semirelief. Some relief sculpture combines two or more types.

High Relief. Figures in high relief project from their background more than half of their implied thickness. High relief is often called by its Italian name, *alto-rilievo.*

Low Relief. Figures that stand out from their background less than half of their suggested thickness are in low relief. When the work is well done, they appear to stand out more than they actually do. The frieze of the Parthenon is the most famous example of low-relief sculpture (see PARTHENON). Sometimes low relief may be nearly flat, as in the design on a coin. Low relief is also known by its French name, *bas-relief.*

Half Relief, or Semirelief. Figures in half relief stand out half their thickness. Half relief is a little higher than low relief, but lower than high relief. It is often called by its Italian name, *mezzo-rilievo.*

History. Sculptors have carved figures in relief for thousands of years. Peoples of the stone ages often carved or scratched figures and designs in relief. The Assyrians, Egyptians, and Greeks used all forms of relief sculpture in their palaces and temples.

Relief sculpture is used in many ways today. It is almost the only form used in making coins and medals. As in all sculpture, the subject matter, design, and execution of relief reflect the development of civilization, the religious trends, and the art of the time in which it is made.   FLORENCE HOPE

See also CAMEO; ENGRAVING; INTAGLIO.

Relief Sculpture is one of the most ancient art forms. The frieze that surrounded the Parthenon in Athens showed a Panathenaic procession in low relief. It began with a group of horsemen and charioteers, *left.* Egyptian low relief in the Temple of Seti I at Abydos, *below left,* dates from the 1300's B.C. Lorenzo Ghiberti produced masterpieces of relief sculpture in creating the bronze doors of the Baptistery in Florence, Italy, *below.* Individual panels picture a series of Biblical subjects. Roman sculpture from the A.D. 100's appears in high relief on a frieze from Trajan's Forum in Rome, *right.* Intricate Maya carvings in both high and low relief cover a huge boulder at Quirigua, Guatemala, *below right.* The sandstone monument, which may have been an altar, dates from the A.D. 500's.

RELIEF, in economics, is assistance of various kinds given to persons who are in need. Relief for the poor is based on the theory that society must help persons who are not able to take care of themselves.

In the United States, relief is administered through federal agencies set up under the Social Security Act; through public-assistance and general-assistance programs, provided by state and local governments; and through private organizations.

The *Social Security Act,* passed in 1935, provides pensions for most workers upon retirement from their jobs. It also provides federal funds to help pay the costs of state *public-assistance programs.* These federal funds are available for relief only to specified groups, including the aged, the blind and disabled, dependent children, and needy mothers. Persons who do not fit into these specified groups may receive help from *general-assistance programs,* paid for by state and local governments.

As a result of federal financial aid, most states have various types of public-assistance programs. All states have programs for aged persons, blind persons, and needy children. All but Nevada have public assistance for the disabled. Each state sets up its own rules in administering funds and defining need. Persons 65 years old or over who need help may get old-age assistance for general expenses. The federal government requires that aid cannot be withheld from any citizen, regardless of when he became a citizen. In 1960, the Kerr-Mills Act provided a program to help pay unusually large medical expenses for the needy aged not on old-age assistance. In 1965, this program was extended to apply to needy, eligible persons of all ages. All the states except Alaska and Arizona now have such programs. Each state determines who is eligible for benefits.

In the early 1970's, about 2,100,000 persons were receiving old-age assistance. On the average, each person received $76 a month. About 7,400,000 needy children in 2,800,000 families received aid at a monthly average of $70 per child. About 80,000 blind persons qualified for an average payment of $104 per month. About 1 million totally and permanently disabled persons received payments that averaged about $98 a month.

In addition to cash payments, recipients also get medical care in many instances. Such care is also provided for medically needy persons who have enough money for normal living needs, but not for unusually high medical bills. In the early 1970's, the amount of such medical payments was about $6¾ billion a year.

All states have general assistance programs. But the effectiveness of the programs varies greatly. General assistance may be granted for many reasons, including the unemployment, death, or disability of a person who supports a family. In the early 1970's, about 450,000 families were receiving an average of about $109 per month for general assistance.

In addition to these public programs, much relief in the United States is furnished by private agencies and charities. These private programs often take care of immediate or emergency needs, because they can sometimes act more quickly than the more formal government agencies. Many private charities, particularly those of religious groups, also give long-term relief.

In Canada, public-assistance programs are much like those in the United States. Public-assistance programs are administered by the provinces, although generally

they are partly financed by the federal government.

History. Throughout history, various persons and groups recognized the need for helping the poor. At one time, churches were the chief organizations extending charity to those in need. In 1531, an English law licensed beggars to ask for alms. In 1601, a law provided for taxing each parish to help support the poor. This law was the first to recognize that the state was responsible for its dependent persons.

Early laws written to give aid to the poor were called *poor laws.* During the 1800's, France, Germany, Italy, Norway, and Sweden recognized the needy as state wards. Their governments passed poor laws. The first poor relief in the United States was patterned after the poor laws brought over by the English colonists. During colonial days, most of the needy were given relief in their own homes. This system was known as *outdoor relief.* Later, many communities set up poorhouses, and poor relief became mostly a matter of placing the needy in institutions. This system was called *indoor relief.*

After 1870, the problem of relief began to be considered more scientifically. The churches continued their support, private organizations sprang up to provide charity, and community chests collected voluntary donations to aid the poor in many cities. Members of communities felt a duty to provide for the poor. They also became convinced that city, state, and national governments should write laws to assure proper relief.

The state laws of the times divided the needy into distinct classes and aided them according to their special needs. Later, the federal government became active in assisting the poor. Under the Federal Emergency Relief Administration, established in 1933, federal government aid took the form of helping states to finance their relief laws. These federal laws were not broad enough to ease the poverty caused by the depression of the 1930's. The government undertook various projects to relieve the serious situation. The Works Progress Administration, founded in 1935, provided work for skilled and unskilled laborers and white-collar workers. Another method used in the 1930's was the distribution of food stamps to needy persons. The stamps entitled a person to certain food products. The government bought many of the foods from producers as surplus foods. Today, surplus foods are distributed by the government in several ways to needy groups.

Great Britain, the United States, Canada, and many other countries have made thorough studies of the conditions that cause poverty. These countries have made radical changes in relief systems so that those on relief may maintain their self-respect. Those who favor social security believe it is better to make cash payments to the poor, sick, and aged, instead of keeping these persons in government institutions.   ROBERT J. MYERS

See also SOCIAL SECURITY; NEW DEAL; SOCIAL WORK; CARE; POVERTY.

RELIEF CORPS, NATIONAL WOMAN'S. See WOMAN'S RELIEF CORPS, NATIONAL.

RELIEF MAP is a small-scale model of a region. It shows the physical features of the region, such as mountains, valleys, and plains. The features may be shown by lines, shadings, and colors. Relief maps are sometimes made of clay or other material.

RELIGION

RELIGION. There have been thousands of definitions of religion. But the many religions in the world cannot be defined by simple statements. Some scholars define religion as belief in one or more gods, or in supernatural beings. But this would not include all religions, because some religions may mean a way of living rather than a way of believing.

Religion could perhaps be best defined as man's attempt to achieve the highest possible good by adjusting his life to the strongest and best power in the universe. This power is usually called God.

In general, religion is a group undertaking, although every person tries to follow his own religious beliefs in his personal life. It is possible for a person to develop his own private religion. But it would be about as difficult for him as educating himself with no outside help. Most religions are organized systems of beliefs based on traditions and teachings.

Religion can be compared with science, which works to discover facts and use them. Religion seeks to discover values and to attract men to them through worship and discipline.

Every religion includes *ethics*, or codes of conduct. But religion is more than ethics. Ethics asks: "How should we behave toward other people?" Religion asks: "How should we relate ourselves to the greatest power in the universe?"

Religion has been one of the most powerful forces in history. Millions of persons have died for their religious beliefs. Many nations have gone to war to spread or defend their faiths. But there has never been a people that did not have some form of religion.

Religions of the World

Eleven major religions are practiced in the world today. Each of them includes various groups that may practice their religion in different ways. But all have certain basic beliefs, traditions, and philosophies.

Christianity is the most widespread religion in the world. It has about a billion followers, most of whom live in Europe and North and South America. Christian beliefs are founded on the teachings of Jesus Christ as set forth in the New Testament. They are also based on the Hebrew Bible, or Old Testament. Christian doctrines teach God's love for men and stress the importance of brotherly love.

Christianity began as a movement of Jews in Palestine who believed that Jesus of Nazareth was the savior for whom their people had been waiting. They called Jesus *the Christ*, or Messiah, and became known as Christians. Their religion soon spread to people in all parts of the world. Christianity has about 300 denominations today. See CHRISTIANITY; JESUS CHRIST.

Judaism was one of the first religions to emphasize *ethical monotheism*, or the belief in One God who is just and good. The Jewish religion centers around this belief. The Hebrew Bible contains the sacred books of Judaism. Many persons believe that Abraham was the first Jew. Judaism took definite form under the leadership of Moses in the 1200's B.C. Jews have always considered Palestine their religious home. But most of them have lived in other countries since A.D. 70, when the Romans destroyed Jerusalem. Today, there are about

Praying hands and beautiful works of art symbolize religion for peoples in all parts of the world. Religion helps man answer such basic questions as the meaning of his life, the meaning of death, and the unknown forces in the world around him.

Stained glass windows in Ulm Cathedral, photographed by Don Zeilstra. "Praying Hands" by Albrecht Dürer

RELIGION

14 million Jews. About 5¾ million live in the United States and about 2¼ million in Israel. See JEWS; JUDAISM.

Islam is the faith taught by Mohammed (570?-632). The word *islam* means *peace* and *submission,* and is usually taken to mean *peace through submission to God. Moslems* (followers of Islam) believe there is one God and that Mohammed was His Prophet. The Arabic word for God is *Allah.* Islam built upon Judaism and Christianity, claiming to be the goal toward which they led. The *Koran* has Allah's revelations to Mohammed. There are about 465 million Moslems in the world. Most of them live in Africa, the Middle East, and Indonesia. See ISLAM; MOHAMMED; MOSLEMS.

Hinduism is the traditional religion of India. Hindus believe in a supreme and absolute power called *Brahman.* They say that the goal of all human life is to be united with Brahman. In that state, men will take part in perfection. But Hindus believe that man's soul must be reborn again and again until it becomes pure enough to be united with Brahman (see TRANSMIGRATION OF THE SOUL). Hindus worship three gods whom they consider reflections of Brahman. These are the Creator, *Brahma;* the Preserver, *Vishnu;* and the Destroyer, *Siva.*

Scholars have traced the beginnings of Hinduism to about 2500 B.C. Most of the world's Hindus live in India, where the religion has about 408 million followers. See BRAHMAN; HINDUISM; SIVA; VISHNU.

Buddhism developed from Hinduism. It was founded by Gautama Buddha (563?-483? B.C.). The word *Buddha* means *Fully Enlightened* or *Awakened One.* The Buddhist goal in life is *Nirvana,* a state of complete peace and love. Buddhists are taught to follow an *Eightfold Path* of righteous living to achieve Nirvana.

Buddhism began in India, but had gradually disappeared there by about A.D. 1000. It spread eastward to Tibet, China, Japan, and southeastern Asia. The total number of Buddhists is estimated at about 165 million. Most live in China. See BUDDHA; BUDDHISM.

Jainism, like Buddhism, grew out of Hinduism. Mahavira (599?-527 B.C.) founded the religion in India. Jains do not worship any particular deity. They believe that after the soul has inhabited many bodies, it frees itself and lives happily and peacefully. Jainism stresses ethical purity, love, and kindness. It teaches that even the lowest insect must be considered sacred, and forbids its followers to kill or injure any living creature. About 2¼ million persons, almost all of whom live in India, practice Jainism today. See JAINISM.

Martha-Mary Chapel, Sudbury, Mass.—F.P.G., courtesy PPG Industries, Inc. "Showplaces of America" series.

Christianity centers on the belief that Jesus Christ is the Son of God. The crucifix, *above*, represents His death on the cross. Christian houses of worship range from the simple wooden church in Sudbury, Mass., *left*, to such cathedrals as New York City's St. John the Divine, *right*.

Judaism centers on the belief in One God who is just and good. The *menorah*, a seven-branched candlestick, symbolizes Jewish faith. A young boy reads from the *Torah*, the first five books of the Hebrew Bible, as he takes part in a Sabbath service. Men wear skullcaps called *yarmulkas* to show their reverence for God.

Confucianism is one of the three great religions of China. The others are Taoism and Buddhism. Confucius (551?-479? B.C.) was the founder of Confucianism. The Chinese often call him the *first Teacher*. Some scholars consider Confucianism a system of ethics rather than a religion, because Confucius taught more about how men should act toward one another than about God. But Confucianism also has a religious side. Confucius believed in a Supreme Being, called *Shang Ti*, to whom he prayed. The *Five Classics* contain the teachings of Confucius. Most Chinese have followed Confucianism somewhat. See CONFUCIANISM; CONFUCIUS.

Taoism (pronounced *DOW izm*). Tradition says that Lao Tzu (*the Old Master*) founded Taoism in China during the 500's B.C. But scholars have so little information about his life that many doubt that he ever lived. Some believe that Taoism developed in the 300's B.C. as a product of many thinkers. The *Tao Te Ching* (*The Way and Its Power*) is the sacred book of Taoism. It stresses a way of life that is quietly, but happily, in harmony with nature. It considers humility one of the highest virtues. In practice, Taoism includes much magic and superstition. Taoism has about 52 million followers, most of whom live in China. See LAO TZU; TAOISM.

Shinto is the native religion of Japan. The word means the *way of the gods*. The beginnings of Shinto have been traced back to the origins of Japanese civilization, about 2,500 years ago. Shinto teaches a reverent loyalty to beloved places and traditional Japanese ways of life. Shintoists worship many gods, including national heroes of the past and nature gods. In a form of Shinto called *New Religions*, individual sects or groups have programs of education and worship. *State Shinto* taught that the emperor descended from the Sun God and should be worshiped as a god. The government and emperor abandoned State Shinto in 1947. See SHINTO.

Sikhism is the religion of about 8 million persons, almost all of whom live in India. It blends Hinduism and Islam. Its founder, Guru Nanak (1469-1538), accepted Islam's belief in one God and various Hindu doctrines, such as the transmigration of the soul. *Sikh* means *disciple*. See SIKHISM.

Zoroastrianism was founded by Zoroaster, an ancient Persian prophet who was born before 600 B.C. The religion centers around *Ahura Mazda*, the god of righteousness and light. It teaches that people can attain eternal reward in heaven by supporting Ahura Mazda in his battle against the powers of evil. The *Zend-Avesta* contains the sacred writings of Zoroastrianism. Zoroastrian doctrines of heaven, hell, and the devil had some influence on Christianity. There are only about 161,000 Zoroastrians in the world today. They are known as *Parsis*, and most of them live in the Bombay region of India. See ZOROASTRIANISM; PARSIS.

Other Religions. The *Bahá'í Faith* stresses the oneness of humanity. It teaches that the world is really one country created by one God, and that all men are its citizens. The faith was founded in Persia (now Iran) in 1863 by Husayn Alí, called *Bahá'u'lláh*. He followed Alí Muhammad, called the *Báb*, and urged the formation of a union of all the nations in the world. The faith's principles were set forth by Bahá'u'lláh in books such as *Hidden Words*, *Seven Valleys*, and *The Book of Iqan*. The faith has about 29,000 centers in more than 300 countries and territories. See BAHÁ'ÍS.

Many religions exist among the tribal peoples of Africa, Asia, Australia, North and South America, and the Pacific Islands. Most of these tribal religions center on the practical needs of the people, such as food, and the fertility and health of crops, animals, and people. Religious ceremonies and rituals usually accompany the main agricultural activities, such as planting crops, and the important stages in the life of men and women.

Tribal peoples do not worship the sun or rain, or their *totems* (objects of special importance). Their "images" and "idols" represent symbols of spiritual or ethical principles. Anthropologists have discovered that tribal religions often contain ethical and moral ideas that are similar to those of the major religions. Tribal religions often express, sometimes crudely and on a limited scale, the same truths as the major religions express on a wider scale.

Although tribal peoples have no written sacred literature, they carefully observe their ceremonies and rituals and pass them on to their children. Anthropologists can learn a great deal about prehistoric religions by studying the religions of these tribes today.

Religious Beliefs and Practices

The Deity. Sooner or later, most persons come to believe that their lives depend on forces in the world more powerful than themselves. They identify these powers, regard them with awe, and seek good relations with them. These forces then become their *deities* (gods). But some persons do not believe that there is a God. They are called *atheists* (see ATHEISM). Others, called *agnostics*, do not deny God, but say that it is impossible for man to know whether there is a God and a spiritual world (see AGNOSTIC).

Many tribal peoples believe that a vague, general, powerful, living, but impersonal force exists in the world. Melanesian tribes in the Pacific Islands call this force *mana*, and anthropologists often apply this word to similar beliefs of other peoples. Some tribal peoples also believe in *animism* (see ANIMISM). They say that everything in nature, even stones, rivers, trees, and mountains, has its own spirit. They try to please these spirits so that the spirits will not harm them. On a higher level, some peoples accept *polytheism*, or the belief in many gods (see POLYTHEISM). They worship the basic powers of nature, including the sun, storms, and the earth, rather than particular objects such as trees,

Three Lions

Eastern Orthodox Christianity makes use of *icons*, representations of Christ, the Virgin Mary, or saints, as objects of reverence, *above*. An Eastern Orthodox priest encourages a woman to show her love of Christ by kissing a cross, *right*. The bearded priest wears a traditional golden robe.

stones, and other things in nature. For example, the ancient Greeks worshiped Zeus, the god of lightning; Apollo, the god of sun; and many other gods.

Most major religions today reject the idea of many gods. They accept monotheism, and say that all the world's powers are expressions of a single Supreme Being. Christianity, Judaism, Islam, and Zoroastrianism believe that God is all-good and all-powerful, and rules the world with a conscious purpose. They think of Him as pure spirit with no body at all. Taoism, Buddhism, Hinduism, and some forms of Confucianism teach that personality traits of any sort suggest man rather than God. See GOD.

Codes of Conduct. Every religion teaches its follow-ers how they should behave. Some religious codes tell people how to act toward God. For example, Judaism forbids the worship of idols, and Islam commands its followers to pray five times every day. Other codes speak of man's relationship with man.

The various religions differ on many points as to what their believers should or should not do. Judaism commands its followers not to eat pork, or to serve meat and milk at the same meal. Hindus may not eat beef, and Buddhists are generally vegetarians. However, the great religions agree on most ethical matters. All condemn murder, theft, adultery, and dishonesty. All teach that selfishness is evil, and that love is the goal of human relationships. All stress some form of golden rule, treating others as we would have them treat us.

In early religions, men were concerned only with the

MAJOR RELIGIOUS BODIES IN THE UNITED STATES

NAME	MEMBERSHIP
*Adventists:	
Advent Christian Church	29,838
Church of God General Conference (Abrahamic Faith)	6,700
*Seventh-day Adventists	407,766
African Orthodox Church, The	6,000
American Rescue Workers	5,785
Bahá'í Faith (*Bahá'ís)	†
*Baptists:	
*American Baptist Association	786,536
*American Baptist Convention	1,454,965
Baptist General Conference	101,226
Baptist Missionary Association of America	183,342
Conservative Baptist Assn. of America	300,000
Duck River (and Kindred) Associations of Baptists	8,492
Free Will Baptists, The National Assn. of	200,000
General Baptists (General Association of)	65,000
*National Baptist Convention of America	2,668,799
*National Baptist Convention, U.S.A., Inc.**	6,300,000
National Baptist Evangelical Life and Soul Saving Assembly of U.S.A.	57,674
*National Primitive Baptist Convention, Inc.	1,523,000
North American Baptist General Conference	55,080
Primitive Baptists	72,000
Progressive National Baptist Convention, Inc.	521,692
Regular Baptist Churches, The General Association of	192,495
Separate Baptists in Christ	7,496
*Southern Baptist Convention	11,487,708
United Baptists	63,641
United Free Will Baptist Church, The	100,000
Bible Way Churches of Our Lord Jesus Christ World Wide, Inc.	30,000
*Brethren (German Baptists):	
Brethren Church (Ashland, Ohio)	17,114
*Brethren, Church of the	185,198
National Fellowship of Brethren Churches	32,307
Plymouth Brethren	33,250
Brethren in Christ Church (River Brethren)	8,954
Buddhist Churches of America	100,000
Christadelphians	15,800
Christian and Missionary Alliance, The	120,330
*Christian Church (Disciples of Christ)	1,444,465
Church of Christ (Holiness) U.S.A.	9,289
Church of Christ, Scientist (*Christian Scientists)	†
Church of Illumination, The	9,000
Church of Our Lord Jesus Christ of the Apostolic Faith, Inc.	45,000
Church of the Living God	45,320
*Church of the Nazarene	372,943
*Churches of Christ	2,400,000

NAME	MEMBERSHIP
Churches of Christ in Christian Union	8,100
*Churches of God:	
Church of God (Anderson, Ind.)	147,752
Church of God and Saints of Christ	38,127
Churches of God in North America (General Eldership)	36,042
Churches of God, Holiness	25,600
Churches of the New Jerusalem (*Swedenborgians)	7,460
Congregational Christian Churches, National Association of	110,000
Conservative Congregational Christian Conf.	16,219
*Eastern Orthodox Churches:	
Albanian Orthodox Archdiocese in America	40,000
American Carpatho-Russian Orthodox Greek Catholic Church, The	104,600
Antiochian Orthodox Archdiocese of Toledo, Ohio, and Dependencies in North America	30,400
Antiochian Orthodox Christian Archdiocese of New York and All North America, The	100,000
Armenian Apostolic Church of America	125,000
Armenian Church of North America, Diocese of the (including Diocese of California)	300,000
Bulgarian Eastern Orthodox Church	86,000
*Greek Orthodox Archdiocese of North and South America	1,875,000
Romanian Orthodox Episcopate of America, The	50,000
Russian Orthodox Catholic Church in North and South America, The Ex-archate of the	152,973
Russian Orthodox Church Outside Russia	55,000
Russian Orthodox Greek Catholic Church of America, The	1,000,000
Serbian Eastern Orthodox Diocese in the United States and Canada	65,000
Syrian Orthodox Church of Antioch (Archdiocese of the U.S.A. and Canada)	30,000
Turkish Orthodox Church in America, Patriarchal Exarchate	8,200
Ukrainian Orthodox Church in America	87,475
Ukrainian Orthodox Church of America (Ecumenical Patriarchate)	45,000
*Episcopal Church, The	3,330,272
*Ethical Culture Movement	6,000
Evangelical Congregational Church	29,582
Evangelical Covenant Church of America, The	67,522
Evangelical Free Church of America, The	63,735
Evangelistic Associations:	
Apostolic Christian Churches of America	9,100
Christian Congregation, Inc., The	46,224
Free Christian Zion Church of Christ	22,260
Missionary Church, The	17,145

*Has a separate article in WORLD BOOK.   †Membership statistics not available.   **Membership reported by religious body.
Source: *Yearbook of American Churches.* Copyright © 1971, National Council of Churches of Christ in the U.S.A.

NAME	MEMBERSHIP
Hungarian Reformed Church in America	11,250
Independent Fundamental Churches of America	122,388
*Jehovah's Witnesses	359,146
Jewish Congregations (*Jews)	5,780,000
*Latter Day Saints, Reorganized Church of Jesus Christ of	200,113
Latter-day Saints, Church of Jesus Christ of (*Mormons)	2,073,146
*Lutherans:	
*American Lutheran Church, The	2,559,588
Apostolic Lutheran Church of America	6,994
Church of the Lutheran Brethren of Am.	7,968
Evangelical Lutheran Synod	16,017
*Lutheran Church in America	3,135,684
*Lutheran Church—Missouri Synod, The	2,786,102
Synod of Evangelical Lutheran Churches	21,656
Wisconsin Evangelical Lutheran Synod	376,319
*Mennonites:	
General Conference of Mennonite Brethren Churches	13,171
*Hutterites (Hutterian Brethren)	3,405
Mennonite Church	85,343
Mennonite Church, The General Conference	35,613
Old Order Amish Church	21,500
*Methodists:	
*African Methodist Episcopal Church	1,166,301
*African Methodist Episcopal Zion Church	940,000
African Union First Colored Methodist Protestant Church, Inc.	8,000
Christian Methodist Episcopal Church	466,718
Evangelical Methodist Church	9,311
*Free Methodist Church of North America	64,394
Primitive Methodist Church, U.S.A.	11,945
Reformed Zion Union Apostolic Church	16,000
Union American Methodist Episcopal Church	27,560
*United Methodist Church, The	10,824,010
*Moravian Church:	
Moravian Church in America	59,415
Unity of the Brethren	6,142
New Apostolic Church of North America	21,000
North American Old Roman Catholic Church	18,500
*Old Catholic Churches:	
Christ Catholic Exarchate of Americas and Europe	5,513
North American Old Roman Catholic Church	59,422
Old Roman Catholic Church (English Rite)	21,466
*Pentecostal Churches:	
Apostolic Overcoming Holy Church of God	75,000
*Assemblies of God	625,027
Christian Church of North America, General Council	8,000
Church of God (Cleveland, Tenn.)	257,995
Church of God, Inc., The (Original)	18,000
Church of God, The	75,290
Church of God in Christ, The	425,000
Church of God of Prophecy, The	48,708
International Church of the Foursquare Gospel	89,215
International Pentecostal Assemblies	6,500
Open Bible Standard Churches, Inc.	30,000
Pentecostal Assemblies of the World, Inc.	45,000
Pentecostal Church of God of America, Inc.	115,000
Pentecostal Free-Will Baptist Church, Inc.	13,500
Pentecostal Holiness Church, Inc.	66,790
United Holy Church of America	28,980
United Pentecostal Church, Inc.	200,000
*Polish National Catholic Church of America	282,411
*Presbyterians:	
Associate Reformed Presbyterian Church (General Synod)	28,273

NAME	MEMBERSHIP
Cumberland Presbyterian Church	92,368
Orthodox Presbyterian Church, The	14,125
*Presbyterian Church in the U.S.	957,569
Reformed Presbyterian Church, Evangelical Synod	14,927
Reformed Presbyterian Church of North America	6,185
Second Cumberland Presbyterian Church in U.S.	30,000
*United Presbyterian Church in the United States of America, The	3,165,490
*Quakers:	
Friends United Meeting (The Five Years Meeting of Friends)	69,149
Ohio Yearly Meeting of Friends Church (Evangelical Friends Alliance)	7,632
Oregon Yearly Meeting of Friends Church	6,343
Religious Society of Friends (Gen. Conf.)	31,498
Religious Society of Friends (Kansas Yearly Meeting)	8,227
Reformed Bodies:	
*Christian Reformed Church	284,737
Reformed Church in America	380,133
Reformed Episcopal Church	7,085
*Roman Catholic Church, The	47,872,089
*Salvation Army, The	331,711
Spiritualists, International General Assembly of (*Spiritualists)	164,072
Triumph the Church and Kingdom of God in Christ	50,080
*Unitarians:	
*Unitarian Universalist Association	265,408
United Brethren in Christ	24,061
*United Church of Christ	1,997,898
*Volunteers of America	32,760
*Wesleyan Church, The	82,358

MAJOR RELIGIONS OF THE WORLD

Number of members in each religion

CHRISTIAN

Roman Catholic
581,000,000

Protestant
316,000,000

Eastern Orthodox
122,000,000

NON-CHRISTIAN

Islam
465,000,000

Hinduism
408,000,000

Confucianism
358,000,000

Buddhism
165,000,000

Shinto
68,000,000

Taoism
52,000,000

Judaism
14,000,000

Source: *World Christian Handbook, 1968*, Abingdon Press

RELIGION

other persons in their groups. Later, religions taught love and service for all men. A world-wide stress on ethical teaching occurred between 1000 and 500 B.C., with the Hebrew prophets preaching in Palestine and Zoroastrianism developing in Persia, Buddhism and Jainism in India, and Confucianism in China.

Life and Death. Most religions teach that there is something in man that survives bodily death. Hinduism, Jainism, and Sikhism believe that the soul is *reincarnated* (reborn) into many bodies before it becomes good enough to be united with the infinite. Buddhism also believes in reincarnation. But its various branches differ in their beliefs as to what part of man passes from body to body, and where the soul finally goes. Christianity, Islam, and Zoroastrianism teach that a man will be judged and sent to heaven or hell. Judaism, Confucianism, Taoism, and Shinto are less definite in their teachings about life after death. But they generally believe that something in man endures beyond death, even though the living cannot understand how.

Worship. Early peoples worshiped their gods as a way of keeping on good terms with them. They praised the gods and offered sacrifices of the things they believed the gods enjoyed. Today, people worship as a means of showing their love and admiration for what they believe to be the noblest Being in the universe.

Worship usually involves symbols and ceremonies. *Symbols* serve as reminders of religious ideas. For example, a cross represents Christ's crucifixion. It reminds Christians of Christ's love for men, and of the importance of sacrifice for others. *Ceremonies* are actions and displays that accompany worship. Processions, bowing, kneeling, and singing help people express their feelings for what they consider highest and best.

Most religions have temples set aside for worship.

Confucianism centers on the ethical teachings of Confucius. Instead of images of him, shrines contain tablets that bear his name, *left.* Followers believe that his teachings lead to perfection in man's relationships with other men.

Dmitri Kessel, courtesy *Life* Magazine. © 1955 Time Inc.

Christians worship in churches or cathedrals, Jews in synagogues or temples, and Moslems in mosques.

Organization is an essential part of religion. Each religion has fixed holy days, orders of services, and religious practices that its followers are required to observe. Clergymen, such as Protestant *ministers*, Roman Catholic *priests*, and Jewish *rabbis*, receive extensive training in the doctrines and beliefs of their religions. They make sure that the traditions of the religion are not lost or made a matter of personal whim. In some religions, including Christianity, Buddhism, and Jainism, individuals may join monastic orders.

Some religions are organized from the top down. That is, a leader heads the entire group and makes all the final decisions. For example, the pope is the leader of the world's Roman Catholics. Other religions, such as Congregational Christianity, are organized from the bottom up. The members make all important decisions.

The Influence of Religion

Religion and the Individual. Almost all religions place great emphasis on the individual. They expect each member not only to attend services or take part in group affairs, but also to carry out religious beliefs and teachings in his personal life. Often, religious teachings influence all aspects of a person's life. For example, Jainism forbids its followers to kill any living creature. As a result, a Jain eats no meat. He must constantly be on his guard not to destroy even the smallest ant. Many Jains wear masks over their mouths to keep from breathing in insects and killing them accidentally.

All religions try to offer their followers a set of values by which to live. Through their stress on ethical conduct, they give the individual a framework for judging right from wrong and for living a good life. Through their emphasis on a Supreme Being, they give the individual a reason for living a good life.

Religion and Government in primitive societies are usually combined. The tribal chief serves as the priest or religious leader. More advanced societies usually distinguish between church and state, or religion and government. Many nations, including the United States, offer equal opportunities to all religions. In other nations, one religion enjoys a special place above the others. Examples include the Anglican Church in England, Islam in Pakistan, Judaism in Israel, the Lutheran Church in Sweden, and the Roman Catholic Church in Spain. A church that is especially favored by a government is sometimes called a *state church*. In some countries, the church is really an arm of the state. Most, but not all, countries with state churches grant religious freedom to members of other faiths. Amendment 1 of the Constitution ensures freedom of religion in the United States.

Throughout history, religion has been closely related to government. The Christian church dominated all Europe during the Middle Ages. It often controlled state policies. Between the 700's and 1200's, the Moslems conquered most of the Middle East, North Africa, and Spain, and spread their religion throughout these lands. The Thirty Years' War began in 1618 as a civil war between Roman Catholics and Protestants in the German states. The partition of India into the states of India and Pakistan in 1947 resulted from religious differences between Hindus and Moslems.

Buddhism centers on *the middle way*, accepting the things of this world, but neither craving them nor shunning them altogether. Temples in such cities as Bangkok, Thailand, have statues of Buddha in contemplation. The Wheel of Doctrine, *above*, symbolizes the path to enlightenment.

RELIGION

Religion and Education. Organized religion depends on education for its existence. Each generation must teach its religion to the next generation. Much religious education takes place in the home, where children see their parents observing religious practices. But most religions stress the importance of formal religious education in church or school. Many countries that have state churches offer religious instruction in public schools. In the United States and Canada, various religious groups conduct their own schools. Roman Catholic, Jewish, and Protestant parochial schools teach both religious and *secular* (nonreligious) subjects. Most Protestants and Jews prefer public schools for secular instruction. They leave religious instruction to Saturday or Sunday schools and special after-school classes in religious history and traditions.

The study of the Bible was one of the first forms of universal education in the United States. The Pilgrims declared in the Mayflower Compact that every member of the new community should have a voice in its decisions, and that these decisions should be guided by Scripture. This meant that everyone had to be taught to read the Bible. See RELIGIOUS EDUCATION.

Religion and the Arts. Religion has always provided a main source of inspiration in all the arts. Some of the most beautiful buildings in the world are cathedrals, churches, temples, and mosques. Some of the greatest music is sacred in nature. Scriptures and religious legends have furnished countless subjects for painting, sculpture, poetry, drama, and the dance. Examples of religious works of art in Western culture include: in architecture, the Parthenon and the great cathedrals of Europe; in music, Bach's masses and Handel's oratorios; in sculpture, Michelangelo's *David* and *Moses;* in painting, the works of Giotto, Raphael, and El Greco; and the writings of Dante and Milton.   HUSTON C. SMITH

Related Articles. See the Religion section of the articles on various countries, such as ISRAEL (Religion); FRANCE (Religion). Additional related articles in WORLD BOOK include:

MAJOR RELIGIONS OF THE WORLD

Buddhism	Islam	Sikhism
Christianity	Jainism	Taoism
Confucianism	Judaism	Zoroastrianism
Hinduism	Shinto	

THEOLOGY

Allah	Foreordination	Philosophy
Angel	Free Will	(Philosophy
Annunciation	Freethinker	and Religion)
Archangel	God	Polytheism
Atheism	Heaven	Predestination
Brahman	Hell	Purgatory
Devil	Immortality	Resurrection
Elohim	Jehovah	Siva
Ethics	Pantheism	Spiritualism

David Douglas Duncan, courtesy
Life Magazine. © 1955 Time Inc.

Islam centers on belief in one God, Allah. His revelations to His Prophet, Mohammed, are contained in the Koran, above.

Hinduism centers on belief in the sacredness of all living things. Many Hindus give offerings to statues of local deities, such as Nandi, the sacred bull, at the city of Mysore, India.

Theology	Transmigration of	Trinity
Transfiguration	the Soul	Virgin Mary
	Transubstantiation	Vishnu

RELIGIOUS LEADERS

See the complete lists of biographies in the following articles: APOSTLE; BIBLE; CARDINAL; POPE: PROPHET; PROTESTANT; ROMAN CATHOLIC CHURCH; SAINT. See also the articles on these religious leaders:

Buddha	Jesus Christ	Mohammed
Confucius	Lao Tzu	Zoroaster

RELIGIOUS OFFICIALS

Abbot	High Priest	Patriarch
Archbishop	Levite	Pope
Bishop	Magi	Prelate
Caliph	Metropolitan	Priest
Cardinal	Minister	Rabbi
Chaplain	Monk	Sanhedrin
Dalai Lama	Monsignor	Vicar
Friar	Nun	
Hierarchy	Panchen Lama	

RELIGIOUS PRACTICES

Baptism	Drama (Medieval Dra-	Hymn
Bar Mitzvah	ma; Religious Plays)	Kosher
Bas Mitzvah	Fast	Marriage
Catechism	Feasts and Festivals	Mass
Communion	Funeral Customs	Novena
Confirmation	Grace	Prayer
Coronation	Hajj	Sacrament

SACRED WRITINGS

Bible	New Testament	Ramayana
Koran	Old Testament	Talmud
Mahabharata	Pentateuch	Veda

ANCIENT RELIGIONS

Assyria (Religion)	Indian, American
Aztec (Religion)	(Religion)
Babylonia (Religion)	Mythology
Egypt, Ancient (Religion)	Persia, Ancient (Religion)
Greece, Ancient (Religion)	Phoenicia (Religion)
Inca (Religion)	Roman Empire (Religion)

PRIMITIVE RELIGIONS

Animal Worship	Animism	Devil Worship

Fetish	Nature Worship	Taboo
Fire Worship	Sun Worship	Voodoo

OTHER RELATED ARTICLES

Ancestor	Freedom of Religion	Painting (Religious
Worship	Gnosticism	Subjects; pictures)
Bahá'ís	Heresy	Religious Education
Church and	House of David	Revivalism
State	Manichaeism	Theocracy
Druses	Mysticism	Theosophist

Outline

I. Religions of the World
A. Christianity	E. Buddhism	I. Shinto
B. Judaism	F. Jainism	J. Sikhism
C. Islam	G. Confucianism	K. Zoroastrianism
D. Hinduism	H. Taoism	L. Other Religions

II. Religious Beliefs and Practices
A. The Deity   D. Worship
B. Codes of Conduct   E. Organization
C. Life and Death

III. The Influence of Religion
A. Religion and   C. Religion and
    the Individual   Education
B. Religion and   D. Religion and
    Government   the Arts

Questions

Why is religion considered more than a matter of learning to live and work with one's fellowmen?

What are some codes of conduct that all the great religions agree upon?

What are the sacred books of (1) Islam? (2) Confucianism? (3) Taoism?

What do Hindus believe about life after death?

How do symbols and ceremonies contribute to worship?

What is the difference between an atheist and an agnostic regarding a belief in God?

Why is education important to religion?

Name three countries with state churches. Which churches are they?

Reading and Study Guide

For a *Reading and Study Guide on Religion*, see the RESEARCH GUIDE/INDEX, Volume 22.

RELIGION, FREEDOM OF. See FREEDOM OF RELIGION.

Tribal Religions often center on the belief in spirits that live in all things. Many peoples believe that they must please these spirits by giving gifts or worshiping them.

RELIGIOUS EDUCATION

RELIGIOUS EDUCATION involves instruction in the beliefs of a particular religion. This type of education is the work of organized religions, through their school and religious organizations. Religious education may also be defined as general education that follows religious instructions and ideals.

Public Schools in the United States have sometimes offered religious instruction to students through various arrangements. But many persons feel that such instruction violates the principle of the separation of church and state.

Various court decisions have affected religious education in the public schools. In 1948, the Supreme Court of the United States ruled on the McCollum case. The Court held that religious instruction could not be conducted within public school buildings, because it would violate the provisions of the Constitution for complete separation of church and state. The majority opinion of the Supreme Court held that Amendment 1 to the Constitution "rests upon the premise that both religion and government can best work to achieve their lofty aims if each is left free from the other within its respective sphere." See CHURCH AND STATE.

Since the late 1940's, there has been new interest in religious education given during school hours but outside the school. Churches or religious organizations pay the cost of such instruction. The school merely arranges for the time. A great number of communities release pupils from regular school hours so that they may attend such classes in the faith of their choice. These classes are taught by special teachers provided by the religious groups. These groups also provide the lesson materials.

There are differences of opinion as to the merits of this system. Some parents say their children are embarrassed by it. If they belong to no particular church, they may not wish to attend these classes. In that case their classmates may point to them as "different." Other parents feel it is not the function of the school to teach the doctrines of the church, or to provide the time for such instruction.

Private Education. Many religious groups have their own educational buildings. Roman Catholic and some Protestant groups maintain grade schools, high schools, and colleges. Such schools offer both secular and religious courses. Some Jewish elementary schools, high schools, and colleges have been established. Jewish synagogues and temples offer instruction in religious subjects and Hebrew to children after school hours and on Sunday mornings. The various religious groups educate their own leaders for teaching their doctrines. See PAROCHIAL SCHOOL.

The Roman Catholic Church conducts catechism classes for children at least once a week, usually on Saturday or Sunday morning. They present oral and written instruction in the doctrines of the Catholic faith. Many Protestant churches offer similar classes. Some of these classes, held in a series, are concluded by a ceremony called *confirmation*.

In Protestant churches, one of the chief methods for religious education is the Sunday school. The modern Sunday school uses specially prepared programs and lessons, such as the International Sunday School Lessons. These courses present graded lesson materials.

Other material includes religious history and background, problems in living, and ideals as taught in the Bible and interpreted today. Some churches also sponsor *Vacation Bible schools*. These schools usually offer religious education for one or more weeks during summer vacation.

Children who do not attend church seldom receive any formal religious education. However, their parents may educate them in their own religious beliefs and teach them from the Bible.

Career Opportunities. Many persons have chosen religious education as a vocation because of the satisfaction that comes from teaching young people the rules and standards of a good life. Anyone who plans to work in this field needs intelligence, imagination, leadership, friendliness, tolerance, fair play, and good insight into character. The degree of formal education and training needed varies with the individual position.

Many opportunities are available to a person who is interested in religious education. Some churches have a director of religious education who is responsible for planning and directing the church's overall program of religious education. He usually works with the pastor of the church. He directs and supervises the Sunday school and other activities such as adult classes and teacher training classes. A person in this position has usually studied religious education. Sometimes he has attended a seminary and has been graduated as an ordained minister (see SEMINARY).

Educators in this field may also work with young people. The director of children's work handles the religious program of children up to the age of 12. A director of youth work plans and guides the study, worship, and recreation of junior and senior high-school students. Other work directly connected with the church includes supervising or teaching in weekday church schools and instructing Sunday school classes.

Religious education also includes such work as publishing, editing, or writing religious literature. Many churches and religious organizations sponsor regular publications. Some may be magazines or newspapers on a national level. Others may be intended for local or parish work. Some groups publish books and pamphlets for general use or for educational purposes. So-called "inspirational" novels may also form part of educational programs. Many newspapers and magazines publish columns written by religious educators.

Persons interested in religious education may teach religion classes in colleges, lead educational programs for such organizations as the YMCA, or teach in missionary schools.

The clergy and various religious orders offer the best opportunities for religious education. Churches may give training for students interested in this type of work. Usually, a person attends college for a general background, and continues specific study at a seminary. There he studies religion and related subjects, as well as educational techniques. With this training, he can preach, instruct, and counsel, as well as perform other duties that are connected with the field of religious education.   HOWARD R. BURKLE

See also CATECHISM; SUNDAY SCHOOL.

RELIGIOUS FESTIVALS. For examples, see FEASTS AND FESTIVALS and its list of Related Articles.

RELIGIOUS FREEDOM. See FREEDOM OF RELIGION.

RELIGIOUS LIFE is a term for the way of life that some people choose for becoming as holy as possible and for being of the greatest possible service to others. Those who adopt this manner of life are called monks, nuns, brothers or sisters—or simply religious. Some, especially men, may be priests or ministers. But most followers of the religious life are not clergymen.

In all the major religions, followers of the religious life devote themselves exclusively to holiness and service. Unlike ascetics and hermits, who also strive for holiness, they belong to religious orders (see ASCETIC; HERMIT). The members of many orders live together in a community under a religious superior. Most monks live in monasteries, and most nuns live in convents. After one or more years of training and testing, candidates are admitted into the community. In most cases, the candidate vows to remain in the community until he dies. Generally, a final commitment is made only after several years of living under temporary vows or promises.

All religious communities were founded to advance the spiritual life of their members. *Contemplative* orders concentrate on this role and have an organized daily routine with ascetic practices and many hours of prayer. *Active* communities engage in social and spiritual work in schools, hospitals, and orphanages. But even the most active community is basically dedicated to promoting the holiness of its members.

Christian Religious Life

Religious life among Christians started with the practice and teachings of Jesus. His voluntary poverty, His *celibacy* (remaining unmarried), and His obedience to God's will became the pattern for the religious life.

The Roman Catholic Church. Persecution in the early Christian church prevented the development of organized religious orders in the Roman Empire. However, many hermits practiced poverty, remained unmarried, and lived alone in the desert. St. Paul the Hermit and St. Anthony of Thebes were dominant figures in this early stage of the religious life. Both lived in Egypt.

In the early 300's, St. Pachomius organized a religious community in south Egypt. He wrote a *rule* (program of life) for monks who wished to live together under a superior. Shortly before his death, there were 40 monasteries with 2,000 monks under his direction. Later in the 300's, St. Basil of Caesarea adopted the rule of Pachomius and made his monasteries in Asia Minor homes of charity. The monasteries included orphanages, hospitals, farms, and places of rest.

St. Benedict of Nursia was the father of Christian monasticism in the West. His policies of the 500's became the pattern for religious life in Europe and America. The Benedictine approach emphasized attachment to a single monastery, community living, and labor. Eastern monasticism, on the other hand, stressed austere physical living and severe discipline. Today, Eastern Orthodox religious life still favors the pattern of St. Pachomius and St. Basil, and the Roman Catholic Church prefers that of St. Benedict.

During the early 1200's, St. Francis of Assisi began a new practice in religious life by encouraging his followers to travel about the countryside, preaching and helping the needy. Also around 1200, St. Dominic established the Order of Preachers to teach in schools and colleges. In 1534, St. Ignatius Loyola founded the Jesuits "to extend the Kingdom of Christ" to all parts of the world. Early Jesuits included missionaries such as St. Francis Xavier in India, and such explorers as Jacques Marquette in America.

During the 1500's and 1600's, as a result of the Protestant Reformation and an expansion of learning, new Roman Catholic orders were established to try to meet every humanitarian need. St. Angela Merici founded the Ursulines in Italy. Louise de Marillac and St. Vincent de Paul started the Sisters of Charity in France. St. Jean Baptiste de la Salle founded the Chris-

SOME LEADING CHRISTIAN RELIGIOUS ORDERS

Popular Name	Official Name	Religion	Founder	Place Founded	Date
Benedictines	Order of St. Benedict	Roman Catholic	St. Benedict	Italy	529?
Carmelites	Order of Our Lady of Mount Carmel	Roman Catholic	St. Berthold	Palestine	1100's
Christian Brothers	Brothers of the Christian Schools	Roman Catholic	St. Jean Baptiste de la Salle	France	1680
Cowley Fathers	Society of St. John the Evangelist	Anglican	R. M. Benson	England	1866
Dominicans	Order of Friars Preachers	Roman Catholic	St. Dominic	France	1215
Franciscans	Order of Friars Minor	Roman Catholic	St. Francis of Assisi	Italy	1209
Jesuits	Society of Jesus	Roman Catholic	St. Ignatius Loyola	France	1534
Monastic Brotherhood	None	Eastern Orthodox	Sts. Pachomius, Basil, Theodore, and Athanasios	Egypt, Asia Minor, and Greece	300's–1000's
Redemptorists	Congregation of the Most Holy Redeemer	Roman Catholic	St. Alphonsus Liguori	Italy	1732
Salesians	Society of St. Francis de Sales	Roman Catholic	St. John Bosco	Italy	1859
Sisters of Charity	Many branches	Roman Catholic	Sts. Vincent de Paul and Louise de Marillac	France	1633
Trappists	Order of Cistercians of the Strict Observance	Roman Catholic	St. Robert of Molesme	France	1098
Wantage Community	Community of St. Mary the Virgin	Anglican	William J. Butler	England	1848

tian Brothers in France as a community of teachers.

Today, there are about 1½ million members of Catholic religious communities throughout the world. About 1 million are women. The United States has 96 orders of priests, 400 orders of nuns, and 36 orders of brothers. The total U.S. membership is more than 200,000.

Vatican Council II, which met from 1962 to 1965, urged religious communities to adapt themselves "to the changed conditions of our time." As a result, the communities started a period of adjustment. Encouraged by the Vatican, women in the communities have adapted their clothing and many of their customs to the practical needs of modern life. The practice of poverty in wealthy societies and of obedience in democratic cultures is being modified. A balance has not yet been reached between the demands of the times and the unchangeable principles of Christian perfection.

The Eastern Orthodox Churches regard monasticism as an essential feature of their tradition. Until the 1900's, Eastern Orthodox monks and nuns rarely took part in teaching, preaching, or the ministry. Practically all Eastern Orthodox religions follow the teachings of St. Basil. Two characteristics of Eastern Orthodox monasteries are liturgical worship and fasting. Membership in these monasteries and convents is about 30,000, of whom two-thirds are women.

Of the estimated 550 Orthodox monasteries in Europe and Asia, the most famous is probably the monastic republic of Mount Athos in Greece. There are 20 monasteries on the mountain. Eleven of them follow the *cenobitic* rule, and nine observe the *idiorrhythmic* rule—the approximate ratio for Eastern Orthodox monasticism in general. The cenobitic rule calls for community life under an abbot elected for life. The idiorrhythmic rule provides for monasteries directed by trustees who are elected annually. It gives monks greater freedom in matters of poverty and daily activities.

Protestant Churches. Protestant leaders did not encourage religious life under vows during the Reformation of the 1500's. However, a Lutheran Augustinian monastery at Möllenbeck, Germany, existed until 1675. Protestant groups called Pietists, such as the Bohemian Brethren, organized in 1722 in Moravia, formed partially monastic communities that later influenced European and American Protestantism.

By the mid-1800's, certain Protestant denominations had re-established religious communities. A Lutheran community of deaconesses was organized in Germany in 1836. In England, an Anglican group for men was founded in 1842, and one for women was set up in 1845. In 1940, the Taizé community in France was formed under Lutheran and Reformed sponsorship. Today, there are several thousand members in about 100 Protestant religious communities throughout the world. Most of these communities are Episcopalian.

Non-Christian Religious Life

Hinduism. The closest Hindu equivalent to Christian religious life is the *ashram*, the fourth and last stage of a Hindu's life. With advancing age, a Hindu, alone or with his wife, may retire from active life. He prays, practices severely simple living, and finally reaches the state of *sannyasi*, the highest level of morality.

Buddhism. Buddha made monasticism an inseparable part of his creed. He planned his religion as a monastic order headed by himself. As Buddhism expanded, laymen were included in the religion. But they had to affirm their belief in the *Sangha* (monastic order) as strongly as their faith in Buddha and his creed.

According to Buddha, "There are two kinds of gifts, the gift of material things and the gift of *Dharma* (the law). Of these two, the gift of the law is preeminent." An example of the first kind of gift-giving would be monks or nuns living in a community where they own material things in common. An example of the second type would be monks and nuns teaching the methods they used to attain *nirvana* (perfect happiness).

There were several thousand Buddhist monasteries in China before the Chinese Communists conquered the country in the 1940's. Buddhist monasticism has been changed drastically since the Communist take-over of China, North Vietnam, and Tibet. The Communists have allowed some monasteries to function in these countries—if the members cultivate an assigned portion of land and raise a quota of crops.

In non-Communist Asia, Buddhist monasticism varies. The greatest differences exist between the Hinayana and Mahayana orders. Hinayana communities have a stricter daily life, and their members spend much time in meditation. Most of these communities are in Southeast Asia. Mahayana communities are more active in welfare and education, and are centered in Japan and China.

Islam developed a form of religious life during the 700's through the Sufi movement. Following the example of the Christian monks of Arabia, members of the Sufi group met regularly to recite the *Koran* (Islamic Bible) and worship together. Gradually, the scattered ascetics organized into religious orders. Almost every Moslem country encouraged the growth of these communities. One of the earliest was the Qadiriya, started by Abd al-Qadir al-Jilani in the 1100's and now centered in Baghdad. Many suborders came from the Qadiriya, including the Rifa'iya in Iraq. This group is known for such activities as eating glass, walking through fire, and playing with serpents.

The Cishtiya are the most influential Moslem order in the world. They attempt to aim all their feelings toward establishing union with *Allah* (God). To this end, they recite the names of Allah silently and aloud, practice mystic contemplation, and remain in spiritual confinement for 40 days at a time. Some groups of ascetics combine Islam and Hinduism in ritual customs that almost amount to a new religion.   JOHN A. HARDON

Related Articles in WORLD BOOK include:

RELIGIOUS ORDERS

Benedictine	Jesuit	Sacred Heart of Jesus,
Capuchin	Knights of	Society of the
Carmelite	Saint John	Saint Lazarus, Order of
Carthusian	Knights Templars	Sister of Charity
Cistercian	Little Sisters	Sister of Mercy
Dominican	of the Poor	Trappist
Franciscan	Paulist	Ursuline

OTHER RELATED ARTICLES

Abbot	Friar	Paul of the Cross,
Anthony of Thebes,	Monasticism	Saint
Saint	Monk	Tonsure
Celibacy	Nun	

RELIGIOUS TOLERANCE. See FREEDOM OF RELIGION.

REMARQUE, *reh MARK*, **ERICH MARIA** (1898-1970), a German-American author, wrote realistic, suspenseful novels about the horrors and effects of war. Remarque's *All Quiet on the Western Front* (1929) is one of the most famous war stories of all time. It relates the shattering experiences of a group of German soldiers in World War I.

Remarque followed this success with *The Road Back* (1931) and *Three Comrades* (1937), stories of the confusion in postwar German society and the hardships faced by veterans. He continued the war theme in *Arch of Triumph* (1946), a novel about a German doctor who fled to Paris to escape the Nazis at the beginning of World War II. *Spark of Life* (1952) is a story of human suffering and courage in a Nazi concentration camp. *The Night in Lisbon* (1964) also describes suffering during World War II.

Remarque was born in Osnabrück, Germany. He fought in World War I, and was wounded several times. In 1933, the Nazis publicly burned Remarque's books because of their antigovernment and antimilitarist themes. The Nazis took away his citizenship in 1938. Remarque lived in Switzerland from 1931 to 1939. He moved to the United States in 1939, but often returned to Switzerland. He became a U.S. citizen in 1947.   WERNER HOFFMEISTER

REMBRANDT, *REM brant* (1606-1669), was The Netherlands' greatest artist. Rembrandt's output was tremendous. Scholars credit him with about 600 paintings, 300 etchings, and 1,400 drawings. Many other works have been lost. Unlike some other great artists, he wrote almost nothing about his art.

The range of Rembrandt's subjects is extraordinary. His works include landscapes, nudes, portraits, scenes of

National Gallery of Art, Washington, D.C., Widener Collection.

Descent from the Cross shows how Rembrandt used strong contrasts in light and shadow to increase the dramatic impact of his pictures. The painting also reveals the artist's genius for portraying people from the Bible in a powerful yet human manner.

Rembrandt's Etching *The Ratkiller* was completed in 1632, the year he established his reputation as a leading artist in The Netherlands. The etching shows Rembrandt's ability to portray common people and scenes from everyday life dramatically.

The British Museum, London, England

everyday life, animals and birds, historical and mythological subjects, and works inspired by stories from the Old and New Testaments. Throughout his career, Rembrandt also made about 100 known portraits of himself. They form a unique autobiography.

Rembrandt's reputation rests on his power as a storyteller, his warm sympathy, and his ability to show the innermost feelings of the people he portrayed. His use of light and shadow creates an atmosphere that enables us to share his sensitive response to nature and profound understanding of man's inner life. Few artists match his

Rembrandt's Self-Portraits form a vivid record of his life. The portrait, *left*, was completed in 1629. The portrait, *right*, was finished in 1658, after he was forced to declare bankruptcy.

Maurithaus Museum, The Hague, Netherlands; The Frick Collection, New York City

REMBRANDT

genius for showing the human aspect of Biblical characters. He was equally capable of suggesting the divine spark which rests in every man.

Early Years. Rembrandt was born in Leiden on July 15, 1606. His full name was Rembrandt Harmenszoon van Rijn. He first studied art with an obscure Leiden painter from about 1621 to 1624. Then he studied with Pieter Lastman in Amsterdam. About 1625, Rembrandt returned to Leiden to paint on his own.

Leiden Years: 1625-1631. Most of Rembrandt's early works are small, precisely finished pictures of Biblical and historical subjects. The influence of Lastman can be seen in the lively gestures and expressions of his figures and in his vivid colors and glossy paint. However, Rembrandt rapidly surpassed his teacher's ability to tell a story. He also used light and shadow better than anyone else to heighten the drama of his works. Light and shadow became Rembrandt's principal means of pictorial expression.

Rembrandt quickly achieved local success. He began to teach in 1628, and his strong personality continued to attract students and followers throughout his entire career.

Early Amsterdam Years: 1632-1640. About 1632, Rembrandt moved to Amsterdam. He remained there for the rest of his life, except for a few short trips within The Netherlands. In 1634, he married Saskia van Uylenburgh. They had four children, but only one, Titus (1641-1668), survived infancy.

In 1632, Rembrandt painted the *Anatomy Lesson of Professor Tulp*. It is reproduced in the article WORLD, HISTORY OF (The Age of Reason). This group portrait immediately established his reputation as the most fashionable portrait painter in Amsterdam. Rembrandt became wealthy, and eagerly collected works of art. In 1639, he bought a large, heavily mortgaged house.

Rembrandt's paintings *Blinding of Samson*, *Danae*, and *Rape of Ganymede* show the exciting subjects he favored during these years. They, like most of his other works during this period, emphasize dramatic movement, emphatic gestures, sharp contrasts of light and shadow, and striking color accents.

The Last Years: 1640-1669. Rembrandt's most famous picture, *The Night Watch*, was painted in 1642. According to a legend, the men who commissioned the portrait were not satisfied with it and refused the painting because Rembrandt would not change it in any way. Because he would not change to please public taste, the tale continues, he soon lost patrons and friends and spent his last years penniless and in total obscurity. However, evidence proves that Rembrandt received a high price for *The Night Watch*, and that he continued to receive important public and private commissions during the last years of his life. These commissions included *Aristotle Contemplating the Bust of Homer*, *Portrait of Jan Six*, *Conspiracy of Claudius Civilis*, and *The Syndics*.

However, tragedy did strike Rembrandt in 1642 when his beloved wife, Saskia, died. Also, the mature Rembrandt did not enjoy the wide popularity he had as a young painter. Although he still ranked as one of his country's leading artists, he ran short of money. The house he purchased in 1639 was too expensive. Rembrandt also collected works of art on a scale he could not afford. Most important, he began to paint more and more for himself. His late majestic Biblical paintings were not commissioned works. They were done to satisfy his own inner needs. An example, *Jacob Blessing the Sons of Joseph*, is reproduced in color in the PAINTING article.

During this period, Rembrandt's art gained steadily in spiritual depth and pictorial richness. His wonderful light now seemed to glow from within his works. The shadows became more intense and vibrant. In place of earlier sensational effects, his work shows solemn restraint, calmness, and tenderness. When man is represented, the thoughtful rather than active side of his nature is stressed. *Man with a Magnifying Glass*, an example from this period, is reproduced in color in the PAINTING article. Rembrandt's landscape etchings and drawings during these years have an unmatched sense of space and fresh air.

Rembrandt was forced to declare bankruptcy in 1656. His house and possessions were sold at auction in 1657 and 1658. But when he died on Oct. 4, 1669, he left his surviving relatives a fairly large inheritance.

For other examples of Rembrandt's work, see the pictures with the articles ETCHING; JESUS CHRIST; and SAMARITAN.   SEYMOUR SLIVE

See also PAINTING (The 1600's and 1700's).

REMEMBRANCE DAY is a Canadian holiday that honors the memory of the men and women who died in World Wars I and II and in the Korean War. Remembrance Day is observed each year on November 11.

Remembrance Day replaced Armistice Day in 1931. The red poppy of Flanders Fields serves as the symbol of Remembrance Day.

REMINGTON, FREDERIC (1861-1909), an American painter, sculptor, and writer, is best known for his action-filled paintings of the western plains. They include *Cavalry Charge on the Southern Plains*, *A Dash for the Timber*, and *The Last Stand*. He also illustrated stories of western life and created bronze statuettes on western themes. Among his most famous statuettes are *Bronco Buster*, *Wounded Bunkie*, and *Coming Through the Rye*, also called *Off the Range*. His sculptures were made with the same skill and feeling as his paintings. He wrote and illustrated *Pony Tracks* (1895), *Sundown Leflare* (1899), *Men With the Bark On* (1900), *John Ermine of Yellowstone* (1902), and *The Way of an Indian* (1906).

Remington was born in Canton, N.Y., and studied art at Yale University and in New York City. He moved to the West at the age of 19 to seek adventure and fortune. He lived and worked with cowboys, and for a short time with friendly Indians.

Remington learned to love the West. He wanted to record what he saw there in his drawings, paintings, and sculpture. Remington's works are realistic, colorful, and

Frederic Remington
Brown Bros.

The Remora Uses a Sucker on Its Head to Attach Itself to Large Fish Such as the Tiger Shark.

true to the life he saw. They are in the Remington Art Memorial, Ogdensburg, N.Y., and Whitney Gallery of Western Art, Cody, Wyo.   EDWIN L. FULWIDER

See also BRIDGER, JAMES (picture); HIAWATHA (picture); WESTERN FRONTIER LIFE (Art; color picture, A Stagecoach); WESTWARD MOVEMENT (picture, Hardy Explorers).

REMÓN, JOSÉ. See PANAMA (Recent Developments).

The *Bronco Buster* by Frederic Remington shows the action-filled style he used in his sculptures of life in the Old West.

The George F. Harding Museum

REMORA, *REM oh ruh,* or SHARK SUCKER, lives in all tropical seas and far out in the open oceans. The remora has an odd sucker on the top of its head that looks like the sole of a rubber boot. This sucking organ is a modified first dorsal fin. The remora uses it to attach itself to the bodies of large fish such as sharks. These remarkable fishes have been found attached to barracuda, tarpon, and other fishes, and to large turtles and whales. Known as an ocean "hitch-hiker," the remora partakes of the food of its host.

The remora is 2 or 3 feet long, slender, and flattened toward the head. A black band runs along the middle of its side and contrasts sharply with lighter shades above and below. Others have black and yellow colors. The *beau gregorys* have bright blue heads and yellow tails. Some are striped lengthwise, and others vertically. *Shark sucker* is another name for the remora.

Scientific Classification. The remora belongs to the remora family, *Echeneidae.* The common remora is genus *Echeneis,* species *E. naucrates.*   LEONARD P. SCHULTZ

REMOTE CONTROL. See RADIO CONTROL.

REMSEN, IRA (1846-1927), an American chemist, did much to promote the rapid development of science in the United States. As a teacher, research worker, and writer, he gave respectability to a career in chemistry. He proved that young scientists could be trained in the United States, and started a spirit of research that spread throughout the nation. In 1879, Remsen founded the *American Chemical Journal,* the first American journal in the field of science. It helped promote research in chemistry for 35 years.

Born in New York City, Remsen received an M.D. degree at 21. He then studied chemistry. At 30, he became the first professor of chemistry at Johns Hopkins University. See also SACCHARIN.   HERBERT S. RHINESMITH

REMUS. See ROMULUS AND REMUS.

REMUS, UNCLE. See HARRIS, JOEL CHANDLER.

Renaissance

Detail from *The Return of the Ambassadors* by Vittore Carpaccio, Gallerie dell' Accademia, Venice (Alinari)

Renaissance Men took a new interest in the world around them. People traveled to many lands to trade goods and exchange ideas. Here, a party of English ambassadors arrives in Venice.

RENAISSANCE, *REN uh sahns* or *ren uh SAHNS,* is the name given to a period of history that lasted about 300 years between the Middle Ages and modern times. It began in Italy about 1300. The Renaissance spread throughout Europe during the 1400's and 1500's. It swept away customs and institutions that had dominated Europe for almost a thousand years. The new ideas and attitudes that grew up still influence our lives.

When the Renaissance began, Europe was divided into great feudal estates owned by wealthy noblemen (see FEUDALISM). Most people were serfs who farmed the land for feudal lords. Almost every part of life centered

around religion, and the Catholic Church was the most powerful force in Europe. As the Renaissance advanced, kings and princes took over the feudal lands and built strong national governments. Trade and commerce increased. Many persons moved from the farms to the growing towns and cities. The Protestant Reformation weakened the power of the Catholic Church and split Christianity into many faiths.

Probably the greatest achievements of the Renaissance came in scholarship and the arts. The people of the Renaissance looked back on the Middle Ages as a time of ignorance and superstition. They tried to model their own civilization on the ways of life of ancient Greece and Rome. Scholars found and translated ancient writings that had been lost during the Middle Ages. Artists invented new techniques to make their works as beautiful and lifelike as those of the ancient masters. Writers broke with the religious thinking of the Middle Ages. Like the Greeks and Romans, they made man, rather than God, their center of interest.

Historians of the 1800's believed that learning had died during the Middle Ages, and was born again in the 1300's and 1400's. They named this period the *Renaissance*, a French word meaning *rebirth*. Later historians believed this name was a mistake. Some said there had been no rebirth at all, because society had actually changed gradually throughout the Middle Ages. Others argued that there had been not one, but several, "renaissances" during the Middle Ages. Today, most historians agree that the changes that took place between 1300 and 1600 were not a complete break with the Middle Ages. But these changes brought widespread and lasting results. For this reason, historians say, the period deserves to be called the *Renaissance*.

This article describes the new spirit and interests that flourished in the Renaissance, especially as seen in the arts and literature. For information on other developments of the period, see the discussions of the Renaissance in the articles EDUCATION, HISTORY OF; EXPLORATION AND DISCOVERY; SCIENCE; and TRADE. See also MIDDLE AGES and REFORMATION.

The Spirit of the Renaissance

The Renaissance was an age of adventure and curiosity. Men became fascinated with the world about them. They set out on dangerous voyages to explore unknown lands. They made scientific studies of plants and animals, and tried daring experiments in astronomy and physics. Most of all, they studied man himself.

Everything that concerned man and his life on earth became important to the people of the Renaissance. This emphasis on man formed a philosophy known as *humanism* (see HUMANISM). During the Middle Ages, most men had thought of themselves as parts of a group rather than as individuals. They were born into a certain class in society, such as the nobility or the peasant class. They never thought of living or working in any other way than according to the traditions of their class. During the Renaissance, a person's class in society became less significant. Men began to put importance on the individual. They took pride in their own accomplishments and began to judge others on the basis of merit rather than birth. Any person skilled in many fields of knowledge was called a "universal man."

Artists, architects, poets, and playwrights used bold new forms and techniques to show the spirit of the age. In their works, they tried to glorify man, and at the same time to win fame for themselves. Artists of the Middle Ages had been unknown craftsmen. Renaissance artists gained the respect and admiration of emperors and popes.

Painting became more realistic than it had been during the Middle Ages. Most medieval painters had limited themselves to religious subjects. Renaissance painters favored portraits, landscapes, and scenes from everyday life. Even in religious paintings, Renaissance artists made their figures look like real people. They often dressed Biblical figures in clothing of their own day.

Sculpture reflected a new understanding of human anatomy. Throughout the Middle Ages, sculpture had been used merely to ornament buildings. Figures were so heavily draped that the human form could barely be seen. Now, sculptors created statues that stood free of any architectural background. They often carved nude figures, and showed muscles and joints accurately.

Architecture centered on man and his needs. Renaissance architects paid as much attention to houses, palaces, and public buildings as they did to designing churches. They tried to make their buildings comfortable for the people who used them.

Renaissance literature emphasized individual personality. New forms, such as essays and biographies, became important. Most medieval literature had been written in Latin. Renaissance writers began using *vernacular* (national) languages such as French and Italian.

The Renaissance in Italy

During the Middle Ages, Italy's location on the Mediterranean Sea made the country an important center of trade. As commerce increased, Italy's many city-states grew wealthy. A new middle class, made up of merchants and bankers, came into power. These men encouraged the growth of learning, and became the chief supporters of art and culture.

Throughout the 1300's, Italian artists and writers searched for new styles to express the new ideas of their time. Renaissance leaders of the 1400's mastered various techniques that helped them perfect the styles that had developed. Renaissance art and literature reached their highest point in Italy during the 1500's. Historians call this period the *High Renaissance*.

The 1300's. The Renaissance began in the city of Florence in central Italy. The painters, sculptors, architects, and writers who lived there included some of the greatest artists the world has ever known. The Medici family, who ruled Florence, helped make it one of the most beautiful cities in Europe (see MEDICI).

Three Florentine men led the way toward a new style in art and literature. They were the painter Giotto (1266?-1337) and the writers Petrarch (1304-1374) and Giovanni Boccaccio (1313?-1375).

Giotto broke away from the stiff, decorative style of medieval painting. He made his figures look like real men and women with strong human feelings. His best-known works are *frescoes* (wall paintings) of the lives of Jesus Christ, the Virgin Mary, and St. Francis of Assisi. Giotto was also a skilled architect and sculptor. The *campanile* (bell tower) that he designed for the Cathedral of Florence rises almost 300 feet high.

Petrarch influenced two important movements in literature. One was the revival of the *classics* (ancient Greek and Roman literature). The other was the development of literature written in the Italian language. Petrarch collected ancient manuscripts, and urged scholars to study both Greek and Latin. He wrote Latin

Tinsley Helton, the contributor of this article, is Associate Professor of English at the University of Wisconsin at Milwaukee.

RENAISSANCE

works in the style of the Roman writer Marcus Tullius Cicero. His love poems, written in Italian, served as models for poets for more than 200 years.

Boccaccio was influenced by his friend Petrarch. Like Petrarch, he studied ancient literature and wrote several books in Latin. But Boccaccio's fame rests on *The Decameron*, a collection of short stories written in Italian. These stories present a lively picture of Italian life during the 1300's.

The 1400's brought many improvements in techniques of painting, sculpture, and architecture. Classical writings influenced Italian literature more than ever.

Painting. Florentine painters of the 1400's discovered better methods of mixing paints. They also made their works more realistic. Masaccio (1401-1428) was probably the greatest painter of the early 1400's. He worked out scientific laws of *perspective* to give his paintings an appearance of depth (see PERSPECTIVE). He used *chiaroscuro* (contrasts of light and shade) to model his figures and set them off from the background (see CHIAROSCURO). Masaccio's works influenced many other painters, including Paolo Uccello (1397-1475) and Antonio del Pollaiuolo (1433?-1498). The Dominican monk Fra Angelico (1400?-1455) combined the new technique of perspective with the decorative style of the Middle Ages. This resulted in deeply moving pictures that reflected a strong religious faith.

Sculpture. Donatello (1386?-1466) made the first important advances in Renaissance sculpture. His powerful and realistic statues show great knowledge of human anatomy. Donatello's *David* was the first statue cast in bronze since ancient times. Lorenzo Ghiberti (1378-1455) blended medieval grace with Renaissance realism. He won fame for the *relief* (raised) sculpture he designed for the doors of the Baptistery in Florence (see RELIEF [picture]). Luca della Robbia (1400?-1482) was the first well-known artist to work with colored and glazed terra cotta sculpture (see TERRA COTTA).

Architecture. The bold, inventive skill of Filippo Brunelleschi (1377?-1446) dominated Italian architec-ture. Brunelleschi studied Roman ruins to learn the principles of classic architecture. The huge dome he designed for the Cathedral of Florence was one of his greatest works. No other architect had been able to build a dome large enough to cover the vast cathedral.

Literature and Scholarship. Latin overshadowed Italian as the literary language of the 1400's. Italian poets imitated the style and rhythm of classical poetry. Many prose writers modeled their works on those of Cicero, as Petrarch had urged them to do.

Three important achievements aided the spread of learning: (1) Rulers and popes began to gather great libraries. The library of Pope Nicholas II, one of the largest, included almost 9,000 books. (2) Scholars founded academies throughout Italy to study and translate ancient literature. Their studies included Hebrew, Arabic, and Egyptian works as well as Greek and Roman literature. (3) Johannes Gutenberg (1395?-1468?) of Germany invented movable type about 1440. Soon printing presses were set up in many parts of Europe. Education and communication became more widespread than ever before. See PRINTING (History).

The 1500's are known as the High Renaissance. During the 1400's, painters, sculptors, and architects had worked to perfect the techniques of their art. Now they also achieved beauty and harmony in their works.

Rome replaced Florence as Italy's cultural center. The popes hired artists from all parts of Italy to beautify the city. St. Peter's Church became a symbol of Rome's importance. Pope Julius II began rebuilding the church in 1506. Many of the greatest artists of the time worked on its plans and decorations.

Michelangelo (1475-1564) stands out as the leading artist of the High Renaissance. He achieved greatness as a painter, a sculptor, and an architect. His remarkable skill as a painter may be seen in the frescoes of the Sistine Chapel in the Vatican (see SISTINE CHAPEL). Famous examples of his sculpture include the *Pietà* in St. Peter's Church and *David* in the Florence Academy. Michelangelo's greatest achievement in architecture was probably the dome he designed for St. Peter's. It served as a model for many later domes.

Leonardo da Vinci (1452-1519), Michelangelo's closest rival in the arts, represented the Renaissance ideal of a "universal man." He is best known for his

Renaissance Clothes were often made of richly-embroidered fabrics. People dressed elaborately for special occasions.

paintings of the *Mona Lisa* and *The Last Supper*. But he also won fame as an architect, an engineer, a musician, and a sculptor. In addition, Leonardo wrote works on anatomy, mathematics, and astronomy.

Another genius of the High Renaissance was Raphael (1483-1520). Like Michelangelo, Raphael worked on architectural plans for St. Peter's Church. He also painted frescoes for the Vatican, including the famous *School of Athens*. Raphael's many beautiful paintings of the Madonna and Child show perfect balance and symmetry (see MADONNA AND CHILD).

Many other artists helped make the 1500's one of the most creative periods in Italian history. Among them was a group of talented painters who lived in Venice. Such Venetian artists as Giovanni Bellini (1430?-1516) and Titian (1477?-1576) used brilliant colors to paint a world of beauty.

Italian writers of the 1500's used the vernacular in many of their works. Cardinal Pietro Bembo (1470-1547) wrote *On the Mother Tongue* to prove that Italian was better for literature than Latin. Outstanding prose works increased the importance of Italian as a literary language. These works include *The Courtier* by Baldassare Castiglione (1478-1529) and *The Prince* by Niccolò Machiavelli (1469-1527). Ludovico Ariosto (1474-1533) popularized Italian poetry in his poem *Orlando Furioso* (*Roland Insane*).

The Renaissance Spreads

As political, social, and economic conditions changed in various European countries, Renaissance attitudes began to take hold. The growth of printing helped spread the ideas of the Italian humanists. Scholars and artists flocked to the great Italian masters.

The Renaissance had reached most European nations by about 1500. At first, the people of these nations copied Italian Renaissance forms. Then they started to use the new principles to develop their own styles.

France came under the influence of the Renaissance during the late 1400's. In 1494, the French began a series of invasions of Italy that continued through most of the 1500's. French kings and noblemen hired dozens of Italian artists and scholars to serve in their courts. Gradually, the French began to adapt Italian ideas to their own national tastes.

Francis I, who became king in 1515, promoted Renaissance art in France. He housed a group of Italian painters and architects in his castle at Fontainebleau. This group and the French artists they taught became known as the *School of Fontainebleau*. In 1546, Francis hired Pierre Lescot (1510?-1578) to rebuild the Louvre palace in Paris in a classical Renaissance style. The sculptor Jean Goujon (1510?-1568?) decorated the building with statues based on Greek models.

Throughout the 1500's, the region around the Loire Valley was a center of Renaissance art. The *châteaux* (castles) built there by French kings are outstanding examples of French Renaissance architecture. They combine classical decorations with delicate, graceful French features.

Many leading Renaissance writers lived and worked at the kings' castles in the Loire Valley. They included the poet Pierre de Ronsard (1524-1585) and the prose writer François Rabelais (1494?-1553?). Ronsard wrote lyric poems on love and nature. He led a group of seven poets known as the *Pléiade*. Rabelais' hilarious stories poke fun at the church, the universities, and other institutions. His best-known work is *Gargantua and Pantagruel* (see GARGANTUA AND PANTAGRUEL).

Germany and The Netherlands. The most important Renaissance achievements in Germany and The Netherlands came in scholarship and painting. Germany took the lead in printing scholarly books after Johannes Gutenberg set up the first printing press in the mid-1400's. In painting, Flemish artists of the 1400's developed the technique of oil painting. In the 1500's, artists used oils to paint more realistically than before.

Desiderius Erasmus (1466?-1536) of The Netherlands was the greatest Renaissance scholar in northern Europe. He published studies of the Old and New Testaments to give scholars a better understanding of the Bible. His writings also aimed at bringing Christian thought into harmony with Greek philosophy. Erasmus worked for reforms in the Roman Catholic Church. But he refused to take part in the Protestant Reformation begun by Martin Luther (1483-1546) in 1517.

German and Flemish painters of the 1500's combined a native interest in detail with an understanding of

Painting of a wedding scene by an unknown artist, Galleria dell' Accademia, Florence (Alinari)

Events of the Renaissance

c. 1300 The Renaissance began in Italy with Giotto's paintings and writings by Petrarch and Giovanni Boccaccio.

1337-1453 France and England fought the Hundred Years' War, a series of wars broken by truces and treaties.

1346 Gunpowder was probably used for the first time in Europe during the Battle of Crécy.

1347-1350 The Black Death swept over Europe, destroying about a fourth of the population.

1378-1417 The Great Schism divided the Roman Catholic Church. Two Italians and a Frenchman claimed to be the legitimate pope.

c. 1440 Johannes Gutenberg, a German printer, invented movable type for printing.

c. 1450 The Renaissance spread to northern Europe. Desiderius Erasmus of The Netherlands became one of the leading Renaissance scholars during the 1500's.

c. 1485 England came under the influence of the Renaissance after the Wars of the Roses, which ended in 1485. The English Renaissance achieved its highest expression in the late 1500's with the plays of William Shakespeare.

1490's Spain began a golden age of art and learning. Miguel de Cervantes, author of *Don Quixote*, was the greatest Spanish writer of the Renaissance.

1492 Christopher Columbus discovered America.

1498 Vasco da Gama, a Portuguese explorer, became the first European to sail around Africa and reach India.

1515 Francis I became king of France, and promoted Renaissance art and learning.

1517 Martin Luther, a German monk, began the Protestant Reformation in Germany.

1519-1522 Spanish ships made the first voyage around the world. Ferdinand Magellan, the Portuguese navigator who commanded the voyage, died before it ended.

1532 *The Prince*, a book on political science by Niccolò Machiavelli, was published five years after his death.

1543 Nicolaus Copernicus, a Polish astronomer, demonstrated that the earth and the planets revolve around the sun.

1588 The English defeated the Spanish Armada, dealing a severe blow to Spain's prestige.

c. 1600 The Italian physicist Galileo founded modern experimental science.

STRATFORD-UPON-AVON •

John Cabot explored North America in 1497.

OXFORD •

• BRISTOL   LONDON •

ENGLAND

Sir Francis Drake sailed around the world from 1577 to 1580.

• PLYMOUTH

Jacques Cartier discovered the Gulf of St. Lawrence in 1534.

ST. MALO •

POITIERS •

The Hundred Years' War began with the English invasion of Normandy in 1337. The English won the battles of Crécy, Poitiers, and Agincourt. But the French won at Orléans and by 1453 had regained all of France except Calais.

ATLANTIC OCEAN

"Don Quixote," one of the greatest novels ever written, ridiculed the knights of the Middle Ages. Miguel de Cervantes, its author, was born in Alcalá de Henares, Spain.

• ALCALÁ DE HENARES

• MADRID

PORTUGAL

SPAIN

ARAGON

Vasco da Gama sailed around Africa to India in 1498.

• LISBON

CASTILE

Ferdinand Magellan began a voyage around the world in 1519.

Christopher Columbus sailed to America in 1492.

• SEVILLE

• SANLÚCAR

• PALOS

• CÁDIZ

GRANADA

Amerigo Vespucci voyaged to the West Indies and South America from 1497 to 1503.

by Seymour Fleishman
for World Book

William Shakespeare expressed the spirit of the Renaissance in his brilliant plays. Many were first performed at the Globe Theatre in London.

Protestant Reformation began in 1517 when Martin Luther nailed his Ninety-Five Theses to the door of All Saints' Church in Wittenberg.

• THORN

POLAND

• ROTTERDAM

WITTENBERG •

Copernicus and Galileo paved the way for modern science with experiments in astronomy and physics. Copernicus was born in Thorn (now Toruń), Poland. Galileo came from Pisa, Italy.

• CALAIS

• AGINCOURT

• CRÉCY

• COLOGNE

PRAGUE •

• ROUEN

• PARIS

MAINZ •

Printing Presses appeared in many parts of Europe after Johannes Gutenberg of Mainz invented movable type.

• FONTAINEBLEAU

• ORLÉANS

HOLY ROMAN EMPIRE

VIENNA •

The Black Death struck again and again in a series of epidemics that killed hundreds of thousands of persons.

Joan of Arc led the French to victory over the English in the Battle of Orléans in 1429. Later, the English burned her at the stake in Rouen.

• VENICE

FRANCE

• AVIGNON

GENOA •

The Medici, a family of bankers, ruled Florence during the 1400's and 1500's. Lorenzo the Magnificent, the most famous Medici, made Florence the most powerful city in Italy.

• MARSEILLE

PISA •

• FLORENCE

• SIENA

Great Italian Artists of the Renaissance included Michelangelo, Leonardo da Vinci, and Raphael. All three worked in Rome and Florence.

ITALY

• ROME

ADRIATIC SEA

Trade and Commerce expanded during the Renaissance. Major ports in the Mediterranean area included Venice, Genoa, Pisa, and Marseille. The Hanseatic League, a powerful organization of German cities, controlled most of North Europe's trade.

NAPLES •

The Great Schism in the Catholic Church lasted from 1378 to 1417. Two papal courts were set up, one at Rome and one at Avignon.

224C

RENAISSANCE

Italian Renaissance techniques. As a result, they created realistic portraits, landscapes, and scenes from everyday life. The two leading German painters of the Renaissance were Albrecht Dürer (1471-1528) and Hans Holbein the Younger (1497?-1543). They went to Italy to study the principles of Renaissance art. Pieter Breughel the Elder (1525?-1569) was the outstanding Flemish painter of the 1500's. He became known for his superb landscapes and paintings that captured lively scenes of peasant life.

England. Renaissance learning reached England after the Wars of the Roses, which ended in 1485. King Henry VII invited many Italian humanists to England. These men encouraged English scholars to study ancient literature and philosophy.

Two English humanists, John Colet (1467-1510) and Sir Thomas More (1477?-1535), helped spread Renaissance ideas. Colet founded St. Paul's School in London. He modeled it on the Renaissance schools of Italy. More's most famous book was *Utopia*. It criticizes the society of the day by contrasting it with an ideal society in which no evil exists. More wrote his book in Latin, and based it on *The Republic* by the ancient Greek philosopher Plato.

The English Renaissance achieved its highest expression in literature, particularly in drama. William Shakespeare (1564-1616), Christopher Marlowe (1564-1593), and other brilliant dramatists became the spokesmen of the age. Their plays blend old ideas with new ones. They show the intense curiosity and bold self-confidence of Renaissance men.

Spain enjoyed a golden age of art and literature during the 1500's. It grew rich and powerful as a result of conquests in Europe and explorations in America. Spanish rulers became generous supporters of the arts. They encouraged artists to use Renaissance styles. The most impressive monument of the Spanish Renaissance is probably the Escorial, a palace and monastery built by Philip II (see ESCORIAL).

Many Spaniards studied in Italy, and returned home to teach at the great universities of Salamanca and Alcalá. Spanish scholars took particular interest in ancient Greek, Hebrew, and Aramaic literature. They published many important works on the Bible.

Three men stand out as the leading figures of the Spanish Renaissance. They are El Greco (1541?-1614), a painter; Miguel de Cervantes (1547-1616), a novelist; and Lope de Vega (1562-1635), a playwright. El Greco developed an original style of painting that reflects both Greek and Italian influences. Cervantes wrote the masterpiece *Don Quixote*. Many critics have called it the greatest novel ever written. Lope de Vega turned out hundreds of plays on a variety of topics. He has become a symbol of the energy and creativity of the Renaissance.

By the Mid-1600's, Renaissance achievements had become part of European life. New styles developed, but Renaissance ideals have continued to influence Western thought to the present day. Renaissance emphasis on the individual has played an important part in the growth of democracy. And Renaissance man's determination to explore his world has its counterpart in today's explorations of outer space.   TINSLEY HELTON

224d

Related Articles in WORLD BOOK include:

ARCHITECTS

Alberti, Leon B.	Brunelleschi, Filippo
Bramante, Donato	Jones, Inigo

PAINTERS

Bellini	Grünewald, Matthias
Botticelli, Sandro	Holbein
Breughel	Piero della Francesca
Da Vinci, Leonardo	Pollaiuolo, Antonio del
Dürer, Albrecht	Raphael
Fra Angelico	Titian
Giotto	Uccello, Paolo
Greco, El	Veronese, Paolo

SCULPTORS

Cellini, Benvenuto	Donatello	Goujon, Jean
Della Robbia	Ghiberti, Lorenzo	Michelangelo

WRITERS

Ariosto, Ludovico	More, Saint Thomas
Boccaccio, Giovanni	Petrarch
Cervantes, Miguel de	Rabelais, François
Erasmus, Desiderius	Ronsard, Pierre de
Machiavelli, Niccolò	Shakespeare, William
Marlowe, Christopher	Tasso, Torquato
Montaigne, Michel de	Vega, Lope de

OTHER RELATED ARTICLES

See the sections on the Renaissance in the various articles on national literatures, such as FRENCH LITERATURE (The Renaissance). See also the discussions of the Renaissance in the following articles:

Architecture	Furniture	Philosophy
Clothing	Jewelry	Science
Dancing	Literature	Sculpture
Democracy	Mathematics	Shelter
(Development)	Music	World, History of
Education	Painting	

Outline

I. **The Spirit of the Renaissance**
II. **The Renaissance in Italy**
   A. The 1300's
   B. The 1400's
   C. The 1500's
III. **The Renaissance Spreads**
   A. France
   B. Germany and The Netherlands
   C. England
   D. Spain
   E. By the Mid-1600's

Questions

What are three ways in which society changed during the Renaissance?

What does the word *Renaissance* mean? Why is it used for this period of history?

In what city did the Renaissance begin?

How was the Renaissance interest in man reflected in (1) painting? (2) literature? (3) architecture?

How did the development of printing influence the spread of the Renaissance?

What is *humanism?*

What were the contributions of (1) Giotto? (2) Donatello? (3) Petrarch?

What does the term "universal man" mean? Who was an example of such a man?

Who were important Renaissance leaders in the following countries: (1) England? (2) Spain? (3) The Netherlands?

How have Renaissance achievements influenced our lives today?

Reading and Study Guide

For a *Reading and Study Guide on the Renaissance*, see the RESEARCH GUIDE/INDEX, Volume 22.

RENAL ARTERY. See KIDNEY.

RENAL VEIN. See KIDNEY.

RENAN, *ruh NAHN*, **ERNEST** (1823-1892), was a French historian and religious scholar. He became famous for his *Life of Jesus* (1863), the first of a series of books on the early history of Christianity. Renan was born at Tréguier. He studied for the priesthood, but lost his belief in the teachings of the church. He became an expert in ancient languages of the Near East, and, in 1862, was made professor at the College of France. He also wrote a *History of the People of Israel.* FRANCIS J. BOWMAN

RENDEZVOUS, in space. See SPACE TRAVEL (table: Space Travel Terms).

RENNES, *ren* (pop. 180,943; met. area 192,782; alt. 100 ft.), is an industrial and trade center in northwestern France. It lies at the meeting point of the Ille and Vilaine rivers. Rennes is the capital of the department of Ille-et-Vilaine.

RENNET. See CHEESE (Separating the Curd).

RENNIN. See FERMENTATION; STOMACH.

RENO, *REE no*, Nev. (pop. 72,863; met. area 121,068; alt. 4,490 ft.), the state's second largest city, lies along the Truckee River. For location, see NEVADA (political map). Reno is often called the *Biggest Little City in the World,* because of its fame as a tourist and gambling center.

Nevada laws make it easy for persons from other states to obtain divorces, and Reno's courts are always crowded with such cases. Reno also ranks as an important business city. It serves as the state's chief distributing, banking, and shopping center.

Railroad men established Reno in 1868. The Nevada Historical Society and one of the campuses of the University of Nevada are in Reno. Reno has a council-manager form of government. It is the seat of Washoe County. LUCIUS BEEBE

RENO, MARCUS ALFRED (1834-1889), was an American army officer who became known for his role in the Battle of the Little Bighorn. In this battle, called "Custer's Last Stand," Indians killed General George A. Custer and all the men under his immediate command. A bitter controversy began after the battle, and Major Reno was accused of cowardice. For an account of the battle and the dispute, see CUSTER, GEORGE ARMSTRONG.

Montana Historical Society,
Helena, Montana

Marcus Alfred Reno

In 1878, two years after the battle, Reno asked that a court of inquiry investigate the charges against him. A court of inquiry, unlike a court-martial, does not actually try a person. Reno was cleared of the charges in 1879. But later that same year, he was court-martialed on several other charges, including drunkenness. The court convicted him, and Reno received a dishonorable discharge in 1880.

In 1967, the Army ruled that Reno's dismissal had been unjust. The Army corrected his record to show he had been honorably discharged. Reno was reburied in the Custer Battlefield National Cemetery in Montana.

Reno was born in Carrollton, Ill. He graduated from the United States Military Academy in 1857 and served in the cavalry during the Civil War. JAMES D. SHACTER

RENOIR, *ruh NWAHR*, **PIERRE AUGUSTE** (1841-1919), a French Impressionist painter, is famous for his pictures of young girls and children, and intimate portraits of French middle-class life. He loved to show gay groups in sensuous surroundings, and often used his friends as models. His *Oarsmen at Chatou* and *Children's Afternoon at Wargemont* appear in color in the PAINTING article. He frequently painted his wife and babies.

In the 1870's, Renoir and Claude Monet together

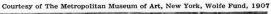

Brown Bros.

Pierre Auguste Renoir, a leading Impressionist painter, became known for his rough brush strokes and vivid colors. In *Madame Charpentier and Her Children,* painted in 1878, Renoir used blurred outlines and soft lighting to make his figures graceful and charming.

developed the broken color technique of the Impressionists. Instead of mixing paints completely, they left small dabs of different colors side by side, permitting the eye to blend them together. But Renoir was more interested in rich color effects and solidity of form than Monet. Renoir also preferred figure painting to landscapes. During the 1870's, he painted a large number of portraits on commission. Perhaps his most famous is *Mme. Charpentier and Her Children*. While many Impressionists brought Japanese qualities into their paintings, Renoir revived the rococo style of such painters as Jean Honoré Fragonard and Jean Antoine Watteau.

Renoir traveled to Italy in 1880, and his study of Renaissance painters there led him to a new appreciation of the importance of line. He returned to France, where he gave up his broad, coloristic manner and spent several years concentrating on drawing. He painted a famous series, *The Bathers*, during this time.

The happy quality of Renoir's later work does not show the agony he suffered from arthritis, which finally crippled his hands. He had brushes tied to his hands and developed a final style of painting in broad brush strokes and vivid colors.

Renoir was born in Limoges, France. He was apprenticed to learn porcelain painting after he showed an early talent for drawing. He painted window shades and fans in Paris. He studied at Charles Gleyre's studio, where he met Monet and other young painters who were to form the Impressionist group. He was influenced also by Edouard Manet and the color methods of Eugène Delacroix. ROBERT GOLDWATER

See also DELACROIX, EUGÈNE; MANET, EDOUARD; MONET, CLAUDE; IMPRESSIONISM.

RENSSELAER POLYTECHNIC INSTITUTE is a private coeducational school of engineering and science at Troy, N.Y. Founded by Stephen Van Rensselaer in 1824, it is the oldest school of engineering and science in the United States. It granted the first degree in engineering in 1835.

The courses at Rensselaer are grouped under the schools of architecture, engineering, humanities and social sciences, and science. There is also a graduate school. Rensselaer has a program with 16 liberal arts colleges which offer three years of liberal arts schooling followed by two years of engineering at Rensselaer. The institute also maintains a graduate center at Hartford, Conn., which offers additional study in science and engineering for persons associated with industrial firms in that area. For enrollment, see UNIVERSITIES AND COLLEGES (table). STEPHEN E. WIBERLEY

RENT, in everyday speech, usually means a payment for the use of something. People speak most often of renting a house, a piece of land, or a room. But it also is possible to rent such things as a boat, a typewriter, an automobile, an airplane, or a masquerade costume.

The word *rent*, in economics, has a special, technical meaning. Economic rent applies only to land. If one piece of land is more fertile than another, it will produce a larger yield per acre in proportion to the tools and labor used on it. A piece of land which yields just enough to pay all the costs of cultivating it, including wages for the work, is barely worth cultivating. Such a piece of land is called *marginal land*. The difference

between the yield from a good piece of land and the yield that could have been obtained with the same expenditure from the same amount of marginal land is called *economic rent*.

Why Rent Exists. If all land had the same quality, and if enough of it existed for everyone, there would be no such thing as rent. No one would pay for the use of land if he could have equally good land for nothing. But when there is not enough good land to go around, the owners of the better land can charge a rental for its use. This rental will roughly equal the probable selling price of the extra product obtained by using this particular piece of fertile land rather than a piece of marginal land.

Economists point out that rent depends on the presence of people. Persons who advocate the single tax argue that because all people give added value to land by their presence, they should share in its rents through high taxes on land. Others believe that the person who has the foresight or good luck to buy desirable land should receive all the rent. See SINGLE TAX.

How Rent Is Determined. To understand how rent develops, imagine that a small, fertile island has just been discovered. The first man to arrive takes a part of the most fertile land. The second man to arrive finds equally good land, both in fertility and in location. Accordingly, no economic rent and no money payment results immediately.

As more settlers arrive, the best land is all taken up, and soon only inferior land is left. Labor and capital applied to the inferior land do not result in as many bushels per acre as they would on the better land. Suppose that labor and capital applied on the poorest land worth cultivating (the marginal land) yield 10 bushels of wheat per acre, and that the same amount of labor and capital applied to the best land would yield 30 bushels per acre. Under these conditions, the best land yields a rent (surplus product) of 20 bushels per acre. If wheat sells for a dollar a bushel, the owners of the best land could demand a money rent of about $20 per acre for the use of their land.

The Selling Price of Land is determined by figuring out how much money it would take to yield an amount of interest equal to the rent from the land. If each acre will yield its owner an income of $20 per year, and if the rate of interest on money is 5 per cent, it would take $400 to earn an interest equal to the income from the land. The land should therefore sell at $400 per acre. But if the rate of interest were only 4 per cent, the land would be worth $500 per acre.

In practice, the actual price at which land will sell is not so easily determined. Buyer and seller must consider the conditions likely to prevail in the future. Farm produce prices and interest rates may go up or down. Settlers may come to the land and increase rental values. Railroads may be built which will decrease the difference in desirability of nearby and far-off lands. Many possibilities must be considered by both purchaser and seller. WILLIAM TUCKER DEAN

See also LEASE.

REORGANIZATION ACT OF 1946. See HOUSE OF REPRESENTATIVES (Committees).

REORGANIZED CHURCH OF JESUS CHRIST OF LATTER DAY SAINTS. See LATTER DAY SAINTS, REORGANIZED CHURCH OF JESUS CHRIST OF.

REPAIRMEN AND MECHANICS are workers who keep the machines of modern life running smoothly and efficiently. In industry, repairmen and mechanics operate, adjust, repair, and maintain the complicated machinery that produces airplanes, automobiles, electronic equipment, and thousands of other products. These experts also service radios, television sets, automobiles, home appliances, and many other machines.

Career Opportunities exist for all classes of repairmen and mechanics. But the greatest demands are for automobile and airplane mechanics, office-machine servicemen, and radio and television servicemen. Future job prospects seem better than ever. Technological advances have actually increased the demand for repairmen and mechanics.

Automobile Mechanics make up the largest group of maintenance and repair employees. Most of them work in auto-repair shops and in the service departments of automobile dealers. Many work for trucking and bus companies. Others help maintain vehicles owned by dairies, bakeries, or other business firms.

Various trade schools offer shop courses in body repairing and mechanics. It is usually possible to specialize in one type of mechanics, such as engine or wheel alignment. Most mechanics learn their trade on the job, regardless of their education. Newcomers start as assistants, and work their way up. It takes about four years to train a qualified mechanic.

Airplane Mechanics usually work for airlines, where they maintain or overhaul aircraft. Airline mechanics must have about three years' training. Many airlines train their own mechanics. Apprentices must have a high-school or technical-school education, with courses in mathematics, physics, chemistry, and machine shop.

Office-Machine Servicemen need various skills, depending on the types of machines they repair, maintain, or install. Machines may range from relatively simple typewriters and adding machines to complicated data-processing machines. Most servicemen receive their training from the companies that build the machines.

Radio and Television Servicemen usually either own their own repair shops or work in such shops. Most of them receive their training in vocational or technical schools. Television repairmen need more training in electronics than do radio repairmen. ALANSON H. EDGERTON

See also the Careers section of various articles in WORLD BOOK on industries mentioned in this article, such as AUTOMOBILE; TELEVISION.

REPARATIONS. See DAWES PLAN; WAR DEBT.

REPEAL means wiping out a law already on the books. A legislative body has the power not only to pass new laws, but also to do away with laws that have been passed earlier. Sometimes, the legislature may pass an act which directly states that an earlier law is repealed. Such an act is known as an *express repeal*. Sometimes, a new law may simply make it quite clear that an older one no longer applies. In this case, the repeal is known as a *repeal by implication*. A new law will sometimes conflict only with a certain portion of an earlier one. The new law is understood to repeal by implication those parts of the earlier law that are inconsistent with it.

To avoid confusion, legislatures often enact an *express repeal* of a law which has already been repealed by implication. For example, the passage by Congress of the Kansas-Nebraska Bill had the effect of repealing the Missouri Compromise. But Congress later passed a second bill specifically declaring the Missouri Compromise "void and inoperative." PAYSON S. WILD, JR.

REPLEVIN, *ree PLEHV in*, is a legal action used to recover goods or chattels that have been unlawfully taken or illegally retained. For example, when two cows broke down a fence and destroyed part of one farmer's cornfield, he drove them into his barn. He refused to return them to their owner until he was paid for his damaged corn. The farmer who owned the cows appealed to the court for an order, or *writ*, directing the sheriff to seize the cows and return them to him. This action in law is called a *replevin*.

A *writ of replevin* directs the sheriff to seize the property described, and to return it at once to the party from whom it was taken. In his application for replevin, the plantiff must assure the court by bond, or in some other way, that he will pay any damages found to be due to the defendant. If the action is decided in favor of the plaintiff, he is entitled to recover his property. If the actual property itself cannot be recovered, he is entitled to its value in cash, together with such damages as the court may allow. WILLIAM TUCKER DEAN

REPORT CARD. See GRADING.

REPORTER. See FOREIGN CORRESPONDENT; JOURNALISM; NEWSPAPER; WAR CORRESPONDENT.

REPOUSSÉ. See EMBOSSING; SCULPTURE (The First Sculptors).

REPPLIER, *REP leer*, **AGNES** (1858-1950), an American writer, was best known for her skillfully written essays. All of her writings, even those on the most serious subjects, show her delightful sense of humor. In her many books, she discussed her life, literary interests, and interest in Philadelphia, her home town. Her books include *The Fireside Sphinx* (1901), *Philadelphia* (1907), and *Americans and Others* (1912). She also wrote *In Our Convent Days* (1905), an autobiography of her school days, and several biographies, which include *Père Marquette* (1929). FREDERICK J. HOFFMAN

REPRESENTATIVE is the name used to refer to a member of the lower house of the Congress of the United States (the House of Representatives), or a member of the lower house of a state legislature. See also ADDRESS, FORM OF; CONGRESSMAN; HOUSE OF REPRESENTATIVES.

REPRESENTATIVE GOVERNMENT is the name given to a system of government carried on by elected representatives of the people. It "derives its just powers from the consent of the governed." A representative government is the opposite of a dictatorship.

REPRESENTATIVES, HOUSE OF. See HOUSE OF REPRESENTATIVES.

REPRIEVE, *ree PREEV*, is the temporary suspension of a sentence passed on a criminal. Reprieves are sometimes granted to permit consideration of new evidence, or a further investigation of the case. The chief executive of a state or country usually grants reprieves. A reprieve is not a pardon (see PARDON). It makes no change in the sentence, but merely changes the date when the sentence goes into effect. A delay or reprieve granted to a prisoner by the court which passed the sentence is often called a *stay of execution*. FRED E. INBAU

REPRISAL. See MARQUE AND REPRISAL.

Norman Myers, Photo Researchers

A. W. Rakosy

REPRODUCTION

Sexual Reproduction varies greatly among animals and plants. But it always involves the uniting of male and female sex cells.

REPRODUCTION is the process by which man, animals, and plants create more of their own kind. The survival of all species of living things depends on reproduction. If any species—human beings, dogs, or tulips —stopped reproducing, it would disappear after all its members had died.

There are two main kinds of reproduction—*sexual reproduction* and *asexual reproduction.* In sexual reproduction, a new *organism* (living thing) is formed from the joining of two sex cells. These cells come from two different parents in most cases. In asexual reproduction, a new organism develops from parts of, or from parts produced by, only one parent. Human beings and most higher animals and plants reproduce sexually. Most lower animals and plants reproduce asexually.

Sexual reproduction is the most complicated kind of reproduction. Animals and plants that reproduce sexually have reproductive organs that produce sex cells. These cells are called *gametes.* A male gamete is called a *sperm,* and a female gamete is called an *egg.* When a male gamete and female gamete unite, the sperm *fertilizes* the egg. The fertilized egg then develops into a new individual. Gametes and the process by which they unite vary greatly among different kinds of animals and plants.

The way a new organism develops after fertilization depends on chemical information in tiny structures called *chromosomes.* Each cell of the organism contains

The contributor of this article, Charles R. Botticelli, is Associate Professor of Biology at Boston University.

228

chromosomes. The chromosomes cause a fertilized human egg to develop into a human being, a fertilized dog egg to grow into a dog, and a fertilized tulip egg to become a tulip.

Animals and plants that reproduce asexually do not have reproductive organs. Asexual reproduction involves any of a number of different processes. Some animals and plants simply split in two to form a new organism. Each half then grows into an adult. Other organisms give off parts of their bodies, and these parts develop into new organisms. Some simple animals and plants produce tiny structures called *spores* that grow into adult organisms.

Human Reproduction

Human reproduction differs from reproduction in animals and plants because it involves more than just a *biological* (life) process. Among human beings, sex and reproduction involve love and other deep feelings. Moral standards govern sexual behavior in most societies, and individual members of the societies are expected to follow those standards.

This article describes the biological process of reproduction among human beings, animals, and plants. For a discussion of sex as it is related to the lives of children, teen-agers, and adults, see the WORLD BOOK article on SEX.

The Male Reproductive System. The male *genitals* (sex organs) are mostly outside the body. A man or boy has a finger-shaped organ called a *penis* between his legs. Behind the penis hangs a small sack called the *scrotum.* The scrotum contains two oval-shaped sex or-

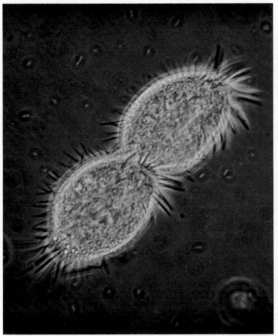

Eric V. Gravé

Jerome Wexler, Photo Researchers

Asexual Reproduction may simply involve a one-celled animal splitting in two, *left*, or a plant, *right*, sending out a slender growth called a *runner*.

gans called *testicles* or *testes*. The testicles consist of a complicated system of tubes in which millions of sperm are produced and stored. A tube called the *vas deferens* carries sperm from each testicle to a tube called the *urethra*. A whitish fluid called *semen* is produced by the *prostate gland* and the *seminal vesicles*, and is mixed and stored with the sperm in the vas deferens. The semen, which contains the sperm, is released through the urethra. The urethra runs through the penis. Sperm from the testicles and urine from the bladder are both discharged from the body through the penis, but always at different times.

The Female Reproductive System. All the female reproductive organs are inside the body. A woman or girl has small folds of skin called the *vulva* between her legs. The vulva covers the opening to a narrow canal called the *vagina*. The vagina leads to the *uterus,* a hollow, pear-shaped organ. Two organs called *ovaries* produce and store female sex cells. The ovaries are near the base of the abdomen. They are oval-shaped and about the size of a walnut. Normally, the ovaries release one egg about every 28 days. The release of an egg from an ovary is called *ovulation.* After ovulation occurs, the egg enters a narrow tube called a *Fallopian tube* or *oviduct.* The Fallopian tubes are not connected to the ovaries, but lie close to them. The tubes carry the eggs from the ovaries to the uterus, which is located between the ovaries.

One of the main differences between the male and female reproductive systems involves the way in which sex cells are produced and released. The testicles produce and store millions of sperm that can be re-

leased at almost any time. The ovaries produce a few thousand eggs, but only a few hundred of them are released during the female's lifetime. Usually, only one egg at a time is released as part of a monthly process called the *menstrual cycle*.

During the menstrual cycle, changes take place in the uterus. The soft inner lining of the uterus develops many tiny blood vessels and thickens. It reaches its full thickness shortly after an egg has been released from an ovary. If the egg is fertilized, it attaches itself to the lining of the uterus and starts to develop. If the egg is not fertilized by a sperm within about 12 hours, it dies. The unfertilized egg, together with the inner lining and blood vessels of the uterus, is then slowly discharged through the vagina in a process called *menstruation*. Menstruation lasts several days. The menstrual cycle occurs every month unless an egg is fertilized. See MENSTRUATION.

Fertilization may occur after a male and female have *sexual intercourse*. Intercourse takes place when a man and woman lie close together and the penis is placed in the woman's vagina. The penis usually hangs limp. But when a male becomes sexually excited, special tissues in the penis fill with blood, and the organ becomes stiff and erect. During intercourse, semen containing millions of sperm is *ejaculated* (discharged) from the penis into the vagina. Each sperm has a head and a long, threadlike tail. The sperm wriggle their tails to travel from the vagina into the uterus, and some then enter the Fallopian tubes. If an egg is passing through one of the Fallopian tubes, one of the sperm is likely to fertilize it.

228a

REPRODUCTION

To fertilize an egg, a sperm must get through the outer covering of the egg. The sperm and the egg then unite. Only one of the millions of sperm released by the man is necessary for fertilization. The other sperm die and are absorbed by the female's body. Fertilization almost always takes place in a Fallopian tube, but it may occur in the uterus.

The ovaries release only one egg each month, and an egg lives only about 12 hours. Therefore, for fertilization to take place, intercourse must occur at about the time of ovulation.

Pregnancy begins when a fertilized egg attaches itself to the lining of the uterus. The egg then starts to develop according to the chemical information in the chromosomes from both the egg and the sperm (see HEREDITY). From the time the fertilized cell begins dividing until about the third month of its development, it is called an *embryo*. For detailed information about the embryo and its development, and a photograph of a human embryo, see EMBRYO.

One of the first steps in the development of the embryo is the formation of a structure called the *placenta*. The placenta consists of tissues and blood vessels that surround the embryo and connect it to the uterus. The *umbilical cord* connects the embryo and the placenta. The umbilical cord is a "life line" that carries oxygen and nourishment from the mother to the developing child. It also carries carbon dioxide and other wastes back to the mother.

At first, the human embryo appears similar to the embryos of many kinds of animals. It begins to resemble a human being after about five weeks. After about two months, nearly all the internal organs have formed, and the growing organism is called a *fetus*. After about three months, the fetus looks much like a human baby. The mother can feel the fetus moving after about four months. Growth and development continue until about nine months after fertilization. The baby is then ready to be born.

Birth begins when the muscles of the uterus become

HUMAN REPRODUCTION

In human reproduction, a sperm from the father unites with and fertilizes an egg from the mother. A baby then develops in the mother's uterus, and is born nine months later.

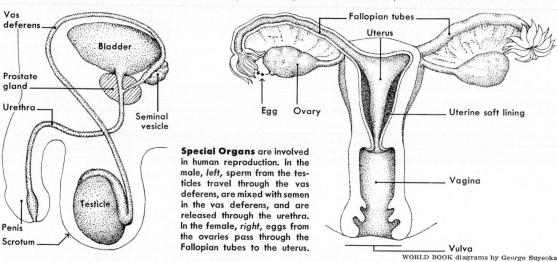

Special Organs are involved in human reproduction. In the male, *left*, sperm from the testicles travel through the vas deferens, are mixed with semen in the vas deferens, and are released through the urethra. In the female, *right*, eggs from the ovaries pass through the Fallopian tubes to the uterus.

WORLD BOOK diagrams by George Suyeoka

A Human Life Begins when a sperm gets through the outer covering of an egg and fertilizes it. In this photo, taken through a microscope, a sperm, *arrow*, can be seen near the center of a fertilized egg. Other sperm are swimming around the egg.

A Tiny Embryo starts to develop after a fertilized cell attaches itself to the inner lining of the uterus. Four days after fertilization, the embryo consists of about 100 cells. After about five weeks, it begins to look like a human baby.

Dr. Landrum B. Shettles, Columbia-Presbyterian Medical Center, New York, N.Y.

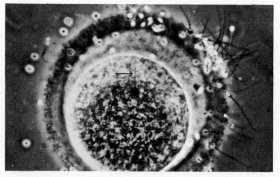

active. This muscle activity causes the mother to have *labor pains*. The muscle action is mild at first, but gradually becomes stronger and more frequent. It finally forces the baby out of the uterus, through the vagina, and out of the mother's body.

After the baby has been born, the physician cuts and ties the umbilical cord, leaving a permanent scar called the *navel*. Muscle action in the uterus continues until the placenta, now called the *afterbirth*, is discharged through the vagina.

Sometimes a fertilized egg splits into two parts, and each part develops into a fetus. This process results in the birth of two babies called *identical twins*. Identical twins are of the same sex and are similar in appearance because both of them develop from the same fertilized egg.

Occasionally, two eggs are released by an ovary at about the same time. If both eggs are fertilized, *fraternal twins* are born. Because fraternal twins develop from different eggs and sperm, they may be of different sexes

and look no more alike than ordinary brothers and sisters.

If a fertilized egg splits into three or more parts, the mother will give birth to identical triplets, quadruplets, or quintuplets. If more than two eggs are released at about the same time and all are fertilized, fraternal triplets, quadruplets, or quintuplets will be born. See MULTIPLE BIRTH.

Animal Reproduction

Animals reproduce both sexually and asexually. Their reproductive processes vary greatly. Some resemble the human reproductive process, but others are completely different.

Sexual Reproduction in Animals. There are several methods of sexual reproduction among animals. Almost all animals that reproduce sexually have special organs or tissues that produce either sperm or eggs. In order for the sperm to reach the eggs, both gametes must be released close to one another at about the same time.

THE BIRTH OF A BABY

The birth process, called *labor*, results from muscle action forcing the baby out of the uterus. These plaster models illustrate the process. At the beginning of labor (1), the head of the baby points toward the opening of the uterus. As the muscles contract, the head turns and (2) passes through the vagina. The baby is born (3) when its head comes out of the vagina. A baby is helpless and requires love and attention from its parents.

WORLD BOOK photo by Joel Cole, Presbyterian-St. Luke's Hospital

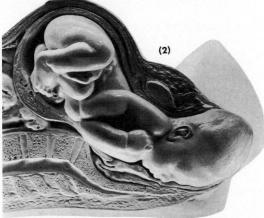

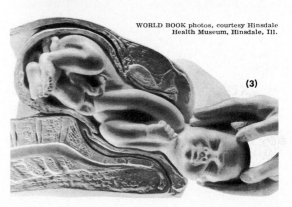

WORLD BOOK photos, courtesy Hinsdale Health Museum, Hinsdale, Ill.

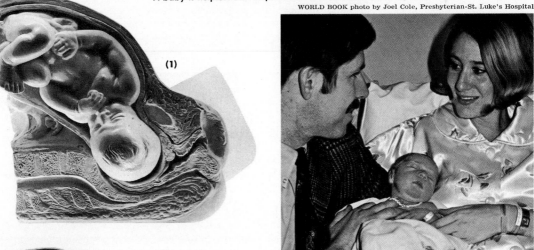

REPRODUCTION

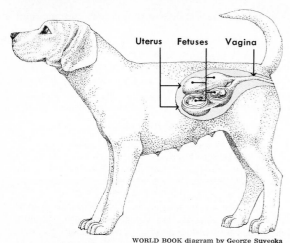

Uterus   Fetuses   Vagina

WORLD BOOK diagram by George Suyeoka

Among Most Mammals, including dogs, fertilization and the early development of the young take place in the mother's body. The birth process is similar to that in humans.

The main differences in sexual reproductive processes involve the ways in which eggs and sperm are released, and the places where fertilization takes place.

Among most higher animals—including almost all mammals, birds, and reptiles—the male releases sperm into the female opening that leads to the reproductive organs. If fertilization takes place, it occurs inside the female's body, and the process is called *internal fertilization*. The process varies among different species of animals.

Among most fish and *amphibians* (animals that live both on land and in water), the males and females both release their gametes into the water. Millions of eggs and sperm are released, but only a small number unite. This process is called *external fertilization* because it takes place outside the female's body.

Salmon reproduce by external fertilization. In some species, the female salmon digs a nest in the bottom of a stream or lake. The male and female then swim next to each other and release their sperm and eggs over the nest. Any eggs that become fertilized begin to develop. Those that are able to survive develop into adult salmon. The process of external fertilization varies with different kinds of animals.

The chances of an egg being fertilized are much greater with internal fertilization than with external fertilization. If gametes are released outside the female's body, they are likely to become separated, to be eaten by other animals, or to die without being fertilized. Inside the female's body, eggs and sperm are protected from such dangers. Animals that reproduce by external fertilization produce far more eggs than those that reproduce by internal fertilization. A female gorilla, for example, releases only one egg each month, but a female frog releases millions of eggs a year.

Among most species of animals that reproduce by internal fertilization, the young are fed and protected by the mother. Among most species that reproduce by external fertilization, the young receive little or no protection or nourishment from the mother.

Among most mammals, the developing organism grows inside the female and receives nourishment directly from her through a placenta. After a certain length of time, the young are born alive. This type of internal development is called *viviparity*.

Most reptiles and birds, though they have internal fertilization, lay their fertilized eggs in shells outside their bodies. Each egg contains enough food material to feed the young organism until it hatches. The development of an embryo in an egg outside the female's body is called *oviparity*. Some fish, amphibians, and reptiles produce eggs that remain inside the female until the young hatch, but are not nourished directly by her. This process is called *ovoviviparity*.

In some species of animals, both eggs and sperm are produced by the same organism. These animals, which include earthworms and some types of sponges, are called *hermaphrodites*. With some hermaphrodites, two gametes from the same animal can fertilize each other. This process is called *self-fertilization*. But with most hermaphrodites, self-fertilization is prevented by (1) the eggs and sperm developing at different times, or (2) the position of the organs that produce the gametes. These animals usually must unite with others of their species for fertilization to take place.

Among some other animals, including honeybees and wasps, an egg can develop into an adult organism without being fertilized. This reproductive process is called *parthenogenesis*. Many animals that reproduce by parthenogenesis can also reproduce by other sexual processes.

Asexual Reproduction in Animals. There are a number of general methods of asexual reproduction in animals. The simplest method, called *binary fission*, involves the splitting of a one-celled organism—an ameba, for example—into two cells. The new cells grow to the size of the original cell, and then each of them splits into new organisms.

A process similar to binary fission occurs in planarians and some other multicelled animals. In this process, called *fragmentation*, the animal breaks into two or more parts, and each part develops into a complete new adult. The missing parts of each fragment grow through a process called *regeneration*. A few animals that do not reproduce through fragmentation can replace lost parts through regeneration. They include lobsters and starfish.

Some animals develop as an outgrowth of a parent organism. This asexual method of reproduction, called *budding*, is common among some sponges. In some cases, the bud separates from the parent after a time. In others, the bud stays attached and develops its own buds, which also remain attached to the parent.

A fourth method, *sporulation*, occurs when an organism produces and releases one-celled structures called *spores*. Each spore develops into a complete new organism. Malaria parasites reproduce through sporulation.

Plant Reproduction

Plants, like animals, reproduce both sexually and asexually. Asexual reproductive processes in plants resemble those in animals. But sexual reproduction

228d

Richard Boolootian

External Fertilization is common among fish. A female grunion, *center,* burrows about halfway into the sand to lay its eggs. A male deposits sperm which sink down and fertilize the eggs.

the ovary. The tissue hardens and forms a seed coat that protects the embryo. The seeds of different plants vary greatly in size and shape.

The seed is carried away from the adult plant in one of a number of ways. For example, the seeds of some plants are blown away by the wind. Many of them settle in a place where they can survive and develop, and the embryos grow into adult plants.

For more information on how plants reproduce sexually, see FLOWER (The Parts of a Flower; How Flowers Reproduce; diagrams); PLANT (Sexual Reproduction).

Asexual Reproduction in Plants can involve the same processes of binary fission, budding, and sporulation that take place among animals. Additional asexual reproductive processes also occur in plants. These processes are called *vegetative propagation.* In many plants, parts cut from a parent plant will grow into a complete new plant. See PLANT (Vegetative Propagation).   CHARLES R. BOTTICELLI

Related Articles in WORLD BOOK include:

Alternation of Generations
Ameba (picture: How
   Amebas Reproduce)
Animal (How Animals
   Reproduce)
Biogenesis
Breeding
Cell
Conjugation
Egg
Embryo
Fish (How Fish Reproduce)
Fission (Cellular
   Fission)
Gametophyte
Genetics
Germ Cell

Gestation
Heredity
Hermaphrodite
Incubation
Insect
Menstruation
Multiple Birth
Plant (How Plants
   Reproduce)
Pollen and Pollination
Seed
Spontaneous Generation
Stem (Reproduction by
   Stems)
Sterility
Tree (How Trees Reproduce; illustration)

among plants involves processes not found in animal reproduction.

Sexual Reproduction in Plants. The most common examples of plants that reproduce sexually are flowering plants. The reproductive organs of these plants are in the flower itself. The male reproductive organ is a long, slender structure called a *stamen.* At the tip of the stamen is a small sacklike part called the *anther.* The female reproductive organ is called a *pistil.* It consists of a round base called an *ovary,* a tube leading up from the ovary called a *style,* and a flattened structure at the top of the style called a *stigma.*

The reproductive process begins when cells within an anther and an ovary divide. The resulting cells in the anther develop a thick covering and become dustlike *pollen grains* that form sperm. The cells in the ovary form an egg.

Pollen is carried from an anther to a stigma by a process called *pollination.* The pollen may be carried by the wind, by water, or by insects or other animals. Many plants have both pistils and stamens, and so pollen can be carried from a stamen to a pistil on the same plant. This process is called *self-pollination.*

After a pollen grain reaches a stigma, it forms a tube through the style. A sperm from the pollen grain travels down the tube and into the ovary, where it fertilizes an egg. An embryo then develops from the fertilized egg. A structure called an *endosperm* forms around the embryo and supplies it with nourishment. After a short time, the embryo and endosperm stop growing, and both become surrounded by tissue from

Outline

I. Human Reproduction
   A. The Male Reproductive System   D. Pregnancy
   B. The Female Reproductive System E. Birth
   C. Fertilization
II. Animal Reproduction
   A. Sexual Reproduction in Animals
   B. Asexual Reproduction in Animals
III. Plant Reproduction
   A. Sexual Reproduction in Plants
   B. Asexual Reproduction in Plants

Questions

What are the two main types of reproduction?
What are the two kinds of gametes?
How is oviparity different from viviparity?
Why do animals that reproduce through internal fertilization release fewer eggs than those that reproduce through external fertilization?
What are the four main methods of asexual reproduction in animals?
How many sperm are needed to fertilize a human egg?
What causes identical twins? Fraternal twins?
What are the names of the male and female reproductive organs in flowering plants?
What begins the birth process in humans?
What is a hermaphrodite?

Reading and Study Guide

For a *Reading and Study Guide on Reproduction,* see the RESEARCH GUIDE/INDEX, Volume 22.

REPTILE, *REP til,* is a member of the class of animals which includes the snakes, lizards, turtles, crocodilians, and the tuatara. The crocodilians include alligators, crocodiles, the gavial of Asia, and the caymans of tropical America. The tuatara, a large reptile, looks like a lizard and lives on islands off the coast of New Zealand. It is the last survivor of a whole group of ancient reptiles.

About 6,000 different kinds of reptiles live throughout the world. They are of many different sizes, shapes, and habits, because the reptiles have gone through many changes since their ancestors lived millions of years ago. The reptiles seen today resemble the twigs of a great tree of reptile life. They are not new branches, but descend directly from ancient animals. The four large separate limbs are the turtles, crocodilians, tuatara, and the snakes and lizards together. The huge dead limbs include such reptiles as the dinosaurs.

Scientists do not yet know exactly why one reptile branch died out while another survived. The lizards and snakes together form the only large branch today. This branch includes about 95 per cent of all the different kinds of living reptiles. Fossil remains do not show that they ever held greater importance than now. The same thing cannot be said of turtles, crocodilians, and the tuatara. Fossil beds in many parts of the world are strewn with shells of many kinds of turtles that are now extinct. Today, only 25 species of crocodilians survive, but there once were more.

The reptiles belong to the vertebrates, or animals with backbones. They are midway between the fishes and the mammals. The fishes cannot live apart from the water, and the amphibians must spend the first part of their life there. The reptiles were the first to break away from the water and live on land. Most reptiles hatch their young from eggs, but many reptiles produce live young.

Reptiles, being cold blooded, cannot keep their temperature much above or below the temperature around them. They cannot stay active in winter, and so cannot live in many of the cooler parts of the earth.

Scientific Classification. Reptiles are in the phylum *Chordata.* They belong to the subphylum *Vertebrata,* and make up the class *Reptilia.*   CLIFFORD H. POPE

Related Articles in WORLD BOOK include:

Alligator	Gavial	Lizard
Crocodile	Herpetology	Snake
Dinosaur	Life (table: Length of	Tortoise
Fossil	Life of Animals)	Turtle

REPTILES, AGE OF, refers to the early Mesozoic Era in the earth's history. During this period, the reptiles reached their greatest importance. Dinosaurs, flying reptiles, and many other huge reptile forms lived at this time.

REPTON, HUMPHREY (1752-1818), was an English landscape gardener. He made his greatest contributions to landscape architecture by publishing books on his observations. He is credited with introducing the informal style that has become identified with English landscape gardening. His books include *Sketches and Hints on Landscape Gardening* (1794) and *An Inquiry into the Changes of Taste in Landscape Gardening, with Some Observations on Its Theory and Practice* (1806). Repton was born at Bury St. Edmunds.   ROBERT E. EVERLY

REPUBLIC is the form of government in which the citizens elect representatives to manage the government. The people give their elected representatives authority to maintain power for specific terms of office. The word *republic* may also refer to a country that has a republican form of government.

Not all republics are alike. In some, a single political party, the army, or some other group may be so powerful that the people may have only limited control. A republic of this sort is not a democracy. But a republic in which the people actually have supreme power may be called a *representative* or *indirect democracy.* In a representative democracy, the people elect delegates to an assembly. The delegates pass the laws, and other citizens chosen by the people enforce the laws. The people maintain control by voting in regularly scheduled elections for officials that carry out their wishes. A republic of this type is probably the nearest thing to pure democracy that a large country can manage.

In 509 B.C., Rome established one of the world's earliest known republics. But the Roman republic ended in 27 B.C., when Augustus named himself emperor. The United States is an outstanding example of a successful republic. When founded in 1776, the United States was the only major country with that form of government.

Switzerland declared its independence in 1815. Since then, it has become one of the most democratic of the world's republics. Other European republics include France, Italy, Austria, Finland, and West Germany. Great Britain prefers to keep the forms of monarchy, but it meets all the qualifications of a republic. Some members of the British Commonwealth of Nations, such as India, are republics, and their chief of state is a president. Others, such as Canada, are constitutional monarchies whose head is the British monarch.

Most Latin American countries, such as Mexico, are republics. However, in some of them a single leader or group actually holds most of the power. Liberia, founded in 1847, is the oldest republic in Africa. Many of the newer African nations are also republics. The Philippines is a leading Asian republic.

Russia and several other countries include the term *republic* in their official names, but are not republics in the true sense. The citizens have so little power over their government officials that such countries are actually dictatorships.   WILLIAM EBENSTEIN

See also DEMOCRACY; GOVERNMENT.

REPUBLIC, THE. See PLATO.

REPUBLIC STEEL CORPORATION is one of the largest steel-producing companies in the United States. It is a leading producer of alloy and stainless steels, carbon sheets and bars, pipe, and wire. Republic also manufactures steel kitchens, lockers, building products, tubing, nuts and bolts, and other metal products.

Republic operates 8 basic steel and 27 fabricating plants in the United States. It also owns coal and iron ore mines, and lake freighters. The Republic Steel Corporation was formed in 1930 through a merger of four steel companies. Additional steel companies have merged with Republic since that time. Company headquarters are in Cleveland. For Republic's sales, assets, and number of employees, see MANUFACTURING (table, 100 Leading U.S. Manufacturers).

Critically reviewed by the REPUBLIC STEEL CORPORATION

From *Thomas Nast* by Albert Bigelow Paine, permission of Harper & Row

The Elephant As a Republican Symbol first appeared in this 1874 cartoon by Thomas Nast in *Harper's Weekly*. The elephant in the cartoon represented the Republican vote. Nast used the elephant many times as a Republican symbol, and it soon came to stand for the Republican Party.

REPUBLICAN PARTY

REPUBLICAN PARTY is one of the two principal political parties of the United States. The other is the Democratic Party. Since the mid-1880's, the Republican Party has often been called the *G.O.P.* (Grand Old Party). This nickname comes from *Grand Old Man*, the nickname of William E. Gladstone, a powerful British statesman of the 1880's.

The Republican Party has greatly influenced the nation's history and politics. It won 14 of the 18 presidential elections from 1860, when Abraham Lincoln was elected, to 1932. But from 1932 through 1968, the Republicans won only 3 of the 10 presidential elections.

The policies of the Republican Party, like those of other parties, have changed through the years. At first, Republican candidates got most of their support from people who opposed slavery. To gain wider support, the party passed land legislation that appealed to farmers. Republicans won the backing of businessmen by endorsing sound money policies and high tariffs. By the late 1800's, the party had become a firm alliance of the agricultural West and the industrial East.

During the 1920's, the Republican Party became known as the "party of prosperity." The party fell out

---

George H. Mayer, the contributor of this article, is Professor of History at the University of South Florida and author of The Republican Party, 1854-1964.

of power during the Great Depression of the 1930's. It regained the presidency in 1952 when General Dwight D. Eisenhower, a great national war hero of World War II, won an easy election victory.

The party suffered a major setback in 1964 when Barry M. Goldwater, leader of the conservative Republicans, lost overwhelmingly in his bid for the presidency. Then, in 1968, Richard M. Nixon topped off a remarkable political comeback—for both himself and the party—when he won election as President.

This article describes chiefly the history of the Republican Party. For information about the party's national convention and organization, see the WORLD BOOK articles on POLITICAL CONVENTION and POLITICAL PARTY.

Origin of the Republican Party dates back to the strong antislavery opposition to the Kansas-Nebraska Bill of 1854. As passed by Congress in May, 1854, the bill permitted slavery in the new territories of Kansas and Nebraska if the people there voted for it.

Antislavery meetings throughout the North had condemned the Kansas-Nebraska Bill. On Feb. 28, 1854, Alvan E. Bovay, a leading Whig, had held such a meeting in Ripon, Wis. The meeting passed a resolution declaring that a new party—the Republican Party—would be organized if Congress passed the Kansas-Nebraska Bill.

Bovay held a second meeting in Ripon on March 20, after the Senate had passed the Kansas-Nebraska Bill.

REPUBLICAN PARTY

The 53 men at this meeting appointed a committee to form the new party. On July 6, 1854, at a party meeting in Jackson, Mich., the delegates formally adopted the name *Republican*.

The new party had chiefly sectional appeal. Few Southern voters supported the Republicans, because almost all Southerners wanted to expand slavery, not restrict it. Many Northerners supported the party. But some feared that the extreme antislavery views of such Republican leaders as Senator Charles Sumner of Massachusetts threatened the Union.

The Election of 1856. As their first presidential candidate, the Republicans chose John Charles Frémont, a dashing young explorer and soldier. During the campaign, antislavery and proslavery groups fought in Kansas. The chief campaign issue became "bleeding Kansas." Democrats predicted that the South would secede from the Union if the antislavery Frémont won.

The voting reflected the sectional appeal of the parties. Frémont won 11 Northern states. His Democratic opponent, James Buchanan, carried 19 states—including every Southern state except Maryland—and won the election.

Changes in Party Policy. After the Republican defeat in 1856, party leaders realized that they could not win the presidency on just the slavery issue. To broaden their appeal, Republicans endorsed construction of a transcontinental railroad and federal aid to improve harbors and rivers. The party also promised to open Western land for settlement, to raise tariff rates, and to permit slavery where it already existed.

In 1860, the Republicans chose Abraham Lincoln, a lanky, self-educated Illinois lawyer, as their presidential candidate. Lincoln had received national attention by expressing moderate antislavery views in a series of debates with Illinois Senator Stephen A. Douglas, a Democrat.

Lincoln easily won the election, even though he received only about 40 per cent of the popular vote. The Democrats had split over the slavery issue. Northern Democrats nominated Douglas as their candidate, and Southern Democrats chose Vice-President John C. Breckinridge.

The Civil War began in April, 1861. Most Southerners believed the election of Lincoln justified secession. In 1860 and 1861—both before and after the shooting started—11 Southern states left the Union.

Above all, Lincoln wanted to save the Union. But many Republicans—the so-called Radical Republicans—made the abolition of slavery their main goal. Many Northern Democrats supported Lincoln and the war and were called War Democrats.

Lincoln tried to bring all groups of both parties together, but he succeeded only partly. By 1864, Lincoln's chances of re-election looked doubtful. To stress the national character of the war—and to gain more supporters—the Republican Party used the name *Union Party*, or *National Union Party*, in the 1864 election. The party nominated Andrew Johnson, a War Democrat, for Vice-President. With the help of Northern victories just before the election, Lincoln won a second term.

On April 9, 1865, shortly after Lincoln's second term began, the war ended when General Robert E. Lee

REPUBLICAN PRESIDENTIAL AND VICE-PRESIDENTIAL CANDIDATES

Year	President	Vice-President	Year	President	Vice-President
1856	John C. Frémont	William L. Dayton	1920	*Warren G. Harding*	*Calvin Coolidge*
1860	*Abraham Lincoln*	*Hannibal Hamlin*	1924	*Calvin Coolidge*	*Charles G. Dawes*
1864	*Abraham Lincoln*	*Andrew Johnson*	1928	*Herbert Hoover*	*Charles Curtis*
1868	*Ulysses S. Grant*	*Schuyler Colfax*	1932	Herbert Hoover	Charles Curtis
1872	*Ulysses S. Grant*	*Henry Wilson*	1936	Alfred M. Landon	Frank Knox
1876	*Rutherford B. Hayes*	*William A. Wheeler*	1940	Wendell L. Willkie	Charles L. McNary
1880	*James A. Garfield*	*Chester A. Arthur*	1944	Thomas E. Dewey	John W. Bricker
1884	James G. Blaine	John A. Logan	1948	Thomas E. Dewey	Earl Warren
1888	*Benjamin Harrison*	*Levi P. Morton*	1952	*Dwight D. Eisenhower*	*Richard M. Nixon*
1892	Benjamin Harrison	Whitelaw Reid	1956	*Dwight D. Eisenhower*	*Richard M. Nixon*
1896	*William McKinley*	*Garret A. Hobart*	1960	Richard M. Nixon	Henry Cabot Lodge, Jr.
1900	*William McKinley*	*Theodore Roosevelt*	1964	Barry M. Goldwater	William E. Miller
1904	*Theodore Roosevelt*	*Charles W. Fairbanks*	1968	*Richard M. Nixon*	*Spiro T. Agnew*
1908	*William Howard Taft*	*James S. Sherman*	1972	*Richard M. Nixon*	*Spiro T. Agnew*
1912	William Howard Taft	James S. Sherman			
1916	Charles Evans Hughes	Charles W. Fairbanks			

Names of elected candidates are in italics.
Each candidate has a separate biography in WORLD BOOK.

ADMINISTRATIONS IN OFFICE

☐ Republican Party   ■ Democratic Party

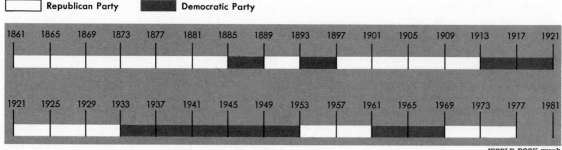

WORLD BOOK graph

F. W. Inversetti

The Birthplace of the Republican Party was this schoolhouse in Ripon, Wis. At a meeting there on March 20, 1854, 53 men appointed a 5-man committee to organize the new political party.

The New York Public Library

Abraham Lincoln easily outruns his opponents—John Bell, John C. Breckinridge, and Stephen A. Douglas, *left to right*—in this 1860 presidential campaign poster.

surrendered to General Ulysses S. Grant. Five days later, Lincoln was assassinated.

The Radical Republicans and Reconstruction. Johnson hoped to follow Lincoln's moderate plan of Reconstruction. But the Radical Republicans in Congress favored harsh punishment for the South. See RECONSTRUCTION.

The Radicals dominated Congress after the congressional elections of 1866. They divided the South into five military districts, deprived former Confederate soldiers of the right to vote, and gave the vote to former slaves.

The dispute over Reconstruction hardened political loyalties along sectional lines. Most Northern Republicans supported the Radical Republicans who, by 1868, felt strong enough to drop the Union Party label. Many Northern Democrats also backed Republican policies. But Southerners rejected Republican leadership. As a result, Reconstruction led to the birth of the Democratic "Solid South."

The Republicans nominated Grant, the great Union war hero, for President in 1868, and he won an easy victory. Grant won re-election in 1872, but by this time many voters had become alarmed over corruption in both business and government. A depression in 1873 helped the Democrats win a sweeping victory in the congressional elections of the next year.

In 1876, the Republicans nominated a cautious reformer, Rutherford B. Hayes. A group of conservative Republicans called *Stalwarts* opposed Hayes because he favored civil service reform and friendly relations with the South. Hayes and his followers became known as *Half Breeds*. Samuel J. Tilden, the Democratic candidate, won more popular votes than Hayes, but the electoral vote was disputed. A special commission declared Hayes the winner by one vote. The Democrats accepted the verdict only because the Republicans had promised informally to end Reconstruction and withdraw the remaining federal troops from the South. Hayes kept the promise.

Political Inactivity marked the 1880's and 1890's. Both major parties failed to face the problems resulting from the rapid industrialization that followed the Civil

Culver Pictures

In the Republican Party Split of 1912, "Teddy" Roosevelt and William Howard Taft pulled apart. The division of the party helped the Democratic candidate Woodrow Wilson win the presidency with about 40 per cent of the popular vote.

War. Many industrial monopolies set high prices for their products and services. Economic power became centered with a few wealthy business leaders, and farmers and wage earners suffered increasingly hard times.

In 1880, Republican James A. Garfield won the presidency. He was assassinated in 1881, after less than four months in office, and Vice-President Chester A. Arthur, a Stalwart, succeeded him. Arthur surprised his fellow Stalwarts by supporting civil service reform. In 1883, Congress passed the Pendleton Act, which established the merit system in the civil service.

232a

In 1884, the Republican candidate, James G. Blaine, narrowly lost to Grover Cleveland. The party made the protective tariff its chief campaign issue in 1888 and won the presidency with Benjamin Harrison. In 1890, the McKinley Tariff pushed tariffs higher than they had ever been before. Dissatisfaction with the tariff helped Cleveland defeat Harrison in 1892.

The Money Issue dominated the election of 1896. A third party, the Populist Party, had appeared during the early 1890's. The Populists demanded that the government increase the amount of money in circulation by permitting unlimited coinage of silver. They believed such action would help farmers and wage earners and improve the nation's economy. Many Democrats joined the Populists in their demand for silver coinage. In 1896, the Democratic Party nominated William Jennings Bryan, the leading silver spokesman, for President. The Republican candidate, William McKinley, supported a currency backed by gold and won the election.

Economic conditions improved rapidly during the late 1890's. The U.S. victory in the Spanish-American War also gained support for the Republicans. McKinley defeated Bryan again in 1900. But six months after beginning his second term, McKinley was assassinated. Vice-President Theodore Roosevelt succeeded him.

The Party Splits. "Teddy" Roosevelt supported much reform legislation. He brought suits against several large monopolies and crusaded for honesty in government. He also sponsored a conservation policy, laws to protect the public from impure food and drugs, and legislation to regulate railroad rates.

In 1908, Roosevelt chose his friend, Secretary of War William Howard Taft, to succeed him and continue his policies. Taft easily beat Bryan, who ran for the third time as the Democratic nominee.

Taft brought many more suits against monopolies than Roosevelt had. But Taft, by nature quieter and more conservative than Roosevelt, lost favor with Republican progressives. He faced open hostility from the progressives after signing into law the high Payne-Aldrich Tariff in 1909. By 1912, Taft no longer led a united party, and the progressives turned to Roosevelt, who wanted to be President again. After the Republicans renominated Taft, Roosevelt left the party and formed the Progressive, or "Bull Moose," Party. The Republican split helped Woodrow Wilson, the Democratic candidate, win the election.

The Republicans began to reunite after their defeat, and in 1916, most of them supported the party candidate, Charles Evans Hughes. But some Republicans backed Wilson because he had promoted progressive legislation and had kept the nation out of World War I (1914-1918). Wilson won re-election by a close margin. A month after he took office for the second time, the United States went to war against Germany.

By the congressional elections of 1918, the Republicans had reunited, and they gained control of Congress. After the war, the Republican-controlled Senate rejected American membership in the League of Nations (see LEAGUE OF NATIONS).

During the Roaring 20's, the Republicans won every presidential and congressional election. In 1920, the party's candidate, Warren G. Harding, promised a return to "normalcy." Americans, weary of wartime controls and world problems, wanted just that—and Harding won in a landslide.

The nation's economy boomed during the 1920's as business and industry expanded. Successive Republican administrations helped big business by keeping government spending and taxes as low as possible and by raising tariffs.

After Harding's death in 1923, congressional investigations revealed corruption in several government departments during his Administration. But the exposures did not prevent Harding's successor, Vice-President Calvin Coolidge, from easily winning the 1924 election. Coolidge's conservative Administration seemed to reflect the largely antiforeign, anti-immigration, antilabor mood of the nation.

In 1928, the Republicans turned to Herbert Hoover, Coolidge's secretary of commerce. Hoover easily defeated his Democratic opponent, Alfred E. Smith, but Smith carried most of the largest cities.

Soon after Hoover took office in 1929, the worst stock-market crash in the nation's history occurred. The Great Depression followed. Hoover tried to stop the depression but could not do so, and he lost badly in 1932 to the Democratic candidate, Franklin D. Roosevelt. Hoover's defeat reduced the Republican Party to a hard core of businessmen, Midwestern farmers, and conservative workers.

From 1933 to 1953, the Republican Party was the minority party. Roosevelt led the nation through the Great Depression with a massive federal program called the New Deal (see NEW DEAL). The Republicans, far outnumbered in both houses of Congress, took little action against Roosevelt's policies. The Republican platform of 1936 criticised the New Deal, but Roosevelt won reelection by a landslide over Alfred M. Landon.

By the election of 1940, World War II (1939-1945) had started. The Republicans nominated Wendell L. Willkie and continued to attack the New Deal, but Roosevelt easily won a third term. The United States entered the war in 1941. Roosevelt defeated Thomas E. Dewey in 1944 and became the only man to be elected President four times.

During the 1930's and 1940's, many Republicans accepted the idea of federal welfare programs and of U.S. leadership in world affairs. They also accepted American membership in the United Nations, established in 1945.

Vice-President Harry S. Truman became President after Roosevelt's death in 1945. The Republicans expected to win the 1948 election easily and nominated Dewey again, but Truman won a surprise victory.

The Eisenhower Years. Dwight D. Eisenhower easily won the 1952 election for the Republicans, defeating Adlai E. Stevenson. The World War II hero carried four Southern states and broke the Democratic Solid South for the first time in more than 20 years. Great numbers of voters turned to Eisenhower for reasons other than his immense popularity. Many voted Republican because of dissatisfaction with the government's conduct of the Korean War (1950-1953). Others believed the widespread charges that the Democrats had harbored Communists in high government posts. Eisenhower won re-election in 1956 by a landslide, again over Stevenson.

Eisenhower, a moderate Republican, won support from his own party and from many Southern Democrats. His Administration encouraged private enterprise, and Congress extended social security benefits and passed the first civil rights act since Reconstruction.

Nixon—From Defeat to Victory. Vice-President Richard M. Nixon won the Republican presidential nomination in 1960. He narrowly lost the election to his Democratic opponent, John F. Kennedy. After Kennedy's assassination in 1963, Vice-President Lyndon B. Johnson succeeded to the presidency.

In 1964, the Republicans nominated Barry M. Goldwater, who stood for an extreme form of conservatism. Johnson defeated him overwhelmingly.

Johnson continued Kennedy's policies, and Congress passed additional civil rights legislation and other laws to help disadvantaged Americans. Johnson sought to build what he called the Great Society. Conservative Republicans and conservative Southern Democrats joined forces to oppose much of his program. By 1966, Johnson's program had been overshadowed by the Vietnam War. The war divided the nation into "hawks," who supported the U.S. role in the war, and "doves," who opposed it.

For the 1968 presidential election, the Republicans turned to Nixon again. The Democrats nominated Vice-President Hubert H. Humphrey. A third party, the American Independent Party, nominated George C. Wallace, a Southern Democrat who strongly opposed civil rights legislation. Nixon won even though he received only about 43 per cent of the popular vote.

An economic recession began during the late 1960's. In 1971, Nixon ordered wage and price controls to help stem rising prices and increasing unemployment. In 1972, business increased and inflation slowed. Nixon also greatly reduced the number of U.S. troops in Vietnam. He expanded relations between the United States and China and withdrew U.S. opposition to China's membership in the United Nations.

Nixon won the Republican presidential nomination in 1972. The Democrats nominated George S. McGovern, who based his campaign on a promise to immediately end U.S. involvement in the Vietnam War. Nixon won the election in November.   GEORGE H. MAYER

Related Articles in WORLD BOOK include:

Free Soil Party	President of the United States
Liberal Republican Party	Progressive Party
Mugwump	Reconstruction (Congress
Nast, Thomas	Takes Control)
Political Convention	United States, History of
Political Party	Whig

REPUBLICAN RIVER. See NEBRASKA (Rivers).

REQUIEM. See MASS.

RESACA DE LA PALMA, BATTLE OF. See MEXICAN WAR (Principal Battles).

RESCUE from difficult and dangerous situations requires quick, sure action. In an emergency, every moment counts, and the steps taken may make the difference between saving or losing lives and property.

People react differently to emergencies. But everyone realizes that there is little time to think when people are in trouble. Every individual should know the basic rules of first aid so that he will have this information to guide his actions when necessary. It is also important to keep handy the telephone numbers of various agencies, including the fire department and the police.

In case of disasters, such as floods, earthquakes, tornadoes, and shipwrecks, the resources of an entire nation are often called into action.   JOHN J. FLOHERTY

Related Articles in WORLD BOOK include:

Fire Fighting	Police	Safety
First Aid	Red Cross	

Wide World   Wide World

Daring Rescue Workers save many lives. Firemen perform various rescue jobs, including saving people who have fallen through thin ice, *left*. Helicopters aid U.S. Army rescue teams. One helicopter lifts a downed "chopper" to safety in South Vietnam, *right*, as a soldier stands guard.

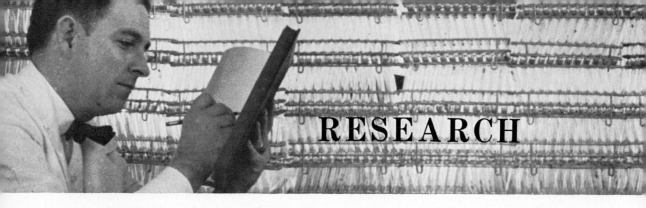

RESEARCH

RESEARCH is the use of systematic methods to evaluate ideas or to discover new knowledge. It usually means an organized, scientific investigation. Research includes investigations to determine the temperature of distant stars, to learn if life exists on other planets, or to test the effectiveness of a new drug. Researchers may also study how to make metal strong at high temperatures, how to produce an inexpensive color television set, or how to cure cancer and heart disease.

Many important products and developments have come from research. These include television, automatic dishwashers, magnetic tape recorders, and stereophonic sound. In transportation, research has helped give us diesel locomotives, jet airplanes, long-wearing automobile tires, and rockets that can travel into space. Farmers have benefited from automatic milking machines, mechanical corn pickers, and synthetic fertilizers. Medical research has provided penicillin, polio vaccine, and the sulfa drugs.

By developing new products and processes, research has made it possible for workers to produce more goods and services in less time. Higher productivity has given workers not only higher wages, but also a shorter work week. These and many other results of research are some of the most important reasons why many nations enjoy the highest standard of living in history.

Research plays an important part in many fields besides science and industry. Improvements in education, government, history, and social planning stem largely from research. The future of mankind may be determined by results of research in all these areas.

Kinds of Research

There are two main reasons for conducting research: (1) to discover or learn more about the basic laws of nature, and (2) to apply this basic knowledge to the solution of practical problems. The first kind of research is called basic, or fundamental, and the second is applied, or directed.

Basic, or **Fundamental, Research** aims at a better understanding of the universe in which we live. It tries to answer such questions as "What is magnetism?"; "What are the forces that hold together the nucleus of an atom?"; "Why is one metal harder than another?"; or "How do plants use the energy of the sun?"

A scientist often conducts basic research because of his own curiosity. He need not have any practical goal in mind. But basic research has great importance, because it supplies the fundamental knowledge for all applied research.

Basic research is exceedingly difficult, if not impossible, to plan or direct. Its results are usually unpredictable. Basic research consists of exploring the unknown. Each new step is planned and chosen from the results of the previous step. But the results of basic research can have far-reaching effects in the lives of all mankind. For example, the atomic bomb resulted from basic research on the structure of the atom. Basic research on the transmission and detection of electromagnetic waves led to radio, radar, and television.

Applied, or **Directed, Research** aims at some specific objective, such as the development of a new product, process, or material. This kind of research is an application of basic knowledge directed toward a specific end result. For example, the application of a fundamental knowledge of magnetism resulted in the magnetic tape recorder. The use of basic knowledge of mathematics and electronics led to the high-speed electronic computer. Other well-known results of applied research include dial telephones, fluorescent lights, and synthetic fibers such as rayon, nylon, and Dacron.

Applied research may also include the improvement of products and processes already in use. For example, steel manufacturers conduct research on furnaces they use to make steel. They try to find ways to improve their design so as to increase production or lower costs. Automobile manufacturers conduct research to reduce engine noise or to decrease the amount of exhaust fumes that may pollute the air. Because of its importance to industry, by far the larger portion of all research is in the field of applied research.

Research Methods

In applied research, it is usually possible to plan and organize the research program. In some cases, researchers can even predict the probability of success. Methods for conducting an applied-research program vary in many details. But most programs include three steps: (1) definition of the problem, (2) collection and analysis of material, and (3) discovery of a solution.

Definition of the Problem, in applied research, means not only a careful statement of the specific problems. It also includes any limiting conditions, the ultimate objective of the research, and the proposed method of attacking the problem. The definition of the problem may be only a few sentences long, or it may be a statement of hundreds of words. A painstaking definition can result in a better understanding of the problem to be solved. It often saves months of useless effort.

For example, a manufacturer of power lawn mowers might want to improve his product so as to increase his sales. As a first step in defining the problem, he

Research Finds Answers to problems in science, industry, business, government, and daily living. These thousands of test tubes symbolize the painstaking care and the careful experimenting used by researchers in their hunt for knowledge.

Courtesy of Eli Lilly and Company

makes a customer survey that shows that the excessive noise of his lawn mower is causing him to lose sales. Therefore, his *specific problem* is to reduce the noise of his lawn mowers. In order to reach his *ultimate objective* of increasing sales, he decides that he cannot increase his selling price. Therefore, any improvements from research must not increase the manufacturing cost. This is the *limiting condition* on the changes he can make in the lawn mower.

A research worker further analyzes the problem and discovers that there are two main sources of noise—the engine and the spinning cutting blades. The researcher then outlines his *method of attack*, setting down the specific steps he will take in trying to reduce noise from these two sources.

Collection and Analysis of Material. The research worker collects important information that relates to his problem. He may gather part of this information by studying technical journals and books to see what is already known about the problem. A number of services provide *abstracts*, or summaries of major facts, from long, complicated articles. The researcher may gather other information by a careful examination of the properties or characteristics of related products or processes. Analysis of this material often leads to possible solutions of the problem.

In the lawn mower problem, the research worker would first search all the literature on noise and noise reduction for the results of any studies that might relate to his specific problem. This would include looking through books, issued patents, and magazines and other periodicals. He would also look for publications on the effect of noise on human beings that would give him information on the kind of noise that most annoys people.

Discovery of a Solution. After collecting and analyzing related material, the research worker develops possible solutions to the problem. At this stage, he often uses mathematical and statistical methods. High-speed computers have greatly reduced long computations in exploring solutions.

The selection of the most likely solutions often calls for experiments. For this purpose, the research worker uses such equipment as the electron microscope, the nuclear research reactor, and stress and strain gauges. Testing the most likely solutions usually requires further experiments.

Finally, the researcher carefully analyzes the experimental tests of the most probable solutions. With the goals of his research clearly in mind, he can choose the best solution or solutions to his problem.

In the lawn mower problem, the researcher found that he could do little to obtain a quieter gasoline engine. However, he could reduce the noise reaching the user by mounting the engine on rubber and enclosing it in an inexpensive metal box. Also, a simple change in the shape of the cutting blades made it possible to slow the rotation speed of the blades, thus decreasing the noise. The final result was a lawn mower that was quieter than any other on the market. The changes were possible with almost no increase in cost.

Research in Action

Agriculture. Research opens new frontiers in agriculture by helping to develop new instruments and processes. Through research, farming is being placed more and more on a scientific and regulated basis. Studies in problems of crop rotation and crossbreeding have produced larger and hardier fruits and vegetables. Research has provided special fertilizers that improve soils and give greater crop yields. Some new chemicals, such as insecticide sprays, protect crops. Other chemicals speed plant growth.

Agricultural engineers, biologists, botanists, and agronomists conduct research in agriculture. Farmers themselves help through cooperative programs. The federal governments of the United States and Canada and most state and provincial governments support research in agriculture. For example, the U.S. Department of Agriculture has many regional laboratories and field experimental stations (see AGRICULTURE, DEPARTMENT OF). Canada's Department of Agriculture has similar centers. Universities and research foundations often maintain greenhouses and farms for research in agriculture. Companies that produce farm materials and equipment also support this work. See AGRICULTURE (How Science Helps Agriculture).

Biological Sciences and Medicine. Research in the biological sciences and medicine constantly produces important scientific advances. For example, the Salk vaccine greatly reduced the number of cases of polio. Another vaccine for controlling Asiatic influenza was developed when the need became evident. Antibiotics of various kinds control and prevent infection. Work on nutrition results in new baby foods, improved animal feeds, and special diets for the sick. Research provides the means for better hospital care, including new surgical techniques and equipment.

Bacteriologists, biochemists, dietitians, doctors, and others conduct research in the biological sciences and in medicine. The United States government supports part of this work through the Department of Health, Education, and Welfare (see HEALTH, EDUCATION, AND WELFARE, DEPARTMENT OF). The Department of National Health supports and conducts much medical research in Canada. Universities, research foundations, and industry, particularly the *pharmaceutical*, or drug, companies, also support this research. Pharmaceutical companies sometimes spend up to 40 per cent of their earnings on research leading to new medical products.

Business operates on an advanced scientific basis as a result of research in economics, human relations, markets, and marketing. The study of relations between employers and employees improves the way of life of

235

RESEARCH

persons at all levels of business. Research has helped reduce drudgery, provide more leisure, and give workers a greater sense of accomplishment. Computers and mechanical controls speed operations and improve business accuracy. In studying the selling and buying of products, market research tries to predict the sales of items that may not even exist today. Advanced techniques in market research lead to better ways of distributing and selling (see ADVERTISING [Research]).

Business executives, economists, industrial engineers, psychologists, statisticians, and others conduct research in the field of business. Most of them work in industrial offices and laboratories, and at large universities. A director of research often is a member of a company's board of directors.

Education. Major advances at all levels of education result from research. For example, research in elementary schools and high schools showed that learning by straight memorization was inefficient. The research led educators to believe that students learn better and faster when they take an active part in their lessons and are motivated to learn. Educational research has also resulted in improved ways to teach such subjects as reading and spelling. Extensive research deals with methods for educating handicapped children. In colleges and universities, research on courses of study in science, engineering, and the humanities leads to better use of the student's time. Research in classroom methods explores many new teaching devices, such as television.

Educators, psychologists, sociologists, and other specialists conduct research in education. Support comes from universities and colleges, large foundations, and governments.

Industry and Engineering. Thousands of companies of all sizes maintain research laboratories or support research conducted by other organizations. This research results in thousands of new products and processes. It makes many kinds of the same product available to consumers. It developed *automation*, or timesaving automatic production methods (see AUTOMATION).

Industries rapidly apply new research tools and findings, such as nuclear reactors, to industrial uses. Many companies devote part of their research efforts to the development of new weapons for the U.S. Department of Defense (see DEFENSE, DEPARTMENT OF).

Engineers, mathematicians, and physical, chemical, and biological scientists work together to solve difficult industrial research problems. Industry itself pays for most of this research. The Department of Defense and other federal agencies contribute to industrial research to meet their own goals, and to aid basic studies in selected areas.

Mathematics and Physical Sciences. Research in mathematics advances rapidly, partly because of the contributions of high-speed computers. Researchers have invented whole new systems of mathematics to meet the needs of an age of space exploration.

Competition between the United States and Russia in launching satellites has stimulated research in many fields. Chemical studies of the properties of matter lead to new metals, such as titanium, molybdenum, and zirconium. These metals have unique properties that fill requirements created by rocket- and satellite-building programs. Exact measurements from geologists provide information about the earth necessary for these programs, and for other research activities. Research in physics expands at a rapid rate in such areas as nuclear physics, solid state physics, and ultrasonics. This research made possible nuclear power plants and transistor radios.

Mathematicians, astronomers, chemists, geologists, and physicists conduct research in the physical sciences. Their work takes place in university, government, and industrial laboratories, and in independent research institutions. Support for these projects comes primarily from industry, and from the federal governments of the United States and Canada.

Social Sciences. Anthropologists provide detailed information on peoples and cultures of all parts of the world. Social psychologists and sociologists constantly improve methods for describing and analyzing community life. Research in the social sciences has resulted

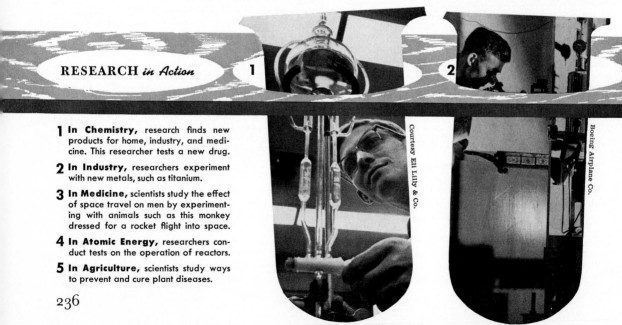

RESEARCH *in Action*   1   2

1 In Chemistry, research finds new products for home, industry, and medicine. This researcher tests a new drug.

2 In Industry, researchers experiment with new metals, such as titanium.

3 In Medicine, scientists study the effect of space travel on men by experimenting with animals such as this monkey dressed for a rocket flight into space.

4 In Atomic Energy, researchers conduct tests on the operation of reactors.

5 In Agriculture, scientists study ways to prevent and cure plant diseases.

Courtesy Eli Lilly & Co.

Boeing Airplane Co.

in such varied developments as guidance clinics for married couples and the recovery of art treasures from ancient civilizations.

Research in the social sciences often proves more difficult than similar work in the physical sciences. The large number of factors that must be studied and the difficulty of conducting experiments help cause this problem. For example, a chemist conducting research in a laboratory can isolate the factors he wants to study and remove all others. But a sociologist conducting research on juvenile delinquency must consider a young person's home life, school, neighborhood conditions, and many other factors that might affect him. These social factors are often difficult to identify and to separate from one another.

But researchers in the social sciences often use tools and information developed in the physical sciences. For example, high-speed data-processing equipment and advanced statistical methods help social scientists pinpoint the characteristics of a community, such as population and income. Archaeologists borrow techniques from physicists to find the age of remains.

Social scientists in all fields receive their support primarily from universities. Governments and foundations also give some help.

Research Institutions

Associations and Societies. Associations of industries that produce similar products often conduct research. This research aims at developing improved products or processes, or at standardizing a certain product. Groups of companies select and plan this kind of research, and benefit from it. For example, industrial groups may work with the research laboratories of the National Bureau of Standards (see NATIONAL BUREAU OF STANDARDS). This cooperation has produced valuable studies of the composition of petroleum and the improvement of automobile tires.

Professional societies, such as organizations of chemists, engineers, psychologists, or physicists, cover specific areas of knowledge. Sometimes these societies conduct basic research to find new knowledge, or applied research to benefit members of the groups. Societies also contribute to research by publishing journals that report research results. For example, the American Chemical Society publishes such journals as *Analytical Chemistry* and *Industrial and Engineering Chemistry*.

Foundations include great funds or trusts created by public-spirited men and women, and institutions such as the National Science Foundation, created by the U.S. government. They support and stimulate research in such institutions as universities, industrial companies, and private research organizations. They do not usually conduct research themselves. The foundations primarily support basic research, and are a principal source of funds for basic research in the United States. Canada also has several foundations that support research, including the Banting Research Foundation and the J. P. Bickell Foundation. See FOUNDATIONS.

Research Organizations. Many research organizations operate as part of various industries or of agencies of the federal government. Some employ thousands of workers. In the United States, government research organizations include the Public Health Service, the Atomic Energy Commission, and the regional laboratories of the Department of Agriculture. In Canada, important federal research organizations include the National Research Council and Atomic Energy of Canada Limited, a government-owned company.

Industrial research laboratories have produced such products as synthetic fibers through research in chemistry. Research by industry in chemistry and physics resulted in the transistor. Research by government made possible atomic energy and space exploration.

Independent research institutions serve industry, government, and the general public on a contract basis. They supplement the work of industry and government. Independent research institutions include the Battelle Memorial Institute, the Illinois Institute of Technology Research Institute, and the Stanford Research Institute.

Universities in all parts of the world provide pri-

RESEARCH

mary centers for basic research, and make many significant contributions to applied research. University research in atomic structure and nuclear fission led to improved scientific tools and new knowledge. These findings made possible the nuclear reactor and atomic power. Most of the basic information that resulted in high-speed computers came from university laboratories.

History

The search for knowledge is as old as man himself. Since the beginning of history, curiosity about the world and the desire for better things has led man to new knowledge and improvements in living. Prehistoric men discovered many of the tools and methods that made civilization possible. The ancient Babylonians, Egyptians, Greeks, and Romans accumulated a great store of knowledge about the world.

True research began in Europe during the 1500's. Before this time, men usually kept practical discoveries and theoretical knowledge separate. But men such as Galileo investigated nature, performed experiments, and discovered scientific laws. These men often worked as lone pioneers. Francis Bacon, an English philosopher and statesman, made one of the first pleas for organized research. He stressed the methodical collection of facts and the formulation of scientific laws from these facts.

Bacon's dream of organized research did not come true until the 1800's. The United States became one of the first leaders of this kind of research. Americans produced a number of inventions, many of which helped establish great industries. One of the greatest of these men, Thomas A. Edison, invented the electric-light bulb, the phonograph, and the motion-picture camera and projector. Edison's workshops and labora-

Pan American Petroleum Corp.

A Biological Researcher studies a tank filled with marine plants and animals to learn how life develops in the sea.

Field Museum of Natural History

Research in Archaeology provides clues to the life of ancient man. Here, researchers study relics in a museum.

Harvester World, International Harvester Co.

Library Research is important to basic and applied research. Libraries provide vital background information.

WORLD BOOK photo, courtesy Leo Burnett Co., Inc.

Motivation Research is used in advertising to find out why people buy. This researcher is testing two advertisements.

238

tories inspired many industries and universities to establish organized research programs and laboratories. For example, the Bell Telephone Company set up a research laboratory in the late 1800's, one of the first of its kind in the world. Many leaders saw that research had national importance. President Woodrow Wilson organized the National Research Council in 1916. Canada's National Research Council was founded the same year. These groups work to encourage and support organized research.

World War II stimulated a tremendous effort in all kinds of research. In the United States, the Office of Scientific Research and Development organized research. Men and women from many scientific and engineering fields worked together as teams. This teamwork helped perfect radar, rockets, and the atomic bomb.

Since World War II, research has expanded rapidly. Every industry encourages and supports research. With the help of government support, research laboratories and programs at universities and colleges continue to grow. The governments of all major countries are putting more and more stress on research, because of the expanding needs of an age of space exploration and atomic energy. See SCIENCE (History).

Careers in Research

Research is generally conducted by scientists, engineers, and scholars. These specialists usually have had advanced training in such fields as aerodynamics, astronomy, biology, chemistry, geology, mathematics, physics, psychology, or sociology.

Personal Qualities. In addition to formal training, a good research worker needs a high degree of curiosity, creativity, and imagination. Research is usually a painstaking process. The researcher must have patience and perseverance, because he must often make many attempts at solving a problem before he is successful. A research worker should have intellectual curiosity, and the ability to depart from standard methods to solve a problem. Above all, the successful researcher must be able to develop and try new ideas.

Research often requires the cooperation and assistance of scientists and workers in many fields. A research worker must be able to work with others. He must also be able to express himself well, so that he can communicate his findings to his teammates and to others who may use his results.

Opportunities. Industrial and independent research laboratories offer careers to college graduates with bachelor of science degrees in chemistry, engineering, physics, and other branches of science. Directors of research usually have doctor's degrees in their fields of specialization. Many organizations have training programs that may lead to executive positions. Former research workers occupy top management positions in industry.

Governments offer numerous career opportunities in research. Many jobs exist in fine, well-equipped government laboratories.

Universities need research workers in all professional fields and areas of knowledge. University research positions include basic research, as well as applied research in science, engineering, medicine, social science, and the humanities. The opportunity to work on a university campus has many recognized benefits, including the availability of good equipment and well-stocked libraries. HALDON A. LEEDY

Related Articles. THE WORLD BOOK ENCYCLOPEDIA contains information on research in articles on various branches of knowledge. See such articles as AGRICULTURE; BUSINESS; ENGINEERING; INDUSTRY; SCIENCE; SOCIAL SCIENCE, with their lists of Related Articles. See also the following articles:

Advertising (Research)	Merrill-Palmer Institute
Agricultural Experiment Station	Motivation Research
	Museum
Agricultural Research Service	National Academy of Education
American Council of Learned Societies	National Academy of Sciences
Battelle Memorial Institute	National Bureau of Standards
	National Science Foundation
Experimentation, Scientific	RAND Corporation
Instrument, Scientific	Stanford Research Institute
Invention	Statistics
Laboratory	Universities and Colleges
Library	(Research and Laboratory Work)

For advice on how to prepare a written or oral research report, see the section *How to Do Research* in the RESEARCH GUIDE/INDEX, Volume 22.

Outline

I. **Kinds of Research**
    A. Basic, or Fundamental, Research
    B. Applied, or Directed, Research
II. **Research Methods**
    A. Definition of the Problem
    B. Collection and Analysis of Material
    C. Discovery of a Solution
III. **Research in Action**
    A. Agriculture
    B. Biological Sciences and Medicine
    C. Business
    D. Education
    E. Industry and Engineering
    F. Mathematics and Physical Sciences
    G. Social Sciences
IV. **Research Institutions**
    A. Associations and Societies
    B. Foundations
    C. Research Organizations
    D. Universities
V. **History**
VI. **Careers in Research**

Questions

Why is research important in everyday life?

How does basic research differ from applied research?

What are two examples of applied research in industry?

In what ways do governments help research?

How do we benefit from agricultural research?

How has research helped fight disease?

What famous philosopher made one of the first pleas for organized research? When?

What are six important products or developments that have come from research?

Why is research in the social sciences often more difficult than similar work in the physical sciences?

What qualities are essential for a good research worker?

RESEARCH COUNCIL, NATIONAL. See NATIONAL ACADEMY OF SCIENCES.

RESERPINE. See RAUWOLFIA SERPENTINA.

RESERVATION, or RESERVE. See INDIAN, AMERICAN (Indians Today).

RESERVE OFFICERS TRAINING CORPS

RESERVE OFFICERS TRAINING CORPS (ROTC) trains students in schools, colleges, and universities to become officers in the United States armed services. It seeks to develop students for positions of military leadership during national emergencies. Qualified students take ROTC training in addition to their regular school or college work. All such training is given on campus, except for six weeks of field training between the student's junior and senior years in college.

Students enrolled in an ROTC unit are organized along military lines. One student serves as cadet commander, and others hold staff or command positions below him. The commissioned officer directing the unit usually has the title of professor of military science (for Army units), naval science (for Navy units), or air science (for Air Force units). His staff includes officers and enlisted men who teach courses, and others who handle the administration of the unit.

Army ROTC consists of two divisions. *Junior* units provide three years of basic military training in high schools. *Senior* units enroll students for two or four years in military schools, colleges, and universities. Course work includes drills, lectures, demonstrations, and field trips. The first two years of the senior course may be required for qualified male students. The last two years are voluntary. In the Advanced ROTC Course program, students may enter in their junior year. Instead of the regular first two-year program, they attend a qualifying basic training course in the summer before entering the advanced course. Students earn $50 a month in their junior and senior year training. The Army grants commissions as second lieutenant in the Army reserve to students who complete the four-year program and a summer of field training. It offers regular Army commissions to students designated as *Distinguished Military Graduates*. Each year the Army obtains about half of its new career officers in this manner. Upon graduation, the new officers may serve six months or two years on active duty, depending on the needs of the Army. The Army has ROTC units in over 280 colleges and universities and in about 580 high schools.

Navy ROTC, or Naval Reserve Officers Training Corps, has units in over 50 colleges and universities and in over 75 high schools. The senior course level has two types of training. The *regular NROTC* program provides selected high-school graduates with a four-year education paid for almost entirely by the government. These students must take two summer cruises as part of their ROTC course work. Upon graduation, they receive commissions as ensigns in the regular Navy or as second lieutenants in the regular Marine Corps. Under the Navy's *contract NROTC* program, students have the same course work as do those in the regular program. But they pay their own tuition, and receive a monthly subsistence of $50 during their last two years. They serve two years of active duty after receiving commissions as ensigns in the naval reserve. Graduates of the regular NROTC must serve for four years.

Air Force ROTC has both junior and senior programs that resemble those of the Army ROTC. College students take four years of part-time military training, and some summer field training at an Air Force base. They receive $50 a month during their last two years. Many graduates take flight training after graduation, including about 35 hours of flight operations and 35 hours of ground school. The newly appointed second lieutenants in the Air Force reserve must serve four years of active duty. Distinguished Military Graduates are offered commissions in the regular Air Force. In 1969, the Air Force began admitting women to ROTC programs at some universities. Air Force ROTC operates in over 170 universities and colleges and in about 145 high schools.

History. The ROTC has its origin in the Land Grant Act of 1862. The act authorized grants of public land to state colleges if they offered part-time military training for all able-bodied male students. The first actual reserve commissions were granted to students in 1908. The National Defense Act of 1916 established the first Army ROTC units. It set up an Officers Reserve Corps to be composed of men trained in the ROTC and in training camps. By the fall of 1916, the Army had enrolled about 40,000 students. In 1926, the Navy established its ROTC program, and set up units at six colleges and universities. The Air Force began its ROTC program in 1947, when it became an independent military service. In the late 1960's, the ROTC program of the Army, Navy, and Air Force had an enrollment of 382,000 students in about 1,300 high schools, colleges, and universities. CHARLES B. MACDONALD

RESERVES. See AIR FORCE, UNITED STATES (Air Force Reserves); ARMY, UNITED STATES (Regulars, Reserves, and National Guard Men); NAVY, UNITED STATES (Regulars and Reserves).

RESERVOIR is a place where large quantities of water are stored to be used for irrigation, power, and water supply. A reservoir may be either natural or artificial. Natural lakes form reservoirs from which many cities obtain their water supply.

An artificial reservoir is one that is built by man. Engineers can make a reservoir by building a dam across a narrow valley or by digging a basin in a level tract of land. Examples of reservoirs that are made by building dams are those of the Tennessee Valley Authority, Lake Mead behind Hoover (Boulder) Dam, and the reservoir behind Grand Coulee Dam. The size of a reservoir is measured in acre feet. Each acre foot contains 325,829 gallons.

A small reservoir that stores rain water for household uses is called a *cistern*. It is an underground basin that

ROTC Units train university and college students for positions as commissioned officers in the Air Force, Army, and Navy.

East Texas State College Photo Service

Black Star

Overflow Water from the Owyhee Reservoir and Dam in southeast Oregon rushes into the "Glory Hole" spillway, *center.*

may be built round or square, and any size desired. Cisterns should be lined with concrete to keep out underground water that contains organic matter, and surface water. But rain water gathers impurities as it passes through the air. Therefore, it should pass through a *filter* (screen) before entering the cistern.

Some small cities store their water in large tanks supported on a high framework. The framework is built higher than the highest buildings to create enough pressure to force the water to the tops of the buildings. Such tanks are often called *standpipes*.   R. G. HENNES

See also AQUEDUCT; DAM; IRRIGATION (How Water Reaches the Crops); WATER; WATER POWER.

RESHEVSKY, SAMUEL. See CHESS (Famous Players).

RESHT. See RASHT.

RESIN, *REZ in.* Resins form a class of vegetable substances used in varnishes, medicines, soaps, and paints. Natural resins have largely been replaced by synthetic resins (see RESIN, SYNTHETIC).

Natural resins may be divided into three main groups: (1) those that flow from plants as the result of wounds; (2) those extracted from wood by solvents; and (3) fossil resins found with the preserved remains of animals and plants. A scale insect of the acacia tree also produces a resin, which is called *lac.*

Resins do not dissolve in water. *Soft* resins are soluble in benzene or ether. *Hard* resins may be dissolved in vegetable oils after heating.

Gum resins, such as asafetida, aloe, myrrh, and the gum of the balsam tree are often used in medicines. *Rosin,* a resin obtained from several varieties of pine trees, is used in paints, varnishes, and soap. *Oleoresins* are resins combined with essential oils that are used in turpentine and tar.   C. L. MANTELL

Related Articles in WORLD BOOK include:

Amber	Balsam	Lac	Rosin
Balm of Gilead	Gum Resin	Mastic	

RESIN, SYNTHETIC, is any one of a large group of chemical compounds that includes most of our common

plastics. These resins may be made as fibers or films, or molded into a great variety of shapes, ranging from pocket combs to automobile bodies. Manufacturers use these compounds in paints and adhesives and as coatings for cloth, paper, and metal.

Synthetic resins are made up of many simple molecules linked together to form large, complex ones. Scientists call them *high polymers. Polymer* comes from the Greek words *poly,* meaning *many,* and *meros,* meaning *part.* The nature of synthetic resins is determined by the chemicals they contain and by the patterns of the new molecules. If long, fibrous molecules form, the substance is tough but dissolves easily and softens when heated. If the molecules form long chains with many crosslinks, the resin is hard, brittle, and sets when it is heated. If few crosslinks form, the resin usually is elastic, like rubber. Resins with short chainlike molecules are gummy or waxlike.

Manufacturers use coal, petroleum, limestone, wood, salt, air, and water to make synthetic resins. Complicated chemical processes change these common materials into a variety of chemicals such as alcohol, formaldehyde, glycerol, phenol, ethylene, ammonia, and urea. These substances are then combined in many ways to form the complex molecules of the resins.

Synthetic polymers vary greatly in composition, properties, and uses. Manufacturers often alter the original properties before making them into marketable items. They do this by combining or compounding the substances with fillers, colors, lubricants, and other materials and by heat treatment.   W. NORTON JONES, JR.

Related Articles in WORLD BOOK include:

Bakelite	Plastics	Silicone
Molecule	Polymer	Urea

RESISTANCE. See ELECTRIC CURRENT; STRENGTH OF MATERIALS.

RESONANCE. See SOUND (Resonance).

RESONANT JET. See JET PROPULSION (Pulsejet).

RESONATOR, *REZ oh NAY tur,* is the name of any device that *resounds* in response to a sound or musical tone. A hollow cylinder will act as a resonator. The body of a stringed instrument such as a guitar is a resonator.

RESORCINOL is a compound used in making ointments, dyes, and other useful chemical compounds. It is a colorless, crystalline phenol with the chemical formula $C_6H_4(OH)_2$ and is also known as *metadihydroxybenzene.* Resorcinol is prepared by fusing benzenedisulfonic acid with sodium hydroxide.

Resorcinol is added to ointments used to treat skin diseases such as acne and eczema. Hexylresorcinol is a general antiseptic. Chemists use resorcinol to make dyes such as *eosin,* a dye used in red ink. It is also important in resin adhesives.   JAMES S. FRITZ

RESOURCES, NATURAL. See NATURAL RESOURCES.

RESPIGHI, *res PEE gee,* **OTTORINO** (1879-1936), was one of the best-known Italian composers of the early 1900's. His style combines the impressionism of Claude Debussy, the colorful orchestration of Rimsky-Korsakov, and an Italian flair for melody. He helped revive interest in older music, as evidenced by his *Gregorian Concerto* (1922). His tone poems, *The Fountains of Rome* (1917) and *The Pines of Rome* (1924), are popular. Respighi was born in Bologna.   WILLIAM FLEMING

241

RESPIRATION

RESPIRATION is the taking in of oxygen and the giving off of carbon dioxide. All but a few living things must perform this function to maintain life. The *breathing* of human beings and of many animals is one form of respiration, called *external respiration*. The exchange of gases between the blood and other tissues in the body is another form of respiration, called *internal respiration*, or *tissue respiration*. A third form of respiration, called *cellular respiration*, occurs within the cell itself.

All living cells need oxygen in order to carry out their various functions. These functions stop quickly if the supply of oxygen fails. All living cells also produce carbon dioxide as a waste product. The carbon in food is combined with oxygen to form carbon dioxide plus heat and energy.

Respiration is necessary for cells of plants as well as those of animals. Plant leaves absorb oxygen and give off carbon dioxide, so that the "breathing" of a plant may be compared with that of a human being. However, in plants, an opposite process called *photosynthesis* occurs at the same time. In this process, the plant absorbs carbon dioxide and gives off oxygen (see PHOTO-SYNTHESIS).

External Respiration

In human beings and many animals, breathing continues constantly without conscious effort. A person can try to hold his breath for a while, but soon he reaches a point when he can no longer do so. Then the automatic, rhythmic breathing starts again.

Organs of Breathing. The lungs are the chief organs of breathing. They are two almost pyramid-shaped structures that lie in the chest, or *thoracic*, cavity. The spongy lung tissue is divided into many small air sacs called *alveoli*. The thin walls of the alveoli are filled with a network of tiny blood vessels called *capillaries*. Another organ important in respiration is the powerful, dome-shaped muscle called the *diaphragm*, which forms the floor of the chest cavity. Of equal importance are the ribs that form the chest cage and the muscles that move them.

Process of Breathing. Breathing is made up of two separate acts, *inspiration* (breathing in) and *expiration* (breathing out). The chest muscles act to expand and contract the chest cavity, causing the lungs to fill or empty. A pause occurs between inspiration and expiration. The pause is shorter during fast breathing.

Inspiration. For a person to breathe in, his chest must expand. The lungs fill the chest cavity completely, no matter how large it is. So when the chest expands, the lungs do also. This expansion lowers the air pressure inside the lungs, creating a slight vacuum that pulls air in from the atmosphere. To do this, the diaphragm contracts, pulling its dome downward. This provides more room in the chest cavity. At the same time, the muscles surrounding the ribs contract. The ribs move upward and outward, making the chest cavity expand frontward.

Expiration results when the process of inspiration is reversed. The muscles act to force out air, just as it is forced out when a bellows is closed. First, the diaphragm relaxes and resumes its dome shape, reducing the space in the chest. Then the rib muscles relax, lowering the ribs to make the chest cavity smaller. These combined actions squeeze the air out of the lungs.

Capacity of the Lungs. During ordinary breathing, each breath lets out and replaces about one-seventh of the air in the lungs. The new air mixes with the old air in the lungs. A person breathing quietly inhales and exhales about a pint of air at each breath. This amount, called *tidal air*, is enough for ordinary body functioning. When a person needs more air, such as when exercising, he can inhale about 4 quarts of air in each breath. This is known as the *vital capacity*.

Regulation of Breathing. Breathing is regulated by the brain. A group of cells in the brain form the *respiratory center*, which is extremely sensitive to carbon dioxide. When there is a slight increase in carbon dioxide in the blood, the center speeds up the impulses it sends to the muscles of respiration. This causes faster breathing. When the amount of carbon dioxide returns to normal, breathing also becomes normal.

How Blood Obtains Oxygen from the Air. When a person breathes in, air enters the alveolar sacs. Here, forming part of the wall of each tiny sac, is one of the richest networks of blood vessels in the whole body. The vessels are so small that the red blood cells are almost in single file as they pass through. Oxygen from the air passes through the exceedingly thin membrane that lines the air sac, and enters the red blood cells. Carbon dioxide from the blood escapes into the air sac and is expelled when the person breathes out. The blood carries the oxygen to the heart, which pumps it to all parts of the body. See BLOOD (Carrying Oxygen).

Internal Respiration

The blood stream acts as a transportation system, carrying oxygen to all the cells and carbon dioxide away from them. The exchange of these gases between the blood cells and the tissue cells is internal respiration.

The heart pumps blood containing oxygen to even the remotest parts of the body. As the blood flows through the body capillaries, the oxygen passes through the thin vessel walls into the tissue fluid and cells. At the same time, it picks up carbon dioxide and carries it back to the lungs to be discharged from the body.

Cellular Respiration

Cellular respiration is the name for certain chemical processes inside the cells. In these processes, oxygen is burned with various foods to give the cells energy. Living cells contain substances called *respiratory enzymes* that cause respiration to take place in the cells. Through an extremely intricate process, the enzymes act on oxygen and the foods in the cells to produce energy. Carbon dioxide is one of the waste products of cellular respiration.   ARTHUR C. GUYTON

Related Articles in WORLD BOOK include:

Artificial Respiration	Gill	Nose (with diagram)
Chest	Iron Lung	Sigh
Diaphragm	Lung	Windpipe

See also *Respiratory System* in the RESEARCH GUIDE/INDEX, Volume 22, for a *Reading and Study Guide.*

RESPIRATOR. See IRON LUNG.

RESPONSE. See LEARNING (How We Learn); REFLEX ACTION.

REST. See HEALTH (Rest and Sleep); SLEEP.

REST, in music. See MUSIC (The Language of Music).

HOW WE BREATHE

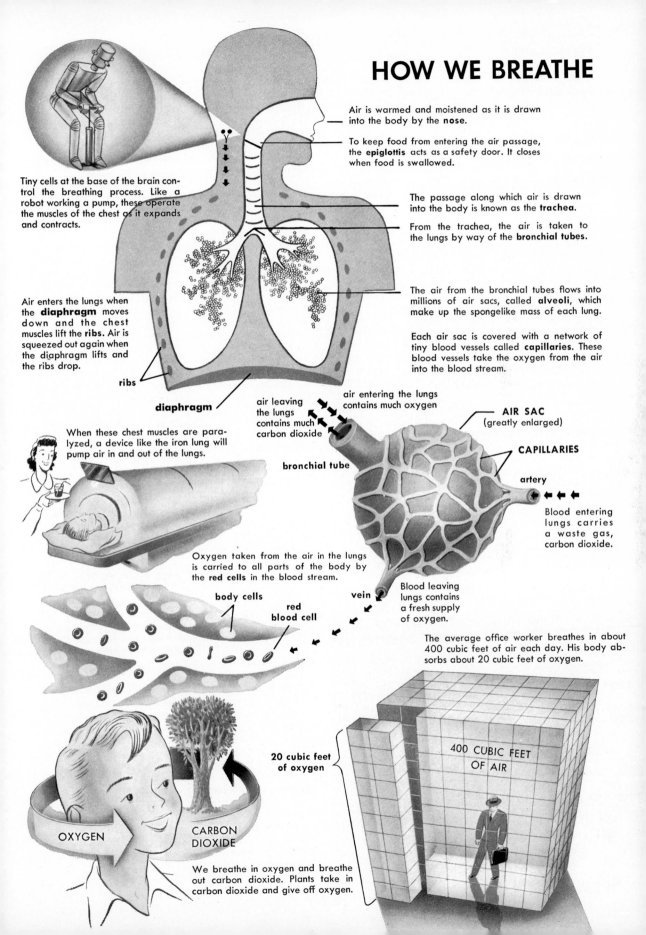

Tiny cells at the base of the brain control the breathing process. Like a robot working a pump, these operate the muscles of the chest as it expands and contracts.

Air is warmed and moistened as it is drawn into the body by the **nose**.

To keep food from entering the air passage, the **epiglottis** acts as a safety door. It closes when food is swallowed.

The passage along which air is drawn into the body is known as the **trachea**.

From the trachea, the air is taken to the lungs by way of the **bronchial tubes**.

The air from the bronchial tubes flows into millions of air sacs, called **alveoli**, which make up the spongelike mass of each lung.

Each air sac is covered with a network of tiny blood vessels called **capillaries**. These blood vessels take the oxygen from the air into the blood stream.

Air enters the lungs when the **diaphragm** moves down and the chest muscles lift the **ribs**. Air is squeezed out again when the diaphragm lifts and the ribs drop.

ribs

diaphragm

air leaving the lungs contains much carbon dioxide

air entering the lungs contains much oxygen

AIR SAC (greatly enlarged)

CAPILLARIES

When these chest muscles are paralyzed, a device like the iron lung will pump air in and out of the lungs.

bronchial tube

artery

Blood entering lungs carries a waste gas, carbon dioxide.

Oxygen taken from the air in the lungs is carried to all parts of the body by the **red cells** in the blood stream.

body cells

red blood cell

vein

Blood leaving lungs contains a fresh supply of oxygen.

The average office worker breathes in about 400 cubic feet of air each day. His body absorbs about 20 cubic feet of oxygen.

20 cubic feet of oxygen

400 CUBIC FEET OF AIR

OXYGEN

CARBON DIOXIDE

We breathe in oxygen and breathe out carbon dioxide. Plants take in carbon dioxide and give off oxygen.

RESTAURANT

RESTAURANT, *REHS toh ruhnt,* is a business establishment that serves meals to the public. Food restores the human body, so the place which serves food was named from the French word *restaurer,* meaning *to restore.*

In the 1600's, men gathered at the local inn to talk over the affairs of the world. They found that food and drink encouraged conversation. Through conversation, they learned of other cities and other countries, and gained new ideas. Gradually the eating part of the inn, called a *tavern,* began serving persons who were not staying at the inn. In time the tavern became a separate business. In England it was called a *coffeehouse,* and in France a *café,* meaning *coffee.*

The word *restaurant* was not used until after about 1750. At first it referred only to the eating section of a hotel, or to a coffeehouse patronized by the rich. But by the 1900's, the name had come to be used for several types of eating places. Today it is applied to almost any place that serves food and beverages.

Restaurants in the United States range from the small hamburger stand to the most expensive night club. They include hotel dining rooms, neighborhood restaurants and tearooms, sandwich shops, lunchrooms, cafeterias, automats, roadside eating places, and fountain lunches.

The sandwich shop as a rule does not serve standard meals. Its business is *à la carte,* which means *from the card.* The "card" in this case is the *menu,* or list of foods offered. It is sometimes called the *bill of fare.* The sandwich shop usually serves only simple dishes and desserts.

A *cafeteria* displays its food so that the patron may see what he is getting. He need only take his tray around the cafeteria counter and serve himself, or point out the items he wants. The first cafeteria in the United States, the Exchange Buffet, opened in New York City in 1885. The *automat* is a type of cafeteria that arose in Germany but has been popular in New York City. The various foods are behind windows ranged around the walls of the restaurant. To obtain a serving of a certain food, the customer drops one or more coins in the slot at the window. The window opens, and he takes his food.

The *fountain lunch* is popular with persons from all walks of life. The most common variety of fountain lunch is found in most drugstores. The name comes from the fact that such a place usually has a soda fountain. The first fountains served only soft drinks and ice cream. Gradually they started serving sandwiches, and today some feature entire meals. Fountains are particularly popular with office workers for noontime meals. They are also popular for between-meal snacks.

Chain restaurants have become widespread in both England and the United States. Often a single chain operates restaurants in a number of cities and towns. Many food-serving drugstores belong to chains. One of the most notable chain restaurants in the United States opened in New York City in 1948. It occupies four floors of a Rockefeller Center building, and is one of the largest service restaurants in the world. About 1,300 persons can be seated at one time. Dishwashing machines operate automatically. All the thousands of pieces of china, glassware, and silver can be washed in an hour.

Career Opportunities. There are many different kinds of work in the restaurant business, and many men and women are needed. Large hotels have restaurants that often employ a *chief steward,* or overseer. He is called a *maître d'hôtel.* Such a person must supervise every job in the kitchen and dining room. He has many responsibilities, from the planning and buying of all the food to the fixing of menu prices.

Large restaurants also hire dietitians. Such persons are skilled in the planning of meals and menus and in a knowledge of all types of foods and of food values. They must plan meals that both appeal to the appetite and give balanced nourishment. They also must choose foods that will appeal to their particular type of customers. A college education helps a person prepare for such work. Usually a study of home economics is necessary.

Every restaurant must employ a cook, or perhaps many cooks with one chief cook. The cook must know how to prepare many different dishes. The reputation of the restaurant depends largely on the tastiness of the meals served. Some restaurants serve only simple foods. Others serve foods and dishes that can be found in all parts of the world. Sometimes they become famous for the unusual foods they serve. Cooks in fashionable restaurants are usually called *chefs.*

Restaurants also provide work for many waiters and waitresses. Such persons must be able to stand hard work and sometimes long hours. In some restaurants they receive tips from the customers in appreciation of their services. The tip is usually 15 per cent of the price of the customer's meal. Many waiters make much more money from tips than from their wages.

Restaurants also sometimes employ hostesses, who supervise the seating of patrons. Many other persons are needed, including dishwashers, bus boys who clear the tables, and porters.   HELEN MARLEY CALAWAY

See also AUTOMAT; CAFETERIA; FOOD (pictures).

RESTAURANT EMPLOYEES INTERNATIONAL UNION. See HOTEL AND RESTAURANT EMPLOYEES AND BARTENDERS INTERNATIONAL UNION.

Roadside Restaurants throughout the United States provide convenient places for people to eat and relax while traveling.
Howard Johnson's

RESTIGOUCHE RIVER, *RESS tih goosh,* forms part of the boundary between the Canadian provinces of Quebec and New Brunswick. It is over 100 miles long (see NEW BRUNSWICK [physical map]). The Restigouche ranks as one of the most famous trout and salmon streams in the world. It flows through much forested wilderness. The Indian word *Restigouche* means *the river which divides like a hand.* The name refers to the five branches of the river, the Matapedia (meaning *musical*), Upsalquitch (*blanket*), Kedgwick (*large*), Patapedia (*little*), and Wagan (*knife*).   W. S. MACNUTT

RESTORATION was the period in English history that followed the return of the House of Stuart to the throne. The Puritan leader Oliver Cromwell, who had ruled as Lord Protector, died in 1658. His son Richard, who succeeded him, was a weak ruler, and civil war threatened England. But General George Monk seized control of the government, and restored the Stuart Prince Charles to the throne. The prince had lived in exile after the execution of his father Charles I in 1649. A new Parliament, elected in 1660, abolished Cromwell's government and restored the monarchy in the name of Charles II.

The English welcomed Charles back to the throne. On his journey to London, people everywhere greeted him with wild enthusiasm. His reign was dated back to the execution of Charles I, instead of the actual year of the restoration. Parliament re-established the Anglican Church as the official church of England and returned the property that had been taken from it. Parliament also passed many laws against the Puritans. Their worship was severely restricted, and their political rights were greatly limited.

During the Restoration period, extreme reaction set in against the strict morality of the Puritans. The court of Charles II became known for immorality and loose living. Men were valued not for their wisdom or integrity, but for their cleverness and wit.

The Restoration marked the return of royal power, but governmental power actually was divided between the king and Parliament. This division of power ended three years after Charles' death. The "Glorious Revolution" of 1688 sharply limited the king's power and gave Parliament greater power.   W. M. SOUTHGATE

Related Articles in WORLD BOOK include:

Charles (II) of England	Furniture (Late Jacobean,
Cromwell, Oliver	or Restoration)
England (The Restoration)	Monk, George
English Literature	Oates, Titus
(The Classical Age)	

RÉSUMÉ. See VOCATIONS (Getting a Job).

RESUMPTION OF SPECIE PAYMENTS. See SPECIE PAYMENTS, RESUMPTION OF.

RESURRECTION, *REZ uh REK shun,* is the return of the dead to life in bodily form. The Egyptians and other ancient peoples believed in a life after death. The belief in bodily resurrection finds expression in the Old Testament, and was defended by the Pharisees among the Jews at the time of Christ. The clearest picture of the Resurrection is given in the New Testament. Here the Gospel writers described Jesus' return to life. The best proof that Jesus did rise from the dead is the effect the event had on His followers. Only faith in a living leader can explain the courage and enthusiasm of the early Christians. The same faith is the reason that Christianity is so firmly followed to this day.

Museo del Prado, Madrid

The Resurrection, painted by El Greco, shows a serene Christ rising above figures overcome by awe and fear.

A discussion of resurrection in general is given by St. Paul the Apostle in I Corinthians 15. St. Paul asks, "How are the dead raised up? and with what body do they come?" Men have never found an answer to satisfy them completely, nor does St. Paul attempt to provide one. The Gospels describe Jesus after His resurrection as being glorified in His body. Jesus looked much as He did before His death. Most Christians believe that on the last day of the world all the dead will come to life. They call the day Judgment Day, because God will judge everyone.   FULTON J. SHEEN and MERVIN MONROE DEEMS

See also EASTER.

RESURRECTION PLANT is the name of several different plants that can be dried, but turn green again when they are watered. The dried stems curl into a tight ball. But they spread out when the plant is put into water. A common plant of this type is the *rose of Jericho,* a

245

A **Resurrection Plant** may look dry and dead, *left,* but moisture revives its greenness within a short time, *right.*

member of the mustard family. It is an annual plant, native to eastern Mediterranean regions. The mature plant loses its leaves and curls up like a ball with its seed pods inside, and blows across the land.

Another resurrection plant is *bird's-nest moss.* This plant reproduces by means of spores.

Scientific Classification. The rose of Jericho belongs to the mustard family, *Cruciferae.* It is genus *Anastatica,* species *A. hierochuntica.* Bird's-nest moss belongs to the selaginella family, *Selaginellaceae.* It is classified as genus *Selaginella,* species *S. leptophylla.* H. D. HARRINGTON

RESUSCITATOR, *ree SUSS uh TAY tur,* is a machine used to revive persons suffering from conditions that interfere with normal breathing. These conditions may result from paralysis, or may be the effects of shock, drowning, or inhaling gas or smoke. Most resuscitators have tight-fitting masks through which oxygen is forced into the lungs. One type, called the *bellows,* or *positive pressure, resuscitator,* blows oxygen into the lungs at pressures above atmospheric pressure. Another type

forces oxygen into the lungs at an increased pressure, then sucks it out at reduced pressure. An *inhalator* provides oxygen through a face mask at atmospheric pressure. It is used in addition to manual methods of artificial respiration. The *pulmotor,* an early type of resuscitator, is rarely used.

The *iron lung,* or *respirator,* works on the outside of the chest, using the principle of the bellows. By creating a vacuum, the iron lung forces the lungs to draw in air. When the vacuum is destroyed, the patient's chest contracts and forces the air out of his lungs, imitating normal breathing. BENJAMIN F. MILLER

See also IRON LUNG.

RESZKE, *RESH keh,* is the family name of two brothers who became famous opera singers. Both were born in Warsaw, Poland.

Jean de Reszke (1850-1925) was an operatic tenor. His first teacher was his mother. Later, he studied with Italian teachers. He made his operatic debut as a baritone at Venice in 1874. But it soon became obvious to him that baritone roles did not suit his voice. He left the stage for two years to perfect himself in tenor parts. De Reszke's first appearance as a tenor started him on a brilliant career. He was in constant demand in Europe. Later, he also sang in New York City with the Metropolitan Opera Company. Perhaps his greatest role was Tristan in Wagner's *Tristan and Isolde.* After he retired from the stage, he taught in France.

Edouard de Reszke (1853-1917), was a celebrated operatic bass. He trained largely in Italy, and made his debut in 1876 in Paris as the king in Verdi's *Aida.* Verdi himself conducted the performance. From 1891 to 1902, De Reszke sang with the Metropolitan Opera Company. He sang lyric, dramatic, and comic roles with equal ease. He spent his last years in Poland in poverty. SCOTT GOLDTHWAITE

RETAILER. See DISTRIBUTION.

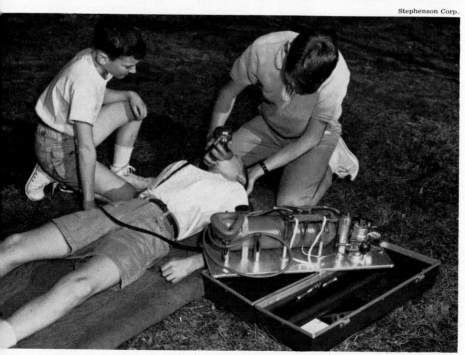

The Resuscitator has saved many lives by reviving persons whose breathing has been stopped by illness or injury. Oxygen flows from the resuscitator tank, through a face mask, into the stricken person's lungs.

RETAILING is the selling of goods in small quantities to household or ultimate consumers. The *retailer* serves as the last link in the series of middlemen through which goods move on their way from the manufacturer or farmer to consumers. Retailers combine most of the important functions of distribution (see DISTRIBUTION). They buy goods, and know more about consumer demand than any other middleman. They sell, and influence consumer selections. They store goods at places accessible to consumers. They divide larger lots of merchandise into units that consumers want. They finance by carrying goods in stock and paying operating expenses. They assume risks in owning goods and extending credit.

Retailers may be classified on the basis of (1) *ownership*, such as independent or chain; (2) *functions* carried out, such as self-service or cash-and-carry; (3) *location*, such as neighborhood or downtown; and (4) *goods handled*, such as general store or specialty shop.

The first retailers in the American colonies were trading posts where people bartered goods obtained from the Indians for products from Europe.

Types of Retailing

Specialty Stores usually handle a complete assortment of one line or a limited number of closely related lines of merchandise. Such stores can often supply any needs in their special lines. They handle such merchandise as books, sporting goods, electrical appliances, jewelry, hardware, or furnishings.

Department Stores developed in the United States during the late 1800's. Such stores have been described as city models of country general stores, because of the many lines of goods they carry. In their early days, they were often a consolidation of many small specialty stores under the same roof. In other cases, they developed as a result of expansion in the number of lines carried by dry-goods and furniture stores. A department store separates and departmentalizes each line of goods from the others. See DEPARTMENT STORE.

Mail-Order House is an American institution. It is a large concern selling a great range of merchandise directly to ultimate consumers by mail without the use of personal salesmen. Mail-order houses developed rapidly during the period from 1870 to 1900, when parcel post, improved express and freight service, and improved facilities for catalog printing made them more practicable. Since about 1910, mail-order houses have established branches and chains of retail department stores. See MAIL-ORDER BUSINESS.

Chain Stores, have been described as "mass distribution." They have had their greatest growth in the United States, beginning about 1860. Such organizations consist of a group of stores, sometimes several thousand in number, operating under the same ownership and management. Their greatest growth has been in groceries, drugs, automotive supplies, and clothing. The chief advantage of chain-store retailing is that the management can save money by buying and selling in large quantities. In recent years, *supermarkets* (chain groceries) have branched out in many other shopping lines. See CHAIN STORE.

Consumers' Cooperatives have had a steady growth in recent years, chiefly in rural areas. They market such products as groceries, oil, and gasoline. Several success-

ful consumers' cooperatives have developed in suburban areas. Their chief attraction to consumers is the patronage dividend based on the volume of purchases over a given period. See COOPERATIVE.

Direct Retailing, or house-to-house selling, accounts for a large volume of the retailing trade. The salesman may carry a small stock, or he may show samples, take orders, and make deliveries later. He has a smaller overhead and can offer the consumer greater convenience.

Vending Machines have also had a steady growth. They sell many types of small-sized, popular-demand, standard-quality merchandise such as candy, cigarettes, and soft drinks. They may be found at places where many persons pass or where they are convenient to a buyer when the desire arises for a particular article of merchandise. See VENDING MACHINE.

Careers in Retailing

Retailing offers opportunities for service to the public. Almost everything that is used in daily life is at some time bought and sold. Salesmen may work long hours for small pay. But top salesmen and sales managers often have high incomes. Many colleges offer courses in retailing, covering retail financing, advertising, sales promotion, buying, merchandising, management, and personnel administration. Graduates frequently begin in their own business after leaving college. Retail organizations often conduct their own training programs, and teach men and women how to sell and to assume management positions.   JOHN H. FREDERICK

See also DISCOUNT HOUSE.

RETAINER is a formal agreement between a lawyer and a client in which the lawyer agrees to take the client's case. This type of agreement is called a *special* retainer. There is also a *general* retainer, in which the lawyer agrees to act for the client whenever his services are needed. When a client retains a lawyer he usually pays him a *retaining fee*, which may also be called a retainer. After a lawyer has accepted a retaining fee he is legally bound to represent his client in the case. He cannot take a retaining fee from the other party to the case. A lawyer who accepts a general retainer cannot perform services for anyone else that would be against his client's best interests.   THOMAS A. COWAN

RETARDATION. See MENTAL RETARDATION.

RETARDED CHILDREN, NATIONAL ASSOCIATION FOR. See HANDICAPPED (table: Organizations).

RETCHING. See VOMITING.

RETICULUM. See RUMINANT.

RETINA. See EYE.

RETINITIS. See BLINDNESS (Diseases).

RETIREMENT PENSION. See PENSION.

RETRACTABLE LANDING GEAR. See AIRPLANE (Landing Gear).

RETREAT. See BUGLE (illustration).

RETRIEVER is a hunting dog trained to *retrieve* (find and bring back) game that has been shot. The dog has a coat of *guard hairs* (outer hairs), and an undercoat that protects it from water and cold. The retriever is a strong swimmer and has a fine sense of smell. It takes training easily. Dog breeders in the United States classify retrievers as sporting dogs. The five recognized breeds of

The Black Labrador Retriever is one of the most popular hunting dogs among the various breeds of retrievers.

retrievers are the *Chesapeake Bay*, the *curly-coated*, the *flat-coated*, the *golden*, and the *Labrador*. Each breed has an article in WORLD BOOK. MAXWELL RIDDLE

See also DOG (pictures; table: Sporting Group).

RETROLENTAL FIBROPLASIA (RLF), *REHT ruh LEHN tuhl FY bruh PLAY zhuh*, is an abnormal condition of the eyes of premature infants that causes almost complete blindness. In this condition, fibrous scar tissue forms a curtain behind the eye lens, shutting out light. RLF was discovered in 1940. During the 1950's, scientists found that excessive oxygen in the incubators caused the disease. Too much oxygen hinders growth of the tiny blood vessels that supply oxygen and food to the eye. Today, few premature babies get the disease.

RETROROCKET. See SPACE TRAVEL (Terms).

RETTING. See FLAX (Processing); HEMP; JUTE.

RÉUNION, *ree YOON yun* or *ray oon YOHN*, is an island in the Indian Ocean, about 400 miles east of the Malagasy Republic. For location, see WORLD (color map). Of volcanic origin, it covers 969 square miles. Saint Denis (pop. 65,614) is the capital.

Réunion's important products are vanilla, tobacco, tea, sugar cane, perfumes, and corn. The population of 472,000 consists largely of French Creoles, with some Indians and Chinese. Discovered by the Portuguese in the early 1500's, it was not settled until the French took possession in 1642. They named it *Bourbon*. The island received its present name in 1848. Since 1946, it has been an overseas department of France. EDWARD W. FOX

REUTER, *ROY tehr*, **BARON VON** (1816-1899), PAUL JULIUS REUTER, established Reuters, the first news service to furnish political and general news to European newspapers. After trying unsuccessfully to start an agency in Paris, Reuter began in 1849 to operate a pigeon post between the terminal points of the German and Belgian-French telegraph lines. Later, he settled in London, where he established Reuters as an agency to relay financial reports. Reuter was born in Kassel, Germany. See also REUTERS. JOHN TEBBEL

REUTERS, *ROY tehrz*, is an international news-gathering agency. It was owned by the British press until 1946. But since then Reuters has been in partnership with the national press organizations of Australia, New Zealand, and India. In addition, a close relationship exists with the newspapers of South Africa and Canada. Under an arrangement with the Associated Press, Reuters also serves many newspapers in the United States (see ASSOCIATED PRESS). Paul J. von Reuter founded Reuters as a financial service in Germany in 1849 (see REUTER, BARON VON). Later he moved to London, and started his news service in 1858. The Civil War was the first big news covered by Reuters. EARL F. ENGLISH

REUTHER, WALTER PHILIP (1907-1970), was president of the United Automobile Workers (UAW) from 1946 until his death in 1970. He began his work in the union when it was formed in 1935. Under his leadership, it pioneered in negotiated welfare and pension programs, guaranteed employment, and wage increases tied to productivity. He became an important labor spokesman.

Reuther was president of the Congress of Industrial Organizations (CIO) from 1952 to 1955. He led CIO negotiations in the no-raiding and merger agreement with the American Federation of Labor. After the merger in 1955, he was head of the AFL-CIO Economic Policy Committee and a member of the executive committee and executive council. He left these posts in 1967. Reuther's union withdrew from the AFL-CIO in 1968. In 1969, the UAW and the Teamsters formed the Alliance for Labor Action to organize nonunion workers. Reuther was born in Wheeling, W.Va. JACK BARBASH

REVAL. See TALLINN.

REVEILLE. See BUGLE (illustration).

REVELATION, *REHV uh LAY shuhn*, is the last book of the New Testament. In the English version it is called *The Revelation of Saint John the Divine*. It is also known as the *Apocalypse of John*. The Apostle John was supposed to have written it while he was in exile on the island of Patmos. Scholars now think, however, that it may have been written about A.D. 95 by some other man who used John's name. The material in the book comes from Christian, Jewish, and Babylonian sources. But the original text of the book was in Greek.

The first part of the Book of Revelation contains a message to the churches. The second part contains a series of visions of the future. The book was probably intended as encouragement to the persecuted Christians of western Asia Minor. They had refused to worship the emperor and were in great peril. The book was intended to show that Christ and His followers would soon be victorious over their enemies. FREDERICK C. GRANT

See also APOCALYPSE; FOUR HORSEMEN OF THE APOCALYPSE.

REVELS, HIRAM R. See NEGRO (Emancipation).

REVENUE, INLAND. See INLAND REVENUE.

REVENUE, INTERNAL. See INTERNAL REVENUE.

REVENUE CUTTER SERVICE. See COAST GUARD, UNITED STATES (History).

REVERE, *ree VEER*, Mass. (pop. 43,159; alt. 15 ft.), is a residential and resort city six miles northeast of Boston. Its amusement parks and greyhound race track, and its excellent beach facing Massachusetts Bay, attract thousands of visitors every summer. At the time of its settlement, shortly before 1630, it was known as Rumney Marsh and was part of Boston. It separated from Boston in 1739, and was named Revere in 1871. It has a mayor-council government. WILLIAM J. REID

PAUL REVERE

Culver

On His Famous Midnight Ride, Paul Revere dashed across the countryside to warn the people that the British were coming.

REVERE, PAUL (1735-1818), was an American patriot who, in April, 1775, carried news to Lexington of the approach of the British. He warned the patriot leaders Samuel Adams and John Hancock of their danger, and called the men of the countryside to arms. His exploit inspired Henry Wadsworth Longfellow's "Paul Revere's Ride," one of the most popular poems in American literature. Revere later made great contributions during the Revolutionary War and aided the industrial growth of the United States.

His Early Life. Paul Revere was born on Jan. 1, 1735, in Boston, Mass., the son of a silversmith. His family was of French Huguenot descent, and Paul's father changed the family name from Rivoire "merely on account that the Bumpkins should pronounce it easier." Paul studied at North Grammar School in Boston, and learned the silversmith's trade. In 1756, he served for a short time in the French and Indian War. Then he married Sarah Orne, and entered his father's business.

The Patriot. Revere soon became interested in the movement for independence. He engraved a number of political cartoons that received wide attention. As the leader of the Boston craftsmen, he met such revolutionary leaders as Samuel Adams and John Hancock. Revere was one of the 50 workers who took part in the Boston Tea Party on Dec. 16, 1773.

Revere also served as a special messenger for the Boston patriots. He was so familiar to the British in this role that his name appeared in London journals before his famous ride. Two days before the ride took place, he galloped to Concord to warn patriots there to move their military supplies.

Paul Revere's Ride. In 1775, General Thomas Gage, the British commander in chief of the Massachusetts

Bay Colony, was instructed to enforce order among the colonists. He ordered Lieutenant Colonel Francis Smith to Concord with a detachment of 700 men to destroy the supplies there and to arrest Adams and Hancock.

Smith began to assemble his force on Boston Common on the evening of April 18. His orders were secret, but the patriots had learned about them. Joseph Warren, a patriot leader, sent Revere and William Dawes to warn Adams and Hancock in Lexington and the patriots in Concord. They arranged for a signal to be flashed from the steeple of the Old North Church. Two lanterns would mean that the British were coming by water, and one, by land. Contrary to Longfellow's account, the signal was not sent to Revere. Instead, Revere directed that the signal be sent to friends in Charlestown.

Revere left Boston at about 10 P.M., and arrived in Lexington at midnight, riding a borrowed horse. He warned Adams and Hancock. At 1 A.M., Revere, William Dawes, and Dr. Samuel Prescott left for Concord. A British cavalry patrol surprised them on their way. Prescott and Dawes escaped, but Revere was captured. Only Prescott got through to Concord. The British released Revere, and let him return to Lexington without his horse. There he joined Adams and Hancock, and they fled to safety in Burlington. But Revere returned to Lexington to rescue valuable papers in Hancock's trunk. When the British arrived in Lexington on April 19, they found the minutemen waiting for them.

Revolutionary Soldier. From 1776 to 1779, Revere commanded a garrison at Castle William in Boston Harbor. In 1779, he commanded artillery in the disastrous Penobscot Expedition, an attempt to invade British territory in Maine. This move cost Massachu-

PAUL REVERE

PATRIOT

Besides his famous "midnight ride," Revere was active in many important events before, during, and after the Revolution. He was closely associated with Adams and Hancock.

CRAFTSMAN

The son of a silversmith, he learned the trade so well that many of his works are now regarded as masterpieces of his craft. He was known as a good businessman.

He was a Lt. Colonel of a Massachusetts artillery regiment.

He played an important part in the Boston Tea Party.

He worked hard for ratification of the Constitution.

"The Boston Massacre" was one of his famous engravings.

He cast bullets and cannon during the war—and, later, church bells.

He invented a process for rolling sheet copper.

---

setts almost its entire trading fleet and more than 1,000,000 pounds in inflated currency. Revere was accused of cowardice and insubordination in the disputes that followed the expedition, but a court-martial cleared him. He left the service in some disrepute, however.

Craftsman and Industrialist. When the war started, Revere learned to manufacture gunpowder. He designed and set up a mill at Canton, Mass. He also designed and printed the first issue of Continental paper currency, and he made the state seal still used by Massachusetts. Revere cast bronze cannon for the army.

After the war, Revere returned to his silversmith trade in Boston. Craftsmen still copy the graceful lines of his work. He marked his own work with the name *Revere* in a rectangle or with the initials *P.R.* He developed considerable skill in engraving copper plates for printing and engraving. He cast cannon and bells in bronze, and many of his bells are still used in New England. He made the copper fittings for the frigate U.S.S. *Constitution* ("Old Ironsides").

Revere was the first American to discover the process of rolling sheet copper, and built the first copper-rolling mill in the United States. Until his time, all sheet copper had to be imported.   ROBERT J. TAYLOR

See also ANTIQUE (picture: Paul Revere Sugar Bowl and Stand); BOSTON (The Freedom Trail; picture: Paul Revere's House); BOSTON MASSACRE (picture); UNITED STATES, HISTORY OF (picture: Paul Revere's Cartoon). For a *Reading and Study Guide on Paul Revere*, see the RESEARCH GUIDE/INDEX, Volume 22.

REVERSING FALLS OF SAINT JOHN. The odd sight of a river current flowing backward over a falls may be

seen in the Saint John River at Saint John, New Brunswick, just before the river enters the Bay of Fundy. Here the Reversing Falls are formed as the river valley becomes a narrow gorge. At low tide the river falls 17 feet in going through this gorge to the harbor below. At high tide, however, a *bore*, or rushing tide, sweeps in from the bay and makes the level of the harbor water 5 feet higher than the level of the river. The current through the gorge then flows upstream and up over the falls. Steamers can pass the gorge only for a brief period, between the ebb and the flood.   W. S. MacNUTT

See also NEW BRUNSWICK (picture).

REVERSION. See ATAVISM.

REVIEWING. See CRITICISM; BOOK REVIEW.

REVIVAL OF LEARNING. See HUMANISM; RENAISSANCE.

REVIVALISM is a Protestant approach to religion that emphasizes individual religious experience rather than the doctrines of a church. In the United States, revivalism has been associated with frontier camp meetings, outdoor religious services, and fervent, emotional preaching (see CAMP MEETING).

Periods of revivalism occurred in Europe among German Pietists and English Methodists during the 1700's. The first major revival movement in the United States was the Great Awakening, which began in the 1720's. It took place primarily within Congregational and Presbyterian denominations along the East Coast (see GREAT AWAKENING). A second Great Awakening occurred from about 1790 to about 1810. During the mid-1800's, the Baptists and Methodists were the chief denominations that used revivalistic methods. The leading revivalists of this period included Peter Cartwright and Charles G. Finney.

During the late 1800's and early 1900's, many preachers, including Dwight L. Moody and Billy Sunday, brought frontier revivalism to growing U.S. cities. In the mid-1900's, the revivalist tradition has been carried on by such preachers as Billy Graham.   ROBERT L. FERM

See also CARTWRIGHT, PETER; FINNEY, CHARLES G.; GRAHAM, BILLY; MOODY, DWIGHT L.; SUNDAY, BILLY.

REVOLUTION is a term that generally refers to a fundamental change in the character of a nation's government. Such a change may or may not be violent. Revolutions may also occur in other areas, including cultural, economic, and social activities. People who work to replace an old system with a new one are called revolutionaries.

Kinds of Revolution. A political revolution may change various ways of life in a country, or it may have no effect outside the government. For example, the Russian Revolution of 1917 not only deposed the czar but also began major social changes, such as the elimination of private property. On the other hand, the Revolutionary War in America (1775-1783) changed a political system without causing basic social changes.

Some revolutions last for many years. The Chinese Communists fought for 22 years before defeating the Nationalist Chinese government in 1949. This revolution involved widespread guerrilla warfare, a popular form of combat among modern revolutionaries. See CHINA (History); GUERRILLA WARFARE.

Some political movements that appear to be revolutions do no more than change a country's rulers. Many Latin-American political uprisings have replaced dictators without making fundamental changes in governmental systems. Political scientists call such movements *rebellions* rather than revolutions. However, a rebellion may lead to a political or social revolution. See COUP D' ÉTAT; JUNTA.

Many revolutions involve illegal uprisings, but some occur after a legal transfer of power within the existing system. For example, Adolf Hitler took power as dictator of Germany soon after the country's president had appointed him chancellor.

Some of history's most widespread revolutions did not have political beginnings. The Industrial Revolution of the late 1700's and early 1800's changed the basic nature of Western society from rural to urban (see INDUSTRIAL REVOLUTION). The invention of the telephone, and other advances in technology and communications during the late 1800's and the 1900's, have also caused revolutions in industry and everyday life.

Causes of Revolution. Most revolutions occur because serious problems have caused widespread dissatisfaction with an existing system. Poverty and injustice under cruel, corrupt, or incapable rulers may contribute to revolution. But in most cases, social problems alone do not cause revolutions. They lead to despair rather than a willingness to fight for something better. Revolutions need strong leaders who can use unsatisfactory conditions to unite people under a program that promises improvements.

Many revolutions occur after rulers begin to lose confidence in themselves and yield to various demands from their rivals. Such compromises by rulers, or rapidly improving social conditions, create a *revolution of rising*

expectations as people begin to see hope for a better life. If changes do not keep pace with their expectations, the people lose faith in their rulers and start listening to revolutionary leaders. The French Revolution of 1789 and the Russian Revolution both began after the rulers agreed to the people's demands for representative assemblies. The Hungarian Revolution of 1956 occurred after the government released some of its strongest opponents from prison.

Not all revolutions have led to improved conditions. Some revolutionaries have worked for change only to gain political power for themselves. A number of conservative rulers have called themselves revolutionaries simply to convince the public that they support social and economic changes.   GUENTER LEWY

See also FRENCH REVOLUTION; REVOLUTION OF 1848; REVOLUTIONARY WAR IN AMERICA; RUSSIA (History).

REVOLUTION, CENTURY OF, is the name given the hundred years beginning with the American Revolutionary War. It was a period of world-wide revolt against tyrannical governments, and of progress in liberty and constitutional government.

REVOLUTION OF 1830. See JULY REVOLUTION.

REVOLUTION OF 1848 was actually a series of popular uprisings which spread through all the countries of Europe at the end of the 1840's. Liberals and socialists led the risings against undemocratic rulers. The unrest increased emigration to the United States.

The great revolutionary movement began in France in February, 1848. French republicans demanded that King Louis Philippe establish a government that would benefit the working class. Angry citizens invaded the French Assembly. They forced the king to flee, and proclaimed the Second French Republic. The disagreements about reforms for the working people continued and, in June, there were bloody street battles in Paris. Later in 1848, Louis Napoleon was elected president of the Republic.

The February Revolution in France encouraged uprisings in Germany, Austria, and Italy. The people of Vienna rose against Prince Metternich and forced him to flee the country. By the end of March, 1848, the people of Hungary had won a new and liberal constitution. Emperor Ferdinand of Austria was forced to abdicate. He was succeeded by Francis Joseph, who adopted more liberal policies. In Italy, citizens drove the hated Austrian troops from some of the Italian cities. Sardinia was granted a constitution. In Germany, the people wanted a constitutional government and a united country, which would include German-speaking Austria. But a constitutional assembly which met at Frankfurt failed when King Frederick William IV of Prussia refused to accept the crown of the proposed new Germany. German unity was not reached until the early 1870's.

The Revolution of 1848 is important for its influence on the course of European development. The uprising in France marked the beginning of a new class struggle. A powerful movement known as socialism took up the rights of the workers. The Frankfurt Assembly popularized the idea of German unity. The Revolution also was an important step in bringing about the dual monarchy of Austria-Hungary.

See also METTERNICH, PRINCE VON.

Revolutionary War

MINUTEMAN
AT LEXINGTON

THE BATTLE OF BUNKER'S HILL by John Trumbull

REVOLUTIONARY WAR IN AMERICA gave birth to a new nation. Thirteen British colonies won their freedom and became the independent United States of America. The war began on April 19, 1775, when a group of colonists fought British soldiers at Lexington, Mass. Hours later in nearby Concord, colonists fired "the shot heard round the world" when they battled British troops near a bridge. The war lasted eight years.

The news of war shocked people in both the American colonies and England. But ill-feeling between the British government and its colonies had been gradually developing for more than 10 years. After gaining control of the French empire in North America in 1763, the British had tried to restore their authority over the American colonies and to tax them more heavily. The Americans, who had enjoyed a large measure of self-

government, wanted even greater freedom from British control. They refused to pay the Stamp Tax of 1765 and the Townshend duties on imports in 1767. Citizens of Boston organized a "tea party" in 1773 to dump incoming tea into the harbor rather than pay a tax on it. Britain sent troops to support its authority.

The First Continental Congress demanded that the British abandon their efforts to make Massachusetts bow to British authority. It asked Britain to admit that parliament had no right to tax the colonists for revenue. But the British government considered Massachusetts and its neighbors to be in rebellion. British troops in Boston were ordered to take swift action.

The Second Continental Congress adopted the Declaration of Independence on July 4, 1776. Ties between the colonies and the mother country had now been cut.

THE LIBERTY BELL
AT PHILADELPHIA

Reproduced by permission of the Yale University Art Gallery

Battle of Bunker Hill in 1775, the war's first major battle, actually took place on Breed's Hill, near Boston. The British drove the patriots from the hill after three assaults.

Britain launched a great offensive to crush the rebellion. A British army under Lt. Gen. William Howe assembled at New York. Gen. George Washington, who had taken command of the Continental Army, slowly withdrew his men in face of the British attacks. The patriots forced Lt. Gen. John Burgoyne and his army to surrender at Saratoga in 1777. They gained an active ally in 1778, when France recognized the independence of the United States and entered the war. Spain declared war on Britain in 1779, and Holland did so in 1780.

Faced by so many enemies, Britain found it difficult to assemble an army powerful enough to destroy the patriot forces. Lt. Gen. Charles Cornwallis tried to conquer the Southern States after Lt. Gen. Sir Henry Clinton captured Charleston, S.C., in 1780. But he found himself checked by Maj. Gen. Nathanael Greene

in the far south. Cornwallis then concentrated his forces at Yorktown, Va. A French fleet cut him off there, and Washington's army of American and French soldiers attacked. On Oct. 19, 1781, Cornwallis' army surrendered at Yorktown in the war's last major action.

The Revolutionary War did not involve large numbers of men. It was a small war compared with modern ones. The size of the fighting forces rarely exceeded 15,000 men. Both the patriots and the *redcoats*, or British soldiers, relied chiefly upon the musket and bayonet. But some Americans used rifles. Britain also hired mercenaries, or soldiers paid to fight its battles, notably the *Hessians* from Germany. At sea, American privateers captured British ships. About a fourth of the colonists supported the redcoats. These Loyalists, or Tories, stirred the bitter hatred of the patriots.

253

POLITICAL CONFLICTS
AND ECONOMIC RIVALRY

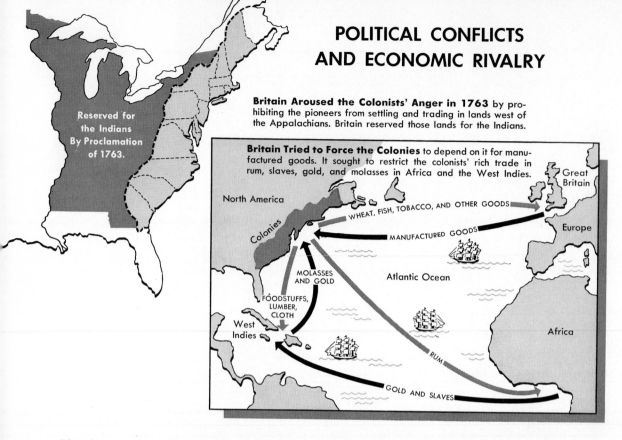

Reserved for the Indians By Proclamation of 1763.

Britain Aroused the Colonists' Anger in 1763 by prohibiting the pioneers from settling and trading in lands west of the Appalachians. Britain reserved those lands for the Indians.

Britain Tried to Force the Colonies to depend on it for manufactured goods. It sought to restrict the colonists' rich trade in rum, slaves, gold, and molasses in Africa and the West Indies.

Great Britain

North America

Europe

Colonies

WHEAT, FISH, TOBACCO, AND OTHER GOODS

MANUFACTURED GOODS

MOLASSES AND GOLD

Atlantic Ocean

FOODSTUFFS, LUMBER, CLOTH

West Indies

Africa

RUM

GOLD AND SLAVES

After the surrender at Yorktown, Great Britain gave up all hope of conquering the patriots. On Sept. 3, 1783, it recognized the new republic in the Treaty of Paris, formally ending the Revolutionary War.

Causes of the War

After the French and Indian War ended in 1763, the British gained the entire French empire in North America (see FRENCH AND INDIAN WARS). At this time, the American colonists were undoubtedly loyal to their "mother country." Yet, only 12 years later, the Americans rebelled against British rule. Historians do not entirely agree on the reasons for this change of attitude. But, as John Adams later wrote: "The Revolution was effected before the war commenced. The Revolution was in the minds and hearts of the people."

Political Conflicts. Space and time helped set the colonies apart from the British Isles. The colonists found that industry, thrift, and courage brought greater rewards in America than in England. They did not have to depend upon others for a livelihood. The colonists could care properly for their families and felt that the future would be bright. They were apt to be self-reliant, optimistic, and independent-minded. Social position and wealth usually determined what a person could or could not do in English society. For example, a poor person in England could hardly hope to own land. But the colonists could easily obtain land.

The typical American of the 1700's belonged to a farm-owning family. People living in towns or villages were usually craftsmen or tradesmen who earned good wages. The American colonies had aristocratic planters

and merchants. But these men enjoyed neither the respect nor the power of members of the British aristocracy. Their influence was diminishing as war approached. The colonists tried to gain control of their local affairs. In Connecticut and Rhode Island, they controlled the legislative, executive, and judicial branches of government. In the other colonies, they dominated the legislative branch. Through this control, they chipped away at the authority of British-appointed officials. See COLONIAL LIFE IN AMERICA.

Economic Rivalry. British laws controlled the overseas trade of the colonies. The colonists did not bitterly resent this restriction until the Revolutionary crisis began developing. They were not seriously offended by British laws that limited colonial manufacturing. The colonists evaded these laws if they had to do so. British officials were often lax in enforcing laws, and the more energetic ones could often be bribed.

British policy regarding the colonies took a sharp turn in 1763. Political leaders in London decided to maintain a standing army in North America, and proposed to support this army by taxing the colonists. They began to enforce acts covering colonial trade and navigation. As a result, parliament passed the Sugar Act of 1764 and the Stamp Act of 1765. It also tried to manage Indian affairs from London, and to slow down the westward expansion of the colonies. The British hoped to tighten their grip, and the Americans resisted.

Events Leading to the Revolution

War exploded in the colonies as a result of an order by the British cabinet to Lt. Gen. Thomas Gage, commander in chief in North America. On Apr. 14, 1775, Gage received orders to use force in Massachusetts. He sent 700 troops to destroy military supplies that the patriots had gathered at Concord. The opening clash between redcoats and militiamen erupted on April 19. But a series of acts preceding this bloodshed provided the immediate cause of war.

Acts of 1763. The first such important act was the British decision to keep a standing army in North America. The British government did not consult the colonists about this move. It had intended that the army provide protection against French, Spanish, and Indian attacks. But the army became available for use against the colonists.

The proclamation of Oct. 7, 1763, aroused further American discontent. It recognized the Indians as owners of the lands they had occupied. It also prohibited settlement west of the Appalachian Mountains. The British hoped to prevent Indian wars, and to keep Americans on the seacoast from manufacturing goods for settlers who pushed beyond the mountains. Pioneers who wanted to settle in the Mississippi Valley deeply resented the order. Colonial land speculators who hoped to obtain estates in the west for their children also bitterly opposed the proclamation. The British later softened these restrictions. But the colonists came to believe that these limits were unjust and illegal.

The Navigation Acts became more serious grievances. British Prime Minister George Grenville (1712-1770) ordered customs officers to enforce strictly the laws regulating colonial shipping (see NAVIGATION ACT). In 1764, Grenville also pushed through parliament the Sugar, or Revenue, Act. This law levied a three-penny tax on each gallon of molasses brought to the colonies from West Indies islands of other countries. Grenville hoped to persuade the colonists to buy molasses from planters in the British West Indies. He also wanted to collect taxes from colonists who continued to buy molasses from the French and the Spaniards. The British could have seriously hurt colonial commerce if they had enforced the Sugar Act. But in 1766 the British government reduced the duty to one penny a gallon on all molasses, British or foreign.

The Quartering and Stamp Acts. In 1765, Grenville prodded parliament into passing two other laws that further angered the colonists. The Quartering Act required Americans to provide quarters, fuel, candles, cider or beer, and transportation for British troops stationed in the colonies. Many colonists considered the law an illegal way of taking money from them without their consent. The Stamp Act required colonists to buy tax stamps and place them on newspapers, playing cards, diplomas, and various legal documents. It came as the final blow to the angry colonists. They refused to allow stamps to be sold, crying that "Taxation without representation is tyranny!" Faced with general defiance, parliament repealed the Stamp Act in 1766. But at the same time, parliament passed the Declaratory Act, which claimed full British authority over the American colonies. See STAMP ACT.

The Townshend Acts. Another crisis occurred in 1767, chiefly because of the Townshend Acts. Chancellor of the Exchequer Charles Townshend persuaded parliament to place duties on tea, paper, lead, and paint imported into the colonies. He assumed that the colo-

nists, feeling internal taxes to be unconstitutional, would have no legal objections to taxes for revenue collected in their ports. But most colonists considered the Townshend taxes to be the same in principle as the hated Stamp Tax. They began a boycott, refusing to buy British goods. Parliament repealed the Townshend duties in 1770, except for the tax on tea. It kept that tax to show that Britain claimed the right to levy taxes for revenue.

The Boston Massacre. Before Britain gave in to other demands of the colonists, serious unrest developed in Boston. The British had sent troops to garrison the city. A fatal clash between redcoats and townspeople occurred on the night of March 5, 1770, on King's Street (now State Street). Some boys had been throwing snowballs at a British sentry. An uproar resulted and, in the clash that followed, a mob of men and boys threatened the soldiers with clubs and stones. The British troops fired into the crowd, killing three men and wounding eight others. Two of the wounded later died. See BOSTON MASSACRE.

Committees of Correspondence. The foremost leaders of the opposition to British policies included Samuel Adams and James Otis. In 1772, Adams persuaded Boston to appoint a committee of correspondence to explain to other towns and to the world the rights of the colonies, and to show how Britain had violated these rights. Committees were established throughout New England. See COMMITTEES OF CORRESPONDENCE.

The Tea Act. In 1773, parliament passed the Tea Act. It enabled the English East India Company to pay the Townshend tax and still sell tea cheaper in the colonies than could the Dutch, who had been smuggling tea into colonial ports. The colonial leaders felt that Americans would buy English tea because of its lower price. But then they would lose their argument of taxation without representation. Energetic leaders in Boston organized the *Boston Tea Party.* On Dec. 16, 1773, a band of colonists disguised as Indians raided British ships in Boston harbor, lifted boxes of tea from their holds, and tossed them overboard. See BOSTON TEA PARTY.

A Revolutionary Cartoon pictured a horse, representing the 13 American colonies, throwing its rider, Britain's King George III.
Library of Congress

British Troops landed in Boston after Great Britain decided to keep a standing army in the American colonies.

Quartering Act forced colonists to provide quarters, fuel, candles, and transportation for British soldiers.

Navigation Laws greatly restricted colonial trade. They covered the types of goods colonists could import, the duties they had to pay, and the methods of transporting such goods.

The Intolerable Acts. The British government decided that something drastic had to be done to assert its authority. It passed the Intolerable, or Coercive, Acts in 1774. These new laws closed Boston harbor to commerce until the city showed repentance for its "tea party." The laws also provided for increased British authority in Massachusetts. Boston and Massachusetts refused to pay for the destroyed tea. When Gage, who was governor of the colony, arrived in Boston with troops, colonists rioted outside the city. Gage avoided immediate conflict. He informed the British cabinet that Massachusetts had revolted and asked for orders.

The First Continental Congress met in Philadelphia in September, 1774, to defend American rights. It denounced many laws passed by parliament since 1763 as violations of the rights of British colonists. It agreed not to import any goods from Britain or Ireland after Dec. 1, 1774, and not to export anything to the British Isles or the West Indies after Sept. 10, 1775, unless the abuses had been corrected. The congress wanted only liberty for the colonies. The movement for full independence from Britain soon began to develop. Patrick Henry sounded the rallying cry: "I know not what course others may take; but as for me, give me liberty, or give me death!" See CONTINENTAL CONGRESS.

The Restraining Act. Parliament declared Massachusetts, Rhode Island, and Connecticut to be in rebellion. It passed the Restraining Act, barring colonists there from fishing on the Grand Banks of Newfoundland and from trading abroad, except with Britain and the British West Indies. It encouraged the use of force.

The cabinet then ordered Gage to arrest the colonial leaders in Massachusetts, break up the "mobs," organize a Tory militia, and use the troops in Boston. Gage sent troops from Boston on the fateful night of Apr. 18, 1775. But Paul Revere rode across the countryside, warning his fellow patriots of the danger.

Men, Battlefronts, and Strategy

At first glance, the colonists could hardly hope to win the war that followed. They could not challenge the British fleet that loosely blockaded the Atlantic Coast. The British army in the colonies, although small, consisted of regular soldiers led by experienced officers. The British had cash and credit to support their troops.

The colonists had more than enough manpower to defend themselves. They did not have to transport supplies across the ocean. They knew the terrain, and could easily retreat to places where the British had difficulty reaching them. The colonists had a special advantage: the good chance that Britain's enemies in Europe would help them. These enemies—France and Spain—eventually did declare war on Britain.

Men Under Arms. British military forces included (1) the regulars, or redcoats; (2) the Loyalists, or Tories; (3) mercenaries, or hired soldiers of other countries; and (4) the Indian tribes, particularly the Six Nations and the Cherokee, that aided the British. The mercenaries were called *Hessians*, because many of them came from Hesse-Cassel, a German state. At peak strength, the British army had about 50,000 men. The British navy reached its peak strength of 468 ships in 1783.

The fighting forces of the patriots consisted of militiamen and volunteers in the Continental Army. The *minutemen* were militiamen ready to act at a moment's notice (see MINUTEMAN). The Continental Army reached a peak strength of 20,000 men. The Continental Navy at its height had about 50 ships, aided by about 2,000 privateers (see PRIVATEER).

The chief weapons of the war included rifles, muskets, and cannon. Some patriots fired the Pennsylvania rifle, which proved more accurate than the smoothbore musket. Later, the French Charleville musket, an improved flintlock, became an almost standard weapon of the Continental Army. The redcoats fired the "Brown Bess," a 14-pound, flint-action smoothbore musket with

The Stamp Act required the colonists to buy tax stamps, *left*, for newspapers, playing cards, diplomas, and legal documents. American resistance forced repeal of the law.

a 14-inch bayonet. Both sides usually massed in close ranks and fired volleys by platoons.

War Leaders. On June 15, 1775, Congress appointed George Washington as "general and commander in chief of the forces raised and to be raised in the defense of American liberty." His principal commanders included Maj. Gens. Benedict Arnold, Horatio Gates, Nathanael Greene, Henry Knox, the Marquis de Lafayette, Charles Lee, Casimir Pulaski, and Friedrich von Steuben. Commodore Esek Hopkins commanded the Continental Navy. Captains Joshua Barney, John Paul Jones, and Thomas Truxtun also served on the sea. The Comte de Rochambeau commanded some of the French troops aiding the patriots.

King George III ruled Great Britain during the war. Lord North served as prime minister until 1782, when the Marquis of Rockingham succeeded him. The principal British field commanders included Lt. Gens. John Burgoyne, Sir Guy Carleton, Sir Henry Clinton, Charles Cornwallis, and William Howe. Vice-Admiral Richard Howe, William's brother, led the British fleet from 1776 to 1778. See the separate biographies of the military leaders in WORLD BOOK listed in the *Related Articles* section of this article.

Battlefronts and Strategy. The battle scene stretched from Quebec in the north to Florida in the south. The scene extended from the Atlantic Coast as far west as what is now southwestern Illinois. The strategy of the British at first called for a quick strike that would overrun New England and cut it off from the other

THE COLONISTS FIGHT BACK

The Boston Tea Party occurred when colonists disguised as Indians raided three British ships and threw their cargoes of tea into the harbor rather than pay a tax on them.

Committees of Correspondence set up by colonial leaders informed the world through pamphlets and letters about the British abuses of American rights and liberties.

Old North Church's two lanterns signaled the route the British would take to Concord.

Robert Lawson from Paul Revere and I

Fight at Concord Bridge, by Frederick Coffey Yohn

colonies. The British planned to seize naval bases in Rhode Island and New York so they could command the Atlantic Coast with their sea power. Later, the redcoats attacked the middle colony-states. The French fleet threatened the British in American waters. After 1778, the redcoats carried on a war of endurance in the New York area. Then they invaded the south.

In the beginning, the colonists concerned themselves chiefly with meeting British threats. Then they fought to drive out the British completely, or else to make the war so costly that the British would have to give up. In most battles, the patriots outnumbered the British, but were inferior to them in discipline and training. As the war progressed, American officers acquired skill, and American soldiers gained experience.

The First Battles (1775-1776)

After the opening shots at Lexington, the patriots fought a running battle at Concord. Then they laid siege to Boston, where the British had headquarters. An American expedition invaded Canada, seized Montreal, and tried to capture Quebec. British plans to occupy the Carolinas met disaster. On July 4, 1776, the Second Continental Congress adopted the Declaration of Independence.

Lexington and Concord. On Apr. 18, 1775, Lt. Gen. Thomas Gage ordered his redcoats to destroy the patriots' main supply depot at Concord, Mass. The move was to be secret. But Joseph Warren, a doctor, found out the British plans. He quickly sent Paul Revere and William Dawes to ride the 16 miles to Lexington on the road to Concord and arouse the patriots. "The regulars are out!" Revere warned John Hancock and Samuel Adams. The two colonial leaders, who had been hiding from the British, fled.

The redcoats arrived at Lexington in the early dawn

of Apr. 19, 1775. Capt. John Parker (1729-1775) and his band of minutemen faced them on the village green. "Don't fire unless fired on," Parker commanded, "but if they mean to have war, let it begin here." No one knows who fired the first shot. But 8 colonists were killed and 10 wounded. One Britisher was wounded.

The British then marched on and destroyed the military supplies stored at Concord. Minutemen opposed their advance, and a skirmish followed. But the shots already fired at Lexington had brought out many of the colonists. Farmers, businessmen, mechanics, merchants, and planters streamed forward to join the cause of liberty, forcing the British to withdraw to Boston. See CONCORD, BATTLE OF.

Bunker Hill. In Boston, the British found themselves besieged by New England militiamen. The patriots could not hope to drive the redcoats away from the city, except by bombarding them from a hill overlooking it. They intended to fortify Bunker Hill, but decided to occupy Breed's Hill, closer to Boston.

On June 17, 1775, the British attempted to drive the patriots away from the hill. Col. William Prescott, commanding a force of militiamen, is said to have ordered: "Don't fire until you see the whites of their eyes." British troops under Maj. Gen. William Howe mounted three frontal charges before the colonists fled (see BUNKER HILL, BATTLE OF).

Even before this battle, the patriots had decided that they needed a unified army. The Second Continental Congress voted to organize a continental army, and chose George Washington to command it. Washington took command on July 3. He laid plans to attack the redcoats, but did not try to carry them out until March, 1776. His men then fortified Dorchester Heights, which towered above Boston to the south. Howe realized that, with enemy artillery on the hill,

258

THE START OF THE WAR

Clashes at Lexington and Concord, a loss at Bunker Hill, the British evacuation of Boston, and the Declaration of Independence marked the opening period of the war. The British also invaded the Carolinas, and Americans seized Montreal in Canada.

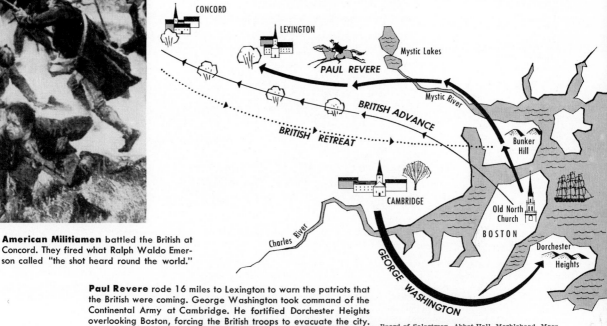

American Militiamen battled the British at Concord. They fired what Ralph Waldo Emerson called "the shot heard round the world."

Paul Revere rode 16 miles to Lexington to warn the patriots that the British were coming. George Washington took command of the Continental Army at Cambridge. He fortified Dorchester Heights overlooking Boston, forcing the British troops to evacuate the city.

Board of Selectmen, Abbot Hall, Marblehead, Mass.

The Spirit of '76, by Archibald M. Willard in the 1870's, portrays colonists rallying to the cause of independence. Patriots from all ranks joined in the war for liberty.

Winter at Valley Forge tested the valor of the patriots. Washington and Lafayette led the army through several months of bitter cold and a shortage of food and clothes.

Brown Bros.

——— HIGHLIGHTS OF THE REVOLUTIONARY WAR ———

1775

Apr. 19 Minutemen and redcoats clashed at Lexington and Concord.
June 17 The British drove the Americans from Breed's Hill in the Battle of Bunker Hill.
July 3 Washington assumed command of the Continental Army.
Nov. 13 The patriots occupied Montreal in Canada.
Dec. 30-31 American forces failed to seize Quebec.

1776

Feb. 27 The patriots drove the Loyalists from Moore's Creek Bridge.
Mar. 3 The Continental fleet captured New Providence Island in the Bahamas.
Mar. 17 The British evacuated Boston.
July 4 The Declaration of Independence was adopted.
Aug. 27 The redcoats defeated the patriots on Long Island.
Sept. 15 The British occupied New York City.
Oct. 28 The Americans retreated from White Plains, New York.
Nov. 16 The British captured Fort Washington.
Dec. 26 Washington mounted a surprise attack on Trenton.

1777

Jan. 3 Washington gained victory at Princeton.
Aug. 6 The redcoats forced the patriots back at Oriskany, but then had to evacuate.
Aug. 16 The patriots crushed the Hessians near Bennington.
Sept. 11 The British won the Battle of Brandywine.
Sept. 19 Gates' forces checked Burgoyne's army in the First Battle of Freeman's Farm.
Sept. 26 The British occupied Philadelphia.
Oct. 4 Washington's forces met defeat in the Battle of Germantown.
Oct. 7 The patriots repulsed the British in the Second Battle of Freeman's Farm.
Oct. 17 Burgoyne surrendered at Saratoga.
Dec. 19 Washington's army retired to winter quarters at Valley Forge.

1778

Feb. 6 The United States and France signed an alliance.
June 28 The Battle of Monmouth ended in a draw.
July 4 George Rogers Clark captured Kaskaskia.
Dec. 29 The redcoats entered Savannah.

1779

Feb. 23-25 George Rogers Clark captured Vincennes.
June 21 Spain declared war on Great Britain.
July 15 Anthony Wayne's troops stormed Stony Point.
Sept. 23 John Paul Jones' *Bonhomme Richard* captured the British ship *Serapis*.

1780

May 12 Charleston fell after a British siege.
July 11 French troops arrived in Newport to aid the American cause.
Aug. 16 The British defeated the Americans at Camden.
Oct. 7 American frontiersmen stormed the British positions on Kings Mountain.

1781

Jan. 17 Patriots won a victory at Cowpens, S.C.
Mar. 15 Cornwallis clashed with Greene at Guilford Courthouse, N.C.
Sept. 15 The French fleet drove a British naval force from Chesapeake Bay.
Oct. 19 Cornwallis' forces surrendered at Yorktown.

1782

Mar. 20 Lord North resigned as British prime minister.
July 11 The British evacuated Savannah.
Nov. 30 The Americans and British signed a preliminary peace treaty in Paris.
Dec. 14 The British left Charleston.

1783

Apr. 19 Congress ratified the preliminary peace treaty.
Sept. 3 The United States and Great Britain signed the final peace treaty in Paris.
Nov. 25 The British left New York City.

260

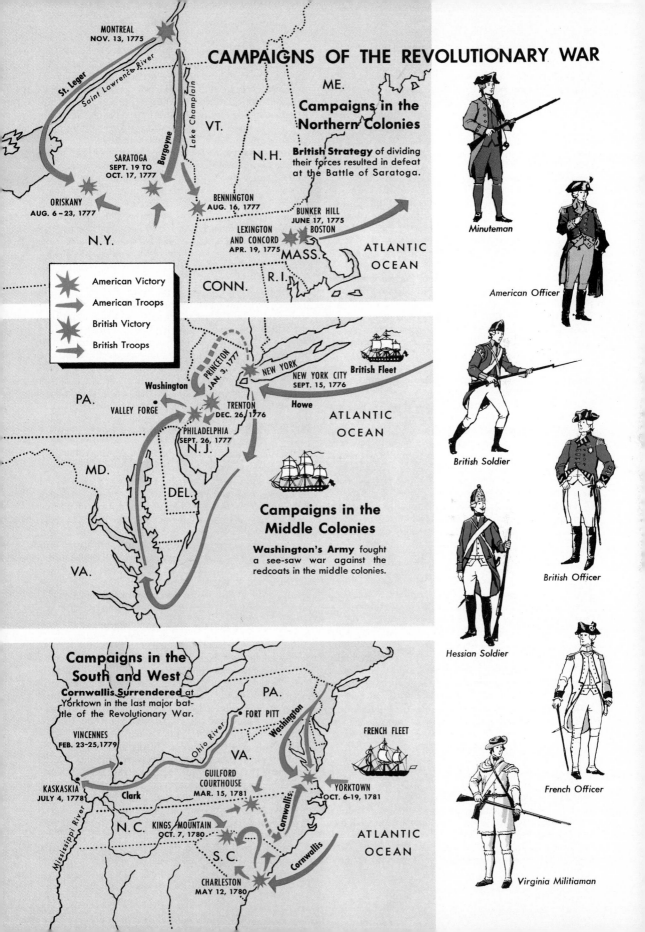

CAMPAIGNS OF THE REVOLUTIONARY WAR

Campaigns in the Northern Colonies

British Strategy of dividing their forces resulted in defeat at the Battle of Saratoga.

MONTREAL
NOV. 13, 1775

St. Leger

Saint Lawrence River

Lake Champlain

Burgoyne

SARATOGA
SEPT. 19 TO
OCT. 17, 1777

ORISKANY
AUG. 6–23, 1777

BENNINGTON
AUG. 16, 1777

BUNKER HILL
JUNE 17, 1775
BOSTON

LEXINGTON
AND CONCORD
APR. 19, 1775

ME.

VT.

N. H.

N. Y.

MASS.

CONN.

R. I.

ATLANTIC OCEAN

★ American Victory
→ American Troops
✦ British Victory
→ British Troops

PRINCETON
JAN. 3, 1777

NEW YORK

NEW YORK CITY
SEPT. 15, 1776

British Fleet

Howe

Washington

PA.

VALLEY FORGE

TRENTON
DEC. 26, 1776

PHILADELPHIA
SEPT. 26, 1777

N. J.

MD.

DEL.

VA.

ATLANTIC OCEAN

Campaigns in the Middle Colonies

Washington's Army fought a see-saw war against the redcoats in the middle colonies.

Campaigns in the South and West

Cornwallis Surrendered at Yorktown in the last major battle of the Revolutionary War.

VINCENNES
FEB. 23–25, 1779

FORT PITT

PA.

Ohio River

Washington

FRENCH FLEET

VA.

GUILFORD
COURTHOUSE
MAR. 15, 1781

YORKTOWN
OCT. 6–19, 1781

KASKASKIA
JULY 4, 1778

Clark

Cornwallis

N. C.

KINGS MOUNTAIN
OCT. 7, 1780

Mississippi River

Cornwallis

S. C.

ATLANTIC OCEAN

CHARLESTON
MAY 12, 1780

Minuteman

American Officer

British Soldier

British Officer

Hessian Soldier

French Officer

Virginia Militiaman

he could not stay in the city. On March 17, his army and a small fleet sailed for Halifax, N.S.

King George III and his cabinet reacted to the news of war by declaring all the colonies to be in rebellion. Parliament passed the Prohibitory Act, which authorized a naval blockade of the colonies. The British relieved Gage of his command, and appointed Maj. Gen. Sir Guy Carleton to command the redcoats in Canada and Lt. Gen. William Howe to lead the British forces in the American colonies. They enlisted troops in Britain, and hired thousands of mercenaries in Germany.

Canada Invaded. As one American army covered Boston, another swept into Canada. The colonists hoped to prevent the British from using Canadian bases. Early in May, 1775, Cols. Ethan Allen and Benedict Arnold, and Allen's Green Mountain Boys, seized the British stronghold at Ticonderoga on the route between New York and Canada (see GREEN MOUNTAIN BOYS). From Ticonderoga, American forces advanced to Crown Point, which the British had left. The two victories provided the colonists with vitally needed cannon, and also opened the way for an invasion of Canada. The patriots hoped the French-Canadians would aid them.

In the fall of 1775, two American expeditions marched northward toward Canada. Benedict Arnold commanded a force that followed the Kennebec River in Maine and the Chaudière River in Canada. Brig. Gen. Richard Montgomery led the other expedition. By November, Montgomery had occupied Montreal, and swept down the St. Lawrence River. Carleton escaped from Montreal by disguising himself as a fisherman. A British ship picked him up and took him to Quebec, where he assumed command of the city's defenses. Arnold and his 1,000-man force pushed through the woods of Maine and camped on the outskirts of Quebec.

Montgomery and Arnold realized that they could not wisely carry on a winter siege, because enemy reinforcements would soon arrive. The two commanders decided to storm the city from two sides. They attacked during a violent snowstorm in the early hours of Dec. 30 and 31, 1775, but the British repulsed both assaults. Montgomery was killed, and Arnold was seriously wounded.

Arnold and other commanders continued to besiege Quebec until May, 1776, when a 10,000-man British army began to land in Canada. The Americans retreated down the St. Lawrence to Lake Champlain. With Carleton's forces in hot pursuit, they gradually fell back to Ticonderoga. Later, the patriots made other plans to invade Canada. But these plans were never carried out, and Canada remained a British possession.

Assaults in the South. The patriots encountered more success in the south than they did in the north. In 1776, they forced the Earl of Dunmore, last British governor of Virginia, to flee. Dunmore assembled a small fleet in Chesapeake Bay, and collected an army of redcoats, Tories, and escaped Negro slaves. He raided the coast of Virginia and destroyed much property. But the patriots crushed his small army at Great Bridge on Dec. 11, 1775. Discouraged, Dunmore finally led his ships and men to New York and joined the main British forces there in the summer of 1776.

The British also met disaster in North Carolina. Josiah Martin, the last royal governor of the colony,

called on the Loyalists to take up arms. He hoped that British warships and troops would support them. But the British squadron he expected failed to appear in time. When more than 1,000 Tories answered Martin's call and marched toward Wilmington, American militiamen met them at Moore's Creek Bridge. On Feb. 27, 1776, the Loyalists tried to sweep through the patriots, but the Americans routed them.

Independence Declared. The Howe brothers had the authority to pardon patriots who laid down their arms. Many Americans vainly hoped that they also had the power to make concessions. Then the patriots heard that Britain had set up a naval blockade and had begun to hire mercenaries. This news spurred many Americans toward full independence. Revolutionary governments replaced colonial ones in the 13 colonies. The patriots had been fighting for their rights within the British Empire. Now they wondered whether they should not fight for full independence.

On June 7, 1776, Richard Henry Lee of Virginia offered a resolution announcing that "These United Colonies are, and of right ought to be, free and independent States." Many delegates held back. Finally, on July 2, delegates from 12 colonies passed Lee's resolution. On July 4, the Second Continental Congress approved the Declaration of Independence (see DECLARATION OF INDEPENDENCE). But the great trial still lay ahead. Thomas Paine summed up the fearful test with the famous words: "These are the times that try men's souls . . . Tyranny, like hell, is not easily conquered; yet we have this consolation with us, that the harder the conflict, the more glorious the triumph."

The War at Sea. The patriots could not hope to match the powerful British fleet. But they promptly began to build small warships. They also commissioned privateers to attack enemy merchant vessels. In 1775, the Continental Congress organized a navy and marine corps. The warships of this navy and those of the separate colonial fleets damaged British commerce and captured supplies intended for the British army. Commodore Esek Hopkins, the navy's first fleet commander, led an American squadron in seizing New Providence Island in the Bahamas. But a British fleet under Rear Adm. Samuel Graves supported the redcoats in Boston, raided American ports, and captured merchant ships.

The Middle Years (1776-1778)

Both sides scored important gains during the second period of the war. New York fell to the invading redcoats. Washington won victories in his campaign in New Jersey. The British occupied Philadelphia, but met disaster in the north. When Lt. Gen. John Burgoyne surrendered at Saratoga, the great American victory helped convince the French that they could safely enter the war on the side of the United States.

The New York Campaign. British strategy in 1776 included a two-pronged attack on New England. Carleton's forces would advance through the Lake Champlain-Hudson River passageway. Howe would seize New York and strike northward. The British hoped to push the New Englanders out of the war, then conquer the Middle Atlantic and Southern States. But Carleton failed even to reach Ticonderoga. A strong fleet under Benedict Arnold hindered the British advance on Lake Champlain. With the approach of winter, Carleton

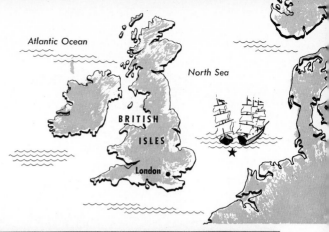

Atlantic Ocean

North Sea

BRITISH

ISLES

London

Brown Bros.

decided not to take further military action until 1777.

Washington placed about a third of his troops on Long Island to face Howe's powerful force. Howe's surprise attack on Aug. 27, 1776, drove the Americans into entrenchments above the East River. Howe paused briefly before attacking again, and Washington quietly withdrew to Manhattan. On September 15, Howe's redcoats landed on Manhattan and forced the patriots back. Many of Washington's militiamen deserted him, but he fought desperately before retreating. The British executed young Capt. Nathan Hale during the New York campaign. Hale had crossed the British lines in disguise to obtain military information for Washington, but was captured. "I only regret that I have but one life to lose for my country," Hale cried.

In October, Howe sent troops up Long Island Sound to attack the Continental Army from the rear. Washington fell back to White Plains. Howe stormed his right flank there on October 28, but met heavy resistance. The Americans then retreated to hilly ground. Howe marched westward to attack Fort Washington in northwest Manhattan. The 3,000 patriots in the fort surrendered on November 16 after a brief struggle.

Princeton and Trenton. The loss of Fort Washington opened the way to New Jersey. British forces under Maj. Gen. Charles Cornwallis quickly poured in. Washington had left part of his army to protect New England. The rest sought safety behind the Delaware River.

Howe did not pursue Washington. Instead, he ordered his men into winter quarters, and assigned Maj. Gen. Sir Henry Clinton to seize Newport, R.I. The British had assigned Hessian troops to garrison Trenton, N.J. Washington's reinforced army launched a three-column attack on the Hessians. Men under Col. John Glover (1732-1797) ferried one attacking force across the ice-clogged Delaware River on Christmas night, 1776. These troops assembled swiftly, then silently marched toward Trenton. They took the Hessians by surprise and captured 1,000 prisoners on December 26.

After some hesitation, Washington took his entire army across the Delaware. But Cornwallis' stronger army advancing toward Trenton endangered the American positions there. Washington marched south, then east around Cornwallis during the night of Jan. 2, 1777.

263

THE END OF THE WAR

The Treaty of Paris in 1783 formally ended the war. It provided for liberal American boundaries extending from the Atlantic Coast to the Mississippi River and from the Great Lakes to the 31st parallel in the south.

Flintlock Musket with a bayonet was the chief weapon of the war. A soldier carried his cartridges of paper, black powder, and lead balls in a leather box slung over his shoulder.

★ Quebec

Montreal ★
Lake Champlain

Ticonderoga ★
Saratoga ★
Bennington ★

N.H.

MASS.
Bunker Hill ★

Concord ★
Lexington

★ Oriskany

N.Y.

CONN.

White Plains

R.I.
Long Island

Valley Forge
PA.

Princeton

New York
Monmouth
Trenton

Germantown
Philadelphia
Brandywine

N.J.

MD.

DEL.

NORTHWEST
TERRITORY

Ohio River

VA.

Yorktown

Vincennes ★

Kaskaskia ★

Claimed by
Virginia

Guilford Courthouse ★

N.C.

Important
Battles
of the War ★

Mississippi River

Claimed by
North Carolina

Kings Mountain ★

Cowpens ★ ★ Camden

S.C.

Charleston

Claimed by
Georgia

GA.

Savannah ★

Burgoyne's surrender led France to join the patriots (1777).

First shots at Lexington preceded the Battle of Bunker Hill (1775).

Washington crossed the Delaware to fight a brilliant campaign (1776).

Cornwallis surrendered his army in the war's last major battle (1781).

George Rogers Clark's men sailed down the Ohio River in flatboats. Their campaign helped to check Indian attacks in the Ohio Valley.

Battle of Kings Mountain marked a turning point in the south (1780).

The following day, he won a brilliant victory at Princeton, defeating some redcoats marching to join Cornwallis. Washington then hurried eastward to Morristown, where his men spent the rest of the winter.

Fighting in Pennsylvania. In the spring of 1777, the British changed their strategy. Lt. Gen. John Burgoyne took command of the British army advancing from Canada, replacing Carleton. The British hoped he would establish a connection with Lt. Gen. William Howe at the end of the campaign. Under their plan, Burgoyne would march to Albany, N.Y., while Howe invaded Pennsylvania. But Howe and Burgoyne were not ordered to work together.

Transports protected by Vice-Adm. Richard Howe's fleet sailed for Philadelphia in July. The 15,000 redcoats aboard, under William Howe, landed at the head of Chesapeake Bay on August 25. Meanwhile, Washington had organized an almost new army, partly supplied with equipment sent secretly by France.

The opposing armies clashed at Brandywine Creek, southwest of Philadelphia, on September 11. Howe pretended to launch a frontal attack, and sent his Hessians against Chads's Ford. But he also sent Cornwallis' men around the patriots' right flank. The sur-

prised American troops under Maj. Gen. John Sullivan fell back in disorder. The Hessians pushed forward across the creek, but Maj. Gen. Nathanael Greene ably covered the American retreat until darkness made the British pursuit ineffective. Howe's success enabled him to occupy Philadelphia on September 26 with no opposition. The Continental Congress fled to York, Pa.

Washington mounted a surprise attack at Germantown, directly north of Philadelphia, on October 4, but made no headway. Howe then opened the Delaware River to British shipping. No further battles between Washington and Howe occurred in 1777. The American Army went into winter quarters at Valley Forge, about 25 miles west of Philadelphia, on December 19. The ill-fed, ill-clothed, and ill-housed Americans suffered through several months of bitter cold. Only about half of the men had shoes or socks. See VALLEY FORGE.

Defeat at Saratoga. Burgoyne's 7,700-man army of British, Hessians, Tories, and Indians swept southward toward Albany. It captured Ticonderoga on July 6, 1777, without a struggle. British forces under Col. Barry St. Leger advanced down Lake Ontario and surrounded

MAJOR BATTLES OF THE REVOLUTIONARY WAR

Name	Place	Date	Commander American	Commander British	Casualties American	Casualties British	Results
Bennington	Vermont-New York border	Aug. 16, 1777	Stark	Baum Breymann	80	900	British defeat encouraged the patriots in their campaign against Burgoyne.
Bonhomme Richard vs. *Serapis*	North Sea	Sept. 23, 1779	Jones	Pearson	150	110	The British warship *Serapis* surrendered.
Brandywine	Pennsylvania	Sept. 11, 1777	Washington	Howe	1,000	576	An American retreat enabled the British to occupy Philadelphia.
Bunker Hill	Massachusetts	June 17, 1775	Prescott	Howe	371	1,054	The patriots were driven from their positions overlooking Boston.
Camden	South Carolina	Aug. 16, 1780	Gates	Cornwallis	600	300	An entire American army was almost destroyed.
Freeman's Farm (First Battle)	New York	Sept. 19, 1777	Gates	Burgoyne	300	600	The British advance southward was halted.
Freeman's Farm (Second Battle)	New York	Oct. 7, 1777	Gates	Burgoyne	150	700	The patriots repulsed a second attack.
Germantown	Pennsylvania	Oct. 4, 1777	Washington	Howe	1,073	520	An American near-victory turned into a loss.
Guilford Courthouse	North Carolina	Mar. 15, 1781	Greene	Cornwallis	1,100	406	The British decided to abandon North Carolina.
Kings Mountain	South Carolina	Oct. 7, 1780	Sevier Shelby	Ferguson	90	1,100	An American victory delayed the British advance northward.
Lexington and Concord	Massachusetts	Apr. 19, 1775	Parker and others	Smith	95	273	The British destroyed the patriots' military supplies.
Long Island	New York	Aug. 27, 1776	Washington	Howe	1,400	400	The British forced the Americans from Long Island.
Monmouth	New Jersey	June 28, 1778	Washington	Clinton	361	400	The redcoats repulsed an American attack.
Montreal	Quebec	Nov. 13, 1775	Montgomery	Carleton	0	50	The patriots captured the city of Montreal.
Princeton	New Jersey	Jan. 3, 1777	Washington	Cornwallis	100	300	The British decided to withdraw from western New Jersey.
Quebec	Quebec	Dec. 30-31, 1775	Montgomery	Carleton	500	18	The Americans failed to seize Quebec.
Saratoga	New York	Sept. 19-Oct. 17, 1777	Gates	Burgoyne	150	7,000	Burgoyne's surrender led to France joining the war against Britain.
Trenton	New Jersey	Dec. 26, 1776	Washington	Rall	4	900	The patriots crushed the Hessians in a surprise assault.
Yorktown	Virginia	Oct. 6-19, 1781	Washington	Cornwallis	262	8,700	The British surrendered in the war's last major battle.

Surrender at Yorktown in 1781 ended most of the fighting in the Revolutionary War. Louis van Blarenberghe, a Frenchman, witnessed the surrender ceremony and painted this scene showing British soldiers leaving their defenses to lay down their arms. American and French soldiers formed ranks on each side of the defeated redcoats.

Fort Stanwix on the upper Mohawk River. In the bloody Battle of Oriskany, St. Leger's troops forced back patriots who tried to relieve the fort, but then had to retreat with the arrival of American reinforcements.

Burgoyne continued to advance southward. But American militia under Brig. Gen. John Stark defeated two detachments of Hessians near Bennington, Vt., on August 16. Opposing Burgoyne's army were troops under Maj. Gen. Philip Schuyler and, later, Maj. Gen. Horatio Gates.

The growing, 6,000-man American army occupied fortified ground at Bemis Heights, north of Albany. The troops were entrenched in lines that stretched into woods on the west. Although Burgoyne had about 8,500 men, he dared not make a frontal attack. On September 19, he tried to break through the woods on the American left flank. But his troops were forced back in the First Battle of Freeman's Farm. Burgoyne refused to retreat toward Canada. On October 7, he led 1,650 British soldiers in another thrust on the American left flank in the Second Battle of Freeman's Farm. The patriots again drove him back. Burgoyne finally began to retreat. He now found himself surrounded by an American army of 17,000 men. On October 17, Burgoyne agreed to terms with Gates at Saratoga, and about 6,000 British troops laid down their arms.

France Joins the War. The news of Burgoyne's surrender had sweeping political results. It persuaded the British government that it must make concessions to the patriots. The British sent a commission headed by the Earl of Carlisle to Philadelphia to offer the Americans dominion status. But the news of the surrender prompted France to enter the war. On Feb. 6, 1778, King Louis XVI signed two treaties with Benjamin Franklin and other American diplomats. In these pacts, France recognized the United States as an independent nation and agreed to a military alliance. The Continental Congress ratified the treaty on May 4, and also refused the terms offered by the Carlisle commission. Large-scale French aid, including an army and a powerful fleet, soon began arriving in the United States. Some Frenchmen, such as the Marquis de Lafayette, had been serving with the Americans for many months.

Forced to face a new enemy, Britain temporarily went on the defensive in America. General Sir Henry Clinton succeeded Howe as commander in chief. He abandoned Philadelphia on June 18 and, with most of his army, marched across New Jersey toward New York City. Washington attacked the British on June 28 at Monmouth Court House with an experienced and revived army. But neither side won an advantage in the battle, and Clinton's troops reached New York safely.

The End of the War (1778-1783)

The final battles of the war took place in the south and west. Naval warfare gained in importance. Exhausted by eight years of fighting on battlefields 3,000 miles from home, the British agreed to a peace treaty in 1783 that formally ended the war.

Clark's Campaign. In 1777, Indians of the northwest had savagely attacked new American settlements in Kentucky. The state of Virginia assigned Lt. Col. George Rogers Clark to protect the settlers. Clark realized that the capture of Detroit would make it easier

to defend "the dark and bloody ground" of the northwest. The British had been using Detroit as a base to supply the Indians. In 1778, Clark and 175 men marched into the Illinois country and captured Kaskaskia, Vincennes, and other French villages. But British troops recaptured Vincennes. Clark took the offensive and forced the British to surrender at Vincennes on Feb. 25, 1779. Clark did not have enough men to reach Detroit, and Tories and Indians led by Simon Girty continued to terrorize much of the Ohio and Indiana country. But at the end of the war, American settlements in Kentucky and Tennessee were stronger than they had been when it began.

Victories at Sea. Throughout the war, American and British ships fought for control of the seas in the Atlantic Ocean and Caribbean Sea. The American fleets consisted of the Continental Navy, the navies maintained by 11 states, and about 2,000 privateers. The patriots could not effectively challenge British ships-of-the-line, or battleships. But their swarms of privateers inflicted heavy damage on British commerce. Privateers captured about 600 enemy vessels. The infant United States Navy captured or destroyed nearly 200 British ships. Captain John Paul Jones in the 18-gun *Ranger* even ventured into the waters about the British Isles. On Sept. 23, 1779, Jones in command of the *Bonhomme Richard* captured the British 44-gun *Serapis* after a bloody, bitter fight. Called on to surrender at the peak of battle, Jones cried: "I have not yet begun to fight!"

The League Against Britain. After France entered the war in 1778, Britain had to fight on many fronts. Spain declared war on the British on June 21, 1779. It hoped to capture Gibraltar and other British possessions. In December, 1780, Holland joined the war.

The British army in New York City did not conduct any large-scale offensives after 1778. Washington's troops remained near the city, but they did not have enough strength to storm it. Washington had to give up plans for an attack when he discovered that the largest French ships under Adm. Comte d'Estaing could not cross the sandbar at the mouth of New York harbor.

Early in 1779, Clinton's army began a series of raids in the Northern States. He captured Stony Point on the Hudson River. But Maj. Gen. Anthony Wayne and his men sailed down the river in small boats and recaptured the fort after a brilliant bayonet attack on July 15. Clinton also tried to win over American leaders to the British cause. As early as May, he began corresponding with Maj. Gen. Benedict Arnold, who took command of the American fort at West Point, N.Y., the next year. Arnold plotted to turn the fort over to the British. But the patriots seized and later executed Major John André, whom the British had sent across the American lines on Sept. 23, 1780, to meet with Arnold. Arnold escaped to New York City.

The British gained little through the efforts of their Indian allies. Cherokee warriors raided southern frontier towns. But American backwoodsmen invaded their villages and punished them severely. Indians and Loyalists harried the frontiers of New York and Pennsylvania, and inflicted heavy losses on the patriots in the Cherry and Wyoming valleys. But they suffered heavily when American troops swept through their land.

The War in the South. Clinton decided to limit his

267

operations in the north, and attacked the far Southern States. Savannah, Ga., fell to invading British forces on Dec. 29, 1778. The patriots, supported by the French, tried unsuccessfully to recapture the city. Encouraged, Clinton led a large army against Charleston, S.C., in the spring of 1780. He captured Charleston on May 12, together with the city's commander, Maj. Gen. Benjamin Lincoln, and a 5,400-man army. The redcoats then quickly overran South Carolina and Georgia. Clinton returned to New York City, left Cornwallis in command, and ordered him not to run any major risks.

Major General Horatio Gates became commander of American forces in the south. As he prepared to attack a British outpost in Camden, S.C., Cornwallis suddenly confronted him. In the battle that followed on Aug. 16, 1780, the American militia quickly fled. The regulars fought desperately, but were forced to withdraw.

The losses at Charleston and Camden discouraged many patriots. But Thomas Sumter, Francis Marion, and Andrew Pickens launched a series of guerrilla attacks against the British. In September, 1780, Cornwallis invaded North Carolina. On October 7, Col. Isaac Shelby's 900 American frontiersmen destroyed a force of 1,100 Loyalists under Maj. Patrick Ferguson, covering Cornwallis' left flank. The loss, sustained at Kings Mountain, S.C., forced the British to retreat.

In October, Maj. Gen. Nathanael Greene was appointed commander of the American army in the south. Brigadier General Daniel Morgan's troops won a victory at Cowpens, S.C., on Jan. 17, 1781. Cornwallis pursued Morgan northward, eager to avenge the defeat. He followed Morgan, now joined by Greene, to the southern border of Virginia. Greene attacked Cornwallis at Guilford Courthouse on March 15. Cornwallis held his own, but decided to withdraw to Wilmington, N.C. From there his men marched into Virginia. Greene now began an offensive to drive the British from the Carolinas and Georgia. By the summer of 1781, the patriots had captured all British posts in the far Southern States except Wilmington, Charleston, and Savannah. The British abandoned all three by December, 1782.

Surrender at Yorktown. Cornwallis violated the spirit of Clinton's orders by marching into Virginia in late April, 1781. He hoped to make the state his center of operations. But Clinton wanted to attack the Maryland-Delaware peninsula and Philadelphia. By August, Cornwallis had decided to use Yorktown, Va., as his base.

Washington stood ready to attack New York when he heard that a 24-ship French fleet under Adm. François de Grasse would sail to the United States from the West Indies. The French then decided to move their fleet into Chesapeake Bay. Lieutenant General Jean de Rochambeau, in command of French troops in America, put his men under Washington. The combined army of patriots and French soldiers headed for Virginia.

The 19-ship British fleet, based in New York City under Rear Adm. Thomas Graves, challenged De Grasse's force at the mouth of Chesapeake Bay. The British failed to win an advantage, and returned to New York City. French ships from Newport then joined De Grasse's fleet to seal off the bay. Washington's army of about 17,000 men surrounded Yorktown on September 28, and began attacking Cornwallis' position on

October 6. Washington started a siege operation early in October. De Grasse held off the British fleet while Washington's troops besieged Cornwallis for three weeks. Without supplies and with no hope of escape, Cornwallis abandoned a desperate scheme for cutting his way out by land, and decided to surrender his 8,000 soldiers and sailors. As the British band played an old tune, "The World Turned Upside Down," Brig. Gen. Charles O'Hara, acting for Cornwallis, gave his sword to Maj. Gen. Benjamin Lincoln on October 19. "I have the Honor to inform Congress, that a Reduction of the British Army . . . is most happily effected," Washington wrote the Continental Congress. News of the surrender reached the congress on October 22. "Cornwallis is taken!" cried a watchman as he spread the tidings to the people.

Clinton's 7,000-man army aboard a British fleet, sailing to rescue Cornwallis, turned back when it heard the news. When the prime minister, Lord North, heard of the crushing defeat at Yorktown, he is said to have cried: "O God! It is all over." He resigned his position, and the new British cabinet decided to open peace negotiations with the patriots. But occasional fighting between the patriots and the redcoats continued for more than a year, chiefly in the south and west.

Results of the Revolution

The Revolutionary War gave birth to the United States of America. It eventually brought new political institutions in many parts of the world, and a number of basic cultural, social, and economic changes. Thomas Paine declared that the war "contributed more to enlighten the world, and diffuse a spirit of freedom and liberality among mankind, than any human event . . . that ever preceded it."

War Losses. The patriots had to pay dearly for their "glorious triumph." Estimates of American battle deaths range from 4,435 to 12,000. The patriots suffered comparatively heavy losses from hardship and disease. Yet these casualties are not large compared with those resulting from modern wars, because the number of men who fought remained relatively small. The cost of the war to the United States has been estimated at about $101 million. Historians do not know the cost of the war to Britain in casualties and money.

The Home Front. Congress and the states printed paper money freely to finance the war. Congress issued about $200 million in continental currency. By 1780, this money was worthless. During the war, some merchants sold goods imported from abroad, and many farmers actually profited from the war. But inflation, destruction and plunder by armies, and disruption of trade inflicted losses on many families. At the end of the war, the states and the congress faced large public debts.

The war also brought a financial strain to Britain. British political leaders worried about national bankruptcy, but the economy withstood the strain. British merchants were able to sell goods in the United States after the war as they had before the war.

France could not afford the cost of the war. The financial deficits that developed during the fighting in America helped bring bankruptcy and revolution to the country in 1789 (see FRENCH REVOLUTION).

The Peace Treaty. Peace negotiations began in Paris in April, 1782. Richard Oswald and Henry Strachey served as the chief British negotiators. Benjamin Franklin, John Adams, John Jay, and Henry Laurens represented the United States.

The British wanted to deal with the Americans separately from the French and Spanish. They agreed to a preliminary treaty on November 30. The agreement would become effective after Britain had reached terms with its other enemies. The United States ratified the preliminary peace treaty on Apr. 19, 1783.

The final peace treaty, signed on September 3, established liberal American boundaries. Under the treaty, United States territory extended from the Atlantic Coast to the Mississippi River in the west, and from the Great Lakes and the 49th parallel in the north to the 31st parallel in the south. The final treaty also gave Americans the right to fish on the Grand Banks off the coast of Newfoundland. It pledged that Congress would "earnestly recommend" to the states that they restore rights and property taken from the Loyalists. The last redcoats in the United States evacuated New York City on November 25.

The United States government gave land and money to those who had fought in the war. Statues and national shrines were dedicated to honor many of these patriots. These shrines include Independence Hall, the Washington Monument, the Bunker Hill Monument, Morristown National Historical Park, and Valley Forge.

The Revolutionary War delivered a blow to the European colonial system. In the years to come, the United States would stand as a shining example of a nation created by a colonial people, free and governed by its own representatives.　　　JOHN R. ALDEN

Related Articles. See the History sections of the articles on the states that fought in the Revolutionary War, such as MASSACHUSETTS (History). See also the following:

BACKGROUND

Boston Massacre
Boston Port Bill
Boston Tea Party
Committees of
　Correspondence

Committees of
　Safety
Continental
　Congress
Declaration of
　Independence

Intolerable Acts
Minuteman
Navigation Act
Stamp Act
Writ of Assistance

AMERICAN MILITARY LEADERS

Allen, Ethan
Arnold, Benedict
Barry, John
Clark, George R.
Clinton, George
Dearborn, Henry
Gates, Horatio
Greene, Nathanael
Hale, Nathan

Hopkins, Esek
Jones, John Paul
Knox, Henry
Lee, Charles
Lee, Henry
Marion, Francis
Moultrie, William
Putnam, Israel
Putnam, Rufus

St. Clair, Arthur
Schuyler, Philip J.
Stark, John
Ward, Artemas
Warner, Seth
Warren, Joseph
Washington, George
Wayne, Anthony

AMERICAN CIVILIAN LEADERS

Adams, John
Adams, Samuel
Deane, Silas
Franklin, Benjamin
Hancock, John
Henry, Patrick

Jay, John
Jefferson, Thomas
Lee, Richard Henry
Livingston,
　Robert R.
Mason, George

Morris, Robert
Otis, James
Paine, Thomas
Revere, Paul
Salomon, Haym

BRITISH MILITARY LEADERS

André, John
Burgoyne, John
Carleton (family)

Clinton, Sir Henry
Cornwallis, Charles
Gage, Thomas

Howe (family)
St. Leger, Barry

BRITISH CIVILIAN LEADERS

Burke, Edmund　　　George (III)　　　North, Lord

OTHER BIOGRAPHIES

Brant, Joseph　　　　　　　　　De Kalb, Johann

Girty, Simon
Grasse, François J. P.
Jouett, Jack
Kosciusko, Thaddeus
Lafayette, Marquis de
Pitcher, Molly

Pulaski, Casimir
Rochambeau, Comte de
Ross, Betsy
Rutledge (John)
Steuben, Baron von

OTHER RELATED ARTICLES

Army, U.S. (History)
Brother Jonathan
Bunker Hill, Battle of
Cabal
Cincinnati, Society of the
Daughters of the
　American Revolution
Flag (Flags of the
　United States; pictures)
Fort Ticonderoga
Green Mountain Boys
Hessian
Marine Corps, U.S.
　(History)

National Park System
Navy, U.S. (History)
Paris, Treaties of
Patriots' Day
Privateer
Sons of Liberty
Sons of the American
　Revolution
United States, History of
United States Constitution
Valley Forge
White Plains, Battle of
Wyoming Valley Massacre
Yankee Doodle

Outline

I. Causes of the War
　A. Political Conflicts　　B. Economic Rivalry
II. Events Leading to the Revolution
　A. Acts of 1763
　B. The Navigation Acts
　C. The Quartering and
　　Stamp Acts
　D. The Townshend Acts
　E. The Boston
　　Massacre
　F. Committees of
　　Correspondence
　G. The Tea Act
　H. The Intolerable Acts
　I. The First Continental
　　Congress
　J. The Restraining Act
III. Men, Battlefronts, and Strategy
　A. Men Under Arms
　B. War Leaders
　C. Battlefronts and
　　Strategy
IV. The First Battles (1775-1776)
　A. Lexington and
　　Concord
　B. Bunker Hill
　C. Canada Invaded
　D. Assaults in the South
　E. Independence Declared
　F. The War at Sea
V. The Middle Years (1776-1778)
　A. The New York Campaign
　B. Princeton and Trenton
　C. Fighting in Pennsylvania
　D. Defeat at Saratoga
　E. France Joins the
　　War
VI. The End of the War (1778-1783)
　A. Clark's Campaign
　B. Victories at Sea
　C. The League Against
　　Britain
　D. The War in the South
　E. Surrender at
　　Yorktown
VII. Results of the Revolution
　A. War Losses
　B. The Home Front
　C. The Peace Treaty

Questions

What were the basic causes of the Revolutionary War?
What were some of the events leading to the war?
Where was "the shot heard round the world" fired?
What was the last major battle of the war?
Why did the colonists resent British attempts to restore authority over them after 1763?
What did John Adams mean when he wrote: "The Revolution was effected before the war commenced"?
Why did it seem in 1775 that the colonists must struggle stubbornly to win the Revolutionary War?
What was the part of ships in the war?
In what ways was the Revolutionary War much more than a conflict between England and the colonies?
What event in the war encouraged France to form an open military alliance with the colonies?

Reading and Study Guide

For a *Reading and Study Guide on the Revolutionary War in America*, see the RESEARCH GUIDE/INDEX, Volume 22.

REVOLVER

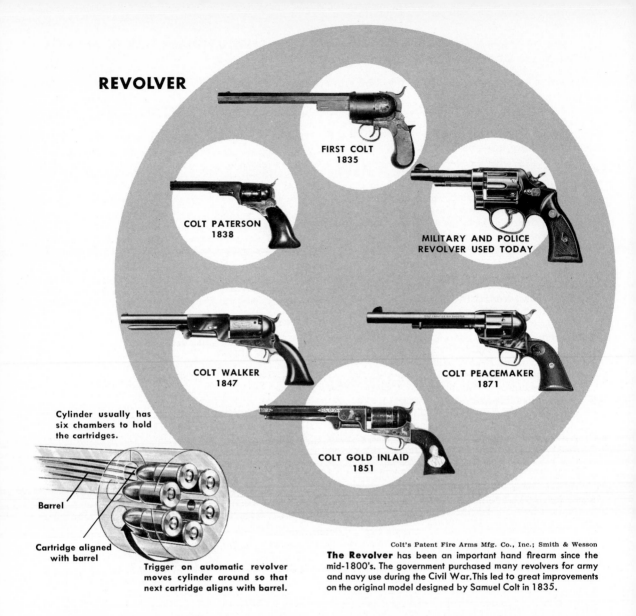

FIRST COLT
1835

COLT PATERSON
1838

MILITARY AND POLICE
REVOLVER USED TODAY

COLT WALKER
1847

COLT PEACEMAKER
1871

COLT GOLD INLAID
1851

Cylinder usually has
six chambers to hold
the cartridges.

Barrel

Cartridge aligned
with barrel

Trigger on automatic revolver
moves cylinder around so that
next cartridge aligns with barrel.

Colt's Patent Fire Arms Mfg. Co., Inc.; Smith & Wesson

The Revolver has been an important hand firearm since the mid-1800's. The government purchased many revolvers for army and navy use during the Civil War. This led to great improvements on the original model designed by Samuel Colt in 1835.

REVOLVER is a hand firearm that has had an important place in recent history. In its simplest form, a revolver consists of a fixed *barrel* (tube), a firing mechanism, and a revolving cylinder that carries loaded cartridges into alignment with the firing mechanism and the rear of the barrel. The cylinder has several chambers for cartridges evenly spaced around its axis. Revolvers usually have five or six chambers, and are often called *six-shooters*.

A revolver is *cocked* when a new chamber is aligned with the barrel and firing mechanism. There are two ways to cock a revolver. In a *single-action* revolver, the user pulls back the hammer by hand. He then pulls the trigger to fire. In a *double-action* revolver, squeezing the trigger once cocks the hammer and then fires the weapon.

A typical single-shot revolver has a cylinder with six chambers arranged around a central axis. The cylinder may swing out so that it can be easily loaded. The chambers are loaded with six cartridges. When the cylinder is closed, the revolver is ready for firing. The action of cocking causes the cylinder to rotate, aligning the next chamber with the barrel.

Most modern revolvers use rimmed ammunition loaded with smokeless powder. The ammunition contains either plain lead or metal-jacketed lead bullets. Most ammunition made in the United States has a jacket made of an alloy containing 95 per cent copper and 5 per cent zinc. Some revolver ammunition has steel jackets.

The idea for a revolver dates back as far as the early 1500's. But the first person to design a revolver simple and rugged enough for long and hard use was an American inventor, Samuel Colt. He designed his weapon in 1835, and was granted a patent for it a year later. Critically reviewed by DEPARTMENT OF THE ARMY

See also BULLET; COLT, SAMUEL; FIREARM; PISTOL.

REWRITE MAN. See JOURNALISM (The Newspaper).

REX CAT. See CAT (Rex Cats).

REXROTH, KENNETH (1905-   ), is an American poet. Since 1940, he has called for freedom from traditional styles in poetry, which he considers artificial. This attitude led many critics to call Rexroth the forerunner of the *beat* movement of the 1950's. Beat writers attacked the use of what they considered outmoded traditions in art.

Rexroth's poems generally show he has a more complex, interesting, and informed mind than most Beat writers. *The Dragon and the Unicorn* (1952) is a book-length story poem that explores the nature of love. *In Defense of the Earth* (1956) contains love poetry, poems directed toward young people, and translations of Japanese poetry. Rexroth is also a painter and essayist and has translated poems from the Japanese, Chinese, Greek, and Latin. He was born in South Bend, Ind. MONA VAN DUYN

REY, JEAN (1902-   ), a Belgian statesman, served as chief administrator of the European Community from 1967, when it was established, until 1970. From 1958 to 1967, Rey had been in charge of the European Economic Community's relations with nonmember countries. See EUROPEAN COMMUNITY.

Rey began his political career in 1935 as a city councilman in Liège, his birthplace. He represented Liège in Parliament in 1939 and from 1946 to 1958. Rey spent 1940 to 1945 as a prisoner of war in Germany. He became convinced that the only way to prevent future wars in Europe was by uniting the European countries. After the war, Rey urged adoption of international trade and work agreements. He served as Belgium's minister of reconstruction from 1949 to 1950, and as minister of economic affairs from 1954 to 1958.

REYKJAVÍK, *RAKE yuh VEEK* (pop. 81,026; met. area 93,953; alt. 45 ft.), is the capital and only large city of

Reynolds' *The Age of Innocence* shows the artist's skill in painting sensitive and appealing portraits of young children.

Oil painting (1788), The National Gallery, London

Iceland. It is a seaport on the southwestern coast, at the head of Faxaflói, a bay. For location, see ICELAND (map). The city is the trading center of Iceland as well as the center of government and education. It has many schools, a university, an observatory, a theater, and a national library.

Water from nearby hot springs is used to heat all buildings in Reykjavík. The water is first piped to large concrete tanks on a hill outside the city. It is then piped into the buildings by flow of gravity.

During World War II, British and American troops protected Reykjavík and all Iceland from possible attack by Germany. A $7 million fertilizer plant was opened nearby in 1954.   RICHARD BECK

REYNARD. See Fox.

REYNOLDS, SIR JOSHUA (1723-1792), was one of the greatest English portrait painters. He probably achieved greater fame and fortune than any other. Thomas Gainsborough rivaled him in the quality of his work, but not in social success or financial reward. Reynolds became the first president of the Royal Academy, and was knighted by King George III in 1768. In 1784, he was made "painter to the king."

Noblemen and wealthy men sought Reynolds' company, and he became a close associate of the leading literary figures of his time. In 1764, he helped found the London Literary Club with such writers as Samuel Johnson, James Boswell, Oliver Goldsmith, and Edmund Burke. He wrote well himself on the theory of art.

Reynolds followed Anton Van Dyck in painting fashionable portraits. He was also influenced by the Venetian painters, but he could not equal either Van Dyck or the Venetians in drawing or in composition. He turned out an enormous number of portraits at high prices. Reynolds' most famous works include portraits of Samuel Johnson, David Garrick, Laurence Sterne, and Oliver Goldsmith. Other well-known paintings by Reynolds include *The Age of Innocence, Mrs. Siddons as the Tragic Muse, The Infant Hercules, The Strawberry Girl,* and *Garrick Between Comedy and Tragedy.*

Reynolds was born in Plympton Earl in Devonshire, England, on July 16, 1723. He was educated by his father, a schoolmaster and clergyman. In 1740, Reynolds went to London, where he studied with Thomas Hudson. In 1746, he established himself in London as a portrait painter.   L. D. LONGMAN

REZA KHAN PAHLAVI, *reh ZAH KAHN PA lah vee,* or PAHLEVI (1877-1944), was the *shah* (king) of Iran (Persia) from 1925 to 1941. He centralized the government, built railroads and industry, decreed compulsory education, and tried to modernize his country. When World War II broke out, Reza tried to maintain neutrality and did not suppress the Nazis in his country. Russia and England forced him to abdicate in 1941, and he died in exile in South Africa in 1944.

Reza was born in an obscure village in Mazanderan province. He became an army officer. In 1921, he led his army into Teheran, the capital, and took over the government. He became prime minister in 1923 and shah in 1925.   SYDNEY N. FISHER

See also IRAN (Reza Khan and Progress).

RFC. See RECONSTRUCTION FINANCE CORPORATION.

R.F.D. See RURAL DELIVERY.

271

The Rhea is often called the South American ostrich, although it is much smaller than the real ostrich.

takes place in only about 1 of 20 Rh-negative women married to Rh-positive men. If the mother's blood is tested and observed for antibodies during pregnancy, a doctor may treat the trouble in one of two ways. He may replace the baby's blood with fresh blood, or he may inject the mother with a vaccine shortly after the birth of her first child to prevent Rh disease with later children. WILLIAM DAMESHEK

See also LANDSTEINER, KARL; TRANSFUSION, BLOOD.

RHADAMANTHUS, RAD uh MAN thus, was a son of Zeus (Jupiter) and Europa. He was the ruler of the happy kingdom of the Islands of the Blest. After his death, he became one of the three judges who decided if dead souls were to pass on to happiness in the Elysian Fields or if they were to suffer in Tartarus (see ELYSIAN FIELDS; TARTARUS). JAMES F. CRONIN

RHAMPHORHYNCHUS. See PTERODACTYL.

RHAPSODY, RAP soh dih, is the name given to certain musical compositions and poetic works. Such works are usually emotional, somewhat disconnected, and ecstatic in nature. In ancient Greece, an epic poem intended to be recited was called a rhapsody.

RHEA. See BOEHMERIA.

RHEA, REE uh, is a large South American bird that cannot fly. It looks like a small ostrich, and it is often called the South American ostrich. However, it has three toes on each foot, while the ostrich has two. The rhea also has larger wings and more feathers on its neck and head than the ostrich. The common rhea stands about 5 feet tall and weighs about 50 pounds.

Rheas live on the plains of southern Brazil, Uruguay, Paraguay, and Argentina. They usually live in flocks of from 20 to 30 birds, generally in brush-covered land near water where they can bathe and swim. They eat leaves, roots and insects.

Rheas have unusual nesting habits. The male scrapes a shallow hole in the ground and lines it with dry grass. Then he leads several hens to the nest, and each hen lays an egg. This process may be repeated several times, and a nest may contain as many as 30 eggs. The male then sits on the eggs until they hatch. He also cares for the young birds.

Scientific Classification. Rheas belong to the order *Rheaformes*. They make up the rhea family, *Rheidae*. The common bird is classified as genus *Rhea*, species *R. americana*. RAYMOND A. PAYNTER, JR.

See also OSTRICH.

RHEA, REE uh, was the goddess of the growth of natural things in Greek mythology. She was called *Cybele* in Phrygia and *Magna Mater* (Great Mother) in Rome. The Megalensian Games started in her honor in 191 B.C. Rhea was the daughter of Uranus (Heaven) and Gaea (Earth). She married Cronus, or Saturn (see SATURN). Among her children were Hera (Juno), Zeus (Jupiter), Pluto, Poseidon (Neptune), and Demeter (Ceres). JAMES F. CRONIN

RHEE, SYNGMAN (1875-1965), a Korean statesman, became the first president of the Republic of Korea in 1948. He left office in 1960, soon after his election to a fourth term, because of widespread riots following unfair election practices.

Rhee was born in Hwanghae province, and was educated in Seoul. Imprisoned from 1897 to 1904 for leading student demonstrations for independence, he wrote the book *Spirit of Independence* (1904). He

RH FACTOR is a substance in the red blood cells of most persons. When this substance combines with a particular member of a group of proteins called *agglutinins*, it causes the red blood cells to *agglutinate* (clump). This reaction may produce serious illness or death. Persons who have the Rh factor are known as Rh-positive. Those who do not have the Rh factor are Rh-negative. Karl Landsteiner and Alexander Wiener, who found the factor in rhesus monkeys in 1940, named it *Rh* for the monkey.

No naturally occurring agglutinin reacts with the Rh factor. But if an Rh-negative person receives a transfusion of Rh-positive blood, an antibody called *anti-Rh* may build up in his blood plasma (see ANTIBODY). This antibody can act as an agglutinin with Rh-positive blood. Thus, if the person receives a second transfusion of Rh-positive blood, the anti-Rh will attack the Rh-positive red blood cells and cause agglutination.

The Rh factor is inherited. The child of an Rh-negative mother and an Rh-positive father may be Rh-positive. Before birth, some of the baby's blood cells may enter the mother's blood. Then the mother may build up Rh antibodies. The antibodies may return to the baby's blood. This reaction usually does not cause trouble for the first child. But the number of antibodies in the mother's blood may build up enough to harm a second Rh-positive child. This may result in severe anemia, brain damage, or death. A severe reaction then went to the United States and studied at George Washington, Harvard, and Princeton universities. Rhee lived in exile in Honolulu for 20 years. He returned to Korea after Japanese forces surrendered in World War II, but went back to Hawaii to live following his resignation in 1960.   GEORGE E. TAYLOR

RHEIMS, or **REIMS.** See REIMS.

RHEINGOLD, DAS. See OPERA (Das Rheingold).

RHENIUM, *REE nih um,* is a rare, costly, silvery-white metal. It is found in small amounts in such minerals as *gadolinite,* and *molybdenite.* Rhenium has one of the highest melting points of the chemical elements. Because it withstands high temperatures, rhenium is a valuable ingredient in certain *alloys* (mixtures of *metals*). It is sometimes mixed with tungsten or platinum to make heat-resistant electrical equipment. It is also used in making *filaments* (fine wires) for *mass spectrographs* (light instruments). The German scientists Walter Noddack, Ida Tacke, and Otto Berg discovered rhenium in 1925. It has the chemical symbol Re. Its atomic number is 75, and its atomic weight is 186.2. It melts at 3180° C. and boils at 5627° C.   ALAN DAVISON

RHEOSTAT, *REE oh stat,* is a device used to regulate and control electric current. Many different kinds of rheostats are used with motors, radio transmitters, generators, and other types of electrical equipment. Some are made of resistance wire and some of carbon. A simple rheostat consists of a wire wound around a cylindrical piece of insulating material. A metal arm that can be moved along the turns of the wire touches each turn as it moves. The current passes through the wire and then into the movable arm. The more turns of wire on the rheostat, the greater its resistance will be, and the smaller the amount of current which will flow through it.   PALMER H. CRAIG

By Moving the Slide Along the Resistance Coil of the rheostat, one can regulate the amount of current.

Press Syndicate

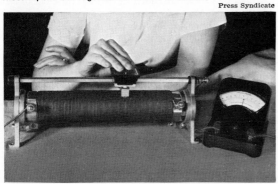

RHESUS MONKEY. See MONKEY (Old World Monkeys; picture).

RHETORIC. See ORATORS AND ORATORY.

RHEUMATIC FEVER is a serious disease that occurs in children and young adults. It was once called *acute inflammatory rheumatism.* Doctors have estimated that about 250,000 persons in the United States contract rheumatic fever each year.

Cause. Doctors believe that a special group of streptococci called the *A beta-hemolytic streptococci* cause rheumatic fever. These are the same organisms

that cause streptococcal sore throat (see STREPTOCOCCUS). But no one knows exactly how they attack the body to cause rheumatic fever.

Symptoms. The disease usually begins with vague, mild pains in the muscles. Because they are so mild and occur in children, people have called them "growing pains." Soon the pains become intense and the person's joints swell. The disease may subside in a few weeks, or may continue for many months, or even years.

Rheumatic Heart Disease. Rheumatic fever is one of the greatest causes of heart diseases in young persons, although some may recover fully without heart damage. Usually at some stage of the disease doctors find that the patient's heart has been affected. In some persons, the involvement may be so minor that it can only be found by using an electrocardiogram. In others, it seriously affects the muscles and valves of the heart.

Frequently the disease damages the heart valves so they cannot completely close. Then when the heart pumps blood out into the great body vessels, some of it flows back. Doctors call the sound of this back-flowing blood a *murmur* (see HEART MURMUR). But sometimes the heart valves heal. However, large scars may form that partially shut off the flow of blood between the heart chambers. Doctors call this condition *stenosis.* Surgery often will correct either of these conditions.

Treatment. To persons with rheumatic fever, complete rest in bed is essential until all signs of fever and inflammation are gone. Doctors often use drugs of the salicylate group (aspirin is one) to ease the pain. ACTH and Cortisone are also used.

When the patient is allowed out of bed, his activities are gradually increased. Because of modern methods of treatment, few children develop so much heart damage that normal activity must be curtailed. Usually, they attend regular school and enter into all but the most strenuous activities.   ALAN C. SIEGEL

See also HEART (Rheumatic Fever).

RHEUMATISM, *ROO muh tiz'm,* is any painful condition that involves the muscles, joints, or connective tissues such as tendons and ligaments. The word comes from the Greek word *rheumatismos,* meaning a *flowing of mucus.* Doctors have found that changes in character of the mucus in body tissues is responsible for many rheumatic diseases.

Muscular rheumatism is probably one of the most common forms. It involves the muscles rather than the joints of the body. The muscle stiffness that occurs during influenza or colds, or when a person's arms or legs have been overstrained, are types of muscular rheumatism. *Wryneck* (a stiff neck) and lumbago are other common forms (see LUMBAGO).

Rheumatic fever is a kind of rheumatism that particularly affects young persons. It often causes heart disease (see RHEUMATIC FEVER). Other kinds of rheumatism include *arthritis,* in which the joints become inflamed and swollen, and *bursitis,* an inflammation of the lubricating spaces near the joints (see ARTHRITIS; BURSITIS). Several kinds of severe rheumatism are called *collagen diseases.* These affect all parts of the body. They are named for the protein, collagen, that makes up the fibers of all connective tissue.   JOSEPH LEE HOLLANDER

RHINE OF AMERICA. See HUDSON RIVER.

German Railroads Information Office

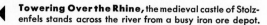

RHINE RIVER is the most important inland waterway in Europe. It is about 700 miles long, and drains an area of more than 75,700 square miles. The river rises in eastern Switzerland. It forms part of the borders of Switzerland, Liechtenstein, Austria, France, and Germany. It flows through Germany and The Netherlands, and empties into the North Sea. To Germans, the Rhine is a symbol of their national history and strength. In Richard Wagner's operas, the Nibelungen ring, a magic ring of Rhine gold, gives its possessor power over all the world.

The Course of the Rhine. Two glacier-fed mountain torrents rise and flow eastward in the high Alps of eastern Switzerland, close to the Italian border. One is the *Vorder* Rhine, and the other is the *Hinter* Rhine. From their union, the Rhine hurries along the edge of Austria and the miniature state of Liechtenstein to Lake Constance, 1,306 feet above the sea. This lake frees the river of its mountain mud and sends it westward, a deep, transparent green, to tumble over a fall 70 feet high at Schaffhausen. From there the Rhine winds between Germany and Switzerland to Basel. This city serves as landlocked Switzerland's principal port. At Basel, the Rhine, now 225 yards wide, turns to the north.

North of Basel the Rhine flows between the Black Forest on the east and the Vosges Mountains on the west. It follows a course down the middle of a plain which is about 20 miles wide and 180 miles long. In the southern part of the plain, the Rhine serves as the boundary between France and Germany. From Basel,

The Rhine River Flows from the Alps to the North Sea.

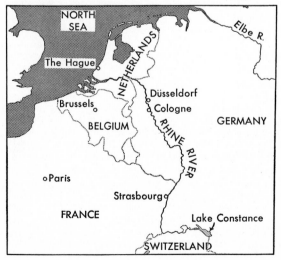

the river gradually widens, and at Bingen, it leaves the plain and plunges into a narrow gorge through the Rhenish Slate Mountains. Here is the rock where the legendary Lorelei sat, and lured boatmen to destruction with her song. There are dozens of hills around which center legends of the heroic Roland, Siegfried, and other historic and mythical figures (see Lorelei; Mouse Tower). At Bonn, river and valley widen again as the Rhine enters the North German Plain on its journey to The Netherlands and its broad delta leading into the North Sea.

Along its course, the Rhine receives the waters of the Neckar, Main, Lahn, Ruhr, and Lippe rivers from the east. The Nahe and Moselle rivers flow into it from the west. Man-made canals from the Rhine to the Rhône, Marne, Ems, Weser, Elbe, and Oder rivers make the Rhine part of a great inland navigation system. The Ludwig Canal connects the Rhine to the Danube River. Below Basel, the Rhine's major ports are Strasbourg, Karlsruhe, Mannheim, Cologne, and Duisburg, the gateway to the industrial Ruhr Valley. Rotterdam is the Rhine River's chief port in The Netherlands.

The Rhine in History. The Rhine has been important in European history ever since Julius Caesar built a timber bridge across it. For 400 years the Rhine was the boundary between the Romans and the Germanic tribes. On the west bank of the Rhine grew up the Roman cities of Cologne, or Köln (Colonia Agrippina), Bonn (Bonna), Koblenz (Confluentes), Mainz (Maguntiacum), all in Germany; Strasbourg (Argentoratum), in France; and Basel (Basilia), in Switzerland. During the Middle Ages, the Rhine was under German rule from Basel to The Netherlands. But when France gained a foothold on its western shore, in 1648, at the close of the Thirty Years' War, a struggle began which lasted into the 1900's. Louis XIV made gains in the Rhine Valley, and Napoleon restored the old Roman boundaries of France. Even after Napoleon was defeated, Alsace, which borders the Rhine from Switzerland to beyond Strasbourg, was left in French hands. But Germany seized it again in 1870.

The same territory was battled over once more during World War I. The Treaty of Versailles returned Alsace and Lorraine to France, again extending that country's domain to the Rhine. Germany signed an agreement not to fortify the Rhineland. In 1936, Hitler repudiated this agreement and began to militarize the region. During World War II, heavy fighting occurred along the Rhine in the last part of the European struggle. After the war, the river again became one of the busiest waterways in the world.   Frank O. Ahnert

RHINITIS, *rye NY tihs,* is an inflammation of the mucous membranes that line the interior portions of the nose. This condition occurs most frequently as *acute rhinitis,* or the common cold. As *allergic rhinitis,* it is a common result of hay fever, which resembles the common cold. In a condition called *atrophic rhinitis,* the mucous membranes wear away so that they are quite thin. During the late stages of this disease, bad-smelling crusts develop on the membranes. See also Cold, Common; Hay Fever.   Noah D. Fabricant

Freight Barges and Passenger Steamboats sail past the massive rock where legend says the water nymph Lorelei lived and lured sailors to destruction. The rock stands along the Rhine River between the German cities of Mainz and Koblenz.

RHINOCEROS

RHINOCEROS, *ry NAHS ur uhs*, is a huge animal that ranks as one of the largest land creatures. The rhinoceros has an immense, solid body, and short, clumsy legs. Its thick skin hangs loosely, and has almost no hair. Depending on the kind, the rhinoceros has one or two slightly curving horns that project from its long nose. The horns continue to grow throughout the life of the rhinoceros. The name *rhinoceros* comes from two Greek words and means *nose-horned*.

The animal has three toes on each foot. Each toe ends in a separate hoof. On each front foot is a fourth toe that is *rudimentary*, or no longer used. This makes the rhinoceros different from the hippopotamus, which has four developed toes. The hippopotamus is a relative of the hog, and the rhinoceros is more nearly related to the horse.

The rhinoceros eats grass, leafy twigs, and shrubs. In captivity, which it endures well, it enjoys bread, fruits, and sweets. Wild rhinoceroses live only in Africa, in southeastern Asia, and on a few large islands near the Asiatic coast. In prehistoric times, they also roamed over Europe, North America, and northern Asia.

Kinds of Rhinoceroses. There are five distinct kinds of rhinoceroses. The one most often seen in zoos and in menageries is the *Indian rhinoceros*, the largest of the three kinds that live in Asia. It stands about 5 feet 8 inches high at the shoulder, and weighs about 2 tons. It has one great blue-black horn, very thick at the base and usually about a foot long. Once in a great while the animal may stand over 6 feet and up to $6\frac{1}{2}$ feet, with a horn 2 feet long. The skin of the rhinoceros is sprinkled with round knobs. It hangs in such definite folds that the huge beast looks as though it were wearing armor plate. But the thick hide can be pierced by a knife or bullet. The animal lives in marshy jungles among growths of reeds and tall grass, on which it feeds morning and evening. The ancients of Oriental countries knew this rhinoceros well. It was even used in the games of the circus in Rome before the time of Christ. Specimens have become so rare that they are now protected by law.

The similar one-horned *Javan rhinoceros* once ranged from eastern Bengal into Burma, and southward to Java and the islands of Borneo and Sumatra. It is now nearly extinct.

The *Sumatran* species is smaller than any other rhinoceros, and has two horns. It stands from 4 to $4\frac{1}{2}$ feet tall, and weighs about a ton. It is quite hairy, especially on the tail and ears. This species may also be found in Borneo and on the Malay Peninsula. Both the Javan

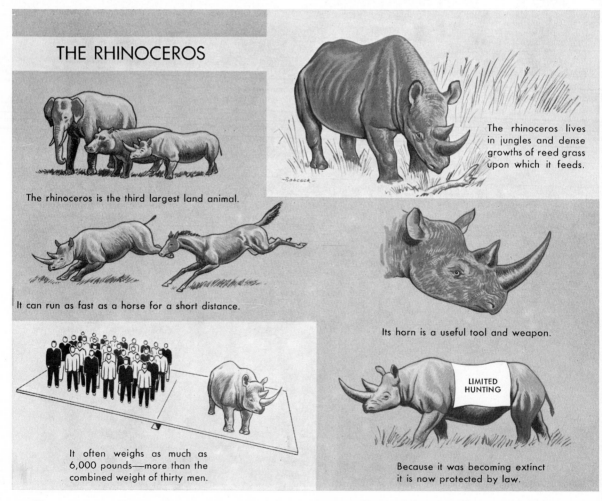

THE RHINOCEROS

The rhinoceros is the third largest land animal.

It can run as fast as a horse for a short distance.

It often weighs as much as 6,000 pounds—more than the combined weight of thirty men.

The rhinoceros lives in jungles and dense growths of reed grass upon which it feeds.

Its horn is a useful tool and weapon.

LIMITED HUNTING

Because it was becoming extinct it is now protected by law.

Towers, Black Star

The Wrinkled Face of a two-horned rhino looks little like that of the horse, which is its relative. Rhinoceros hunters use high-powered rifles and steel-tipped shells to pierce the tough skin of this heavy but speedy animal.

and Sumatran rhinoceroses are found in forested hills.

The two African species are two-horned. They are known as the *black rhinoceros* and the *white rhinoceros*, although they are almost the same bluish-gray color. *Long-lipped* (for the black) and *square-mouthed* (for the white) are better names for them. The black rhinoceros has a front horn that is sometimes as much as $3\frac{1}{2}$ feet long. It uses this horn for defending itself. The rear horn may be the same length or shorter. The digging horn is so strong that the animal easily uproots and overturns bushes and small trees with it. Then it feeds on the leaves. This rhinoceros lives on dry plains that are covered with tall brush. It remains hidden by day, and wanders about at night in search of food and water.

The white rhinoceros is the largest of all the rhinoceroses. It stands about 5 feet 8 inches tall. In some cases, it may be over 6 feet tall and 15 feet long. It weighs about $3\frac{1}{2}$ tons. The horns of the female are longer but more slender than those of the male. This is also true for the black rhinoceros. A record white-rhinoceros horn measured 62 inches. The white rhinoceros was once nearly extinct. It is now increasing in numbers in Uganda. Both species are protected by law. Limited hunting of the black rhinoceros is usually allowed by special license.

Hunting the Rhinoceros. The Indian rhinoceros lives in jungles and thickets of grass and reeds that may grow 20 feet high. Sometimes, it is tracked to its hiding place with an elephant. At times, a hunter on foot follows its well-beaten track to a drinking place, and surprises it wallowing shoulder-deep in a mudhole. It is more common, however, to beat the animal out with a line of elephants. Hunters are stationed at intervals along the edge of the jungle to shoot it when it breaks from cover. The animal is quiet and harmless unless it is provoked, and prefers to seek safety in flight. But, if it is wounded or badly confused, it may turn and charge. The African black rhinoceros has been hunted for sport so much that it is becoming rare. Although this large animal appears clumsy, it can move swiftly. For a short distance, it can run as fast as a horse.

Scientific Classification. Rhinoceroses make up the family *Rhinocerotidae.* The Indian rhinoceros is genus *Rhinoceros,* species *unicornis;* the Javan is *R. sondaicus;* the Sumatran is *Didermocerus sumatrensis;* the black is *Diceros bicornis;* the white is *D. simus.*   THEODORE H. EATON, JR.

See also ANIMAL (color pictures: Animals of the Grasslands).

RHINOCEROS BEETLE. See BEETLE (pictures).

RHINOCEROS IGUANA. See IGUANA.

RHIZOID. See MOSS; PLANT (Liverworts and Mosses).

RHIZOME, *RYE zohm,* or ROOTSTOCK, is a long, horizontal, underground stem that looks like a root. It serves as a special organ for storing food. Many spring-flowering perennial plants such as blue flag and wild ginger have a *rhizome.* See also BULB; ORRISROOT.

Old Slater Mill, a Historic Textile Mill, Stands in Pawtucket

RHODE ISLAND is the smallest state in the Union. It covers only 1,214 square miles—843 square miles less than Delaware, the second smallest state. In spite of its size, Rhode Island is an important industrial state. It ranks high among the states in textile and jewelry production. Rhode Island's nickname is *Little Rhody*. Providence is Rhode Island's capital and largest city.

Rhode Island lies on beautiful Narragansett Bay, an arm of the Atlantic Ocean. The bay makes the state a leading vacationland and an important defense center. Thousands of vacationers come to Rhode Island each summer to enjoy boating, fishing, and other water sports. Giant naval bases lie along Narragansett Bay at Newport and Quonset Point. The Newport base is one of the permanent ports of the United States Atlantic Fleet.

Narragansett Bay almost cuts Rhode Island in two. The bay extends 28 miles inland from southern Rhode Island. The state has 36 islands, most of which are in the bay. Aquidneck, the largest island, was officially named *Rhode Island* in 1644. Towns on the mainland were called *Providence Plantations*. As a result, Rhode Island's official name is *State of Rhode Island and Providence Plantations*. Thus, the smallest state has the longest official name.

About 85 per cent of Rhode Island's people live in the Providence-Pawtucket-Warwick metropolitan area. Only California and New Jersey have a greater percentage of urban residents. About a fifth of Rhode Island's people live in Providence itself, second to Boston among New England's largest cities.

The people of Rhode Island have played important parts in the history and industrial development of the United States. Roger Williams, who founded Providence in 1636, worked for religious and political freedom. Under his leadership, Rhode Islanders gained fame for their love of personal liberty. In 1776, Rhode Island became the first of the 13 original colonies to formally declare independence from Great Britain. But it was the last colony to ratify the U.S. Constitution. Rhode Island delayed ratification for three years—until 1790—when the Bill of Rights was ready to be added to the Constitution.

Samuel Slater of Rhode Island founded the American textile industry. He built the first American textile machines during the late 1700's. Nehemiah and Seril Dodge, Rhode Island brothers, started the jewelry industry in America. Rhode Island men also were prominent in boatbuilding, fishing, shipping, and whaling.

For the relationship of Rhode Island to other states in its region, see NEW ENGLAND.

RHODE ISLAND ⚓ *LITTLE RHODY*

Cliff Walk Winds Past *The Breakers,* **the Cornelius Vanderbilt Estate in Newport**

Rhode Island (blue) ranks as the smallest of all the 50 states. It is one of the New England States (gray).

The contributors of this article are William D. Metz, Chairman of the Department of History at the University of Rhode Island; Marion I. Wright, Professor of Geography at Rhode Island College; and Joseph M. Ungaro, Managing Editor of the Providence Journal *and* Evening Bulletin.

FACTS IN BRIEF

Capital: Providence.

Government: *Congress*—U.S. senators, 2; U.S. representatives, 2. *Electoral Votes*—4. *State Legislature*—senators, 50; representatives, 100. *Counties*—5 (Rhode Island has no county governments). *Cities and Towns*—39 with local governments.

Area: 1,214 square miles (including 165 square miles of inland water but excluding 14 square miles of Atlantic coastal water), 50th and smallest in size among the states. *Greatest Distances*—(north-south) 48 miles; (east-west) 37 miles. *Coastline*—40 miles.

Elevation. *Highest*—Jerimoth Hill, 812 feet above sea level; *Lowest*—sea level along the Atlantic Coast.

Population: *1970 Census*—949,723; 39th among the states; density, 782 persons to the square mile; distribution, 87 per cent urban, 13 per cent rural. *1960 Census*—859,488.

Chief Products: *Agriculture*—apples, beef cattle, broilers, dairy products, eggs, greenhouse and nursery products, hogs, potatoes. *Fishing Industry*—clams, flounders, lobsters. *Manufacturing*—food and related products, jewelry, machinery, metal products, primary metals, textiles. *Mining*—sand and gravel, stone.

Statehood: May 29, 1790, the 13th state.

State Motto: *Hope.*

State Song: "Rhode Island." Words and music by T. Clarke Brown.

Constitution of Rhode Island was adopted in 1842. It became effective on May 2, 1843. Until then, a royal English charter of 1663 served as Rhode Island's constitution. An *amendment* (change) to the state constitution may be proposed by the Rhode Island legislature or by a constitutional convention. To become law, amendments proposed in the legislature need the approval of a majority of the legislators twice—once before and once after an election. The amendments are then submitted to the people in a regular election. Three-fifths of those voting must approve the amendments. To call a constitutional convention, a majority vote by the legislators and voters is needed. Amendments proposed by a constitutional convention require the approval of a majority of the voters in a regular election.

Executive. The governor of Rhode Island holds office for two years. He may be re-elected any number of times. The governor receives a yearly salary of $30,000. The state has no official residence for its governor. For a list of all the governors of Rhode Island, see the *History* section of this article. Rhode Island voters also elect the lieutenant governor, attorney general, secretary of state, and state treasurer to two-year terms. The governor, with the state senate's approval, appoints most other key executive officials. These officials include the directors of administration, business regulation, employment security, health, labor, natural resources, public works, and social welfare.

Legislature of Rhode Island is called the *General Assembly*. It consists of a 50-member senate and a 100-member house of representatives. Voters in each of Rhode Island's 50 senatorial districts elect one senator. Voters in each of the state's 100 representative districts elect one representative. Senators and representatives serve two-year terms.

The legislature meets annually, beginning on the first Tuesday of January. Regular and special legislative sessions have no time limit. But legislators are paid for only 60 working days during regular sessions.

In 1966, the legislature *reapportioned* (redivided) the senate and the house of representatives. For a discussion of reapportionment in Rhode Island, see *The Mid-1900's* section of this article.

Courts. The supreme court of Rhode Island has a chief justice and four associate justices. The General Assembly elects the justices to life terms. The justices choose a chief justice from among their group. Rhode Island's next lower court, the superior court, has a presiding justice and 10 associate justices. The governor, with the senate's consent, appoints superior court justices to life terms. Other Rhode Island courts include a family court, a district court, and 39 probate courts. The governor appoints family court judges to life terms, and district court judges to 10-year terms. These appointments also need the senate's approval. City and town councils appoint probate judges.

Local Government. Rhode Island and Connecticut are the only states that have no county governments. Five of Rhode Island's 8 cities and 10 of its 31 towns have *home rule*. That is, they can write and amend their charters without permission from the legislature. Rhode Island *towns* are similar to *townships* in other states. They are geographic districts that may include several communities under one government. Rhode Island has many unincorporated villages.

Most large Rhode Island cities have the mayor-council form of government. These cities include Central Falls, Cranston, Pawtucket, Providence, Warwick, and Woonsocket. East Providence and Newport use the council-manager form of government.

The town meeting is the most common form of government in Rhode Island towns. Dating from colonial days, the town meeting is one of the purest examples of democracy. Voters at annual town meetings participate directly in governmental decisions. They elect officials, approve budgets, pass laws, and decide other business.

Taxation provides about three-fourths of the state government's income. Almost all the rest comes from federal grants and other U.S. government programs. Sales and gross receipts taxes bring in the largest part

Eric M. Sanford

Old Colony House in Newport was built in 1739. On May 4, 1776, colonists stood on the balcony to announce Rhode Island's independence from Great Britain. The building served as a hospital for French and for British forces during the Revolutionary War. Then, from 1790 to 1900, it was the meeting place for Rhode Island's General Assembly.

The State Seal

Symbols of Rhode Island. On the seal, the state motto, *Hope*, is printed above an anchor, a symbol of hope. The date is the year Roger Williams founded Providence, the state's first permanent white settlement. The seal was adopted in 1875. The state flag, adopted in 1877, has 13 gold stars that represent the 13 original colonies. The white field symbolizes the white uniforms worn by Rhode Island soldiers during the Revolutionary War.

Flag and flower illustrations, courtesy of Eli Lilly and Company

of the state's revenue. Other major sources of revenue include taxes on alcoholic beverages, cigarettes, corporation income, gasoline, horse racing, inheritances, insurance, personal income, and public utilities. The state also receives income from license and motor vehicle registration fees.

Politics. Rhode Island became a Republican state shortly before the Civil War. Most Rhode Island voters favored the antislavery and pro-Northern policies of the Republican Party. The growth of cities, usually favorable to the Democratic Party, helped Rhode Island become a two-party state during the 1920's.

Rhode Island voters supported the Republican presidential candidate in every election from 1856 to 1908. They voted for Woodrow Wilson, a Democrat, in 1912, but supported Republicans in the next three elections. Since 1928, the state has voted Democratic in all presidential elections except 1952, 1956, and 1972. For the state's electoral votes and voting record in presidential elections, see ELECTORAL COLLEGE (table).

In state and congressional elections, Rhode Islanders usually voted for Republicans from the 1860's to the 1920's. Since the 1920's, they have generally favored Democratic candidates for the state legislature and for Congress. Rhode Islanders follow no general party pattern in choosing their governor, and often elect a governor and a lieutenant governor from different parties.

The State Capitol is in Providence, the capital of Rhode Island since 1900. Earlier capitals were Newport, East Greenwich, Bristol, South Kingstown, and Providence (at the same time, 1663-1854); and Newport and Providence (at the same time, 1854-1900).

Rhode Island Development Council

The State Flag

The State Bird
Rhode Island Red

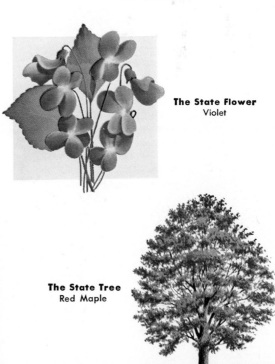

The State Flower
Violet

The State Tree
Red Maple

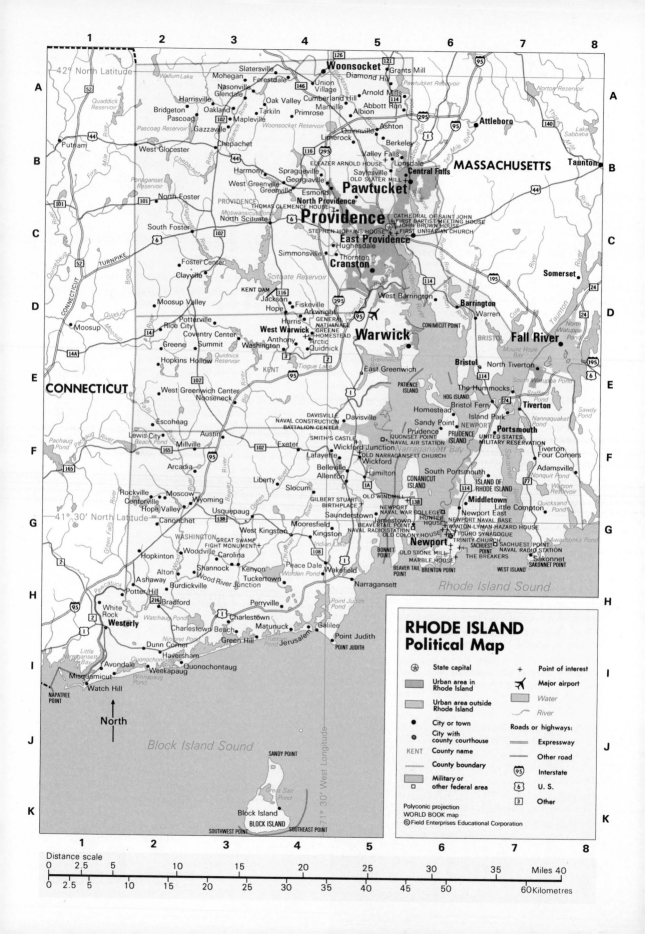

RHODE ISLAND
Political Map

Legend:
- ⊛ State capital
- Urban area in Rhode Island
- Urban area outside Rhode Island
- ● City or town
- ⊙ City with county courthouse
- KENT County name
- County boundary
- Military or other federal area
- + Point of interest
- ✈ Major airport
- Water
- River

Roads or highways:
- Expressway
- Other road
- 95 Interstate
- 6 U.S.
- 3 Other

Polyconic projection
WORLD BOOK map
ⓒ Field Enterprises Educational Corporation

North

Distance scale

Miles 0 2.5 5 10 15 20 25 30 35 40

Kilometres 0 2.5 5 10 15 20 25 30 35 45 50 60

Population

949,723	...Census...	1970
859,488	"	1960
791,896	"	1950
713,346	"	1940
687,497	"	1930
604,397	"	1920
542,610	"	1910
428,556	"	1900
345,506	"	1890
276,531	"	1880
217,353	"	1870
174,620	"	1860
147,545	"	1850
108,830	"	1840
97,199	"	1830
83,059	"	1820
76,931	"	1810
69,122	"	1800
68,825	"	1790

Metropolitan Area

Fall River (Mass.) 149,976
(137,417 in Mass.;
12,559 in R.I.)
Providence-
Warwick-
Pawtucket ...914,110
(792,515 in R.I.;
121,595 in Mass.)

Counties

Bristol ....45,937..D 7
Kent ....142,382..E 4
Newport ...94,228..F 6
Providence 581,470..C 3
Washington 85,706..G 2

Cities and Towns

Adamsville ....F 8
Albion ....A 5

Allenton ....F 5
Alton ....H 2
Anthony ....E 4
Arcadia ....F 3
Arctic ....E 4
Arkwright ....D 4
Arnold Mills ......A 5
Ashaway ...1,559..H 2
Ashton ....B 5
Austin ....I 1
Avondale ....I 1
Barrington .17,554▲.B 6
Belleville ....F 5
Berkeley ....B 5
Block Island ....K 4
Bradford ...1,333..H 2
Bridgeton ....A 2
Bristol ...17,860▲○E 7
Bristol Ferry .....E 7
Burdickville ......H 2
Burrill-
ville* ....10,087▲.A 3
Canonchet ....G 2
Carolina ....H 3
Centerville ....G 2
Central
Falls ....18,716..B 6
Charlestown .2,863▲.H 3
Chepachet ....B 3
Clayville ....D 3
Coventry* ..22,947▲.E 5
Coventry Center ...E 4
Cranston ...74,287..D 5
Cumber-
land* ....26,605▲.A 5
Cumberland Hill ...A 5
Davisville ....F 5
Diamond Hill ......A 5
Dunn Corner ......I 2
East Green-
wich ......9,577▲○E 5
East Provi-
dence ...48,207..C 6
Esmond ....B 4
Exeter ....3,245▲.F 4
Fiskeville ....D 4
Forestdale ....A 4

Foster* ....2,626▲.C 2
Foster Center .....C 2
Galilee ....I 4
Georgiaville ......B 4
Glendale ....A 3
Glocester* ..5,160▲.B 3
Green Hill ....I 4
Greene ....E 2
Greenville ....B 4
Hamilton ....F 5
Harmony ....B 4
Harris ....D 4
Harrisville .1,053..A 3
Haversham ....I 2
Homestead ....F 6
Hope ....D 4
Hope
Valley ....1,326..G 2
Hopkins Hollow ....E 2
Hopkinton ..5,392▲.H 2
Hughesdale ....C 5
Island Park ....F 7
Jackson ....D 4
Jamestown ...2,114
(2,911▲)..G 6
Jerusalem ....I 4
Johnston* ..22,037▲.C 5
Kenyon ....H 3
Kingston ...5,601..G 4
Lafayette ....F 5
Liberty ....G 4
Limerock ....B 5
Lincoln* ..16,182▲.B 5
Little
Compton ..2,385▲.G 8
Lonsdale ....B 5
Manville ....A 5
Mapleville ....A 3
Matunuck ....I 4
Middle-
town ....29,290▲.G 6
Misquamicut ....I 2
Mohegan ....A 3
Mooresfield ....G 5
Moosup Valley .....D 2
Moscow ....G 2
Narragansett 7,138▲.H 5

Narragan-
sett Pier* .2,686..H 5
Nasonville ....A 3
New
Shoreham* ...489▲.K 4
Newport ...34,562.○G 6
Newport
East .....10,285..G 6
Nooseneck ....E 3
North Foster ......C 2
North Kings-
town* ....29,793▲.F 5
North Provi-
dence ....24,337▲.C 5
North Scituate ....C 4
North Smith-
field* ....9,349▲.A 4
North Tiverton ....E 7
Oak Valley ....A 4
Oakland ....A 3
Pascoag ...3,132..A 3
Pawtucket .76,984..B 6
Peace Dale, see
Wakefield
[-Peace Dale]
Perryville ....H 4
Point Judith ......I 5
Ports-
mouth ...12,521▲.F 7
Potter Hill ....H 2
Potterville ....D 3
Primrose ....A 4
Provi-
dence ...179,116.○C 5
Prudence ....F 6
Quidnick ....E 4
Quinnville ....B 5
Quonochontaug .....I 2
Rice City ....D 2
Richmond* ..2,625▲.H 2
Rockville ....H 2
Sakonnet ....G 7
Saunderstown ......G 5
Saylesville ....B 5
Scituate* ...7,489▲.D 3
Shannock ....H 3
Simmonsville ......C 4

Slatersville ......A 4
Slocum ....G 4
Smith-
field* ...13,468▲.B 4
South Foster ......C 3
South Kings-
town* ....16,913▲.H 4
South Portsmouth ..F 7
Spragueville ......B 4
Summit ....E 3
Tarkiln ....A 3
The Anchor-
age* .....3,441..G 6
The Hummocks ......E 7
Thornton ....C 5
Tiverton ..12,559▲.E 7
Tiverton
Four Corners .....F 7
Tuckertown ....H 4
Union Village .....A 4
Usquepaug ....G 3
Valley Falls ......B 5
Wakefield [-Peace
Dale] ....6,331..H 4
Warren ...10,523▲.D 7
Warwick ...83,694..E 6
Watch Hill ....I 2
Weekapaug ....I 2
West Barrington ...D 6
West Glocester ....B 2
West Greenville ...B 4
West Green-
wich* ....1,841▲.E 2
West Greenwich
Center ....E 2
West Kingston ...○G 4
West
Warwick ..24,323▲.D 4
Westerly ..13,654
(17,248▲)..I 1
White Rock ....H 1
Wickford ....F 5
Wickford Junction ..F 5
Wood River
Junction ....H 3
Woonsocket 46,820..A 4
Wyoming ....G 3

○County courthouse
*Does not appear on the map; key shows general location.
▲Entire town (township), including rural area

Source: Latest census figures (1970). Places without population figures are unincorporated areas and are not listed in census reports.

A Row of Old Storefronts built in 1880 adds charm to downtown Newport. The Newport Casino stands behind the stores. The Casino was built in 1880 as a social center for the city's wealthy residents. It now houses the National Lawn Tennis Hall of Fame.
John T. Hopf

RHODE ISLAND/*People*

The 1970 United States census reported that Rhode Island had 949,723 persons. The population had risen 10 per cent over the 1960 census figure, 859,488.

Rhode Island has only eight cities. All other communities in the state are called towns. The cities, in order of size, are Providence, Warwick, Pawtucket, Cranston, East Providence, Woonsocket, Newport, and Central Falls. See the separate articles on Rhode Island cities listed in the *Related Articles* at the end of this article.

Almost a fifth of Rhode Island's people live in Providence. About 85 per cent of the people live in the Providence-Warwick-Pawtucket Standard Metropolitan Statistical Area (see METROPOLITAN AREA). Part of this metropolitan area extends into Massachusetts. Part of the Fall River, Mass., metropolitan area extends into Rhode Island. For the populations of these metropolitan areas, see the map index of *Rhode Island*.

Most Rhode Islanders were born in the United States. They include descendants of settlers from Canada and most European countries. Roman Catholics make up the state's largest religious body. Other large religious groups in Rhode Island include Baptists, Episcopalians, Jews, Lutherans, Methodists, and members of the United Church of Christ.

POPULATION

This map shows the *population density* of Rhode Island, and how it varies in different parts of the state. Population density is the average number of persons who live on each square mile.

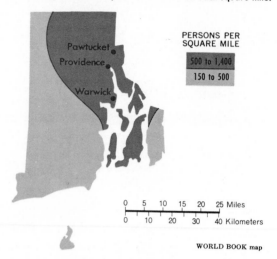

PERSONS PER SQUARE MILE
500 to 1,400
150 to 500

WORLD BOOK map

Crowds of Shoppers stroll along Westminster Street in downtown Providence, the state's largest city. Rhode Island has a strongly urban character. About 85 of every 100 Rhode Islanders live in the Providence-Warwick-Pawtucket metropolitan area.

Thomas D. Stevens

284

Schools. In colonial times, many Rhode Island ministers established schools to teach boys. Girls and very young boys attended *dame schools*, which were taught by women. In 1640, the people of Newport founded a free school to educate poor children.

Rhode Island's first statewide law establishing public schools was passed in 1800. The law was discontinued in 1803, but was adopted again in 1828. Also in 1828, the Rhode Island legislature set up the state's first permanent public-school fund.

A commissioner of education and a nine-member board of regents direct Rhode Island's public-school system. The governor appoints the board members to four-year terms. The regents appoint the commissioner, who serves a three-year term. School committees and superintendents head the local school districts.

Rhode Island children must attend school between the ages of 7 and 16. For the number of students and teachers in Rhode Island, see EDUCATION (table).

Libraries. Rhode Island's first library was founded in Newport in 1700 by Thomas Bray, an English minister. The Redwood Library and Athenaeum, established in Newport in 1747, is the oldest library still operating in the state.

Today, Rhode Island has 75 public libraries, 11 university and college libraries, and 42 special libraries. The largest library, the Providence Public Library, has eight branches. Its many valuable collections include the George W. Potter and Alfred M. Williams Memorial on Irish Culture and the Harris Collection on the Civil War and Slavery. The libraries of Brown University house over a million volumes. The John Hay Library of the university has one of the world's most complete collections of writings by and about Abraham Lincoln. The John Hay Library also includes the famous Harris

Collection of American Poetry and Plays. The Rhode Island State Library in Providence owns a special law collection for use by government officials and the public. Other special libraries in the state include those of the Newport Historical Society and the Rhode Island Historical Society in Providence.

In 1964, Rhode Island established a Department of State Library Services. This department administers state and federal funds for libraries in Rhode Island.

Museums. The Museum of Art at the Rhode Island School of Design in Providence displays water colors and oils by many famous artists. The Roger Williams Park Museum and Roger Williams Planetarium has science displays and exhibits of animals and plants. It also owns a large collection of Indian relics. The South County Museum near Wickford displays tools used by American colonists. Other museums include the Haffenreffer Museum of Anthropology in Bristol, the Museum of Primitive Cultures in Peace Dale, the Betsey Williams Cottage in Providence, and the Westerly Museum and Art Gallery.

--- **UNIVERSITIES AND COLLEGES** ---

Rhode Island has nine universities and colleges accredited by the New England Association of Colleges and Secondary Schools. For enrollments and further information, see UNIVERSITIES AND COLLEGES (table).

Name	Location	Founded
Barrington College	Barrington	1900
Brown University	Providence	1764
Bryant College	Providence	1916
Providence College	Providence	1917
Rhode Island, University of	Kingston	1892
Rhode Island College	Providence	1854
Rhode Island School of Design	Providence	1877
Salve Regina College	Newport	1947
Seminary of Our Lady of Providence	Warwick	1959

Leon Kowal, Alpha

Rhode Island School of Design in Providence offers instruction in both the fine and applied arts. The school is nationally known for its work in textile and industrial design. It also maintains an art museum. The school was founded in 1877.

RHODE ISLAND / *A Visitor's Guide*

Thousands of vacationers visit Rhode Island's coastal resorts each year. The resorts offer swimming, boating, fishing, and beautiful scenery. Rhode Island's leading resort centers include Block Island, Narragansett Pier, Newport, and Watch Hill. Tourists also can visit many historic sites, colonial buildings, and old churches.

© John T. Hopf

Music Festival in Newport

Arthur Griffin

Birthplace of Gilbert Stuart in North Kingstown

F. Moscati, *Town and Country*

Gold Room in the Marble House in Newport

PLACES TO VISIT

Following are brief descriptions of some of Rhode Island's most interesting places to visit.

Cliff Walk, in Newport, is a three-mile path through scenes of contrasting beauty. On one side of the walk is the rocky Atlantic coast. On the other side are many beautiful mansions. The most famous of the mansions is *The Breakers,* a 70-room house built for Cornelius Vanderbilt in 1895. A nearby mansion called *Marble House* is one of the most ornate buildings in the United States. It was built for William K. Vanderbilt in 1892.

Colonial Buildings rank among Rhode Island's most interesting landmarks. They include the *Gilbert Stuart Birthplace,* built in North Kingstown in 1751, and the *General Nathanael Greene Homestead,* built in Coventry in 1770. Stuart was the foremost painter of portraits of George Washington. Greene was one of the greatest patriot leaders of the Revolutionary War. Other Rhode Island colonial buildings, with the location and original completion date of each, include *White Horse Tavern* (Newport, 1673); *Wanton-Lyman-Hazard House* (Newport, 1675); *Smith's Castle* (near Wickford, 1678); *Clemence Irons House* (Johnston, 1680); *Eleazer Arnold House* (Lincoln, 1687); *Old Colony House* (Newport, 1739); *Stephen Hopkins House* (Providence, about 1743); *Hunter House* (Newport, 1748); *Armory of the Kentish Guards* (East Greenwich, 1774); *John Brown House* (Providence,

286

ANNUAL EVENTS

Many of Rhode Island's most popular annual events include boat races, fishing contests, and tennis tournaments. The annual Newport Music Festival is held in late July and early August. It features Metropolitan Opera stars. Other annual events include:

January-March: New Year's Day Swim in Newport (January); St. Patrick's Day Parade in West Warwick (March).

April-June: Rhode Island Ceramic Show in Cranston (April); Rhode Island Heritage Month, statewide (May); Newport-Bermuda Yacht Race and Newport-Annapolis Yacht Race, Newport (alternate years, June).

July-September: South County Heritage Festival in Wakefield (July); Narraganset Indian Tribe August Pow-Wow in Charlestown; Invitational Tennis Tournament at Tennis Hall of Fame in Newport (August); U.S. Atlantic Tuna Tournament in Galilee (September).

October-December: Oliver H. Perry Day Celebration in Newport (November); Newport House Tours (December).

© John T. Hopf

Touro Synagogue in Newport

Rhode Island Development Council

The U.S. Atlantic Tuna Tournament in Waters off Block Island

1786); and *Old Windmill* (Jamestown, 1787).

Houses of Worship also rank among Rhode Island's points of interest. *Old Narragansett Church* (1707) in North Kingstown is the oldest Episcopal church in the northern United States. *Touro Synagogue* (1763) in Newport is the oldest existing synagogue in the United States. Other churches include *Trinity Church* (an Episcopal church in Newport, 1726); *First Baptist Meeting House* (Providence, 1775); *Beneficent Congregational Church* (Providence, 1810); *Cathedral of St. John* (an Episcopal church in Providence, 1810); *First Unitarian Church* (Providence, 1816); and *Cathedral of Saints Peter and Paul* (a Roman Catholic church in Providence, 1886).

Old Slater Mill, in Pawtucket, was one of the first successful textile mills in North America. It was built in 1793 by Samuel Slater, the founder of the American textile industry. The mill is now a textile museum. It has been called the *Cradle of American Industry*.

Old Stone Mill, in Newport, is a roofless stone tower. Most historians believe English colonists built the tower in the mid-1600's. It was once thought that Vikings built the tower about A.D. 1000.

State Parks. Rhode Island has 20 state parks. For information on these parks, write to Chief, Division of Parks and Recreation, Department of Natural Resources, 83 Park Street, Providence, R.I. 02903.

RHODE ISLAND / *The Land*

Land Regions. Rhode Island has two main land regions. They are, from east to west, (1) the Coastal Lowlands, and (2) the Eastern New England Upland.

The Coastal Lowlands cover more than half the Rhode Island mainland, the islands in Narragansett Bay, and the land east of the bay. The Coastal Lowlands are part of a larger land region of the same name that covers the entire New England coast. Many sandy beaches and plains line the shores of Rhode Island's lowlands. The shore west of Point Judith has sandy beaches, lagoons, and salt ponds. Rocky cliffs are found on the islands and the shore along the bay. Inland, the land rises to form higher elevations. East of Narragansett Bay, the slopes are low, round, and have few trees. West of the bay, they are rugged and forested.

The Eastern New England Upland covers the northwestern third of Rhode Island. The entire Eastern New England Upland extends from Maine to Connecticut. The portion in Rhode Island is often called the *Western Rocky Upland*. This region has gently sloping hills, and a higher elevation than the Coastal Lowlands. The land rises from about 200 feet above sea level in the east to more than 800 feet in the northwest. Lakes,

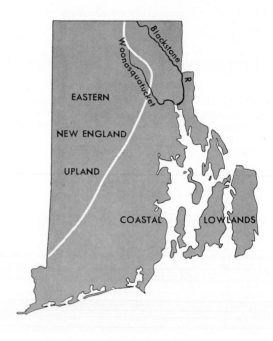

BLOCK ISLAND

Farm Buildings stand in a wooded area near Chepachet in the Eastern New England Upland region of northern Rhode Island.
© John T. Hopf

The Rocky Atlantic Coast borders Cliff Walk, a winding footpath in Newport. This area lies in the Coastal Lowlands.

Eric M. Sanford

288

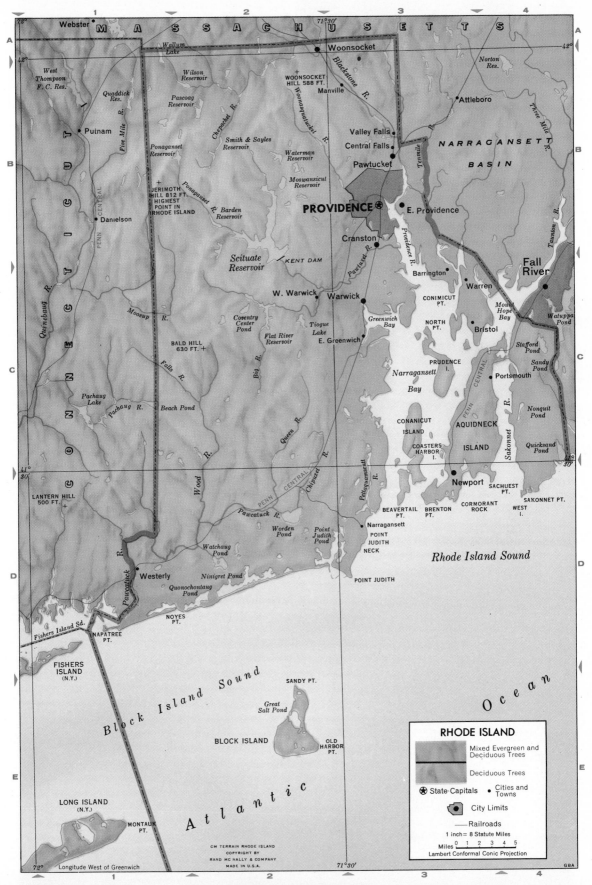

MASSACHUSETTS

Webster

Wallum Lake

Woonsocket

West Thompson F. C. Res.

Wilson Reservoir

WOONSOCKET HILL 588 FT.

Manville

Woonasquatucket R.

Blackstone R.

Norton Res.

Attleboro

Three Mile R.

Quaddick Res.

Pascoag Reservoir

Chepachet R.

Putnam

Fine Mile R.

Ponaganset Reservoir

Smith & Sayles Reservoir

Waterman Reservoir

Valley Falls

Central Falls

Pawtucket

Tenmile R.

NARRAGANSETT BASIN

JERIMOTH HILL 812 FT. HIGHEST POINT IN RHODE ISLAND

Danielson

Ponaganset R.

Barden Reservoir

Moswansicut Reservoir

PROVIDENCE

E. Providence

Cranston

Taunton R.

Scituate Reservoir

KENT DAM

Pawtuxet R.

Providence R.

Barrington

Warren

Fall River

Watuppa Pond

W. Warwick

Warwick

CONIMICUT PT.

Mount Hope Bay

Moosup R.

Coventry Center Pond

Big R.

Flat River Reservoir

Tiogue Lake

E. Greenwich

Greenwich Bay

NORTH PT.

Bristol

Stafford Pond

BALD HILL 630 FT.

Falls R.

Narragansett Bay

PRUDENCE I.

Sandy Pond

Pachaug Lake

Pachaug R.

Beach Pond

Queen R.

CONANICUT ISLAND

AQUIDNECK ISLAND

Portsmouth

Sakonnet R.

Nonquit Pond

Quicksand Pond

COASTERS HARBOR I.

LANTERN HILL 500 FT.

Wood R.

Chipaud R.

Pettaquamscutt R.

Newport

SACHUEST PT.

BEAVERTAIL PT.

BRENTON PT.

CORMORANT ROCK

SAKONNET PT.

WEST I.

Pawcatuck R.

Worden Pond

Point Judith Pond

Narragansett

POINT JUDITH NECK

Rhode Island Sound

Watchaug Pond

Westerly

Ninigret Pond

Quonochontaug Pond

POINT JUDITH

Pawcatuck R.

NOYES PT.

Fishers Island Sd.

NAPATREE PT.

FISHERS ISLAND (N.Y.)

Block Island Sound

SANDY PT.

Great Salt Pond

BLOCK ISLAND

OLD HARBOR PT.

Ocean

LONG ISLAND (N.Y.)

MONTAUK PT.

Atlantic

CM TERRAIN RHODE ISLAND
COPYRIGHT BY
RAND MC NALLY & COMPANY
MADE IN U.S.A.

Longitude West of Greenwich

RHODE ISLAND

Mixed Evergreen and Deciduous Trees

Deciduous Trees

⊛ State Capitals

• Cities and Towns

City Limits

Railroads

1 inch = 8 Statute Miles

Miles 0 1 2 3 4 5

Lambert Conformal Conic Projection

GBA

Specially created for **World Book Encyclopedia** by Rand McNally and World Book editors

Mohegan Bluffs on Block Island tower more than 200 feet above the Atlantic Ocean. These clay cliffs are on the southern end of the island.

Arthur Griffin

Leon Kowal, Alpha

Stone Lighthouse on Point Judith was built in 1816. Point Judith, a sandy finger of land five miles south of Narragansett, has been the scene of violent storms that have wrecked many ships.

reservoirs, and ponds nestle among the region's many hills. These hills include 812-foot Jerimoth Hill, the highest point in Rhode Island. Rhode Island has no mountains.

Islands. Rhode Island includes 36 islands. They range in size from 45.23-square mile Aquidneck Island (officially named Rhode Island) to Despair, a clump of rocks in Narragansett Bay. Block Island (officially New Shoreham) covers about 11 square miles. It lies in the Atlantic, about 10 miles south of the Rhode Island mainland. Bridges and ferry service connect the largest islands and the mainland.

Coastline. Rhode Island has a 40-mile general coastline. If the tidal shoreline of the state's bays and islands were included, the coastline would measure 384 miles. The largest bay, Narragansett Bay, extends 28 miles inland. The many arms of Narragansett Bay include Greenwich and Mount Hope bays.

Rivers and Lakes. Three of Rhode Island's chief rivers—Providence, Sakonnet, and Seekonk—are really salt-water arms of Narragansett Bay. Several fresh-water rivers flow into the bay. These include the Pawtuxet, Pettaquamscutt, Potowomut, and Woonasquatucket. One river, the Blackstone, becomes the Pawtucket and then the Seekonk before flowing into the bay. The Pawcatuck River flows through southwestern Rhode Island and forms part of the Rhode Island-Connecticut border. Other important rivers include the Chepachet, Ponaganset, and Wood.

Most of the state's inland rivers are small but swift. Many break into waterfalls. Water was once the major source of power for Rhode Island's mills and factories.

Many lakes, ponds, and reservoirs dot the Rhode Island countryside. Scituate Reservoir, the state's largest inland body of water, supplies water for Providence and nearby communities. Other large bodies of water include Watchaug Pond and Worden Pond.

Newport Naval Base spreads across the peninsulas and inlets of Coasters Harbor Island. The United States Naval War College is in the foreground. Rhode Island's jagged coastline provides safe harbors for many fishing boats and pleasure vessels.

© John T. Hopf

RHODE ISLAND / *Climate*

Warming winds from Narragansett Bay help give Rhode Island a mild climate. January temperatures in Rhode Island average 30° F., and July temperatures average 70° F. The state's highest temperature, 102° F., was recorded at Greenville on July 30, 1949. The lowest temperature, −23° F., was recorded at Kingston on Jan. 11, 1942.

Yearly *precipitation* (rain, melted snow, and other forms of moisture) in Rhode Island averages about 44 inches. Snowfall averages about 31 inches a year. The state has a growing season of about 200 days.

Damaging hurricanes, often accompanied by tidal waves, sometimes lash the Rhode Island coast. The worst hurricanes came in 1815, 1938, 1944, and 1954.

Elizabeth Potter

Fresh Breezes Fill the Sails of boats on Point Judith Pond. Rhode Island's mild climate lures many sportsmen to sail on the calm bays and inlets along the state's Atlantic Coast.

SEASONAL TEMPERATURES

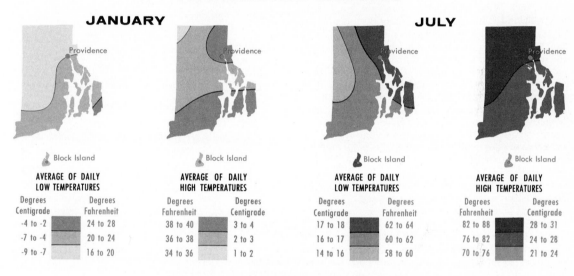

JANUARY

Providence

Block Island

AVERAGE OF DAILY LOW TEMPERATURES

Degrees Centigrade		Degrees Fahrenheit
-4 to -2		24 to 28
-7 to -4		20 to 24
-9 to -7		16 to 20

Providence

Block Island

AVERAGE OF DAILY HIGH TEMPERATURES

Degrees Fahrenheit		Degrees Centigrade
38 to 40		3 to 4
36 to 38		2 to 3
34 to 36		1 to 2

JULY

Providence

Block Island

AVERAGE OF DAILY LOW TEMPERATURES

Degrees Centigrade		Degrees Fahrenheit
17 to 18		62 to 64
16 to 17		60 to 62
14 to 16		58 to 60

Providence

Block Island

AVERAGE OF DAILY HIGH TEMPERATURES

Degrees Fahrenheit		Degrees Centigrade
82 to 88		28 to 31
76 to 82		24 to 28
70 to 76		21 to 24

AVERAGE YEARLY PRECIPITATION
(Rain, Melted Snow, and Other Moisture)

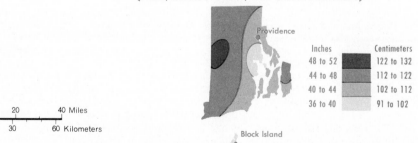

Providence

Inches		Centimeters
48 to 52		122 to 132
44 to 48		112 to 122
40 to 44		102 to 112
36 to 40		91 to 102

```
0        20        40 Miles
|----|----|----|----|
0        30        60 Kilometers
```

Block Island

WORLD BOOK maps

MONTHLY WEATHER IN BLOCK ISLAND AND PROVIDENCE

	JAN	FEB	MAR	APR	MAY	JUNE	JULY	AUG	SEPT	OCT	NOV	DEC	Average of:
BLOCK ISLAND	38	37	43	51	61	69	75	75	70	61	51	41	High Temperatures
	26	25	31	39	48	57	63	63	57	48	39	29	Low Temperatures
	12	11	12	11	11	9	9	9	8	9	10	11	Days of Rain or Snow
	12	10	12	12	11	10	10	9	8	8	10	11	Days of Rain or Snow
PROVIDENCE	37	37	45	55	66	75	80	79	72	62	51	39	High Temperatures
	21	20	29	37	47	56	62	60	53	43	34	24	Low Temperatures

Temperatures are given in degrees Fahrenheit.

Source: U.S. Weather Bureau

Manufacturing is by far Rhode Island's most important economic activity. The tourist industry ranks second, followed by agriculture. The Providence area is Rhode Island's chief manufacturing center. The thousands of tourists who visit Rhode Island contribute about $60 million a year to the state's economy.

Natural Resources. Forests cover about two-thirds of the state. But forest products add little to the state's economy. Rhode Island has few large mineral deposits.

Forests. More than 60 kinds of trees grow in Rhode Island. They include the ash, birch, cedar, elm, hickory, maple, oak, pine, poplar, and willow. Beautiful tulip trees grow in Providence County and Warwick. Pin and post oak trees are found near the north shore of Wickford harbor. Canoe, or paper, birches thrive in northern Rhode Island.

Soil. Rhode Island's richest soil is found along Narragansett Bay. Miami stony loam covers the bay's basin and tableland. This firm brown soil holds moisture for an entire growing season. Glocester stony loam is the state's least fertile soil. This light brown sand covers much of western and northern Rhode Island.

Minerals. Westerly granite is Rhode Island's best-known mineral. Its hardness and fine grain make it an excellent building material. Deposits of this granite lie mainly in southwestern Rhode Island, near the town of Westerly. The Coastal Lowlands have large sand and gravel deposits, and the Narragansett Bay region has some coal of poor quality. This coal is no longer mined. Other minerals found in Rhode Island include limestone and sandstone.

Plant Life. Many kinds of seaweed grow along the Rhode Island coast. Fresh-water seaweeds, including waterweed and pickerelweed, thrive in ponds and streams. Eelgrass, a fertilizing seaweed, grows in small bodies of salt water. Asters and cattails bloom in the marshland of Charlestown and South Kingstown. Scarlet pimpernel grows on the cliffs of Newport. Red deer grass, white daisies, and wild carrots are found in meadows. Woodland flowers of Rhode Island include dogwoods, mountain laurels, rhododendrons, trilliums, and violets.

Animal Life of Rhode Island includes deer, foxes, minks, muskrats, otters, rabbits, raccoons, and squirrels. Barred owls, blue jays, catbirds, flickers, robins, ruffed grouse, and screech owls live in the woodlands. Gulls, loons, ospreys, terns, and other shore birds make their homes along the Rhode Island coast. Game birds include partridges, pheasants, quail, wild ducks, and woodcocks.

Fresh-water fish in the state's waters include bass, eels, perch, pickerel, and trout. Salt-water fish include bluefish, butterfish, flounder, mackerel, menhaden, sea bass, striped bass, swordfish, and tuna.

Manufacturing accounts for about 98 per cent of the value of goods produced in Rhode Island. Goods manufactured there have a *value added by manufacture* of about $1½ billion a year. This figure represents the value created in products by Rhode Island industries, not counting such costs as materials, supplies, and fuel.

The textile industry is Rhode Island's most important manufacturing activity. The state's textile mills make

PRODUCTION OF GOODS IN RHODE ISLAND

Total value of goods produced in 1969—$1,506,207,000

Manufactured Products 98%
Agricultural Products 1%
Fish and Mineral Products 1%

Note: Percentages are based on farm income, value added by manufacture, and value of fish and mineral production.

Sources: *Statistical Abstract of the United States, 1971,* U.S. Bureau of the Census; and other government publications

EMPLOYMENT IN RHODE ISLAND

Total number of persons employed in 1970—346,000

	Number of Employees
Manufacturing	121,000
Wholesale & Retail Trade	68,000
Government	55,000
Mining & Community, Business & Personal Services	52,000
Finance, Insurance & Real Estate	16,000
Transportation & Public Utilities	16,000
Construction	15,000
Agriculture	3,000

Sources: *Statistical Abstract of the United States, 1971,* U.S. Bureau of the Census; U.S. Bureau of Employment Security

cotton, nylon, rayon, woolen, and worsted fabrics, and lace. Central Falls, Pawtucket, and Providence are among the cities that turn out a wide variety of textiles. Woonsocket is the state's chief center of woolen and worsted textile production. Rhode Island mills account for about half the lace made in the United States. Factories process and dye large quantities of textiles made in other states.

Other leading manufactured products include machinery, metal products, and primary metals. Providence is one of the nation's leading jewelry-manufacturing centers. Factories also make apparel; chemicals; clay, glass, and stone products; food and related products; and instruments. Boatyards on Narragansett Bay build small boats and yachts. Printing and publishing are also important in Rhode Island.

Agriculture accounts for about 1 per cent of the value of goods produced in Rhode Island. Rhode Island farm products have a value of about $20 million yearly. The state has about 1,000 farms. They average about 100 acres in size.

Dairy products bring in over a fourth of Rhode Island's farm income. Milk is the state's most valuable dairy product. Greenhouse and nursery products rank next in importance. Sales of ornamental trees and shrubs and other nursery products earn about a fourth of Rhode Island's agricultural income.

Vegetables account for about one-fifth of the state's farm income. Vegetable farms are especially produc-

288d

tive in Kent, Newport, and Providence counties, where cities provide ready markets. Potatoes are by far the leading vegetable crop. Poultry products earn nearly a fifth of Rhode Island's farm income. The state's leading poultry products are eggs and *broilers* (chickens between 9 and 12 weeks old). The Rhode Island Red, a famous breed of chicken, was developed in the Rhode Island town of Little Compton. Apples and peaches are Rhode Island's most valuable fruits.

Fishing Industry. Lobsters are Rhode Island's most valuable shellfish. Fishermen also catch hard-shelled and soft-shelled clams. They catch bluefish, sea bass, swordfish, tuna, and other deep-sea fish in the waters off Block Island. Other valuable fishes include butterfish, cod, flounder, porgy, squid, and whiting.

Mining. Sand and gravel are the state's most valuable mineral products. They are mined in most parts of Rhode Island. The state also produces granite and limestone.

Electric Power. Steam turbines produce almost all the state's electric power. Hydroelectric plants generate less than 1 per cent. For Rhode Island's kilowatt-hour production, see ELECTRIC POWER (table).

Transportation. Newport and Providence were international shipping centers from colonial days until the 1830's. Their importance as shipping centers declined with the development of railroads.

Rhode Island's first railroad began operating between Providence and Boston in 1835. Today, railroads operate on about 160 miles of track in Rhode Island. Four railroads provide freight service, and passenger trains serve Kingston, Providence, and Westerly. Roads and highways total about 5,000 miles, and most of these are surfaced. The Rhode Island portion of Interstate Highway 95 was completed in 1969. It extends from the Connecticut border, near Ashaway, to Providence. Interstate 295, which skirts Providence to the north and west, was also completed in 1969. Rhode Island has six public airports. The biggest one is the Theodore Francis Green Airport in Warwick.

Communication. Over 20 newspapers and about 25 magazines are published in Rhode Island. The state's leading newspapers, in order of circulation, include the *Providence Journal* and *Evening Bulletin*, the *Pawtucket Times*, and the *Woonsocket Call and Evening Reporter*.

Rhode Island's first newspaper, the *Rhode Island Gazette*, began publication in 1732. Its publisher, James Franklin, was the brother of Benjamin Franklin. In 1758, James Franklin's son, also named James, founded the *Newport Mercury*. In 1934, the *Mercury* became a weekly edition of the *Newport News*, and its name was changed to the *Newport Mercury and News*.

Rhode Island's first radio stations, WEAN and WJAR, began broadcasting from Providence in 1922. The state's first television station, WJAR-TV, started operating there in 1949. Rhode Island now has 21 radio stations and 2 television stations.

Manufacturing, Rhode Island's chief economic activity, is centered in and around Providence. In this factory, workers carefully sort and test transistor parts.

FARM AND MINERAL PRODUCTS

This map shows the areas where the state's leading farm and mineral products are produced. The major urban areas (shown in red) are the state's important manufacturing centers.

WORLD BOOK map

HISTORIC RHODE ISLAND

Old Slater Mill, built in Pawtucket in 1793, was one of the first successful textile mills in North America.

Roger Williams founded Rhode Island's first white settlement at Providence in 1636.

Pawtucket ●

PROVIDENCE ★

Rhode Island Shipyards built hundreds of merchant and whaling vessels from the middle 1600's to the late 1800's.

Dorr's Rebellion of 1842, though crushed by state troops, helped remove voting requirements that kept city people from the polls.

Rhode Island Red Chickens were developed at Little Compton. The breed resulted from experiments begun in 1854 by William Tripp and John Macomber.

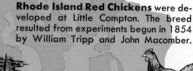

Gas Lamps using gas made from coal were introduced in the United States in 1806 by David Melville of Newport.

Great Swamp Fight near Kingston in 1675 was the first major victory of British settlers over the Indians in King Philip's War.

Kingston ●

Newport ●

Little Compton ●

Slave Traders brought thousands of captives to Rhode Island ports until 1774, when the colony outlawed slaves.

Great Britain Was Challenged in 1769 when Rhode Islanders burned the *Liberty* in one of the first acts of rebellion in the colonies.

Indian Days. A few thousand Indians lived in what is now Rhode Island before the white man came. The Indians belonged to five tribes of the Algonkian Indian family—the Narraganset, Niantic, Nipmuck, Pequot, and Wampanoag. The Narraganset Indians were the most numerous tribe in the Rhode Island area. They were peaceful people who hunted, fished, and farmed.

Exploration. Miguel de Cortereal, a Portuguese navigator, may have sailed along the Rhode Island coast in 1511. Giovanni da Verrazano, an Italian navigator working for France, explored Narragansett Bay in 1524. Some historians believe Verrazano named Rhode Island when he wrote that it resembled the Island of Rhodes in the Mediterranean Sea. Other historians believe the Dutch navigator Adriaen Block named the region. In 1614, Block called an island in Narragansett Bay *Roodt Eylandt* (Red Island). Block used this name because of the red clay on the island's shore.

Settlement. In 1636, Roger Williams established Rhode Island's first permanent white settlement, at Providence. Williams, a minister, had been driven out of Massachusetts because he called for increased religious and political freedom. Massachusetts leaders feared Williams as a threat to their colony's security. Williams founded Providence on land he bought from Canonicus and Miantonomo, two Narraganset Indian chiefs. Williams established a policy of religious and political freedom.

In 1638, William Coddington, John Clarke, Anne Hutchinson, and others left Massachusetts in search of religious freedom. They founded the settlement of Pocasset on Aquidneck Island. The settlers separated after political and religious differences developed among them. Mrs. Hutchinson and her followers stayed at Pocasset and renamed it Portsmouth. Coddington, Clarke, and their followers moved south and founded Newport in 1639.

In 1643, Samuel Gorton, John Greene, and others founded a fourth Rhode Island settlement, Warwick. They had left Providence because they believed true liberty was possible only under established English law. Providence was largely independent of English law.

Williams proposed that the four Rhode Island settlements unite for protection against neighboring colonies. He obtained a charter from the English Parliamentary Commission in 1644, and the four settlements united under this charter in 1647.

In 1663, King Charles II of England granted Rhode Island a second charter, called the *Charter of Rhode Island and Providence Plantations*. This charter remained the law of Rhode Island until 1843.

King Philip's War. Roger Williams respected the rights of Indians and maintained peace with them. But trouble began in nearby Massachusetts Bay Colony and Plymouth Colony when young Indian chiefs replaced older ones. The young chiefs feared further English settlement as a threat to their lands. In 1675, the Wampanoag chief King Philip (Metacomet) began killing New England colonists. The same year, troops from Massachusetts, Plymouth, and Connecticut defeated the Indians in the Great Swamp Fight near Kingston, R.I. The Indians then burned towns and

---

IMPORTANT DATES IN RHODE ISLAND

1524 Giovanni da Verrazano sailed Narragansett Bay.

1636 Roger Williams founded Providence.

1638 William Coddington, John Clarke, Anne Hutchinson, and others settled on Aquidneck Island.

1647 The settlements of Providence, Portsmouth, Newport, and Warwick were united after England granted Roger Williams a charter in 1644.

1663 England granted Rhode Island its second charter.

1774 Rhode Island prohibited the importation of slaves.

1776 Rhode Island declared its independence from England.

1790 Rhode Island became the 13th state when it ratified the U.S. Constitution on May 29.

1842 Dorr's Rebellion helped bring about a more liberal state constitution.

1938 A disastrous hurricane struck Rhode Island.

1966 The Rhode Island legislature reapportioned the senate and the house of representatives.

1969 Newport Bridge over Narragansett Bay was completed, linking Newport with Jamestown.

1971 The state legislature approved a personal income tax for the first time.

---

murdered colonists in Rhode Island. The colonists killed King Philip in 1676 near Mount Hope (present-day Bristol). The war ended in southern New England that year, but continued in Maine and New Hampshire until 1678. See INDIAN WARS (King Philip's War.)

The Early 1700's was a period of great prosperity in Rhode Island. The fertile coastal regions and the islands in Narragansett Bay made excellent farm and grazing land. Many Rhode Islanders developed large plantations somewhat like those of the South. Slaves worked the land and took care of cattle, horses, and sheep. In addition to crops and livestock, Rhode Island plantations produced great quantities of cheese. Plantation owners developed a fine breed of saddle horse called the Narragansett Pacer.

During the 1700's, Newport merchants owned large fleets of ships. These vessels were used to export plantation products to the other English colonies in America and to the West Indies. The plantation owners and merchants increased their profits by investing in the rum trade and the African slave trade. In spite of the profitable slave trade, Rhode Island was the first colony to prohibit the importation of slaves. It did so in 1774.

The Revolutionary War. During the 1760's, Great Britain passed a series of laws that caused unrest in Rhode Island and the other American colonies. Most of these laws either imposed severe taxes or restricted colonial trade. The people of Rhode Island were among the first colonists to take action against British rule. Their many acts of rebellion included the burning of the British ship *Liberty* at Newport in 1769.

After the Revolutionary War began in Massachusetts in 1775, hundreds of Rhode Islanders joined the patriot forces. Stephen Hopkins and other Rhode Island men were among the chief organizers of the Continental Navy. Esek Hopkins became the first commander in chief of the navy. Nathanael Greene rose to fame as one of the great leaders of the Continental Army.

British troops occupied Newport from December, 1776, to October, 1779. The British also raided other

Rhode Island communities during the war. But no major battles of the Revolutionary War took place on Rhode Island soil.

On May 4, 1776, Rhode Island became the first colony to declare its independence from Great Britain. New Hampshire had adopted an independent constitution in January, 1776. But New Hampshire did not sign its declaration of independence until July.

Rhode Island ratified the Articles of Confederation (the forerunner of the United States Constitution) on July 9, 1778. On May 29, 1790, Rhode Island became the last of the 13 original colonies to *ratify* (approve) the U.S. Constitution. Rhode Island delayed ratification until the amendments called the Bill of Rights were ready to be added to the Constitution. These amendments placed limits on the powers of the federal government and guaranteed individual liberties. Even with the Bill of Rights, many Rhode Islanders opposed joining the Union. The Rhode Island convention ratified the Constitution by a slim 34 to 32 vote.

Industrial Growth began in Rhode Island during the late 1700's. Textile manufacturing was the state's first important industry. The first hand-operated cotton-spinning jenny in the United States was built in Providence in 1787. The first water-powered machines for spinning cotton were built in Pawtucket in 1790 by Samuel Slater. Power spinning had begun in England, but the English kept the process secret. They wanted to prevent people in other countries from learning how to manufacture cloth and thread by machine. Textile workers were even forbidden to leave England. But Slater, who had worked with textile machines in England, escaped disguised as a farmer. He came to the United States and was hired by Moses Brown, a Providence businessman. Slater built the power machines from memory.

The Rhode Island textile industry grew rapidly for several reasons. The textile makers had power spinning, an abundance of water power, nearby markets in Boston and New York City, and excellent transportation. The Jefferson Embargo of 1807, which prohibited importing textiles, also aided the industry.

Other Rhode Island industries also began and grew during the late 1700's. In 1794, Nehemiah Dodge of Providence found a way to cover cheap metals with precious metals. Dodge and his brother Seril founded the American jewelry industry, and Rhode Island became the country's jewelry-making center. Newport, Providence, and Warren were leading whaling centers from 1775 to 1850. Whale oil and candles made from the head oil of sperm whales became profitable products. The fishing industry was another important business of the period.

Dorr's Rebellion. Rhode Island cities grew rapidly during the early 1800's. Thousands of Canadians, Europeans, and Rhode Island farmers came to the cities to work in textile mills. But Rhode Island laws did not keep pace with the growth of cities. For example, most city people were denied the right to vote. Rhode Island was still governed by its 1663 charter, which restricted voting to landholders or their eldest sons. Rural areas had the greatest representation in the state legislature,

even though cities had the largest populations. These conditions led to a political struggle and an uprising called *Dorr's Rebellion.* Thomas Dorr and his followers tried to form their own government. Their revolt failed, but it was partly responsible for the adoption of a more liberal state constitution in 1842. The new constitution became effective in 1843. It gave voting rights to native-born Rhode Island men of legal age who paid taxes of $1 a year or served in the militia. The constitution also increased city representation in the legislature. See DORR'S REBELLION.

The Late 1800's. More than 24,000 Rhode Islanders served in the Union Army and Navy during the Civil War (1861-1865). The most famous one was Major General Ambrose E. Burnside, who commanded the Army of the Potomac for a brief period. Burnside later served as governor of Rhode Island and as a United States senator.

Prosperity continued in Rhode Island after the war. The state's population almost doubled between 1870 and 1900. The textile industry developed world-wide markets, and other industries also expanded. Newport became the home of the Newport Naval Station in 1883 and of the Naval War College in 1884. The station is now part of the Newport Naval Base, and the college is the navy's highest educational institution. Also in the late 1800's, Newport won fame as the summer home of many wealthy railroad and banking families.

The Early 1900's. During World War I (1914-1918), Rhode Island's factories made chemicals, munitions, and other war materials. Shipyards in Newport and Providence built combat and cargo ships.

The Rhode Island textile industry began a steady decline during the 1920's. Many textile plants moved to the South, where labor and transportation costs were low. The increased manufacture of machine tools, machinery, and metal products helped make up the loss. But then the Great Depression of the 1930's further slowed Rhode Island's economic growth. Conditions improved as the depression eased in the late 1930's.

In 1938, Rhode Island suffered one of its worst natural disasters. A hurricane and tidal wave struck the state, killing 258 persons and causing $100 million in property damage.

The Mid-1900's. During World War II (1939-1945), war industries helped stimulate the state's recovering economy. The U.S. Navy established Quonset Point Naval Air Station in 1941, creating many jobs. Quonset huts, a famous type of World War II shelter, were first built at Quonset Point that year.

Rhode Island's economy lagged after the war. Employment fell as wartime industries closed and textile mills continued to move to the South. By 1949, more than 17 per cent of the state's workers were unemployed. Rhode Island revived its economy during the 1950's and 1960's by expanding the electronics, chemical, machinery, and plastics industries. By the end of the 1960's, the state had a varied economy, and unemployment had dropped to about 3 per cent. The textile industry remained important, but Rhode Island's economy no longer depended largely on it.

During the 1960's, the tourist industry became increasingly important to Rhode Island's economy. New roads and freeways opened much of the state to tourists. In 1969, a $71-million bridge was completed across

	Party	Term			Party	Term
Under Articles of Confederation				30. Charles C. Van Zandt	Republican	1877-1880
1. William Greene	None	1778-1786		31. Alfred H. Littlefield	Republican	1880-1883
2. John Collins	None	1786-1790		32. Augustus O. Bourn	Republican	1883-1885
				33. George P. Wetmore	Republican	1885-1887
Under United States Constitution				34. John W. Davis	Democratic	1887-1888
1. Arthur Fenner	Anti-Federalist	1790-1805		35. Royal C. Taft	Republican	1888-1889
2. Henry Smith	Unknown	1805		36. Herbert W. Ladd	Republican	1889-1890
3. Isaac Wilbur	Unknown	1806-1807		37. John W. Davis	Democratic	1890-1891
4. James Fenner	*Dem.-Rep.	1807-1811		38. Herbert W. Ladd	Republican	1891-1892
5. William Jones	Federalist	1811-1817		39. D. Russell Brown	Republican	1892-1895
6. Nehemiah R. Knight	*Dem.-Rep.	1817-1821		40. Charles W. Lippitt	Republican	1895-1897
7. William C. Gibbs	*Dem.-Rep.	1821-1824		41. Elisha Dyer	Republican	1897-1900
8. James Fenner	*Dem.-Rep.	1824-1831		42. William Gregory	Republican	1900-1901
9. Lemuel H. Arnold	†Nat. Rep.	1831-1833		43. Charles D. Kimball	Republican	1901-1903
10. John Brown Francis	Democratic	1833-1838		44. Lucius F. C. Garvin	Democratic	1903-1905
11. William Sprague	Democratic	1838-1839		45. George H. Utter	Republican	1905-1907
12. Samuel Ward King	Rhode Island Party	1840-1843		46. James H. Higgins	Democratic	1907-1909
13. James Fenner	Law and Order	1843-1845		47. Aram J. Pothier	Republican	1909-1915
14. Charles Jackson	Liberation	1845-1846		48. R. Livingston Beeckman	Republican	1915-1921
15. Byron Diman	Law and Order	1846-1847		49. Emery J. San Souci	Republican	1921-1923
16. Elisha Harris	Whig	1847-1849		50. William S. Flynn	Democratic	1923-1925
17. Henry B. Anthony	Whig	1849-1851		51. Aram J. Pothier	Republican	1925-1928
18. Philip Allen	Democratic	1851-1853		52. Norman S. Case	Republican	1928-1933
19. Francis M. Dimond	Democratic	1853-1854		53. Theodore F. Green	Democratic	1933-1937
20. William W. Hoppin	Whig and Know-Nothing	1854-1857		54. Robert E. Quinn	Democratic	1937-1939
21. Elisha Dyer	Republican	1857-1859		55. William H. Vanderbilt	Republican	1939-1941
22. Thomas G. Turner	Republican	1859-1860		56. J. Howard McGrath	Democratic	1941-1945
23. William Sprague	Democratic & Conservative	1860-1863		57. John O. Pastore	Democratic	1945-1950
24. William C. Cozzens	Democratic	1863		58. John S. McKiernan	Democratic	1950-1951
25. James Y. Smith	Republican	1863-1866		59. Dennis J. Roberts	Democratic	1951-1959
26. Ambrose E. Burnside	Republican	1866-1869		60. Christopher Del Sesto	Republican	1959-1961
27. Seth Padelford	Republican	1869-1873		61. John A. Notte, Jr.	Democratic	1961-1963
28. Henry Howard	Republican	1873-1875		62. John H. Chafee	Republican	1963-1969
29. Henry Lippitt	Republican	1875-1877		63. Frank Licht	Democratic	1969-1973
				64. Philip W. Noel	Democratic	1973-

*Democratic-Republican   †National Republican

Narragansett Bay between Jamestown and Newport. Completion of the Rhode Island section of Interstate Highway 95, also in 1969, allowed motorists to travel across the state from Connecticut to Massachusetts without a traffic light along the way.

Also during the 1960's, the University of Rhode Island began to develop a scientific research center at Saunderstown on Narragansett Bay. The center includes the *Trident*, a 180-foot research ship used for oceanographic studies. The U.S. Public Health Service has a shellfish laboratory at the center, and the U.S. Bureau of Sports Fisheries and Wildlife has a biological laboratory there. The center is also the site of the nation's first state-owned nuclear reactor.

Destructive hurricanes struck Rhode Island again in the 1940's and 1950's, though none was so severe as the 1938 hurricane. During the 1960's, the U.S. Army Corps of Engineers built a large hurricane barrier across the Providence River. This dam, completed in 1966, protects the downtown section of the city of Providence from hurricanes.

The Rhode Island legislature passed many new laws in the mid-1900's. The state held its first direct primary election in 1948. In 1951, the legislature repealed the poll tax and gave home rule to cities and towns. A 1963 law provided for lending textbooks to students in private schools. In 1964, the state set up a program to help pay medical bills for needy persons over 65.

The Rhode Island Supreme Court ruled in 1962 that the state House of Representatives must be *reapportioned* (redivided) to provide equal representation based on population. A constitutional convention met in 1964 to act on reapportionment of both the house and the senate and to consider other issues. In 1965, the legislature appointed a special commission to draw up a temporary reapportionment plan. The legislature used this plan to reapportion itself in 1966. In 1967, the constitutional convention proposed a new constitution. The constitution, which included a new reapportionment plan, was rejected by Rhode Island voters in 1968.

Rhode Island Today. In the 1970's, Rhode Island is continuing its industrial growth. Unemployment in the state is below the national average.

Rhode Island hopes to become a world center for oceanographic research. The University of Rhode Island's complex at Saunderstown has developed into one of the finest research centers in the nation. The addition of a National Marine Medicine Institute has been proposed for the center.

One of Rhode Island's chief problems is to find new sources of income to pay for the rising costs of education, highways, and welfare. The state's industrial growth has increased pollution. Many Rhode Islanders fear that pollution not only threatens their health, but may also prevent further growth of the tourist trade in the state.

WILLIAM D. METZ, JOSEPH M. UNGARO, and MARION I. WRIGHT

Related Articles in WORLD BOOK include:

BIOGRAPHIES

Brown (family)	Greene, Nathanael
Brown, Joseph R.	Hopkins, Esek
Burnside, Ambrose E.	Hopkins, Stephen
Cohan, George M.	Hutchinson, Anne M.
Corliss, George H.	Pastore, John O.
Ellery, William	Philip, King
Gray, Robert	Slater, Samuel
Green, Theodore F.	Williams, Roger

CITIES

Cranston	Pawtucket	Warwick
Newport	Providence	

HISTORY

Colonial Life in America	Indian Wars
Dorr's Rebellion	Revolutionary War in
Flag (color picture: Flags	America
in American History)	

OTHER RELATED ARTICLES

Baptists	Newport Naval Base
Cotton (History)	Quonset Point
Narragansett Bay	Naval Air Station
New England	

Outline

I. **Government**
A. Constitution
B. Executive
C. Legislature
D. Courts
E. Local Government
F. Taxation
G. Politics
II. **People**
III. **Education**
A. Schools
B. Libraries
C. Museums
IV. **A Visitor's Guide**
A. Places to Visit
B. Annual Events
V. **The Land**
A. Land Regions
B. Islands
C. Coastline
D. Rivers and Lakes
VI. **Climate**
VII. **Economy**
A. Natural Resources
B. Manufacturing
C. Agriculture
D. Fishing Industry
E. Mining
F. Electric Power
G. Transportation
H. Communication
VIII. **History**

Questions

What American industries began in Rhode Island?
What were the causes and the results of Dorr's Rebellion?
What is Rhode Island's biggest income-producing activity?
What is *The Breakers?*
Why did Roger Williams move to Rhode Island?
What are Rhode Island's two main land regions?
What is unusual about local government in Rhode Island?
What is often called the *Cradle of American Industry?*
Why did Rhode Island wait so long to ratify the U.S. Constitution?
What is Rhode Island's official name? How did Rhode Island get this name?

Books for Young Readers

ALDERMAN, CLIFFORD L. *The Rhode Island Colony.* Macmillan, 1969.
BEALS, CARLETON. *Colonial Rhode Island.* Nelson, 1970.
CARPENTER, ALLAN. *Rhode Island.* Childrens Press, 1968.
CORBETT, SCOTT. *Rhode Island.* Coward-McCann, 1969.
EATON, JEANETTE. *Lone Journey: The Life of Roger Williams.* Harcourt, 1944.
MONJO, F. N. *Slater's Mill.* Simon & Schuster, 1972. Fiction. A novel about the founder of the first cotton-spinning mill in the American colonies.
SIMISTER, FLORENCE P. *Pewter Plate.* Hastings, 1957. Fiction. *Girl with a Musket.* 1959. Fiction. *Daniel and Drum Rock.* 1963. Fiction. Novels about American Revolutionary days in Rhode Island.

Books for Older Readers

COLEMAN, PETER J. *The Transformation of Rhode Island, 1790-1860.* Brown Univ. Press, 1963.
ERNST, JAMES E. *Roger Williams: New England Firebrand.* AMS Press, 1932.
LIPPINCOTT, BERTRAM. *Indians, Privateers and High Society.* Lippincott, 1961. A history of Rhode Island.
MONAHON, CLIFFORD P. *Rhode Island: A Students' Guide to Localized History.* Teachers College Press, 1965.
Providence Journal-Bulletin Rhode Island Almanac. The Providence Journal Company. An annual publication.
Rhode Island Yearbook. Rhode Island Yearbook Foundation, Providence, R.I. An annual publication.
SCHOFIELD, WILLIAM G. *Ashes in the Wilderness.* Paperback Library, 1971. Fiction. A novel about King Philip's War.

RHODE ISLAND, UNIVERSITY OF, is a state-controlled, coeducational, land-grant institution at Kingston, R.I. The university has colleges of agriculture, arts and sciences, business administration, engineering, home economics, and pharmacy. It also has a graduate library school and a school of nursing. The university includes the Division of Engineering Research and Development, the Agricultural Experiment Station, the Narragansett Marine Laboratory, and the Bureau of Government Research. Elementary and secondary education courses are offered. The university grants bachelor's, master's, and doctor's degrees, and a diploma in dental hygiene. The university was founded as a college in 1892. For enrollment, see UNIVERSITIES AND COLLEGES (table). FRANCIS H. HORN

RHODE ISLAND COLLEGE. See UNIVERSITIES AND COLLEGES (table).

RHODE ISLAND SCHOOL OF DESIGN. See UNIVERSITIES AND COLLEGES (table).

RHODES, *roads,* is one of the Dodecanese Islands in the Aegean Sea. It lies 12 miles off the southwestern coast of Asia Minor (see GREECE [map]). Rhodes (also called *Ródhos*) has an area of 540 square miles, and a population of about 64,000. A range of mountains runs lengthwise across the island and rises to a height of 3,986 feet above the sea. Orchards, farms, and vineyards in the fertile valleys produce oranges, olives, tobacco, and grapes. Sponges are the chief export.

In early days, Rhodes was a wealthy and independent state of Greece. It was the home of many poets, artists, and philosophers. A great statue of Helios, called the *Colossus of Rhodes,* was one of the Seven Wonders of the Ancient World (see SEVEN WONDERS OF THE WORLD). In 1310, the Knights Hospitallers of Saint John occupied Rhodes and held it until 1522. Then the Turks took it, and Rhodes declined in glory and grandeur.

Italy occupied Rhodes during the Turko-Italian War of 1911-1912. After the war, Turkey lost Rhodes and

13 other Aegean Islands to Italy. Since 1935, Rhodes has been a hospital and munitions center. After World War II, Italy ceded Rhodes and the rest of the Dodecanese Islands to Greece. The capital of Rhodes and of the other Dodecanese Islands is the city of Rhodes (or Ródhos). HARRY N. HOWARD

RHODES, CECIL JOHN (1853-1902), was a British diamond king, statesman, and empire builder. He did more than any other man of his time to enlarge the British Empire.

Early Life. Rhodes was born in Hertfordshire on July 5, 1853, the son of a clergyman. He attended a grammar school, but poor health kept him from entering college. In 1870, he went to Natal, South Africa, where one of his brothers was a planter. Rhodes stayed with his brother for a year and then went to work in the diamond mines at Kimberley. In two years, he made a fortune.

WORLD BOOK photo
Cecil Rhodes

The climate of South Africa restored his health, and Rhodes determined to have the education his illness had prevented. From 1876 to 1881, he spent half of each year at Oxford University. During these years, he also combined most of the diamond mines in Kimberley into one company, the De Beers Consolidated Mines. Rhodes soon controlled almost all the diamonds produced in the world.

Gains Rhodesia. In 1881, Rhodes was elected to the assembly of the Cape Colony. At once, he set out to advance British imperial authority in South Africa. He forced the annexation of Bechuanaland (now Botswana) in 1884. Four years later, he forced the Matabele tribe to surrender most of its land to Great Britain. This great territory later became the state of Rhodesia (see RHODESIA; ZAMBIA). The British South Africa Company was put in charge of the territory. Rhodes became the leading official in this company.

In 1890, Rhodes became premier of the Cape Colony. In this office, he planned and promoted the Cape-to-Cairo Railroad, which was to cross Africa from south to north, but he did not succeed. He planned for the day when the British would control all South Africa.

Conflict with the Dutch. Rhodes saw that British rule in South Africa could only be enlarged at the expense of the Dutch. The Dutch had been settled in South Africa for hundreds of years and had large possessions there. But Rhodes did not hesitate to interfere in the politics of Dutch Transvaal. He was largely responsible for the Jameson Raid, in which Rhodesian troops attacked the Transvaal (see JAMESON, SIR LEANDER STARR). This incident was badly planned and caused much unfavorable comment. Rhodes resigned as premier of the Cape Colony following the raid, and withdrew to Rhodesia to wait for a better time to carry out his plans for expansion.

Rhodes was at Kimberley in 1899 when the Boer War finally broke out. He assisted in the defense of the city and helped direct the course of the war. But he died of tuberculosis before the war was over.

His Character. Cecil Rhodes was a man of vast ambitions and plans for the greatness of the British Empire. He spent his wealth freely when he thought he could advance the empire. When Rhodes found that he was going to die, he only worked harder at his plans. A tyrant by nature, he was ruthless in carrying out his plans.

Rhodes' will was an important part of his life work. He left his fortune to public service. A large gift to Oxford University established the Rhodes Scholarships (see RHODES SCHOLARSHIP). ANDRÉ MAUROIS

RHODES, COLOSSUS OF. See SEVEN WONDERS OF THE WORLD.

RHODES, JAMES FORD (1848-1927), an American historian, received a Pulitzer prize in 1918 for *A History of the Civil War, 1861-1865*. He also wrote a nine-volume *A History of the United States from the Compromise of 1850*. Many critics felt it did not do justice to the South or to labor, but the book became a standard work. Rhodes was born in Cleveland, Ohio, and studied at New York University, the University of Chicago, and in Europe. He entered business in 1870, but retired in 1885 to devote himself to historical study. MERLE CURTI

RHODES SCHOLARSHIP is an award that entitles students from the British Commonwealth, South Africa, West Germany, and the United States to two years' residence and study at Oxford University in England. The scholarship may be extended a third year. Rhodes scholars receive about 1,300 pounds (about $3,120) a year, which includes living expenses and tuition. The scholarship was established in 1902 with money left by Cecil John Rhodes, the English colonial statesman. His aim was to strengthen the British Empire and to bring about a closer union among English-speaking peoples.

Rhodes' will states that the selected students are not to be mere bookworms. They must be all-around men of high character and superior scholarship, with outdoor and athletic tastes, unmarried, and between the ages of 18 and 24. The method of selection is by committees in the various countries.

The scholarships are given out each year. Annually, Canada receives 11; South Africa, 8 or 9; Australia, 6; Rhodesia, 3; India, 2; and New Zealand, 2; Bermuda, Jamaica, Malta, and Pakistan each get 1. One scholarship is given every third year to the British Caribbean (from 1961); to Ceylon (from 1958); to Ghana (from 1959); to Malaya (from 1960); and to Nigeria (from 1961). The United States receives 32 scholarships annually. The United States awards were suspended in 1939 because of World War II, but appointments continued to be made in the British Commonwealth. Awards were resumed in the United States in 1946. West Germany receives two awards yearly. The German awards also were stopped in 1939, but resumed in 1970.

Candidates from the United States must be citizens who have lived in the country for at least five years. They must also have completed at least two years' work at some recognized four-year college or university of the United States. The nation is divided into eight districts for purposes of selection. Competition is held in each state before a selection committee. Successful state candidates then go before the district committee, which selects four district representatives. THOMAS J. McLERNON

See also RHODES, CECIL JOHN; OXFORD UNIVERSITY.

RHODESIA

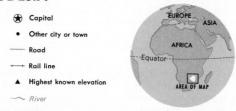

- ⊛ Capital
- • Other city or town
- — Road
- ← → Rail line
- ▲ Highest known elevation
- ∼ River

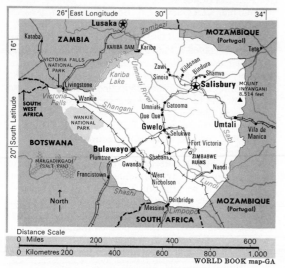

WORLD BOOK map-GA

RHODESIA is a self-governing British colony in southern Africa that declared itself independent in 1965. Rhodesia was the first colony to break away from Great Britain without consent since the American Colonies declared their independence in 1776. No country officially recognizes Rhodesia's independence.

Rhodesia's declaration of independence stems from its constitutional history and its racial situation. As in neighboring South Africa, the vast majority of the people are black Africans. But the whites, who make up only about 4 per cent of the population, control the country. The British tried during the 1960's to give the Africans more power. But the white Rhodesians then declared Rhodesia independent. Led by the United Nations, many countries applied political and economic pressure to try to force them to give in.

Rhodesia is a little bigger than Montana. It lies in the tropics, but the climate is pleasant because of the high altitude. The famed Victoria Falls lies on the Zambezi River on Rhodesia's northern border. Rhodesia's national parks have many wild animals. Rhodesia is a leading mineral and tobacco producer. Salisbury is the capital and Bulawayo is the largest city.

Government. Rhodesia adopted a new constitution in 1970. The constitution declares Rhodesia a republic and provides for a president as head of state. The president is elected to a five-year term. The constitution also provides for a two-house parliament made up of a

Kenneth Kirkwood, the contributor of this article, is Rhodes Professor of Race Relations at Oxford University.

23-member Senate and a 66-member House of Assembly. Members are elected to five-year terms.

The Senate has 10 European members and 10 African chiefs. European members are elected by an electoral college of European members of the House of Assembly. An electoral college of tribal chiefs elects the African members. Three additional members, either European or African, are appointed by the president.

The House of Assembly consists of 50 European members elected by non-African voters, and 16 African members. Half the African members are elected by qualified African voters and half by electoral colleges made up of tribal chiefs. The number of black members may be increased to 50 when black Rhodesians pay more than 24 per cent of Rhodesia's income taxes. But most black Rhodesians are poor. Citizens over 21 years of age may vote. But strict economic and educational requirements prevent many black Rhodesians from voting.

People. About 94 out of every 100 Rhodesians are Africans. About 4 of every 100 are Europeans, and the rest are Asians and *Coloureds* (persons of mixed ancestry). Over three-fourths of the Africans live in rural areas. Most of the Europeans, Asians, and Coloureds live in cities and towns. The Mashona and Matabele are the largest African tribes. The Mashona speak a language called *Chishona* and the Matabele speak *Sindebele*.

Most of the Africans are farmers. They live in small thatched huts on reservations that cover about 40 per cent of Rhodesia. A government body holds reservation land on behalf of the Africans. Africans can purchase individual pieces of land only in certain specified areas. Most farmers can raise only enough food for their families. Their main crop, maize, is pounded into flour to make a dish called *mealie porridge*.

Many Africans work on European farms or go to South Africa to work in mines. Others work in cities and towns. There, they live in special sections called *African townships*. The Europeans include farmers, who own most of the high *veld* (grasslands), and business and professional men. About 37 of every 100 acres in Rhodesia are reserved for Europeans.

Land. Most of Rhodesia is a high, rolling plateau from 3,000 to 5,000 feet above sea level. The High Veld, a central plateau about 400 miles long and 50 miles

---
FACTS IN BRIEF

Capital: Salisbury.

Official Language: English.

Area: 150,804 square miles.

Population: *Estimated 1973 Population*—5,792,000; distribution, 80 per cent rural, 20 per cent urban; density, 38 persons to the square mile. *1969 Census*—5,070,400. *Estimated 1978 Population*—6,780,000.

Chief Products: *Agriculture*—cattle, coffee, cotton, maize, sugar, tea, tobacco, wheat. *Manufacturing and Processing*—chemicals, clothing and footwear, iron and steel, metal products, processed foods, textiles. *Mining*—asbestos, chrome, coal, copper, gems, gold.

Flag: The flag has three vertical stripes—green, white, and green from left to right. The Rhodesian coat of arms in the center includes a gold pickax symbolizing mining, a green shield symbolizing agriculture, and a red lion between two thistles from the coat of arms of Cecil Rhodes. See FLAG (picture: Flags of Africa).

Money: *Basic Unit*—Rhodesian dollar.

292

wide, crosses the country from northeast to southwest. The Middle Veld lies on either side of the High Veld. The Low Veld consists of sandy plains in the Zambezi, Limpopo, and Sabi river basins. Mt. Inyangani (8,514 ft.) is the highest point in Rhodesia.

Rhodesia's summer season lasts from October to April, and is hot and wet. The winter, from May to September, is cool and dry. October and November are the hottest months and June and July are the coolest. Temperatures range between 54° and 85° F., and rainfall varies from 15 inches a year in the west to 50 inches in the east.

Economy. During 1966 and 1967, Great Britain and the United Nations banned trade with Rhodesia. South Africa and Mozambique continued trading with Rhodesia, but most other nations stopped. Rhodesia is among the world's leading tobacco producers. Tobacco was its most valuable export. Farmers also grow sugar, corn, cotton, peanuts, tea, wheat, and raise cattle.

Rhodesia is a leading gold, asbestos, and chrome producer. A smelter at Que Que extracts iron from ore mined in the area. Coal comes from the Wankie region. The country also has copper, tin, and precious stones.

The Kariba Gorge hydroelectric development on the Zambezi is one of the world's largest. The dam forms Kariba Lake, which covers 2,000 square miles. The Kariba power plant supplies electricity to most of Rhodesia. It is operated jointly by Rhodesia and Zambia.

History. Bushmen paintings and ancient tools found in the region indicate that Rhodesia had Stone Age inhabitants. By the A.D. 800's, the people were mining large amounts of minerals for trade. Shona people, ancestors of the present-day Mashona, established their rule in the 1000's or 1100's. They built stone structures at Zimbabwe, and ruins of these structures can be seen near Fort Victoria. During the 1400's, a branch of the Shona, known as the Karanga, established an empire called Mwanamutapa and made Zimbabwe the capital. See ZIMBABWE.

The World-Famous Victoria Falls, on the Rhodesia-Zambia border, sends up a cloud of spray that can be seen for 10 miles.

European

In the late 1400's, a dispute arose among the empire's rulers. It split the kingdom into a northern section, Mwanamutapa, and a southern section, Changamire, which had Zimbabwe as its capital. Portuguese traders intervened in Mwanamutapa and by 1630 took control of it. Nguni warriors from what is now South Africa conquered Changamire in the early 1800's and extended their rule into the northern region.

Portuguese explorers introduced Christianity to the area in the 1500's, but few people accepted it until the 1850's when Robert Moffat, a Scottish missionary, set up a mission there. In 1888, a branch of the Nguni, the Matabele, granted mineral rights in the area to Cecil Rhodes, a British financier. By 1893, Rhodes' British South Africa Company occupied most of the region. In 1895, the company named its territory Rhodesia.

The British crushed tribal uprisings in 1896 and 1897, and reports of gold brought more Europeans to the area. In 1898, Great Britain recognized Southern and Northern Rhodesia as separate territories. In 1922, the white settlers of Southern Rhodesia voted for self-government, and Southern Rhodesia became a self-governing British colony in 1923. In 1953, Britain set up the Federation of Rhodesia and Nyasaland, which included Southern Rhodesia, Northern Rhodesia (now Zambia), and Nyasaland (now Malawi).

In 1961, Britain and Rhodesia approved a new constitution. But the leading African party boycotted the first election, because it felt too few Africans could qualify to vote. The boycott helped Ian Smith defeat Sir Edgar Whitehead, who supported the 1961 constitution. Later, the government banned two African parties, the Zimbabwe African People's Union and the Zimbabwe African National Union. Both parties demanded a greater part in government for Africans.

The Rhodesian government demanded independence in 1964. But Britain declared that Southern Rhodesia must first guarantee the African majority a greater voice in the government. Rhodesian talks with Britain finally broke down. On Nov. 11, 1965, Prime Minister Ian Smith declared Rhodesia independent. Britain claimed that this was an illegal action. By January, 1966, it had banned all trade with Rhodesia. On Dec. 1, 1966, Smith and British Prime Minister Harold Wilson met to discuss the conflict. But Rhodesia rejected British proposals for a settlement. On December 16, the United Nations imposed compulsory economic sanctions against Rhodesia. In 1967, some fighting broke out between government troops and African nationalists.

Smith and Wilson met again in late 1968, but could not reach an agreement. In 1969, Rhodesian voters—mostly Europeans—approved a new constitution that would prevent the black African majority from ever gaining control of the government. The constitution went into effect in 1970.

Rhodesia declared itself a republic on March 2, 1970. The United Nations Security Council condemned Rhodesia's action. It asked all nations with consulates in Rhodesia to close them.   KENNETH KIRKWOOD

RHODESIA AND NYASALAND, FEDERATION OF,
was a federated territory in central Africa from 1953 to
1963. It belonged to Great Britain. It consisted of the
self-governing colony of Southern Rhodesia and the
protectorates of Northern Rhodesia and Nyasaland.
Great Britain created the federation in 1953, hoping to
develop one economically strong state.

The federation was governed by a British governor-
general, but a prime minister actually headed the
government. The prime minister presided over a cabinet
selected from the federal assembly. The assembly had
59 members, including 12 Africans and 3 Europeans
who were especially elected to represent the interests
of the Africans. Salisbury, the largest city in the federation, served as the capital.

Africans opposed formation of the federation, because the whites kept control of the governments even
though they were in the minority. African nationalist
groups gradually gained a voice in the governments of
Nyasaland and Northern Rhodesia. They demanded
full independence. A constitutional conference in 1960
gave Africans a majority in the Nyasaland legislature.
Great Britain granted Northern Rhodesia a new constitution in 1962. White voters approved a new constitution for Southern Rhodesia in 1961, but the Africans demanded more representation in the government.

Great Britain agreed to dissolve the federation on
Dec. 31, 1963. In 1964, Nyasaland became the independent nation of Malawi and Northern Rhodesia
gained independence as Zambia. Southern Rhodesia
became the self-governing country of Rhodesia, but did
not receive full independence from Great Britain. In
1965, Rhodesia declared itself independent from Britain. Malawi and Zambia remained in the British Commonwealth.   HIBBERD V. B. KLINE, JR.

See also MALAWI; RHODESIA; ZAMBIA.

RHODESIAN MAN. See PREHISTORIC MAN (Homo
Sapiens; color picture).

RHODESIAN RIDGEBACK is a medium-sized hound
raised in southern Africa. It is also called an *African
lion hound*, because it was originally bred to hunt lions
and hold them at bay. The Rhodesian ridgeback has a
ridge on its back formed by hair that grows in a direction opposite to the rest of the coat. The coat has a
wheatlike color, and sometimes has a red tint. The dog
stands about 27 inches tall. Most weigh from 65 to 75
pounds.   OLGA DAKAN

RHODIUM, *ROH dee uhm*, is a hard, silvery-white
element belonging to the platinum group of metals.
William Wollaston, a British scientist, first isolated
the metal in 1803. Rhodium is obtained as a by-product of nickel manufacture in Canada. South Africa and
Russia also produce small quantities of the metal.

Industry uses rhodium as a coating to prevent wear
and corrosion on high-quality scientific equipment
and electrical parts. Rhodium with platinum metal
makes an alloy used in thermocouples.

Rhodium has the symbol Rh. Its atomic number is
45, and its atomic weight is 102.905. It is not soluble in
acids and melts at 1966° C. (±3° C.).   J. GORDON PARR

RHODOCHROSITE. See MANGANESE (Sources).

RHODODENDRON, *ROH doh DEN drun*, is the name
of a group of trees and shrubs that belong to the heath

Greater Eureka C of C
The Rhododendron Produces Large Clusters of Flowers.

family. The name means *rose tree*. The group includes
several species which are known for the beauty of their
flowers and for their evergreen leaves. One of the best
known is the *great rhododendron*, which is also called
great laurel and *rose bay*. It grows widely in the Allegheny
Mountains. There the interlocking branches form almost impassable thickets. This rhododendron rarely
grows higher than 35 feet. Its white or rose-colored
flowers grow in a large cluster.

Another species, the *mountain rose bay*, is a common shrub in Virginia. It produces brilliant, lilac-
purple flowers. Other species are found in the Pacific
Coast region. Some magnificent specimens grow in the
mountainous regions of India. Washington and West
Virginia have adopted the rhododendron as their flower.

Scientific Classification. The rhododendrons belong
to the heath family, *Ericaceae*. The great rhododendron is
genus *Rhododendron*, species *R. maximum*. The mountain
rose bay is *R. catawbiense*.   J. J. LEVISON

See also NORTH CAROLINA (color picture: Mount
Mitchell); WEST VIRGINIA (picture: The State Flower).

RHODOPE MOUNTAINS. See BULGARIA (The Land).

RHOMBOID, *RAHM boyd*, is a plane figure with two
parallel sides of equal length, and the other two sides
a different, but also equal, length. Its sides are not at
right angles to each other. See also RHOMBUS.

RHOMBUS, *RAHM bus*,
is the name given to a
plane figure with two pairs
of straight, parallel sides,
all of equal length. Usu-
ally, its sides are not at
right angles to each other.
See QUADRILATERAL.

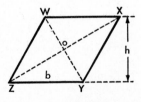

Its area is found by multiplying base by altitude, or
$A = bh$. The diagonals WY and XZ are perpendicular
to each other. Using the two triangles ZWX and XYZ
in the figure, you can show that the area of a rhombus
is half the product of its diagonals.   ROTHWELL STEPHENS

RHÔNE RIVER, *roan,* an important commercial waterway of France, is also famous for the beauty of its valley. The river rises in the Rhône glacier of Switzerland, at an altitude of over 5,000 feet. Glacial clay picked up by the river in the Swiss Alps makes the water of the Rhône almost milky. But during the Rhône's course through Lake Geneva, it loses most of the glacial clay at the bottom of that lake. The clear blue of the river, after leaving Lake Geneva, inspired the English poet Lord Byron to describe it as "the blue rushing of the arrowy Rhône."

After the Rhône leaves Switzerland and enters France, it flows southwestward to Lyon. It then winds south and empties through a large delta into the Gulf of Lions, an arm of the Mediterranean Sea.

The Rhône is over 500 miles long, and navigable for about 300 miles. Chief branches are the Saône, the Isère, and the Durance. A canal near the mouth of the

The Rhône River Flows Through Southern France.

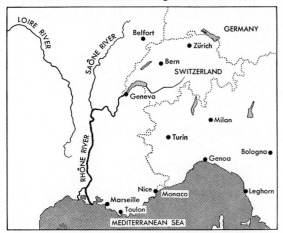

Rhône connects this river with France's largest Mediterranean port, Marseille. In 1949, French engineers completed the Génissiat Dam on the Rhône River, on the French-Swiss border near Bellegarde.

Greek and Latin civilizations followed the Rhône Valley to Lyon, and up its tributaries. JACK R. VILLMOW

RHUBARB, or PIEPLANT, is one of the few perennial vegetables. It originally came from Mongolia, but is grown both in Europe and America. The plant forms a large, yellow storage root and a mass of feeder roots underground. The roots produce buds from which grow long, thick leafstalks with large leaves. People use the reddish, juicy stalks for food. A person may become ill from eating the leaves because they contain the poisonous oxalic acid salts (see OXALIC ACID).

Although rhubarb is technically a vegetable, people usually prepare it as a dessert food, often as pie fillings and sweet sauces. Stores sell frozen and canned rhubarb, but many people prefer to eat the vegetable's fresh stalks. Rhubarb contains some vitamin C, and has laxative qualities.

Rhubarb plants produce many seeds, but plants from the seeds are not always like the parent plant. Growers plant pieces of the big storage root that have several buds from which new plants grow. Each plant lasts

5 to 8 years. Rhubarb is relatively free from insect attack and suffers from few diseases.

Scientific Classification. Rhubarb belongs to the buckwheat family, *Polygonaceae.* It is genus *Rheum,* species *R. rhaponticum.* ARTHUR J. PRATT

RHUMB LINE. See GREAT-CIRCLE ROUTE.

RHUMBA, or RUMBA, is a ballroom dance in four-four time. Its strong quick-quick-slow rhythm is usually subjected to complex syncopation. Accentuated body movements rather than foot movements characterize the dance. Rhumba had its roots as a Spanish and African folk dance. The ballroom dance originated in Cuba and became known in the United States in the early 1930's. The various forms of the ballroom rhumba are performed throughout the West Indies. WALTER SORELL

RHYME, also spelled RIME, means echoing or repeating sounds in poetry. It usually occurs at the ends of lines:

> Marching along, fifty-score strong,
> Great-hearted gentlemen singing this song.

This is an example of end-rhyme. *Strong* in the first line rhymes with *song* in the second. In addition, the first line has internal rhyme. *Along* rhymes with *strong.*

In masculine rhyme, the end sounds of stressed syllables are repeated, as in *strong* and *song.* But in feminine rhyme, two or three syllables are echoed or repeated. For example, *water* and *daughter,* or *dreamingly* and *seemingly.*

In perfect rhyme, the stressed vowel and the following sounds are repeated exactly. But different sorts of imperfect rhyme are often used: (1) rhyme in which the

Rhubarb Plants produce reddish, juicy stalks which are used in pies and in sauces. Although rhubarb is a vegetable, it is popular as a dessert. Stores sell frozen and canned rhubarb.

J. Horace McFarland

stressed vowels are not the same (as in *forever* and *river*); (2) rhyme in which the consonants following the vowels are different (as in *goes* and *clothes*); (3) rhyme in which the end-sound of a stressed syllable is repeated in an unstressed syllable (as in *sing* and *dancing*). In so-called eye-rhyme, the words only look as if they rhyme (as in *brow* and *glow*).

Rhyme becomes a noticeable and often delightful feature when poetry is read aloud. Rhyme draws attention to the verses as they are read, and it gives form to the stanzas. It may also emphasize the meaning of the rhyming words.

Rhyme is used only accidentally in prose, and it is not necessary in poetry (see PROSE; BLANK VERSE; FREE VERSE). In some parts of the world, the art of poetry makes little or no use of rhyme. Present-day poets are free to use rhyme as they wish.   CHARLES W. COOPER

See also POETRY (Metrical Patterns); ALLITERATION.

RHYTHM, *rith'm*, is the natural swing felt in dancing, music, and language. The word comes from the Greek word *rhythmos*, meaning *measured motion*. In dancing, rhythmic patterns and variations are created by physical motions of shorter or longer duration and of greater or lesser emphasis. In music, rhythmic figures and phrases come from an arrangement of tones, organized according to their duration and stresses, or accents. In language, rhythm is the rise and fall of sounds according to syllables, vocal inflections, physical speech accents, and pauses. Modern English and German are of the language type that has physically stressed, or accented, syllables. Greek and Latin are of the language type that uses long and short syllables or inflections to give stress. In poetry, both types organize syllables into rhythmic patterns called *feet*, which are grouped into many different poetic forms.

In all the arts, rhythm is the element that provides a universal means of communication.   GRANT FLETCHER

See also DANCING; LANGUAGE; METER (poetry); MUSIC (Rhythm; Notation).

RHYTHM BAND describes a group of performers playing *percussion instruments* (instruments that produce musical tones when struck). Elementary schools in the United States use rhythm bands as a method of teaching children about basic rhythm in music. Children learn to sing, tap, or play the characteristic rhythm of a melody. The purpose of these bands is to develop a feeling and response to rhythms of all kinds. Some rhythm band instruments, such as the xylophone, triangle, chimes, gong, or cymbals, may be made commercially. Children may also make their own instruments, using such materials as old brake drums, suspended horseshoes, and lard tubs covered with inner tubes stretched and nailed over their tops. In some schools, rhythm band members dress in costumes and play for parents' groups.   RAYMOND KENDALL

RHYTHM METHOD. See BIRTH CONTROL.

RIAL, *RYE al*, is a coin that serves as the basic monetary unit of Iran (formerly Persia). One rial can be subdivided into 100 *dinars*. Iran issues *copper-nickel* coins worth 1, 2, 5, and 10 rials, and paper notes worth 10, 20, 50, 100, 200, and 1,000 rials. The name of the coin comes from the old French and Spanish words for *royal*. It is sometimes incorrectly called *real*, which was the name for a silver coin of Spain (see REAL). For its value in dollars, see MONEY (table).   BURTON HOBSON

RIALTO BRIDGE. See VENICE.

RIB is any one of the 24 bones that enclose the chest in the human body. There are 12 ribs on each side of the body, each connected to the *vertebral column* (backbone) by small joints called *costovertebral joints*. In the front of the body, the uppermost seven ribs on each side connect to the *sternum* (breastbone), and are called *true ribs*. The five lower ribs, called *false ribs*, do not connect directly to the sternum. Each of the upper three false ribs is attached to the rib above with *cartilage* (gristle). The lowest two ribs are attached only to the backbone. They are known as *floating ribs*. The spaces between the ribs, called *intercostal spaces*, contain arteries, veins, muscles, and nerves.

Most *vertebrates* (animals with backbones) have ribs, although the number of ribs varies considerably. For example, in mammals, the number varies from 9 pairs, as in some whales, to 24 pairs, as in two-toed sloths.

The ribs perform two functions in the body. They form a cage around the chest cavity that protects the heart and lungs. They also move up and down and, to-

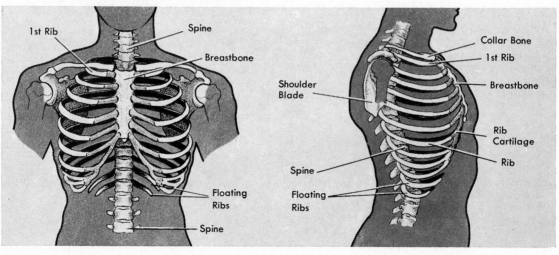

gether with the diaphragm, control the movement of air in and out of the lungs. When the ribs move up, the chest cavity enlarges and air is sucked into the lungs. When they move down, air is forced out of the lungs.

A hard blow on the chest can fracture a rib. Fractured ribs cause sharp pain when the injured person breathes, and tenderness when pressure is applied to the fracture area. A person who has injured his chest should call a doctor.   MARSHALL R. URIST

See also HUMAN BODY (Trans-Vision color picture).

RIB GRASS. See PLANTAIN.

RIBAUT, *REE BOH,* **JEAN** (1520?-1565), a French colonizer, led an expedition to America in 1562 to found a Huguenot colony. He built Fort Charles, where Port Royal, S.C., now stands. He then returned to France, and left the settlement in care of 26 colonists, who later abandoned it. In 1565, Ribaut took charge of a French Protestant settlement at Fort Caroline, on the Saint Johns River in Florida. Spaniards later captured Ribaut and his men and stabbed Ribaut to death. He was born in Dieppe, France.   J. CARLYLE SITTERSON

RIBBENTROP, *RIB un trawp,* **JOACHIM VON** (1893-1946), was Adolf Hitler's top diplomatic agent. He served as foreign minister of Germany from 1938 to 1945. He helped engineer the seizure of Austria, the partition of Czechoslovakia, and alliances with Italy and Japan. He made a deal with Joseph Stalin of Russia in August, 1939, which safeguarded Germany's eastern border in exchange for concessions to Russia. After World War II, he was tried and hanged for war crimes.

Ribbentrop was born in Wesel, Germany. He studied in France, and worked in both the United States and Canada. His familiarity with different languages helped him greatly in diplomacy. In 1935, he gained from England a naval treaty which gave Germany equality in submarines.   WILLIAM A. JENKS

RIBBON FALLS is a beautiful waterfall that looks like a narrow ribbon as it drops 1,612 feet straight down in the Yosemite Valley. It is fed by a tiny creek that rises in the mountains above the valley. The water drops down a narrow gorge to empty into the Merced River, which flows through the valley. Ribbon Falls goes dry in early August after the dry California summer. It becomes a thundering torrent during May and June. See also WATERFALL (chart).   C. LANGDON WHITE

RIBBON WORM is any of a group of worms with a long slender *proboscis* (snout). The proboscis lies in a tubular space above the mouth and can be thrown out quickly and wrapped around the prey. In some ribbon worms, the proboscis has daggerlike *stylets*. In others, it has *nematocysts* (fine stinging threads). Ribbon worms feed on other animals such as worms and mollusks, both living and dead. They are not harmful to man. Most ribbon worms live in the ocean, but a few live in moist earth and fresh water. They range in size from less than an inch to many feet long. Some are brilliantly colored and some are dull.   J. A. McLEOD

Scientific Classification. Ribbon worms make up the phylum *Rhynchocoela* (*Nemertinea*).

RIBERA, JUSEPE DE (1591-1652), was a Spanish painter. Many of his paintings show Christian martyrdoms and saints doing penance. Until 1635, Ribera's style showed the influence of the Italian painter Michelangelo Caravaggio. Ribera then used somber colors and placed realistic figures in simple, diagonal compositions.

Between 1635 and 1639, influenced by the Italian painters Correggio and Titian, he used brighter colors and more complex compositions. Elements of these earlier styles are found in his work after 1639.

Ribera was born in Játiva, near Valencia, Spain. In 1616, he settled in Naples, Italy, then a Spanish territory. He became very successful and never returned to Spain. The Italians nicknamed him *Lo Spagnoletto* (Little Spaniard).   MARILYN STOKSTAD

RIBICOFF, ABRAHAM A. (1910-   ), a Connecticut Democrat, has served in many high government posts. He has served in the U.S. Senate since 1963. He was secretary of health, education, and welfare in President John F. Kennedy's Cabinet (1961-1962).

Ribicoff also served in the Connecticut House of Representatives from 1938 to 1942, and in the U.S. House of Representatives from 1949 to 1953. He was governor of Connecticut from 1955 to 1961.

Ribicoff was born in New Britain, Conn., and was graduated with honors from the University of Chicago Law School in 1933. He practiced law and served as a police court judge before entering politics. As governor, he led a traffic safety program. As a senator, he called for legislation to require certain safety features on automobiles.   ALBERT E. VAN DUSEN

RIBOFLAVIN. See VITAMIN; NUTRITION (Vitamins).

RIBONUCLEIC ACID. See NUCLEIC ACID.

RICARDO, DAVID (1772-1823), was the leading British economist of the early 1800's. He helped establish the theories of *classical economics,* which stresses economic freedom through free trade and free competition.

In his book *Principles of Political Economy and Taxation* (1817), Ricardo defined the conditions that would enable a nation's economy to reach its greatest potential. He believed that the accumulation of capital was the key to rapid economic growth. He argued that allowing businessmen to seek high profits would bring about a rapid accumulation of capital.

Ricardo considered labor to be the most important source of wealth. But he also thought that population growth would push wage rates down to a level that would barely support the people. As the economy expanded and the population continued to grow, land rent would rise. This would reduce profits, the accumulation of capital would slow down, and economic growth would end. But Ricardo believed that by this time industrialization would have spread throughout the world and peak production would be a reality.

Ricardo's theories influenced other economists. His theory of comparative advantage is still the basis for the modern theory of international trade (see INTERNATIONAL TRADE). Karl Marx was influenced by Ricardo's *labor theory of value,* which held that the value of a commodity is determined by the amount of labor needed in its production. Henry George, a land reformer, developed Ricardo's theory of rent into a detailed study of progress and poverty. John Stuart Mill, a British philosopher and economist, used Ricardo's ideas as the basis for a philosophy of social reform.

Ricardo was born in London, and made a fortune on the stock exchange while still in his 20's. He served in Parliament from 1819 until his death.   DANIEL R. FUSFELD

RICE

Thomas Melvin, Pix

RICE is one of the world's most important food crops. About half the people of the world eat this valuable grain as their chief food. Most of these people live in Asia, where rice is even more important than wheat is to the people of Europe and the United States. Many Asians eat rice three times a day, and often have little else to eat. People in India and Japan eat an average of from a half to two-thirds of a pound of rice daily. Some of them eat more than a pound daily. In the United States, the average is only about eight pounds of rice a year for every person.

Oriental peoples often eat rice cakes at certain festivals as symbols of happiness and long life. In Japan, the emperor celebrates an important religious ceremony at the beginning of the rice-growing season. The custom of throwing rice at weddings probably came from India. In Italy, people celebrate the harvesting of rice crops with festivities. Rice-harvest festivals are also held at Crowley, La., and Winnie, Tex.

Rice is a cereal grass related to such plants as oats, rye, wheat, and barley. However, rice grows in many

Nelson E. Jodon, the contributor of this article, is an agronomist with the U.S. Department of Agriculture Rice Experiment Station at Crowley, La.

places too warm and too wet for some of these other crops. Because rice needs a constant supply of water, farmers plant it in flooded fields or in unflooded fields where rainfall is heavy. When the plants are young, the fields look like bright green lakes. As the grain ripens, the straw-colored heads of the plants show among the more or less dry leaves.

A grain of rice has a rough outer *hull* (shell) that is not good to eat. The kernel within this fairly loose covering is surrounded by a series of brownish skins called *bran coats*. These contain most of the vitamins and minerals. The bran coats stick tightly to the *kernel* (center). We eat the hard, starchy kernels.

Uses of Rice

As a Food. Cooks usually prepare rice by boiling or simmering the kernels in water. Sometimes the kernels are steamed. During cooking, the kernels swell to two or three times their original size because they soak up water. To save vitamins and minerals, rice should not be cooked in more water than it will absorb.

Many persons eat rice with meat, fish, or poultry. They flavor the kernels with butter, gravies, or sauces. Chop suey and several oriental dishes are usually served with rice. Soups, curries, puddings, and cas-

298

serole dishes often combine rice, seasonings, and spices with other foods. The kernels are *puffed* or *flaked* into ready-to-eat breakfast cereals. Flour made from rice is sometimes used in flour mixes.

Rice kernels without hulls contain about 80 per cent starch, 8 per cent protein, and 12 per cent water. The kernels have few minerals, but they contain the vitamins thiamine, niacin, and riboflavin. Although rice contains less protein than wheat contains, rice protein is superior in quality.

Before cooking, the grains must be *milled*. Milling removes the hulls and usually takes off the bran coats with the valuable vitamins and minerals. Persons whose main food is *polished* (or completely milled) rice, often suffer from vitamin-deficiency diseases such as beriberi (see BERIBERI). To make up the vitamin and mineral losses, many millers mix regular kernels with kernels that have been coated with vitamin and mineral preparations. They sell this product as *enriched rice*. In the United States, millers prepare *quick-cooking* rice by partly cooking milled rice and then drying it in heated air. Quick-cooking rice is also enriched. *Brown rice* is rice that has not had the bran coats removed by milling.

Beverages. The Japanese use fermented rice kernels to make an alcoholic drink called *sake* (rice wine). In several Asian countries, people use rice to make beer as well as wine. In the United States and Europe, brewers sometimes use rice in making beer.

By-Products. Commercial milling machines remove the hulls and bran coats from rice kernels. This process produces powdery by-products called *bran* and *polish*. Rice bran is obtained as the outer bran coats are rubbed off. Polish includes the inner bran coats and some starch from the kernel. The bran and polish are used for livestock feeds. In some regions, oil extracted from the bran is used in making soap and margarine. *Starch* made from rice has very fine particles. It is used chiefly in cosmetics and in laundry starch.

The Japanese often pack rice *hulls* around fragile articles to prevent breakage during shipping. In many places, hulls serve as an inexpensive fuel for steam engines that power rice mills. Asian farmers often burn hulls to warm their homes, or use them in making adobe-type bricks (see ADOBE). Rice *straw* (the dried stalks) is used in Asia to make sandals, hats, and raincoats, and to thatch roofs. Philippine farmers sometimes grow mushrooms on beds of rice straw.

Kinds of Rice

Cultivated Rice. Farmers throughout the world raise between 7,000 and 8,000 kinds of cultivated rice. Farmers in the United States grow about 15 varieties of rice.

Most of the world's rice crop grows with water standing on the fields. Such rice is called *lowland, wet,* or *irrigated* rice. In the United States, rice grows in artificially flooded fields. Farmers in countries with plentiful rainfall raise rice on land too hilly to be flooded. Such rice, called *upland, hill,* or *dry* rice, grows in regions of Africa, Asia, and South America. Certain rice varieties grow best on lowlands and others on uplands. Some varieties grow well in either place.

Some kinds of *very early* rice ripen within 80 days after planting. But some late varieties require more than 200 days. Rice grown in the United States ripens in from 110 to 150 days.

During the 1960's, researchers developed a type of plant that makes possible higher rice yields than ever before. They crossbred a high-producing *dwarf* (short) variety with an ordinary tall variety. The new short, sturdy plant is so highly productive, especially when fertilized, that it has been called "miracle rice." Wind and rain do not cause it to fall down and spoil, as often happens with ordinary rice. Food specialists hoped the new rice would help reduce food shortages in countries using rice as a basic food. However, no single variety is suitable for growing everywhere. As a result, rice breeders in many countries are working to develop new varieties to meet local needs.

The best rice varieties have fairly hard, glassy kernels that can be milled without much breakage. Most cultivated varieties have brownish inner kernels from $\frac{2}{10}$ to $\frac{4}{10}$ of an inch long. Rice growers in the United States classify rice by grain length as *short* or *pearl, medium,* and *long*.

All rice has the same food value. But long grain rice costs more because more of the long kernels break during milling. Some persons prefer long kernel rice because it cooks dry, with the kernels separated from each other. The most expensive rice, called *scented* or *aromatic* rice, has long grains that cook dry. This rice tastes somewhat like popcorn. Many people like short or medium grain rice because it cooks moist and firm. Left-over rice of this type can be used for a later meal, because it stays soft.

Some Asian farmers prefer to eat *glutinous* or *waxy* rice. The milled kernels of this rice appear white and waxy. The rice cooks to a sticky paste and is used for cakes and confections. Although this rice is called glutinous, neither it nor any other rice contains gluten.

Wild Rice usually has red bran coats. People in India eat it on certain religious occasions and they believe it is helpful in treating certain diseases.

A grass plant called *Canada, wild,* or *Indian,* rice grows along lake shores in Canada and the Great Lakes region of the United States. This plant is called *wild* rice because of its growth habits. It is used in the same

FOOD VALUE OF RICE

STARCH
80 per cent

WATER
12 per cent

PROTEIN
8 per cent

USDA

299

PLANTING

Sowing Rice. Farmers sometimes *broadcast* (scatter) the seeds on flooded fields, such as this one in Japan, *left*. Later, they thin out the young plants.

Transplanting. Many farmers grow young rice plants in well-fertilized nurseries, such as this one in China, *below*. After 30 or 40 days, workers, such as these in India, *opposite page*, transplant clumps of young plants from nurseries into the soupy soil of paddies.

Three Lions

Charbonnier, Photo Representatives

way as ordinary rice, although it is not a true rice.

Other kinds of wild grasses have *rice* in the common name, but they are not used for food.

The Rice Plant

Appearance. Rice plants grow from 2 to 6 feet tall and look much like other cereal plants. At first, a single shoot appears. Then one, two, and often many more *tillers* (offshoots) develop. Each stalk has at least five or six hollow joints, and there is a leaf for each joint. The leaf blade is long, pointed, flat, and rather stiff. The highest joint grows a branched *panicle* (head) much like that of the oat plant. Each panicle bears from 50 to 300 *spikelets* (flowers) from which the grains develop.

Enemies. Moth larvae called *stem borers* sometimes live in the stems of rice plants. Other insects suck the plant juices or chew the leaves. Birds eat ripening grain or newly sown seeds. Bird enemies of rice include the bobolink (sometimes called the ricebird) and the Java sparrow or paddybird. Fungi, tiny roundworms, viruses, and bacteria infect the plants and cause disease. A fungus disease called *blast* causes the panicles to break. Weeds, such as *barnyard grass* (*jungle rice*), *sedges*, and *red rice*, are common in rice fields.

Dusts and sprays are used against some diseases and insects. But farmers can best control diseases by growing varieties that resist disease. In the United States, airplanes spray chemicals to kill certain weeds and grasses. Noisemakers are used to frighten away birds.

Growing Rice

Rice grows in many types of soil, including some that are too heavy and wet for most other crops. The best crops grow in river valleys, on deltas, and on coastal plains where the soil holds water well. Most rice soils are low in nitrogen and phosphorus, so fertilizers containing

these elements must be added to produce good crops. Crops are very small where rice is grown every year with little or no fertilizer. Yields are only 800 to 1,200 pounds per acre. Rice grows well at temperatures between 70° and 100° F. It needs an average temperature of at least 75° F. during the growing season, and an average rainfall of at least 45 inches unless irrigation is used. Usually, *nonirrigated* or *upland* rice yields less per acre than irrigated rice.

Few rice farms in Asia are larger than 10 to 15 acres, and most of them are only 2 to 3 acres. Most Asian farmers use the same primitive methods and crude tools that their ancestors used. Some have water buffalo or oxen for plowing, but the rest must grow their crops using hand labor.

In the United States and a few countries of South America, profitable rice farms range from 300 to over 1,000 acres. Despite their size, such farms require few laborers, because the work is done almost completely with the aid of modern farm machinery.

The Rice Field. Farmers grow lowland rice in fields divided into smaller parts by dirt walls called *dikes* or *levees*. An area surrounded by a dike is called a *paddy* or *cut*. The dikes range from 1 to 2 feet high and from 4 to 6 feet wide. On fairly level land, farmers build dikes in straight or wavy lines. On hilly land, they follow the slopes and form terraced paddies that rise like steps. The dikes hold water on the fields.

Rice growers often irrigate their fields before working up the soil for planting. They plow the paddies and turn the weeds under the soil or mud.

Planting Rice. Farmers may sow rice on dry land by planting the seeds in rows of small dirt hills, or by using a machine called a *drill* that plants several rows at a time. Sometimes they *broadcast* (scatter) the seeds on the ground and then plow them into the soil.

Lowland rice can also be broadcast onto muddy land.

In the United States, low-flying airplanes sometimes broadcast sprouted seeds onto flooded fields.

In many places outside the United States, farmers broadcast seeds very thickly over small patches of well-fertilized, wet or dry soil. They carefully tend these nursery beds and, after 30 or 40 days, transplant the *seedlings* (young plants) to the flooded fields. Usually they push a clump of from one to six stalks into the soupy mud. The clumps are spaced over the field, sometimes in rows.

Farmers in the Northern Hemisphere usually begin to plant rice in April or May, but they may start nurseries earlier. In some parts of Asia and South America, farmers produce two rice crops a year on the same land.

Cultivating lowland rice consists mainly of controlling the water supply and weeding the rice fields. When the young plants are a few inches tall, workers carefully flood the paddies with water. They keep 2 to 6 inches of water on the field until the grain begins to ripen. Then the water is drained off through openings in the levees so the soil can dry by harvest time.

Irrigation controls weeds, because flooding kills many weeds. In Ceylon, China, India, and Japan, workers also pull weeds by hand. Cultivating upland rice usually involves only weeding.

Harvesting and Threshing begin when the straw- or yellow-colored heads of ripe rice bend down. In most countries, workers harvest by hand. They use knives or sickles to cut the stalks. They tie the stalks in sheaves, and leave them in the sun to dry. Some farmers have simple foot-powered threshing machines. But in some places men or animals trample the sun-dried sheaves to thresh the grains from the stalks. Or the sheaves may be hit against wide-spaced screens so the separated grains fall through openings in the screens.

THE RICE PLANT

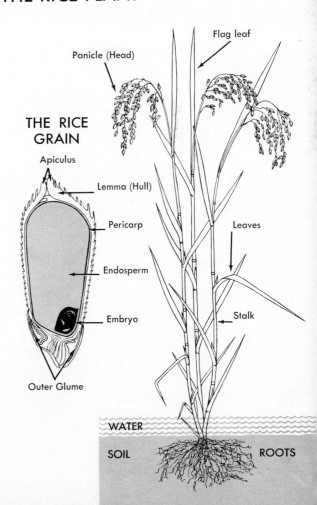

THE RICE GRAIN

Flag leaf

Panicle (Head)

Apiculus

Lemma (Hull)

Pericarp

Leaves

Endosperm

Embryo

Stalk

Outer Glume

WATER

SOIL

ROOTS

HARVESTING

Gathering in the Grain takes place when the rice turns yellow or straw-colored. The ripe grains are full and firm, and the heads droop over. Most of the world's rice is harvested by hand with sickles. In Java, the farmers use knives and snip off the heads one by one.

LEADING RICE-GROWING COUNTRIES

Tons of rice grown in 1969

China (Communist) *100,310,000 tons	🌾🌾🌾🌾🌾🌾🌾🌾🌾🌾🌾🌾🌾🌾🌾🌾🌾🌾🌾🌾
India 69,446,000 tons	🌾🌾🌾🌾🌾🌾🌾🌾🌾🌾🌾🌾🌾🌾
Pakistan 23,443,000 tons	🌾🌾🌾🌾
Japan 19,295,000 tons	🌾🌾🌾
Indonesia 18,276,000 tons	🌾🌾🌾
Thailand *11,874,000 tons	🌾🌾
Burma 9,204,000 tons	🌾🌾
Brazil 6,173,000 tons	🌾
Korea (South) 6,092,000 tons	🌾
Vietnam (South) 5,638,000 tons	🌾

*1968, latest available information

Source: FAO

LEADING RICE-GROWING STATES

Tons of rice grown in 1969

Arkansas 1,236,000 tons	🌾🌾🌾🌾🌾🌾🌾🌾🌾🌾🌾🌾
Texas 1,082,000 tons	🌾🌾🌾🌾🌾🌾🌾🌾🌾🌾🌾
California 1,070,000 tons	🌾🌾🌾🌾🌾🌾🌾🌾🌾🌾🌾
Louisiana 1,039,000 tons	🌾🌾🌾🌾🌾🌾🌾🌾🌾🌾🌾

Source: U.S. Department of Agriculture

In the United States and some parts of South America, combines harvest and thresh the grain in the fields. The threshed grain is dried by heated air. Farmers usually leave the stalks in the field to decay and serve as fertilizer. Sometimes they bale the straw for livestock feed and bedding.

How Rice Is Milled

The dried, threshed grain, still enclosed in its hull, is called *paddy* or *rough rice*. Farmers usually sell the rough rice to millers, who remove the hulls with machines and produce the polished rice we eat.

Hulling. In Asia and South America, farmers sometimes pound some of their rough rice in crude mortars or grind it between stones to remove the hulls. Usually these crude methods do not remove the inner skins, or bran coats, and the *undermilled* kernels have the brownish color of bran. *Brown rice* is especially high in food value, because the skins contain most of the oil, minerals, and vitamins. But brown rice spoils when the oil turns rancid. Commercial rice mills use machines to remove the hulls from the kernels. Other machines rub off most of the bran coats.

In southern Asia, millers *parboil* the rough rice before milling. They soak the paddy rice in heated water, steam it under pressure, and dry it. This makes the kernels less likely to break. The yellowish parboiled kernels store better, and retain more vitamins and minerals. In the United States, patented parboiling processes produce *malekized* (converted) rice. These products are used the same as raw white rice.

Polishing. Millers also use machines to polish and smooth the kernels between revolving bands of felt or soft leather. This process rubs off bran coats and some of the kernel starch. In the United States and Europe,

Powerful Combines harvest rice in the United States. They can harvest and thresh two or more acres of rice an hour.

Farmers Winnow Rice to separate the rice hulls from the kernels. Portuguese farmers remove the hulls by pounding or grinding the grain. They toss the mixture into the air. The kernels fall to the ground, and the wind blows away the hulls.

millers often add talc and a glucose solution to produce a glossy, transparent coating on the kernels. This adds to their appearance and helps preserve them.

Grading. Kernels often break during hulling and polishing. Millers use machines to sort the broken and unbroken kernels for sale as different grades of rice. In the United States, the most expensive grade, *head rice*, consists chiefly of perfect kernels. *Second head rice* has more of the larger broken pieces. Both are used as food, and may be sold as *fancy* or *choice*, depending on the color and the presence of weed seeds. *Screenings* (finely broken pieces) are ground and used in flour mixes and in the distilling and brewing industries.

Where Rice Is Raised

About 650 billion pounds of rice are produced throughout the world each year. This is about 184 pounds for each person on the earth. Rice grows as far south as Argentina and as far north as Austria.

In Asia. The countries of Asia produce over nine-tenths of the world's rice supply, or about 590 billion pounds a year. About one-half of the world's rice exports go to Asian countries that do not raise enough to feed their own people.

Mainland China and India lead the world in rice production. Rice also grows in other countries of the Far East, some countries of the Middle East, and in Russia. Burma, mainland China, Thailand, and the United States are the leading rice exporters. Ceylon, India, Japan, and the Philippines are the leading importers. Farmers in Japan and Formosa harvest high yields of 3,600 to 5,100 pounds of rough rice per acre. They use productive varieties, chemical fertilizers, and adequate pest and weed controls.

In the United States, farmers harvest about 9 billion pounds of rice a year, an average of about 4,300 pounds per acre. The U.S. ranks among the leading rice exporters, although it furnishes only a little over 1 per cent of the total rice crop.

In Other Countries. Italy and Spain have unusually good rice crops, and Italy grows more rice than any other country in Europe. Egypt and the Malagasy Republic raise the most rice in Africa. Many Central American and South American countries raise rice.

History

Rice probably grew originally in southeast Asia thousands of years ago. The Bible does not mention rice, but ancient records show that the Greeks learned of it around 326 B.C. when Alexander the Great invaded India. The Moors introduced the crop into Spain during their conquest of that country in the A.D. 700's. The Spaniards brought rice to Italy during the 1400's, and Spanish colonists took it to the West Indies and South America in the early 1600's.

Legend says that rice was brought to the U.S. in the late 1600's, when a ship from Madagascar, damaged by storms, took refuge in the Charleston, S.C., harbor. Before sailing, the ship's captain presented the governor of the colony with a sack of seed rice. For almost 200 years, South Carolina was the leading rice producer in the United States. By 1839, rice was grown in all states south of the Ohio River and east of the Mississippi, as well as in Illinois and Virginia. In 1889, Louisiana became the leading rice state. Crowley, La., became known as the *Rice Center of America* because of its many rice mills. Texas began to grow upland rice as early as 1863, but did not become commercially important as a rice producer until 1899, after irrigation methods were introduced. Commercial production began in Arkansas in 1905, in California in 1912, and in Mississippi in 1949.

Scientific Classification. Rice is in the grass family, *Gramineae*. Genus *Oryza*, species *O. sativa* is the kind most commonly cultivated for food. Over 4,000 varieties grow in India alone. Glutinous rice is a variety of *O. sativa*. Red rice is a wild variety of *O. sativa*.   NELSON E. JODON

See also GRAIN WEEVIL; WILD RICE. For pictures of rice culture, see ARKANSAS; CHINA; INDONESIA; JAPAN; THAILAND; VIETNAM.

Outline

I. **Uses of Rice**
  A. As a Food   B. Beverages   C. By-Products
II. **Kinds of Rice**
  A. Cultivated Rice   B. Wild Rice
III. **The Rice Plant**
  A. Appearance   B. Enemies
IV. **Growing Rice**
  A. The Rice Field   D. Harvesting and
  B. Planting Rice   Threshing
  C. Cultivating
V. **How Rice Is Milled**
  A. Hulling   B. Polishing   C. Grading
VI. **Where Rice Is Raised**
  A. In Asia   C. In Other Countries
  B. In the United States
VII. **History**

Questions

What are some uses of rice besides for food?

How does rice farming in Asia differ from rice farming in the United States?

How did an accident start the U.S. rice industry?

What continent produces most of the world's rice?

Why is a lowland-rice area divided by dikes?

303

RICE, ELMER (1892-1967), was an American dramatist who championed moral, social, and personal freedom. His many plays reflect his belief that it is better to love than to hate, to question than to accept, to be free than to be bound.

Rice is best known for two plays. *The Adding Machine* (1923) is an expressionistic satire on the growing mechanization of man. Rice used distorted settings and nonrealistic acting to show the tortured mind of the chief character, Mr. Zero. *Street Scene* (1929), a Pulitzer prize winner, gives a naturalistic picture of life in a crowded big-city apartment house. Rice's other plays include *Counsellor-at-Law* (1931); *We, the People* (1933); and *Dream Girl* (1945). Rice also wrote novels and an autobiography, *Minority Report* (1963).

Rice was born Elmer Leopold Reizenstein in New York City. He studied law, but became a playwright after his *On Trial* (1914) became a hit.   MARDI VALGEMAE

See also EXPRESSIONISM (Expressionist Drama).

RICE, GRANTLAND (1880-1954), was the first United States newspaperman to gain fame by writing about sports. He wrote about Bobby Jones, Jack Dempsey, Bill Tilden, Helen Wills, and other sports champions during the 1920's. Rice also wrote five books of verse about sports. His autobiography, *The Tumult and the Shouting*, was published in 1954. Grantland Rice was born in Murfreesboro, Tenn.   PAT HARMON

RICE, HENRY MOWER (1817-1894), was a frontier Indian trader, an Indian commissioner, and one of the first United States senators from Minnesota. He was born in Waitsfield, Vt. In 1839, he moved to Minnesota as an Indian trader, and became a partner in various frontier trading firms. His knowledge of Indians led to his appointment as commissioner to make treaties with them. Through his treaties, the Chippewa tribes gave up most of the state of Minnesota. Rice was a U.S. senator from 1858 to 1863. He represents Minnesota in Statuary Hall in Washington, D.C.   W. B. HESSELTINE

RICE UNIVERSITY is a privately controlled, coeducational university in Houston, Tex. It has undergraduate programs in architecture, arts and sciences, and engineering, and graduate programs in many departments. Rice grants bachelor's, master's, and doctor's degrees. The university's research facilities include a space science research center, nuclear accelerator, and computer equipment.

Rice University was chartered in 1891, and classes were first held in 1912. Its full name is William Marsh Rice University. For enrollment, see UNIVERSITIES AND COLLEGES (table).   CAREY CRONEIS

RICE WEEVIL. See GRAIN WEEVIL.

RICEBIRD. See BOBOLINK.

RICH, ROBERT. See WARWICK, EARL OF (Robert Rich).

RICHARD was the name of three English kings who ruled between 1189 and 1485. All died violent deaths.

Richard I (1157-1199) ruled from 1189 to 1199. He is known in history as Richard the Lion-Hearted, or Richard Coeur de Lion. He was a son of Henry II, the first king of the Plantagenet dynasty (see PLANTAGENET). After Richard became king, he joined Philip Augustus of France in a crusade to the Holy Land. He captured Acre (now 'Akko), but could not retake Jerusalem.

During the crusade, Richard aroused the hatred of Leopold V, duke of Austria. In 1192, while Richard was on his journey home, Leopold seized him. Leopold kept Richard in a castle on the Danube River as a prisoner of the Holy Roman emperor, Henry VI. It is said that while Richard lay in prison his favorite minstrel, Blondel, made himself known to his master by singing outside the castle. Richard was later delivered to Henry, who released him in 1194 after a ransom was paid.

Detail of an engraving (1743) by George Vertue; The Newberry Library, Chicago

Richard I

Richard returned to England in 1194, but did not really rule. He left the government to the care of a minister and fought in a war with Philip Augustus of France. In 1199, Richard was killed during the siege of a French castle, and his brother John became king.

During his entire reign, Richard spent little more than six months in England, and he performed no real service for the good of his country. He was a brave and vigorous man, sometimes cruel, but often gallant and generous. He was a *troubadour* (lyric poet), and some of his songs have been preserved. See also FLAG (color picture: Historical Flags [Early English Flags]).

Richard II (1367-1400) was 10 years old when he succeeded his grandfather, Edward III, as king. He was the son of Edward, the Black Prince, and a nephew of John of Gaunt, duke of Lancaster (see JOHN OF GAUNT). From the beginning of Richard's reign, Gaunt was the real ruler. Gaunt taxed the people so heavily that a rebellion under Wat Tyler broke out in 1381 (see WAT TYLER'S REBELLION). Richard showed considerable spirit and courage in putting down the rebellion.

Richard was a tyrant. He was guilty of great extravagance and of playing favorites. Because of his conduct, he won the hatred of all classes. The breaking point came when he seized

Detail of an illuminated manuscript (about 1389) by an unknown artist; St. John's College, Cambridge, England

Richard II

the estates of his cousin, Henry Bolingbroke, John of Gaunt's son, in an attempt to ruin the House of Lancaster. Bolingbroke rallied an army and in 1399 forced Richard from the throne. Bolingbroke then became King Henry IV (see HENRY [IV] of England). Richard died in prison. He was probably murdered.

Richard III (1452-1485), duke of Gloucester and brother of Edward IV, became the last Plantagenet king in 1483. His reign brought on the revolt that ended the Wars of the Roses (see WARS OF THE ROSES).

In the spring of 1483, Edward IV died, and his elder son became King Edward V at the age of 12. The young king was left in the care of Richard, who was named protector of the realm. The Woodvilles, the family of the young king's mother, attempted to seize power. In crushing their conspiracy, Richard found that he might himself become king and reached for the opportunity. He was crowned early in July, 1483, after Parliament had declared him rightful king. Edward V and his younger brother Richard were put in the Tower of London.

National Portrait Gallery
Richard III

Some scholars believe that King Richard had the boys killed. But no proof of such a crime exists, and the fate of the youths is still a mystery.

Richard governed well, but the people grew tired of civil disturbances. Powerful Lancastrian nobles plotted against him. With their help, Henry Tudor, earl of Richmond, of the House of Lancaster, invaded England from his exile in France. His forces won the Battle of Bosworth Field in 1485, killing Richard. Henry Tudor became king as Henry VII. PAUL M. KENDALL

See also LANCASTER; SHAKESPEARE, WILLIAM (Synopses of Plays); YORK.

RICHARD, GABRIEL. See MICHIGAN (Education).

RICHARD, *REE shard,* **MAURICE** (1921-), ranks among the leading goal scorers in National Hockey League (NHL) history. Only Gordie Howe and Bobby Hull bettered Richard's total of 544 regular-season goals. In 1944-1945, Richard became the only NHL player to score 50 goals in a 50-game season. His skating speed and fast shots earned him the nickname "Rocket."

Richard played right wing for the Montreal Canadiens from the 1942-1943 season through the 1959-1960 season. He helped lead the Canadiens to eight Stanley Cup championships. He shattered Nels Stewart's then existing scoring record by 220 goals. Richard's 421 assists brought his regular-season point total to 965. He was born in Montreal. HERMAN WEISKOPF

RICHARD II. See SHAKESPEARE, WILLIAM (Types of Plays; tables).

RICHARD III. See SHAKESPEARE, WILLIAM (Synopses of Plays).

RICHARD THE LION-HEARTED. See RICHARD (I).

RICHARDS, BOB. See TRACK AND FIELD (Famous Track and Field Champions).

RICHARDS, DICKINSON WOODRUFF, Jr. (1895-), an American physician, shared the 1956 Nobel prize in medicine and physiology, for developing a way to diagnose heart diseases by means of a catheter. The *catheter,* a thin tube, is inserted into the heart. This allows a doctor to study the heart and decide what treatment is needed. Richards was born in Orange, N.J. See also FORSSMANN, WERNER.

RICHARDS, I. A. (1893-), a British critic, published *The Meaning of Meaning* (1923) with C. K. Ogden. This book strongly influenced the semantic movement (see SEMANTICS). It shows Richards' use of psychology in dealing with language. Richards became a leader in the attempt to make literary criticism scientific in *Principles of Literary Criticism* (1924), *Science and Poetry* (1925), *Practical Criticism* (1929), and *The Philoso-*

RICHARDSON, HENRY HOBSON

phy of Rhetoric (1936). In 1932, he began working with Basic English, a form of English with an 850-word vocabulary. He wrote a Basic English version of Plato's *Republic* (see BASIC ENGLISH). Ivor Armstrong Richards was born in Cheshire, England. He taught English at Harvard University from 1944 to 1963. JOSEPH E. BAKER

RICHARDS, LAURA ELIZABETH HOWE (1850-1943), an American author, wrote books for adults and nonsense verse and stories for children. She won the Pulitzer prize in 1917 for *Julia Ward Howe,* a biography of her mother. She also wrote an autobiography, *Stepping Westward* (1931). Mrs. Richards had a genius for writing nonsense verses, collected under such titles as *Tirra Lirra* (1932) and *The Hottentot and Other Ditties* (1939). She was born in Boston, Mass. Her mother, Julia Ward Howe, wrote "The Battle Hymn of the Republic" (see HOWE). EVELYN RAY SICKELS

RICHARDS, SIR WILLIAM BUELL (1815-1889), a Canadian lawyer and statesman, served as the first chief justice of the Supreme Court of Canada from 1875 to 1879. His judicial career began in 1853 when he was appointed to the Court of Common Pleas. He rose to become chief justice of this court in 1873, and then was called to head the newly established Supreme Court. He also served as attorney general of Canada, holding that office from 1851 to 1853. Richards was born in Brockville, Ont., Canada. J. E. HODGETTS

RICHARDSON, ELLIOT LEE (1920-), became United States secretary of health, education, and welfare in 1970. He had previously had extensive experience in public service. From 1957 to 1959, Richardson was an assistant secretary in the Department of Health, Education, and Welfare (HEW). He served as undersecretary of state for 18 months in 1969 and 1970.

From 1959 to 1961, Richardson was U.S. attorney in his home state of Massachusetts. He served as lieutenant governor of Massachusetts from 1964 to 1967 and as Massachusetts attorney general from 1967 to 1969. As the state's lieutenant governor, Richardson promoted reforms in education, health, and welfare.

Dept. of HEW
Elliot L. Richardson

Richardson was born in Boston and graduated from Harvard University Law School in 1947. Between periods of public service, Richardson practiced law in Boston. CLARK R. MOLLENHOFF

RICHARDSON, HENRY HOBSON (1838-1886), was the first American architect to achieve international fame. He dominated U.S. architecture during the 1870's and 1880's.

Richardson established the Romanesque Revival as a major architectural style. But he was chiefly interested in reworking Romanesque and other earlier styles to create new arrangements of forms and spaces. His most notable buildings are straightforward and massive, with surfaces of rough stone and closely fitted brick and shingles. For a picture of his famous Marshall Field and

305

RICHARDSON, JOHN

Commission on Chicago Historical and Architectural Landmarks

Richardson's Glessner House shows the influence of Romanesque architecture in its massiveness and rough stone surface.

Company Wholesale Warehouse (1887) in Chicago, see ARCHITECTURE (The 1800's).

Richardson was born on a plantation near New Orleans. He first gained national prominence by winning the design competition for the Trinity Church in Boston in 1872. DAVID GEBHARD

RICHARDSON, JOHN. See CANADIAN LITERATURE (English-Canadian Literature).

RICHARDSON, LEWIS FRY. See WEATHER (Scientific Advances).

RICHARDSON, SAMUEL (1689-1761), an English writer, is considered one of the founding fathers of the novel. He wrote three novels: *Pamela; or, Virtue Rewarded* (1740), *Clarissa; or, The History of a Young Lady* (1747-1748), and *Sir Charles Grandison* (1753-1754). These works are too long to be much read today, but their influence has been enormous.

Richardson's books brought various important, and in some ways new, elements to the novel. Each of his novels has a genuinely unified plot rather than disconnected episodes. The characters maintain a consistent point of view, without interference by the author. The works established the theme of courtship leading to marriage as a basic plot of the novel.

All three novels are written in the form of letters. Indeed, the idea for the form of *Pamela* originated from a manual of model letters written by Richardson. *Pamela* was published anonymously and was a sensational success. All the novels have a breathless quality that sweeps the reader along from letter to letter to see what happens next.

It is easy to mock the somewhat dubious, often priggish morality of Richardson's novels. Indeed, *Pamela* inspired several witty parodies by writers of his time. Nevertheless, Richardson set the novel firmly in what became its main direction: a detailed description of real people in common situations of domestic life.

In particular, Richardson's novels treat women's concern for security, marriage, and a proper social role.

This reflects how, with the rise of the new middle class, women with conscious individual identities and problems were coming to the forefront. This tendency has grown since Richardson's time, and in him, as in many later novelists, women have found a sympathetic and sensitive spokesman.

Richardson was born in Derbyshire. He started his own printing business in 1719, and later became one of London's most successful publishers. IAN WATT

RICHELIEU, *REE shuh LYOO*, **CARDINAL** (1585-1642), ARMAND JEAN DU PLESSIS, and DUC DE RICHELIEU, was one of the ablest of French statesmen. For more than 18 years, he was the actual ruler of France. He succeeded in strengthening the French monarchy.

Richelieu was born in Paris and was educated for a career in the army. He came from a family of the minor nobility, which for many years had served in the armies of France. Richelieu's father fought with distinction in the religious wars. King Henry III rewarded the father by offering the office of bishop of Luçon to his eldest son. Richelieu, the third son, accepted the position to keep the bishop's income in the family.

Becomes Bishop. Richelieu was more than five years under the age required for his position as bishop when he took the post in 1606. The next year, he was consecrated by the pope. As bishop, Richelieu proved himself able and energetic. But he was extremely ambitious and soon became impatient for higher office. In 1614, he was elected to represent the clergy of Poitou in the *States-General* (Parliament) of France. His great charm and tact soon made him a trusted friend of Marie de' Medici, the mother of King Louis XIII.

By 1616, he had become a member of the Royal Council of Louis XIII. But this appointment lasted only a short time. King Louis distrusted his mother's power and began to fear for his throne. He arranged the murder of his prime minister, the Marquis d'Ancre, and exiled Richelieu and the queen mother in 1617.

Most Powerful Man in France. Pope Gregory XV made Richelieu a cardinal in 1622. In 1624 he regained a place in the king's council. He served with great skill and ability and soon became the leading influence in the French government. He ruled France from 1624 to 1642 in the interests of Louis XIII.

Richelieu first sought to make a friendly alliance with England. He arranged the marriage of the Prince of Wales and Henrietta Maria, the sister of Louis XIII. He then turned to the situation in France. He wanted to make the royal power supreme throughout the country. He determined to humble the proud feudal nobles of France and to put down the rebellious Huguenots.

Religious Wars. Richelieu was not himself intolerant in religious matters. He made no attempt to take freedom of worship away from the Huguenots, and made war upon them only as enemies of the king. He led the royal army in person at the siege of La Rochelle. This Huguenot stronghold, aided by the English, held out for 15 months, but surrendered in October, 1628. Richelieu destroyed the political privileges which the Huguenots had received by the Edict of Nantes. But he did not interfere with their right to worship.

Richelieu then turned his attention to the nobles. He considered their independence the greatest obstacle to a centralized state in which the king held all the power. In 1626, he called out the army to destroy all fortified castles not needed for defense against invasion. His action weakened the nobility.

His Influence in Europe. Richelieu's greatest interest was in foreign affairs. He wanted to make France strong at home and abroad.

When he came to power, Europe was struggling in the Thirty Years' War. He saw an opportunity for France in the confusion. He dreamed of making France "the heart of all Christian states," both Protestant and Catholic.

To thwart the powerful Hapsburg Empire, Richelieu decided to support The Netherlands and the various German princes in their attack on Austria

Brown Bros.
Cardinal Richelieu

from the north. He also planned to help the Italians attack the Hapsburgs and the Spaniards from the south. But troubles inside France delayed Richelieu's plans.

From 1628 to 1631, Richelieu fought both Spain and Savoy over the French claim to the duchy of Mantua. Under his direction, Louis XIII led 36,000 men across the Alps and established Charles Gonzaga, Duke of Nevers, as the ruler of Mantua. To keep Sweden at war with the Hapsburgs, Richelieu gave Sweden $120,000 for past efforts in the war, and promised $400,000 a year for six years, or until a general peace was made. Sweden agreed to keep 36,000 men in the field.

Richelieu thus saved France the enormous expense of a war, but he accomplished the purpose of a war by paying Sweden to fight his enemy. He did not live to see the full results of his plans to humble Spain and Austria. But when he died in 1642, France had won parts of Alsace and Lorraine.

Richelieu was a man of learning and wanted to be a great writer. He wrote many works. But his greatest contribution to literature was his support and protection of literary men, and the founding of the French Academy in 1635.   RICHARD M. BRACE

Related Articles in WORLD BOOK include:

Codes and Ciphers (History)	Louis (XIII)
Diplomacy (History)	Mazarin, Jules Cardinal
French Academy	Sorbonne
Huguenots	States-General
	Thirty Years' War

RICHELIEU RIVER is a Canadian stream, also known as the CHAMBLY, the SAINT JOHN, and the SOREL. The Richelieu rises in Lake Champlain, near the Quebec-Vermont border. It flows north for 80 miles and meets the St. Lawrence River at Sorel, between Montreal and Trois Rivières. Ships travel the river from Sorel southward to Chambly. The river has two canals, at St. Ours, (south of Sorel) and at Chambly. The Richelieu is a transportation artery, carrying chiefly lumber and grains. It was named after Cardinal Richelieu, the French statesman.   MURRAY G. BALLANTYNE

RICHFIELD, Utah (pop. 4,471; alt. 5,310 ft.), is near the geographic center of the state (see UTAH [political map]). It lies in the broad Sevier River Valley. Grain, beet, and alfalfa fields, and livestock ranches cover the valley. Cheese and beet sugar are among the leading

products of the city and valley. The town was a frontier outpost for many years after it was settled in 1864. In 1867, the settlers were driven out by Indians, but resettled in 1870. Richfield has a council-manager government. It is the seat of Sevier County.   A. R. MORTENSEN

RICHLAND, Wash. (pop. 26,290; alt. 360 ft.), is the administrative and residential center of the Hanford Atomic Energy Works, to the north. Before World War II, Richland had about 500 residents. It grew rapidly during and after the war as the Hanford Works expanded. The federal government put up most of the buildings.

Richland and the neighboring towns of Pasco and Kennewick are called the Tri-Cities. All are residential areas for workers at the Hanford plutonium plant. They lie on the Columbia River near the junction of the Yakima and Snake rivers (see WASHINGTON [political map]). Richland and Kennewick form a metropolitan area of 93,356 persons. Richland has a mayor-council government.   HOWARD J. CRITCHFIELD

RICHLER, *RIHK lehr*, **MORDECAI** (1931-   ), is a Canadian novelist. As a boy, Richler lived in a poor Jewish district of Montreal, where he was born. His experiences there provided the background for *Son of a Smaller Hero* (1955) and *The Apprenticeship of Duddy Kravitz* (1959).

Richler has done much of his writing in Europe, and *The Acrobats* (1954) and *A Choice of Enemies* (1957) have European settings. In *Cocksure* (1968) and *St. Urbain's Horseman* (1971), Richler wrote about Canadians living in Europe. Both these novels combine humor, satire, and shrewd observations about sophisticated, urban society. Richler also writes short stories and motion-picture and television scripts.   CLAUDE T. BISSELL

RICHMOND is one of the five boroughs of New York City. See NEW YORK CITY (Richmond); STATEN ISLAND.

RICHMOND, Calif. (pop. 79,043; alt. 10 ft.), on the northeast shore of San Francisco Bay, is a principal west coast port. For location, see CALIFORNIA (political map). Its harbor has three major terminals facing on deep water. The San Rafael-Richmond bridge (5½ miles) is one of the world's longest high-level bridges.

During World War II, four large shipbuilding plants operated in Richmond. The sites and buildings were converted to peacetime industrial production after the war. Richmond has over 120 major industries. Among them are oil refining, steel fabrication, chemicals, and food processing. Richmond was first settled as a community in 1899 when the Santa Fe railroad established its yards and shops there. The city has a council-manager government.   GEORGE SHAFTEL

RICHMOND, Ind. (pop. 43,999; alt. 940 ft.), lies on a fork of the Whitewater River, about 70 miles east of Indianapolis (see INDIANA [political map]). Richmond claims to produce more lawn mowers and bus bodies than any other city. It also makes bedding, dies, drills, gears, insulation, piston rings, and tools. Richmond grows over 11 million roses annually. The city is the home of Earlham College. It was settled in 1806. An explosion in downtown Richmond in 1968 killed 41 persons and injured more than 225. The explosion caused about $21 million in damage. Richmond has a mayor-council government.   PAUL E. MILLION, JR.

RICHMOND

RICHMOND, Va. (pop. 249,621; met. area 518,-319; alt. 160 ft.), is the state capital and a trade and cultural center. It has some of the largest cigarette factories in the world. The city is also rich in historic interest. It served as a capital of the Confederate States of America during the Civil War. Richmond is said to have more monuments and museums than any other city in the South.

Location, Size, and Description. Richmond lies on the James River, about 125 miles west of the Atlantic Ocean and 100 miles south of Washington, D.C. The city covers about 40 square miles, and its metropolitan area totals over 730 square miles. Richmond is the seat of Henrico County. For location, see VIRGINIA (political map).

Built originally on seven hills, the city now spreads out over picturesque, rolling country. Handsome homes surrounded by beautiful flower gardens face broad, tree-lined streets. Parks and playgrounds, which number about 60, add beauty to the city. William Byrd and Maymont are the most extensive parks, and most residents consider them the most beautiful. Residential suburbs extend westward along both banks of the James River, and northward across hilly terrain.

Government activity centers about the state Capitol in Capitol Square. The building, designed by Thomas Jefferson from the model of a Roman temple in Nîmes, France, has influenced the architecture of many public buildings in the United States. Jean Antoine Houdon's famous statue of George Washington stands in the center of the Capitol's rotunda. Virginians usually consider it the state's most precious art treasure. In surrounding niches are busts of seven other Presidents born in Virginia. They are Thomas Jefferson, James Madison, James Monroe, William Henry Harrison, John Tyler, Zachary Taylor, and Woodrow Wilson. One niche holds an Houdon bust of the Marquis de Lafayette, the French soldier who aided the colonists in the Revolutionary War. See VIRGINIA (picture: State Capitol).

A bronze equestrian statue by Thomas Crawford stands in Capitol Square. Six nine-foot bronze figures of important Virginia statesmen flank its stone base. Statues of Robert E. Lee, "Stonewall" Jackson, Jefferson Davis, and other leaders of the Southern Confederacy stand along Monument Avenue.

Several historic buildings still stand in Richmond. Old St. John's Church, built in 1741, is one of the oldest wooden buildings surviving in Virginia. In this church in 1775, Patrick Henry made his famous speech for colonial freedom, in which he proclaimed, "Is life so dear or peace so sweet as to be purchased at the price of chains and slavery? Forbid it, Almighty God! I know not what course others may take, but as for me, give me liberty or give me death!"

Jefferson Davis lived in the White House of the Confederacy, now also known as the Museum of the Confederacy. Items in this museum include Lee's sword and the original Great Seal and provisional constitution of the Confederacy. The Virginia Historical Society is another museum containing Civil War relics.

The red brick John Marshall House, occupied by the chief justice from 1790 until his death in 1835, still stands. The Edgar Allan Poe Shrine is a gray stone cottage said to be the oldest house in Richmond. It dates back to 1686. Many of Poe's manuscripts are on display there.

The Carillon Tower in Byrd Park is Richmond's memorial to its World War I dead. The Hall of Memory, a huge World War II memorial, opened on the north bank of the James River in 1956. Hollywood Cemetery, named for its magnificent holly trees, is the burial place of statesman John Randolph, Confederate President Davis, and United States Presidents Monroe and Tyler.

Cultural Activities. Richmond is the home of the Presbyterian School of Christian Education, the University of Richmond, and Virginia Union University. Richmond also has Virginia Commonwealth University, and Union Theological Seminary. More than 50 public and several private schools serve the younger students of the city.

Valentine Museum and the Virginia Museum of Fine Arts attract many visitors. The artmobile of the Virginia Museum began running in 1953. It is the first state-sponsored traveling art museum in the country.

The Virginia State Library is a storehouse of information on early Virginia history. During the winter, many people attend grand opera in the Mosque Theater. Others go to plays at the theater of the Virginia Museum of Fine Arts.

Industry. Richmond has developed a variety of industries in addition to its tobacco factories, which turn out 115 billion cigarettes and 21 million pounds of tobacco annually. There is much printing, bookmaking, and manufacturing of paper. Richmond also produces baking powder, drugs and medicine, fertilizer, iron, steel, and such chemical products as cellophane, nylon, and rayon.

Transportation and Communication. Six railroads serve Richmond. Truck, bus, and air lines also connect Richmond with other cities. Water freight service is provided on the James River to and from Hampton Roads. The Richmond-Petersburg toll road was opened in 1958.

The *Richmond Times-Dispatch* and *Richmond News-Leader* rank as two of the most influential newspapers published in the South. Virginia's first television station, WTVR, opened in Richmond in 1948.

Government. Richmond has a council-manager form of government. The people elect the nine-member council, and it elects one of its members as mayor to preside at council meetings. The council also elects the city manager, the city attorney, and the school board. The city manager appoints the heads of the bureau of budget and bureau of purchasing, and administrative heads of such departments as finance, public works, public utilities, public welfare, and public health. The Virginia general assembly elects judges of the courts of record, and they appoint judges of the municipal courts of Richmond.

History. Richmond's history dates back to 1607, the year of the first permanent English settlement in the United States, made at Jamestown. At that time, an exploring party led by captains Christopher Newport and John Smith visited the site of Richmond. Richmond was surveyed in 1737, and named for Richmond, England. The community was incorporated in 1742, at which time it had 250 residents.

Two conventions met in Richmond in 1775. One elected delegates to the Second Continental Congress in

Monument Avenue, a beautiful residential street in Richmond, is lined with monuments to leaders of the Confederacy. Among the men honored on this street are Robert E. Lee, Jefferson Davis, and Thomas J. (Stonewall) Jackson.

Richmond Chamber of Commerce

Philadelphia. The other appointed a Committee of Safety, proposed the enlisting of troops, and set up a plan to help finance the Revolutionary War.

In 1779, Virginia moved its capital from Williamsburg to Richmond, a more centrally located place. About 680 people then lived in Richmond.

Two years later, Benedict Arnold, an American who had turned traitor to his country, attacked the town. Arnold's troops burned the cannon factory, several important buildings, and many valuable government papers. When Arnold attempted another raid on the town, Governor Thomas Jefferson and the general assembly moved to a safer place, thus making Richmond no longer an important military objective for the British.

In 1782, Richmond was incorporated as a town. Virginia ratified the United States Constitution at a convention held in Richmond in 1788. Chief Justice John Marshall presided over the treason trial of Aaron Burr in the Capitol in Richmond in 1807.

Trade with the Piedmont region of Virginia became possible with the opening of the James River Canal in 1840. Richmond's trade greatly expanded with the extension of railroads into that region a little later. From the 1830's to the outbreak of the Civil War, Richmond

served as one of the centers of the domestic slave trade. For 30 cents a day, slave merchants housed and fed all slaves intended for sale. Robert Lumpkins' slave jail was the most famous institution of this kind in the city. After the Civil War, it became a Negro school.

Virginia voted to secede from the Union in April, 1861. In May, the capital of the Confederacy moved to Richmond from Montgomery, Ala. Union and Confederate armies fought several fierce battles over the possession of the city. Richmond National Battlefield Park was the site of some of these battles. The Confederate capital moved to Danville, Va., on April 3, 1865, in the last days of the war.

President Jefferson Davis was attending services at St. Paul's Church when he learned that Petersburg had fallen and that Richmond would have to be abandoned. Richmond was evacuated, and the residents burned part of their own city rather than let it fall intact to the Union army.

The destroyed part of the city was rebuilt after the war. For many years, tobacco-processing was almost the only industry of Richmond. But during the 1900's, Richmond attracted a wide variety of industries in order to diversify its economy. FRANCIS B. SIMKINS

The Edgar Allan Poe Shrine in Richmond, built in 1686, is said to be the oldest house in the city. The little stone cottage contains many papers and relics of the famous poet. He once lived and worked in Richmond.

Ewing Galloway

The White House of the Confederacy in Richmond was the home of Jefferson Davis during the Civil War. The mansion is now a museum, and exhibits General Lee's sword and many other Confederate relics.

Virginia State Chamber of Commerce

RICHMOND, UNIVERSITY OF

RICHMOND, UNIVERSITY OF, is a privately controlled liberal arts institution in Richmond, Va. It is related to the Baptist Church. The university has two coordinate colleges—Richmond College for men and Westhampton College for women. It also includes the coeducational University College, a graduate school, and schools of business and law. Courses lead to bachelor's and master's degrees, and the J.D. degree in law. Richmond College has a cooperative program in forestry with Duke University. The University of Richmond was founded in 1830 as Dunlora Academy. It was chartered as Richmond College in 1840 and assumed its present name in 1920. For enrollment, see UNIVERSITIES AND COLLEGES (table). E. BRUCE HEILMAN

RICHMOND COLLEGE. See UNIVERSITIES AND COLLEGES (table [New York, City University of]).

RICHMONDTOWN is a village in the southeastern part of Staten Island in New York City. The Dutch made the first settlement there in 1661. Richmondtown became the county seat of Richmond County in 1729. When the county became one of the five boroughs of New York City in 1898, the city took over the administration of the county government. In 1939, the Staten Island Historical Society began making the entire village an early colonial restoration. The project includes moving, rebuilding, and restoring more than 30 buildings. New York City and private individuals and organizations are financing the project. Completion is scheduled for the mid-1970's. WILLIAM E. YOUNG

RICHTER, CONRAD (1890-1968), an American novelist, won the Pulitzer prize in 1951 for *The Town* (1950). In 1961, he won the National Book Award for fiction for *The Waters of Kronos* (1960) and was elected to the National Institute of Arts and Sciences. Most of his novels concern pioneer life. He collected frontier stories in *Early Americana* (1936). He wrote *The Sea of Grass* (1937), *The Trees* (1940), and *The Fields* (1946), all dealing with frontier life. He also wrote *A Simple Honorable Man* (1962) and *The Grandfathers* (1964). He was born in Pine Grove, Pa. JOHN O. EIDSON

RICHTER, *RICK tur,* **HANS** (1843-1916), was one of the founders of modern orchestral conducting. He became noted for his broad and powerful interpretations of German music, and conducted several Bayreuth festivals. He influenced the development of a broad musical public in England, where he conducted the Halle Orchestra in Manchester from 1897 until 1911. He was born in Györ, Hungary. IRVING KOLODIN

RICHTER, JOHANN PAUL FRIEDRICH (1763-1825), was an outstanding humorous writer of the German Romantic movement. He became widely known under the name of JEAN PAUL. A master of satire, Richter possessed a rich imagination, and wrote difficult but delightful prose. His first great success was the romance *The Invisible Loge* (1793). He also wrote *The Titan* (1800-1803) and *Introduction to Aesthetics* (1804). Richter was born in Wunsiedel, Bavaria. GOTTFRIED F. MERKEL

RICHTER MAGNITUDE is a number that indicates the strength of an earthquake. Scientists calculate Richter magnitude by using information obtained from a *seismograph,* an instrument that records an earthquake's ground motion. Charles F. Richter, an American *seismologist* (scientist who studies earthquakes), developed this system of measuring earthquakes in 1935. The system is sometimes called the *Richter scale.*

The highest Richter magnitude ever recorded was 8.9—in the Pacific Ocean near the Colombia-Ecuador border in 1906 and in Japan in 1933. The San Francisco earthquake of 1906 measured 8.3. Those magnitudes were calculated on the basis of instruments in use at the time. The Alaska earthquake of 1964 measured 8.4.

More than 1,000 earthquakes with a magnitude of at

The Restoration of Richmondtown Will Make This Historic Town Look as It Did in Colonial Days.

least 2 occur daily. But seismologists consider earthquakes of magnitude 5 or less as minor because few cause serious damage. An earthquake of magnitude 7 or more can cause great damage and kill many people if the shocks are centered in a populated area.

Each number on the Richter scale represents an earthquake 10 times as strong as one of the next lower magnitude. For example, an earthquake of magnitude 7 is 10 times as strong as one of magnitude 6.

Although each earthquake has only one magnitude, its damage varies from place to place. Seismologists use various other scales to measure the damage of an earthquake. For example, the *Modified Mercalli Intensity Scale* (M.M.) classifies earthquakes into 12 categories ranging from those barely felt to ones that cause tremendous damage. ALBERT J. RUDMAN

See also EARTHQUAKE; SEISMOGRAPH; SEISMOLOGY.

RICHTHOFEN, BARON (1833-1905), FERDINAND VON RICHTHOFEN, a German geologist and geographer, pioneered in the study of *geomorphology* (land forms). He exerted a major influence on present-day geography. His five-volume report, *China, The Results of Personal Journeys* (1879-1883), made him famous as a scientific traveler. Richthofen was born in Karlsruhe, Germany. He became interested in geography after training and working in geology. He taught geography at the universities of Bonn, Leipzig, and Berlin. J. RUSSELL WHITAKER

RICHTHOFEN, MANFRED VON. See WAR ACES.

RICKENBACKER, EDWARD VERNON (1890-   ), was the leading American air ace in World War I. He shot down 22 enemy planes and 4 balloons. In 1938, he became president of Eastern Air Lines. He resigned from this post in 1959, but stayed on as chairman of the board of directors until 1963.

Rickenbacker was born in Columbus, Ohio. He was forced to leave school at the age of 13 when his father died. He studied by taking correspondence courses. One of his first successes was as an automobile mechanic and racing driver. After winning an international reputation in automobile racing, Rickenbacker enlisted in the Army in 1917. He served as a staff driver and

Eastern Air Lines
"Eddie" Rickenbacker

as an engineering officer before becoming a pilot.

After World War I, Rickenbacker worked with several automobile firms and owned the Indianapolis Speedway for 18 years. As president of Eastern Air Lines for 21 years, he led the company to prosperity.

On a World War II inspection trip for Secretary of War Henry Stimson in 1942, Rickenbacker and seven others were forced down in the Pacific some 600 miles north of Samoa. They drifted on rubber rafts for 24 days before they were rescued. ROBERT B. HOTZ

RICKER COLLEGE. See UNIVERSITIES AND COLLEGES (table).

RICKETS is a bone disease that occurs mostly in children under 3 years of age. It may be caused by a lack of calcium and vitamin D or by the inability of the body to use those substances properly. The bones are so soft

that they bend into abnormal shapes. They may develop bumps called *knobs*. Rickets results in conditions called bowlegs, knockknees, chicken breast, funnel chest, rosary ribs, and knobbed forehead. As the child grows, bones harden, but the abnormal shape usually remains.

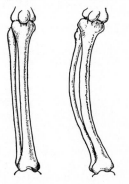
RICKETS
Normal Lower   Lower Leg Bones
Leg Bones   Affected by Rickets

Some of the symptoms of rickets are sweating, especially on the head, weakness, flabbiness, pain in the bones, and misshapen bones. Doctors use X rays to diagnose rickets.

Eating foods that are rich in calcium and vitamin D usually prevents rickets. Calcium can be obtained by drinking plenty of milk and eating green vegetables each day. The best sources of vitamin D are sunlight and fish oils.

A child can sometimes be cured of rickets by exposing him to plenty of sunlight and by giving him substances rich in vitamin D, such as cod-liver oil or halibut-liver (haliver) oil. J. F. A. McMANUS

See also COD-LIVER OIL; VITAMIN (Vitamin D).

RICKETTS, HOWARD TAYLOR. See RICKETTSIA.

RICKETTSIA, *rick EHT see uh*, is one of a group of disease-producing organisms. They are generally smaller than bacteria. When rickettsiae are introduced into the blood stream of human beings by bites of ticks or lice, they cause diseases such as Rocky Mountain spotted fever, typhus, and dengue (see ROCKY MOUNTAIN SPOTTED FEVER; TYPHUS). Rickettsiae resemble viruses, because they cannot survive outside of living cells. They are named for Howard Taylor Ricketts (1871-1910), an American pathologist. H. WORLEY KENDELL

RICKOVER, HYMAN GEORGE (1900-   ), an American naval officer, pioneered in developing the U.S.S. *Nautilus*, the first nuclear-powered submarine. In 1965, he received the Enrico Fermi Medal, highest U.S. atomic science award. He wrote his views on education in *Education and Freedom* (1959).

In 1947, Rickover became head of the Naval Reactors Branch of the U.S. Atomic Energy Commission. He also served as head of the Nuclear Power Division of the U.S. Navy. He was promoted to the rank of vice-admiral in 1959. Rickover reached compulsory retirement age in 1964, but he continued to serve in the Navy's nuclear propulsion program. Born in Warsaw, Poland, Rickover came to the United States with his family when he was 4 years old. RALPH E. LAPP

RICKSHA. See JINRIKISHA.

Hyman G. Rickover
U.S. Navy

a MILL   and a WALK   and a KEY   = MILWAUKEE

A Picture Riddle Is Called a Rebus.

RIDDLE, *rid'l*, is a form of puzzling question, or enigma, which is to be solved by guessing. Sometimes it is a statement which has a hidden meaning to be discovered or guessed. A riddle has come to mean anything puzzling, uncertain in its meaning, or complicated.

Riddles have always been popular. They are a type of folklore and are collected by students of language. The earliest riddles were presented by ancient oracles and bards, and were of a serious character. They were genuine enigmas and sometimes called *sense riddles*. Modern riddles are less serious and may be described as *conundrum* puns. A conundrum is a kind of riddle based upon some imagined likeness between things that are quite unlike. The answer to the puzzling question often involves a pun, or play upon words (see Pun).

Ancient Riddles. The Bible contains riddles. A good one is found in the story of Samson in Judges 14. Samson returned to a young lion he had killed. In the carcass he found honey and a swarm of bees. He offered the following riddle to the young men at his wedding feast:

Out of the eater came forth meat,

And out of the strong came forth sweetness!

The young men secretly wormed the answer out of Samson's bride. When they replied, "What is sweeter than honey, and what is stronger than a lion?" Samson knew they had cheated. He took a terrible revenge, killing 30 men and leaving his wife.

The ancients made riddles about the sun, the moon, the rainbow, and especially the wind. "What flies forever and rests never?" was a riddle referring to the wind. In Greek mythology we find the famous riddle asked by the Sphinx, "What has one voice and yet becomes four-footed and two-footed and three-footed?" Oedipus guessed the answer, "Man," who crawls on all fours when a baby, then learns to stand erect, and in old age walks with a cane. The myth goes on to say that the Sphinx was so grieved that she killed herself.

The early peoples took their riddles seriously. Homer, the great Greek poet, is said to have died of humiliation because he could not answer a riddle. Ancient Norse mythology mentions a riddle contest between the god Odin and a giant. It is said that Lycerus, king of Babylon, and Nectanebo, king of Egypt, waged a war of riddles. Lycerus is supposed to have won, through the aid of Aesop, author of the Fables.

Medieval Riddles. By the Middle Ages riddling had become a popular pastime. The following is a riddle of this period:

What is it that never was and never will be?

(A mouse's nest in a cat's ear.)

Not quite so old, perhaps, is the familiar riddle of our childhood:

When is a door not a door?

(When it is ajar.)

Another nursery rhyme riddle is:

Little Nanny Etticoat

In a white petticoat

And a red nose;

The longer she stands

The shorter she grows.

The answer is "a candle."

Most of the riddles of today are conundrums. The following are a few examples:

What has eyes but can't see? (potato)

What kind of fruit is red when it is green? (blackberry)

A houseful, a hole full; you cannot catch a bowlful! (smoke)

What has four or more wheels and flies? (garbage truck)   WALTER H. HOLZE

See also CHARADE; REBUS.

RIDDLE OF THE SPHINX. See RIDDLE; SPHINX.

RIDEAU CANAL, *rih DOH*, is a Canadian waterway connecting the Ottawa River at Ottawa with Lake Ontario at Kingston. It consists of the Rideau and Cataraqui rivers, several lakes, and some short canals. It is 123 miles long, and has 47 locks, each 134 feet long, 33 feet wide, and 5 feet deep. One branch of the canal, known as the Tay branch, extends to the town of Perth, and has two locks. The Rideau Canal was completed in 1832. It was designed to offer a safe route for gunboats and military supplies between Montreal and the Great Lakes.   D. M. L. FARR

RIDEAU FALLS. See OTTAWA (Location; map).

RIDEAU HALL. See OTTAWA (What to See and Do in Ottawa; picture).

RIDER COLLEGE. See UNIVERSITIES AND COLLEGES (table).

RIDGE AND VALLEY REGION. See UNITED STATES (The Appalachian Highland).

RIDGWAY, MATTHEW BUNKER (1895-   ), became the first United States Army officer to hold supreme commands in both the Pacific and Atlantic areas. In 1951, he succeeded General Douglas MacArthur as supreme commander for the Allied Powers in Japan, and as supreme commander for the United Nations forces in the Far East. The following year, Ridgway succeeded General Dwight D. Eisenhower as supreme commander of Allied forces in Europe. From 1953 to 1955, Ridgway was United States Army Chief of Staff.

Ridgway was born in Fort Monroe, Va., and was graduated from the U.S. Military Academy in 1917. He served in China, Nicaragua, the Panama Canal Zone, and the Philippines. Ridgway was with the War Department War Plans Division when World War II began. He led the 82nd Airborne Division in the invasions of Sicily, Italy, and Normandy, and

Wide World
Matthew B. Ridgway

later commanded the 18th Airborne Corps in Europe. After the war, Ridgway became commander of the Mediterranean theater and the Caribbean command. In 1949, he went to Washington, D.C., as army deputy chief of staff. The next year Ridgway was appointed commander of the United States Eighth Army in Korea.

In 1955, Ridgway retired. He became chairman of the Mellon Institute of Industrial Research in Pittsburgh, Pa., serving until 1960.   MAURICE MATLOFF

RIDING. See HORSE (How to Ride).

RIDING MOUNTAIN NATIONAL PARK. See CANADA (National Parks).

RIDLEY, NICHOLAS (1500?-1555), an English bishop, was a martyr of the Protestant Reformation. Many regarded him as the master spirit among the English reformers. He helped compile the first Book of Common Prayer of 1549, and the Forty-Two Articles of Religion in 1553. These later became known as the Thirty-Nine Articles (see THIRTY-NINE ARTICLES). Ridley supported Lady Jane Grey's unsuccessful claim to the throne, and in 1553 Queen Mary imprisoned him in the Tower of London. In 1554 Ridley was condemned for heresy, and the following year he was burned at the stake at Oxford.

Ridley was born in Northumberland, and was graduated from Pembroke College, Cambridge University. In 1547 he became bishop of Rochester, and in 1550, bishop of London.   GEORGE L. MOSSE

RIEL, *ree ELL*, **LOUIS** (1844-1885), led uprisings against the Canadian government in 1869-1870 and 1885. He led protesting *métis* (persons of mixed French and Indian descent), who feared the land they had settled would be taken over by new settlers. Riel was hanged as a traitor after the second revolt.

The first uprising began after the Canadian government decided to buy Hudson's Bay Company land in what is now Manitoba and open the land to new settlers. The métis in the Red River Valley feared that they would lose their land to the new settlers. Riel protested in vain. In 1869, métis led by Riel captured Fort Garry (present-day Winnipeg). Government troops ended the revolt of the métis in 1870. Riel fled and was classed as an outlaw. But the government set aside land for the métis, and established the Province of Manitoba.

Louis Riel

Culver

Riel was elected to the Canadian House of Commons in 1873 and 1874, but was denied his seat. He was given a pardon in 1875 on the condition that he leave Canada for five years. But Riel suffered a mental breakdown in 1875 and was in insane asylums from 1876 until 1878. Then he moved to Montana. He became a United States citizen in 1883.

During this time, hundreds of métis had moved from the Red River Valley to what is now Saskatchewan. In 1884, the métis again feared they would lose their land to new settlers. Riel helped the métis form a provisional government in March, 1885. Fighting broke out, and government troops defeated the métis. Riel surrendered, was convicted of treason, and was hanged. His death caused an outburst of racial hatred between French Canadians and English Canadians that weakened Canadian unity. Riel was born in St. Boniface, Manitoba.   P. B. WAITE

See also RED RIVER REBELLION; SASKATCHEWAN REBELLION.

RIEMANN, GEORG FRIEDRICH. See FOURTH DIMENSION.

RIEMENSCHNEIDER, *REE mun shny dur*, **TILMAN** (1460?-1531), was one of the best-known sculptors of his day in Germany. Riemenschneider carved in both stone and wood. Most of his sculpture is concerned with religious subjects. Riemenschneider's work is noted for its quiet religious feeling. His major sculpture is also known for its accurate portrayal of the subject's physical appearance, whether the subject is a person or an object.

Riemenschneider was born in Thuringia. He studied his trade in several German cities before settling in Würzburg. He spent most of his life there, becoming a prominent citizen and a member of the Würzburg city council.   ROBERT R. WARK

RIENZI, *ree EN zee*, **COLA DI** (1313?-1354), was a famous Roman patriot. His career shows how power can turn a freedom-loving patriot into a tyrant.

Rienzi was born in Rome, where he received a good education and became a notary. The way the nobles of his time oppressed the common people made him sick at heart, and the nobles hated and feared him. In 1347, he became powerful enough to call a meeting of the people on Capitol Hill to demand a new government. Soon he became a *tribune*, or defender of the people, and received the powers of a dictator.

Rienzi ruled wisely for a time, but he began to want more and more power. Soon he became unpopular, and the people lost confidence in him. After ruling seven months, he fled to Naples. There, Emperor Charles IV imprisoned him. In 1354, Rienzi was released and returned to Rome. The people welcomed him, and he regained his lost power. But he again acted with the cruelty of a tyrant. He was killed while trying to put down a riot.   FRANKLIN D. SCOTT

RIESENGEBIRGE. See SUDETES MOUNTAINS.

RIF is a mountainous region on the northern coast of Morocco. It stretches for about 180 miles along the coast of the Mediterranean Sea. The inhabitants, called *Riffs* or *Riffians*, are Hamites of the Moslem faith (see HAMITE). They have frequently revolted against the government of Morocco. Abd-el-Krim, the most famous Riff leader, tried to overthrow the Spanish administration in the 1920's. He succeeded at first, but French and Spanish troops later defeated him. Many Riffians fought with Francisco Franco in the 1930's during the Spanish Civil War.   VERNON ROBERT DORJAHN

RIFLE is a gun that is held against the shoulder when firing. Soldiers use rifles in battle, and sportsmen use them to hunt game and to compete in shooting matches.

Military rifles and sporting rifles differ greatly. Military rifles are ruggedly built and are designed to work under the harshest conditions. Most military rifles are semiautomatic or automatic. An automatic rifle can fire bullets rapidly one after another with one squeeze of the trigger. Most hunting and target rifles are operated by hand after each firing and are designed for beauty as well as accuracy.

The Parts of a Rifle

All rifles have four basic parts: (1) the barrel, (2) the stock, (3) the action, and (4) the sights.

The *barrel* is a strong steel tube with spiral grooves called *rifling* cut along the inside. The front end of the barrel is called the *muzzle*, and the rear end is the *breech*.

The *stock* of a rifle helps keep the rifle steady when firing. The butt of the stock is placed against the shoulder when firing. The front end extends under the barrel. Stocks of military rifles are made of wood, plastic, or fiberglass. Many sporting rifles have stocks made of expensive wood with decorative or grip-aiding carving called *checkering*.

The *action* is the basic machinery of the rifle. It includes the parts that feed a cartridge into the firing chamber, fire the bullet, and eject the used cartridge.

The *sights* are used to aim the rifle. When aimed properly, the rear sight, front sight, and target should be in alignment. Many sporting rifles have *telescopic sights* that make distant targets appear closer. On military rifles, these sights are used only for sniping.

How a Rifle Works

A rifle is ready to fire when a cartridge has been fed into the *firing chamber*. Then the rifle is aimed and the trigger squeezed. The *hammer* or *firing pin* strikes the rear end of the cartridge and ignites the *primer*. The primer in turn ignites the propellant powder in the cartridge. The powder burns rapidly, creating pressure that drives the bullet down the barrel.

The rifling in the barrel makes the bullet spin. Without spin, a bullet will not stay pointed forward in flight, but will tumble over and over. The spinning motion increases the accuracy of a bullet.

Kinds of Rifles

Rifles are classified by the type of action (manually operated, automatic, or semiautomatic); the name of the designer or manufacturer (for example, Remington or Winchester); or the *caliber*. The caliber may refer to the inside diameter of the barrel or the diameter of the bullet used in the rifle. The caliber is measured in *millimeters* or in decimal fractions of an inch.

There are three kinds of repeating rifles with hand-operated actions—*bolt-action*, *lever-action*, and *slide-action*. These rifles have *magazines* (cartridge holders) that feed cartridges into the firing chamber. The action on two other kinds of rifles—*semiautomatic* and *automatic*—is operated by some of the forces caused by the explosion of a cartridge in the firing chamber.

Bolt-Action Rifles have an action that resembles a bolt used to lock a door. When the bolt on the rifle is pulled back, the used cartridge is thrown out and the hammer is cocked. When the bolt is moved forward, it pushes a new cartridge into the firing chamber.

Lever-Action Rifles are loaded by moving a lever under the breech down and back up. The down movement throws out the used cartridge and cocks the hammer. The up movement inserts a new cartridge into the firing chamber.

Slide-Action Rifles, also called *pump-action rifles*, are loaded with a back-and-forth movement of a rod and handle beneath the front part of the barrel. When the handle is pulled back, the breech opens and the used cartridge is thrown out. A live cartridge is inserted when the handle is pushed forward.

Automatic and Semiautomatic Rifles are used mainly by soldiers and policemen. When any rifle is fired, gas is formed by the burning powder in the firing chamber. The expanding gas drives the bullet out of the barrel. In most modern automatic and semiautomatic rifles, some of this gas operates the action. When a cartridge is fired, a fresh cartridge is moved out of the magazine into the firing chamber, and the firing mechanism is cocked. A completely automatic rifle fires one bullet after another when its trigger is held back.

The M16 rifle is one of two models of automatic rifles used by the U.S. armed forces. It weighs 7.6 pounds

PARTS OF A RIFLE   A Bolt-Action Repeating Rifle can be fitted with a small telescope called a *scope* to make distant targets appear closer. The bolt-action rifle is the most popular kind of repeating rifle.

WORLD BOOK illustration by Tom Morgan

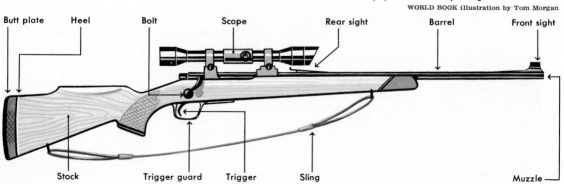

Butt plate   Heel   Bolt   Scope   Rear sight   Barrel   Front sight

Stock   Trigger guard   Trigger   Sling   Muzzle

when loaded with a 20-cartridge magazine. The M16 can be set to fire one shot at a time, or 20 shots in a single burst.

The M14 rifle, also used by the U.S. armed forces, weighs about 11 pounds when loaded. The M14 can fire one shot at a time, or 20 shots in about 9 seconds. The .30-caliber cartridge used in the M14 is longer and heavier than the .223-caliber cartridge used in the M16. As a result, the M14 has a greater range than the M16.

Rifle Cartridges

Rifle cartridges are enclosed in a *casing* (metal covering) made of brass or steel. Cartridges vary in size according to the caliber of the rifle. The names of some cartridges include the year the cartridge was put into use. The 30-06 is a 30-millimeter cartridge chosen for use by the U.S. Army in 1906. The classification of some other cartridges includes the caliber and *velocity* (speed) of the bullet. The bullet from a .250-3000-caliber cartridge has a velocity of 3,000 feet per second.

History

Modern rifles developed from the crude, muzzle-loading firearms of the 1400's. Rifling of barrels was invented in Europe about 1500. *Smooth-bore* firearms (weapons without rifling) could not be depended on to hit targets more than 100 steps away.

The jaeger rifle of central and northern Europe was the first accurate rifle. The jaeger—the German word *Jaeger* means *hunter*—was developed about 1665. Ger-

FAMOUS RIFLES Early rifles were used for hunting, target shooting, and warfare. The same type of rifle was used for all three purposes. Today's automatic and semiautomatic rifles are used mainly by the military, and repeating rifles with hand-operated actions are used for hunting and target shooting.

The Remington Arms Co., Inc.

The Flintlock Rifle had to be reloaded through the muzzle after each firing. This rifle was made from 1816 to 1846.

Gun Digest Co.

The Buffalo Rifle was made by the Sharps Rifle Company in 1874. One trigger cocked the rifle, and the other fired it.

The Remington Arms Co., Inc.

The Beals Revolving Rifle could be fired six times without reloading. This repeating rifle was made from 1866 to 1872.

Gun Digest Co.

The Mauser M1898 was a bolt-action military rifle. It was the model for the American Springfield rifle used in World War I.

Colt Industries

The M16 Rifle can fire 20 bullets in six seconds. The M16 is an official rifle of the United States armed forces.

HOW RIFLING WORKS

Rifling is the wide spiral grooves that are cut along the *bore* (inside) of a rifle barrel, *right*. The thin, slightly raised bore surfaces are called *lands*. When the rifle is fired, the grooves give a spinning motion to the bullet. This spinning motion makes the bullet stay on course in flight and increases its range. Friction from the lands marks the bullet, *far right*.

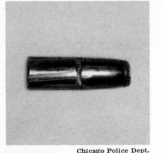

Sharps Arms Co.

Chicago Police Dept.

WORLD BOOK diagram by Tom Morgan

Rifle barrel   Bullet   Land   Groove   Bore

man immigrants brought jaegers to Pennsylvania in the early 1700's and gave them new features, including longer barrels. The Pennsylvania-made Kentucky rifle developed from the jaeger. Some Kentucky rifles were used during the American Revolutionary War (1775-1783).

Rifles used round bullets until the 1850's, when the more accurate Minié bullets became popular. Minié bullets had hollow bases and pointed tips and were used during the U.S. Civil War (1861-1865).

Improvements of the late 1800's included repeating rifles, smokeless explosive powder, and *jacketed* bullets, which have a tough metal cover over a lead or steel core.   WARREN PAGE

Related Articles in WORLD BOOK include:

Ammunition	Firearm	Musket
Bullet	Garand Rifle	Shotgun
Carbine	Gunpowder	Sniperscope
Cartridge		

RIFT VALLEY. See GREAT RIFT VALLEY.

RIG-VEDA. See VEDA.

RIGA, *REE guh* (pop. 680,000; alt. 30 ft.), is the capital and chief industrial and shipping center of Latvia, a republic of Russia. It lies on the Dvina River, about 8 miles from the Gulf of Riga. For location, see LATVIA (map). Albert von Apeldern, Bishop of Livonia, founded Riga in 1201.

From 1918 to 1940, when Latvia was independent, the University of Riga was the center of Latvian culture. Russian forces seized Riga in 1940, but were driven out by the Nazis. The Nazis held Riga until 1944, when the Russians again took control.   FRANCIS J. BOWMAN

RIGA, GULF OF. See ESTONIA (Location).

RIGEL, *RY jel,* or *RY gel,* is a bright star in the constellation Orion. It is at least 15,500 times brighter than the sun. Rigel is also a giant star, with a diameter 35 times as large as that of the sun. Its mass is 33 times that of the sun. It is about 540 light-years from Earth. See also ASTRONOMY (How to Use a Star Map).

RIGGING. See SAILING (Rigging).

RIGHT ASCENSION. See ASTRONOMY (table: Terms).

RIGHT-HAND RULE. See ELECTRIC MOTOR (Basic Principles).

RIGHT OF ASSEMBLY. See ASSEMBLY.

RIGHT OF POSSESSION. See TITLE.

RIGHT OF PRIVACY. See PRIVACY, RIGHT OF.

RIGHT OF SEARCH. Under international law, a nation at war has the right to visit and search merchant ships of neutral nations. The search must be carried out by the officers of a warship. The purposes are to determine the true nationality of the vessel, and to find out whether the vessel is engaged in unneutral service or in carrying contraband of war (see CONTRABAND). In peacetime, the right of search may be exercised to enforce revenue laws or prevent piracy.

In making the search, the ship's papers are first examined. These papers name the ship, its master, or captain, the port it sailed from, and the port for which it is bound. The papers should describe the cargo, and should certify that the officers have met the customs regulations of the country from which the ship has sailed.

If the papers are correct, the search usually ends. But if suspicion is aroused, the cargo may be examined. Any officer who refuses to stop his ship and allow it to be searched runs the risk of having both ship and cargo confiscated. The Hague Conference of 1907 and the London Conference of 1909 tried to set limits to the right of search. Conference members agreed that the mail of neutral nations should be free from search. But all sides disregarded these agreements in wartime.

During the period of Prohibition in the United States, some countries agreed to extend their territorial limits to the number of miles that could be covered in one hour's sailing from their coasts. These agreements made it easier to search for smuggled articles, and they remain in force. For other purposes the limits are 3 miles and 12 miles, depending on the kind of search. By a 1939 statute, the President may authorize a search for revenue purposes over an area as far as 62 miles from the U.S. coast.   TELFORD TAYLOR

RIGHT OF WAY. See EASEMENT; RAILROAD (Right of Way); ROADS AND HIGHWAYS (Planning).

RIGHT-TO-WORK LAW provides that a person need not belong to a labor union to get or keep a job. It also provides that he may not be denied a job because he belongs to a union. Twenty states, most of them in the South, have such laws.

Right-to-work laws have the effect of barring closed shop, union shop, and maintenance-of-membership agreements between employers and unions. In the *closed shop*, the employer can hire only members of the union. In the *union shop*, all employees must join the union after they have worked there for a certain period. *Maintenance-of-membership clauses* require that employees who are union members retain membership until the union contract expires.   MELVIN WARREN REDER

RIGHT WING refers to a conservative, traditional group or political party. In some legislative bodies, the conservatives sit to the right of the speaker. Radical and liberal groups form the *left wing*, with middle-of-the-road groups making up the *center*. This custom originated with the French National Assembly of 1789. In that assembly, nobles took the honored seats to the king's right.

See also CONSERVATISM.

RIGHTS, BILL OF. See BILL OF RIGHTS.

RIGHTS OF MAN, DECLARATION OF THE, is a French document that sets forth the principles of human liberty and the rights of individuals. The first two articles of the declaration state that all men are free and equal in "liberty, property, security, and resistance to oppression." The other 15 articles of the declaration summarize the democratic political thought concerning both the limitations of government and the rights of citizens.

The French National Assembly adopted the Declaration of the Rights of Man and of the Citizen on Aug. 27, 1789, during the French Revolution. The refusal of King Louis XVI to approve the declaration helped bring about increased revolutionary activity in October, 1789.

The writers of the declaration were influenced by the United States Declaration of Independence, bills of rights in United States state constitutions, and the democratic writings of the French philosopher Jean Jacques Rousseau.   ROBERT B. HOLTMAN

RIGOLETTO. See OPERA (Rigoletto).

RIIS, *rees,* **JACOB AUGUST** (1849-1914), was an American newspaperman and social reformer. He worked as a police reporter for the *New York Tribune* and the *New York Evening Sun* for more than 20 years. During this time, he exposed graft, vice, and crime in the slum areas of New York City. Sometimes called *America's first photojournalist,* Riis used his camera to prove the truth of his writings. His photographs and writings helped better the living conditions of the poor. See PHOTOGRAPHY (Major Advancements).

Riis became instrumental in establishing playgrounds and parks. His efforts in 1888 resulted in the abolition of Mulberry Bend, one of the worst tenement sections in New York City. The Jacob A. Riis Neighborhood House for social work was founded on the site (see PLAYGROUND). Riis devoted his later years to writing, lecturing, and social work. His writings include *How the Other Half Lives* (1890); *The Making of an American* (1901), which was his own story; and *Theodore Roosevelt, the Citizen* (1904).

Riis was born on May 3, 1849, in Ribe, Denmark. He came to the United States when he was 21.   JOHN TEBBEL

RIJEKA, *ree YEH kah* (pop. 116,000; alt. 328 ft.), is a port in Yugoslavia. It is also called FIUME. The city lies on the Gulf of Kvarner (Quarnero) near the northern end of the Adriatic Sea. For location, see YUGOSLAVIA (color map).

Rijeka's chief export is lumber. The city is also a manufacturing center for chemicals, leather, machinery, and tobacco goods.

After about 400 years under Austria, Rijeka was annexed by Hungary in 1779. Both Italy and Yugoslavia claimed the city after World War I. In 1919, while negotiations were still in progress, an Italian force led by Gabriele d'Annunzio seized the city. The 1920 Treaty of Rapallo made Rijeka a free city (see FREE CITY). In 1922, however, Italy once again took over the city.

By the terms of the Treaty of Rome, signed in 1924, Rijeka was given to Italy, and its suburb Susak to Yugoslavia. The World War II Allied treaty with Italy gave Rijeka to Yugoslavia.   JOSEPH S. ROUCEK

See also D'ANNUNZIO, GABRIELE; RAPALLO, TREATIES OF; YUGOSLAVIA (After World War I).

RIKSDAG. See SWEDEN (Parliament).

RIKSMÅL. See NORWAY (Language).

RILEY, JAMES WHITCOMB (1849-1916), won fame as the *Hoosier Poet.* He wrote much verse in pure English, but he wrote his most popular works in the dialect of his home state, Indiana. Among his works are *The Old Swimmin' Hole and 'Leven More Poems* (1883), *Rhymes of Childhood* (1890), *Poems Here at Home* (1893), and *Book of Joyous Children* (1902).

Riley, the son of a lawyer, was born on Oct. 7, 1849, in Greenfield, Ind. He left home after receiving a grammar school education, and worked for a time as a sign painter. He next joined a medicine show as an actor. In his spare time he composed songs and revised plays for the company. Riley came to know very well

James Whitcomb Riley
Riley Memorial Association

the dialect and the peculiarities of the country folk of Indiana, and he began to write poems about them.

Returning to Greenfield, Riley worked on the local paper, then on the *Anderson* (Ind.) *Democrat.* In 1877, he joined the *Indianapolis Journal.* He began to contribute poems to several papers under the name "Benj. F. Johnson of Boone." These verses soon made him famous. He traveled about the country with Bill Nye, lecturing and reading his poems.   PETER VIERECK

See also INDIANA (Places to Visit).

RILKE, *RIL kuh,* **RAINER MARIA** (1875-1926), was one of the most important lyric poets in German literature and a major representative of the symbolism movement. His poems are characterized by richness of imagery and melody and fine shades of meaning. They have a tone of self-examination and prophecy.

RILLIEUX, NORBERT

Rilke's cycle of poems *The Book of Hours* (1905) expresses a longing for a mystic union with God. *New Poems* (1907, 1908) contains works that try to express the essence, or "idea," of an object or experience. Rilke's novel *The Notebooks of Malte Laurids Brigge* (1910) portrays the loneliness and confusion of a young poet searching for identity in turbulent Paris. The *Duino Elegies* (1923) and *Sonnets to Orpheus* (1923) are poems that praise human existence.

Rilke was born in Prague. He spent much of his life wandering through Europe.   WERNER HOFFMEISTER

RILLIEUX, *RIL ee yew,* **NORBERT** (1806-1894), was an American engineer who revolutionized the sugar industry. He made the first practical multiple-effect vacuum evaporator, a major improvement in the *vacuum pan process* of manufacturing sugar. This process removes the water from the sugar cane without damaging the sugar. In one chamber of Rillieux's machine, the sugar cane juice was boiled until it became syrup. Then, in a connected chamber, the hot vapor from the first chamber boiled the syrup until it became grains of sugar. This double use of the same heat greatly reduced the cost. Other products, including soap, gelatin, some glues, and condensed milk, are now manufactured through a process based on Rillieux's invention.

Rillieux was born in New Orleans, the son of a French engineer and a free Negro woman. He studied in Paris and became an engineering teacher there in 1830. In the 1840's, he installed his invention on many sugar plantations in the United States. He returned to Paris permanently in the 1850's.   EDGAR ALLAN TOPPIN

RIMBAUD, *ram BOH,* **ARTHUR** (1854-1891), was a French poet. He wrote his major poems during five turbulent years between the ages of 15 and 20. The poem that first won him recognition was "Le Bateau ivre" ("The Drunken Boat," 1871). Looking at a toy boat in a park pool, Rimbaud makes it sail in his imagination through luminous oceans and dazzling landscapes.

Rimbaud's major collection of free verse and prose poems is *Les Illuminations*. It was published in 1886, long after the poet had abandoned literature to become a trader in Ethiopia. The work shows what the world might have looked like after the Deluge to a person not bound by preconceived habits and impressions. *Une Saison en enfer* (*A Season in Hell*, 1873), is an autobiographical account of the most tormented moment in Rimbaud's young life, when he lost faith in reality and madness hovered over him. Rimbaud freed himself of this torment, just as he freed himself of the emotional entanglement with poet Paul Verlaine, which had caused the anguish. Rimbaud and Verlaine were close friends and traveled together in 1873 and 1874.

In a famous letter, Rimbaud stated his poetic principle: that the only real subject of poetry was the exploration of self through "a systematic derangement of all the senses;" the poet must search for a more dynamic use of language: "the alchemy of the word." Rimbaud was born in Charleville.   ANNA BALAKIAN

See also VERLAINE, PAUL.

RIMSKY-KORSAKOV, *RIM skih-KAWR suh koff,* **NICHOLAS** (1844-1908), a Russian composer, became famous for his colorful and brilliant orchestration. His symphonic suite *Scheherazade*, based on the book *Ara-*

Culver
Nicholas Rimsky-Korsakov

bian Nights, is an example of his powers.

Rimsky-Korsakov wrote 15 operas, but only excerpts from them have remained popular. These include "Song of India" from *Sadko*, "Flight of the Bumblebee" from *Tsar Sultan*, and "Hymn to the Sun" from *The Golden Cockerel*. His other works include three symphonies, several choral works, and a book on instrumentation.

Rimsky-Korsakov was born in Tikhvin, Novgorod. He attended the naval college in St. Petersburg (now Leningrad), and then entered the navy as a career. While an officer on a three-year cruise, he composed his first symphony.

At the age of 27, Rimsky-Korsakov became a professor of orchestration and composition at the Conservatory of Saint Petersburg. He was mainly self-taught, but he achieved professional standing through disciplined study. The composer Igor Stravinsky studied under him. Rimsky-Korsakov belonged to a group of Russian nationalist composers called "The Five."   JOYCE MICHELL

RINDERPEST, *RIN der pest,* or **CATTLE PLAGUE,** is a highly contagious, acute disease of cattle and other members of the ox family. Symptoms are a sudden loss of milk in cows, fever, prostration, bloody diarrhea, loss of flesh, and ulcerations of the mouth. The cause is an invisible virus. Death usually occurs in four to seven days. The death rate is as high as 98 per cent.

The disease hindered the development of western civilization for many hundreds of years. It swept over Europe from the East with every war. The last European outbreak occurred in Belgium following World War I. The disease has never reached the United States, and is chiefly confined to Oriental countries.   D. W. BRUNER

RINEHART, MARY ROBERTS (1876-1958), was an

American novelist and playwright. Her mystery stories, such as *The Circular Staircase* (1908) and *The Man in Lower Ten* (1909), have clever plots and a blend of horror and humor. She also wrote a play, *The Bat*, with Avery Hopwood, which became a stage success in 1920. Mrs. Rinehart was born in Pittsburgh, Pa., where she studied nursing. She used this training as material for several of her books.   HERBERT R. BROWN

Harris & Ewing
Mary Roberts Rinehart

RINFRET, THIBAUDEAU (1879-1962), served as chief justice of Canada from 1944 to 1954. During this time, appeals to the Judicial Committee were abolished, and the Supreme Court became the final court of appeal. Rinfret's understanding of common law and the civil code, the two systems of law used, smoothed over this period. Rinfret was born in Montreal. He was graduated from McGill Law School.   J. E. HODGETTS

318

An Intaglio Ring, dug up from the ruins of ancient Troy, has a noble Grecian image hollowed out of the stone.

Key Rings worn by the ancient Romans, above, had small usable keys attached to them. Modern key rings are not worn on the finger, but have a number of keys hanging from them. A portrait of the Emperor Trajan's wife adorns the ancient Roman thumb ring, *left*.

Rings of Long Ago include: (1) ancient Egyptian ring; (2) gold ring from Mycenae; (3) Egyptian signet ring; (4) Roman gilded bronze ring; (5) Grecian gold ring; (6) Brahman gold signet ring; (7) Anglo-Saxon betrothal ring; (8) Jewish marriage ring; (9) papal ring, 1400's; (10) betrothal ring, 1600's; (11) wedding rings of Luther and Katharina; (12) Merovingian ring.

RING is a small band, round or nearly round in shape. People generally wear rings on their fingers. Most rings are made of gold or other precious metals. Other materials such as ivory or plastics also may be used. Rings may be plain, engraved and decorated, or set with stones. The most popular precious stone used in ring settings is the diamond. But the amethyst, turquoise, topaz, pearl, emerald, ruby, and sapphire are also widely used. People often use personal initials to form the decoration of a ring. A ring which contains a seal is called a *signet ring*.

The custom of wearing rings is probably as old as man. But the earliest rings known are those found in the tombs of ancient Egypt. The exchange of rings may be symbolic of love or marriage. A ring may also be a sign of authority. Many rings have no special significance, and are worn simply as personal ornaments.

Rings Worn as Ornaments. Some people have worn rings in the nose or ear. Rings still adorn noses, ears, arms, ankles, and toes of the members of certain tribes of Africa and the islands of the South Pacific. People of the Orient sometimes wear toe rings. But in other countries, it has long been the custom to wear rings only on the fingers or in the ears (see EARRING). Until the 1300's, people commonly wore rings on their thumbs.

Wedding and Engagement Rings. The Romans probably began the use of engagement, or betrothal, and wedding rings. Most married persons wear the wedding ring on the third finger of the left hand because of an old, but untrue, belief that a vein runs directly from this finger to the heart. However, Germans and many members of the Eastern Orthodox Churches wear the wedding ring on the right hand. Both husband and wife may wear wedding rings.

Rings as Symbols of Authority. A ring has long been a symbol of a ruler's authority. Kings gave their rings to trusted servants. The ring gave the wearer the power of king's messenger. In the Bible, Pharaoh placed his signet ring on Joseph's finger when he set him over all Egypt (Gen. 41:42).

The ring of the pope is especially interesting. He receives it when he is crowned. It bears his name and a picture of Saint Peter in a boat, so it is sometimes called the *fisherman's ring*. All papal documents, called *briefs*, must be stamped with this signet. When a pope dies, his ring is broken. A new one is made for the next pope. When the pope names a cardinal, he gives him a huge thumb ring. Bishops of the Roman Catholic Church also wear special rings.   WILLIAM M. MILLIKEN

See also JEWELRY.

RING OF THE NIBELUNG, THE

RING OF THE NIBELUNG, *NEE buh loong,* **THE,** is a group of four operas by Richard Wagner. The cycle consists of: *Das Rheingold, Die Walküre, Siegfried,* and *Die Götterdämmerung.* The plot of these operas deals with both men and gods, and is based on Scandinavian and Germanic mythology and on ancient legends, especially material in several poems in the Elder (Poetic) Edda, and in the *Volsunga Saga.* The operas are not only highly dramatic, but also symbolic in theme.

The leading characters include Brünnhilde, a warrior maiden and daughter of Wotan (Odin), chief of the ancient gods, and Siegfried, a fearless hero. The story centers around the struggle for the possession of a hoard of gold. A Nibelung, or dwarf, steals the gold from the Rhine maidens, and makes a ring from part of the hoard. Wotan steals the treasure from the Nibelung and gives it into the custody of Fafnir, a giant turned into a dragon. The angry Nibelung puts a curse of death on the ring.

Siegfried slays Fafnir and gains the treasure. He also succeeds in rescuing Brünnhilde from her mountain prison, and the two fall in love. But Gunther, a half-brother of one of the Nibelungs, gives Siegfried a magic potion that makes him forget Brünnhilde. Later Siegfried's enemies kill him, and Brünnhilde rides her horse into the funeral pyre. In the end, the gold is returned to the Rhine maidens.   RICHARD BECK

See also NIBELUNGENLIED; OPERA (Das Rheingold; Die Götterdämmerung; Nibelungen Ring; Siegfried; Valkyrie); VOLSUNGA SAGA.

RINGLING BROTHERS were five American brothers who built a small troupe of performers into the world's largest circus. The oldest four brothers, **Albert C.** (1852-1916), **Otto** (1858-1911), **Alfred T.** (1861-1919), and **Charles Edward** (1863-1926), are all believed to have been born in McGregor, Iowa. Their father, a

The Five Ringling Brothers built up the world's largest, most famous, and most spectacular circus in the early 1900's.

harness maker, had settled there after coming from Germany. Later, the family moved to Baraboo, Wis., where the fifth brother, **John** (1866-1936), was born.

The brothers showed talent as musicians, jugglers, and clowns. They started giving shows in Baraboo and in neighboring towns. By 1884, they had saved enough money to start a wagon show with a trained horse and a dancing bear. Four years later, they bought their first elephant, and by 1890 the circus traveled by train.

In 1906, the brothers bought the Forepaugh-Sells Circus. The next year they bought the Barnum & Bailey Circus, but did not combine it with their own show until 1919. Charles Ringling directed the circus for many years. John Ringling succeeded him, and was one of the richest men in the world until the stock market crash of 1929 wiped out his fortune. **John Ringling North** (1903-   ), the son of John Ringling's sister, directed the circus from 1937 to 1943. **Robert E. Ringling** (1897-1950), son of Charles Ringling, was in charge from 1943 to 1946, when North again acquired control. In 1967, he sold the circus to Judge Roy Hofheinz and Irvin and Israel Feld.

See also CIRCUS; FLORIDA (Museums; Places to Visit [Circus Winter Quarters]; color picture: Circus Quarters Near Venice); WISCONSIN (Places to Visit [Circus World Museum]).

RINGWORM is a general name for several kinds of skin diseases that are caused by tiny plants, or fungi. Itching may or may not be a symptom. Common ringworm of the skin is often seen on children. It begins as a small red area the size of a split pea. This grows larger, and sometimes reaches the size of a silver dollar. The inside of the area clears, and the eruption appears as a red, scaly ring. There may be one or several patches. This form of ringworm occurs on the non-hairy parts of the body. It is infectious, but it can usually be easily cured if treated with local applications of fungicidal compounds as advised by a physician. The spots of this type of ringworm often disappear without treatment after a few weeks, but they may persist for months. Body ringworm may attack persons of any age. Flat yellowish or brownish patches may appear on the patient's neck, back, chest, or abdomen.

Ringworm of the hands and feet is another common ailment, and has three types. A soft white area between the toes, especially the part next to the little toe, may be *interdigital* ringworm, commonly called *athlete's foot.* It may not cause discomfort, but is sometimes followed by the *vesicular* form, which causes eruptions of blisters on the hands and feet. *Keratotic* ringworm is less common but more persistent than these forms. This disease is usually limited to the palms of the hands and soles of the feet. The affected areas are dry, slightly thickened, and slightly reddened.

There may also be ringworm of the hairy parts of the body. Children are especially susceptible to ringworm of the scalp, which they sometimes contract from other children or from dogs and cats. Epidemics of ringworm of the scalp may occur in schools. Ringworm of the bearded part of the face is called *barber's itch.*

When ringworm appears in a family, each affected person should be careful to use only his own comb, towels, washcloths, and other personal articles. The disease is highly infectious.   THOMAS H. WELLER

See also ATHLETE'S FOOT; ITCH.

The Harbor of Rio de Janeiro is one of the most beautiful in the world. Famed Sugar Loaf
Mountain, *right*, stands out among the other small mountainous islands in the bay.

RIO DE JANEIRO, *REE oh duh juh NAY roh* (pop.
4,031,000; alt. 30 ft.), often called *Rio*, is the second
largest city of Brazil. Only São Paulo is larger. Rio de
Janeiro lies on Guanabara Bay, on the Atlantic Ocean.
Pão de Açúcar (Sugar Loaf), a 1,230-foot-high peak,
rises in the bay. Rio's other striking landmark is a huge
concrete statue of Christ the Redeemer. This statue
stands atop 2,310-foot Corcovado (Hunchback) Mountain.

The blue sea, dazzling white beaches, green parks,
and gray mountains help make Rio de Janeiro one of
the most beautiful cities in the world. Broad, tree-
shaded boulevards lined by patterned black and white
mosaic sidewalks add to the city's charm.

Rio de Janeiro is famous for *Carnival*, a yearly festival
held before Ash Wednesday. During Carnival, streets
and buildings are decorated with gaily colored bunting
and lights. Almost everyone dresses in colorful costumes,
and dances and sings in the streets.

Location and Size. Rio de Janeiro lies on a narrow
strip of land between the mountains, the bay, and the
ocean, on the southeast coast of Brazil. Some of the
city extends into the valleys of the nearby mountains.

Rio de Janeiro covers about 60 square miles. For location, see BRAZIL (political map).

General Description. The city has many old, narrow
streets and low stucco buildings, built when it was a
Portuguese colonial city. But its fine harbor, busy commercial life, and new buildings make it a progressive,
modern metropolis.

Avenida Rio Branco, one of the main thoroughfares
in the city's business section, is more than 100 feet wide.
It is bordered by brazilwood trees and skyscrapers. The
mile-long avenue begins at a plaza called Praça Mauá,
the landing place for persons entering the city by ship.
It meets Avenida Beira Mar, which curves south along
the shore for several miles. Beira Mar is bordered on
one side by magnificent beaches such as Flamengo,
Botafogo, Copacabana, Ipanema, and Leblon, and on
the other side by modern apartment buildings.

Several granite hills, some more than 3,000 feet high,
separate the city into districts. Tunnels run through
some of these hills and connect the districts with one
another.

Parks and Gardens. Rio's 135-acre Botanical Garden, founded by King John VI of Portugal in 1808, has

RIO DE JANEIRO

over 5,000 kinds of plants. Other parks include Boa Vista and Tijuca.

Public Buildings. A group of stately buildings stands at the southern end of Avenida Rio Branco. These buildings include the Municipal Theater, or Opera House; the National Library; and Monroe Palace. The Monroe Palace was named for President James Monroe of the United States. The palace was built for the Brazilian exhibit at the St. Louis Exposition of 1904, and later was moved to Rio.

Nearby is the Ministry of Education and Health Building, an example of the city's modern architecture. Many of the new buildings are made of reinforced concrete. Several stand on stilts so that the ground level is open, and have louvers (ventilating boards) on the outside walls to protect the windows from the hot sun.

Three interesting buildings stand south of the central part of the city. Catete Palace was formerly the official home of the president of Brazil, and São Joaquim is the residence of the Archbishop of Rio de Janeiro. Guanabara Palace, which now belongs to the city, once was a royal palace.

Nearly all the people are Roman Catholics. One of

Statue of Christ the Redeemer, in Rio de Janeiro, stands on top of Corcovado (Hunchback) Mountain, which rises 2,310 feet above the city. The 100-foot statue is made of concrete, and is the work of Paul Landowski. The figure looks like a giant white cross when it is floodlighted at night.

Underwood-Stratton

the most beautiful Catholic churches is Candalária, in the center of Avenida Getúlio Vargas. Each October, many persons make a pilgrimage to the hilltop Church of Our Lady of Penha, reached by a flight of 365 steps. Other Roman Catholic churches include the Franciscan Church and Convent, the Benedictine Church, and the Imperial Chapel of Our Lady of Glory.

One of Rio de Janeiro's most spectacular buildings is the Maracanã Stadium, built in 1950. It can hold more than 150,000 spectators at sports events and other public activities.

Trade and Industry. Rio de Janeiro is a great port. About 4,500 ships enter Guanabara Bay every year. The city has about 5,000 industrial plants. Manufactures consist mostly of goods for local use, such as clothing, glassware, foodstuffs, medicines and drugs, furniture, and tobacco products.

Education. Rio de Janeiro has two universities. The national government founded the University of Brazil in 1920. Catholic University was established by the Roman Catholic Church in 1941. The Oswaldo Cruz Institute is famous for biological research. The National Library is said to be the largest in South America. It has more than 1 million books, and many other publications.

Government of Rio de Janeiro is headed by a mayor and a city council. The president of Brazil appoints the mayor for a term of four years. Fifty aldermen, who make up the council, are elected for four years. The mayor directs and supervises municipal public services, and can appoint and dismiss public servants. The city council has authority to provide for its own organization, and fixes the salaries of the mayor and the aldermen.

History. During the late 1400's, Spain and Portugal agreed upon a line of demarcation that divided between them all of the lands that were eligible for colonization (see LINE OF DEMARCATION). When American lands were explored, Portugal gained much of the territory that is now known as Brazil because of this line. Portugal held Brazil as a colony until 1822. A Portuguese navigator is believed to have discovered the bay of Rio de Janeiro on Jan. 1, 1502. He supposedly named the bay *Rio de Janeiro*, or *River of January*, because of the date and because he mistakenly thought the bay was the outlet of a great river.

French explorers, led by Admiral Nicolas Duran de Villegaignon, established a settlement on the bay in 1555. Ten years later, the Portuguese built a fort in Rio. They drove out the French in 1567. The Portuguese then built homes, churches, and stores on the site of their earlier settlement. They called it St. Sebastian of Rio de Janeiro. The local Indians called the first structure put up by the Portuguese *carioca* (the white man's house), and the people of Rio de Janeiro ever since have called themselves *cariocas*.

In 1807, during the Napoleonic Wars, France invaded Portugal at Lisbon. The Portuguese ruler, Prince John (later King John VI), fled with his court to Rio de Janeiro rather than surrender to the French. In Rio they established a government-in-exile for the entire Portuguese empire. During this period, which lasted from 1808 to 1821, the city served not only as the capital of Brazil, but also of all parts of the Portuguese empire.

Brazil proclaimed itself an independent monarchy in 1822, with Rio de Janeiro as its capital. The Brazilian emperors Pedro I and Pedro II, son and grandson of John VI, established their courts there. In 1891, Brazil became a republic under a federal arrangement providing for the division of the country into 20 states. Rio de Janeiro was not included, but was placed in a separate federal district similar to that of the District of Columbia in the United States.

The city grew from a population of 522,600 in 1890 to 1,157,863 in 1920. In 1922, the city leveled Morro de Castelo, the hill on which Rio originally stood, making room for more buildings to accommodate the population increase. Displaced soil from the hill was dumped in the bay, and Santos Dumont Airport was built on this new land. Brasília replaced Rio de Janeiro as Brazil's capital in 1960.   GEORGE I. BLANKSTEN

See also BRAZIL (color pictures); LATIN AMERICA (pictures).

RÍO DE LA PLATA, *REE oh thay lah PLAH tah,* is an estuary, or funnel-shaped bay, formed by the Paraná and the Uruguay rivers on the southeastern coast of South America. The bay extends northwestward from the Atlantic Ocean for about 170 miles. A great volume of water flows into the bay from the Paraná and Uruguay rivers, and there is a powerful current. Many dangerous shallows make sailing risky all along the river's course. The natural harbor of Montevideo, in Uruguay, lies near the 140-mile-wide mouth of the bay. On the Argentine side, at Buenos Aires and La Plata, huge docks have been built and deep channels have been dredged.

In 1516, Juan Díaz de Solís became the first white man to enter the bay. It was named Río de la Plata (Silver River) by Sebastian Cabot, the Italian navigator. Cabot probably chose the name because of the silver ornaments the Indian residents there wore at the time.   BOSTWICK H. KETCHUM

RÍO DE ORO. See SPANISH SAHARA.

RIO GRANDE, *REE oh GRAND,* the sixth longest river in North America, flows for 1,885 miles through the southwestern part of the United States. It forms the international boundary between the United States and Mexico for about 1,240 miles, or almost two-thirds of the common border. Early Spanish explorers gave the river its name. *Rio Grande* means *large river.* Mexicans call the river *Río Bravo* (*bold river*) or *Río Bravo del Norte* (*bold river of the north*).

Upper Course. The Rio Grande rises on the Continental Divide in the southern Rocky Mountains in southwestern Colorado. It flows southeast through the San Luis Valley Reclamation Project. At Alamosa, the river turns south. It crosses into New Mexico, and flows from north to south through the center of the state. In northern New Mexico, the Rio Grande, fed by mountain streams, passes through a series of basins separated by narrow valleys. The Rio Grande's valley widens above Albuquerque, and the river flows out upon a dry plateau. Here Elephant Butte Dam impounds the river for about 40 miles. Further downstream is the Caballo Reservoir. Both these lakes store water for the Rio Grande Reclamation Project at Las Cruces. The American Dam controls the waters of the Rio Grande north of El Paso at the Texas, New Mexico, and Mexico borders.

Middle Course. From El Paso to the Gulf of Mexico, the Rio Grande forms the international boundary. The river flows southeast from El Paso to Presidio, where it turns abruptly north to pass around the mountainous Big Bend country. Beyond the Big Bend, the Rio Grande flows eastward until the Pecos River joins it. Then it turns southeast for the rest of its course. Amistad

Rio Grande

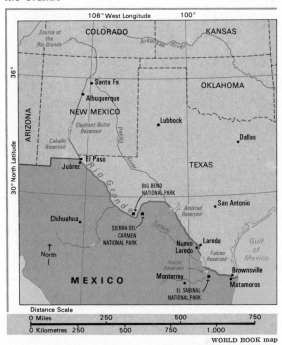

WORLD BOOK map

Texas Highway Department

The Rio Grande forms most of the boundary between the United States and Mexico. It flows from Colorado to the Gulf of Mexico.

RIO GRANDE COLLEGE

Dam spans the river about 12 miles northwest of Del Rio, Tex. The dam forms Amistad Reservoir, which extends upstream 86 miles. During its middle course, the Rio Grande flows through very dry country. The river itself may be dry in late summer, because of little rainfall and the amount of water used for irrigation. Railroads cross the border at El Paso and Presidio.

Lower Course. The Rio Grande widens between Eagle Pass and Laredo, both important railroad crossings. About 50 miles below Laredo, the Salado River, a major tributary from Mexico, joins the Rio Grande. Falcon Dam, about 20 miles below the mouth of the Salado River, forms Falcon Reservoir, which extends upstream more than 35 miles. At Rio Grande City is the Los Olmos Reservoir on another tributary, the Río Los Olmos. Lake El Azúcar lies across the Rio Grande at Camargo in Mexico.

Further downstream, at Mission, is Mission Reservoir. These lakes, built jointly by the United States and Mexico, hold back floodwaters for the lower valley's irrigation projects. Between Rio Grande City and Brownsville, farmers grow citrus fruits, vegetables, and cotton in the irrigated valley. A railroad crosses the border at Brownsville. In 1936, a 17-mile canal was built from Brownsville to Laguna Madre, with jetties through the barrier beach to the Gulf of Mexico. Most of the river is too shallow for boats.   John H. Garland

See also Elephant Butte Dam; Falcon Dam; Pecos River; Rio Grande Project; River (chart).

RIO GRANDE COLLEGE. See Universities and Colleges (table).

RIO GRANDE PROJECT is a federal flood-control, power, and irrigation project that extends along the Rio Grande from Elephant Butte Reservoir in southern New Mexico into southern Texas. Congress authorized the project in 1905. Elephant Butte Dam, a major dam, was completed in New Mexico in 1916 (see Elephant Butte Dam). The United States Bureau of Reclamation has built four diversion dams and more than 1,000 miles of canals and ditches at a cost of about $26 million. The Rio Grande Project irrigates 196,538 acres in New Mexico and Texas.

RIO MADEIRA. See Madeira River.

RÍO MUNI. See Equatorial Guinea.

RIO NEGRO, *NAY groh,* is the largest stream entering the Amazon River from the north. This South American river is named the Rio Negro (Black River) because its waters carry black mud. The Rio Negro rises in southeastern Colombia and flows 1,400 miles southeast to join the Amazon. Ocean steamers sail up to Manaus in Brazil, 10 miles above the river's meeting point with the Amazon. From there, river steamers can sail 423 miles up to the rapids. There is little trade on the river because it flows through a wilderness that is inhabited by primitive Indians. For location of the river, see Brazil (physical map).   Marguerite Uttley

RIO PACT. See Pan-American Conferences (Stronger Ties).

RÍO TINTO, *TEEN toh,* is a river in southern Spain. It flows southward about 70 miles to Huelva Harbor on the Atlantic Ocean. *Río Tinto* are the Spanish words for *Red River.* Copper deposits give the water a reddish color.

RIOT is a noisy, violent outbreak of disorder by a group of people. Rioters often harm other persons and damage property. Rioting or urging people to riot is a crime in most countries and in all the states of the United States. However, the precise legal definition of a riot differs from place to place.

Rioting cannot always be easily distinguished from vandalism, disorderly conduct, or other similar offenses. But most riots involve hundreds or thousands of people, and follow an aggravation of already severe economic, social, or political grievances. A riot may break out spontaneously, or it may be carefully planned through conspiracy. Few riots—unlike revolts or rebellions—are aimed at overthrowing a government or removing specific leaders. However, a riot may set forces in motion that bring about such a result.

A riot may break out during a demonstration. In a demonstration, many people gather merely to protest publicly against some policy of the government, an industry, a university, or some other institution. But when passions run high, the massing together of thousands of persons and the efforts of police to keep order can lead to violence. In the United States, the Constitution guarantees everyone the right to *dissent* (disagree) peacefully, as an individual or in a group (see Freedom of Speech). But when dissent changes into disruption of order and is accompanied by violence that injures others, a riot begins.

Causes of Riots

Riots have occurred throughout the world since the beginning of history. In ancient Rome, the poor rioted several times to press their demands for lower rents and lower food prices. In England, during the early 1800's, workers called *Luddites* staged a series of riots in which they destroyed labor-saving machines, which they feared would replace them. In Mexico City in 1968, rioting students fought with police over various issues, including alleged police brutality during student demonstrations.

The specific issues that trigger riots vary. However, the underlying causes of many riots are similar. Many riots occur because some groups of people believe they do not have an equal chance for economic, political, or social advancement. Members of most minority groups live in this situation (see Minority Group). Large numbers of people in such groups may feel they are mistreated by individuals or by government agencies or other organizations that strongly influence their lives. They may become depressed because they feel they cannot help make major decisions that affect themselves and their community. People who believe their grievances are being ignored often become defiant and have a smoldering desire to display their feelings.

Members of a majority group may also become rioters if they fear a minority. They may attack members of the minority to keep them in an inferior social or economic position. Most lynch mobs in the Western and Southern United States were composed of mem-

Marvin E. Wolfgang, the contributor of this article, is Chairman of the Department of Sociology at the University of Pennsylvania, and coauthor of Subculture of Violence. *He served in 1968-1969 as Director of Research for the National Commission on the Causes and Prevention of Violence.*

bers of dominant, majority groups (see LYNCHING).

Many social scientists classify riots into two groups: (1) *instrumental riots* and (2) *expressive riots*.

Instrumental Riots occur when groups resort to violence because of discontent over specific issues. Throughout history, most riots have been of this type. The violence results from attempts to change certain policies or to improve certain conditions. Most labor riots, especially those in the past, fall into this category. During the 1800's and early 1900's, for example, laborers in the United States fought vigorously to improve working conditions in mines, on railroads, and in factories. Union disputes with management often resulted in violence. Other instrumental riots include prison, antidraft, antiwar, and student riots.

Instrumental riots often indicate that the organizations being attacked have not listened effectively to or acted upon grievances previously voiced through orderly channels. But most people condemn the use of violence to achieve even the most desirable goals.

Expressive Riots occur when many people in a minority group use violence to express dissatisfaction with their living conditions. Studies of urban riots of the 1960's show that Negroes in the riot areas had many grievances. They were extremely discontented about their few job opportunities, bad housing, and inferior schools, and the use of what they felt was excessive force by the police. Several of the riots were triggered by arrests or other routine police actions that people of the black ghettos considered police brutality. These police actions brought large crowds into the streets in protest. In a short time, thousands of people were milling around. The small number of police at the scene could not control them.

The resulting riots became chiefly symbolic gestures

of widespread discontent. For some rioters, however, they became opportunities to loot stores for personal gain. For others, the riots were little more than destructive play. In trying to restrain the rioters and promote a return to order, the police sometimes used more force than many people thought necessary. Such action caused many rioters to become even more violent. See NEGRO (Unrest in the Cities).

Major Riots in the United States

Before the 1960's, most riots in the United States were instrumental riots. High and unfair taxation was a leading cause of such riots. During the 1760's and 1770's, American colonists rioted against tax collectors and other British-appointed officials (see BOSTON TEA PARTY; REVOLUTIONARY WAR IN AMERICA [Events Leading to the Revolution]). For information on other riots resulting from taxation, see SHAYS' REBELLION; WHISKEY REBELLION.

Anti-Catholic and anti-immigrant riots were common during the 1800's. Many native-born Americans strongly disliked immigrants, especially Irish Roman Catholics and Orientals. In the mid-1850's, members of the Know-Nothing, or American, Party opposed the Roman Catholic Church. The Know-Nothings feared rising Irish Catholic political power. In the mid-1850's, they attacked Irish Catholics in several cities, including Baltimore, Louisville, New Orleans, and St. Louis. The uprisings took several lives.

Many Chinese immigrants were victims of mob violence during the economic depression of the 1870's. Large numbers of native-born Americans believed that the immigrants were taking their jobs and forcing down

Labor Riots broke out frequently in the United States during the late 1800's and early 1900's. In 1916, rioting during a steel strike in Youngstown, Ohio, caused extensive property damage, *below.*

wages. Anti-Chinese riots in California and other states resulted in several deaths and the passage of laws prohibiting Asians from entering the United States. See KNOW-NOTHING; ORIENTAL EXCLUSION ACTS.

In 1863, during the Civil War, antidraft riots broke out in New York City. They were among the most destructive riots in United States history. Armed mobs swarmed through the downtown area to protest the drafting of men into the Union army. The rioters set buildings on fire, looted shops and homes, and shot Negroes, policemen, and federal troops. More than 1,000 persons were killed or wounded.

Labor riots of the late 1800's and early 1900's caused great bloodshed. Dozens of persons were killed in riots in several cities during the great railroad strikes of 1877 (see LABOR [The Knights of Labor]). The Haymarket riot of 1886 in Chicago erupted when someone threw a bomb into a group of anarchists who were protesting police tactics against strikers at an industrial plant (see HAYMARKET RIOT). In 1919 workers' efforts to unionize the steel industry were marked by violence at plants in Indiana, Ohio, and Pennsylvania. In 1934, a dispute between unions and management in the cotton-textile industry led to riots in Georgia, South Carolina, Alabama, Rhode Island, Connecticut, and several other states. These riots took about 20 lives.

Race riots in the United States have been especially violent and destructive. Violence aimed at Negroes and abolitionists broke out in several Northern cities before the Civil War. After the war, in 1866, white Southerners attacked Negroes in New Orleans and Memphis. During the early 1900's, attempts to segregate Southern Negroes and keep them from voting led to lynchings in rural areas and riots in cities.

During World War I (1914-1918), many Negroes moved to the North to work in defense factories. White persons feared that Negroes would take their jobs and move into their neighborhoods. The blacks claimed that white law officers treated them unfairly. These grievances led to many clashes between whites and Negroes. The worst one occurred in 1917 in East St. Louis, Ill., where a riot took the lives of 39 Negroes and 9 whites. A riot in Chicago in 1919 caused 38 deaths and over 500 injuries. Racial violence broke out during World War II (1939-1945). The most destructive riot occurred in 1943 in Detroit, where 34 persons died.

The 1960's. Many riots erupted in United States cities during the 1960's, largely as a result of the economic deprivation and social injustices suffered by ghetto Negroes. The most destructive riots included those in the Watts section of Los Angeles in 1965, in Detroit and Newark in 1967, and in Cleveland in 1968. The Detroit riot was the most violent. It led to 43 deaths, more than 600 injuries, about 7,000 arrests, and property damage of about $45 million.

After the Detroit riot, President Lyndon B. Johnson established the National Advisory Commission on Civil Disorders to study the causes of urban riots. The commission put much of the blame on the racial prejudice and discrimination of whites against blacks. In 1968, Johnson established a related commission, the National Commission on the Causes and Prevention of Violence.

In 1968, riots broke out during the Democratic National Convention in Chicago. Thousands of young people assembled in downtown Chicago. Many were protesting the nation's part in the Vietnam War. They were also demonstrating for the presidential nomination of Senator Eugene J. McCarthy of Minnesota, a major critic of the war. Other demonstrators included revolutionists and anarchists who dissented from society generally. Several bloody clashes took place between demonstrators and the police, but no one was killed.

During the late 1960's, student riots occurred in many cities throughout the world, including New York City, Montreal, Mexico City, Berlin, London, Paris, and Tokyo. Most of these riots were planned by middle-class students who demanded a greater voice in the administration of their schools. In the United States, militant black students also used violence in efforts to enforce their demands, which included the addition of Afro-American history and culture courses.

A chief tactic of the students was to seize a university building and control it until the school gave in to their demands. City or campus police often used force to remove the rebels. This action tended to create sympathy for the rebels among other students, and to strengthen resentment against the university administration.   MARVIN E. WOLFGANG

See also MACE.

Brown Bros.

Rip Van Winkle fills his pipe and listens patiently while his wife scolds him for his easygoing manner and way of living.

RIP VAN WINKLE is one of America's best-known and best-loved folklore characters. In the *Sketch Book* (1819), Washington Irving wrote the story of this cheerful ne'er-do-well who prefers hunting and fishing to farming and his wife's nagging. On one of his jaunts, Rip joins in drunken revels and falls asleep for 20 years. When he awakens and returns to his village, he finds his wife has died, and everything changed in American political life. He is at first ridiculed. But his children recognize him, and the village people reinstate him. The story blends folklore and European legend. Joseph Jefferson, an American actor, won fame playing Rip in a play he wrote with Dion Boucicault.   B. A. BOTKIN

See also IRVING, WASHINGTON (picture).

RIPARIAN RIGHTS, *rih PAIR ih un*, are the legal rights of a landowner whose property borders or forms the bed of a stream or river. Each riparian owner has a right to the flow of water in the stream, and to use it reasonably. His permission is required for any increase or decrease in the flow, any move to change the flow's direction, or any action that would make the water dirty. The riparian owner may own the land extending to the center of the bed of a stream, or only to the usual high watermark along a navigable stream.

In western states with scarce water supplies, riparian rights are either limited or do not exist. In these states, reasonable use of water by riparian owners has been replaced by the right of *prior appropriation*. This right gives legal use of the water to the person who takes it first. Other persons may use any remaining water. The term *riparian* comes from the Latin word *ripa*, which means *riverbank*.   ROBERT E. SULLIVAN

RIPLEY, GEORGE. See BROOK FARM.

RIPLEY, ROBERT LEROY (1893-1949), an American cartoonist, became famous by collecting odd and unusual facts. He started a cartoon feature, *Believe It or Not*, in December, 1918. It still appears in more than 350 newspapers throughout the world. Many of the cartoons were collected in two *Believe It or Not* books. Ripley was born in Santa Rosa, Calif.   DICK SPENCER III

RIPON COLLEGE is a private, coeducational liberal arts school at Ripon, Wis. Liberal arts courses include languages and literature, history and philosophy, the social and physical sciences, mathematics, music, art, and drama. Ripon was founded in 1851. For enrollment, see UNIVERSITIES AND COLLEGES (table).

RIPOSTE. See FENCING.

RIPUARIAN. See FRANK.

RITCHIE, SIR WILLIAM JOHNSTONE (1813-1892), served from 1879 to 1892 as the second chief justice of

Robert Ripley gathered odd and unusual facts from all parts of the world for his famous cartoon series, *Believe It or Not.*
Culver

the Supreme Court of Canada. His judgments often displayed his astonishing legal knowledge and his capacity for careful argument. Ritchie originally opposed the creation of a supreme court of Canada, but he accepted appointment to it in 1875. He was born in Nova Scotia of a family that had the reputation of contributing more eminent men to the legal profession than any other in Canada.   J. E. HODGETTS

RITSCHL, ALBRECHT (1822-1889), a German theologian, influenced many liberal European, British, and American preachers and teachers. He tried to show that the "values" of Jesus' teachings could be true even though modern science questioned many basic parts of the New Testament. He wrote many books, including *Justification and Reconciliation* (1872). Ritschl was born in Berlin.   L. J. TRINTERUD

RITTENHOUSE, DAVID (1732-1796), of Philadelphia, was a leading astronomer, mathematician, and clockmaker. In 1769, he measured the earth's distance from the sun. Astronomers used his measurements to determine the distance of other planets from the sun. Rittenhouse built a precise model of the solar system in 1770. In 1782, he built a pendulum that made clocks more accurate. He became the first director of the United States Mint in 1792. He was president of the American Philosophical Society from 1791 to 1796, and was elected to the British Royal Society in 1795. He was born in Germantown, Pa.   S. K. STEVENS

RITTER, JOSEPH CARDINAL (1892-1967), archbishop of St. Louis, became a cardinal of the Roman Catholic Church in January, 1961. He was ordained a priest in 1917. He became bishop of Indianapolis in 1934, and archbishop in 1944. In 1946, he was named archbishop of St. Louis, and soon integrated the city's Catholic schools. Ritter was a leading American liberal at the Vatican Council of the early 1960's. He was born in New Albany, Ind., and studied for the priesthood at St. Meinrad Seminary in Indiana.   THOMAS P. NEILL

RITTER, KARL (1779-1859), a German geographer, did much to make geography a scientific study. He wrote *Earth Science in Relation to Nature and to the History of Man* (1817-1818). Its 19 volumes describe the surface and resources of Asia and Africa, and show how they influenced the progress of races and nations. He also wrote *Europe, a Geographical, Historical, and Statistical View* (1804-1807), developing similar ideas for Europe.

Ritter was born in Quedlinburg, Germany, and studied in Halle. He served as a tutor in Frankfurt, lived in Göttingen and Berlin, and traveled throughout Europe. In 1820, he became the first professor of geography at the University of Berlin.   J. RUSSELL WHITAKER

RITTY, JAMES (1836-1918), an American restaurant owner, invented the cash register. While traveling to Europe in 1878, he saw a device for counting the revolutions of the ship's propellers. When he returned home, he devised a similar machine to record business transactions. In 1879, he and his brother John built and patented a gear-operated adding machine. Later they built a simpler paper-punch register. The Rittys sold the business in 1881. James Ritty was born in Dayton, Ohio.   ROBERT P. MULTHAUF

RIVADAVIA, BERNARDINO. See ARGENTINA (Early Struggles).

RIVER. Many interesting things can be learned about a river by observing a dirt roadway after a heavy rain. Drops of water collect into little rills. These unite with others to form larger rills, and a number of these unite and form a main stream that carries the water into the ditch. Each tiny stream wears a channel, or bed, in the soft earth. The raindrops that flow in one stream are separated from those flowing in another by a little ridge or a tiny hill. The top of the ridge forms a "watershed" in the little landscape. No matter how large a river may be, it has been formed in much the same way as the stream flowing down the road.

Parts of a River

A river usually begins far up in the mountains or hills. Its source is generally a small spring or a melting glacier. As the river flows on, other streams join it and it continues to increase in size. The river wears itself a channel. The bottom of the channel is known as the *bed* of the stream, and the sides are the *banks*. The *right* bank of a river is on the right when you are looking downstream, and the *left* bank is on your left. A river and all its *tributaries*, or branches, make up a *river system*. A *distributary* is a river branch flowing *out* of the main stream and not rejoining it. The area from which a river system drains is called the river *basin*.

The basin of the Mississippi River, for instance, includes the section of the United States that is drained by the river and its tributaries. The volume, or size, of a river depends upon the area of its basin and the amount of rainfall in the region. Ridges of land that separate rivers and river systems are called *divides*.

The Course of a river is usually divided into three parts—the upper, middle, and lower courses. These parts are usually of different length, and each has distinctive characteristics of a river.

In the *upper course* the slope, called the *gradient*, of the channel is steep, and the current is swift. The slope is usually more than 50 feet to the mile. The channel has been worn down rapidly and the banks have a steep slope. Sometimes the banks are nearly straight up and down. The water carries much sand and gravel and sometimes fairly large, heavy rocks. These are carried swiftly along by the current. They constantly wear away the bed of the stream. The current is so swift that it removes most of the obstacles in its course, and the channel has few small curves. The channels of the tributaries are usually worn down to the level of the main channel, and form deep ditches, or ravines.

The river enters its *middle course* when it leaves the mountains or hills in which it rises and enters the lower lands, where the slope is more gentle. The slope now is usually no more than 10 feet, and often less than 2 feet, to the mile.

The current is not swift enough to carry the heavy material that it has brought down. This material is deposited, or dropped, on the bottom of the channel. For this reason, the beginning of the middle course of many rivers has gravel beds. Since the channel wears more slowly, the slope of the banks is more gentle and the valley is broader. The current has lost much of its speed and must flow around obstacles such as heavy stones or

◀ **The Illinois River** winds through the farm land of central Illinois and empties into the Mississippi River.

LONGEST RIVERS

Approximate length is given in miles

WESTERN HEMISPHERE

River		Length
Colorado	(North America)	1,450
Arkansas	(North America)	1,450
Paraguay	(South America)	1,500
Nelson	(North America)	1,600
Araguaia	(South America)	1,630
Tocantins	(South America)	1,700
Orinoco	(South America)	1,700
São Francisco	(South America)	1,800
Purús	(South America)	1,850
Rio Grande	(North America)	1,885
St. Lawrence	(North America)	1,900
Yukon	(North America)	1,979
Madeira	(South America)	2,000
Missouri	(North America)	2,315
Mississippi	(North America)	2,348
Paraná	(South America)	2,450
Mackenzie	(North America)	2,635
Amazon	(South America)	3,900

Cooper, Black Star

The Amazon River flows from the Andes Mountains through the tropical jungles of Brazil into the Atlantic Ocean. Taxi boats, like these at Iquitos, Peru, ply the Amazon, the second longest river in the world.

EASTERN HEMISPHERE

1,700	(Asia)	Euphrates; (Asia) Indus
1,725	(Europe)	Danube
1,750	(Asia)	Salween
1,770	(Asia)	Syr Darya
1,840	(Asia)	Irtysh
2,290	(Europe)	Volga
2,310	(Australia)	Murray-Darling
2,360	(Asia)	Yenisey
2,500	(Asia)	Ob
2,600	(Africa)	Niger
2,600	(Asia)	Mekong
2,645	(Asia)	Lena
2,700	(Asia)	Hwang Ho
2,700	(Asia)	Amur
2,718	(Africa)	Congo
3,100	(Asia)	Yangtze
4,160	(Africa)	Nile

Ewing Galloway

The Nile rises in East-Central Africa and flows northward into the Mediterranean Sea. It is the longest river in the world. Boats with *lateen sails* (triangular) carry goods and passengers along the Nile.

RIVER

snags. The middle course of the Mississippi illustrates this movement. Obstacles in the middle of the channel collect deposits of silt or mud until these deposits finally reach the surface and form islands. Islands in the upper part of the stream are formed by rocks that the current has been unable to carry along or wear away.

The *lower course* of a river differs only a little from the middle course. The current is somewhat slower, and the continuous deposit of silt raises the bed of the stream. The slope now is only a few inches a mile. The river often overflows the low banks and forms wide flood plains. When these plains are drained, they make productive farms. In the case of the Mississippi, this process of raising the river bed has continued until the river near its mouth is higher than the surrounding countryside. Disastrous floods often occur when the banks break, so the banks must be protected by levees (see LEVEE).

Cataracts and Canyons. Rivers frequently flow over rocks that are not equally hard. When this happens, the softer rock is worn away, leaving the hard rock as an obstacle or obstruction. These conditions usually exist in places where the current is swift, and rapids or cataracts are formed in the river. The cataracts of the Nile River and the rapids in the St. Lawrence River are good illustrations.

When the soft rock lies under a hard layer, a falls such as Niagara is formed. In mountainous regions, the swift current sometimes wears a deep channel with vertical walls, forming a canyon. The Grand Canyon of the Colorado River and the Grand Canyon of the Yellowstone River were formed in this way. The speed of such torrents sometimes reaches 40 miles an hour.

Estuaries and Deltas. A river flowing slowly into a sea that is protected from great waves and high tides drops its silt at its mouth and builds up land there. Such a piece of land is an alluvial plain called a *delta* (see DELTA). The Mississippi and the Nile have large deltas. When the bed of the river in its lower course slopes into the sea, it forms a drowned valley. The tides extend up into the river mouth. The silt is carried away and the mouth of the river remains a broad estuary, like the Gulf of St. Lawrence and the Río de la Plata. Such estuaries form good harbors. Some of the greatest seaports are formed in this way.

The Work of Rivers

Rivers have always been important to man. In early days, they were his chief form of transportation. Today, *navigable rivers* (rivers wide and deep enough for large boats) are vital to transportation.

Rivers also provide water for farmlands and electric power for industries. Many rivers have been dammed to store water for irrigation and to turn the turbines of electric generators. The power of waterfalls is also harnessed to provide electrical energy.

Some rivers are important for the fish they contain. Various minerals, such as gold and quartz, are often taken from river beds.　　　　　LOYAL DURAND, JR.

Related Articles. See the Rivers and Lakes sections in the various country, state, and province articles, such as ALABAMA (Rivers and Lakes). See also the following articles:

AFRICA

Congo River	Nile River	Vaal River
Limpopo River	Orange River	Zambezi River
Niger River	Ubangi River	

ASIA

Abana River	Mekong River
Amu Darya	Narmada River
Amur River	Ob River
Brahmaputra River	Salween River
Euphrates River	Shatt al Arab
Ganges River	Si-kiang
Hooghly River	Sutlej River
Hwang Ho	Syr Darya
Indus River	Tigris River
Irrawaddy River	Ural River
Irtysh River	Yalu River
Jordan River	Yangtze River
Jumna River	Yenisey River
Lena River	

AUSTRALIA

Murray River	Ord River
Murrumbidgee River	

CANADA

Assiniboine River	Peace River
Athabasca River	Red River of the North
Chaudière River	Restigouche River
Churchill River	Richelieu River
Columbia River	Saguenay River
Detroit River	Saint John River
Fraser River	Saint Lawrence River
Kootenay River and District	Saint Marys River
Mackenzie River	Saskatchewan River
Miramichi River	Skeena River
Montmorency River	Slave River, or
Moose River	Great Slave River
Nelson River	Stikine River
Niagara Falls and	Winnipeg River
Niagara River	Yukon River
Ottawa River	

CENTRAL AMERICA

Chagres River

EUROPE

Adige River	Oder River
Aisne River	Oka River
Arno River	Piave River
Avon, River	Po River
Clyde, River	Prut River
Danube River	Rhine River
Dee, River	Rhône River
Derwent, River	Río Tinto
Dnepr River	Rubicon
Dnestr River	Ruhr River
Don River	Saône River
Doon, River	Sava River
Douro River	Schelde River
Dvina River	Seine River
Ebro River	Severn, River
Elbe River	Shannon, River
Garonne River	Somme River
Guadalquivir River	Spree River
Humber, River	Tagus River
Inn River	Tay, River
Isère River	Thames, River
Liffey, River	Tiber River
Loire River	Torne River
Main River	Trent, River
Marne River	Tweed, River
Mersey, River	Ural River
Meuse River	Vistula River
Moselle River	Volga River
Neman River	Volturno River
Neva River	Weser River

HOW RIVERS HAVE INFLUENCED MAN

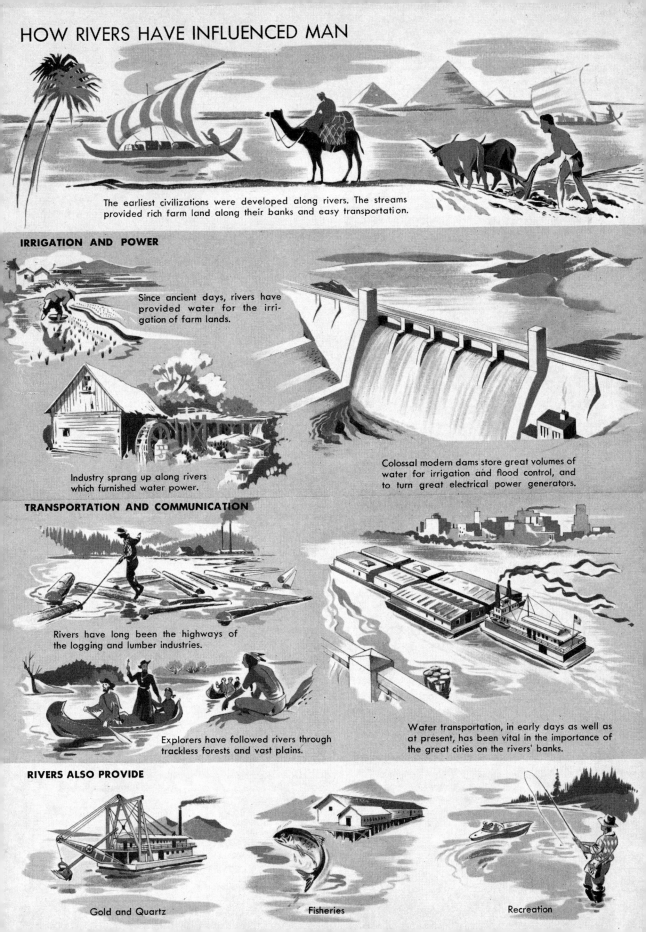

The earliest civilizations were developed along rivers. The streams provided rich farm land along their banks and easy transportation.

IRRIGATION AND POWER

Since ancient days, rivers have provided water for the irrigation of farm lands.

Industry sprang up along rivers which furnished water power.

Colossal modern dams store great volumes of water for irrigation and flood control, and to turn great electrical power generators.

TRANSPORTATION AND COMMUNICATION

Rivers have long been the highways of the logging and lumber industries.

Explorers have followed rivers through trackless forests and vast plains.

Water transportation, in early days as well as at present, has been vital in the importance of the great cities on the rivers' banks.

RIVERS ALSO PROVIDE

Gold and Quartz

Fisheries

Recreation

RIVER

North America

See the articles listed under Canada, Central America, and United States in this section.

South America

Amazon River	Orinoco River	São Francisco,
Araguaia River	Paraguay River	Rio
Iguaçu River	Paraná River	Tapajós
Madeira River	Purús River	Tocantins River
Magdalena River	Rio Negro	Uruguay River

United States

Alabama River	Mohawk River
Allegheny River	Monongahela River
Apalachicola River	Niagara Falls and River
Arkansas River	Ohio River
Aroostook River	Pecos River
Ausable River	Pee Dee, or Yadkin, River
Bighorn River	Penobscot River
Brazos River	Platte River
Canadian River	Potomac River
Chattahoochee River	Powder River
Colorado River	Rappahannock River
Colorado River (Texas)	Raritan River
Columbia River	Red River
Connecticut River	Red River of the North
Coosa River	Rio Grande
Cumberland River	Roanoke River
Delaware River	Rock River
Detroit River	Sabine River
East River	Sacramento River
Genesee River	Saint Marys River
Gila River	Salt River
Green River	San Joaquin River
Housatonic River	Sangamon River
Hudson River	Savannah River
Humboldt River	Schuylkill River
Illinois River	Scioto River
James River	Shenandoah River
Kanawha River	Snake River
Kennebec River	Susquehanna River
Kentucky River	Suwannee River
Klamath River	Tennessee River
Kuskokwim River	Tombigbee River
Lackawanna River	Trinity River
Lehigh River	Wabash River
Licking River	White River
Merrimack River	Willamette River
Miami River	Wisconsin River
Minnesota River	Yazoo River
Mississippi River	Yellowstone River
Missouri River	Yukon River
Mobile River	

Other Related Articles

Alluvial Fan	Delta	Oxbow Lake
Alluvium	Divide	Pothole
Basin	Erosion	Silt
Bayou	Floods and	Styx
Bore	Flood Control	Valley
Canyon	Lagoon	Water Power
Dam	Levee	Waterfall

RIVER—————. Some rivers, particularly those in Great Britain, have names starting with the word *River*, such as River Clyde. See the separate articles for these rivers under the name following the word *River*, for example, CLYDE, RIVER.

RIVER HORSE. See HIPPOPOTAMUS.

RIVERA, *ree VAY rah*, **DIEGO** (1886-1957), was one of the most controversial of Mexico's artists. Early in his career he became a Communist. His favorite themes,

Brown Bros.; European

Diego Rivera, *above,* played an outstanding role in the birth of mural art in Mexico. He drew his themes from his country's revolution and its social problems. The mural, *right,* in Mexico's presidential palace, shows his style.

revolution and labor, appear in his murals in the Ministry of Education in Mexico City. Rivera also became noted for his paintings of children. He was born in Guanajuato, and studied in Europe. When he returned to Mexico, he helped lead a successful campaign to permit Mexican artists to decorate the walls of government buildings.   ROBERT C. SMITH

RIVERA, FRUCTUOSO. See URUGUAY (Civil War).

RIVERA, JULIO ADALBERTO. See EL SALVADOR (National Development).

RIVERA, MIGUEL PRIMO DE. See PRIMO DE RIVERA, MIGUEL.

RIVERS, LARRY (1923-   ), is an American painter. His works suggest the speed, fragmentation, diversity, and rapidly-changing qualities of modern life. Many include passages that look unfinished. Some show parts of the same figure from several points of view.

Rivers' *Washington Crossing the Delaware* shows the artist's individual approach to traditional American subjects.

The Museum of Modern Art, New York City

Rivers likes to take familiar American themes, such as cigarette advertisements or the painting of Washington crossing the Delaware, and paint them as lively, active scenes. The figures in Rivers' paintings are deliberately unidealistic, as in his series showing elderly Civil War veterans lying in bed under Confederate flags. However, his paintings are not satirical, but have an amusing, ironical tongue-in-cheek flavor.

Rivers was born in New York City. He studied with the painter Hans Hofmann.　　　ALLEN S. WELLER

See also PAINTING (picture: *Forty Feet of Fashion*).

RIVERSIDE, Calif. (pop. 140,089; alt. 875 ft.), is a manufacturing, agricultural, and educational center about 50 miles east of Los Angeles (see CALIFORNIA [map]). Chief products include aircraft engines and instruments, aluminum products, food-packing equipment, metal cookingware, and paint. Riverside lies in a region of great citrus groves, and serves as an important distributing point for navel oranges. The city is the home of a branch of the University of California, the La Sierra campus of Loma Linda University, California Baptist College and Riverside City College. Founded in 1870, Riverside was incorporated in 1883. It is the seat of Riverside County, and has a council-manager government. With San Bernardino and Ontario, Riverside has a metropolitan area of 1,140,609.　　GEORGE SHAFTEL

RIVETING is a method of joining two metal plates with threadless aluminum, iron, or steel bolts called *rivets*. A rivet has a rounded head at one end.

In riveting, a worker called a *rivet boy* heats rivets in a small portable forge. When the rivets become red hot, the rivet boy removes them from the forge with small tongs and throws or passes them to another worker called the *holder up*. The holder up inserts the rivets in holes that have been drilled or punched in two metal plates. The rivets are long enough to extend through both plates. The holder up places an *anvil* or *bucking bar* against the rounded head of the bolt. Then another worker, called the *riveter*, uses a pneumatic hammer to close and shape the *tail*, or open end of the rivet. When rivets are compressed and joined in this way, they become double-ended bolts that hold the plates firmly together.

Ordinarily, only one row of rivets is used. This is called *single* riveting. Riveters sometimes use *double* riveting, or two rows, when extra strength is needed. Workmen can punch holes in soft metals. But they must drill the rivet holes in thick pieces or hard metals.

Sometimes devices other than pneumatic hammers are used to shape and close rivets. Machine shops often use large hydraulic presses for riveting. A *riveting machine* has the anvil and the hammer joined together by a hinge or solid yoke. The anvil holds the rivet in place, and the hammer closes and shapes the tail.

In *cold heading*, riveters use soft iron rivets that are shaped and closed while cold. The cold forming of the soft metal increases its strength. The aircraft industry commonly uses cold heading on the aluminum wing and body surfaces of airplanes.

Welding has replaced riveting for many uses. But riveting is still the accepted method in making boilers and erecting structural steel for buildings. It is also necessary in shipbuilding. WILLIAM G. N. HEER

RIVIER COLLEGE is a school for women at Nashua, N.H. It is conducted by the Catholic Sisters of the Presentation of Mary. Rivier has schools of arts and sciences, with departments of education, home economics, business administration, and nursing. For the enrollment of Rivier College, see UNIVERSITIES AND COLLEGES (table).

RIVIERA, *ree VYEH rah*, is a narrow strip of land on the Mediterranean. The region runs from Hyères in southern France to La Spezia in northwestern Italy. The Alps rise back of the Riviera. Travelers from many parts of the world have basked in the warm sunshine of the Riviera for both health and pleasure. Balmy southern breezes drift in from the sea throughout the year, and the Alps shut off the cold north and east winds.

A chain of French and Italian towns lies on the Riviera. They are connected by an excellent road that

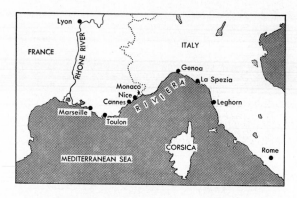

The Riviera Lies on the Mediterranean.

follows an ancient Roman highway. A railroad also links the towns together. The towns are colorful with brightly painted houses and green, fragrant gardens. The people of the Riviera cultivate flowers, dates, bananas, pomegranates, and prickly pears.

The Riviera towns include Nice and Menton, in France; Monaco and Monte Carlo, in Monaco; and Bordighera, Ospedaletti, San Remo, Rapallo, Genoa, and La Spezia, in Italy. BENJAMIN WEBB WHEELER

See also CÔTE D'AZUR; FRANCE (picture); MONACO; NICE.

RIYADH, *ree YAHD* (pop. 225,000; alt. 1,897 ft.), is the capital of Saudi Arabia. It also serves as the capital of the political division of Nejd. *Riyadh* is Arabic for *many meadows.* The city lies in east-central Saudi Arabia on the Nejd Plateau (see SAUDI ARABIA [map]).

The vast, whitewashed royal palaces and great mosque dominate this ancient city. Riyadh also serves as a trading center and an agricultural market for the dates, grain, and vegetables grown in the oasis nearby. The Saudi Arabian government railway connects Riyadh with Ad Dammām, a city on the Persian Gulf.

Riyadh is at least 3,000 years old. Between 1902 and 1925, the Arab leader Ibn Saud used the city as a base to conquer neighboring provinces and form what is now Saudi Arabia. DOUGLAS D. CRARY

RIZAL. See PASAY.

RIZAL, *ree ZAHL,* **JOSÉ** (1861-1896), was a member of the Young Filipino Party, which demanded reforms in the Spanish administration of the Philippine islands. He fled to Europe, and on his return was banished to the island of Mindanao. In December, 1896, he was arrested and shot. Rizal was born near Manila. He won fame for his work in medicine and economics and for his poetry and political satires. DONALD E. WORCESTER

RIZZIO, DAVID. See MARY, QUEEN OF SCOTS.

RLF. See RETROLENTAL FIBROPLASIA.

RNA. See NUCLEIC ACID; CELL (Producing Proteins; RNA—The Master Copy).

ROACH. See COCKROACH.

ROACH is a fish of the carp family that lives in fresh waters of Europe. This fish usually grows about 5 inches long, but may reach a length of 12 inches. It is silvery, with a greenish back. The name *roach* is also given to a large American minnow called the *golden shiner.*

Scientific Classification. The roach belongs to the carp family, *Cyprinidae.* The European roach is genus *Rutilus,* species *R. rutilus.* CARL L. HUBBS

Jane Burton, Bruce Coleman Ltd.
The Roach is a slow-swimming fish that lives along the banks of fresh-water streams and rivers. It is found only in Europe.

ROAD MAP is a drawing that shows the locations and names of cities and towns, and the roads and highways that connect them.

Reading a Road Map is somewhat like being in an airplane and looking down on the land below. But a road map usually shows a larger area than can be seen clearly from an airplane.

Most road maps include a legend in one corner that lists the symbols used on the map. These legends usually provide the following kinds of information: (1) how to tell roads with different kinds of surfaces; (2) how to tell which roads are better than others; (3) how to determine the differences between local, state, and interstate road numbers; (4) how to find the distances between various towns, cities, and other points of interest; (5) how to judge the sizes of cities and towns on the map; and (6) how to identify other important landmarks.

For general information on using a map, see MAP (How to Read a Map).

HOW TO USE A ROAD MAP

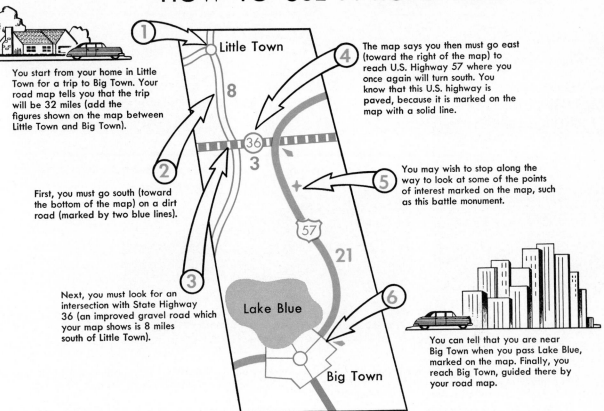

You start from your home in Little Town for a trip to Big Town. Your road map tells you that the trip will be 32 miles (add the figures shown on the map between Little Town and Big Town).

First, you must go south (toward the bottom of the map) on a dirt road (marked by two blue lines).

Next, you must look for an intersection with State Highway 36 (an improved gravel road which your map shows is 8 miles south of Little Town).

The map says you then must go east (toward the right of the map) to reach U.S. Highway 57 where you once again will turn south. You know that this U.S. highway is paved, because it is marked on the map with a solid line.

You may wish to stop along the way to look at some of the points of interest marked on the map, such as this battle monument.

You can tell that you are near Big Town when you pass Lake Blue, marked on the map. Finally, you reach Big Town, guided there by your road map.

Sources of Road Maps. Gasoline service stations provide the greatest distribution of free road maps for motorists. Oil companies give away millions of maps each year through stations that sell their products. Large map-making companies compile and publish most of the road maps. Automobile clubs also prepare road maps for their members. State highway departments often publish and give away free road maps of their own states. Map manufacturers estimate that approximately 200 million road maps are used by motorists throughout the world each year.

History. Beginning in the 1880's, bicycling clubs began to publish some road maps. But as a rule, early motorists had to depend on written instructions from their automobile clubs. Directions of this kind might say something like "drive $3\frac{1}{2}$ miles until you come to a little white church, then take the left fork in the road."

Road maps were first published in large quantities for sale to the public about 1910. William B. Akin, a Pittsburgh, Pa., advertising man, generally is credited with developing the idea of the free road map in 1914. As a result of his idea, an oil company distributed many free road maps the following year. DUNCAN M. FITCHET

See also ROADS AND HIGHWAYS.

ROAD RUNNER is a swift-footed bird of the cuckoo family. It lives in the southwestern United States and in northern Mexico. It is also called the *chaparral cock* or *hen, ground cuckoo,* and *snake killer.* The name *road runner* refers to its habit of racing down a road in front of travelers. The road runner is the state bird of New Mexico.

The road runner is nearly two feet long, and has long legs with two toes at the front and two in the back. It builds its nest of sticks in low trees or bushes. The female lays from two to nine whitish eggs. The road runner eats insects, mice, lizards, snails, young snakes, and some fruits. It is noted for its attacks on snakes.

Scientific Classification. The road runner belongs to the cuckoo family, *Cuculidae.* It is genus *Geococcyx,* species *G. californianus.* HERBERT FRIEDMANN

See also BIRD (color picture: Birds That Help Us).

A Road Runner with a whip-tailed lizard in its bill perches on a cactus branch before flying to its nearby nest.
Wide World

ROADS AND HIGHWAYS

Local Road

Secondary Road

Primary Highway

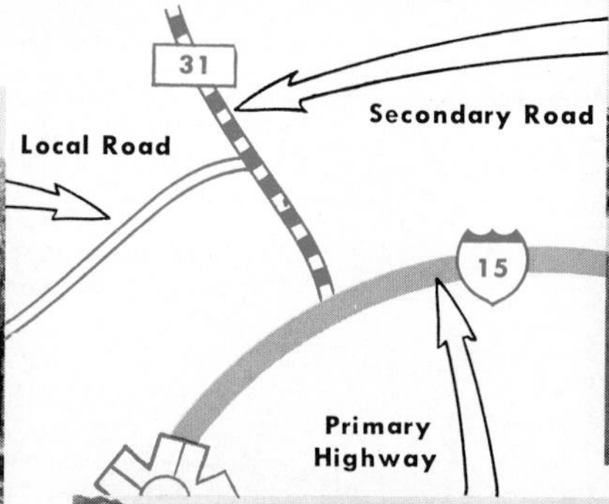

Illinois State Division of Highways

California State Division of Highways

Illinois State Division of Highways

ROADS AND HIGHWAYS are strips of land that provide routes for travel by automobiles and other wheeled vehicles. Roads usually connect urban areas with each other and rural areas with urban areas. Roads within towns and cities are called *streets* (see STREET).

Roads and highways are vital lifelines. Without adequate roads, farmers could not ship their products to market. Trucks could not carry manufactured products from one area to another. Good roads and highways provide escape routes to and from cities and towns in case of a disaster. Good roads carry millions of passenger automobiles that travel on business and pleasure.

Kinds of Roads and Highways

There are more than 3,160,000 miles of U.S. surfaced and unsurfaced roads and highways. Every year the United States spends billions of dollars to build new roads and to improve existing roads. Canada has about 450,000 miles of surfaced and unsurfaced roads.

Local and Secondary Roads make up about three-fourths of the roads in the United States. *Local roads* carry traffic within a local area. *Secondary roads* link small communities and connect local roads to main highways leading to more distant places. Most local and secondary roads are built and maintained by local governments, such as counties and townships.

Primary Highways. The most important roads generally are those that carry the greatest number of automobiles, trucks, and buses. These main roads, called *primary highways*, connect the larger communities. Most of these are built and cared for by state governments.

The federal government helps the states pay the

cost of building and improving primary and secondary roads and streets. The routes are selected by the states.

Some highways with four or more traffic lanes are divided in the center with a strip of land, called a *median strip*. This strip separates lines of traffic going in opposite directions and helps prevent collisions.

Another important factor in safety and smooth traffic flow is the principle of *controlled access*. This means that a vehicle can enter or leave a main highway only at certain locations called *interchanges*. These interchanges are usually located at main crossroads. *Grade separations*

──── **Roads and Highways in the United States** ────
(Excludes Streets)

Year	Miles		
	SURFACED	UNSURFACED	TOTAL
1909	190,000	2,010,000	2,200,000
1921	387,000	2,538,000	2,925,000
1930	694,000	2,315,000	3,009,000
1940	1,340,000	1,650,000	2,990,000*
1950	1,678,619	1,311,417	2,990,036*
1955	1,942,413	1,102,852	3,045,265
1960	2,165,468	950,657	3,116,125
1961	2,179,499	947,726	3,127,225
1962	2,228,570	915,767	3,144,337
1963	2,252,647	892,858	3,145,505
1964	2,271,886	880,691	3,152,577
1965	2,302,119	881,101	3,183,220
1966	2,321,154	866,561	3,187,715
1967	2,336,433	847,278	3,183,711*
1968	2,361,855	790,192	3,152,047*
1969	2,391,325	770,401	3,161,726*

*Total mileage in these years, is less than in previous years for three reasons: (1) roads were straightened by rebuilding in new locations; (2) cities and towns expanded and former roads became streets; and (3) unused roads were abandoned.

Source: Federal Highway Administration

This article was critically reviewed by the Federal Highway Administration.

are often used to separate crossing streams of traffic. In a grade separation, one of the intersecting highways crosses over the other on a bridge. The two are connected by sloping, curved roadways called *ramps*.

With controlled access, no driveways from homes or commercial establishments connect directly with the main highway. Minor roads and streets run over or under the road without connecting to it. Minor roads may also dead-end at the highway or connect with a service road that runs parallel to the highway.

Freeways, sometimes called *superhighways*, are main highways with full access control and grade-separated interchanges. Those with four or more lanes are divided by a median strip. Freeways in congested parts of big cities are often *elevated* (built above surface streets) or *depressed* (built below surface streets). The term *freeway* refers only to the free flow of traffic. Motorists may have to pay a toll to travel on these roads.

Expressways are similar to freeways but sometimes have only partial access control. *Parkways* are roads resembling freeways. But they are built in park-like surroundings with attractive landscaping and scenery. Most parkways are limited to passenger cars.

Federal Interstate Highway System is a 42,755-mile network of freeways scheduled for completion in the 1970's. The official name for this network is the *National System of Interstate and Defense Highways*. When this system is completed, it will connect more than 90 per cent of the U.S. cities with populations over 50,000. It will carry about 20 per cent of all road and street traffic in the United States. The map with this article shows this highway system.

Main Paved State Highways
(Excludes City Streets)

Year	Miles		
	TOTAL	MORE THAN 2 LANES	DIVIDED ROADS
1957	356,106	15,429	8,516
1959	370,679	19,565	12,450
1961	379,287	23,295	16,448
1963	386,692	27,484	21,310
1965	394,125	33,139	27,104
1967	405,206	37,878	32,641
1968	407,196	40,538	35,373
1969	392,767*	43,138	38,041

*Total mileage in 1969 is less than in previous years because of the transfer of some state primary (main) roads to the secondary system.

Source: Federal Highway Administration

Highways and their continuations through cities are numbered by the states to help guide people. These numbers appear along roads on black-and-white shield-shaped "U.S." route signs. The interstate highway system is marked with red, white, and blue shield-shaped signs. In the "U.S." and interstate systems, east-west routes have even numbers and north-south routes have odd numbers. The lowest numbered "U.S." routes are in the north and east. The lowest numbered interstate routes are in the south and west.

How Roads and Highways Are Built

Planning. Highway planners study everything from the long-range needs of a state or the entire country to a particular section of a single route. This planning

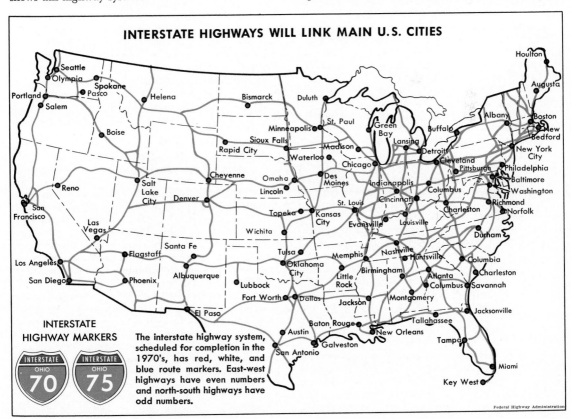

INTERSTATE HIGHWAYS WILL LINK MAIN U.S. CITIES

INTERSTATE HIGHWAY MARKERS

The interstate highway system, scheduled for completion in the 1970's, has red, white, and blue route markers. East-west highways have even numbers and north-south highways have odd numbers.

Federal Highway Administration

335

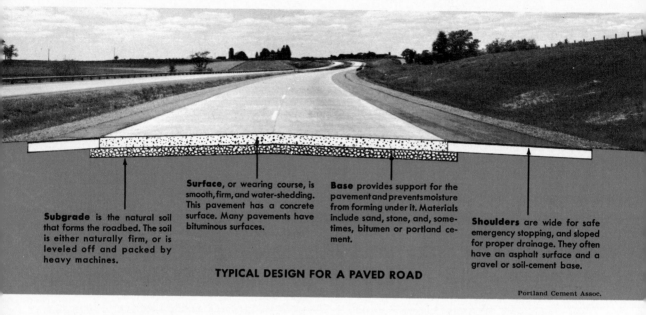

Subgrade is the natural soil that forms the roadbed. The soil is either naturally firm, or is leveled off and packed by heavy machines.

Surface, or wearing course, is smooth, firm, and water-shedding. This pavement has a concrete surface. Many pavements have bituminous surfaces.

Base provides support for the pavement and prevents moisture from forming under it. Materials include sand, stone, and, sometimes, bitumen or portland cement.

Shoulders are wide for safe emergency stopping, and sloped for proper drainage. They often have an asphalt surface and a gravel or soil-cement base.

TYPICAL DESIGN FOR A PAVED ROAD

Portland Cement Assoc.

determines what the highway needs are, as well as how these needs can best be fulfilled and paid for.

The United States needs better roads, capable of carrying more traffic with greater safety and speed, and lower vehicle-operation costs. As a result, much U.S. highway work is devoted to improving present roads or replacing them. Relatively few new roads are being built. Most of the new roads are freeways and highways serving new suburban developments.

In planning a system or a route, planners must learn: (1) where people live, (2) where they want to go, (3) how they get there, (4) where goods are produced, (5) what markets the goods are sent to, and (6) how the goods reach their final users. Traffic counts tell how many and what kinds of vehicles travel on a road, and when traffic is heaviest. From these and other facts about the past and present, planners can forecast the future. They can predict probable future growth in population and industry, changes in land use, and how such growth and change will affect highway needs.

Highway engineers have drawn up standards for various kinds of roads, highways, and bridges. These standards govern the thickness and kind of foundation and surfacing for different kinds of traffic; the number of lanes needed; the sharpness of curves; and the steepness of hills. For example, engineers agree that most highway lanes should be at least 11 feet wide.

In planning a new road or rebuilding an existing one, maps must be drawn if they are not already available. Aerial photography is widely used today for this work. These maps show the location of other roads, railroads, towns, farms, houses, and other buildings. They also show such natural features as rivers, lakes, forests, hills, and the slope of the land. The types of soil may also be identified.

Using these maps, engineers locate new highways and make detailed drawings called *plans*. The plans show the exact boundaries of the *right-of-way*. This is land needed for road pavement, shoulders, ditches, and side slopes. The plans also show the exact location, grades,

and curves of the pavement, and the location of bridges and culverts.

Bypasses are built to take motorists around cities. Motorists traveling some distance often do not want to drive through small towns or the centers of large cities that lie on their routes. Those traveling from one part of a city to another also usually prefer to avoid downtown traffic. The bypass helps these motorists avoid city traffic, and reduces traffic congestion for those who want to drive into town. Bypasses today are usually built as freeways, sometimes with service roads on one or both sides to serve local traffic. In large cities, a bypass may be called a *circumferential* or a *beltway*.

Intersections are crossings of one road by another. Most intersections are at the same level, so that vehicles going east and west have to take turns crossing with vehicles going north and south. Sometimes roads intersect at odd angles and it is especially difficult to make a safe crossing. At such places, the traffic engineer may put *islands* in the paved area to keep traffic in the proper paths. The best and safest kind of intersection is the grade-separated interchange. One common type of interchange is called a *cloverleaf*, because its curved inner ramps form the pattern of a four-leaf clover. A simpler kind is called a *diamond* because its ramps form that shape. Diamonds often connect a major highway and a secondary road. When two freeways intersect, more complex interchanges are sometimes needed. These may require a number of bridges and many ramp roadways.

Grading. The first job in building a new highway is to clear the right-of-way. There may be trees to cut down and stumps to pull up. Sometimes buildings have to be torn down or moved. The right-of-way then is ready for rough grading. Here is where other big machines begin to work. Huge earth movers, which can dig up a roomful of dirt in one scoop, are used. They cut into the hills, carry the earth along, and drop it into the valleys to make a road with gentle grades.

Sometimes, the right kind of earth to be used for

336

the foundation of the road must be hauled in, perhaps from some distance away. While the grading is going on, *culverts*, or pipes to carry away rain water, are put in place under the road or under driveway entrances. Ditches are cut at the roadsides to carry rain water to the culverts. After the right-of-way is shaped roughly for traffic lanes, shoulders, and ditches, it is smoothed and packed down to the required level and shape.

Surfacing begins after grading is completed. The surface is of definite thickness and is of stronger materials than the earth underneath. The kind and thickness of road surfaces depend largely on the weight and amount of traffic expected to use them.

In some places, different kinds of earth or soil are mixed together to form a surface. Certain chemicals, lime, cement, or *bitumens* (asphalts and tars) may also be mixed with soil to act as a binder and to make it harder and more durable. On most of the low-traffic surfaced roads, however, the surfaces are of gravel, crushed rock, oyster shells, or other mineral materials. These types of surfacing may be given a thin coating of bitumens known as *seal coat*.

Roads that carry heavy traffic must have a durable surface, called *pavement*. An intermediate type of pavement is called *bituminous macadam*. This is made by placing crushed stone or gravel on the roadbed, packing it down firmly, and filling the spaces with a bitumen. Better types of bituminous pavements are made with sand, gravel, or crushed stone premixed with bitumens. They are laid with a paving machine, and then rolled hard and smooth. Bituminous pavement is sometimes referred to as *blacktop*.

Another hard surfacing material is portland cement concrete. It is made with sand, portland cement, water, and gravel or crushed stone. In both kinds of pavement —bituminous and portland cement concrete—the *aggregate* (stone and sand) forms the body of the material and the bitumen or portland cement serves as a binder.

Lighting. Good lighting helps cut accidents for both vehicles and pedestrians. On most roads and highways, nearly all the light comes from the headlights of

the trucks and cars. But on busy streets and at dangerous rural locations, overhead lights are used. Highway lights usually are placed on poles spaced about 200 feet apart along both sides of the highway. Reflectors for the lamps are designed specifically to shine most of the light down on the roadway without glaring into the eyes of drivers.

Roadside Improvement. Roadsides are often planted with special grasses or vines to keep the earth from washing into the ditches. Often roadsides are beautified with trees and bushes. Such planting and landscaping help break the monotony of travel and make the countryside more attractive. Many states have laws which prohibit putting billboards and other commercial signs close to the road. Most states provide turnouts from highways where picnics can be held or where tourists can admire a scenic view.

Tests and Research. Most highway testing falls into one of five groups: soils, materials, equipment, construction, or research. Soil testing is done to find out how soils change when they are dry or wet. Tests show how heavy a load the soil can support.

As roads are built, they are inspected continually and tests are made on materials being used. Even after a road or highway is finished, drilling machines take sample *cores* out of the pavement. These samples are removed from the pavement much as you take the core out of an apple. Pavement cores show how thick the finished pavement is. Tests on the cores also tell how strong the pavement is.

The federal government cooperates with the state highway departments in a national program of highway research and development. The program includes every aspect of highway work, from planning to traffic control and road maintenance.

How Roads and Highways Are Maintained

Repairing Damage and Resurfacing. Roads and highways gradually wear out. The work of repairing

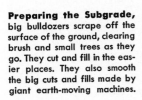

Preparing the Subgrade, big bulldozers scrape off the surface of the ground, clearing brush and small trees as they go. They cut and fill in the easier places. They also smooth the big cuts and fills made by giant earth-moving machines.

and resurfacing is called *maintenance*. Maintenance also includes removing ice and snow, painting stripes on pavement, cutting grass, putting up signs, and caring for roadside shoulders, roadsides, and bridges.

Gravel and other similar type roads have to be smoothed quite often. Every few years, gravel and similar surfaces require new coverings to replace the material that has blown, washed, or worn away.

Surfaces and edges of bituminous materials are repaired by patching with new material where worn spots develop from travel or because of weak spots in the ground underneath. Most bituminous surfaces have to have a new seal coating from time to time. Every 10 or 15 years many of them are resurfaced completely.

Concrete pavements are repaired by digging out broken places and putting in new concrete. Cracks are often repaired by filling them with asphalt. Many older concrete pavements are resurfaced completely. In some cases, sections, or slabs, of concrete pavement settle unevenly into the ground. These slabs sometimes are *mud-jacked* back into place. This is done by drilling holes through the slab, then pumping in liquid asphalt or cement under great pressure. As the liquid is forced in, it pushes the pavement back up into place.

Clearing Ice and Snow. Most roads and highways must serve all year around. So they must be kept free from snow and ice in the winter. In some places *snow fences* are put up. These are thin pickets wired together and placed parallel to the road, on the side from which

Money Spent for Roads and Highways in the U.S.
(Excludes Streets)

Year	Dollars
1921	$ 996,000,000
1930	1,681,000,000
1940	1,767,000,000
1950	3,011,000,000
1960	7,139,000,000
1966	10,050,000,000
1967	10,464,000,000
1968	11,272,000,000
1969	11,793,000,000
1970 (estimate)	12,846,000,000

Source: Federal Highway Administration

the storm winds usually blow, and about 50 to 100 feet from the road. Snowdrifts then form between the fence and the road instead of piling up in the road.

Trucks with V-shaped or straight blade plows attached to the front clear the roads when it starts to snow. In deep drifts, special snowplows are needed. Some of the most powerful are called *rotary plows*. They have a big screw at the front which chews into the snowdrifts and pulls the snow back into a large fan. This shoots the snow to one side of the road.

Often roads and highways which are slippery from ice and snow must have salt, chemicals, sand, or cinders spread on them to keep them passable.

How Roads and Highways Are Paid For

Roads and highways are built and maintained by the various governments—federal, state, county, township.

Blacktop Pavement Being Laid on a State Highway. Asphalt cement and crushed stone were heated and mixed in the contractor's plant. This mix then was carried by truck to the proj- ect. It was dumped into a mechanical paving machine, *left*, which lays the pavement to the desired thickness. A compacting machine, *right*, rolls the pavement smooth and hard.

The Texas Co.

Concrete Pavement Being Laid by an "Equipment Train."
(1) Concrete is poured into forms on top of the base course.
(2) A spreader levels off the concrete. (3) Finishers smooth the surface. (4) Men with brushes roughen the surface slightly so automobile tires can get a good grip on it. (5) The pavement is covered with heavy paper so it will not dry too rapidly.

State and Local Financing. State and local communities pay for road building and maintenance with tax receipts. Much of this money comes from taxes levied on highway and road users. Every state levies taxes on motor fuel and charges fees for registering motor vehicles. In some states, trucks and buses pay special fees. For example, some states levy a *weight-distance* or a *ton-mile* tax. This tax requires trucks to pay a set amount, based on the tonnage of the load and the number of miles it is carried.

Most highway-user taxes are spent only for roads and streets. Using this tax money for other purposes is called *diversion*. For example, some states set aside part of their motor fuel tax money for welfare or education. Constitutional amendments in many states prohibit diversion.

Most states give part of the taxes they collect from highway users to local governments, to be spent on local roads. The local governments provide whatever additional money they need for roads, usually from general funds raised by property taxes.

State and local governments often borrow money to build roads. These loans, made by selling *bonds*, are repaid with money collected from taxes. States sometimes set aside part of their motor fuel tax money to repay these loans.

The cost of building many bridges and *turnpikes* (toll highways) is paid by the travelers who use them. Motorists pay a flat fee for crossing toll bridges. Fees for using turnpikes usually depend on how far the motorist travels. Large vehicles such as trucks and trailers usually pay more than passenger cars.

Federal Financing. Since 1916, the federal government has been aiding states in building and improving the nation's highways. This aid reflects the federal government's interest in adequate roads for mail delivery, interstate commerce, national defense, and the general welfare of the country.

The federal-aid program was greatly expanded by legislation passed by Congress in 1956 and later years. Federal aid for primary and secondary roads and streets totals almost $1\frac{1}{2}$ billion a year, and the states must

Rural Roads in the Early 1900's were often filled with ruts and bumps. In rainy weather or during the spring thaw, automo-biles often sank to their axles in sticky, oozing mud. Today, many rural roads have hard gravel or bituminous surfaces.

contribute an equal amount. In addition, the 1956 legislation provided financing for the federal interstate highway system. This system is expected to cost about $70 billion. The federal government is paying 90 per cent of the cost and the states 10 per cent. To finance the interstate program, Congress established a highway trust fund. This fund receives money from taxes on motor fuel, tires and inner tubes, retread rubber, new trucks and buses, and an annual tax on heavy vehicles. Construction or improvement of the roads is done by the states, with federal aid. The roads belong to the state or local governments, which must maintain them. See GASOLINE TAX.

History of Roads and Highways

The First Roads. Roads are so old that we are not sure of the origin of the word *road*. Most experts think it came from the Middle English word *rode*, meaning *a mounted journey*. This may have come from the Old English *rad*, from the word *ridan*, meaning *to ride*.

In England, hundreds of years ago, certain main roads were higher than the surrounding ground. This was because earth was thrown from the side ditches toward the center. Because they were higher, they were called *highways*. These roads were under protection of the king's men and were open to all travelers. Private roads were known as *byways*.

The first roads in the world probably followed trails and paths made by animals. These trails and paths led from feeding grounds to watering places. Men followed these trails to hunt for animals. Men also made their own trails and paths in searching for water, food, and fuel. Explorers followed these trails as they investigated new lands.

Early roads were built in the Near East soon after the wheel was invented. This was about 3500 B.C. As trade developed between villages, towns, and cities, other paths, or trade routes, were made. One such early system of roads was the Old Silk Trade Route which ran over 6,000 miles, connecting China with Rome and pre-Christian Europe. Merchants used this ancient route to carry Chinese silk across Turkestan, India, and Persia.

The first road markers were piles of stones at intervals. Trails through forests were marked by *blazing* trees, or cutting a piece from the bark of the tree.

The Egyptians, Carthaginians, and Etruscans all built roads. But the first really great road builders were the Romans. They knew how to lay a solid base and how to give the road a pavement of flat stones. The Romans knew that the road must slope slightly from the center toward both sides to drain off water. This gave the road a *crown*. The Roman road builders knew also that there must be ditches along the sides of the road to carry water away. Roman roads were built mainly to get soldiers from one part of the empire to another. These roads ran in almost straight lines and passed over hills instead of cutting around them. The Romans built more than 50,000 miles of roads in their empire and some of them still are in use today. See APPIAN WAY (picture); ROMAN EMPIRE (color picture: How the Romans Built a Road).

In the Middle Ages, most roads in Europe were merely clearings in the forests. There was little reason to build good roads, because most of the travel was on horseback. The cleared way was sometimes quite wide, so that robbers hiding in the woods could not leap out suddenly upon travelers. Later, when more and more wheeled vehicles, such as wagons, came into use, the roads still remained in poor shape. Usually they were just one mudhole after another. Roads with smooth surfaces were rare in England until the 1600's.

At this same time, in South America from the 1200's to the 1500's the Inca Indians built a network of 10,000 miles of road connecting their cities.

In Europe, the one man who did more for road building than anyone else up to his time was John Loudon McAdam, a Scotsman. McAdam began building roads in England in the early 1800's. He is remembered for the surface he developed for roads. This kind of surface is called *macadam* and is used to this day. See MCADAM, JOHN LOUDON; INDUSTRIAL REVOLUTION (Roads).

Early American Roads. The first settlers in North America found a wilderness. They located their homes along the rivers and bays and used the water for transportation. As new settlers went inland, they usually built crude roads to the nearest wharf. Until after the War of 1812, travel was mainly on foot or on horseback. See TRAILS OF EARLY DAYS.

The first extensive hard-surfaced road was completed in 1795. This road was called the Lancaster (Pa.) Turnpike. It was 62 miles long and was surfaced with hand-broken stone and gravel. In the next 40 years, many turnpikes were built. Most surfaces were of earth, gravel, or broken stone. Some roads were covered with logs or planks, laid crosswise. Where logs were used, the roads were called *corduroy roads*. Both corduroy roads and plank roads were very bumpy. In 1830, it looked as though a great period of road building would begin. But in that year, the steam locomotive was successfully operated and rapid development of railroads began. People became convinced that the railroad was the best means for travel over long distances. From 1830 to 1900, there was little change in the surfacing materials for roads and highways. Even in cities, only wood blocks, brick, and cobblestones were used (see STREET [History]).

Modern Roads. By 1900, because of the development of the United States, there was a growing demand for good roads. It was mainly for roads extending for a few miles from the railroads so farmers could get their produce to the rails. But with the ever-growing use of the automobile after 1900, the demand arose for good roads to all places. The first concrete road was laid in Detroit in 1908. By 1924, the United States had over 31,000 miles of concrete roads. In 1925, the system of numbering highways, suggested by Wisconsin highway engineer A. R. Hirst in 1917, was adopted.

In the 1920's, a nationwide campaign for road building was carried on. Then came the depression of the 1930's and the war years of the 1940's, when little more than necessary road maintenance was accomplished. In the 1950's, many groups joined in an effort to improve roads and highways. These included automobile clubs, truckers' groups, farm organizations, motor-vehicle manufacturers, and civic organizations. By the early 1970's, much progress had been made on the Federal Interstate Highway System, scheduled for completion in the 1970's.

Critically reviewed by the FEDERAL HIGHWAY ADMINISTRATION

Related Articles. See the Transportation section in the various state, province, and country articles. See also the following articles in WORLD BOOK:

SOME ROADS AND HIGHWAYS

Alaska Highway	National Road
Appian Way	Oregon Trail
Boston Post Road	Pan American Highway
Burma Road	Pennsylvania Turnpike
Columbia River	Pulaski Skyway
Highway	Simplon Pass and Tunnel
Dixie Highway	Trails of Early Days
El Camino Real	Trans-Canada Highway
Lincoln Highway	

CONSTRUCTION AND MAINTENANCE

Asphalt	Electric Light	Street
Bridge	Eminent Domain	Traffic
Bulldozer	Gravel	Tunnel
Cement and Concrete	Lighting	Viaduct
Easement	Snowplow	

OTHER RELATED ARTICLES

Automobile	Safety (Transportation)
Bus	Star Route
Freeway	Superhighway
Gasoline Tax	Telford, Thomas
Interstate Commerce	Toll
McAdam, John Loudon	Transportation
Police	Truck and Trucking
Road Map	Turnpike

Outline

I. **Kinds of Roads and Highways**
  A. Local and Secondary Roads
  B. Primary Highways
  C. Federal Interstate Highway System
II. **How Roads and Highways Are Built**
  A. Planning   E. Surfacing
  B. Bypasses   F. Lighting
  C. Intersections G. Roadside Improvement
  D. Grading   H. Tests and Research
III. **How Roads and Highways Are Maintained**
  A. Repairing Damage and Resurfacing
  B. Clearing Ice and Snow
IV. **How Roads and Highways Are Paid For**
  A. State and Local Financing
  B. Federal Financing
V. **History of Roads and Highways**

Questions

How do local roads and primary highways differ?
What is a macadam road? Why is it so called?
Where was the first concrete road in the U.S.?
What are the most widely used methods to collect money for the states to spend for roads?
Are odd or even numbers used to mark "U.S." highways running north and south?
Name four necessary considerations in highway planning.

ROADSIDE AMERICA. See PENNSYLVANIA (Places to Visit).

ROANOKE, *ROH uh nohk,* Va. (pop. 92,115; met. area 181,436), an industrial, trade, and transportation center, is one of the largest cities in Virginia. The name *Roanoke* comes from the Indian word *Raw-enoke,* meaning *shell money.*

The city lies on the Roanoke River between the Blue Ridge and Allegheny mountains (see VIRGINIA [political map]). It is 905 feet above sea level. Mill Mountain rises in the city to a height of 2,000 feet.

Roanoke is the home of Hollins College, Roanoke College, and the Roanoke Technical Institute. Cultural facilities include a symphony orchestra, a fine arts center, and a library.

Roanoke is a convention center and a railroad center. The Norfolk and Western Railway has its headquarters

Roanoke is the industrial, trade, and railroad center for a rich agricultural and coal-mining area in southwestern Virginia.
Fairchild Aerial Surveys, Inc.

there. The city also has electrical equipment and electronics plants, flour mills, furniture factories, iron and steel plants, lumber mills, plastics factories, and textile mills.

Roanoke is a young city compared with Virginia's Tidewater and Piedmont cities. In 1881, it was the small pioneer settlement of Big Lick, named after a large salt marsh where deer fed. In 1882, two railways made a junction at Big Lick. The town was renamed Roanoke in 1882. It has a council-manager government. For the monthly weather in Roanoke, see VIRGINIA (Climate). FRANCIS B. SIMKINS

ROANOKE COLLEGE. See UNIVERSITIES AND COLLEGES (table).

ROANOKE ISLAND. See LOST COLONY.

ROANOKE RIVER runs through Virginia and North Carolina. The river rises in the Blue Ridge Mountains in southwestern Virginia, and flows in a general southeasterly direction for about 380 miles. It empties into Albemarle Sound, North Carolina. The river's chief hydroelectric installations include the John H. Kerr Reservoir and Dam, near Clarksville, Va.; and the Smith Mountain Dam and Reservoir, southeast of Roanoke.

ROARING FORTIES. See PREVAILING WESTERLY.

ROARING 20'S. See UNITED STATES, HISTORY OF (The Roaring 20's).

ROASTING. See COOKING (Roasting).

ROB ROY (1671-1734) was a famous Scottish outlaw whose real name was ROBERT MACGREGOR. He was known as "the Robin Hood of Scotland." Sir Walter Scott wrote the famous novel *Rob Roy* about him. *Roy* is the Gaelic word for red, and Macgregor was called Rob Roy because of his red hair and ruddy complexion.

Rob Roy was born in Glengyle, the son of a younger brother of the chieftain of the Macgregor clan. He inherited land from his father, and raised cattle for the English market. He organized a band of armed clansmen to prevent outlaws from running off with his cattle. His band also protected the cattle of other landowners.

In the meantime, Rob Roy had borrowed money from his neighbor, the Duke of Montrose, and he could not pay it back. The duke drove him off his property. In revenge, Rob Roy became an outlaw. He called himself Campbell, which was his mother's name, and led his band in raids on the duke's cattle. His men also stole cattle and rent money from tenants of the duke.

The English tried for a long time to capture Rob Roy. He gave himself up in 1722. He was imprisoned and sentenced to exile, but later was pardoned. KNOX WILSON

ROBALO. See FISHING (table: Game-Fishing World Records [Snook]).

ROBBER BARONS. See UNITED STATES, HISTORY OF (The Rise of Big Business).

ROBBER CRAB. See HERMIT CRAB.

ROBBERY means stealing money or goods from a person by violence or threats. This crime is classed as a *felony*, and is punishable by imprisonment. The value of the property taken has little influence in determining the legal penalty, so long as the property is of value to its owner. Robbery with a gun is usually considered more serious than simple robbery. Robbery on a street or highway is often called *highway robbery*.

Robbery occurs only when a thief uses force or threats

to obtain something from a person. It is *larceny* if money is taken from a man's pocket without his knowing it. If a thief enters a home while the owner is asleep or away, the crime is called *burglary*. FRED E. INBAU

See also BANDIT; BURGLARY; FELONY; LARCENY; PIRATE.

ROBBIA, DELLA. See DELLA ROBBIA.

ROBBINS, FREDERICK CHAPMAN (1916-), shared the 1954 Nobel prize for physiology and medicine with John Enders and Thomas Weller. The men received the prize for developing tissue culture techniques for poliomyelitis viruses. Robbins was born in Auburn, Ala. He received his M.D. degree from Harvard University. In 1952, Robbins became a professor of pediatrics at Western Reserve (now Case Western Reserve) University and director of the pediatrics and contagious diseases department at Metropolitan General Hospital in Cleveland, Ohio. HENRY H. FERTIG

ROBBINS, JEROME (1918-), is an American dancer and *choreographer* (dance composer). He became well known to dance audiences in 1944, when he created his first ballet, *Fancy Free.* He achieved more widespread fame as director of the musicals *West Side Story* (1957) and *Fiddler on the Roof* (1964). In both, he blended the acting, singing, and dancing into a unified work of art. He returned to the ballet with the creation of *Les Noces* in 1965. Many of Robbins' ballets are based on American subjects. Others are abstract in nature and modern in style. They often include jazz rhythms.

Robbins was born in New York City. He was a member of Ballet Theatre from 1940 to 1948 and associate artistic director of the New York City Ballet from 1949 to 1963. In 1966, using a grant from the federal government, he began an experimental project to develop a new form of American musical theater. SELMA JEANNE COHEN

ROBERT I. See BRUCE, ROBERT.

ROBERT COLLEGE. See TURKEY (Education).

ROBERTS, SIR CHARLES GEORGE DOUGLAS (1860-1943), was a Canadian poet, short-story writer, and novelist. The best feature of his work is his exact observation of the landscape and wildlife of his country.

Sir Charles Roberts
Trans-Canada Press

Roberts' first book of poems, *Orion* (1880), published when he was 20 years old, laid the foundation of a distinctive Canadian literature form. He later produced more verse, some novels, and many short stories. Roberts was born near Fredericton, N.B. DESMOND PACEY

ROBERTS, FREDERICK SLEIGH (1832-1914), EARL ROBERTS OF KANDAHAR, PRETORIA, AND WATERFORD, was a famous British general. He was born in Cawnpore (now Kanpur), India, the son of a British general. After a military education, he served as an officer in the Indian Army for 25 years. He gained special distinction in dealing with transport and supply problems. In 1880, Roberts led a famous march to relieve Kandahar, which was being attacked by the Afghans. In 1885, he was made commander in chief of the Indian Army.

During the Boer War, Roberts became commander in chief of the British Army in South Africa. The British situation was doubtful when he took command. By using more mounted troops and improving the transport system, he increased the army's mobility. These changes and Roberts' campaign strategy brought victory.

When the war was almost over, Roberts returned to England to become commander in chief of the British Army and to receive an earldom. He retired from active duty in the army in 1914. Beloved by his troops, he was known as "Bobs." See also BOER WAR.   JAMES L. GODFREY

ROBERTS, KENNETH LEWIS (1885-1957), an American novelist and essayist, was noted for his series of historical novels. His writing reflects his interest in American history and his lively quarrel with modern American life. He disliked liberal politics, advertising, shoddy manufacturing, and the use of sex or obscenity as a fictional theme. Roberts was born in Kennebunk, Me., and was graduated from Cornell University.

Harold Stein
Kenneth L. Roberts

His works include the historical novels *Arundel* (1930), *Rabble in Arms* (1933), *Captain Caution* (1934), *Northwest Passage* (1937), *Oliver Wiswell* (1940), and *Lydia Bailey* (1947). His best-known works of nonfiction include *Europe's Morning After* (1921), *Black Magic* (1924), *Florida* (1925), and *For Authors Only* (1935). In 1957, Roberts received a special Pulitzer prize citation for his literary work.   BERNARD DUFFEY

ROBERTS, OWEN JOSEPHUS (1875-1955), served as a justice of the Supreme Court of the United States from 1930 to 1945. President Calvin Coolidge appointed Roberts to prosecute the "oil scandal" cases arising from the leasing of public lands to the oil industry in 1924 (see TEAPOT DOME). In 1930, President Herbert Hoover appointed Roberts an associate justice of the Supreme Court. Roberts was born in Philadelphia. He was graduated from the University of Pennsylvania in 1898.   H. G. REUSCHLEIN

ROBERT'S RULES OF ORDER. See PARLIAMENTARY PROCEDURE (In Organizations).

ROBERTS WESLEYAN COLLEGE. See UNIVERSITIES AND COLLEGES (table).

ROBERTSON, JAMES. See WATAUGA ASSOCIATION.

ROBERTSON, OSCAR (1938-   ), became one of the greatest scorers and passers in basketball history. He was named an All-America guard three times while playing at the University of Cincinnati. Robertson joined the professional Cincinnati Royals of the National Basketball Association (NBA) in 1960, and was named the NBA's most valuable player in 1964. He was traded to the Milwaukee Bucks of the NBA in 1970.

Robertson, who is called "The Big O," stands 6 feet 5 inches tall and weighs over 200 pounds. Robertson has averaged about 30 points per game, both as a college and a professional player. He has also led the NBA several times in *assists* (passes to teammates that result in field goals). Robertson was born in Charlotte, Tenn.   HERMAN WEISKOPF

ROBERVAL, SIEUR DE (1500?-1560?), JEAN FRANÇOIS DE LA ROCQUE, was one of the first French explorers and colonists in Canada. King Francis I made him a viceroy and lieutenant-general of Canada in 1541. Roberval organized a colonizing expedition, followed Jacques Cartier to Canada, and landed in Newfoundland in 1542 with about 200 colonists. Cartier returned to France because he was unwilling to serve under Roberval. Roberval proceeded up the Saint Lawrence River, and spent the winter at Charlesbourg Royal (now a suburb of Quebec). After months of hardships, Roberval returned to France in 1543 with the few surviving colonists. Later, he again tried his luck, but without success. He was murdered in 1560 or 1561.   JEAN BRUCHÉSI

ROBESON, *ROHB sun,* **PAUL** (1898-   ), an American Negro actor and bass-baritone, appeared in many concerts in Europe and America. He starred in *The Emperor Jones* in 1923. The production in which he played Othello in 1943 and 1944 had the longest run of any Shakespearean play on record. His other successes include roles in *The Hairy Ape*, *Black Boy*, and the motion picture *Show Boat*. Robeson lost popularity when he became a champion of communism. He was born in Princeton, N.J.   MARY VIRGINIA HEINLEIN

ROBESPIERRE, *ROBES peer* (1758-1794), became the most famous and controversial leader of the French

Brown Bros.
Robespierre

Revolution. In the name of democracy, he supported a Reign of Terror that sent thousands to their death on the guillotine. Finally, he met the same fate. Robespierre was born at Arras, France. His full name was MAXIMILIEN FRANÇOIS MARIE ISIDORE DE ROBESPIERRE. He distinguished himself in school and became a lawyer. He read Jean Jacques Rousseau's works devoutly. In 1789, he was elected by the people of Arras to serve in the States-General. There, he became the spokesman for the lower middle classes and artisans.

Wide World
Oscar Robertson became a star guard for the **Cincinnati Royals** and later the Milwaukee Bucks of the NBA.

ROBESPIERRE

Election to the Convention. At first, Robespierre favored a democratic monarchy. But, after the king proved untrustworthy, he advocated a democratic republic. The people of Paris expressed their confidence in him by electing him to the powerful Paris Commune and also to the new National Convention.

In the convention, Robespierre led the Jacobin attack on the Girondists, moderate republicans who were in control (see JACOBIN). He helped force them to vote for the execution of the king, and charged them with mismanagement. Aided by Paris extremists, Robespierre's Jacobins ousted the Girondists from power in June, 1793.

Committee of Public Safety. The next month, Robespierre was elected by the convention to the powerful 12-man Committee of Public Safety. These men, all Jacobins, resorted to a Reign of Terror. Thousands were executed on the guillotine as enemies of the republic. No one person dominated the committee, and Robespierre cannot be blamed for all the violence. He and several associates tried to continue the Terror in 1794 to change France into a republic of virtuous people. They proposed to wipe out immorality by force.

His Death. The ferocity of the Terror increased in June and July, 1794. Robespierre's fellow Jacobins organized a plot against him. On July 26, Robespierre, in a brilliant speech before the convention, seemed to call for an end of the Terror. But he threatened unnamed deputies. The next day, the conspirators persuaded the convention to order his arrest. He escaped, a Paris uprising misfired, and his jaw was shattered in a scuffle at the time of his capture. In this condition, his head swathed in bandages, he was sentenced by the convention to die on the guillotine. The execution took place on July 28.   RAYMOND O. ROCKWOOD

Related Articles in WORLD BOOK include:

French Revolution	Jacobin	States-General
Girondist	Louis (XVI)	Tuileries
Guillotine	Reign of Terror	

ROBIDOUX was the family name of four brothers who were fur traders, explorers, and founders of two cities. They were four of the six sons of Joseph Robidoux, who moved from Canada to St. Louis, Mo., in 1750. All four of the brothers were born in St. Louis.

Joseph Robidoux (1783-1868) traded from 1809 to 1822 at the present site of Council Bluffs, Iowa. He sold his holdings to the American Fur Co. and agreed, for an annual payment of $1,800, not to re-enter the fur trade for three years. At the end of that period, he established a new post where the Blacksnake Creek enters the Missouri River. He prospered as a trader there. In 1842, he had his land surveyed into lots and organized the town of St. Joseph, Mo.

François Robidoux (1788-1856?) was a signer of the original petition for the incorporation of St. Louis. He worked out of his brother Joseph's trading post, trapping and trading in the Indian villages.

Louis Robidoux (1796-1862) began trading out of Missouri over the Santa Fe Trail probably as early as 1822. He settled in Santa Fe about 1824 and became prosperous there. About 1838, he began trading with California. He moved there in 1844 and bought about 30,000 acres on the Santa Ana River. He farmed there on a large scale. He later broke up his estate, and sold

G. Ronald Austing

The American Robin may have two or three broods a year. Each brood consists of three to six young. The male and female help each other feed the newly hatched birds.

much of it to farmers. Riverside, Calif., was built, under Robidoux' patronage, on land that he had once owned.

Michel Robidoux (1798- ?) worked mostly as a trapper. He ranged from the Gila River region in New Mexico and Arizona to Wyoming.   WILLIAM P. BRANDON

ROBIN is a well-known North American thrush that grows about 9 to 10 inches long. The male has a brownish orange-red breast, brownish gray upper parts, and a blackish head. Its white throat is streaked with black and its outer tail feathers are tipped with white. The female is usually slightly smaller than the male and of duller color. Robins are the state birds of Connecticut, Michigan, and Wisconsin.

Robins live in North America from Georgia to Alaska. In winter, they may fly as far south as Mexico. But they are among the last birds to leave northern regions in autumn. Often they linger until November, and sometimes remain throughout the winter. When they winter in the south, robins are among the first birds to return north in spring. The first spring robin is a popular sign that winter will soon be over.

Robins are friendly and gay. They like to live in open areas near people. John Burroughs, the American naturalist, called the robin "the most native and democratic" of American birds. Few birds have more dignity and beauty, or a lovelier song. During the mating season, the males fill the air with joyful, ringing notes. Their song sounds as if they were singing "cheerily, cheerily, cheerily."

Robins frequently return to the same place each year to build their nests. Their favorite nesting places are in the fork between two branches, on a horizontal branch, or on a shelf or ledge of a barn or house. They form a cup-shaped structure from grass stems, roots, twigs, rags, string, and paper. They use mud to hold the nest together. Then they line it with dry grasses. The female does most of the work in building the nest. The male often accompanies her on trips to and from the nest. The female lays and incubates three to six delicate blue eggs for about two weeks. When the young hatch, the male helps feed them. Robins may have two or three broods during the spring and summer.

These birds are greedy eaters, and about half of their diet consists of fruit. They prefer wild fruit, and farmers can help protect valuable crops by planting wild fruit-bearing shrubs and trees nearby. Robins also eat insects. Robins probably cause some harm because they eat useful earthworms.

The European robin, also called the *redbreast*, is smaller than the American robin. But its plumage is similar. It also is a thrush. According to an old English legend, this "pious bird with the scarlet breast" mercifully picked a thorn from the crown of Christ as He was on His way to Calvary. As the bird carried the thorn in its beak, a drop of blood fell from the thorn to its breast, dyeing it red.

Scientific Classification. Robins belong to the family *Turdidae*. The common American robin is genus *Turdus*, species *migratorius*. The European redbreast is *Erithacus rubecula*.   GEORGE J. WALLACE

See also BIRD (color pictures: Favorite Songbirds, Birds' Eggs).

ROBIN GOODFELLOW. See PUCK.

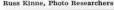

The European Robin lives throughout Europe and the British Isles. The female is smaller than the male, but they have the same colors. The European robin is about half as large as the American robin.

ROBIN HOOD

ROBIN HOOD was a legendary English hero of the common people, much as King Arthur was a hero of the upper classes. The old ballads show Robin Hood as an outlaw living in Sherwood Forest, in Nottinghamshire. His followers included Maid Marian, Friar Tuck, Little John, and a jolly band of yeomen (see FRIAR TUCK; LITTLE JOHN). Robin Hood was a gentlemanly outlaw. He divided the stolen money with the needy.

Robin Hood's gentleness toward women continued to his death, as is shown in the ballad of his death. Feeling ill, he went with Little John to Kirkley Monastery to be bled. The prioress opened a vein in his arm, but then she locked him in his room. Robin summoned Little John with his horn. In his grief, Little John wanted to burn down the monastery, but Robin wouldn't allow a

N. C. Wyeth illustration from *Robin Hood*.
Reprinted by special permission of David McKay, Publishers

Robin Hood, *left,* was a legendary outlaw of Sherwood Forest. He stole from the rich and gave money to the poor. Stories claim that Robin Hood was an expert marksman with a bow and arrow.

woman to be harmed. He shot one more arrow to show where his grave should be, and died.

Scholars have long discussed whether there ever was a real Robin Hood. But early historians spoke of him as living in the 1100's and 1200's, and he is mentioned in *Piers Plowman* (late 1300's). One series about him, *Lytell Geste of Robin Hood,* forms one of the earliest ballad collections known.

Robin Hood appears as a character in more recent literature. Sir Walter Scott introduced him as Locksley in *Ivanhoe.* Alfred, Lord Tennyson made him the central figure in his drama *The Foresters.* Howard Pyle wove the old tales into the *Merry Adventures of Robin Hood,* and Reginald De Koven used them in the comic opera *Robin Hood.*　　　　　　　　　　　　　KNOX WILSON

See also LITERATURE FOR CHILDREN (picture: Robin Hood).

ROBINS AIR FORCE BASE, about 18 miles southeast of Macon, Ga., is the site of the U.S. Air Force Continental Air Command headquarters. The command sup-

ports and directs Air Force Reserve activities. Established in 1942, the post was named for Brig. Gen. Augustine W. Robins, former chief of Army Air Corps Materiel. The base covers nearly 7,250 acres.

ROBINSON, BILL (1878-1949), was an American Negro tap dancer and one of the most famous entertainers of his time. Born Luther Robinson in Richmond, Va., he changed his name to Bill, but was often called "Bojangles." He danced in vaudeville, night clubs, and in such motion pictures as *The Little Colonel* and *Rebecca of Sunnybrook Farm.* He starred in the stage play *The Hot Mikado.* To honor his 60th year on the stage, Mayor William O'Dwyer of New York City proclaimed that April 26, 1946, be celebrated as "Bill Robinson Day."　　　　　　　　LILLIAN MOORE

See also DANCING (Exhibition Dancing).

ROBINSON, BOARDMAN (1876-1952), was an American artist, mural painter, and illustrator. He is best known for his mural paintings in Rockefeller Center in New York City and for his illustrations for Fyodor Dostoevsky's novel *The Brothers Karamazov.* His work is characterized by vitality and clarity. Born in Nova Scotia, Robinson studied in Boston and in Paris, France. In 1914, he traveled in Russia. He wrote *Cartoons of the War* (1915) and, with John Reed, *The War in Eastern Europe* (1916).　　　　　　EDWIN L. FULWIDER

ROBINSON, EDWIN ARLINGTON (1869-1935), an American poet, became best known for short poems in which he presents character studies. Three of his 13 volumes of poetry won Pulitzer prizes—*Collected Poems* in 1922, *The Man Who Died Twice* in 1925, and *Tristram* in 1928.

Robinson's characters are citizens of the imaginary community of Tilbury Town. Among the most familiar characterizations are those in "Richard Corey," "Miniver Cheevy," "Flammonde," and "Mr. Flood's Party." In these poems, the characters seem doomed to failure and suffering. Yet Robinson was not a pessimistic writer. He indicated clearly that his characters suffer because they ask too much from life and themselves.

Robinson's continuing theme of the need for humility and complete self-honesty also appears in his philosophical poem "The Man Against the Sky" (1916). Robinson also wrote long narrative poems. *Merlin* (1917) and *Lancelot* (1920), along with *Tristram,* form a connected series telling the legends of King Arthur.

Robinson was born in Head Tide, Me. Through the assistance of President Theodore Roosevelt, who admired his poetry, Robinson became a clerk in the New York Custom House in 1905. Robinson resigned in 1909 to devote himself to writing.　　　CLARK GRIFFITH

ROBINSON, JACKIE (1919-1972), became the first Negro player in modern American major-league baseball when he joined the Brooklyn Dodgers in 1947. In 10 major-league seasons, he batted .311. He helped the Dodgers win six National League pennants and defeat the New York Yankees in the 1955 World Series. Born Jack Roose-

United Press Int.
Jackie Robinson

velt Robinson in Cairo, Ga., Robinson began his career in athletics as a football star for the University of California at Los Angeles. He retired from baseball when the Brooklyn Dodgers traded him to the New York Giants in January, 1957. Robinson won the Spingarn medal in 1956. He was elected to the National Baseball Hall of Fame in 1962. ED FITZGERALD

ROBINSON, JAMES HARVEY (1863-1936), an American historian, influenced the writing and teaching of history by emphasizing man's scientific and social achievements. He wrote *An Introduction to the History of Europe* (1902), and collaborated with C. A. Beard on *The Development of Modern Europe* (1907). One of Robinson's most popular books was *The Mind in the Making* (1921). Robinson was born in Bloomington, Ill. He served as professor of history at Columbia University from 1895 to 1919. MERLE CURTI

ROBINSON, JOSEPH TAYLOR (1872-1937), was the Democratic candidate for Vice-President of the United States in 1928. He and presidential candidate Alfred E. Smith lost to Republicans Herbert C. Hoover and Charles Curtis. Robinson was elected governor of Arkansas in 1912. But shortly after he took office, the state legislature elected him to fill a vacancy in the U.S. Senate. He served as Senate majority leader from 1933 until his death. Robinson was born in Lonoke County, Arkansas. He studied law at the University of Virginia.

Wide World
Joseph T. Robinson

IRVING G. WILLIAMS

ROBINSON, RAY (1920-), won fame as one of the greatest boxers in history. He got his nickname, "Sugar Ray," after a sportswriter described him as "the sweetest fighter ... sweet as sugar." Robinson held the welterweight title from 1946 to 1951 and then won the middleweight championship five times.

Robinson defeated Jake LaMotta in 1951 to win his first middleweight title. That same year he lost it to Randy Turpin and then won it back. He retired as undefeated champion in 1952 but returned to the ring in 1954. In 1955, he regained the title by defeating Bobo Olson. Gene Fullmer won the title in 1957. Robinson won it back and lost it to Carmen Basilio that same year. In 1958, he again regained the title. In 1959, the National Boxing Association stripped Robinson of the title because he failed to defend it within a year. Robinson retired in 1965. He had won 175 of his 202 professional fights, 109 of them by knockouts.

Robinson was born in Detroit. He grew up in New York City. Robinson's real name is Walker Smith, Jr. BILL GLEASON

See also BOXING (pictures).

Wide World
Ray Robinson

ROBINSON, SIR ROBERT (1886-), a British organic chemist, received the 1947 Nobel prize for chemistry. He found the structure and behavior of many important natural substances, including the red and blue pigments of flowers; alkaloids, such as morphine and strychnine; hormones; and penicillin. He also developed methods for making many of these substances artificially.

Robinson was born near Chesterfield, England, and served as professor of organic chemistry at Sydney (Australia), Liverpool, Manchester, St. Andrews, and London universities. In 1929, he became a professor at Oxford University. HENRY M. LEICESTER

ROBINSON CRUSOE is an imaginary story about a sailor who is marooned on a desert island in the Caribbean Sea. Daniel Defoe wrote this novel in 1719. He based the story partly on the experiences of a Scottish sailor, Alexander Selkirk. But Defoe's realistic account

Illustration from the Windemere edition of the *Life and Adventures of Robinson Crusoe* by Daniel Defoe, illustrated by Milo Winter.
© 1942, Rand McNally & Co.
Robinson Crusoe, after being shipwrecked and stranded on an island, sees in the sand a footprint that is not his own.

of Crusoe's life is much more interesting, and has become one of the most popular books in English.

The book explains how Crusoe cleverly manages to make himself comfortable while he lives on the island. He tames wild goats, makes his own clothes, and builds a house for himself. After living alone for a long time, Crusoe rescues a man from cannibals. He calls the man *Friday* because he met him on that day. Friday becomes Crusoe's trusted friend and servant. The term, "man Friday," has come to mean any trusted servant. Finally, after 28 years, a ship visits the island and takes the two men back to England. GEORGE A. WICKES

See also DEFOE, DANIEL; SELKIRK, ALEXANDER.

ROBOT, *ROH buht,* is a device that can do certain jobs automatically, and does not need a person to operate it. An example is an "electric eye" door opener,

Bill De Luga, *Chicago Daily News*

A Robot Called "Mr. Mobar" moves at the touch of a button by its 16-year-old builder. The robot was a science fair project.

which automatically opens the door when an object approaches it (see ELECTRIC EYE).

The word *robot* comes from the Czech word *robotit*, which means *to drudge*. It came into use after the production of a play by the Czech dramatist Karel Čapek called *R.U.R.* The initials that make up the play's title stand for *Rossum's Universal Robots*. In this play, the robot was a mechanical man. The word has been applied to all devices that seem to act like mechanical men.   RAYMOND F. YATES

Related Articles in WORLD BOOK include:

Automation	Computer	Servomechanism
Calculating Machine	Electronics	

ROBUSTI, JACOPO. See TINTORETTO.

ROC, *rahk,* was a mythical bird of enormous size, known from the stories in the *Arabian Nights*. It resembled an eagle, but was incomparably greater in size. It was large enough to seize an elephant in its talons. In the *Arabian Nights*, Sinbad the Sailor tells of seeing the roc's egg, which was 50 paces in circumference. The bird was assumed to live on the island of Madagascar. Marco Polo heard the people of the island report that at a certain season of the year the bird appeared from the south. See also ELEPHANT BIRD.   I. J. GELB

ROCHAMBEAU, *RAHSH um boh,* **COMTE DE** (1725-1807), JEAN BAPTISTE DONATIEN DE VIMEUR, a French general, came to America in 1780 with French troops to serve under General George Washington in the Revolutionary War. In 1781, he helped plan the Battle of Yorktown and the defeat of Lord Cornwallis.

Rochambeau was born in Vendôme, the younger son of a French nobleman. He studied for the priesthood.

But, in 1742, he began a long and distinguished career as a soldier. His bravery and skill in the War of the Austrian Succession and the Seven Years' War won him steady advancement. As inspector-general of the army, Rochambeau made many important military reforms later used successfully during the French Revolution and by Napoleon.

Brown Bros.

Comte de Rochambeau

On his return from America in 1783, Rochambeau was appointed governor of Picardy and Artois. He served in the French Revolution, and was promoted to Marshal of France in 1791. Imprisoned during the Reign of Terror, Rochambeau narrowly escaped being executed. Napoleon later restored his rank.   RAYMOND O. ROCKWOOD

ROCHAS, BEAU DE. See GASOLINE ENGINE (Development of the Gasoline Engine).

ROCHDALE PRINCIPLES. See COOPERATIVE (Consumer Cooperatives).

ROCHE, MAZO DE LA. See DE LA ROCHE, MAZO.

ROCHELLE SALT, or sodium potassium tartrate, has the chemical formula $NaKC_4H_4O_6 \cdot 4H_2O$. It comes in granular, powdered, or crystallized form, depending on how it is processed. Rochelle salt is used in the manufacture of cheese and in silvering mirrors. In medicine, it serves as a laxative. The crystals are used in electronics systems. See also PIEZOELECTRICITY; SALTS; SEIDLITZ POWDERS; TARTARIC ACID.

ROCHESTER, Minn. (pop. 53,766; met. area 84,104; alt. 990 ft.), is famous as the home of the Mayo Clinic. William W. Mayo and his sons, Charles and William, established this medical center in 1889. The clinic treats over 200,000 patients each year (see MAYO; MAYO CLINIC). Rochester has extensive hospital and hotel facilities to serve those who come for medical treatment. A large state mental hospital is also there.

Rochester lies in southeastern Minnesota, about 65 miles southeast of Minneapolis. For location, see MINNESOTA (political map). The city serves as the trade center for surrounding dairy and truck farms. It has one of the largest pea- and corn-canning plants and the largest diversified dairy-products processing plant in the world. A huge plant that manufactures business machines opened in Rochester in 1957. Other important products include electrical equipment, and sheet steel products. Four airlines, a railroad freight line, and a network of highways serve the city. Rochester has a civic auditorium, two radio stations, and a television station. The city is the seat of Olmsted County, and has a mayor-council government.   HAROLD T. HAGG

ROCHESTER, N.H. (pop. 17,938; alt. 230 ft.), is an industrial city on the Cocheco River in southeastern New Hampshire (see NEW HAMPSHIRE [political map]). The chief products made in Rochester are bricks, fiber, lumber, woolen goods, and shoes. The Cocheco and Salmon Falls rivers supply water power. An agricultural fair is held in the city every year. Rochester was incorporated as a city in 1891, and has a mayor-council form of government.   J. DUANE SQUIRES

ROCHESTER, *RAH chehs tur,* N.Y. (pop. 296,233; met. area 882,667; alt. 515 ft.), is a leading industrial, commercial, educational, and cultural center. More than half the city's people earn their living in manufacturing industries. Rochester lies along the Genesee River near its outlet into Lake Ontario. It is 70 miles northeast of Buffalo (see NEW YORK [political map]).

Description. Rochester, the third largest city in the state, is located on a broad, level plateau in the heart of the picturesque Genesee Valley. Two waterfalls within the city limits supply Rochester with an enormous amount of electric power. Rochester lies on the route of the New York State Barge Canal System.

The Genesee River divides Rochester into two almost-equal parts. Thirteen bridges cross the river. The city has one of the best park systems in the country, and many beautiful residential sections. Scenic attractions include the nearby Finger Lakes. See FINGER LAKES; GENESEE RIVER.

Industries. Rochester was first known as *The Flour City.* In the mid-1800's, it developed into the nursery-products center of the country, and became known as *The Flower City.* People later called it *The Kodak City,*

Pat Murphy, Tom Stack & Associates

Rochester, New York's third largest city, lies on the Genesee River. The river's upper falls, *above,* are near the downtown area.

ROCHESTER INSTITUTE OF TECHNOLOGY

because the Eastman Kodak Company is located there. Rochester claims to be *The City of Many Industries.*

Rochester leads the world in the manufacture of photographic film, cameras, optical goods, dental equipment, thermometers, mail chutes, and enameled steel tanks. It ranks high in the manufacture of men's clothing, shoes, buttons, television sets, leather goods, telephone apparatus, electrical supplies, railway signals, machinery, printing and lithography, malt, and soft drinks. The city has over 1,000 manufacturing plants.

Transportation and Communication. Trains, buses, airplanes, and boats serve Rochester. The city has its own bus lines. There are eight radio stations, four television stations, and several newspapers.

Cultural Activities. The University of Rochester ranks high among the universities of the country. Perhaps the best-known part of the university is the Eastman School of Music. Rochester is also the home of several other institutions. They include Nazareth College, Rochester Institute of Technology, St. Bernard's Seminary, and St. John Fisher College.

The George Eastman House of Photography is a center for the study of the history and uses of photography. The Rundel Memorial Building houses the public library and historical collections. The city also has the Memorial Art Gallery and the Rochester Museum and Science Center, which includes a museum and a planetarium.

The city is the home of the Rochester Philharmonic Symphony Orchestra and the Rochester Oratorio Society. Each summer the city sponsors free operas "under the stars" at Highland Park Bowl. The Community War Memorial, built in 1955, has an auditorium that seats 9,000.

History. The French established a post near the present site of Rochester in 1710. But the settlement was really established by New Englanders under the leadership of Nathaniel Rochester in 1812. It was incorporated as the village of Rochesterville in 1817, and chartered as the city of Rochester in 1834. Rochester is the seat of Monroe County. The city has a city-manager form of government. WILLIAM E. YOUNG

ROCHESTER, UNIVERSITY OF, is a privately controlled university at Rochester, N.Y. Its coeducational divisions include the College of Arts and Science, the Eastman School of Music, the School of Medicine and Dentistry, the University School of Liberal and Applied Studies, the College of Education, the College of Engineering, the School of Business Administration, the Institute of Optics, and the Graduate School. Courses lead to bachelor's, master's, and doctor's degrees. The university was founded in 1850. For enrollment, see UNIVERSITIES AND COLLEGES (table). See also EASTMAN SCHOOL OF MUSIC. C. W. DE KIEWIET

ROCHESTER INSTITUTE OF TECHNOLOGY is a private, coeducational institution in Rochester, N.Y. It has a school of applied science and colleges of business, continuing education, engineering, fine and applied arts, general studies, graphic arts and photography, and science. Courses at the institute lead to associate's, bachelor's, and master's degrees. The institute was founded in 1829. For enrollment, see UNIVERSITIES AND COLLEGES (table). PAUL A. MILLER

ROCK

ROCK is the hard, solid part of the earth's crust. In many areas, the rock is covered by a layer of soil in which plants or trees may grow. Soil itself is made up of tiny bits of rocks usually mixed with organic materials from plants and animals. Rock also lies beneath the oceans and under the polar icecaps.

Where highways cut through hills, you can often see layers of rock in the exposed hillsides. When the rock is removed to make way for the highway, construction men often break it up and use the pieces to build up the road's foundation.

Rivers frequently cut deep channels through the rock. Great cliffs of rock line many seashores, such as in Maine and Norway. In desert regions, rock cliffs and pinnacles may rise high above sandy plains.

Most rocks are *aggregates*, or combinations, of one or more minerals. Basalt, for example, contains crystals of the minerals plagioclase and pyroxene. Some rocks appear to be dense and massive, and have no mineral grains. But if you examine a very thin slice of such rock under a microscope, you can see grains of minerals.

Rocks and minerals are useful to us in many ways. Builders use granite, marble, and other rocks in construction work. Cement made from limestone and other rocks binds crushed stone into strong, long-lasting concrete for buildings, dams, and highways.

Saturday Evening Post photo by Gene Lester © 1958 Curtis Publishing Co.

"Rock Hounds" Hunt for Rocks to add to their collections. These hobbyists are examining petrified wood in Utah. Interesting rocks can be found almost anywhere.

Sorting and Classifying Rocks is an important part of rock collecting. Rock samples should be numbered and catalogued to make it easier to identify and locate them.

United Press Int.

IGNEOUS

RHYOLITE
Colorado

PERIDOTITE
Arkansas

GRANITE
Minnesota

OBSIDIAN
Oregon

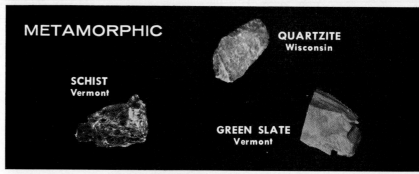

METAMORPHIC

QUARTZITE
Wisconsin

SCHIST
Vermont

GREEN SLATE
Vermont

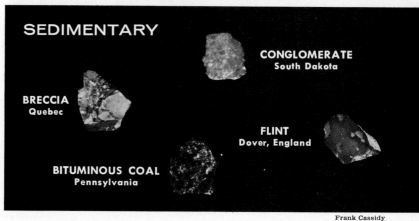

SEDIMENTARY

CONGLOMERATE
South Dakota

BRECCIA
Quebec

FLINT
Dover, England

BITUMINOUS COAL
Pennsylvania

Frank Cassidy

Metals such as aluminum, iron, lead, and tin come from rocks that we call *ores*. Ores also supply such radioactive elements as radium and uranium. Ore deposits may lie close to the earth's surface, or thousands of feet underground. In some regions, deposits of iron or copper ores make up entire mountains.

Some rocks contain valuable nonmetallic minerals such as borax and graphite. Asbestos rock has a fibrous mineral that we use to insulate our homes. All gems, except amber, coral, and pearl, come from rocks. Diamonds mined in Africa and Arkansas come from a rock called *peridotite*. Emeralds are found in black limestone in Colombia.

Geologists trace the history of the earth by studying rocks (see GEOLOGY). They find oil deposits by studying different rock layers. Other scientists study *fossils* (remains of plants and animals found in rock) to learn about the kind of life that existed millions of years ago (see FOSSIL).

Thousands of young people and adults enjoy collecting rocks and minerals as a hobby. The hobbyists call themselves "rock hounds." They trade rocks and minerals just as stamp collectors trade stamps. A collector in Los Angeles may trade with fellow hobbyists in his local rock and mineral club, or with other collectors as far away as New York City, Montreal, or Vienna. There are about a thousand rock and mineral clubs in the United States and Canada. These clubs hold regular meetings, sponsor study groups and exhibits, and organize field trips to collecting areas. Sometimes they

COMMON ROCKS

IGNEOUS ROCKS

GABBRO
New York

PUMICE
Utah

BASALT
Michigan

ROCK	COLOR	STRUCTURE
Basalt	Dark, greenish-gray to black.	Dense, microscopic crystals, often form columns.
Gabbro	Greenish-gray to black.	Coarse crystals.
Granite	White to gray, pink to red.	Tightly arranged medium-to-coarse crystals.
Obsidian	Black, sometimes with brown streaks.	Glassy, no crystals, breaks with a shell-like fracture.
Peridotite	Greenish-gray.	Large, pipelike formations.
Pumice	Grayish-white.	Light, glassy, frothy, fine pores, floats on water.
Rhyolite	Gray to pink.	Dense, sometimes contains small crystals.
Scoria	Reddish-brown to black.	Large pores, looks like furnace slag.
Syenite	Gray to pink and red.	Coarse crystals, resembles granite but has no quartz.

METAMORPHIC ROCKS

DOLOMITIC MARBLE
Massachusetts

PINK MARBLE
Georgia

	COLOR	STRUCTURE
Gneiss	Gray and pink to black and red.	Medium to coarse crystals arranged in bands.
Marble	Many colors, often mixed.	Medium to coarse crystals, may be banded.
Quartzite	White, gray, pink, buff.	Massive, hard, often glassy.
Schist	White, gray, red, green, black.	Flaky particles, finely banded, feels slippery, often sparkles with mica.
Slate	Black, red, green, purple.	Fine grains, dense, splits into thin, smooth slabs.

SEDIMENTARY ROCKS

SHALE
Colorado

SANDSTONE
New York

LIMESTONE
Florida

	COLOR	STRUCTURE
Breccia	Gray to black, tan to red.	Angular pieces of rock, held together by natural cement.
Clay	White, red, black, brown.	Fine particles, dusty when dry, muddy and sticky when wet.
Coal	Shiny to dull black.	Brittle, in seams or layers.
Conglomerate	Many colors.	Rounded pebbles or stones held together by natural cement.
Flint	Dark gray to buff.	Hard, breaks with a sharp edge.
Limestone	White, gray, and buff to black and red.	Forms thick beds and cliffs. May contain fossils.
Sandstone	White, gray, yellow, red.	Fine or coarse grains cemented together in beds.
Shale	Yellow, red, gray, green, black.	Dense, fine particles, soft, splits easily, smells like clay.

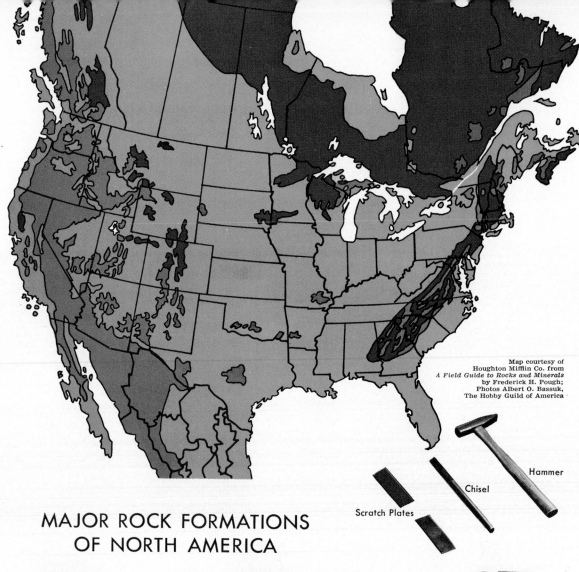

Map courtesy of
Houghton Mifflin Co. from
A Field Guide to Rocks and Minerals
by Frederick H. Pough;
Photos Albert O. Bassuk,
The Hobby Guild of America

Hammer

Chisel

Scratch Plates

MAJOR ROCK FORMATIONS
OF NORTH AMERICA

Magnifying Glass

 SEDIMENTARY ROCKS

 METAMORPHIC ROCKS

 IGNEOUS ROCKS

 PLUTONIC ROCKS
(A TYPE OF IGNEOUS)

INTERESTING FACTS ABOUT ROCKS

Balanced Rock, in the Garden of the Gods near Colorado Springs, Colo., is an enormous block of sandstone delicately balanced on a small base.

Bendable Rock. Most rocks cannot be bent or squeezed out of shape. But thin slabs of itacolumite, a rare kind of sandstone found in India and North Carolina, can be bent by hand because of their crystalline structure.

Eight Elements make up more than 98 per cent of all the rocks in the world. These elements are found in about the following percentages: oxygen (46.5), silicon (27.6), aluminum (8.0), iron (5.0), calcium (3.6), sodium (2.8), potassium (2.6), and magnesium (2.0).

Floating Rock. Pumice is a rock that floats on water. It was once volcanic lava filled with gases. When the gases escaped, they left millions of tiny holes that filled with air.

Rock of Gibraltar is a huge block of limestone that broke away from the mainland of Europe.

help develop collections for local museums.

The three main kinds of rocks are: (1) igneous rocks, (2) sedimentary rocks, and (3) metamorphic rocks.

Igneous Rock

Deep within the earth there exists *molten*, or melted, rock material called *magma*. Magma is under great pressure and is extremely hot (1380° to 2000° F.). This hot material sometimes rises to the earth's surface through *fissures*, or cracks, caused by earthquakes and other deep movements of the earth's crust. Or, the intense heat and pressure of the magma weakens the rocks above it until they give way to its force. *Igneous rocks* form when magma cools and solidifies. Scientists divide igneous rocks into two groups: extrusive rocks and intrusive rocks.

Extrusive Rocks form when magma is *extruded*, or

forced out, onto the surface of the earth. The magma may penetrate the surface as a volcano that erupts great masses of hot lava, cinders, and ash, or pours forth great rivers of molten rock. *Lava* is the name for magma that reaches the surface.

Exposure to the cooler surface temperatures causes the lava to harden in a few hours. The minerals it contains do not have time to form large crystals. It may harden so quickly that it forms *obsidian*, a smooth, shiny *volcanic glass; pumice*, a finely porous rock frothy with air bubbles; and *scoria*, a rough rock that looks like furnace slag. Lava that hardens more slowly forms rocks with tiny mineral crystals. These *finely crystalline* rocks include dark-colored *basalts* and light-colored *felsites*.

Sometimes a volcano throws lava from the earth with great violence. The masses of lava form lumps of rock that range in size from tiny particles of *volcanic dust* to *volcanic bombs* that may be an inch to several feet in diameter. Pieces that become bound together by natural cement are called *agglomerate* rocks or *volcanic breccias*.

Intrusive Rocks form from magma that does not rise all the way to the surface of the earth. It may push up the surface rock in the shape of a huge blister. Or, it may fill in the folds caused when mountains form. Sometimes it spreads out in sheets between layers of older rocks. Beneath the surface, the molten rock cools and hardens slowly. Rocks formed in this way have coarse mineral grains and crystals that can be seen with the unaided eye. These *coarsely crystalline* rocks include the *granites, syenites,* and *gabbros.*

Sedimentary Rock

Sedimentary rock consists of materials that once were part of older rocks or of plants and animals. These rocks were deposited millions of years ago as *strata* (layers) of loose material. Most of the deposits occurred on ocean floors, but some appeared on land and in fresh water. As time passed, the loose materials changed into solid rocks. Geologists divide these rocks into three groups, according to the type of material from which they were formed. These groups are (1) clastic sediments, (2) chemical sediments, and (3) organic sediments.

Clastic Sediments are rock fragments that range in size from coarse boulders and cobbles, through pebbles and gravels, to fine grains of sand and particles of silt and clay. Rocks break and crumble into fragments by a natural process called weathering (see EROSION [Weathering]). These fragments are carried about and deposited, chiefly by running water, but sometimes by wind and glaciers. Eventually, layers build up and then a *lithification* (stone-forming process) takes place. Sometimes pressure *compacts* (squeezes) the water from the deposits. This locks the particles together and forms rocks called *siltstone* from silt, and *shale* from clay. Natural chemical substances *cement* (bind) grains of sand together to form *sandstone*. Sometimes waterworn boulders, cobbles, and pebbles become cemented together to form *conglomerate* rocks. Broken and angular pieces become cemented to form *breccias.*

Chemical Sediments are deposits of minerals that were once dissolved in water. The evaporation of the water causes minerals to crystallize, leaving deposits of *rock salt* (sodium chloride), *phosphate rocks* (calcium phosphate), and *gypsum* (calcium sulfate). Many *limestone* beds form from calcite (calcium carbonate) crystals, and some deposits of *iron ore* form from the crystallization of dissolved iron oxide. Dissolved silica makes beds of flint rocks. See CRYSTAL AND CRYSTALLIZATION.

Organic Sediments are the shells, skeletons, and other parts of plants and animals. Shellfish take calcite from water and use it to build their shells. Coral polyps use the same mineral to build coral reefs (see CORAL). Coral reefs and piles of shells harden to form *fossiliferous limestone*. The shells of one-celled animals called *foraminifera* make *chalky limestone* such as that found in the famous white cliffs of Dover, England. Coal formed from ferns and other marsh plants that became buried in swamps and decayed. These deposits of organic matter changed into beds of peat and coal (see COAL [How Coal Was Formed]).

Metamorphic Rock

Metamorphic rock is rock that has changed its appearance, and sometimes its mineral composition. These changes may be caused by hot magma, pressure and heat from mountain-building movements in the earth, or the chemical action of liquids and gases. All kinds of rock, including igneous and sedimentary, have gone through such *metamorphism* to produce metamorphic rocks. Granite, for example, is an igneous rock that contains quartz, feldspar, and mica. Metamorphism causes feldspar and quartz crystals to form layers between which mica crystals often lie in wavy bands. The new rock is called *gneiss*. Metamorphism recrystallizes the calcite in limestone to form *marble*. The quartz grains in sandstone become more tightly packed to form *quartzite*. Soft shales and clays harden to form *slate*, a rock that easily splits into smooth slabs. Felsites and impure sandstones, limestones, and shales change into *schists* that glisten with mica and other minerals such as hornblende, chlorite, and garnet.

Rocks as a Hobby

Collecting Rocks. You can find interesting rocks and minerals in many places near your home. Good "hunting grounds" include mines, quarries, building excavations, ocean cliffs and beaches, and the rocky sides of road cuts and riverbanks. You can easily start a collection by gathering loose rocks, but a few simple tools will help in obtaining specimens.

The most important tool is a *mineral hammer* that has both square and pointed ends for pounding and loosening specimens embedded in solid rocks. A chisel helps loosen crystals. By examining rocks through a low-power magnifying glass you can choose the most desirable specimens. Many collectors carry a pocket magnet to help identify rocks containing magnetite. A *streak plate* (piece of unglazed porcelain) aids them in recognizing minerals by streak colors. A pocket knife makes a handy tool for testing mineral hardness. All this equipment can be bought inexpensively at a hardware store or from a mineral dealer. A knapsack or a small fruit basket makes a good carrying case. All rock specimens should be wrapped in newspaper or tissue paper for protection.

As you collect specimens, identify each with a label. The label should tell the location and date of collection, and what kind of rock or mineral it may be. Later you can transfer the information about the rocks and minerals to a permanent record book.

Identifying Rocks may seem hard at first. But it soon becomes easy to recognize common types. Many beginners buy inexpensive *reference collections* of rocks or minerals from rock and mineral dealers. These collections identify common rocks and minerals. You can compare unknown rocks with known specimens.

All minerals have important characteristics, such as chemical composition and streak color, that help identify them. Experts also study the formations in which certain rocks are found, and the physical characteristics of the rocks.

Chemical Composition may be determined by certain chemical tests for the mineral elements. For example, a simple chemical test for calcite in limestone is to pour soda pop over the rock. The pop, a weak acid, fizzes vigorously on limestone.

Streak Color is the color of the powder obtained by rubbing a mineral across a hard, rough surface such as unglazed porcelain or a file. The powder color often differs from the color of the mineral mass. For example, pyrite (ferrous sulfide) looks yellow in rocks. But its streak color is black. Many minerals have a typical streak color.

Formations and Physical Characteristics. You can often identify rocks by knowing where they are found and how they look. For example, you usually can recognize sedimentary rocks because they lie in *stratified*, or layered, formations. Sedimentary rocks often contain fossils, and many have markings such as old mud cracks or ripple marks caused by waves. Except for volcanic glass, all igneous rocks are solid and crystalline. Some appear dense, with microscopic crystals, and others have larger, easily seen crystals. They occur in volcanic areas, and in intrusive formations that geologists call batholiths, laccoliths, sills, dikes, and stocks. Many metamorphic rocks have characteristic bands, and can be split easily into sheets or slabs. See also MINERAL (Identifying Minerals).

Displaying Rocks. The size of the rocks in your collection will depend on the available storage space. Some persons collect small *micromounts*, that can be kept in small boxes and viewed under a low-power microscope. Others prefer larger specimens of the size found in museum collections. Probably the best size for storage ranges from 2 inches by 3 inches to about 3 inches by 4 inches. Crystals, of course, would be smaller. You can trim rocks to the desired size by using your hammer, but be careful not to damage choice crystals. Dirty specimens can be cleaned by washing with soap and water, and brushing with a stiff brush. Specimens containing rock salt cannot be washed, because the salt dissolves in water. Usually, you can brush or blow the dirt from such specimens.

After cleaning your specimens, you can catalogue them by painting a small white spot on each rock and writing a number on the spot in India ink. This allows you to refer to the corresponding number in your record book for information about each one.

A chest of drawers or a set of bookshelves makes an ideal storage unit. Put your rocks in shallow cardboard trays. You might keep very small specimens and crystals in cardboard boxes or trays that have partitions. Small exhibits of choice specimens make attractive displays on mantels or shelves, or in glass-front cases.

Rock Collections. Many public museums in larger cities of the United States, Canada, and Europe exhibit excellent collections of rocks and minerals. Museums connected with state geological surveys, usually located at state capitals, have exhibits of fossils, minerals, and rocks found in the state. Some of the best-known rock and mineral collections are in the following places: American Museum of Natural History, New York City; British Museum, London; California Academy of Sciences, San Francisco; Field Museum of Natural History, Chicago; Cranbrook Institute of Science, Bloomfield Hills, Mich.; Harvard University Museum, Cambridge, Mass.; Royal Ontario Museum, Toronto; and the Smithsonian Institution, United States National Museum, Washington, D.C. DAVID E. JENSEN

Related Articles in WORLD BOOK include:

FAMOUS ROCK FORMATIONS

Garden of the Gods	Mount Rushmore	Palisades
Giant's Causeway	National	Stone Mountain
Gibraltar	Memorial	

IGNEOUS ROCKS

Basalt	Lava	Porphyry	Syenite	Travertine
Granite	Obsidian	Pumice	Tachylyte	

METAMORPHIC ROCKS

Gneiss	Mica Schist	Slate
Marble	Quartzite	Soapstone

SEDIMENTARY ROCKS

Chalk	Coal	Flint	Sandstone
Clay	Coral	Limestone	Shale

OTHER RELATED ARTICLES

Boulder	Gem	Ore
Cliff	Geode	Petrology
Corrosion	Geology	Quarrying
Crystal and	Gravel	Sand
Crystallization	Hardness	Silt
Crystalline Rocks	Loess	Soil
Earth	Metamorphism	Syncline
Emery	Mineral	Taconite
Erosion	Mining	Tektite
Fossil	Mountain	Volcano

Outline

I. **Igneous Rock**
    A. Extrusive Rocks   B. Intrusive Rocks
II. **Sedimentary Rock**
    A. Clastic Sediments   C. Organic Sediments
    B. Chemical Sediments
III. **Metamorphic Rock**
IV. **Rocks as a Hobby**
    A. Collecting Rocks   C. Displaying Rocks
    B. Identifying Rocks   D. Rock Collections

Questions

What are the three major kinds of rocks?
What is streak color? What does it tell about minerals?
What rocks are used for building materials?
Where are good places to collect rocks?
What kind of rocks can be bent by hand?
What rock do we use to help insulate our homes?
How can soda pop be used to test for calcite?
How do rocks help scientists study the earth's history?
How can collecting rocks be an educational hobby?

Reading and Study Guide

For a *Reading and Study Guide on Rocks and Minerals*, see the RESEARCH GUIDE/INDEX, Volume 22.

ROCK, THE. See ALCATRAZ (picture); GIBRALTAR.

ROCK BEAUTY. See FISH (color picture: Tropical Salt-Water Fishes).

ROCK CORNISH HEN. See CHICKEN (Crossbreds).

ROCK CRYSTAL. See QUARTZ.

ROCK ISLAND, Ill. (pop. 50,166; alt. 570 ft.), lies on the Mississippi River, just west of Moline (see ILLINOIS [political map]). Like Moline, it is known for the manufacture of farm tools. Rock Island and Moline, together with Davenport, Iowa, have a metropolitan area population of 362,638. The Rock Island Arsenal, which produces arms and shells for the U.S. Army, stands on Rock Island in the Mississippi River. Augustana College is in Rock Island. Sac and Fox Indian villages once stood in this region. The Black Hawk War (1832) was fought for the possession of them. Rock Island, originally called Stephenson, was founded in 1833. The city has a council-manager government. It is the seat of Rock Island County.   PAUL M. ANGLE

ROCK MUSIC is the leading form of popular music in many parts of the world. During its early days in the 1950's, rock was called *rock 'n' roll.* Both terms probably came from the *lyrics* (words) of "There's Good Rockin' Tonight," a blues song of the early 1950's.

The Rock Sound comes largely from Negro blues and gospel music. Some critics consider Chuck Berry, a black composer and blues singer, the single most important influence on rock music. Folk music and country and western music also helped create the rock sound.

Rock music has a strong, often superficially monotonous rhythm and uses the electric guitar as the dominant instrument. The electric guitar is capable of producing a remarkable range of sounds at almost any degree of loudness. The intense loudness of much rock music is one of its most distinctive features.

Jim Marshall, Photon West

A Rock Music Concert may be performed against a background of swirling patterns of color called a *light show.* The musicians in most rock groups play the electric guitar, electric bass, or drums. Some groups have a lead singer who plays no instrument.

When performing in person, rock groups generally use one or more electric guitars, an electric bass, drums, and sometimes such traditional instruments as saxophones, trumpets, and piano. Many rock recordings offer a much broader range of musical effects than musicians can produce in live performances. Recording engineers and musicians achieve these effects with a variety of electronic sound equipment.

Rock Lyrics. Many critics consider rock a rebellion against traditional popular songs that emphasize unrealistic and sentimental lyrics. These critics believe that young people especially become attracted to rock because the young people believe many of its lyrics describe the realities and problems of the world around them.

Rock lyrics deal with many subjects. A number of rock songs describe the problems of growing up or of the generation gap. Some of the lyrics describe the effects of drugs, and others deal frankly with sex. Social protest is the basis of many rock songs about such issues as civil rights, dissent, poverty, and the Vietnam War.

Influence. For many people, rock music symbolizes a distinct way of life. These people identify the music with the rejection of traditional middle-class values. Many rock critics consider the music the leading form of communication among young people. Rock expresses (1) young people's ideas for a better world and (2) youthful discontent with social injustices. Some people relate rock music to the use of drugs, the wearing of unusual clothing and hair styles, and liberal views about sex.

The influence of rock has appeared in several other forms of music. Some musical comedies, notably "Hair" (1967), emphasize rock songs. Rock groups have performed with symphony orchestras, and composers have written operas and religious works in the rock style. The rock sound has been added to country and western music, jazz, and traditional popular music. Many motion pictures have used music written and performed by rock musicians.

Rock music became the greatest commercial success in the history of modern music. Since the late 1950's, it has almost completely dominated the rankings of best-selling records in the United States, Canada, and Western Europe. Many rock composers and performers became wealthy while still in their teens. Hundreds of radio stations play only rock music, and dozens of recording companies make only rock records.

History. Elvis Presley, a young country and western singer, was the first important rock soloist. He recorded a series of hit rock songs in 1955 and 1956, beginning with "Heartbreak Hotel" and "Hound Dog." Presley's style combined the elements that became the foundation of rock—Negro blues, the electric guitar, a strong beat, and special electronic recording effects. Bill Haley and His Comets became the first famous rock band. Their recording of "Rock Around the Clock" from the motion picture *Blackboard Jungle* (1955) was the first international rock hit.

Radio played an important role in spreading rock music during the mid-1950's. Television had replaced radio as the chief producer of drama and variety enter-

354a

tainment. Many radio stations turned to playing rock music to capture an audience. Disc jockeys who played the records over the air became powerful forces in promoting the popularity of rock performers.

The success of such folk groups as the Kingston Trio and the Weavers during the late 1950's and early 1960's showed that a tremendous market existed for music dealing with serious themes. The concern with social problems became an important part of rock music, especially in the songs of Bob Dylan, an American singer and composer.

During the 1960's, the Beatles, an English rock quartet, helped reshape rock with their witty, sophisticated lyrics and many experiments in musical styles. In the late 1960's, rock festivals lasting several days attracted thousands of young people in the United States, Canada, and Western Europe. Several books evaluated rock music as a cultural and social phenomenon. Some colleges introduced courses in which students analyze lyrics of rock songs as both social messages and poetry. RALPH J. GLEASON

See also BEATLES; DYLAN, BOB; POPULAR MUSIC.

ROCK OF AGES. See HYMN.

ROCK OF CHICKAMAUGA. See THOMAS, GEORGE H.

ROCK OIL. See PETROLEUM.

ROCK RIVER rises in the south-central part of Wisconsin, and flows 300 miles southwest to join the Mississippi River, near Rock Island, Ill. The river has swift rapids which furnish water power to four Wisconsin cities: Watertown, Jefferson, Janesville, and Beloit. At Janesville, a huge rock juts into the water. The Indian chief Black Hawk is said to have made his last speech there (see BLACK HAWK). JAMES I. CLARK

ROCK SALT. See SALT (Salt from Mines).

ROCKEFELLER is one of the most famous names in American business, finance, and philanthropy. Three members of the family also became active in politics.

John Davison Rockefeller (1839-1937) was once the world's richest man. He made his fortune in the oil business and later became a famous philanthropist.

Many people have criticized the business methods that Rockefeller used in developing his vast industrial empire. But his contributions to the welfare of mankind form an equally important part of his record. Rocke-

feller was a thinker as well as a planner and enterpriser, and he brought these abilities to philanthropy as he previously had to business.

Rockefeller gave away about $550 million during his lifetime. Most of it went to foundations and organizations, including the Rockefeller Foundation, Rockefeller University, the General Education Board, and the Laura Spelman Rockefeller Memorial (see ROCKEFELLER FOUNDATION; FOUNDATIONS; ROCKEFELLER UNIVERSITY; GENERAL EDUCATION BOARD).

Rockefeller, the son of a peddler, was born in Richford, N.Y., near Ithaca. When he was 14 years old, his family moved to Cleveland, where he attended high school. Rockefeller started work at 16 as a clerk in a small produce firm. He then formed a partnership in a grain commission house. He used the profits to enter the oil business at 23.

At that time, oil production and refining had little organization. Wide price variations and wasteful practices occurred frequently. Rockefeller set out to make the industry orderly and efficient. He realized that to do this he had to establish centralized control. Fifteen years later, he achieved his goal of having the flow of oil products from producer to consumer controlled by one company—the Standard Oil Company.

Standard Oil, which was established in 1870, grew out of several oil companies owned by Rockefeller, his younger brother William, and some associates. By the end of the 1870's, it owned the chief refineries in Cleveland, New York City, Pittsburgh, and Philadelphia.

Rockefeller also concentrated on the transportation and distribution of crude petroleum and its refined products. He built tank cars and distribution systems. His dealings with railroads involved rebates and other types of privileged treatment (see REBATE). In 1882, Rockefeller organized the Standard Oil Trust. He now controlled almost all U.S. oil refining and distribution and much of the world's oil trade.

The vastness of Rockefeller's holdings—plus public criticism of his methods—caused the Ohio Supreme Court to dissolve the Standard Oil Trust in 1892. A holding company, the Standard Oil Company of New Jersey, replaced the trust. In 1911, the Supreme Court of the United States ordered the firm to dissolve. See STANDARD OIL COMPANY; TRUST; HOLDING COMPANY.

From 1895 to 1897, Rockefeller gradually retired

Wide World

John D. Rockefeller, *left,* became famous for his philanthropies. In his later years, Rockefeller often gave shiny new dimes as mementos to strangers he met. At his death, his heirs included, *left to right,* his son, John D., Jr., and his grandsons David, Nelson, Winthrop, Laurance, and John D. III. The Rockefellers became active in business, government, and philanthropic work.

from active business. By that time, he had started his philanthropic activities. For example, he helped found the University of Chicago in 1890. By 1910, his gifts to that institution totaled $35 million. Rockefeller spent the rest of his life establishing the foundations through which he gave his money to the public.

John Davison Rockefeller, Jr. (1874-1960), was the only son of John D. Rockefeller. He became a business associate of his father after graduating from Brown University. He devoted most of his life to extending the philanthropic work started by his father. Rockefeller donated $8½ million to buy land for United Nations headquarters in New York City. He also built Rockefeller Center, a landmark of New York City; and provided the funds to restore the historic city of Williamsburg, Va. (see NEW YORK CITY [Manhattan; A Visitor's Guide]; WILLIAMSBURG).

John Davison Rockefeller III (1906-   ) is the oldest son of John D. Rockefeller, Jr. He became chairman of the board of trustees of the Rockefeller Foundation in 1952. Rockefeller helped found the Lincoln Center for the Performing Arts in New York City and later became its chairman. He also founded the Population Council, which conducts research on population problems throughout the world. Rockefeller is chairman of the President's Commission on Population Growth and the American Future. He was born in New York City and graduated from Princeton University.

Nelson Aldrich Rockefeller (1908-   ), son of John D. Rockefeller, Jr., was elected governor of New York in 1958 and won re-election in 1962, 1966, and 1970. He previously had held several posts in the federal government. In 1940, President Franklin D. Roosevelt appointed Rockefeller, a Republican, coordinator of inter-American affairs. From 1944 to 1945, Rockefeller served as assistant secretary of state. He was undersecretary of health, education, and welfare from 1953 to 1954 and special assistant to President Dwight D. Eisenhower from 1954 to 1955. Rockefeller was born in Bar Harbor, Me., and graduated from Dartmouth College. During the 1930's, he took part in his family's business and philanthropic activities. He campaigned for the Republican presidential nomination in 1964 and 1968.

Nelson A. Rockefeller

Laurance Spelman Rockefeller (1910-   ), son of John D. Rockefeller, Jr., became known for his activities in conservation and recreation. He donated more than 5,000 acres of land for the Virgin Islands National Park and contributed land and money for other parks. He developed vacation resorts in several states. Rockefeller became president of the American Conservation Association in 1958 and chairman of the New York State Council of Parks in 1963. He was born in New York City and graduated from Princeton University.

Winthrop Rockefeller (1912-   ), son of John D. Rockefeller, Jr., became the first Republican governor of Arkansas since 1874. He was elected in 1966 and

again in 1968, but in 1970 he lost his bid for a third term. Rockefeller was born in New York City and attended Yale University. He moved to Arkansas in 1953 and became active in land development, home construction, and industrial development, as well as in politics. From 1955 to 1964, he served as chairman of the Arkansas Industrial Development Commission and brought much new industry into the state.

David Rockefeller (1915-   ) is the youngest son of John D. Rockefeller, Jr. In 1969, he became chairman of the Chase Manhattan Bank, the nation's second largest bank. He previously had served as president of the bank for eight years. Rockefeller encouraged U.S. investments in developing countries. In 1953, he became chairman of the Rockefeller Institute for Medical Research (now Rockefeller University). He was born in New York City, graduated from Harvard University, and earned a Ph.D. at the University of Chicago.

John Davison Rockefeller IV (1937-   ), son of John D. Rockefeller III, became secretary of state of West Virginia in 1969. In 1972, he was the Democratic candidate for governor of West Virginia. He had previously served in the West Virginia House of Delegates from 1967 to 1969. Rockefeller was born in New York City and graduated from Harvard University. During the 1960's, he served as special assistant to the director of the Peace Corps and in the U.S. Department of State. Rockefeller went to West Virginia in 1964 as a field worker in the Action for Appalachian Youth Program.   W. H. BAUGHN

ROCKEFELLER FOUNDATION is a nonprofit organization chartered in 1913 to promote "the well-being of mankind throughout the world." The present program of the foundation is concerned with the extension and application of knowledge in the fields of medical education, public health, medical and biological research, agriculture, the social sciences, and humanities. Aid is given through grants to qualified agencies and to the training of personnel in related fields.

John D. Rockefeller originally provided an endowment of $100 million for the foundation. Later, he increased it to more than $183 million.

The policies of the organization are controlled by a self-perpetuating board of trustees who receive no pay. Its offices are at 111 W. 50th Street, New York, N.Y. 10020. For the assets of the foundation, see FOUNDATIONS (table). Critically reviewed by THE ROCKEFELLER FOUNDATION

ROCKEFELLER UNIVERSITY is one of the most important institutions in the United States devoted to research and teaching in biology and medicine. It was incorporated in 1901 as the Rockefeller Institute for Medical Research. John D. Rockefeller had pledged $200,000 for preliminary work in medical research in the interest of "humanity and science." Later gifts brought the endowment close to $90 million.

In 1954, the institute became a graduate university granting Ph.D. and D.M.S. degrees. Since 1954, research grants and contracts have been accepted from government and private sources. Research at the university is published in scientific journals throughout the world. Headquarters are at 66th Street and York Avenue, New York, N.Y. 10021.   FRANK L. HORSFALL, JR.

See also ROCKEFELLER (John D.).

ROCKET

ROCKET is a type of engine that can produce more power for its size than any other kind of engine. A rocket can produce about 3,000 times more power than an automobile engine of the same size. The word *rocket* is also used for the vehicle driven by a rocket engine.

Man uses rockets of many sizes. Rockets two or three feet long shoot fireworks into the sky for Fourth of July celebrations. Rockets that carry giant missiles thousands of miles to bomb enemy targets are usually 50 to 100 feet long. Larger and more powerful rockets lift man-made moons called *satellites* into orbit around the earth. The Saturn V rocket that carries men to the moon stands more than 360 feet high.

A rocket can produce great power, but it burns fuel rapidly. For this reason, a rocket must have a large amount of fuel to work for even a short time. The Saturn V rocket burns more than 560,000 gallons of fuel during the first $2\frac{3}{4}$ minutes of flight.

Rockets become very hot as they burn fuel. The temperature in some rocket engines reaches 6000° F., about twice the temperature at which steel melts.

Rockets can be used for only a few kinds of jobs. Imagine an automobile with a rocket engine. If the car did not melt from the heat of the rocket, it could travel much faster than an ordinary car. But instead of burning a few gallons of gasoline every hour, it would burn hundreds of gallons of fuel every minute. Such problems limit the use of rockets. Man uses them chiefly for scientific research, space travel, and war.

Men have used rockets in war for hundreds of years. During the 1200's, Chinese soldiers fired rockets against attacking armies. British troops used rockets to attack Fort McHenry in Maryland during the War of 1812 (1812-1814). After watching the battle, Francis Scott Key described "the rockets' red glare" in "The Star-Spangled Banner." During World War I (1914-1918), the French used rockets to shoot down enemy airplanes. Germany attacked London with rockets during World War II (1939-1945). Today's rockets can destroy jets and missiles flying faster than the speed of sound many miles above the earth.

Scientists use rockets for exploration and research in the atmosphere and in space. Rockets carry scientific instruments high in the sky to gather information about the air that surrounds the earth. Since 1957, rockets have shot hundreds of satellites into orbit around the earth. These satellites take pictures of the earth's weather and gather other information for scientific study. Rockets also carry scientific equipment far into space to explore the moon, the planets, and even the space among the planets.

Rockets provide the power for man's flights into space, which began in 1961. In 1969, rockets carried man to his first landing on the moon. In the future, rockets may carry men to Mars and the other planets.

The contributors of this article are Wernher von Braun, Vice-President for Engineering and Development of Fairchild Industries and former Deputy Associate Administrator of the National Aeronautics and Space Administration, and Frederick I. Ordway, Professor of Science and Technology Applications at the University of Alabama in Huntsville.

NASA

The Giant Saturn V Rocket that carried the first men to the moon rises from its launch tower. Rockets are the only vehicles that can launch men and machines into space.

356

A basic law of motion—discovered in the 1600's by the English scientist Sir Isaac Newton—describes how rockets work. This law states that for every action, there is an equal and opposite reaction (see MOTION [Newton's Laws of Motion]). Newton's law explains why the flow of air from a toy balloon *propels* (drives forward) the balloon in flight. A powerful rocket works in much the same way.

A rocket burns special fuel in a *combustion* (burning) chamber and creates rapidly expanding gas. This gas presses out equally in all directions inside the rocket. The pressure of the gas against one side of the rocket balances the pressure of the gas against the opposite side. The gas flowing to the rear of the rocket escapes through a nozzle. This exhaust gas does not balance the pressure of gas against the front of the rocket. The uneven pressure drives the rocket forward.

The flow of gas through the nozzle of a rocket is the *action* described in Newton's law. The *reaction* is the continuous *thrust* (pushing force) of the rocket away from the flow of exhaust gas.

Rocket Propellant. Rockets burn a combination of chemicals called *propellant*. Rocket propellant consists of (1) a fuel, such as gasoline, kerosene, or liquid hydrogen; and (2) *an oxidizer* (a substance that supplies oxygen), such as nitrogen tetroxide or liquid oxygen. The oxidizer supplies the oxygen that the fuel needs to burn. This supply of oxygen enables the rocket to work in space, which has no air.

Jet engines also work by means of an action-reaction process. But jet fuel does not contain an oxidizer. Jet engines draw oxygen from the air and, for this reason, cannot function outside of the earth's atmosphere. See JET PROPULSION.

A rocket burns propellant rapidly, and most rockets carry a supply that lasts only a few minutes. But a rocket produces such great power that it can hurl heavy vehicles thousands of miles into space.

A rocket burns the most propellant during the first few minutes of flight. During that time, the rocket's speed is held down by air friction, gravity, and the weight of the propellant. Air friction drags on the rocket as long as the rocket travels through the atmosphere. As the rocket climbs higher, the air becomes thinner and the friction decreases. In space, no air friction acts on the rocket. Gravity pulls a rocket toward the earth, but the pull decreases as the rocket travels farther from the earth. As a rocket burns its propellant, the weight it must carry becomes less.

Multistage Rockets consist of two or more sections called *stages*. Each stage has a rocket engine and propellant. Engineers developed multistage rockets for long flights through the atmosphere and for flights into space. They needed rockets that could reach greater speeds than were possible with single-stage rockets. A multistage rocket can reach higher speeds because it lightens its weight by dropping stages as it uses up propellant. A three-stage rocket can reach about three times the speed of a single-stage rocket.

The first stage, called the *booster*, launches the rocket. After the first stage has burned its propellant, the vehicle drops that section and uses the second stage. The rocket continues using one stage after another. Most space rockets have two or three stages.

Launching a Rocket. Space rockets require specially equipped launch sites. All launching activity at a site centers around the launch pad, from which the rocket is fired. A launch site also has (1) assembly buildings, where engineers complete the final steps of rocket construction; (2) service structures, where workers check the rocket before launching; and (3) a control center, where scientists direct the launch and flight of the rocket. Tracking stations, located around the world, record the path of the rocket's flight.

Engineers prepare a rocket for launching in a step-by-step process called the *countdown*. They schedule each step for a specific time during the countdown and launch the rocket when the countdown reaches "zero." Undesirable weather or some other difficulty may cause a *hold*, which temporarily stops the countdown.

HOW A MULTISTAGE ROCKET WORKS

A two-stage rocket carries a propellant and one or more rocket engines in each stage. The first stage launches the rocket. After burning its supply of propellant, the first stage falls away from the rest of the rocket. The second stage then ignites and carries the payload into earth orbit or even farther into space.

WORLD BOOK diagram

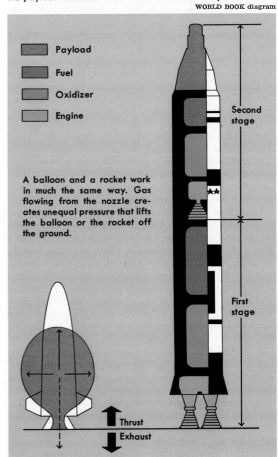

Payload

Fuel

Oxidizer

Engine

A balloon and a rocket work in much the same way. Gas flowing from the nozzle creates unequal pressure that lifts the balloon or the rocket off the ground.

Second stage

First stage

Thrust

Exhaust

Man uses rockets chiefly to provide high-speed transportation, both within the earth's atmosphere and in space. Rockets are especially valuable for (1) military use, (2) atmospheric research, (3) launching probes and satellites, and (4) space travel.

Military Use. Rockets used by the military vary in size from small, battlefield rockets to giant guided missiles that can fly thousands of miles.

The *bazooka* is a small rocket launcher carried by soldiers for use against armored vehicles. A man using a bazooka has as much striking power as a small tank (see BAZOOKA). Armies use larger rockets to fire explosives far behind enemy lines and to shoot down enemy aircraft. Fighter airplanes carry guided missiles to attack other planes and ground targets. Navy ships use guided missiles to attack other ships, land targets, and planes.

One of the most important military uses of rockets is to propel a type of long-range guided missile called an *intercontinental ballistic missile* (ICBM). Such a missile can travel thousands of miles to bomb an enemy target with nuclear explosives. A set of powerful rockets launches an ICBM and propels the missile during the early part of its flight. Then the rockets stop firing, and the ICBM coasts the rest of the way to its target. See GUIDED MISSILE.

Atmospheric Research. Scientists use rockets to explore the earth's atmosphere. *Sounding rockets*, also called *meteorological rockets*, carry such equipment as barometers, cameras, and thermometers high into the atmosphere. These instruments collect information about the atmosphere and send it by radio to receiving equipment on the earth. This method of collecting information and sending it great distances by radio is called *telemetry* (see TELEMETRY).

Rockets also provide the power for experimental research airplanes. Engineers use these planes in the development of spacecraft. By studying the flights of such planes as the rocket-powered X-15, engineers learn how to control vehicles flying many times faster than the speed of sound. They also learn how high speeds and high altitudes affect man.

Launching Probes and Satellites. Rockets that carry research equipment on long voyages to explore the solar system are called *probes*. *Lunar probes* gather information about the moon. They may fly past the moon, orbit it, or land on its surface. *Interplanetary probes* take one-way journeys into the space among the planets. *Planetary probes* collect information about the planets. A planetary probe travels in orbit around the sun with the planet it is exploring. The first planetary probes explored Mars and Venus. Someday, probes will probably reach all the planets.

Rockets lift artificial satellites into orbit around the earth. Some orbiting satellites gather information for scientific research. Others relay telephone conversations and radio and television broadcasts across the oceans (see COMMUNICATIONS SATELLITE). The armed forces use satellites for communications and to guard against surprise missile attack. They also use satellites to photograph enemy missile sites.

Rockets that launch probes and satellites are called

carrier rockets or *launch vehicles*. Most of these rockets have from two to four stages. The stages lift a satellite to its proper altitude and give it enough speed—about 18,000 miles per hour—to stay in orbit. An interplanetary probe must reach even greater speed—about 25,000 miles per hour—to escape the pull of earth's gravity and continue on its voyage.

Space Travel. Rockets provide the power for spacecraft that orbit the earth and travel to the moon and the planets. These rockets, like the ones used to launch

NASA

Sounding Rockets, such as this Astrobee 1500, collect information about the atmosphere. Radio equipment in the rocket sends data from high altitudes to the earth for scientists to study.

U.S. Army

A Military Rocket called a Tow missile is fired at an enemy target by a two-man crew. Various kinds of rockets have been used as weapons for hundreds of years by many armies.

probes and satellites, are called carrier rockets or launch vehicles.

The first space launch vehicles were military rockets or sounding rockets that engineers changed slightly to carry spacecraft. For example, they added stages to some of these rockets to increase their power. Today, engineers sometimes attach smaller rockets to the first stage of a launch vehicle. These *piggyback boosters* provide additional thrust to launch heavier spacecraft.

The Saturn V rocket, which carries United States astronauts to the moon, is the most powerful U.S. launch vehicle. Before launch, it weighs more than 6 million pounds and stands about 363 feet tall. It can send a spacecraft weighing more than 100,000 pounds to the moon. The Saturn V uses 11 rocket engines to propel its three stages.

In the future, scientists plan to use many other kinds of rocket-powered spacecraft. If *reusable shuttle vehicles* are successfully developed, they will fly into space and return to the earth for repeated journeys. They will carry people and supplies to and from space stations that will orbit the earth. Smaller rocket-powered vehicles called *space tugs* may provide transportation over short distances, such as from a shuttle vehicle to a space station or from one satellite to another. Such vehicles may also provide power for space probes launched to the planets from earth orbit. See SPACE TRAVEL.

Other Uses. Rockets have been used for many years as distress signals from ships and airplanes and from the ground (see SIGNALING). Rockets also shoot rescue lines to ships in distress. Small rockets help heavily loaded airplanes take off. These rockets are called *JATO* (*jet-assisted take-off*) *units*. Rockets have long been used in fireworks displays for the Fourth of July and other celebrations (see FIREWORKS). Scientists even use rockets to "seed" clouds with chemicals in an effort to control the weather (see WEATHER [Attempts to Control the Weather]).

Sovfoto

A Russian Rocket sits on its pad before launching the Soyuz IX space flight. When the towers on each side of the pad are raised, technicians can work on all parts of the rocket.

NASA

An Orbiting Astronomical Observatory Satellite is prepared by technicians for launch. The nose cone, *right center*, protects the satellite while its Atlas-Centaur rocket lifts it into orbit.

NASA

An Atlas-Centaur Rocket lights up its launch pad during lift off. These rockets place such scientific satellites as the Orbiting Astronomical Observatory in orbit around the earth.

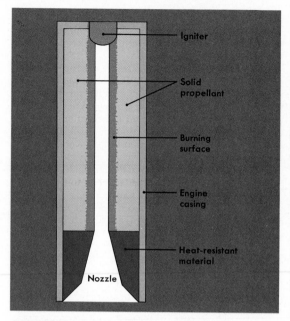

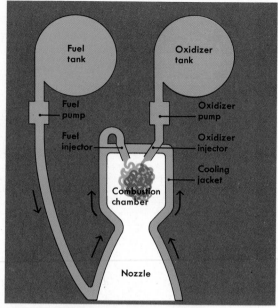

A Solid-Propellant Rocket burns a solid material called the *grain*. Engineers design most grains with a hollow core. The propellant burns from the core of the grain outward. Unburned propellant shields the engine casing from the heat of combustion.

A Liquid-Propellant Rocket carries fuel and an oxidizer in separate tanks. The fuel circulates through the engine's cooling jacket before flowing into the combustion chamber. This circulation preheats the fuel for combustion and helps cool the rocket.

There are four basic kinds of rockets: (1) solid-propellant rockets, (2) liquid-propellant rockets, (3) electric rockets, and (4) nuclear rockets.

Solid-Propellant Rockets burn a rubbery or plastic-like material called the *grain*. The grain consists of a fuel and an oxidizer in solid form. Unlike some liquid propellants, the fuel and oxidizer of a solid propellant do not burn upon contact with each other. The propellant must be ignited in one of two ways. It may be ignited by the burning of a small charge of black powder. The propellant also may be ignited by the chemical reaction of a liquid chlorine compound sprayed onto the grain.

The temperature in the combustion chamber of a solid-propellant rocket ranges from 3000° F. to 6000° F. In most of these rockets, engineers use high-strength steel or titanium to build chamber walls that can stand the pressure created at such high temperatures. They also may use fiber glass or special plastic materials.

Solid propellants burn faster than do other propellants, but they produce less thrust. Solid propellants remain effective for long periods of storage and present little danger of exploding until ignited. They do not require the pumping and blending equipment needed for liquid propellants. On the other hand, it is difficult to stop and start the burning of a solid propellant. Astronauts on space flights must stop and start the burning of propellant to control the flight of their spacecraft. One method used to stop the burning of solid propellant involves blasting the entire nozzle section from the rocket. But this method prevents restarting of the rocket.

Solid-propellant rockets are used chiefly by the armed forces. Military rockets must be ready to fire instantly, and solid propellants can be stored better than other kinds of propellants. Solid-propellant rockets provide the power for ICBM's, including the Atlas, Titan II, and Minuteman II, and for such smaller missiles as the Hawk, Talos, and Terrier. Solid-propellant rockets are used as boosters for carrier rockets, as JATO rockets, and as sounding rockets. They are also used in fireworks displays.

Liquid-Propellant Rockets burn a mixture of fuel and oxidizer in liquid form. These rockets carry the fuel and the oxidizer in separate tanks. A system of pipes and valves feeds the two propellant elements into the combustion chamber. Either the fuel or the oxidizer flows around the outside of the chamber before blending with the other element. This flow cools the combustion chamber and preheats the propellant element for combustion.

Methods of feeding the fuel and oxidizer into the combustion chamber include using (1) pumps or (2) high-pressure gas. The most common method uses pumps. Gas produced by burning a small portion of the propellant drives the pumps, which force the fuel and oxidizer into the combustion chamber. In the other method, high-pressure gas forces the fuel and oxidizer into the chamber. The supply of high-pressure gas may come either from nitrogen or some other gas stored under high pressure, or from the burning of a small amount of the propellant.

Some liquid propellants, called *hypergols*, ignite when the fuel and the oxidizer contact each other. But most

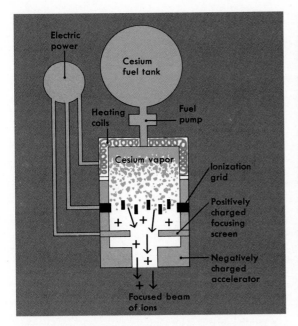

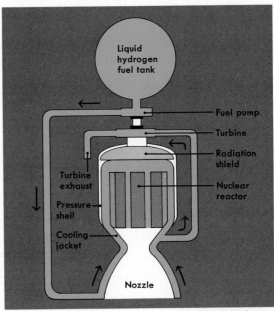

WORLD BOOK diagrams

An Ion Rocket is a kind of electric rocket. Heating coils in the rocket change a fuel, such as cesium, into a vapor. A hot platinum or tungsten *ionization grid* changes the flowing vapor into a stream of electrically charged particles called *ions*.

A Nuclear Rocket uses the heat from a nuclear reactor to change a liquid fuel into a gas. Most of the fuel flows through the reactor. Some of the fuel, heated by the nozzle of the rocket, flows through the turbine. The turbine drives the fuel pump.

liquid propellants require an ignition system. An electric spark may ignite the propellant, or the burning of a small amount of solid propellant in the combustion chamber may do so. Liquid propellants continue to burn as long as the mixture of fuel and oxidizer flows into the combustion chamber.

Thin, high-strength steel or aluminum is used to construct most tanks that hold liquid propellant. Most combustion chambers in these rockets are made of steel or nickel.

Liquid propellants burn more slowly than do solid propellants, and they produce greater thrust for each pound of propellant. It also is easier to start and stop the burning of liquid propellants than that of solid propellants. The burning can be controlled merely by closing or opening valves. But liquid propellants are difficult to handle. If the propellant elements blend without igniting, the resulting mixture will explode easily. Liquid propellants also require more complicated rocket construction than do solid propellants.

Scientists use liquid-propellant rockets for most space launch vehicles. For example, liquid-propellant rockets provide the power for the three stages of the Saturn V launch vehicle.

Electric Rockets use electric power to produce thrust. These rockets include (1) arc jet rockets, (2) plasma jet rockets, and (3) ion rockets. They can operate much longer than can other rockets, but they produce less thrust. An electric rocket could not lift a spacecraft out of the earth's atmosphere, but it could propel a vehicle through space. Scientists are working to develop electric rockets for long space flights of the future.

Arc Jet Rockets heat a propellant gas with an electric spark called an *electric arc*. The spark can heat the gas to a temperature three or four times as great as that produced by a solid- or liquid-propellant rocket.

Plasma Jet Rockets are a type of arc jet rocket. The flow of propellant gas created by an electric arc contains some electrically charged particles. The mixture of the gas and these particles is called a *plasma*. Plasma jet rockets use an electric current and a magnetic field to increase the speed at which the plasma flows from the rocket.

Ion Rockets produce thrust with a flow of electrically charged particles called *ions*. A part of the rocket called the *ionization grid* produces ions as a special gas flows over the surface of the grid. An electric field speeds the flow of the ions from the rocket.

Nuclear Rockets heat fuel with a *nuclear reactor*, a machine that produces energy by splitting atoms. The heated fuel becomes hot, rapidly expanding gas. Such rockets can produce two or three times more power than do rockets that burn solid or liquid propellant. Scientists are working on the development of nuclear rockets for space travel.

In nuclear rockets, liquid hydrogen is pumped to the reactor through a jacket surrounding the rocket engine. This pumping process helps cool the rocket, and it also preheats the liquid hydrogen. Hundreds of narrow channels pass through the nuclear reactor. As the liquid hydrogen flows through these channels, heat from the reactor changes the fuel into rapidly expanding gas. The gas flows through the rocket's exhaust nozzle at speeds up to 22,000 miles per hour.

Early Rockets. Scientists believe the Chinese invented rockets, but they do not know exactly when. Historians describe "arrows of flying fire"—believed to have been rockets—used by Chinese armies in A.D. 1232. By 1300, the use of rockets had spread throughout much of Asia and Europe. These first rockets burned a substance called *black powder*, which consisted of charcoal, saltpeter, and sulfur. But for several hundred years, the use of rockets in fireworks displays outranked their military use in importance.

During the early 1800's, Colonel William Congreve of the British Army developed rockets that could carry explosives. Some of these rockets weighed as much as 60 pounds and could travel 1½ miles. British troops used Congreve rockets against the United States Army during the War of 1812. Austria, Russia, and several other countries also developed military rockets during the early 1800's.

An English inventor, William Hale, improved the accuracy of military rockets. He substituted three fins for the long wooden tail that had been used to guide the rocket. United States troops used Hale rockets in the Mexican War (1846-1848). During the American Civil War (1861-1865), each side used rockets in some battles.

Rockets of the Early 1900's. A Russian high-school teacher, Konstantin E. Tsiolkovsky, first stated the correct theory of rocket power. He described his theory in a scientific paper published in 1903. Robert H. Goddard, an American scientist, became the father of the modern rocket. In 1926, Goddard conducted the first successful launch of a liquid-propellant rocket. The rocket climbed 184 feet into the air at a speed of about 60 miles per hour.

During the 1930's, rocket research went forward in Germany, Russia, and the United States. Hermann Oberth led a small group of German engineers and scientists that experimented with rockets. Leading Russian rocket scientists included F. A. Tsander and I. A. Merkulov. Goddard remained the chief researcher in the United States.

During World War II, German rocketeers under the direction of Wernher von Braun developed the powerful V-2 guided missile. Germany bombarded London and Antwerp, Belgium, with hundreds of V-2's during the last months of the war. American forces captured many V-2 missiles and sent them to the United States for use in research. After the war, von Braun and more than 200 other German scientists came to the United States to continue their rocketry work. Some other German rocket experts went to Russia.

High-Altitude Rockets. For several years after World War II, scientists in the United States benefited greatly by conducting experiments with captured German V-2's. These V-2's were the first rockets used for high-altitude research.

The first high-altitude rockets designed and built in the United States included the WAC Corporal, the Aerobee, and the Viking. The 21-foot WAC Corporal reached altitudes of about 45 miles during test flights in 1945. Early models of the Aerobee climbed about 75 miles. In 1949, the United States Navy launched the

火箭兵

Chinese Warriors fired rockets in battle during the A.D. 1200's. The use of rockets as weapons and fireworks spread from China throughout much of Asia and Europe during the next century.

Robert H. Goddard, *left,* an American rocket pioneer, inspects a gasoline- and oxygen-powered rocket as his assistants look on. This rocket was built under Goddard's supervision in 1940.

Viking, an improved liquid-propellant rocket based chiefly on the V-2. The Viking measured more than 45 feet long, much longer than the Aerobee. But the first models of the Viking rose only about 50 miles.

Rockets developed by the United States armed forces during the 1950's included the Jupiter and the Pershing. The Jupiter had a range of about 1,600 miles, and the Pershing could travel about 450 miles. The U.S. Navy conducted the first successful launch of a Polaris underwater missile in 1960. United States space scientists later used many military rockets developed during the 1950's as the basis for launch vehicles.

Rocket-Powered Airplanes. On Oct. 14, 1947, Captain Charles E. Yeager of the U.S. Air Force made the first *supersonic* (faster than sound) flight. He flew a rocket-powered airplane called the *X-1*. A rocket engine also powered the *Skyrocket*, which set an airplane altitude record of 15 miles in 1951 and a speed record of 1,325 miles per hour in 1953. Another rocket plane, the X-15, raised the altitude record to more than 67 miles in 1963. It set the speed record of 4,520 miles per hour—more than six times the speed of sound—in 1967. See AIRPLANE (tables: Altitude Records, Speed Records—Land Planes).

The Space Age began on Oct. 4, 1957, when Russia launched the first artificial satellite, *Sputnik I*, with a three-stage rocket. On Jan. 31, 1958, the United States Army launched the first American satellite, *Explorer I*, into orbit with a Juno I rocket. On April 12, 1961, a Russian rocket put a man, Major Yuri A. Gagarin, into orbit around the earth for the first time. On May 5, 1961, a Redstone rocket launched Commander Alan B. Shepard, Jr., the first American to travel in space. For more information about rockets in space, see SPACE TRAVEL. WERNHER VON BRAUN and FREDERICK I. ORDWAY

ROCKET / Study Aids

Related Articles in WORLD BOOK include:

Alabama (Places to Visit [Space and Rocket Center; picture])	Guided Missile
	Heat Shield
American Institute of	Inertial Guidance
Aeronautics and Astronautics	Jet Propulsion
Artillery	Space Travel
Bazooka	Telemetry
Congreve, Sir William	Von Braun, Wernher
Goddard, Robert H.	Yeager, Charles E.

Outline

I. How Rockets Work
  A. Rocket Propellant   C. Launching a Rocket
  B. Multistage Rockets

II. How Rockets Are Used
  A. Military Use   D. Space Travel
  B. Atmospheric Research   E. Other Uses.
  C. Launching Probes
    and Satellites

III. Kinds of Rockets
  A. Solid-Propellant Rockets   C. Electric Rockets
  B. Liquid-Propellant Rockets   D. Nuclear Rockets

IV. History

Questions

What makes a rocket move?
Where does a rocket get the oxygen it needs?
What is a *multistage rocket?* A *booster?*

What was the contribution of Robert H. Goddard to rocket development? Of Konstantin E. Tsiolkovsky?
What is a *countdown?*
How do jet engines differ from rockets?
What is a *sounding rocket?* A *planetary probe?*
How will scientists use electric rockets?
Who probably invented rockets?
What are the two basic parts of rocket propellant?

ROCKET, THE, was the first steam locomotive to be built along the lines of modern engines. Two Englishmen, George and Robert Stephenson, built the locomotive in 1829. *The Rocket* reached a speed of $29\frac{1}{2}$ miles an hour on its trial run and received a prize of £500 (about $2,500) from the Liverpool and Manchester Railway. The locomotive obtained its name, not because of its speed, but because a British engineering journal said that passengers would be more foolhardy to ride on the train than they would be to ride on a military rocket. The Stephensons took up the challenge and called their engine *The Rocket*. FRANKLIN M. RECK

See also LOCOMOTIVE; STEPHENSON (family).

ROCKET ENGINE. See AIRPLANE (Rocket Engines).

ROCKET SOCIETY, AMERICAN. See AMERICAN INSTITUTE OF AERONAUTICS AND ASTRONAUTICS.

ROCKFORD, Ill. (pop. 147,370; met. area 272,063; alt. 715 ft.), is a manufacturing center and the second largest city in Illinois. The city lies on both banks of the Rock River, 17 miles south of the Wisconsin border. It is about halfway between Chicago and Dubuque, Iowa (see ILLINOIS [political map]).

Rockford is the largest *screw product* (fasteners, nuts, bolts) producer in the United States and one of the largest machine-tool centers in the world. Furniture, hardware, farm implements, automobile parts, and precision instruments and machinery, are also among the more than 300 types of products made there. Four freight railroads serve Rockford, but no passenger trains stop there. The city is also served by three airports and several truck and bus lines.

Rockford was founded in 1834. In 1836 it received a town charter. It became a city in 1852. Its original settlers were chiefly from New England, but large numbers of Swedes came here after 1850. Rockford has a mayor-council government. The city is the seat of Winnebago County. PAUL M. ANGLE

ROCKFORD COLLEGE is a private, liberal arts, coeducational college at Rockford, Ill. Courses lead to bachelor's and master's degrees. There is an evening division and an annual summer session. Rockford was founded in 1847. Until 1955 it was a coordinate college, uniting Rockford College (for women) and Rockford Men's College. For enrollment, see UNIVERSITIES AND COLLEGES (table).

ROCKHURST COLLEGE is a coeducational school in Kansas City, Mo. It is conducted by members of the Society of Jesus, a Roman Catholic order. The college grants bachelor's degrees in business administration, engineering science, and liberal arts. Rockhurst offers preprofessional training in dentistry, law, and medicine. It also has an evening division and a summer session. Rockhurst was founded in 1910. For the enrollment of Rockhurst College, see UNIVERSITIES AND COLLEGES (table). MAURICE E. VAN ACKEREN

ROCKNE, KNUTE

ROCKNE, *RAHK nee,* **KNUTE,** *noot,* **KENNETH** (1888-1931), was one of the greatest of all American football coaches. He served as the head football coach at Notre Dame University from 1918 until his death. Rockne won fame for his insistence on good sportsmanship, and for his clever football strategy. He perfected the famous "Rockne system" of offensive football, which made the forward pass and fast, deceptive plays popular in college football. His football teams won 105 games, tied 5, and lost 12.

University of Notre Dame
Knute Rockne

Rockne was born in Voss, Norway, and came to the United States in 1893. He studied chemistry and played football at Notre Dame. He was graduated in 1914, and then served as a chemistry instructor and assistant football coach for four years. He was killed in an airplane crash in Kansas.   FOREST EVASHEVSKI

ROCKS, THE. See NEW BRUNSWICK (Places to Visit).

ROCKWELL, NORMAN (1894-   ), is an American illustrator. His paintings of everyday people and situations usually tell stories, often humorous ones. But they show careful observation and technical skill. He is a meticulous craftsman, whose works portray homely incidents, well-defined character, and a wealth of supporting detail.

Rockwell gained great popularity as a cover illustrator for *The Saturday Evening Post* and other magazines. He also did art work for many advertisers. He illustrated the "Four Freedoms" of the Atlantic Charter in a well-known series of paintings.

Rockwell was born in New York City. Later, he lived in Arlington, Vt. He studied at the Chase School of Art, the National Academy of Design, and the Art Students League. His work first appeared in *Boys' Life, St. Nicholas, American Boy,* and other magazines and books for children.   NORMAN L. RICE

ROCKY MOUNTAIN COLLEGE. See UNIVERSITIES AND COLLEGES (table).

ROCKY MOUNTAIN GOAT looks like a goat, but it is not a true goat. Like the chamois, it is more closely related to the antelope family. It does not appear to be intelligent, nor as impressive or graceful as the mountain sheep. A suit of dense, woolly underfur with an overcoat of long white hair covers its body. This coat keeps it warm in its cold, windy home high in the mountains where trees will not grow.

The *billy* (male goat) stands from 3 to $3\frac{1}{2}$ feet at the shoulder and weighs about 200 pounds. A long beard gives it a dignified look. Its slender, backward-curving black horns may be as much as a foot long. The *nanny* (female goat) has smaller horns and a shorter beard. Both the male and female Rocky Mountain goat have small black hoofs.

The nanny produces one kid, or often twins, in May or June. Mountain goats live in the northern Rocky Mountains from Cook Inlet, Alaska, south through western Canada as far as Washington, Idaho, and Montana. They eat herbs, including grasses and sedges, and the leaves and twigs of shrubs. They are sure-footed, expert climbers on rocky cliffs and slopes. Each male goat prefers to be alone except during the November mating season.

Scientific Classification. The Rocky Mountain goat belongs to the bovid family, *Bovidae*. It is genus *Oreamnos*, species *O. americanus*.   VICTOR H. CAHALANE

See also ANIMAL (color picture: Animals of the Mountains).

ROCKY MOUNTAIN NATIONAL PARK, a mountain playground in northern Colorado, is one of the most magnificent sections of the Rocky Mountains. The federal government made it a national park in 1915. It covers over 260,000 acres of the highest and most rugged mountain country in the United States. It has more than 100 peaks over 10,000 feet high. The highest

Cotton Fiber Paper Manufacturers

Norman Rockwell became known for his humorous paintings of everyday life in the United States. His work has appeared in many popular American magazines.

Longs Peak in Rocky Mountain National Park towers over beautiful Nymph Lake. Slim pines line the shoreline and reflect in the crystal-clear water. The spectacular scenery in this mountain playground attracts thousands of tourists every summer.

is Longs Peak (14,256 feet). Rocky Mountain National Park has two main entrances, Estes Park on the east, and Grand Lake on the west.

Naturalist Enos Mills has been called "the father of Rocky Mountain National Park." It was through his efforts that the park was established. He built his log cabin in a valley that looked up to Longs Peak.

About 150 lakes lie within the boundaries of Rocky Mountain National Park. They reflect the snowy mountain peaks in summer, and become frozen blocks of ice in winter. The lakes and streams abound in trout, and fishing draws many thousands of visitors. The park is noted for its wildlife, including Rocky Mountain sheep (bighorn), elk, deer, black bears, and many smaller animals. More than 200 varieties of birds have been seen in the park, and more than 700 species of flowering plants have been identified there.

Rocky Mountain National Park once was a home for the Arapaho Indians and a rich source of furs for trappers. JAMES J. CULLINANE

ROCKY MOUNTAIN SHEEP. See BIGHORN.

ROCKY MOUNTAIN SPOTTED FEVER is a serious, often fatal, disease. One of the *Rickettsia*, which are germs slightly larger than viruses, causes the disease. This germ infects wood ticks, which bite man and other mammals. When the tick bites a person, it transfers the rickettsia to that person's blood stream. Doctors first discovered Rocky Mountain spotted fever in the Rocky Mountain area of the United States, but it occurs throughout the country. About 600 cases of the fever are reported every year, usually in late spring or early sum-

mer. It begins with chills and fever, and severe pains in the leg muscles and the joints. Then a rash develops. Rocky Mountain spotted fever resembles many of the typhus diseases (see TYPHUS).

Aureomycin, chloromycetin, and other antibiotics are effective in treatment. There are two vaccines that give immunity for a short time. Recovery from the fever gives complete immunity. AUSTIN EDWARD SMITH

See also RICKETTSIA.

Rocky Mountain Spotted Fever is a serious disease transmitted to humans by this wood tick.

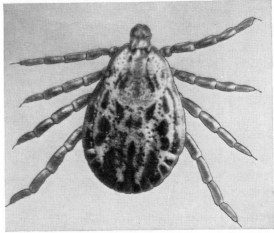

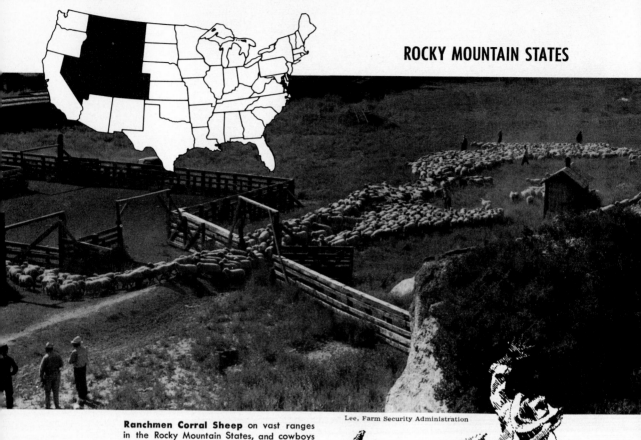

Ranchmen Corral Sheep on vast ranges in the Rocky Mountain States, and cowboys test their skill at staying on "buckin' broncos."

Lee, Farm Security Administration

ROCKY MOUNTAIN STATES include Colorado, Idaho, Montana, Nevada, Utah, and Wyoming. Arizona and New Mexico are also sometimes considered Rocky Mountain States, as well as Southwestern States. The region takes its name from the rugged, snow-capped Rocky Mountains. Fewer persons live in the Rocky Mountain States than in the state of Michigan. But the region occupies more than a fourth of the United States.

The Rockies have influenced the development of the region and the lives of its people in many ways. Winds sweep in from the Pacific Ocean and drop rain and snow on the mountains. Snow melts and forms streams that run down the mountainsides. This water provides moisture for growing crops and grasses.

Agriculture is the second largest industry in the Rocky Mountain States. Beef cattle, dairy cattle, and sheep roam the vast ranges. Wyoming produces more sheep and wool than any other state except Texas. Farmers raise large crops of wheat, cotton, corn, alfalfa, sugar beets, peas, beans, and potatoes. Great dams, including Hoover, Parker, and Davis on the Colorado River and American Falls Dam on the Snake River, provide water for irrigation and power. The Mormons

M. John Loeffler, the contributor of this article, is Professor of Geography at the University of Colorado.

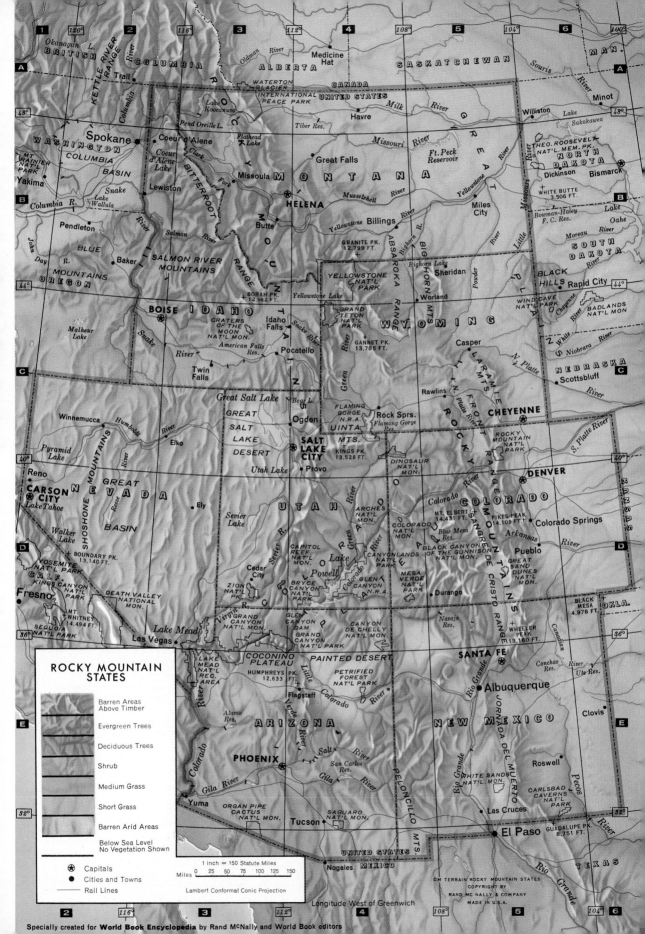

Idaho Potatoes, From the Snake River Plain, rank as one of the most famous products of the Rocky Mountain states.

A Famous Winter Sports Center, the region boasts such noted winter resorts as Aspen, Colo., and Sun Valley, Ida.

Valuable Rocky Mountains Timber is floated to sawmills to be processed into fence posts, poles, mine supports, and lumber.

Colorful Wild-West Rodeos and rugged mountain scenery, such as that found in Yellowstone and Grand Canyon national parks, attract thousands of tourists.

who settled in Utah pioneered in modern methods of irrigation in the United States.

Rich veins of minerals, including copper, gold, silver, lead, and zinc run through the mountains. Prospectors hunting for gold and silver first opened the Rocky Mountain region to settlement. Today, petroleum and natural gas earn the largest share of mining income. The Colorado Plateau yields uranium-bearing ore. The Atomic Energy Commission's raw-materials division built its western headquarters at Grand Junction, Colo.

Manufacturing is important but not too widespread, because the mountains make transportation costs high. Also, manufacturers must ship their products long distances to large market towns. The chief manufactures include primary metals, such as iron and steel; processed foods; and chemicals. Factory workers make furniture, poles, fences, and boxes from spruce, aspen, fir, and pine cut from mountain forests. The town of Eureka, Mont., is called "The Christmas Tree Capital of the World," because it markets about 3,000,000 Christmas trees every winter.

Glaciers and rushing rivers have gouged deep valleys, and canyons such as Yellowstone Canyon in Yellowstone National Park. Every year, crowds of sightseers explore the scenic wonders of Yellowstone and other spectacular sights, including Zion, Bryce, Hells, and Grand canyons. Winter-sports enthusiasts ski and toboggan on snowy mountain slopes. Sun Valley, Ida., and Aspen, Colo., have won world fame as winter-resort centers. Visitors also enjoy colorful rodeos, such as the annual Frontier Days event at Cheyenne, Wyo. Cowboys exhibit their skills at bronc riding, roping and branding cattle, and lariat throwing.

The Land and Its Resources

The United States acquired parts of Colorado, Montana, and Wyoming from France in the Louisiana Purchase of 1803. In 1848, at the end of the Mexican War, Mexico ceded to the United States land that makes up present-day Nevada and Utah, and parts of New Mexico and Arizona. Idaho became a United States possession in 1846 under the terms of the Oregon treaty with Great Britain.

Land Regions of the Rocky Mountain States are (1) the Basin and Range Region, (2) the Plateau Region, (3) the Rocky Mountains, and (4) the Great Plains.

The Basin and Range Region stretches from Nevada and western Utah through southern Arizona to southwestern New Mexico. In Nevada, the region forms a great highland area, with mountains to the east and west. The Great Salt Desert, one of the country's driest areas, covers more than 4,000 square miles in western Utah. Southern Arizona and southwestern New Mexico have broad mountains, plains, and deep valleys.

The Plateau Region includes the Columbia Plateau in southwestern Idaho and northern Nevada, and the Colorado Plateau which extends from eastern Utah and western Colorado through northern Arizona and western New Mexico. The Snake River has cut fertile valleys through the plateau in Idaho. Deep lava bedrock lies under northern Nevada. Swift streams have chiseled deep canyons in the region.

The Colorado Plateau in Utah, Colorado, and Arizona consists of mountains, flat-topped hills called *mesas*, gorges, and deep canyons. The beauty of Utah's Zion, Bryce, and Cedar Breaks canyons rivals the grandeur of Arizona's Grand Canyon.

The Rocky Mountains stretch from northern Idaho and Montana southeast to central New Mexico. These mountains were formed millions of years ago when hot, rock-making materials pushed the earth's crust skyward thousands of feet above sea level.

High in the Rockies lies a north-south watershed called the Continental Divide (see DIVIDE). Streams to the west of it flow into the Pacific Ocean. Waters to the east reach the Atlantic Ocean. Large rivers that supply water for most of the region rise in the mountains. The Snake River begins in western Wyoming, the Missouri in western Montana, and the Colorado in the range west of Denver.

Valuable timber covers the Rockies in Idaho. Glacier-gouged lakes lie hidden among the rugged, snowy peaks. Dense forests grow below the timber line on the Rockies in Montana. Much of the region is a primitive wilderness. Geysers and hot springs are scattered throughout one of the nation's most beautiful natural wonders, Yellowstone National Park. Established in 1872, Yellowstone was the first national park in the United States. Hundreds of streams flow from Utah's Rockies.

The Colorado Rockies include 55 peaks that rise 14,000 feet or more. Skiers, mountain climbers, and other winter-sports lovers visit ski lodges in the region.

The Great Plains extend from eastern Montana to

Sparkling Mountain Lakes, such as Lake Josephine in Glacier National Park, attract fishing, boating, and camping enthusiasts.
Bob and Ira Spring

ROCKY MOUNTAIN STATES

southeastern New Mexico. Occasional mountains and wide river valleys break the gently rolling highlands in Montana. Here lie colorful badlands of clay and stone formations carved by the wind and rain through thousands of years (see BADLANDS). Tough grass covers the region's dry land in Wyoming. Columns of lava rock called *buttes* tower above the plains. Farmers grow a variety of crops in the irrigated Wyoming basins. Irrigation has also turned the dry Colorado and New Mexico plains into fertile farm land.

Climate. The Rocky Mountain States have great differences in climate, depending on altitude. Low stretches of hot, dry desert make up parts of Arizona, New Mexico, Nevada, and Utah. Sections in the Rockies are generally cool, with much rainfall. High peaks in this mountain chain often force ocean winds to drop their moisture on the western side of the mountains. This gives the eastern Great Plains region comparatively little rain.

Average January temperatures range from about 10°F. in the mountain areas of northwestern Wyoming, northeastern Utah, and northern Colorado to about 50°F. in southwestern Arizona. January temperatures in Wyoming drop as low as −60°F. July temperatures average about 60°F. in northern Montana and along a belt running southward to the Rockies in central New Mexico. They average about 90°F. in southwestern Arizona.

The average yearly rainfall varies from about 50 inches in the Rockies at the Idaho-Montana border to about 5 inches in southwestern Arizona. The average annual snowfall ranges from 1 inch in many parts of the desert and Great Plains region to 200 inches in the mountain areas of Colorado and New Mexico. Between 40 and 50 feet of snow often cover mountain slopes that face the wind. Warm winter winds, called *chinooks*, blow from the mountains to the lowlands, causing temperatures to rise suddenly. These warm winds are sometimes called "snow eaters," because they melt large quantities of snow in a short time. See CHINOOK.

Activities of the People

The People. Archaeologists have discovered bones and other evidence that men lived in the Rocky Mountain region about 15,000 years ago. Cave dwellers left crude drawings on rocks and walls. The Spanish explorers who first reached the region found great numbers of Indians living there. These included the Arapaho, Bannock, Crow, Nez Percé, Paiute, Shoshoni, and Ute tribes. Today, about 190,000 of their descendants live in the Rocky Mountain States.

In 1540, the Spanish explorer Francisco Vásquez Coronado led an expedition north from Mexico. One of the party, García López de Cárdenas, discovered the famous Grand Canyon. Many other Spanish explorers passed through the region before 1804, when the United States sent Meriwether Lewis and William Clark to explore and map the mountainous wilderness.

In the middle 1800's, a group of Mormons led by Brigham Young settled in the Great Salt Lake area in Utah. They were members of the Church of Jesus Christ of Latter-day Saints who had been driven west because of their religious beliefs (see MORMONS). The Mormons

pioneered in irrigating the hard, sun-baked soil.

In 1858, the discovery of gold in Colorado started the slogan, "Pikes Peak or Bust." Thousands of gold seekers rushed there in search of quick fortunes (see GOLD RUSH). The next year, prospectors found a rich vein of silver ore at Virginia City, Nev. Prospector Henry Comstock claimed these deposits, known as the Comstock Lode. Miners soon exhausted many rich ore reserves, and boom towns were deserted overnight. Many of these "ghost" towns lie in scattered areas throughout the region.

Congress passed the first Homestead Law in 1862, and farmers, cattlemen, sheepmen, miners, and trappers poured into the area (see HOMESTEAD ACT).

Today, the people of the Rocky Mountain region are about evenly distributed between rural and urban areas. People in the most densely populated farm districts live in irrigated river valleys. The farms here are small but intensively cultivated. In many sections of the region, the population density is less than one person to the square mile. Cities have grown up near mountain passes. The major cities, including Boise, Carson City, Cheyenne, Denver, Helena, and Salt Lake City, are bustling transportation, marketing, and manufacturing centers.

Agriculture is the second largest industry in the region. During the early 1800's, settlers learned that the land could be farmed by dry farming or by irrigation (see DRY FARMING; IRRIGATION).

Cattle Raising has been the most important farm activity since the pioneers pushed west beyond the Rockies. Livestock graze on vast tracts of pasture grasses that spread over about half of the land. Montana ranks among the leading beef-producing states. Wyoming stands second after Texas in the production of sheep and wool. Vast herds of beef and dairy cattle also graze the plains and mountain slopes of Colorado and Utah. Rocky Mountain farmers receive about 15 per cent of their income from the sale of milk, butter, cheese, and other dairy products.

Field Crops. Wheat is the leading crop of the region. Many kinds of spring and winter wheat grow in the plains areas, including red spring and durum. Montana ranks among the leading wheat-growing states. Cotton is the second main income-producing crop. Most of the irrigated land devoted to cotton spreads over southern New Mexico, southern Arizona, and southeastern Nevada. Farmers harvest quantities of barley and alfalfa in Montana and Idaho. These states and Colorado are among the 10 leading sugar producers. Most of the sugar comes from sugar beets, grown in the South Platte and Arkansas valleys in Colorado, on the Snake River plain in Idaho, and in Montana and Utah.

Idaho, Colorado, Wyoming, and Montana rank among the 10 top bean states. Idaho's most famous crop is potatoes, grown on the Snake River plain.

Fruits. Rocky Mountain orchards produce more cherries than any other fruit. Utah and Idaho rank high in the production of sweet black cherries. Farmers in this region also grow plums, strawberries, currants, grapes, peaches, pears, apples, and cantaloupes.

Manufacturing and Processing. Manufacturing ranks first in the value of production among the primary industries in the region. But manufacturing plants

366

are not widespread, because of long distances from markets, high transportation costs, and the lack of a large, dependable water supply. Colorado manufactures more consumer goods than any other Rocky Mountain state.

Primary Metals, such as iron and steel, are the region's chief manufacture. Freight cars carry iron ore from Wyoming and Utah to furnaces and mills in Pueblo, Colo. Pueblo's ore-smelting and metal-refining plants have earned it the nickname of the *Pittsburgh of the West*. Important steel products of the region include rails and structural steel. Colorado and Utah have uranium mills that refine ore from the Colorado Plateau and other areas.

Food Processing. Most large Rocky Mountain cities have plants that freeze or can poultry, vegetables, and fruits. The larger towns and cities have slaughterhouses for cattle and sheep. Great numbers of animals are shipped to Denver, one of the nation's chief meat-packing centers. Thousands of workers help produce sugar from sugar beets grown throughout the region.

Forest Products. Sawmills in Idaho and Colorado produce lumber, fence posts, telephone poles, and mine supports. The largest white-pine sawmill in the world, at Lewiston, Ida., cuts about 200 million board feet of lumber a year. Idaho and Colorado also have important pulp and paper mills.

Other Manufactures of the region include furniture, chemicals, fertilizers, and electronic equipment.

Mining is the third most important industry of the Rocky Mountain States. Petroleum and natural gas bring the largest income, followed by copper. Oil fields in nine Wyoming counties supply the major share of petroleum. Most of the petroleum and natural gas produced by Colorado, Wyoming, Utah, New Mexico, and Arizona comes from fields explored in the 1950's.

Seven Rocky Mountain States—Arizona, Colorado, Idaho, Montana, Nevada, New Mexico, and Utah—rank among the 10 leading copper-producing states (see COPPER). Arizona mines account for about nine per cent of the world's copper. Silver comes from every Rocky Mountain state. Idaho stands first in the United States in silver production, and has the country's largest silver mine, in Shoshone County. The Rocky Mountain region also supplies large quantities of lead, zinc, and gold.

Colorado has about 250 mines that yield top-grade uranium-bearing ore. Soft-coal reserves lie under about a fourth of Colorado. Utah is the only state that mines gilsonite, or natural rock asphalt. Other minerals in the Rocky Mountain States include mercury, molybdenum, potash, gypsum, and kaolin, a clay used in making pottery.

Transportation. Caravans of pioneers on horseback and in jostling covered wagons rode the Oregon Trail into the Rocky Mountain region. This road stretched from Missouri to the Northwest. Others came by way of the Emigrant Trail, parallel to the Humboldt River.

Stagecoaches replaced the covered wagons, and carried travelers through the region until about 1870, when railroads first crossed the open country. The mountains and deserts hampered railroad construction. Even today, major railroads and highways extend around the Rockies, rather than over them.

Large aircraft fly over the Rockies, but small planes

avoid them. Dozens of airports serve the major airlines. In 1919, the Tucson Municipal Airport became America's first city-owned airport. Many ranchers have private landing fields for planes which they use for pleasure, and for seeding and spraying their crops.

Regional Cooperation involves chiefly the search for a sufficient and reliable water supply for farms, homes, and industry. In the late 1950's, Idaho, Montana, Wyoming, Nevada, and Utah, as well as Oregon and Washington, established the Columbia Interstate Compact Commission. This agency helps to apportion the water supplied to each state by water-power projects.

The federal government approved the Upper Colorado River Basin Project in 1956. Four large multiple-purpose dams—Flaming Gorge in northeastern Utah, Glen Canyon in northern Arizona, Navajo in northern New Mexico, and Curecanti in Colorado—are scheduled to be built by the year 2000. These dams will regulate the flow of the river and provide additional water for the states of Wyoming, Colorado, Utah, and New Mexico.

Interstate organizations also cooperate in soil and wildlife conservation, sanitation, recreation, transportation, and commerce.   M. JOHN LOEFFLER

Related Articles. For additional information on the Rocky Mountain States, see the separate article on each state in this region with its list of Related Articles. Other related articles in WORLD BOOK include:

HISTORY AND GOVERNMENT

Comstock Lode	Pioneer Life in America
Indian, American	Pony Express
Indian Wars	State Government
Lewis and Clark Expedition	Trails of Early Days
Louisiana Purchase	Western Frontier Life
Mexican War	Westward Movement

PHYSICAL FEATURES

Butte	Great Salt Lake
Colorado River	Mesa
Desert	Rocky Mountains
Glen Canyon Dam	Yellowstone
Great Basin	National Park

Outline

I. **The Land and Its Resources**
   A. Land Regions   B. Climate
II. **Activities of the People**
   A. The People   D. Mining
   B. Agriculture   E. Transportation
   C. Manufacturing   F. Regional Cooperation
      and Processing

Questions

How did the Mormons pioneer in the development of the region's agriculture?

What industry brings the Rocky Mountain States their greatest income?

What city in the region has the nickname, "The Pittsburgh of the West"? Why?

What was the Comstock Lode?

What has delayed the development of manufacturing plants throughout the Rocky Mountain region?

What is the leading agricultural crop of the area?

What are chinooks? Why are they called "snow eaters"?

What natural wonder in the Rocky Mountain area was set aside as the country's first national park?

Where is the country's largest silver mine?

Where is "The Christmas Tree Capital of the World"?

The Rocky Mountains tower high above the famous Canadian resort in Banff, Alberta, above. The Rockies stretch over 3,000 miles across the western part of the North American continent, from northern New Mexico to northern Alaska.

ROCKY MOUNTAINS. The Rockies are a well-named group of jagged, snow-capped peaks which run through the western part of North America. This chain of mountains extends over 3,000 miles, and is about 350 miles wide in some places. The Rockies begin in northern New Mexico and extend as far as northern Alaska. From New Mexico, the mountain chain stretches through Colorado, Utah, Wyoming, Idaho, Montana, and Washington. At the International Border, the part of the range known as the Canadian Rockies passes through the provinces of Alberta and British Columbia, and the Northwest Territories and Yukon Territory of Canada. The Rockies are part of the Cordilleran chain which reaches from Cape Horn to the Arctic Circle. The Sierra Madre Oriental of Mexico and the Andes of South America form the southern part of this chain.

Many persons include in the Rocky Mountains peaks and ranges which are really not part of that chain. Geographers do not include in the Rockies proper such

ranges as the Sierra Madre in Mexico, the Sierra Nevada, Cascade, and Coast ranges in the United States, and the Coast, Gold, and Selkirk ranges of Canada.

Most of the peaks of the Rockies were formed millions of years ago in a great upheaval of the earth's crust. The sides of the mountains have been found to contain the fossil skeletons of animals that once lived in the sea, and rocks that were formed in the hot interior of the earth. In the southern half of the Rockies, there are mountains which were once volcanoes. Evident signs of volcanic activity are also found in the huge lava sheets of Idaho and the geysers of Yellowstone National Park. Since the time the Rockies were formed, the peaks have been cut into their sharp spires and angled faces by the forces of the wind, the rain, and the glaciers. The glaciers hollowed out the valleys between the peaks of the Rockies, and thus show geologists the history of the mountains. The glaciers and streams also exposed the great mineral riches of the Rocky Mountains, including gold, silver, lead, and copper, as well as bituminous (soft) coal, oil shale, and phosphate rock.

Grasslands cover the lower Rocky Mountain slopes. Forests of pine and spruce below the timber line give way to sparse grasses and low shrubs higher up. Animals found in the Rockies include grizzly bears, bighorn sheep, pumas, Rocky Mountain goats, antelope, and caribou. Cattle and sheep graze on mountain pastures during the summer. Farmers raise such crops as potatoes and wheat in fertile mountain areas.

The Rockies are famous for their scenic beauty and natural wonders. Several national parks of the United States are located in the Rockies, including the oldest and largest, Yellowstone National Park, and the Rocky Mountain National Park of Colorado. Such mighty rivers as the Columbia, the Missouri, the Arkansas, the Colorado, and the Rio Grande begin in the Rocky Mountains.

In the United States, the Rockies are divided into two distinct parts by a plateau in Wyoming called the Laramie Plains. Engineers of the first railroad to the Pacific found this plateau while they were searching for a place where they could lay their tracks across the Rockies without climbing heavy grades. In southern Wyoming the plateau is over 250 miles long and about 100 miles wide. It runs through the mountains from east to west, and is located at a height of about 7,000 feet above sea level.

That part of the Rocky Mountain system which lies south of the Laramie Plains is the highest and broadest of the chain. It covers Colorado and eastern Utah, and also the somewhat lower and more compact mountains of New Mexico. This section is referred to as the *Southern Rockies* of the United States. In Colorado there are 55 peaks of the Rockies which rise over 14,000 feet above sea level. Ten peaks in Utah and New Mexico are over 13,000 feet.

North of the Laramie Plains, the direction of the Rockies range turns northwest. These mountains are narrower and slightly lower than in the south, and they constitute the *Northern Rockies* of Wyoming, Montana, Idaho, and Washington.

The Canadian Rockies include dozens of peaks more than 11,000 feet high, and several more than 12,000 feet. Mount Robson, in British Columbia, is 12,972 feet high. In Alberta, some of the finest scenic areas of the Rockies have been made into Canadian national parks, including the famous regions around Banff and Lake Louise. The principal peaks of the Canadian Rockies are in British Columbia. As the range extends north through Alaska, the Rockies gradually become lower until they disappear in a series of ice-covered hills at the Arctic Circle.   LOYAL DURAND, JR.

Related Articles in WORLD BOOK include:

Bighorn	Mount	Rocky Mountain
Bitterroot Range	Assiniboine	Goat
Continental Divide	Mount Evans	Teton Range
Divide	Pikes Peak	Wasatch Range

ROCOCO, *roh KO koh,* is a style of art that flourished in western Europe from about 1720 to 1780. The style was especially important in France. Rococo artists used irregular flowing curves, shimmering surfaces, and elaborate ornamentation in their works. The word *rococo* comes from a French word meaning a fanciful rock or shell design.

Rococo developed out of an ornate style called *baroque.* Rococo art is more delicate, and usually on a

The Art Institute of Chicago

Rococo Vase made in France in 1754 shows a painting in the style of François Boucher.

smaller scale than baroque. Rococo often has a feeling of weariness and relaxation. The baroque style is heroic and energetic. Compare the baroque painting *Elevation of the Cross* by Peter Paul Rubens with *The Swing,* a rococo painting by Jean Fragonard. The paintings are reproduced in color in the PAINTING article.

The rococo style was used in painting, sculpture, architecture, and the design of furniture, textiles, porcelain, and clothing. François Boucher, Fragonard, and Antoine Watteau were the leading French rococo painters. They painted classical mythology subjects in playful, intimate, make-believe outdoor settings. Aristocratic ladies and gentlemen were often represented in their paintings. Other leading rococo painters included Giovanni Tiepolo of Italy and Thomas Gainsborough of England. In architecture, the richness of rococo ornamentation reached its greatest splendor in the palaces, monasteries, and churches of southern Germany and Austria (see GERMANY [Arts]).   ALLEN S. WELLER

See also ARCHITECTURE (The 1700's); PAINTING (The 1600's and 1700's); FRAGONARD, JEAN HONORÉ; BAROQUE.

ROD. See EYE (The Eyeball).

ROD is a unit for measuring length in the English system. One rod is equal to $5\frac{1}{2}$ yards, $16\frac{1}{2}$ feet, or $\frac{1}{320}$ mile. One square rod is equal to $\frac{1}{160}$ acre.

The Legal Rod in the 1500's was the total length of the left feet of 16 men who lined up to be measured.

Ford Motor Co.

RODENT

RODENT is an animal with front teeth especially suited to gnawing hard objects. Squirrels, beavers, and rats are rodents. Squirrels can break the shells of nuts with their front teeth. Beavers can gnaw through tree trunks, and rats can gnaw through some wood and plaster walls. The many kinds of rodents include gophers, hamsters, mice, and porcupines.

All rodents have two top and two bottom front teeth called *incisors*. They wear away at the tips, but do not wear out until late in the animal's lifetime because they keep growing until the animal is old. The incisors wear faster in the back than in front. As a result, they have a chisellike edge, well-suited to gnawing. Rodents also have back teeth which they use for chewing.

Rodents are *mammals* (animals that feed their young milk). There are more individual rodents than there are individuals of all other kinds of mammals combined. Rodents live in almost all parts of the world.

Mice are the smallest rodents and capybaras of South America are the largest. Some capybaras are up to 4 feet long. Most rodents are *herbivorous* (plant eaters). But rats and some other rodents will eat almost any food they can find.

Rodents are both helpful and harmful to man. Some rodents eat harmful insects and weeds, and some have valuable fur. Man uses mice and rats in scientific research. But some rodents, especially mice and rats, damage crops and other property. Rats and mice also carry serious diseases, such as plague and typhus.

Scientific Classification. Rodents make up the order *Rodentia* in the class *Mammalia* and the phylum *Chordata*. To learn where the order fits into the whole animal kingdom, see ANIMAL (table: A Classification of the Animal Kingdom). WILLIAM V. MAYER

Related Articles. See the following articles on rodents:

Agouti	Flying	Kangaroo Rat	Porcupine
Beaver	Squirrel	Lemming	Prairie
Capybara	Gerbil	Marmot	Dog
Cavy	Gopher	Mountain	Rat
Chinchilla	Guinea Pig	Beaver	Squirrel
Chipmunk	Hamster	Mouse	Vole
Coypu	Jerboa	Muskrat	Woodchuck
Dormouse	Jumping Mouse	Pack Rat	

RODEO, *ROH dee oh* or *roh DAY oh*, is an exciting show that presents the features of a Western roundup. It is a contest of superiority among cowboys. They come to the rodeo at their own expense, and pay an entry fee for the events in which they participate. They receive money only if they perform well enough to win a prize.

Famous rodeos include Frontier Days in Cheyenne, Wyo.; the Roundup in Pendleton, Ore.; and the Stampede in Calgary, Alta. (see ALBERTA [color picture]). The events listed below are approved by the Rodeo Cowboys Association.

Bareback Riding is the original sport of the West. In this thrilling, dangerous event, the rider does not have reins to control his horse. The cowboy must stay on the horse for 10 seconds while the animal jumps,

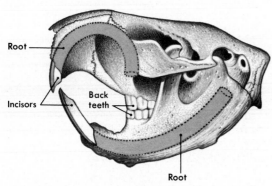

WORLD BOOK illustration by Tom Dolan

All Rodents have chisellike upper and lower front teeth called *incisors.* They can be seen in the beaver skull *above.*

The Wood Rat, a common rodent, eats mainly roots, stems, seeds, and leaves. It can live without drinking much water.

U.S. Dept. of the Interior

A Bronco-Buster must stay mounted for at least 10 seconds spurring the horse as often as possible. He may grip the reins with only one hand. The other hand must remain free.

Bob Taylor

Bob Taylor

A Rodeo puts cowboys through the paces of an old-time Western roundup. Roping is one of the many tests of skill in which cowboys compete for points to decide the national champion.

plunges, and bucks. He must also spur the horse.

Saddle-Bronc Riding resembles bareback riding, except that the cowboy uses a saddle, a halter, and one rein. He must hold on with only one hand, spur the horse, and stay on for 10 seconds. *Pickup men* ride alongside and take off the rider after this time.

Bull Riding. In this event, the cowboy holds onto a long rope that has been looped around the middle of a bull's body. A bull ride lasts 8 seconds, and the cowboy is not required to spur the animal. Rodeo clowns distract the bull and protect the cowboy after he has completed his ride or been thrown off the bull.

Calf Roping. The cowboy rides a horse in this event. He must throw a rope around a running calf, stop his horse, dismount, throw the calf to the ground, and tie three of its feet. A champion rider can do all this in from 12 to 15 seconds.

Steer Wrestling, or *bulldogging,* is the only event that does not come from the original Western roundups. A Texas cowboy named Bill Pickett is generally credited with devising this spectacular stunt. Pickett would plunge from the back of a speeding horse onto the neck of a running steer. He would then grasp the steer by the head and twist the animal to the ground. An expert cowboy can do this in 3 to 8 seconds.   EDDIE G. COLE

See also BRONCO; COWBOY (picture: Roping a Calf); and the Annual Events sections in the following articles: ALBERTA; COLORADO; MONTANA; NEVADA; WYOMING.

RODGERS, RICHARD (1902-   ), is a noted American composer of popular music. He wrote the music for *Oklahoma!* (1943), a musical comedy that ran nearly six years in New York City. He and his associates shared Pulitzer prizes for *Oklahoma!* and *South Pacific.*

Rodgers was born in New York City. He attended Columbia University. While there, he began to work with Lorenz Hart. Their first professional success was *A Connecticut Yankee,* in 1927. Together they wrote 29 musical shows and nearly 400 songs. The shows include *Present Arms, On Your Toes,* and *Pal Joey.* After Hart's death in 1943,

Bettmann Archive

Richard Rodgers

Rodgers worked with Oscar Hammerstein II (see HAMMERSTEIN [Oscar II]). Rodgers composed the music for *Oklahoma!, Carousel, South Pacific, The King and I, Me and Juliet,* and *The Sound of Music.*   GILBERT CHASE

RODIN, *roh DAHN,* **AUGUSTE** (1840-1917), is ranked by many as the greatest sculptor of the 1800's. Rodin greatly admired the Italian sculptors Donatello and Michelangelo. Like Michelangelo, Rodin dealt almost entirely with the human figure. Perhaps no sculptor since Michelangelo has created figures with such emotional intensity as Rodin did.

Rodin created an enormous amount of sculpture, and it covers a wide range of human vitality, passion, and suffering. Rodin was primarily a modeler in clay and wax rather than a carver in stone. He built up his forms

Auguste Rodin, *right,* was one of the foremost of modern sculptors. *The Thinker, below,* is his most noted figure.

The Metropolitan Museum of Art, New York; Brown Bros.

371

into irregular, flowing masses and surfaces that carry a vigorous sense of movement to each part. Rodin tried to capture from the living model those fine shades of pose and action that express the individual character of the body. He created many works that he deliberately left incomplete or fragmentary. But even these have a boldness that makes them completely satisfying works in themselves. See HAND (picture).

Rodin was born in Paris. He did not win public recognition for many years, and had to earn his living designing popular sculpture and sculptural ornament for commercial firms. Indifference and misunderstanding greeted his first sculpture exhibits. Gradually, however, appreciation for his work began to spread. By 1880, a large number of influential artists, critics, and public figures recognized his genius.

In 1880, Rodin was commissioned by the French government to create a large sculptural door for the Museum of Decorative Art in Paris. The subject was the "Inferno" from Dante's *Divine Comedy*. The door was never finished, but Rodin did many figures for it. Later he developed many of them as independent sculptures. The best known include *The Thinker* and *The Kiss*. His most important later works include the monumental group *The Burghers of Calais* and the monument to Balzac. The Balzac statue appears in color in the FRANCE (Arts) article. Rodin's *Orpheus* appears in color in the SCULPTURE article. MARCEL FRANCISCONO

RODNEY, CAESAR (1728-1784), was an American statesman. With Thomas McKean, George Read, and John Dickinson, he was most responsible for Delaware's participation in the American Revolutionary War. As a delegate to the Continental Congress in 1776, he voted for independence, riding 80 miles on horseback in order to arrive in time. Rodney was born in Dover, Del. His experience in many county offices prepared him for the provincial assembly. Except for 1771, he served there from 1761 to 1776. Rodney led opposition to British laws during this period, and was elected to the Continental Congresses of 1774 and 1775. In 1777, he commanded the Delaware militia. The next year, he was elected president of the state for a three-year term. A statue of Rodney represents Delaware in Statuary Hall. See also DOVER. CLARENCE L. VER STEEG

RODÓ, *roh DOH*, **JOSÉ ENRIQUE** (1872?-1917), was a Uruguayan thinker and essayist. He believed in the human spirit's infinite capacity to renew itself, but he feared that humanity was pursuing material goals at the expense of the spirit. In his essay *Ariel* (1900), Rodó warned Latin-American youth to avoid the excessive materialism he saw in the United States and to devote part of its energy to higher, spiritual goals. His message, often misinterpreted as approving hatred of the United States, remains an active force in Latin-American thought today. Rodó figures in the Latin-American literary movement of *Modernism* as the master of the literary essay.

Rodó was born in Montevideo, Uruguay. He attended the University of Montevideo, and served in the Uruguayan parliament for three terms. MARSHALL R. NASON

RODRIGO DÍAZ. See CID, THE.

RODZINSKI, *roh JIN skih*, **ARTUR** (1894-1958), was a well-known American conductor. He directed major orchestras in Los Angeles, Philadelphia, Cleveland, Chicago, and New York. He also served as the guest conductor of many other important orchestras. Rodzinski was born in Split, Yugoslavia. He came to the United States in 1926. From 1943 to 1947, he conducted the New York Philharmonic. IRVING KOLODIN

ROE. See CAVIAR; SPAWN.

ROE, SIR ALLIOTT VERDON- (1877-1958), was the first Englishman to design, build, and fly an airplane. In 1910, he founded A. V. Roe & Company, Ltd., which became one of the world's largest aircraft firms. Roe was born in Manchester. He worked for an automobile firm before entering aviation. He made short flights in his aircraft, but did not succeed financially until Louis Blériot's flight across the English Channel in 1909 showed that airplanes might become important. ROBERT B. HOTZ

ROE DEER. See DEER (table: Some Members of the Deer Family).

ROEBLING, *ROBE ling*, is the family name of two American civil engineers, father and son, who built the Brooklyn Bridge and other bridges in the United States.

John Augustus Roebling (1806-1869) pioneered in designing suspension bridges. He started the first wire-rope and cable factory in the U.S. He designed the Brooklyn Bridge, using large cables composed of parallel strands of steel wire with a continuous soft-wire wrapping as protection against weather. Roebling died after his foot was crushed while he was making surveys for the Brooklyn Bridge. He was born in Mühlhausen, Germany.

Washington Augustus Roebling (1837-1926) became chief engineer on the Brooklyn Bridge after his father's death. During construction of the bridge foundations, he was stricken with caisson disease, which left him an invalid the remainder of his life (see BENDS). He directed the completion of the bridge by inspecting the work with field glasses from his sickroom window. He was born in Saxonburg, Pa. ROBERT W. ABBETT

ROEMER, OLAUS. See LIGHT (Speed of Light).

ROENTGEN. See RADIATION (Effects of Exposure); ION AND IONIZATION.

ROENTGEN, *RUNT gun*, **WILHELM KONRAD** (1845-1923), a German physicist, in 1901 won the first Nobel prize in physics for his discovery of X rays. Experimenters using *Crookes tubes* (evacuated glass tubes through which an electric current was passed) found that photographic plates near the tubes became fogged. Investigating the fogging in 1895, Roentgen covered a Crookes tube with black paper. He found that a fluorescent substance nearby glowed when he turned on the current.

Roentgen assumed that unknown, invisible rays, which he called *X rays*, were coming from the tube. These rays passed through some substances, such as flesh, but were stopped by others, such as metal or bone. Because of this characteristic, Roentgen found he could take a photograph of the bone structure of his hand with the rays. The use of X rays revolutionized medical and surgical techniques, and provided new insights into the structure of the atom.

Roentgen was born in Lennep (now Remscheid), Germany. Roentgen was a professor at the University of Würzburg when he made his famous discovery. For many years, X rays were called *Roentgen rays* in his honor.   SIDNEY ROSEN

See also X RAYS.

ROETHKE, *REHT kee,* **THEODORE** (1908-1963), an American poet, received the Pulitzer prize for poetry in 1954 for *The Waking: Poems 1933-1953.* Roethke shifted his style often between his first published work, *Open House* (1941), and his last collection, *The Far Field* (1964). His early poems had the concentrated quality of the poetry of Emily Dickinson. His next works showed the meditative mysticism of T. S. Eliot's poems. His later poems showed the influence of William Butler Yeats.

United Press Int.
Theodore Roethke

Roethke's concerns, however, remained constant. His field was the inner life rather than the political or social life. He looked for a sense of self in memories of childhood and for a sense of life in the examination of growing things. His father's greenhouse revealed for him nature (rooting, blossoming, dying) and art (grafting stems, forcing bloom). Roethke also wrote poems for children. He was born in Saginaw, Mich.   MONA VAN DUYN

ROGATION DAYS, *roh GAY shun,* are the Monday, Tuesday, and Wednesday before Ascension Day, as celebrated in the Roman Catholic, Anglican, and Protestant Episcopal Churches. On Rogation Days, the priests and people sing or recite prayers known as the *litanies.* Often the singing is done in a public procession. The week in which the days occur is sometimes called *Rogation Week.* The name comes from the Latin *rogare,* meaning *to ask.* The chief purpose of these prayers is to ask the blessing of God upon the year's crops.   FULTON J. SHEEN and MERVIN MONROE DEEMS

See also ASCENSION DAY; LITANY.

ROGERS, ROBERT. See ROGERS' RANGERS; PONTIAC (picture).

ROGERS, WILL (1879-1935), started life as a cowhand, and went on to become a stage and motion-picture star, and a noted homespun philosopher. He is still regarded as one of the greatest ropers of all time. But it was the shrewd, homely witticisms he made while performing his tricks that won him fame and fortune.

A talented writer, Rogers' short comments on the news appeared in about 350 daily newspapers. In 1926, he toured Europe as President Calvin Coolidge's "ambassador of good will." The following year, his admirers chuckled over his *Letters of a Self-Made Diplomat to His President* (1927). But Rogers was at his best giving a performance. His usual opening, "All I know is what I read in the papers," became a byword during the 1920's.

William Penn Adair Rogers was born on a ranch near Oologah, Indian Territory (now Oklahoma). His parents had some Cherokee Indian blood. Rogers attended Kemper Military Academy in Boonville, Mo., for two years ("One in the guardhouse and one in the 4th grade," he said later). He left school in 1898, and became a cowboy in the Texas Panhandle. Rogers drifted off to Argentina and later turned up in South

Wide World
Will Rogers, the cowboy philosopher, became famous for his homespun humor and his shrewd, timely comments on current events.

Africa as a member of Texas Jack's Wild West Circus.

Rogers made his first stage appearance in New York City in 1905. He first reached real fame in the Ziegfeld Follies of 1916. In 1918, he started his motion-picture career. In 1934, he made his first appearance in a stage play in Eugene O'Neill's *Ah, Wilderness!* Rogers married Betty Blake, an Arkansas schoolteacher, in 1908. They had four children. Rogers was killed in a plane crash near Point Barrow, Alaska, while on a flight to the Orient with Wiley Post. Statues of the cowboy philosopher stand in the Statuary Hall Collection in the Capitol in Washington, D.C., and at the Will Rogers Museum in Claremore, Okla.   HARRIET VAN HORNE

See also OKLAHOMA (Places to Visit).

ROGERS, WILLIAM PIERCE (1913-   ), became secretary of state under President Richard M. Nixon in January, 1969. A long-time friend and political associate of Nixon, Rogers had previously served as U.S. attorney general under President Dwight D. Eisenhower from 1957 to 1961. He organized the civil rights division of the attorney general's office.

Rogers was born in Norfolk, N.Y., and graduated from Colgate University and Cornell University Law School. He was an assistant district attorney in New York County before entering the Navy in World War II. After the war, he served as counsel for two Senate investigating committees, and later was an assistant attorney general. In 1967, Rogers served on the United States delegation to the United Nations.   DAVID S. BRODER

William P. Rogers
Department of State

373

ROGERS ACT. See FOREIGN SERVICE (The Rogers Act).

ROGERS COLLEGE. See UNIVERSITIES AND COLLEGES (table).

ROGERS' RANGERS scouted for the British Army during the French and Indian War (1754-1763). Robert Rogers (1731-1795) led the rangers. He won fame as a daring commander whose men would follow him anywhere. During the French and Indian War, Rogers' Rangers carried out many bold raids. But his men were rowdy and undisciplined, and in constant trouble with their superior officers. Rogers was born in Massachusetts, and served as an Indian trader and explorer. In 1756, he became captain of a company of rangers. By 1758, he had been promoted to major and given command of nine companies of rangers. Rogers faced constant financial trouble in later years, and died in poverty. He remained loyal to Great Britain during the Revolutionary War. MERRILL JENSEN

ROGET, *roh SHAY,* or *rahzh AY,* **PETER MARK** (1779-1869), was a British physician and scholar. He became best known as the compiler of Roget's *Thesaurus of English Words and Phrases* (1852). This book has been a source of synonyms for more than 100 years. Roget was born near London. He received a medical degree from the University of Edinburgh, and lectured on anatomy and physiology throughout England. Roget also lectured and wrote about physics, mathematics, and electricity. He made a slide rule, and worked on a calculating machine. G. E. BENTLEY

ROGIER, CHARLES. See BELGIUM (Independence).

ROHDE, RUTH BRYAN OWEN. See OWEN, RUTH B.

ROJANKOVSKY, *ROH jan KAWF skee,* **FEODOR** (1891-1970), was a Russian-American artist and illustrator of books for children. In 1956, Rojankovsky won the Caldecott medal for illustrating John Langstaff's *Frog Went A-Courtin'*.

Rojankovsky was born in Latvia and studied at the Academy of Fine Arts in Moscow. The Russian Revolution interrupted his career, but in 1925 he went to Paris, hoping to illustrate books for children. He stayed there until 1941, when he came to the United States. His first illustrations published in Paris appeared in Esther Averill's *Daniel Boone.* Rojankovsky also illustrated *The Tall Book of Mother Goose,* Rudyard Kipling's *Just-So Stories,* and Esther Averill's *Cartier Sails the St. Lawrence.* RUTH HILL VIGUERS

ROLAMITE is a nearly frictionless mechanism that can perform a variety of mechanical jobs. A simple rolamite device consists of two rollers that are held tightly in the loops of an *S*-shaped flexible band. The ends of the band are attached to a frame. When the rollers are pushed, they roll with little friction along the band from one end to the other. The movement of the rollers can operate switches and valves to control other machines. Different devices with more rollers and bands can be made from the simple rolamite principle.

ROLAND, *ROH lund,* was the hero of the great French epic poem, *Song of Roland,* written about 1100. In Italian romances, Roland is known as *Orlando.* He was probably a Frankish count named *Hruolandus* who died in an ambush staged by Basque mountaineers in 778.

The French epic tells that Charlemagne defeated the Saracens in Spain. Through treachery, he was persuaded to withdraw beyond the Pyrenees, leaving his nephew Roland in command of the rear guard. An army of 100,000 Saracens attacked Roland's force. Too proud to send for help, Roland fought until all his companions fell. Alone and wounded, he blew his enchanted horn. Charlemagne heard the call and returned with his army only to find Roland dead, his face turned toward the fleeing enemy. ARTHUR M. SELVI

ROLAND DE LA PLATIÈRE, *raw LAHN duh lah PLAH TYAIR,* **MARIE JEANNE** (1754-1793), known as MADAME ROLAND, was a political adviser and hostess to the Girondist group during the French Revolution (see GIRONDIST). She was intelligent, ambitious, and attractive. With her husband, Jean-Marie Roland de la Platière, a minor government official, she took an active interest in the revolutionary movement which began in 1789. By 1791, they had moved from their country home near Lyon to Paris. Roland became minister of interior under the Girondists in 1792. Madame Roland helped him administer this office, and also served as hostess to many of the leaders of the Girondist group.

Brown Bros.
Madame Roland

Unfortunately for party unity, Madame Roland disliked some members of the Girondists. Her dislike of Georges Jacques Danton helped alienate him from the party. When the Girondist leaders were arrested in June, 1793, Madame Roland also went to prison. After a political trial, she was executed by the guillotine in November, 1793. Her husband, who had escaped arrest, committed suicide when he learned of her death. The *Memoirs* she wrote in prison explained her beliefs and became very popular. Madame Roland was born in Paris. RICHARD M. BRACE

ROLE PLAYING is a method of teaching and learning. A real-life problem, such as a disagreement between people, is described. Members of a group act out roles. Each tries different ways of behaving in the situation. Other members of the group observe the effects of the behavior. Then the group discusses what happened and often suggests other ways of handling the problem.

Role playing, sometimes called *sociodrama,* was perfected in the 1930's and has been used in schools, industry, social work, and adult education. Doctors use a form of role playing, called *psychodrama,* to treat mentally ill patients. Role playing helps people understand the feelings of others. It also allows people to test new solutions to problems. MALCOLM S. KNOWLES

See also MENTAL ILLNESS (Special Techniques).

ROLFE, JOHN (1585-1622), an early English settler at Jamestown, Va., was married to the famous Indian princess, Pocahontas. Their marriage in 1614 made the Indians friendly and brought peace to the Jamestown colony.

Rolfe was born at Heachum, England. He was shipwrecked near the Bermuda Islands in 1609 while on his way to Virginia, but he reached there in 1610. He dis-

The Marriage of John Rolfe and Pocahontas took place in Virginia. It is thought to have been the first marriage between an Indian and an Englishman. The marriage greatly improved relations between the Indians and the Virginia settlers.

Ayer Collection, Newberry Library

covered a method of curing tobacco that made it popular in England. As a result, tobacco became the basis of Virginia's economy.

Rolfe took Pocahontas to England, and she died there in 1617. After her death, he returned to Virginia and became a member of the Virginia council. He was killed by Indians in the massacre of 1622. Rolfe and Pocahontas had a son, Thomas. JOSEPH CARLYLE SITTERSON

See also POCAHONTAS.

ROLL SULFUR. See BRIMSTONE.

ROLLAND, *raw LAHN*, **ROMAIN** (1866-1944), a French author, won the 1915 Nobel prize for literature. His reputation is based on his 10-volume novel *Jean-Christophe* (1904-1912), the story of a young German-born musician. Rolland called the work a *roman-fleuve*, by which he meant that its form corresponded to the unpredictable whims of life, rather than to any preconceived design or plot. In *Jean-Christophe*, Rolland criticized modern civilization and commented on the artist's place in society. The novel expresses Rolland's idealism, his opposition to egotism and hypocrisy, and his love of courage, sincerity, and enthusiasm.

Rolland was born in Clamecy in Burgundy. He taught in Paris from about 1900 to 1912. He wrote a series of biographies of famous musicians, artists, and writers, and several plays. Rolland was living in Switzerland when World War I began in 1914. He remained there during the war, and appealed to intellectuals on both sides to work for peace. EDITH KERN

ROLLER is a brightly colored bird. It looks like a jay, but is more closely related to the motmots and kingfishers. Like them, it has toes which are partially grown together. The roller gets its name from the male's habit of tumbling in the air when it is trying to attract the attention of the female. The *common roller* spends its summers in southern Europe and flies to North Africa for the winter. It nests in holes in the ground, and the female lays pure white eggs.

Scientific Classification. Rollers belong to the roller family, *Coraciidae*. The common roller is genus *Coracias*, species *C. garrulus*. HERBERT FRIEDMANN

See also BIRD (color picture: Birds of Other Lands).

ROLLER BEARING. See BEARING (Kinds of Bearings; pictures).

ROLLER SKATING is the exciting sport of skating on wheeled skates. Millions of persons throughout the United States, Canada, and many other countries enjoy roller skating. Almost every American child skates on sidewalks and playgrounds. Skating to music at indoor rinks is a popular year-round sport. The United States has more than 4,000 roller rinks, and about 20 million Americans enjoy roller skating every year.

Roller skating has also developed into an organized

Jim Collins

Wide World

Wide World

Roller Skating Is an Exciting Sport for both children and adults. Many children learn to skate in playgrounds or on sidewalks. Experienced skaters may perform skating dances set to music or compete in sports events, such as a roller derby.

375

sport, with contests for speed skating, figure skating, and dancing. The Girl Scouts in the United States award merit badges to members for roller skating.

The origin of roller skating is uncertain. In 1760, a man named Joseph Merlin demonstrated in London a pair of roller skates he had invented. Indoor roller skating became popular in England by the mid-1800's. James Plimpton, an American, invented an improved skate in 1863. Beginning in the 1800's, roller skating had alternate periods of popularity and disfavor. It has gained steadily in popularity since the 1930's.

Equipment

Roller Skates. For outdoor skating, most people wear skates with steel wheels. These skates usually clamp to the shoes and have a strap that goes around the ankle. For indoor skating, skaters usually wear skates with attached boots. These may have wood, fiber, or plastic wheels mounted on rubber cushions. The cushions make the wheels flexible so the skaters can turn by leaning to one side or the other. Both outdoor and indoor skates may have ball bearings.

Rinks. Most indoor rinks have skating surfaces made of maple or some other hard wood. A growing number of rinks have asphalt floors. The floors of most rinks are coated with a thin layer of plastic, which is replaced every few months. This coating protects the floor from wear, and keeps the skate wheels from slipping.

Roller Skating as a Sport

The two main kinds of competitive skating are (1) artistic skating and (2) speed skating. The United States Amateur Roller Skating Association conducts and sponsors such skating contests throughout the country. It has headquarters at 120 West 42nd Street, New York City, N.Y. 10036. There are also roller-derby and roller-skating hockey contests. Roller-skating hockey, a game that is played much like ice hockey, is becoming increasingly popular in some areas (see ROLLER-SKATING HOCKEY).

Artistic Roller Skating may be divided into (1) school-figure skating, (2) free skating, and (3) dancing. In *school-figure skating*, the skaters must complete 64 different maneuvers. They skate on a series of circles painted on the floor. Many of the figures are similar to those performed in ice skating (see ICE SKATING). In *free skating*, the skaters create their own routines of jumps and spins. They can compete as individuals, with partners, or in teams of four persons. They are judged on the originality, beauty, and technical skill of their routines.

In *dancing*, a man and woman skate together as a team and follow a series of standard steps. They are judged on their timing with the music, and on their grace and skill.

Speed-Skating Contests are usually held on rinks, although many schools and communities hold outdoor contests. Distances range up to five miles for men, and one mile for women. Children race over much shorter distances.

Roller Derby is a speed-skating sport. Teams consist of five men and five women. The male members of each of two teams compete for 12 minutes, then the women

skate for the same period. A player scores points by *lapping* an opposing player. This means that he passes the opponent after skating one more lap than the opponent has skated. Players are allowed to block each other in this rough sport.　　　　　　　　　　　　O. H. NELSON

See also HOCKEY.

ROLLER-SKATING HOCKEY is played in much the same way as ice hockey, but the players wear roller skates. The rink is about 60 feet wide by 90 feet long. Goals 5 feet wide and 4 feet high stand halfway between the sidelines of the rink. The game usually consists of two periods of 20 minutes each. See also HOCKEY (How to Play Hockey).

ROLLING MILL. See IRON AND STEEL (How Steel Is Shaped and Used).

ROLLINS COLLEGE is a privately controlled, coeducational school at Winter Park, Fla. It has schools of liberal arts and sciences, music, secretarial studies, and commercial art. It grants bachelor's degrees in arts, science, and music. There is a fine shell collection on the campus. Rollins was founded in 1885. For enrollment, see UNIVERSITIES AND COLLEGES (table).

ROLLO. See NORMAN; NORMANDY.

RÖLVAAG, *ROLL vahg,* **OLE EDVART** (1876-1931), was a Norwegian-American novelist. His fame rests on *Giants in the Earth* (1924-1925), a classic novel about life on the American frontier. The book describes the hardships of Norwegian farmers in the Midwest during the late 1800's. Rölvaag continued his story in *Peder Victorious* (1928) and *The Blessed Day* (1931). His novels were written in Norwegian.

Rölvaag was born in Dønna, near Bodø, Norway. He came to the United States in 1896, farmed for a short time, and then attended colleges in the United States and Norway. He became a U.S. citizen in 1908. From 1907 until his death, he was professor of Norwegian at St. Olaf College in Northfield, Minn.　　RICHARD B. VOWLES

Harper & Bros.
Ole Rölvaag

ROMAINS, *roh MAN,* **JULES** (1885-1972), was the pen name of LOUIS FARIGOULE, a French dramatist and novelist. He wrote several satirical plays. The best known of these is *Dr. Knock* (1923), a comedy about a successful fraud. Romains was even better known as a novelist. His series of novels published under the general title of *Men of Good Will* (1913-1946) is one of the great achievements of French literature. These novels demonstrate Romains' philosophy of *unanimism*, according to which the experiences and emotions of groups are more important than those of individuals.

Romains' other works include the books of poems *Song of Ten Years* and *The Unanimistic Life* (1908); the novels *The Regenerated City* (1906) and *The Boys in the Back Room* (1938); and the plays *The Army in the Town* (1911) and *The Dictator* (1926). He was born at St. Julien-Chapteuil. He became active in politics and journalism in the 1930's.　　JOHN W. GASSNER

ROMAN ALPHABET. See ALPHABET.

ROMAN CALENDAR. See CALENDAR (History).

A Roman Catholic Priest blesses the wedding rings and sprinkles them with holy water during the marriage ceremony. Catholics believe that marriage is one of seven sacraments established by Jesus Christ.

ROMAN CATHOLIC CHURCH is that body of Christians which accepts the pope as its head on earth. It looks upon him as the representative of Christ and as the successor of Saint Peter in a direct line. It believes that special powers given by Christ to Peter have descended to the pope. It also believes that the pope is infallible in all matters of faith and morals when he speaks *ex cathedra*, or by virtue of his office. Decrees on these matters, when defined by the pope or by him and the bishops in council, are held of necessity to be free from error. Roman Catholics believe that by special protection of the Holy Spirit their church has kept unchanged the doctrines laid down by Jesus Christ. They also believe that it is impossible for error to creep into the official teachings and doctrines of the Roman Catholic Church concerning faith and morals.

Organization

The Hierarchy, or governing body of the Roman Catholic Church, is headed by the sovereign pontiff, or pope. Under him are the Sacred College, or College of Cardinals; several congregations, or ecclesiastical committees; patriarchs; archbishops; bishops; apostolic delegates; vicars and prefects; abbots; and other prelates. The Sacred College is the supreme council of the church. Its members are cardinal bishops, cardinal priests, and cardinal deacons. Its most important duty is to elect a new pope when a pope dies. About 20 lower congregations carry on the central administration of the church.

The Priesthood. The church believes in a body of priests who link God and man in a special way. They perform especially the function of offering sacrifice for the living and for the dead. They also bring the tokens of God's grace to men in the sacraments which they administer. These priests are set aside by the bishops, who are the direct successors of the Apostles. The church demands celibacy of the priesthood in those parts of the world where Latin is its official language, and where Western customs prevail. It believes that an unmarried clergy may serve God with more freedom and with an undivided heart. The law requiring celibacy is for purposes of discipline only. Among Roman Catholics of certain Eastern rites, a married parochial clergy is the rule, and only those priests are required to be celibate who are also monks. Even in eastern Europe and the Near East, where these customs are in force, a bishop must be unmarried or a widower. The positive side of the obligation not to marry is a solemn promise to God to preserve perfect chastity. This is required of all the Latin clergy in the preliminary steps to their priestly ordination, and this has been the rule of the Roman Church, of universal application in the West, at least since the days of Pope Gregory I (590-604).

The Doctrines

The Apostles' Creed and its variants, the Nicene Creed, the Athanasian Creed, and the Creed of Constantinople, set forth the basic doctrines and beliefs of the Roman Catholic Church. In the 1500's, after the Council of Trent, Pope Pius IV issued the most minute statement of doctrines. His statement is actually a summary of the other creeds, as was the creed published by Pope Paul VI in 1968. The Roman Catholic Church accepts the Bible, both the Old and New Testaments, as the word of God. But it accepts as its rule of faith the entire body of truths delivered by Jesus Christ to the Apostles and their successors. These were not at first committed to writing, and Roman Catholics do not expect to find all of Christ's teachings explicitly set forth in the Bible.

The Sacraments of the church are of great importance to Roman Catholics. The church teaches that Jesus Christ instituted the seven sacraments. An individual can receive three of the sacraments—Baptism, Confirmation, and Holy Orders—only once.

The Constitution on Sacred Liturgy, published by the Second Vatican Council, stated "The purpose of the sacraments is to sanctify man, to build up the body of Christ and finally, to give worship to God. Because they are signs they also instruct."

Anointing of the Sick, formerly *Extreme Unction*, is given, not at the moment of death, but as soon as there is some danger of death from sickness or old age. This sacrament destroys the remains of sin and all venial sins the soul repents.

Baptism is given to infants as well as to adults. For children it is held to wash away the original sin which remains attached to human nature from the fall of Adam. It sets up a sonship of the recipient with God by infusing sanctifying grace. With adults it also washes away all sins previously committed.

Confirmation confers the Holy Spirit upon the Christian person and obliges him to live, by word and example, the Christian life.

Holy Eucharist is a sacrament which truly and substantially contains the body, blood, soul, and divinity of the Lord Jesus Christ under the species (appearance) of bread and wine. It is brought into existence by the consecration at Holy Mass, where bread and wine are substantially changed into the living body and blood of Christ. It continues to exist as the adorable "Blessed Sacrament" as long as the appearances remain and it is thus preserved (only under the appearance of bread) in the tabernacle of the altar. It becomes the nourishment of the faithful in Holy Communion. It was instituted by Jesus Christ at the "Last Supper" on the eve of His Passion. A law of the Church obliges every Roman Catholic who has reached the age of reason to partake of this sacrament in Holy Communion at least once a year, at Paschal or Easter time. Many Roman Catholic theologians counsel more frequent communion, even daily communion, as do the authorities of the Church.

Penance has three stages. The first is sorrow for sin and a determination to amend. The second is confession or accusation of one's self to a priest, who is vowed to eternal secrecy. The third is the acceptance of certain penitential acts which are imposed by the priest. At this point the priest pronounces forgiveness in the name of God. All Roman Catholics believe that God ratifies this forgiveness and restores His friendship if the penitent is truly sincere.

Holy Orders. By this sacrament, the clergy are differentiated from the laity. They are admitted into the definite service of Christ. At the same time, they receive the spiritual powers necessary for the exercise of their respective orders.

Marriage is a sacrament instituted by Jesus Christ to sanctify the lawful union of man and woman and to give them the graces necessary for their state. This bond, for a Catholic, cannot be dissolved by any power on earth once it has been validly entered into and consummated. Separation may be granted on account of circumstances occurring after the marriage, but not dissolution of the marriage.

Other Beliefs and Ceremonies. The most sacred and solemn function of the church is the Mass. This is the commemoration, continuation, and consummation of the Sacrifice of the Cross.

Roman Catholics believe in life eternal. They believe in purgatory, the place of purification for the soul after death, where satisfaction is made for the temporal punishment due to sin. Here grave sins whose guilt has been removed after repentance but for which there is still a debt of satisfaction owed, and venial sins that have not been repented, are satisfied.

All the saints of the church are honored, but special veneration is given to Mary, the Mother of Christ. In 1950, Pope Pius XII proclaimed the doctrine of the Assumption of Mary to heaven. Roman Catholics believe that, by her intercession, Mary can obtain many spiritual blessings from her Son. They believe that other saints, especially Joseph, Mary's husband, may also intercede, but none are so close to God as is the Virgin Mary.

History

Growth. The bishopric in Rome was one of the first in the Christian Church. Roman authorities persecuted the church in Rome during its early years. But in the 300's, an edict of Constantine and Licinius gave it freedom, and it gained more influence in society at large. Bishoprics were established in various parts of the empire, but the one at Rome remained supreme.

The papacy met opposition on more than one occasion. In the 800's, a schism began in the church itself. Two hundred years later, as a result of this schism, the Eastern churches broke away from the Roman communion (see EASTERN ORTHODOX CHURCHES). In the 1500's, the Protestant Reformation caused another divi-

The Roman Catholic Mass was first celebrated in America by a priest who accompanied Columbus on his second voyage. Columbus is kneeling behind the man holding the cross. The crew kneels to thank God for a successful journey.

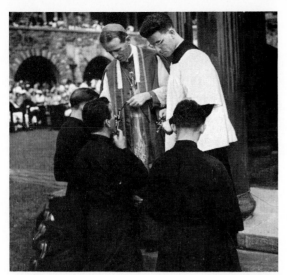

Pinney, Black Star

Roman Catholic Missionaries of the Catholic Foreign Mission Society (Maryknoll) take part in a farewell ceremony.

sion within the church. But these movements did not have a lasting effect on the growth of the Catholic Church, particularly in countries of southern Europe.

During the Middle Ages, the church had worldly as well as religious power. It held much territory at times. But the civil rulers never looked with favor upon this part of the church's activities. Long and bitter struggles took place between the church and the Holy Roman emperors. It was not until the Concordat of Worms in 1122 that the spiritual and temporal powers of both church and emperors were strictly defined. The establishment of the modern kingdom of Italy in the 1800's took away the civil powers of the church. But temporal power was restored in 1929 by a concordat and treaty which Pius XI made with the Italian Government (see PAPAL STATES).

The Church in America. Twelve priests went with Columbus on his second voyage in 1493, and in 1512 the first episcopal see was set up at San Domingo. In 1522 the second see was established at Santiago de Cuba. In 1530 the third was founded at Mexico City.

The Roman Catholic missionaries who pioneered in what are now the southeastern and southwestern parts of the United States were mainly Spanish Dominicans, Franciscans, and Jesuits. They established themselves during the 1500's to the 1700's. During the same period, French priests found their way to the Northeast, to Maryland and Pennsylvania, and along the Mississippi River.

The first Roman Catholic diocese in the United States was established in Baltimore, Md., in 1789. The Basilica of the Assumption of the Blessed Virgin Mary, the first Roman Catholic cathedral built in the United States, was dedicated in Baltimore in 1821.

The Church Today has more members throughout the world than any other Christian church. It has about 581 million followers. For membership in the United States, see RELIGION (table).

In 1959, Pope John XXIII announced he would call a worldwide church council to deal with the renewal and updating of the church. The council, called the Second Vatican Council, met from 1962 to 1965. For a discussion of council actions on various aspects of church life, see VATICAN COUNCIL.   FULTON J. SHEEN

Related Articles in WORLD BOOK include:

BIOGRAPHIES

See the separate articles POPE with its table, The Popes; CARDINAL with its tables, Canadian-born Cardinals and American-born Cardinals; SAINT. See also the following articles:

Baraga, Frederic	Merton, Thomas
Bossuet, Jacques B.	Neumann, John N.
Coughlin, Charles E.	Parsons, Robert
Damien de Veuster, Joseph	Peter the Hermit
Duns Scotus, John	Pire, Dominique G.
Eck, Johann	Savonarola, Girolamo
Erasmus, Desiderius	Serra, Junípero
Fénelon, François de S.	Seton, Elizabeth A.
Flanagan, Edward J.	Sheen, Fulton J.
Grosseteste, Robert	Teilhard de
Hubbard, Bernard R.	Chardin, Pierre
Jiménez de Cisneros, Francisco	Tetzel, Johann
Lanfranc	Thomas a Kempis
Maritain, Jacques	Torquemada, Tomás de

DOCTRINES, BELIEFS, AND CEREMONIES

Advent	Feasts and	Missal
Annunciation	Festivals	Novena
Anointing of	Holy Water	Purgatory
the Sick	Holy Year	Rogation Days
Apostles' Creed	Immaculate	Rosary
Ave Maria	Conception	Sacrament
Baptism	Indulgence	Ten Commandments
Canon Law	Lent	Transubstantiation
Canonization	Limbo	Trinity
Communion	Litany	Viaticum
Confirmation	Liturgy	Virgin Mary
Excommunication	Mass	

HIERARCHY

Abbot	Hierarchy	Nun	Religious
Archbishop	Knights Templars	Nuncio	Life
Archdiocese	Legate	Patriarch	Sacred
Bishop	Metropolitan	Pope	College
Cardinal	Monk	Priest	Vicar
Friar	Monsignor		

HISTORY

Church and State	Jesuit	Pisa, Council of
Constance Missal	Lateran	Reformation
Counter	Middle Ages	Trent, Council of
Reformation	Nicene Councils	Vatican City
Eucharistic Congress	Papal States	Vatican Council
Inquisition	Peter's Pence	Western Church

ORGANIZATIONS

Catholic Conferences, United States	Catholic Youth Organization
Catholic Library Association	Knights of Columbus
	National Council of Catholic Youth
Catholic Women, National Council of	Newman Apostolate

OTHER RELATED ARTICLES

Breviary	Concordat	Index Librorum	Old Catholic
Bull	Encyclical	Prohibitorum	Churches
Conclave			

For a *Reading and Study Guide on the Roman Catholic Church*, see the RESEARCH GUIDE/INDEX, Volume 22.

ROMAN CIRCUS. See ROMAN EMPIRE (Family Life).

THE ROMAN EMPIRE

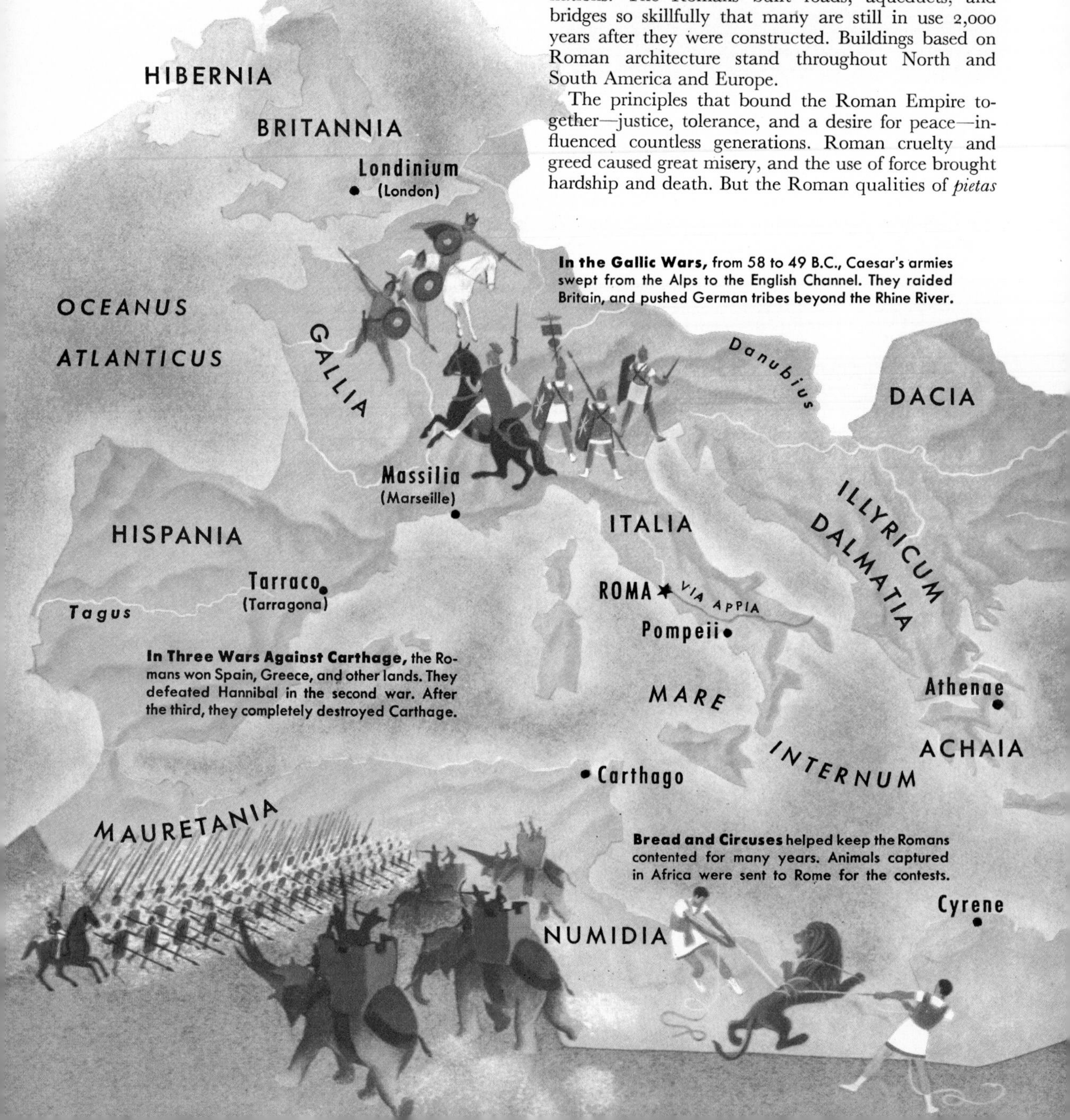

At its greatest size, in A.D. 117, the Roman Empire stretched from northern Britain to the shores of the Red Sea and the Persian Gulf.

ROMAN EMPIRE, at its height, included most of Europe, the Middle East, and the northern coastal area of Africa. Its millions of people spoke many languages and worshiped different gods. But they were united by the military power and government of the Romans. The city of Rome grew from a farming village in central Italy to become the capital of the huge empire.

The Roman Empire fell apart almost 1,500 years ago, but it still influences our lives. More than 300,000,000 persons speak languages directly related to Latin, the Roman tongue. Many words in English and in other languages come from Latin. Roman law provided the basis of the law of most European and Latin-American nations. The Romans built roads, aqueducts, and bridges so skillfully that many are still in use 2,000 years after they were constructed. Buildings based on Roman architecture stand throughout North and South America and Europe.

The principles that bound the Roman Empire together—justice, tolerance, and a desire for peace—influenced countless generations. Roman cruelty and greed caused great misery, and the use of force brought hardship and death. But the Roman qualities of *pietas*

HIBERNIA

BRITANNIA

Londinium
● (London)

In the Gallic Wars, from 58 to 49 B.C., Caesar's armies swept from the Alps to the English Channel. They raided Britain, and pushed German tribes beyond the Rhine River.

OCEANUS

ATLANTICUS

GALLIA

Danubius

DACIA

Massilia
(Marseille) ●

ITALIA

ILLYRICUM
DALMATIA

HISPANIA

Tarraco ●
(Tarragona)

Tagus

ROMA ★ VIA APPIA

Pompeii ●

Athenae
●

In Three Wars Against Carthage, the Romans won Spain, Greece, and other lands. They defeated Hannibal in the second war. After the third, they completely destroyed Carthage.

MARE

INTERNUM

ACHAIA

● Carthago

MAURETANIA

Bread and Circuses helped keep the Romans contented for many years. Animals captured in Africa were sent to Rome for the contests.

Cyrene
●

NUMIDIA

(sense of duty), *gravitas* (seriousness of purpose), and *dignitas* (sense of personal worth) remain ideals for people everywhere.

The Land and Its Resources

Location and Size. The boundaries of the Roman Empire changed many times during its 1,300-year history. In general, however, Rome ruled all the lands around the Mediterranean Sea, which the Romans called *Mare Internum* (Inland Sea) or *Mare Nostrum* (Our Sea). The Romans ruled the region south and west of the Rhine River and Danube River. This territory included present-day Spain, Portugal, France, parts of Belgium and The Netherlands, and most of England and Wales. Switzerland and Austria and such Balkan countries as Yugoslavia, Bulgaria, Albania, and Greece also came under Roman rule. In the East, the Roman Empire controlled Asia Minor (present-day Turkey) and the lands along the eastern Mediterranean, including Syria, Lebanon, Israel, and Jordan. The southern parts of the empire, bordered by the Sahara Desert, included Egypt as far south as the First Cataract (waterfall) of the Nile River, and a narrow strip of

All Roads Led to Rome for hundreds of years. The Arch of Titus commemorated the Roman conquest of Jerusalem. Titus helped complete the work on the Colosseum, *background*.

Heraclea

PONTUS EUXINUS
(Black Sea)

Great Cities developed in all parts of the Roman Empire. In A.D. 330, Constantine moved the capital from Rome to a new city, Constantinople, on the site of Byzantium.

Sinope   **Trapezus**

CONSTANTINOPLE ★

Nicomedia

Pergamum

Ephesus   **Tarsus**

Antiochia
(Antioch)   *Euphrates*   *MESOPOTAMIA*

Tyrus
(Tyre)

Trajan's Wars added vast territories to the Empire. He conquered Dacia, north of the Danube, by 107. Ten years later, he had marched to the Persian Gulf. But his conquests were costly, and later rulers had to give them up.

Hierosolyma
(Jerusalem)

Alexandria

Nilus

Cleopatra, Queen of Egypt, charmed two Roman conquerors, Caesar and Antony. She killed herself in 30 B.C., when she could not sway a third Roman general, Augustus.

AEGYPTUS

land along the northern shore of Africa (modern Tunisia and northern Libya, Algeria, and Morocco). Rome also controlled the islands in the Mediterranean.

The Roman Empire reached its greatest size during the reign of the Emperor Trajan. At his death in A.D. 117, it included about 2½ million square miles. This was about five-sevenths the size of the United States.

Natural Resources. The vast area of the Roman Empire provided the people with many different natural resources. The rich soil of Egypt, North Africa, and Sicily produced grain for the entire empire. The level plains of Gaul (France) and southeastern Europe also proved valuable for farming. Farmers used much of the poorer land around the Mediterranean for grape vines and olive trees, or for pastureland.

The lands of the empire yielded many minerals, including the gold, silver, and lead of Spain. Cyprus supplied copper, and tin came from Britain. The Balkan countries supplied iron ore and gold, and Greece and Italy contributed marble for Rome's building projects.

The forests of Asia Minor and Central Europe provided great quantities of lumber for construction. The Mediterranean Sea yielded fine catches of fish.

Climate. Most of the Roman Empire surrounding the Mediterranean Sea enjoyed a climate somewhat like that of southern California, mild in winter and hot in summer. Moderate rain fell in winter, and summers were dry. The climate of this area may have been somewhat colder and wetter in ancient times than it is now. In the areas of the empire farther away from the sea, the climate was probably much as it is today.

Life of the People

The empire included so many different peoples for so long that it is difficult to describe them or their way of life. There was no "average Roman." Within the empire lived barbaric Germanic tribesmen, cultured Greeks, Jewish scholars, and Egyptian farmers. Many of these people, particularly those in the East, continued to live as their ancestors had lived before the Roman conquests. The way of life which came to be known as "Roman" included features of many cultures.

The People. The word *Roman* included all persons who possessed Roman citizenship, regardless of language, race, culture, or place of birth. For example, St. Paul was a Jew from Tarsus in Cilicia, but he was also a Roman citizen.

The population varied greatly from time to time, depending on the size of the empire. Scholars estimate that about 54 million people lived in Roman lands at the time Christ was born. Of this number, 6 million lived in Italy and a little less than a million in Rome itself.

Roman society had two main divisions—citizens and noncitizens. About 1 of every 10 persons in the Roman Empire at the time of Christ was a citizen. Citizens included (1) the ruling class of *senatorial aristocracy;* (2) *equites* (knights), a group of wealthy businessmen; and (3) *plebeians* (lower classes). At first, only persons who actually came from the city of Rome could be citizens. But the government gradually extended the rights and duties of Roman citizenship to people throughout the empire. Freedmen (freed slaves) received incomplete citizenship.

Noncitizens included (1) *peregrini* (aliens), including privileged groups of allies called *socii;* and (2) slaves. Roman slaves included prisoners of war, persons captured and sold by pirates, children sold by their parents, and condemned criminals. Slaves had no legal rights. They ranged from cultured Greek teachers to uneducated mine and farm workers.

Language. Latin was the official language of the Roman Empire. It was spoken in all parts of the empire, and formed a common bond among the different peoples. Latin endured long after the empire fell, both as a separate language, and in changed form in the Romance languages (see LATIN LANGUAGE; ROMANCE LANGUAGE).

Many other languages were spoken within the empire. In the East, the educated classes spoke Greek. The common people spoke Coptic in Egypt and Aramaic in the Middle East. In the West, the common people of Gaul and Britain spoke several Celtic dialects. The Germans near the Rhine and Danube rivers spoke an early form of German. In the old territory of Carthage in Africa, some people still spoke Phoenician.

Family Life. Roman households were large and closely knit. They included not only the father, mother, and children, but also married sons and their families, and slaves. The father, or *paterfamilias*, held supreme authority over the household, and served as the chief priest in family worship.

Roman women had no legal rights, but they were held in high respect. They managed most household affairs, and were free to move about the city and to attend public functions.

Children were taught by their parents and household tutors. Boys of wealthy families started school at the age of 6. Girls learned about domestic tasks from their mothers. Boys assumed adult responsibilities at the age of 16 or 17. Girls married at about the same age. Parents usually picked husbands for their daughters and wives for their sons.

Shelter. An early Roman house consisted of a single four-sided room called the *atrium* (see ATRIUM). Later,

Roman Bakers sold round loaves of bread in shops open to the street. The baker's sign showed a mule turning a mill to grind grain.

ENTERTAINMENT

At the Circus, charioteers raced at breakneck speed around the pillars that marked each end of the race course.

At the Colosseum, gladiators fought lions or each other. Such contests drew thousands of spectators. Beneath the wooden floor, slaves worked machines that pulled animal cages up to the level of the sand-covered arena.

the Romans built more elaborate houses by adding rooms along the sides of the atrium. These extra rooms served as bedrooms and dining rooms, and the atrium became a reception hall. Still later, wealthy families added a garden enclosure, the *peristylium,* at the back of the house, with rooms opening off from it. These large houses were usually built of concrete, and were surfaced with brick or stone. They were simply but elegantly furnished. The Romans invented a central heating system, but not many people could afford it. Charcoal braziers furnished heat in most houses. Water was piped into wealthy homes.

Poorer people in farm areas lived in simple huts made of sun-dried brick. In the cities, the poor lived in concrete buildings six or seven stories high.

Food. The Romans usually ate three meals a day: *ientaculum* (breakfast), *prandium* (lunch), and *cena* (dinner). Sometimes a fourth—*merenda*—was served as a midafternoon snack. Breakfast, a light meal, generally consisted of bread dipped in wine, or eaten with honey, olives, or cheese. Lunch was also simple, often with a meat or egg dish, fruit, and wine. Dinner, the most elaborate meal, sometimes lasted well into the night. Guests reclined on couches as they enjoyed several different dishes. A typical Roman dinner might include an appetizer of eggs, fish, and salad greens; a main course of meat or chicken and vegetables; and dessert of pastry or fruit and nuts.

Bread was the chief food of the Roman diet. Other basic foods included fish, poultry, pork, eggs, vegetables, and fruits. Herbs and spices added variety to meals. Like the Greeks, the Romans used olive oil instead of butter, and honey instead of sugar. Most Romans drank wine mixed with water.

Clothing. Roman dress, like that of the Greeks, was worn draped over the body. Both men and women wore the *tunica,* a short-sleeved garment that hung to the knees. Over this, Roman men who were citizens wore the *toga,* an oblong drape with rounded corners. The style and color of the toga varied according to the wearer's age and position (see TOGA). Both citizens and noncitizens wore cloaks of various shapes. Women wore the *stola,* a long outer tunic fastened with clasps. A *palla* (cloak), was worn outdoors. In later years, the Romans wore the *dalmatica,* a long-sleeved tunic. Clothing was homemade, of wool, and styles seldom changed.

Both men and women wore sandals. Women were fond of jewelry and elaborate hair styles. Sometimes they dyed their hair, powdered it with gold dust, or added false blond hair imported from Germanic tribes.

Recreation. The Romans observed many holidays, most of them religious festivals. In Caesar's time, in the 40's B.C., there were more than 100 holidays a year. Some involved special religious sacrifices or home celebrations (see LUPERCALIA; SATURNALIA). Most of them featured public entertainment at government expense. Poorer citizens became so fond of the great spectacles that the poet Juvenal described their only needs in life as *panem et circenses* (bread and circuses).

Chariot races, probably the most popular entertainment, were held in a vast oblong arena called a *circus.* The Circus Maximus in Rome eventually seated more than 180,000 spectators. There were many other arenas, both in Rome and in the provinces. People bet on their favorite charioteers.

The Romans also enjoyed entertainment at the amphitheater. Gladiators fought each other, or with wild beasts. Condemned criminals and Christians were sometimes thrown to wild animals. The floor of the arena was often flooded with water for mock naval battles called *naumachia.* The greatest of all the amphitheaters was the Colosseum in Rome (see COLOSSEUM; GLADIATOR).

The Romans often attended the theater, where they watched Roman and Greek plays. But they preferred

ROMAN EMPIRE

the *mimus*, a form of low farce, and *pantomimus*, masked dancing.

The people spent much time at the baths. These huge establishments often included pools and hot and cold baths, gymnasiums, art galleries, and libraries. Other amusements included hunting and fishing; games resembling checkers and backgammon; and variety shows with acrobats, dancers, and magicians.

City Life. Rome was the greatest city of the Roman Empire. For a description and map, see ROME (The Ancient City). Many other cities also served as administrative and commercial centers. In the East, these included Alexandria, in Egypt; Antioch, the ancient capital of Syria; and Ephesus and Pergamum in Asia Minor. Western provinces were governed from various cities, including Carthage (now Tunis, Tunisia), Lugdunum (Lyon, France), Massilia (Marseille, France), and Tarraco (Tarragona, Spain). Athens had little commercial importance, but it remained a center of education. In the later days of the empire, Byzantium (later renamed Constantinople, and now Istanbul, Turkey) grew in size and influence.

Most provincial cities copied many features from Rome. Public buildings stood grouped together in a *forum*, with residential areas and shops surrounding it (see FORUM, ROMAN). Ruins of aqueducts, streets, temples, and amphitheaters still stand in many parts of the Mediterranean world.

Life in cities of the empire was busy and varied. The streets hummed with schoolchildren, women shoppers, and busy workmen and slaves. Peoples from all parts of the empire mingled in the markets, the forum, the amphitheaters and circuses, and the baths.

Country Life. Roman farms varied in size from a few acres to huge estates worked by hundreds of slaves. Wealthy Romans often owned both city and country houses. Even when Rome governed a great empire, agriculture was regarded as the only fit occupation for a gentleman. Such works as Cato's *De Agricultura* (On Farming) and Virgil's *Georgics* show how the Romans loved life in the country.

Life on the farm demanded hard work from all members of the household. On the principal festival days—seedtime and harvesttime—farm families asked the gods of the field and sky to bless their crops. The farmers, or *pagani*, remained faithful to their farm gods and farm feasts throughout Roman history. They were the last to accept Christianity. Because of this, non-Christians were called *pagans*.

Work of the People

Agriculture formed the basis of economic life in the Roman Empire. Greeks and other eastern Mediterranean peoples usually handled the thriving industries and commercial ventures. The system of capitalism developed by the early Romans encouraged free competition and individual enterprise. Later, the government controlled many aspects of the economy, and giant businesses engaged in agriculture, banking, and trade, as well as manufacturing.

Agriculture. The main farming areas of the Roman Empire included Italy, Egypt, North Africa, Sicily, and Gaul. Farmers grew wheat, barley, millet, and many kinds of vegetables and fruits. Olive trees yielded olives for food and oil, and vineyards supplied grapes for wine. Flocks of sheep and goats grazed on the hillsides of Italy, and throughout the rocky lands of Greece and Asia Minor. The Romans also raised hogs, poultry, donkeys, horses, and mules.

The earliest farms averaged only a few acres in size. Later, wealthy Romans took over large amounts of land to form great estates called *latifundia*. Slaves did much of the work on these farms. But during the empire, tenant farmers called *coloni* took their place.

The Romans rotated their crops, irrigated and fertilized their fields, and used oxen and donkeys as beasts of burden. Their most important contribution to agriculture was to teach the peoples of Mediterranean lands the advanced knowledge of crops and methods that had been developed in the Middle East.

Manufacturing. By conquering neighboring nations, the Romans obtained the manufactured products of other peoples. Throughout the Roman Empire, slaves and craftsmen made such products as pottery and building materials for local use. Alexandria, Miletus, and Pergamum produced linen and wool. People in Phoenicia and on the island of Cos raised silkworms and wove silk. Alexandria gained fame for its perfumes and silver plate, and Corinth produced fine bronzeware. Syria became well known for purple dye and glassware. Pergamum gave its name to parchment, which it manufactured in quantity (see PARCHMENT).

Mining ranked among the most important heavy industries. The great building projects of the empire required large supplies of construction materials, especially marble. The Romans considered Parian marble (from the island of Paros) the best. Other marble came from Greece and northern Italy. The Romans mined iron and silver in Spain, gold in Dalmatia, and copper in Cyprus. They imported tin from Britain and Gaul.

The Romans used slaves, condemned criminals, and prisoners of war in their mines. They often made these people live below ground until they died.

Trade. Merchants carried food, raw materials, and manufactured goods from one end of the Roman Em-

Metropolitan Museum of Art

A Roman Girl with Her Puppy. Roman sculptors made realistic statues. They were among the first to model children to look like children instead of like small adults.

A ROMAN HOUSE

On the Inside, *above,* a wealthy Roman's house was simply furnished, but gleamed with luxurious tile and marble. Fresco paintings decorated the walls. A Roman received guests in the atrium, *foreground.* A pool called the *impluvium* caught rain water that fell through an opening in the roof.

On the Outside, *below left,* the house presented a simple appearance. The small shops usually had no doors to the inside of the house. The floor plan, *below right,* is from a house at Pompeii. Bedrooms, dining rooms, and other living quarters surrounded the peristylium, behind the atrium.

Plan of a Roman House

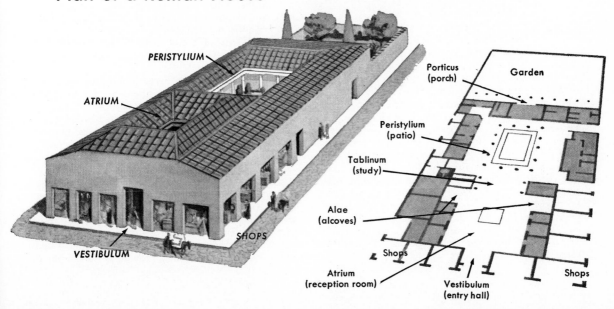

PERISTYLIUM

ATRIUM

VESTIBULUM

SHOPS

Porticus (porch)

Garden

Peristylium (patio)

Tablinum (study)

Alae (alcoves)

Shops

Atrium (reception room)

Vestibulum (entry hall)

Shops

pire to the other. Italy imported grain and exported wine, oil, and manufactured goods. From Arabia, Roman traders brought perfumes, drugs, and precious stones. Africa contributed gold dust, ivory, and ebony. Silk came from China, and amber and furs from Baltic countries. India supplied ivory, ebony, and spices.

Transportation. The Romans traveled about more easily, quickly, and safely than any other people before them or after them until the 1700's. Ships sailed the Mediterranean Sea to all points along the coasts, and also traveled to Britain and to the East. Merchant ships were usually sailing vessels, while *galleys* (warships) were propelled chiefly by oars (see GALLEY).

On land, the famous Roman road system linked all parts of the empire. The army built most of the roads for its own use, but all the people traveled on them. Wealthy persons hired carriages and drivers, but most Romans walked or rode horses or mules. The oldest Roman road, the *Via Appia* (Appian Way), stretched from Rome to the seaports of Tarentum (Taranto) and Brundisium (Brindisi) in the southeast (see APPIAN WAY). The *Via Flaminia* (Flaminian Way) connected Rome with Ariminum (Rimini) in the northeast (see FLAMINIAN WAY). Many other roads crossed the empire.

Communication. The Romans sent news by sea if possible, because it traveled faster than by land. The government established a postal system on land, but it was used only for official correspondence. Businesses and wealthy individuals provided their own messenger systems. Both government and private messengers traveled over the roads, either in relays or by changing horses at posting-houses.

News in Rome was circulated in the *Acta Diurna*, a government newspaper posted throughout the city. It reported new laws and important events, and listed births and deaths. In many cities, the Romans posted announcements of special interest on their buildings. They also hung tablets carved with notices. Craftsmen pictured their trades on signboards to identify their shops. For example, the sign of a bush designated a wineshop. These were among the earliest forms of advertising (see ADVERTISING [Earliest Uses]).

Activities of the People

Roman cultural achievements were almost all patterned on Greek models. But Roman culture was not just a copy of Greek culture. Virgil's *Aeneid* and Livy's *History*, for example, both emphasize the traditional Roman qualities of patriotism and faith in Rome's destiny. By imitating Greek accomplishments in education, the arts, and science, the Romans preserved and passed on much that might otherwise have been lost.

Education. In the early days, parents taught their children reading, writing, and moral standards. Fathers taught their sons to be good farmers and soldiers, and mothers taught their daughters how to run a household. Later, the Romans adopted Athenian methods of education. Upper-class boys and sometimes girls attended schools away from home. Courses included literature, especially Greek; *rhetoric* (the art of persuasion); oratory; and physical exercises. After Rome conquered Greece, wealthy young Roman men often spent a year or two in Athens, studying philosophy.

Usually, no special buildings were constructed as schools. Teachers held classes wherever they could find space and shelter. They maintained strict discipline, but gave their students many holidays.

Religion. In earliest times, gods such as Janus, Jupiter, Juno, Mars, and Vesta symbolized the powers of nature. There were thousands of lesser gods, because the Romans believed that a different god represented every object, as well as many events in a person's life. For example, there was a god of the door, a god of gold coins, and a goddess of fever. Household worship centered around the Lares and Penates (see LARES AND PENATES). Religious ceremonies at the many festivals were performed with strict care. Many decisions depended on the observations of augurs and sibyls (see AUGUR; SIBYL).

As Roman power expanded, the influence of Greek religion became strong. The Romans adopted such Greek gods as Apollo and Aesculapius, and identified many Roman gods with Greek ones. Ceres became the same as the Greek goddess Demeter, and Venus the same as Aphrodite. The Romans established 12 *Dii Majores*, or greater gods, and adopted many of the Greek myths about them. See MYTHOLOGY.

By the time of Augustus, about 20 B.C., people found little satisfaction in the old religion. The ideas of Greek philosophers, especially the Stoics and the Epicureans, caused people to question former beliefs (see EPICURUS; STOIC PHILOSOPHY). Augustus and later emperors tried unsuccessfully to revive the old religion, and even declared themselves divine. People turned to Oriental religions such as the worship of Cybele, and to the cults of Isis, Mithras, and Serapis (see ISIS; MITHRAS; SERAPIS). Greek mystery religions attracted many persons (see MYSTERIES).

Finally, Christianity began to gain converts. After severe persecution under such emperors as Nero and Diocletian, Christians received freedom of religion under Constantine in A.D. 313. Christianity became the state religion under Theodosius I about 392.

The Arts. In the arts, the Romans owed much to the Etruscans and the Greeks. In the fields of architecture and portrait sculpture, however, they produced original works of great power.

Architecture. The Romans copied the basic forms of Greek architecture, but made their buildings much larger and more ornate. They also added two important contributions, the arch and concrete. The Romans did not invent the semicircular arch, but they were the first to realize its possibilities. They made concrete by mixing lime and volcanic earth to form an unusually strong, hard material. By using the arch to support and reinforce the concrete, the Romans built imposing vaults and domes, such as that of the Pantheon (see PANTHEON). Aqueducts still standing throughout the Mediterranean area are monuments to Roman achievements in engineering (see AQUEDUCT).

Sculpture and Painting. Greek artists carved most of the sculpture that decorated Roman homes and public buildings. They were expert technicians, but their work had lost its earlier imagination and taste. However, Roman sculptors made beautiful portrait busts that depict men and women with remarkable realism. They also worked out giant reliefs to commemorate Roman victories. The reliefs provide picture-books of episodes in Roman history. The greatest of these was the *Ara Pacis* (Altar of Peace), erected by Augustus to celebrate the peace he had brought. Carvings on arches and columns often told the stories of military exploits. These monuments include the Arch of Titus, Trajan's Column, and the Column of Marcus Aurelius. The arches of Septimius Severus and Constantine show major changes from realistic sculpture.

The Romans liked decorative painted murals in their homes. Frescoes found in the ruins of Pompeii and Herculaneum show that Roman painters preferred landscapes, still-lifes, and scenes from mythology and everyday life.

Literature. The Greeks greatly influenced early Roman writers. But the works of such Romans as Cicero, Virgil, and Livy reached a high peak of excellence, and influenced Western writing for hundreds of years. Letter-writing and satire originated as literary forms in Roman times. See LATIN LITERATURE.

The Sciences did not interest the Romans, although they made use of Greek knowledge. Pliny the Elder wrote a scientific encyclopedia, the *Historia Naturalis* (Natural History), which gathered together the knowledge of the ancient world on every conceivable scientific subject. Later, in the Middle Ages, Pliny's work became a kind of scientific Bible. The astronomical theories of Ptolemy, an Alexandrian, also had wide influence in medieval times (see PTOLEMY). A Roman application of Ptolemaic astronomy, the calendar worked out under Julius Caesar, remained in use in Europe until 1582 (see JULIAN CALENDAR).

Government

The Romans were great statesmen, and have influenced the ideas and practices of government for hundreds of years. They were the first to impose central authority upon a large area, and at the same time preserve local city government.

Rome remained the center of government throughout most of the long history of the Roman Empire. In the early days, a series of kings ruled. Their power was limited by a council of advisers called the *Senate*, and by an assembly of citizens, the *Comitia Curiata*.

The Republic. Rome was a republic from 509 to 27 B.C. But not all citizens had equal rights. Patricians enjoyed full citizenship, but plebeians could not hold public office or marry into patrician families. The plebeians struggled from the beginning of the republic to improve their position, and finally won complete equality in 287 B.C. See PATRICIAN; PLEBEIAN.

Two *consuls*, elected every year, governed the Roman republic as chief executives. They had the *imperium* (absolute power to command), but either consul could veto the acts of the other. Even with those checks, the consuls enjoyed almost unlimited power in civil and military affairs. The consuls were aided by other magistrates such as the *praetors* (judicial officials); *quaestors*, with financial duties; and *censors*, who supervised the census and public morals. The *Senate*, which had advised the early kings, continued under the republic as a powerful advisory body. The 300 senators, usually former magistrates, were chosen for life by the consuls. An assembly called the *Comitia Centuriata* elected the consuls and other important magistrates. The patricians controlled this assembly, so the plebeians

set up their own group, the *Concilium Plebis*. The resolutions passed by this assembly, called *Plebiscita*, did not have the force of law until 287 B.C., but they gave the plebeians a legal means of expressing their demands. Powerful officials called *tribunes of the plebs* presided over the plebeian assembly (see TRIBUNE).

Distinctions between plebeians and patricians gradually disappeared, and two new ruling classes arose. A small number of wealthy families, both patrician and plebeian, replaced the old aristocracy. This new group, the *nobiles*, ruled through the Roman Senate, and became known as the *senatorial class*. A second group, the *equites*, consisted of wealthy businessmen who gained control over the courts and tax collections.

The Empire. Augustus became *princeps* (ruler) of Rome in 27 B.C. After that, supreme authority rested with the emperor, aided and advised by the Senate. However, Rome preserved the forms of republican government. The emperor held office as consul or some other magistrate, and the Senate went through the motions of electing him. Actually, he was chosen either by his predecessor or by the army. A vast civil service carried on much of the day-to-day business of the government. As time went on, the Senate lost power, and the Roman government became an absolute monarchy.

The Provinces had little voice in the government, but local officials were permitted to manage local affairs. Central authority rested in the hands of a Roman governor, appointed by the Senate or, later, by the emperor. The governor (called by such titles as *proconsul, legate, procurator,* or *prefect*) was aided by a staff of military and administrative assistants. Under the republic, the provinces often suffered from the greed of Roman tax-collectors. Exploitation decreased under the empire, and public works increased.

Law was one of the great Roman contributions to Western civilization. It forms the basis for the civil law of many European and Latin-American countries, and many of its principles and terms are part of English and American common law.

Three main principles of Roman law influenced later legal systems. One was the concept of *single sovereignty*, or the idea that all law must come from a single central source. A second, the concept of *universality*, grew out of the theory that all men have basic characteristics in common. The Romans taught that certain laws were fair, not because the state ordered men to observe them, but because they depended on the nature of human society. The third great concept of Roman law, the idea of *equity*, is expressed in the saying "Circumstances alter cases." The Romans believed that laws should be flexible enough to fit particular cases.

One of the most important achievements of the Roman legal system was the *codification* (classification) of its many laws. The plebeians were the first to demand that the laws of Rome be written down so that everyone might know them. In 450 B.C., the government published these laws on 12 tablets. A thousand years later, scholars drew up a final Roman legal code under the Emperor Justinian (see JUSTINIAN CODE; TWELVE TABLES, LAWS OF THE).

The Army was originally made up of citizens whose duty it was to serve in time of war. By Caesar's time,

THE ROMAN ARMY

Roman Legions provided the military power that made the Roman Empire great. Legions and auxiliary troops conquered new territory and maintained a constant guard on the frontiers.

The Army's Engineers built bridges and roads throughout the empire to help speed the troops. Roman soldiers, like those of today, used boats to support temporary pontoon bridges.

A Roman Soldier's Armor included a crested helmet, leather breastplate, leg protectors called *greaves*, and a shield made of wood and leather. He fought with an iron-headed javelin, a dagger, and a sword.

When Besieging City Walls, Roman soldiers often fitted shields together to form a *testudo* (tortoise). Under this protection, they could withstand heavy blows from above while digging under enemy fortifications.

How The Romans Built a Road

Cutting Through Mountains and Spanning Streams, well-built Roman roads followed straight lines whenever possible. Ditches and sloping sides improved drainage. Some Roman roads are still in use.

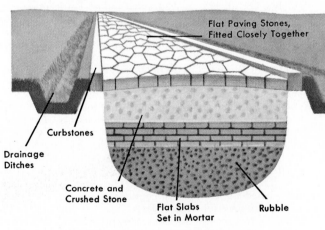

Flat Paving Stones, Fitted Closely Together

Curbstones

Drainage Ditches

Concrete and Crushed Stone

Flat Slabs Set in Mortar

Rubble

in the 40's B.C., most soldiers were professionals in a standing army. Their training and discipline made the Roman army one of the greatest forces of all time.

At the time of Augustus, about 20 B.C., some 250,000 men served in the army. The main division, a *legion*, included about 6,000 infantry and 120 cavalry (see LEGION). Smaller groups included the *cohort*, the *maniple*, and the *century*. Legionaries were Roman citizens who enlisted for 20 years. Attached to every legion was an *auxiliary*, a force of the same size made up of noncitizens drafted for 25-year terms. Auxiliaries also included cavalry regiments called *alae*.

The Roman army formed a civilizing force, as well as a conquering one. When soldiers were not fighting or patrolling the frontiers, they built roads, bridges, and walls (see ROMAN WALLS). Their camps served as centers of Roman influence in faraway places. The Latin word for camp, *castra*, is the root of many place names, such as Chester, England.

City cohorts lived in Rome and served as police and fire brigades. The most important was the Praetorian (Imperial) Guard. This hand-picked force of about 10,000 men served the emperor and at times gained enough power to overthrow him and choose his successor. See PRAETORIAN GUARD.

History

Legendary Rome. No one knows how or when Rome was founded. One legend says that the Trojan warrior Aeneas set up a kingdom in Italy after the fall of Troy in the 1100's B.C. Another tradition describes how two of his descendants, Romulus and Remus, founded the city of Rome in 753 B.C. Probably neither of these stories is true. But it is fairly certain that a people called the Latins lived on the site of Rome as early as the 700's B.C. Excavations show that Rome was a simple farming community until about 600 B.C.

According to tradition, seven kings ruled early Rome. They were Romulus, Numa Pompilius, Tullus Hostilius, Ancus Marcius, Lucius Tarquinius Priscus, Servius Tullius, and Lucius Tarquinius Superbus. During the 500's B.C., the Etruscans ruled Rome. These pro-

gressive people built a wall around the city, drained nearby swamps, and laid the first sewer. See ETRUSCAN.

The Early Republic (509-264 B.C.). The Romans rose against the harsh Etruscan king Tarquinius Superbus, and declared Rome a republic in 509 B.C. But hostile peoples still surrounded Rome and other cities on the little plain of Latium. The Etruscans lived north of the Tiber River. Tribes of Aequians, Hernicans, and Volscians made their homes in the Apennine foothills to the east and south. During the 400's B.C., Rome and its neighboring cities formed the Latin League to fight their common enemies. Horatius, Coriolanus, and Cincinnatus were heroes of this period of struggle.

─────── **IMPORTANT DATES IN ROMAN HISTORY** ───────

753 B.C. According to tradition, Romulus and Remus founded Rome.

509 B.C. The Romans drove out the Etruscans and established a republic.

390 B.C. The Gauls raided Italy and destroyed Rome.

264-241 B.C. The Romans defeated the Carthaginians in the First Punic War.

218-201 B.C. The Second Punic War ended in defeat for Hannibal and the armies of Carthage.

146 B.C. Roman forces destroyed Carthage.

55-54 B.C. Julius Caesar invaded Britain.

49 B.C. Julius Caesar made war on the Roman Senate.

44 B.C. Brutus and a group of conspirators assassinated Caesar.

27 B.C. Augustus became the first Roman emperor.

A.D. 43 Claudius conquered Britain.

70 Titus captured and destroyed Jerusalem.

79 Mount Vesuvius erupted, destroying Pompeii.

249 Decius ordered persecution of the Christians.

293 Diocletian divided the empire into four prefectures and set up two capitals.

313 Constantine's Edict of Milan granted religious toleration to the Christians.

330 Constantine moved the capital to Byzantium.

395 The East and West Roman Empires split apart.

410 The Visigoths captured and sacked Rome.

455 Vandal tribes attacked Rome.

476 Odoacer deposed Romulus Augustulus, the last Roman emperor in the West.

Spanish Tourist Office

A Roman Bridge almost 2,000 years old still spans the Tagus River at Alcántara, Spain. Roman masons set blocks of granite in its 170-foot-high arches without using mortar. They built a fortified gateway in the middle of the bridge.

The Roman Forum, shown in an etching by Giovanni Piranesi about 1750, was the center of government. It became half-buried in rubble after Rome fell. Only two-thirds of the arch of Septimius Severus, *left*, stood above ground. Shrubbery sprouted from the temples of Vespasian and Saturn, *right*.

The Senate met in the *Curia*, which probably stood left of and behind the arch of Septimius Severus. Senators gave advice on religion, finance, and foreign policy.

The Romans also fought the Gauls, who invaded Italy in 390 B.C. The Gauls burned Rome and occupied it for seven months. They left only after the Romans had paid them a large ransom. In 340 B.C., the cities of the Latin League attacked Rome, because they were jealous of its growing power. After two years of warfare, Rome conquered its former allies and became master of Latium. By 300 B.C., after more warfare against the Gauls and Etruscans, Rome controlled almost all the peninsula up to present-day Florence.

Rome also fought a series of wars with the Samnites, a group of mountain tribes in the central Apennines. They conquered the Samnites in 290 B.C. After a series of struggles with the Greek cities of southern Italy, Rome established its power as the head of an Italian Confederacy that included almost all Italy.

Rome used both military and political methods in its march to power. To hold conquered territory, the Romans built excellent roads and established frontier forts called *coloniae* (colonies). These military outposts grew into peaceful towns where trade flourished. The Latin language and Roman culture soon spread throughout Italy.

Overseas Expansion (264-133 B.C.) drew the Romans into conflict with powerful peoples outside Italy. By 264 B.C., Rome had become one of the most powerful nations of the western Mediterranean. Its only major rival was Carthage, a former Phoenician colony on the coast of northern Africa in what is now Tunisia.

The Punic Wars. Rome and Carthage clashed in struggles called the Punic Wars. The first clash came in Sicily, in a struggle for the Greek city of Messina. Hamilcar Barca ably led the forces of Carthage, but Rome won the first war after 23 years of fighting. At the end of the war, in 241 B.C., Sicily became the first Roman province. Three years later, Rome annexed the islands of Sardinia and Corsica.

The Second Punic War, which began in 218 B.C., was the most desperate struggle that Rome ever fought. The Carthaginian general Hannibal, Hamilcar Barca's son, marched from Spain over the Pyrenees and the Alps into the Po Valley. He won four brilliant victories, and led his armies up and down Italy for the next 13 years. He never reached a decisive victory, because the Romans refused to meet him again in open battle. Gradually the Romans reconquered their lost territory. Hannibal's brother, Hasdrubal, led another army from Spain to Italy to rescue Hannibal. But the Romans defeated his forces at Metaurus in 207 B.C. (see ARMY [Famous Land Battles]). Under the leadership of Scipio (Africanus Major), Roman armies then invaded Africa and defeated Hannibal at Zama in 202 B.C. Rome had broken the strength of Carthage. It gained Spain in this war, although the Romans did not subdue the fierce Spanish tribesmen until 133 B.C. Carthage's prosperity revived in the next 50 years, and Rome declared war again in 149 B.C. After three years of siege, Rome destroyed Carthage. See PUNIC WARS.

Wars in the East. Rome had also begun to expand into the eastern Mediterranean. The Romans fought

Courts met in public buildings called *basilicas*. The basilica style, with a central nave, side aisles, and curved enclosure at one end, became the model for church architecture in all parts of the world.

two wars (215-196 B.C.) with Philip V of Macedonia, because he had helped Hannibal. Rome also invaded Asia in 192 B.C. and defeated Antiochus III of Syria, an ally of Philip, in the Battle of Magnesia.

Greece at this time was torn by quarrels among its city-states. Perseus, who had succeeded his father, Philip V, as king of Macedonia, took advantage of Greek discontent to provoke a war with Rome. Rome easily crushed Perseus in 168 B.C. The Romans suppressed further Greek and Macedonian revolts in 148 B.C., and made Macedonia the first eastern Roman province. Two years later, the Romans destroyed the city of Corinth, completing their conquest of Greece.

A Century of Revolution (133-27 B.C.). Rome now dominated the whole Mediterranean world. But trouble at home followed peace abroad. Two tribunes, the brothers Tiberius and Gaius Gracchus, tried to help the poorer classes by starting land reforms (see GRACCHUS). The ruling classes resisted the reforms, mobs killed the Gracchi, and their laws were abolished. A new Popular party tried to make reforms by constitutional means. This party weakened the Senate's power, but did not restore authority to the popular assemblies. In the end, only army commanders had real power.

One such commander was Marius, who had won fame in Spain, Africa, and northern Italy. The people elected him consul six successive times. Meanwhile, in 90 B.C., Rome's Italian allies, called *socii*, rose in revolt and tried to set up their own independent state. Another powerful general, Sulla, led the Roman armies that crushed the socii in the so-called Social War. Marius and Sulla then struggled for power, at the same time fighting enemies outside Italy such as Jugurtha and Mithridates. Mithridates had built up a powerful kingdom in Asia. But two able Roman generals, Lucullus and Pompey, destroyed his power, and greatly extended Roman domination in the East. The Roman world soon reached to the frontiers of Parthia and Armenia, and included Syria and most of Asia Minor.

After Marius died in 86 B.C., Sulla gained control of Rome. A reign of terror followed. The government posted daily *proscriptions* (lists of condemned persons). Sulla died in 78 B.C., and new struggles broke out. Julius Caesar, Pompey, and Crassus set up a three-man rule, called a *triumvirate*.

Caesar won new territory in Europe after gaining brilliant military victories in Gaul and Spain. He described his battles in Gaul in *De Bello Gallico (Commentaries on the Gallic War)*. In eight years of fighting, Caesar conquered Celtic tribes between the Rhine River and the Atlantic Ocean. This Roman advance laid the Latin foundations for the Middle Ages.

By 49 B.C., the Senate feared the power of Caesar and ordered him to give up his command. Caesar refused and led his troops across the Rubicon River in defiance of the Senate (see RUBICON). Caesar, by winning a civil war against Pompey, established himself as sole ruler of Rome for the next five years. During the war, Caesar went to Egypt, where he met Queen Cleopatra (see CLEOPATRA).

391

ROMAN EMPIRE

A group of republican die-hards, led by Brutus and Cassius, murdered Caesar in 44 B.C., because they feared his power. But his death could not restore the republic. Octavian, Caesar's great-nephew and adopted son, joined Mark Antony and Lepidus in a second triumvirate. Octavian gained supremacy in their clash for power after winning the Battle of Actium in 31 B.C. (see ACTIUM, BATTLE OF).

Establishment of the Empire. In 27 B.C., Octavian took the name of Augustus and became the first emperor of Rome. He and his successors retained republican titles and forms of government, but Rome was actually a monarchy. Augustus introduced many reforms, and the resulting peace and prosperity won the people's admiration and respect. Art and literature reached a high point in the *Augustan Age*. In many ways, the early empire was an improvement over the late republic. The emperor ended heavy taxation in the provinces, and responsible officials replaced the amateurs who had controlled public administration.

The Pax Romana (27 B.C.-A.D. 180). The reign of Augustus marked the beginning of the *Pax Romana* (Roman peace), which lasted for 200 years. No country was strong enough to wage a major war on Rome, or to pose a serious threat to the frontiers. Commerce flourished, and the standard of living rose.

Scholars often write the history of the first 100 years of the empire in terms of the personal lives of the emperors. Many were inferior men. But competent administrators gave the Roman government an automatic efficiency that carried it through the reigns of both good and bad emperors.

During the reign of Tiberius, while Pontius Pilate was governor of Judea, Jesus Christ was put to death. Christ's teachings began to spread, and in A.D. 64, the Emperor Nero condemned Christians on the charge of setting fire to Rome. In A.D. 70, the Romans crushed a Jewish revolt and destroyed Jerusalem.

Prosperity reached its greatest height in the A.D. 100's. The "five good emperors"—Nerva, Trajan, Hadrian, Antoninus Pius, and Marcus Aurelius—reigned in turn from A.D. 96 to 180. Their learning and devotion to duty made them loved as well as respected.

During its first 200 years, the empire successfully defended its frontiers. Augustus in his will asked that the frontiers should remain as he left them. In general, his request was followed. Exceptions included Claudius' annexation of Britain in A.D. 43, and Trajan's addition of Dacia in 107 and Mesopotamia in 115.

Military Crisis (180-285). Warfare lasting 100 years followed the 200 years of peace. Rome found itself threatened in both east and west by barbarian tribes. To meet these threats, the empire doubled the size of its army. The increased drain on men and resources caused an economic crisis. For almost 100 years, the army put emperors on the throne and removed them at will. During one 67-year period, there were 29 emperors and claimants to the throne, only four of whom died natural deaths. These "barracks emperors" engaged in almost continuous fighting, and usually lived in camps near the frontiers.

Great changes took place outside the empire during this period. In the East, the vigorous Sassanid Empire

won control of Persia. In the West, German tribes formed powerful new federations and pressed hard on the frontiers. The drain on Rome's strength was so great that the government could not defend all its provinces. Parts of the empire formed governments of their own to defend themselves.

Reforms in Government (284-337) held the empire together for another 200 years. In 293, Diocletian grouped the provinces into four divisions called *prefectures* for more centralized rule. Because he felt the empire could no longer be ruled by one man, he divided it into east and west parts. Diocletian set up one capital for himself at Nicomedia in Asia Minor, and chose a

---
EMPERORS OF ROME

Name	Reign†	Name	Reign†
*Augustus	27 B.C.-A.D. 14	Tacitus	275-276
*Tiberius	14-37	Florian	276
*Caligula	37-41	Probus	276-282
*Claudius	41-54	Carus	282-283
*Nero	54-68	Carinus (W)	283-284
Galba	68-69	Numerianus (E)	283-285
Otho	69	*Diocletian (E)	284-305
Vitellius	69	Maximian (W)	286-305
*Vespasian	69-79	Constantius I (W)	305-306
*Titus	79-81	Galerius	305-311
*Domitian	81-96	Severus	306-307
Nerva	96-98	*Constantine	306-337
*Trajan	98-117	Licinius	308-324
*Hadrian	117-138	Maximinus	310-313
*Antoninus Pius	138-161	Constantius II	337-361
*Marcus Aurelius	161-180	Constantine II	337-340
Commodus	180-192	Constans	337-350
Pertinax	193	*Julian	361-363
Didius Julianus	193	Jovian	363-364
*Septimius Severus	193-211	Valentinian I (W)	364-375
Caracalla	211-217	*Valens (E)	364-378
Macrinus	217-218	Gratian (W)	364-378
Elagabalus	218-222	Valentinian II (W)	375-392
Severus		Eugenius	392-394
Alexander	222-235	*Theodosius I	379-395
Maximinus			
Thrax	235-238	**Emperors of the West**	
Gordian I and		Honorius	395-425
Gordian II	238	*Valentinian III	425-455
Pupienus	238	Petronius	
Balbinus	238	Maximus	455-457
Gordian III	238-244	Majorian	457-461
Philippus	244-249	Libius Severus	461-467
Decius	249-251	Anthemius	467-472
Gallus	251-253	Olybrius	472-473
Aemilianus	253	Glycerius	473-474
Valerian	253-260	Julius Nepos	474-475
*Gallienus	253-268	Romulus	
Claudius II	268-270	Augustulus	475-476
*Aurelian	270-275		

*Has a separate article in THE WORLD BOOK ENCYCLOPEDIA.
†Between 283 and 395, Rome was usually ruled by two or more emperors at once. Sometimes the eastern (E) and western (W) portions of the empire were ruled by separate emperors. At other times, as many as four emperors ruled the empire.

soldier named Maximian to rule the west from Milan.

This arrangement did not last long. A series of struggles took place between rivals for the throne. Constantine, who became emperor in 306, ruled both the East and West Roman Empires after 324. He introduced administrative reforms, doubled the size of the army, and created a new mobile force as a reserve. In 313, Constantine issued the Edict of Milan, making Christianity legal. And, in 330, he created a new capital at Byzantium, later renamed Constantinople.

The Roman Republic ruled only the area shown in red before the Punic Wars began in 264 B.C. But the Romans took to the seas and won the land shown in green in 130 years. When Trajan died in A.D. 117, they had conquered all the territory shown in orange.

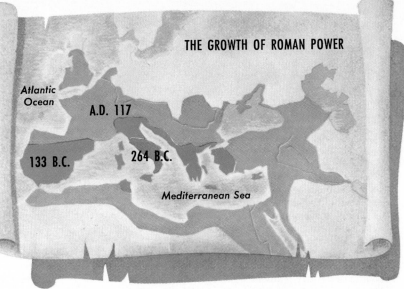

THE GROWTH OF ROMAN POWER

Atlantic Ocean

A.D. 117

133 B.C.   264 B.C.

Mediterranean Sea

The Empire Was Too Large for one man to rule. It was split into two parts in 395. Each empire had two prefectures (divisions). By that time, Christianity was the state religion of both empires.

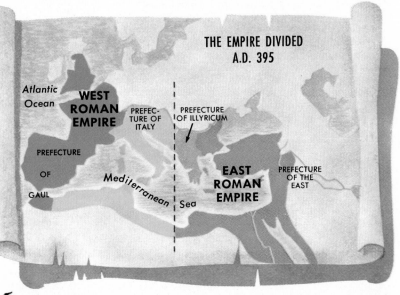

THE EMPIRE DIVIDED
A.D. 395

Atlantic Ocean

WEST ROMAN EMPIRE

PREFEC- TURE OF ITALY

PREFECTURE OF ILLYRICUM

PREFECTURE OF GAUL

Mediterranean   Sea

EAST ROMAN EMPIRE

PREFECTURE OF THE EAST

Barbarian Tribes gradually won control of France, Spain, and northwestern Africa. In 476, a Germanic tribal chieftain named Odoacer forced out Romulus Augustulus, the last Roman Emperor in the west.

THE FALL OF THE WEST ROMAN EMPIRE
A.D. 476

Atlantic Ocean

ANGLES
SAXONS   ALAMANNI
JUTES   LOMBARDS
                  BURGUNDIANS
FRANKS   OSTROGOTHS

KINGDOM OF ODOACER

VISIGOTHS

VANDALS   Mediterranean Sea

EAST ROMAN EMPIRE

ROMAN EMPIRE

Decline and Fall of Rome (337-476). Another period of great disorder followed Constantine's death in 337. The only living, growing force within the western provinces seemed to be the Christian Church. The people no longer provided enough soldiers to defend the empire, and hired barbarians filled the armies. The burden of supporting a greatly increased army and civil service taxed the resources of the empire to the breaking point. Prices rose, trade declined, and men left the cities for the simpler security of farm life. The government tried unsuccessfully to fix wages and prices, and to force men to stay in the towns. After Theodosius died in 395, the two parts of the empire split apart.

The West Roman Empire grew steadily weaker. In 410, the Goths burst into Italy and swept on to Rome itself, capturing and looting the once mighty city. The Huns advanced into Gaul, but a combined force of Romans and Visigoths defeated them at Châlons-sur-Marne (see ARMY [Famous Land Battles]). In 455, the Vandals plundered Rome for two weeks. The last emperor of Rome was a youth named Romulus Augustulus, recalling Rome's first king and first emperor. In 476, the German chief Odoacer finally deposed Romulus.

German chieftains and their peoples began carving kingdoms out of the provinces of the empire. The Vandals swept through the heart of the empire and took northern Africa. Jutes, Angles, and Saxons landed in Britain, and the Franks under Clovis invaded northern Gaul. In the south, the Goths seized Italy and Spain. Roman rule in the East withstood the crisis and survived until 1453. For the history of the East Roman Empire, see BYZANTINE EMPIRE.   CHESTER G. STARR

Related Articles in WORLD BOOK include:

BIOGRAPHIES

See the table *Emperors of Rome* with this article. For biographies of Roman authors, see the Related Articles at the end of LATIN LITERATURE. Other biographies in WORLD BOOK include:

Agrippina the Younger	Gracchus (family)
Antony, Mark	Marius, Gaius
Brutus, Marcus Junius	Octavia
Caesar, Gaius Julius	Pilate, Pontius
Cassius Longinus, Gaius	Plotinus
Catiline	Pompey the Great
Cato (family)	Porphyry
Cincinnatus, Lucius Q.	Regulus, Marcus Atilius
Coriolanus, Gaius Marcius	Roscius, Quintus
Crassus, Marcus Licinius	Scipio (family)
Fabius (family)	Spartacus
Gaius	Sulla, Lucius Cornelius
Galen	

BUILDINGS AND WORKS

Appian Way	Catacombs	Pantheon
Aqueduct	Colosseum	Roads and
Arcade	Column	Highways
Atrium	Flaminian Way	Roman Walls
Basilica	Forum, Roman	Shelter (History)

CITIES AND REGIONS

Galatia	Latium	Pompeii
Gaul	Mauritania	Rome (Ancient City;
Herculaneum	Numidia	pictures)

CONTRIBUTIONS TO CIVILIZATION

Ancient	Julian Calendar	Latin Literature
Civilization	Justinian Code	Law (Law in
Architecture	Latin Language	Ancient Rome)

Library (History)	Painting	Twelve Tables,
Music (History)	Roman Numerals	Laws of the
Mythology	Sculpture	

DAILY LIFE

Augur	Education	Lupercalia
Baths and Bathing	(History)	Pontifex
Battering-Ram	Fairs and	Saturnalia
Chariot	Expositions	Sibyl
Clothing (Cloth-	Food (Early	Textile (Greek
ing Through	Civilizations)	and Roman)
the Ages)	Furniture (Rome)	Toga
Drama (Roman	Gladiator	Triumph
Drama)	Lares and Penates	

GOVERNMENT

Comitia	Fasces	Praetor
Consul	Legion	Praetorian Guard
Decemvirs	Lictor	Quaestor
Dictator	Patrician	Tribune
Equestrian Order	Plebeian	Triumvirate

HISTORY

See the History sections of articles on countries which Rome ruled, such as ENGLAND (History). See also:

Actium,	Etruscan	Romulus
Battle of	Flag (color pictures:	and Remus
Barbarian	Historical Flags	Rubicon
Byzantine	of the World)	Sabine
Empire	Numa Pompilius	Servius Tullius
Cannae	Punic Wars	Tarpeian Rock

Outline

I. The Land and Its Resources
  A. Location and Size   C. Climate
  B. Natural Resources

II. Life of the People
  A. The People   C. Family Life   E. Country Life
  B. Language   D. City Life

III. Work of the People
  A. Agriculture   D. Trade
  B. Manufacturing   E. Transportation
  C. Mining   F. Communication

IV. Activities of the People
  A. Education   C. The Arts
  B. Religion   D. The Sciences

V. Government
  A. The Republic C. The Provinces E. The Army
  B. The Empire   D. Law

VI. History
  A. Legendary Rome   F. The Pax Romana
  B. The Early Republic   G. Military Crisis
  C. Overseas Expansion   H. Reforms in
  D. A Century of Revolution   Government
  E. Establishment of the   I. Decline and Fall
     Empire   of Rome

Questions

Why was there no "average Roman"?

What was the *Pax Romana?*

Why is Roman law still important in the Western world?

What are some important contributions the Romans made to man's knowledge?

How did the Romans govern their provinces?

What present-day countries were once ruled by Rome?

Why did Roman armies build roads?

Why were non-Christians called *pagans?*

Reading and Study Guide

For a *Reading and Study Guide on the Roman Empire,* see the RESEARCH GUIDE/INDEX, Volume 22.

ROMAN FORUM. See FORUM, ROMAN.

ROMAN GODS. See MYTHOLOGY.

ROMAN LAW. See LAW (Law in Ancient Rome); JUSTINIAN I; ROMAN EMPIRE (Law).

ROMAN MYTHOLOGY. See MYTHOLOGY.

ROMAN NUMERALS are symbols that stand for numbers. They are written in certain capital letters of the English, or Latin, alphabet. The Roman-numeral system was the most popular form of writing numbers until the widespread use of Arabic numerals in the late 1500's. Today, the Roman system is used to number the faces of clocks, to list important topics in outlines, and to record dates on monuments and public buildings.

All Roman numerals are written with seven basic symbols. These are I (1), V (5), X (10), L (50), C (100), D (500), and M (1,000). There is no zero. All other numbers are written by combining these seven symbols.

Roman numerals are written from left to right, using the principle of addition. A person first writes the thousands, then the hundreds, then the tens, and finally the units. To write 2,763, first write MM (2,000), then DCC (500+200=700), next LX (50+10=60), then III (3). The number 2,763 appears as MMDCCLXIII.

All 4's and 9's use the principle of subtraction. Thus, 4 is written as IV, or 5 minus 1, and 9 is written IX, or 10 minus 1. This principle usually applies to any number beginning with a 4 or 9, such as 40=XL, 90=XC, 400=CD, 900=CM. But sometimes the principle of subtraction is not used. In the pictures on this page, for example, 400=CCCC. In Roman numerals, a smaller numeral appearing before a larger numeral indicates that the smaller numeral is subtracted from the larger one. To write larger numbers, a *vinculum*, or bar, is sometimes placed over a number to multiply it by 1,000. For example, 13,524 is written as $\overline{XIII}DXXIV$.

It is simple to add and subtract with Roman numerals. But the system is inconvenient and clumsy for other types of calculation. It has been replaced by the easier Arabic-numeral system.   HOWARD W. EVES

See also ARABIC NUMERALS; NUMERATION SYSTEMS (History).

Using Roman Numerals seems difficult to those of us who work arithmetic problems with Arabic numerals. To illustrate, a *marionette* (puppet) Roman soldier confidently starts solving a multiplication problem, *top.* He becomes angry as he struggles with it, *above,* and then gets the wrong answer, *below.* Actually, Romans and others who worked with Roman numerals usually used an abacus to multiply.

Ormond Gigli, *Life* © 1957 Time, Inc.

—— **ROMAN NUMERALS FROM 1 TO 10,000,000** ——

1........I	120................CXX
2........II	130...............CXXX
3........III	140................CXL
4........IV	150.................CL
5........V	160................CLX
6........VI	170...............CLXX
7......VII	180..............CLXXX
8.....VIII	190................CXC
9.......IX	200.................CC
10........X	300................CCC
11........XI	400.................CD
12......XII	500..................D
13.....XIII	600.................DC
14.....XIV	700................DCC
15......XV	800...............DCCC
16.....XVI	900.................CM
17....XVII	1,000................M
18...XVIII	2,000...............MM
19.....XIX	3,000..............MMM
20.......XX	4,000...............M$\overline{V}$
30.....XXX	5,000................$\overline{V}$
40.......XL	10,000................$\overline{X}$
50........L	15,000...............$\overline{XV}$
60.......LX	25,000...............$\overline{XXV}$
70.....LXX	50,000.................$\overline{L}$
80....LXXX	100,000................$\overline{C}$
90......XC	1,000,000.............$\overline{M}$
100.......C	5,000,000..........$\overline{MMMMM}$
110......CX	10,000,000 $\overline{MMMMMMMMM}$

ROMAN WALLS

ROMAN WALLS were barriers that the Romans built where no natural territorial boundaries existed. By A.D. 100, they had built a line of walls in what is now Romania and Germany. They later built Hadrian's Wall and the Antonine Wall along the northern edge of the province of Britain. These walls were named for two Roman emperors, Hadrian and Antoninus Pius, and are the most famous Roman walls.

The walls discouraged raids and revolts. But their main purpose was to remind the tribes on both sides that the Romans were masters. The walls also made it

Stone Walls surrounding the ruins of ancient Pevensey Castle in Sussex date from about A.D. 250. This Roman strong point was built on what was once a group of small islands off the shore. The sea receded hundreds of years ago.

Camera Press, Pix

The Roman Wall built across northern England by the Emperor Hadrian in the A.D. 120's consisted of fortified sites joined together by a great wall. The ruins in some places are still 5 to 6 feet high and wide enough to walk on.

easier for the Romans to control trade and to collect taxes.

Hadrian's Wall was built in the A.D. 120's by units of the fleet and the army. It extended 73 miles, from the mouth of the Tyne River to the Solway Firth. Parts of the wall are still standing today. It was about 10 feet wide at its base and 20 feet high. For half its length, it was all stone. The rest was stone and turf. Forts stood about a mile apart along the wall, with small watch towers every third of a mile. A wide ditch lay in front of the wall, with a wider ditch 10 feet deep behind it.

The Antonine Wall was built in the A.D. 140's, north of Hadrian's Wall in a narrower part of Scotland. It was a simpler wall, made of turf, and it stretched for 37 miles.

The Romans allowed Hadrian's Wall to decay until 211, when they could no longer defend the Antonine Wall. Then they rebuilt Hadrian's Wall carefully. They rebuilt it twice more in the 300's, and defended it until nearly 400.   RAMSAY MACMULLEN

ROMANCE, *roh MANS*, is a story of adventure. A romance is not necessarily a love story, although many persons think of love and romance as the same. It may be in either prose or verse. Originally, *romance* meant any composition in the language of the common people of any of the countries where dialects of classical Latin were spoken. These dialects were called the Romance languages. Tales of adventure were the most popular early modern writings in these languages. Thus, the name gradually narrowed to its present meaning.

Adventure tales are far older than the Romance languages. The ancient Greek stories of adventure in prose and in verse were forerunners of the modern romance. The earliest of these is the *Odyssey*, with its frankly mythical adventures. The *Iliad*, on the other hand, is more realistic, yet still a romance. Later Greek romances introduced many themes which became popular in medieval and early modern stories. The separation of lovers and their final reunion was a favorite theme.

During the medieval period, the popular European romances were in verse, recited by wandering minstrels who went from court to court as beggarly entertainers. They wove marvelous tales around the names of national or local heroes. Great stories grew up about Charlemagne, Roland, Alexander, Arthur, Richard the Lion-Hearted, and the heroes of the Trojan War. These were passed on from one bard to another, each changing or adding to the material as he saw fit. In the days of chivalry, love became a principal theme, in addition to heroic deeds. It was usually the artificial, worshipful love of a knight for a noble lady.

Gradually prose began to replace poetry in romances. The legend of King Arthur was put into English prose by Sir Thomas Malory in his *Morte Darthur*. But the stories of the Spanish Cid and the French Roland remained in verse. The romance gradually led to the novel. Some of the greatest novels are correctly called romances. Sir Walter Scott's *Ivanhoe* is one of the great historical romances. Most of Robert Louis Stevenson's tales are pure romances of adventure, and Nathaniel Hawthorne is considered one of the best romance writers. Many short stories may also be classed as romances.   J. N. HOOK

ROMANCE LANGUAGE is any of several languages that developed from Latin. The Romance tongues include French, Italian, Spanish, Portuguese, and Romanian. Other Romance, or Romanic, languages are Sardinian and Rhaeto-Romance (the general name for a group of languages, including Romansh, spoken in certain parts of Switzerland, the Tyrol, and Friuli).

The Romance group also includes Provençal, the language spoken in southern France. Provençal was the language of the troubadours, who were the poets of the 1100's (see TROUBADOUR). The lyrics of more than 400 Provençal poets have come down to us. Most of their poems were love lyrics, but some had moral, religious, or political themes written to popular melodies. The use of Provençal as a literary medium began to decline soon after A.D. 1200.

Romance languages grew up because Rome sent colonists to settle the countries it had conquered. The soldiers, tradesmen, and farmers who colonized these conquered countries took their language with them, but it was not the Latin of the classics studied in school today. It was *popular*, or *vulgar*, Latin, the everyday speech of ordinary people. This popular Latin often adopted words or features of pronunciation from the language of the conquered country. For example, the Latin word for *hundred*, *centum*, became *cent* in French, *ciento* in Spanish, and *cento* in Italian. The varieties of popular Latin formed in this way eventually developed into separate languages.   ROBERT A. HALL, JR.

Related Articles in WORLD BOOK include:

French Language	Portuguese Language
Italian Language	Spanish Language
Latin Language	

ROMANESQUE ARCHITECTURE was the style of building used in western Europe from about A.D. 1050 to 1200. During this age of feudalism, there were few cities. Men depended on castles or monasteries for pro-

tection. These structures provide some of the best examples of Romanesque architecture.

The architecture of this period was usually heavy and sometimes crude, because its builders at first had little skill. In the 1100's, Romanesque builders in England, Italy, and southern France achieved great mastery, especially in their monastic churches.

Builders usually constructed Romanesque churches in the shape of a Latin cross. Most of these churches are rather dark and often low. The builders often used stone *vaults*, or roofs constructed on the principle of the arch (see ARCH). Lower side aisles flanked a higher central aisle, or *nave*. Thick walls and heavy *piers*, or columns, between nave and side aisles, characterized Romanesque churches. Builders usually used round arches for windows, doors, and the spaces between the piers. Sculptors often carved figures on these piers and arches (see SCULPTURE [picture: Prophet Isaiah]). Artists also decorated the walls of Romanesque churches with frescoes portraying religious stories.

Later, architects attempted to build higher, brighter churches. This development led to the growth of Gothic architecture.   BERNARD LEMANN

See also ARCHITECTURE (Romanesque; pictures).

ROMANESQUE FURNITURE. See FURNITURE (Romanesque).

ROMANESQUE PAINTING. See PAINTING (Romanesque Painting).

French Government Tourist Office

Romanesque Churches have rounded arches and massive stone exteriors. The Church of St. Sernin in Toulouse, *above*, is the largest Romanesque church in France. It was built in the 1000's.

Fresco (1100's) by an unknown artist; chapel at Berzé-la-Ville, France

Romanesque Frescoes decorate the interior of many churches with scenes from Bible stories and the lives of the saints. The fresco above portrays episodes from the life of Saint Blaise.

ROMANIA

Mountainous Romania now welcomes tourists from Western countries. Poiana Braşov, *left*, in the Carpathian Mountains is Romania's leading resort for winter sports.

ROMANIA is a mountainous country in southeastern Europe. It is nearly as large as Oregon, but it has about 10 times as many people as that state. Romania is one of the least economically developed countries in Europe. But industry in Romania has been expanded since the 1950's.

Romanians are a dark-complexioned, slender people who are known for their gypsy music and their brightly colored, embroidered clothing. Most of the people of

Alvin Z. Rubinstein, the contributor of this article, is Professor of Political Science at the University of Pennsylvania.

FACTS IN BRIEF

Capital: Bucharest.

Official Language: Romanian.

Government: Socialist Republic (Communist dictatorship).

Divisions: 39 districts. The city of Bucharest has district status.

Area: 91,699 square miles. *Greatest Distances*—(east-west) about 450 miles; (north-south) about 320 miles. *Coastline*—143 miles along the Black Sea.

Elevation: *Highest*—Moldoveanu Mountain, 8,343 feet above sea level; *Lowest*—sea level.

Population: *Estimated 1973 Population*—20,929,000; distribution, 58 per cent rural, 42 per cent urban; density, 228 persons to the square mile. *1966 Census*—19,103,163. *Estimated 1978 Population*—22,105,000.

Chief Products: *Agriculture*—barley, cattle, corn, fruit, hogs, oats, rye, sheep, sugar beets, wheat. *Manufacturing and Processing*—cement, chemicals, food, refined petroleum, textiles, wine. *Mining*—bauxite, coal, copper, crude petroleum and natural gas, iron, lignite, salt.

Flag: The blue, yellow, and red vertical stripes are the colors found in the coats of arms of Moldavia and Walachia. Romania's coat of arms is in the center. See FLAG (color picture: Flags of Europe).

National Holiday: August 23.

Money: *Basic Unit*—leu. See MONEY (table: Values).

Romania live in small towns and work on farms.

Romania has been a Communist country since 1947. A strict Communist government rules the country. Romania's official name is REPUBLICA SOCIALISTĂ ROMÂNIA (SOCIALIST REPUBLIC OF ROMANIA). Bucharest, a city of about 1⅓ million persons, is the capital.

The Land

Romania may be divided into six natural land regions: Moldavia, Dobruja, Walachia, Banat, Transylvania, and Bucovina.

Moldavia is in northeastern Romania. It stretches from the Carpathian Mountains east to the Prut River. The western part of Moldavia is full of high mountains and sheltered valleys, while most of the eastern part of the region is a level plain.

Dobruja is a strip of land which lies in southeastern Romania along the coast of the Black Sea. Dobruja is a fertile and marshy river plain, crisscrossed with canals and streams. The Danube delta is in Dobruja.

Romania Lies in Southeastern Europe.

398

Walachia lies along much of the southern border of Romania. The western part of Walachia is called *Oltenia*, and the eastern part, *Muntenia*. Much of Walachia is a fertile flatland along the Danube River.

In southwest Romania is a region called *Banat*, which means *frontier province*. Banat slopes northwestward from the Transylvanian Alps to fertile plains.

A region called *Transylvania* is in northwestern Romania along the Hungarian border. It is a high, fertile plain, separated from the rest of Romania by the Carpathian Mountains and Transylvanian Alps.

Bucovina is a heavily forested, mountainous region between Transylvania and Moldavia.

Mountains. The Carpathian Mountains and Transylvanian Alps form a semicircle through the center of the country, from its northwest corner to its southeast corner. The mountains separate the plains of Moldavia and Walachia in the east and south from the Transylvanian plateau in the northwest.

Rivers. The Danube River (called Dunărea in Romania) and its branches drain most of the country. The Danube runs along much of the southern border of Romania. Then it swings northward and meets the Prut River, which separates Romania from Russia. Many small streams flow southeast from the Transylvanian Alps and empty into the Danube. Some rivers flow northwest from the Bihor Mountains.

Climate. Winters in Romania are cold, and a thick blanket of snow covers the country for several months. The average January temperature is 30° F.; the average July temperature, 70° F. Rainfall averages 20 inches on the plains and from 20 to 40 inches in the mountains.

The People

Most Romanians are descendants of the ancient Dacians, Roman colonists, and such invading tribes as the Goths, Huns, and Slavs. Romania's present-day population includes Hungarians, Germans, Bulgars, Turks, and Russians. The Romanian language comes from Latin, and is similar to Italian. Romanians use many Slavic, Greek, and Turkish words.

The Communist party does not rule as harshly as it did between 1945 and 1960, but it still tightly controls the people's lives. Romanians cannot travel freely abroad. Tourists from other countries must obtain government approval before they can talk privately with Romanian citizens. Romanians cannot publicly criticize the government. Living standards are improving slowly in the cities, where the government has built many new apartment buildings. But life in rural areas is drab. Rural roads are poor, there are few telephones, and television is rare. Rural educational standards and wages are lower than those in the cities.

Industry. Before World War II, the Romanian economy was based primarily on agriculture, forestry, and the petroleum industry. However, since the 1950's the Communist government has increased Romania's industrial output through a series of long-term economic plans. The plans have emphasized heavy industrial production, such as iron and steel; chemicals; and machine-building, instead of consumer goods. Taking metals such as aluminum, copper, lead, and zinc from ores and preparing them for use is also important.

Romania is the second largest petroleum and natural gas producer in Europe. The principal oil-producing regions are around Ploești and Buzău, in southeastern Romania. Pipelines carry oil from these regions to Constanța, on the Black Sea, and to Giurgiu, on the Danube River. Such valuable minerals as bauxite, coal, copper, lead, manganese, silver, and zinc are mined in the mountains. Romania also has deposits of uranium.

Almost half of Romania's national income comes from industry and mining. About 18 per cent of the working people work in factories. But in spite of rapid industrialization, the country's economy is one of the least developed in Europe. After 1945, the government took over ownership and operation of all industries.

Agriculture and Forestry provide about 30 per cent of the national income. About 60 per cent of the working people work on farms. Major crops include corn, potatoes, sugar beets, and wheat. Farmers grow corn and wheat on the fertile plains. Fruits, such as apples, apricots, cherries, and plums, are grown in the foothills of the Carpathian Mountains. Cattle, pigs, and sheep are the chief livestock. After World War II, the government took over most farms. It decides what to plant, how much to grow, and what prices to pay farmers.

Forests of beech, fir, oak, pine, and willow trees cover more than a fourth of Romania. Timber-processing plants produce paper, cellulose for paper and explosives, and lumber for building and for handicrafts.

Transportation and Communication. The government owns and operates the transportation systems. Romania has about 6,800 miles of railroads and about 45,000 miles of highways. River shipping is increasing. Brăila and Galați are the leading Danube River ports. Constanța is Romania's only port on the Black Sea. A government-owned airline links Bucharest to major European cities. The government-operated radio network has 31 stations and the television network has 30 stations.

Foreign Trade. Until the early 1960's, more than 80 per cent of Romania's foreign trade was with Russia and other Communist countries. Since 1962, however, Romania has expanded its trade with such western European countries as France, Italy, and West Germany. By 1967, more than 40 per cent of Romania's trade was with non-Communist countries. Chief exports are petroleum, timber, food products, and manufactured products. Imports consist mainly of machinery and other

Romania Has Few Automobiles. Motorcycles are also rare because they are expensive. Many of the people ride bicycles.
Eastfoto

ROMANIA

equipment, and raw materials such as iron ore, coal, and rubber.

Social and Cultural Achievements

Education. Romanian law requires that children attend school for at least eight years. The government controls the schools and education is free. In the mid-1960's, about 3 million pupils attended primary schools, and about 300,000 attended secondary, technical, and vocational schools. About 130,000 students attended Romania's 46 institutions of higher education. Leading universities are located in Bucharest, Iaşi, Cluj, Galaţi, Braşov, and Timişoara. Almost all Romanians can read and write.

Communist beliefs are emphasized in the schools, but the government gave more attention to Romanian history and culture in the late 1960's. Higher education was being reorganized to stress the training of the scientists and technicians needed to modernize Romania.

The Arts. Romania has rich literary and musical traditions. Prior to World War I, its literature consisted primarily of ballads, folk tales, and poems. Romanian novelists, such as E. Lovínescu and Titu Maiorescu, became widely known between World War I and World War II. When the Communists took over, writers had to present Communist ideas in their works. As a result, literature became dull. In the 1960's, however, the Communists have permitted novelists and playwrights to deal realistically with life and society. Dumitru Radu Popescu became the most prominent writer of the 1960's. His novel *The Blue Lion* openly questions the lawfulness of the Communist government.

Much Romanian music is based on gypsy melodies. Georges Enesco (1881-1955), a Romanian composer, included gypsy melodies in his *Romanian Rhapsodies*. He also wrote three symphonies, and an opera, *Oedipus*.

Religion. Most Romanians belong to the Romanian Orthodox Church, which has its own leader, called the *Patriarch*. Other faiths include the Adventist, Baptist, Calvinist, Islamic, Jewish, and Lutheran. The government closely supervises all churches in Romania, and forbids Communists to take part in religious activities.

Government

National Government. The Romanian Communist Party—the country's only political party—controls the government. The government carries out policies set by the central committee, the party's ruling council. The chief government officials are party members and all candidates for election must obtain the party's approval. The party's general secretary is the most powerful political leader in Romania.

According to the constitution, Romania's one-house legislature, the Grand National Assembly, is the most important governing unit. The people elect the 465 assembly members to four-year terms. Each member repre-

---

ROMANIA MAP INDEX

Cities and Towns

Adjud	8,347	A 4
Agnita	10,865	B 3
Aiud	16,536	A 2
Alba Iulia	22,215	A 2
Alexandria	21,898	C 3
Anina	14,063	B 1
Arad	126,440	
	*137,444	A 1
Babadag	7,343	B 5
Bacău	73,414	A 4
Baia Mare	62,658	A 2
Baia-Sprie	13,182	A 2
Băicoi	9,120	B 3
Băileşti	18,490	B 2
Balş	9,174	B 3
Beiuş	8,744	A 2
Bîrlad	41,060	A 4
Bistriţa	25,519	A 3
Blaj	15,775	A 2
Bocşa Romînă*	16,015	B 1
Botoşani	35,220	A 4
Brad	15,532	A 2
Brăila	138,940	
	*144,759	B 4
Braşov	164,479	
	*264,537	B 3
Breaza	12,733	B 3
Bucharest (Bucureşti)	1,372,937	
	*1,518,725	B 4
Buhuşi	15,341	A 4
Buşteni	10,781	B 3
Buzău	56,349	B 4
Buziaş	5,554	B 1
Calafat	9,483	C 2
Călan*	11,761	B 2
Călăraşi	35,684	B 4
Călimăneşti	6,735	B 3
Caracal	22,714	B 3
Caransebeş	18,194	B 2
Carei	19,686	A 2
Cernavodă	11,259	B 5
Cîmpia Turzii	17,457	A 2
Cîmpina	22,902	B 3
Cîmpulung	24,877	B 3
Cîmpulung Moldovenesc	15,031	A 3
Cisnădie	14,979	B 3
Cluj	186,483	
	*223,519	A 2
Codlea	13,075	B 3
Comăneşti	14,653	A 4
Constanţa	152,324	
	*202,024	B 5
Corabia	14,502	C 3
Covasna	7,831	B 4
Craiova	150,098	
	*174,669	B 2
Cristuru Secuiesc	5,942	A 4
Cugir*	15,575	B 2
Curtea de Argeş	16,424	B 3
Dej	26,984	A 2
Deva	26,969	B 2
Dorohoi	16,699	A 4
Dr. Petru Groza*	5,754	A 2
Drăgăşani	11,589	B 3
Dumbrăveni	8,452	A 3
Eforie*	6,617	B 5
Făgăraş	22,934	B 3
Fălticeni	17,839	A 4
Feteşti	21,412	B 4
Focşani	35,094	B 4
Găeşti	8,962	B 3
Galaţi	152,204	B 5
Gheorghe Gheorghiu-Dej, see Oneşti		
Gheorgheni	13,828	A 3
Gherla	12,766	A 2
Giurgiu	39,199	C 3
Gura Humorului	9,081	A 3
Hunedoara	68,207	B 2
Huşi	20,715	A 5
Iaşi	162,063	
	*196,167	A 4
Isaccea	5,059	B 5
Jimbolia	13,633	B 1
Lipova	11,705	A 1
Luduş*	11,794	A 3
Lugoj	35,364	B 1
Lupeni	29,340	B 2
Măcin	8,147	B 5
Mangalia*	12,674	C 5
Mărăşeşti	6,795	B 4
Medgidia	27,981	B 5
Mediaş	46,384	A 3
Miercurea Ciuc	15,329	A 3
Mizil	10,334	B 4
Moineşti	18,714	A 4
Moreni	11,659	B 3
Năsăud	6,620	A 3
Nucet	2,768	A 2
Ocna Mureş	12,126	A 2
Odorhei	18,244	A 3
Olteniţa	18,623	B 4
Oneşti (Gheorghe Gheorghiu-Dej)	35,663	A 4
Oradea	124,026	
	*136,375	A 1
Orăştie	12,822	B 2
Oraviţa	9,912	B 1
Orşova	8,112	B 2
Panciu	7,948	B 4
Paşcani	18,689	A 4
Petrila	24,796	B 2
Petroşeni	35,187	B 2
Piatra Neamţ	45,852	A 4
Piteşti	60,113	B 3
Ploeşti	147,695	
	*191,663	B 4
Predeal	6,680	B 3
Pucioasa	11,212	B 3
Rădăuţi	18,580	A 3
Reghin	23,295	A 3
Reşiţa	56,653	B 1
Rîmnicu Sărat	22,336	B 4
Rîmnicu Vîlcea	23,867	B 3
Rîşnov	9,700	B 3
Roman	39,012	A 4
Roşiori de Vede	21,747	B 3
Săcele	22,809	B 3
Salonta	17,754	A 1
Satu Mare	68,246	A 2
Sebeş	13,715	B 2
Sfîntu-Gheorghe	20,768	B 3
Sibiu	110,474	B 3
Sighet	29,771	A 2
Sighişoara	25,109	A 3
Şimeria	9,365	B 2
Şimleu Silvaniei	12,324	A 2
Sinaia	11,976	B 3
Sînnicolau Mare	11,428	A 1
Siret	8,018	A 4
Slănic	7,307	B 3
Slatina	19,250	B 3
Slobozia	12,443	B 4
Sovata	7,582	A 3
Strehaia	9,768	B 2
Suceava	37,697	A 4
Tecuci	28,454	B 4
Timişoara	175,421	
	*194,159	B 1
Tîrgovişte	29,763	B 3
Tîrgu Jiu	30,805	B 2
Tîrgu Mureş	86,464	A 3
Tîrgu Neamţ	12,877	A 4
Tîrgu Ocna	11,647	A 4
Tîrgu Secuesc	9,502	A 4
Tîrnăveni	20,349	A 3
Topliţa	10,993	A 3
Tulcea	35,561	B 5
Turda	42,307	A 2
Turnu Măgurele	26,409	C 3
Turnu Severin	45,397	B 2
Urlaţi	9,145	B 4
Urziceni	9,291	B 4
Vălenii de Munte	7,380	B 4
Vaslui	17,960	A 4
Vatra Dornei	13,815	A 3
Vişeu de Sus	16,601	A 3
Vulcan	21,979	B 2
Zalău	15,144	A 2
Zărneşti	17,628	B 3
Zimnicea	13,231	C 3

*Population of metropolitan area, including suburbs.
*Does not appear on map; key shows general location.

Physical Features

Argeşul R.		B 3
Arieşul R.		A 2
Barladul R.		A 4
Bega Canal		B 1
Bihor Mts.		A 2
Bistriţa R.		A 3
Black Sea		B 5
Buzău R.		B 4
Caliman Mts.		A 3
Carpathians (Mts.)		A 4
Ciucul Mts.		A 3
Codrul Mts.		A 2
Crasna R.		A 2
Crişul Alb R.		A 1
Crişul Repede R.		A 2
Dîmboviţa R.		B 3
Danube (Dunărea) R.		B 4
Harghitei Mts.		A 3
Ialomiţa R.		B 4
Iron Gate (Pass)		B 2
Jijia R.		A 4
Jiu R.		B 2
Lake Razelm		B 5
Lake Sinoe		B 5
Moldova R.		A 4
Moldoveanu (Peak)		B 3
Motrul R.		B 2
Mouths of the Danube		B 5
Mureşul R.		A 3
Negoi (Mtn.)		B 3
Oltetul R.		B 2
Oltul R.		A 3
Pietrosu (Mtn.)		A 3
Prut R.		B 5
Rodnei Mts.		A 3
Roşul Pass		B 2
Siretul R.		A 4
Someşul R.		A 2
Suceava R.		A 4
Teleorman R.		B 3
Tîrnava Mică R.		A 3
Transylvanian Alps (Mts.)		B 3
Varf Mandra (Mtn.)		B 2
Vedea R.		B 3

Source: Latest census (1966).

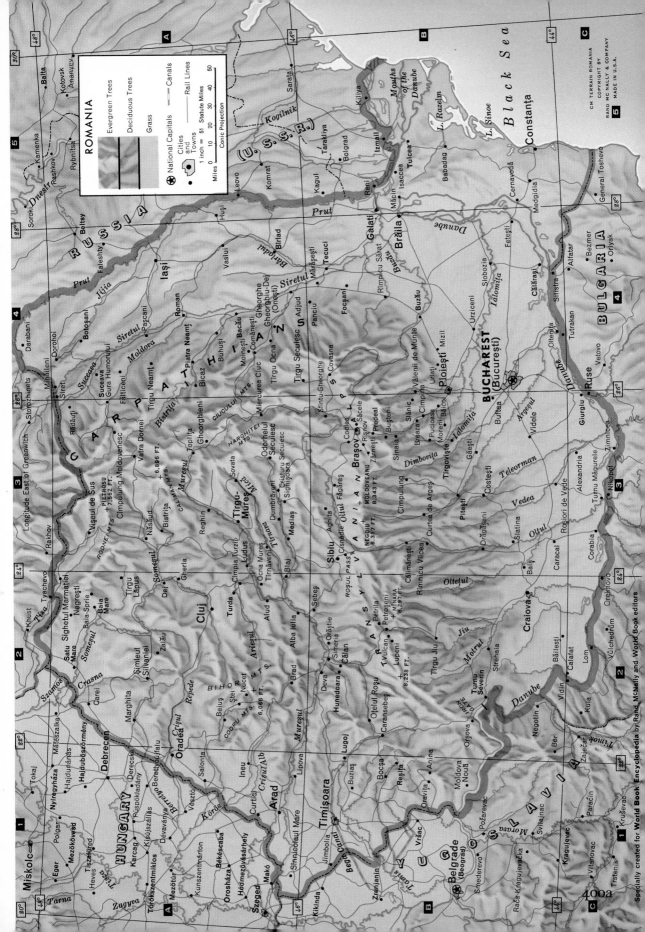

ROMANIA

Evergreen Trees
Deciduous Trees
Grass

☆ National Capitals
⦿ Cities and Towns
• Cities and Towns

Canals
Rail Lines

1 inch = 51 Statute Miles

Miles 0 10 20 30 40 50

Conic Projection

Black Sea

Mouths of the Danube

BULGARIA

(U.S.S.R.)

RUSSIA

HUNGARY

YUGOSLAVIA

CARPATHIAN MTS

TRANSYLVANIA

BUCHAREST
(Bucureşti)

400a

ROMANIA

sents 40,000 persons. The assembly elects the 17-member State Council. It meets for only a few days each year, so the State Council handles most legislation. The president of the State Council is head of state. The assembly also elects the 31-member Council of Ministers to administer the government. It elects the Supreme Court, which administers the court system. All persons 18 years of age or older may vote.

District Government. Romania is divided into 39 administrative districts. Bucharest has special district status. A people's council governs each district.

History

Early Days. In the 300's B.C., people called the Dacians occupied the region now known as Romania. The Roman emperor Trajan conquered the Dacians between A.D. 100 and 106. Roman colonists settled the region, bringing their customs and language. The name *Romînia* described this part of the Roman Empire.

Middle Ages. In the late 1200's, the Romanians founded two independent territories which were ruled by local princes. These territories were Moldavia and Walachia. They frequently took part in wars fought in the area among the Poles, Hungarians, Turks, and Russians. By the 1500's, the princes, known locally as the *hospodars*, were paying tribute to the Turkish (Ottoman) Empire. In exchange, the Turks allowed the princes to manage their own territories.

Moldavia and Walachia won back their independence in the late 1500's, when Michael the Brave of Walachia united the two territories. But Turkey regained control after Michael was assassinated.

The Unification of Romania. The princes of Moldavia and Walachia were on close terms with Russia by the early 1700's. To punish them, the Ottoman rulers sold the positions and duties of the princes to wealthy Greeks. The Greeks controlled all phases of Romanian life, and imposed heavy taxes on the people. Several Russo-Turkish wars took place in Moldavia and Walachia. The province of Bucovina was lost to Austria in 1775, and the province of Bessarabia was lost to Russia in 1812. The Turkish sultan replaced the Greeks with local princes in 1821.

In 1828, the Russians invaded Moldavia and Walachia, and occupied the country until 1834. In that year, Moldavia and Walachia received Organic Statutes, or constitutions. They were written with the help of the Russians. Considerable progress was made during the next twenty years in all phases of national life. A strong unification movement developed. In 1856, after the Crimean War, Russia was forced to give up southern Bessarabia to Moldavia.

In 1859, Moldavia and Walachia elected Prince Alexander John Cuza as their common ruler. The union of the principalities was recognized by other countries in 1861. The new country of Romania was still somewhat under the control of the Turks, but it gained a great deal of independence in local affairs. Cuza's harsh methods angered many persons. The people forced him to abdicate in 1866.

Romanian Independence. The next ruler was Karl of Hohenzollern, a German prince, who took the throne in 1866 as Prince Carol. The Congress of Berlin, a meeting

—————— IMPORTANT DATES IN ROMANIA ——————

300's B.C. Dacians occupied the area that is now known as Romania.

A.D. 100's Romans conquered Dacians.

300's to 1200's Goths, Huns, and Slavs invaded the area.

1200's Principalities of Moldavia and Walachia founded.

1859 Principalities of Moldavia and Walachia elected the same prince, Alexander John Cuza, to govern them.

1861 Union of Moldavia and Walachia recognized.

1916 Romania entered World War I on Allied side.

1947 Romanian monarchy ended with abdication of King Michael.

1948 Communists set up a Soviet-type dictatorship.

1952 New Communist constitution adopted. It provided for state control of industry and natural resources, and collectivized farming.

1955 Romania joined the United Nations.

1964 Romanian Communist Party declared that Romania's policies would be independent of those of Russia.

1965 Romania adopted a new constitution.

held in 1878 at the end of the Russo-Turkish Wars, recognized Carol as the king of a completely independent Romania.

The Congress took the region of southern Bessarabia from Romania and gave it to Russia. But it also took northern Dobruja from the Ottoman Empire and gave it to Romania. Carol I ruled until 1914. During his reign, parliamentary government became established in Romania.

The Second Balkan War was fought in 1913. Romania joined the nations fighting against Bulgaria, and received southern Dobruja from Bulgaria at the end of the war.

World War I. King Carol died in 1914 and his nephew, Ferdinand I, became king. When World War I began, both sides sought Romania's friendship. At first, Romania remained neutral. However, it wanted to acquire the Austro-Hungarian provinces of Banat, Bucovina, and Transylvania, which had large Romanian populations.

On Aug. 27, 1916, Romania joined the Allies. But Germany and the other Central Powers soon defeated Romania. They forced Romania to sign a peace treaty with them in May, 1918. Later in 1918, Romania again entered the war on the Allied side. In the peace settlement, Romania received the three Austro-Hungarian provinces, and Bessarabia from Russia.

After World War I, the Romanian people demanded land reforms. The government divided the estates of the *boyars* (large landowners) and sold them in small lots to individual farmers. A new constitution adopted in 1923 confirmed the land reforms. King Ferdinand died in 1927, and his five-year-old grandson became King Michael I. Michael's father, Prince Carol, had given up his rights to the throne in 1925.

Iuliu Maniu led the National Peasant Party to power in 1928. The world-wide depression that started in 1929 brought severe economic distress to Romania. The depression intensified the people's dissatisfaction with the government. Many people turned to the new Communist and Fascist parties. The Fascist Iron Guard was the most important of these parties. It was an extreme nationalist group that favored an alliance with Germany and Italy.

In 1930, the Romanian parliament repealed the law which kept Carol from the throne, and proclaimed him King Carol II. In 1938, a new constitution replaced the constitution of 1923. It made King Carol a dictator, enlarged his powers, reduced the authority of the parliament, and provided for the abolition of political parties.

World War II. King Carol tried to keep Romania neutral in World War II. But after the Germans defeated France, King Carol had to give Bessarabia and northern Bucovina to Russia. Germany and Italy forced him to give southern Dobruja to Bulgaria, and northern Transylvania to Hungary. This angered the Romanian people and they forced King Carol to abdicate on Sept. 6, 1940. Carol's son, Michael, again became king, but he had no real power. General Ion Antonescu, who was appointed premier on Sept. 4, 1940, became dictator.

Antonescu cooperated with the Germans, who occupied the country in 1940. In June, 1941, Romania joined Germany in attacking Russia and won back

Eastfoto

Romania's Wheat Harvest provides one of the nation's most valuable farm crops each year. Most of the farmland in Communist Romania is now in collectivized farms owned by the government. The Dudesti state farm, *above*, is located near Bucharest.

Slanting Windows of a cathedral, built at Curtea de Argeş in 1512, create an illusion that the corner towers are leaning.

Black Star

Bessarabia and northern Bucovina. After the tide of war turned against Germany, King Michael overthrew Antonescu in August, 1944. He signed an armistice with the Allies and returned Bessarabia and northern Bucovina to Russia. Romania then entered the war on the Allied side. As a reward, Russia took northern Transylvania from Hungary and returned it to Romania. Russian troops entered Romania in 1944. Some Russian troops remained until the late 1950's.

After World War II, a coalition government controlled by the Russians ran the country until the peace treaty was signed on Feb. 10, 1947. In the meantime, the Communist party took over Romania's government in 1946. All non-Communists in opposition groups were imprisoned or killed. The presence of Russian troops and the control exerted by the Communist-run secret police assured a Communist victory in elections held in 1946. In December, 1947, King Michael was forced to give up his throne. Communist leaders proclaimed Romania a *People's Republic.* A constitution modeled on that of Russia was adopted in 1948.

By 1952, Romania was a Russian *satellite.* That is, Russia controlled Romania's government and its policies. Georghe Gheorghiu-Dej was made premier. A new constitution was adopted in 1952. It was similar to the 1948 constitution, but it emphasized Romania's dependence on Russia even more strongly. In 1955,

401

Embassy of the Socialist Republic of Romania

Bucharest, Romania's Capital, has wide boulevards, many parks, and attractive buildings.

Questions

What minerals are mined in Romania?
How is agriculture organized in Romania?
What land regions of Romania are most mountainous?
When did Romania join the Allies in World War II?
What did Russia then give Romania?
What was the Iron Guard?
What two territories united to form Romania?
To what church do most Romanians belong?
What state does Romania correspond to in size?
What is the source of the Romanian language?

Gheorghiu-Dej became head of the Communist Party. Romania joined the Warsaw Pact, a Russian-dominated military alliance, in 1955. Romania also became a member of the United Nations in 1955.

In the 1960's, Romania asserted more independence from Russia. In 1962, it opposed Moscow's efforts to keep the Eastern European Communist countries tied economically to Russia through the Council for Economic Assistance (COMECON). Romania insisted that every Communist country should be free to develop its own trade in the most profitable markets. Since 1962, it has expanded its trade with non-Communist countries. Romania and the United States signed a trade agreement and exchanged ambassadors in 1964. The Romanian government declared that each Communist country has the right to conduct its own affairs, free from Russian interference.

This policy gained strength in 1965 when Romania adopted a new constitution, which emphasized Romanian control of its own affairs. A vigorous new leader, Nicolae Ceausescu, was elected general secretary of the Romanian Communist Party when Gheorghiu-Dej died in 1965. Ceausescu became head of state in 1967.

Despite Russian opposition, Romania established diplomatic relations with West Germany in January, 1967. Romania was the only Communist country that took a neutral position on the Arab-Israeli war of June, 1967. In 1968, the Romanian delegation walked out of a 67-nation Communist meeting in Budapest, Hungary, charging that the meeting was controlled by Russia. In 1969, President Richard M. Nixon visited Romania while he was on a world tour. It was the first visit by a U.S. president to a Communist country since 1945.   ALVIN Z. RUBINSTEIN

Related Articles in WORLD BOOK include:

BIOGRAPHIES

Brancusi, Constantin   Ionesco, Eugène
Carol   Michael
Ceausescu, Nicolae   Steinberg, Saul
Coanda, Henri M.

ROMANOV, *ROH muh noff,* was the name of the imperial family which ruled Russia from 1613 to 1917. The Romanovs came from Lithuania or Germany. They became Russian landholders and reached a high position when Czar Ivan IV married Anastasia Romanovna in 1547. Her nephew became leader of the church. His son Michael was elected czar in 1613 (see CZAR). Michael's son, Alexis I, acquired the Ukraine and brought the church under czarist control.

Fifteen more Romanov rulers followed. The most famous was Peter the Great. The imperial family died out in 1762, but the rulers kept the Romanov name down to Nicholas II, who was deposed in 1917. He and his immediate family were executed in July, 1918, but other members of the Romanov family escaped from Russia and survived.   WALTHER KIRCHNER

Related Articles in WORLD BOOK include:
Alexander (czars)   Duma   Peter I, the Great
Catherine (II)   Nicholas (czars) Russia (History)

ROMANS, EPISTLE TO THE, the sixth book of the New Testament, was written by the Apostle Paul about A.D. 58. The theme of the *epistle* (letter) is Christ's part in salvation. It teaches that people can be saved only through faith in Christ and service to God. It warns that all men are under the power of sin and tells the church how to prevent pitfalls and how to solve its problems. The epistle has been called the *Constitution of Christianity.* See also PAUL, SAINT.   W. W. SLOAN

ROMANS OF ASIA. See ASSYRIA.

ROMANSH, or **ROMANSCH.** See SWITZERLAND (Language).

402

ROMANTICISM is a style in the fine arts and literature. It emphasizes passion rather than reason, and imagination and inspiration rather than logic. Romanticism favors full expression of the emotions, and free, spontaneous action rather than restraint and order. In all these ways, romanticism contrasts with another style called *classicism* (see CLASSICISM). Periods of romanticism usually develop as a revolt against classicism. Artists and writers throughout history have shown romantic tendencies. But the term *romantic movement* usually refers to the period from the late 1700's to the mid-1800's.

The Qualities of Romanticism

Romantics believe man's creative powers work best when the imagination is unrestrained. The English romantic poet Samuel Taylor Coleridge created his poem "Kubla Khan" from a dream. A classical poet would not consider a dream a proper subject for a work of art.

Romanticism stresses freedom for the individual. It rejects restricting social conventions and unjust political rule. In literature, the romantic hero, such as Lord Byron's "Don Juan," is often a rebel or outlaw.

Just as the romantic hero is in revolt against social conventions, the romantic artist is in revolt against classical ideas of good form. In the drama, for example, the romantic rejects the classical unities of time, place, and action. He allows events in his play to range widely in time and space. Jean Racine's play *Phèdre* is rigidly classical in form. Johann Wolfgang von Goethe's play *Faust* is romantic.

Romanticism in the Arts

Romanticism in Literature. During the romantic movement, most writers disliked their world. It seemed commercial, mechanized, and standardized. To escape from society, the romantics turned their interest to remote and faraway places, the medieval past, folklore and legends, and nature and the common man. They were also drawn to the supernatural and the morbid.

Many romantic characteristics were united in the *Gothic novel*. This was a type of horror story, filled with violence and supernatural effects, and set against a background of gloomy medieval Gothic castles. The Gothic novel influenced the American writers Nathaniel Hawthorne and Edgar Allan Poe. The novels of Sir Walter Scott of Scotland and James Fenimore Cooper of the United States reveal the typically romantic interest in the past. *Grimm's Fairy Tales*, collected by Jakob and Wilhelm Grimm, are famous examples of the romantic interest in legends and folklore.

Many typically romantic characteristics appear in the poetry of William Wordsworth of England. Wordsworth preferred a dreamy, "vacant and pensive mood" to an organized, scientific search for truth. He believed we learn more by communing with nature than by reading books. He also believed conversations with simple peasants teach us more about moral truths than do discussions with learned philosophers and theologians.

Romanticism in Painting. Romantic painters often used bold lighting effects and deep shadow to reveal the personality of their subjects. Classical forms and themes were abandoned for faraway exotic subjects such as the Oriental scenes painted by Frenchman Eugène Delacroix. Dramatic scenes of nature were also popular subjects. Compare Nicolas Poussin's classical painting

St. John on Patmos with the romantic painting *Stoke-by-Nayland* by John Constable. Both paintings appear in color in the PAINTING article.

Romanticism in Music. Romantic composers modified the formalism of classical music, and aimed at lyric expression and emotion. Many composers gave their works a nationalistic character by using folk songs as themes. Romantic composers include Franz Schubert of Austria; Felix Mendelssohn, Robert Schumann, Richard Wagner, and Carl Maria von Weber of Germany; and Frédéric Chopin of Poland.

Romanticism and Society. The French philosopher Jean Jacques Rousseau taught that man is naturally good, but has been corrupted by the institutions of civilization. He taught the idea of the *noble savage*, a concept in which primitive people lead ideal lives because they are unspoiled by the evils of Western civilization. Influenced by this concept and by a belief in freedom, the romantics opposed political tyranny and often took part in liberal and revolutionary activities. The revolutions in America and France in the late 1700's were influenced by romantic ideals.

Many of Rousseau's theories influenced educational theory and practice. Romanticism also became associated with economic and social reform, especially in the United States.   W. T. JONES

Related Articles. There is a separate biography in WORLD BOOK for each person discussed in this article. For the historical development of romanticism, see:

Drama (Romanticism)	Literature (Romanticism)
English Literature (The Romantic Age)	Music (The Early 1800's)
French Literature (The 1800's)	Painting (The 1800's)
German Literature (1750-1830)	Russian Literature (The Age of Romanticism)
Latin-American Literature (Romanticism)	Sculpture (1600-1900)
	Spanish Literature (Romanticism)

ROMBERG, SIGMUND (1887-1951), was a famous composer of operettas. They include *Maytime; Blossom Time*, based on the life and music of Franz Schubert; and *The Student Prince*. He wrote more than 70 musical shows, among them *Rose of Stamboul*, *The New Moon*, *The Desert Song*, and *Up in Central Park*. His musical comedies include *Follow Me* and *Over the Top*.

Romberg was born in Hungary, and studied at the University of Bucharest. He trained as an engineer, but also studied music in Vienna. He came to the United States in 1909. Romberg's theatrical career began when he became a staff composer for the Winter Garden Theater in New York City, writing music for *The Passing Show*. He gained his first success with *The Midnight Girl* in 1913. He settled then in New York City, but later moved to Hollywood, where he wrote music for motion pictures. Many of his operettas were made into motion pictures. GILBERT CHASE

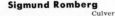
Sigmund Romberg
Culver

Pictorial Parade

An Air View of Rome looking northeast shows Saint Peter's Church, *center*, the world's largest Christian church. The city lies on the Tiber River.

ROME

ROME is the capital of Italy and one of the world's great historic cities. It has been an important center of civilization for more than 2,000 years. Because of Rome's long history, it is called the *Eternal City*. Rome is also one of the most beautiful cities in the world. Its ancient monuments and magnificent churches and palaces stand as reminders of Rome's past glory. Gleaming new buildings are a sign of the city's modern-day importance.

Rome ruled the ancient Western world as the capital of the mighty Roman Empire. For hundreds of years, Rome was the supreme power of Europe, northern Africa, and western Asia. Ancient Rome's influence can still be seen today in such fields as architecture, government, language, and law.

As the home of the popes, Rome also became the center of the Roman Catholic Church. During the 1500's and 1600's, the popes brought a new splendor to Rome. They hired great artists who gave the city beautiful buildings and priceless works of art. Today, thou-

sands of visitors come every year from all parts of the world to enjoy these masterpieces, and to see the ruins of ancient Rome.

Visitors also enjoy the colorful life of sunny Rome. They stroll through the city's fashionable shops and open-air markets, and ride in horse-drawn carriages. Like the Romans, visitors enjoy relaxing at sidewalk cafes or in the many beautiful squares. The people of Rome are friendly and proud of their city. They are happy to help strangers find their way or select the most delicious foods in restaurants, or just to chat.

--- **FACTS IN BRIEF** ---

Population: 2,455,302.

Area: 582 square miles; metropolitan area, 756 square miles.

Altitude: 66 feet above sea level.

Climate: *Average temperature*—January 45° F.; July, 78° F. *Average annual precipitation* (rainfall, melted snow, and other forms of moisture)—38 inches.

Government: *Chief executive*, mayor (4-year term). *Legislature*, 80-member City Council (4-year terms).

Founded: 753 B.C. (according to legend).

Maria Corda Costa, the contributor of this article, is Associated Professor of Education at the University of Rome.

404

Rome lies on both banks of the Tiber River in central Italy, 17 miles east of the Tyrrhenian Sea. The city is on about 20 hills, but its outskirts have some wide stretches of flat ground. These hills include the famous seven hills on which ancient Rome was built —the Aventine, Caelian, Capitoline, Esquiline, Palatine, Quirinal, and Viminal hills.

Today, the ruins of ancient buildings cover most of the Aventine, Caelian, and Palatine hills. The Palatine also has a modern public park. Crowded commercial districts spread over the Esquiline and Viminal hills. The Italian presidential palace and some government buildings stand on the Quirinal, the tallest of the seven hills. The streets of ancient Rome extended from the Capitoline, a center of Roman life. Today, this hill has famous art museums, the City Council building, and a square designed by Michelangelo, the great Renaissance artist.

Throughout the city are many beautiful squares connected by busy streets. The heart of Rome is around the *Piazza Colonna* (Colonna Square). Banks, hotels, luxury shops, office buildings, restaurants, and theaters make it the busiest place in the city. Rome's mile-long main street, the *Via del Corso* (Way of the Course), runs through the Piazza Colonna and links two other squares to the north and south. The street got its name because it was used as a horse-racing course during the Middle Ages. The horses ran without riders while Romans cheered from balconies lining the street.

Vatican City, the administrative and spiritual center of the Roman Catholic Church, lies in northwestern Rome. The Vatican, as it is sometimes called, is the smallest independent state in the world. It covers only 108.7 acres, or about a sixth of a square mile. See VATICAN CITY.

Rome is also one of the world's most important art centers. Actors, musicians, painters, sculptors, and writers take part in the city's busy cultural life.

Parks and Gardens. Romans enjoy the city's many public parks and gardens on the grounds of magnificent old *villas* (large estates). The villas were once owned by wealthy families. The great Villa Borghese, which was opened to the public in 1902, is the finest of these parks. Its hills, meadows, and woods seem like natural countryside. It also has a large zoo.

Many campers visit the Villa Ada, the old home of Italian kings. The Villa Glori, a park honoring Italy's war dead, is covered with pine trees. The Villa Sciarra has famous fountains and rare plants. Gardens on top of the Janiculum Hill are especially popular with children.

Music and Theater. The National Academy of Santa Cecilia has one of Rome's leading symphony orchestras. Other orchestras include the Rome Philharmonic and the Radiotelevisione Italiana.

Romans, like most Italians, love opera. The city has two opera seasons. The Opera House offers performances from January to June. In July and August, operas are presented at the Baths of Caracalla, the ruins

ROME

...... City Limits

Administrative Area of Rome

✈ Major Airport

INNER ROME

Rail Line and Station

Major Street

Park

Area of Ancient Rome

Baths of Caracalla......23
Campidoglio..........19
Capitoline Museum......18
Castel San Angelo.......2
Colosseum............21
English Cemetery.......24
Gallery of Modern Art...6
Garibaldi Monument....26
Madama Palace.......15
Mausoleum of Augustus...3
National Museum
  of the Villa Giulia.....5
Opera House..........11
Piazza Colonna........14
Piazza del Popolo.......4
Quirinal Palace........12
St. John Lateran,
  Basilica of..........22
St. Mary Major,
  Basilica of..........10
St. Peter's Church........1
Termini Station..........9
Tiber Island...........20
Trevi Fountain..........13
U.S. Embassy..........8
Venezia Palace........16
Victor Emmanuel
  Monument..........17
Villa Sciarra...........25
Villa Medici...........7

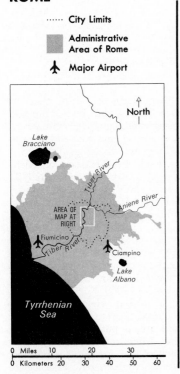

0 Miles 10 20 30
0 Kilometers 20 30 40 50 60

WORLD BOOK map-FGA

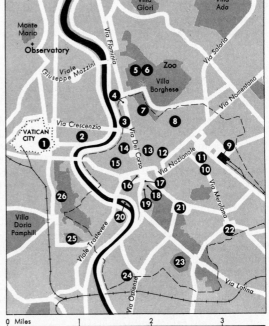

0 Miles 1 2 3
0 Kilometers 1 2 3 4 5

The Streets of Rome are jammed with heavy traffic. One of the busiest streets, the famous Via Veneto, has many fashionable shops and cafes.

of ancient public baths. Rome's many theaters offer plays and musical comedies, including productions by companies from other countries.

Museums and Art Galleries. Countless visitors come to see Rome's priceless art collections. Many of the finest paintings and statues are displayed in the Vatican Palace. They include masterpieces by such famous artists as Leonardo da Vinci, Michelangelo, and Raphael. Some of Michelangelo's greatest paintings decorate the ceiling and front wall of the Vatican's Sistine Chapel. See MICHELANGELO (pictures).

The oldest art collection in Rome, begun in 1471, is in the Capitoline Museum. It includes many fine sculptures of ancient Rome. The National Museum of the Villa Giulia has a splendid collection of art from central Italy dating from pre-Roman times. Greek and Roman sculptures, and articles from ancient civilizations are exhibited in the National Roman Museum. The Borghese Collection in the Villa Borghese includes works by almost every master of the Renaissance. The national Gallery of Modern Art has masterpieces chiefly of the 1800's and 1900's.

Churches, Palaces, and Fountains. Saint Peter's Church in Vatican City is the world's largest Christian church. It is an outstanding example of Renaissance architecture. Michelangelo helped design the church during the 1500's. Many famous art masterpieces can be seen inside (see SAINT PETER'S CHURCH). Other well-known churches of Rome also date from the Renaissance, and from earlier and later periods.

The most famous of Rome's many palaces is the Venezia Palace, built during the mid-1400's. The Italian dictator Benito Mussolini established his office there in the Fascist period of the 1920's and 1930's. The palace now houses an art museum. The Madama Palace, once owned by the powerful Medici family, has been the seat of the Italian Senate since 1871. The Italian president's official residence is the Quirinal Palace, formerly the home of popes and the kings of Italy.

Rome has many magnificent fountains that are considered great works of art. The Trevi Fountain, completed in 1762, is the most popular with visitors from other countries. A legend says that visitors who throw coins into this fountain will someday return to the city. See FOUNTAIN (picture, Fountain of Trevi).

Schools. The University of Rome, founded in 1303, is Italy's largest university (see ROME, UNIVERSITY OF). Various religious societies of the Roman Catholic Church operate a number of schools in Vatican City. There, students from many countries attend seminaries to become priests, or take university graduate studies. Some seminaries have been established for students from one country only. For example, the North American College has graduated about 1,800 American priests since it was founded in 1859.

Roman children must attend school between the ages of 6 and 14, which takes them through junior high school. They may also attend public schools at the next level of education. These schools include senior high schools and schools of fine arts, teacher training, and technical job training. Students pay small fees to

A Summer Opera Theater is provided by ruins of the Baths of Caracalla. These ruins date from the early A.D. 200's.

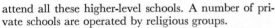

The University of Rome, founded in 1303, is the largest university in Italy. About 50,000 men and women study there.

The Sport Palace, built for the 1960 Summer Olympic Games, is in a newly developed area on Rome's southwestern outskirts.

attend all these higher-level schools. A number of private schools are operated by religious groups.

The Vatican Library, established in the 1400's, is one of the most important libraries in the world. It owns many old Latin manuscripts (see VATICAN LIBRARY). Rome also has nine public libraries with a total of about three million books. Five other libraries are operated by Roman Catholic orders.

Sports. Soccer, a form of football, is Rome's most popular sport. Huge crowds attend club and international soccer matches in the Olympic Stadium. Horse shows are held in the *Piazza di Siena* (Siena Square) and the Capannelle and Tor di Valle Hippodromes. Other popular sports include basketball, boxing, and tennis.

Economy. Rome is not a heavily industrialized city. Most Romans earn their living in nonindustrial jobs, such as those in commerce and government. Many Romans work in restaurants and in the building trades. Tourism also provides a large part of the city's income. Only about a fifth of Rome's workers are employed in industry. The city's factories produce textiles, processed foods, and other products. Most of the factories are in the northwestern part of Rome.

Motion-picture production is an important part of Rome's economy. The city is one of the film capitals of the world. Motion-picture companies of Italy and other countries have produced many famous films in Rome's studios and streets.

"All roads lead to Rome" is a well-known saying, and Rome is a major transportation center of Italy. Railways and roads connect Rome with cities in most parts of the country. Airlines link the city with the rest of Italy and other parts of the world. Rome's central railroad station is one of the largest and most beautiful in the world. This huge building, completed in 1950, stands on the ruins of a house of the A.D. 100's. The Metropolitana, Rome's subway, runs southwest from the railroad station to a new office district on the outskirts of the city. Buses, streetcars, taxis, and trolley buses also serve Rome.

Rome has many daily newspapers, of which the most important are *Il Messaggero* (The Messenger), *Il Tempo* (The Time), and *Paese Sera* (Country Evening). The Vatican publishes the official newspaper of the Roman Catholic Church, *L'Osservatore Romano* (The Roman Observer). Many other specialized newspapers are published in Rome, including *Corriere dello Sport* (Sport Courier). Some papers are official dailies of political parties. These include *Il Popolo* (The People) of the Christian Democratic party and *L'Unità* (Unity), the largest Communist party paper in the Free World. Italy's radio and television system, Radiotelevisione Italiana, has its headquarters in Rome.

Government. Rome is governed by a City Council of 80 members, elected every four years. The council members elect one of their group as mayor, and 18 of the group to the City Executive Committee. The mayor and the members of this committee all serve four-year terms. The mayor heads the committee as well as the general city administration. Fifteen departments direct the city's affairs, including health, markets, public works, and transportation.

Colosseum

FPG

Roman Forum

Weldon King, FPG

ANCIENT ROME

WORLD BOOK map -FGA

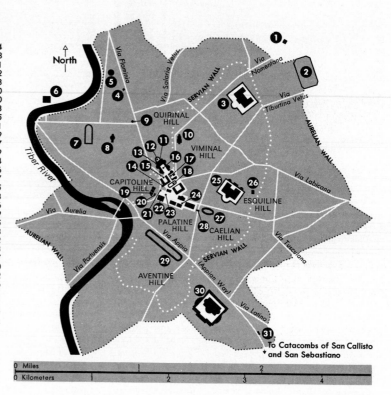

0 Miles
0 Kilometers

Arch of Constantine

John V. Mills, Black Star

Pantheon

Wide World

Remains of the splendors of ancient Rome may be seen throughout the city, especially in an area east of the Tiber River. Since the 1800's, the Italian government has cleared the main sites of the ruins and surrounded them with trees and gardens. Thousands of tourists visit these attractions yearly.

Forums. The centers of ancient Roman life were open market places called *forums*, where public meetings were held. The Roman Forum, the most important of these areas, was the center of Roman government. Ruins there include the *Curia* (Senate House), the triumphal Arch of Septimius Severus, the Temple of Saturn, and the Basilica Julia, an assembly hall.

Most streets of ancient Rome were narrow and crooked, but a few were wide and beautiful, with high arches and white marble buildings. The chief street, the *Via Sacra* (Sacred Way), crossed the Roman Forum. Victorious emperors and generals returning from war paraded over its lava pavement. See FORUM, ROMAN; ROMAN EMPIRE (picture, The Roman Forum).

Many Roman rulers built forums of their own. The ruins of five of these forums still stand—those of Augustus, Julius Caesar, Nerva, Trajan, and Vespasian. Trajan's Forum is the finest. Most of its buildings, including the Basilica Ulpia and the Temple of Trajan, are in ruins. But Trajan's Column, a hundred feet tall, is almost whole. It has carvings of scenes from Trajan's wars. Nearby stand the Markets of Trajan, a large semicircle of three-storied shops. One of the shops has been rebuilt to show how it looked in ancient times. See TRAJAN.

The Colosseum is one of the chief landmarks of Rome. In this huge, half-ruined amphitheater, Romans watched trained fighters called *gladiators* battle each other or fight wild animals. The audiences also saw persecuted Christians killed by lions. See COLOSSEUM.

Baths. Only wealthy Romans could afford to own private baths, but the city had many public ones. During the time of the emperors, the public baths became luxurious meeting places. They looked like great square-shaped swimming pools, and were surrounded by gardens, columned marble porches, and libraries. The bath buildings had facilities for warm and cold baths, steam baths, and massages.

The most splendid remains of baths are those of Cara-calla and of Diocletian. The Baths of Caracalla, which date from the early A.D. 200's, are especially impressive. They were decorated with precious marble, statues, and *mosaics* (pictures formed of bits of colored glass, stone, or wood). Few of these decorations remain. But the ruins provide an effective background for the operas that are now presented there in summer. The Baths of Diocletian, completed in the early A.D. 300's, were the largest of all Roman baths. They could serve 3,000 persons at a time. Most of the site has been built over, but some rooms can still be seen.

The Catacombs were systems of underground passages and rooms used as Christian burial places and chapels. The early Christians dug them from the A.D. 100's to the early 400's, and hid there during periods of persecution. The catacombs are decorated with paintings on walls and ceilings, and Christian symbols. The most famous catacombs include those of San Callisto, San Sebastiano, and Sant' Agnese. See CATACOMBS.

Other Remains. The Pantheon is the best preserved of all the remains of ancient Rome. The Romans built it as a temple in honor of all their gods (see PANTHEON). The triple Arch of Constantine, built about A.D. 315, also is well preserved. It includes three connected arches, side by side, richly decorated with sculpture.

The ruins of the *Domus Aurea* (Golden House) are in a popular public park. This building was the palace of Emperor Nero. The ruins, which lie mainly underground, occupy a large area. Paintings cover some of the walls. The well-preserved Column of Marcus Aurelius, built during the A.D. 100's, honors Roman victories in battle. It has carvings of war scenes. Stairs inside the hollow marble column lead to the top, where a statue of Saint Paul has stood since 1589.

The Mausoleum of Augustus, begun about 28 B.C., is the tomb of Augustus and the principal members of his family. Augustus, the first Roman emperor, built the nearby *Ara Pacis* (Altar of Peace) after establishing the *Pax Romana* (Roman Peace), which lasted 200 years. These buildings stood on the *Campus Martius* (Field of Mars), which had been used for military training. During the A.D. 200's, barbarian tribes attacked the empire, and Rome built the Aurelian Wall and other walls for defense. Many parts of these walls are still standing.

Catacombs of San Sebastiano
Italian Government Travel Office

Trajan's Column
Stockpile

Early Days. A legend says that Rome was founded by twin brothers in 753 B.C. For an account of this story, see ROMULUS AND REMUS. Rome expanded, and became the supreme power of the Western world. For the history of Rome through the fall of the West Roman Empire in A.D. 476, see ROMAN EMPIRE (History).

After Rome fell to Germanic tribes, most of the once-splendid city became an unhealthful area of marshes. During the mid-500's, Emperor Justinian I of the Byzantine Empire drove the Ostrogoths from Rome. He re-established Roman rule of the city as a Byzantine territory, but the decay of Rome continued. See BYZANTINE EMPIRE.

Rome had far-reaching importance as the official center of the Christian Church. During the 700's, the popes greatly increased their political power. When invading Lombards threatened Rome, Pope Stephen II asked for help from Pepin the Short, king of the Franks. Pepin saved Rome twice, and gave the city and nearby lands to the pope in 756. Pepin's son Charlemagne later expanded these *Papal States*, as they were called. See PAPAL STATES; PEPIN THE SHORT.

Feudal Times and the Renaissance. For hundreds of years after the 800's, Rome was torn by struggles among kings and princes. Various European rulers tried to control the powerful popes, especially by influencing papal elections. In 1305, through the efforts of King Philip IV of France, a French archbishop was elected pope. The new pope, Clement V, moved his court to Avignon, France. It was returned to Rome in 1377. See POPE (The Troubles of the Papacy).

During this period, Cola di Rienzi, a Roman patriot, rebelled against the nobles. He established a democratic republic in 1347. But Rienzi soon became cruel and greedy for power, and was later killed in a riot.

Rome became one of the most splendid cities of the Renaissance. In 1527, raiding German and Spanish troops destroyed and stole many of the city's treasures, and killed thousands of Romans. Soon afterward, the job of rebuilding Rome began. During the rest of the 1500's and the 1600's, the popes built hundreds of magnificent buildings. They appointed the finest painters and sculptors, including Michelangelo, to design and decorate the structures.

The 1800's. In 1798, after Napoleon conquered the Italian peninsula, the victorious French troops entered Rome. Napoleon ended the pope's political power in 1809. He made the Papal States a part of his empire. Napoleon also declared Rome as the second city of his empire, after Paris. Pope Pius VII fought these changes, and Napoleon arrested him. After Napoleon's downfall, the Papal States were returned to the pope in 1815.

During the early 1800's, movements for unity and freedom from foreign rule swept the Italian peninsula. But the popes opposed these movements. In 1848, revolutionists made Rome a republic, and Pope Pius IX fled the city. French troops captured Rome in 1849, and restored the pope to power the next year.

In 1861, when Victor Emmanuel II became king of a united Italy, Rome was not yet a part of the new kingdom. Italian volunteers tried to take Rome in 1867, but French defenders stopped them. In 1870, after the French troops had left, Victor Emmanuel entered the city practically without bloodshed. He ended the pope's political power and made Rome his capital. In protest, Pius IX shut himself up in the Vatican and refused to deal with the government. All popes after him followed the same policy until 1929. That year, the government established Vatican City as an independent state, and officials of the Roman Catholic Church recognized Rome as Italy's capital.

Plan of the Seven Churches of Rome, 1575 by Antoine Lafrery, from Gabinetto Nazionale delle Stampe, Rome, Italy

Map of Rome in 1575 shows seven old churches of the city. The drawing was made during the Holy Year of Jubilee declared in 1575 by Pope Gregory XIII. The four churches in which the holy year was celebrated are marked by crosses.

The **1900's** have been a period of widespread construction in Rome. New buildings and roads have been built, and the city has restored many ancient buildings and monuments. During the 1920's and 1930's, the Fascist dictator Benito Mussolini promoted much poorly planned construction. It has led to severe traffic jams and other city problems today. Mussolini completed a new University of Rome campus in 1935, and began a huge central railroad station in 1938. The work was halted by World War II (1939-1945). Rome suffered little damage during the war. The railroad station was completed in 1950 according to improved new plans.

In 1936, Mussolini began building the *Esposizione Universale di Roma* (Universal Exhibition of Rome, or E.U.R.). This world's fair was to have opened in 1942, and plans called for its buildings to form a government center later. The construction was interrupted by the war, and was resumed in 1951. This E.U.R. project included government and private office buildings, and apartments, museums, and restaurants.

In 1955, Rome's subway linked the 1,075-acre E.U.R. with the new railroad station. Some of the 1960 Summer Olympic Games were held near the E.U.R. in the city's new Sport Palace. By the late 1960's, the E.U.R. was almost completed, and many large companies and government agencies operated there.   MARIA CORDA COSTA

ROME/Study Aids

Related Articles in WORLD BOOK include:

Outline

I. The City Today
    A. Parks and Gardens
    B. Music and Theater
    C. Museums and Art Galleries
    D. Churches, Palaces, and
       Fountains
    E. Schools
    F. Sports
    G. Economy
    H. Government

II. The Ancient City
    A. Forums
    B. The Colosseum
    C. Baths
    D. The Catacombs
    E. Other Remains

III. History

Questions

Why is Rome called the *Eternal City?*
On how many hills was Rome built?
Where were public meetings held in ancient Rome?
What is the largest church in the world?
What is Rome's most popular sport?
What great painter decorated the Sistine Chapel?
How did the Via del Corso get its name?
Between which two points does Rome's subway run?
What were the catacombs? What were they used for?
What is the legend of the Fountain of Trevi?

ROME, N.Y. (pop. 50,148; alt. 445 ft.), is called the *Copper City*, because of its many manufactured copper products. More than a tenth of all the copper used in

the United States is fabricated there. The city lies in central New York, about 15 miles northwest of Utica (see NEW YORK [political map]). With Utica, it forms a metropolitan area of 340,670 persons.

Rome stands on the site of Fort Stanwix. Some persons believe that the Stars and Stripes flew there for the first time in battle on Aug. 2, 1777. But most historians believe it was the Cambridge, or Grand Union, flag that flew there (see FLAG [Flags in American History]). Rome has a mayor-council government.   WILLIAM E. YOUNG

ROME, ANCIENT. See ROMAN EMPIRE; ROME (The Ancient City); CITY (picture).

ROME, UNIVERSITY OF, is a coeducational state university in Rome, Italy. It was established in 1303 by Pope Boniface VIII. The Italian government took over control of the school in 1870 and made it a royal, then state, university. There are faculties of architecture, economics and commerce, education (Magistero), engineering, law, letters and philosophy, mathematics and physics, medicine and chemistry, pharmacy, political science, and statistical sciences. The university was moved from the center of Rome to the eastern part of the city in 1935. The departments of architecture, engineering, economics and commerce, and education are in other parts of the city.   LIVIO OLIVIERI

ROME-BERLIN AXIS. See AXIS.

ROMEO AND JULIET. See SHAKESPEARE, WILLIAM (Synopses of Plays).

ROMMEL, *RAHM ul,* **ERWIN** (1891-1944), a German field marshal, became one of the most brilliant generals of World War II. He commanded the Afrika Korps until the British forces stopped him in Egypt in 1942. His clever tactics earned him the nickname of "The Desert Fox." In 1944, he commanded a German army that opposed the Allied invasion of Normandy. He lost his command because he reported to Adolf Hitler that it was futile for Germany to continue the war. He was implicated in the plot to kill Hitler in July, 1944. Rommel was given his choice of trial or poison. His selection of death by poison spared Hitler much embarrassment. Rommel was born in Swabia.   LESTER B. MASON

ROMNEY, GEORGE WILCKEN (1907-   ), became secretary of housing and urban development in 1969 under President Richard M. Nixon. He had served as governor of Michigan from 1963 to 1969.

Romney was elected governor after taking a leading role at the constitutional convention that remodeled Michigan's government. He was re-elected in 1964 and 1966. Romney's administration increased state programs in civil rights and education, modernized the state tax structure, and ended the financial problems that had plagued Michigan. In 1964, Romney refused to support the Republican presidential candidate, the conservative Senator Barry M.

George W. Romney
State of Michigan

Goldwater of Arizona. In 1967, Romney became a front-runner for the 1968 Republican presidential nomination. He withdrew from the race for the nomination in February, 1968, after public opinion polls showed Nixon far in the lead.

Romney was born in Chihuahua, Mexico, of American parents. At the age of 5, he returned with his family to the United States. He attended the University of Utah and George Washington University. From 1930 to 1962, Romney followed a business career and became president of American Motors Corporation. Under his leadership, the company developed and marketed America's first successful compact automobile, the Rambler. Romney also held high positions in the Church of Jesus Christ of Latter-day Saints.   DAVID S. BRODER

ROMULO, *ROH muh loh,* **CARLOS PENA** (1901-   ), a Filipino diplomat and author, became Philippine secretary of foreign affairs in 1969. He had previously held several important government posts. Romulo served as Philippine ambassador to the United States in 1952 and 1953, and from 1955 to 1962. He was his country's representative at the United Nations (UN) from 1945 to 1955, and president of the UN General Assembly in 1949. In 1957, Romulo represented the Philippines on the UN Security Council. He served as president of the University of the Philippines from 1962 to 1969. Romulo also served as secretary of education from 1966 to 1969.

Romulo was born in Manila and educated at the University of the Philippines and Columbia University. For 20 years, he edited a chain of Philippine newspapers. He won a Pulitzer prize in 1942 for his reporting on a tour of the Far East.   GEORGE E. TAYLOR

ROMULUS (?-716 B.C.?) **AND REMUS** (?-753 B.C.?) were the legendary founders of Rome. According to legend, they were twin sons born to Rhea Silvia, daughter of Numitor, king of Alba. Their father was Mars, the god of war. Rhea Silvia was a vestal virgin (see VESTA). She was sentenced to be buried alive for breaking her vows.

Early Years. The story tells that the two children were thrown into the Tiber River in a basket, but were cast ashore at the foot of the Palatine Hill. A she-wolf cared for the boys until the shepherd Faustulus found them and took them to his home. He reared them with his own children and they grew up to be strong, handsome men who showed their high birth. As young men, they aided King Numitor, who had been driven from his throne by his brother Amulius. Romulus and Remus drove out Amulius and returned the throne to King Numitor.

Founding of Rome. Soon afterward, Romulus and Remus decided to build a new city along the Tiber River, at the spot where their lives had been saved by the wolf. They quarreled about its exact location and asked the gods to decide. The gods decided in favor of Romulus. He began to mark out the boundaries for the wall of the city. But Remus was still jealous, and leaped over the boundary. Romulus became angry and killed his brother. He was sorry as soon as he had killed Remus. As king of Rome, Romulus kept an empty chair beside him to show that his dead brother shared his power.

Young men came to Rome from all directions. But there were few women. The Romans were forced to steal their wives from the neighboring Sabine tribe. This caused war. After the Romans won several battles, the Sabines united with the Romans (see SABINE).

Romulus died in a mysterious manner. He was reviewing his army after a successful battle, when the sky became dark. A storm arose, and lightning flashed around his head. The people were frightened and fled. When they returned, Romulus had disappeared. The Romans believed that Mars had carried him to the gods' dwelling place. They renamed him Quirinus and worshiped him (see QUIRINUS).   THOMAS A. BRADY

ROMULUS AUGUSTULUS. See ODOACER.

RONCALLI, ANGELO GIUSEPPE. See JOHN (XXIII).

RONDO, *RAHN doh,* is a form of musical composition in which the principal section or theme is repeated at least three times in the same key. Contrasting sections appear between the principal themes. Because it constantly returns to the main idea, this form is cyclic, and so is called a *rondo.* If *A* represents the principal section or theme, and *B* and *C* the contrasting sections, the sequence of sections might be ABACA, or ABACABA, and so on.   RAYMOND KENDALL

RONSARD, *ron SAHR,* **PIERRE DE** (1524-1585), often called the Prince of Poets, led an influential group of French poets called the *Pléiade.* The *Sonnets for Helene* (1578), perhaps his best-known work, explored the joys and sorrows of love in masterful and descriptive verse. Ronsard's *Odes* (1550-1552) were inspired by Greek and Latin poetry. He wrote many volumes of love poetry and the moral and philosophical *Hymnes* (1555-1556). In *Discours* (1562-1563), he wrote stirring attacks against the Protestant movement during the religious wars that shook France in the 1560's.

Ronsard was born in the family manor house near Vendôme, and trained to be a diplomat. He turned to literature after he became partially deaf.   JOEL A. HUNT

See also FRENCH LITERATURE (The Pléiade).

ROOD. See WEIGHTS AND MEASURES (Miscellaneous).

ROOF is the cover of any building. The term also includes the materials which support the roof. Climate often determines the design of roofs. Ancient Syrians and Egyptians used flat roofs because of the hot sun and the lack of rain. Steep, sloping roofs covered the homes of central Europe, to help drain off heavy rains.

There are many variations of flat and sloping roofs. A *gable* roof has two sides sloping up to a center ridge. The *hip* roof has four sides sloping up from all four walls. The *lean-to* is a single slope over a small building, usually set against a larger building. A *gambrel* roof has two added ridges parallel to the center gable ridge, making steep slopes below each side of the upper, flatter slopes. *Mansard* roofs also have ridges below the center one, but on four sides, like the hip roof. Water is drained beyond the walls of a building by the *eaves* (overhang) of the roof.   TALBOT HAMLIN

See also ARCHITECTURE (pictures); DOME; HOUSE; SHELTER.

ROOF OF NORTH AMERICA. See COLORADO (Land Regions).

ROOF OF THE WORLD. See TIBET; PAMIRS, THE.

ROOK is the most common European member of the crow family. It is smaller than the raven, and larger than the jackdaw. It differs from other members of its family in having a purple gloss on its black plumage, and in its habit of feeding entirely on insects and grain. Upon reaching maturity, it sheds the feathers of its face, which then becomes a grayish-white. The migrating habits of rooks vary. Those in central Europe remain in their homes the year round. Those farther north fly southward when winter comes. During the nesting season, they gather in communities of many hundreds, known as rookeries. Tame rooks sometimes learn to imitate human speech. They are known for their cunning. See also CROW.

Scientific Classification. The rook belongs to the crow family, *Corvidae*. It is classified as genus *Corvus*, species *C. frugilegus*.   GEORGE J. WALLACE

ROOKERY. See ROOK; SEAL (Seal Rookeries).

ROOKWOOD POTTERY is a kind of earthenware or artware that shows American ideas and methods in pottery work. The pottery includes a large variety of vases, bowls, bookends, candlesticks, flower holders, novelties, art tiles, and some dinnerware. Mrs. Bellamy Storer founded the Rookwood Pottery in 1880.

Most of the clays used in this type of pottery come from the Ohio River Valley. The first Rookwood ware had a stone or coarse earthen body, which was decorated in glaze shades of brown and sea green. Later Rookwood pottery includes beautiful tints of all colors, many types of ornamentation, and famous glazes.

The three classes of Rookwood pottery include the cameo (or ornamented ware), the dull-finished ware, and the richly glazed ware.   EUGENE F. BUNKER, JR.

ROOM. See INTERIOR DECORATION; HOUSE.

ROOM-AND-PILLAR MINE. See COAL (Underground Mining Systems).

ROOSA, STUART ALLEN (1933-   ), is a United States astronaut. He was a crewman on the Apollo 14 space mission, which made a manned landing on the moon in February, 1971. Roosa piloted the command module as it orbited above the moon. His fellow astronauts, Edgar D. Mitchell and Alan B. Shepard, Jr., piloted the lunar module to the moon's surface.

Roosa was born in Durango, Colo., on Aug. 16, 1933. He joined the Air Force in 1953 and served as a fighter pilot and as a test pilot. Roosa earned a degree in aeronautical engineering from the University of Colorado in 1960 and graduated from the Aerospace Research Pilot School in 1965. Roosa became an astronaut in 1966.   WILLIAM J. CROMIE

ROOSEVELT, ELEANOR

ROOSEVELT, ELEANOR (1884-1962), the wife of President Franklin D. Roosevelt, became a distinguished public figure in her own right. She was probably the most active first lady in American history. Mrs. Roosevelt, a niece of President Theodore Roosevelt, won fame for her humanitarian work.

Mrs. Roosevelt was christened ANNA ELEANOR ROOSEVELT. But her family called her Eleanor, and she almost never used her real first name. In 1905, she was married to Franklin D. Roosevelt, a distant cousin. She began to work politically in his behalf after a polio attack crippled him in 1921. While Roosevelt was governor of New York and later President, she frequently made fact-finding trips for him. During World War II, Mrs. Roosevelt traveled to Europe, Latin America, and other parts of the world. She began to work with young people and the underprivileged, and fought for equal rights for minority groups.

From 1945 to 1951, Mrs. Roosevelt served as a delegate to the United Nations General Assembly. In 1946, she was elected chairman of the UN's Human Rights Commission, part of the Economic and Social Council. She helped draft the Universal Declaration of Human Rights (see HUMAN RIGHTS, UNIVERSAL DECLARATION OF). In 1961, she returned to the General Assembly. Her books include *This Is My Story* (1937), *This I Remember* (1950), *On My Own* (1958), and *Tomorrow Is Now* (published in 1963, after her death).   FRANK FREIDEL

See also ROOSEVELT, FRANKLIN DELANO.

Karsh, Ottawa

Eleanor Roosevelt

TYPES OF ROOFS

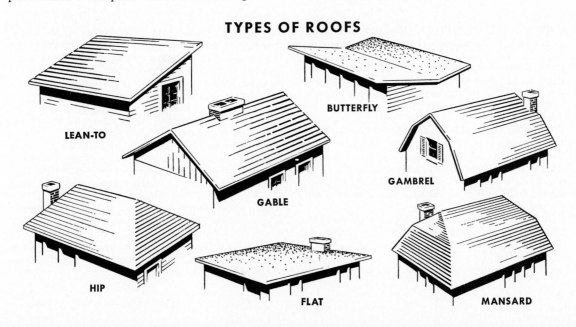

LEAN-TO

BUTTERFLY

GABLE

GAMBREL

HIP

FLAT

MANSARD

COOLIDGE
30th President
1923 — 1929

HOOVER
31st President
1929 — 1933

FRANKLIN
DELANO
ROOSEVELT

Franklin D. Roosevelt

32ND PRESIDENT
OF THE
UNITED STATES
1933-1945

ROOSEVELT, FRANKLIN DELANO (1882-1945), served as President for more than 12 years, longer than any other man. He was the only President elected four times. Roosevelt led the United States through its worst depression and through its worst war. He died just 83 days after becoming President for the fourth time.

Roosevelt took office as President at the depth of the Great Depression. About one of every four workers in the United States had lost his job. Many families had no money to buy food. Others had lost their homes because they could not pay their mortgages. Millions of Americans feared what would happen next. In Roosevelt's inaugural address, he called for faith in America's future. "The only thing we have to fear is fear itself," he declared boldly.

A new era in American history began under Roosevelt. He called his program the *New Deal*. For the first time, the federal government took strong action to help make the United States prosperous. Roosevelt said he wanted to help the average American, whom he called the "forgotten man." He promised relief for unemployed workers. He said he would aid farmers. Under his leadership, the government put stronger controls on business companies than ever before. It spent billions of dollars on relief and public works to "prime the pump" of business activity. Dozens of new government agencies were set up. Many were known by their initials, such as CCC, TVA, and NRA. Roosevelt himself became widely known by his initials, F.D.R.

Probably no other President since Abraham Lincoln has been so bitterly hated or so deeply loved. Critics charged that Roosevelt's policies gave the federal government too much power. They accused him of taking over many rights that belonged to the states under the Constitution. Many Americans thought that government controls over business might destroy the free enterprise system and lead to socialism. But millions believed that Roosevelt was the friend and protector of the common man. Their faith was the key to Roosevelt's success in politics.

TRUMAN
33rd President
1945 — 1953

EISENHOWER
34th President
1953 — 1961

The start of World War II in 1939 divided Roosevelt's presidency into two parts. Until the German invasion of Poland that year, the government worked hard to end the depression. The war then became the chief concern of Roosevelt and the United States.

Born into a wealthy family, Roosevelt entered politics because he believed it offered great opportunity for public service. Before he was elected President, he served in the New York state senate, as Assistant Secretary of the Navy, and as governor of New York.

Roosevelt had a colorful personality. He was known for his friendly smile, flashing eyes, and genial manner. He had two famous "trademarks." These were the glasses that he wore clipped to the bridge of his nose, and the cigaret holder that jutted upward at a jaunty angle from his mouth. He was a fine speaker, with a warm, pleasing voice.

People in all parts of the world admired Roosevelt for his personal courage. Although he was crippled by polio at the age of 39, he refused to give up his career of public service. As he struggled to regain the use of his legs, his physical appearance changed. As a young man, Roosevelt had been slender and more than 6 feet tall. After his illness, he became stocky and heavy-set. Roosevelt could never again stand without help. He had to learn to walk with leg braces and crutches. But a little more than 11 years after being stricken, he was elected President of the United States.

Early Life

Boyhood. The Roosevelt family traced its beginnings to Klaes Martensen van Roosevelt. Van Roosevelt was a Dutch landowner who in the 1640's had settled in New York City (then New Amsterdam). Van Roosevelt was also an ancestor of Theodore Roosevelt, the 26th President of the United States. Franklin and Theodore were fifth cousins.

Franklin Delano Roosevelt was born on Jan. 30, 1882, on his father's estate, "Springwood," in Hyde Park, N.Y. He was the only child of James and Sara Roosevelt. James Roosevelt was a wealthy vice-president of the Delaware and Hudson Railway. His wife was a member of the wealthy Delano family. The estates of both the Delanos and the Roosevelts overlooked the Hudson River. When Franklin was born, his mother was 28 years old and his father was 54.

Franklin's parents brought him up with loving firmness. His mother made him live by a rigid schedule. She set definite times for such daily activities as eating, studying, and playing. Sara Roosevelt was a domineering woman. Even after her son was grown and had children of his own, she would tell him to put on his rubbers before going outdoors in rainy weather. James Roosevelt made sure his son had all the advantages that wealth could buy. But he taught Franklin that being wealthy also brought with it the responsibility of helping persons who were not so lucky.

Education. From the time he was 3 years old, Franklin's parents usually took him on their yearly trips to Europe. He studied under governesses and private tutors until he was 14. He learned to speak and write both German and French. Roosevelt attended a public school only once—for six weeks, during a family trip in Germany. His mother thought the experience might improve his German. He was 9 years old at the time.

At the age of 14, Roosevelt entered the Groton School, a preparatory school in Groton, Mass. He made good grades, but was shy and had few close friends. He was graduated from Groton in 1900.

Roosevelt enrolled that same year at Harvard University. He majored in history and earned fair grades. He joined intramural rowing and football teams. He also was elected secretary of the Freshman Glee Club. Roosevelt was proud of his appointment in 1903 as an editor of the *Harvard Crimson*, the school newspaper. His college activities helped him make friends more easily.

Roosevelt was graduated from Harvard in 1903. But he continued his studies for another year. In 1904, he entered the Columbia University Law School. He passed the bar examination in 1907. But he had little interest in the study of law and left school that year before receiving a degree. Roosevelt worked as a clerk for a law firm in New York City for the next three years. However, he showed no enthusiasm for legal work.

Roosevelt's Family. Roosevelt and his distant cousin, Eleanor Roosevelt (1884-1962), had known each other slightly since childhood. He began to court her seriously while at Harvard. In 1903, after they became engaged, Roosevelt told his mother of his plans to marry. Sara Roosevelt did not want another woman in her son's life. She tried to change his mind, and even took him on a Caribbean cruise in hope that he would forget Eleanor. But Roosevelt went ahead with his plans. He and Eleanor were married on March 17, 1905. President Theodore Roosevelt, Eleanor's uncle, gave the bride away. See ROOSEVELT, ELEANOR.

While the Roosevelts were on their honeymoon, his mother rented a house for them and furnished it completely. Eleanor was disappointed to learn that she could not furnish her own home. But, rather than anger

─── **IMPORTANT DATES IN ROOSEVELT'S LIFE** ───

1882 (Jan. 30) Born in Hyde Park, N.Y.
1905 (March 17) Married Eleanor Roosevelt.
1913 Appointed Assistant Secretary of the Navy.
1920 Ran unsuccessfully for Vice-President of the United States.
1921 Stricken with polio.
1928 Elected governor of New York.
1932 Elected President of the United States.
1936 Re-elected President.
1940 Re-elected President.
1944 Re-elected President.
1945 (April 12) Died in Warm Springs, Ga.

her mother-in-law, she accepted the arrangement. She learned to take the older woman's interference silently, and to go her own way quietly. Roosevelt never seemed to mind his mother's attempts to dominate him.

The Roosevelts had six children. They were Anna Eleanor (1906-   ); James (1907-   ); Franklin Delano, Jr. (died in infancy, 1909); Elliott (1910-   ); Franklin Delano, Jr. (1914-   ), and John (1916-   ). James and Franklin, Jr., both served in the United States House of Representatives.

Roosevelt was a great companion to his children. He enjoyed swimming, sailing, and sledding with them. He often competed with them in races and contests. The Roosevelts called their children "the chicks."

Entry into Politics

State Senator. In 1910, Roosevelt accepted an invitation from state Democratic leaders to run for the New York senate. He joined the Democratic party chiefly because his father had been a Democrat. Roosevelt's task seemed impossible. The Republicans had controlled his district for more than 50 years. Roosevelt called for clean government and declared his opposition to "big-city bosses." He surprised veteran politicians by winning the election.

Roosevelt entered the state senate at the age of 29. He soon became known as a bold and skillful political fighter. At that time, U.S. Senators were elected by the state legislatures. Roosevelt led a group of Democratic legislators in a successful revolt against a candidate chosen by the party bosses. His action angered Tammany Hall, the Democratic organization in New York City (see TAMMANY, SOCIETY OF).

Assistant Secretary of the Navy. In 1912, Roosevelt supported Woodrow Wilson against his cousin Theodore Roosevelt in the presidential election. Wilson became President and in 1913 appointed Franklin Roosevelt as Assistant Secretary of the Navy. Roosevelt was delighted with his new post. "I now find my vocation combined with my avocation in a delightful way," he said. Politics was his "vocation," or work. His "avocation," or hobby, was ships and naval history.

Josephus Daniels was Secretary of the Navy and Roosevelt's immediate superior. He taught Roosevelt much about national politics, and especially about ways to get along with Congress.

In 1914, Roosevelt ran for nomination as a candidate for the United States Senate. He lost by a wide margin, chiefly because Tammany Hall opposed him.

After the United States entered World War I in April, 1917, Roosevelt wanted to enter military service. But Daniels persuaded him to stay at his desk. Roosevelt worked on many wartime projects, including a plan to lay antisubmarine mines in the North Sea. He became known as a man who "got things done." In 1918, he toured European battlefields and conferred with military leaders overseas. Roosevelt had become a national figure.

Candidate for Vice-President. In 1920, the Democratic national convention nominated Governor James M. Cox of Ohio for President. In order to "balance the ticket," the delegates wanted a vice-presidential candidate from an eastern state. Partly for this reason, the convention nominated Roosevelt.

Cox and Roosevelt campaigned on a platform calling for U.S. membership in the League of Nations. But the Senate had blocked American membership in the League. In addition, most voters were indifferent to the League. The Republican candidates, Senator Warren G. Harding of Ohio and Governor Calvin Coolidge of Massachusetts, defeated Cox and Roosevelt easily.

The defeat did Roosevelt little harm. He was only 38, and had established himself as a leader among progressive Democrats. In 1920, he became a vice-president of the Fidelity and Deposit Company of Maryland, a surety-bonding firm. He took charge of the company's New York City office.

Crippled by Polio

Tragedy Strikes. The Roosevelt family had a summer home on Campobello Island, off New Brunswick, Canada. On Aug. 9, 1921, Roosevelt fell into the water while sailing. He became chilled. The next day, he felt tired. He went swimming to refresh himself. "I didn't feel the usual reaction . . . ," Roosevelt wrote later. He meant that he did not feel refreshed after swimming. "When I reached the house, the mail was in, with several newspapers I hadn't seen. I sat reading for a while, too tired even to dress." The next morning, Roosevelt recalled, "my left leg lagged . . . Presently it refused to work, and then the other."

By August 12, Roosevelt could not stand or even move his legs. He suffered severe pain. His back, arms, and hands became partially paralyzed. He could no longer hold a pen to write. He did not know for certain that he had a severe case of polio, but he suspected the truth. "While the doctors were unanimous in telling me that the attack was very mild . . . ," he recalled, "I had, of course, the usual dark suspicion that they were just saying nice things to make me feel good." Later, lying in bed in New York City, Roosevelt showed his withered legs to his children. He explained how polio had damaged his muscles. He wanted them to understand his illness.

In January, 1922, Roosevelt's condition suddenly became worse. He remained cheerful despite more weeks of severe pain. One day, Josephus Daniels visited Roosevelt in the hospital. Roosevelt beckoned him close to the bed, then struck Daniels on the chest so hard it made him stagger. "You thought you were coming to see an invalid," Roosevelt said with a laugh, "but I can knock you out in any bout."

Many persons thought Roosevelt's political career had ended. His mother urged him to retire. But he continued his political activity—writing letters, issuing statements, and holding conferences in his home. He received encouragement and help from his wife and from his aide, Louis Howe.

He began to fight back against the disease that had crippled him. He regained the use of his hands, and the paralysis left his back. By exercising regularly, Roosevelt developed great strength in his arms and shoulders. After many months, using gymnasium equipment, he began trying to learn to walk again. He had several bad falls, but he did not give up.

As a result of being crippled, Roosevelt developed a fear of fire. He worried that he might some day be trapped by fire, and be unable to escape. Because of this fear, Roosevelt learned to drag himself along the floor, using his arms and hands. His legs improved a little, but he never again could walk unaided, or without braces.

The Warm Springs Foundation. In addition to his other exercises, Roosevelt went swimming as often as he could. "The water put me where I am, and the water has to bring me back," he said. He was referring to the swim he had taken just before the first polio attack. Now, swimming gave him a chance to exercise his legs.

In 1924, Roosevelt began to spend several months of each year at Warm Springs, Ga. Many polio victims had been helped by swimming in the pool of warm mineral water there. At the springs, Roosevelt met patients who could barely afford the cost of polio treatment. In 1926, he bought the springs and 1,200 acres of land around them. The next year, with a group of friends, he established the Georgia Warm Springs Foundation. The foundation provides low-cost treatment for "polios," as Roosevelt affectionately called his fellow victims. See WARM SPRINGS FOUNDATION, GEORGIA.

Return to Politics

By April, 1922, Roosevelt could walk a little. He wore braces on his legs and used crutches. While learning to walk again, he devoted more and more time to politics. Aided by Louis Howe, he corresponded with Democratic leaders throughout the country.

Roosevelt made a spectacular return to national politics in 1924. He nominated Governor Alfred E. Smith of New York for President at the Democratic national convention. He ignored the advice of friends who said he should not support a Roman Catholic for the presidency. The nominating speech was Roosevelt's first major public appearance since his polio attack. Thundering cheers greeted him as he walked slowly to the podium, aided by his son James. Smith did not get the nomination. But Roosevelt gained importance as a Democratic leader and as a man who had conquered personal tragedy.

In 1928, again with Roosevelt's support, Smith won the Democratic nomination for President. Smith asked Roosevelt to run for governor of New York. At first, Roosevelt refused to run. He wanted to continue his polio treatments at Warm Springs. But Smith insisted, feeling that Roosevelt's candidacy would strengthen his own chances. Roosevelt finally consented. He barely defeated his Republican opponent, Albert Ottinger, the attorney general of New York. Smith lost the presidential election to Herbert Hoover, and did not even carry New York.

Governor of New York. As governor, Roosevelt supported a variety of progressive legislation. He obtained tax relief for farmers. After the Great Depression began in October, 1929, he established the first system of relief for the unemployed in New York. He brought about tighter control of public utilities. He also created a power authority to develop the water power of the Saint Lawrence River. Other laws modernized the state prison system and established old-age pensions. A broad conservation and reforestation program also went into effect.

In 1930, Roosevelt won re-election by about 725,000 votes, a record for the state at that time. The victory proved that he was popular with voters.

Election of 1932. Roosevelt had gained wide public respect for his work as governor by 1932. Early that year he began to seek the Democratic presidential nomination. James A. Farley, Democratic party chairman in New York state, directed his campaign. In a nationwide radio address, Roosevelt outlined a program to meet the economic problems of the nation. Such a program, he said, had to be built for the average American, whom he called the "forgotten man." The Democratic national convention nominated Roosevelt on the fourth ballot. John Nance Garner of Texas, the Speaker of the House of Representatives, was chosen for Vice-President. The Republicans renominated President Herbert Hoover and Vice-President Charles Curtis.

Roosevelt flew to the convention in Chicago to ac-

The President and Mrs. Roosevelt worshiped together at St. Thomas Episcopal Church in Washington, D.C.

Swimming helped Roosevelt after he contracted polio in 1921. He backed the annual "March of Dimes" campaigns to fight the disease.

As Assistant Secretary of the Navy, Roosevelt made many inspection tours. In 1918, during World War I, he visited an American base in France.

Triumph Over Polio. In his first major public appearance after being stricken, Roosevelt nominated Alfred E. Smith for President in 1924.

cept the nomination. It was the first time a presidential nominee had made an acceptance speech at a national convention. Roosevelt promised a "new deal" to lead the nation out of the depression. He said he would set up economic safeguards to prevent future depressions.

During the election campaign, Roosevelt visited 38 states. He wanted to show the voters that he was physically able to be President. He promised to provide relief for the unemployed, to help the farmers, and to balance the budget. He also said he would end Prohibition (see PROHIBITION). In the election, Roosevelt received 472 electoral votes to only 59 for Hoover. Many persons sang a popular song, "Happy Days Are Here Again," to celebrate Roosevelt's victory. This tune had been the Democratic campaign song.

On Feb. 15, 1933, Giuseppe Zangara, a mentally ill bricklayer, tried to assassinate Roosevelt in Miami, Fla. Roosevelt escaped injury, but the shots fired by Zangara killed Mayor Anton J. Cermak of Chicago. Zangara, who said he had visions of killing a "great ruler," was executed on March 20, 1933.

Roosevelt's First Administration (1933-1937)

Roosevelt became President on March 4, 1933, at the age of 51. The inauguration was the last held in March. Under Amendment 20 to the Constitution, all later inaugurations have been held in January.

The depression had grown steadily worse. Thousands of unemployed workers were standing in bread lines to get food for their families. Many farmers and city workers had lost their homes. Even more were about to lose them because they could not pay their mortgages.

The Banking Crisis. About three weeks before Roosevelt took office, a banking panic began. It spread throughout the country as anxious depositors hurried

─── ROOSEVELT'S FIRST ELECTION ───

Place of Nominating Convention. Chicago
Ballot on Which Nominated..... 4th
Republican Opponent......... Herbert Hoover
Electoral Vote................. 472 (Roosevelt) to
                                      59 (Hoover)
Popular Vote................... 22,815,785 (Roosevelt) to
                                      15,759,266 (Hoover)
Age at Inauguration........... 51

to their banks to get cash and gold. The panic created "runs" that ruined many banks. On the day before Roosevelt's inauguration, more than 5,000 banks went out of business.

On March 6, 1933, Roosevelt declared a "bank holiday." He closed all banks in the United States until officials of the Department of the Treasury could examine every bank's books. Banks in good financial condition were to be supplied with money by the Treasury and allowed to reopen. Those found in doubtful condition were kept closed until they could be put on a sound basis. Many banks that had been badly operated never opened again.

The President's action restored confidence and ended the bank crisis. People knew that if a bank opened its doors, it was safe. Few wished to withdraw their money from a bank they knew was sound. See BANK HOLIDAY.

The "Hundred Days." On March 9, 1933, Congress began a special session called by Roosevelt. The President at once began to submit recovery and reform laws for congressional approval. Congress passed nearly all the important bills that he requested, most of them by large majorities. This special session of Congress came to be known as the "Hundred Days." It actually lasted 99 days, from March 9 to June 16. Important laws passed during this period included the Agricultural Adjustment Act (AAA), the Tennessee Valley Authority (TVA) Act, and the National Industrial Recovery Act (NIRA). See NEW DEAL (Leading New Deal Agencies).

On March 12, Roosevelt gave the first of his famous "fireside chats," speaking to the nation by radio. He explained what action had been taken and what he planned for the immediate future.

Many of the advisers who helped Roosevelt during his presidential campaign continued to aid him after he entered the White House. From time to time they included Adolf A. Berle, Harry L. Hopkins, Raymond Moley, Samuel I. Rosenman, and Rexford G. Tugwell. A newspaperman once described the group as "Roosevelt's Brain Trust." The name stuck.

Roosevelt's Cabinet included Frances Perkins as Secretary of Labor. She was the first woman ever

United Press Int.

Taking Office as President on March 4, 1933, Roosevelt told Americans that "the only thing we have to fear is fear itself." James Roosevelt stood between his father and Herbert Hoover, *extreme right*, whom Roosevelt succeeded.

The "Fireside Chats." Roosevelt made many informal reports by radio to the American people. He was the first President to use radio effectively to win public support. He also became the first President to appear on television.

named to a Cabinet post. Harold L. Ickes, a Chicago lawyer who had been chairman of the National Progressive League for Roosevelt and Garner, was named Secretary of the Interior. Henry Morgenthau, Jr., became Secretary of the Treasury in 1934.

The New Deal, as Roosevelt called his reform program, included a wide range of activities. The President described it as a "use of the authority of government as an organized form of self-help for all classes and groups and sections of our country."

Unemployment Legislation. At first, Roosevelt favored only emergency measures. At his request, Congress appropriated $500,000,000 for relief to states and cities through the Federal Emergency Relief Administration. In the winter of 1933-1934, the government started a relief program called the Civil Works Administration (CWA). The CWA supplied funds to local authorities

--------- **VICE-PRESIDENTS AND CABINET** ---------

Vice-President	*John N. Garner
	*Henry A. Wallace (1941)
	*Harry S. Truman (1945)
Secretary of State	*Cordell Hull
	*Edward R. Stettinius, Jr. (1944)
Secretary of the Treasury . . .	William H. Woodin
	*Henry Morgenthau, Jr. (1934)
Secretary of War	George H. Dern
	Harry H. Woodring (1937)
	*Henry L. Stimson (1940)
Attorney General	Homer S. Cummings
	Frank Murphy (1939)
	*Robert H. Jackson (1940)
	Francis Biddle (1941)
Postmaster General	*James A. Farley
	Frank C. Walker (1940)
Secretary of the Navy	Claude A. Swanson
	Charles Edison (1940)
	*Frank Knox (1940)
	*James Forrestal (1944)
Secretary of the Interior . . .	*Harold L. Ickes
Secretary of Agriculture . . .	*Henry A. Wallace
	Claude R. Wickard (1940)
Secretary of Commerce	Daniel C. Roper
	*Harry L. Hopkins (1939)
	Jesse H. Jones (1940)
	*Henry A. Wallace (1945)
Secretary of Labor	*Frances Perkins

*Has a separate biography in WORLD BOOK.

such as mayors of cities and governors of states. These funds made possible such public projects as building streets, roads, bridges, and schoolhouses; cleaning up parks; or doing other useful tasks. A number of persons criticized the CWA. They said many CWA employees merely raked leaves or held other useless jobs.

Roosevelt ended the CWA after a few months. But other employment relief programs were more permanent. The Civilian Conservation Corps (CCC) operated from 1933 until 1942. The CCC gave work and training to 500,000 young men. It achieved great success with its programs of flood control, forestry, and soil conservation. The Works Progress Administration (WPA) was established in 1935 to provide work for persons without jobs. It employed an average of 2,000,000 workers annually between 1935 and 1941.

All these government projects cost a great deal of money—much more than the government was collecting through taxes. The deficit was made up partly by raising taxes and partly by borrowing. The government borrowed money by selling government bonds. The national debt rose higher than ever before.

Other Reforms. During Roosevelt's first year in the White House, Congress passed laws to protect the investments of persons who buy stocks and bonds. Other legislation helped the oil and railroad industries, small businessmen, and homeowners. In December, 1933, Amendment 21 to the Constitution ended Prohibition. The Social Security Act of 1935 provided unemployment relief and old-age assistance. The National Labor Relations Act of 1935 gave workers the right to bargain collectively (see LABOR [Collective Bargaining]).

Opposition to the New Deal. By 1935, some New Deal measures were meeting strong opposition, chiefly from businessmen. The WPA and the National Labor Relations Act received heavy criticism. Critics charged that these measures wasted money and favored unions.

Good Neighbor Policy. Roosevelt described his foreign policy as that of a "good neighbor." This phrase came to be used to describe the U.S. attitude toward the countries of Latin America. Under Roosevelt's Good Neighbor Policy, the United States took the lead in promoting good will among these nations.

417

The Platt Amendment of 1901 had given the United States the right to intervene in the affairs of Cuba (see CUBA [United States Control]). On May 31, 1934, the government repealed this amendment. It also withdrew American occupation forces from some Caribbean republics, and settled long-standing oil disputes with Mexico. Reciprocal trade treaties were signed with some Latin-American countries between 1934 and 1937. These countries included Brazil, Colombia, Costa Rica, Cuba, El Salvador, Guatemala, Haiti, Honduras, and Nicaragua (see RECIPROCAL TRADE AGREEMENT). In 1935, the United States signed treaties of nonaggression and conciliation with six Latin-American countries. The desire for hemispheric ties soon spread to include Canada. The United States and Canada signed several reciprocal trade agreements.

Roosevelt also used personal diplomacy. In July, 1934, he took a trip to Cartagena, Colombia, and became the first President to visit South America. In 1936, he attended the Inter-American Conference for the Maintenance of Peace, in Buenos Aires, Argentina. On the way home, he visited Montevideo, Uruguay.

Relations with Russia. Roosevelt hoped that trade could be resumed between the United States and Russia. Partly for this reason, his administration recognized the Soviet government of Russia in November, 1933. Relations between the two countries had been broken off after the Russian Revolution of 1917. In 1933, for the first time in 16 years, the United States and Russia exchanged diplomatic representatives.

Election of 1936. The Democratic national convention renominated Roosevelt by acclamation in 1936. The delegates also renominated Vice-President Garner. The Republicans picked Governor Alfred M. Landon of Kansas for President and Frank Knox, publisher of the *Chicago Daily News*, for Vice-President.

In the campaign, the Republicans charged that Roosevelt had not kept his promise to balance the budget. Roosevelt replied by pointing to the action taken by his administration to fight the depression and return the nation to prosperity.

Roosevelt won re-election in a landslide. He received 523 electoral votes to 8 for Landon, and carried every state except Maine and Vermont.

Roosevelt's Second Administration (1937-1941)

The Supreme Court. According to the United States Constitution, only Congress has the power to make laws binding upon every American. The Constitution also states that Congress may "regulate" various activities, such as interstate commerce. However, Congress is too large and has too many other duties to do an effective job of regulating. So the courts have held that Congress may delegate its regulatory power to various government agencies.

——— ROOSEVELT'S SECOND ELECTION ———
Place of Nominating Convention. Philadelphia
Ballot on Which Nominated.....1st
Republican Opponent.........Alfred M. Landon
Electoral Vote.................523 (Roosevelt) to
8 (Landon)
Popular Vote.................24,751,597 (Roosevelt) to
16,697,583 (Landon)
Age at Inauguration............54

But when is a rule a mere regulation, and when is it a law? This difficult question arose over the regulations of some New Deal agencies. In 1935, a chicken dealer sued the government to nullify the National Industrial Recovery Act. The case eventually went to the Supreme Court. The Court ruled the act unconstitutional because it delegated lawmaking powers to the National Recovery Administration (NRA). This decision ended the NRA, one of the chief New Deal projects. See NATIONAL RECOVERY ADMINISTRATION.

The Agricultural Adjustment Act, the Railroad Retirement Act, and a number of other New Deal measures were also declared unconstitutional. The President feared his whole program might be defeated by the nine Supreme Court justices.

In 1937, shortly after his second inauguration, Roosevelt proposed a reorganization of the Supreme Court. Congress approved six of the seven major changes recommended by the President. In the seventh, Roosevelt proposed that when a Supreme Court justice reached the age of 70, a younger man should be appointed to sit with him on the Court. The total number of justices was not to exceed 15.

Roosevelt's opponents charged he was trying to "pack" the Supreme Court with judges who would always favor the New Deal. While Congress was debating the President's proposal, the Supreme Court approved some legislation considered essential to the New Deal program. The controversy died down. By 1944, so many justices had retired or died that all but two Court members were Roosevelt appointees.

Attitude Toward Japan. In the mid-1930's, President Roosevelt realized that Japanese attacks on China were a threat to world peace. He tried to arouse the nation to the danger. In October, 1937, he called on peaceful countries to unite and "quarantine" war in the same way that doctors quarantine, or isolate, a contagious disease.

Roosevelt and Secretary of State Cordell Hull believed that the United States needed a policy that would help the country arm for defense. The President tried to strengthen the army and the navy, although Congress often opposed him. He refused to recognize the Japanese puppet state of Manchukuo in northern China. He believed Japan should respect American rights in the Pacific and Far East. The President demanded that Japan apologize and pay for the sinking of the American gunboat *Panay* in 1937. The Japanese met his demands at once.

Neutrality Acts of the 1930's reflected the desire of many Americans to isolate the United States from other nations (see ISOLATIONISM). Congress passed the first Neutrality Act in 1935. It prohibited the United States from furnishing weapons or supplies to any nation at war. President Roosevelt said he hoped that any future neutrality laws "might provide for greater flexibility." But in 1936 and 1937, Congress approved other legislation to keep America free of "foreign entanglements."

Roosevelt opposed the neutrality laws because they treated all nations the same—whether a country had attacked another country, or had been attacked itself. These laws made it all but impossible for the United States to aid any friendly nation. Roosevelt wanted to give "all aid short of war" to nations opposing the Axis powers—Germany, Italy, and Japan. He believed that an Axis victory would endanger democracy everywhere.

World War II began on Sept. 1, 1939, when Germany invaded Poland. Still, many Americans did not agree that the situation was as dangerous as Roosevelt believed. These "isolationists" thought the United States could stay out of the war.

As tension increased, Americans became more concerned about the war in Europe. Some isolationists accused Roosevelt of *warmongering*, or trying to get America into the war.

Shortly after German troops attacked Poland, Congress passed the Neutrality Act of 1939. This law made it possible for a nation fighting the Axis to buy war supplies from the United States. But it had to furnish its own ships to carry the weapons. In November, 1941, Congress repealed two sections of the act. These sections had kept American vessels out of war zones and had forbidden them to carry guns.

Election of 1940. The Democratic party broke precedent in 1940 by nominating Roosevelt for a third consecutive term. Secretary of Agriculture Henry A. Wallace was chosen as his vice-presidential running mate. The Republicans nominated Wendell L. Willkie of Indiana, a corporation president, to oppose Roosevelt. They picked Senator Charles L. McNary of Oregon for their vice-presidential candidate. Willkie supported Roosevelt's foreign policy, and favored many of the New Deal programs for social reform. But he opposed the controls which the Democratic administration had put on business.

To obtain the support of both Republicans and Democrats for his military program, Roosevelt appointed two Republicans to his Cabinet in 1940. Henry L. Stimson became Secretary of War. He had held this office under President William Howard Taft, and had been Secretary of State under President Hoover. Stimson replaced Harry H. Woodring, who was regarded as an isolationist. Newspaper publisher Frank Knox became Secretary of the Navy.

The Republicans based their campaign on the tradition that no President had ever sought three terms in succession. Roosevelt defended his administration's programs. He promised to try to keep the nation out of war. In June, France had surrendered to Germany. The defeat of the French army, believed by many to be the strongest in the world, shocked the United States. Most Americans decided that Roosevelt's leadership and experience were needed for another term. Roosevelt carried 38 of the 48 states, and won 449 electoral votes to 82 for Willkie.

Roosevelt's Third Administration (1941-1945)

The Eve of War. By the time Roosevelt took his third presidential oath of office, the United States was giving Great Britain all aid short of war. In the summer of 1940, Britain gave the United States 99-year leases on several naval bases in the Atlantic. The British navy

———————— ROOSEVELT'S THIRD ELECTION ————————

Place of Nominating Convention . Chicago
Ballot on Which Nominated 1st
Republican Opponent . . . . Wendell L. Willkie
Electoral Vote . . . . 449 (Roosevelt) to
             82 (Willkie)
Popular Vote . . . . 27,243,466 (Roosevelt) to
             22,304,755 (Willkie)
Age at Inauguration 58

received 50 old American destroyers in return. The United States adopted its first peacetime selective service, or draft, law in September.

In August, 1941, Roosevelt met British Prime Minister Winston Churchill on a cruiser anchored off Newfoundland. The two men adopted a declaration that became known as the *Atlantic Charter*. They pledged not to seek gains, "territorial or otherwise"; to respect the right of every nation to choose its own form of government; to guarantee freedom of the seas; and to conduct peaceful world trade. See ATLANTIC CHARTER.

In a speech on Jan. 6, 1941, Roosevelt declared that all men are entitled to freedom of speech, freedom of worship, freedom from want, and freedom from fear. These basic rights came to be called the *Four Freedoms* (see FOUR FREEDOMS). On March 11, Congress passed the Lend-Lease Act. This law authorized the government to provide war supplies to any nation at war with the Axis powers. See LEND-LEASE.

Relations with Japan became increasingly tense. Germany, Italy, and Japan had signed a mutual aid pact in 1940. Beginning in 1941, the United States tried to stop Japanese aggression in Southeast Asia. The government reduced trade with Japan, and issued warnings from time to time. Roosevelt described this policy as "babying the Japanese along."

America Goes to War. On Sunday, Dec. 7, 1941, Secretary of State Hull conferred with two Japanese diplomats. While they talked, Japanese planes attacked the U.S. Pacific Fleet which lay at anchor in Pearl Harbor, Hawaii (see PEARL HARBOR NAVAL BASE).

President Roosevelt addressed Congress the next day. He said December 7 was "a date that will live in infamy." The United States declared war against Japan. Four days later, on December 11, Germany and Italy declared war on the United States. America then declared war on those countries.

Most Americans realized that the nation faced a serious situation. The war extended across both the Atlantic and Pacific oceans. The navy had been crippled by the attack on Pearl Harbor. But the draft had given the army more than a million men with at least a year's military training.

A great decision confronted the President after Pearl Harbor. He had to decide where to strike first. On the West Coast, many people felt that Japan was the chief foe. In the East, many wanted Germany defeated first.

Roosevelt conferred with Churchill in the White House in December, 1941, and January, 1942. The two leaders realized that the United States could not strike an effective blow against Japan until the navy had recovered from its losses at Pearl Harbor. In addition, German scientists were developing new weapons that could mean defeat for the Allies. Both the British and the Russians wanted to see Germany defeated as soon as possible. For these reasons, Roosevelt and Churchill decided that Germany, the most powerful enemy nation, must be defeated first.

Roosevelt suggested the name *United Nations* for the alliance that fought Germany, Italy, and Japan. This alliance formed the basis for the peacetime United Nations organization that later was established in 1945. See UNITED NATIONS.

For a description of life in the United States and Canada during World War II, see WORLD WAR II (The Home Front in the United States and Canada).

North African Invasion. On Nov. 7, 1942, the Allies invaded North Africa. It was the greatest landing operation in history up to that time. After the landings began, Roosevelt spoke by radio to the French people in their own language. He explained that the Allies had to drive the Germans out of French territory in North Africa. Roosevelt was the first President to give a radio address in a foreign language. See WORLD WAR II (The North African Campaign).

The Big Three. President Roosevelt left the United States many times during the war for conferences with Allied leaders. He was the first President to leave the country in wartime. Early in 1943, he met with Churchill in Casablanca, Morocco. The two leaders announced that they would accept only unconditional surrender by the Axis nations. In other conferences, Roosevelt discussed problems of war and peace with both Churchill and Premier Joseph Stalin of Russia. They came to be known as the "Big Three." Roosevelt also conferred with Generalissimo Chiang Kai-shek of China in 1943.

Early in the war, the Russians asked for a "second front" against the Germans in Western Europe. Churchill believed the Allies should first attack the Germans in Africa or in other places where they were relatively weak. He also feared that Russia would take control of Eastern Europe after the war. In November, 1943, the Big Three met at Teheran, Iran. During and after this conference, Roosevelt worked to get Churchill and Stalin to agree on major war aims. At Teheran, he refused to have lunch with Churchill before meeting with Stalin. The President did not want Stalin to think he and Churchill had made a separate agreement. See TEHERAN CONFERENCE.

Life in the White House was relaxed and informal during Roosevelt's presidency. His many grandchildren stayed in the Executive Mansion from time to time. They often romped with the President before the day's work began. Mrs. Roosevelt had a swing put up for them in a tree on the White House grounds.

An indoor swimming pool was installed so the President could continue to exercise his crippled legs. In the summer of 1934, the executive offices in the West Wing of the White House were enlarged, and a new Cabinet Room was added. The East Wing was also enlarged and remodeled.

The Roosevelts entertained a great deal until the Japanese attack on Pearl Harbor. Their guest lists often included as many as 1,500 persons. In 1939, King George VI and Queen Elizabeth became the first British monarchs to visit the United States. They stayed at the White House as guests of the Roosevelts.

Many changes in White House routine were made after the United States entered World War II. The Roosevelts reduced their entertaining. Wartime security regulations went into effect. Machine guns were set up on the White House roof, and Secret Service agents took over a special office in the East Wing. Engineers built a bomb shelter in the White House basement. Prime Minister Churchill, a frequent wartime visitor, had his own map room on the second floor.

Election of 1944. In June, 1944, the Republicans nominated Governor Thomas E. Dewey of New York

THE WORLD OF

WORLD EVENTS

1933 Adolf Hitler became chancellor of Germany.

1935-1936 Italian forces under Benito Mussolini conquered Ethiopia.

1936 Edward VIII of Britain abdicated to marry an American divorcée, Mrs. Wallis Simpson.

1936-1939 Rebels led by Francisco Franco defeated the Loyalists in the Spanish Civil War.

1939 The German invasion of Poland marked the start of World War II.

1941 Japan attacked Pearl Harbor seven weeks after Hideki Tojo became premier.

1944 Allied armies landed in Normandy and began their assault on Hitler's "Fortress Europe."

1945 The "Big Three" met at Yalta, in the Crimea.

★   ★   ★

U.S. population was about 140,000,000 in 1945, the year Roosevelt died in office. The United States flag had 48 stars while he was President. No new states joined the Union during his administration.

NATIONAL EVENTS

1933 The New Deal began with the "Hundred Days." Congress passed emergency laws to end the depression.

1933 Amendment 21 to the Constitution, permitting the sale of liquor, ended Prohibition.

Amendment 21
1933

1935 Congress passed the Social Security Act.

1935 The National Industrial Recovery Act was declared unconstitutional by the U.S. Supreme Court.

1937 Roosevelt tried to "pack" the Supreme Court with justices of his own choosing. The unsuccessful attempt caused a national controversy.

1940 Congress approved the Two-Ocean Navy Act.

1940 The Selective Service and Training Act, America's first peacetime draft law, was passed by Congress.

1940 The American people broke tradition by electing Roosevelt to a third term as President.

1941 The Lend-Lease law, providing arms for Great Britain, made America the "Arsenal of Democracy."

1944 Congress approved the Servicemen's Readjustment Act, or "GI Bill of Rights," to help returning veterans.

1944 Roosevelt won election to a fourth term as President.

PRESIDENT FRANKLIN D. ROOSEVELT

Tojo

Mussolini

World War II

Hitler

World War II began in 1939 with the German invasion of Poland. The Japanese attack on Pearl Harbor in 1941 brought America into the war.

Social Security Act was passed by Congress in 1935. It provided for assistance to the aged and unemployed.

Public Works projects, including schools, bridges, and hospitals, gave employment to thousands of men during the depression years.

The "Bank Holiday," Roosevelt's first official act, closed banks in 1933. It helped end the bank crisis.

First Nuclear Chain Reaction was achieved in December, 1942, at the University of Chicago.

"Good Neighbor Policy," proclaimed by Roosevelt in 1933, sought to strengthen friendly ties among nations of the Western Hemisphere.

ROOSEVELT, FRANKLIN DELANO

for President and Governor John W. Bricker of Ohio for Vice-President. Roosevelt had not said whether he would run for a fourth term. He finally declared that he wanted to retire, but felt it was his duty to run again. Roosevelt said he wanted to avoid a wartime change in leadership. Many Democratic leaders felt that he might not live through a fourth term. But the President easily won renomination. Senator Harry S. Truman of Missouri was nominated for Vice-President. See TRUMAN, HARRY S. (Vice-President).

In the campaign, the Republicans argued that no man should be President for 16 years. The Democrats answered by saying that America should not "change horses in mid-stream." Republicans charged that Roosevelt was in poor health. The President replied by driving around New York City in an open car for four hours during a rainstorm—and then making a major speech. Roosevelt won an easy victory. He carried 36 of the 48 states, and received 432 electoral votes to 99 for Dewey.

Roosevelt's Fourth Administration (1945)

Roosevelt's inaugural address of January, 1945, was one of the shortest in American history. It lasted only six minutes. The President declared that Americans had learned "we cannot live alone at peace, that our own well-being is dependent on the well-being of nations far away . . ."

Roosevelt was in poor health when he started his fourth term. A series of colds had bothered him for more than a year. He had lost about 15 pounds. In the fall and winter of 1944, he had been busy directing his legislative program and dealing with increasingly difficult international problems. The election campaign of 1944 had weakened him further.

─────── ROOSEVELT'S FOURTH ELECTION ───────

Place of Nominating Convention. Chicago
Ballot on Which Nominated 1st
Republican Opponent . . . . Thomas E. Dewey
Electoral Vote . . . . 432 (Roosevelt) to
99 (Dewey)
Popular Vote . . . . 25,602,505 (Roosevelt) to
22,006,278 (Dewey)
Age at Inauguration 62

───

The "Big Three"—Winston Churchill of Great Britain, Roosevelt, and Joseph Stalin of Russia—held two conferences during World War II. Roosevelt appeared aged and weary at the Yalta Conference in February, 1945, two months before his death.

United Press Int.

— HIGHLIGHTS OF ROOSEVELT'S ADMINISTRATIONS —

1933 Congress enacted New Deal recovery measures during the "Hundred Days."
Prohibition was repealed.
1935 The Social Security Act and the first Neutrality Act were passed.
1937 Roosevelt's "court-packing" recommendations started the Supreme Court controversy.
1939 The United States began selling arms to friendly countries on a "cash-and-carry" basis.
1940 Congress passed the Selective Service Act.
1941 The Atlantic Charter was issued.
(Dec. 7) Japan attacked Pearl Harbor.
1942 Twenty-six nations signed the Declaration of the United Nations.
1943 Roosevelt and Churchill announced the goal of unconditional surrender by the Axis powers. Roosevelt, Churchill, and Stalin conferred in Tehran, Iran.
1944 (June 6) The Allies invaded Normandy, France.
1945 Roosevelt, Churchill, and Stalin met at Yalta, in the Crimea.

───

Yalta Conference. Two days after his fourth inauguration, Roosevelt left to meet Churchill and Stalin at Yalta, a famous resort in the Crimea in southern Russia. On Feb. 11, 1945, the three leaders issued the Crimea Declaration. It repeated the principles of the Atlantic Charter and the Casablanca conferences. The leaders mapped the final assault on Germany and the postwar occupation of that country. They also planned a meeting in San Francisco to lay the foundations for the peacetime United Nations organization. In a secret agreement, Russia promised to enter the war against Japan after the surrender of Germany. In return, Russia was to receive the Kuril Islands and other concessions. Critics later charged that Roosevelt had been cheated by Stalin. See YALTA CONFERENCE.

While reporting to Congress on the Yalta meeting on March 1, Roosevelt made one of his rare public references to his physical handicap. "I hope that you will pardon me for this unusual posture of sitting down . . . ," he said, "but . . . it makes it a lot easier for me not to have to carry about 10 pounds of steel around at the bottom of my legs."

During the next few weeks, Roosevelt began to have doubts about the good will of the Russians. He was anxious, he told Churchill, about "the development of the Soviet attitude."

Death. On March 29, 1945, the President left for a rest at Warm Springs. He had prepared a speech for broadcast on April 13. Roosevelt had written: "The only limit to our realization of tomorrow will be our doubts of today. Let us move forward with strong and active faith."

April 12 began as usual. The President read newspapers and mail that had been flown from Washington. He planned to attend a barbecue in the afternoon. Before the barbecue, Roosevelt was working at his desk while an artist, Mrs. Elizabeth Schoumatoff, painted his portrait. Suddenly he fell over in his chair. "I have a terrific headache," he whispered. These were Roosevelt's last words. He died a few hours later of a cerebral hemorrhage. As news of his death spread, a crowd gathered in front of the White House, silent with grief. Millions of people in all parts of the world mourned the dead President.

Roosevelt was buried at Hyde Park. His home and library there have been set aside as the Franklin D. Roosevelt National Historic Site.   FRANK FREIDEL

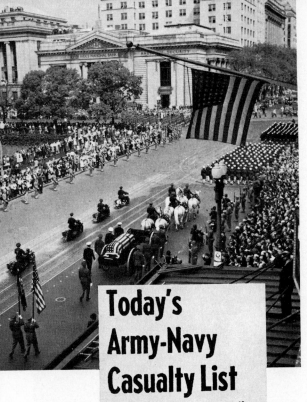

Today's
Army-Navy
Casualty List

Washington, Apr. 13.—Following are the latest casualties in the military services, including next-of-kin.

ARMY-NAVY DEAD
ROOSEVELT, Franklin, D., Commander-in-Chief, wife, Mrs. Anna Eleanor Roosevelt, the White House.
Navy Dead
DECKER, Carlos Anthony, Fireman 1c. Sister, Mrs. Elizabeth Decker Metz, 16 Concord Pl., Concord, S. I.
SEILER, Edwin Norton, Lt. Mother

United Press Int.; Culver

Casualty List of April 13, 1945, was headed by President Roosevelt. Thousands of mourners lined the streets of Washington, D.C., to honor the nation's wartime commander in chief.

Related Articles in WORLD BOOK include:

Agricultural Adjustment
    Administration
Bank Holiday
Churchill, Sir Winston
Dewey, Thomas E.
Four Freedoms
Garner, John N.
Hopkins, Harry L.
Hull, Cordell
Landon, Alfred M.
National Recovery
    Administration

New Deal
New York (Places to Visit)
President of the U.S.
Roosevelt, Eleanor
Roosevelt, Campobello
    International Park
Teheran Conference
Truman, Harry S.
Wallace, Henry A.
Willkie, Wendell L.
World War II
Yalta Conference

Outline

I. Early Life
  A. Boyhood
  B. Education
  C. Roosevelt's Family

II. Entry into Politics
  A. State Senator
  B. Assistant Secretary
     of the Navy
  C. Candidate for
     Vice-President

III. Crippled by Polio
  A. Tragedy Strikes
  B. The Warm Springs
     Foundation

IV. Return to Politics
  A. Governor of New York
  B. Election of 1932

V. Roosevelt's First Administration (1933-1937)
  A. The Banking Crisis
  B. The "Hundred Days"
  C. The New Deal
  D. Good Neighbor Policy
  E. Relations with Russia
  F. Election of 1936

VI. Roosevelt's Second Administration (1937-1941)
  A. The Supreme Court
  B. Attitude Toward Japan
  C. Neutrality Acts
  D. Election of 1940

VII. Roosevelt's Third Administration (1941-1945)
  A. The Eve of War
  B. America Goes to War
  C. North African
     Invasion
  D. The Big Three
  E. Life in the White
     House
  F. Election of 1944

VIII. Roosevelt's Fourth Administration (1945)
  A. Yalta Conference
  B. Death

Questions

What illness almost ended Roosevelt's career?
What were the two critical periods during which Roosevelt served as President?
What was Roosevelt's first federal office?
What was the *New Deal?*
How did the "bank holiday" help end the financial crisis of 1933?
Why was Roosevelt criticized for his proposal to reorganize the Supreme Court?
How did Roosevelt first use the phrase "good neighbor"? What did the phrase come to mean?
What were the "Hundred Days"?
How did Roosevelt try to end unemployment?
Why was Roosevelt's election in 1940 unique?

Reading and Study Guide

For a *Reading and Study Guide* on Franklin D. Roosevelt, see the RESEARCH GUIDE/INDEX, Volume 22.

Books to Read

BURNS, JAMES M. *Roosevelt: The Lion and the Fox.* Harcourt, 1956. *Roosevelt: The Soldier of Freedom.* 1970. Won a Pulitzer prize.
CAVANAH, FRANCES. *Triumphant Adventure: The Story of Franklin Delano Roosevelt.* Rand McNally, 1964. For young readers.
FREIDEL, FRANK. *Franklin D. Roosevelt: The Apprenticeship.* Little, Brown, 1952. *Franklin D. Roosevelt: The Ordeal.* 1954. *Franklin D. Roosevelt: The Triumph.* 1956.
LEUCHTENBURG, WILLIAM E. *Franklin D. Roosevelt and the New Deal, 1932-1940.* Harper, 1963.
SCHLESINGER, ARTHUR M., JR. *The Age of Roosevelt.* 3 vols. Houghton, 1957-1960.
SHERWOOD, ROBERT E. *Roosevelt and Hopkins.* Rev. ed. Harper, 1950. Won a Pulitzer prize.
THOMAS, HENRY. *Franklin Delano Roosevelt.* Putnam, 1962. For young readers.

ROOSEVELT, NICHOLAS J. (1767-1854), an American inventor and engineer, pioneered in developing steam navigation. Roosevelt became associated with Robert Fulton, and in 1811 he built the steamer *New Orleans* at Pittsburgh, Pa. He traveled in the *New Orleans* down the Ohio and Mississippi.

Born and educated in New York City, Roosevelt early developed a love for mechanics. In 1782, he built a model boat which was propelled by side-paddle wheels turned by springs. After an unsuccessful attempt at copper mining, he became interested in building steam engines, and established a foundry at Belleville, N.J. In 1798, he built a steamboat at his foundry in cooperation with Robert R. Livingston and John Stevens, but it was not a success. Roosevelt was a great-granduncle of President Theodore Roosevelt.   JOHN H. KEMBLE

ROOSEVELT, QUENTIN. See ROOSEVELT, THEODORE (Second Marriage; World War I).

CLEVELAND
24th President
1893 — 1897

McKINLEY
25th President
1897 — 1901

THEODORE
ROOSEVELT

Theodore Roosevelt

26TH PRESIDENT
OF THE UNITED STATES
1901-1909

Chicago Historical Society

ROOSEVELT, THEODORE (1858-1919), was the youngest man ever to become President. He took office at the age of 42. Roosevelt had been Vice-President for only six months when President William McKinley was assassinated in September, 1901. Roosevelt won wide popularity, and millions of Americans affectionately called him "Teddy" or "T.R." In 1904, the voters elected him to a second term as President. He ran for President a third time in 1912, as the "Bull Moose" party candidate, but lost to Woodrow Wilson.

Roosevelt was a man of great energy, and practiced what he called the "strenuous life." He enjoyed horseback riding, swimming, hunting, hiking, and boxing. He often expressed enthusiasm for something by describing it as "bully." Cartoonists liked to draw Roosevelt with his rimless glasses, bushy mustache, prominent teeth, and jutting jaw. One cartoon showed him with a bear cub. Soon, toymakers were producing stuffed animals that are still known as "teddy bears."

As commander of the fearless Rough Riders, Roosevelt became a national hero during the Spanish-American War in 1898. He led this famous cavalry regiment against the Spaniards in Cuba. Roosevelt came home and won election as governor of New York. Two years later, he was elected Vice-President.

As President, Roosevelt used his power of leadership to help the United States meet challenges at home and abroad. "I did not usurp power," Roosevelt said, "but I did greatly broaden the use of executive power."

Roosevelt fought for reforms that would benefit the American people. He became known as a "trust buster" because he tried to limit the power of great business corporations. During his administration, Congress passed laws to regulate the railroads, to protect the public from harmful foods and drugs, and to conserve the nation's forests and other natural resources.

In foreign relations, Roosevelt worked to make the United States a world leader. He felt that this leadership must be supported by strong armed forces. He expressed his foreign policy as: "Speak softly and carry a big stick." Roosevelt strengthened the U.S. Navy, began the construction of the Panama Canal, and kept European nations from interfering in Latin America. He helped end the Russo-Japanese War, and became the first American to receive the Nobel prize for peace.

While Roosevelt was President, millions of Americans traveled by bicycle—even women in their sweeping, ankle-length skirts. But automobiles, along with electric lights and telephones, started to come into widespread use. Guglielmo Marconi sent the first radio message

424

across the Atlantic Ocean, and a telegraph cable was laid across the Pacific to the Philippines. The air age was born when the Wright brothers flew the first successful airplane. Roosevelt enjoyed taking a ride in one of the early models.

Roosevelt regarded public life as a great stage. As President, he joyfully held the center of that stage. When Roosevelt left office, he wrote: "I do not believe that anyone else has ever enjoyed the White House as much as I have." He was probably right.

Early Life

Boyhood and Education. Theodore Roosevelt was born in New York City on Oct. 27, 1858. He was the second of the four children of Theodore and Martha Bulloch Roosevelt. "Teedie," as the family called him, was younger than his sister Anna, and older than his brother Elliott and his sister Corinne.

Roosevelt's ancestors, the Van Roosevelts, had come to America from Holland in the 1640's. One of these ancestors, Klaes Martensen van Roosevelt, settled in New York, which was then called New Amsterdam. Klaes was also an ancestor of Franklin D. Roosevelt, the 32nd President of the United States. Most of the Van Roosevelts were wealthy landowners and businessmen.

Theodore Roosevelt's mother came from a prominent Georgia family. One of her brothers was an admiral in the Confederate Navy. She sympathized with the South during the Civil War. Her husband, an importer of plate glass, supported the North. But the Roosevelts did not let their differences keep them from providing a happy home life for their family.

Like his father, Teedie had great energy, curiosity, and determination. He enjoyed an active childhood although he was puny and frequently ill. He suffered greatly from asthma. While playing with friends one day, he discovered that he also was nearsighted. The other children easily read an advertisement on a billboard some distance away. "Not only was I unable to read the sign, but I could not even see the letters," Roosevelt wrote later. From then on he wore glasses.

Theodore loved both books and the outdoors. He combined these interests in nature study. His bureau drawers smelled of dead mice and birds, and so, often, did Theodore. When he was 10, and again when he was 14, Theodore went with his family on year-long trips abroad. He visited Europe and the Middle East.

When Theodore was about 12, his father told him that he would need a strong body to give his mind a chance to develop fully. The next year, while alone on a trip to Maine, Theodore was tormented by two mischievous boys. He felt ashamed because he was not strong enough to fight back. Roosevelt's father built a gymnasium in the family home, and Theodore exercised there regularly. He overcame his asthma, and built up unusual physical strength.

Roosevelt studied under tutors until he entered Harvard University in 1876 at the age of 18. He earned good grades in college. Once he asked so many questions during a natural history lecture that the professor exclaimed: "Now look here, Roosevelt, let me talk. I'm running this course!" Roosevelt was graduated from Harvard in 1880.

First Marriage. In October, 1879, Roosevelt met Alice Hathaway Lee (1861-1884). She was the daughter of a wealthy official of a Boston investment firm. Roosevelt courted Alice during his senior year at Harvard. They were married on his 22nd birthday.

A double tragedy struck on Feb. 14, 1884. Alice Roosevelt died two days after the birth of a daughter, also named Alice (1884-   ). On the same day, Roosevelt's mother died of typhoid fever.

Political and Public Activities

State Legislator. After graduation from Harvard in 1880, Roosevelt did not know what to do for a living. His father, who had died in 1878, had left him some money. But Theodore needed to earn more in order to live comfortably. "I had enough bread," he wrote later. "What I had to do . . . was to provide the butter and jam." He enrolled in the Columbia University Law School, but the courses did not interest him. While studying law, he wrote *The Naval War of 1812*, a technically excellent but dull book.

Roosevelt decided to enter politics as a means of public service. He joined a Republican club in New York City. He recalled that his friends "laughed at me, and told me that politics were 'low . . .' I answered that . . . the people I knew did not belong to the governing class, and that the other people did—and that I intended to be one of the governing class."

In the fall of 1881, at the age of 23, Roosevelt won election to the New York state assembly. He wore sideburns and dressed elegantly. The other legislators thought he looked like a "dude." But his intelligence, courage, and energy won their respect. He was re-elected twice, in 1882 and 1883.

Party Leader. In 1882, Roosevelt served briefly as leader of the Republican minority in the assembly. State party bosses expected him to follow orders, but he refused to obey blindly. The bosses removed him as minority leader. However, Roosevelt remained the most influential man in the assembly. He worked closely with Governor Grover Cleveland, a Democrat, and became interested in civil service reform.

Rancher and Writer. After the death of his wife and mother in 1884, Roosevelt left politics. He bought two cattle ranches on the Little Missouri River in the Dakota Territory. The hard life and endless activity of a rancher helped him recover from his sorrow. Wearing cowboy clothes, Roosevelt often spent 14 to 16 hours a day in the saddle. He hunted buffalo and other wild

Woman's Roosevelt Memorial Association

Roosevelt's Birthplace in New York City is now a memorial. "Teddy" was a weak, sickly child. His father installed a gymnasium in the house, and the boy exercised there regularly.

── IMPORTANT DATES IN ROOSEVELT'S LIFE ──

1858 (Oct. 27) Born in New York City.
1880 (Oct. 27) Married Alice Hathaway Lee.
1882-1884 Served in the New York state assembly.
1884 (Feb. 14) Mrs. Alice Roosevelt died.
1886 (Dec. 2) Married Edith Kermit Carow.
1889 Appointed to the U.S. Civil Service Commission.
1897 Named Assistant Secretary of the Navy.
1898 Led the Rough Riders in the Spanish-American War.
1899 Elected governor of New York.
1900 Elected Vice-President of the United States.
1901 (Sept. 14) Became President of the United States.
1904 Elected to full term as President.
1912 Defeated for President on the "Bull Moose" ticket.
1919 (Jan. 6) Died at his home in Oyster Bay, N.Y.

animals, tended cattle, and even helped law officers capture a band of outlaws.

Roosevelt wrote steadily. In one period of less than three months, he completed a biography of Senator Thomas Hart Benton of Missouri. He also wrote a book called *The Winning of the West*.

Severe snowstorms in the winter of 1885-1886 destroyed most of Roosevelt's cattle. He returned to New York City in 1886 and at the request of Republican leaders, ran for mayor. He was badly defeated.

Second Marriage. During several trips home from his ranches, Roosevelt had visited a childhood friend, Edith Kermit Carow (1861-1948). They were married on Dec. 2, 1886, and lived in Sagamore Hill, Roosevelt's home in Oyster Bay, Long Island, N.Y. Edith Roosevelt had a strong influence on her husband. He came to depend on her advice. "Whenever I go against her judgment, I regret it," he said.

The Roosevelts had five children: Theodore, Jr. (1887-1944); Kermit (1889-1943); Ethel Carow (1891-); Archibald Bulloch (1894-); and Quentin (1897-1918). Mrs. Roosevelt reared Alice Roosevelt, Theodore's daughter by his first wife, as her own child. Roosevelt loved to play with his children.

Civil Service Commissioner. Benjamin Harrison won the Republican nomination for President in 1888. Roosevelt went on a speaking tour for Harrison, who was elected in November. Partly as a reward for Roosevelt's service, Harrison appointed him to the Civil Service Commission. Roosevelt brought publicity to the commission, which previously had attracted little attention. He improved the merit system by establishing examinations for some Civil Service jobs. Roosevelt

opposed the practice of handing out government jobs to reward political friends. Many Republicans resented his attitude. But President Grover Cleveland reappointed him in 1893.

Police Commissioner. In 1895, Roosevelt gladly accepted the post of president of the Board of Police Commissioners in New York City. For the next two years, he fought to stamp out dishonesty on the police force. Sometimes he patrolled the streets at night to check on policemen suspected of illegal activities.

A National Figure

Assistant Secretary of the Navy. In 1895, some friends asked Roosevelt if he might be a candidate for President. "Don't you dare ask me that!" Roosevelt exclaimed. "Don't you put such ideas into my head . . .I must be wanting to be President. Every young man does. But I won't let myself think of it. . .If I do. . .I'll be careful, calculating, cautious, and so . . .I'll beat myself. See?"

Roosevelt campaigned vigorously for William McKinley, the Republican candidate for President in 1896. McKinley won, and Roosevelt asked him for a government appointment. McKinley did not want this brash young man in Washington, but Roosevelt had powerful support. The President finally made him an Assistant Secretary of the Navy.

Roosevelt believed that sea power was the decisive factor in world history. He worked to strengthen the navy. He also believed that war for a righteous cause brought out the finest virtues in both men and nations. "No triumph of peace is quite so great as the supreme triumphs of war," he said soon after taking office. "The diplomat is the servant, not the master, of the soldier."

The Rough Riders. Since 1895, Cuban rebels had been revolting against their Spanish rulers. Many Americans demanded that the United States help the Cubans. On Feb. 15, 1898, the U.S. battleship *Maine* was blown up in Havana harbor. Roosevelt tried to rush preparations for war against Spain. He became impatient with McKinley's attempts to avoid war. In private, Roosevelt complained that the President had "no more backbone than a chocolate éclair."

On April 25, 1898, the United States declared war on Spain. Roosevelt immediately resigned as Assistant Secretary of the Navy so he could fight. Even before resigning, he had started to recruit men for a cavalry regiment. This unit became the First Volunteer Cavalry Regiment. Under Roosevelt's command, it won fame as the Rough Riders. Most of the men were former college athletes and western cowboys.

426

On July 1, 1898, American troops attacked a ring of fortified hills surrounding Santiago, Cuba. Colonel Roosevelt led his men in a charge up Kettle Hill, which flanked the Spanish blockhouse on San Juan Hill. He and the Rough Riders became nationally famous. Twenty years later he declared: "San Juan was the great day of my life." See SPANISH-AMERICAN WAR.

Governor of New York. The Republicans faced defeat in New York in 1898 because of a scandal over state canal contracts. The state party leader, Senator Thomas C. Platt, did not like Roosevelt. But Platt knew that Roosevelt's reputation might save the Republicans. Roosevelt agreed to run for governor. He won, largely because of his war record.

As governor, Roosevelt did not break with Platt. Neither did he follow Platt's wishes. He described this policy to a friend: "I have always been fond of the West African proverb: 'Speak softly and carry a big stick, you will go far.' " Roosevelt became an efficient, independent administrator. He supported mild reform legislation, including a law affecting civil service in the state. He angered large business interests by approving a bill for the taxation of corporation franchises.

Vice-President. McKinley's renomination in 1900 seemed certain. Roosevelt had no wish to oppose the President, who he knew had nationwide support. But Roosevelt wondered whether he himself might get the nomination in 1904. As the Republican national convention drew near, a movement began to nominate him for Vice-President.

Roosevelt felt that being Vice-President would take him out of active politics. In this way, his chances for the presidential nomination in 1904 would be weak-

ened. Roosevelt also knew that Senator Platt wanted to get rid of him as governor of New York. Roosevelt felt he might not win a second term as governor in opposition to Platt. He finally consented to be McKinley's running mate. The Republicans nominated both men by acclamation. In the election, McKinley and Roosevelt defeated their Democratic opponents, William Jennings Bryan and former Vice-President Adlai E. Stevenson.

On Sept. 6, 1901, only six months after his second inauguration, President McKinley was shot by an assassin. The tragedy occurred at the opening ceremonies of the Pan American Exposition in Buffalo, N.Y. Doctors told Roosevelt that McKinley would probably recover. But, while vacationing in the Adirondack Mountains, Roosevelt learned that McKinley was near death. He hurried to Buffalo, traveling about 20 hours by carriage and train. McKinley died before Roosevelt arrived. That same day, Sept. 14, 1901, Roosevelt took the oath of office as President. See MCKINLEY, WILLIAM (Assassination).

Roosevelt's First Administration (1901-1905)

Roosevelt became President just six weeks before his 43rd birthday. He kept all the members of McKinley's Cabinet. He said he would continue McKinley's policies "absolutely unbroken." But Roosevelt had too much originality to follow another man's plans.

Most businessmen feared Roosevelt because of some reforms he had introduced as governor of New York. Several of these reforms had brought about stricter

Roosevelt the Rancher. Roosevelt quit politics in 1884, after his mother and first wife died. He bought two ranches in the Dakota Territory and lived the rugged life of a cowboy. He sometimes tended cattle for 16 hours a day.

government control over industry. Early in his administration, Roosevelt tried to convince businessmen that he would not interfere with them. He also tried to persuade conservative Republican leaders that he was not dangerous. But he never won them over completely. They considered much of his legislation dangerously progressive, even socialistic. The Republicans controlled Congress throughout Roosevelt's presidency. But because of conservative opposition, Roosevelt had increasing difficulty getting Congress to act on his recommendations.

"Trust Buster." Many Americans had become worried about the *trusts*, or large business monopolies. These trusts were increasing rapidly in both number and power. The trusts had increased productivity and had raised the standard of living. But prices had also risen, and the people blamed the trusts. In his first message to Congress, in December, 1901, Roosevelt expressed this feeling. "Captains of industry . . . have on the whole done great good to our people," he said. But he also pointed to "real and grave evils." Roosevelt recommended that "combination and concentration should be, not prohibited, but supervised and, within reasonable limits, controlled."

In 1902, the government sued the Northern Securities Company on charges of trying to reduce competition. This firm had been formed by J. P. Morgan and other financiers to control key railroads in the West. Roosevelt said he did not want to use the power of the government to ruin Morgan. Rather, he wanted to keep order among all the great economic forces in the nation. The Supreme Court upheld the government's view in 1904. It dissolved the Northern Securities Company.

During Roosevelt's presidency, the government filed suits against 43 other corporations. In major cases, the government ended John D. Rockefeller's oil trust and James B. Duke's tobacco trust. Many persons called Roosevelt a "trust buster." But the President declared that he wanted the government to regulate, not "bust," the trusts.

Friend of Labor. Roosevelt wanted the government to act justly toward labor unions as well as toward business. Government intervention in labor disputes was not new. But it had usually favored management.

In May, 1902, about 140,000 members of the United Mine Workers went on strike in the hard-coal fields of Pennsylvania. Public opinion favored the strikers, who demanded more pay and better working conditions. As the strike continued, coal supplies began to run low in eastern cities. Many hospitals and schools had no fuel. Winter was approaching.

Roosevelt had no legal authority to intervene in the strike. But he called a conference of leaders of both sides. He proposed that the strike be settled by arbitration. The miners agreed, but the mineowners refused. Roosevelt threatened to have the army seize and operate the mines. At Roosevelt's request, J. P. Morgan helped reach a compromise with the mine owners. The miners got a pay raise the next March. Roosevelt said later that he had tried to give the miners a "square deal." He often used this phrase to refer to his policy of social reform. In 1903, Congress established the Department of Commerce and Labor (see LABOR, DEPARTMENT OF).

Foreign Policy. Roosevelt believed that the govern-

428

WORLD EVENTS

1902 The British defeated the Dutch in the Boer War in South Africa.

1905 Japan defeated Russia in the Russo-Japanese War. Roosevelt won the Nobel peace prize for helping to end the conflict.

1905 Albert Einstein, a 26-year-old physicist, published his theory of relativity.

1907 Delegates from 44 nations attended the second conference on world disarmament at The Hague in The Netherlands.

★　★　★　★　★　★

NATIONAL EVENTS

U.S. population was about 90 million in 1909, the year Roosevelt left the presidency. Oklahoma joined the Union during Roosevelt's administration. It became the 46th state in 1907.

There were 45 stars in the United States flag when Roosevelt became President.

1903 Congress established the Department of Commerce and Labor.

1903 Roosevelt sent a message over the newly completed cable across the Pacific Ocean.

1903 A six-man tribunal upheld U.S. claims in the Alaska boundary dispute with Great Britain.

1906 The San Francisco earthquake destroyed much of the city and killed about 700 persons.

1907 A financial panic started when prices dropped suddenly on the New York City stock market.

1908 The first "Model T" Ford went on the market.

ment needed a "big stick," or threat of force, to carry out its foreign policies. He used this policy in relations with Europe and Latin America.

The Venezuela Affair. The Monroe Doctrine held that the United States should keep European powers out of the Western Hemisphere. Roosevelt upheld this doctrine in what was known as the Venezuela Affair.

Venezuela had borrowed large sums of money in Europe. In December, 1902, German and British ships blockaded Venezuelan ports to force payment of the debts. Roosevelt feared that Germany planned to seize Venezuelan territory. He warned the Germans that he might have to use force if they took any part of Venezuela. The Germans withdrew their warships. Later, Roosevelt helped settle the dispute peacefully.

The "Roosevelt Corollary." In 1904, Santo Domingo (now the Dominican Republic) found it could not pay its debts to several European countries. Again, Roose-

PRESIDENT THEODORE ROOSEVELT

Russo-Japanese War

OKLAHOMA

The Wright Brothers launched the air age when they made the first airplane flight.

U.S. Forest Service was established in 1905 under a national conservation program.

The Panama Canal Zone was obtained by the United States from Panama in 1903.

Federal Food and Drugs Act of 1906 protected the public against impure foods.

U.S. GOVERNMENT INSPECTION

First Wireless Telegraph message to flash across the Atlantic was sent in 1901.

"Great White Fleet" of U.S. warships sailed on a 14-month good-will tour in 1907.

velt feared European intervention. He announced that the United States might be forced "in flagrant cases of . . . wrongdoing or impotence, to the exercise of an international police power." This policy was called the "Roosevelt Corollary" of the Monroe Doctrine.

Roosevelt ordered American officials to take over the customs system of Santo Domingo in 1904. American control continued for 28 months, and brought order to Santo Domingo's finances.

The Panama Canal. Between 1902 and 1905, Roosevelt persuaded Congress to approve building 10 battleships and 4 armored cruisers for the U.S. Navy. He believed the larger fleet would give the nation greater influence in international affairs. But the fleet would need to shift rapidly between the Atlantic and Pacific oceans. A canal across Central America seemed necessary.

In 1903, Roosevelt began negotiating with Colombia for the purchase of a strip of land across Panama, a province of Colombia. When rebels in Panama set up a revolutionary government, Roosevelt sent troops to keep Colombian forces from attacking them. Within three days, the United States recognized the Republic of Panama. Less than two weeks later, the United States and Panama signed a treaty for the construction of a canal. Roosevelt said he was prouder of the Panama Canal than of any other accomplishment of his administration. He visited Panama in 1906—the first President to travel to a foreign country while in office. See PANAMA CANAL (picture).

The Alaskan Boundary Dispute. No one cared about the exact boundary between Canada and Alaska until gold was discovered in the Klondike in 1896. Then Canada claimed a line which gave it control of important routes to the gold fields. The United States disputed the claim. Early in 1902, Great Britain asked that the matter be settled by arbitration. At first, Roosevelt

429

refused. But then he agreed that the dispute should be settled by a tribunal of six "impartial jurists" appointed by both countries. In 1903, the tribunal ruled in favor of the United States.

Conservation. Roosevelt made notable achievements in conservation. He told Congress that "the forest and water problems are perhaps the most vital internal problems of the United States." To discourage the waste of natural resources, Roosevelt added more than 125 million acres to the national forests. Congress passed the Reclamation Act of 1902, which provided for the reclamation and irrigation of dry western lands. Roosevelt also started 25 irrigation or reclamation projects. The largest was the Theodore Roosevelt Dam in Arizona. See CONSERVATION (National Policy); ROOSEVELT DAM.

Life in the White House was never dull during Roosevelt's presidency. The Roosevelt children and their friends became known as the "White House Gang." The President sometimes joined in their games. One day, he heard that the gang was preparing an "attack" on the White House. He sent a message to the children through the War Department, ordering them to call it off. Once Roosevelt scolded his sons for decorating a portrait of President Andrew Jackson with spitballs. But he allowed the boys to bring their pets, including a pony and snakes, into the White House.

The President often played tennis on the White House lawn with friends. These friends came to be known as the "tennis cabinet." The group also went horseback riding and hiking. More than once, on winter hikes, Roosevelt and his friends swam across the Potomac River through chunks of floating ice.

In 1902, the White House was remodeled and enlarged. The east and west wings were built. Workmen installed new plumbing, heating, and electrical systems.

Edith Roosevelt was an efficient and gracious White House hostess. She carefully kept out of politics. The President's daughter by his first marriage was called "Princess Alice" by newspaper reporters. In 1906, Alice married Nicholas Longworth. Their wedding took place in the White House, and was one of the biggest social events in Washington in many years.

Election of 1904. The Republicans unanimously nominated Roosevelt for President at their 1904 national convention. They chose Senator Charles W. Fairbanks of Indiana for Vice-President. The Democrats nominated Judge Alton B. Parker of the New York supreme court for President, and Henry G. Davis of West Virginia for Vice-President.

During the election campaign, Roosevelt called on the voters to support his "square deal" policies. Parker appealed for an end to what he called "rule of individual caprice" and "usurpation of authority" by the President. Roosevelt won the election by more than $2\frac{1}{2}$ million popular votes. No earlier President had won by so large a margin.

Roosevelt's Second Administration (1905-1909)

Domestic Problems. Roosevelt believed that laws were badly needed to control the nation's railroads. The Elkins Act of 1903 had prohibited railroads from making *rebates*, or returning sums of money, to favored shippers. But the act had not stopped such practices, which often put rival shippers out of business. Roosevelt demanded legislation to curb the abuses. In 1906, Congress passed the Hepburn Railway Rate Act despite conservative opposition. The act did not end the rebates, but it was a step in that direction.

The food and drug industries were also affected by reforms. In 1906, Roosevelt read Upton Sinclair's new novel *The Jungle*. It described unsanitary conditions in the meat-packing industry. Roosevelt ordered an investigation, and received what he called a "sickening report." He threatened to publish the report if Congress did not correct the situation. That same year, Congress passed the Meat Inspection Act and the Food and Drugs Act. See PURE FOOD AND DRUG LAWS.

In 1907, the stock market slumped. A financial panic spread throughout the country. Businessmen blamed Roosevelt and his progressive legislation. But most historians believe that speculation and inefficient business management actually caused the panic. Prosperity returned by 1909.

Friction with Japan. In 1905, Roosevelt helped end the Russo-Japanese War. He brought representatives of

Edith Carow Roosevelt hired a secretary to handle White House social matters so that she could spend more time with her family.

Sagamore Hill, the President's spacious home in Long Island, N.Y., was Roosevelt's "summer White House" while he was Chief Executive.

Frick Art Reference Library; Charles Phelps Cushing

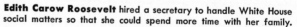

Vice-President.............*Charles W. Fairbanks
Secretary of State.........*John Hay
                           *Elihu Root (1905)
                           Robert Bacon (1909)
Secretary of the Treasury....Lyman J. Gage
                           Leslie M. Shaw (1902)
                           George B. Cortelyou (1907)
Secretary of War..........*Elihu Root
                           *William Howard Taft (1904)
                           Luke E. Wright (1908)
Attorney General.........*Philander C. Knox
                           William H. Moody (1904)
                           *Charles J. Bonaparte (1906)
Postmaster General........Charles E. Smith
                           Henry C. Payne (1902)
                           Robert J. Wynne (1904)
                           George B. Cortelyou (1905)
                           George von L. Meyer (1907)
Secretary of the Navy.......John D. Long
                           William H. Moody (1902)
                           Paul Morton (1904)
                           *Charles J. Bonaparte (1905)
                           Victor H. Metcalf (1906)
                           Truman H. Newberry (1908)
Secretary of the Interior.....Ethan A. Hitchcock
                           James R. Garfield (1907)
Secretary of Agriculture.....James Wilson
Secretary of Commerce
    and Labor................George B. Cortelyou
                           Victor H. Metcalf (1904)
                           Oscar S. Straus (1906)
                           *Has a separate biography in WORLD BOOK.

Place of Nominating Convention..Chicago

Ballot on Which Nominated......1st

Democratic Opponent..........Alton B. Parker

Electoral Vote...................336 (Roosevelt) to
                                 140 (Parker)

Popular Vote....................7,623,486 (Roosevelt)
                                 to 5,077,911 (Parker)

Age at Inauguration.............46

States (see GENTLEMAN'S AGREEMENT). In 1908, Japan and the United States signed the Root-Takahira Agreement. In this pact, the two nations promised not to seek territorial gains in the Pacific, and to honor the Open-Door Policy in China (see OPEN-DOOR POLICY).

In 1907, Roosevelt decided to display American naval power. He sent 16 new battleships on a good-will tour of the world. These ships became known as the *Great White Fleet* because they were painted white. The fleet received enthusiastic welcomes in Japan and other countries. Roosevelt viewed the tour as a part of "big stick" diplomacy.

European Power Balance was maintained with Roosevelt's help. In 1905, Germany demanded a share in the control of Morocco, which was dominated by France. Two alliances of nations—one headed by Germany, the other by France and Great Britain—came close to war. Roosevelt persuaded Germany to attend an international conference in Spain in 1906. At the conference, the United States sided with France and Britain. Germany backed down on its demand.

A Party Split developed among the Republicans as Roosevelt neared the end of his presidency. Conservative Republicans put up increased resistance to Roosevelt's progressive policies. For his part, Roosevelt fought harder for "political, social, and industrial reform." But during his last year in office, he got little Congressional action. His Republican opponents dared to resist him because they believed he would leave office in 1909.

Roosevelt had declared after his election in 1904 that he would "under no circumstances" run for President again. He decided to keep this pledge. He selected William Howard Taft, his secretary of war, to succeed him. At the Republican national convention of 1908, he persuaded most of the delegates to support Taft for President. In this way, he assured Taft's nomination. Taft won an easy election victory over the Democratic candidate William Jennings Bryan. See TAFT, WILLIAM HOWARD (Election of 1908).

Later Years

After leaving the presidency in March, 1909, Roosevelt sailed for Africa to hunt big game. Some conservative Congressmen wished "health to the lions." But Roosevelt and his party brought down 296 big-game animals, including 9 lions. When Roosevelt arrived home in June, 1910, he found himself the center of national attention. Progressive Republicans felt that Taft had betrayed them. They turned to Roosevelt.

"Bull Moose" Candidate. Roosevelt tried to bring together the progressive and the conservative wings of the Republican party. But he failed. He had become identified too closely with the progressives.

Russia and Japan together in Portsmouth, N.H. Then the President served as mediator in the peace talks that led to the Treaty of Portsmouth. In 1906, Roosevelt received the Nobel prize for peace. He was the first American to win a Nobel prize.

As the victors in the war, the Japanese demanded compensation payments from Russia. During the peace talks, Roosevelt had opposed this demand. His attitude angered the Japanese and also Japanese-Americans in the United States. Their anger grew in 1906, when the San Francisco school board decided to segregate children of Japanese descent.

Relations between the United States and Japan became more strained. Roosevelt feared a Japanese attack on the Philippines. Many Americans thought war with Japan was near. But the President persuaded the San Francisco school board to end its segregation policy. He also negotiated a *Gentleman's Agreement* with Japan to keep Japanese laborers out of the United

Loving Grandfather. Roosevelt called his granddaughter, Edith Derby, "the dearest one-year-old baby I have ever known."
Theodore Roosevelt Collection, Harvard College Library

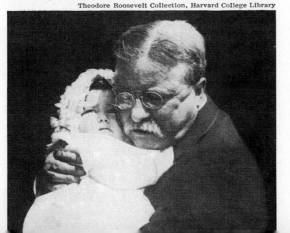

In 1910, while on a speaking tour of the West, Roosevelt proclaimed a policy of "New Nationalism." This became the policy of the progressive Republicans. Roosevelt declared that the President must be the "steward of public welfare." He frightened conservatives with his views on private property. He said that private property was "subject to the general right of the community to regulate its use to whatever degree the public welfare may require it."

In 1912, Roosevelt gave in to pleas that he run for a third term as President. He said that his statement in 1904 had meant not running for a third *consecutive* term. Roosevelt won several victories in primary elections. These victories indicated that he was the popular choice of the party. But President Taft controlled the party machinery, and was renominated by the Republican national convention. Roosevelt and his followers formed the Progressive party, or *Bull Moose* party. The name came from Roosevelt's reply when a reporter asked how he felt. "I feel as strong as a bull moose," he said.

On Oct. 14, 1912, a saloonkeeper named John N. Schrank tried to assassinate Roosevelt. Schrank shot Roosevelt just before he made a speech in Milwaukee. A glasses case in Roosevelt's pocket deflected the bullet and probably saved his life. Even with the bullet in his chest, Roosevelt insisted on making the speech. He recovered from the wound in about two weeks. Schrank was committed to a mental hospital.

Roosevelt's candidacy split the Republican vote. The Democratic candidate, Governor Woodrow Wilson of New Jersey, easily won the election. See WILSON, WOODROW (Presidential Candidate).

World War I began in 1914. Roosevelt called for American preparedness against a "strong, ruthless, ambitious, militaristic . . . Germany." He developed an intense dislike of Wilson, mostly because the President did not lead the nation into war immediately. After the United States entered the war in 1917, Roosevelt asked Wilson for permission to raise a division of troops to fight in France. Wilson refused the request.

Roosevelt's sons served in France. Quentin, an aviator, was killed in an air battle with a German pilot.

Death. In 1913 and 1914, Roosevelt had explored the River of Doubt in the Brazilian jungle. He contracted a form of jungle fever, and returned weak and prematurely aged. Early in 1918, Roosevelt underwent operations to remove abscesses on his thigh and in his ears. The abscesses resulted from the jungle fever. He lost the hearing in his left ear. At about this time, Roosevelt revealed that he had been blind in his left eye since 1905. He lost the sight in the eye while boxing with a military aide in the White House.

Roosevelt opposed American membership in the League of Nations, which he felt would limit the United States in foreign relations. It seemed possible that he would receive the Republican presidential nomination in 1920. But Roosevelt died unexpectedly of a blood clot in the heart on Jan. 6, 1919. He was buried at Sagamore Hill in Oyster Bay, N.Y. His first wife had been buried in New York City. His second wife died in 1948 and was buried beside him in Oyster Bay.

In 1962, Congress authorized the establishment of Roosevelt's home at Oyster Bay and his birthplace in New York City as National Historic Sites. His ranches at Medora, N.Dak., form part of the Theodore Roosevelt National Memorial Park. Roosevelt is one of the four Presidents whose faces are carved on the side of Mount Rushmore in South Dakota.   FRANK FREIDEL

Related Articles in WORLD BOOK include:

Bird (Refuges and Sanctuaries)	Parker, Alton Brooks
Conservation (National Policy)	President of the United States
Fairbanks, Charles Warren	Progressive Party
McKinley, William	Roosevelt, Theodore, Jr.
Mount Rushmore National Memorial	Rough Riders
North Dakota (Annual Events; color picture)	Spanish-American War
Panama Canal (picture)	Square Deal
	Taft, William Howard
	Trust
	White House (History)

Outline

I. Early Life
    A. Boyhood and Education   B. First Marriage
II. Political and Public Activities
    A. State Legislator   E. Civil Service
    B. Party Leader   Commissioner
    C. Rancher and Writer   F. Police Commissioner
    D. Second Marriage
III. A National Figure
    A. Assistant Secretary   C. Governor of New
        of the Navy   York
    B. The Rough Riders   D. Vice-President
IV. Roosevelt's First Administration (1901-1905)
    A. "Trust Buster"   D. Conservation
    B. Friend of Labor   E. Life in the White House
    C. Foreign Policy   F. Election of 1904
V. Roosevelt's Second Administration (1905-1909)
    A. Domestic Problems   C. European Power
    B. Friction with Japan   Balance
                                     D. A Party Split
VI. Later Years
    A. "Bull Moose"   B. World War I
        Candidate   C. Death

Questions

As a boy, how did Roosevelt build up his strength?
What was the "White House gang"?
What phrase did Roosevelt use to describe his foreign policy? What did this phrase mean?
Why did Roosevelt become known as a "trust buster"?
How did the "Bull Moose" party get its name?
What did Roosevelt consider to be the greatest accomplishment of his administration?
How did Roosevelt first win national fame?
What did the "Roosevelt Corollary" proclaim?
Who was "Princess Alice"?
What did Roosevelt call "the great day of my life"?

Reading and Study Guide

For a *Reading and Study Guide on Theodore Roosevelt*, see the RESEARCH GUIDE/INDEX, Volume 22.

Books to Read

BUSCH, NOEL. *T. R.: The Story of Theodore Roosevelt and His Influence on Our Times*. Reynal, 1963. For young readers.

CAVANAH, FRANCES. *Adventure in Courage: The Story of Theodore Roosevelt*. Rand McNally, 1961. For young readers.

CHESSMAN, GEORGE W. *Theodore Roosevelt and the Politics of Power*. Ed. by Oscar Handlin. Little, Brown, 1969.

HAGEDORN, HERMAN. *The Roosevelt Family of Sagamore Hill*. Macmillan, 1954.

MOWRY, GEORGE E. *The Era of Theodore Roosevelt, 1900-1912*. Harper, 1958.

PRINGLE, HENRY F. *Theodore Roosevelt: A Biography*. Rev. ed. Harcourt, 1956.

ROOSEVELT, THEO-DORE, JR. (1887-1944), the oldest son of President Theodore Roosevelt, became an American soldier, statesman, explorer, and writer. During World War I, he commanded an infantry regiment and won the Distinguished Service Cross. After the war, he helped organize the American Legion. Roosevelt served in the New York assembly, and then as Assistant Secretary of the Navy

United Press Int.
Theodore Roosevelt, Jr.

from 1921 to 1924. In 1925, he led the Field Museum expedition to Asia, and later wrote books on his explorations and on American colonial policies. He worked efficiently as governor of Puerto Rico from 1929 to 1932. He died in 1944 while commanding World War II infantry troops in France. Roosevelt was born at Oyster Bay, N.Y. See also AMERICAN LEGION.   HARVEY WISH

ROOSEVELT CAMPOBELLO INTERNATIONAL PARK covers about 2,700 acres on Campobello Island in New Brunswick, Canada (see NEW BRUNSWICK [physical map]). President Franklin D. Roosevelt's summer home is in the park. Roosevelt received the house in 1910 as a wedding gift. He and his family often spent their vacation there. Roosevelt was stricken with poliomyelitis at Campobello Island in 1921. During the 1950's, the house was made to look as it did when Roosevelt lived in it.

The United States and Canada dedicated the park in 1964. A joint U.S.-Canadian commission administers the park. The Franklin D. Roosevelt International Bridge links Campobello Island and Lubec, Me.

ROOSEVELT DAM is part of the Salt River irrigation project in south-central Arizona. It is a rubble-masonry arch-gravity dam. It is 280 feet high, and has a crest length of 723 feet. Its reservoir is approximately 23 miles long and can store 1,398,430 acre-feet of water. The Salt River project supplies water to 350,000 acres of nearby land. The irrigation system has 201 pumping plants. The dam is also used for flood control and power production. The United States Bureau of Reclamation built Roosevelt Dam in 1911. It was officially named the Theodore Roosevelt Dam in 1959.   T. W. MERMEL

ROOSEVELT UNIVERSITY is a privately controlled coeducational school in downtown Chicago. It has colleges of arts and sciences, business administration, and education. It also includes a college of continuing education, the Chicago Musical College, a graduate division, and a division of labor education. Day and evening courses lead to bachelor's and master's degrees.

The school was named for President Franklin D. Roosevelt. Activities are centered in the 18-story Auditorium Building, an architectural masterpiece designed in the 1880's by Dankmar Adler and Louis Sullivan. Founded in 1945 as Roosevelt College, the school became Roosevelt University in 1954. For enrollment, see UNIVERSITIES AND COLLEGES (table).   ROLF A. WEIL

ROOSTER. See CHICKEN.

ROOSTERFISH. See FISHING (table: Game-Fishing World Records).

ROOT, in mathematics, is a quantity that yields a given quantity when it is taken as a factor a specified number of times (see FACTOR). The number of times the root is taken as a factor is called its *index*. Roots are named from their indexes. Thus, 3 is a *fourth* root of 81, because $3 \times 3 \times 3 \times 3 = 81$. Roots with indexes of 2 and 3 are also called *square roots* and *cube roots*, respectively. The positive nth root of a positive number p is indicated by $\sqrt[n]{p}$. Thus, $\sqrt[4]{81} = 3$. The symbol $\sqrt{}$ is called a *radical sign*. When no index is shown, the index 2 is understood.

A root in algebra is a quantity which, when substituted for the variable in an equation, satisfies the equation. For example, 3 is a root of $x + 2 = 5$, because if 3 is substituted for the variable x, the equation correctly reads $3 + 2 = 5$. See also ALGEBRA; CUBE ROOT; SQUARE ROOT.   HOWARD W. EVES

ROOT. In most plants, roots are the parts that grow in the ground and draw in water and dissolved minerals (salts) from the soil. But some plants have their roots in water, or even in air. Roots are one of the three organs that most plants must have in order to grow. The other two organs are the stems and leaves.

Parts of a Root. Most root systems have many branches. The smaller *rootlets* are covered with tiny *root hairs*. The part of the root where root hairs grow keeps advancing as the root tip lengthens. This part always stays about $\frac{1}{4}$ inch behind the tip. Root hairs grow from the outermost tissue of the rootlet, called the *epidermis*. The hairs are only as thick as a single plant cell. Each

The Tip of a Root is well equipped to absorb water and salts. Root hairs increase the root's absorbing area. Pipelines in the core carry the water and salts up the stem quickly. A root cap protects the delicate tip as the root pushes through the soil.

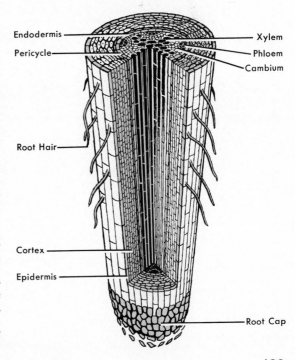

Endodermis

Pericycle

Root Hair

Cortex

Epidermis

Xylem

Phloem

Cambium

Root Cap

ROOT

hair is like a tiny mouth. It "drinks" in water and dissolved minerals from the tiny spaces around the particles of soil. This watery solution continuously flows from the soil through the root hairs. Then it enters the *cortex* (spongy tissue) of the root, and finally the center cylinder of the root. From there, the water and minerals are carried to the rest of the plant.

Wherever roots grow, they must have oxygen to live. The upper parts of the plant, the leaves and stem, cannot supply this oxygen, so the roots must get air through the soil or water. Roots of trees that grow partly under water need some special way of getting air. One example of such a tree is the cypress of the southeastern United States. Around its base are cone-shaped "knees" sticking up through the water. These knees grow out from the root system. Air filters through the tissues of these knees and into the roots beneath the water.

Types of Roots. The chief work of the roots is to hold the plant in place, and to supply it with water and nourishing salts from the soil. Roots that form first, and grow directly from the stem, are called *primary roots*. Branches of the primary roots are called *secondary roots*, and branches of these are *tertiary roots*.

Roots with different forms have special names. A primary root that grows much larger than any of its branches is called a *taproot*. Sometimes taproots grow very thick, and store up food for the rest of the plant. These are *fleshy roots*, and may be seen in carrots or

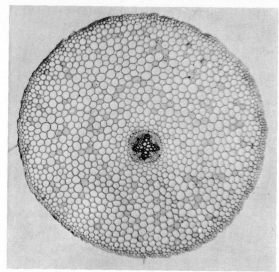

Frank Ballard

Cross-Section of a Young Root shows a central core, which carries water, food, and salts, surrounded by a fleshy cortex, and a single-celled outer layer called the *epidermis*.

turnips. Clustered, thick, primary roots, like those of the sweet potato, are called *fascicled roots*. Threadlike roots, as in grasses, are *fibrous*. Roots that live one year are called *annuals;* those that live two years are *biennials;*

Root Systems of plants vary greatly. Plants that need much water usually have thick, bushy root systems. Those that grow in dry places send out branched roots that grow to great depths. Small plants get enough water with shallow roots.

Brooklyn Botanic Garden

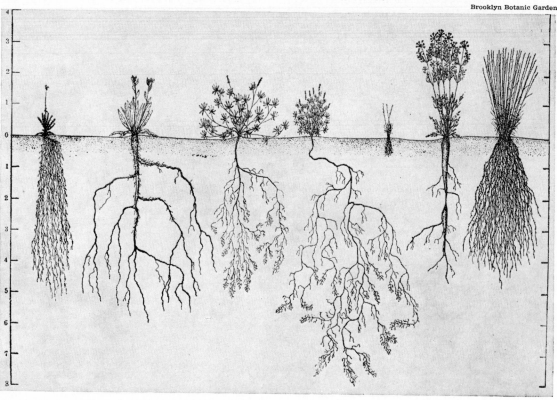

and those that live longer than two years are *perennials*.

Roots may also grow on the stem, or in other unusual places. These are called *adventitious roots*. They grow on plants that need extra support for their stems. For example, a corn plant has arching "prop" roots that reach out from the base of the stem into the ground. The most unusual roots of this type grow on the banyan tree of the tropics. These roots start downward from the branches toward the earth. Finally they form added trunk and root systems and help support the trunk.

Roots are called *soil roots*, *aerial* or *air roots*, or *water roots*, depending on where they grow. Poison ivy and other plants that are anchored in the ground sometimes develop extra air roots. Still other plants, such as many kinds of orchids, grow entirely in the air. The water hyacinth has roots especially suited for the water. *Parasitic roots*, such as on mistletoe and dodder, get food from other plants. ARTHUR W. GALSTON

See also CARROT; DANDELION (picture); GERMINATION; PLANT (Roots; pictures); TREE (The Roots).

ROOT, ELIHU (1845-1937), was an American lawyer, statesman, and Cabinet officer. His great contribution was his tireless effort to assure international peace. He won the 1912 Nobel peace prize. Though Root was one of the main critics of the League of Nations, he helped plan the Permanent Court of International Justice, or World Court, which the League sponsored. For nearly 10 years, he battled to have the U.S. join the court. But the isolationists in the Senate proved too powerful for him and eventually caused him to retire from politics. Long after he had retired, he continued to urge the United States to join the World Court.

Root was one of the ablest lawyers the United States has produced. Most of his clients were giant corporations, and he is said to have earned enormous fees. At one time, he sought the Republican nomination for President of the United States. But many party leaders thought he was too closely identified with large corporations, and he lost the nomination.

Wide World
Elihu Root

Root was born at Clinton, N.Y. His father taught at nearby Hamilton College. After attending Hamilton, Root studied law at New York University. He started practicing in New York City, and in 1873 became famous as counsel for "Boss" Tweed, who was charged with political corruption (see TWEED, WILLIAM MARCY).

Root gained national political prominence in 1899 when President William McKinley appointed him secretary of war. As secretary, he planned the Army War College and introduced the General Staff. In 1905, President Theodore Roosevelt named him secretary of state. He served with distinction until 1909, when the New York legislature elected him to the U.S. Senate. He served in the Senate until 1915. H. G. REUSCHLEIN

ROOT-TAKAHIRA AGREEMENT. See ROOSEVELT, THEODORE (Friction with Japan).

ROOTSTOCK. See RHIZOME.

Columbia Rope Co.
Ropes Are Different in Construction according to their uses. *At the top* is the common 3-strand rope; *in the center* is a 4-strand which will support a much greater weight; and *at the bottom* is the "cable-laid" rope which has great elasticity.

ROPE. The ropes that hold a huge ship to a dock and lift tons of cargo aboard are made from thousands of tiny plant fibers. *Cordage* (rope) ranges in size from small lines about an inch around to huge cables more than 20 inches around.

About nine-tenths of the fibers that are made into rope come from the abacá plant and the agave, or century, plant. Ropes made from abacá fibers are known as *Manila*, and ropes manufactured from agave fibers are called *sisal*.

Manila is a strong, hard fiber that comes from the leaf stems of the stalk of the abacá. The abacá plant looks much like a banana tree. The fiber gets its name from Manila, in the Philippines, where the abacá plant grows. Manila has great natural resistance to wind, rain, and sun. The tough, sheathlike protection of the fiber cells of the abacá plant makes Manila rope very strong. It is also resistant to rubbing. These qualities make Manila valuable for use on ships. Manila fiber is preferred for most kinds of rope that receive long, hard usage. See ABACÁ.

Sisal, a hard fiber, is about three-fourths as strong as Manila. But it is the most widely used substitute for Manila. Sisal is a whiter, shinier fiber than Manila. It comes from the leaf of the agave plant, which grows in the West and East Indies and in parts of Africa. Sisal also is made into tying twines for use in factories and stores. See CENTURY PLANT; SISAL.

Henequen, True Hemp, Jute, and Coir are soft fibers that may also be used to make rope.

Henequen is very much like sisal. It is often called *Mexican sisal* because it grows in Mexico. It is not so strong as other sisals, and is used mostly to make lower

435

Fibers for Making Rope feed into a ropemaking machine from huge bobbins. The machine twists the fibers into heavy strands, which are then twisted into the finished rope. The rope winds into great coils for shipment as it leaves the machine.

grades of rope, such as binder twine for agricultural use, and tying twines.

True Hemp is found between the bark and the pith in the stem of the *Cannabis sativa* plant. It is used mostly for small tarred cordage such as ratlines, marlines, and houselines. True hemp is produced in many European countries, Asia, and the United States. See Hemp.

Jute has less strength than Manila, sisal, or hemp. But it has other qualities that make it useful. It is used for tying twines and cordage. The fiber comes from the jute plants of India. See Jute.

Coir comes from the outer husk covering of the coco-nut. It grows in India and is used chiefly in making *coir rope*, which is water resistant.

Nylon Rope has replaced other types of rope for many uses because it is stronger, lighter in weight, and resistant to mildew.

Rope Manufacture. Fibers are made into rope by machinery. They come to the factory in bales weighing about 275 pounds. First the fibers are prepared by separating them, laying them straight, and combing them into ribbons. Repeated combing reduces the width of the ribbon for spinning into yarn. Two or more yarns are twisted into strands. Then the strands are twisted, or *laid*, together to form the rope. Most ropes are made of three strands. The number of yarns varies.

Strength of Rope depends on its size and the material from which it is made. A Manila rope that measures 1½ inches around can hold a weight of 2,650 pounds. A Manila rope measuring 7 inches around can lift 41,000 pounds.

Wire Ropes are made from steel wire twisted together. They are widely used for cables, for ship rigging, and in operating derricks of oil and salt wells. They are also widely used in industry. Wire ropes are made by twisting a number of individual wires together to form a strand. The strands are then twisted around a hemp core to form a wire rope. The hemp core is often replaced with a wire strand to make the rope stronger.

Wire rope has several advantages over fiber rope. It is stronger and wears better, and can be adapted to a greater variety of uses. It is also easier to estimate its exact strength. H. J. LINDQUIST

See also FIBER; KNOTS, HITCHES, AND SPLICES; OAKUM.

ROQUE. See CROQUET.

ROQUEFORT, *ROHK fert*, is a strong-tasting cheese made from sheep's milk to which one of the blue or blue-green *Penicillium* molds has been added. True Roquefort cheese comes from Roquefort, France. There, manufacturers cure the cheese in natural caves that have the right atmospheric conditions for proper curing. The milk supplies the distinctive flavor. Roquefort cheese may be used in salad dressings. It is also served with fruits as an appetizer.

ROQUER, EMMA DE. See CALVÉ, EMMA.

RORAIMA FALLS, *roh RY mah*, refers to several seasonal waterfalls on Mount Roraima on the Brazil-Guyana-Venezuela border. In the dry season, the falls are reduced to a trickle, and sometimes they almost entirely disappear. MANOEL CARDOZO

RORQUAL, *RAWR kwul*, is a term used for toothless whales with grooves on their throats and undersides, and a small fin on their backs. The blue, finback, humpback, pygmy finner, and sei whales are rorquals.

A rorqual has from 60 to 90 grooves. Each groove is one or two inches deep. The grooves extend from the chin to the navel, and cover from 45 to 60 per cent of the whale's underside. RAYMOND M. GILMORE

See also WHALE.

RORSCHACH INK-BLOT TEST. See MENTAL ILLNESS (Diagnosis).

ROSA, MONTE. See MONTE ROSA.

ROSAMUND (1140?-1176?) was the mistress of King Henry II of England. Her full name was ROSAMUND CLIFFORD. She is generally called "fair Rosamund" in the many legends about her life. One story says that Henry's wife, Eleanor of Aquitaine, poisoned her because of jealousy.

ROSARIO, *roh SAHR ee oh* (pop. 671,852; alt. 86 ft.), is the second largest city in Argentina. Only Buenos Aires, 150 miles to the southeast, is larger. Rosario lies on the west bank of the Paraná River. For location, see ARGENTINA (political map). Rosario serves as an important industrial and trading center. Most of the railroads that serve Rosario bring grain into the city from surrounding agricultural areas.

Rosario was for many years a center of transcontinental transportation and shipping, because of its river

location, and because it lies on the eastern edge of the Argentine Pampa. Its position as a shipping center began to decline in the mid-1950's. Newer shipping methods being introduced in Argentina make less use of the river systems. Many shipping firms that formerly operated in Rosario moved to Buenos Aires and other large cities in Argentina during the late 1950's.

Rosario was founded in 1725. It is a well-developed city, with broad streets and many parks. One of its large parks has a zoo, an exposition building, and a race track. Rosario has a branch of the University of the Litoral, a famous Argentine school. The best school of painting in Argentina is also located in the city. The Fuentes Palace is perhaps the most elaborate building in Rosario. GEORGE I. BLANKSTEN

ROSARY is a string of beads, made of wood, metal, or stone, by which prayers are counted as an aid to memory. The rosary commonly used in the Roman Catholic Church consists of a circle of 50 small beads. Four large beads divide the small beads into equal sections. A pendant, composed of two large beads, three small ones, and a crucifix, hangs from the rosary. On the large beads is said the Lord's Prayer, or the *Our Father*. The small beads are for prayers to the Virgin Mary, or the *Hail Mary*. On the crucifix is said the *Apostles' Creed*.

While the prayers are being said, the mysteries of the faith are reflected upon. At the end of each group of *Hail Marys*, a short verse of praise, or a *doxology*, is repeated. The complete rosary consists of going around the ordinary form of beads three times and reflecting upon 15 mysteries.

Prayer beads are of ancient origin, and were probably first used by the Buddhists. Both Buddhists and Moslems make use of them in their prayers. Saint Dominic is said to have introduced their use into the Roman Catholic Church. FULTON J. SHEEN

ROSARY COLLEGE is a coeducational Roman Catholic liberal arts college in River Forest, Ill. It is conducted by the Dominican Sisters. The college confers the degrees of Bachelor of Arts, Bachelor of Music Education, and Master of Arts in Library Science. The college was founded as Saint Clara Academy in Sinsinawa, Wis., in 1848. It was chartered as a college in 1901, and moved to its present location in 1922. For the enrollment of Rosary College, see UNIVERSITIES AND COLLEGES (table).

ROSARY HILL COLLEGE is a Roman Catholic liberal arts school for women in Buffalo, N.Y. It was founded in 1947 and is run by the Congregation of the Sisters of Saint Francis of Penance and Christian Charity. Rosary Hill grants bachelor's degrees in arts, science, and music. For the enrollment of Rosary Hill College, see UNIVERSITIES AND COLLEGES (table).

ROSAS, JUAN MANUEL DE. See LATIN AMERICA (Self-Government).

ROSCIUS, *RAHSH ih us*, **QUINTUS** (126? B.C.-62? B.C.), a Roman actor, was so famous in his day that his name came to stand for "great actor." He excelled in both comic and tragic parts, and founded a school for actors. One of his pupils was the orator Cicero, who later defended him in a famous speech. Roscius was born a slave, not far from Rome. He became rich through his acting, and bought his freedom. MARSTON BALCH

ROSE

ROSE. The rose, one of the most beautiful of all flowers, is a symbol of fragrance and loveliness. Its name calls to mind pictures of the sweetbrier, or wild rose, the loveliest wild flower of the country roadsides.

Flower experts recognize two main classes of cultivated roses. The first kind blooms once a year, usually in early summer. It includes the yellow briers, damask roses, moss roses, and many climbers. The second kind blooms more than once in a single season. Roses of this kind are known as *perpetual roses*, or *summer and autumn roses*. Examples of the perpetuals are the teas, hybrid teas, floribundas, hybrid perpetuals, polyanthas (baby ramblers), China roses, and rugosas.

The teas and hybrid teas are so named because their flowers often smell like tea or fruit. Others have a "rose" scent, or have little odor. They come in many different colors, but never in blue. Hybrid teas were developed from the ever-blooming teas, and the hardier hybrid perpetuals. Hybrid perpetuals are bushes from 3 to 6 feet high. Polyanthas are low bushes that bear clusters of small flowers. Some have an unusual orange-scarlet color. Floribundas were developed from the hybrid teas and polyanthas. The flowers, borne in clusters, come in a wide range of colors and forms.

The climbing and rambler roses can be trained on trellises and fences. Others creep over the ground, and may cover steep banks. Some climbers have large flowers, but true ramblers have clusters of small flowers. Climbers have to be hardy. Those with the small flowers are usually the hardiest.

Another important group is the shrub roses. The rugosas grow large bushes, 6 to 15 feet tall, with thorny stems. They usually have fragrant flowers. The sweetbrier and its cultivated forms are tall, graceful bushes, with fragrant leaves.

When the rose plant grows wild, it is an erect or climbing shrub. It bears thorns and single flowers with five petals. The flowers of the cultivated varieties are generally double, and some forms have been grown without thorns.

Roses grow in many parts of the world, but do especially well in temperate and mild climates, like those of southern France and the Pacific Coast.

Roses grow in so many different kinds of soil and climate, and thrive so well under cultivation, that thousands of different varieties have been developed. Botanists disagree on the right way to divide them into different species. Estimates of the number of rose species range from 30 to 250.

Best Roses. There are thousands of different varieties of roses. Some are popular year after year. Others disappear because plant breeders produce better ones. The American Beauty rose was once very popular but has now dropped out of the trade. It was a hybrid perpetual, famous for its large fragrant flowers of carmine-crimson. It gave the name of the color American Beauty red. The flower was first grown in France. Its correct name is Mme. Ferdinand Jamin, but it was called American Beauty so it would sell better. Now roses are grown which are considered superior to the American Beauty.

Following are some of today's best varieties:

Hybrid Teas. Crimson Glory, finest dark red
Eclipse, long, yellow buds
Christopher Stone, fragrant red
Charlotte Armstrong, recognized as the best red rose since 1935
Mme. Henri Guillot, raspberry-pink, deepening with age
Peace, a magnificent yellow with pink shadings at the edges of the petals
Good News, peach-pink
Tallyho, crimson, shading to rose-red
Rubaiyat, light rose-red

The Rose Has Become a Symbol of fragrance and beauty; no other flower has had so many poetic tributes paid to it.

A Rosebush Laden with Flowers lends color and charm to this simple home, and perfumes the air with its fragrance.

J. Horace McFarland

The Lovely Frau Karl Druschki is a hybrid perpetual rose that blooms all summer. The bush is large and hardy.

Climbers. Mrs. Arthur Curtiss James, yellow
   Dr. J. H. Nicholas, long stem, large, rose-pink
   Paul's Scarlet, and New Dawn, soft pink
Hybrid Perpetuals. Frau Karl Druschki, taffy-white
Floribundas. Donald Prior, clear red
   Red Pinocchio, dark red
   Floradora, cinnabar red
   Fashion, coral pink
   Vogue, coral red
   Goldilocks, yellow

The *moss rose* is one of the type known as cabbage roses. It is a clear pink and is very fragrant. It is called moss rose because its calyx and stem are rough, like moss. There is also a false mallow called moss rose. The *rose moss* is not a rose, but a portulaca of the purslane family. It is a popular annual. Its flowers have five petals, and are glistening yellow, red, or white in their color. The Christmas rose belongs to the crowfoot, or buttercup, family. It is genus *Helleborus*, species *niger*. The Lenten rose is a closely related species of Helleborus.

How to Grow Roses. Most roses are grown from slips, that is, cuttings. New varieties usually start as seedlings. The best cultivated sorts seldom bear seeds, and, if there are seeds, only a few are good. In double roses, the parts of the flower that produce seeds have changed to extra petals, and hence few seeds are possible.

The plot for a rose garden should be protected from cold winds, and open to sunlight several hours a day. A deep, rich loam is usually the best soil for roses. But hybrid roses will grow in sandy and gravelly soil. Any soil must be well drained. Roses do not grow well in wet ground. Sometimes they need artificial drainage.

A few weeks before planting, the soil should be mixed with about one third its bulk of rotted manure to a

depth of two feet. The rose roots should not be allowed to touch the fresh manure.

The time for planting depends on the kind of rose and on the location. Some hardy roses can be planted in autumn, but the general rule is to plant in the spring. When the plants are received from the nursery, see that the wind does not dry out the roots before they are planted. If necessary, cover them with burlap or similar material, and keep them damp. The holes should be deep enough to let the roots point downward and slant outward. They must not lie flat. The gardener should be careful to arrange the plants so that the beds are easy to water and weed. A good rule is to have the beds not over five feet wide. The plants should be from ten inches to two and a half feet apart. The exact distance depends on their spreading habits. A hoe and a sharp steel rake should be used to keep the soil loose and the weeds out. However, plants should not be cultivated deeply.

The rose is the national flower of Iran. Several states and a Canadian province have also chosen the rose as their official flower. The District of Columbia has taken the American Beauty rose. Georgia has chosen the Cherokee rose. This is a white Chinese rose. The wild rose is the flower of Iowa, North Dakota, and Alberta. A series of battles in English history are called the Wars of the Roses (see WARS OF THE ROSES). The rose is also the flower for the month of June.

The Rose Family is one of the most important of the plant kingdom. There are about 2,000 species of trees, shrubs, and herbs in the rose family. Some of the loveliest flowers and most valuable fruits belong to it. Its members include the apple, pear, quince, berries, peach, apricot, plum, and cherry. Its many ornamental plants include the meadowsweet, mountain ash, and haw-

Black Spot Is a Common Rose Disease. The fungus attacks the foliage, causing the leaves to turn yellow and fall off.

Cornell College of Agriculture

thorn. Plants of this family also give us many useful products. Several fine woods are used in cabinetmaking. Attar, an oil from rose petals, is used to make toilet water and perfumes (see ATTAR; ROSE WATER). The fruits of some rose plants, called *hips*, are sometimes used in jellies and other foods.

Plants of the rose family have regular flowers. Each has five petals, a calyx with five lobes, many stamens, and one or more carpels. They bear seeds, so they are classed as *angiosperms*. The sprouts have two seed leaves, so they belong to the *dicotyledonous* plants.

Scientific Classification. Roses belong to the rose family, *Rosaceae*. They make up the genus *Rosa*. The moss rose is genus *Rosa*, species *R. centrifolia*, variety *muscosa*. The climbing rose is *R. setigera*.   ALFRED C. HOTTES

Related Articles in WORLD BOOK include:

Angiosperm	Crab Apple	Peach
Apple	Eglantine	Pear
Apricot	Flower (color	Plum
Attar	picture: Summer	Pome
Blackberry	Garden Flowers)	Quince
Bramble	Hawthorn	Raspberry
Bridal Wreath	Loquat	Spiraea
Cherry	Mountain Ash	Strawberry
Cinquefoil		

ROSE, MAURI (1906-   ), an automobile racing driver, won the Memorial Day Indianapolis Speedway 500-mile race in 1947 and 1948. He shared first place in 1941 as the relief driver for Floyd Davis. Rose drove in the Indianapolis race each year from 1937 to 1951, and in seven of those races drove the full 500 miles without relief. He was noted for his ability to pass other cars on turns. Rose retired after the 1951 race, and became an experimental engineer. He was born in Columbus, Ohio.   RICHARD G. HACKENBERG

ROSE, URIAH MILTON (1834-1913), was a noted American lawyer. In 1907, he served as an American delegate to the International Peace Conference at The Hague. He was born at Bradfordsville, Ky., and was graduated in 1853 from Transylvania Law School. He settled in Arkansas and helped develop that frontier community. He set a high standard of honesty and service for the legal profession. Arkansas placed a statue of him in Statuary Hall in 1917. JOHN A. GARRATY

ROSE BOWL. See FOOTBALL (College); PASADENA.

ROSE CHAFER, often called the ROSE BUG, is a beetle about $\frac{1}{3}$ of an inch long. It is light brown, and has long, spiny legs. It feeds on many plants and is often found on roses, ornamental plants, grapes, and various fruit trees. The beetles eat the blossoms of grapes and roses, and often apples. They also attack many fruits. The insect is particularly destructive in localities where there are large areas of grassland. The rose chafer lives throughout the eastern and central regions of the United States.

After feeding for three or four weeks, the beetles disappear. The females de-

Alexander B. Klots

The Rose Chafer

posit their eggs in the soil. These eggs hatch, and the larvae feed upon the roots of grass. Nearly full-grown by fall, they go below the frost line for the winter. The larva, which looks like a white grub, comes near the surface in the spring and becomes a pupa. There is only one generation each year.

When the beetles are very numerous, the best means of preventing injury is to cover small plants with cloth, or to pick the beetles off by hand. Large numbers can be collected in a pan containing water and kerosene. Commercial plantings of grapes, apples, and other fruit may be protected by cultivating all nearby areas during May and June to destroy any eggs that may have been laid. Insecticides may also be applied on the plants to destroy the beetles.

Scientific Classification. Rose chafers belong to the family *Scarabaeidae*. They are classified as genus *Macrodactylus*, species *M. subspinosus*.   R. E. BLACKWELDER

ROSE-HULMAN INSTITUTE OF TECHNOLOGY is a privately controlled engineering school for men in Terre Haute, Ind. B.S. degrees are offered in chemical, civil, electrical, and mechanical engineering. The school was founded in 1874. For enrollment, see UNIVERSITIES AND COLLEGES (table).

ROSE MOSS. See PORTULACA.

ROSE OF JERICHO. See RESURRECTION PLANT.

ROSE OF LIMA, SAINT (1586-1617), was the first American to be declared a saint, or *canonized* (in 1671). She was born in Lima, Peru, and her life was modeled upon that of Saint Catherine of Siena. In 1606 she became a Dominican of the third order. Saint Rose of Lima practiced extreme mortification and penance. She was gifted with remarkable mystical experiences and visions. She is the Patroness of South America. August 30 is her feast day.   FULTON J. SHEEN

ROSE OF SHARON, or SHRUBBY ALTHEA, is a large hibiscus shrub with lovely rose, purple, white, or blue flowers about 3 inches wide. The flowers appear in September, when few other shrubs are in bloom. It does well under unfavorable conditions, either in the city or in the country. The shrub comes from eastern Asia and grows in many American gardens. It grows about 12 feet high and has large three-lobed leaves. Gardeners have developed a number of different forms. The rose of Sharon may be grown in pots and later transplanted.

Scientific Classification. The rose of Sharon belongs to the mallow family, *Malvaceae*. It is classified as genus *Hibiscus*, species *H. syriacus*.   J. J. LEVISON

See also HIBISCUS.

ROSE WATER is a clear, colorless solution made from fresh rose flowers and used in making perfumes and certain medicines. Rose water has a fragrant odor much like that of fresh rose blossoms. It is made by distilling the fragrant parts of the flowers, such as the petals and sepals, with water. This is done by placing the flowers in water, boiling the water, and separating the vapor into a vessel. The vapor is then condensed back into a liquid, which is rose water.   PAUL Z. BEDOUKIAN

ROSE WINDOW. See WINDOW.

ROSECRANS, WILLIAM STARKE (1819-1898), was a Union general in the Civil War. He commanded forces in western Virginia in 1861, and at Corinth, Miss., in 1862. He became commander of the Army of the Cumberland in 1862. He fought in the battle of Stones River, and later forced the Confederates out of Chattanooga.

But he was defeated at Chickamauga in 1863 and lost his command. Born in Delaware County, Ohio, Rosecrans was graduated from the U.S. Military Academy in 1842. After the war, he served as minister to Mexico in 1868. He represented California in Congress from 1881 to 1885.　　　　　　　　T. HARRY WILLIAMS

ROSEFISH is an important food fish found from Iceland to New Jersey and off the northern shores of Europe. It is also called *Norway haddock*. The greatest numbers of rosefish come from the New England and Greenland coasts. The rosefish has an orange-red color, a spiny head, and may grow 2 feet long.

Scientific Classification. The rosefish belongs to the family *Scorpaenidae*. The North Atlantic rosefish is genus *Sebastes*, species *S. marinus*.

ROSEMARY is an evergreen shrub of the mint family noted for the fragrance of its leaves. It is a native of the Mediterranean region. Rosemary grows 4 to 8 feet high. It bears lustrous dark-green leaves and tiny, pale blue flowers. In masses, blossoming rosemary looks like bluegray mist blown over the meadows from the sea. Its name comes from the Latin *rosmarinus*, meaning *sea dew*. Rosemary yields an oil that is used in perfumes. Cooks use the plant for seasoning. The plant is an emblem of fidelity and remembrance. In *Hamlet*, Ophelia remarks, "There's rosemary, that's for remembrance."

Scientific Classification. Rosemary belongs to the mint family, *Labiatae*. It is classified as genus *Rosmarinus*, species *R. officinalis*.　　　　　　　　J. J. LEVISON

ROSEMONT COLLEGE. See UNIVERSITIES AND COLLEGES (table).

The Rose of Sharon is a favorite shrub for ornamental purposes, because of its large and attractively colored flowers.

ROSENBERG, ALFRED (1893-1946), was the philosopher of the German Nazi movement. His *Myth of the Twentieth Century* (1930) stressed "Aryan" racial superiority and the cult of the great leader. He wanted to replace Christianity with a Germanic pagan religion. Born of German parents in Estonia, he returned to Eastern Europe during World War II as minister for Germany's eastern occupied territories. He pressed for extermination of the Jews. After the war, Rosenberg was executed for war crimes.　　　　LESTER B. MASON

ROSENBERG, ETHEL GREENGLASS (1915-1953) and **JULIUS** (1918-1953), were two American citizens, husband and wife, who were executed as spies. They were the first Americans given a death sentence for espionage by a United States civil court. Their acts of espionage occurred during wartime, but their trial and execution took place during peacetime.

Ethel and Julius Rosenberg were born and grew up in New York City. They were married in 1939, shortly after Julius was graduated from the College of the City of New York. After their marriage, Ethel worked briefly as a typist for the United States Bureau of the Census. She gave up this job when Julius obtained a civilian position with the U.S. Signal Corps.

Julius was fired from the Signal Corps in 1945 on charges that he belonged to the Communist party, which he denied. Between 1946 and 1950, he worked with his brother-in-law, David Greenglass, in a small surplus war-material business. Greenglass had previously worked on the atomic bomb project at Los Alamos, N. Mex., in 1944 and 1945.

Klaus Fuchs, a physicist who had worked at Los Alamos, exposed the spy ring in 1949, when he confessed to British authorities that he had spied for Russia. Then in 1950, Greenglass was arrested and indicted on charges of spying. He incriminated the Rosenbergs, and they also were arrested. The Rosenbergs were accused of obtaining information concerning atomic weapons, fuses, gunfire mechanisms, and other military matters, and giving it to Russian agents. They were tried by jury in March, 1951, and found guilty. Judge Irving Kaufman sentenced them to die in the electric chair.

The case was appealed to the Supreme Court of the United States. Protests against the death penalty and questioning the evidence were organized in the United States and Europe. But the Supreme Court denied all appeals, and President Dwight D. Eisenhower twice denied pleas for clemency. The Rosenbergs were executed on June 19, 1953. Greenglass was sentenced to prison. He was released in 1960.　　RICHARD L. WATSON, JR.

ROSENKAVALIER. See OPERA (Some of the Famous Operas).

ROSENTHAL, MORIZ (1862-1946), a Polish pianist, became noted for the great technical skill, full tone, and brilliance of his playing. At the age of 10, he began to study with Rafael Joseffy in Vienna. Five years later, he studied with the composer Franz Liszt in Weimar.

Rosenthal made his American debut in 1888. Later, he lived in Vienna, where he was court pianist. After 1933, he lived in New York City. He was the coauthor of *School of Advanced Piano Playing*. He was born in Lemberg, Poland.　　　　　　ROBERT U. NELSON

ROSENWALD, JULIUS (1862-1932), was an American businessman and philanthropist. He contributed about $63 million to Negro education, Jewish philanthropies, and a wide range of educational, religious, scientific, and community organizations and institutions. Rosenwald established the Museum of Science and Industry in Chicago (see MUSEUM OF SCIENCE AND INDUSTRY).

He once said it was easier to make $1 million honestly than to give it away wisely. He tried to aid groups rather than individuals and to make his gifts in such a way as to stimulate contributions from others. He donated money through the Julius Rosenwald Fund and other separate donations. He disliked perpetual endowments, and ordered that all of the Julius Rosenwald Fund be spent within 25 years of his death.

Rosenwald was born and educated in Springfield, Ill. He entered the clothing business at age 17, and joined Sears, Roebuck and Company in 1895. He was president of Sears from 1909 to 1924. ROBERT H. BREMNER

ROSENWALD FUND, JULIUS was a sum of money set aside to improve the opportunities and living conditions of Negroes in America. Julius Rosenwald, an American merchant and philanthropist, created the fund in 1917. The fund contributed to the building of more than 5,000 rural Negro schools.

In 1928, the fund was reorganized and its program enlarged. The program then included the formation of clinics and other organized medical services to improve the health of Negroes in low income groups. The program also promoted projects in general education and child study and in the social sciences and public administration. The fund aided many famous Negro artists, writers, and musicians.

Rosenwald did not believe in perpetual endowments. He felt social conditions change too rapidly to store up large sums of money for the future. The Julius Rosenwald Fund ended in 1948, after $22½ million had been donated to various causes. CARTER ALEXANDER

ROSES, WARS OF THE. See WARS OF THE ROSES.

ROSETTA STONE, *roh ZET uh,* gave the world the key to the long-forgotten language of ancient Egypt. A French officer of Napoleon's engineering corps discovered it in 1799. He found the stone half buried in the mud near the Rosetta mouth of the Nile River. The Rosetta Stone was later taken to England, where it is still preserved in the British Museum.

On the stone is carved a decree by Egyptian priests to commemorate the crowning of Ptolemy V Epiphanes, king of Egypt from 203 to 181 B.C. The first inscription is in ancient Egyptian hieroglyphics. The second is in Demotic, the popular language of Egypt at that time. At the bottom of the stone the same message is written again in Greek. See HIEROGLYPHIC.

The stone is made of black basalt, 11 inches thick. It is about 3 feet 9 inches high and 2 feet 4½ inches across. Part of the top and a section of the right side of the Rosetta Stone are missing.

The language of ancient Egypt had been a riddle to scholars for many hundreds of years. The Rosetta Stone solved the riddle. A French scholar named Jean François Champollion studied the stone. He first translated the Greek portion. Using this text as a guide, he next studied the position and repetition of proper names in the Greek text and was able to pick out the same names in the Egyptian text. This enabled him to learn the meaning of the Egyptian hieroglyphic characters.

Champollion had a thorough knowledge of Coptic, the modern Egyptian language, and this enabled him to recognize many Egyptian words in the upper part of the inscription. After much work, Champollion could read the entire text. In 1822, he published a pamphlet, *Lettre à M. Dacier,* containing the results of his work. This pamphlet enabled scholars to read the literature of ancient Egypt. JOSEPH WARD SWAIN

ROSEVILLE, Mich. (pop. 60,529; alt. 615 ft.), is a residential suburb northeast of Detroit. Its industries produce aircraft parts, conveyors, hardware, machine tools, and truck bodies. Roseville was incorporated as a village in 1925. It merged with the township of Erin in 1957 to form the city of Roseville. It has a council-manager form of government. For location, see MICHIGAN (political map). WILLIS F. DUNBAR

ROSEWOOD is the name of several kinds of attractive wood of the botanical genus *Dalbergia*. It is used either as solid wood or as veneer in making ornamental furniture and musical instruments. Its ability to take a high polish and its rich color make rosewood valuable. Its color runs from dark reddish-brown to purplish-brown. Its name comes from the roselike odor of the wood when it is sawed. It is sometimes called *blackwood*. Rosewood grows in Brazil, Central America, Southern Asia, and Madagascar.

Scientific Classification. Rosewoods are in the pea family, *Leguminosae*. They are genus *Dalbergia*. HARRY E. TROXELL

The Hieroglyphics on This Fragment of Stone, known as the Rosetta Stone, were translated by scholars. They provided the key to the language used in ancient Egypt.

United Press Int.

The Blast of the Shofar on Rosh Hashanah calls on Jews to examine their deeds and repent their sins.

ROSH HASHANAH, ROHSH *hah SHAH nah,* is the Jewish New Year celebration. It is a solemn festival when Jews pray for forgiveness and long life. It falls on the first day of the Hebrew month of Tishri, and lasts two days. Reform Jews and Israelis celebrate it for one day. The holiday usually comes in September.

Rosh Hashanah begins the Ten Days of Penitence that end on Yom Kippur, the Day of Atonement (see YOM KIPPUR). According to tradition, Rosh Hashanah is a Day of Judgment, when the fate of each person is inscribed in the Book of Life. But penitence and prayer can change the verdict before it is sealed on Yom Kippur. Jews attend solemn synagogue services on Rosh Hashanah. The *shofar,* or ram's horn, is blown as a call for repentance. On the first day of the festival, many Orthodox Jews take part in a ceremony called *tashlik.* They symbolically cast away their sins in rivers.

In many Jewish homes, the father recites a blessing for a sweet year over an apple dipped in honey. Round, smooth loaves of bread symbolize a wish for a smooth year. Many Jews send New Year's cards to their friends and families. The traditional greeting is "May you be inscribed for a happy year." LEONARD C. MISHKIN

ROSH HODESH, *ROHSH HOH desh,* is the Hebrew term for the start of a new month. Hebrew months are based on the moon. Ancient Hebrews celebrated the *new moon* (beginning of a month) as a holiday. Many Jews today recite special blessings for Rosh Hodesh.

ROSICRUCIAN ORDER, ROH *zih* KROO *shun,* is an international fraternity. Members of the Rosicrucian Order study the mysteries and scientific laws of the world. The organization traces its traditional origin back to about 1500 B.C., when the Pharaohs of Egypt formed a society of thinkers and scientists. These scholars learned much about science and philosophy. Many Greek men of wisdom inherited their knowledge. Members of the ancient society made discoveries in chemistry and medicine that are still in use today.

The Rosicrucian Order was founded in the United

Brown Bros.

The Legend of Betsy Ross tells how she made the first flag of the United States. The house, *left*, called the *Betsy Ross House*, stands on Arch Street in Philadelphia. It may be the home she lived in.

11, his 84-year-old grandmother told him the story of how she made the first official United States flag. As the story goes, a committee headed by General George Washington visited Mrs. Ross in June, 1776. George Ross, a signer of the Declaration of Independence and an uncle of Betsy Ross' first husband, was a member of the committee. These men asked Mrs. Ross to make a flag according to the rough design they gave her. Washington wanted six-pointed stars in the flag, but the seamstress persuaded him to make the stars five-pointed. No proof has been found that this incident actually happened. But it is known that Betsy Ross was an official flagmaker for the Pennsylvania Navy. The stars-and-stripes design she may have sewed was adopted by Congress on June 14, 1777. WHITNEY SMITH, JR.

See also FLAG (First United States Flags); PHILADELPHIA (Independence Hall National Park).

ROSS, EDMUND GIBSON (1826-1907), was an American statesman. Although he opposed President Andrew Johnson, he voted in the Senate against convicting Johnson during the impeachment trial in 1868. This vote wrecked Ross' career, but won him a reputation for political courage. He was born in Ashland, Ohio. In 1856, he led free-state settlers to Kansas. He served in the United States Senate from 1866 to 1871, and as governor of the New Mexico territory from 1885 to 1889. ARTHUR A. EKIRCH, JR.

ROSS, GEORGE (1730-1779), a Pennsylvania lawyer, signed the Declaration of Independence. From 1768 to 1776, he served in the Pennsylvania assembly, where he opposed the governor. He helped draft Pennsylvania's first constitution in 1776. Ross also served as a delegate to the Continental Congress from 1774 to 1777. In 1779, he was commissioned an admiralty judge of the state of Pennsylvania. He served until his death that year. Ross was born in New Castle, Del. ROBERT J. TAYLOR

ROSS, HAROLD WALLACE (1892-1951), founded *The New Yorker* magazine, and edited it until his death. Intended as a publication for and about New York City, it became a national magazine with a reputation for good writing, clever cartoons, and penetrating observations. Ross was born in Aspen, Colo. He left high school to become a newspaperman. During World War I, he helped edit the service publication *Stars and Stripes*. He founded *The New Yorker* in 1925. I. W. COLE

ROSS, SIR JAMES CLARK (1800-1862), was a British polar explorer. He led an expedition to the Antarctic from 1839 to 1843 and discovered the Ross Ice Shelf, Victoria Land, and Mount Erebus, an active volcano. He reached 78° 10' south latitude, the southernmost point reached by man until 1900. His uncle, Sir John Ross, and Sir William Edward Parry trained him during six Arctic voyages in search of the Northwest Passage between 1818 and 1834. Ross discovered the North Magnetic Pole in 1831 while serving under his uncle. Ross was born in London. JOHN E. CASWELL

ROSS, JOHN. See NORTHWEST PASSAGE.

ROSS, JOHN (1790-1866), a chief of the Cherokee Indians, led the Cherokee during their most difficult period. He is best known for resisting the United States government's attempt to move the Cherokee west of the Mississippi River. His Indian name was *Cooweescoowee*, meaning *large white bird*. During the 1830's, he opposed a Cherokee group that favored the move. But his efforts failed, and in 1838 he began to lead his people west. The following year, he was chosen chief of the united Cherokee Nation west of the Mississippi River.

Ross was born in Tennessee of a Scottish father and a part-Cherokee mother. He attended the Kingston Academy in Tennessee. In 1809, he joined the Cherokee. Rose Cottage, his home in Park Hill, Okla., has been restored as a memorial. WILLIAM H. GILBERT

ROSS, NELLIE TAYLOE (1880-   ), an American politician and public official, was the first woman governor in the United States. She was elected to succeed her husband, William B. Ross, as governor of Wyoming after his death in 1924. She served as governor from 1925 to 1927. In 1933, President Franklin D.

Nellie Tayloe Ross

Harris & Ewing

Roosevelt named Mrs. Ross director of the United States Mint, a position she held until 1953. She was the first woman to hold that post. For several years she served as a vice-chairman of the Democratic National Committee in charge of activities for Democratic women. Mrs. Ross was born in St. Joseph, Mo. F. JAY TAYLOR

ROSS, ROBERT. See WAR OF 1812 (Campaigns of 1814).

444

ROSS, SIR RONALD (1857-1932), a British physician, won the 1902 Nobel medicine prize for research that led to the discovery of how to combat human malaria. When Ross began his research in 1894, the malaria parasite was known, but no one understood how humans became infected. After searching for two years, Ross found the parasite in the stomach of a mosquito that had fed on the blood of a malarial patient. In 1898, he succeeded in transmitting bird malaria by mosquito bites. In 1899, scientists used human volunteers and confirmed Ross's belief that the *Anopheles* mosquito carried human malaria. Born in Almora, India, Ross worked in India most of his life.   MORDECAI L. GABRIEL

ROSS DAM was built in a narrow gorge of the Skagit River north of Seattle, Wash. The arch-type dam, one of the world's highest, is a unit of the Seattle power system. Ross Dam is 540 feet high, 1,300 feet long, and forms a 24-mile-long lake which can store 1,405,000 acre-feet of water. The dam is part of a project that also includes Diablo Dam.   T. W. MERMEL

See also DIABLO DAM.

ROSS DEPENDENCY is a wedge-shaped section of Antarctica that includes Ross Sea, Ross Ice Shelf, and McMurdo Sound. The dependency covers about 160,-000 square miles. It is uninhabited except for scientific personnel. New Zealand has governed the area since 1923. *Little America*, the base set up by Richard E. Byrd in 1928, is located there.   EDWIN H. BRYAN, JR.

ROSS ICE SHELF. See ANTARCTICA (Exploration).

ROSS SEA. See ANTARCTICA (West Antarctica).

ROSSETTI, *roh SET ih,* **CHRISTINA GEORGINA** (1830-1894), was an English poet. Many of her poems are melancholy and deal with symbolic religious themes. But one of her best works is the nonreligious "Goblin Market" (1862). Miss Rossetti wrote it in an exciting, fast-paced style that makes the poem particularly effective when read aloud. Her other works include *Sing-Song* (1872), a collection of nursery rhymes; and two volumes of religious prose—*Annus Domini* (1874) and *Seek and Find* (1879).

Miss Rossetti was born in London. She lived a quiet, religious life and never married. She refused several marriage proposals because of religious differences. Her brother Dante Gabriel Rossetti was a famous English poet and painter.   JAMES DOUGLAS MERRITT

ROSSETTI, *roh SET ih,* **DANTE GABRIEL** (1828-1882), was one of the most famous English poets and painters of the 1800's. Rossetti was a central figure in the Pre-Raphaelite Brotherhood, an art movement he helped

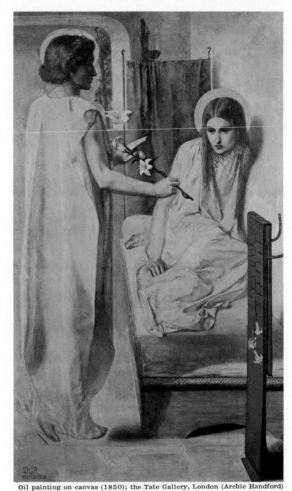

Oil painting on canvas (1850); the Tate Gallery, London (Archie Handford)

Rossetti's Painting *The Annunciation* shows the angel Gabriel telling the Virgin Mary that she will be the mother of Jesus. The painting's moody quality is typical of Rossetti's style.

found in 1848 (see PRE-RAPHAELITE BROTHERHOOD).

Rossetti's poetry is noted for its flowery language, vivid descriptions, and fantastic and symbolic themes. He had almost no training as a painter, and his works show little technical ability. But his best pictures are noted for their rich colors.

Many of Rossetti's poems and paintings were inspired by Elizabeth Siddal, whom he married in 1860. She died less than two years later, and the grief-stricken Rossetti buried the only manuscript of his poems with her. He agreed in 1869 to have the manuscript removed from her grave, and it was published in 1870 as *Poems*. The collection made Rossetti known as a major poet. In 1881, he published *Ballads and Sonnets*. His best-known poems include "The Blessed Damozel," "Sister Helen," and a series of love sonnets, *The House of Life*. He also translated many European works into English.

Rossetti was born in London, the son of an Italian political refugee. His sister Christina also was a famous poet.   JAMES DOUGLAS MERRITT

Portrait by William Holman
Hunt (Bettmann Archive)

Dante Gabriel Rossetti

Drawing by Dante Gabriel
Rossetti (Bettmann Archive)

Christina Rossetti

ROSSINI, GIOACCHINO ANTONIO

ROSSINI, *rohs SEE nee,* **GIOACCHINO ANTONIO** (1792-1868), was an Italian opera composer. His *The Barber of Seville* (1816) is perhaps the greatest farce opera ever written.

Rossini was born in Pesaro and received advanced musical training in Bologna. His second opera, *La Cambiale di matrimonio* (1810), made him an important force in Italian music. This was the first of his operas to be performed. For the next 13 years, Rossini wrote comic and tragic operas, sometimes as many as three or four a year. The most popular ones include *The Italian in Algiers* (1813), *The Turk in Italy* (1814), *Otello* (1816), *Cinderella* (1817), *Moses in Egypt* (1818), *The Lady of the Lake* (1819), and *Semiramide* (1823). They are noted for their rich and catchy melodies, surging vitality, and expert vocal writing. Rossini composed many of the great female roles in his tragic operas for his first wife, Isabella Colbran.

Brown Bros.
Gioacchino Rossini

In 1824, Rossini moved to Paris, then the opera capital of the world. In 1826 and 1827, he revised two of his Italian operas for French words. He then composed—to French texts—the masterly comic *Le Comte Ory* (1828) and his serious masterpiece *William Tell* (1829), with its famous overture.

Rossini composed no operas after 1829, partly because he was often in poor health, and partly because he did not like the new operatic styles. His compositions after that year include the religious work *Stabat Mater* (1842) and many small instrumental and vocal pieces that he called *Péchés de vieillesse* (*Sins of Old Age*). Rossini had intelligence, wit, and humor, and became a famous host in Paris. The evenings of musical concerts at his city and suburban homes attracted the highest society. HERBERT WEINSTOCK

ROSTAND, *raws TAHN,* **EDMOND** (1868-1918), was a famous French playwright and poet. He wrote his plays in verse, and showed great skill and imagination. His most famous play, *Cyrano de Bergerac* (1897), is regarded as a classic of the modern theater.

He was born in Marseille, the son of a journalist. He studied in Marseille and Paris. He became a lawyer, but soon turned to literature. Rostand published a small volume of poems in 1890. His poetic play, *The Romancers,* was produced in Paris four years later. Three other plays followed in quick succession before he won his greatest success with *Cyrano de Bergerac.*

Brown Bros.
Edmond Rostand

Culver

Edmond Rostand's *Cyrano de Bergerac* is a famous romantic play based on the life of a French soldier and author of the 1600's. José Ferrer, *above left,* played the hero with the long nose in a revival of the play in 1953.

Rostand's play *L'Aiglon* (1900) tells the story of Napoleon II. The play starred the great actress Sarah Bernhardt. He completed a symbolic barnyard comedy, *Chantecler,* in 1910. Its hero, a rooster, is a dreamer who follows high ideals of courage and honor. Rostand was elected to the French Academy in 1902. He died before completing his last dramatic work, *The Last Night of Don Juan.* JOHN W. GASSNER

See also CYRANO DE BERGERAC, SAVINIEN DE.

ROSTOCK, *RAHS tahk* (pop. 198,396; alt. 195 ft.), is an East German seaport and industrial center on the Baltic Sea. For location, see GERMANY (political map). The city lies at the mouth of the Warnow River and has been an important shipping point for hundreds of years. It is the chief port of entry for East Germany's petroleum supplies. Rostock's factories produce machinery, motors, submarines, chemicals, and airplanes. A railroad ferry runs from suburban Warnemünde to Denmark.

Founded in the 900's, Rostock was a member of the Hanseatic League during the Middle Ages (see HANSEATIC LEAGUE). The University of Rostock was founded in 1419. JAMES K. POLLOCK

ROSTOV-ON-DON, or ROSTOV, *rahs TAWF* (pop. 789,000; alt. 100 ft.), is one of Russia's most important cities. Rostov (Rostov-na-Donu in Russian) lies on the Don River, 25 miles from where it empties into the Sea of Azov (see RUSSIA [political map]). The city is the gateway to the Caucasus (see CAUCASUS MOUNTAINS). Rostov is a railroad and industrial center and a river port. It has one of the largest farm-machinery plants in Europe.

Rostov was founded in 1780. It began a long period of development as a trading center in the 1800's. German forces occupied Rostov in 1942 after a long, bitter battle. Russian forces retook the city from the Germans in 1943. THEODORE SHABAD

446

ROSWELL, *RAHZ well,* N. Mex. (pop. 33,908; alt. 3,555 ft.), is the center of a great cattle-raising and farming area. It lies in the Pecos Valley in southeastern New Mexico (see NEW MEXICO [political map]). For information about the monthly temperature and rainfall in Roswell, see NEW MEXICO (Climate).

Roswell has good railway, air, and bus services. It is the distribution center for surrounding cotton and alfalfa lands which depend upon irrigation from artesian wells. The city lies near Bottomless Lake State Park, with the Carlsbad Caverns on the south, and the White and Sacramento mountains on the west.

Van C. Smith, an early settler, named the city's post office for his father, Roswell Smith, in 1871. John Chisum, the "cattle king" of the Pecos Valley, lived near Roswell. The settlement was on the Goodnight-Loving cattle trail from Texas to Colorado. Roswell is the home of the New Mexico Military Institute and Walker Air Force Base. The seat of Chaves County, it has a council-manager government. FRANK D. REEVE

Steel brazed with copper sculpture. The Cleveland Museum of Art, Gift of the Cleveland Society for Contemporary Art

Theodore Roszak's *Mandrake* **is typical of the fierce, menacing birdlike forms that appear in many of the sculptor's works.**

ROSZAK, *ROH zak,* **THEODORE** (1907-   ), is an American sculptor. Since 1945, Roszak has created welded metal forms that are violent and expressionistic in appearance. His works in this style frequently deal with menacing, fossilized savage birds and animals. He described these works as "blunt reminders of primordial strife and struggle."

Roszak was born in Posen, Poland, and moved to Chicago with his family in 1909. He studied at the Art Institute of Chicago, the National Academy of Design, and Columbia University. His earliest works were paintings. From 1935 to 1945, he produced sculptured abstract works, severely geometrical and impersonal in style. Roszak taught at Sarah Lawrence College from 1941 to 1956. DOUGLAS GEORGE

ROT is a plant disease in which the plant rots, or decays, because of fungi or bacteria that may infect the plant and kill the cells. There are many varieties of this disease. A few common varieties are bitter rot, potato rot, brown rot, black rot, and dry rot. *Bitter rot* is found mostly in apples, although it may also attack quinces and pears. This disease is caused by a fungus which destroys the fruit, twigs, and limbs. In the fruit, the fungus causes a brown spot which gets larger and deeper and may give the fruit a bitter taste.

Potato rot is a dangerous disease because it can destroy an entire crop and cause a potato famine.

Brown rot destroys peaches and other stone fruits such as the plum and cherry. Small brown spots are found on the fruit. These grow until the entire fruit is infected.

Black rot attacks cultivated plants, such as the sweet potato, apple, grape, pear, and quince. Several fungi cause black rot. The disease produces dark-brown spots in the infected parts.

Dry rot is a disease that is common to timber. Any of several types of fungi cause dry rot. Dry rot also attacks some fruits and vegetables.

Rot is dangerous to plant life because it can quickly spread. It is difficult to control. WILLIAM F. HANNA

ROTA (pop. about 1,000) is an island in the Pacific Ocean, about 30 miles northeast of Guam. It is part of the Mariana Islands. Rota covers 33 square miles and rises to 1,168 feet. Some sugar plantations are located there. The island, along with most of the Marianas, became a United States trusteeship after the end of World War II. See also MARIANA ISLANDS.

ROTARY INTERNATIONAL is the world-wide organization of all Rotary Clubs. It supervises member clubs, and works for the advancement of Rotary throughout the world. A Rotary Club is a group of men, each in a different profession or business in a community.

All Rotary Clubs base their activities on the same general objectives. Rotarians take part in community welfare, foster good citizenship, promote high business and professional standards, improve rural-urban understanding, and advance international peace, understanding, and good will. Each year, the Rotary Foundation makes grants that give more than 500 young people an opportunity to study in other countries.

The official Rotary magazine is *The Rotarian.* Its Spanish-language edition is called *Revista Rotaria.*

Rotary International has a cogwheel for an emblem.

Paul P. Harris (1868-1947), a lawyer in Chicago, organized the first Rotary Club in 1905. It was named *Rotary* because members met in rotation at their places of business. There are more than 13,300 clubs in about 145 countries, with about 637,000 members. Rotary headquarters are at 1600 Ridge Ave., Evanston, Ill. 60201. GEORGE R. MEANS

ROTARY PRESS. See PRINTING (Running the Presses).
ROTARY WING AIRCRAFT. See HELICOPTER; AUTOGIRO; CONVERTIPLANE.
ROTATION OF CROPS. See CROPPING SYSTEM.
ROTC. See RESERVE OFFICERS TRAINING CORPS.
ROTENONE, *ROH tee nohn,* is a poisonous substance taken from the root of the derris and cube plants. It is much used in garden sprays because it is poisonous to cold-blooded creatures, but is fairly harmless to warm-blooded animals. Truck gardeners often use rotenone because this poison kills insects but will not harm the people who may later eat the vegetables.

447

ROTH, PHILIP

Rotenone is commonly used in home gardens. It is also used to control animal parasites, including cattle grubs in dairy cattle, and fleas, lice, and ticks. It is used in fruit sprays to control certain pests.

Indians in South America use crushed cube roots to catch fish. Although the rotenone in the roots kills the fish, the Indians can safely eat them.   W. V. MILLER

ROTH, PHILIP (1933-   ), is an American novelist and short-story writer. He is particularly noted for fiction about the psychology and morality of Jewish society and Jewish family life in the United States. Roth gained prominence with *Goodbye, Columbus* (1959),

Bob Peterson, *Life* magazine © Time Inc.

Philip Roth

a short novel about suburban country-club life. His novel, *Portnoy's Complaint* (1969) caused widespread discussion because of its frank analysis of the psychological atmosphere of Jewish family life and because of its detailed sexual episodes.

Many critics have praised Roth as a satirist. They also have praised his ability to describe details that symbolize various aspects of American society and his accuracy in transcribing the flavor of everyday speech. Roth's other novels include *Letting Go* (1962) and *When She Was Good* (1967). Several of his short stories were published with *Goodbye, Columbus*. Roth was born in Newark, N.J.   MARCUS KLEIN

ROTHSCHILD is the name of a family of bankers, financiers, and philanthropists. For many years they formed one of the banking powers of Europe.

The family was first connected with large financial dealings when Mayer Amschel Rothschild (1743-1812), son of a Jewish merchant of Frankfurt am Main, Germany, opened a money-exchange house. He invested the wealth of an Austrian nobleman, and handled the money so well that he soon handled investments for many royal families. When he died, he left his five sons a family banking house and enormous fortunes.

Amschel Mayer Rothschild (1773-1855), the oldest son, took control of the family bank in Frankfurt. He was succeeded by his sons. Salomon Mayer Rothschild (1774-1855), the second son, established part of the family banking firm in Vienna, while Nathan Mayer Rothschild (1777-1836), the third son, started the London branch of the family firm. Karl Mayer Rothschild (1788-1855), the fourth son, founded a branch bank in Naples, and James Mayer Rothschild (1792-1868), the youngest son, founded the Paris branch of the firm.

These banks greatly influenced European affairs. They sometimes supported wars and sometimes prevented them by refusing the necessary loans. They helped to start national education systems in France and Germany, and aided in the industrial development of many European countries.

Lionel Rothschild (1808-1879), a son of Nathan Rothschild, led in freeing British Jews from discrimination. Between 1847 and 1857, he was elected four times to

Parliament, but was not allowed to take his seat because he would not take an oath supporting Christianity. Finally in 1858, he secured passage of an act which freed Jewish members of Parliament from taking such an oath. He sat in the House of Commons from 1858 to 1868 and from 1869 to 1874.

Nathan Mayer Rothschild (1840-1915), the first English Baron Rothschild, was a member of the House of Commons. In 1885, he became the first Jew ever to be admitted to the House of Lords.

Lionel Walter Rothschild (1868-1937) was a zoologist. He served in the House of Commons, and was elected to the Royal Society in 1911.   CHARLES F. MULLETT

ROTIFER, *ROH tuh fer*, is a microscopic animal that commonly lives in still, fresh water. Its shape may resemble that of a tiny worm. The name *rotifer* means *wheel bearer*, and comes from the circles of projections, that are called *cilia*, located on the animal's head (see CILIA). The rotifer uses these cilia to swim and to sweep food into its mouth. The animal gives off a sticky cement, which holds it in place while it feeds. Its food consists chiefly of microscopic plants and animals.

Rotifers are not made of separate cells like other animals, but of masses of protoplasm with many nuclei. The males help in producing young, but the females can also reproduce by themselves. This second kind of reproduction is called *parthenogenesis*. Rotifers can live many years in a dry condition. Winds and birds carry the dried animals to distant places.

Scientific Classification. Rotifers belong to the phylum *Rotifera*. The common rotifer is genus *Rotifer*, species *R. vulgaris*.   RALPH BUCHSBAUM

Greatly Enlarged Glass Models of Rotifers show the graceful forms of these tiny animals. The stationary rotifer, *left,* uses its cilia to swim. The tube-building rotifer, *right,* plainly shows the round, bricklike makeup of the lower part of its body.

American Museum of Natural History

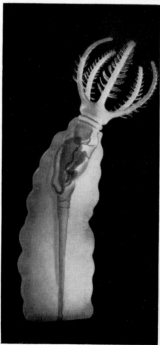 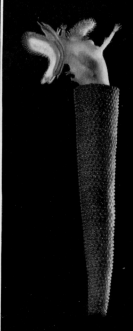

The Center of Rotterdam, which was almost completely destroyed by German bombing raids during World War II, has been rebuilt since the war ended. This view shows a part of the *Lijnbaan*, a large, modern shopping center built since the war.

Rotkin, PFI

ROTOGRAVURE. See PRINTING (Printing by Gravure); PHOTOENGRAVING AND PHOTOLITHOGRAPHY (Gravure Photoengraving).

ROTOR, *ROH tur*, is the rotating part of a machine. For example, the rotor of a steam turbine revolves as the steam strikes the rotor blades. Other machines that have rotors include electric motors, electric generators, and centrifugal pumps. See also ELECTRIC GENERATOR (Parts of a Generator); TURBINE (Turbine Terms).

ROTOR SHIP is a seagoing vessel driven by the action of air currents on revolving metal cylinders. The ship has two large cylinders mounted in the usual position of the smokestacks. They have discs on each end which are larger around than the cylinders. The cylinders turn on masts at a rate of 125 times a minute. Anton Flettner of Germany built the first rotor ship in 1926. The rotor ship has never become important, because it is so much slower than propeller-driven ships. ROBERT H. BURGESS

ROTTEN BOROUGH. See BOROUGH.

ROTTERDAM (pop. 710,871; met. area 1,056,038) is the second largest city in The Netherlands. Rotterdam lies on both banks of the Nieuwe Maas, as this part of the Rhine River is called, near the mouth of the Lek River. The city lies 13 miles southeast of The Hague (see NETHERLANDS [map]). Three-fifths of Rotterdam lies about 8 feet below sea level. The remainder is 15 feet above sea level. Rotterdam is the largest port in Europe and the second largest in the world. Many shipping firms have headquarters there. A canal about 17 miles long connects the city to the North Sea.

The most famous church in Rotterdam is St. Laurens, which was built during the 1400's. This fine Gothic building, which was bombed during World War II, contained a great organ and many monuments to Dutch naval heroes. The church was rebuilt after the war.

The fine zoological and botanical gardens of Rotterdam were founded in 1857. Art lovers from many parts of the world have visited the Boymans Museum, which has a collection of paintings by Dutch masters.

Rotterdam was incorporated as a city in 1299. It grew so rapidly that its boundaries were constantly extended. During the 1800's and 1900's, the city began to take on great importance as a port and trading center. The chief industry now is shipbuilding. Factories produce cigars, alcoholic beverages, paints, sugar, and chemicals.

German bombs destroyed the entire center of Rotterdam in 1940 (see NETHERLANDS [picture]). Toward the end of World War II, the Nazis destroyed the harbor quays. Rotterdam engineers repaired the harbor and expanded its facilities. Since the war, large sections of Rotterdam have been rebuilt. In one of its rebuilt areas, Rotterdam has a modern shopping center called the Lijnbaan. BENJAMIN HUNNINGHER

See also PORT (table).

ROTTWEILER, *ROT wile ur*, is a stocky dog with short, coarse black hair. The dog has tan or mahogany marks on its head, chest, and legs. Rottweilers resemble Doberman pinschers. When full-grown, they stand about 27 inches high. Rottweilers were developed

WORLD BOOK photo by E. F. Hoppe

Powerful Rottweilers Once Guarded Roman Herds.

449

in one of the valleys of southern Germany, near the village of Rottweil. They are descended from the camp dogs that followed Roman armies in their conquest of southern Germany about 1,900 years ago. The Romans used these dogs to herd the cattle and sheep that provided meat for the armies. OLGA DAKAN

ROUAULT, *roo OH*, **GEORGES** (1871-1958), was a French artist. He was a deeply religious man with strong moral convictions, and his works show his hatred of hypocrisy, poverty, sin, and war.

Rouault was born in Paris. From 1885 to 1890, he worked for a maker of stained-glass windows. Rouault's paintings, with their hard black outlines and brilliant, intense color, show the influence of stained-glass designing. About 1905, Rouault was briefly associated with a group of painters called the fauves (see FAUVES). The bold brushstrokes and dramatic color contrasts of the fauves became important parts of his style. From about 1903 to 1916, Rouault painted religious subjects, portraits of sad clowns, and satirical pictures of prostitutes and corrupt judges. All these works reflect misery and pain.

From 1916 to 1927, Rouault worked chiefly on a series of about 60 aquatints and etchings. This series, called *Miserere*, was published in 1948 and ranks as one of the greatest achievements in modern printmaking. From 1927 until his death, Rouault continued to paint

Oil painting on canvas (1938); Museum of Art, Carnegie Institute, Pittsburgh, Pa. (WORLD BOOK photo by Elton Schnellbacher)

Rouault's *The Old King* resembles a stained-glass window with its thick black lines enclosing areas of bright color.

clowns and religious pictures, but chose fewer satirical subjects. GREGORY BATTCOCK

ROUEN, *roo AHN* (pop. 120,471; met. area 369,793; alt. 90 ft.), is a trading center and river port on the Seine River, about 70 miles northwest of Paris (see FRANCE [political map]). Manufactures include silk, cotton, and woolen materials, hosiery, ammunition, chemicals, and refined petroleum. The English burned Joan of Arc at the stake in Rouen in 1431. EDWARD W. FOX

ROUGE. See COSMETICS.

ROUGET DE LISLE, CLAUDE JOSEPH. See MARSEILLAISE.

ROUGH RIDERS is the nickname for a famous American regiment that fought under Theodore Roosevelt's leadership in the Spanish-American War of 1898. The official name of the regiment was the First United States Volunteer Cavalry. About 1,000 men, all "good shots and good riders," were recruited for the unit. It soon became known by the nickname *rough riders*, a popular name for western cowboys. Leonard Wood commanded the Rough Riders when the regiment was first formed. Later, Roosevelt became colonel in command.

The Rough Riders had their greatest day on July 1, 1898, during the battle of San Juan Hill in Cuba. Roosevelt led his men in a victorious charge up "Kettle Hill," which is near San Juan Hill. Many Americans died in the charge, but those who survived were hailed as heroes. The fame of the Rough Riders later helped Roosevelt in his political activities. FRANK FREIDEL

ROULETTE, *roo LET*, is one of the most popular games at gambling casinos. Roulette equipment consists of a table with a built-in wheel and a small ball. The wheel lies flat. It has small *compartments* (pockets) that are alternately black and red and are numbered from 1 to 36. There are also two green pockets numbered on opposite sides of the wheel. These are 0 (zero) and 00 (double zero). Each number and color on the wheel has a corresponding space on the table.

Players put their money or chips on any number or combination of numbers, or simply on either color. The man in charge, the croupier (pronounced *KROO pih ur*), spins the wheel. As the wheel turns, he releases the ball in the opposite direction. The ball comes to rest in one of the compartments, marking the winning number and color. The odds against winning vary from 35 to 1, with a bet on one number; to even money (1 to 1), with a bet on a color only. Winnings vary according to the odds. JOHN SCARNE

ROUMANIA, a variant of Romania. See ROMANIA.

ROUND is a musical composition for several voices or instruments. Three or four voices begin to sing the same words and music at different times. "Three Blind Mice" is one example of a round. See also CANON.

ROUND HILL SCHOOL. See BANCROFT, GEORGE.

ROUND TABLE was a famous table in the legends of King Arthur. Merlin, a magician, supposedly created it. According to legend, the table was made of marble, but it could be folded magically and carried in a coat pocket. The table was round so that no one could argue over the order in which Arthur's knights should be seated. According to legend, the Round Table remained at Camelot, the location of Arthur's court. Some persons believe that Camelot is Caerleon-on-Usk, Wales. A table, once thought to be the original Round Table, hangs in a former castle in Winchester, England.

King Arthur's Knights sit at a round table in this illustration from a French version of the King Arthur legend.

Culver

The stories of King Arthur and his knights played an important part in the literature of medieval chivalry. In 1470, Sir Thomas Malory, an English writer, collected all the legends in one book, *Le Morte Darthur*. Many later writers retold the romantic tales. Alfred, Lord Tennyson, poet laureate of England in the 1800's, told about the knights of the Round Table in his loosely organized epic, *Idylls of the King*. See KNIGHTS AND KNIGHTHOOD (Knighthood in Literature); MALORY, SIR THOMAS.

Arthur and Merlin are two of the most important characters in the legends that surround the Round Table. Arthur was a historical figure who lived about A.D. 500. The early legends of King Arthur tell of his marriage to Guinevere. They also describe his many battles with other kings, giants, the Roman invaders, and his discontented subjects. A real Merlin supposedly lived about 470. He was a Welsh bard who entered the service of Arthur during the Saxon invasion. He went mad after watching a horrible battle near Solway. Thereafter he lived in caves, singing to himself.

The legend of Merlin, creator of the Round Table, appears in Spanish, French, German, and English stories. He was known as a poet and a prophet as well as a magician. He was supposedly the son of a fierce demon and a Welsh princess. Merlin began to show his marvelous powers while still a child. During the time of the Saxon invasion, he called two dragons out of the ground. They represented the Saxons and the Britons. As the dragons fought, Merlin sang a series of verses predicting the future of England down to the time of Geoffrey of Monmouth in the 1100's.

According to legend, Merlin arranged for the birth of Arthur by bringing together King Uther Pendragon and Igrayne, Duchess of Cornwall. Later the magician helped Arthur become king. Merlin also provided Arthur with a famous sword, *Excalibur*, which he received from the Lady of the Lake. Arthur lost his throne be-cause of his treacherous nephew Modred. The nephew stirred up a rebellion in the kingdom while Arthur was away fighting another war. When Arthur returned to Camelot, a bitter battle was fought between the rebels and the loyal subjects. The king killed Modred but was severely wounded himself. Arthur's friends carried him to a barge and took him to the Valley of Avalon to be healed of his wounds. It is believed that Arthur never returned to Camelot. But legends say he will some day come back to rule over England again.

Other Characters. Sir Lancelot was one of the most romantic figures of this period. He was noted for his gentleness as well as for his fierce fighting ability. But Lancelot fell in love with Queen Guinevere, and had to flee from Camelot when Arthur found out about their love. The stories of the Round Table tell of the adventures of many other famous knights, including Gawain, Kaye, Pellinore, Tristram, Tor, Percivale, Bors, and Bedivere. The name Elaine, mentioned many times in these stories, refers to several different women. One was the half sister of Arthur and the mother of Modred. Another was the daughter of King Pelles, and the mother of Sir Galahad. But the most famous Elaine was the "lily maid of Astolat," who died for love of Sir Lancelot. She was made famous by Tennyson in his poem "Lancelot and Elaine."

The Holy Grail. One of the goals of the knights of the Round Table was to find the Holy Grail, the cup Jesus was said to have used at the Last Supper. A special seat at the Table, called *The Siege Perilous*, was reserved for the knight who could find this holy cup. The son of Lancelot, Sir Galahad, at last found the Grail and won The Siege Perilous.   KNOX WILSON

See also ARTHUR, KING; GALAHAD, SIR; HOLY GRAIL; LANCELOT, SIR; LAUNFAL, SIR.

ROUNDHEAD was a name given to the opponents of the Royalist followers of the English King Charles I. They were called Roundheads because they had their hair cut close to their heads, in contrast to the Royalists who wore wigs of long, flowing curls. Most of the Roundheads were Puritans, who, by cutting their hair short, wished to show their disapproval of the bewigged aristocrats.   J. SALWYN SCHAPIRO

See also CAVALIER; PURITAN.

ROUNDUP. See COWBOY (The Roundup).

ROUNDWORM is one of a group of long, cylinder-shaped worms, many of which live in the intestines of man and animals. Some roundworms live in plants. These species that live in plants and animals are called *parasites* and may sometimes cause serious disease (see PARASITE). But some parasites are not very harmful. Many other species of roundworms live in oceans, lakes, streams, and in the soil.

Ascaris is a parasitic roundworm that lives in the intestines of man, and sometimes of pigs and horses. This roundworm is light cream in color and has four white lines running along the length of the worm. Its covering is thick and tough. The body is pointed at both ends. The female may grow 16 inches long or more, and is always longer than the male. But most roundworms are much smaller than this. At the front or *anterior* end of the worm there is a *mouth*, and near the rear or *posterior* end there is an *anus*, where the wastes are

ROUS, FRANCIS PEYTON

given off. In the male, the posterior part of the body is curved under. Food is taken in through the mouth and absorbed in the intestine. The worm feeds on food already digested in the host's intestine.

Almost all roundworms reproduce by laying eggs. However, the vinegar eel gives birth to live young (see VINEGAR EEL). A roundworm may lay as many as 10,000 to 20,000 eggs in a day. The female ascaris can lay as many as 200,000 eggs a day. The eggs are tiny and oval shaped. They are sometimes found on vegetables that have not been properly cleaned. The eggs are sometimes swallowed and hatched inside the intestines. The roundworms may travel to other parts of the body, such as the liver and appendix.

Scientific Classification. Roundworms are in the animal subkingdom *Metazoa*. They are the phylum *Aschelminthes*, and make up the class *Nematoda*. JAMES A. MCLEOD

See also NEMATODA; PINWORM; WORM (picture).

ROUS, FRANCIS PEYTON (1879-1970), an American medical researcher, proved that viruses cause some types of cancer. In 1910, Rous ground up a cancerous tumor from a chicken and filtered out everything larger than a virus. The resulting liquid produced cancer when injected into other chickens. For many years, scientists scoffed at Rous's discovery. They believed that cancer could not be caused by a virus because the disease is not contagious. In 1966, Rous shared the Nobel prize in medicine and physiology for his work.

Rous was born in Baltimore and earned an M.D. from Johns Hopkins University in 1905. He joined

United Press Int.
Francis Peyton Rous

the Rockefeller Institute for Medical Research (now Rockefeller University) in 1909 and worked there for more than 60 years. In 1915 and 1916, during World War I, Rous helped develop a method of storing blood for transfusions. This technique made possible the establishment of blood banks. ISAAC ASIMOV

ROUSSEAU, *roo SOH*, **HENRI** (1844-1910), was a French artist who painted some of the most unusual pictures in early modern art. He is called a *primitive* painter because he had no professional training.

The bold colors and decorative patterns of Rousseau's paintings resemble many works by artists called *impressionists* and *nabis*. But unlike such artists, Rousseau portrayed each detail precisely and polished the surfaces of his canvases to a high gloss. Rousseau took many of his subjects—such as a wedding party or a patriotic celebration—from French middle-class life. But he also loved to paint realistic figures and objects in fantastic or mysterious relationships. Rousseau's *The Sleeping Gypsy* is reproduced in the PAINTING article. Such pictures strongly influenced the surrealism movement of the 1920's (see SURREALISM).

Rousseau was born in Laval. He worked as a minor customs official in Paris until about 1885, when he retired to devote his life to painting. ALBERT BOIME

ROUSSEAU, *roo SOH*, **JEAN JACQUES** (1712-1778), a French philosopher, was the most important writer of the Age of Reason, a cultural movement of the 1700's. Rousseau's political philosophy influenced the development of the French Revolution. His theories also have had great impact on education and literature as well as on political philosophy.

Throughout his life, Rousseau suffered from severe emotional distress, marked by feelings of deep inferiority and guilt. Rousseau's actions and writings reflect his attempts to overcome his sense of inadequacy and find an acceptable identity in a world that seemed to reject him constantly. He needed love, but seemed unable to have a satisfactory relationship with a woman. He needed friends, but spoiled his friendships with his suspicious and hypersensitive nature. He has been called a perfect example of an outsider in society.

Pastel portrait on paper (1753) by Maurice Quentin De La Tour; Musée Antoine Lécuyer, Saint-Quentin, France
Jean Jacques Rousseau

Early Life. Rousseau was born on June 28, 1712, in Geneva, Switzerland. His personality problems probably originated in childhood. Rousseau's mother died giving birth to him, and his father made him feel guilty about her death. The father alternated between affection and rejection toward his son and finally abandoned him when he was 10 years old. Rousseau ran away from Geneva in 1728 and began a wandering, adventurous life in which he tried many jobs. He either failed in them or quit them. He succeeded only in the work he did alone—copying music scores or writing.

When Rousseau was about 17, he converted from Protestantism to Roman Catholicism. For this act, he felt shame and guilt all his life. Soon after his conversion, he settled down near Chambéry, France, with Louise de Warens, a wealthy widow 12 years older than he. Rousseau described the happiness of their early relationship in his famous autobiography, *Confessions*. However, their relationship later became an increasing agony to him. He finally left her in 1740. In 1741, Rousseau went to Paris seeking fame.

The turning point in Rousseau's life came in 1749, when he read about a contest being sponsored by the Academy of Dijon. The academy was offering a prize for the best essay on "Whether the renaissance of the sciences and the arts has contributed to purifying morals." As he read about the contest, Rousseau suddenly realized that his vocation was to oppose society as it then existed and point out new paths for it to follow. Rousseau submitted an essay, "Discourse on the Sciences and the Arts" (1750), attacking the arts and sciences for corrupting mankind. He won the prize—and the fame he had so long desired.

Later Life. Rousseau became more vain, inconsiderate, and suspicious as he grew older. He reconverted to Protestantism in 1754. In 1757 and 1758, he quarreled bitterly with his former friends, a group of philosophers called the *philosophes* (see PHILOSOPHES). In 1762, the French government condemned one of Rousseau's works, *Émile*, charging that its views on religion attacked traditional Christian doctrine. Rousseau fled to Switzerland to escape persecution. In 1766, he accepted an invitation of refuge in England from the Scottish philosopher David Hume. But Rousseau had a quarrel with Hume and returned to France in 1767.

Beginning in 1770, Rousseau concentrated on writing autobiographical works in which he tried to justify his life and conduct. The most important of these writings was the *Confessions*, which Rousseau began in 1764 and completed in 1770. It was published in 1782, after his death. In *Rousseau, Judge of Jean Jacques* (1789), a series of dialogues, Rousseau attempted to answer charges by his critics. His last work was the beautiful and calm *Reveries of the Solitary Stroller* (1782).

His Ideas. Rousseau expressed his criticism of society in several essays, including "Discourse on the Origin of Inequality" (1755) and "Letter to d'Alembert on Spectacles" (1758). His *Julie, or the New Heloise* (1761) is a romantic novel as well as a novel of social criticism. In *The Social Contract* (1762), a landmark in the history of political science, Rousseau gave his views on government and the rights of citizens. In *Émile* (1762), Rousseau stated his belief that children should be taught with sympathy and an appeal to their interests, rather than through discipline and strict lessons. However, he also felt that children's thoughts and behavior should be manipulated and controlled.

Rousseau believed that man is not a social being by nature. He felt that when men lived in a state of nature, isolated and without language, they were good—that is, they had no motive or impulse to hurt one another. But as soon as men began to live together in society, they became evil. According to Rousseau, society corrupts men by bringing out their inclinations toward aggression and egotism.

Rousseau believed that society should be reorganized into communities in which all persons would be completely controlled. He invented a system for behavioral control that foreshadowed some modern theories of psychological conditioning and behavior. He also outlined the institutions for a democracy in which all persons would participate and be involved. This democracy would use training, guidance and propaganda, censorship, and reduction of privacy to eliminate special-interest groups and to control ideas. Rousseau did not advise that men return to a state of nature. He wanted a simple agricultural society in which men's desires could be limited, their sexual and ego drives controlled, and all their energies directed toward total involvement in community life. Some of his ideas greatly influenced Robespierre, a leader of the French Revolution, and the socialists and communists of the 1800's and 1900's.

His Literary Influence. Rousseau was one of the first writers to support romanticism, a movement that dominated the arts from the late 1700's to the mid-1800's. In his personal life and writings, he captured the spirit of romanticism by prizing feeling over reason, and impulsiveness and spontaneity over self-discipline. Rousseau introduced true and passionate love into the novel, popularized descriptions of nature, and created a lyrical and eloquent prose style. With his *Confessions*, he started a fashion for intimate autobiographies. Lester G. Crocker

See also Age of Reason; Romanticism.

ROUSTABOUT. See Circus (On Tour).
ROUTES OF TRADE. See Trade Route.
ROUTT, JOHN L. See Colorado (History).
ROVING. See Wool (Shearing and Manufacture).
ROWAN, *RO an*, **ANDREW SUMMERS** (1857-1943), a U.S. Army lieutenant, brought information about the military situation in Cuba to the U.S. government from the Cuban rebel, General Calixto García y Íñiguez, in 1898. Elbert Hubbard's "A Message to Garcia" vividly but incorrectly described his adventure.

Rowan disguised himself as an English sportsman and made use of the Spanish he had learned during service in Chile. For his exploit, he received the Distinguished Service Cross in 1920, 11 years after he had retired from the Army. He was born in Gap Mills, W.Va. He was graduated from the United States Military Academy in 1882. H. A. DeWeerd

See also García y Íñiguez, Calixto.

ROWAN, CARL THOMAS (1925-   ), an American newspaperman, was director of the United States Information Agency (USIA) in 1964 and 1965. He was the first Negro to serve on the National Security Council. He also served as deputy assistant secretary of state for public affairs from 1961 to 1963 and as ambassador to Finland in 1963 and 1964. In 1965, he became a columnist for the *Chicago Daily News*.

Rowan was an outstanding reporter for the *Minneapolis Tribune* from 1948 to 1961. He received Sigma Delta Chi national journalism awards in 1954, 1955, and 1956. His books include *South of Freedom*

Harris & Ewing
Carl T. Rowan

(1952), *Go South in Sorrow* (1957), and *Wait Till Next Year* (1960). Rowan was born in Ravenscroft, Tenn. He attended Oberlin College and received a master's degree from the University of Minnesota. Eric Sevareid

ROWAN TREE. See Mountain Ash.
ROWE, NICHOLAS. See Poet Laureate.

ROWING is the act of propelling a boat with oars. Many persons find rowing on lakes, rivers, and lagoons a pleasant form of exercise. Rowing races have also developed into well-organized amateur sporting events.

Types of Rowing. In racing, there are two main kinds of rowing: (1) sculling and (2) sweep-oar rowing.

In *sculling*, each oarsman, or *sculler*, uses two oars. Both the boat and the oars are called *sculls*. The various sizes of scull craft include *single* sculls, for one man; *double* sculls, for two men; and *quadruple* sculls, for four men. A few eight-place sculls, known as "centipedes," have also been built.

In *sweep-oar rowing*, each man uses only one oar. Sweep oars are much larger and longer than sculling oars. The boats used in this form of rowing hold two, four, six, or eight men, and are called *pairs*, *fours*, *sixes*, and *eights*. Eights, and some fours, are designed to hold an additional crewman, known as the *coxswain*. He steers the boat by pulling on tiller ropes to turn a rudder.

ROWLAND, HENRY AUGUSTUS

The coxswain may also direct the timing of the oar strokes for the *stroke*, the oarsman who sits closest to him in the boat. The stroke sets the pace for the other oarsmen.

Racing rowboats are lighter, and more fragile than ordinary rowboats. For this reason, they are called *shells*. There are no rules limiting the length, width, or shape of a shell. A single scull may weigh 30 pounds or less. An eight shell may be 60 feet long, 2 feet wide, and weigh about 285 pounds.

History. Rowboats with rudders for steering were in use before 3000 B.C. The ancient Greeks and Romans traveled in huge rowboats called *galleys* (see GALLEY). These boats had long rows of oars which were often placed one above the other. The vikings were other early peoples who made skillful use of rowboats (see VIKING).

Thomas Doggett, an English comedian, helped originate boat racing in the 1700's. He offered a trophy known as the "Doggett Coat and Badge" to the winner of a race held for boatmen on the River Thames. Later, the *regatta*, or racing meet, became an important sporting event at many universities. The first race, between Oxford University and Cambridge University, took place in 1829. In the United States the oldest intercollegiate regatta is held by Harvard University and Yale University. It started in 1852.

Famous regattas are now held annually throughout the United States and in many parts of the world. A number of these are open to contestants from all nations. The Henley Royal Regatta, an outstanding English event that started in 1840, is held each year at Henley-on-Thames. Other famous races include the Intercollegiate Racing Association Regatta at Syracuse, N.Y., and the Royal Canadian Henley at St. Catharines, Ont.   R. HARRISON SANFORD

Photoreporters, Inc.

Rowing in a Race, the oarsmen stroke to the count of the coxswain, who sits facing them. He also steers the shell.

ROWLAND, *ROH lund,* **HENRY AUGUSTUS** (1848-1901), was an American physicist. He invented the concave grating for spectrum analysis, and built an improved ruling and dividing engine for making precise rulings on glass or metal surfaces. In his Berlin experiment in 1876, he proved that electrostatic charges of electricity in motion produce a magnetic field similar to the field produced by an electric current in a wire. He also determined the mechanical equivalent of heat, and the value of the *ohm*, the unit for measuring resistance to the flow of an electric current (see OHM).

Rowland was born on Nov. 27, 1848, in Honesdale, Pa., and was graduated from Rensselaer Polytechnic Institute. He was a professor of physics at Johns Hopkins University from 1875 to 1901.   CARL T. CHASE

ROXAS Y ACUÑA, *RRAW hahs ee ah KOO nyah,* **MANUEL** (1892-1948), served as the first president of the Philippine Republic, after it received its independence from the United States on July 4, 1946. He fought the Japanese in World War II, first as a colonel and then as a guerrilla on the island of Mindanao. The Japanese captured him and forced him to serve as a minor official under the puppet government of Jose P. Laurel. Roxas used his position to shield the spy ring he formed to aid the United States.

Roxas was born in Capiz (now Roxas), on Panay Island. He studied law at the University of the Philippines and became governor of his home province. As speaker of the House of Representatives, he achieved fame as a champion of independence.   GEORGE E. TAYLOR

See also PHILIPPINES (History).

ROY, GABRIELLE (1909-   ), a French-Canadian novelist, won fame with *Bonheur d'Occasion*, a novel of life in the slums of Montreal. In 1947, the book was translated into English as *The Tin Flute*. Miss Roy was born in St. Boniface, Man. She studied in a convent and at the Teachers' Training College in Winnipeg. She taught school, went to Europe, and began to write when she returned to Canada in 1939. Her books include *Where Nests the Water Hen* (1951), *The Cashier* (1955), and *Street of Riches* (1957).   DESMOND PACEY

ROY, MAURICE CARDINAL (1905-   ), a Canadian religious leader, was named a cardinal of the Roman Catholic Church in 1965 by Pope Paul VI. At the time of his elevation, Roy was archbishop of Quebec and primate of Canada. He was ordained a priest in 1926. During World War II, he served overseas for five years as a chaplain in the Canadian Army. He was born in Quebec City.   THOMAS P. NEILL

ROY, ROB. See ROB ROY.

ROYAL ACADEMY OF ARTS is an association of artists in London, England. King George III founded the academy in 1768. Sir Joshua Reynolds, a great portrait painter, was its first president. The academy operates several art schools and organizes exhibitions of paintings.

Critically reviewed by the ROYAL ACADEMY OF ARTS

ROYAL AIR FORCE. See AIR FORCE.

ROYAL ARCANUM, *ahr KAY num,* **SUPREME COUNCIL OF THE,** is a fraternal benefit society of the United States and Canada, founded in 1877 in Boston, Mass. The society combines a fraternal union with benefits for members providing home protection and disability, old age, and life insurance. Its 45,000 members make up 425 councils. The Supreme Council of the Royal Arcanum accepts male and female members up to 60 years of age. Its headquarters are at 10 Batterymarch St., Boston, Mass. 02110.   WILLIAM J. MOIR

ROYAL BOTANIC GARDENS, KEW. See FLOWER (Famous Flower Gardens).

ROYAL CANADIAN AIR FORCE. See AIR FORCE (Major Air Forces of the World).

Royal Canadian Mounted Police perform the *Musical Ride,* a series of complex movements including the "Dome," *top.* The RCMP badge, *left,* has a motto in French that means *Maintain the Right.* Mounties patrol Canadian highways and often assist motorists, *right.*

ROYAL CANADIAN MOUNTED POLICE (RCMP) is the national law enforcement department of Canada. The fame of the Mounted Police has spread throughout the world since the force was organized in 1873. Today, the Mounted Police travel in motor vehicles instead of on horses. But the heroic men on horseback still live in the many books and motion pictures about them. The badge of the Royal Canadian Mounted Police bears the organization's motto, *Maintiens le droit* (Maintain the right).

Organization and Duties. The Royal Canadian Mounted Police enforces federal law throughout Can-

ada. It is the only police force in the Northwest Territories and the Yukon. Members of the Royal Canadian Mounted Police serve as provincial police in all provinces except Ontario and Quebec, which have their own police forces. They also provide police protection in some municipalities.

More than 8,800 men serve in the RCMP. Applicants must be Canadian citizens or British subjects, at least 19 years of age, and have at least an 11th-grade education. Recruits receive six months training at Regina, Sask. They are graduated as *constables.*

The force also maintains the Canadian Police Col-

ROYAL CANADIAN MOUNTED POLICE BADGES OF RANK

Officers

Commissioner

Deputy Commissioner

Assistant Commissioner

Chief Superintendent

Superintendent

Sub-Inspector

Inspector

Enlisted Men

Corps Sergeant Major

Sergeant Major

Staff Sergeant Major

Staff Sergeant

Sergeant

Corporal

WORLD BOOK illustration by Tom Morgan

Mounted Police Use Snowmobiles as well as airplanes to patrol the vast, thinly populated areas of the Northwest Territories and the Yukon Territory in northern Canada.

Royal Canadian Mounted Police

Checking Gun Registrations is the responsibility of one of the 11 sections of the RCMP Identification Branch. The branch handles all police identification matters in Canada.

Malak, Miller Services

lege. Senior members of the force and policemen invited from other countries study the latest methods of crime prevention and detection there.

The Royal Canadian Mounted Police maintains about 2,630 land motor vehicles, including cars, trucks, and snowmobiles. It has police dogs and horses, but the horses are used only for ceremonial purposes. The force also has air and marine divisions. The air division stations aircraft at strategic points throughout Canada. The marine division operates more than 35 ships and boats on Canada's two coasts, the St. Lawrence River, and the Great Lakes.

The solicitor general of Canada oversees the force. A commissioner directs its activities from headquarters in Ottawa. The Royal Canadian Mounted Police has 12 police divisions with headquarters in the provincial capitals. Five other divisions deal with administration, training, and with the force's air and water operations.

Uniform. The working uniform of today's Mounted Policeman includes a cloth cap, brown *tunic* (jacket), brown leather gloves, dark blue trousers with a broad yellow stripe, oxford shoes, and side-arm equipment. At ceremonies, Mounted Policemen still wear their famed uniforms with wide-brimmed hats, scarlet dress tunics, breeches tucked into high boots, and spurs.

The color of the dress tunic is the only part of the uniform that has never changed. Scarlet was chosen because Indians considered it a symbol of justice and fair dealing. The Indians respected the British soldiers who came to Canada's western plains before the Mounted Policemen. The soldiers wore scarlet coats.

Mounted Policemen of 1873 wore gray riding

ROYAL CANADIAN MOUNTED POLICE

breeches, loose-fitting tunics, black riding boots, and spurs. Their hats were either white cork helmets or caps shaped like pillboxes. By 1878, the loose-fitting jacket was replaced by a short, tight-fitting tunic. Blue breeches with a yellow stripe replaced gray breeches.

About 1900, broad-brimmed hats became part of the uniform. Mounted Policemen had complained that the helmets were hot and that the pillbox caps did not protect them from the blazing prairie sun. Brown boots replaced the black ones. New side-arm equipment consisted of a belt with shoulder strap and holster on the right side. When the force became the Royal North-West Mounted Police, royal blue shoulder straps and collar patches were added to the tunic. Since that time, changes have been made to bring the uniform to what it is today.

History. In 1869, Canada's Dominion government acquired the great, unsettled territory of the Canadian Northwest. The Red River Rebellion and other smaller uprisings made it difficult to open the territory to permanent settlers. Criminal bands roamed the forest lands and took the law into their own hands. The government decided that the area must be controlled.

A mounted police force was organized in 1873. The name first proposed was the North-West Mounted Rifles. But the United States protested the idea of an armed force patrolling the international boundary. Because of the protest, the force was named the North-West Mounted Police to avoid misunderstanding.

The first members of the force were trained during

The Early Royal Canadian Mounted Police were called the North-West Mounted Police. The force was established in 1873 to eliminate illegal trade in whiskey, collect customs duties, calm growing unrest among Canadian Indians, and fight lawlessness in western Canada.

Canadian Pacific

the winter of 1873-1874. The following summer, about 300 men rode west to the plains between the Manitoba border and the Rocky Mountains. The men established posts there, and quickly halted the smuggling of whisky from across the border. The Indians feared the police at first, but later came to respect the rugged men in the scarlet jackets. The N.W.M.P. soon established law and order on the plains.

In 1885, the Northwest Rebellion broke out in what is now central Saskatchewan. The North-West Mounted Police helped the militia stop the uprising, and later aided many settlers who wanted to establish homes on the prairies. During the gold rush to the Klondike in the late 1890's, the N.W.M.P. helped maintain order in the Yukon gold camps.

King Edward VII officially recognized the North-West Mounted Police in 1904 when he granted it the prefix *Royal*. The force became the Royal Canadian Mounted Police in 1920 when it merged with the Dominion Police and took over federal law enforcement.

The Royal Canadian Mounted Police agreed to enforce provincial law in Saskatchewan in 1928. In 1932, they also began serving as police in Manitoba, Alberta, New Brunswick, Nova Scotia, and Prince Edward Island.

During World War II, the Royal Canadian Mounted Police maintained Canada's internal security. Men from its ranks also served with the Canadian army overseas. In 1950, the RCMP took over provincial law enforcement in British Columbia and Newfoundland.   Critically reviewed by the ROYAL CANADIAN MOUNTED POLICE

See also CANADA, GOVERNMENT OF (color picture).

ROYAL COLONY. See COLONIAL LIFE IN AMERICA (Types of Colonies).

ROYAL CROWN COLA COMPANY. See SOFT DRINK (Leading Soft Drink Companies).

ROYAL DUTCH AIRLINES. See AIRLINE.

ROYAL GEOGRAPHICAL SOCIETY is a British organization composed of persons interested in new geographical facts and discoveries. In July, 1830, several hundred British subjects founded the society in London. It now has over 7,200 members in many countries. The society has a library and map room, which are open to the public. It promotes exploration and geographic research. The organization has headquarters at 1 Kensington Gore, London S.W. 7, England.   L. P. KIRWAN

ROYAL GORGE is a canyon of the Arkansas River, extending about 10 miles from Canon City, Colo. The gorge is more than 1,000 feet deep. It is the most remarkable chasm in the world through which a railroad passes. The canyon is only 30 feet wide at some points. Many bridgelike structures had to be built along the walls of the gorge for the railroad tracks. This roadway provides a water-level route through a mountainous section of the Rockies. The highest suspension bridge in the world, 1,053 feet above the water, spans the gorge at the top. See also ARKANSAS RIVER.   TIM K. KELLEY

ROYAL HOUSEHOLD OF GREAT BRITAIN includes officials who conduct the private business of the monarch and supervise all branches of court life. They have few powers of government. The *lord chamberlain* supervises the household. The *lord steward* controls household finances, and supervises the treasurer and the comptroller of the household. The *master of the horse*

cares for the royal stables. The queen's chief attendant is the *mistress of the robes*. She attends the queen on all state occasions. The *ladies of the bedchamber* are the queen's personal attendants. The original household offices, such as marshal, steward, and chamberlain, are hereditary in some families. These officials act only on ceremonial occasions.   I. J. SANDERS

ROYAL INSTITUTION is a scientific society, founded in England in 1799. King George III granted the society a charter in 1800. Its purpose is to encourage scientific study and to spread technical knowledge. The society has about 1,500 members.

Many brilliant scientists have been connected with the institution. These include Thomas Young, who worked out the wave-motion theory of light; Sir Humphry Davy, who invented the safety lamp for use in mines; and Michael Faraday, who did important work in the field of electrical research. The institution receives funds from private contributions. The public may attend its lectures. It has headquarters at 21 Albemarle St., London W. 1, England.   WATSON DAVIS

ROYAL JELLY. See BEE (Life of the Honeybee).

ROYAL MAUSOLEUM. See HAWAII (Places to Visit).

ROYAL MILITARY COLLEGE OF CANADA, in Kingston, Ont., is a college for cadets in the Canadian Armed Forces. Graduates receive a bachelor's degree in arts, science, or engineering, and a commission as an officer in the Canadian Armed Forces.

Royal Military College of Canada, with Royal Roads Military College, near Victoria, B.C., and Collège militaire royal de Saint-Jean, in St. Jean, Que., make up the Canadian Military Colleges. Cadets can begin college at any of the three schools. But they must spend their last two years at Royal Military College. Royal Military College cadets attend classes in the fall, winter, and spring. In summer, they are trained for their chosen element of the Canadian Armed Forces.

Royal Military College was founded in 1874. It is maintained and administered by the Canadian Department of Defence. For enrollment, see CANADA (table: Universities and Colleges).   WILLIAM P. HAYES

See also CANADA, ARMED FORCES OF.

ROYAL OAK, Mich. (pop. 85,499; alt. 661 ft.), is a residential community about 10 miles north of Detroit (see MICHIGAN [political map]). Nearby automobile plants employ most of the city's workers. Products of Royal Oak include metal stampings, farm machinery, tractor transmissions, and fabricated steel. Royal Oak has the Detroit Zoological Park, famous for its cageless exhibits. The Shrine of the Little Flower, made famous by Father Charles E. Coughlin, lies near Royal Oak.

The city was organized as a township in 1832, and incorporated as a city in 1921. Royal Oak has a commission-manager government.   WILLIS F. DUNBAR

ROYAL PALM is a common sight in tropical America. A tall, graceful tree, its trunk resembles a pillar. A cluster of feather-like leaves crowns its top. The royal palm grows in southern Florida, the West Indies, and Central America. See also PALM (picture).

Scientific Classification. The royal palm is in the palm family, *Palmae*. It makes up the genus *Roystonea*.

ROYAL SOCIETY is the oldest scientific society in the world and probably the most famous. The full title of the organization is *The Royal Society of London for Improving Natural Knowledge*. It grew out of weekly meetings which London scientists held as early as 1645. In 1660, the society was officially organized with the approval of King Charles II.

The British government soon recognized the importance of the society. In 1671, it gave the society the responsibility of directing the Royal Observatory at Greenwich. Later undertakings of the society included correcting the calendar in 1752, perfecting a way to protect British ships from lightning, and the measurement of a degree of latitude. The society directed many scientific expeditions, and worked out comparisons between the metric and English systems of weights and measurements. Today, the society does important work in many schools and scientific institutions in Great Britain. It has headquarters in London.   WATSON DAVIS

ROYAL SOCIETY OF CANADA was founded in Montreal, Canada, in 1882, to encourage interest in arts and sciences. Membership is open only to Canadians who have made important contributions in the arts, sciences, or literature. There are about 600 members. The society has done important work in the interest of the Canadian public. Its research is published annually in volumes called *Transactions*. The society awards medals for research, and scholarships to aid research. Headquarters are in the National Library Building, 395 Wellington Street, Ottawa 4, Ont.

Critically reviewed by the ROYAL SOCIETY OF CANADA

ROYAL WATER. See AQUA REGIA.

ROYALIST. See ENGLAND (The Civil War).

ROYALTY, a commission. See WRITING (Novels).

ROYALTY. See KING, with its Related Articles.

ROYCE, JOSIAH (1855-1916), an American philosopher, was the leading representative of a movement called *idealism*. Royce emphasized the religious aspect of philosophy and the need for a philosophical interpretation of religion. He developed a philosophy of loyalty that included a system of ethics, a theory of self-knowledge, and a theory of human society.

According to Royce, men gain self-knowledge through interaction with others, not in isolated contemplation. He urged men to be "loyal to loyalty." Royce believed that man's deepest problems can be solved by harmonizing conflicting interests through a commitment to a higher loyalty. For example, he regarded Christianity as the religion of loyalty that binds its followers together in a "beloved community."

Royce was born in Grass Valley, Calif. He taught at Harvard University from 1882 until his death. His best-known works include *The Spirit of Modern Philosophy* (1892), *The World and the Individual* (two volumes, 1900-1901), *The Philosophy of Loyalty* (1908), and *The Problem of Christianity* (1913).   JOHN E. SMITH

See also IDEALISM (In Philosophy).

ROZELLE, PETE (1927-   ), became commissioner of the National Football League (NFL) in 1960, and played a leading part in expanding professional football. In 1961, he helped persuade Congress to pass a law allowing professional sports leagues to grant television rights to a single network. This law allowed professional leagues to sign multimillion-dollar contracts for television. Television coverage did much to publicize the game. In 1966, Rozelle helped arrange a merger of the National and American football leagues, which ended their costly competition for outstanding players.

Alvin Ray Rozelle was born in South Gate, Calif.

He was general manager of the Los Angeles Rams before he became commissioner.   HERMAN WEISKOPF

RUANDA-URUNDI, *roo AHN dah oo ROON dee*, was a United Nations trust territory in east-central Africa administered by Belgium. The territory covered 20,916 square miles, and about 4,900,000 persons lived there. Usumbura (now Bujumbura) was the capital. In UN-supervised elections in 1961, Ruanda proclaimed itself a republic and Urundi established a monarchy. On July 1, 1962, the election results took effect and Ruanda became independent as RWANDA, and Urundi as BURUNDI. Kigali is the capital of Rwanda, and Bujumbura is the capital of Burundi.

Batwa pygmies were the earliest inhabitants of Ruanda-Urundi. The *Bahutu*, a Bantu people, came from the Congo basin and forced the Batwa into the forests (see BANTU). Then about 300 years ago, the tall *Watusi* from Ethiopia conquered the Bahutu and ruled the area.

British explorers Richard F. Burton and John H. Speke searched in the area for the source of the Nile in 1858. Henry M. Stanley and David Livingstone explored around Lake Tanganyika in 1871. German explorers arrived later. Germany made Ruanda-Urundi part of German East Africa in 1899. The League of Nations gave Belgium a mandate over Ruanda-Urundi in 1923, and the United Nations made it a Belgian trusteeship in 1946.   HARRY R. RUDIN

See also BURUNDI; KIGALI; RWANDA.

RUBÁIYÁT, *roo BYE YAHT,* is the title of a poem written by the Persian poet Omar Khayyám in the early A.D. 1100's. The word *rubáiyát* is an Arabic term which means a collection of *quatrains* (four-line stanzas).

The poem has many different moods. Some stanzas complain about the shortness of life and the injustice of the world. Others praise wine, pleasure, spring, flowers, or love. The 16th and 21st verses are typical of the beauty and philosophy of the *Rubáiyát*.

> The Worldly Hope men set their Hearts upon
> Turns Ashes—or it prospers; and anon,
>   Like Snow upon the Desert's dusty Face,
> Lighting a little hour or two—is gone.
>
> Ah, my Beloved, fill the Cup that clears
> To-day of past Regrets and future Fears:
>   To-morrow!—Why, To-morrow I may be
> Myself with Yesterday's Sev'n thousand Years.

The 12th stanza is probably the most quoted.

> A Book of Verses underneath the Bough,
> A Jug of Wine, a Loaf of Bread—and Thou
>   Beside me singing in the Wilderness—
> Ah, Wilderness were Paradise enow!

The *Rubáiyát* of Omar Khayyám has been translated into English by several authors. But the work of Edward FitzGerald is by far the most popular. FitzGerald did more than translate the verse from the Persian language. He created a genuine English lyric poem with delicate imagery and a clear, simple style. But at the same time, the poem is a faithful reproduction of the spirit of the Persian writer. FitzGerald's translation covers about 100 of the quatrains that have been credited to Omar Khayyám.   FRANZ ROSENTHAL

See also FITZGERALD, EDWARD; OMAR KHAYYÁM.

RUBBER is one of our most interesting and most important raw materials. *Natural rubber* comes from the juice of a tree. *Synthetic rubber* is made from chemicals.

Rubber is especially useful for several reasons. It holds air, keeps out moisture, and does not conduct electricity. But its chief importance to us is that it is *elastic*. When you stretch a rubber band and let it go, its elasticity makes it quickly spring back to its original shape. A rubber ball bounces because of this same springiness. Your rubber heels absorb shock when you walk because they have elasticity.

We depend so much on rubber that it would be almost impossible to get along without it. This is not the case with most other materials. If we lack one material, we can usually substitute another. A house can be built of wood, brick, stone, concrete, glass, or metal. Clothes can be made of cotton, silk, wool, or other fibers.

But what about the tires of an automobile, truck, or bus? It is hard to imagine making them of anything but rubber. Only rubber is elastic, airtight, water-resistant, shock-absorbing, and long-wearing.

During World War II, the Japanese captured the chief rubber-growing lands of southeastern Asia. They cut off almost all the natural-rubber supply from the Allies. Inventors tried to make tires from wood, leather, and steel springs. These tires did not work. Luckily, scientists found ways to make synthetic rubber for use in tires and other products. As a result, cars, trucks, and buses continued to run throughout the war. Without

The Natural Rubber Bureau

Rubber Can Be Made by Nature or by Man. These trees, *left*, on a Liberian plantation produce natural rubber. A giant chemical plant in Louisiana, *right*, makes synthetic rubber.

synthetic rubber, the Allies could not have won the war.

Manufacturers make between 40,000 and 50,000 rubber products. A typical automobile has about 550 rubber parts. Some cars, of course, use less rubber than this, and some use more. Many cars and buses even have springs made of rubber instead of steel.

Uses of Rubber

About 65 per cent of the rubber used in the United States goes into tires and tubes. These are used on automobiles, airplanes, buses, trucks, tractors, and con-

INTERESTING FACTS ABOUT RUBBER

Akron, Ohio, is called "the Rubber Capital of the World." It produces more rubber products than any other city.

"Champion" Rubber Trees can produce more than 20 pounds of rubber a year.

Consumption of rubber in the United States is 10 times as great per person as in the rest of the world.

Rubber can be made so elastic that it will stretch more than nine times its normal length.

Rubber Plantations throughout the world cover about 14½ million acres. This is more than the areas of Delaware, Maryland, and New Jersey combined.

Shasta Dam in California has a rubber conveyor belt 9 miles long.

Synthetic Rubber is made from chemicals obtained from such raw materials as petroleum, natural gas, coal, coke, grain, and potatoes.

Thomas A. Edison once made rubber from the latex of a giant goldenrod plant.

Tire and Tube Manufacturing accounts for about 65 of every 100 pounds of rubber used in the United States.

World's Largest Tire in regular production contains more than 1,700 pounds of natural rubber. It is used to carry oil-drilling equipment over the deserts of Saudi Arabia.

The Firestone Tire & Rubber Co.

USES OF RUBBER

HOME USES

DOOR MATS AND NONSKID MATERIALS

RUBBER BANDS

MATTRESSES AND CUSHIONS

JAR RINGS

WRINGERS

SPORTS SHOES

ICE-CUBE TRAYS

GALOSHES

FOOD COVERS

GLOVES

BOTTLE NIPPLES

PLAY USES

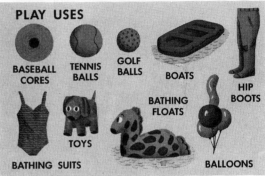

BASEBALL CORES

TENNIS BALLS

GOLF BALLS

BOATS

HIP BOOTS

BATHING FLOATS

TOYS

BATHING SUITS

BALLOONS

INDUSTRIAL USES

TIRES AND INNER TUBES

BATTERY BOXES

TRANSMISSION BELTS

CONVEYOR BELTS

TANK CAR LININGS

ELECTRICAL INSULATION

HOSE

WATERTIGHT BEARINGS

PAVEMENT EXPANSION JOINTS FOR BRIDGES

CATERPILLAR TREADS

OTHER USES

WATER BOTTLES

AIRPLANE WING DE-ICERS

PIPES

PAINT

FLOORING

OXYGEN MASKS

DIVING SUITS

ERASERS

RAINCOATS

Rubber Received Its Name when, in 1770, English chemist Joseph Priestley found it would rub off pencil marks.

Schoenfeld Collection, Three Lions

The Famous Mackintosh Raincoats, made of rubber between two layers of cloth, came on the market in 1823.

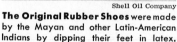

Shell Oil Company

The Original Rubber Shoes were made by the Mayan and other Latin-American Indians by dipping their feet in latex.

struction machinery. About one tenth is used for mechanical products such as gaskets, sealing devices, belting, and printing rollers.

Manufacturers use rubber to make waterproof aprons, boots, raincoats, gloves, and hats, and to give elasticity to other types of clothing and household fabrics. Hard-rubber goods include hair combs and automobile storage-battery cases. Doctors use rubber hot-water bottles, ice bags, syringes, elastic tapes, and surgeon's gloves. Hearing aids, iron lungs, oxygen tents, and many other pieces of equipment have rubber parts.

Swimmers wear rubber bathing suits and caps, goggles, and ear stoppers, and sun-bathe on rubber rafts. Many sports are played with rubber balls that range in size from small golf balls to large beach balls. Other rubber products include thread, bottle stoppers, toys, jar rings, elastic bands, rubber-based paints, erasers, and floor coverings.

Air pockets in sponge and foam rubbers make them springy. Manufacturers use such kinds of rubber for cushions, mattresses, pillows, and upholstery padding. They are also used as an insulating material. For example, some shoes have a layer of foam rubber next to the leather to keep out the cold.

Rubber cement can be used to hold pieces of paper together, but the pieces can be pulled apart easily. This cement is made of a solution of raw natural rubber in a solvent such as gasoline or benzol. The solvent evaporates, and the sticky rubber holds the paper together.

The Development of Rubber

First Uses. When the early European explorers came to Central and South America, they saw the Indians playing with bouncing balls made of rubber. According to an early Spanish historian, Christopher Columbus found the Indians of Haiti using balls "made from the gum of a tree." But later historians doubt this account, because it was written more than a hundred years after Columbus made his voyage.

The explorers learned that the Indians made "waterproof" shoes from *latex*, the milky white juice of the rubber tree. They spread the latex on their feet and let it dry. The Indians also made waterproof bottles by smoothing latex on a bottle-shaped clay mold. They dried the latex over a fire, and then washed out the clay.

The South American Indians called the rubber tree *cahuchu*, which means *weeping wood*. The drops of latex oozing from the bark made them think of big white tears. A French explorer, Charles Marie de La Condamine (1701-1774), gathered samples of hardened latex in Peru in 1735, and took them back to France. The French called this new material *caoutchouc*, the French pronunciation of the Indian name *cahuchu*. Variations of the French spelling are used as the word for rubber in most European countries. In 1770, the English chemist Joseph Priestley discovered that the material could be used as an eraser to *rub* out pencil marks. From this use, we get the name *rubber*.

The Rubber Industry Begins. By the late 1700's, scientists had found that hardened latex dissolved in turpentine made a waterproofing liquid for cloth. In the early 1820's, the English inventor Thomas Hancock (1786-1865) built what he called a "pickle machine" to knead scraps of rubber into a solid mass. His inventions and experiments led to the development of present-day rubber processing. In 1823, Charles Macintosh (1766-1843), a Scottish chemist, began manufacturing the "mackintosh" raincoats that became world-famous. He made them with a layer of rubber between two layers of cloth. Manufacturers in Europe and the United States began to make many rubber products, including elastic bands, raincoats, hoses, tubes, and shoes.

Discovery of Vulcanization. Early rubber products became sticky in hot weather, and stiff and brittle in cold weather. In 1839, Charles Goodyear, a Connecticut inventor, discovered a way to make rubber stronger and give it resistance to heat and cold. He accidentally spilled a sulfur-rubber mixture containing other ingredients on a hot stove while conducting an experiment. The rubber compound was "cured" by the heat, and

The First Vulcanization took place in 1839 when Charles Goodyear dropped a rubber-sulfur mixture on a hot stove.

Solid Rubber Tires were used in England in the 1800's. Thomas Hancock put them on Queen Victoria's carriage in 1846.

Pneumatic, or Air-Filled, Tires were first made successfully by John Dunlop of Great Britain in 1888.

stayed tough and firm in heat and cold. The process of heating sulfur-rubber mixtures became known as *vulcanization*, after Vulcan, the Roman god of fire. With vulcanized rubber, manufacturers could make dependable products, and the rubber industry grew rapidly. Vulcanized rubber was elastic, airtight, and watertight. It could be used to make tight seals between the moving parts of machinery.

The First Plantations. At first, manufacturers used only wild rubber. Most of it came from the Amazon Valley of Brazil, although some was from latex-bearing vines in Africa. At the request of the British government, an amateur botanist named Henry A. Wickham (1846-1928) took about 70,000 seeds of the *Hevea brasiliensis* tree from Brazil to England in 1876. About 2,500 of the seeds sprouted in a greenhouse at Kew Gardens near London. The seedlings were taken to Ceylon and Malaya for replanting on plantations. Almost all the plantation trees in the Far East come from these seedlings. The British, Dutch, and French developed plantations in Indonesia, Thailand, Indochina, and other countries of the Far East.

The invention of the automobile in the late 1800's created a tremendous demand for rubber. Planters in Malaya and Ceylon set out 100,000 acres of hevea trees in 1905, or almost twice as many as they previously had planted since 1876. By 1914, the yearly production of plantation rubber had exceeded that of wild rubber. Later, plantations were established in Africa, South and Central America, and the Philippines.

Development of Synthetic Rubbers. The importance of rubber in wartime became obvious during World War I. Armies needed rubber-tired vehicles to carry troops and supplies. The Germans were cut off from their natural-rubber supplies by the Allied blockade, and began to make synthetic rubber. But it did not work well. Experiments in producing synthetic rubber continued in the 1920's, chiefly by scientists in Germany and the United States.

When World War II began in 1939, Germany was manufacturing two chief types of synthetic rubber: (1) *Buna S*, made from *butadiene* (a gas) and *styrene* (a liquid made from coal tar and petroleum); and (2) *Buna N*, made from butadiene and acrylonitrile (a liquid ob-

tained from acetylene and hydrocyanic acid). Before 1939, experimenters in the United States made small amounts of several types of synthetic rubber to find a substitute for natural rubber. But the estimated cost of making these synthetic rubbers was much higher than that of natural rubber. For this reason, manufacturers still produced most products from natural rubber.

The United States produced only about 9,000 tons of synthetic rubber in 1941. The Japanese captured the rubber-growing lands of the Far East in 1942. This cut off nine-tenths of the natural-rubber supply to the United States. Almost overnight, the United States developed a great synthetic-rubber industry. The government built plants to produce Buna S and the styrene and butadiene needed for it. Rubber manufacturers and chemical companies operated the plants and pooled their knowledge about synthetic rubber. They worked with the government to develop ways to make as much synthetic rubber as they could, and as quickly as possible.

By the end of World War II in 1945, rubber production capacity in the United States had jumped to about 1,200,000 tons a year. The United States government sold its synthetic-rubber manufacturing plants to private companies in 1955.

The Rubber Industry

Production and Uses. About nine-tenths of the world's natural rubber grows on plantations in the Far East, chiefly in Malaysia and Indonesia. Other Far Eastern rubber-producing countries include Brunei, Burma, Cambodia, Ceylon, India, South Vietnam, and Thailand. Africa grows about 7 per cent of the world's supply of natural rubber, chiefly in Liberia, Nigeria, and Zaire. The remaining rubber supply comes from South America. Most Brazilian rubber comes from

461

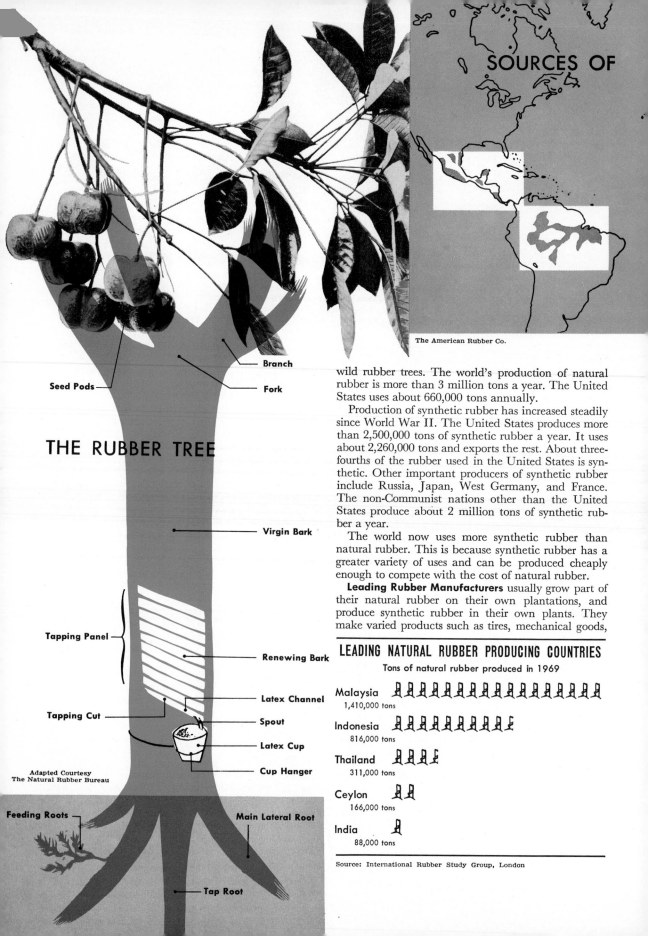

THE RUBBER TREE

Seed Pods

Branch

Fork

Virgin Bark

Tapping Panel

Renewing Bark

Latex Channel

Tapping Cut

Spout

Latex Cup

Cup Hanger

Adapted Courtesy
The Natural Rubber Bureau

Feeding Roots

Main Lateral Root

Tap Root

SOURCES OF

wild rubber trees. The world's production of natural rubber is more than 3 million tons a year. The United States uses about 660,000 tons annually.

Production of synthetic rubber has increased steadily since World War II. The United States produces more than 2,500,000 tons of synthetic rubber a year. It uses about 2,260,000 tons and exports the rest. About three-fourths of the rubber used in the United States is synthetic. Other important producers of synthetic rubber include Russia, Japan, West Germany, and France. The non-Communist nations other than the United States produce about 2 million tons of synthetic rubber a year.

The world now uses more synthetic rubber than natural rubber. This is because synthetic rubber has a greater variety of uses and can be produced cheaply enough to compete with the cost of natural rubber.

Leading Rubber Manufacturers usually grow part of their natural rubber on their own plantations, and produce synthetic rubber in their own plants. They make varied products such as tires, mechanical goods,

LEADING NATURAL RUBBER PRODUCING COUNTRIES
Tons of natural rubber produced in 1969

Malaysia
1,410,000 tons

Indonesia
816,000 tons

Thailand
311,000 tons

Ceylon
166,000 tons

India
88,000 tons

Source: International Rubber Study Group, London

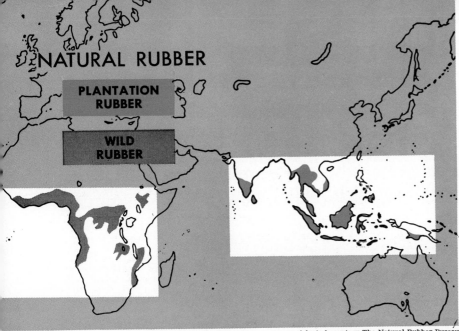

NATURAL RUBBER

PLANTATION RUBBER

WILD RUBBER

Natural rubber comes chiefly from rubber trees grown on plantations in southeastern Asia. Some rubber is also obtained from wild rubber plants, chiefly in Africa and in Central and South America.

Adapted courtesy The Natural Rubber Bureau

industrial products, shoe materials and footwear, aircraft parts, and rubberized textiles. Some companies also produce, for their own use and for sale to other firms, raw materials used to make synthetic rubber. The big rubber companies produce plastics as well as rubber, because synthetic rubbers and plastics are much alike chemically. The five largest rubber companies in the United States are described below. For sales, assets, and number of employees of the four largest, see MANUFACTURING (table: 100 Leading U.S. Manufacturers).

Firestone Tire & Rubber Company is the second largest rubber manufacturer in the United States. Founded in 1900 by Harvey S. Firestone, the company has plants in Akron and 22 other U.S. cities. It operates subsidiaries and plants in 22 other countries. Company headquarters are in Akron.

General Tire & Rubber Company, the fifth largest rubber manufacturer, was founded by William O'Neil in 1915. The company has 41 plants in the United States and plants in 18 other countries. Company headquarters are in Akron.

B. F. Goodrich Company, the fourth largest rubber manufacturer, was founded in 1870 by B. F. Goodrich.

The company has plants in Akron and 25 other U.S. cities. It operates subsidiaries and plants in 14 other countries. Company headquarters are in Akron.

Goodyear Tire & Rubber Company is the largest rubber manufacturer in the United States. The company was founded in 1898. It has 36 plants in the United States and 39 plants in other countries. Company headquarters are in Akron.

WORLD PRODUCTION OF RUBBER

Year	Natural Rubber (Tons)	Synthetic Rubber* (Tons)
1900	50,000	—
1910	107,000	—
1920	383,000	—
1930	923,000	—
1940	1,587,000	48,000
1950	2,083,000	643,000
1960	2,221,000	2,231,000
1969	3,147,000	6,066,000

*Russia included from 1953; Communist China, from 1961.
Sources: FAO; International Rubber Study Group, London

LEADING SYNTHETIC RUBBER PRODUCING COUNTRIES

Tons of synthetic rubber produced in 1969

United States
2,520,000 tons

Russia
772,000 tons

Japan
580,000 tons

Germany (West)
322,000 tons

France
303,000 tons

Sources: FAO; International Rubber Study Group, London

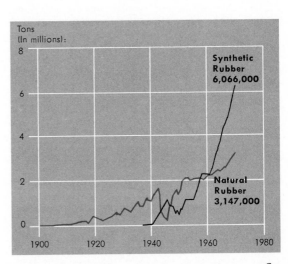

Tons (In millions):

Synthetic Rubber 6,066,000

Natural Rubber 3,147,000

THE PRODUCTION OF NATURAL RUBBER

Growing a Rubber Tree starts with planting a root, *above*, on which a bud has been grafted. The bud sprouts into a young rubber tree, *right*. Grafting enables rubber companies to produce trees that yield more rubber than those grown directly from seeds.

Tapping the Tree, *left*, is done by plantation workers with sharp tools called *gouges*. Latex oozes from a cut in the bark and flows through a spout to a cup. Workers pour latex from the cups into pails and carry it to collection stations, *right*, for weighing.

Uniroyal, Inc., formerly United States Rubber Company, the third largest rubber manufacturer, operates plants in 41 U.S. cities. It has subsidiaries and plants in 23 other countries, with headquarters in New York City. It was formed in 1892 by the consolidation of nine separate companies.

Natural Rubber

Latex is found in many kinds of trees and plants. You can see latex oozing from the broken stem of a dandelion or from a cut branch of goldenrod. Latex is still something of a mystery to scientists. They know that it is not a sap, but they are not sure of its use to the plant. Scientists believe that it acts as a protective substance when a plant is wounded.

Chemical analysis shows that about 30 to 35 per cent of latex consists of pure rubber. Water makes up another 60 to 65 per cent. The remainder consists of small amounts of other materials such as resins, proteins, sugar, and mineral matter. Latex holds little *globules* (particles) of rubber in the same way that milk holds butterfat. Latex spoils easily, and must be processed into *crude rubber* as soon as possible after tapping. This is done by separating the natural rubber in the latex from water and other materials. About 99 of every 100 pounds of natural rubber comes from the latex of the *Hevea brasiliensis*. This is the tree that we call the *rubber tree*.

The Rubber Tree. The hevea tree grows best in hot, moist climates in deep, rich soils. The finest rubber-growing regions lie within a *rubber belt* that extends about 700 miles on each side of the equator. Almost all natural rubber comes from huge plantations of rubber trees in the Far East.

The rubber tree cultivated on plantations grows straight and slender, about 60 to 70 feet tall. It has smooth, light-colored bark and shiny, dark leaves. When its pale yellow blossoms fade, seed pods grow in their place. Each pod contains three brownish, speckled seeds about an inch long. The latex containing the rubber flows through a series of tubes in the tree's

cambium layer, the outer wood layer directly under the bark. When this layer is pierced, the milky white latex oozes out. Botanists work continually to improve the hevea tree. By grafting and careful breeding, they have developed trees that produce more than six times as much natural rubber as the wild hevea. They hope to increase the yield of latex by giving hormones and vitamins to the tree.

Rubber has also been collected from *landolphia* vines that grow in Africa. In Mexico, *guayule* bushes have been cultivated for their rubber, but they produce only a small amount. In Brazil, a small amount of rubber comes from wild hevea trees. Other rubber-bearing trees include the *manihot* tree, also found in Brazil, and the trees of the genus *Castilloa* found in Central America, Colombia, and Ecuador.

Tapping the Tree. Rubber plantations employ workers called *tappers* who collect latex from the trees. A tapper starts tapping trees at daybreak, because the latex flows most freely in the cool morning air. He carries a *gouge*, a long, sharp knife with a curved blade. The tapper cuts a narrow groove in the bark of a tree about four feet above the ground. The groove slants diagonally downward about halfway around the trunk. At the bottom of the cut, the tapper attaches a V-shaped metal spout, and below it, a small cup. Latex oozes from the cut and flows down the groove through the spout. The spout directs the juice, drop by drop, into the cup. The tapper then moves to another tree and cuts it in the same way. He taps about 350 trees on one round of tapping. This task takes about three hours. After tapping his last tree, the tapper makes a second round to collect the latex. At each tree he collects about a teacupful of latex. He empties the cups into a large pail and carries the latex to the plantation's collecting station. There, the latex is turned into crude rubber.

Some plantations tap the trees every other day. Other plantations tap every day for 15 days, and then allow the trees to "rest" for 15 days. On each tapping, the

Baling and Shipping take place after the latex has been processed into crude rubber. The rubber passes through rollers that squeeze out the water, and then is pressed, *left*, into 224-pound bales. On this Liberian plantation, workers load the bales on riverboats, *right*, that carry them to the port of Monrovia where the rubber is shipped on freighters to the United States.

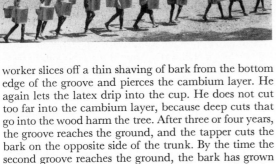

The Firestone Tire & Rubber Co.

worker slices off a thin shaving of bark from the bottom edge of the groove and pierces the cambium layer. He again lets the latex drip into the cup. He does not cut too far into the cambium layer, because deep cuts that go into the wood harm the tree. After three or four years, the groove reaches the ground, and the tapper cuts the bark on the opposite side of the trunk. By the time the second groove reaches the ground, the bark has grown back on the first groove, and it can be tapped again.

Workers begin to tap rubber trees about five to seven years after planting. But younger trees do not give so much rubber as they do about the tenth year, when they are fully grown. Rubber trees in Sumatra yield their full capacity of latex for about 25 to 30 years. About a hundred trees grow on one acre, and each full-grown tree produces from one to four gallons of latex a year. An acre of trees on a large, well-developed plantation may yield more than 1,500 pounds of dry crude rubber a year.

Separating the Latex. Most plantations make crude rubber from latex by *coagulation*. Tappers pour latex from their collecting pails into tanks, and add an equal amount of water. They strain the diluted latex through sieves to remove dirt and bits of bark or twigs that may have fallen in during the tapping process. Formic acid is then added to the strained latex to make it *coagulate*, or form solid particles. Acid thickens latex in much the same way that vinegar curdles milk. The rubber particles rise to the surface of the liquid and form a doughy white mass of crude rubber.

Processing Crude Rubber. Workers feed the crude rubber through rollers that squeeze out the water. One type of roller produces sheets of crude rubber that have a ribbed appearance. These sheets are hung to dry for several days in a hot smokehouse. The smoke turns the rubber brown, and kills molds and bacteria that would rot it. The workers press the dried sheets into 224-pound bales for shipment to market. This form of crude rubber is called *ribbed smoke sheet*.

Pale crepe rubber is formed by passing the doughy mass through rollers that roughen and crinkle the sheets so that they look like thick crepe paper. The rubber is constantly washed while being rolled. The sheets hang in heating rooms and turn pale yellow while they dry. The sheets keep this color if a chemical preservative is added to the latex. Workers bale the pale, crinkled sheets for shipment. *Crepe rubber* is often used in the soles of shoes. *Amber crepes, brown crepes,* and *flat-bark crepes* come from poorer quality sheets that have had less careful preparation.

The oldest method of making crude rubber from latex is by drying the latex over a smoky fire. This method still supplies the small amount of rubber that comes to market in the form of large, black balls called *biscuits*. To form a biscuit, a worker dips a wooden paddle into the fresh latex and holds it over a smoky fire. After the heat and smoke dry the latex, he re-dips the paddle and smokes a new coating. Gradually, he builds up many layers of dried latex until he forms a large biscuit of crude rubber.

Processing Latex. Sometimes, all the latex collected on plantations is not coagulated. Workers place part of the fresh latex in machines called *separators*, similar to those used by dairies to separate cream from milk. These machines remove part of the water from the latex. Ammonia or some other preservative keeps the latex from coagulating and prevents spoiling. The preserved liquid latex is sent to market in drums or tanks. Rubber manufacturers use latex to make articles such as surgeon's gloves, foamed-latex mattresses, and furniture upholstery.

Manufacturing Rubber Products

Manufacturers obtain bales of dry rubber from plantations and from synthetic-rubber manufacturing plants. Latex comes to them in big tanks on ships and in tank cars. Manufacturers usually process natural and synthetic rubber in much the same way, although latex requires different steps.

Plasticization involves only dry rubber. It is a series

465

of processes that makes dry rubber softer and more *plastic*, or easier to mold.

Workers first slice the big bales into small pieces of rubber that they can handle easily. The lower grades of natural rubber receive a thorough washing in a wringerlike machine called a *wash mill*. Then the rubber slices are fed into mixing mills and other machines that *plasticize*, or soften, them into a doughlike mass. Manufacturers plasticize the rubber faster by heating it and adding materials called *plasticizers* and *softeners*. Machines for plasticizing include (1) roll mills, (2) internal mixers, and (3) plasticators.

Roll Mills usually consist of two rotating cylinders that turn toward each other at different speeds. The slices of rubber are placed on rolls that pass between the rotating cylinders. The pressure of the rolls squeezes and flattens the slices into a doughy sheet that sticks to the slow-moving cylinder. Cutting the sheet and doubling it back on top of the rolls makes it possible to rework the rubber several times until it reaches the desired degree of softness.

Internal Mixers work more rapidly than roll mills, and plasticize larger batches. One type, called the Banbury mixer, works somewhat like a roll mill. But the two rotating cylinders knead the rubber inside an enclosed chamber. Instead of being smooth, each cylinder has a spiral-shaped ridge along its surface. Thus, the rubber is kneaded in two ways: (1) by the two cylinders as the rubber passes between them, and (2) by the spiral-shaped ridge on the cylinder as it squeezes the rubber against the chamber wall. It operates much like the mixer that a baker uses to knead dough.

Plasticators operate on the same principle as meat grinders. Each has a large barrel-like chamber enclosing two *threaded*, or spirally grooved, rolls called *screws*. As the screws rotate, they work a continuous strip of rubber between their threads and the inside of the cylinder.

Compounding and Mixing. Compounding means adding carefully measured amounts of various ingredients to plasticized rubber and to latex. The compounding "recipe" helps control the elasticity, strength, and other properties of the final product. The chief ingredients used in compounding dry rubber are (1) sulfur, (2) accelerators, (3) pigments, (4) antioxidants, (5) reclaimed rubber, and (6) fillers.

Sulfur is the principal ingredient most commonly used to bring about *vulcanization*, a process that takes place later in rubber manufacturing.

Accelerators are added to the rubber to speed vulcanization. They also improve the properties of the final product, and help make it uniform throughout. A variety of chemicals serve as accelerators.

Pigments, such as carbon black, make the rubber stronger and give it greater resistance to wear (see Carbon).

Antioxidants protect rubber against chemical changes and the harmful effects of heat, sunlight, and air. Some chemicals prevent cracking caused by ozone and oxidation (see Oxidation; Ozone).

Reclaimed Rubber is obtained by treating waste rubber, such as old tires, with heat and chemicals. This treatment makes rubber compounds softer and easier to handle so they can be reworked on mills and other equipment. They can then be revulcanized. In some places, reclaimed rubber is used in place of crude rubber.

Fillers may be added to dry rubber to increase its volume and to make a stronger, more flexible product. *Neutral*, or *inert*, fillers such as clay make the compound easier to handle, but do not increase its strength.

Shaping. Manufacturers use several methods to shape rubber into final products. These include (1) calendering, (2) extrusion, (3) molding, and (4) dipping.

Calendering means rolling rubber into sheets. It is done on a machine that has two to five rolls mounted one above the other. A conveyer belt carries the rubber from a roll mill to the top roll of the calender. The rubber passes between each pair of rotating rolls. They press it into a continuous sheet that comes off the lowest roll. Steam or cold water runs through the rolls to regulate the temperature. If the rolls are too hot, the rubber sheets will blister. If the rolls are too cold, the sheets will be too rough. Workers adjust the spacing between the rolls to form sheets as thin as one or two thousandths of an inch, or as thick as two tenths of an inch. They cut the sheets into sizes and patterns, or stock them in layers to make many products. These include rubber flooring, toys, bed sheets, baby pants, and mechanical goods such as wrapping tapes, washers, rings, and discs.

Extrusion is the final step in the processing of some rubber products. The word *extrude* means to push out. *Tube machines* push soft rubber through a hole, much as toothpaste is squeezed from a tube. The shape of extruded rubber depends upon the shape of the hole through which the rubber is pushed. Extruded products include hoses, inner tubes, and rubber strips used on refrigerator doors and automobile windshields. Extruded products are vulcanized after they have been formed.

Molding produces shoe soles and heels, rubber tires, hot-water bottles, mattresses, hard-rubber articles, and industrial products such as gaskets and fittings. Workers prepare pieces of rubber in the approximate size and shape of the finished product. They put the pieces in molds shaped to form the final product. Many products are formed in molds and vulcanized at the same time. During vulcanization, the rubber takes the exact shape of the mold in which it has been placed.

Dipping is used only to make products from liquid latex. Products made by dipping include rubber gloves

HOW A SPONGE RUBBER BALL IS MADE

Making a ball is like baking a cake. First, rubber is compounded with bicarbonate of soda, *left*. The rubber is placed in a mold the size of the finished ball, *center*. Heat makes the rubber rise like a cake, *right*.

MAKING SYNTHETIC RUBBER

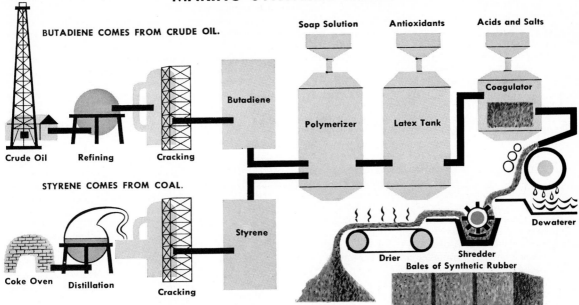

BUTADIENE COMES FROM CRUDE OIL.

Crude Oil　Refining　Cracking　Butadiene

Soap Solution　Antioxidants　Acids and Salts

Polymerizer　Latex Tank　Coagulator

Dewaterer

STYRENE COMES FROM COAL.

Coke Oven　Distillation　Cracking　Styrene

Drier　Shredder
Bales of Synthetic Rubber

and toy balloons. Workers dip molds, usually made of metal, glass, or ceramic materials, into tanks of latex. They drain the excess latex, and dry the mold at low temperatures. By repeating this process, they build up several layers on the mold.

Vulcanization is usually the last step in preparing a final product. It gives strength, hardness, and elasticity to rubber by treating it with heat and vulcanizing agents such as sulfur. During vulcanization, the heat causes the sulfur to combine with the rubber and cure it. This makes the rubber stronger and more durable. Generally, the more sulfur that is added, the firmer the vulcanized compound will be. A compound containing one-third sulfur and two-thirds rubber vulcanizes to form *ebonite*, or hard rubber. Manufacturers use benzoyl peroxide instead of sulfur to vulcanize silicone rubbers. Scientists know of many other vulcanizing agents, including tellurium, selenium, and certain benzene compounds. These agents are seldom used commercially, because they cost more than sulfur.

Vulcanization may take from a few minutes to several hours. Small products such as toys and shoe soles require about 5 to 7 minutes, but large products such as tires take from 45 to 60 minutes. Compounds containing accelerators and sulfur vulcanize faster than plain sulfur compounds without accelerators.

Manufacturers vulcanize and shape molded products at the same time by heating the molds under pressure. They vulcanize extruded and sheet products on pans in hot-air or steam chambers. Dipped products are vulcanized in hot water, hot air, or open steam before being removed from the molds. Foam products in molds are vulcanized in steam chambers or boiling water.

Sponge Rubber may be made either from dry rubber or from latex. *Blowing* produces one type of sponge rubber from dry rubber. During vulcanization, the chemicals that have been added turn to gas and "blow" tiny bubbles of air in the rubber compound. When the rub-

ber *gels*, or sets, in the mold, the bubbles are trapped in it. Blown sponge rubber may be either hard or soft.

Foam rubber is a type of sponge rubber made by whipping air into latex, much as a cook whips air into egg whites. Vulcanization takes place after the foam gels in a mold. Foam rubber has millions of tiny cells filled with air. Some types may be nine-tenths air and only one-tenth rubber. Foam rubber is widely used for automobile cushions, mattresses, pillows, upholstery, and foam strips for surgical use.

Synthetic Rubber

Rubberlike materials made from chemicals were called synthetic rubbers because they were intended as substitutes for natural rubber. Synthetic rubber has a close relationship to plastic. In fact, it can be described as a "rubberlike plastic." In the polyurethane family, for instance, there is no real dividing line between polyurethane rubbers and polyurethane plastics. For this reason, chemists use the word *elastomer* for any substance, including rubber, that stretches easily to several times its length, and returns to its original shape.

Manufacturers group synthetic rubbers into two classes: general-purpose and special-purpose. General-purpose rubbers can be used in place of natural rubber. Special-purpose rubbers improve upon nature. They have special properties such as great resistance to grease, air, and extreme temperatures, that make them better than natural rubber for certain uses.

General-Purpose Synthetic Rubbers. The most important general-purpose rubber is styrene-butadiene rubber (SBR). It usually consists of about three parts butadiene and one part styrene. Chemists make butadiene, a gas, from alcohol or from gaseous products obtained during petroleum refining. The butadiene must be compressed into liquid form for use in manufacturing rubber. Styrene is a liquid manufactured from coal tar or petroleum.

RUBBER

Styrene and butadiene usually come to the synthetic-rubber plant in tank cars or tank trucks. Sometimes they are piped in directly from the plants that produce them. Correct amounts of styrene and butadiene are pumped into a big tank containing a mixture of soap and water. The mixture is heated or cooled depending on the type of SBR being made. A catalyst causes the styrene and butadiene to combine with each other (see CATALYSIS). Gradually, with stirring, the ingredients change to a milky white fluid, also called *latex*. This synthetic latex looks much like natural latex from rubber trees.

Workers pump the latex into another tank where antioxidants are added. Acids and salts are added in a third tank called a *coagulator*. The salts and acids coagulate the latex. The rubber forms into lumps that float on top of the liquid. Washing the lumps removes extra chemicals. After drying, the lumps may be packed as loose crumbs or pressed into big bales of dry rubber.

American rubber companies produce about four times as much SBR as all other types of synthetic rubber combined. Manufacturers use SBR rubbers to make such products as tires, shoes, foamed sponge rubber, backings for rugs, air springs, and rubber parts for automobiles.

Special-Purpose Rubbers. Contact with gasoline, oils, sunlight, and air harms natural rubber. Special-purpose synthetic rubbers resist these "enemies" better than natural rubber or SBR do. Also, some of these special-purpose rubbers have greater resistance to heat and cold. They cost more than natural rubber or SBR, but their special properties make them worth the difference. Special-purpose rubbers include (1) butyl rubber, (2) cis-polyisoprene rubber, (3) neoprene rubber, (4) nitrile rubber, (5) polysulfide rubbers, (6) polyurethane rubbers, and (7) silicone rubber.

Butyl Rubber holds air and gases much better than natural rubber. It has wide use in inner tubes and in linings of tubeless tires. It resists aging, heat, and the harmful effects of acids, and does not conduct electricity. The chief ingredients of butyl rubber include isobutylene (a gas) and isoprene (a liquid). Both are by-products of petroleum refining.

Cis-Polyisoprene Rubber may eliminate our reliance on distant plantations for natural rubber. Its chemical composition is almost the same as natural rubber. It works just as well as natural rubber for products such as heavy truck tires and heavy motor mountings. Chemists have produced only a small amount of this rubber, which is prepared from isoprene.

Neoprene Rubbers resist oxygen, sunlight, oil, gasoline, and other chemicals better than natural rubber does. Their chief uses include gasoline hose, insulation for wire and cables that come in contact with oil, and gaskets for use as seals against oil or gas. Neoprene rubber is made from acetylene gas, which is produced from coal and limestone (see ACETYLENE).

Nitrile Rubber (Buna N) has an especially high resistance to the harmful effects of gasoline, grease, oil, wax, and solvents. It withstands heat (up to 350°F.) much better than natural rubber and most synthetic rubbers. Nitrile rubber is used in gasoline hoses, paper, leather products, and many types of cloth. It contains varying proportions of butadiene and acrylonitrile. Acrylonitrile comes from the chemical reaction between acetylene and hydrocyanic acid.

Polysulfide Rubbers, such as Thiokol, have unusually good resistance to softening and swelling in gasoline and greases. They also resist aging, air, and sunlight. Their chief uses include the lining of gasoline hoses, and for printing plates and rollers. Ethylene dichloride and sodium polysulfide are the main ingredients of polysulfide rubbers.

Polyurethane Rubbers resist age and heat, and withstand remarkable stresses and pressures. They can be made so tough that they will outlast natural rubber as materials for tires. Manufacturers use them in limited amounts, chiefly for upholstery, foam-rubber mattresses, and insulating materials. Polyurethane foams come in a great variety of types, from flexible to rigid, and from dense to light. The ingredients of polyurethane rubbers include ethylene, propylene, glycols, and adipic acid.

Silicone Rubbers keep their rubberlike properties at much higher and lower temperatures than natural rubber or any other type of synthetic rubber. They can be used at temperatures ranging from −130°F. to 600°F. Other rubbers become brittle and useless at such temperatures. Manufacturers use silicone rubbers in such products as seals, gaskets, and other parts of jet planes and machinery exposed to high temperatures. Silicone rubbers are made of oxygen and silicon, with a hydrocarbon added to the silicon.

The Chemistry of Rubber

The Chemistry of Natural Rubber has presented a challenge to scientists since its discovery. Why did vulcanization make rubber stronger and tougher? Could rubber be made synthetically?

In 1826, Michael Faraday, an English physicist and chemist, discovered that rubber is a hydrocarbon. That is, it belongs to a large family of substances composed of hydrogen and carbon. Other well-known hydrocarbons include gasoline, motor oil, natural gas, and oil of turpentine. This explains why so many synthetic rubbers are made from petroleum products. See HYDROCARBON.

In 1860, another Englishman, Greville Williams, heated some rubber and obtained a colorless liquid that he called *isoprene*. Each isoprene molecule contains five carbon atoms and eight hydrogen atoms (C_5H_8). The atoms in the isoprene molecule always form a definite pattern. Four of the carbon atoms form a chain. The fifth carbon atom branches off from one of the carbons in the *chain*. Three hydrogen atoms surround the fifth carbon atom to form a *methyl group*. The following chemical symbols show the arrangement of the five carbon and eight hydrogen atoms in the isoprene molecule:

468

In natural rubber, thousands of tiny isoprene molecules link together in a giant, chainlike molecule, the rubber molecule. Chemists call such chainlike molecules *polymers*, meaning "many parts." They call single molecules, such as isoprene, *monomers*.

The particular chainlike structure of the rubber polymer explains why rubber is elastic. Polymer molecules of unstretched rubber fold back on themselves somewhat like irregular coils. Stretching the rubber straightens the chain of folded molecules. Releasing the rubber lets the chain return to its coiled position.

The sulfur that combines with the rubber during vulcanization sets up "cross links" between the rubber chains. The chains in unvulcanized rubber can slip. Therefore, the rubber will not have elasticity. During vulcanization, the cross links bind the chains together so they cannot slip past one another. This gives elasticity and strength to the vulcanized product. However, if the cross linking is carried too far, the cross links tend to stop the unfolding of the chains. This reduces the elasticity of the rubber. The number of cross links increases according to the amount of sulfur that is added to the rubber compound. With large amounts of sulfur, the rubber becomes stiffer, tougher, and less stretchable, until it turns into hard rubber.

Chemists believe that the characteristics of many rubberlike substances depend on the way their atoms are joined together. For example, they know that each carbon atom in a rubber molecule can combine with four other atoms. When the carbon atom holds four other atoms, it can hold no more. It is then said to be *saturated*. If it holds less than four atoms, it is *unsaturated*. Unsaturated atoms can hook on to other atoms.

Natural rubber has many unsaturated carbon atoms. Oxygen atoms from the air gradually attach themselves to the carbon atoms. This breaks down the rubber polymers so that the rubber becomes brittle and loses elasticity. The addition of antioxidants during compounding prevents this action.

Scientists have not discovered all the answers to the chemistry of rubber. For example, they once believed that sulfur atoms attached themselves to unsaturated carbon atoms during vulcanization. But the sulfur reaction that makes rubber hard now seems more complicated than this. In many other ways, the chemistry of natural rubber remains a mystery.

The Chemistry of Synthetic Rubber. For years, chemists tried in vain to duplicate the true rubber polymer with isoprene monomers. One big problem was to join isoprene monomers end to end to build up a long chainlike polymer, as in rubber. The carbon atoms in the center of the isoprene monomer are unsaturated. The problem was to prevent the atoms in the center from connecting with one another. Otherwise, the polymer would branch out at the side instead of joining at the end to form a long chain.

Scientists finally discovered how to approximate the giant polymer of natural rubber. The process for making synthetic rubber was difficult to discover, but is now rather simple.

Isoprene monomers make a difficult building block. This is why scientists made the first successful synthetic rubbers from the monomers of other hydrocarbons. These monomers included butadiene (C_4H_6), styrene ($C_2H_3C_6H_5$), isobutylene (C_4H_8), acrylonitrile (C_2H_3CN), and chloroprene (C_4H_5Cl). Each of these building blocks can be made in several different ways, from a wide variety of raw materials. Silicone rubbers are quite different from the other synthetic rubbers. The chain of the polymer is made of silicon and oxygen atoms instead of carbon.

Research in rubber is directed mainly toward making better synthetic rubbers to provide improved rubber products for home and industrial use. In addition, many unusual types of rubber will be required for the new age of atomic energy and space travel. As the new supersonic planes and missiles fly higher and faster, they require rubber parts that can withstand temperatures from $-120°F.$ to $700°F.$ Chemists hope to develop rubbers that increase protection against nuclear radiation in atomic plants.

Research also tries to develop better processing methods. Scientists hope to vulcanize rubber by the use of atomic radiation. Some new synthetics, including certain kinds of polyurethanes, do not need vulcanization at all.   HARVEY S. FIRESTONE, JR.

Related Articles in WORLD BOOK include:

Outline

I. **Uses of Rubber**
II. **The Development of Rubber**
III. **The Rubber Industry**
    A. Production and Uses
    B. Leading Rubber Manufacturers
IV. **Natural Rubber**
    A. The Rubber Tree   D. Processing Crude
    B. Tapping the Tree   Rubber
    C. Separating the Latex E. Processing Latex
V. **Manufacturing Rubber Products**
    A. Plasticization   C. Shaping
    B. Compounding and   D. Vulcanization
        Mixing   E. Sponge Rubber
VI. **Synthetic Rubber**
    A. General-Purpose Synthetic Rubbers
    B. Special-Purpose Rubbers
VII. **The Chemistry of Rubber**
    A. The Chemistry of Natural Rubber
    B. The Chemistry of Synthetic Rubber
    C. Research

Questions

Who first used the name "rubber"? Why?

What accident led to the discovery of vulcanization? Who made this discovery?

What country first developed general-purpose synthetic rubber?

What event brought about the first successful mass production of synthetic rubber?

What countries grow most of the world's natural rubber?

What is the world's greatest rubber-manufacturing city?

What is latex? Why is it said to be something of a mystery?

How are rubber trees tapped? Why is tapping done early in the morning?

At what age do rubber trees produce the most rubber? What is crude rubber?

How are "biscuits" of rubber formed?

How does the chemical structure of rubber explain its elasticity?

What country produces the most synthetic rubber?

469

RUBBER PLANT

RUBBER PLANT is the common name for a house plant that is related to the fig. The rubber plant can grow well in house heat and lack of humidity. It grows tall rapidly and lives a long time. The leaves are large and broad and may grow from 2 to 12 inches long. The upper surface of the leaf is a shiny, dark green color, and the under side is dull and lighter green. The rubber plant requires little care. It will grow well if the soil in the pot is rich in minerals and the plant is given enough sunlight, water, and room. The plant should be placed outdoors during the summer so that it will get enough sunlight to last during the winter months. A rubber plant may grow so tall that it may be necessary to cut it back to make it branch. Sometimes a new plant can be grown from the tip of the stem that is cut off.

Rubber plants are often attacked by scale insects. These pests can be destroyed by spraying the plants

J. Horace McFarland

The Attractive Rubber Plant is frequently grown in pots in the home. It has thick, glossy, rubberlike leaves.

with nicotine. Commercial rubber does not come from these rubber plants, but from a tropical tree that belongs to the castor-bean family.

Scientific Classification. Rubber plants are in the mulberry family, *Moraceae*. The common rubber plant is genus *Ficus*, species *F. elastica*. The more decorative rubber plant is the fiddle fig, *F. lyrata*.   MARCUS MAXON

RUBEL, IRA. See PRINTING (Developments in Platemaking).

RUBELLA. See GERMAN MEASLES.

RUBELLITE. See TOURMALINE.

RUBENS, PETER PAUL (1577-1640), was the greatest Flemish painter of the 1600's. In addition to his paintings, Rubens made designs for book illustrations and tapestries, and occasionally for architecture and sculpture. He was also a noted scholar and a respected diplomat.

Detail of an oil self-portrait
on canvas (1640);
Kunsthistorisches Museum, Vienna

Peter Paul Rubens

His Life. Rubens was born in Siegen, Germany, of Flemish parents. After his father died in 1587, his mother returned with her children to her native city of Antwerp. There, Rubens studied under local painters. He moved to Italy in 1600 to study art. In Italy, he was employed as a painter by Vincenzo Gonzaga, duke of Mantua. In 1603, the duke sent Rubens to Spain as a member of a diplomatic mission. After returning to Italy, he continued his painting and his art studies.

Rubens went back to Antwerp in 1608, to visit his sick mother, but she died before he arrived. In Antwerp, Rubens was offered several important commissions for paintings, and he decided to remain in the city. In 1609, he married Isabella Brant, a member of a prominent Antwerp family. They had three children.

Also in 1609, Rubens became court painter to the Brussels court of Archduke Albert and the Infanta Isabella. Rubens' fame as a painter spread, and noblemen throughout Europe sought his services. He also received many commissions from churches.

To carry out his commissions for large-scale works, Rubens trained several young artists to be his assistants. However, he still completed much of the work himself. Rubens never claimed any of his assistants' pictures as his own unless he had retouched them thoroughly. His most famous assistant was the Flemish artist Anton Van Dyck.

After his wife died in 1626, Rubens accepted several diplomatic assignments involving peace negotiations between England and Spain. His assignments took him to Madrid in 1628 and to London in 1629. King Charles I of England knighted Rubens for his skill in diplomacy.

Rubens married again in 1630 and gradually withdrew from political life. His second wife was a beautiful 16-year-old girl, Hélène Fourment. Hélène, like Rubens' first wife, was a member of a prominent Antwerp family. Rubens painted her many times. They had five children. After 1635, Rubens spent much time at his country estate near Brussels. The beautiful landscape scenes he painted there reflect his love for Flanders.

His Art. The most important influence on Rubens' style was the ancient Roman sculpture he studied in Italy. He was also influenced by the paintings and sculptures of such Italian Renaissance artists as Michelangelo, Raphael, Tintoretto, Titian, and Paolo Veronese. Among the artists of his own time, Rubens especially admired Michelangelo Caravaggio and Annibale Carracci.

Rubens was the most important baroque artist of northern Europe. His paintings are known for their vast

Rubens' *Coronation of Marie de Médicis,* was one of a series of pictures painted by the artist to glorify Queen Marie de Médicis of France and her late husband, King Henry IV. The painting shows the drama, rich color, and vitality that characterized Rubens' baroque style.

scale, brilliant colors, and emotional intensity. Rubens completed an enormous number of works. In one commission during the 1620's, he painted 24 large pictures on the life of Marie de Médicis, the widow of King Henry IV of France. From 1630 to 1635, he painted nine huge canvases for the Banqueting House at Whitehall in London. In the mid-1630's, he organized the artists of Antwerp to decorate structures in the city according to his designs to celebrate the visit of a new Spanish governor.

Rubens' subjects include hunting scenes, Biblical episodes, stories from classical mythology, portraits and self-portraits, and landscapes. *Elevation of the Cross* is an example of his baroque style. It is reproduced in color in the PAINTING article. JULIUS S. HELD

See also BAROQUE; DANIEL (picture); NEW TESTA-MENT (picture).

RUBICON, *ROO bih kahn,* is a stream near Rimini, Italy, that Julius Caesar made famous when he was governor of Gaul. The Rubicon was part of the boundary between Roman Italy and the Roman province of Cisalpine Gaul (the Po valley). Caesar and other Roman governors were forbidden to cross the boundary with troops. Caesar was commanding troops in Gaul when the Roman Senate, fearing his power, ordered him to give up his command. Caesar refused, and led his men across the Rubicon on Jan. 10, 49 B.C. This action symbolized the start of Caesar's successful drive for the leadership of Rome. The expression *to cross the Rubicon* means to make a decision that cannot be changed.

The name Rubicon comes from the Latin word *rubeus* meaning *red.* The stream got its name because its waters are colored red by mud deposits. It may be the same as the present-day Fiumicino River. CHESTER G. STARR

See also CAESAR, GAIUS JULIUS.

RUBIDIUM, *roo BIH dee uhm,* is a soft, silvery-white metallic element. The German scientists Gustav Kirchhoff and Robert Bunsen discovered it in 1861. Rubidium occurs abundantly in the earth's crust. But, it is so widely distributed that its production is limited. It is usually obtained from minerals used for lithium production. Industry uses rubidium as a catalyst, and in making photocells and vacuum tubes.

Rubidium has the chemical symbol Rb. Its atomic number is 37, and its atomic weight is 85.47. Rubidium oxidizes readily in air and is a fire hazard. It dissolves in acids and melts at 38.89° C. J. GORDON PARR

RUBINSTEIN, ANTON GREGOR (1829-1894), was a Russian pianist and composer. His tours throughout Europe and America made him the most famous pianist of his time. Few of his many compositions are played today. Rubinstein was born near Balta, in the Ukraine. At 10, he made his first public appearance in Moscow. While still a child, he traveled through Europe. Audiences everywhere received his playing with enthusiasm.

When Rubinstein was 16, he began to teach in Vienna. Two years later he went to St. Petersburg (now Leningrad). There the Grand Duchess Helen became his patroness and gave him many opportunities to be heard in public. In 1858, he became court pianist and concert conductor. The following year, he became director of the Royal Russian Musical Society, and four years later he founded the St. Petersburg Conservatory. He served as its director until 1867, and again from 1887 to 1890. Rubinstein came to the United States in 1872 and toured the country. ROBERT U. NELSON

Anton Rubinstein
Brown Bros.

RUBINSTEIN, ARTHUR

Natl. Concert & Artists
Arthur Rubinstein

RUBINSTEIN, ARTHUR (1889-   ), is an American pianist of Polish descent. He made his first American tour in 1906. He began to tour widely in 1913. After World War II broke out, he lived in California for many years, but then returned to Europe. Rubinstein was born in Łódz, near Warsaw. He studied in Berlin and appeared at 12 as a soloist with the Berlin Symphony Orchestra. For a short time, he studied with Ignace Jan Paderewski. He became an American citizen in 1946.   ROBERT U. NELSON

RUBLE, *ROO b'l,* or ROUBLE, is the monetary unit of Russia. The ruble is divided into 100 *kopecks* (see KOPECK). The real value of Russian currency is difficult to determine, since there is no free international exchange. For the value of the ruble in dollars, see MONEY (table: Values of Monetary Units).

Chase Manhattan Bank Money Museum
Ruble Is Russia's Basic Monetary Unit.

Russian currency in circulation includes treasury notes (paper money) in values of 1, 3, and 5 rubles. Copper-nickel coins are used in denominations of 1 ruble and 10, 15, 20, and 50 kopecks. Copper-zinc coins are made in values of 1, 2, 3, and 5 kopecks. BURTON H. HOBSON

RUBY is the red gem variety of the aluminum oxide mineral *corundum.* It is the rarest, and, in large sizes, the costliest of the gems. Sapphires and fancy sapphires are other color varieties of this mineral. Corundum is colorless when pure, but a trace of chromium oxide impurity gives it the red color of the ruby. This color may range from a light red or rose, known as pink sapphire, to the most highly valued deep bluish red, called *pigeon blood.* The finest rubies come from Burma, and paler ones come from Ceylon. Those of Thailand are a yellower red. Small, poor-quality rubies have been found in North Carolina.

A large perfect Burma ruby may be worth several times as much as a diamond of the same size. Corundum is one of the hardest minerals known. Synthetic or artificial rubies and sapphires have the same hardness and composition as the real stone. Millions of carats of the synthetic stone are made each year for use as gems.

Their value is as low as a few cents a carat, but they have not hurt the market for the real stone. The expert can easily tell the synthetic product from the natural stone. Garnets are often sold under misleading names such as Arizona ruby and Cape ruby.

The ruby is the birthstone for July and the symbol for the fortieth wedding anniversary.   FREDERICK H. POUGH

See also CORUNDUM; GARNET; GEM (Imitation and Artificial Gems; color picture); SAPPHIRE.

RUBY, JACK. See KENNEDY, JOHN FITZGERALD (The Death of Oswald); WARREN REPORT.

RUDDER. See AIRPLANE (Parts of an Airplane); SHIP (The Chief Parts of a Ship).

RUDOLF LAKE. See LAKE RUDOLF.

RUDOLPH, LUCRETIA. See GARFIELD, JAMES A. (Garfield's Family).

RUDOLPH, WILMA. See TRACK AND FIELD (Famous Track and Field Champions).

RUE, *roo,* is the French word for *street.*

RUFF is a sandpiper native to the Eastern Hemisphere. During the mating season, the male develops a tuft of feathers on his neck that he can erect into a ruff. The birds range in color from black and chestnut to

Field Museum of Natural History, Chicago
The Ruff Is a Sandpiper found in the Eastern Hemisphere. The male develops a large "ruff" of neck feathers at mating time.

buff and whitish. The female, called a *reeve,* has more modest plumage than the male. Ruffs are occasionally seen on the East Coast of North America.

Scientific Classification. The ruff belongs to the sandpiper family, *Scolopacidae.* It is classified as genus *Philomachus,* species *P. pugnax.*   GEORGE E. HUDSON

RUFFED GROUSE is a thickly feathered grouse of North America. It is famous for the drumming sounds the male bird makes with his wings. He picks some special log for his drumming and goes to it daily early in the morning. For many years, naturalists thought that the bird drummed by beating his wings against the log, against his breast, or against each other. They now believe that he merely beats the air with his wings. At first the sounds are dull and well spaced, but as the bird warms to his work, the drumming becomes a long roll. The sound can be heard for a great distance, and

472

may seem to be as loud a quarter of a mile away as it does close by.

The male grows about 17 inches long. A thick collar of feathers around the bird's neck gives him his name. These feathers are a gleaming black and can be lifted outward until they look like a ruff.

The ruffed grouse makes its nest at the foot of a tree. The nest may be formed from leaves, and may contain from nine to 14 eggs. The birds do not fly south in the autumn. In winter, the leg feathers of the grouse grow longer for warmth, and a weblike structure grows between its toes which allows it to walk over the surface of snow. The ruffed grouse is the state bird of Pennsylvania.

Scientific Classification. Ruffed grouse belong to the grouse family, *Tetraonidae*. They are genus *Bonasa*, species *B. umbellus*.   JOSEPH J. HICKEY

See also BIRD (color picture: Game Birds); GROUSE.

RUFFIN, EDMUND (1794-1865), was a noted Virginia farmer and a strong supporter of slavery. He favored *secession* (withdrawal) from the Union, and was given the honor of firing the first shot on Fort Sumter, S.C., where the Civil War was started in 1861.

Ruffin was born in Prince George County, Virginia. He experimented in crop rotation and with improved plowing, drainage, and fertilizing methods. He wrote about his theories and experiments, and helped bring about important changes in farming methods in the South. Ruffin founded the *Farmer's Register*, an agricultural journal, in 1833, and headed the Virginia State Agricultural Society from 1852 to 1854. Ruffin was so disturbed when the South lost the Civil War that he committed suicide.   FRANK L. KLEMENT

RUGBY FOOTBALL is a fast, rough game played by two teams of players. Each team tries to score by kicking, passing, or carrying the ball until they can kick it over the opponent's goal or touch it down behind the opponent's goal line. The team that scores the most points wins the game.

There are two main versions of rugby football—*rugby union* and *rugby league*. Amateur teams of 15 players each play rugby union. Thirteen-man amateur or professional teams play rugby league.

American football developed from rugby, and the two games are similar in many ways. In both games, the players may kick, pass, and run with an oval ball. And opposing players may tackle the ball carrier. But American football consists of *plays* (planned maneuvers) separated by brief periods of inaction. Rugby football features almost continuous play.

Like American football, rugby football involves rough play such as kicking and tackling. However, rugby players wear little protective equipment. The rugby players wear only thin shirts, shorts, knee-length stockings, and cleated shoes. Some players wear shin guards.

Rugby Rules

Rugby games are divided into two *halves* (periods), usually of 40 minutes each. There is a rest period of not more than 5 minutes between halves, and the teams change goals for the second half. In rugby union the referees may add up to 3 minutes of playing time for *stoppages* (times-out) caused by injuries. Injured players who leave the field during a game cannot resume play

without permission of the referee. Substitute players cannot replace others during a match.

The Field is a rectangle, up to 75 yards wide between two *touch lines* and up to 110 yards long between the two *goal lines*. Goal posts 18 feet 6 inches apart and over 11 feet high stand on each goal line. Each set of goal posts has a crossbar 10 feet above the ground.

The Ball is an air-filled bladder covered with leather. The rugby union ball is 11 to $11\frac{1}{4}$ inches long and from 24 to $25\frac{1}{2}$ inches around the center. It weighs from $13\frac{1}{2}$ to 15 ounces. The rugby league ball is slightly smaller.

The Officials include a *referee* and two *touch judges*. The referee controls the game, and his judgment is final. He enforces the rules, and serves as timekeeper and scorekeeper. The touch judges signal when and where the ball goes *in touch* (out of bounds), and may help decide whether a kick at goal is successful.

The Team. A 15-man rugby union team has 1 fullback, 4 three-quarter backs, 2 halfbacks, and 8 forwards. A rugby league 13-man team has 6 forwards.

At certain points in a game, the forwards link themselves together tightly and lower their heads to make a formation called a *scrum* or *scrummage*. In this position, the two opposing lines of forwards form a tunnel into which the ball is tossed. The man in the center of the scrum, the *hooker*, tries to *heel* (kick) the ball back out of the formation to a teammate.

The halfbacks include the *scrum half* and the *standoff*. The scrum half tosses the ball into the scrummage, and receives the ball if his forwards manage to heel it

The Rugged Forwards on Rugby Teams leap high and fight hard to get the ball for their team when it is thrown into play.
Keystone

RUGBY FOOTBALL

The Kick-Off

Scoring a Goal

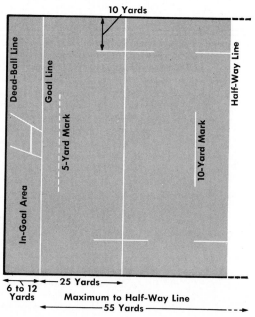

Scoring a Try

back. The stand-off "stands off" from the scrum to link up with the three-quarter line of backs. He is also called the *fly half* in rugby union and the *outside half* in rugby league. The three-quarter backs include two *wingers* and two *centers*. With the stand-off, these players form the team's attacking unit. They try to advance the ball down the field and score. The fullback is the last line of defense. He tries to stop the attacking team and intercept the ball.

Scoring in rugby football includes a *try* and a *goal*. A player scores a try when he touches the ball down in the opponent's in-goal area. This counts 3 points. After scoring a try, a player on the scoring team may

convert it into a goal. To *convert* a try (score a *conversion*), he place-kicks the ball over the crossbar from a point opposite the spot where his team scored the try. Defensive players must stand behind their own goal line while he kicks. A successful conversion adds 2 points, so a converted try counts 5 points.

There are two kinds of goals, a *dropped goal* and a *penalty goal*. Each counts 3 points in a rugby union and 2 points in a rugby league. A player scores a dropped goal by drop-kicking the ball over the crossbar while it is in play. He scores a penalty goal by drop-kicking or place-kicking over the crossbar on a penalty kick.

In a rugby union, a player who is awarded a free kick

THE RUGBY UNION FIELD

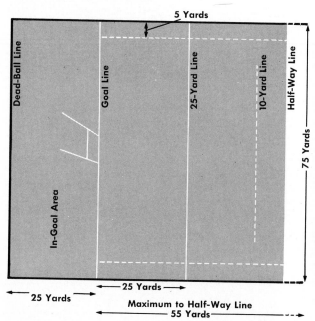

THE RUGBY LEAGUE FIELD

Scrum

Handing Off

Place Kick

Drop Kick

Punt

Tackling

Passing

for a *fair catch* can score a *goal-from-a-mark*. A fair catch occurs when the player catches the ball after an opponent kicks it. He makes a mark with his heel, and calls, "Mark." Opposing players then stand at the mark, and the player who made the fair catch must drop-kick or place-kick the ball over the crossbar from the spot at which he caught the ball.

How to Play Rugby Football

The Kickoff starts a rugby football game, and also starts play in the second half. A player place-kicks the ball from the center spot on the halfway line. The receiving team stands behind the 10-yard line.

The team that gets the ball then tries to move it over the opponent's goal line by running with it, or passing or kicking it to other team members. They often *dribble* (nudge the ball ahead) with their legs or feet as they run downfield. Players cannot pass the ball *forward* (toward the opponent's goal). When a player is tackled and downed, he must release the ball. But play continues, and any player may pick up the ball or kick it. When the ball goes out of bounds, or play stops for another reason, the team that did not cause the stoppage puts the ball in play in a scrum.

The wing man on the team that did not stop play tosses it in between the two lines of forwards, and each group tries to heel the ball out to its backs. The back who receives the ball from the scrum then starts downfield with his fellow backs, running, kicking, or passing the ball laterally. Players ahead of a teammate who is advancing the ball are *offside*. They cannot play the ball until the man with the ball has passed them. Usually, the backs run downfield, dodging opponents, then kicking or passing off to a teammate when an opponent is about to tackle them. A player with the ball may avoid a tackle by *handing off* his opponent. That is, he may push the opponent away with the palm of his hand. But he cannot strike or punch.

In rugby union, players also form a *loose scrum* of one or more players on each team. When a ball carrier is tackled and downed, he must let the ball go "loose."

The forwards then form a scrum around the ball. Players are penalized if they *knock on* (hit the ball toward the opponent's goal line with hand or arm).

History

Many people believe that rugby began at Rugby School, England, in 1823. In 1871, 21 clubs in London formed the Rugby Football Union. In 1871-1872, the Scots formed a union, and Oxford and Cambridge played the first university match at Oxford.

In 1877, the rules were revised to reduce the number of players in a team from 20 to 15. In 1893, the strictly amateur Rugby Union refused to allow payment to players in northern England. Players in some northern counties then formed the Northern Union. In 1922, they changed its name to the *Rugby League*, and began playing with 13 players on a team.

Both forms of rugby are now played in Australia, Britain, France, New Zealand, and South Africa.

See also FOOTBALL; SOCCER.

RUGBY SCHOOL is a famous English public school founded in 1567 at Rugby, England, through a bequest of Laurence Sheriffe. England's "public" schools are not free schools. They are endowed institutions for secondary education. Rugby's playground was one of the founding places of Rugby football. The school became one of England's leading public schools under Thomas Arnold, who was headmaster in 1828. Arnold is the popular headmaster in the book *Tom Brown's School Days*, by Thomas Hughes. Rugby's average enrollment is more than 500. R. W. MORRIS

RUGG, HAROLD ORDWAY (1886-1960), an American educator, aroused nationwide controversy through his efforts to reform the teaching of social studies. He served as professor of education at Teachers College, Columbia University, from 1920 until 1951. After his retirement in 1951, Rugg lectured in Egypt and served as a visiting professor at the University of Puerto Rico. He was born at Fitchburg, Mass., and received degrees from Dartmouth College and also from the University of Illinois. JOHN S. BRUBACHER

473

RUGS AND CARPETS are floor coverings used in homes and other buildings. They are useful for many reasons. They add warmth and comfort to a room. They soften noises and protect floors. They also add beauty. A carefully chosen rug or carpet not only adds its own color and loveliness, but also sets the feeling and tone for a whole room. It can fit together various furniture styles. It can blend the colors used in decorating the room. It can add to the beauty of other furnishings.

The terms *rug* and *carpet* are often used interchangeably. But generally, a rug covers only part of a floor and is not fastened down. A carpet covers the entire floor. Carpets are made in various widths, such as 9, 12, or 15 feet. Rugs may be made in prefinished standard sizes, such as 9 feet by 12 feet, or cut from rolls of carpet. *Broadloom* refers to carpets made on wide looms or machines more than 6 feet wide. It is simply a term of measurement and does not refer to any quality, style, or method of construction.

How Rugs and Carpets Are Made

Weaving Rugs and Carpets. Woven rugs and carpets used today are produced mechanically on big machines called *looms.* Oriental rugs are woven on looms, too, but they are made by hand. Rugmakers use much the same steps in both kinds of weaving. These steps are much like the ones used for making cloth. See WEAVING.

Long threads of cotton, wool, or silk are stretched from the back of the loom to the front. They form the *warp* (lengthwise foundation threads) of the rug. The crosswise foundation threads are called the *weft.* On most handmade rugs, the warp threads are fastened to the loom at both ends. Thus, the handmade rug can be only as large as the warp and weft. On power looms, the warp threads unwind from large spools as they are needed. The carpet can be as long as the weaver wants.

The *pile*, or surface material, is added to the warp threads. The pile contains the rug's design. On Oriental rugs, the pile is formed by tying tufts of wool, silk, or camel's hair to the warp threads. The weaver leaves the loose ends of the knotted yarn sticking out on the side facing him. This becomes the top of the rug. The ends of warp threads become the fringes at the ends of the rug. On machine-made rugs, long threads of yarn are woven through the warp in a definite pattern to form the pile. After one row of the pile has been added, by either process, a weft thread of the same material as the warp is woven in, over and under the warp threads. The row of pile threads and the row of weft thread are pressed tightly together with a blunt instrument called a *comb.* Row after row of pile and weft threads are added until the rug is completed.

On machine-made rugs, the pile may be a tuft with loose ends. Or it may be a loop of yarn. For some carpeting, the machine-made loop is cut after the weaving is completed. Cutting a loop leaves two tufts.

Other Ways of Making Rugs. Many rugs are not woven. Rugs made from scraps of cloth are called *rag rugs.* Many rag rugs are made by braiding. The rugmaker starts by tearing the rags into long, thin strips. Then he sews together the ends of the strips to form long bands of cloth. The band for a braided rug may be an inch wide, or even less. The rugmaker then braids the bands together. When the rugmaker has a long enough braid, he sews the flat sides together to form the rug. Many color combinations are possible. Braided rugs are usually made in simple round or oval shapes.

Another kind of handmade rug is made by pushing tufts of yarn through a cloth backing. These rugs are called *hooked* or *embroidered* rugs, depending on whether the yarn is punched through the rug with a hook or is used in an embroidery needle. Persons who make these rugs at home follow designs printed or drawn on the backing. The designs show where to use the different colored yarns or threads.

Oriental Rugs

Many of the skills of modern rugmaking can be traced back to the first methods of making Oriental rugs. These beautiful rugs are still made in the same way that they were hundreds of years ago.

The Art of Oriental Rugmaking has been handed down from father to son for hundreds of years. Ancient processes are used in shearing, bleaching, picking, and spinning the wool to make the yarn. Dyeing the wool is a part of the process that requires great skill. The dyes used are made from leaves, roots, barks, and certain insects.

Weaving an Oriental rug takes a long time. Often it is a family enterprise. A designer creates the pattern and colors for the rug. Dyers follow the designer's instructions in making the colors. Weavers produce the rug under the direction of a master weaver. The width of the rug determines how many weavers work on it. One man may make a narrow rug, and eight or ten

Metropolitan Museum of Art

Embroidered Rugs that were made in early America are valuable as collector's items today. The Caswell Carpet, *above*, was made in 1835 by Zeruah Higley Guernsey of Castleton, Vt.

Bucilla

Cotton-Tufted Rugs have a backing of burlap or similar material. Tufts are made from loops of cotton yarn. Then they are sewed separately onto the backing. The rugs are long-wearing and washable.

Nahigian Bros.

Oriental Rugs are costly and beautiful. Weaving them is a slow and painstaking process. The prayer rug, *left,* is a Kermanshah, one of the finest antique Persian weaves.

Modern Design is often used in hooked rugs. *Eastward, below,* was designed by the painter Irene Rice Pereira and made by Gloria Finn. It was hooked with a punch needle.

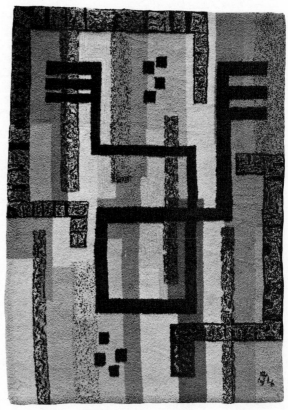

MACHINE-MADE RUGS AND CARPETS

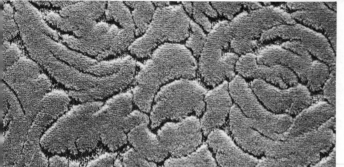

The Carpet Institute

Bigelow-Sanford Carpet Co.

Looped Cotton Rugs and Carpets are moderately priced. They come in bright colors. The small-size rugs can be washed in home washing machines.

Sculptured Wool Carpets are given a pattern by *sculpturing* the pile, or trimming it to different heights. The surface then has a single-colored design.

Fiber Rugs are made from such materials as wood, paper, or grass. They can be used on either side, and this means that they will wear well for a long time.

Deltox Rug Co.

will work on a wide one. They knot each tuft of pile in place, and see that all knots are about the same size. Then they weave two weft threads through the warp and hammer the weft and the row of knots with a blunt comb. Next, they trim the row of knots to the same depth as the pile already on the loom.

The commercial value of an Oriental rug depends on the size and closeness of the weave. Tightly woven rugs are more valuable, because they wear better. Antique Oriental rugs are also valued for rarity and beauty.

Kinds of Oriental Rugs. There are six distinct groups of Oriental rugs—Persian, Turkish, Turkmen, Caucasian, Chinese, and India rugs. Each group has many subdivisions. Rugs are usually named for the towns where they are woven. A rug's name indicates its type, but not the quality or closeness of its weave. Experts can tell the region, and often the town, where a rug was made by inspecting its design and weave.

Persian rugs are made in Iran (formerly Persia). Among the best-known Persian weaves produced today are the Sarouk, the Kerman (or Kirman), and the Keshan. Beautiful antique Persian rugs come from Tabriz, Kermanshah, Feraghan, and Laver. Leading names in the *Turkish* rug group are Ghiordes, Koula, and Ladik. Famous *Turkmen* rugs, from the region of central Asia called Turkestan, include the Bokhara, the Khiva, and the Samarkand. Beautiful patterns among *Caucasian* Oriental rugs are the Cabistan, the Daghistan, the Kazak, and the Karabagh. Fine *India* rugs come from the ancient cities of Agra and Lahore. *Chinese* Oriental rugs have designs and lotus-flower patterns woven into backgrounds of blue, red, or yellow. They are named for the dynasties during which they were made, rather than for places or regions.

Most modern Oriental rugs imported into the United States today are *washed* in a mild chemical solution to soften and give luster to the pile.

Prayer Rugs with beautiful designs come from all the

Moslem regions of Asia. The designs of all prayer rugs include an arrow or some pointed shape that indicates the head and foot of the rug. Moslems face Mecca as they kneel to pray, and so they place the prayer rug with the pointed design directed toward Mecca.

Modern Rugs and Carpets

Rugs and carpets are made today in factories on power-driven looms, or on tufting or knitting machines. The U.S. rug and carpet industry produces about $1,000,000,000 worth of floor coverings each year. Leading rug- and carpet-producing states are Georgia, Pennsylvania, North Carolina, South Carolina, and Virginia.

Loom-Made Rugs are divided into three main types, *Wilton*, *Axminster*, and *velvet*. A fourth type, *chenille*, is no longer produced in the United States. It is manufactured only in limited quantities in England.

Wilton rugs are woven on a Jacquard loom. This kind of loom raises a yarn of the correct color to the surface of the rug to make a pattern. All yarns except the pattern yarn are buried under the surface of the rug. Only the desired color shows in the design. This method of weaving gives the rug great depth, springiness, and strength. From three to six different colored yarns may be used in making the pattern. There is also a way of

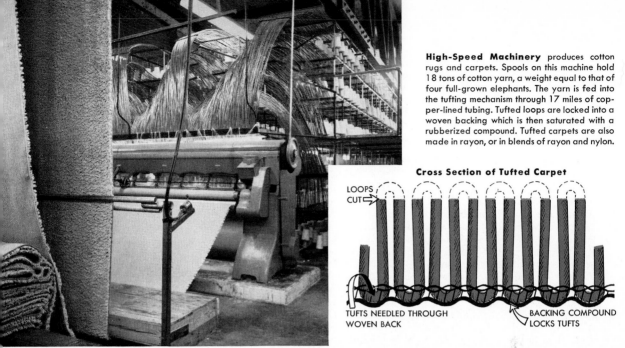

Cross Section of Tufted Carpet

LOOPS
CUT→

TUFTS NEEDLED THROUGH WOVEN BACK

BACKING COMPOUND LOCKS TUFTS

Photographs Courtesy of Bigelow-Sanford Carpet Co.

Cross Section of Axminster Weave

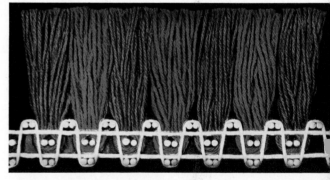

Cross Section of Wilton Weave

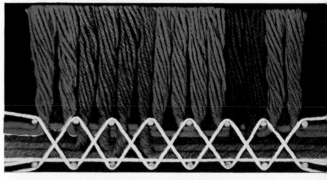

Cross Section of Velvet Weave

adding color on a Jacquard loom by using *moresque* strands, in which several colors are spun together.

Axminster rugs are named for the town in England where they were first made, in the 1700's. In an Axminster rug, the pile yarn is attached to the backing, one tuft at a time. The tuft is knotted to the backing, but most of the yarn is on the surface of the rug. Almost any number of colors can be used in making an Axminster, because each tuft comes from a separate spool.

Velvet rugs are made with the simplest of all rug weaves. They are woven on looms much like those used for making regular cloth. A layer of pile yarn loops is bound to a layer of jute with linen or cotton threads. Then the pile loops are cut, forming a smooth surface. Velvet rugs are usually made of just one color. Patterns are sometimes printed on the surface of solid-color velvet rugs. If the loops in velvet are left uncut, the weave is sometimes called *tapestry* weave.

Tufted Rugs are the leading type produced in the United States. A variety of colorful designs and textures can be produced by this method. In this high-speed process, pile yarns are sewed to a prewoven backing by a wide machine using hundreds of needles. The tufts are then firmly attached to the backing with a rubberized latex compound. The backing may be made of jute or synthetic fibers. Both natural and synthetic fibers are used in the tufts.

Knitted Rugs are produced in many different styles. Knitting machines use features of both loom and tufting processes. Knitting machines produce rugs faster than looms but slower than tufting machines.

Care and Cleaning

Rugs and carpets should be cleaned with a carpet sweeper or a vacuum cleaner. Sweeping with a broom usually only raises the dust and dirt and moves it to some other part of the rug. Spots and stains should be removed quickly.

Even with regular vacuum cleaning, dirt gets stuck below the surface of the pile, next to the warp and weft. Dirt also clings to the pile itself. Wall-to-wall carpeting can be professionally cleaned on the floor without being taken up and relaid. But rugs should be sent out to a professional cleaner at regular intervals. The cleaner vacuums and washes both sides of the rug with more powerful machines than are used in homes.

History

In prehistoric times, men put animal skins on the floors of their caves, huts, and tents. They used the skins for the same reasons that we use rugs and carpets today—for warmth, comfort, and quiet. When man learned to weave, he used *textiles* in place of skins. Rugs and other textiles were among the first means of adding beauty and color to homes.

Some museums have fragments of rugs that were probably made nearly 3,500 years ago. No one knows exactly where rugweaving began, but it was probably somewhere in Asia. Egyptian temples were decorated with rugs, but these were flat textiles, without piles. The art of Oriental rugmaking, with deep piles, developed in the Near East.

The Moors brought the art of rugweaving to Europe when they conquered Spain in the 700's. Tapestry weaving began a little later, in the south of France. By the 1450's, a carpetmakers' guild had been organized in Paris. Two popular styles of French rugs were already well known at that time. One is the *Aubusson* tapestry. The other is the *Savonnerie*, woven with a deep pile in the hand-knotted Oriental technique. Both types used the same general colors and patterns.

Weaving got its first real start in England in the 1300's, when Edward III invited Flemish weavers to the country. They made expensive tapestries that were used as wall hangings. The people continued to cover their floors with inexpensive rushes. But rugweaving was well established by the late 1500's.

In North America, early settlers made their own floor coverings from rags. Colonists imported woven rugs from England. Trading ships brought rugs from the Orient. The American Indians learned to make beautiful rugs (see INDIAN, AMERICAN [color picture: The Navahos]).

About 1800, Joseph Marie Jacquard, a weaver of Lyon, France, invented the loom that bears his name. This loom arranged the different colors of yarn to go into a pattern through a device like the roll for a player piano. In 1839, a power loom for making carpets was invented in Lowell, Mass. Erastus Bigelow perfected the loom two years later. Halcyon Skinner, another American, perfected a power-driven Axminster loom in 1876. Many improvements have been made since then.

Today, both natural and synthetic fibers are used to make rugs and carpets. The natural fibers are wool and cotton. Synthetic fibers are *acrylics* and *modacrylics*, *nylon, polypropylene olefin, rayon,* and *acetate.*

Critically reviewed by the AMERICAN CARPET INSTITUTE

Related Articles in WORLD BOOK include:

Carpet Beetle	Jacquard, Joseph M.	Turkestan
Flower (color picture:	Philippines (picture)	(picture)
Flowers in Art)	Tapestry	Weaving
Islamic Art (picture)		

RUHR, *roor,* is a coal-mining and industrial region in northwestern Germany. Several branches of the Rhine River run through the region, including the Ruhr River, from which it takes its name. The area most commonly known as the Ruhr is rectangular in shape, with corners roughly at Hamm, Lüdenscheid, Mönchen-Gladbach, and Wesel. The Ruhr covers about 1,770 square miles. People sometimes refer to a greater Ruhr area, which includes the Cologne and Bonn regions.

The People and Their Work. The Ruhr is one of the most crowded sections of Europe. It has a population of about 5,700,000, excluding the Cologne and Bonn areas. Dortmund, Duisburg, Düsseldorf, Essen, and Wuppertal are large industrial cities in this region. The entire area along the Ruhr River from Duisburg to Dortmund forms practically one continuous city.

The Ruhr includes one of the largest concentrations of industry in the world. It has great coal fields and a great transportation network that includes railroads and river and canal developments. The region's industries produce chemicals, iron and steel, and textiles.

History. The Ruhr became important to German industry in the mid-1800's. Its huge coal fields and fine transportation facilities made it important as a coal-mining area. In 1871, Germany won control of most of Alsace and Lorraine after the Franco-Prussian War.

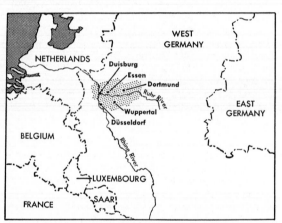

The Ruhr Is the Shaded Area Around Essen.

This made iron ore from Lorraine available to German industries without customs duties. Industrialists in the Ruhr area began to bring in ore from Lorraine, and the region developed into an industrial center rather than simply a mining area. Firms such as Krupp and Thyssen developed many phases of the Ruhr's industries.

Germany lost Lorraine after World War I. For a time it seemed likely that the Ruhr would again become only a mining district. But the German government paid huge sums to iron manufacturers for the loss of Lorraine. With this money, the industrialists built smelting works that could process iron ore from Sweden.

By 1922, Germany had fallen behind in paying France and Belgium for damages caused during World War I. French and Belgian troops occupied the Ruhr in January, 1923, as a means of forcing Germany to make its payments. But the German government encouraged Ruhr workers to follow a policy of passive

Jacob van Ruisdael's Painting, *The Mill,* is an example of landscape painting at its best. The paintings and etchings by this Dutch artist have made scenes of windmills and canals in The Netherlands familiar to people throughout the world.

resistance and to produce as little as possible during the occupation.

The French took harsh steps to increase German production. But all their measures failed. The decrease in production of the Ruhr soon affected the economic life of France and Germany disastrously. Both countries headed toward national bankruptcy. The occupation cost Germany about $833 million, and France lost about $200 million worth of coal.

On Sept. 27, 1923, Germany finally ended its passive resistance in the Ruhr. At the same time, France saw that it was useless to occupy the Ruhr any longer. Under the terms of the Dawes Plan, French and Belgian troops left the region by Aug. 1, 1925.

Adolf Hitler came to power in Germany in 1933. He harnessed the industries of the Ruhr to supply the Nazi war machine. During World War II, Allied bombers made many devastating raids on the Ruhr. American armies captured it, and British troops occupied the area.

In 1949, the United States, Great Britain, France, the Benelux countries, and West Germany set up an organization called the International Ruhr Authority to allocate Ruhr coal, iron, and steel. This organization was dissolved in 1952, when the European Coal and Steel Community was established (see EUROPEAN COMMUNITY).   JAMES K. POLLOCK

RUHR RIVER rises in Westphalia, West Germany, and flows 144 miles through the famous Ruhr Valley. It joins the Rhine River near Duisburg. See RUHR.

Another Ruhr (Roer) River rises on the Belgian frontier and flows northeast and northwest through Germany for 67 miles. It enters the Maas (Meuse) River at Roermond, The Netherlands.   JOHN D. ISAACS

RUISDAEL, *ROIS dahl,* or **RUYSDAEL, JACOB VAN** (1628?-1682), was a great Dutch landscape painter. While other artists stressed the placid nature of the Dutch countryside, Ruisdael painted stormy seas, waterfalls, melancholy ruins, and clouded skies pierced by sudden rays of light. Romantic painters of the 1800's greatly admired his poetic approach to nature, and often imitated his style and subject matter.

Ruisdael was born in Haarlem of a family of painters. He became a member of the painters' guild in 1648. He later moved to Amsterdam, where he did his best work. He studied medicine, and began to practice in 1676 because his work did not sell. His *View of Haarlem* appears in color in the PAINTING article.   JULIUS S. HELD

RUITER, MICHEL ADRIAANS-ZOON DE. See RUYTER, MICHEL ADRIAANS-ZOON DE.

RUIZ, *roo EES,* **JUAN** (1283?-1350?), ranks among Spain's important poets on the strength of a single known work. His *Book of Good Love* (*Libro de buen amor,* 1330-1347), a collection of stories in verse and song, is the most entertaining and human book in medieval Spanish literature. "Good love" in the title stands for love of God and the Virgin Mary, a popular topic in medieval Spain. But the work is more a praise of human love than spiritual love. See SPANISH LITERATURE (Early Medieval Literature).

Ruiz was born in Alcalá de Henares and was archpriest of Hita, a small town in Castile. He probably suffered a long prison term by order of the Archbishop of Toledo. Ruiz' book mingles mock allegories, tales from medieval French literature, and references to classical authors with realistic episodes apparently based on his own travels and amorous adventures.   PETER G. EARLE

RUIZ CORTINES, ADOLFO

RUIZ CORTINES, ADOL-FO (1891-   ), served as president of Mexico from 1952 to 1958. A civil servant for 30 years, he was governor of Veracruz from 1944 to 1948 and secretary of the interior under President Miguel Alemán.

Wide World
Adolfo Ruiz Cortines

As president, Ruiz Cortines fought dishonesty and corruption in reforming the civil service. He also consolidated gains made by Alemán's administration in developing agriculture and industry. In 1954, Ruiz Cortines helped make it easier for Mexicans to cross the border for seasonal agricultural work in the United States. He directed reform of the government of Mexico City, and effectively met the crisis caused by an earthquake in 1957. Ruiz Cortines was born in Veracruz on Dec. 30, 1891. HAROLD E. DAVIS

RULES COMMITTEE. See HOUSE OF REPRESENTATIVES (Committees; Transacting Business); UNITED STATES, GOVERNMENT OF (How a Bill Becomes Law).

RULES FOR SPORTS. See the sections on rules in the various sport articles, such as BASEBALL (The Rules); BASKETBALL (How to Play Basketball).

RULES OF ORDER. See PARLIAMENTARY PROCEDURE.

RUM. See ALCOHOLIC DRINK (Distilled Liquors).

RUMANIA. See ROMANIA.

RUMBA. See RHUMBA.

RUMELIA, *roo MEAL yuh*, is the name of a former Turkish region in the Balkan Peninsula, made up of ancient Thrace and part of Macedonia. In 1878, the Congress of Berlin made Eastern Rumelia a partially self-governing province of Turkey. In 1885, Eastern Rumelia became part of Bulgaria.

RUMEN. See RUMINANT.

RUMFORD, COUNT. See THOMPSON, BENJAMIN.

RUMINANT is the name given to a grazing animal that chews its cud and has split hoofs. Such animals as

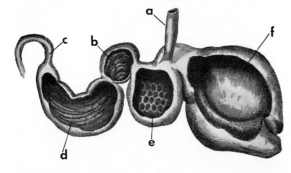

The Stomach of a Ruminant usually has four compartments. These are, *left to right*, the abomasum, omasum, reticulum, and rumen. Food enters the stomach through the esophagus, *a*. It passes from the rumen, *f*, into the reticulum, *e*, where it is softened. The reticulum forms the food into a cud, and returns it to the mouth. The animal chews the cud, and swallows it. The cud passes through the rumen and reticulum to the omasum, *b*. Then it moves through the abomasum, *d*, and enters the intestines through the duodenum, *c*.

the ox, sheep, cow, camel, llama, deer, goat, antelope, and giraffe are ruminants. The ruminant has an odd way of digesting food. It swallows its food, usually grass, after chewing it only slightly. The food then goes down the *esophagus* (food pipe), into the stomach.

Except for camels and some others, most ruminants have a stomach that has four separate *cavities* (compartments). Each cavity helps digest food. The first cavity is called the *rumen*, or *paunch*. Most of the food collects there after being swallowed. Some food passes directly into the second cavity, called the *reticulum*. The reticulum has tiny pockets in its walls that look like a honeycomb. Food stored in the rumen passes into the reticulum, where it is softened and formed into soft masses called *cuds*. As the animal rests, the muscles of the reticulum send the food back to the mouth to be chewed and mixed with saliva. The animal chews with a roundish motion of the jaw and swallows again. The cud passes through the rumen and reticulum to the third cavity, the *omasum*, and finally into the fourth cavity, the *abomasum*. In the abomasum, the food mixes with the stomach juice. From the stomach, the food passes into the intestine, where digestion is completed. The digested food is then absorbed through the lining of the intestine and passes to all parts of the body through the blood stream.

The ruminant chews its food with its molars. It does not have any biting teeth, or incisors, in the upper jaw. The lower teeth bite against the hard upper gum.

Scientific Classification. Ruminants are in the class *Mammalia*. They are in the order *Artiodactyla*, and make up the suborder *Ruminantia*.   L. B. AREY

RUML, *RUM'l*, **BEARDSLEY** (1894-1960), an American financial expert and merchant, proposed the *withholding tax*, a system of income tax payments. This system was adopted by the United States Congress in 1943. Ruml was born in Cedar Rapids, Iowa, and he was graduated from Dartmouth College. He obtained a Ph.D. at the University of Chicago, and became dean of social sciences there. In 1934, he went to R. H. Macy & Co., Inc., as treasurer, and served as chairman of the board from 1945 to 1949.   W. H. BAUGHN

RUMMY is the name for a group of card games all played generally in the same way. The cards are dealt one at a time until 10 cards have been dealt to each player. The rest of the deck is placed face down on the table. The object of the game is to get sequences of three or more cards in the same suit, or three or four of a kind in the same denomination—for example, the ace, king, and queen of hearts, or three tens. Such groups are *melded* by laying them face up in front of the player.

Each player in turn draws a card from the deck or discard pile. If a player can meld, he does so. A play is completed by discarding one card, placing it face up beside the deck to form the *discard pile*. In some rummy games, the cards in the discard pile are so arranged that each card is visible. Any card in the pile may then be taken by a player, provided he also takes all cards which may be on top of it. He must also be able to meld some cards, using the card he drew from the discard pile. Players may play on the cards melded by other players by placing their cards before them, face up.

When a player uses or discards the last card in his hand, he *rummies*, and the game is over. Picture cards count 10 each, others count 5 each. The ace counts 15, unless used in a sequence as 1. Cards remaining in the hands of the other players count for the winner.

Gin Rummy is best played by two persons. Four or six may play by taking sides and using a separate deck of cards for each couple. If two play, 10 cards are dealt to each player, the 21st card being turned face up beside the deck. All face-up cards in the discard pile are placed on top of each other. Only the top card may be taken by a player. At no time does a player have more or less than 10 cards in his hand.

The object of the game is to meld an entire hand if possible. If a player can meld everything, with only one card left over to discard, he "goes gin." If he melds and retains 10 points or less in unmatched cards remaining in his hand, he "knocks." He then scores the difference between his unmelded cards and all the cards remaining in his opponent's hand. The opponent may "lay off" on the winner's cards first. When a player gins, he gets the amount of his opponent's cards plus 25 points. If a player can go 11-card gin without discarding the final card he drew, he scores 50 points plus points from his opponent's hand. If he knocks and finds his opponent has a smaller, unmelded count than himself, the opponent wins 10 points. There are more than a dozen variations of gin rummy.   LILLIAN FRANKEL

RUMP PARLIAMENT was a name given the English Parliament during the civil war of the middle 1600's. It had only about 60 members. The other members had been excluded from Parliament by troops of the Puritan leader Oliver Cromwell.

Civil war broke out in 1642 between the forces of King Charles I and those of the *Long Parliament* (see LONG PARLIAMENT). Later, members of Parliament disagreed on the conduct of the war. On Dec. 6, 1648, soldiers led by Colonel Thomas Pride surrounded the House of Commons. They arrested 47 members of Parliament who opposed the trial of the king, and excluded many others. This action was called *Pride's Purge*. The remaining members became known as the *Rump Parliament*, because they were the *rump* (end) of the larger body. They brought about the execution of Charles I in 1649.

The Rump Parliament fought later against many demands made by Cromwell's army. Cromwell entered Parliament in 1653 at the head of a troop of soldiers, and ordered it dissolved. The Rump Parliament met twice after Cromwell's death. In 1660, after the members expelled by Colonel Pride had been recalled, the Long Parliament dissolved itself and ordered the election of a new Parliament.   W. M. SOUTHGATE

See also CHARLES (I) of England; CROMWELL, OLIVER.

RUNDLE, ROBERT T. See ALBERTA (The Missionaries).

RUNDSTEDT, *ROONT shtet,* **KARL RUDOLF GERD VON** (1875-1953), was a German field marshal during World War II. He was Germany's most experienced general at the start of the war. He led his army successfully in the Polish and French campaigns of 1939-1940. But Adolf Hitler interfered so much during his invasion of Russia in 1941 that he gave up his command and took over the German army of occupation in France. Hitler retired him from command in July, 1944, but called him back to direct "The Battle of the Bulge," Germany's last desperate effort in the West. Rundstedt was born at Aschersleben, Germany.   LESTER B. MASON

RUNE, *roon,* is any one of the characters of the earliest written alphabet used by the Teutonic peoples of Europe. The term *rune* comes from a Gothic word meaning *secret*. The runes were associated with secrecy or mystery because only a few persons knew them. Heathen priests probably first used the characters in their charms and magic spells. But later, runic characters were scratched on monuments, slabs, coins, and jewelry. The runes were made almost entirely of straight lines, arranged singly or in combinations of two or more.

The oldest runic inscriptions date back to the A.D. 200's. But the characters are believed to have been used even before the time of Christ. Most of the runes discovered were written earlier than the A.D. 1000's. Most authorities believe that the runic characters were copied from Greek and Roman coins carried to northern Europe by the Greeks, Etruscans, or Phoenicians. This may account for the two different theories of the origin of the Teutonic alphabet. Some say that the runes came from the Roman alphabet, and others claim that the characters are based on Greek letters. Traces of their use occur most often in Denmark, Norway, and Sweden. But other runic characters were discovered in Germany, France, Spain, and England.

Norsemen believed that their chief god Odin invented runic characters. Christian missionaries introduced the Latin alphabet because the runes were identified with heathen worship.   WILLIAM A. MCDONALD

RUNE STONE. See KENSINGTON RUNE STONE.

RUNNING is probably the oldest sport known to man. Men have always competed in some form of foot racing. Eventually, running developed into an organized sport with separate running events. The Olympic Games of ancient Greece included foot races over various distances. Some of these races are still run today.

Foot races have become an important part of track

Letters of the Runic Alphabet Were Used for Writing Ancient Anglo-Saxon Inscriptions.

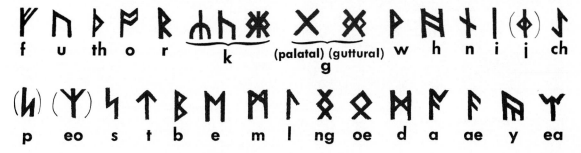

and field meets among colleges and nations. In the United States, the Amateur Athletic Union governs all amateur runners and keeps the official records for all races. The International Olympic Committee establishes the rules for the Olympic Games.

All foot races are classified by distance. The divisions are (1) sprints, or dashes; (2) middle-distance races; and (3) long-distance races. Hurdle and relay races have separate divisions.

Sprints are run at 100, 220, and 440 yards, and 100, 200, and 400 meters. Indoor sprints often include races at 50, 60, and 70 yards. In sprint races, the competitor runs the full distance at top speed. The most exciting race is probably the 100-yard dash.

Middle-distance races are run at more than 440 yards. They include races from 880 yards to 2 miles, and from 800 meters to 3,000 meters. The mile run is probably the most popular middle-distance race. Long-distance runs may cover more than 15 miles.   FRED RUSSELL

See also OLYMPIC GAMES; TRACK AND FIELD.

RUNNYMEDE, *RUN ih meed,* is an English meadow on the south bank of the River Thames, about 36 miles southwest of London. On June 15, 1215, the barons of England forced King John to grant the *Magna Carta,* which limited the powers of the king, at Runnymede. In 1965, a memorial to President John F. Kennedy was dedicated at Runnymede. See also MAGNA CARTA; LAW (picture: A Monument to the Magna Carta).

RUNYON, DAMON (1880-1946), was an American writer. His first collection of stories, *Guys and Dolls* (1932), told the comic adventures of New York City gamblers, gangsters, and characters of the sporting world. He told these and later stories in imaginative slang, and they became popular. His books include *Tents of Trouble* (verse, 1911), *Guys and Dolls* (1932), *Blue Plate Special* (1934), *Money from Home* (1935), *Take It Easy* (1938), and *My Wife Ethel* (1939).

Runyon was born in Manhattan, Kans. After serving in the Spanish-American War, he worked from 1900 to 1910 on newspapers in the West. In 1911, he became a sports writer for the *New York American.* E. HUDSON LONG

RUPEE, *roo PEE,* is the chief monetary unit of India and the basic unit in India's decimal currency system. It is divided into 100 smaller units called *paise.* Paise are

Western Publishing Co., Inc.

The One-Rupee Note of India has a watermark showing three lions, the country's national emblem. Mahatma Gandhi, who helped free India from British control, is also pictured.

circulated in the form of nickel, copper-nickel, or bronze coins. Ten million rupees, or 100 *lacs,* are called a *crore.* The monetary systems of Ceylon, Mauritius, Nepal, and Pakistan are also based on rupees. But all of these rupees have different values. For the value of the rupee in dollars, see MONEY (table: Values).   BURTON H. HOBSON

RUPERT'S LAND is the name once given to the great part of Canada drained by rivers flowing into the Hudson Bay. The area was named for Prince Rupert, first governor of the Hudson's Bay Company, which received title to the land from Charles II of England. The company's control ended in 1870 when Rupert's Land became part of the new Dominion of Canada. The Canadian Northwest was at first called "Rupert's Land and the Northwest Territory" (see NORTHWEST TERRITORIES [History]). The territory is rich in mineral and other wealth.   R. A. J. PHILLIPS

RUPP, ADOLPH (1901-   ), was one of the top college basketball coaches in the United States. Rupp coached the University of Kentucky basketball team to 879 victories—more than any other college coach had won. Under Rupp, Kentucky won the National Collegiate Athletic Association (NCAA) championship in 1948, 1949, 1951, and 1958. His Kentucky teams also won 27 Southeastern Conference championships. Rupp became coach at Kentucky in 1930, and retired in 1972. That same year, he became president of the Memphis Tams of the American Basketball Association.

Adolph Frederick Rupp was born in Halstead, Kans. He played guard on the University of Kansas basketball team from 1921 to 1923. Rupp's coach at Kansas, Forrest C. (Phog) Allen, ranked as the college coach with the most victories until January, 1968, when Kentucky, under Rupp, won its 772nd game.   NICK CURRAN

RUPTURE. See HERNIA.

RURAL CREDIT. See FARM CREDIT ADMINISTRATION.

RURAL DELIVERY is a mail service for persons who live in rural areas of the United States. The rural carriers use automobiles to deliver the mail. They place letters and packages in mailboxes by the side of the road. Each carrier travels a certain route, and each route has a number. About 31,000 rural carriers serve 35½ million persons and travel more than 1,868,000 miles a day.

Before 1896, there was no rural delivery system. Farmers' organizations, especially the National Grange, were active in getting Congress to provide money for free delivery of mail to rural areas. In 1896, the first rural deliveries were made in West Virginia. The system was called Rural Free Delivery (R.F.D.). The number of delivery routes increased during the early 1900's. In 1917, the service was extended to most rural areas.

The development of the rural delivery system was important to the development of farm areas. For the first time, the farmer could receive his newspaper daily by mail. The system led to parcel-post service and the development of great mail-order firms.

Critically reviewed by the U.S. POSTAL SERVICE

See also POST OFFICE (picture: Rural Free Delivery).

RURAL ELECTRIFICATION ADMINISTRATION (REA) is an agency of the Department of Agriculture that helps bring electricity to rural areas of the United States and its territories. It lends money to organizations so they can build and operate electric power systems. The REA also helps to extend and improve telephone service in rural areas in this same manner. It also provides engineering advice and management assistance to help borrowers.

Electrification Program. When the REA was established in 1935, fewer than 11 out of every 100 farms in the United States had electric service. By the late 1960's, however, more than 98 out of every 100 farms had electricity. Half of the electrified farms are served by REA-financed electric systems, and about 90 per cent of these REA borrowers are cooperatives. The cooperatives sign up prospective members, organize under state laws, and then apply to the REA for a loan. To receive a loan, a cooperative must show that its members will buy enough electricity to repay the borrowed money.

The REA has loaned more than $6\frac{3}{4}$ billion for electrification, and REA borrowers operate about $1\frac{3}{4}$ million miles of electric power lines. These lines provide electric service to more than 6 million customers in the United States, Puerto Rico, and the Virgin Islands. About 150,000 customers are added each year.

Telephone Programs. In 1949, the REA received authority to lend money to rural telephone systems. The 1950 census showed that only about one-third of the farms in the U.S. had telephone service. Much of this service was old-fashioned and deficient. In the late 1960's, over three-fourths of the nation's farms had telephones, and most of these were modern, dial models.

The REA has loaned more than $1\frac{1}{2}$ billion to about 900 telephone systems. These systems provide new or improved telephone service to about 2 million subscribers in nearly all the states. About one-third of the borrowers are commercial telephone companies.

History. President Franklin D. Roosevelt established the REA by executive order in 1935. In 1936, Congress approved the Rural Electrification Act. This act provided for a 10-year REA electrification loan program, which was extended indefinitely in 1944. Congress determines the amount of money the REA can lend each year. In 1944, it fixed the interest rate on loans at 2 per cent, and set the maximum repayment period at 35 years. The REA became an agency of the Department of Agriculture in 1939. An administrator appointed by the President with the approval of the Senate heads the REA.

Critically reviewed by the RURAL ELECTRIFICATION ADMINISTRATION

RURAL LIFE. See FARM AND FARMING.

RURAL SCOUTING. See BOY SCOUTS (Rural Scouting).

RURIK. See RUSSIA (Early Days).

RUSH is the common name for a group of grasslike plants that generally grow in marshes. The true rushes belong to one family. They have round stems with three rows of leaves, and their tiny flowers are greenish or brown. The small seed pod contains many dustlike brown seeds. The common rush is a wiry, dark-green plant that often grows on damp paths and lawns. Most other species grow in marshes or damp prairies. Rushes are used to weave baskets, mats, and chair seats. At one time, the pith of the stems was used for wicks in candles, called *rushlights*. Various plants called rushes are not true rushes. *Scouring rushes* (horsetails) are related to the ferns (see HORSETAIL). *Bulrushes* are actually sedges (see BULRUSH).

Scientific Classification. Rushes belong to the rush family, *Juncaceae*. The common rush is classified as genus *Juncus*, species *J. tenuis*.   RICHARD W. POHL

RUSH, BENJAMIN (1745-1813), was an American physician and a prominent figure in the public life of his time. He was the most influential physician in the United States, but his ideas were highly controversial. His faith in the curing power of bloodletting and in purging with calomel was extreme even for his day. But his efforts to improve the treatment of the mentally ill were advanced and humane.

Rush was born on Dec. 24, 1745, in Byberry, Pa. He was graduated from Princeton University at the age of 15. In 1768, he received his degree in medicine from the University of Edinburgh. Later, he practiced in Philadelphia and served as professor of chemistry and medicine at the medical college there. In 1783, Rush became a staff member of the Pennsylvania Hospital. His work there aroused his interest in social reform and, in 1786, he established the first free *dispensary* (clinic) in the United States.

Rush helped found the first American antislavery society, and Dickinson College. He served as a member of the Continental Congress, and signed the Declaration of Independence. During the Revolutionary War, Rush served as surgeon-general in the Continental Army. With James Wilson, he led the successful fight to ratify the federal Constitution. He also helped frame the Pennsylvania state constitution. He served as treasurer of the U.S. Mint from 1797 to 1813.   CAROLINE A. CHANDLER

RUSH, WILLIAM. See SCULPTURE (American).

RUSH-BAGOT AGREEMENT. See MONROE, JAMES (Diplomatic Achievements).

RUSHLIGHT. See RUSH.

RUSHMORE, MOUNT. See MOUNT RUSHMORE NATIONAL MEMORIAL; MOUNTAIN (picture chart).

RUSK, DEAN (1909-   ), served as secretary of state from 1961 to 1969 under Presidents John F. Kennedy and Lyndon B. Johnson. As secretary of state, he became a leading spokesman for the Johnson Administration's Vietnam War policy.

Rusk was born David Dean Rusk on a cotton farm in Cherokee County, Georgia. He graduated from Davidson College in North Carolina in 1931, and studied at Oxford University as a Rhodes scholar in 1933 and 1934. He later became a political science professor and dean of the faculty at Mills College in California.

Rusk joined the Department of State in 1946, and was appointed director of its office of United Nations affairs in 1947. He helped bring the Marshall Plan and the North Atlantic Treaty Organization (NATO) into being. From 1950 to 1952, during the Korean War, Rusk served as assistant secretary of state for far eastern affairs. In 1952, he became president of the Rockefeller Foundation. After resigning as secretary of state in January, 1969, Rusk was made a "distinguished fellow" by the Rockefeller

Dean Rusk

Harris & Ewing

Foundation. In 1970, he became a professor of law at the University of Georgia.   F. JAY TAYLOR

RUSKIN, JOHN (1819-1900), was probably the most influential English critic of the 1800's. His many writings on art, literature, and social issues helped form the tastes of Victorian England.

Ruskin was born in London. While a student at Oxford University, he became a strong supporter of the British artist Joseph M. W. Turner, whose paintings had aroused much controversy. Ruskin's first book, *Modern Painters I* (1843), defended Turner's style (see TURNER, JOSEPH M. W.). Ruskin's other works on art and architecture include four more volumes of *Modern Painters* (1846-1860), *The Seven Lamps of Architecture* (1849), and *The Stones of Venice* (three volumes, 1851-1853).

Ruskin believed that education, morality, and healthy social conditions were needed to produce good art. As a result, he concerned himself with social and economic issues. In lectures, essays, and books, Ruskin questioned the operations and motives of the free enterprise system. He attacked the quality of mass-produced products and encouraged industrial workers to be artistically creative. Ruskin's ideas had little political effect, but they inspired many young people of his day. His writings on social issues include four essays, published as *Unto This Last* (1862), and *Fors Clavigera*, a series of letters to British workers published from 1871 to 1884.

During his last years, Ruskin had periods of depression and insanity. His last important work was an unfinished autobiography, *Praeterita*, written from 1885 to 1889.   AVROM FLEISHMAN

RUSSELL is the family name of a father and his two sons, noted American educators.

James Earl Russell (1864-1945) served as dean of Teachers College, Columbia University, from 1897 to 1927. He built the college from a small school for training practical-arts teachers into a noted general teacher-training institution. He established its reputation by appointing outstanding scholars to the faculty. Russell was born in Hamden, N.Y., and was graduated from Cornell University.

William Fletcher Russell (1890-1956) succeeded his father as dean of Teachers College in 1927, and served until 1954. Under his leadership, the college continued to grow in influence and enrollment. It became almost exclusively a graduate school. Russell helped organize the World Organization of the Teaching Profession in 1947, and served as its president for five years. He was also dean at the University of Iowa. He was born in Delhi, N.Y. He received degrees from Cornell and Columbia universities.

Charles Russell (1893-1957) was president of the State Teachers College in Westfield, Mass., from 1925 to 1938. Later, he became education chairman of the American Museum of Natural History in New York City. He specialized in educational testing. Russell was born in Ithaca, N.Y. He received degrees at McGill and Columbia universities.   GALEN SAYLOR

RUSSELL is the name of one of England's most famous families. Several members became prominent in politics. Bertrand Russell was a noted mathematician and philosopher (see RUSSELL, BERTRAND).

John Russell (1486?-1555), 1ST EARL OF BEDFORD, became a prominent soldier and diplomat during the reign of King Henry VIII. He later received many grants of land, including the abbeys of Tavistock and Woburn and the Covent Garden estate in London. He was born in Kingston.

Francis Russell (1593-1641), 4TH EARL OF BEDFORD, played an important part in Parliament's struggle to limit the power of King Charles I. He built a mansion at Woburn.

William Russell (1613-1700), 5TH EARL OF BEDFORD, switched his support from Parliament to Charles I and back to Parliament during the English Civil War. He became the Duke of Bedford in 1694.

Lord John Russell (1792-1878), EARL RUSSELL, served as prime minister from 1846 to 1852 and from 1865 to 1866. He was elected to the House of Commons in 1813. He helped write and pass the Reform Bill of 1832, which gave the vote to more men. He was born in London.

Hastings William Sackville Russell (1888-1953), 12TH DUKE OF BEDFORD, was a pacifist and defended some of Adolf Hitler's policies during World War II. He was born in Galloway, Scotland.

John Robert Russell (1917-   ), 13TH DUKE OF BEDFORD, was a journalist and farmer in South Africa. He made Woburn a public park in 1955. He was born in London.   VERNON F. SNOW

RUSSELL, BERTRAND ARTHUR WILLIAM (1872-1970), EARL RUSSELL, was a British mathematician and philosopher. He received the 1950 Nobel prize for literature for his writings "as a defender of humanity and freedom of thought."

Russell first gained attention in 1903 with his book *Principles of Mathematics*. In 1910, he and Alfred North Whitehead published *Principia Mathematica*, which opened a new era in the study of the foundations of mathematics. Russell wrote over 40 books on such subjects as philosophy, education, politics, and sex. Among them are *Mysticism and Logic* (1918), *Marriage and Morals* (1929), *The Conquest of Happiness* (1930), *Education and the Social Order* (1932), *Human Society in Ethics and Politics* (1954), and *Has Man a Future?* (1962).

Russell's outspokenness and liberal views involved him in many controversies. During World War I, he was dismissed from Cambridge University and imprisoned because of his pacifist views. In 1940, protests against his radical views on religion and morals caused the College of the City of New York to cancel his appointment as a professor. Attempts to oust him from Harvard University the same year failed. In the early 1960's, Russell led pacifist moves to ban nuclear weapons. He was imprisoned briefly in 1962 for these activities.

Bertrand Russell
United Press Int.

Russell was born near Trelleck, Wales. He was graduated from Cambridge University in 1894, and worked briefly in the British embassy in Paris. Then he went to Germany, where he wrote his first book, *German Social Democracy*, in 1896. He came to the United

States to lecture at Harvard in 1914. He also taught at the University of Peking in China, the University of Chicago, and the University of California.   PHILLIP S. JONES

RUSSELL, BILL (1934-), became one of the finest defensive players in basketball history. A 6-foot 10-inch center for the Boston Celtics, Russell became a master at blocking shots and rebounding. He ranks second only to Wilt Chamberlain among the leading rebounders in the history of the National Basketball Association (NBA).

William Felton Russell was born in Monroe, La. He helped lead the University of San Francisco to a 57 wins and 1 loss record during the 1954-1955 and 1955-1956 seasons. Russell joined the Celtics in the 1956-1957 season and helped lead the team to 11 NBA championships in the 13 years he played. Russell coached the Celtics from 1966 to 1969. He was the first Negro head coach in major league professional sports, and played while coaching. He retired in 1969.   HERMAN WEISKOPF

RUSSELL, CHARLES MARION (1864-1926), an American painter and sculptor, won fame as the *cowboy artist*. He captured the life of the Old West in oil and bronze, portraying Indians, frontiersmen, cowboys, and animals of the plains and mountains. He first won notice about 1891 with his painting *Waiting for a Chinook*. He painted *Lewis and Clark at Ross' Hole* for the Montana House of Representatives. He did many sculptures in wax and clay. His sculptures include *Where the Best of Riders Quit* and *When the Sioux and Blackfeet Meet*.

Russell was born in St. Louis, Mo. At 16, he went to Montana as a cowboy. His statue represents Montana in Statuary Hall in the U.S. Capitol.   JEAN LIPMAN

See also UNITED STATES (The Arts in the United States [color picture: Bronc to Breakfast]).

RUSSELL, GEORGE WILLIAM (1867-1935), was an Irish mystical poet and painter who wrote under the pen name of "A.E." He was one of the group of writers and artists who helped to bring about the Irish Literary Revival. In addition, he was an outstanding essayist and philosopher, and an ardent nationalist. Russell was born in Lurgan, Ireland.   HASKELL M. BLOCK

RUSSELL, HENRY NORRIS (1877-1957), an American astronomer, influenced the growth of theoretical astrophysics in the United States. He pioneered in using atomic physics to analyze the nature of stars. With Ejnar Hertzsprung, he developed a famous diagram that relates the brightness of a star to its surface temperature. Extensive astronomical research has been based on this diagram. It has helped scientists interpret the physical nature and evolution of stars.

Russell was born in Oyster Bay, N.Y. He was graduated from Princeton University. From 1905 to 1947, he served as chairman of the astronomy department and director of the observatory at Princeton. He wrote several books, including *Astronomy* (1926) and *The Solar System and Its Origin* (1935).   HELEN WRIGHT

See also STAR (Studying the Stars [diagram]).

RUSSELL SAGE FOUNDATION

RUSSELL, LILLIAN (1861-1922), an American actress and singer, was the ideal of feminine beauty during "The Gay Nineties." She made her debut in *H.M.S. Pinafore* in 1879. She became famous during the 1880's when she was billed at Tony Pastor's Theatre in New York City as "the beautiful English ballad singer." Her costumes, especially her hats, became the talk of the town. She appeared in leading roles in such shows as *The Great Mogul, Olivette, Patience,* and *The Sorcerer*. She was born Helen Louise Leonard in Clinton, Ia., on Dec. 4, 1861.   WILLIAM VAN LENNEP

RUSSELL, RICHARD BREVARD (1897-1971), a Georgia Democrat, became one of the most influential men in the U.S. Senate. He served as chairman of the Senate Armed Services Committee in 1951 and 1952 and again from 1955 until 1969, when he became chairman of the Senate Appropriations Committee. In 1969, he also was elected president *pro tempore* of the Senate. As chairman of the appropriations group, Russell had great influence on the nation's spending, especially in gaining Senate approval of military budgets. He also was a leading opponent of civil rights legislation.

Russell was born in Winder, Ga., and graduated from the University of Georgia School of Law. After a year in the Navy, he returned to Winder to practice law. Russell was elected to the Georgia House of Representatives in 1921 and became speaker of the House in 1927. In 1930, he was elected governor of Georgia. In 1932, he was elected to complete the term of U.S. Senator William J. Harris, who had died. Russell served in the Senate continuously from 1933 until his death. He was an unsuccessful candidate for the Democratic presidential nomination in 1948 and 1952.

RUSSELL, LORD WILLIAM. See RYE HOUSE PLOT.

RUSSELL CAVE NATIONAL MONUMENT lies near Bridgeport, Ala. The cave contains almost continuous evidence of human life from about 6000 B.C. to about A.D. 1650. Scientists have also found traces of a campfire that burned in the cave about 9,000 years ago. The 310.45-acre monument was established in 1961.

RUSSELL COLLEGE. See UNIVERSITIES AND COLLEGES (table).

RUSSELL SAGE COLLEGE. See UNIVERSITIES AND COLLEGES (table).

RUSSELL SAGE FOUNDATION. See SAGE FOUNDATION, RUSSELL.

485

Red Square in Moscow is the scene of a huge May Day parade every year. Communists set aside the May 1 and 2 holiday to honor working people. The marchers carry Russian flags past 400-year-old Saint Basil's Church. The Communists changed the building from a place of worship to a museum.

The six contributors of this article are all members of the Executive Committee of the Center for Russian Studies at the University of Michigan. These contributors are William B. Ballis, Professor of Political Science; Morris Bornstein, Professor of Economics; Deming Brown, Professor of Russian Literature; George Kish, Professor of Geography; William K. Medlin, Professor of Education; and Arthur P. Mendel, Professor of Russian History.

RUSSIA

Union of Soviet Socialist Republics

RUSSIA, the UNION OF SOVIET SOCIALIST REPUBLICS (U.S.S.R.), is the largest country in the world, and the most powerful Communist nation. Russia covers more than half of Europe and nearly two-fifths of Asia. It takes up more than a seventh of the world's total land area. Russia is larger than four continents—South America, Antarctica, Europe, and Australia—and is almost as large as all of North America. Only China and India have more people than Russia. Moscow, Russia's capital and largest city, is the fourth largest city in the world.

The official name of Russia is the *Union of Soviet Socialist Republics*. In the Russian language, this name is *Soyuz Sovetskikh Sotsialisticheskikh Respublik*. In the Russian alphabet, the initials of these words are C.C.C.P., and they appear on Russian postage stamps. Most people call the country *Russia* or the *Soviet Union*.

A thousand years ago, Russia was a small region in Europe. It grew to its present size by adding territory on all sides. As the country expanded, peoples of many different backgrounds came under Russian rule. These peoples have kept many of their customs and their own languages. As a result, "Russia is not a country, but a world," according to an old Russian saying.

For hundreds of years, Russia was ruled by *czars*, who had complete power over Russian life. The czars kept Russia cut off from the progress being made in Western Europe. By the early 1900's, many other countries had become industrialized, but Russia had little industry. Most Russians were poor, uneducated peasants. They farmed Russia's broad plains with the same kinds of hand tools that their ancestors had used. In spite of their harsh life, the peasants loved their giant land, which they called "Mother Russia." They expressed this love in beautiful and sad songs, and in folk dances and colorful festivals. Many educated Russians produced great works of art under the czars. Anton Chekhov, Fyodor Dostoevsky, and Leo Tolstoy wrote masterpieces of literature. Modest Mussorgsky and Peter Ilich Tchaikovsky composed music of lasting greatness.

In 1917, a revolution drove the czar from power. The *Bolsheviks* (later called *Communists*) seized the government several months later and set up a dictatorship. They brutally took over the factories, farms, and other means of production, and Russia became the first Communist nation. Its economy expanded rapidly. Today, Soviet industrial production ranks second only to that of the United States. Only the United States leads Russia in crop production.

The early Communists hoped to take over the industrialized Western nations by force. Today, Russia believes that Communism can triumph throughout the world without a major war. Russian leaders have stressed *peaceful coexistence* with non-Communist countries. Under this policy, the Soviet Union expects to defeat the Western nations through economic, political, and technological power.

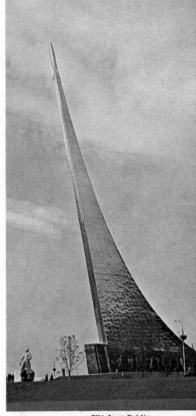

ZFA from Publix

Russia's *Sputnik I,* honored by this monument in Moscow, opened the space age in 1957. It was the first spacecraft to circle the earth.

FACTS IN BRIEF

Capital: Moscow.

Official Language: Russian.

Official Name: Union of Soviet Socialist Republics.

Form of Government: Communist dictatorship; 15 Union Republics. *Head of State*—Chairman of the Presidium of the Supreme Soviet of the U.S.S.R. *Head of Government*—Premier, or Chairman of the Council of Ministers (Cabinet).

Legislature: Supreme Soviet of the U.S.S.R., consisting of two houses—Soviet of the Union (767 deputies, 4-year terms); Soviet of Nationalities (750 deputies, 4-year terms).

Area: 8,649,500 square miles (2,151,000 square miles in Europe and 6,498,500 square miles in Asia). *Greatest Distances*—(east-west) 6,000 miles; (north-south) 3,200 miles. *Coastline*—30,787 miles.

Elevation: *Highest*—Communism Peak, 24,590 feet above sea level. *Lowest*—Karagiye Depression, 433 feet below sea level.

Population: *Estimated 1973 Population*—250,867,000; distribution, 57 per cent urban, 43 per cent rural; density,

29 persons to the square mile. *1970 census*—241,748,000. *Estimated 1978 Population*—264,972,000.

Chief Products: *Agriculture*—barley, beef and dairy cattle, corn, cotton, flax, milk, oats, potatoes, rye, sheep, sugar beets, tobacco, vegetables, wheat, wool. *Fishing*—cod, herring, salmon, sturgeon. *Manufacturing*—chemicals, electrical and electronic equipment, iron and steel, lumber, machinery, paper, petroleum products, processed foods, processed metals, textiles, transportation equipment. *Mining*—bauxite, coal, copper, gold, iron ore, lead, magnesium, manganese, natural gas, nickel, petroleum, platinum, salt, tungsten, zinc.

National Anthem: *Gosudarstveny Gimn Sovetskogo Soyusa* (National Anthem of the Soviet Union).

National Holiday: November 7 and 8, the dates of the Bolshevik Revolution of 1917.

National Motto: *Proletarii Vsekh Stran, Soyedinyaites!* (Workers of All Countries, Unite!)

Money: *Basic Unit*—ruble. One hundred kopecks equal one ruble. For the value of the ruble in dollars, see MONEY (table: Values). See also KOPECK; RUBLE.

The Grand Kremlin Palace, center, in Moscow is the meeting place of the Supreme Soviet of the U.S.S.R., Russia's parliament. Fireworks light the sky every May Day.

RUSSIA/Government

Russia has a long constitution that gives all political power to the people and to their elected representatives. The Constitution mentions the Communist Party only once. However, Russia is completely controlled by the Communists. The men who run the Communist Party run Russia. The government is like a glove, and the party is like a hand inside the glove. The glove moves only the way the hand does. The government simply accepts all Communist Party decisions, puts them into laws and orders, and sees that they are obeyed. When a Russian votes, he or she has only one choice—the person selected by the party. A voter may cross out the name of the party's choice, but almost no one does.

Russia is made up of 15 *union republics*. Each republic, like the entire nation, is governed by a *soviet* (council). This political structure gives Russia its official name, the *Union of Soviet Socialist Republics* (U.S.S.R.). See the separate articles on the union republics listed in the *Russia Map Index*.

The Communist Party of the Soviet Union permits no other political party to oppose it. It has about $13\frac{1}{2}$ million members. Thus, the men and women in the Communist Party make up only about 5 per cent of Russia's population.

A Russian who wants to join the Communist Party must be at least 18 years old. He or she must be recommended by three members of the *primary party organization* (the lowest party unit) that he wishes to join. The recommending members must have been party members for at least five years, and must have known the candidate for at least one year. Both the primary party organization and the party organization on the next higher level must approve the candidate. The candidate then must wait a year before he can be approved as a full member. This whole process permits only those who are most loyal to Communism to join the party.

The Communist Party structure is like a pyramid. At the bottom of the pyramid are about 320,000 primary party organizations. They operate throughout Russia, wherever there are at least three Communists. These groups are set up in such places as factories, farms, government offices, and schools. They have great influence over local political and economic life. To a Russian, the man who heads the local party group is a person to be respected—and sometimes feared. Many of Russia's leaders worked their way to the top from positions in local party organizations.

Most primary party organizations have many members. If an organization has more than 15 members, it elects a *bureau* to conduct its work. If an organization

The Flag of Russia. The red stands for revolution; the hammer and sickle for united peasants and workers; and the star for the Communist Party.

The Coat of Arms carries the motto, "Workers of All Countries, Unite!" The hammer and sickle represent the spread of Communism. The rising sun is a symbol of the dawning of the "new day" of Communism.

488

Russia, the World's Largest Country, is nearly three times as large as the United States, not counting Alaska and Hawaii. Russia extends about 6,000 miles across Europe and Asia.

has more than 150 members, its bureau elects a full-time *secretary* to head the organization. The secretary is released from his regular job and is paid for his party duties. The secretary and his staff make up the *secretariat* of the organization.

Just above the primary party organizations are the *rayon* (district) *party organizations*. The primary groups in each district elect representatives to a *district conference*, held every two years. This conference elects a committee, which, in turn, elects a bureau and a secretariat. The committee, bureau, and secretariat direct the district party between district conferences.

The district organizations operate under the *oblast* (region) *party organizations*. The district groups in each

region elect representatives to a *regional conference*, which is also held every two years. The regional conference also elects a committee, which then chooses a bureau and a secretariat.

On the next party level, in 14 of the 15 union republics, is the *republic party organization*. Each republic organization is made up of representatives from lower party groups in the republic. The representatives meet in a *congress* at least every four years. The congress elects a *central committee*, which also selects a bureau and a secretariat. The Russian Soviet Federated Socialist Republic, the largest republic, has no separate party organization. Its party activities are managed by bodies of the national party organization.

The main organization at the top of the nationwide Communist Party pyramid is the *All-Union Party Congress*. Under party rules, the congress must meet at least every five years. But it does not meet that regularly. The All-Union Party Congress consists of about 5,000 delegates from lower party organizations throughout Russia. It elects a Central Committee to handle its work between congresses. The Central Committee, which has about 400 regular and alternate members, meets at least every six months. It elects a *Politburo* (Political Bureau) and a *Secretariat* to direct its work between meetings. In actual practice, the party congress does not really "elect" the Central Committee, nor does the Central Committee really "elect" the Politburo and Secretariat. The Politburo and the Secretariat select their own members and those of the Central Committee. The Central Committee and the All-Union Party Congress simply approve these selections.

The Politburo of the Central Committee is the most powerful body in Russia. It establishes all important Soviet policies in national and foreign affairs. The Politburo has 15 regular members and 6 alternates. They meet in secret and never reveal their discussions or how they voted. Only their decisions are announced.

The Secretariat of the Central Committee manages the daily work of the Communist Party. The Secretariat

The Palace of Congresses in Moscow is the meeting place of delegates from Communist Party organizations in all parts of Russia. The white marble building was completed in 1961.

Kenneth Katzner

has 11 members, several of whom are also members of the Politburo. The *general secretary* of the Central Committee heads both the Secretariat and the Politburo. He is the most powerful person in the Soviet Union.

The Secretariat is aided by a staff of about 1,000 professional party secretaries called *apparatchiki*. They form a chain of command like that of an army, with the general secretary at the top. The secretaries at each level are selected by those above them in the party structure. They manage the work of all party organizations, and have wide control over Russian life.

Federal Government. The structure of the Soviet government, like that of the Russian Communist party, resembles a pyramid. Each government body is responsible to the one above it. At the top, the main body is a two-house federal parliament, the *Supreme Soviet of the U.S.S.R.* Almost all its members are Communists. The members are elected to four-year terms, and meet twice a year for a week or less. They pass without question all proposed laws, which come from the Communist party's leaders.

One house of parliament, the *Soviet of the Union*, has 767 members called *deputies*. Each deputy is elected from a district of about 300,000 residents. The other house, the *Soviet of Nationalities*, has 750 deputies. Each of the 15 union republics elects 32 deputies. Within the various union republics are 20 *autonomous* (self-governing) republics, 8 autonomous regions, and 10 *okrugs* (national areas). Each of these elects 11, 5, or 1 deputy to the Soviet of Nationalities.

In elections to the Supreme Soviet, there is only one candidate for each position. Several candidates are nominated in the voting districts, but Communist party officials make the final choice. Russian voters must be at least 18 years old.

The Supreme Soviet elects two important bodies, but their members are actually selected by the Communist party's leaders. These bodies are the *Presidium of the Supreme Soviet* and the *Council of Ministers*. The Presidium handles legislative matters between sessions of the Supreme Soviet. Its chairman is considered Russia's head of state, but he has little real power. He is assisted by 15 deputy chairmen (one from each union republic), a secretary, and 16 other members.

The powerful Council of Ministers, or cabinet, is the highest executive body of the Soviet government. Its members are among the highest-ranking Communist party leaders. The council chairman, often called *premier* or *prime minister*, is the actual head of the Soviet government. The dictators Joseph Stalin and Nikita S. Khrushchev held this position while they headed the Communist party. The council also includes 2 first deputy chairmen, 9 deputy chairmen, almost 50 department ministers, and nearly 30 committee chairmen.

Local Government. Each of the 15 union republics and the 20 autonomous republics has a constitution. Each also has a supreme soviet with a presidium, and a council of ministers. Members of the supreme soviets are elected to four-year terms. The lower levels of government, from the autonomous regions down to the smallest districts, have *soviets of working people's deputies*. The members of these soviets are elected to two-year terms. Most soviets elect *executive committees* to handle local work between legislative sessions.

Courts in the Soviet Union differ from those in the Western democracies. Western courts operate according to general ideas of justice. Court rulings in Russia, on the other hand, are based on policies of the Communist party. Soviet courts are under the *procurator-general*, Russia's chief legal officer. He is selected by Communist party leaders and appointed to a seven-year term by the Supreme Soviet of the U.S.S.R.

Russia's highest court is the *Supreme Court of the U.S.S.R.* Each republic also has a supreme court. All supreme court judges are elected by the supreme soviets to five-year terms. Below them, the judges of the *regional courts* are elected, also to five-year terms, by the regional soviets. The lowest courts are the *people's courts*. Judges of the people's court are elected to five-year terms by local voters.

The *Party Control Committee* sees that the rules of the Communist party are followed on all government and party levels. This committee is appointed by the national party's Central Committee. The *Committee on State Security*, an agency of the Council of Ministers, is the government's political police system. It has offices and agents throughout Russia.

Armed Forces of the Soviet Union are the largest in the world. Western military experts estimate that Russia has a total of more than 3 million men in its army, navy, and air force. Required military service begins at the age of 18 and lasts at least two years. See AIR FORCE (Russia); ARMY (Russia); NAVY (Russia).

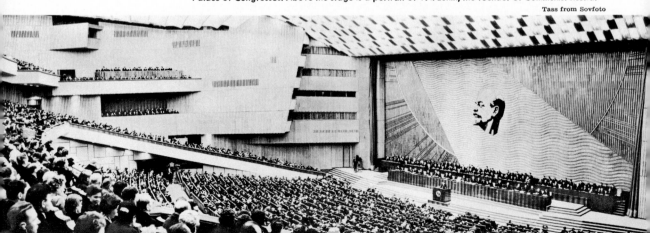

The 23rd All-Union Communist Party Congress met in 1966 in the main auditorium of the Palace of Congresses. Above the stage is a portrait of V. I. Lenin, the founder of Communist Russia.

Tass from Sovfoto

THE STRUCTURE OF POLITICAL POWER IN RUSSIA

The constitution of Russia provides that representatives elected by all the people shall run the government. However, there is only one candidate for each political office in Russia. In addition, the all-powerful Communist Party selects each candidate.

Thus, the Communist Party has complete control over the government. The government simply passes all laws proposed by the party's leaders. The Communist Party allows no other political party in Russia. Its power reaches to all levels of Russian life.

Communist Party of the Soviet Union

HEAD OF THE COMMUNIST PARTY

The general secretary of the Communist Party's Central Committee heads its Politburo and Secretariat. He is the most powerful person in Russia.

POLITBURO OF THE CENTRAL COMMITTEE

The policy-making body of the Communist Party is the Politburo of the Central Committee. It establishes economic programs, determines Russia's relations with other countries, and sets other important policies. The Politburo has 15 regular members. They meet in secret and reveal only their decisions.

SECRETARIAT OF THE CENTRAL COMMITTEE

The day-to-day work of the Communist Party is managed by the Secretariat of the Central Committee. The group has 11 members. Several of them are also members of the Politburo. The Secretariat is aided at all levels of the Communist Party by a staff of about 1,000 professional party secretaries.

ALL-UNION PARTY CONGRESS

The rules of the Communist Party grant supreme power in the party to the All-Union Party Congress. The congress consists of about 5,000 delegates from lower party organizations throughout Russia. It is actually controlled by the party's leaders, and simply approves their decisions. Under the party's rules, the All-Union Party Congress is supposed to meet every five years. But it does not meet that regularly.

CENTRAL COMMITTEE

The Central Committee of the Communist Party handles Communist affairs between sessions of the All-Union Party Congress. The committee meets at least once every six months. It has about 400 regular and alternate members. The party's leaders select the members on the basis of their loyalty to them. The persons they select are then "elected" to the Central Committee by the All-Union Party Congress.

Federal Government

PRESIDIUM OF THE SUPREME SOVIET

The Presidium handles legislation between sessions of the Supreme Soviet of the U.S.S.R., which meets twice a year. It has 33 members. The chairman is considered Russia's head of state.

PREMIER

The premier, or chairman of the Council of Ministers, heads the government of Russia. Joseph Stalin and Nikita S. Khrushchev each headed the government and the Communist Party at the same time.

SUPREME SOVIET OF THE U.S.S.R.

Russia's legislature is the Supreme Soviet of the U.S.S.R. It has two houses—the Soviet of the Union and the Soviet of Nationalities. Members of both houses are elected to four-year terms. They pass all laws proposed by the Communist Party's leaders. The Supreme Soviet "elects" the members of its Presidium and the Council of Ministers after they are selected by party leaders.

SOVIET OF THE UNION

The Soviet of the Union consists of 767 members, who are called *deputies*. Each of the deputies represents a district of about 300,000 persons.

SOVIET OF NATIONALITIES

The Soviet of Nationalities has 750 deputies. Each of the 15 union republics elects 32 deputies. Various regions within the republics elect the rest.

COUNCIL OF MINISTERS

The highest executive body of Russia's government is the Council of Ministers, or cabinet. It controls Russian economic and cultural life through various ministries and committees. It also handles Russia's relations with other countries. The Council of Ministers has about 90 members. They are among the highest-ranking officials of the Communist Party.

RUSSIA Political Map
(UNION OF SOVIET SOCIALIST REPUBLICS)

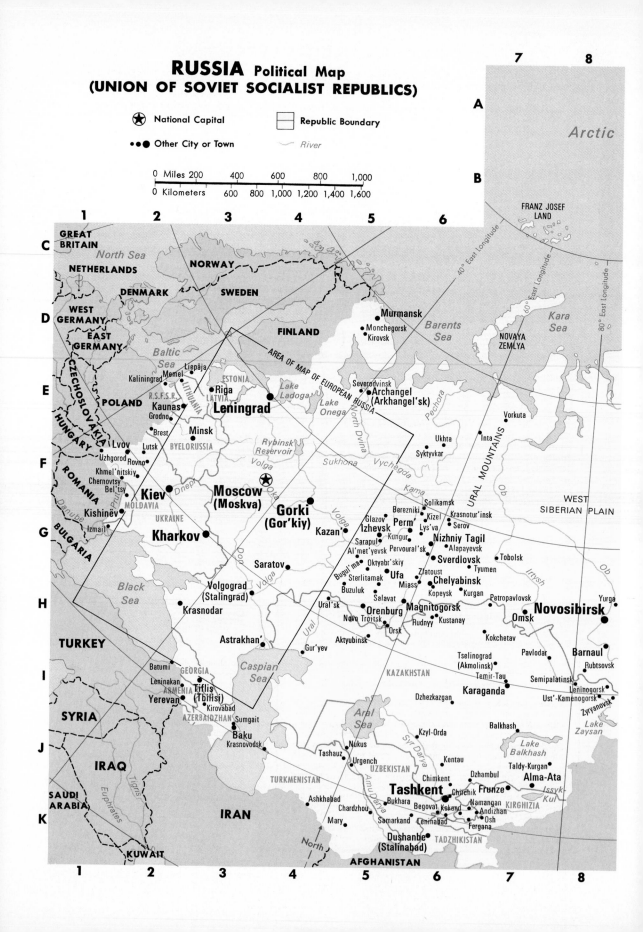

⭐ National Capital   ▭ Republic Boundary

•••● Other City or Town   ～ River

0   Miles 200   400   600   800   1,000

0   Kilometers   600   800   1,000   1,200   1,400   1,600

Arctic

FRANZ JOSEF LAND

GREAT BRITAIN
North Sea
NETHERLANDS
NORWAY
DENMARK
SWEDEN
WEST GERMANY
EAST GERMANY
FINLAND
Murmansk
Monchegorsk
Kirovsk
Barents Sea
Kara Sea
NOVAYA ZEMLYA

Baltic Sea
CZECHOSLOVAKIA
POLAND
Liepāja
Memel
Kaliningrad
ESTONIA
R.S.F.S.R.
Riga
LATVIA
LITHUANIA
Lake Ladoga
AREA OF MAP OF EUROPEAN RUSSIA
Severodvinsk
Archangel (Arkhangel'sk)
Pechora
Vorkuta

HUNGARY
Kaunas
Grodno
Leningrad
Lake Onega
North Dvina
Ukhta
Inta
Syktyvkar

Lvov
Uzhgorod
Rovno
Brest
Lutsk
Minsk
BYELORUSSIA
Rybinsk Reservoir
Volga
Sukhona
Vychegda
URAL MOUNTAINS
Ob
WEST SIBERIAN PLAIN

ROMANIA
Khmel'nitskiy
Chernovtsy
Bel'tsy
Kiev
Dnepr
Moscow (Moskva)
Oka
Kama
Solikamsk
Berezniki
Kizel
Krasnotur'insk
Serov
Tobolsk

Danube
Prut
Kishinëv
MOLDAVIA
UKRAINE
Don
Gorki (Gor'kiy)
Kazan'
Glazov
Izhevsk
Perm'
Lys'va
Kungur
Nizhniy Tagil
Alapayevsk
Sverdlovsk
Tyumen
Irtysh
Ob

BULGARIA
Izmail
Kharkov
Saratov
Volga
Sarapul
Al'met'yevsk
Pervoural'sk
Zlatoust
Chelyabinsk
Kopeysk
Kurgan
Petropavlovsk
Yurga
Novosibirsk

Black Sea
Volgograd (Stalingrad)
Krasnodar
Don
Bugul'ma
Oktyabr'skiy
Sterlitamak
Ufa
Miass
Buzuluk
Salavat
Ural'sk
Orenburg
Magnitogorsk
Rudnyy
Kustanay
Kokchetav
Omsk

TURKEY
Astrakhan'
Ural
Gur'yev
Novo Troitsk
Orsk
Aktyubinsk
KAZAKHSTAN
Tselinograd (Akmolinsk)
Temir-Tau
Pavlodar
Barnaul
Rubtsovsk

Batumi
GEORGIA
Leninakan
Tiflis (Tbilisi)
ARMENIA
Yerevan
Kirovabad
AZERBAIDZHAN
Sumgait
Caspian Sea
Karaganda
Semipalatinsk
Ust'-Kamenogorsk
Zyryanovsk
Lake Zaysan

SYRIA
Baku
Krasnovodsk
Aral Sea
Dzhezkazgan
Balkhash
Lake Balkhash
Taldy-Kurgan
Alma-Ata
Issyk-Kul

IRAQ
Tigris
Euphrates
Nukus
Tashauz
Urgench
UZBEKISTAN
Syr Darya
Kzyl-Orda
Kentau
Chimkent
Dzhambul
Frunze
KIRGHIZIA

SAUDI ARABIA
Ashkhabad
Chardzhou
TURKMENISTAN
Amu Darya
Bukhara
Tashkent
Begovat
Chirchik
Kokand
Namangan
Andizhan
Osh

IRAN
Mary
Samarkand
Leninabad
Fergana
North
Dushanbe (Stalinabad)
TADZHIKISTAN

KUWAIT
AFGHANISTAN

40° East Longitude
60° East Longitude
80° East Longitude

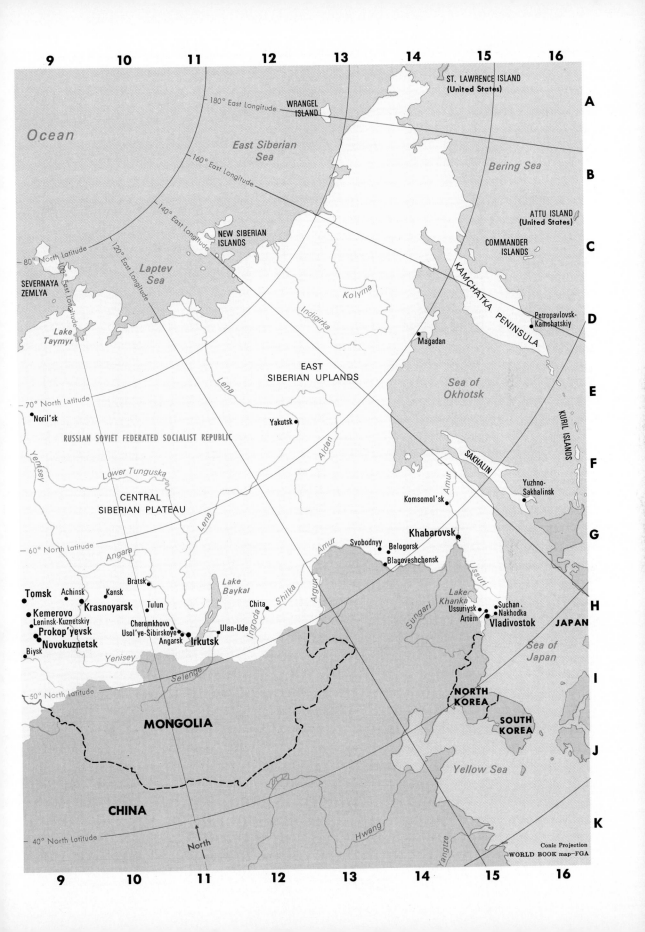

——— RUSSIA MAP INDEX ———

——— Union Republics ———

Map Key	Name	Population	Area (Sq. Mi.)	Capital
I 2	Armenia	2,253,000	11,506	Yerevan
J 3	Azerbaidzhan	4,802,000	33,436	Baku
F 2	Byelorussia	8,744,000	80,155	Minsk
E 3	Estonia	1,294,000	17,413	Tallinn
I 3	Georgia	4,611,000	26,911	Tiflis
J 7	Kazakhstan	12,413,000	1,048,306	Alma-Ata
K 7	Kirghizia	2,749,000	76,641	Frunze
E 3	Latvia	2,285,000	24,595	Riga
E 2	Lithuania	3,026,000	25,174	Vilnius
G 2	Moldavia	3,425,000	13,012	Kishinëv
F 7	Russian Soviet Federated Socialist Republic (R.S.F.S.R.)	127,312,000	6,592,850	Moscow
K 6	Tadzhikistan	2,654,000	55,251	Dushanbe
K 4	Turkmenistan	1,966,000	188,456	Ashkhabad
G 2	Ukraine	45,966,000	233,090	Kiev
J 5	Uzbekistan	10,896,000	173,592	Tashkent

Each republic has a separate article in WORLD BOOK.

Population

1977 Estimate	263,112,000
1972 ”	248,760,000
1970 Census	241,748,000
1959 ”	208,826,650
1939 ”	170,557,093
1926 ”	147,027,915
1917 Estimate	163,000,000
1913 Census	165,713,200
1897 ”	128,200,000

Cities and Towns

Abakan* ...78,000..H 9
Achinsk ...69,000..H 9
Akmolinsk, see Tselinograd
Aktyubinsk 135,000..H 5
Alapayevsk .49,000..G 6
Aleksin ...54,000..P 20
Alma-Ata .652,000..J 7
Almalyk* ...73,000..K 6
Al'met'yevsk 74,000..G 5
Andizhan .169,000..K 7
Angarsk .183,000..H 11
Angren* ...74,000..K 6
Antratsit* ...55,000..T 20
Anzhero-Sud-
zhensk* ..116,000..H 9
Archangel (Arkhan-
gel'sk) .310,000..E 5
Armavir .139,000..U 21
Artëm ...65,000..H 15
Artëmovsk* 77,000..G 3
Arzamas ...57,000..P 22
Asbest* ...74,000..G 6
Ashkhabad 238,000..K 4
Astrakhan' 368,000..U 23
Azov ...56,000..T 20
Baku ...772,000
*1,196,000..J 3
Balakovo ...85,000..R 23
Balashikha* 74,000..P 21
Balashov ...71,000..R 22
Balkhash ...75,000..J 7
Baranovichi 85,000..F 2
Barnaul ..407,000..H 8
Bataysk ...85,000..T 20
Batumi ...100,000..I 3
Begovat ...59,000..K 6
Belaya
Tserkov' ..92,000..R 18
Belgorod .129,000..R 20
Belogorsk ...51,000..G 14
Beloretsk* ...64,000..H 5
Belovo ..116,000..H 9
Bel'tsy ...87,000..F 2
Bendery ...61,000..T 17
Berdichev ..60,000..R 17
Berdyansk ..87,000..G 2
Berezniki .134,000..G 6
Biysk .181,000..I 9
Blagovesh-
chensk .121,000..G 14
Bobruysk .120,000..Q 18
Bor ...49,000..P 23
Borisoglebsk 62,000..R 22
Borisov ...74,000..P 18
Borovichi ...55,000..N 20
Bratsk .122,000..H 10
Brest ...96,000..F 2
Bryanka* ...79,000..G 10
Bryansk .288,000..Q 19
Bugul'ma ...74,000..G 5
Bukhara .102,000..K 5
Buzuluk ...63,000..H 5
Chapayevsk 87,000..R 24
Chardzhou ...88,000..K 5
Cheboksary 178,000..P 23
Chelyabinsk 836,000..H 6
Cherem-
khovo .109,000..H 11
Cherepovets 165,000..N 21
Cherkassy .128,000..S 18
Cherkessk ...57,000..V 21
Chernigov .139,000..Q 18

Cherno-
gorsk* ...61,000..H 9
Chernovtsy 178,000..F 2
Chimkent .219,000..J 6
Chirchik .100,000..K 6
Chistopol'* ..61,000..G 5
Chita .203,000..H 12
Chusovoy* ...63,000..G 6
Daugavpils 89,000..O 18
Derbent* ...59,000..I 3
Dneprodzer-
zhinsk ..224,000..S 19
Dnepro-
petrovsk 816,000..S 19
Dolgo-
prudnyy ..50,000..P 21
Donetsk
(Stalino) 840,000..H 3
Drogobych* 56,000..F 1
Druzhkovka* 50,000..S 20
Dushanbe (Stalina-
bad) .333,000..K 6
Dzerzhinsk 201,000..P 22
Dzhambul 158,000..J 6
Dzhezkaz-
gan ...58,000..I 6
Elektrostal' 117,000..P 21
Engel's .122,000..R 23
Feodosiya ..59,000..U 19
Fergana ...93,000..K 6
Frunze .396,000..J 7
Gatchina ..53,000..M 19
Glazov ...65,000..G 5
Gomel' ..237,000..Q 18
Gorki (Gor'-
kiy) ..1,120,000..G 4
Gorlovka ..343,000..S 20
Grodno .111,000..E 2
Groznyy .331,000..V 22
Gukovo* ...68,000..H 3
Gur'yev .101,000..I 4
Gus'-Khrus-
tal'nyy* ...63,000..P 22
Inta ...51,000..F 7
Irbit* ...49,000..G 6
Irkutsk ..420,000..H 11
Ishimbay* ...53,000..H 5
Ivano-Fran-
kovsk* ...92,000..F 2
Ivanovo ..407,000..O 22
Izhevsk .376,000..G 5
Izmail ...63,000..G 1
Jelgava ...49,000..N 17
Kadiyevka 139,000..S 20
Kalinin .318,000..O 20
Kaliningrad (Königs-
berg) ..270,000..E 2
Kalinin-
grad* ...96,000..F 4
Kaluga .179,000..P 20
Kamenets-Podol'-
skiy* ...52,000..F 2
Kamensk-Shakhtin-
skiy ...71,000..T 21
Kamensk-Ural'-
skiy* .161,000..G 6
Kamyshin ..77,000..S 23
Kansk ...91,000..H 10
Karaganda 498,000..I 7
Kaunas ..284,000..E 2
Kazan' ..821,000..P 24
Kemerovo .364,000..H 9
Kentau ...52,000..J 6
Kerch' ..118,000..U 19
Khaba-
rovsk ..435,000..G 15
Kharkov (Khar'-
kov) ..1,125,000..G 3
Khasavyurt 49,000..V 23
Kherson .235,000..T 18
Khimki ...70,000..P 20
Khmel'nit-
skiy ...87,000..F 2
Kiev ..1,413,000..F 2
Kimry ...50,000..O 21
Kineshma ..94,000..O 22
Kirov .309,000..O 24
Kirovabad 174,000..I 3
Kirovakan* 82,000..I 1

Kirovograd 168,000..S 18
Kirovsk* ...50,000..H 3
Kirovsk ...46,000..D 5
Kiselëvsk* .138,000..H 9
Kishinëv .302,000..G 2
Kislovodsk .84,000..V 21
Kizel ...55,000..G 6
Klaipëda, see Memel
Klin ...69,000..O 20
Klintsy ...52,000..Q 19
Kohtla-
Järve ...66,000..M 18
Kokand .131,000..K 6
Kokchetav .76,000..H 7
Kolomna .131,000..P 21
Kommu-
narsk ..124,000..S 20
Komsomol'sk
-on-Amur, see
Komso-
mol'sk ..209,000..G 14
Königsberg, see
Kaliningrad
Konotop .61,000..R 19
Konstanti-
novka* .103,000..H 3
Kopeysk .166,000..H 6
Korkino* ...83,000..H 7
Kostroma .209,000..O 22
Kotlas ...61,000..M 23
Kovrov ..116,000..P 22
Krama-
torsk ..141,000..S 20
Krasnoar-
meyskaya 53,000..U 20
Krasnodar 407,000..U 20
Krasnodon* 68,000..H 3
Krasno-
gorsk* ...50,000..F 15
Krasno-
kamsk* ...55,000..G 6
Krasnotur'-
insk ...61,000..G 6
Krasno-
vodsk ...48,000..J 4
Krasno-
yarsk ..576,000..H 9
Krasnyy
Luch ..102,000..T 20
Kremen-
chug ..136,000..S 19
Krivoy Rog 510,000..S 19
Kropotkin .62,000..U 21
Kulebaki ...46,000..P 22
Kungur ...70,000..G 6
Kurgan .215,000..H 6
Kursk ..255,000..R 20
Kustanay .118,000..H 6
Kutaisi .159,000..W 21
Kuybyshev 992,000..Q 24
Kuznetsk ...75,000..R 23
Kzyl-Orda .91,000..J 6
Labinsk ...49,000..V 21
Leninabad 100,000..K 6
Leninakan 133,000..I 2
Lenin-
grad ..3,296,000
*3,706,000..E 4
Leninogorsk 70,000..I 8
Leninsk-Kuznet-
skiy ..138,000..H 9
Liepãja ...86,000..E 3
Lipetsk .253,000..Q 21
Lisichansk 120,000..S 20
Lugansk .352,000..S 20
Lutsk ...82,000..F 2
Lvov
(Lwów) 512,000..F 2
Lys'va ...79,000..G 6
Lyubertsy .120,000..P 21
Magadan ...89,000..D 14
Magnito-
gorsk ..357,000..H 6
Makeyevka 414,000..T 20
Makhach-
kala ..165,000..W 23
Margelan* ..89,000..K 6
Mariupol, see Zhdanov
Mary ...59,000..K 5
Maykop ..106,000..V 20
Melekess ...75,000..Q 24
Melitopol' .119,000..T 19
Memel (Klai-
pëda) .131,000..E 2
Mezhdure-
chensk* ...79,000..H 9
Miass ..122,000..H 6
Michurinsk .91,000..Q 21
Mineral'nyye
Vody ...47,000..V 22
Minsk ..772,000..P 17
Mogilëv ..176,000..P 18
Monche-
gorsk ...53,000..D 5
Moscow (Mos-
kva) ..6,507,000..F 4
Mukachëvo* 58,000..F 1
Murmansk 287,000..D 5
Murom ...96,000..P 22
Mytishchi .112,000..P 21
Nakhodka ..96,000..H 15
Nal'chik .119,000..V 22
Namangan 188,000..K 6
Nebit-Dag* 49,000..J 4
Nevinno-
myssk* ...63,000..V 21

Nezhin ...55,000..R 18
Nikolayev .300,000..T 18
Nikopol' .110,000..T 19
Nizhniy
Tagil ..377,000..G 6
Noginsk* .102,000..F 4
Noril'sk .129,000..E 9
Novgorod .107,000..N 19
Novocher-
kassk ..161,000..T 21
Novokuyby-
shevsk* .107,000..H 4
Novokuz-
netsk ..493,000..H 9
Novomos-
kovsk ..126,000..Q 21
Novomos-
kovsk* ...58,000..G 3
Novo-
rossiysk 123,000..U 20
Novoshakh-
tinsk ..107,000..T 21
Novosi-
birsk ..1,064,000..H 8
Novo
Troitsk ..82,000..H 5
Nukus ...56,000..J 5
Odessa ..776,000..T 17
Oktyabr'skiy 79,000..G 5
Omsk ..774,000..H 7
Ordzhoni-
kidze ..219,000..W 22
Orekhovo-
Zuyevo ..117,000..P 21
Orël ..209,000..Q 20
Orenburg .326,000..H 5
Orsha ...89,000..P 18
Orsk ..215,000..H 5
Osh ..119,000..K 7
Osinniki* ...69,000..H 9
Panevëzys .65,000..O 17
Pavlodar .154,000..I 8
Pavlograd* 62,000..G 3
Pavlovo ...60,000..P 22
Pavlovskiy
Posad* ...65,000..F 4
Penza ..333,000..Q 23
Perm' ..796,000..G 6
Pervomaysk 52,000..S 18
Pervou-
ral'sk ..110,000..G 6
Petropav-
lovsk ..166,000..H 7
Petropavlovsk-
Kam-
chatskiy 123,000..D 16
Petroza-
vodsk ..171,000..M 20
Pinsk ...57,000..Q 17
Podol'sk .163,000..P 21
Polevskoy* .54,000..G 6
Polotsk ...61,000..O 18
Poltava ..184,000..S 19
Poti ...46,000..W 21
Priluki ...56,000..R 18
Prokop'-
yevsk ..290,000..H 9
Pskov ..112,000..N 18
Pyatigorsk .81,000..V 22
Ramen-
skoye* ...53,000..F 4
Revda* ...57,000..G 6
Riga
(Rīga) ..680,000..N 17
Rostov-on-
Don ..757,000..T 20
Roven'ki ...60,000..S 21
Rovno ..100,000..F 2
Rubezhnoye 52,000..S 20
Rubtsovsk .142,000..I 8
Rudnyy ...89,000..H 6
Rustavi* ...95,000..I 3
Ryazan' ..311,000..P 21
Rybinsk .212,000..O 21
Rzhev ...59,000..O 20
Salavat ...98,000..H 5
Samarkand 248,000..K 6
Saran'* ...54,000..I 7
Saransk .154,000..Q 23
Sarapul ...91,000..G 5
Saratov ..720,000..P 23
Semipala-
tinsk ..204,000..I 8
Serov ..104,000..G 6
Serpukhov 121,000..P 20
Sevastopol
(Sevas-
topol') ..209,000..U 18
Severodo-
netsk ...74,000..S 20
Severod-
vinsk ..121,000..E 5
Shadrinsk* 65,000..H 6
Shakhtërsk* 72,000..T 19
Shakhty ..209,000..T 21
Shchëkino ..56,000..Q 20
Shchëlkovo* 72,000..F 4
Shostka ...54,000..Q 19
Shuya ...69,000..O 22
Šiauliai* ...82,000..E 2
Simferopol' 223,000..U 18
Slavyansk 113,000..S 20
Slavyansk-na-
Kubani ...52,000..U 20
Smela ...52,000..S 18

Smolensk .196,000..P 19
Snezhnoye ..72,000..T 20
Sochi ..188,000..V 20
Sokol ...50,000..N 22
Solikamsk ..88,000..G 6
Stalinabad, see
Dushanbe
Stalingrad, see
see Volgograd
Stalino, see Donetsk
Stavropol' 177,000..U 21
Sterli-
tamak .162,000..H 5
Stupino ...53,000..P 21
Suchan ...50,000..H 15
Sukhumi ...88,000..V 21
Sumgait .104,000..J 3
Sumy ..140,000..R 19
Sverdlovsk 961,000..G 6
Sverdlovsk* 73,000..H 3
Svobodnyy .62,000..G 13
Syktyvkar .102,000..F 6
Syzran' .169,000..R 24
Taganrog .245,000..T 20
Taldy-
Kurgan .50,000..J 8
Tallinn ..340,000..M 18
Tambov .211,000..R 21
Tartu ...85,000..N 18
Tashauz ...60,000..J 5
Tashkent 1,239,000..K 6
Tbilisi, see
Tiflis
Temir-Tau 150,000..I 7
Ternopol' ..72,000..F 2
Tiflis
(Tbilisi) 842,000..I 3
Tikhoretsk .57,000..U 21
Tiraspol' .91,000..S 17
Tobolsk
(Tobol'sk) 47,000..G 7
Tolyatti .143,000..Q 24
Tomsk .324,000..H 9
Torez ...95,000..T 20
Troitsk* ...86,000..H 6
Tselinograd
(Akmo-
linsk) ..176,000..I 7
Tula ..377,000..Q 20
Tulun ...48,000..H 10
Tyumen' .240,000..G 6
Ufa ..704,000..H 5
Ukhta ...53,000..F 6
Ulan-Ude .227,000..H 11
Ul'yanovsk 294,000..Q 24
Uman' ...59,000..S 17
Ural'sk .123,000..H 4
Urgench ...65,000..J 5
Usol'ye-Sibir-
skoye ...75,000..H 11
Ussuriysk .124,000..H 15
Ust'-Kameno-
gorsk .212,000..I 8
Uzhgorod ..61,000..F 1
Uzlovaya ...52,000..Q 21
Velikiye
Luki ...80,000..O 19
Vichuga ...53,000..O 22
Vilnius ..316,000..O 17
Vinnitsa .163,000..R 17
Vitebsk ..203,000..P 18
Vladimir .211,000..P 21
Vladivostok 397,000..H 15
Volgograd
(Stalin-
grad) ..743,000..T 22
Vologda .170,000..N 22
Vol'sk ...70,000..R 23
Volzhskiy .114,000..T 22
Vorkuta ...65,000..E 7
Voronezh .611,000..R 21
Voskre-
sensk ...59,000..F 4
Votkinsk* ...72,000..G 5
Vyborg ...65,000..M 19
Vyshniy
Volochëk .73,000..O 20
Yakutsk ...95,000..E 12
Yalta ...55,000..U 18
Yangi-
Yul'* ...55,000..K 6
Yaroslavl' .498,000..O 21
Yegor'yevsk 64,000..P 21
Yelets ...96,000..Q 21
Yenakiyevo 94,000..T 20
Yerevan ..665,000..I 2
Yessentuki .53,000..V 21
Yevpatoriya 70,000..U 18
Yeysk ...68,000..T 20
Yoshkar-
Ola ..137,000..P 23
Yurga ...54,000..H 8
Yuzhno-Sak-
halinsk ..92,000..G 16
Zagorsk ...85,000..O 21
Zapo-
rozh'ye .595,000..T 19
Zelënodol'sk 72,000..P 24
Zhdanov
(Mariu-
pol) ..385,000..T 20
Zhitomir .141,000..R 17
Zhukovka ...63,000..Q 19
Zlatoust ..178,000..H 6
Zyryanovsk 57,000..I 8

*Population of metropolitan area, including suburbs.
*Does not appear on map; key gives general location.

Source: Official estimates (1967).

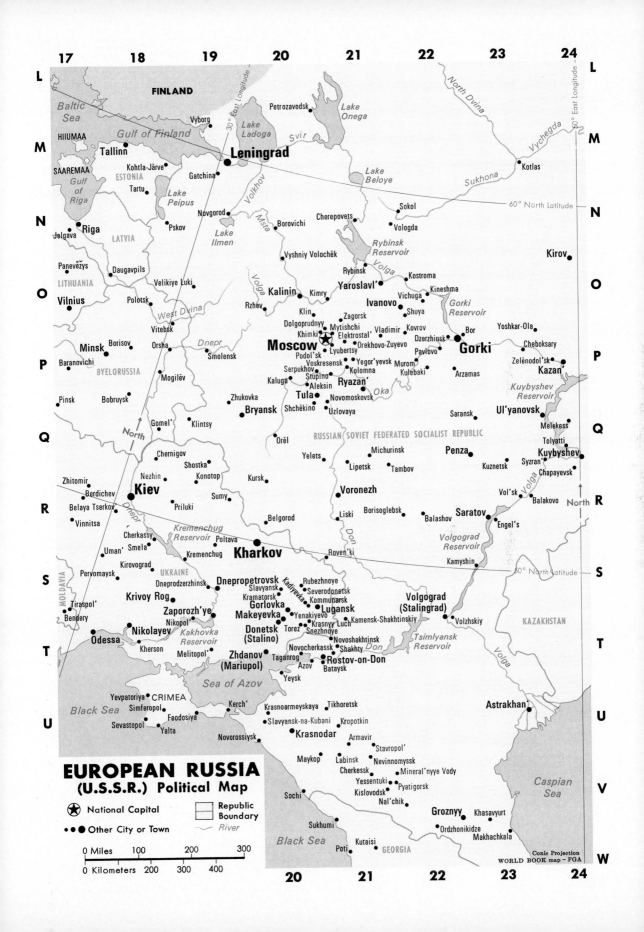

EUROPEAN RUSSIA
(U.S.S.R.) Political Map

⭐ National Capital

•••● Other City or Town

▭ Republic Boundary

〰 River

0 Miles 100 200 300

0 Kilometers 200 300 400

Conic Projection
WORLD BOOK map – FGA

The population of Russia is spread out unevenly across the country. About 75 per cent of the people live in European Russia, which covers about a fourth of the land. European Russia has an average of more than 85 persons to the square mile. Asian Russia averages fewer than 10 persons to the square mile.

Nationalities and Languages. Russia's people have many different backgrounds and speak many different languages. The Soviet census lists over 100 nationality groups in Russia. They are identified mainly by the languages they speak. Soviet republics are set up on the basis of various nationality groups and carry their names, such as *Ukrainian* Soviet Socialist Republic and *Latvian* Soviet Socialist Republic. Most nationality groups are of *Caucasoid* (white) stock. Others are of *Mongoloid* (yellow) stock, or are mixtures of the two races. See LANGUAGE (Language Families).

Slavic Nationality Groups make up more than three-fourths of the total population. They speak different, but closely related, Slavic languages. The ancestors of the Slavs established the original Russian state more than a thousand years ago.

The *Russians* are the largest Slavic group, though all Soviet peoples are generally called Russians. This group, once known as *Great Russians*, makes up about 55 per cent of the nation's population. The Russians live throughout the country, and hold most positions of leadership in the government and Communist party. Russian is the official language, and is taught in all Soviet schools. Almost all Soviet citizens speak Russian as a first or second language. See RUSSIAN LANGUAGE.

The *Ukrainians*, the second largest Slavic group, live in southern European Russia. The *Byelorussians*, some-times called *White Russians*, are the third largest Slavic group. Most of them live in western European Russia. Closely related to the three major Slavic groups are the *Poles* of westernmost Russia.

Turkic Peoples rank second in number to the Slavs. Their languages are also closely related. Some Turkic peoples are Mongoloid. The largest Turkic groups live in Soviet Central Asia, a region between the Caspian Sea and China. The *Uzbeks* are the most numerous and the most advanced people of the region. Their ancestors were among the first settled farmers in the world. Other Turkic groups of Soviet Central Asia include the *Kazakhs*, *Kirghiz*, and *Turkmen*. The *Tuvinians* and *Yakuts* live in Siberia, a huge region that covers most of Asian Russia. The *Azerbaidzhani* live in the Caucasus Mountain region west of the Caspian Sea. The largest Turkic groups of European Russia live in the Volga River Valley. They are the *Bashkirs*, *Chuvash*, and *Tartars*, or *Tatars*. See TARTAR; TURK.

Other Groups. The *Finno-Ugric* peoples live in northern Russia, between the Baltic Sea and central Siberia. The largest of these groups include the *Estonians* near the Baltic Sea; the *Finns* and *Karelians* near Finland; and the *Mari*, *Mordovians*, and *Udmurts* of the Volga Valley. The *Lithuanians* and *Latvians* live near the Baltic Sea and speak related languages.

The *Germans* are widely scattered over many parts of Russia. The ancestors of most of the Germans were settlers who arrived during the 1700's and 1800's. Yiddish-speaking *Jews*, listed as a nationality group by the Soviet census, live mainly in European Russia. The *Moldavians* live near Romania, and are closely related to the Romanians. Their language is much like Romanian, but it

POPULATION AND LANGUAGE

This map shows where the people of Russia live. Each dot represents about 65,000 people. The colors on the map show where the major languages are spoken. The regions in which these languages are spoken closely resemble the individual republics of Russia.

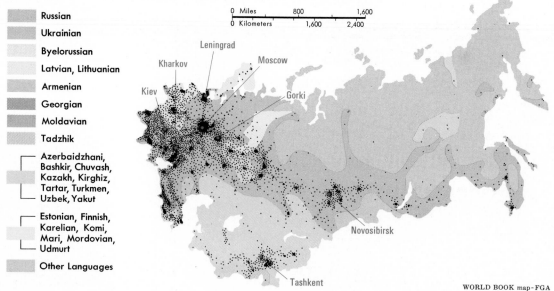

Russian
Ukrainian
Byelorussian
Latvian, Lithuanian
Armenian
Georgian
Moldavian
Tadzhik

Azerbaidzhani, Bashkir, Chuvash, Kazakh, Kirghiz, Tartar, Turkmen, Uzbek, Yakut

Estonian, Finnish, Karelian, Komi, Mari, Mordovian, Udmurt

Other Languages

Leningrad
Kharkov
Moscow
Kiev
Gorki
Novosibirsk
Tashkent

WORLD BOOK map-FGA

is written in the Russian *Cyrillic* alphabet (see ALPHA-BET [The Cyrillic Alphabet]).

The *Armenians* and *Georgians* are the major nationality groups of the Caucasus region. The *Tadzhiks*, whose language resembles Persian, live in the mountain valleys of Soviet Central Asia. Many small Siberian groups are related to American Indians and Eskimos.

Religion. The Russian Orthodox Church was the official Russian church before the Communists rose to power. The Communists were *atheists* (persons who believe there is no God). They looked on religion as an anti-Communist force, and called it the "opium of the people." The Communists destroyed many churches, made museums of others, and arrested or killed many church leaders who refused to follow Communism.

Religious worship survived in the Soviet Union, however, and the persecution gradually decreased. Many religious restrictions were dropped during the early 1940's, after church leaders supported Russia's war effort in World War II. These restrictions were brought back during the late 1950's. The government closed many churches and prohibited religious services outside officially recognized places of worship.

Today, the Communists do all they can to discourage religion through propaganda and education. However, many Russians worship in secret as well as in public. The Russian Orthodox Church probably has between 20 million and 45 million followers, more than any other church in Russia. Moslems are the second largest religious group in Russia. Other religious groups in the country include Buddhists, Evangelical Christian Baptists, Jews, Lutherans, Roman Catholics, and members of the Armenian Church.

Burt Glinn, Magnum

Ukrainian Woman wears government medals awarded for her high farm-production record.

Howard Sochurek

Uzbek Cotton Workers belong to the largest Turkic group in Russia. The Uzbeks live in Soviet Central Asia.

A Leningrad Crowd hurries home from work in the second largest city in the Soviet Union. The population of Leningrad, like that of the entire country, consists mostly of Slavic people.

ZFA from Publix

Soviet Life

Siberian Yakut Woman, of the Mongoloid race, is a geologist. Women make up over half the workers in Russia.

Stan Wayman, *Life*
© 1963 Time Inc.

Estonian Girl wears one of her people's historic costumes in a parade. The Estonians are closely related to the Finns.

The early Communists hoped to achieve a *classless society*—a society with neither rich nor poor people. The government took over all privately owned factories, farms, and other means of production. The Communist slogan was: "From each according to his ability, to each according to his needs." Everyone would serve the government as best he could, and no one would have any special rights.

The Communists have failed to achieve their goal of a classless society. The old classes that had special rights based on inherited rank and wealth have disappeared. However, new classes with special rights have appeared under the Soviet system. These groups include top officials of the Communist party and the government, and some professional persons, including artists, engineers, and scientists. They have automobiles, comfortable apartments and *dachas* (country homes), and other luxuries that most Russians do not have. For the great majority of Russians, living conditions are poor.

Personal Freedom. In the past, especially during the 1930's, the people of Russia lived under extreme terror. The secret police arrested millions of Russians suspected of anti-Communist views or activities. The victims were shot or sent to prison camps.

Today, the Russians live under greater freedom, though few dare criticize the government or the Communist party in front of a stranger. The government allows a limited amount of criticism to go unpunished.

Also, many Russian writers whose views have been officially disapproved are widely popular with the people. But any Russian who opposes party policies too strongly may be expelled from his city, or even sent to a prison labor camp.

The government restricts the people's contacts with the Free World. It allows few Russians to travel outside the country. A person even needs official permission to move into a city or from one apartment to another. On the other hand, the government provides some important free benefits, including medical and hospital care. Higher education is provided for every student with a good record in schoolwork and behavior.

City Life. About half of the people of Russia live in cities and towns. Twenty-nine Russian cities have over 500,000 persons. Seven Russian cities have more than a million persons. They are, in order of size, Moscow, Leningrad, Kiev, Tashkent, Gorki, Kharkov, and Novosibirsk. See the separate articles on the cities of Russia listed in the *Related Articles* at the end of this article.

Russian cities are so crowded that millions of families must share small, plain apartments with one or more other families. A family may wait for years to get its own apartment, which will probably have only one or two rooms.

Russian housewives have a special problem shopping for food and clothing. There is a shortage of meat, and

Soviet Life from Sovfoto

New Apartment Buildings are going up in Moscow and other Russian cities to help reduce the shortage of housing.

Novosti

Gunvor Betting, P.I.P.

Sharing Tiny Apartments is a way of life for millions of Russian families. There is a severe housing shortage, and a family may wait years for its own apartment.

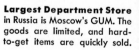

Largest Department Store in Russia is Moscow's GUM. The goods are limited, and hard-to-get items are quickly sold.

it is expensive. Clothing in the stores is plain and lacks variety. Shoppers often go from store to store looking for what they want, much of the time without finding it. They sometimes stand in line for hours before they can be waited on.

Village Life. Every year, about a million Russians leave the villages and move to the cities. Jobs are easier to find in the rural areas, but living conditions there are much worse than in the cities. In the villages, many Russians live in small log huts or in community barracks. Most of the families have no gas, plumbing, or running water, and many do not have electricity. There are fewer stores in the villages than in the cities, and they carry a smaller variety of goods. The quality of education that is provided in the villages is far below that of the cities.

Most Russians in the rural areas work on huge government-controlled farms. A Russian farmer is allowed to cultivate a small plot of land for himself, and to keep a few animals on it. He can sell his own dairy products, meat, and vegetables in the cities for private income.

Family Life. Many Russian mothers spend little time at home with their families. Over half of all Russian workers are women, partly because millions of Russian men were killed during World War II. Like the men, the women work six days a week and do every kind of work. They even lay bricks, dig ditches, and repair streets. About 75 per cent of Russia's doctors are women.

In addition to working, a Russian mother must spend much time away from home to do the shopping.

The government operates about 60,000 nursery schools for children from 2½ months to 3 years old. Each nursery cares for as many as 200 youngsters. The nurseries, as well as kindergartens for children up to 7 years old, help make it possible for Russian mothers to work. Most of the mothers bring in their children at 7:30 A.M. and call for them at 5:30 P.M.

Recreation. Russians are enthusiastic sports fans, and Soviet athletes have won the respect of the world for their skill. Sports training for Russian children begins in nursery school and kindergarten, and continues throughout school. There are also special sports camps and clubs for children and adults. Most factory and office workers take part in daily group exercises. The exercises are broadcast from Moscow twice a day.

Soccer, a form of football, is the most popular sport in Russia. Soccer teams are sponsored by trade unions and other groups. Beginning at the age of 12, children are selected and trained by the various teams. Other popular sports include basketball, hockey, ice skating, skiing, and track and field events. The government strongly encourages sports, and often sends athletic teams outside Russia to compete against teams of other nations. Chess is especially popular, and millions of Russians begin to play the game at an early age. Russian players often win international chess tournaments.

Few Russian Villages have gas, plumbing, or running water. Most of the villages in the Soviet Union have no more than one paved street.

Novosti

Howard Sochurek

Workers on a State Farm eat a noon meal of soup and bread. It was prepared in a field kitchen, *background*, and on an outdoor stove, *right rear*.

During the early 1900's, Russia was largely an underdeveloped country of poor, uneducated peasants. After the Communists seized control, they promoted education strongly. Great numbers of highly trained managers and workers were needed to build up the nation. Russian schools began expanding to meet this need.

Today, Russia has more than 50 million students, and nearly all the people can read and write. Russia is a mighty industrial nation partly because of its educational program. The schools stress science and technology, which includes industrial skills. Soviet achievements in these fields are among the highest in the world.

Russian students know that education is the surest road to success in their country. Students who earn high marks can look forward to important, highly paid careers. But students are graded on more than schoolwork. Their behavior and leadership in group activities in class and after school are also graded. Students who receive low marks in behavior may not be permitted to continue their education.

During the 1930's, Soviet law required children to attend school for four years. Beginning in 1970, 10 years of school were required, from the age of 7 to 17. Russia has no private schools, and education is free. Students buy textbooks, which cost little. About three-fourths of the students in schools of higher education receive government allowances for living expenses.

The same basic courses are given throughout Russia. The Communist party approves all educational programs and policies. Lower education is supervised by ministries of education in the union republics. Higher education is directed by the federal Ministry of Higher and Secondary Specialized Education. All schools stress Communist beliefs. Communism is presented as the best form of society, and other forms receive little attention.

In most schools, pupils are taught in the local language of the republic or region. All republics also have schools that teach in Russian. Parents decide which of these schools their children will attend. In schools that teach in a local language, children begin studying Rus-

Kindergarten Children learn folk dancing under a portrait of Lenin, *background.* The Russians see a picture of the founder of Communist Russia almost everywhere they turn.

Weston Kemp

Howard Sochurek

Young Pioneers, members of a group for Soviet children from 9 through 15 years old, do exercises on the grounds of an old Leningrad palace, their activities center.

Students Learning English are urged to follow the example of their hero Lenin. Russians study English, French, or German from fifth through tenth grade.

Student Uniforms are worn in many Russian schools. Classes meet six days a week.

sian in second grade. From fifth grade through tenth grade, pupils study English, French, or German.

Elementary Grades in Russia are the first four grades. Classes meet six days a week—about $4\frac{1}{2}$ hours daily Monday through Friday, and a shorter period on Saturday. The program includes arithmetic, art, language, music, physical education, and simple work skills. Nature study and Soviet history are started in fourth grade.

Intermediate Grades consist of fifth grade through eighth grade. Classes meet about 30 hours a week, and each subject is taught by a different teacher. Fifth-grade subjects include arithmetic, botany, geography, history, language, and shop work skills. Algebra, geometry, literature, physics, and zoology are taught in sixth grade. Chemistry is started in seventh grade. Eighth-grade courses include anatomy and physiology.

Secondary Grades are the ninth and tenth grades. About 60 per cent of the secondary program consists of mathematics, science, and work skills of various trades. These courses are designed to help meet the government's need for specialists in science and industry. Russian secondary schools also teach history, language, literature, physical education, and social studies. Graduates with high marks receive gold or silver medals. They are freed from required military service so they can continue their education.

Special Schools. After eighth grade, students may attend technical or trade schools. These schools train young people to be skilled technicians and workers in agriculture, engineering, industry, and other fields. Soviet law requires that jobs must be provided for graduates of these technical or trade schools. If a technician receives high marks and then works for

three years, he may be quickly admitted to a higher technical institute.

The Soviet Union has many schools for gifted children who are selected by their teachers. These schools, beginning in first grade, stress the arts, foreign languages, or mathematics and physics. They also cover subjects in the general educational program.

Higher Education. Russia has about 700 specialized institutes and about 40 universities. Almost $3\frac{1}{2}$ million students attend these schools of higher education. From 85 to 90 per cent of them attend specialized institutes. The rest go to universities.

At the institutes, students are trained in agriculture, engineering, medicine, teaching, and other fields. More than two-fifths of the students specialize in engineering. University students are trained chiefly to be researchers, scholars, or teachers. Moscow State University is the oldest and largest university in Russia. It was established in 1755 and has more than 30,000 students.

Most programs in higher education take from 4 to $5\frac{1}{2}$ years of study. After completing their studies, students must work for three years at government-assigned jobs in their fields. Many are sent to underdeveloped areas of Russia, where specialists are needed. The students receive their diplomas after working one year.

After-School Activities are required of Russian children. These activities include crafts, folk dancing, music, sports, and cleaning and repairing the schools. The children also may join organizations supervised by the Communist party. Youngsters from 7 through 9 years old may join the *Little Octobrists*, a group named in honor of the October Revolution of 1917. This organization encourages children to be leaders in such activities as after-school duties, preparing for holiday ceremonies, and organizing plays. Children from 9 through 15 years old may join the *Young Pioneers*. The activities of this group include boat building, home-making, music, painting, and radio operating.

The *Komsomol* (Young Communist League) is an organization for Russians from 15 through 28 years old. Students who do not join the Komsomol may have difficulty being admitted to schools of higher education. The organization is primarily a political movement to gain support and members for the Communist party. The Komsomol works with children's groups and helps spread Communist teachings. Most persons who join the party come from the Komsomol.

Young people also may work on projects at scientific and technical clubs. The clubs' equipment, staff members, and workrooms are provided by Soviet industries. Other clubs operate for young and adult Russians interested in acting, dancing, or music.

Libraries. The Soviet Union has about 370,000 libraries, more than any other country. About 127,000 are general public libraries. Every city, town, and village has a general public library. The rest of Russia's libraries are special libraries, operated by farms, industries, schools, unions, or other organizations. Russia's largest library, the Lenin State Library in Moscow, is one of the biggest in the world. Its collections of books, magazines, and newspapers include about 25 million items. The Library of the Academy of Sciences of the U.S.S.R. in Leningrad has about 20 million volumes. The M. E. Saltykov-Shchedrin State Public Library in Leningrad owns about 17 million volumes.

Museums. There are more than 900 museums in Russia. Every important city and town has at least one museum. The museums deal with the arts, history, and science. Many families spend their holidays visiting local museums, because Russia has a limited number of popular amusements. The State Historical Museum in Moscow is Russia's chief historical museum. Its displays cover Russian history from ancient times until the Revolution of 1917. The Museum of the Revolution, also in Moscow, has exhibits from the revolutionary period to the present time.

Sovfoto

Education Means Success in Russia. These students use a sign that reads: "Do not disturb! We are preparing for exams."

N. Granovsky, Sovfoto

Moscow State University, Russia's largest university, has over 30,000 students. Many of them live in its main building.

E. Kassin, Sovfoto

University Students enjoy a friend's guitar playing at a New Year's party. Although Communist leaders disapprove, young Russians like jazz and the latest Western dances.

The Soviet government operates all communication activities in Russia, including broadcasting, motion-picture production, and publishing. They are controlled by various ministries and committees of the Council of Ministers. The Communist party checks all broadcasts and publications to make sure that they follow party policies. The party also publishes many books, magazines, and newspapers. Moscow is the communication center of the Soviet Union.

Russia has more than 400 radio stations, and there are about 20 radios to every 100 Russians. Many stations broadcast in local languages. The nation has over 90 main television stations, and about 75 TV stations that rebroadcast programs to distant areas. There are only about 3 television sets to every 100 Russians. Television programs consist mainly of movies, music, and sports.

In Russia, motion pictures are an important means of spreading Communist beliefs, as well as entertainment. In most of the movies, the hero or heroine is an eager worker for Communism. Films are produced in about 30 studios. The largest studio is Mosfilm in Moscow. The Soviet Union has about 90,500 movie theaters.

Thousands of newspapers are published in Russia, including those published by factories, farms, and government agencies. The newspapers are printed in more than 50 languages. Twenty-five major newspapers are sold throughout the country. *Izvestia* (News) of Moscow has a daily circulation of more than 8 million copies, more than any other paper in the world. *Izvestia* is the official newspaper of the Soviet government. *Pravda* (Truth), also of Moscow, is Russia's second largest paper. It has a daily circulation of about 7 million copies. *Pravda* is published by the Communist party.

Most of Russia's other major newspapers represent various activities of national life, including the armed forces and trade unions. *Tass* is the official Soviet news agency (see TASS).

Nearly 4,000 magazines are published in Russia. Every year, about 80,000 different books and pamphlets are published in Russia, probably more than in any other country. Russia's huge publishing industry, like the nation's other communication industries, is an important tool for spreading Communist beliefs.

Telephone and telegraph lines cross the huge country. There are about 7,200,000 telephones in the Soviet Union, or about 3 telephones to every 100 Russians.

A Russian Cartoon from *Krokodil* (Crocodile), the official magazine of humor, pokes fun at village managers. The woman, *lower left*, says: "Good gracious! There must be a fire somewhere!" She is told: "Don't get panicky, Auntie! This is only our management watching how the field work is going."

Sovfoto

The Communist Party Newspaper, *Pravda* (Truth), has one of the world's largest circulations. *Pravda* sells about 7 million copies a day.

Homer J. Smith

The Trinity by Andrew Rublev. State Tretyakov Gallery, Moscow

Religious Paintings called *icons* are outstanding examples of Russian art during the Middle Ages.

Act II, *The Cherry Orchard* by Anton Chekhov. Novosti

Masterpieces of Drama written by Anton Chekhov and other great Russian playwrights are presented by the famous Moscow Art Theater.

Novosti

Young Russian Poets such as Yevgeny Yevtushenko attract large audiences to their public readings.

Lenin State Museum (Constantine Manos, Magnum)

Soviet Art follows an official style called *socialist realism*. This painting shows Lenin with a group of Russian workers.

RUSSIA /Arts

Artists in Russia must present the ideas of Communism in their works. Artists' unions and the Communist party carefully control all artistic production. The Soviet government accepts only a simple art style that it calls *socialist realism*. This style stresses the goals and benefits of Soviet life, and ignores the faults. Works difficult to understand are officially discouraged, and artists who criticize Communism may be sent to prison labor camps. Many artists who work within the official restrictions receive large government salaries.

Architecture of old Russia is represented by churches with many-colored, onion-shaped domes. The most famous of these churches is 400-year-old Saint Basil's Church in Red Square in Moscow (see ARCHITECTURE [picture, Saint Basil's Church]). Until the 1950's, Soviet architects designed buildings in a highly decorative

style known in the West as "wedding cake." Since then, the government has encouraged standard, simple designs to help speed its huge housing program.

Literature. The 1800's were years of great literary activity in Russia. Outstanding writers of the period included Anton Chekhov, Fyodor Dostoevsky, Alexander Pushkin, Leo Tolstoy, and Ivan Turgenev.

Since 1917, strict Communist controls have interfered greatly with literary production. Communist Russia has produced only a few great writers. They included Ilya Ehrenburg, Maxim Gorki, Boris Pasternak, and Mikhail Sholokhov. Pasternak and Sholokhov won the Nobel prize for literature. But the Communist party disapproved of Pasternak's views of Soviet life, and forced him to refuse the prize. During the 1960's, the popular poet Yevgeny Yevtushenko demanded

John G. Ross, Photo Researchers

Ballet Dancers of the Bolshoi Theater in Moscow are world famous for their skill and gracefulness.

Louis Renault, Photo Researchers

The Winter Palace in Leningrad, a home of the czars, represents the baroque style of architecture. The palace was built between 1754 and 1762.

Burt Glinn, Magnum

Music by Aram Khachaturian and other Soviet composers is often based on old folk songs of Russia.

Scene from *The Cranes Are Flying*, directed by Mikhail Kalatozov (Novosti)

Motion Pictures are an important means of spreading Communist beliefs in Russia. Most of the leading characters are eager workers for Communism.

more freedom from government control for writers, and was officially criticized several times. See RUSSIAN LITERATURE and the biographies of Russian writers listed in the *Related Articles* with that article.

Music. Mikhail Glinka, who wrote operas during the early 1800's, is considered the father of serious Russian music. Many of Russia's greatest composers wrote during the late 1800's. They included Modest Mussorgsky, Nicholas Rimsky-Korsakov, and Peter Ilich Tchaikovsky. The famous composers Sergei Rachmaninoff and Igor Stravinsky left Russia in the early 1900's. Well-known composers of Communist Russia include Aram Khachaturian, Sergei Prokofiev, and Dimitri Shostakovich. See the biographies of Russian composers listed in the *Related Articles* with the MUSIC article.

Painting. Early Russian artists painted large reli-

gious pictures on church walls, and also smaller religious pictures called *icons* (see ICON). By the mid-1800's, Moscow and St. Petersburg (now Leningrad) had busy art schools, and Russian artists were painting more varied subjects. The two most famous Russian-born painters, Marc Chagall and Wassily Kandinsky, left the country in the early 1900's.

Theater and Ballet in Russia have a long history of high quality. They still present skillful performances under Communism, but have adopted few new ideas. Several fine drama groups developed in Moscow during the late 1800's. The most famous, the Moscow Art Theater, still performs (see MOSCOW ART THEATER). Many experts consider the ballets of Moscow's Bolshoi Theater the highest achievement in Russian arts today. See BOLSHOI THEATER BALLET; DRAMA (Modern Drama).

505

RUSSIA / The Land

Russia is the largest country in the world. It covers more than 8½ million square miles, or over a seventh of all the land on earth. Russia spreads across northern Europe and Asia for about 6,000 miles, from the Baltic Sea to the Pacific Ocean.

Land Regions. Russia is a land of huge *steppes* (grassy plains), thick forests, high mountains, and rugged plateaus. The country has six main land regions: (1) the European Plain, (2) the Ural Mountains, (3) the Aral-Caspian Lowland, (4) the West Siberian Plain, (5) the Central Siberian Plateau, and (6) the East Siberian Uplands. See SIBERIA.

The European Plain is the home of about three-fourths of the Russian people. Most of the nation's industries and much of its richest soils are in this region. The plain is mostly flat to gently rolling, with some low hills. It averages about 600 feet above sea level. At the southern edge of the plain, the Caucasus Mountains rise more than 18,000 feet. The highest point in Europe, 18,481-foot Mount Elbrus, is in the Caucasus. The Caucasus mark the beginning of a series of high mountains that extends eastward along Russia's southern border to Lake Baykal in Siberia. See CAUCASUS MOUNTAINS.

The Ural Mountains form the boundary between European Russia and Siberia. These old, rounded mountains have been worn down by streams to an average height of only about 2,000 feet. Several peaks in the north and south rise above 5,000 feet. In the middle section, the most heavily populated part of the region, the range splits into a series of low ridges. The Urals are a storehouse of great mineral wealth, and have many industries. See URAL MOUNTAINS.

The Aral-Caspian Lowland, or *Soviet Central Asia*, has broad, sandy deserts and low, grassy plateaus. The deserts include the *Kara Kum* (Black Sands) and *Kyzyl Kum* (Red Sands). The Karagiye Depression, 433 feet below sea level, is the lowest point in the Soviet Union. It is on the Mangyshlak Peninsula, which extends into the Caspian Sea. The highest point in Russia, 24,590-foot Communism Peak, also is in the region. It rises in the Pamirs, a rugged mountain system along Russia's southern border. See PAMIRS, THE.

Land Regions of Russia

East Siberian Uplands · Central Siberian Plateau · West Siberian Plain · European Plain · Ural Mountains · Aral-Caspian Lowland

Physical Features

Feature	Grid
Aldan Plateau	D 8
Altai Mts.	E 6
Amgun River (River)	E 8
Amu Darya (River)	C 10
Amur River	D 8
Anadyr Range	C 10
Anadyr River	D 7
Angara River	E 4
Aral Sea	A
Arctic Ocean	A
Argun River	D 7
Atlantic Ocean	B 10
Ayon Island	E 3
Azov, Sea of	B 10
Baltic Sea	B 7
Barents Sea	B 5
Baykal Mts.	D 7
Belyy Island	B 5
Bennett Island	D 10
Bering Sea	B 9
Bering Strait	C 11
Black Sea	E 3
Cape Chelyuskin	B 6
Cape Kanin	C 4
Cape Lopatka	D 9
Cape Navarin	C 10
Cape Olyutorskiy	C 10
Cape Svyatoy	B 8
Cape Zhelaniya	B 7
Caspian Depression	E 4
Caspian Sea	E 4
Caucasus Mts.	E 4
Cherskiy Mts.	C 9
Commander Islands	D 10
Communism Peak	E 5
Crimea (Peninsula)	E 3
Dnepr River	F 3
Dnestr River	C 10
Don River	E 3
Donets Basin	D 7
Dzhugdzhur Mts.	E 4
East Siberian Sea	B 9
Faddeyev Island	A
Franz Josef Land	D 1
Gulf of Anadyr	C 11
Gulf of Shelekhov	E 3
Gydan Mts.	B 10
Irtysh River	D 5
Ishim River	B 7
Issyk-Kul (Lake)	D 5
Japan, Sea of	E 8
Kama River	D 10
Kamchatka Peninsula	E 3
Kara Kum (Desert)	C 4
Kara Kum Canal	B 8
Kara Sea	B 7
Karaganda Basin	C 10
Karagiye Depression	E 4
Karagiye Island	D 10
Khanka Lake	B 8
Khatanga River	B 7
Klyuchevskaya (Volcano)	D 10
Kola Peninsula	C 3
Kolguyev Island	C 4
Kolyma River	C 10
Koryak Mts.	B 9
Korelskiy Island	B 9
Kuril Islands	E 8
Kuril Strait	E 4
Kurybyshev Reservoir	D 4
Kuznetsk Basin	D 6
Kyzyl Kum (Desert)	B 9
Lake Balkhash	E 5
Lake Baykal	D 7
Lake Chany	A 5
Lake Chelkar Tengiz	D 5
Lake Ladoga	E 5
Lake Onega	D 3
Lake Peipus	C 3
Lake Tengiz	B 8
Laptev Sea	E 5
Lena River	C 8
Lenin Peak	C 8
Long Strait	B 10
Lower Tunguska River	D 9
Medvezhi Islands	F 5
Merv (Oasis)	B 10
Mezen River	C 4
Moscow-Volga Canal	D 4
Mt. Belukha	D 6
Mt. Chen	E 4
Mt. Elbrus	E 4
Mt. Karkaraly	E 5
Mt. Piramida	D 6
Mt. Polkan	D 6
Mt. Purpula	D 7
Mt. Sokhondo	C 7
Mt. Yamantau	B 8
Narodnaya (Mtn.)	C 5
Neman River	B 3
New Siberian Islands	B 9
Northern Dvina River	B 9
Novaya Sibir Island	B 9
Novaya Zemlya (Islands)	C 5
Ob River	B 4
Obskaya Guba (Bay)	B 5
Okhotsk, Sea of	D 7
Olenek River	C 8
Olekma River	E 5
Pamirs, The (Mts.)	F 5
Pechora River	C 4
Pur River	B 10
Queen Victoria Sea	C 6
Rybinsk Reservoir	D 4
Sakhalin (Isl.)	D 9
Sayan Mts.	F 5
Severnaya Zemlya (Islands)	B 6
Shantar Islands	B 7
Siberia (Region)	C 6
Sikhote-Alin Mts.	E 8
Snezhnyy Peak	D 7
Stanovoy Mts.	D 8
Syr Darya (River)	E 5
Taymyr Lake	B 6
Taymyr Peninsula	B 6
Taz River	E 5
Tien Shan (Mts.)	C 5
Tobol River	E 5
Turan Lowland	D 4
Ural Mts.	E 4
Ural River	D 4
Ussuri River	F 4
Ust-Urt Plateau	A 3
Valdai Hills	C 3
Vaygach Island	B 4
Verkhoyansk Mts.	C 7
Vilyuy River	B 5
Volga-Baltic Waterway	C 3
Volga-Don Canal	D 4
Volga River	B 3
Volgograd Reservoir	D 4
White Sea	C 3
White Sea-Baltic Canal	D 4
Wrangel Island	B 11
Yablonovyy Mts.	D 7
Yamal Peninsula	B 5
Yana River	C 6
Yenisey River	C 6
Zaysan Nor (Lake)	E 8

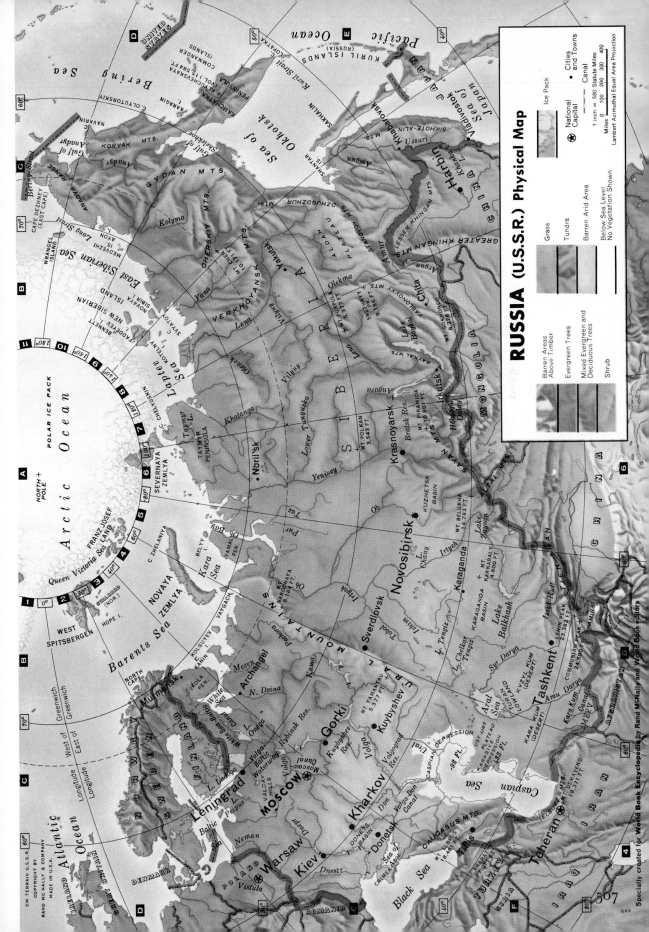

RUSSIA (U.S.S.R.) Physical Map

Legend

National Capital ⊛
Cities and Towns •
Canal
Ice Pack

1 inch = 580 Statute Miles

Miles
0   100 200 300 400
0   100 200 300 400 500
Lambert Azimuthal Equal Area Projection

Grass
Tundra
Barren Arid Area
Below Sea Level No Vegetation Shown

Barren Areas Above Timber
Evergreen Trees
Mixed Evergreen and Deciduous Trees
Shrub

Specially created for World Book Encyclopedia by Rand McNally and World Book editors

507

RUSSIA

The West Siberian Plain is almost entirely flat. It lies north of the Altai Mountains, and is the largest level region in the world. The plain covers more than a million square miles, and in no place is more than 500 feet above sea level. This region is drained by the Ob River system, which flows northward into the Arctic Ocean. Drainage is poor, and much of the plain is marshy.

The Central Siberian Plateau has an average height of about 2,000 feet. The region slopes upward toward the south from coastal plains along the Arctic Ocean. The Sayan and Baykal mountains, which rise more than 11,000 feet, are along the southern edge of the plateau. The plateau has been deeply cut by streams, some of which flow through canyons. This region has a wide variety of rich mineral deposits.

The East Siberian Uplands are mainly a trackless wilderness of mountains and plateaus. The mountains rise as high as 10,000 feet. They form part of a series of ranges that curves along the eastern coast of Asia and continues in offshore islands. The Kamchatka Peninsula has about 25 active volcanoes. Snow-capped Klyuchevskaya, the highest, rises 15,584 feet.

Rivers and Lakes. Russia's longest river, the 2,683-mile Lena, is in Siberia. Other long rivers in Siberia include the Amur, Ob, and Yenisey. These rivers are frozen from seven to nine months a year. The Volga River is the longest river in Europe. It flows 2,290 miles from the Valday Hills, northwest of Moscow, to the Caspian Sea. Most of the Volga is frozen three months a year. Other important rivers of European Russia include the Dnepr, Don, Neman, and Northern and Western Dvina. Soviet Central Asia has few rivers.

The Caspian Sea, a salt lake 92 feet below sea level, is the largest inland body of water in the world. It covers 143,630 square miles in southern Russia between Europe and Asia. Lake Ladoga, which covers 6,835 square miles, is the largest lake entirely in Europe. Lake Baykal in Siberia, more than 5,712 feet deep, is the deepest fresh-water lake in the world. Other large lakes include the salty Aral Sea and Lake Balkhash, both in Soviet Central Asia. See the separate articles on the rivers, lakes, and other physical features of Russia listed in the *Related Articles* at the end of this article.

Burt Glinn, Magnum
Howard Sochurek

The European Plain includes huge steppes (grassy plains) with some of the richest soils in the world. North of the steppes, forests cover much of this region.

The Ural Mountains are rich in iron ore, petroleum, and other minerals. Their low valleys have long been used for travel between Europe and Siberia.

Howard Sochurek
Pictorial Parade

The Aral-Caspian Lowland consists largely of sandy deserts where camel-riding Turkic herdsmen raise sheep. Much cotton is grown with irrigation.

The West Siberian Plain includes much of the forest zone that extends across northern Russia. This flat region becomes marshy toward the north.

Soviet Life from Sovfoto

Central Siberian Plateau  is a cold region of thick forests and swampy Arctic plains. The people raise reindeer for food and transportation.

The East Siberian Uplands 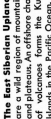 are a wild region of mountains and plateaus. An offshore chain of volcanoes forms the Kuril Islands in the Pacific Ocean.

Burt Glinn, Magnum

Russia is famous for its long, bitter winters, which have had a great influence on the nation's history. Napoleon and Adolf Hitler, both of whom set out to conquer Russia, were defeated partly by the icy winds that roar across the Russian plains. A large part of Russia lies north of the Arctic Circle. Snow covers more than half the country six months a year. Almost half the country has *permafrost* (permanently frozen soil) beneath the ground surface. Most of Russia's coastal waters, lakes, and rivers are frozen much of the year.

Northeastern Siberia is Russia's coldest region. January temperatures average below −50° F. there, and temperatures below −90° F. have been recorded. The region averages 60° F. in July, but sometimes has temperatures of nearly 100° F. This great range between temperature highs and lows—almost 200 degrees—is the widest in the world. Russia's summers are hot or warm, but short. Only the southern deserts have long summers. July temperatures there average about 90° F., and may rise above 120° F.

The heaviest rainfall in the Soviet Union occurs in the Caucasus region. There, some foothills get more than 100 inches of rain a year. Parts of western and central Siberia receive the heaviest snowfall, up to 4 feet a year.

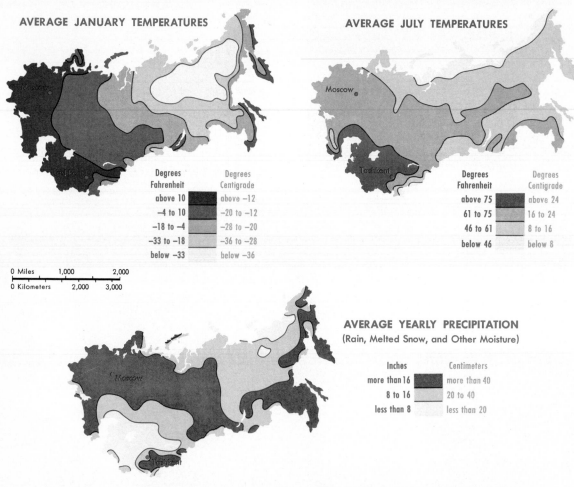

AVERAGE JANUARY TEMPERATURES

Degrees Fahrenheit	Degrees Centigrade
above 10	above −12
−4 to 10	−20 to −12
−18 to −4	−28 to −20
−33 to −18	−36 to −28
below −33	below −36

0 Miles 1,000 2,000
0 Kilometers 2,000 3,000

AVERAGE JULY TEMPERATURES

Degrees Fahrenheit	Degrees Centigrade
above 75	above 24
61 to 75	16 to 24
46 to 61	8 to 16
below 46	below 8

AVERAGE YEARLY PRECIPITATION
(Rain, Melted Snow, and Other Moisture)

Inches	Centimeters
more than 16	more than 40
8 to 16	20 to 40
less than 8	less than 20

Sources: Meteorological Office, London; Ministry of Geology USSR, Moscow

MONTHLY WEATHER IN MOSCOW AND TASHKENT

	JAN	FEB	MAR	APR	MAY	JUNE	JULY	AUG	SEPT	OCT	NOV	DEC	Average of:
MOSCOW	21	23	32	47	65	73	76	72	61	46	31	23	High Temperatures
	9	10	17	31	44	51	55	52	43	34	23	13	Low Temperatures
	11	9	8	9	9	10	12	12	9	11	10	9	Days of Rain or Snow
	10	8	12	10	7	4	1	1	1	5	7	9	Days of Rain or Snow
TASHKENT	37	44	53	65	78	87	92	89	80	65	53	44	High Temperatures
	21	27	37	47	56	62	64	60	52	41	35	29	Low Temperatures

Temperatures are given in degrees Fahrenheit.

WORLD BOOK maps - FGA

Russia's total production ranks second only to that of the United States. Russia is the world's leading example of a socialist, centrally planned economy. The Soviet government owns the nation's banks, factories, land, mines, and transportation and communication systems. It plans and controls the production, distribution, and pricing of almost all goods. Since 1928, Russia's economy has expanded rapidly under a series of plans pushing industrialization. But improvements in living conditions have come slowly. The standard of living still remains far below that of the United States.

Russians work an average of about 40 hours a week. Their salaries are set by the government, and vary among different jobs and industries. For example, coal miners earn about twice as much as most factory workers. Since the mid-1950's, Russian workers have been free to quit their jobs. But a housing shortage discourages them from looking for work in other cities.

Natural Resources. The Soviet Union has some of the most fertile soils in the world. No other nation has so much farmland, so many mineral deposits or forests, or so many possible sources of hydroelectric power. Russia also has a variety of plant and animal life.

Soils. The steppes of Russia have the country's richest soils. These are *chernozem* soils—rich, black topsoils from 3 to 5 feet deep. Chernozem soils cover more than two-fifths of Russia's farmland. They lie in the *Black Earth Belt*, which extends from the western Ukraine to southwestern Siberia. The deserts of Soviet Central Asia lie south of the Black Earth Belt. When irrigated, the sandy desert soils can support plant life. The Caucasus region has rich yellow and red soils with large amounts of clay. North of the Black Earth Belt, soils are either poor or somewhat fertile. Spongy, swampy soils are found in the *tundra*, the low plains along the Arctic Ocean (see TUNDRA).

Minerals. Russia has great supplies of almost every

RUSSIA'S GROSS NATIONAL PRODUCT IN 1969

Total gross national product—$444,000,000,000

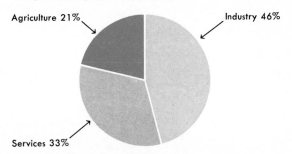

Agriculture 21%
Industry 46%
Services 33%

The Gross National Product (GNP) is the total value of goods and services produced by a country in a year. The GNP measures a nation's total economic performance for the year. It can also be used to compare the economic output and growth of countries.

Production and Workers by Economic Activities

Economic Activities	Per Cent of GNP Produced	Employment*	
		Number of Persons	Per Cent of Total
Manufacturing	37	27,483,000	24
Agriculture, Forestry & Fishing	21	39,540,000	34
Other Services	16	20,698,000	18
Transportation & Communication	11	8,793,000	8
Construction	9	6,342,000	5
Trade	6	6,964,000	6
Government	—	1,744,000	2
Mining	†	2,317,000	2
Utilities & Other	†	1,435,000	2
Total	100	115,316,000	100

*1968, latest information available
†Included in Manufacturing
Source: Joint Economic Committee, Congress of the U.S.

Siberia, Russia's New Economic Frontier, has rich deposits of oil and other minerals. Trucks carry equipment to men who are developing areas that have long been frozen wilderness.

Soviet Life

FARM, MINERAL, AND FOREST PRODUCTS

This map shows where the leading farm, mineral, and forest products of Russia are produced. The map also shows the major manufacturing centers. Most of the cropland and almost all the major industrial centers are in European Russia.

	Crops and Livestock		Mainly Livestock		Mainly Forest

● Major Manufacturing Center

0 Miles   500   1,000

0 Kilometers   1,000   1,500

WORLD BOOK map - FGA

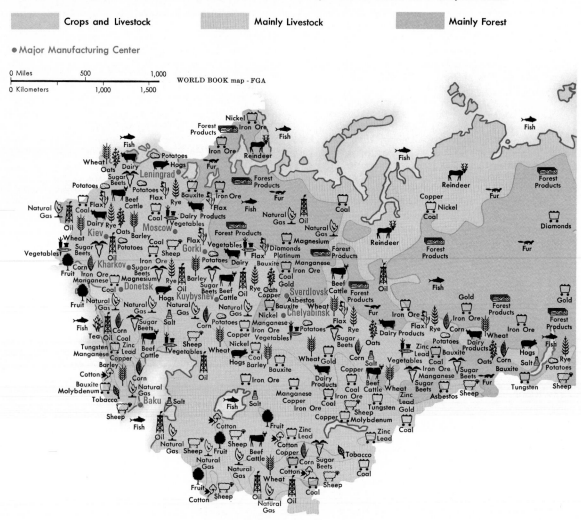

mineral needed for modern industry. Tin is the only important mineral not found in quantities large enough for Soviet needs. Russia has about a third of the world's coal deposits, and huge reserves of petroleum and natural gas. The eastern Ukraine and the Ural Mountains are great storehouses of iron ore. The world's largest deposits of manganese are in the republics of Georgia and the Ukraine. Chromium and nickel are found throughout the Urals. The republic of Kazakhstan has great deposits of copper, lead, and zinc.

Forests cover about a third of Russia's land. The country has about a fifth of the world's timber. A huge forest zone of cone-bearing trees extends more than 5,000 miles across northern Russia, from Finland to the Pacific Ocean. This northern forest consists of fir, larch, and pine trees. Between the forest and the almost treeless steppes is a mixed-forest zone of these cone-bearing trees and such trees as beeches, elms, lindens, maples, and oaks.

Plant Life of Russia's tundra consists of mosses, moss-like plants called *lichens*, and low shrubs. Some small, shrublike birches and willows also grow there. Large areas of the northern forest have marshes and peat bogs, especially in Siberia. The mixed-forest zone has some open grasslands. Long grasses once grew on the steppes, now Russia's major farming region.

Animal Life of the tundra includes reindeer and such small animals as the arctic fox, ermine, hare, and lemming. Huge flocks of waterfowl spend the summer along the Arctic coast. Many large animals roam the forests. They include the brown bear, deer, elk, lynx, and reindeer. Smaller forest animals include the beaver, rabbit, and squirrel. Antelope live in the eastern steppes. Antelope, bear, deer, hyenas, leopards, and tigers live in the deserts or mountains of Soviet Central Asia. Many kinds of fish are found in Russia's coastal waters, lakes, and rivers.

Manufacturing. During the 1920's, Russia was

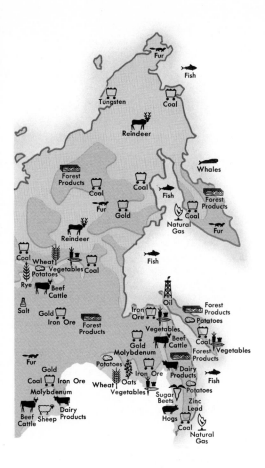

Novosti

Wheat Is Russia's Chief Crop. The Soviet Union produces about 2 billion bushels a year, more than any other country.

items of each to produce, and where to sell them. The quality of consumer goods was almost ignored. Many products were so poorly made and so unattractively styled that few people bought them. In 1965, the government began putting factories on a profit basis. Government agencies now set sales and profit goals for plant managers, instead of production goals. The managers base their production on what their customers want. The factories keep more of their profits to pay bonuses to the better workers and to improve production methods.

The Moscow area is Russia's leading manufacturing center. Its factories produce chiefly automobiles, buses, and trucks. Other products made in Moscow include chemicals, electrical and electronic equipment, processed foods, steel, and textiles. Ships are built and many kinds of industrial equipment are produced in the Leningrad area. The Ukraine is Russia's leading iron and steel region. It also produces a wide variety of machinery. Metal processing and machinery production are important in the Urals, and most Russian oil is refined in the Volga-Urals oil fields. Lumber and paper mills operate in many parts of Russia. Many new industries are being developed in Siberia to make use of the region's great mineral and hydroelectric resources.

Agriculture. Russia has more farmland than any other country. Its farmland covers more than $2\frac{1}{4}$ million square miles—over a fourth of all Russia. Russia and the United States are the world's leading crop-producing countries. Russia has more than twice as much farmland as the United States, but U.S. farmland is generally more fertile. In addition, much of the farmland in the Soviet Union lies near the Arctic Circle, where growing seasons are short, or in regions of light rainfall. American farmers receive higher prices for their products, have better equipment, and use more fertilizers. Many Russian government farm production plans are impractical and interfere with the farm managers'

mainly a farming nation. Today, it is an industrial giant. Only the United States outranks Russia in the value of manufactured products.

In 1928, Russia's Communist leaders began the first of a series of *five-year plans* to promote industry. Each plan set up investment programs and production goals for a five-year period. At first, the government chiefly developed factories that produced heavy-industry products, including chemicals, construction materials, machine tools, and steel. Heavy industry, especially steel-making, expanded rapidly. But housing construction and the production of *consumer goods*, such as clothing, food, and household articles, lagged seriously. During the mid-1950's, the Soviet government began to increase somewhat the production of consumer goods. But the increase still fell far short of the people's needs.

Until 1965, the government took almost all the profits of the nation's factories. Government agencies told factory managers which products to make, how many

Homer J. Smith

Automation in Russia is increasing. This electronic computer was set up to operate an electric power plant in Kharkov.

Sovfoto

Women Oil Field Workers check production figures on their way home after work. Women hold every kind of job in Russia.

job of making the best use of the land and workers.

More than half of Russia's farmland consists of about 9,000 *sovkhozy* (state farms). These farms average about 75,000 acres in size. The average size of U.S. farms is about 350 acres. Russia's state farms are operated like government factories, and the farmworkers receive wages. Less than half the nation's farmland consists of about 39,000 *kolkhozy* (collective farms), which are controlled by the government. These farms average about 15,000 acres in size. In general, more than 400 families live on a collective farm. The farmers are paid lower wages and a share of the production and profits. Families on state or collective farms may farm small land plots for themselves. These farmers grow crops and raise animals, and can sell their products privately.

Barley, rye, and wheat are the main grain crops, and Russia leads all countries in their production. Wheat, the most important crop, is grown in the Ukraine, southwestern Siberia, and northern Kazakhstan. Barley is grown in many regions. Rye is produced in the less fertile, wetter parts of northwestern European Russia. The Soviet Union also leads all countries in the production of flax, potatoes, and sugar beets. Potatoes, the basic food of most of the people, are grown throughout most of Russia. Irrigated regions of Soviet Central Asia produce large crops of cotton. Farmers along the Black Sea coast grow tea plants. Tea is the national beverage. Other important crops in Russia include corn, fruits, oats, tobacco, and vegetables.

Livestock production is the weakest part of Russian agriculture. During the late 1920's and early 1930's, millions of Soviet farmers were forced to join collective farms. In protest, they killed great numbers of farm animals. Livestock production did not reach its earlier levels until the mid-1950's, and its growth since then has been slow. Today, Russians eat about half as much meat as Americans do.

Beef and dairy cattle and hogs are raised chiefly in the Ukraine and in some regions to the north. Sheep graze on the grasslands of Soviet Central Asia and other regions, and wool is an important product. Many farmers raise poultry on their private plots.

Mining. Russia leads all countries in the production of coal, iron ore, lead, manganese, and the platinum-group metals. Russia's largest coal mines are in the Donets River Basin in the Ukraine, and in the Kara-

ganda and Kuznetsk basins in Siberia. The eastern Ukraine and the Urals provide about 85 per cent of the Soviet Union's iron ore. Over 40 per cent of the world's manganese is produced near Nikopol' in the Ukraine, and near Chiatura in Georgia. Platinum is mined in the Urals and in northern Siberia.

The Soviet Union ranks second among all countries in the production of copper, gold, natural gas, nickel, petroleum, and tungsten. It ranks third in the production of bauxite. Bauxite, used in making aluminum, is mined north of Serov in western Siberia and in Kazakhstan. About 85 per cent of the country's natural gas comes from European Russia. Kazakhstan is the nation's leading producer of copper. About 70 per cent of the petroleum comes from the Volga-Urals region, and another 25 per cent comes from the Baku oil fields near the Caspian Sea. Other important minerals mined in Russia include asbestos, diamonds, magnesium, molybdenum, salt, and zinc.

Forest Products. Russia also leads all nations in lumbering. Most timber cut in Russia comes from the European section, which has about a fourth of the nation's forests. The high cost of transportation to the huge forests of Asian Russia has held back the development of forest industries there.

Fishing. In the Barents Sea and White Sea, Russian fishermen catch cod, haddock, herring, salmon, and other fishes. Sturgeon are caught in the Caspian Sea. Russia's famous black *caviar* is the salted eggs of sturgeon. Russian fishermen also fish in the Atlantic and Pacific oceans and in the Baltic and Black seas. Russia ranks second in whaling, behind Japan.

Electric Power. Only the United States produces more electric power than Russia. Fuel-burning plants generate more than four-fifths of Russia's power. Hydroelectric plants and a few nuclear power stations provide the rest. The Soviet Union has about an eighth of the world's undeveloped hydroelectric power. About four-fifths of Russia's undeveloped hydroelectric power is in the Asian section of the country. The world's largest hydroelectric station is near Bratsk, on the Angara River in south-central Siberia. In 1969, Russia began operating a tidal power station northwest of Murmansk, on the Arctic Ocean.

Foreign Trade plays only a small part in the Russian economy. Russia's enormous natural resources provide

514

TRANSPORTATION

This map shows the major roads, rail lines, airports, seaports, and inland waterways of Russia. European Russia has large networks of rail lines and waterways. The rest of Russia depends chiefly on rail lines and air transportation to cover the great distances. Most of Siberia lacks any form of modern transportation. The Russians do not depend on roads so much as people do in North America.

⊷ Major Port	╷ — Major Road
○ Major Airport	←—→ Major Rail Line
	— Major Waterway

Miles 400 800 1,200 1,600 2,000
Kilometers 800 1,200 1,600 2,000 2,400 2,800

WORLD BOOK map — FGA

almost all the important raw materials that the nation needs. Also, the government does not want to become dependent on foreign markets or suppliers. Russia's major exports are iron and steel, lumber, machinery, and petroleum. Its main imports are industrial equipment and consumer goods.

About 70 per cent of Russia's foreign trade is with other Communist countries, especially those of Eastern Europe. This trade is set up largely by the Council for Mutual Economic Assistance (COMECON). COMECON is an economic planning organization made up of Russia and nine other Communist nations. Russian trade with the United States is limited by laws in both countries. But during the early 1970's, the two nations agreed to work for an increase in their trade activities.

Transportation. Railroads carry about 80 per cent of Russia's freight and passenger traffic. Russia has about 81,000 miles of track, more than any other country except the United States. Eleven main rail lines extend from Moscow, Russia's transportation center, to all parts of the country. One rail line connects Moscow with Vladivostok on the Pacific coast, and is Siberia's major railroad. The Trans-Siberian Express runs on this line. It covers the distance, about 5,600 miles, in seven days. In Soviet Central Asia, railways extend from Tashkent to Moscow, Novosibirsk, and other cities.

There are only about 1,300,000 automobiles in Russia, compared with about 89,309,000 in the United States. Russia has about 200,000 miles of hard-surface highways, compared with about 2,700,000 miles in the United States. Trucks are used mainly for short trips, such as hauling freight to and from railroad depots.

Aeroflot, the national airline, is the largest public air-

Novosti

Russia's Largest Airport opened in 1965 at Domodedovo, near Moscow. It can handle about 3,000 passengers an hour.

line in the world. It connects all the major cities of the Soviet Union, and links Russia with about 50 countries. Aeroflot's 6,770-mile flight between Moscow and Havana, Cuba, is the longest nonstop airline route in the world. Russia's largest airport is at Domodedovo, near Moscow.

Inland waterways carry only about 5 per cent of Russia's freight traffic, because most of the rivers are frozen many months every year. Several canals link rivers and seas. The most important canals include the Volga-Don and the White Sea-Baltic. The Moscow Canal connects Moscow with the Volga River.

The harbors of most Russian seaports are also frozen much of the year. Some nearly ice-free ports are on the Black and Baltic seas. The long Arctic coast is icebound about nine months of the year. During the warmer months, ships sail along the Arctic coast from the ports of Murmansk and Archangel in Europe to ports in northern and far eastern Siberia.

Russian history can be thought of as a long tug of war between *Eastern* (Asian) and *Western* (European) forces. Since ancient times, first one side and then the other gained power. Peoples and influences from the East and West changed Russian life many times. As a result, Russia has never been entirely an Eastern or a Western country.

This article traces the major developments of Russian history. To understand more fully who and what made Russia what it is today, read also the articles listed in the *Related Articles* at the end of this article.

Early Days. Beginning about 1000 B.C., the Cimmerians, a Balkan people, lived north of the Black Sea in what is now the southern Ukraine. They were defeated about 700 B.C. by the Scythians, an Iranian people from central Asia. The Scythians controlled the region until about 200 B.C. They fell to invading Sarmatians, another Iranian group. The Scythians and the Sarmatians lived in close contact with Greek colonies—later controlled by the Romans—along the northern coast of the Black Sea. They absorbed many Greek and Roman ways of life through trade, marriage, and other contacts. See CIMMERIAN; SCYTHIAN.

Germanic tribes from the West, called the Goths, conquered the region about A.D. 200. The Goths ruled until about 370, when they were defeated by the Huns, a warlike Asian people. The Huns' empire broke up after their leader, Attila, died in 453. The Avars, a tribe related to the Huns, began to rule the region in the mid-500's. The Khazars, another Asian people, won the southern Volga and northern Caucasus regions in the mid-600's. They became Jews, and established a busy trade with other peoples. See GOTH; HUN.

By the 800's, Slavic groups had established many towns in what is now European Russia. They had also

MIGRATIONS—700 B.C. TO A.D. 700

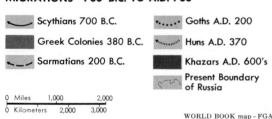

～ Scythians 700 B.C.	·····› Goths A.D. 200
▬ Greek Colonies 380 B.C.	▬▬ Huns A.D. 370
▬ ▬ Sarmatians 200 B.C.	▬ Khazars A.D. 600's
	▱ Present Boundary of Russia

```
0   Miles    1,000        2,000
0   Kilometers   2,000   3,000
```

WORLD BOOK map—FGA

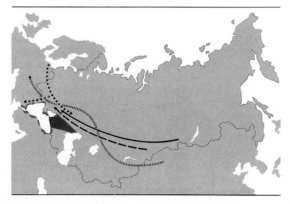

———————— **IMPORTANT DATES IN RUSSIA** ————————

A.D. 800's The first Russian state was established at Kiev.

c. 988 Vladimir I converted the Russians to Christianity.

1237-1240 The Mongols conquered Russia.

c. 1318 The Mongols appointed Prince Yuri of Moscow as the Russian grand prince.

1480 Ivan III broke Mongol control over Russia.

1547 Ivan IV became the first ruler to be crowned czar.

1604-1613 Russia was torn by civil war, invasion, and political confusion during the Time of Troubles.

1613 Michael Romanov became czar. He started the Romanov line of czars, which ruled until 1917.

1703 Peter I founded St. Petersburg and began building his capital there.

1773-1774 Russian troops crushed a peasant revolt.

1812 Napoleon invaded Russia, but was forced to retreat.

1825 The Decembrist revolt, led by discontented army officers, was put down.

1861 Alexander II freed the serfs.

1905 Japan defeated Russia in the Russo-Japanese War. A revolution forced Nicholas II to establish the *Duma* (parliament).

1914-1917 Russia fought Germany in World War I.

1917 A revolution overthrew Nicholas II in March. The Bolsheviks (Communists) seized power in November, and Lenin became dictator. Russia withdrew from World War I.

1918-1920 The Communists defeated their anti-Communist opponents in a civil war.

1922 The Union of Soviet Socialist Republics was established. Joseph Stalin became general secretary of the Communist party and began his rise to power as dictator.

1928 Stalin began the First Five-Year Plan to expand Russia's economy.

Mid-1930's Millions of Russians were shot or imprisoned during the Great Purge ordered by Stalin.

1941 German forces invaded Russia during World War II.

1942-1943 Russia defeated Germany in the Battle of Stalingrad, a major turning point in the war.

1945 Russian troops captured Berlin on May 2. Germany surrendered to the Allies on May 7.

Late 1940's Russia set up the Iron Curtain to cut off contacts between Communist and Western nations. The Cold War developed between East and West.

1953 Stalin died, and Nikita S. Khrushchev became head of the Communist party.

1956 Khrushchev announced a policy of peaceful coexistence with the West. This policy led to a bitter dispute with China over the basic methods of reaching the goals of Communism. Khrushchev also criticized Stalin's rule by terror, and Russian life became freer.

1957 Russia launched *Sputnik I*, the first spacecraft to circle the earth.

1958 Khrushchev became premier of Russia.

1961 Yuri A. Gagarin, a Russian air force officer, became the first man to orbit the earth.

1962 Russia set up missile bases in Cuba, and then removed them under United States pressure.

1964 High-ranking Communists forced Khrushchev to retire. He was replaced by Leonid I. Brezhnev as head of the Communist party and Aleksei N. Kosygin as premier.

1965 Soviet factories were put on a profit basis.

1966 A Russian spacecraft made the first soft landing on the moon. Another reached the planet Venus, and a third went into orbit around the moon.

developed an active trade. No one knows where the Slavs came from. Some historians believe they came during the 400's from what is now Poland. Others think the Slavs were farmers in the Black Sea region under Scythian rule or earlier. See SLAV.

The earliest written Russian history dealing with the 800's is the *Primary Chronicle*, written in Kiev, probably in 1111. It says that quarreling Slavic groups in the town of Novgorod asked a Viking tribe to rule them and bring order to the land. The Vikings were called the *Varangian Russes*. Historians who accept the *Chronicle* as true believe Russia took its name from this tribe. According to the *Chronicle*, a group of related Varangian families headed by Rurik arrived in 862. Rurik settled in Novgorod, and the area became known as the "land of the Rus."

Many historians doubt that the Slavs of Novgorod invited the Vikings to rule them. They believe the Vikings invaded the region. Some historians claim the word *Rus*, from which Russia took its name, was the name of an early Slavic tribe in the Black Sea region. It is known, however, that the first Russian state was established during the 800's at Kiev, an important trading center on the Dnepr River. Whether it was developed by the Vikings is unclear.

The Kievan State. The *Primary Chronicle* states that Oleg, a Varangian, captured Kiev in 882 and ruled as its prince. During the 900's, the other Russian *principalities* (regions ruled by a prince) recognized Kiev's major importance. Kiev lay on the main trade route connecting the Baltic Sea with the Black Sea and the Byzantine Empire. In addition, Kiev's forces defended Russia against invading tribes from the south and east. The Kievan ruler came to be called *grand prince*, and ranked above the other Russian princes.

About 988, Grand Prince Vladimir I became a Christian. He was baptized in the Eastern Orthodox branch of the Christian church, centered in the Byzantine capital of Constantinople (now Istanbul). The Russians were *pagans*, and worshiped idols representing the forces of nature. Vladimir made Christianity the state religion, and most Russians turned Christian. He later became a saint of the Russian Orthodox Church.

Several grand princes were strong rulers, but Kiev's power began to decrease after the mid-1000's. Other Russian princes grew in power, and they fought many destructive wars. In Novgorod and a few other towns with strong local governments, the princes were driven out. Badly weakened by civil wars and without strong central control, Kievan Russia fell to the huge *Tartar* (Mongol) armies that swept across Russia from the east during the 1200's (see TARTAR).

The Golden Horde. In 1237, Batu, a grandson of the conqueror Genghis Khan, led between 150,000 and 200,000 Mongol troops into Russia. These savage Asians destroyed one Russian town after another and killed the people. They destroyed Kiev in 1240. Russia then became part of the Mongol empire. It was included in a section of the empire called the *Golden Horde*. The capital of the Golden Horde was at Sarai, near what is now Volgograd. See MONGOL EMPIRE.

Batu forced the surviving Russian princes to pledge allegiance to the Golden Horde and to pay heavy taxes. From time to time, the Mongols left their capital and wiped out the people of various areas because of their disloyalty. The Mongols also appointed the Russian grand prince and forced many Russians to serve in their armies. But they interfered little with Russian life in general. The Mongols were chiefly interested in maintaining their power and collecting taxes.

The Battle of Kulikovo in 1380 was the first Russian victory over the Mongol forces. It took place near the Don River.

Illustration from the Russian manuscript *Life of St. Sergius* of the 1500's.
Lenin State Library, Moscow

Historical Pictures Service

THE GOLDEN HORDE—ABOUT 1300

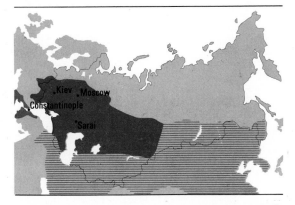

Golden Horde

Other Parts of the Mongol Empire

Byzantine Empire

Present Boundary of Russia

| 0 Miles | 1,000 | 2,000 |
| 0 Kilometers | 2,000 | 3,000 |

WORLD BOOK map – FGA

Illustration from *Voyages du Sr. Adam Olearius* (1633-1639) by Adam Olearius. The Newberry Library

The Bell Tower of Ivan the Great was built during the 1500's in the Kremlin, the walled central area of Moscow.

Peter the Great at Deptford, England by Daniel Maclise (Bettmann Archive)

Peter the Great learned Western ways on a trip through Europe in 1697 and 1698. The czar studied shipbuilding in England.

Catherine the Great saw apparently prosperous peasants during a trip through southern Russia in 1787. But the real peasants had been hidden, and her route falsely beautified.

Deceiving an Empress by R. Caton Woodville. *Illustrated London News*, April 15, 1905 (Mansell)

During the Mongol period, which ended in the late 1400's, the new ideas and reforming spirit of the Renaissance were dramatically changing Western Europe. But under Mongol control, Russia was cut off from these important Western influences. See RENAISSANCE.

The Rise of Moscow. During the early 1300's, Prince Yuri of Moscow married the sister of the Golden Horde's *khan* (ruler). Yuri was appointed the Russian grand prince about 1318. Mongol troops helped him put down threats to his leadership from other principalities. The Mongols also began letting the grand prince of Moscow collect taxes for them. This practice started with Ivan I (called the Moneybag) about 1330. Ivan kept some of the tax money. He bought much land and expanded his territory greatly. Other princes and *boyars* (high-ranking landowners) began to serve in Moscow's army and government. Ivan also persuaded the chief bishop of the Russian Orthodox Church to remain in Moscow. Until then, Kiev had been the spiritual center of Russia.

Moscow grew stronger and richer. But the Golden Horde grew weaker, chiefly because of struggles among the Mongols for leadership. In 1380, Grand Prince Dmitri defeated a Mongol force in the Battle of Kulikovo, near the Don River. The victory freed Moscow of Mongol control for a short period. The Mongols recaptured Moscow in 1382, but the belief that they could not be beaten had been destroyed.

During the late 1400's, Moscow became the most powerful Russian city. Ivan III (the Great) won control of Moscow's main rivals, Novgorod and Tver (now Kalinin), and great numbers of boyars entered his service. In 1480, Ivan made the final break from Mongol control by refusing to pay taxes to the Golden Horde. Mongol troops moved toward Moscow, but turned back to defend their capital from Russian attack.

Ivan the Terrible. After the rise of Moscow, its grand prince came to be called *czar*. In 1547, Ivan IV (the Terrible) became the first ruler to be crowned czar. Ivan made the czar's power over all Russia complete.

Ivan was brutal, extremely suspicious, and perhaps, at times, insane. He formed a special police force, and began a reign of terror in which he ordered the arrest and murder of hundreds of *aristocrats* (princes and boyars). He feared they were planning to kill him. Ivan gave his victims' estates as payment to the *service gentry* (landowners serving in the army and government). He also established strict rules concerning the number of warriors and horses each landowner had to supply to the army. Ivan burned many towns and villages, and killed church leaders who opposed him. In a fit of rage, Ivan even struck and killed his oldest son.

The number of service gentry increased rapidly. But their estates had no value unless the peasants remained on the land and farmed it. Ivan and later czars passed a series of laws that bound the peasants to the land as *serfs*. Serfdom became the economic basis of Russian power. The development of Russian serfdom differed sharply from changes occurring in Western Europe. There, during the Renaissance, the growth of trade led to both the use of money as royal payment and the disappearance of serfdom. See SERF.

Ivan fought Tartars at Astrakhan' and Kazan' to the southeast, and won their lands. Russian forces crossed the Ural Mountains and conquered western Siberia. Ivan also tried to win lands northwest to the Baltic Sea, but he was defeated by Lithuanian Polish, and Swedish armies. See IVAN.

The Time of Troubles developed because of a breakdown of the czar's power after Ivan's death. Theodore I, Ivan's second son, was a weak czar. His wife's brother, Boris Godunov, became the real ruler of Russia. Theodore's younger brother, Dmitri, was found dead in 1591, and Theodore died in 1598 without a male heir. The *Zemskii Sobor* (Land Council), a kind of parliament with little power, elected Boris czar. But a man believed to be Gregory Otrepiev, a former monk, posed as Dmitri. This *False Dmitri* claimed Dmitri had not died, and fled to Lithuania to avoid arrest. In 1604, he invaded Russia with Polish troops. The invaders were joined by large numbers of discontented Russians of all classes. This invasion marked the beginning of the Time of Troubles. Russia was torn by civil war, invasion, and political confusion until 1613.

False Dmitri became czar in 1605, but a group of boyars killed him the next year. Prince Basil Shuisky then became czar. In 1610, Polish invaders occupied Moscow. They ruled through a powerless council of boyars until 1612. Meanwhile, a new False Dmitri and a number of other pretenders to the throne won many followers. Peasant revolts swept through Russia. Landowners and frontier people called *Cossacks* fought each other, and sometimes joined together to fight powerful aristocrats (see COSSACK). The Polish control of Moscow led the Russians to unite their forces and drive out the invaders. They recaptured the capital in 1612.

The Early Romanovs. After the Poles were defeated, there was no one of royal birth to take the throne. In 1613, the Zemskii Sobor elected Michael Romanov czar. The Romanov czars ruled Russia for the next 300 years, until the February Revolution of 1917 ended czarist rule. See ROMANOV.

During the 1600's, Russia won much of the Ukraine and extended its control of Siberia eastward to the Pacific Ocean. During this same period, the Russian Orthodox Church made changes in religious texts and ceremonies. People called *Old Believers* objected to these changes and broke away from the church. This group still follows the old practices today.

Peter the Great. In 1682, a struggle for power resulted in the crowning of two half brothers—Peter I (the Great) and Ivan V—as co-czars. Both were children, and Ivan's sister Sophia ruled as *regent* until Peter's followers forced her to retire in 1689. Peter made close contact with the many Western Europeans living in Moscow, and absorbed much new information from them. He came into full power in 1696, when Ivan died.

Under Peter, Russia expanded its territory to the Baltic Sea in the Great Northern War with Sweden. In 1703, Peter founded St. Petersburg (now Leningrad) on the Baltic, and began building his capital there. After traveling throughout Europe, he introduced Western-type clothing, factories, and schools in Russia. Peter also strengthened the czar's power over the aristocrats, churchmen, and serfs. See PETER I, THE GREAT.

Catherine the Great. After Peter's death in 1725, a series of struggles for the throne took place. The service gentry and the leading noblemen were on opposite sides. Candidates for the throne who were supported by the service gentry won most of these struggles and rewarded their followers. The rulers increased the gentry's

power over the serfs and local affairs. The gentry's enforced service to the state was gradually reduced, and was ended altogether in 1762.

Magnificent royal parties and other festivities, all in the latest Western fashion, took place during the 1700's. The arts were promoted, and many new schools were started, mainly for the upper classes. The Russian Imperial School of Ballet was founded, and Italian opera and chamber music were brought to Russia. It also became fashionable in Russia to repeat the newest Western ideas on freedom and social reform, especially during the rule of Empress Catherine II (the Great). In 1767, Catherine called a large legislative assembly to reform Russian laws, but it achieved nothing.

The great majority of Russians remained in extreme poverty and ignorance during this period. In 1773 and 1774, the peasants' discontent boiled over in a revolt led by Emelian Pugachev, a Cossack. The revolt swept through Russia from the Ural Mountains to the Volga River. It spread almost to Moscow before being crushed

---

CZARS AND EMPRESSES OF RUSSIA

Ruler	Reign	Ruler	Reign
*Ivan IV	1547-1584	Peter II	1727-1730
Theodore I	1584-1598	Anne	1730-1740
Boris Godunov	1598-1605	Ivan VI	1740-1741
Theodore II	1605	Elizabeth	1741-1762
False Dmitri	1605-1606	Peter III	1762
Basil Shuisky	1606-1610	*Catherine II	1762-1796
Michael		Paul	1796-1801
Romanov	1613-1645	*Alexander I	1801-1825
Alexis	1645-1676	*Nicholas I	1825-1855
Theodore III	1676-1682	*Alexander II	1855-1881
Ivan V	1682-1696	*Alexander III	1881-1894
*Peter I	1682-1725	*Nicholas II	1894-1917
*Catherine I	1725-1727		

*Has a separate article in WORLD BOOK.

EXPANSION OF RUSSIA—1360 TO 1917

■ 1360		■ 1689 to 1917	
■ 1360 to 1524		⟅⟆ Present Boundary of Russia	
■ 1524 to 1689			

```
0 Miles      1,000        2,000
0 Kilometers   2,000    3,000
```

WORLD BOOK map-FGA

by government troops. In 1775, Catherine further tightened the landowners' control over the serfs.

Under Catherine, Russia rose to new importance as a major power. Russian armies won most of what is now the republic of Byelorussia from Poland. In wars against the Ottoman Empire (now Turkey), Russia gained the Crimea and other Turkish lands. Catherine died in 1796, and her son, Paul, became czar. See CATHERINE.

Alexander I. Paul's five-year rule ended with his murder in 1801. Alexander I, Paul's son, became czar and talked about freeing the serfs, building schools for all young Russians, and even giving up the throne and making Russia a republic. He established several reforms, such as freeing many political prisoners and spreading Western ways and ideas. But he did nothing to lessen the czar's total power or to end serfdom. Alexander knew that Russia's military strength and position as a major power depended on income provided by serfdom. Under his rule, Russia continued to win territory from the Persians, Swedes, and Turks.

In June, 1812, Napoleon led the Grand Army of France into Russia. Napoleon wanted to stop Russian trade with France's chief enemy, Great Britain, and to halt Russian expansion in the Balkan region. The French swept forward and reached Moscow in September, 1812. Most of the people had abandoned the city, and Napoleon entered without a struggle.

Soon afterward, fire destroyed most of Moscow. Historians believe the Russians themselves set the fire. After 35 days, the French left the city because they feared they might not survive the approaching bitter Russian winter. They began a disastrous retreat with little food and under continual attack by the Russians. Of the estimated 600,000 French troops in Russia, about 570,000 died or were captured. Russia then became a major force in the campaign by several European countries that defeated Napoleon. See NAPOLEON I (Disaster in Russia).

Although Alexander had begun some reforms, harsh rule continued in Russia. Beginning in 1816, many

Napoleon Captured Moscow during his 1812 invasion, but a fire, believed set by the Russians, destroyed most of the city.

Return from Petrovsky Palace by V. V. Vereshchagin
from Lenin State Library, Moscow

young aristocrats became *revolutionaries* (persons who seek to overthrow a government). They formed secret organizations, wrote constitutions for Russia, and prepared to revolt. Alexander died in 1825, and Nicholas I became czar. In December of that year, a group of revolutionaries took action. This group, later called the *Decembrists*, included about 30 army officers and 3,000 soldiers. They gathered in Senate Square in St. Petersburg, and government troops arrived to face them. After several hours, the Decembrists fired a few shots. Government cannons ended the revolt.

Nicholas I. The Decembrist revolt deeply impressed and frightened Nicholas. He removed aristocrats, whom he now distrusted, from government office, and replaced them with professional military men. He tightened his control over the press and education, reduced travel outside Russia, and prohibited organizations that might have political influence. Nicholas established six special government departments. These departments, which included a secret police system, handled important economic and political matters. Through the departments, Nicholas avoided the regular processes of Russian government and increased his power.

In spite of Nicholas' harsh rule, the period was one of outstanding achievement in Russian literature. Nikolai Gogol, Mikhail Lermontov, Alexander Pushkin, and others wrote their finest works. Fyodor Dostoevsky, Leo Tolstoy, and Ivan Turgenev began their careers. Many educated Russians began to debate the values of Westernized Russian life against those of old Russian life. The pro-Western group argued that Russia must learn from and catch up with the West economically and politically. The other group argued for the old Russian ways, including the czarist system, a strong church, and the quiet life of the Russian countryside.

Nicholas became known as the "policeman of Europe" because he sent troops to put down revolutions in Poland and Hungary. Nicholas also posed as the defender of the Eastern Orthodox Church, and fought two wars with the Moslem Ottoman Empire. In the war of 1828 and 1829, Russia gained much territory in the Balkan region. Russia also won the right to move merchant ships through the Turkish-controlled straits connecting the Black Sea with the Mediterranean Sea.

In 1853, the Crimean War broke out between Russia and the Ottoman Empire. Austria, Great Britain, France, and Sardinia came to the aid of the Turks. These countries objected to Russian expansion in the Balkans. Russia was defeated, and signed the Treaty of Paris in 1856. This treaty forced Russia to give up much of the territory it had taken earlier from the Turks. See CRIMEAN WAR; RUSSO-TURKISH WARS.

Expansion in Asia. After its defeat in the Crimean War, Russia began to expand in Asia. In the Far East, Russia won disputed territories from China. In 1858 and 1860, the Chinese signed treaties giving Russia lands north of the Amur River and east of the Ussuri River. By 1864, Russian forces defeated rebel tribes in the Caucasus. Central Asia was won during a series of military campaigns from 1865 to 1876. In 1867, Russia sold its Alaskan territory to the United States for $7,200,000 (see ALASKA [History]).

Alexander II. Nicholas I died in 1855, during the Crimean War. His son, Alexander II, became czar. Russia's defeat in the war taught Alexander a lesson. He realized that Russia had to catch up with the West to remain a major power. Alexander began a series of reforms to strengthen the economy and Russian life in general. In 1861, he freed the serfs and gave them land. He began developing railroads and organizing a banking system. Alexander promoted reforms in education, reduced controls on the press, and began a jury system and other reforms in the courts. He also established forms of self-government in the towns and villages.

But many young Russians believed that Alexander's reforms did not go far enough. Some revolutionary groups wanted to establish socialism in Russia. Others wanted a constitution and a republic. These groups formed a number of public and secret organizations. After a revolutionary tried to kill Alexander in 1866, the czar began to weaken many of his reforms. The revolutionaries then argued that Alexander had never been a sincere reformer at all. During the mid-1870's, a group of revolutionaries tried to get the peasants to revolt. They wanted to achieve either socialism or *anarchism* (absence of government) for Russia (see ANARCHISM). After this effort failed, a terrorist group called the *Will of the People* tried several times to kill the czar. Alexander then decided to set up a new program of reforms. But in 1881, he was killed by a terrorist's bomb in St. Petersburg.

Alexander III, Alexander's son, became czar and soon began a program of harsh rule. Alexander III limited the freedom of the press and of the universities, and sharply reduced the powers of local self-governments. He set up a special bank to help the aristocrats increase their property. He also appointed *land captains* from among the aristocrats, and gave them much political power over the peasants. Alexander started some programs to help the peasants and industrial workers. But their living and working conditions improved very little. See ALEXANDER (of Russia).

Nicholas II became Russia's next, and last, czar in 1894. The revolutionary movement had been quiet until the 1890's, when a series of bad harvests caused starvation among the peasants. In addition, as industrialization increased, discontent grew among the rising middle class and workers in the cities. Discontented Russians formed various political organizations of which three became important. (1) The *liberal constitutionalists* wanted to replace czarist rule with a Western type of parliamentary government. (2) The *social revolutionaries* tried to promote a peasant revolution. (3) The *Marxists* wanted to promote revolution among the city workers. The Marxists followed the socialist teachings of Karl Marx, a German social philosopher (see MARX, KARL).

In 1898, the Marxists established the Russian Social Democratic Labor party. It split into two groups in 1903 —the *Bolsheviks* (members of the majority) and the *Mensheviks* (members of the minority). The Bolshevik leader was Vladimir I. Ulyanov, who used the name Lenin (see LENIN). The Bolsheviks wanted party membership limited to a small number of full-time revolutionaries who would lead the *proletariat* (workers). The Mensheviks wanted the party to have a wider membership and more democratic leadership.

Discontent among the Russian people grew after an economic depression began in 1899. The number of student protests, peasant revolts, and worker strikes increased. The unrest grew further after war broke out with Japan in 1904. Russia's expansion in the Far East

had alarmed Japan. After a series of disputes, the Japanese attacked Russian ships at Port Arthur, a Chinese port leased by the Russians. The small but well-supplied Japanese forces won battles on land and sea, and defeated the Russians in 1905. See RUSSO-JAPANESE WAR.

The Revolution of 1905. On Jan. 22, 1905, thousands of unarmed workers marched to the czar's Winter Palace in St. Petersburg. The workers were on strike, and planned to ask Nicholas II for reforms. Government troops fired on the crowd and killed or wounded hundreds of marchers. After this *Bloody Sunday* slaughter, the revolutionary movement, led mainly by the liberal constitutionalists, gained much strength. More strikes broke out, and peasant and military groups revolted.

In October, 1905, a general strike paralyzed the country. Revolutionaries in St. Petersburg formed a *soviet* (council) called the Soviet of Workers' Deputies. Nicholas then agreed to establish an elected *Duma* (parliament), which could pass or reject all proposed laws. Many Russians were satisfied, but many others were not. The revolution continued, especially in Moscow, where the army crushed a serious uprising in December.

Each of the first two Dumas, which met in 1906 and 1907, was dissolved after meeting a few months. The Dumas could not work with Nicholas and his high-ranking officials, who refused to give up much power. Nicholas illegally changed the election law, and made the selection of Duma candidates less democratic. The peasants and workers were allowed far fewer representatives in the Duma, and the upper classes many more. The third and fourth Dumas cooperated with the czar. They lasted their full five-year terms, from 1907 to 1917. During this period, Russia made important advances in the arts, education, farming, and industry.

World War I. By the time World War I began in 1914, Europe was divided into two tense armed camps. On one side was the *Triple Entente* (triple agreement), consisting of Russia, France, and Great Britain. Russia and France had agreed in 1894 to defend each other against attack. France and Great Britain had signed the *Entente Cordiale* (friendly agreement) in 1904, and Russia had signed a similar agreement with Great Britain in 1907. The Triple Entente developed from these treaties. Opposing the Triple Entente was the *Triple Alliance*, formed in 1882 by Austria-Hungary, Germany, and Italy. See TRIPLE ENTENTE; TRIPLE ALLIANCE.

On Aug. 1, 1914, Germany declared war on Russia, a rival for influence in the Balkans. Soon afterward, Russia changed the German-sounding name of St. Petersburg to Petrograd. German troops crushed the Russians at Tannenberg, Germany. But the Russians defeated an Austrian army in the Battles of Lemberg in the Galicia region of Austria-Hungary.

In 1915, Austrian and German forces drove back the Russians. The next year, Russian troops attacked along a 70-mile front in Galicia. They advanced 60 miles and captured more than 400,000 prisoners. Russian troops moved into the Carpathian Mountains in 1917, but the Germans pushed them back. For the story of Russia in the war, see WORLD WAR I.

The February Revolution. During World War I, the Russian economy could not meet the needs of the soldiers and also those of the people at home. The railroads carried military supplies, and could not serve the cities. The people suffered severe shortages of food, fuel, and housing. Russian troops at the front were loyal, but the untrained soldiers behind the fighting lines became disloyal. They knew they would probably be sent to the front and be killed. The townspeople and these soldiers were tense and angry.

By the end of 1916, almost all educated Russians opposed the czar. Nicholas had removed many capable officials from high government offices, and replaced them with weak, unpopular men. He was accused of crippling the war effort by such acts. Many Russians blamed his actions on the influence of Grigori Y. Rasputin, adviser to the czar and the czarina. The royal couple believed that Rasputin was a holy man who was saving their sick son's life. In December, 1916, a group of noblemen murdered Rasputin. But the officials who supposedly had been appointed through his influence remained. See RASPUTIN, GRIGORI Y.

Early in March, 1917, the people revolted. (The month was February in the old Russian calendar, which was replaced in 1918.) In Petrograd, riots and strikes over shortages of bread and coal grew more violent. Troops were called in to halt the uprising, but they joined it instead. So did the aristocrats, who had turned against the czar. The people of Petrograd turned to the Duma for leadership. Nicholas ordered the Duma to dissolve itself, but the parliament ignored his command. The Duma established a *provisional* (temporary) government consisting of some Duma leaders and other public figures. Prince George Lvov became chairman of the Council of Ministers, or premier. Nicholas had lost all political support, and he gave up the throne on March 15. See NICHOLAS (of Russia).

A new Soviet of Workers' and Soldiers' Deputies was also formed in Petrograd in March. It was a kind of unofficial partner of the provisional government. Many similar soviets were set up throughout Russia. The soviets seriously weakened the government's ability to carry on the war. Many Russian army units refused to fight. In April, Lenin demanded "all power to the soviets," but the soviets were unwilling to take over the government then. In July, however, armed workers and soldiers tried to seize power in Petrograd. They

The February Revolution of 1917 began in Petrograd (now Leningrad). The revolt ended czarist rule within a few days.

failed. Lenin fled to Finland, and his followers escaped or were jailed. Later that month, Alexander F. Kerensky, a socialist, became premier.

The October Revolution. Many powerful Russians blamed Kerensky for failures in the war, and opposed his socialist views. General Lavr Kornilov, the army commander in chief, planned to seize power. Kerensky freed the imprisoned Bolsheviks, and let them arm the Petrograd workers against Kornilov. The general advanced on Petrograd in September, 1917, but his group broke up before reaching the capital. The Bolsheviks were free, however, and now the workers had guns.

Also in September, 1917, the Bolsheviks won a majority in the Petrograd soviet. Lenin returned from Finland in October and convinced the Bolsheviks that they should try to seize power. He hoped a revolution would set off other socialist revolts in Western countries. Lenin's most capable assistant, Leon Trotsky, helped him plan the take-over. On November 7 (October 25 in the old Russian calendar), the armed workers took over important points in Petrograd. Early that evening, the workers and Bolshevik-led soldiers and sailors attacked the Winter Palace, headquarters of the provisional government. They seized the palace, which was weakly defended by students from a military school, and arrested members of the government. After a bloodier struggle in Moscow, the Bolsheviks controlled that city by November 15.

The Bolsheviks formed a new Russian government, headed by Lenin. They spread Bolshevik rule from town to town through the local soviets. For a short time, Lenin let the peasants seize much farmland. He permitted workers to control the factories, and allowed them to play important roles in the local soviets. But the government soon tightened control, and forced the peasants to give the government most of their products. The government also took over Russian industries, and set up central management bureaus to control them. The Cheka, a secret police force, was established. Bolshevik rule became complete.

After the Bolsheviks seized the government, Russia withdrew from World War I and began peace talks with Germany. In March, 1918, Russia signed the Treaty of Brest-Litovsk with Germany. Under the treaty, Russia gave up large areas, mostly in the fertile western and southwestern regions. Much of this land was returned to Russia after Germany surrendered in November, 1918.

In 1918, the Bolsheviks moved the Russian capital back to Moscow. They also changed the name of their Russian Social Democratic Labor party to the Russian Communist Party (Bolsheviks). This name was later changed to the Communist Party of the Soviet Union. The Bolsheviks organized the Red Army, named for the color of the Communist flag. The Communists themselves were called *Reds*. See COMMUNISM.

Civil War. From 1918 to 1920, Russia was torn by war between the Communists and anti-Communists, who were called *Whites*. The peasants believed they would lose their lands to their old landlords if the Whites won, and supported the Reds. The Whites were aided by troops from France, Great Britain, Japan, the United States, and other countries that opposed the Communist government. But these nations provided little help, because they were unwilling to fight another war after

Novosti

Lenin, the first dictator of Communist Russia, led the Bolshevik takeover of the government in the October Revolution of 1917.

Sovfoto

Joseph Stalin, *fourth from right,* one of the cruelest rulers in world history, was dictator of Russia from 1929 to 1953.

World War I. The aid probably did the Communists more good than harm. It allowed them to claim they were defending Russia against invaders. The Whites were poorly organized, and the Reds defeated them.

The Red Army had less success against Polish invaders in 1920. The Polish government claimed that western parts of Byelorussia and of the Ukraine belonged to Poland. Polish troops, aided by the French, defeated the Russians. A treaty, signed in 1921, gave Poland much of the land it claimed.

The New Economic Policy. By 1921, seven years of war, revolution, civil war, and invasion had exhausted Russia. During the civil war alone, more than 20 million Russians had died in epidemics, in the fighting, or of starvation. Agricultural and industrial production had fallen disastrously. A million Russians, many of them skilled and educated, had left the country. The people's discontent broke out in new peasant uprisings, in workers' strikes, and in a sailors' revolt at the Kronstadt naval base near Petrograd.

In 1921, Lenin established the New Economic Policy (NEP) to strengthen the country. This program replaced many of the socialist measures started earlier. Small industries and retail trade were allowed to operate under their own control. The peasants no longer had to give most of their farm products to the government. They could sell freely to customers after paying a tax. The government kept control of heavy industry, the transportation and banking systems, and foreign trade. The economy recovered steadily under the NEP, though the Communists disliked its nonsocialist features.

Formation of the U.S.S.R. In December, 1922, the Communist government established the Union of Soviet Socialist Republics (U.S.S.R.). The union consisted of four *union republics*—the Russian Soviet Federated Socialist Republic (Russian Republic), Byelorussia, Transcaucasia, and the Ukraine. The first republic formed after the Bolshevik revolution, the Russian Republic, has always been the largest and most powerful one.

During the 1920's, three other union republics were established—Tadzhikistan, Turkmenistan, and Uzbekistan. In 1936, Transcaucasia was divided into Azerbaidzhan, Armenia, and Georgia. Kazakhstan and Kirghizia also became union republics in 1936. In 1940, during World War II, Russia gained the union republics of Estonia, Latvia, Lithuania, and Moldavia.

From Lenin to Stalin. Lenin became seriously ill in 1922. A struggle for power developed among members of the *Politburo* (Political Bureau), the policy-making

body of the Communist party's Central Committee. Leon Trotsky ranked after Lenin in power. But the next two most important members of the Politburo—Lev Kamenev and Grigori Zinoviev—joined forces to oppose Trotsky. They chose Joseph Stalin to be their partner. Stalin had become general secretary of the party in 1922. See STALIN, JOSEPH.

After Lenin died in 1924, leading Communists held three different views on how far Russian socialism should go, and also on the need for world revolution. (1) Trotsky and his followers believed in immediately promoting both full socialism in Russia and world revolution. Kamenev and Zinoviev shared this view. (2) A group led by Nicholas Bukharin agreed with Trotsky that Russian socialism depended on world revolution. But Bukharin felt that Russia should continue Lenin's temporary program of weakened socialism because other countries were not ready for revolution. (3) Stalin and his followers agreed with Bukharin's economic policies at first. But they believed that Russian socialism could succeed without world revolution.

Stalin's power in the Communist party grew rapidly. As general secretary, he had the support of the local party secretaries, whose careers depended on his approval. Stalin built up this following carefully behind the scenes. Stalinist groups became stronger at the party *congresses* (meetings), which elected the top Communist bodies and approved Communist programs.

Stalin defeated his rivals one by one. Trotsky lost power in 1925. Stalin then joined the Bukharin group to expel Kamenev and Zinoviev, his former partners, from the party. At the 15th Communist Party Congress in December, 1927, Stalin won a sweeping victory. By then, Stalin, like Trotsky, urged full socialism. The congress adopted measures to begin Stalin's economic program the next year. In 1929, Stalin removed Bukharin and his followers from power. They signed a statement, ordered by Stalin, admitting that Stalin's economic views were correct and theirs were wrong. Stalin had become dictator of the Soviet Union.

Planned Economy. By the mid-1920's, Lenin's New Economic Policy had served its purpose. All factories and other means of production that had closed during the civil war were operating again. Russia's agricultural and industrial production had increased above pre-World War I levels. However, the prices of manufactured consumer goods were rising faster than the prices of farm products. As a result, the peasants held back their grain and other products.

523

RUSSIA

Stalin then proposed the First Five-Year Plan. This socialist program had two major goals. First, the small peasant farms would be combined into large *kolkhozy* (collective farms) controlled by the government. Second, the production of such heavy-industry products as chemicals, construction materials, machine tools, and steel would be expanded rapidly. The 15th Communist Party Congress approved these goals, and the *Gosplan* (State Planning Commission) worked out the details. The First Five-Year Plan started in 1928, and the government began taking over private businesses.

Stalin forced the collective farmers to give most of their products to the government. These products were needed to supply raw materials to industry, to feed the people of the growing manufacturing centers, and to pay for imported machinery. The peasants opposed being forced to join collective farms, and destroyed much of their livestock and crops in protest. As punishment, Stalin sent several million peasant families to prison labor camps in Siberia and Soviet Central Asia during the early 1930's. Farm production lagged, but Soviet industries expanded rapidly.

The Great Purge. Many Russians opposed Stalin's policies during the mid-1930's. To crush this opposition, Stalin began a program of terror called the Great Purge. His secret police arrested millions of persons. Neighbors and even members of the same family spied on one another. Fear spread throughout Russia. Stalin eliminated all real or suspected threats to his power by having the prisoners shot or sent to labor camps. The victims included thousands of Communists. Some were party members Stalin had defeated during his rise to power. Many were old Bolsheviks who had been associated with Lenin. Others were officers of the Red Army.

Stalin staged "trials" at which arrested Communist leaders were forced to confess to "crimes against the people." Most of these *purge trials* took place from 1936 to 1938. Stalin replaced the party leaders he eliminated with young Stalinists he could trust. The secret police enforced strict loyalty to Stalin's policies on all levels of life. Stalin controlled everything that was published, taught, or publicly spoken.

Foreign Policy Before World War II. In 1919, Lenin

The First Five-Year Plan (1928-1932) expanded Russia's economy. These new tractors were supplied for farms near Moscow.
P.I.P.

had established the *Comintern* (Communist International) as part of the world Communist movement. Through this organization, Lenin hoped to control Communist parties in other countries and to promote world revolution. But he feared attack by the more powerful Western, non-Communist countries. Lenin became especially fearful after these nations aided the Whites during the Russian civil war. As a result, Soviet leaders put aside the movement for world revolution during the early and mid-1920's. They concentrated on developing friendly relations with other nations. Their immediate goals were to avoid attack and to strengthen Russia through foreign trade.

During the late 1920's, Russia became more active in the world Communist movement. But soon Russia's fear of attack again became the major concern of Soviet foreign policy. Russia felt itself threatened by two events. First came the Japanese invasion of China in 1931. Second, and even more threatening to Russia, was the rise of Adolf Hitler in Germany. Hitler became dictator of Germany in 1933, and one of his major programs was to destroy Communism. This threat led the Soviet Union to sign many military and political agreements with the Western democracies. In 1934, Russia joined the League of Nations as further protection against invasion by Germany (see LEAGUE OF NATIONS). Soviet leaders also ordered Communists throughout the world to combine with political parties in other countries. These combined groups, called *popular fronts*, opposed the growing parties that supported Hitler.

But Russia still feared and suspected the Western democracies. Stalin felt that various agreements among the Western powers were attempts to strengthen Germany against Russia. In 1938, France, Germany, Great Britain, and Italy signed the Munich Agreement. This agreement forced Czechoslovakia to give much of its land to Germany. See MUNICH AGREEMENT.

German expansion in Europe continued, and war between Germany and the Western powers seemed likely. Probably to escape the war, Russia signed an agreement with Germany on Aug. 23, 1939. This agreement provided that neither nation would attack the other. The two countries agreed secretly that each could conquer various territories without interference from the other. Russia and Germany also agreed secretly to divide Poland between themselves.

World War II began when Hitler's troops invaded Poland from the west on Sept. 1, 1939. Two days later, France and Great Britain declared war on Germany. Russia invaded Poland from the east on Sept. 17, 1939. The Russians, claiming they had to "protect" their borders, soon occupied the region. Also to "protect" their borders, the Russians attacked Finland on November 30. In December, Russia was expelled from the League of Nations for this attack. Russia won much Finnish territory by March, 1940, when Finland surrendered. See RUSSO-FINNISH WARS.

In June, 1940, the Red Army moved into Bessarabia (then part of Romania) and the Baltic countries of Estonia, Latvia, and Lithuania. Russia had lost all these lands after World War I, and now took them back. In August, 1940, the three Baltic countries became separate republics of the U.S.S.R., and Bessarabia became part of the new Moldavian Soviet Socialist Republic.

On June 22, 1941, what the Russians had long feared

took place. A huge German force invaded Russia. The German attack pushed back the heavily outnumbered Red Army. German warplanes destroyed much of the Russian air force, and Hitler's tanks and troops drove deep into Soviet territory. In September, the Germans captured Kiev and attacked Leningrad (formerly Petrograd). By December, the Germans came close to Moscow. The attack on Leningrad lasted until January, 1944, when the Germans were finally driven off.

Great Britain and the other Western Allies welcomed Russia as a partner in the war against Germany. Britain, Canada, and the United States began shipping supplies to Russia. The United States joined the Allies in December, 1941, after the Japanese attack on Pearl Harbor. The supplies sent to Russia by the Allies included billions of dollars' worth of food, raw materials, planes, tanks, and trucks.

The Germans were not prepared for the bitter Russian winter. By early 1942, the Russians had driven them back from the Moscow area and some other battlegrounds. The five-month Battle of Stalingrad (now Volgograd), during the winter of 1942-1943, was a major turning point in the war. By the time the Germans surrendered, about 350,000 of their troops had been killed or captured. See STALINGRAD, BATTLE OF.

After the victory at Stalingrad, the Red Army advanced steadily across Eastern Europe and into eastern Germany. As the Russians swept across Eastern Europe, they freed many countries from German control, including Czechoslovakia, Hungary, Poland, and Romania. In April, 1945, Soviet troops began to attack Berlin. Red Army units joined forces with United States troops at Torgau on the Elbe River. Berlin fell to the Russians on May 2, and Germany surrendered to the Allies on May 7. The war in Europe was over.

More than 20 million Russian servicemen and servicewomen were killed or wounded in World War II. No other country suffered so many military casualties. In addition, millions of Russian civilians died, whole regions of Russia lay in ruins, and much of the Soviet economy was shattered.

In February, 1945, Stalin had met with President Franklin D. Roosevelt of the United States and Prime Minister Winston Churchill of Great Britain at Yalta in Russia. At this conference, Stalin promised to help in the war against Japan (see YALTA CONFERENCE). On August 6, the United States dropped on Japan the first atomic bomb used in warfare. Two days later, Russia declared war on Japan and invaded Japanese-held Manchuria and Koréa. The Russians occupied Manchuria for eight months and took nearly a billion dollars' worth of industrial machinery from the region. Japan's surrender to the Allies on Sept. 2, 1945, marked the end of World War II. For the story of Russia in the war, see WORLD WAR II.

The Cold War. During World War II, Stalin had promised Roosevelt and Churchill to help promote freedom throughout the world. After the war, however, Russia cooperated with its Allies only in dividing Berlin and the rest of Germany into occupation zones. East-West relations in Germany soon became tense. Russia set up a Communist police state in its zone, and blocked Western efforts to unite Germany. See GERMANY (After World War II).

Red Army units remained in the Eastern European countries that they had freed from German control. The Red Army helped establish Communist governments in these nations. The Russians used terrorist methods, such as arresting anti-Communists, bringing them to "trial," and shooting them as "fascists."

The Communists in Eastern European countries formed what seemed to be *coalition* governments. In such governments, two or more political parties share power. But the Communists, supported by Russia, seized important government positions and held the real power. Their strength grew, and they did not permit free elections. By early 1948, Russia controlled seven countries in Eastern Europe. These *satellite* countries were Albania, Bulgaria, Czechoslovakia, Hungary, Poland, Romania, and Yugoslavia. Russia also controlled its East German occupation zone, which surrounded West Berlin. The Russians promised the Western powers freedom to move through East Germany to West Berlin. In June, 1948, however, the Russians blocked all land and water routes to West Berlin. The Western powers then flew food and other supplies to West Berlin daily. The Russians lifted the blockade in May, 1949. See BERLIN AIRLIFT.

Russia cut off nearly all contacts between its satellites and the West. The Soviet barriers against communication, trade, and travel came to be known as the *Iron Curtain*. Extreme distrust grew between East and West. An East-West struggle called the *Cold War* spread through Europe and many other regions of the world. For the story of this struggle, see the article on COLD WAR.

Soviet expansion forced the Western nations to act. In 1947, the United States sent military and economic aid to Greece and Turkey. This aid helped prevent Communists from making those countries Soviet satellites. In 1948, the United States began the Marshall Plan to provide aid to help rebuild war-torn European countries. Russia did not allow its satellites to receive the aid. The West also formed a military union called the North Atlantic Treaty Organization (NATO) for defense against possible Communist attack. See MARSHALL PLAN; NORTH ATLANTIC TREATY ORGANIZATION.

Russia, in turn, strengthened the Communist nations

The Battle of Stalingrad was a turning point in World War II. The Russians defeated attacking Germans in the five-month fight.

Pix from Publix

in the Cold War. In 1947, it established the *Cominform* (Communist Information Bureau) to spread Soviet policies in the satellites. In 1948, however, Yugoslavia broke away from Soviet control (see YUGOSLAVIA [History]). In 1949, Russia set up COMECON (Council for Mutual Economic Assistance) to bring the economies of the satellites under greater control. In 1955, the Warsaw Pact provided for military unity among Russia and its satellites (see WARSAW PACT).

From Stalin to Khrushchev. Russia's rapid industrialization continued after World War II under new five-year plans. Restrictions on the workers and peasants, which had been loosened somewhat during the war, again became severe. For example, workers could not quit or change their jobs without government permission. The collective farms were reorganized and made much larger. Stalin also began a new wave of political arrests and executions. Then, on March 5, 1953, Stalin died after a stroke.

No one man immediately replaced Stalin. A *collective leadership* made up of several men ruled the Soviet Union. For almost two years, Georgi M. Malenkov held the major leadership as premier, or chairman of the Council of Ministers. During this period, a struggle for power developed among Malenkov and other leading Communists. Nikita S. Khrushchev became head of the Communist Party in September, 1953 (see KHRUSHCHEV, NIKITA S.). Also that year, Lavrenti P. Beria, chief of the secret police, was executed secretly on charges of plotting to seize power.

Khrushchev's strength increased steadily, and Malenkov was forced to resign in 1955. Nikolai A. Bulganin became premier, but Khrushchev held the real power. At a closed session of the 20th Communist Party Congress in 1956, Khrushchev bitterly criticized Stalin. He

RUSSIA IN WORLD WAR II

■ Territory Gained by Russia

▨ Farthest Advance of German Forces

▤ Farthest Advance of Russian Forces

⬚ Present Boundary of Russia

| 0 Miles | 1,000 | 2,000 |
| 0 Kilometers | 2,000 | 3,000 |

WORLD BOOK map-FGA

accused Stalin of murdering many innocent people and of faulty leadership.

Khrushchev almost lost power in 1957. Following anti-Communist revolts in Hungary and Poland in 1956, Khrushchev's powerful rivals demanded that he resign. But he took the matter before the party's Central Committee, which included many of his followers. Through the committee, Khrushchev defeated his enemies and forced them to lose all positions of power. In 1958, Khrushchev became premier and also remained party leader.

To strengthen his position further, Khrushchev repeated his attacks on Stalin openly at the 22nd Communist Party Congress in 1961. Buildings, cities, and towns named for Stalin were renamed. Pictures and statues of Stalin were destroyed. The government removed Stalin's body from its place of honor in Lenin's tomb in Moscow, and buried it in a simple grave nearby.

Khrushchev's Policies differed greatly from Stalin's. The secret police did not spread terror, and the government allowed somewhat freer political discussion. The workweek was shortened to about 40 hours, and workers were allowed to quit or change their jobs. Khrushchev also tried to raise the nation's standard of living. Government industrial planning aimed for greater production of clothing, food, household appliances, and other consumer goods. But gains were slow.

Russia's relations with the West improved after Stalin's death. Unlike other Communist leaders, Khrushchev denied that war with the West was necessary for Communism to triumph throughout the world. In 1956, Khrushchev announced a policy of *peaceful coexistence*. He described this policy as avoiding war while competing with the West in the fields of science and economic development. Khrushchev loosened restrictions on communication, trade, and travel across the Iron Curtain. He made friendly visits to several Western countries, including the United States. But Russia still tried to expand its influence by encouraging revolts, riots, and strikes in non-Communist countries.

China believed that war with the West was necessary, and strongly criticized Russia's "soft" policy. A bitter split developed between the two major Communist powers. Their dispute reached a climax at the 22nd Communist Party Congress in Moscow in 1961. The Chinese premier, Chou En-lai, suddenly left the congress and returned to China. Albania, a Russian satellite, supported China, and Russia ended relations with Albania.

Russia took an early lead over the United States in exploring space. Under Khrushchev, the Soviet Union spent huge sums to develop powerful launching rockets. On Oct. 4, 1957, Russia launched *Sputnik I*, the first spacecraft to circle the earth. This achievement marked the beginning of the space age. In 1961, Yuri A. Gagarin, a Russian air force officer, became the first man to orbit the earth. See SPACE TRAVEL (Steps in the Conquest of Space).

The Spy Plane and Cuba. Khrushchev and President Dwight D. Eisenhower of the United States scheduled a meeting in Paris in May, 1960, with British and French leaders. Shortly before the meeting began, the Russians shot down an American U-2 plane over Soviet territory. The pilot, Francis Gary Powers, confessed that he had been spying. Eisenhower admitted that U-2 planes had been taking photographs over Russia for four years. When the Paris meeting began, Khrushchev demanded that Eisenhower apologize. The President refused, and Khrushchev angrily left the conference. The meeting broke up the next day.

Another crisis occurred in October, 1962. The United States learned that Russia had missile bases in Cuba. These bases could have launched atomic attacks against the United States or other parts of the Western Hemisphere. President John F. Kennedy ordered a naval blockade of Cuba to prevent more Russian missiles from reaching the island. He also demanded that Russia remove all the missiles and missile bases. Khrushchev met these demands. See CUBA (The Cuban Missile Crisis).

Khrushchev's Fall from Power. In 1963, Russia, the United States, and Great Britain signed a treaty prohibiting all nuclear weapons tests except those conducted underground. Also in 1963, Russia and the United States set up a direct teletype connection called the *hot line* between Moscow and Washington, D.C. They hoped it would help prevent any misunderstanding from leading to war. The first use of the line came during the Arab-Israeli war in June, 1967. Russia, the United States, and Great Britain agreed in 1964 to reduce their production of nuclear weapon materials.

Although Khrushchev improved Russia's relations with the West, many of his other policies failed. His farm program collapsed, and in 1963 Russia had to buy more than 10 million tons of wheat from the West. Soviet industrialization slowed down. The economy also suffered because the people refused to buy many poorly made products. In addition, the split with China and Khrushchev's withdrawal of the missiles from Cuba drew sharp criticism. On Oct. 15, 1964, pressure from high-ranking Communists forced Khrushchev to retire. He was replaced by Leonid I. Brezhnev as Communist party head, and Aleksei N. Kosygin as premier (see BREZHNEV, LEONID I.; KOSYGIN, ALEKSEI N.).

In 1965, Brezhnev and Kosygin reorganized Russia's economy. Factories were put on a profit basis. Government supervision of the factories was taken from regional agencies and given to federal bodies under the Council of Ministers. (For a discussion of these changes, see the *Manufacturing* section of this article.) A new five-year plan, approved in 1966, eliminated Khrushchev's impractical goals, such as producing more than the United States by 1970. New goals included increasing industrial production by half, the people's income by a third, and farm production by a fourth. This plan, unlike earlier ones, placed almost as much importance on consumer goods as on heavy-industry products.

Russia Today is still the leading Communist power, but the Communist world is no longer united behind the Soviet Union. The bitter dispute with China has become a struggle for influence over other Communist nations and over newly independent countries, especially those in Africa and Asia.

In 1967, war broke out between Israel and Egypt and its Arab allies. Russia had backed the Arabs, and had sent them military equipment and other aid. Israel crushed the Arabs in six days. After the war, Russia rearmed some Arab states and gained more influence in the Middle East and the Mediterranean region.

During the 1960's, Russia lost some control over its Eastern European satellites. But in 1968, Soviet troops invaded Czechoslovakia and crushed a reform movement aimed at giving the people more personal freedom.

In 1969, Russia and China fought a series of armed border conflicts. Late that year, representatives of the two countries met to discuss their border disputes.

During the 1960's and early 1970's, the Vietnam War strained relations between Russia and the United States. American forces aided South Vietnamese troops against the Communists of North and South Vietnam. Russia sent the Communist forces surface-to-air missiles and other weapons. See VIETNAM WAR.

In the late 1960's, a consular treaty between Russia and the United States improved Soviet-U.S. relations. In November, 1969, Russia met with the United States in Helsinki, Finland, for talks on the control of nuclear weapons (see STRATEGIC ARMS LIMITATION TALKS [SALT]). In August, 1970, leaders of Russia and West Germany signed a treaty to outlaw the use or threat of force between the two nations.

President Richard M. Nixon traveled to Russia in 1972 and met with Soviet leaders. Agreements reached during the summit talks included a treaty to limit each country's production of nuclear weapons. The two nations also agreed to work together in such fields as pollution control, medicine, and space exploration.

WILLIAM B. BALLIS, MORRIS BORNSTEIN, DEMING BROWN, GEORGE KISH, WILLIAM K. MEDLIN, and ARTHUR P. MENDEL

RUSSIA/Study Aids

Related Articles in WORLD BOOK include:

BIOGRAPHIES

See the Related Articles of DRAMA; MUSIC; and RUSSIAN LITERATURE. See also the following:

Alexander (of Russia)	Malenkov, Georgi M.
Andropov, Yuri	Mazurov, Kirill T.
Beria, Lavrenti P.	Mikoyan, Anastas
Brezhnev, Leonid I.	Molotov, Vyacheslav
Bulganin, Nikolai A.	Nicholas (of Russia)
Catherine	Peter I, the Great
Gromyko, Andrei A.	Plekhanov, Georgi V.
Ivan	Podgorny, Nikolai V.
Kalinin, Mikhail I.	Polyansky, Dmitri S.
Katushev, Konstantin F.	Ponomarev, Boris N.
Kerensky, Alexander F.	Pugachev, Emelian I.
Khrushchev, Nikita S.	Rasputin, Grigori Y.
Konev, Ivan S.	Shelepin, Alexander N.
Kosygin, Aleksei N.	Shelest, Peter Y.
Lenin, V. I.	Stalin, Joseph
Litvinov, Maxim M.	Suslov, Mikhail A.

Weston Kemp

A Soviet Space Exhibition near Moscow honors Russian cosmonauts and features displays of Soviet spacecraft.

RUSSIA

Trotsky, Leon
Vishinsky, Andrei Y.
Vladimir I

Yakubovsky, Ivan I.
Yepishev, Alexei A.
Zhukov, Georgi K.

Kremlin
Politburo
Ruble
Russian Language
Russian Literature

Soviet
Space Travel
Strategic Arms Limitation Talks
Tass
Warsaw Pact

CITIES

Archangel	Kaliningrad	Moscow	Sevastopol
Astrakhan	Kazan	Murmansk	Smolensk
Baku	Kharkov	Novosibirsk	Sverdlovsk
Dneprope-	Kiev	Odessa	Tashkent
trovsk	Kuybyshev	Omsk	Tiflis
Donetsk	Leningrad	Rostov-on-	Vladivostok
Dushanbe	Lvov	Don	Volgograd
Gorki	Magnitogorsk	Samarkand	Yalta
Irkutsk	Minsk	Saratov	Yerevan

HISTORY

Berlin,	Hungary (History)	Russo-Japanese
Congress of	Mongol Empire	War
Bolshevik	MVD	Russo-Turkish
Cold War	Paris, Treaties of	Wars
Crimean War	Poland (History)	Triple Entente
Czar	Russo-Finnish	World War I
Duma	Wars	World War II

PHYSICAL FEATURES

Altai Mountains	Kara Kum	Novaya Zemlya
Amu Darya	Kara Sea	Ob River
Amur River	Karelian	Oka River
Aral Sea	Isthmus	Okhotsk, Sea of
Azov, Sea of	Kuril Islands	Sakhalin
Caspian Sea	Kyzyl Kum	Stanovoy
Caucasus Mountains	Lake Balkhash	Mountains
Commander Islands	Lake Baykal	Syr Darya
Dnepr River	Lake Ilmen	Ural Mountains
Dneproges Dam	Lake Ladoga	Ural River
Dnestr River	Lake Onega	Volga River
Don River	Lake Peipus	White Sea
Dvina River	Lena River	Wrangel Island
Franz Josef Land	Merv	Yablonovyy
Irtysh River	Mount Elbrus	Mountains
Kamchatka	Neman River	Yenisey River
Peninsula	Neva River	

REGIONS

Bessarabia	Crimea	Karelia	Turkestan
Bucovina	Daghestan	Ruthenia	Tuva
Caucasia	Galicia	Siberia	

UNION REPUBLICS

See the separate article on each union republic listed in the *Russia Map Index.*

PRODUCTS AND INDUSTRY

For Russia's rank in production, see the following:

Agriculture	Fishing	Lumber	Ship
Aluminum	Industry	Manganese	Silver
Barley	Flax	Manufacturing	Sugar
Cattle	Forest and	Nickel	Sugar Beet
Cheese	Forest	Oats	Tea
Chemical	Products	Petroleum	Textile
Industry	Gas (fuel)	Platinum	Tin
Clothing	Gold	Potato	Tobacco
Coal	Horse	Rubber	Tungsten
Copper	Iron and Steel	Rye	Vegetable
Cotton	Lead	Salt	Wheat
Electric Power	Leather	Sheep	Zinc

OTHER RELATED ARTICLES

Asia (Way of Life in
    North Asia)
Astronaut (The Rus-
    sian Cosmonauts)
Ballet (Russian Ballet)
Communism

Dancing (Ballet)
Five-Year Plan
Flag (picture: Historical Flags)
Government (Comparing
    Democracy and Communism)
Iron Curtain

Outline

I. Government
II. People
  A. Nationalities and Languages   B. Religion
III. Way of Life
  A. Personal   B. City Life   D. Family Life
     Freedom   C. Village Life   E. Recreation
IV. Education
  A. Elementary Grades   E. Higher Education
  B. Intermediate   F. After-School Activities
     Grades   G. Libraries
  C. Secondary Grades   H. Museums
  D. Special Schools
V. Communication
VI. Arts
  A. Architecture   C. Music   E. Theater
  B. Literature   D. Painting   and Ballet
VII. The Land
  A. Land Regions   B. Rivers and Lakes
VIII. Climate
IX. Economy
  A. Natural Resources   F. Fishing
  B. Manufacturing   G. Electric Power
  C. Agriculture   H. Foreign Trade
  D. Mining   I. Transportation
  E. Forest Products
X. History

Questions

What is the longest nonstop airline route in the world?
What led to the Russian-Chinese dispute of the 1960's?
What Russian achievement started the space age?
What were some ways in which Russian life differed under Joseph Stalin and under Nikita S. Khrushchev?
How does the Komsomol serve Communism?
How did Soviet factory operations change in 1965?
Why does foreign trade play only a small part in the economy of Russia?
What is the largest inland body of water in the world?
Why is it so important for Russian schoolchildren to receive high marks in behavior?
Who planned the October Revolution of 1917?

Reading and Study Guide

For a *Reading and Study Guide on Russia*, see the RE-SEARCH GUIDE/INDEX, Volume 22.

Books for Young Readers

FOLSOM, FRANKLIN. *The Soviet Union: A View from Within.* Nelson, 1965.
NAZAROFF, ALEXANDER. *The Land and People of Russia.* Rev. ed. Lippincott, 1966; *Picture Map Geography of the USSR.* 1969.
SEEGER, ELIZABETH. *The Pageant of Russian History.* McKay, 1950.
SNYDER, LOUIS L. *The First Book of the Soviet Union.* Rev. ed. Watts, 1965.

Books for Older Readers

FLORINSKY, MICHAEL T. *Russia: A Short History.* 2nd ed. Macmillan, 1969.
KOUTAISSOF, ELISABETH. *The Soviet Union.* Praeger, 1971.
MILLER, JACK. *Life in Russia Today.* Putnam, 1969.
SALISBURY, HARRISON E., ed. *The Soviet Union. The Fifty Years.* Harcourt, 1967.
SETON-WATSON, HUGH. *The Russian Empire: 1801-1917.* Oxford, 1967.
VERNADSKY, GEORGE. *A History of Russia.* 4 vols. Yale, 1943-1959.
WALLACE, ROBERT. *Rise of Russia.* Time Inc., 1967.

RUSSIAN LANGUAGE is the most important Slavic language, both as to the number of persons who speak it and as to its cultural influence. It is the native tongue of about 130 million persons in Russia. It is also the common means of communication between most of the other inhabitants of Russia, who speak more than 100 different languages and dialects. Russian is the official language of Russia.

Russian, or Great Russian, belongs to the eastern branch of the Slavic linguistic family, as do Ukrainian (or Little Russian) and Byelorussian (or White Russian). It is closely related to other Slavic tongues, such as Polish, Czech, Slovak, Slovenian, Serbo-Croatian, Macedonian, and Bulgarian. Russian has three main dialects: northern, central, and southern. Modern literary Russian is based on the central dialect, the speech of Moscow and the surrounding areas. The present literary Russian dialect became fairly stabilized by the end of the 1700's. It has changed little since that time.

Alphabet. The alphabet used in Russia has 33 letters. They form the Cyrillic alphabet, based largely on the Greek alphabet. The letters and their approximate sounds in English are as follows:

Russian		Roman Equivalent	Approximate Sound in English
А	а	a	*far*
Б	б	b	*b*og
В	в	v	*v*ault
Г	г	g	*g*o
Д	д	d	*d*og
Е	е	ye	*y*et
Ё	ё	yo	*y*awl
Ж	ж	zh	a*z*ure
З	з	z	*z*one
И	и	i	*f*eet
Й	й	y	bo*y*
К	к	k	*k*id
Л	л	l	*l*aw
М	м	m	*m*oose
Н	н	n	*n*ot
О	о	o	*aw*e
П	п	p	*p*ot
Р	р	r	*thr*ice (rolled)
С	с	s	*s*oot
Т	т	t	*t*oe
У	у	u	*f*ool
Ф	ф	f	*f*or
Х	х	kh	lo*ch*
Ц	ц	ts	i*ts*
Ч	ч	ch	*ch*urch
Ш	ш	sh	*sch*nauzer
Щ	щ	shch	fre*sh ch*eese
Ъ	ъ	—	indicates a break for syllable and y-sound before vowel following
Ы	ы	y	rh*y*thm
Ь	ь	—	usually softens preceding consonant, with attached y-sound, as *n* in canyon
Э	э	e	m*e*t
Ю	ю	yu	*u*se
Я	я	ya	*y*ard

The letters ъ, ы, and ь never occur at the beginning of a word or syllable. But these letters may be capitalized for signs, titles, and other special uses. In pronunciation, most Russian consonants have two distinct values—an ordinary *hard*, or nonpalatalized, sound, and a *soft*, or palatalized, sound. Soft con-

sonants are pronounced with the tongue raised and touching the hard palate of the mouth, thus adding to the consonant a short *y* sound before the following vowel. The vowels—е, ё, и, ю, and я (as well as ь)—are pronounced *eh, aw, ee, oo,* and *ah,* and normally indicate that the preceding consonant is soft. Thus, ву is pronounced *voo,* and вю is pronounced *vyoo,* or somewhat like the French *vu.* At the beginning of a word or syllable, the soft vowels е, ё, ю, and я indicate a distinct *y* sound preceding the vowel: *ye, yaw, yu, ya.*

Russian spelling, like English, tries to combine an historical principle with a phonetic one. That is, some words retain their traditional spelling, even though they are no longer pronounced as they used to be.

Grammar. Russian belongs to the Indo-European family of languages. Like Latin and Greek, it is highly inflected. Nouns have six cases and three genders. Pronouns and adjectives change their forms to agree with the words they represent or modify. Russian also has special forms for predicate adjectives and for the comparative and superlative forms. Russian verbs have only three tense forms—present, past, and future. Completed, continued, and repetitive actions are expressed by special verb forms called *aspects.* The language has a marked stress. The accent of a given word may change, depending on the grammatical form. The word order in a Russian sentence is not rigid, and is frequently much the same as in English.

Vocabulary. Comparatively few basic words in everyday Russian are easily recognizable as related to English, although many may derive from a common ancestor. In recent years, scientific, technical, and everyday Russian have borrowed a great number of words from Western languages. They include *aeroplan, mekhanik, telefon,* and thousands of others.

History. All the Slavic languages probably developed from a primitive Common-Slavic tongue. Old Church Slavic, the language of the Russian Orthodox Church, resembles Common-Slavic more closely than any other language. This tongue played a role in the history of Russian quite similar to that played by Latin in the history of the Romance languages. A great many words, most of them compound forms with prefixes and suffixes, used in modern Russian, are actually Old Church Slavic in origin. Russian has many word pairs, with the native Russian form used for a word with a concrete, everyday meaning, and the Old Church Slavic used to express an abstract, metaphoric concept. This characteristic resembles word pairs in English, which often consist of a common word derived from Anglo-Saxon *(house)* and a more formal word derived from Latin *(residence).*

The earliest formal literature in Russia was written chiefly in Old Church Slavic, with some native Russian words and forms. The oldest manuscripts, dating back to the 1000's, show evidences of a distinct Russian language. Old Russian legal and business documents were written in the native dialect. By the 1700's, works of literature were written in Russian, and it gradually replaced Old Church Slavic entirely, except for religious use.

OLEG A. MASLENIKOV

See also ALPHABET (The Cyrillic Alphabet).

Novosti Press Agency, Moscow

Russian Literature includes many famous works, such as *The Three Sisters*, a drama by Anton Chekhov. A scene from a production of the play by the Moscow Art Theater is shown above.

RUSSIAN LITERATURE

RUSSIAN LITERATURE includes some of the greatest masterpieces ever written. Russian authors have used all literary forms, but are best known for their novels and poetry. Style, content, and keen character analysis contribute to the excellence of Russian writing. The most famous Russian works show a deep concern for moral, religious, and philosophical problems.

History has had an important influence on Russian literature. The widespread acceptance of Christianity in Russia during the late 900's resulted in literature that consisted mostly of religious works. Themes of the Tartar invasion and conquest dominated Russian literature from the 1200's to the late 1400's. The Tartar occupation kept Russia isolated from Western Europe for more than 200 years. But by the end of the 1600's, translations and imitations of Western European works were appearing in many Russian writings. By the late 1700's, literature had become a major form of social protest against the czars, serfdom, and moral and political corruption. The greatest Russian poetry, prose, and drama were written during the 1800's.

Since the Revolution of 1917, literary activity in Russia has been controlled by the Communist government. Government censors require that literature portray Soviet society as being full of optimism and joy of life. Writers who ignore such regulations face the threat of severe punishment. However, the constant struggle of Russian writers against censorship has led to occasional periods of creative freedom and experimentation.

Early Literature

Religious Literature. The first Russian literature appeared at about the time of the nation's conversion to Christianity in A.D. 988. The literature, like the

new religion, came from the Byzantine Empire and the Slavic kingdoms of Bulgaria and Serbia. The writings were largely religious in the form of sermons, hymns, and biographies of saints. Many of these works, despite their religious themes, were characterized by imagination and vivid details of Russian life. Some works were original, but many were based on Greek writings.

Early Russian literature was written in a mixture of Russian and *Church Slavic*, a related language. Church Slavic came from the Slavic peoples of central and Balkan Europe. The Russians also were Slavs, and could understand the new language without much difficulty. Church Slavic became the official language of the Russian Orthodox Church. Elements of Slavic style were used even in nonreligious literature to give it a more dignified tone.

Most of Russia's first literary works were both written and read by clergymen. Printing was not introduced in Russia until 1564, and so the clergymen copied manuscripts by hand.

Nonreligious Literature. The *chronicles*, which were records of outstanding events, were probably the most important early nonreligious Russian writings. The capital of each *principality* (region ruled by a prince) had its own chronicle. During the 1100's, the chronicle of Kiev, the original capital, carried frequent warnings against the danger of a divided Russia. Later chronicles, particularly those of Moscow, claimed that their principalities had the right to reunite and rule all Russia. Much of a chronicle was dry narrative, but

William E. Harkins, the contributor of this article, is Professor of Slavic Languages at Columbia University and the author of A Dictionary of Russian Literature.

some accounts were vivid descriptions of military or political battles. Others were fantastic stories based on legend rather than fact.

The greatest work of early Russian literature was the *Igor Tale*, written by an anonymous author of the late 1100's. This prose poem, famous for its vivid imagery and nature symbolism, described the unsuccessful campaign of a Russian prince against the Polovetzkians, an Asiatic tribe, in 1185. The *Igor Tale* pleaded for cooperation among the princes to prevent an invasion by foreign forces. This gloomy work turned out to be a correct prophesy. The Tartars invaded Russia in 1223 and again in 1237. By 1240, they had conquered almost the entire country.

The Literature of Tartar Captivity reflected less original thought than did the literature of any other period in Russian history. Tartar rule, which lasted until 1480, provided the dominant theme of the small amount of literature that did appear. The *Zadonshchina* (*Battle of the Don*), an important work of the 1400's, described the first major Russian victory over the Tartars. This work imitated the literary language and imagery of the *Igor Tale*.

Muscovite Literature developed as Moscow rose to power following the final defeat of the Tartars in 1480. All Russian-speaking territories were united into a single state under the grand prince of Moscow. Russia eventually became an empire, and the grand prince became known as czar. Main themes of Muscovite literature included the right of Moscow to rule the Russian land, and the czar's right to absolute authority. One work, the *Domostroy* (*How to Keep House*), advised a man to rule his family with complete authority, while obeying God, the czar, and the state. Other works praised the grandeur and magnificence of the new Russian empire. Writers emphasized style rather than content.

Beginnings of Modern Literature

Western Influences. The 1600's saw an almost complete reshaping of Russian literature. Western Europe, from which Russia had been isolated since the 1100's, began to have a strong influence on Russian writing. Western works, such as anecdotes, fables, moral tales, poetry, and stories of knighthood, were translated and imitated. For the first time, rhymed verse appeared in Russian literature. Russian folklore provided a source for many fairy tales, *satires* (writings that ridiculed persons or their actions), and other works. Some authors discarded Church Slavic, the old literary language, and wrote in Russian.

The greatest writer of the new literature was Avvakum, an archpriest and a strict clergyman. He joined a group opposed to changes made in the ritual of the Russian Orthodox Church in the 1650's, which led to a split in the church. Avvakum's autobiography illustrated his colorful personality and deep religious convictions. His expressive language and vivid descriptions of everyday life make his writings some of the most revealing works of this period.

Simeon Polotsky, a monk who received a Western education in Kiev, was an outstanding author of the period. His most important contribution to literature was the introduction of a rigid syllabic system into Russian verse. Each line of poetry had a fixed number of syllables with regularly placed pauses. Polotsky wrote quaint but serious verse. Many of his works praised the czar and the ruling family. He also wrote several plays on Biblical subjects. Another playwright who was influenced by Western literature was Johann Gregori, a German Lutheran pastor in Moscow. Gregori's crude comedies, based on Biblical stories, became popular.

One of the strongest supporters of Western European influence on Russian literature was Czar Peter I (the Great). He promoted the translation of European works and sent a number of noblemen abroad to study Western ways of life. Several fantastic tales about their adventures were written by anonymous authors.

The complete Westernization of Russian literature took place during the 1700's. Despite the many political changes that occurred in Russia, European culture continued to flourish there. Many French, German, and English works influenced Russian authors.

Prince Antioch Kantemir, a leading poet and diplomat, wrote nine satires in verse supporting Peter the Great's reforms and the spread of Western culture. Kantemir used everyday speech in his works, and the informal language helped his characters appear lively and typically Russian.

Mikhail Lomonosov has been called the founder of modern Russian literature and the forerunner of classicism. His dignified *odes* (lyric poems) praised the czar and the greatness of God. Lomonosov introduced the modern Russian type of verse, featuring a regular pattern of stressed and unstressed syllables. He also established a system of three literary styles. These styles varied among (1) the highest, or most dignified, language; (2) the middle language based on spoken Russian, but without the vulgarisms; and (3) the lowest, or most popular, speech.

The Classical Movement, introduced by Lomonosov's literary reforms, emerged fully in Russia about 1740. Classical writers followed the formal rules of composition developed by the ancient Greeks and Romans. The classical movement stressed the importance of reason and analysis in the interpretation of life. Classicism came to Russia as part of the continual cultural flow from Western Europe.

The most typical Russian classicist was Alexander Sumarokov, who wrote in a variety of forms. His works included fables, plays, satires, and songs. Many of his comedies were amusing, but his tragedies were crude and monotonous.

Vasili Ivanovich Maykov, one of Sumarokov's followers, wrote a mock epic poem called *Elisey, or Bacchus Infuriated* (1771). This realistic work describes the hilarious adventures of a drunken coachman. Another important classicist, Denis Fonvizin, became famous for his satirical comedies. *The Adolescent* (1782), though it has obvious flaws, is considered his finest work. This play attacked the ignorance and cruelty of country landowners. Fonvizin was forced out of literature in the 1780's after Empress Catherine II (the Great) prohibited him from publishing his writings.

An outstanding poet of the 1700's was Gavriil Derzhavin who, like Lomonosov, wrote mostly odes. In

RUSSIAN LITERATURE

Felitsa (1783), Derzhavin praised Catherine and ridiculed the vices of her courtiers. Derzhavin did much to make the ode a fresh poetry of life and feeling. His work marked the turning point in Russian literature from classical to romantic writing.

During the late 1700's and early 1800's, fables were the most popular form of literature in Russia. The nation's greatest writer of fables was Ivan Krylov. His works, typically Russian in their everyday language and humorous characterizations, ridiculed ignorance and vanity.

The Age of Romanticism

Romanticism, which originated in Germany and England, stressed the full expression of emotions in literature. The movement developed as a revolt against the logic and formality used by classical writers. Romantic characteristics began to appear in Russian literature during the late 1700's. But romanticism did not become a significant influence until the early 1800's.

Sentimentalism, one of the strongest early romantic trends, came to Russia from Europe about 1790. The followers of this movement emphasized the importance of feelings and imagination. However, the sentimentalists continued to use classical forms in poetry.

The leading Russian sentimentalist was Nikolai Karamzin. His elegantly written *Letters of a Russian Traveler* (1791-1792) was filled with the excitement of his trip to the West and his meetings with famous writers. *Poor Liza* (1792) was a popular tale about a peasant girl who was abandoned by her lover, a nobleman. Karamzin's *History of the Russian State* (1816-1826) is still an important work of Russian history.

Preromanticism. Another group of writers of the late 1700's are known as preromantics. They showed a greater interest in nature and more love of moods than did the sentimentalists. Leading preromantic writers included Vasili Zhukovsky and Konstantin Batyushkov. Zhukovsky, a gifted poet, translated the works of several German and English romantics. Batyushkov wrote sad, passionate lyrics.

Early Romanticism. A new generation of poets appeared during the 1820's, marking the beginning of the *Golden Age* of Russian poetry. These poets, like the preromantics, combined classical forms with romantic sentiments. However, the early romantics showed a greater concern for individual freedom and an interest in a broader range of subjects. The poets of the Golden Age were strongly influenced by two English authors, William Shakespeare and Lord Byron.

Russia's greatest lyric poet, and the leading writer of early romanticism, was Alexander S. Pushkin. His poems were distinguished by their brief but expressive language. Pushkin's brief style made his works difficult to translate, or to be appreciated in any language except Russian.

Pushkin's narrative poems, like those of Byron, dealt with man's place in society. Many of his main characters, such as the title hero of *Eugene Onegin* (1823-1831), are unable to find a purpose in life. They end up bored and insensitive to love.

In 1825, Pushkin wrote *Boris Godunov*, a historical

IMPORTANT PERIODS IN THE DEVELOPMENT OF RUSSIAN LITERATURE

EARLY RUSSIAN LITERATURE (Late 900's to 1600's)	THE AGE OF ROMANTICISM (Late 1700's to the early 1840's)	THE AGE OF REALISM (Early 1840's to the early 1900's)
Early Russian literature consisted primarily of religious works written by clergymen. Some important nonreligious writings, mostly historical works, also appeared during this period.	The romantic movement in literature developed as a revolt against classicism. Romantic writing featured a new freedom of form and admiration for human emotion.	Realism in literature was a reaction against romantic writing. The realists felt that literature should portray life honestly. Russian realists wrote about social and political problems.

The chronicles
  The *Igor Tale*
  The *Zadonshchina*
	Sentimentalism
	(Late 1700's and early 1800's)
	Nikolai Karamzin
	  Letters of a Russian Traveler
	  (1791-1792)
		Early Realism
		(Early 1840's to the early 1860's)
		Ivan Turgenev
		  Rudin (1856)
		  Fathers and Sons (1862)

BEGINNINGS OF MODERN RUSSIAN LITERATURE (1600 to the late 1700's)	**Preromanticism**
	(Late 1700's and early 1800's)
	Vasili Zhukovsky
	Konstantin Batyushkov
		Alexander Ostrovsky
		  Poverty Is No Crime (1854)
		  The Storm (1860)

Western Europe began to have a strong influence on Russian literature during the 1600's. Russian authors translated English, French, and German writings and imitated Western literary forms.	**Early Romanticism**
	(1820 to the early 1830's)
	Alexander Pushkin
	  Eugene Onegin (1823-1831)
	  Boris Godunov (1825)
		The Period of Great Russian Novels (Early 1860's to the early 1880's)
		Leo Tolstoy
		  War and Peace (1865-1869)
		  Anna Karenina (1875-1877)

Archpriest Avvakum
Prince Antioch Kantemir
Mikhail Lomonosov
	Alexander Griboyedov
	  Woe from Wit (1825)
		Fyodor Dostoevsky
		  Crime and Punishment (1866)
		  The Brothers Karamazov (1880)

The classical movement, which began in Western Europe, appeared in Russia about 1740. Classical writers followed the formal rules of composition developed by the Greeks and Romans.	**Late Romanticism**
	(Early 1830's to the early 1840's)
	Mikhail Lermontov
	  A Hero of Our Times (1840)
		Late Realism
		(Early 1880's to the early 1900's)
		Anton Chekhov
		  Uncle Vanya (1897)
		  Three Sisters (1901)

Alexander Sumarokov
Gavriil Derzhavin
	Nikolai Gogol
	  Taras Bulba (1835)
	  Dead Souls (1842)
		Maxim Gorki
		  The Lower Depths (1902)

drama in blank verse. This play represented an attempt to introduce Shakespeare's type of chronicle play into Russian drama. *The Bronze Horseman* (1833), one of Pushkin's greatest poems, shows the tragedy of an ordinary man sacrificed to the needs of the state.

Pushkin also wrote a novel and several stories. His novel, *The Captain's Daughter* (1836), resembled the historical novels of Sir Walter Scott, a Scottish romantic. One of Pushkin's best stories, *The Queen of Spades* (1834), is about a gambler who goes mad after failing to win a fortune at cards.

Other poets of the Golden Age included Yevgeny Baratynsky, Baron Anton Delvig, and Wilhelm Kuchelbecker. Baratynsky became famous for his precise, original style. His narrative poems include *Eda* (1825), *The Ball* (1828), and *The Gypsy Girl* (1842).

Another important writer of the 1820's was Alexander Griboyedov. His most famous work, *Woe from Wit* (1825), was a satirical comedy written in rhymed verses. The hero, Chatsky, like Pushkin's Eugene Onegin, is unable to fit into the society of his time. Onegin and Chatsky became known as "superfluous" or useless men whose weak natures prevent them from pursuing constructive goals. Later writers used this character type to describe Russian nobles who could not provide strong liberal leadership in support of political and social reforms. The superfluous man appeared in Russian literature several times during the 1800's and early 1900's.

Late Romanticism featured a new freedom of form and style, and an admiration for human feelings and passions. This movement, which began in the 1830's, also stressed the deep significance of dreams, visions, and fantasies. Political and moral corruption were the themes of some late romantic Russian literature. However, censorship had become severe under Czar Nicholas I, whose rule began in 1825. Many works that were critical of Russian society could not be published. The leading writers of this period included Mikhail Lermontov, Fyodor Tyutchev, and Nikolai V. Gogol.

Lermontov was an outstanding poet and novelist. His lyrics expressed intense frustration and boredom with life in Russia. In several of his poems, Lermontov dreamed of an unattainable paradise. Pride and unrestrained desire cause the hero of *The Demon* (1839) to lose this ideal state. Lermontov's *A Hero of Our Times* (1840) was the first psychological novel in Russian literature. The hero, Pechorin, is another superfluous man. He wastes his life in a series of senseless adventures because the strictness of Russian social and political life keeps him from any useful activities except his military duties.

Tyutchev, another brilliant poet, wrote several pessimistic works about man's insignificant place in the universe. Tyutchev's poems include *A Vision* (1829), *Dream on the Sea* (1836), and *Holy Night* (1849).

Gogol was one of Russia's greatest writers. His early works give colorful descriptions of life in the Ukraine, where he was born. *Taras Bulba* (1835), a historical novel, praises the past glory of Ukrainian Cossacks. Literary critics regarded many of Gogol's later works as political satires. But Gogol's main objective was to make fun of man's spiritual weaknesses. The characters

REVOLUTIONARY LITERATURE (Late 1800's to the early 1900's)	SOVIET LITERATURE (1917 to the present)	
The spirit of revolution, which swept through the country during the late 1800's and early 1900's, became an important influence on the works of Russian writers.	Since the Bolshevik Revolution of 1917, the government has attempted to use literature as a propaganda tool. Russian writers have been told to present only favorable descriptions of Soviet life and government censorship has limited the free expression of ideas. The works of many Soviet writers have been published outside Russia.	
Symbolism, a literary trend that began in Russia during the mid-1890's, opposed a realistic portrayal of life in writing.	During the 1920's, several important works were written about the revolution and the civil war that followed from 1918 to 1920.	The 1950's and 1960's were marked by the appearance of several liberal writers who attacked social and political conditions in Russia.
Alexander Blok *The Twelve* (1918)	Isaak Babel *Red Cavalry* (1926)	Poets
Andrey Bely *St. Petersburg* (1913)	Alexei N. Tolstoy *Road to Calvary* (1921-1941)	Yevgeny Yevtushenko Andrey Voznesensky
		Novelists
Post-Symbolism, which began about 1910, was a revolt against the vague works of the symbolists. It stressed simplicity and clarity in literature.	From 1928 to 1932, Russian writers helped promote Soviet industry by producing works that dealt with such subjects as agriculture and manufacturing.	Boris Pasternak *Doctor Zhivago* (1957)
Anna Akhmatova Vladimir Mayakovsky	Valentin Kataev *Time, Forward* (1932)	Alexander Solzhenitsyn *The First Circle* (1968)
	Many works written during the 1930's and 1940's were based on historical events, such as the revolution or the war against Germany from 1941 to 1945.	
	Mikhail Sholokhov *The Quiet Don* (1928-1940)	
	Konstantin Simonov *Days and Nights* (1941)	

RUSSIAN LITERATURE

in *The Inspector-General* (1836) represent common human vices. *The Overcoat* (1842), the story of a pathetic copy clerk, protests the spiritual poverty of man. *Dead Souls* (1842), though never completed, was one of Gogol's most brilliant satires. The hero of the story travels around Russia buying up titles to dead serfs whose names are still in the census. He plans to use the titles in a swindle. This tale, an attack on moral corruption, was misinterpreted by readers of Gogol's day as a criticism of political corruption.

The Age of Realism

During the 1840's, realism emerged as an important literary trend in Russia. Followers of this movement were influenced partly by the teachings of Vissarion Belinsky, a leading literary critic. Belinsky believed that realistic literature should give an honest picture of life and, at the same time, preach social reform. His view that literature should serve the needs of society became an established principle in Russian writing.

Early Realism. The literature of the 1840's and the 1850's had both romantic and realistic traits. Early realists combined romantic sentiments and feelings with realistic portrayals of social and political problems.

Ivan Turgenev, an outstanding novelist and playwright, displayed a deep understanding of Russian society and people. *A Sportsman's Sketches* (1852) helped stir up public sympathy for Russia's serfs. Turgenev described the serfs as kind and dignified, and portrayed landowners as crude and insensitive. In *Rudin* (1856), Turgenev showed the traditional superfluous man as a frustrated liberal. *Fathers and Sons* (1862) was superior to Turgenev's other works in dramatic content and in character analysis. It shows the *nihilists* (radical Russian youths of the early 1860's) as strong-willed, and disrespectful of authority and tradition. They want to change Russian society, but the country is not yet ready for a revolution. The hero, Bazarov, dies inactive and frustrated. One of Turgenev's favorite themes was young love, the subject of *Asya* (1858) and *First Love* (1860). In *First Love*, a boy experiences his first crush, only to learn that the girl is his father's mistress. Turgenev's most successful play, *A Month in the Country* (1850), tells a similar story. A mother and her adopted daughter compete for the love of a young tutor.

Ivan Goncharov, another important novelist, tried to convince Russian liberals that only practical action, not sentiment, leads to social reform. In *Oblomov* (1859), the superfluous man is portrayed as a well-bred landowner whose failure to act keeps him from achieving his youthful dreams. Goncharov showed romantic traits in his sympathetic treatment of Oblomov's gentleness and sensitivity.

Alexander N. Ostrovsky, one of the most popular and most productive Russian dramatists, wrote plays criticizing the middle classes. His use of everyday Russian speech gives his work strong national appeal. Ostrovsky's villains, products of the merchant world, are greedy, dishonest, and dominating. In *Poverty Is No Crime* (1854), a selfish businessman decides that his daughter must marry a wealthy swindler. Ostrovsky's greatest work, *The Storm* (1860), tells the tragic story of a

merchant's wife who is driven to suicide by her domineering mother-in-law.

Sergey Aksakov, another leading writer of the 1850's, based his vivid descriptions of nature and people on childhood experiences. Unlike other Russian realists, Aksakov neither attacked nor defended Russian society in his writings. His works include *Family Chronicle* (1856) and *The Childhood of Bagrov the Grandson* (1858).

The 1860's and 1870's brought an end to romanticism in Russian literature. Russian realists began to write about social conditions in their works. A simplified prose replaced the elegant style of romanticism. The novel became the principal literary form of the period. Many novels had vivid characters but little plot structure.

Count Leo N. Tolstoy, one of Russia's greatest writers of realistic fiction, produced his major novels during the 1860's and 1870's. Tolstoy discarded romantic values of heroism and spiritual love. Instead, he showed a deep concern for the natural stages of human development, such as birth, marriage, and death. Tolstoy's magnificent novel *War and Peace* (1865-1869) captures the color and fire of the French invasion of Russia in 1812. But it also opposes war and reveals Tolstoy's desire for a quiet life in close harmony with nature. In *Anna Karenina* (1875-1877), Tolstoy attacked romantic love as self-indulgence, and encouraged a sense of moral duty and love of family instead. *The Death of Ivan Ilyich* (1886), one of Tolstoy's greatest tales, is a terrifying picture of a man's death and his acceptance of his doom as a natural end to life.

Fyodor M. Dostoevsky, together with Tolstoy, was Russia's greatest novelist. His works are famous for their dramatic portrayals of man's inner conflicts. Dostoevsky's characters experience a violent spiritual struggle between their belief in God and their strong sense of pride and self-centeredness. *Crime and Punishment* (1866), Dostoevsky's most exciting novel, describes the drama of a murderer who is tortured by his conscience. The hero is spiritually redeemed when he finally confesses his crime and accepts the punishment. *The Possessed* (1871-1872), also known as *The Devils* and as *The Demons*, portrays political radicals as ambitious men who turn against God. *The Brothers Karamazov* (1880), Dostoevsky's last and greatest novel, tells about the murder of an evil man by one of his four sons. The symbolic redemption of two of the sons represents the author's faith in the saving power of God.

Late Realism. Alexander III, who became czar in 1881, opposed many of the reforms made by his father, Alexander II. Themes of despair and bitterness, resulting from the czar's harsh rule, appeared in Russian writings of the 1880's and 1890's. Stories and plays became the major literary forms of late realism.

Anton P. Chekhov was a leading writer of short stories and plays. Many of his works deal with the boredom and frustration of life. *Ionych* (1898) tells the story of a sensitive, idealistic doctor who becomes lazy and conceited as he grows older. *Uncle Vanya* (1897) is a drama about an intellectual who realizes that his life, which he thought he had devoted to idealism, has been wasted. *Three Sisters* (1901) describes a family whose members are too lazy to change their dull lives. The decay of the landowning nobility is the subject of Chekhov's last play, *The Cherry Orchard* (1904).

534

Maxim Gorki, the last of the great Russian realists, wrote novels, plays, and stories. His early works, reflecting his Communist philosophy, describe the terrible poverty of the lower classes. Gorki's most famous play, *The Lower Depths* (1902), dramatizes the miserable lives of the inhabitants of a flophouse. A favorite theme of Gorki's later works was the decay of the middle class, shown in his novel *The Artamanovs' Business* (1925). Gorki also wrote three autobiographical novels and a volume of *Reminiscences* based on his memories of famous Russian authors.

Revolutionary Literature

The spirit of revolution dominated Russian literature during the late 1800's and early 1900's. Authors began to develop new and unusual writing styles. Their former interest in peasants and serfs was replaced by a concern for the urban laboring classes. Some writers based their works on religious and philosophical beliefs.

Symbolism in Russian poetry and fiction began in the mid-1890's. The symbolists opposed the realistic portrayal of everyday life and its problems. Russian writers, particularly Tyutchev, Lermontov, and Dostoevsky, as well as several authors of Western Europe, inspired the symbolists. Followers of the new movement returned to the dreams and fantasies of the romantics, and some concentrated on religious and philosophical theories. Leading symbolists included Alexander Blok and Andrey Bely.

Blok, a poet, expressed his religious ideals in his early works. His later poetry describes the ugliness of the world. Blok's most famous work, *The Twelve* (1918), interprets the *Bolshevik* (Communist) revolution of 1917 as a spiritual purification of Russia.

Bely was an outstanding novelist and also a poet. His *St. Petersburg* (1913) pictures the former Russian capital as a place where Eastern and Western philosophies meet and conflict with almost explosive violence.

Leonid Andreyev combined elements of realism and symbolism in his works. He wrote sensational stories with themes of sex, madness, and terror. Andreyev's short novel *Seven That Were Hanged* (1908) is a sympathetic treatment of seven revolutionaries arrested for trying to kill a high official.

Another leading writer of the early 1900's was Ivan Bunin. Although he was not a symbolist, his work, dominated by themes of love and death, resembles the literature of the symbolists. Bunin's masterpiece, *The Gentleman from San Francisco* (1915), is a story about an American millionaire who works too hard and is later unable to enjoy life. Bunin won the Nobel prize for literature in 1933.

Post-Symbolism was a revolt against the vague, philosophical works of the symbolists. It began in Russia about 1910. A number of authors started writing poetry that was uncomplicated and easy to understand. The *acmeists*, one of the most important post-symbolist groups, used clear-cut images and simple language in their writing. Among the leading acmeists were Anna Akhmatova and Osip Mandelstam. The *futurists*, a more radical group, sought new forms of expression in poetry.

Vladimir Mayakovsky, one of the most famous futurists and an outspoken Communist, shocked readers with his strong language and unusual imagery. His

poetry includes *The Cloud in Trousers* (1915) and *Lost in Conference* (1922).

Boris L. Pasternak, another poet associated with futurism, later became one of his country's greatest writers. Pasternak created an original and personal lyric poetry about nature and life. He wrote many works from a child's point of view. Pasternak's collections of poetry include *A Twin in the Clouds* (1914) and *My Sister Life* (1922).

Soviet Literature

The Communist Revolution of 1917 marked the beginning of a new era in Russian literature. The government greatly tightened censorship, which had existed under the czars. Many writers who opposed the Soviet government left the country. Those who remained had to serve the interests of the state and were not allowed to criticize the government. Russian writers have been told to describe Soviet life as happy and prosperous.

From 1917 to 1920. Following the revolution, literary activity decreased considerably. Publishing houses closed, and book production and sales dropped. Newspapers and magazines became political tools of the Communist Party. Printing presses were taken over by the state. The government encouraged the development of a *proletarian* literature to express the interests of Russian workers and peasants. However, few works of value were written during this period.

The Period of Rebirth in Russian literature occurred during the 1920's. The poor writing of the first few years of Communist rule resulted in a more lenient government policy. The government restored a certain amount of literary freedom, and reopened publishing houses. It also permitted literary criticism to resume. A new group of poets and novelists called *fellow travelers* appeared in Russia. Isaak Babel wrote a series of stories called *Red Cavalry* (1926) about the horrible conditions resulting from war. Leonid Leonov, inspired by Dostoevsky, told about the psychological effects of the revolution on the Russian people. His greatest novels are *The Badgers* (1924) and *The Thief* (1927). In the first volume of *Road to Calvary* (1921-1941), Alexei N. Tolstoy described the life of the educated classes during the revolution and the civil war that followed from 1918 to 1920.

The Period of Industrial Literature began in 1928 with Russia's First Five-Year Plan. This plan aimed in part to build up Soviet industry. Writers were expected to produce works concerning economic problems. During this period, *factory* and *production novels* appeared in Russia. They dealt with such subjects as the building of a factory or the organization of collective farming. Most of this literature was inferior, but a few works, such as *Time, Forward* (1932) by Valentin Kataev, were interesting and skillfully written.

The Period of Socialist Realism started in the early 1930's. The government, headed by Joseph Stalin, banned all private literary organizations and established the Union of Soviet Writers. The union, which all professional writers were required to join, endorsed the newly developed theory of *socialist realism*. According to this doctrine, the main purpose of literature is to portray the building of a socialist society. The government-controlled union ordered Soviet authors to produce optimistic works that were easy to understand and similar to the style of such writers as Tolstoy and Chekhov. Censorship already was eliminating undesirable material from authors' manuscripts. But by forcing writers to meet the requirements of socialist realism, the government gained additional control over literature. Writers who ignored the doctrine were expelled from the union. This meant the end of their literary careers. Some writers were imprisoned.

Historical literature became common during the 1930's and early 1940's. One of the finest works about the revolution and the civil war was *The Quiet Don* (1928-1940) by Mikhail A. Sholokhov. This long epic novel tells the story of a young Cossack whose happiness is destroyed by the tragedy of war. Sholokhov also wrote *Virgin Soil Upturned* (1932, 1960), a two-volume novel that describes the problems of peasants living on collective farms. Sholokhov received the Nobel prize for literature in 1965.

World War II. During the war against Germany from 1941 to 1945, the Russian government gave writers somewhat greater freedom. Soviet leaders were more interested in fighting the Germans than in building socialism. Themes of individual suffering and death dominated Russian literature of this period. *Days and Nights* (1941) by Konstantin Simonov was one of many patriotic war novels that appeared. The government reestablished strict controls over literature almost immediately after the war. It also forced several authors out of the Union of Soviet Writers. These writers included Anna Akhmatova and Mikhail Zoshchenko, an outstanding humorist and satirist.

The 1950's and 1960's. The death of Stalin in 1953 was followed by another period of relaxed restrictions in Soviet life and literature. This change became known as *The Thaw*, the name of a short novel written by Ilya Ehrenburg in 1954. In contrast to the policy of describing Soviet life as happy and optimistic, Ehrenburg wrote about frustrated, lonely people. A novel by Vladimir Dudintsev, *Not by Bread Alone* (1956), tells the tragic story of an inventor who suffers poverty and isolation as a result of corruption in the Communist Party. Strict censorship returned after the publication in 1962 of *A Day in the Life of Ivan Denisovich* by Alexander Solzhenitsyn. This short novel describes Soviet labor camps during the tyranny of Stalin's time.

A number of young liberal writers appeared in Russia during the 1960's. One of the most popular young poets was Yevgeny Yevtushenko. Although a Communist, Yevtushenko supports freedom and creativity in Soviet life. In *Babii Yar* (1961), he attacked the prejudice against Jews in Russia. Another young poet, Andrey Voznesensky, became famous for his original style. He centers entire poems around a single word, and uses highly complicated imagery. The major theme of Voznesensky's work is self-analysis through personal experience.

Censorship in Russia has prevented many works from being published, though typewritten or mimeographed copies of some manuscripts have been distributed secretly. Some Russian writers publish works abroad that are never seen in their own country. One of the first

Russian novels to be published outside the Soviet Union was *We* (1924) by Yevgeny Zamyatin. In 1957, Boris Pasternak's novel *Doctor Zhivago* appeared in Western Europe and in the United States, but was never allowed in Russia. Pasternak won the 1958 Nobel prize for his literature, including this novel. He refused the award because of pressure from the Soviet government.

Andrey Sinyavsky published several stories abroad in 1959 under the name of Abram Tertz. His works, including *The Trial Begins*, describe the terrors of life in a police state. In 1966, Sinyavsky was arrested and sent to a labor camp. *The First Circle* by Alexander Solzhenitsyn was published in the West in 1968. This novel tells about the life of political prisoners in a research institute during the Stalin era. The author claimed the manuscript was sent out of Russia without his consent. In 1969, Solzhenitsyn was expelled from the Union of Soviet Writers.   WILLIAM E. HARKINS

Related Articles in WORLD BOOK include:

Outline

Questions

What was the literary language used in early Russia?
What was the greatest work of early Russian literature?
How did Western culture affect Russian literature?
Who was the founder of modern Russian literature and the forerunner of classicism?
What were the characteristics of Russian romanticism?
Who was Russia's greatest lyric poet?
What was the "superfluous" man in Russian literature?
Who were Russia's greatest novelists?
Who were the *acmeists?* The *futurists?*
What is the theory of *socialist realism?*

RUSSIAN ORTHODOX CHURCH. See RUSSIA (Religion); EASTERN ORTHODOX CHURCHES.

RUSSIAN REVOLUTION. See RUSSIA (History).

RUSSIAN SOVIET FEDERATED SOCIALIST REPUBLIC (R.S.F.S.R.) is the largest and most important of the 15 republics that make up Russia. The R.S.F.S.R. has a population of 127,312,000. It covers 6,592,850 square miles, over three-fourths of the area of Russia. It extends from the Arctic Ocean south to the Black Sea, and from the Baltic Sea east to the Pacific Ocean (see RUSSIA [political map]). The Ural Mountains separate European Russia from Siberia. Moscow is the republic's capital and Leningrad is its chief seaport.

The R.S.F.S.R. is the principal manufacturing and agricultural state in Russia. It is also the country's dairy, lumber, steel, and textile center. The republic has vast deposits of oil, coal, copper, gold, iron ore, lead, nickel, platinum, and silver.

The R.S.F.S.R. was the first republic organized after the Russian Revolution in 1917. It was one of the four original republics that united to form the Soviet Union in 1922.   GEORGE KISH

RUSSIAN THISTLE. See TUMBLEWEED.

RUSSIAN WOLFHOUND. See BORZOI; WOLFHOUND.

RUSSO-FINNISH WARS. During World War II, the Soviet Union and Finland fought each other in two wars. They battled in the brief "Winter War" of 1939-1940. The second war, called the "Continuation War," took place from 1941 to 1944. Finland lost both wars.

"The Winter War." Germany conquered Poland in 1939. The Soviet Union claimed it feared a German invasion by way of Finnish territory. It maintained that it needed Finland's Karelian Isthmus, only 25 miles from the Russian city of Leningrad, to protect its bor-

Ski Troops were among the most effective soldiers in the Finnish Army during the Russo-Finnish Wars. The ski troops included Swedish volunteers, *below*.

United Press Int.

RUSSO-JAPANESE WAR

ders from such an attack. The Soviet Union demanded that Finland cede this territory and allow it to set up sea and air defenses along the Finnish coast. The Finns refused to yield. After fruitless negotiations, the Soviet Union broke diplomatic relations with Finland. On Nov. 30, 1939, the Soviet Union attacked Finland without formally declaring war. In the early stages of a harsh winter campaign, the Finns demonstrated that a small army using advantages of terrain and climate could outfight a larger and better-equipped force. But by February, the tide turned. The Finns suffered heavy losses, and received little help from other countries. As a result, on March 12, 1940, Finland had to accept harsh Soviet terms and sign the Peace of Moscow.

The Soviets took even more than they had first demanded. Finland lost one-tenth of its total area, including most of Karelia, the industrialized areas of Lake Ladoga, strategic islands in the Gulf of Finland, and the Petsamo region on Finland's Arctic coast near the Russian port of Murmansk. The Soviet Union also received a 30-year lease on the Hangö Peninsula.

"The Continuation War." Between the first and second Russo-Finnish wars, Finland drifted into a closer relationship with Nazi Germany. In September, 1940, Finnish military leaders secretly agreed to allow German troops and war supplies to enter Finland. On June 22, 1941, Germany invaded the Soviet Union. Finland sought to regain territory it lost in the "Winter War." It joined in the war against the Soviet Union. The Soviet Union immediately bombed Finland.

Great Britain had already declared war on Germany. It now declared war on Finland, in December, 1941. As the war turned against the Germans, Finnish enthusiasm for the war cooled. The Germans made life difficult for the Finnish people. In September, 1944, Finland accepted severe Soviet peace terms. The treaty restored the 1940 border between Finland and the Soviet Union. The Finns lost the Arctic port of Petsamo and nearby nickel mines. They regained the Hangö Peninsula, but had to grant the Soviet Union a 50-year lease on the Porkkala Peninsula, near Helsinki. Finland agreed to pay the Soviet Union $300 million for war damages, and to disarm the German troops remaining in the country. The Soviet Union returned the Porkkala Peninsula to Finland early in 1956. In 1962, Russia agreed to lease to Finland part of the Saimaa Canal lost to the Russians in 1940.   STEFAN T. POSSONY

See also FINLAND (History).

RUSSO-JAPANESE WAR brought recognition to Japan as a major power of the world. Russia's defeat in the war sharpened the dissatisfaction of its people with the corrupt, poorly run government. This discontent flamed into the Russian Revolution of 1905. The Russo-Japanese War began on Feb. 8, 1904, when Japan attacked Port Arthur in Manchuria. It ended on Sept. 5, 1905, with the signing of the Treaty of Portsmouth.

Underlying Causes of the war were the conflicting ambitions of the Russian and Japanese empires. Russia had been expanding its holdings and its interests in the Far East throughout the late 1800's. In 1891, Russia began to build the Trans-Siberian Railway connecting Moscow and Vladivostok. In 1896, Russia signed a treaty with China. The pact allowed Russia to build the Chinese Eastern Railway across Manchuria, and gave Russia partial control of that province. In 1898, Russia leased the Liaotung Peninsula from China and built there the naval base of Port Arthur and the commercial port of Dairen. Russia expanded its influence in Korea during these years. The Boxer Rebellion in China (1900-1901) gave Russia an opportunity to increase its power in Manchuria (see BOXER REBELLION).

These Russian moves disturbed the Japanese, who also wanted to extend their power at the expense of China. After Japan defeated China in a war (1894-1895), the Japanese tried to seize the Liaotung Peninsula, but Russia, Germany, and France prevented it. Japan became angry when Russia leased Liaotung.

The two nations were also rivals in Korea, whose location was important to both Japan and Russia. Japan wanted to gain control of Korean trade and industry. It already owned the Korean railroads and had sent thousands of Japanese settlers to Korea.

Russian and Japanese diplomats made a series of agreements about Korea and Manchuria. But the Russians broke the agreements. The Japanese therefore made an alliance with Great Britain in 1902 and began to prepare for war. The Russians failed to prepare.

Port Arthur Attacked. Japan broke off diplomatic relations with Russia on Feb. 6, 1904. On February 8, Vice-Admiral Heihachiro Togo's fleet attacked without warning Russian ships at Port Arthur. Japan declared war against Russia on February 10. Russia seemed so much more powerful than Japan that most people expected Russia to win the war easily. But Russia had only 80,000 troops in the Far East when the war began. More soldiers and all supplies had to be shipped over 5,000 miles from western Russia on the uncompleted Trans-Siberian Railway. Also, the Russian people did not favor the war, and some people began planning a revolution in St. Petersburg.

Last Battles. Japan had 200,000 troops in North China, and another large army nearby. Japan lay closer to the scene of the fighting, and its people supported the government. Japanese warships and mines soon bottled up most of Russia's Pacific squadron in Port Arthur. The Japanese destroyed or chased away the few Russian ships that tried to escape from there and from Vladivostok in the Battle of the Sea of Japan. Then the Russians ordered the Baltic Fleet, under Admiral Zinovy Rozhdestvensky, to sail to the Far East. This fleet steamed all the way from the Baltic Sea around Africa, across the Indian Ocean, and into the Korean Strait. But the Japanese fleet nearly annihilated it in the Battle of Tsushima Straits in 1905.

The land war went just as badly for the Russians. This was due to poor leadership, the lack of troops and supplies, and to Japanese skill and hard work. Japanese forces under Marshal Iwao Oyama gradually drove the Russian forces back into Manchuria, and defeated them there at the Battle of Mukden in 1905. After a two-month siege, Port Arthur surrendered to Japan. By that time, both countries were ready to stop the war. The Russian government suffered trouble at home, and the Japanese were running out of war funds.

Treaty of Portsmouth. President Theodore Roosevelt of the United States, at the secret suggestion of the Japanese, arranged a peace conference at Portsmouth, N.H., in 1905. The Treaty of Portsmouth gave southern Sakhalin Island to Japan, and forced Russia to remove its troops from Manchuria. Russia also had to give Japan Port Arthur and Dairen, and leave Korea for the Japanese. Russia's defeat was one of the main causes of the Russian Revolution of 1905.   WARREN B. WALSH

RUSSO-TURKISH WARS. The Russian Empire and the Ottoman Empire (now Turkey) engaged in almost constant disagreement for about 300 years after the 1600's. They fought frequent wars during this period. At first, Turkey was the aggressor. The Turks interfered in the southern borderlands of Russia and supported the Crimean Tatars, the ancient enemies of Russia. Until the late 1600's, Russia avoided open, direct war with the Turks, because Turkey was much stronger than Russia. But as Turkey grew weaker, Russia became stronger and began to expand toward the Black Sea and the Balkans. The Turks controlled both of these areas. Turkey then sought mainly to defend itself, although it occasionally took the offensive, especially when it had the support of another country.

Peter the Great and then Catherine the Great of Russia each fought successful wars against Turkey. Peter forced the Turks out of most of what is now the Ukraine. Catherine's armies conquered the Crimea and completed the opening of the southern lands to Russian settlement. She also forced the Turks to allow Russian merchant vessels to sail the Black Sea, and to grant Russia certain privileges with regard to the Orthodox Christians who lived within the Ottoman Empire. Russia later used this as grounds for claiming to be the official protector of these Christians. This claim resulted in much trouble and proved to be one of the causes of the Crimean War in the mid-1800's (see CRIMEAN WAR).

Russia and Austria allied themselves against Turkey in all three wars fought during the 1700's (1736-1739, 1768-1774, and 1787-1792). Russia and Turkey were allies for a brief period in the early 1800's, but this unusual arrangement did not last long. During the 1800's, Russia and Turkey fought four wars: 1806-1812, 1828-1829, 1853-1856, and 1877-1878. At the end of the first war, Russia gained the region of Bessarabia and a special position in the Balkans. The second war gave Russia control of the eastern coast of the Black Sea. The third war, known as the *Crimean War*, ended in a Turkish victory. Russia lost its dominant position in the Balkans and Black Sea area. It regained some of these losses in the fourth war, when the two countries signed the Treaty of San Stefano.

A Turkish alliance with Germany in 1914 led directly to another Russo-Turkish war, which was part of World War I. Russia had hoped to gain Constantinople and the Straits of the Dardanelles. Both Russia and Turkey joined the Allies in World War II.   WARREN B. WALSH

See also BERLIN, CONGRESS OF; CRIMEA.

RUSSWURM, JOHN BROWN (1799-1851), was an early spokesman against slavery and an important figure in an American Negro "back-to-Africa" movement. Russwurm expressed his antislavery views chiefly through *Freedom's Journal*, a newspaper he and Samuel Cornish started in New York City in 1827. The newspaper was the first in the United States to be owned and operated by Negroes. Russwurm soon came to believe that Negroes could never gain full citizenship in the United

States. In 1829, he moved to Liberia, in Africa. Liberia had been founded in 1822 as a place where free Negroes from the United States could settle. Russwurm served as governor of a colony at Cape Palmas, Liberia.

Russwurm was born in Jamaica and raised in Maine. He graduated from Bowdoin College. RICHARD BARDOLPH

RUST is a fungus that is a parasite of plants and is especially harmful to cereal crops. The rust fungus gets its name from the spores it produces which are brownish in color and resemble iron rust. The rust has special organs resembling threads that grow among the cells of the host plant and suck in the food of the plant cells. This may cause the leaves and stems to wither. Badly rusted crops produce only shriveled and worthless grain.

Every species of rust goes through a certain life cycle. Each period or stage in this life cycle is marked by a different type of spore formation. Some rusts have as many as five different types of spores, while others have only two or three. Some species of rusts spend their entire life cycle on one host. These rusts are called *autoecious*. Other species must spend their life cycle on two different hosts. This type is called *heteroecious*. The second host is known as the *alternate host*.

How Rust Attacks. An example of the heteroecious type is the common *black stem* rust which attacks wheat plants. This species of rust has five different kinds of spores and must live its life cycle on two hosts, the wheat plant and the American barberry plant (see BARBERRY). In the spring, small cups filled with spores appear on the lower side of the leaves of the barberry plant. These spores are carried by the wind and spread to wheat plants. The spores germinate and send out threads. These enter the tissues of the wheat plant and there produce reddish spores which are carried to other healthy wheat plants. This is the first stage. The second stage occurs in the fall, when there is a growth of tiny black spores on the stalks and stubble. These black spores sprout in the spring and produce small colorless spores called *sporidia*, which mark the third stage of life. The sporidia cannot grow on the wheat plant and will grow only on the barberry plant. These sporidia are carried by the wind to the barberry. The fourth stage is the development of tiny yellow spores on the upper surface of the barberry leaves. Later, yellow-orange cups containing spores appear on the undersurface of the barberry leaves. This marks the fifth stage. These spores are not able to infect the barberry plants. They must be blown to wheat plants where the life cycle begins again.

Other Types of rusts attack green plants. For example, *asparagus* rust is dangerous to the asparagus crop, *cedar* rust attacks apples, *crown* rust is harmful to oats, and *blister* rust attacks the white pine.

One method of controlling a rust which grows on two hosts is to destroy the alternate host. In the case of black stem rust, wheat crops have been saved by destroying barberry plants. Another method is to breed a rust-resistant plant. Rust is sometimes controlled by destroying the crops affected by the disease. Crop rotation also helps to prevent rust. WILLIAM F. HANNA

RUST is a brownish-red substance that forms on the surface of iron or steel when it is exposed to damp air. The term used alone means *iron rust*, which consists mainly of hydrated iron oxide ($3Fe_2O_3 \cdot H_2O$). Rust is formed by the union of the oxygen of the air with the iron by a process called *oxidation* (see OXIDATION).

Moisture is an important agent in producing the change.

Rust not only corrodes the surface, but also weakens the metal. Long exposure to air and moisture will cause nails to rust off, and rust holes to form in sheet iron. With the exception of special types of rust-resistant steel alloys, articles of iron and steel should be kept in dry places, or their surfaces should be coated with some substance that will resist the action of oxygen. Polished tools may be easily protected if wiped with a cloth soaked in oil. Heavy greases, sprayed-on plastic coatings, or a special chemically coated paper wrapped around metal objects also prevent rust.

Rust may be removed from iron and steel by scrubbing with water, or by the use of a polishing powder, provided the rust has not been forming for too long a time. A thick coat of rust requires the use of an emery wheel, a grindstone, or a file for its removal.

See also CORROSION; TARNISH.

RUST COLLEGE at Holly Springs, Miss., was the first Negro college established after the Civil War. It was founded in 1866 and chartered in 1868. This coeducational school grants B.A. and B.S. degrees. It operates under the auspices of the Methodist Church. For the enrollment of Rust College, see UNIVERSITIES AND COLLEGES (table).

RUSTIN, BAYARD, *BY urd* (1910-   ), is an American civil rights leader. A Quaker and a pacifist, he believes in achieving civil rights by nonviolent means.

Rustin was the chief organizer of the 1963 March on Washington. More than 200,000 persons took part in the march to protest racial injustice in the United States. Rustin also planned the organization of the Southern Christian Leadership Conference, led by Martin Luther King, Jr. In 1947, Rustin helped organize and took part in the first "freedom ride" into the South to protest racial discrimination.

In 1964, Rustin became executive director of the A. Philip Randolph Institute in New York City. This organization works toward economic and social reforms to benefit all Americans, regardless of race. Rustin was born in West Chester, Pa. C. ERIC LINCOLN

RUSTLER. See WESTERN FRONTIER LIFE (Crime).

RUTABAGA, *ROO tuh BAY guh*, is a plant with an edible root that tastes like a turnip. It is also called *Swedish turnip* and *Russian turnip*. Rutabagas are hardier than turnips, but need a growing season from four to six weeks longer. The plant has powdery, blue-green leaves. Its roots are larger, longer, and tougher than those of turnips. Rutabaga can be cooked like turnips.

Scientific Classification. Rutabaga belongs to the mustard family, *Cruciferae*. It is genus *Brassica*, species *B. napobrassica*. S. H. WITTWER

RUTGERS, THE STATE UNIVERSITY, is a university in New Brunswick, N.J. It also has coeducational colleges in Newark and Camden.

The New Brunswick campus has three undergraduate colleges—Douglass College (for women), Livingston College (coeducational), and Rutgers College (coeducational). The campus also has a graduate school; professional schools of education, library science, pharmacy, and social work; University College (evening division); the University Extension Division; the New Jersey Agricultural Experiment Station; and the Institute of Microbiology (see MICROBIOLOGY, INSTITUTE OF).

The Newark campus has the Newark College of Arts and Sciences, schools of business administration and law, and a college of nursing. The Camden College of Arts and Sciences and a school of law are in Camden.

Rutgers was founded in 1766 as Queen's College, and took its present name in 1825 to honor a benefactor. In 1869, Rutgers beat Princeton, 6 to 4, in the first intercollegiate football game. For enrollment, see UNIVERSITIES AND COLLEGES (table). JOHN L. SWINK

RUTH is the name of an Old Testament book and its heroine. It is a charming, beautifully told story.

In the days when the judges ruled Israel, there was a great famine in the land. A man named Elimelech left his home in Bethlehem and moved to the land of Moab. His wife Naomi and their two sons Mahlon and Chilion went with him. Elimelech died soon after, and the sons married Moabite women, Ruth and Orpah. Then the sons died. Naomi resolved to return to Bethlehem, and told her daughters-in-law to go back to their families. Orpah reluctantly did so, but Ruth refused. With touching devotion she said, "Whither thou goest, I will go . . . thy people shall be my people, and thy God my God: Where thou diest, will I die, and there will I be buried" (Ruth 1:16-17). So Naomi took Ruth to Bethlehem and Ruth found work gleaning barley in the fields of Boaz, a rich landowner. Boaz, who was a distant relative by marriage, fell in love with Ruth and eventually married her. Their son became the grandfather of King David. JOHN BRIGHT

RUTH, BABE (1895-1948), won fame as the greatest slugger in baseball history. He set many records, including his 714 regular-season home runs. Ruth had a personality that caught the imagination of fans and helped popularize baseball.

He was born George Herman Ruth in Baltimore, Md. He was raised at St. Mary's Industrial School in Baltimore. One of Ruth's teachers recognized his skill at baseball and helped him start his career in 1914. Later that year, Ruth joined the Boston Red Sox and became a successful pitcher. But by the time the Red Sox traded him to the New York Yankees in 1920, he was playing in the outfield regularly. In 1927, Ruth set a record of 60 home runs in a season. His slugging power made him baseball's biggest attraction. The Yankees' new stadium was nicknamed the *House That Ruth Built*. Ruth hit his 60 home runs during a 154-game season and this record still stands. In 1961, New York Yankees star Roger Maris set another record by hitting 61 home runs during a 162-game schedule.

The Yankees released Ruth after the 1934 season, and he finished his career with the Boston Braves in 1935. He was named to the National Baseball Hall of Fame in 1936. Ruth died of cancer. ED FITZGERALD

See also BASEBALL (The Babe Ruth Era).

RUTHENIA is the Transcarpathian *Oblast* (region) in the Ukrainian Soviet Socialist Republic. Originally a part of Hungary, it belonged to Czechoslovakia before World War II. Ruthenia covers 4,942 square miles. Most of its 1,057,000 residents are Ukrainians. Ruthenia is a mountainous land with thick forests. The chief resources are timber and rock

salt. Most of its people are herdsmen and foresters. The chief city is Uzhgorod. Ruthenia was ceded to Russia in 1945. THEODORE SHABAD

RUTHENIAN. The Ruthenians are Slavic people who live in southeastern Europe. In ancient times, they were called *Scythians* (see SCYTHIAN). During the 1200's and later, they were called *Little Russians* to distinguish them from the *Great Russians* of the Moscow region.

The Ruthenians are a peaceful people who have always been at the mercy of powerful countries. Both Russia and Austria tried for many years to win their favor. During World War I, the Ruthenians tried to set up an independent state, but Poland crushed the movement. Czechoslovakia was one of the few countries which gave equal political rights to Ruthenians.

There are about 40 million Ruthenians. They live chiefly in the Polish and Russian sections of Galicia, in the Soviet Ukraine, in Romania, and in Czechoslovakia. Most of the Ruthenians in Czechoslovakia were taken into Russia after World War II. The Russian government also took over many of the Ruthenians who once lived in Poland.

Most Ruthenians are darker than other Slavic people. The Ruthenians have their own language, but almost all speak Russian as well. WILTON MARION KROGMAN

RUTHENIUM (chemical symbol, Ru) is a rare metallic element. It belongs to the platinum group of metals. Its atomic number is 44, and its atomic weight is 101.07. Ruthenium was discovered by the Russian chemist Karl Klaus in 1844. It has a high melting point of about 2250° C. (4082° F.), and boils at about 3900° C. (7052° F.). It is hard and brittle, and does not dissolve in either water or acids. Ruthenium is useful as a hardener for platinum and palladium. A platinum alloy containing 10 per cent ruthenium makes electrical contacts used in aircraft magnetos. Some ruthenium is added to the hard alloy of osmium used to make pen tips. See also ELEMENT, CHEMICAL. WALTER J. MOORE

RUTHERFORD, ALEXANDER CAMERON. See ALBERTA (A New Province).

RUTHERFORD, ERNEST (1871-1937), BARON RUTHERFORD OF NELSON, a British physicist, worked out the nuclear theory of the atom in 1911. Earlier, he had published his theory of atomic transmutation. He also discovered alpha and beta rays and protons. Because of Rutherford's many contributions to science, he has been called the *father of nuclear science*.

In the nuclear theory of the atom, Rutherford discarded the notion that atoms were like solid "building blocks." He explained that they are constructed much like the solar system. That is, a heavy part, called the *nucleus*, forms the center of each atom. Particles of negative electricity, called *electrons*, form the outer part of the atom, most of which consists of space. Niels Bohr later combined the nuclear theory with the quantum theory in the Bohr theory of atomic structure (see BOHR, NIELS).

In 1902, Rutherford published his *theory of atomic transmutation*. The theory explains that radioactive elements give off electrically charged particles known as alpha and beta rays. This process changes the *parent* (original) atom into a *daughter* atom. Because of the changes, the new atom is in the form of a different chemical element. This achievement won Rutherford the 1908 Nobel prize in chemistry. Rutherford produced the first man-made atomic disintegration in 1919 when he bombarded nitrogen atoms with alpha particles and produced *protons*, positively charged particles from the nucleus of the atom. He described this work in the *Philosophical Magazine*.

Rutherford was born in Nelson, New Zealand, on Aug. 30, 1871. He studied at Canterbury College in New Zealand, and at Cambridge University. He taught at McGill University in Canada, the University of Manchester, and Cambridge. In 1903, he was elected a fellow of the Royal Society. He wrote *Radioactive Substances and Their Radiations* (1912).　　RALPH E. LAPP

See also ATOM (Rutherford's Theory of the Atom).

RUTHERFORDIUM. See ELEMENT 104.

RUTILE, *ROO teel* (chemical formula, TiO_2), is a common titanium-oxide mineral found in the United States, Australia, Brazil, and India. It is an important source of titanium. Most deposits are beach sands. Rutile crystals are usually light brown, but larger crystals are black. Sometimes the crystals have a yellow, blue, or violet tint. The refined white oxide makes the best pigments for white paint. It is also used to color porcelain. Grains of rutile are used to coat welding rods. See also MINERAL (color picture); TITANIUM.　　FREDERICK H. POUGH

RUTIN, *ROO tin*, is a drug used to treat weakened capillaries. It is a yellow powder. Rutin was first made from garden rue, but is now extracted from buckwheat.

RUTLAND. See ENGLAND (political map).

RUTLAND, Vt. (pop. 19,293; alt. 500 ft.), is the state's second largest city. It lies 65 miles southwest of Montpelier (see VERMONT [political map]). Rutland is the trading center for a region of about 100,000 persons. Marble finishing and the manufacture of weighing scales, fire clay, and stone-working machinery are important industries in Rutland. The *Rutland Herald*, established in 1794, is the oldest continuously published newspaper in the state of Vermont. Rutland has a mayor-council government.　　WALTER R. HARD, JR.

RUTLEDGE is the family name of two American patriots and public officials during the Revolutionary War period. They were brothers.

John Rutledge (1739-1800), a well-known lawyer and orator, was one of the first to urge independence for the 13 colonies. He represented South Carolina at the Stamp Act Congress in 1765, and twice in the Continental Congress. Rutledge was chairman of the commission that drew up the South Carolina constitution in 1776.

Rutledge became South Carolina's first executive, as president from 1776 to 1778. He served as governor from 1779 to 1782. He was a member of the convention that framed the United States Constitution, where he spoke often in favor of the slaveholders. From 1790 to 1791, he served as an associate justice of the Supreme Court of the United States. In 1795, President George Washington named him chief justice, but the Senate refused to confirm the appointment. Rutledge was born in Charleston, S.C., and studied law in England. He practiced in Charleston. JERRE S. WILLIAMS

John Rutledge
Chicago Historical Society

Edward Rutledge (1749-1800) was a signer of the Declaration of Independence. Like his brother, he studied law in England and practiced in Charleston, S.C. He served in the Continental Congress from 1774 to 1776, and in the provincial congress. In 1780, the British captured him during the siege of Charleston. After the Revolutionary War, he served in the state legislature. From 1798 to 1800, he was governor. Rutledge was born in or near Charleston.　　ROBERT J. TAYLOR

RUTLEDGE, ANN (1816-1835), became famous as Abraham Lincoln's first sweetheart. Romantic stories of their tragic love affair are based more on legend than on fact. Ann Rutledge was the daughter of the innkeeper in New Salem, Ill., where Lincoln lived for a time. She was engaged to John McNamar, a wealthy settler. He left for the East, and there was doubt that he would return to marry Ann. Meanwhile, she accepted Lincoln's proposal of marriage. But shortly afterward, she became ill and died.　　HELEN E. MARSHALL

RUWENZORI RANGE, *ROO wen ZOOR ee*, is a group of mountains that lies just north of the equator in east-central Africa. It extends between Lake Albert and Lake Edward on the border between Uganda and Zaire. The mountain range is about 75 miles long and 40 miles wide. It rises from thick steaming jungle into dense clouds that hide six snow-capped peaks. The highest elevation is Margherita Peak (16,763 feet). The range is not volcanic, but consists of ancient crystalline rock that moved upward from the earth's crust.

Ancient peoples called the range the *Mountains of the Moon*. Ptolemy, the Alexandrian geographer, first used this name on a map. Melting snows from the range feed some of the farthest Nile headwaters.

In 1889, Henry M. Stanley became the first white man to see the range. He used the local name *Ruwenzori* (rainmaker).　　HARRY R. RUDIN

RUYSBROECK, JAN VAN. See MYSTICISM.

RUYSDAEL, JACOB VAN. See RUISDAEL, JACOB VAN.

RUYTER, *ROY ter*, or **RUITER, MICHEL ADRIAANSZOON DE** (1607-1676), was one of the greatest fighting seamen of The Netherlands. He was an admiral of the Dutch Navy during the three wars between England and The Netherlands in the middle 1600's (see NETHERLANDS [Wars with England and France]). During the first war, he helped Admiral Martin Tromp defeat the English off Dungeness in 1652. When Tromp died, Ruyter became chief in command. In 1666, during the second war, he won the Four Days' Battle. He won all the naval battles of the third war. However, the Dutch lost the war, when the French attacked them on land. In 1676, Ruyter was killed while fighting the French. He was born in Flushing (now Vlissingen). JANE K. MILLER

RUŽIČKA, *ROO zheech kah*, **LEOPOLD** (1887-　　), a Swiss chemist, shared the 1939 Nobel chemistry prize for his work on the structure of important vegetable products known as *higher terpenes*. He found that they consist of large rings of carbon atoms. These products are found in *essential* (odorous) oils. Chemists use his methods in many synthetic and analytical procedures. Ružička was born in Vukovar, Yugoslavia, and was educated in Zurich. He taught at the University of Utrecht and at the Federal Polytechnic Institute in Zurich.　　HENRY M. LEICESTER

RWANDA

- ✪ National Capital
- • Other City or Town
- —— Road
- ⌒ River
- ▲ MOUNTAIN

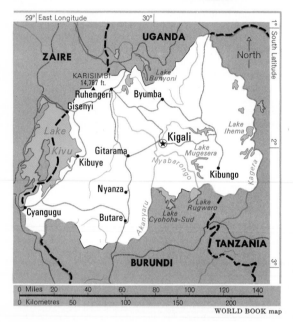

WORLD BOOK map

RWANDA, r WAHN duh, is a small country in east-central Africa, just south of the equator. The country has about the same area and population as the state of Maryland. Rwanda is one of the most crowded countries in Africa.

R. J. Harrison Church, the contributor of this article, is professor of geography at the University of London, and the author of Africa and the Islands *and* West Africa.

The people of Rwanda are divided into two large tribal groups—the Bahutu and the Watusi. The Bahutu are farmers, and the Watusi are cattle owners. The Watusi are dignified people known for their height and for their skill at dancing. For hundreds of years, they controlled what is now Rwanda, and they treated the Bahutu as slaves. But in 1959, when the country was still a United Nations trust territory, the Bahutu rebelled. After bloody fighting, the Watusi king and more than 140,000 of his tribesmen fled the country. They settled in nearby countries, including Urundi (now Burundi), which has a Watusi king. See BURUNDI.

After the king left, the people voted to make the country an independent republic. The Bahutu gained control of the government, but fighting between them and the remaining Watusi continued.

Even though Rwanda is near the equator, it has a cool, pleasant climate. This is because it lies on a series

of high, level *plateaus* (plains). Rwanda is sometimes called the *African Switzerland,* because of its beautiful lakes, valleys, and snow-capped mountains.

Rwanda is one of Africa's poorest countries. It has little industry, no railroads, and poor soil. Starvation is an ever-present danger. The largest town, Kigali, has about 30,000 persons. It is the capital of the REPUBLIC OF RWANDA.

Government. Rwanda is a republic. The president serves as head of state. He is elected to a four-year term, and governs with the aid of a *Council of Ministers* (cabinet). The president appoints the 13 members of the Council of Ministers. The people elect the 44 members of the National Assembly to five-year terms. Rwanda is divided into 10 departments and 141 *communes* (smaller units) for local government.

People. About 84 of 100 Rwandese belong to the Bahutu tribe. The Bahutu are farmers, most of whom can raise only enough food for their own families. Some of them also raise coffee, Rwanda's chief export.

About 15 of 100 persons belong to the Watusi tribe. The Watusi raise cattle for almost all their food and other needs. They live on beef, milk, and milk products, and on blood which they draw from living animals. Some make their clothing from animal hides and hair.

About 30,000 pygmies also live in Rwanda. The pygmies once made their living by hunting, but some of them now live and work in the towns (see PYGMY). Only a few Europeans live in Rwanda. Some are farmers who raise tea; pyrethrum, which is used in making insecticides; and geranium, which provides an oil used in making perfumes. A few Europeans are executives in the mining industry. Others are Christian missionaries.

French and Kinyarwanda are the official languages. Most of the people speak Kinyarwanda, a Bantu language (see BANTU). About half the people practice fetish religions. As part of their religion, they try to protect themselves against evil spirits by using magic and objects they believe to be charms. Most of the other people are Roman Catholics. The Roman Catholic and other Christian churches operate most of the elementary schools in Rwanda. There are several teacher-training colleges and technical schools. A very small university was opened in 1963 in Butare, about 50 miles south of Kigali. Public education is free and compulsory for

--- **FACTS IN BRIEF** ---

Capital: Kigali.

Official Language: French and Kinyarwanda.

Official Name: Republic of Rwanda.

Form of Government: Republic.

Head of State: President (4-year term).

Area: 10,169 square miles. *Greatest Distances*—(east-west) 145 miles; (north-south) 110 miles.

Population: *Estimated 1973 Population*—3,920,000; density, 385 persons to the square mile. *Estimated 1978 Population*—4,520,000.

Chief Products: *Agriculture*—cattle, coffee, geranium, pyrethrum, tea. *Mining*—tin, wolfram.

Flag: The flag has three vertical stripes of red, yellow, and green, with a large black *R* in the center. See FLAG (color picture: Flags of Africa).

Money: *Basic Unit*—franc. See MONEY (table: Values).

542

children from 7 to 16 years of age, but there are not enough classrooms to accommodate all the pupils. About 95 of every 100 Rwandese cannot read or write.

Land. Rwanda covers 10,169 square miles, much of it rugged and mountainous. The highest mountains, in the west and northwest, were formed by volcanoes. Rwanda's western border runs through Lake Kivu. The Kagera River forms the eastern border. The Akanyaru River forms part of the southern border, and the Ruzizi River forms part of the southwestern border. The land rises sharply from Lake Kivu to about 9,000 feet above sea level. The Virunga Mountains rise to about 14,800 feet in the northwest. The heavy rainfall in western Rwanda has *leached* (washed away) most of the chemicals which should enrich the soil. Heavy farming has also caused soil erosion.

The eastern part of Rwanda is a series of plateaus between 5,000 and 7,000 feet above sea level. The plateaus slope down toward the east. Each plateau is bounded on the east by an *escarpment* (steep edge) with a marsh at the foot of the escarpment. Forests once covered the plateaus, but the people have cleared most of this land for farming.

The Rift Valley areas in the west have an average

At a Market Place in Northern Rwanda, farmers and their families trade their produce and visit with their neighbors.

Marilyn Silverstone, Magnum

annual temperature of 73° F. and an average annual rainfall of 30 inches. The mountainous areas in the west have an average annual temperature of 63° F. and an average annual rainfall of 58 inches. The rainfall is even greater on the Virunga Mountains. On the plateaus, the temperature averages 68° F. annually. The annual rainfall is about 47 inches.

Economy. Most Rwandese are farmers. But many farmers can grow only enough food to feed their own families. Coffee is the country's chief export. The farming varies according to the altitude. For example, farmers raise *robusta* coffee on land up to about 4,500 feet above sea level. This coffee is used to make instant coffee. From about 4,500 feet to 6,000 feet, farmers grow coffee *arabica*. See COFFEE (Kinds of Coffee).

European companies operate tin and wolfram mines in north-central Rwanda and several tin mines along the southern border. These minerals account for about one-third of the country's exports. Rwanda has little power and few manufacturing industries. The nation has no railroads. The main highways are surfaced, but there are mostly dirt roads. Kigali and Butare have airfields.

The territories of Ruanda (now Rwanda) and Urundi (now Burundi) cooperated closely for many years. Rwanda's exports were shipped through Burundi mainly to the ocean ports of Dar es Salaam in Tanzania; Lobito in Angola; and Beira in Mozambique. But after the fighting between Bahutu and Watusi, relations between the two countries became strained. Most of Rwanda's exports now are hauled to Kampala, Uganda, and then shipped by train to Mombasa, in Kenya. This makes it difficult and expensive for Rwanda to export and import goods and products.

History. What is now Rwanda was first inhabited by Bahutu farmers and pygmy hunters. About 400 years ago, the Watusi, a warrior tribe with large herds of big-horned cattle, invaded the country from the north. The Bahutu could not defeat the Watusi, so each Bahutu agreed to serve a Watusi "lord." In return, the Watusi agreed to protect his Bahutu servant and allow the Bahutu to use one of his cows. In this way, the Watusi dominated the area until 1959.

Germany conquered the area that is now Rwanda and Burundi in 1897. It ruled this area as part of German East Africa. Belgium occupied the area, then called Ruanda-Urundi in 1916, during World War I. Germany lost its African colonies after the war, and Ruanda-Urundi became a mandated territory under Belgian administration in 1919 (see MANDATED TERRITORY). In 1946, the area became a United Nations trust territory.

Political unrest followed the death of *Mwami* (King) Mutara III in 1959. Bahutu tribesmen finally rebelled against the Watusi, and massacred thousands of Watusi in the bloody uprising. The Watusi mwami and about 140,000 Watusi tribesmen fled to Burundi and other neighboring countries.

In 1961, the people of Ruanda voted to make their country a republic. Ruanda-Urundi became independent as two countries, Rwanda and Burundi, on July 1, 1962. The people of Rwanda then elected Gregoire Kayibanda as the first president. R. J. HARRISON CHURCH

See also BURUNDI; KIGALI; RUANDA-URUNDI.

RYAN, THOMAS FORTUNE (1851-1928), a financier and businessman, became one of the richest men in America. His wealth was estimated at more than $200 million.

Ryan started as an errand boy in Baltimore. He went to New York City in 1872 and became wealthy as a stockbroker. With two partners, he gained control of the New York streetcar system, and in 1886 created the Metropolitan Traction Co., probably the first *holding company* (a company that controls other companies) in America. In 1905, Ryan consolidated with the Interborough Transit Co., which had built a new subway system. Ryan gained control of the Equitable Life Assurance Society in 1905, and later sold it to J. P. Morgan. Ryan was a controller of the Consolidated Tobacco Co., which was found guilty of violating antitrust laws in 1911. He was born in Nelson County, Virginia.   DAVID A. SHANNON

RYDER, ALBERT PINKHAM (1847-1917), is considered one of the most original of American painters. He is best known for his brooding night scenes of the sea and dream-like landscapes. His paintings are based on stories from the Bible, William Shakespeare, and other literary sources. Ryder conceived simple, bold designs and laid his paint on thickly. He worked on each painting for a long time, repainting it until layers of color were built up.

Ryder was born in New Bedford, Mass. Romantic and withdrawn by nature, he worked in seclusion. He did not produce many paintings, but his imaginative style, which often comes close to abstract design, influenced many painters.   ROBERT GOLDWATER

RYE is a cereal grain similar to wheat and barley. The plant has slender seed spikes with long, stiff beards. The dark-colored grains grow in pairs. Like those of

USDA; Frank Cassidy

A Rye Seed Spike, *top,* has long, stiff beards. Rye grains, *above,* grow in pairs. Rye is an important food in many countries.

wheat, the grains fall free from the chaff when threshed. Rye flowers, unlike those of wheat, oats, and barley, open for pollination. They shed their pollen in great golden showers at blossomtime. Because rye pollinates in the open, it is difficult to keep varieties pure. Rye is used to make bread and certain liquors.

Rye has been raised as a grain since the days of ancient Rome. It probably originated from wild species in eastern Europe or Asia. Wild rye still grows in these regions and in northern Africa.

Production. Rye is an important crop in the cool climates of northern Europe, Asia, and North America. In the Southern Hemisphere, comparatively little rye is cultivated. Russia produces the most rye. Other important producers are Czechoslovakia, East Germany, Poland, Turkey, the United States, and West Germany. In North America, most rye is grown in the Dakotas, central Canada, Minnesota, and Nebraska.

The world produces an average of about 1,200,-000 bushels of rye each year. During the past few hun-

The Cleveland Museum of Art

Albert Ryder's Painting
The Race Track or *Death on a Pale Horse, left,* illustrates the moody, mystical quality of his work. The subject was revealed to him in a dream.

dred years, wheat bread has become more popular than rye bread.

Uses. In most countries, rye is used chiefly for human food. The food value of rye is nearly as great as that of wheat. But American farmers feed much of the grain to livestock. Rye hay and *middlings* (medium-sized particles which are a by-product of bran flour milling) are frequently used as stock feed. Young rye plants make good pasture in spring and autumn. But sometimes, cows that graze on rye give milk that has an unusually strong flavor.

Farmers frequently grow rye to improve or to protect the soil. For example, a crop of rye may be raised alternately with other crops to protect the soil. Then, it is called a *cover crop*.

The heavy, black bread of Europe is made from rye flour. Rye does not contain as much gluten as wheat. Because of this, yeast cannot raise rye dough as easily as wheat dough, and rye bread is heavier and more compact than wheat bread. In the United States, bakers usually add much wheat flour to the rye so that the bread is not so dark as that made in Europe.

Distillers use malt made from rye for rye whiskey and Holland gin. Rye straw is long, smooth, and easy to bend. It is used in a variety of ways. Packers use the straw as a packing material. Manufacturers use it to make hats, paper, mats, and mattress stuffing. Rye straw is also used as a thatch in European countries, where thatched roofs are still common. It is particularly suited to such use, because it decays less rapidly than most other kinds of straw.

Construction workers use rye to conserve soil. They plant rye in the raw soil along new roadbeds. The plants grow in the infertile subsoil, and keep it from eroding.

Cultivation. Rye grows well in much poorer soils than those necessary for most cereal grains. Therefore, it is an especially valuable crop in regions where the soil contains sand or peat. Rye plants withstand cold better than other small grains do. Most farmers grow winter ryes, which are planted and begin to grow in autumn. When spring comes, the plants develop and produce their crop.

Like all cereal grains, rye plants are annuals and new seeds must be planted each year. Most American farmers use grain drills to plant rye. These machines plant the seeds in rows. About $1\frac{1}{2}$ to 2 bushels of seed are sown on each acre. In the United States, rye yields an average of about 20 bushels of grain to the acre. In other countries, the crop may yield several times this amount. Because of the low yields, farmers usually grow wheat instead of rye whenever possible.

Ergot. A poisonous fungus, called *ergot*, often destroys rye grain. Ergot replaces the grain with a hornlike blackish body several times longer than the normal grain. These ergot bodies poison livestock and human beings who eat the grain or products made from it. This disease is called *ergotism*. But ergot supplies a valuable drug. Doctors use small doses of drugs made from it to ease migraine headaches, to control bleeding, and as an aid to childbirth.

Scientific Classification. Rye belongs to the grass family, *Gramineae*. It is a member of the genus *Secale* and is species *S. cereale*.   RICHARD W. POHL

See also GRAIN (picture); ERGOT.

LEADING RYE-GROWING STATES AND PROVINCES

Bushels (56 pounds) of rye grown each year

Saskatchewan 7,000,000 bu.	
South Dakota 5,992,000 bu.	
North Dakota 5,050,000 bu.	
Alberta 3,325,000 bu.	
Manitoba 2,731,000 bu.	
Nebraska 2,104,000 bu.	
Minnesota 1,797,000 bu.	
Ontario 1,405,000 bu.	
Georgia 1,364,000 bu.	
Michigan 933,000 bu.	

Based on a 4-year average, 1966-1969

Sources: Dominion Bureau of Statistics; U.S. Department of Agriculture

LEADING RYE-GROWING COUNTRIES

Bushels (56 pounds) of rye grown each year

Russia 478,029,000 bu.	
Poland 321,141,000 bu.	
Germany (West) 117,461,000 bu.	
Germany (East) 69,337,000 bu.	
Turkey 31,052,000 bu.	
Czechoslovakia 28,750,000 bu.	
United States 26,669,000 bu.	
Austria 15,675,000 bu.	
Canada 14,680,000 bu.	
Spain 13,562,000 bu.	

Based on a 4-year average, 1966-1969

Source: U.S. Department of Agriculture

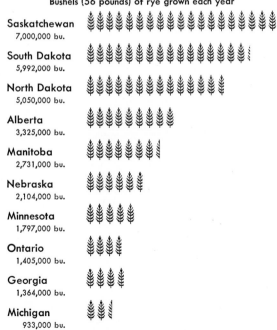

RYE HOUSE PLOT

RYE HOUSE PLOT was a scheme concocted by radical members of the English Whig Party in 1683. They planned to kill Charles II and his brother, James, and place the Protestant Duke of Monmouth on the throne of England. The assassination was to take place at Rye House Farm. The plot failed. Lord William Russell (1639-1683) and Algernon Sidney (1622-1683) were beheaded, although their guilt was not proved.   J. SALWYN SCHAPIRO

RYERSON POLYTECHNICAL INSTITUTE is a private coeducational school in Toronto, Ont. It has divisions of applied arts, arts, business, community services, and technology. Ryerson was the first Canadian school to offer courses in graphic arts management. It grants bachelor's degrees and three-year diplomas.

The school was established in 1948 under provincial control as the Ryerson Institute of Technology. It became self-governing in 1962 and was given its present name in 1964. For enrollment, see CANADA (table: Universities and Colleges).   DONALD L. MORDELL

RYOJUN. See PORT ARTHUR.

RYSWICK, *RIS wick*, **TREATY OF.** In 1697, Louis XIV of France signed a treaty in Ryswick (Rijswijk), Holland, ending the War of the League of Augsburg. In this war, England, Spain, The Netherlands, the Holy Roman Empire, and many small German states fought together against France. The treaty ended a nine years' war, and kept Louis from expanding his power in Europe. It also ended King William's War in North America (see FRENCH AND INDIAN WARS).

Louis agreed to surrender all the places he had seized except Strasbourg and to recognize William III as King of England. Holland won the right to keep troops in the Spanish Netherlands. The duchy of Lorraine was returned to the rule of its duke.   J. SALWYN SCHAPIRO

RYUKYU ISLANDS, *rih OO kyoo*, are a group of more than 100 islands that stretch from Japan to Taiwan between the China Sea and the Pacific Ocean. The Ryukyus have a total land area of 1,464 square miles and a population of 1,150,000. Some of the islands have no people. The Ryukyus can be divided geographically into five groups from north to south—(1) the Osumi Islands, (2) the Tokara Islands, (3) the central Ryukyus including the Amami Islands and Okinawa, (4) the Miyako Islands, and (5) the Yaeyama Islands.

People. Farming is the most important occupation of the islanders, though the soil is rocky and hilly. The people grow rice, but their main food crop is sweet potatoes. They export sugar cane and pineapple. Fishing is another important activity for income and food.

The Ryukyuans speak a language similar to Japanese. Their religion has been influenced by both China and Japan. Burial of the dead in large family tombs and ceremonies honoring ancestors are important parts of the Ryukyuan religion. Ryukyuans also worship things connected with nature, such as trees and fire.

Land and Climate. Most of the Ryukyu Islands are rough and mountainous. The highest elevation above sea level, more than 6,000 feet, is on Yaku Island. Some of the islands have active volcanoes.

The Ryukyus have a warm, wet climate. The average temperature is about 70° F. (21° C.), and the annual rainfall ranges from 53 to 120 inches. Typhoons bring damaging winds and rains in summer and autumn.

546

RYUKYU ISLANDS

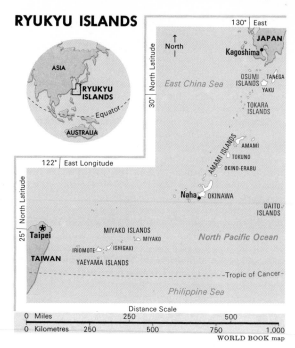

WORLD BOOK map

Winters are usually cloudy and chilly, with less rain.

History. Ancestors of the Ryukyuans probably came from Japan and Taiwan, and possibly from the Philippines. Some scientists believe that prehistoric people may have lived on the islands in the Ice Age.

Chinese and Japanese expeditions stopped in the Ryukyu Islands as early as the A.D. 600's. During the 1400's and 1500's, Okinawa was part of a thriving trade network that linked China, Japan, Korea, and Southeast Asia. China and Japan both claimed the Ryukyus until 1874, when China signed a treaty recognizing Japanese rule. In 1879, the islands became part of two *prefectures* (provinces) of Japan.

After Japan's defeat in World War II, the United States took over the Ryukyus. In 1953, the United States returned the islands north of Okinawa to Japan. United States agencies continued to supervise Okinawa and the southern Ryukyus until 1972, when those islands were returned to Japan.   RICHARD JOSEPH PEARSON

See also OKINAWA.

RYUN, JIM (1947-   ), an American track star, became the world's fastest middle-distance runner. In 1966, as a University of Kansas freshman, Ryun ran the mile in 3 minutes 51.3 seconds, breaking the record held by Michel Jazy of France. Ryun set another record that year by running 880 yards in 1 minute 44.9 seconds. In 1967, he set a 1,500-meter record of 3 minutes 33.1 seconds and lowered his mile record to 3 minutes 51.1 seconds.

James Ronald Ryun was born in Wichita, Kans. In 1964, as a high school junior, he ran the mile in 3 minutes 59.0 seconds. Ryun suffered from mononucleosis while training for the 1968 Olympics. He finished second in the 1,500-meter run, and the next year he retired from track for 19 months. In 1971, in his second race after returning to competition, he equaled the indoor mile record of 3 minutes 56.4 seconds. FRANK LITSKY

See also TRACK AND FIELD (picture).